LABOR RELATIONS LAW
Second Edition

Benjamin J. Taylor
Fred Witney

- Minority group problems under Taft-Hartley and civil rights' legislation

- The *Collyer* doctrine

- Successor employer developments

- Changes in National Labor Relations Board jurisdiction

- The so-called "make-whole" doctrine originally established in *Ex-Cell-O*

- Industrial conflict innovations

- Developments in the public sector

- Developments in the control of internal union affairs established by Landrum-Griffin

These are some of the critical current dilemmas and recent changes in government regulations that are included in the new, revised edition of *Labor Relations Law*. Particular attention is given to how the Nixon National Labor Relations Board applied the Taft-Hartley law. Other new developments of major importance are interwoven in the discussions. Court cases are discussed and analyzed in an understandable way for employers, unions, employees, and the public in general to help each grasp the significance of the decisions or actions.

LABOR
RELATIONS LAW

This up-to-date material is explained in clear easily absorbed language that helps you examine the legal framework of labor relations and probe the ever changing problems that keep it in a state of flux.

BENJAMIN J. TAYLOR holds a Ph.D. from Indiana University, and currently is the Chairman of the Department of Economics at the University of Oklahoma. He has written several articles and books, including *Indian Manpower Resources in the Southwest* and *Arizona Labor Relations Law*.

FRED WITNEY holds his Ph.D. in economics from the University of Illinois. He is Professor of Economics at Indiana University. He has lectured extensively on labor relations and served as labor arbitrator under the auspices of the Federal Mediation Board. *Wartime Experiences of the N.L.R.B.* and *Labor Relations* are among his other books.

Prentice-Hall
Industrial Relations and Personnel Series
DALE YODER, Editor

2nd
edition

LABOR
RELATIONS LAW

BENJAMIN J. TAYLOR

University of Oklahoma

FRED WITNEY

Indiana University

Prentice-Hall, Inc.
ENGLEWOOD CLIFFS, NEW JERSEY

Library of Congress Cataloging in Publication Data

TAYLOR, BENJAMIN J
   Labor relations law.

   (Prentice-Hall industrial relations and personnel
series)
   Bibliography: p.
   Includes indexes.
   1. Collective bargaining—United States. 2. Labor
laws and legislation—United States. I. Witney,
Fred joint author. II. Title.
KF3408.T35 1975   344′.73′0189   74-22054
ISBN 0-13-519637-X

Printed in the United States of America

10 9 8 7 6 5 4 3

Prentice-Hall International, Inc., LONDON
Prentice-Hall of Australia, Pty. Ltd., SYDNEY
Prentice-Hall of Canada, Ltd., TORONTO
Prentice-Hall of India Private Limited, NEW DELHI
Prentice-Hall of Japan, Inc., TOKYO

To the Memory of E. B. McNatt

Professor of Economics Emeritus
University of Illinois

Teacher—Counsellor—Friend

Contents

COLLECTIVE BARGAINING:

V
AREA OF
INDUSTRIAL CONFLICT

Preface

This book is intended for readers in liberal arts and business school curriculums and for business and union people with little legal background. It stresses the institutional framework in which the government structure of collective bargaining is cast. Though the book is not intended for lawyers, members of the legal profession might find it useful to gain an appreciation and an understanding of the impact of government in the field of labor relations. The study deals with the major trends in the law of collective bargaining, the reasons for these trends, and their consequences on the overall functioning of collective bargaining.

The law of labor relations has little meaning in the absence of an understanding of the dynamics of labor unions and collective bargaining. Consequently, attention has been devoted to the labor relations environment in which the legal structure operates. Moreover, where appropriate, there is economic analysis of the problems resulting from the efforts of government to define the rights, duties, and obligations of labor unions and employers in the area of labor relations and collective bargaining. In this manner, it is hoped that the reader will be in a better position to evaluate public policy in labor relations.

The structure of the book strikes a balance between the development of the law of collective bargaining and current problems of labor relations. Through Part Three an analysis is made of the general sweep of events from 1806 through the Wagner Act era. Parts Four and Five highlight the effects of Taft-Hartley and subsequent amendments on the operation of unions and collective bargaining. Part Six deals with the essential features of the Landrum-Griffin Act. Labor relations in the public sector are also dealt with in the last part. Included are texts of major federal labor statutes and a summary at the end of each chapter.

The difficulty of labor relations law, but also its challenge and attraction, is that the law is ever changing and developing. This, of course, is the justification for this second edition. Because the basic structure of the first edition has proved successful, it remains unchanged. What *is* new are doctrines established by the National Labor Relations Board and the courts since the publication of the original volume. In keeping with the goal of the first edition, not all the changes are treated; we have concentrated upon major developments of outstanding significance.

Among those receiving particular attention in the new edition are minority group problems under Taft-Hartley and civil rights' legislation; the *Collyer* doctrine; successor employer developments; changes in National Labor Relations Board jurisdiction; the so-called "make-whole" doctrine originally established in *Ex-Cell-O;* industrial conflict innovations; developments in the public sector; and developments in the control of internal union affairs established by Landrum-Griffin. How the Nixon NLRB has applied Taft-Hartley receives appropriate attention. Additional new developments of major importance are interwoven at the appropriate places.

The authors, of course, are grateful for the reception by the faculty and students of the first edition. As with the first edition, we believe the volume is amenable for a one semester course. Of course, depending upon the interests of the particular faculty member and the background of the class, the course could be limited to certain areas treated in the volume, which is written in a manner providing flexibility to adapt to particular faculty and student needs. In any event, we hope that the new volume will add to the understanding of labor relations law.

As always, we are indebted to more people than we can list. A large number of secretaries provided valuable typing assistance. Some of our colleagues were kind enough to read and comment on various sections of the manuscript. We owe them all a special debt of gratitude. We are especially indebted to Dr. Dale Yoder, to Dr. Karen Koziara, and to Dr. E. B. McNatt who read the entire manuscript and gave us valuable encouragement based on their years of experience with the subject. Our families have suffered the greatest costs of all. We are most grateful for their patience.

BENJAMIN J. TAYLOR
FRED WITNEY

LABOR
RELATIONS LAW

I INTRODUCTION TO COLLECTIVE BARGAINING

PROLOGUE. *This book deals with the evolution and current problems of the law of collective bargaining. What then is collective bargaining and what function does it perform in contemporary society? What is the relationship between labor organizations and collective bargaining? What are some salient features of the history and structure of the American labor union movement? What are the major sources of the law of collective bargaining? The answers to these questions provide the foundation for a meaningful appreciation of the impact of government on collective bargaining.*

1 Nature and Development of Collective Bargaining

THE NATURE OF COLLECTIVE BARGAINING

Collective bargaining means the joint determination by employees and employers of the problems of the employment relationship. Such problems include wage rates and wage systems, hours and overtime, vacations, discipline, work loads, classification of employees, layoffs, and worker retirement. The advent of collective bargaining does not give rise to these problems. Rather they are germane to the industrial relations environment, and exist with or without unionization. In the absence of the organization of workers, the employer solves these problems on a unilateral basis. The framework in which they are settled will be conditioned by the employer's conceptions of fairness, attitudes toward maximization of profit, social responsibility, and knowledge of current labor market conditions. Collective bargaining means that the employer does not unilaterally determine all the conditions of employment. Through this vehicle, the employer and the representatives of his workers attempt to reach a meeting of minds on wages, hours, and other terms and conditions of work. If the parties fail to reach a satisfactory adjustment, the result can be an interruption of production. Collective stopping of work by workers constitutes a strike. The interruption is termed a lockout if the employer controls the timing and duration of the work stoppage. However, the threat of a strike or lockout, and the stoppage itself, are the prods which stimulate management and unions to find a peaceful solution to the problems of employment. Indeed, the strike is an integral part of the collective bargaining process. Without it, collective bargaining does not function effectively as the vehicle of joint determination of the issues of the employment relationship.

Although collective bargaining embraces a wide variety of the problems of employment, the process by no means solves each and every issue of employment. At any one stage in the development of the socioeconomic environment, certain problems of employment appear ill suited for the collective bargaining process. For example, few people thirty-five years ago would have argued that pensions constitute a proper subject for collective bargaining. As the socioeconomic environment changes, the content of bargaining likewise becomes altered. Moreover, at any one time there are a variety of employment issues whch cannot be solved through the framework of collective bargaining. This does not mean that unions should not be consulted in these areas which appear beyond collective bargaining. Progressive managements see the value of taking the union into their confidence on issues that can be solved only imperfectly, if at all, through collective bargaining. In this way, the cooperation of the labor organization is fostered, and the general prosperity of the firm advanced. Few collective bargaining systems require management to consult with the union prior to the investment of new capital in the business. However, since such investment could affect the economic status of its workers, the firm might profit from consultation with their representatives concerning plans for expansion. Workers are becoming increasingly aware of the impact of foreign investment and production on their jobs.

Collective bargaining systems, moreover, cannot provide the answer to each human problem of employment. Many of them still must be disposed of with common sense and fair dealing. Despite the broad character of collective bargaining, the process simply cannot resolve the myriad of human employment problems. Collective bargaining is highly elastic in character. It can accommodate the most difficult of employment problems. But the very nature of collective bargaining makes the process unwieldy for the solution of each and every human problem within the employment relationship. Collective bargaining is ostensibly *collective* in nature. It deals with the problems common to large groups of workers. It can provide for wage systems, but the process will not resolve the question of whether or not John Jones can leave the job two hours early to take his wife home from the hospital. Of course, the union will protect workers who receive arbitrary treatment from management. But this is a negative or defensive mechanism. Human problems should be resolved positively and in a manner which will meet the standards of justice and industrial efficiency. This can best be accomplished outside the formalized structure of collective bargaining.

A balanced view of collective bargaining aids in the understanding of its limitations and potentialities. It cannot solve every human employment problem. Nor does it provide the solution for each and every economic problem confronting the firm, the industry, or the nation. For example, collective bargaining cannot solve the problem of depression-type unemployment. However, union-management relations, of which collective bargaining is a part, can fulfill a much wider mission than is assigned to collective bargaining in contemporary society. In the last analysis collective bargaining is essentially a negative and protective institution. It limits the authority of management, imposes obligations on employers, and assures workers of a series of industrial rights. These, of course, are the historical and traditional purposes of unions.

There is, however, a much wider area in which union-management relations can operate. This area embraces the issues vital to the economic prosperity of the firm, industry, and nation. Matters of plant layout, sales and distribution, plant locale, investment, method of acquisition of new capital, pricing, and the like are commonly regarded as foreign to union-management solution. No labor contract, for example, can effectively provide for the method by which a firm should raise $500,000 of emergency-needed capital. The economic conditions of the particular time must determine such a decision. However, to say that such issues are beyond collective bargaining does not infer that they are beyond union-management dealings. Indeed, consultation between management and unions over such business problems would probably increase the long-run and over-all harmony of the relationship. Such collective *dealings* (not collective *bargaining*) if conducted in good faith should do much to advance the productive potential of American industry and American manpower.[1] It would mean a more mature approach to the economic problems of the firm, the industry, and the nation.

THE MAINSPRINGS OF UNIONISM

The union is the vehicle of collective bargaining. What affects the growth and effectiveness of unions conditions the over-all vitality of the collective bargaining process. This does not mean that the development of unionism and of collective bargaining proceed at the same rate. For a time there can be unions without collective bargaining. Such a condition can arise when employers refuse to recognize unions or negotiate labor contracts even though employees have organized labor unions. However, in the long run, unions and collective bargaining are two sides of the same coin because unions go out of existence if they are not successful in gaining collective bargaining recognition and obtaining contracts. If unions are weak and of ephemeral character, collective bargaining will not be much of a factor in the society. Consequently, the forces surrounding collective bargaining are those which stimulate unionism. What then are the mainsprings of the union movement?

The contemporary economic environment operates to render ineffective the effort of the worker to improve his economic status through individual bargaining. Characteristics of modern industry (including features such as large-scale production, concentration of ownership, and the divorce of ownership from control) have encouraged workers to utilize collective action to improve their standard of living. It is the totality of the economic environment which has served to stimulate the development and growth of the labor movement.

Before the rise of the modern factory system, there was little need for collective bargaining in the United States. When agriculture constituted the nation's leading pursuit, almost every individual owned his own tools and in effect acted as his own employer. This applied not only to agricultural workers but also to workers who performed duties in the small handicraft shops prevalent during the early days of the United States. The need for collective bargaining arises when the worker sells his labor to another person. Its need is intensified when a nation's economy is organized around companies so large that the individual worker loses his importance to the enterprise.

Shortly after the turn of the present century, industry replaced agriculture as the nation's top pursuit. The small handicraft shop gave way to the modern industrial facility, which in some cases employed several thousands of workers. By the beginning of World War I, the vast majority of the nation's labor force was employed in industry. In 1950, out of a labor force of about 63 million, approximately 46 million were employed in nonagricultural industrial facilities and only about 8.5 million earned their living on farms. By 1973 the civilian labor force increased to over 86 million workers. Nearly 78 million are now engaged in nonagricultural employment. However, manufacturing is no longer viewed as the vast employer that it once was. Production workers on manufacturing payrolls number only about 14.5 million. But government and services combined employ over 25 million workers.[2] As a result of this trend, the centers of population of the nation continue to shift from the rural to the urban areas. This change has resulted in many political, sociological, and economic problems.

Still, the mere fact that the American economy shifted from agriculture to industry and is now shifting to services and government employment does not automatically mean the rise of the union movement. The fundamental prerequisite for the emergence of a permanent union movement rests in the development of a permanent working class. In addition, it is necessary that workers recognize the limited alternatives available to them in labor markets. A stable and permanent union movement emerges when workers recognize that their status as workers is not a temporary phenomenon and that they will experience a rising standard of living only insofar as they are able to maintain employment. Periodic rises in the unemployment rate and relatively slow wage advances make union membership attractive to some workers.

This principle of union growth is underscored by American experience. For many years, workers themselves were not greatly interested in collective bargaining: such was their attitude even though the American economy was shifting from agriculture to industry. Why was this the case? While American industry was expanding at a rapid rate and the western frontier was still relatively unexploited, the opportunities for upward occupational mobility for workers and their children were abundant. As a matter of fact, before the exhaustion of the western frontier, a good number of workers were able to push west to begin their own enterprises. All of this meant that many workers believed that their period of service as industrial workers was only an interlude until they found the opportunity to start up their own businesses. As long as this attitude prevailed, there was no definite working class consciousness, and a permanent labor movement was precluded. However, with the maturing of American industry and the declining opportunites of the western frontier, workers became aware that the opportunities for them or their children to advance from the ranks of the employees to the proprietor class were remote. They learned that the attitudes of vested economic interests toward new competition, the large amounts of capital needed to finance a new venture of even modest size, and the growing concentration of ownership of American industrial facilities all served to block elevation to the proprietor class. These forces produced a permanent working class philosophy. The result was a permanent union movement.

It is not only the institutional arrangement of modern industry that stimulates workers to organize into unions. The structure of the contemporary labor and product markets adds to the propensity for unionism. The development of national and international markets provides the framework for wage cutting. Employers in some industries compete vigorously for sales on the basis of lower prices. To protect profit margins and still garner the lion's share of the product market, employers are under constant pressure to reduce wages or to increase productivity. This is particularly true in industries in which labor costs represent a sizable percentage of total costs. Moreover, the opportunity for wage cutting becomes greater in periods of severe unemployment. Labor unions represent the worker's adjustment to this feature of the economic environment. To resist the downward pressure on wages, some workers organize labor unions.

The pressure of economic life requires the complete organization of industries. Once a union gains a foothold in an industry, it is compelled to organize most of its firms. To do otherwise is to invite the demise of the labor organization. Nonunion firms, operating with lower labor standards, may be able to undersell their organized rivals. Such a state of affairs, if unchecked, would eventually result either in the elimination of the union or in the bankruptcy of the firms organized. Clearly, the structure of labor, product, and services markets provides a mainspring toward unionization and of equal importance, widespread organization.

The economic side of collective bargaining is by no means the only stimulus for unionism. It is, of course, possible that unions may provide their members with better pay, vacations, paid holidays, pensions, and the like. However, workers form labor unions not only for economic considerations but also because of psychological and social factors. Not all results of unions find their way into the pay envelope. Workers want to have a voice in the determination of things of importance in the bargaining unit. Personal dignity attaches to the extent to which they accomplish this objective.

An individual is not a well-rounded personality unless he is creative. In modern society, the quality of creativeness attaches itself mainly to the job. But creativeness means more than the mere completion of the particular task. To be creative, the worker must have the opportunity to participate effectively in the determination of the over-all environment in which the job is performed. He must be able to do this without fear of reprisal. He must be convinced that his recommendations will be given serious consideration. A work environment which precludes this demonstration of self-determination on the part of the workers makes for thwarted and troubled personalities. Unions may provide employees with the opportunity to satisfy the psychological need for the development of a well-rounded personality. Collective bargaining offers the vehicle for self-expression and thereby services the psychological needs of workers.

THE EXTENT AND SIGNIFICANCE OF COLLECTIVE BARGAINING

Although little need existed for trade unionism prior to the industrialization of the nation, the rate of growth of the organized labor movement did not keep pace with the country's industrial development. Neither has labor organization in the services and government employment areas proceeded at the same rate. By 1920 about 30 million people were engaged in nonagricultural pursuits. In contrast, the number of workers in trade unions numbered about 5 million. From 1794, the year in which the first union was formed in the United States, until the New Deal period, the figure of 5 million represented the top level of union membership. Union membership declined to less than 3 million during the severe economic depression of the early thirties.

After 1935 union membership increased in large numbers. By 1950 approximately 15 million workers were members of labor unions as compared with the 3 million of 1933. Approximately 20 million workers belonged to labor organizations in 1973. The importance of the labor union movement, however, is not measured by the moderateness of the trade unions in organizing the workers of the nation. Reference to the mere numbers of the labor movement does not provide an accurate standard to evaluate its importance.

Union policy and activities in the highly organized areas affect not only these particular industries but the operation of the entire economy. The modern economy is a highly integrated machine. Anything of importance which takes place in one area of the economy will produce effects throughout industry. Union wage policy in basic steel, for example, could cause repercussions throughout the entire economy. No particular segment of industry is isolated from the effects of changes in wages, costs, and prices in any significant branch of industry. Since labor unions operate in the most vital parts of the nation's economy, they exert an important influence on the entire economic structure.

THE LEGAL CLIMATE

The progress of organized labor during the New Deal period was no accident. It resulted partly from the operation of a legal environment which fostered unionism. New Deal labor laws outlawed employer antiunion practices which for years had stifled unionization. No longer was government an ally to management at the time of labor disputes. A contributory factor making for union progress in the New Deal period was the revival of business activity. However, the growth of unionism was rooted also in the favorable legal environment and not only in improved economic conditions.

The legal climate is one of the principal factors conditioning the effectiveness and the scope of collective bargaining. Unionism flourishes under a favorable legal climate and is retarded in a hostile legal environment. Labor history reveals that public policy toward collective bargaining has not been uniform. When this policy has been favorable, a rapid rate of growth of the labor movement has ensued. The reverse has been the case when the legal environment has been unfavorable. A purpose of this book is to sketch the salient features of the development of the law of collective bargaining. What course the law of labor relations takes in the future will largely determine the position of collective bargaining in our nation. Only through an accurate knowledge of the roots of the law of collective bargaining can we intelligently influence its future development.

In analyzing the character of labor relations law, a careful examination must be made of several sources of that law. Important decisions of the judiciary must be considered. For many years, the courts determined the elements of the law of collective bargaining. The judiciary chartered the legal boundaries of union conduct. Subsequently, statutory law became more important than the common law as the determiner of the content of labor relations law. However, the influence of the courts on the character of labor law is still of great importance. The Supreme Court of the United States, the custodian of the federal Constitution, possesses the power to review all legislation in the light of the standards of the nation's basic document. In short, it has the authority to invalidate statutory law, including labor legislation, on the grounds of conflict with the Constitution. Upon many occasions, the high court utilizes its power of judicial review to strike down legislation calculated to strengthen the union movement. In still other ways the Supreme Court plays an important role in the shaping of the structure of labor relations law.

Action of the legislative branch of government merits close attention. Labor relations legislation ultimately became of paramount importance in the story of the development of organized labor. Since 1932 Congress enacted four major labor relations laws which have set the course of federal labor policy. These laws—Norris–La Guardia, the Wagner Act, Taft-Hartley, and Landrum-Griffin—will provide the framework for much of our subsequent discussion. Important decisions of labor agencies, such as the National Labor Relations Board (NLRB), must also be considered. Labor boards are indeed an important source of labor law. Thus the NLRB interpretation of the Wagner Act and Taft-Hartley largely determines the practical application of these laws. The fact that administrative rulings of labor boards are reviewable by the courts does not detract from their importance in the shaping of labor relations law. Finally, the executive branch of government as a source of labor law must receive attention. Acting within their legal areas of operation, the President of the United States and the governors of the states influence the labor relations environment. During war periods the President historically becomes a particularly important figure in the labor arena. Also the executive branch of government becomes important when the President of the United States and the governors intervene in important strikes. Another important example of executive action occurred in 1962 when President Kennedy issued Executive Order 10988 which provided a measure of protection for federal employees to engage in collective bargaining. Some states followed this precedent and influenced the growth of public employee unions on the state level.

The efforts of Congress and state legislatures to promote unionization were frequently thwarted by the judiciary. The legislative branch of government would have protected the right of employees to self-organization and collective bargaining. However, until 1937, the Supreme Court refused to sanction such legislation, declaring such efforts of Congress and state legislatures to be unconstitutional. Indeed, one of the most interesting aspects of labor relations law is this tussle between the judiciary and the legislative branches of government on the labor issue. Why this lag between the judiciary and the legislative branches occurred will subsequently become evident. Moreover, the effect of this conflict on the development of the union movement will be highlighted.

As never before, a careful analysis of the law of labor relations is necessary. Collective bargaining is in the spotlight. Almost every day the newspapers detail organizational efforts of unions, strikes, and employer responses to union tactics. An understanding of the development and current posture of the law influencing the labor relations environment is required if the nation is to deal intelligently with one of its most important problems.

SUMMARY

Collective bargaining involves the joint determination of work conditions by workers and employers. The process is one part of union-management relations, and there exists the possibility that collective dealings (not *collective bargaining*) between unions and employers in areas regarded normally as beyond collective bargaining may constitute the proper structure for negotiations. Such may be the case in public employment.

Unionism represents the adjustment by workers to the problems of modern industrialism. Since unionism serves the economic, psychological, and social needs of workers on the job, the labor union remains as a persistent and vital institution in contemporary society. The progress of unions has not been uniform. Their growth has been influenced by the socioeconomic and legal complex. After 1935 the power of unions and the extent of collective bargaining have greatly increased. By 1973 the conditions of employment of about 20 million workers were directly determined through collective bargaining. Moreover, the importance of the labor union movement is not measured by mere reference to the absolute numbers of workers in labor unions. Indeed, if membership in all associations that use union tactics is totaled, the import of unionization may be more impressive than is often thought.

This book is concerned with the legal framework in which the collective bargaining process operates. To understand this framework, reference must be made to statutes, court decisions, and rulings by administrative agencies, such as the NLRB. Such an investigation is of vital significance for the power of government can aid or hinder labor organizations.

NOTES

[1] See Alexander R. Heron, *Beyond Collective Bargaining* (Palo Alto: Stanford University Press, 1948).

[2] U.S. Department of Labor, Bureau of Labor Statistics, *Monthly Labor Review*, Vol. 96, No. 10 (October, 1973), pp. 93, 95.

II

LEGAL SUPPRESSION OF COLLECTIVE BARGAINING

PROLOGUE.   *Prior to 1932 the legal climate precluded the growth and effective implementation of collective bargaining. What is the evidence to support this thesis? What forces of government combined to establish a restrictive legal environment for unionism? The answers are to be found in examining the conspiracy doctrine, the use of the injunction in labor disputes, the "yellow-dog" contract, and the application of the antitrust statutes to labor union activities.*

2 Labor Unions: Unlawful Combinations

THE EARLY UNION MOVEMENT: ITS SOCIOECONOMIC CONTENT

The United States ranked second only to Great Britain in industrial activity in the first half of the nineteenth century. The trend of the future was set during this period even though agriculture remained the nation's leading occupation. In 1820, of all workers gainfully employed, about 72 percent earned their living on the nation's farms. Manufacturing and the mechanical arts accounted for only about 12 percent. However, the trend was definite and unmistakable. By 1860, the number of workers gainfully employed in agriculture decreased to about 60 percent, while manufacturing and the mechanical arts accounted for about 18 percent.[1] Indeed, the rapid rise of manufacturing after 1800 is one of the outstanding features in the development of the nation's economy. By 1860 the gross value of manufactured products was around $1,800 million.[2] This was ten times the estimated figure for 1810. In the nation's irresistible march to industrialism, household manufacturing became a casualty. By 1860 the factory generally replaced the household as the locale for manufacturing. The factory turned out cheaper and better products than could be produced in the home. The machine required the factory environment for its effective utilization. Factory methods were first applied to metal and iron products, food, and furniture. The increase in cotton manufacturing was representative of what was to occur in other industries. In 1808 there were but 8,000 spindles in all the nation. In 1860 more than 5 million were in operation. One writer reported that by 1850 "it had become possible for rich and poor alike to dress adequately and attractively in cloth of American manufacture."[3]

Many factors accounted for the rapid rise of American manufacturing.

13

Growing machine technology was the heart of the nation's factory system. For example, mechanical production of cotton was made possible by the invention of the cotton gin, which insured an adequate supply of fiber for the mills. If machines constituted the heart of the factory system, an adequate system of transportation was its arteries, for the development of transportation stimulated the growth of national markets. In 1830 the nation boasted of twenty-three miles of rail transportation. By 1860 this figure increased to 30,626.[4] Railroads connected the East and West and supplemented a rapidly improving river and road transportation system. Thus, in 1812 it took six days to go from Philadelphia to Pittsburgh by stagecoach and at least sixteen days for freight; by 1854 the railroad covered the distance in fifteen hours.[5] The growth of population also contributed significantly to the advance of American industry. The number of people in the United States doubled between 1820 and 1840. This growth broadened the market for factory goods and, of equal importance, provided the labor supply for the nation's factories. Moreover, new sources of capital became available in the early 1820s. Between 1820 and 1840 investment in American factories rose from $50 million to $250 million.[6] The development of natural resources for power and raw materials likewise added impetus to the growth of American industry. Additional factors were also involved: the westward expansion made the nation more dependent on American goods than on England's commodities; business quickly learned of the security of the sheltered market and successfully pressured tariff bills through Congress in the 1820s; and government inducements to business in the form of tax considerations, bounties, and miscellaneous special privileges aided American industrial growth.

The rise of the factory system in this period did more than serve as a harbinger of American industrial greatness. It produced a distinct labor class and thereby created the basis for modern labor problems: the adjustment of workers to the economic and social problems of industrialism. In the colonial era a worker normally passed through the stages of apprentice and journeyman, and eventually became an independent master-craftsman. In this role he performed simultaneously the functions of laborer, employer, capitalist, merchant, and entrepreneur. However, as the factory system arose, the economy took on its contemporary characteristic of specialization of function. And this meant that an increasing number of workers were destined to remain "hired hands" throughout their lives.

As the market for the products of industry widened under the stimulus of an ever-improving transportation system, the economic position of the laboring class was changed. The products made in one locality competed with those turned out in other areas. When an employer found that he was being undersold by a rival producer, he frequently reduced wages to wipe out the price differential and still maintain profit margins. As a matter of fact, many of the strikes in the early 1800s were protests against wage cutting. For example, in Manayunk, Pennsylvania, a textile manufacturing town, there was a strike in 1828 against a 25 percent reduction in pay. Commons in this connection declared, "Even at the old prices, it was said, a spinner could make only 'from $7.50 to $8.50 per week for himself by working the full period of twelve hours daily, and in doing this he actually earned for his employers from $40 to $50 per week.'"[7] Indeed, low wages were the lot for many of the newly created working class. This was particularly true in the New England textile factories which employed large numbers of women and children, groups notorious for their weak bargaining power. In some cases, whole families were employed in the factories, but their earnings were low. Thus, four members of a family between April 25 and May 19, 1832, worked a total of 93 days for a net return of $18.30.[8]

Other conditions of work in the early factories also reflected competitive pressures of product markets. Hours of work were long relative to current standards, frequently ranging from twelve to fourteen per day. The lack of provisions for the prevention of accidents had not advanced to the point of becoming a public issue. Little attention was paid to the establishment of healthy working conditions. In short, in the race to create profitable enterprises, the early factory owners generally had little time to pay attention to the welfare of their employees. Thus, one historian, speaking on the lot of labor in the 1800–1850 period, concludes: "Although the factory system from the beginning brought to society in general increased leisure and many conveniences the value of which can scarcely be measured, the people whose sweat and toil made these changes possible profited little."[9]

Profits and the exploitation of new markets occupied the major proportion of the new factory owner's time. Riches stimulated the desire for still more riches. That the worker shared but little in the fruits of the newly created industrial system was of little concern to the predominantly agriculturally oriented public. Many publicly endorsed the philosophy of Alexander Hamilton, who once declared, "All communities divide themselves into the few and the many. The first are rich and well born and the other, the mass of people who seldom judge or determine right."[10] Social responsibility was not to become an important element of the American industrial system until industry grew to a more secure position in the economy. The precedent for labor unrest was set by the uncertainties of firm and industry survival due to fierce domestic and international competition. The framework for the labor-management strife of contemporary society was erected at the dawn of American industrialism.

CONSPIRACY DOCTRINE APPLIED TO UNIONS

Stimulated by a more rapid rate of socioeconomic change, some workers formed labor unions to protect their vested interests. The American labor movement dates from the early part of the nineteenth century, though ephemeral organizations and sporadic worker protests occurred previously. In the early 1800s organizations of a more permanent character were formed to provide workers with a shield of protection from the consequences of the new industrialism.

Efforts at organization of the early unions were confined largely to the skilled craftsmen of the shoemaking, weaving, hatmaking, and printing trades rather than among the lesser skilled factory workers. This feature of labor union development is easily explained. It is commonly accepted that the conditions of the factory workers were much worse than those of the skilled craftsmen. But many factors operated to forestall the organization of the hired hands of the newly created factories. These workers, unlike the craftsmen, were very easily replaced due to the surplus of such workers. Training for the jobs was practically unnecessary, as witness the large number of children who successfully held down factory jobs. Moreover, a high proportion of the factory workers were women and children, groups which for many reasons were not readily organizable. The factory worker did not possess the necessary insight into the socioeconomic forces released by the growing industrial society. This is not surprising for many of these workers were uprooted from the farms, and had little opportunity except for the most meager type of education. Although the evidence is not clear, one could say with a degree of certainty that a sizable proportion of the early factory workers were illiterate. The craftsmen, of more worldly experience, quickly understood the necessity of effective organization of labor to meet the problems of the new structural arrangement of industry. This is not to say that the factory workers did not protest against working conditions. On the contrary, they participated in many strikes, most frequently carried out against wage cutting. However, these strikes were poorly managed and generally unsuccessful. No union can maintain itself for long when it cannot strike successfully. Thus the early attempts at unionization by unskilled factory workers were usually unsuccessful. Indeed, it was not until the birth of the Congress of Industrial Organizations (CIO) in 1935 that the nation's factory workers organized on a successful and permanent basis. Even then, their success was due to a more favorable government policy, which was not present in earlier years.

Accordingly, the American labor movement first took root among the craft workers. They occupied a strategic position. Employers could not readily replace them, for their skills were not easily learned. For this reason, they had a fair opportunity to win strikes. They were usually considered more permanent followers of a trade, and they quickly discerned the value of a well-disciplined and militant union movement. The early union movement differed sharply from the complex and intricate structure of the modern labor union movement. The early movement was localized in character. The rise of the national union did not take place until toward the end of the first half of the nineteenth century. In this early period there was no industry-wide or semi-industry-wide bargaining. Collective bargaining, where it existed, was carried on between individual employers and local unions. No federations of labor unions, similar to the American Federation of Labor (AFL) or the Congress of Industrial Organizations, were in operation.

In spite of the localized structure of the early movement, the unions engaged in many activities that to this day are pursued by the modern labor union. Many of the early organizations engaged in successful strikes for higher wages. There is also evidence that a sympathetic strike took place in 1799.[11] In addition, the early unions demanded the closed shop, paid out strike benefits, engaged in picketing and boycott activities, and upon occasion disciplined their members.

Of the early unions the shoe and bootmakers' organizations were by far the most aggressive. Many of the other unions had a sporadic existence, the craftsmen binding themselves together to carry out periodic strikes and then dissolving after the strikes were terminated. In contrast, the shoemakers' unions had a permanent existence during the early period. The Philadelphia shoemakers, for example, organized in 1792 and maintained their organization permanently for many years. So successful were these shoemakers' unions that shoemaker employers' associations were established, which in part had as their objective the neutralization of the craftsmen unions. For a time employers resorted to economic pressure tactics calculated to defeat the labor unions. Among the most effective weapons was the employment of replacements willing to work for wages below the scale demanded by unionists.

In 1806 some employers struck upon a new method to deal with the shoemakers' unions. They sought the aid of the courts. This procedure—the solicitation of government aid in labor disputes—remains to this day a persistent element in the industrial relations pattern. It is noteworthy that the precedent was established as early as 1806.

In that year the Philadelphia shoemaker employers charged that unions were conspiracies. As conspiracies, they contended, labor unions were unlawful combinations. A conspiracy, generally defined, is the combination of two or more persons who band together to prejudice the rights of others or of society. Under the doctrine of conspiracy would fall, for example, the plot of a group of people who work together to bring about conviction of an innocent person. Likewise, the conspiracy doctrine would apply to the action of a group that plotted to overthrow an established government. Before conspiracy can be charged, it must be shown that the group has caused or will cause an injustice to other people or to society. An interesting characteristic about the conspiracy doctrine is that conspirators can be indicted and found guilty before they commit any overt act. For example, it is a crime to plot the murder of a person even though the evil plan is not executed. Another feature of importance is that an action by one person, though legal, becomes illegal when carried out by a group. This characteristic of the conspiracy doctrine had particular significance in the labor union conspiracy cases.

How did the employers attempt to prove that labor unions were conspiracies and hence unlawful organizations? How did unions, according to this point of view, prejudice the rights of others or of society? How did employers support the contention that labor unions by regulating wages caused "great damage and prejudice of other artificers, and journeymen in the said act and occupation of a (shoemaker), to the evil example of others, and against the peace and dignity of the Commonwealth of Pennsylvania"?[12]

THE CASE AGAINST THE UNIONS

Employers based their case against the unions partly on the economic doctrines of the classical school of economics. It was to be expected that the people responsible for the prosecution of unionists would be influenced by the economic doctrines of their times.[13] However, the pure elements of classical theory were not realized in practice. This placed a greater burden on the labor factor than was commonly assumed. Resistance by labor to such philosophies resulted because full employment was not the norm of operations.

Control of wages by unions, it was argued, "is an unnatural, artificial means of raising the price of work beyond its standard, and taking an undue advantage of the public."[14] It was contended that the increase of wages by union pressure leads to higher prices of commodities. This in turn results in the reduction of demand for products, causing unemployment in the community. The net effect of the union, therefore, was to cause injury to the community, damage commerce and trade, and prejudice the rights of all workers. So ran the general argument of the prosecution.

In addition, it was argued that nonunion workers were injured by the refusal of unionists to work beside them. It was contended that "A master who employs fifteen or twenty hands is called upon to discharge that journeyman who is not a member of the body; if he refuses they all leave him whatever may be the situation of his business."[15]

In the early trials, much was made of the fact that labor unions were declared unlawful in England by both common law and statutory legislation.[16] Prosecutors urged that English law established a precedent for American courts. In his charge to the jury, the presiding judge in one conspiracy case declared that "the common law of England . . . must be deemed to be applicable. . . ."[17] In other words, the American courts should be bound by the doctrines and laws prevailing in England. The prosecution conceded, however, that workers as individuals had the right to take action to increase their wages. Individual bargaining for higher wages, even individual quitting of work because of dissatisfaction with working conditions, was legal. The charge was that the combining of workers to force higher wages constituted illegal conduct. On many occasions, the principle of conspiracy law was cited where "what may be lawful in an individual, may be criminal in a number of individuals combined, with a view to carrying it into effect."[18] In this connection, the prosecution in the first (1806) conspiracy case declared:

> Let it be well understood that the present action is not intended to introduce the doctrine that a man is not at liberty to fix any price whatsoever upon his own labor. Our position is that no man is at liberty to combine, conspire, confederate, and unlawfully agree to regulate the whole body of workmen in the city. The defendants are not indicted for regulating their own individual wages, but for undertaking by a combination to regulate the price of the labor of others as well as their own.[19]

In summary, the charge against the unions was that (1) labor organizations are conspiracies because they injure society and prejudice the rights of individuals; and (2) unions were declared unlawful in England and English law is a compelling precedent for American courts. These factors led one of the judges in the very first conspiracy case to remark that "a combination of workmen to raise their wages may be considered in a twofold point of view: one is to benefit themselves . . . the other is to injure those who do not join their society. The rule of law condemns both."[20]

CHARACTERISTICS OF THE CONSPIRACY TRIALS

From 1806 until 1842 there were seventeen trials in which labor unions were charged as conspiracies. Of these, shoemakers' unions were involved nine times. In all cases the unionists were charged with engaging in a criminal conspiracy. This meant that if convicted the defendants could have been imprisoned. However, penalties, when assessed, were in the form of small fines. In passing sentence, judges threatened a more serious penalty for second offenses. The effect of the judgments was to discourage union activities.

A Philadelphia court decided the first conspiracy case against a union in 1806. Later trials were held in Pittsburgh, Baltimore, Buffalo, Hudson, and New York. The doctrine established in the Philadelphia case spread to the other cities. Courts always pay close attention to decisions developed in other judicial jurisdictions. Had the Philadelphia court ruled labor unions to be lawful associations, it is likely that few, if any, prosecutions in the other cities would have taken place.

The worker defendants in the conspiracy cases were tried by juries. An analysis of the composition of the juries reveals that the jurors were representative of the merchant and employer groups. For example, in the first conspiracy trial, three of the jurors were grocers, two made their living as innkeepers, one was a tavernkeeper, and the others respectively were designated as "merchant," "hatter," "tobacconist," "taylor," and "bottler." In the early days of our nation property qualifications were generally a prerequisite for jury duty. Workers, who held little or no property, were generally excluded from jury service. This feature undoubtedly influenced the outcome in the conspiracy trials. In addition, the decisions were influenced, not only by the social and economic predilections of the jurors, but by the general background of the judges presiding at the trials. Some of the judges made little effort to conceal their antiunion feelings. For example, one judge, while making his charge to the jury, declared, "If these evils (organization of workers in labor unions) were unprovided for by the law now existing, it would be necessary that laws should be made to restrain them."

IN DEFENSE OF LABOR UNIONS

Competent legal counsel defended the workers brought to trial in the conspiracy cases. Their preparation was such that they could make a thorough presentation of the workers' position. Arguments offered by the defense counsels reflected modern thinking on collective bargaining. The workers involved in the conspiracy cases had the benefit of learned and articulate counsel. Their conviction under the conspiracy doctrine was not attributable to the lack of ability of the defense lawyers. Workers through their lawyers argued that labor unions do not produce the evils so vividly portrayed by the prosecution. No empirical data or evidence was presented to bear out the prosecution's arguments, it was contended. It was also argued that collective action undertaken by workers to raise wages did not set in motion economic forces that resulted in hardship to the community. Defense counsels vigorously, but in vain, pointed to the positive contributions that labor unions could make to the economic and social life of the community. According to the defendants, English law did not apply to American courts for by the Revolution we divorced ourselves from British rule and "have shaken off the supremacy of English law."[21]

Furthermore, the defense objected to being tried under the common law. It was argued that no statute or action by the legislative branch of government outlawed labor unions. Accordingly, why should a court outlaw this form of association when the legislature, the representative branch of government, had not seen fit to take this action? Freedom of action, it was further contended, applied not only to business people in the conduct of their economic activities, but applied equally to workers who sought to advance their position in the economy by collective action. The doctrine of liberty was not reserved for any particular economic group; instead, it equally embraced workers, farmers, and merchants. These arguments, presented in a most lucid and convincing manner, failed to sway the courts, for when the juries were polled, labor unions were indicted as unlawful associations. It seemed for a time that there was no place for them in American economic life.

THE STATE OF AFFAIRS BEFORE
COMMONWEALTH v. HUNT

In spite of the conspiracy cases, workers continued to form labor organizations. Although the negative legal environment was "effective . . . in checking the early trade societies," Selig Perlman, a foremost labor historian, reported that the early trade union movement was retarded even more by the industrial depression which set in after the conclusion of the Napoleonic Wars.[22] By 1836 there were several hundred local trade unions established in leading industrial cities of the East. The structure of the labor movement was taking on a more modern appearance. Before 1842 city centrals were formed in practically every eastern city in which local trade unions operated. National labor organizations also made their appearance during the years in which the courts applied the conspiracy doctrine to organized labor. In addition, in this period the first federation of labor unions in the United States was established. The National Trades' Union, as this federation was called, was organized in New York City in 1834. At its first convention delegates appeared from many of the local unions and city centrals operating in New York, Philadelphia, Boston, Brooklyn, Poughkeepsie, and Newark. The federation sought to unite in one organization every local union, city central, and national labor union in the nation. The National Trades' Union had a striking resemblance to the present national federation, the AFL–CIO. Along with every other unit of the organized labor movement, it was swept away in the depression of 1837.

Thus many workers organized labor unions even though the courts declared their associations unlawful. Apparently, some workers felt that they had too much to gain from their labor unions to disband them because of the declaration of unlawfulness. It may be that workers believed that collective action was the prerequisite for the satisfactory settlement of their employment grievances. As a matter of fact, employees in this period did protest against many economic and political conditions.[23] In addition, significant changes were taking place in the area of political philosophy. The more liberal philosophy of Jackson and Jefferson was displacing the basically conservative doctrines of Alexander Hamilton. More attention was being given to the rights and liberties of individuals. Some writers in this period stressed that liberty and freedom in the area of economic affairs were not the monopoly of any group but were the common heritage of all citizens regardless of occupational status. The poor as well as the wealthy could take action to implement their right "to life, liberty, and the pursuit of happiness." Many workers interpreted the emphasis on liberty and the rights of man as a philosophical justification for organization and collective bargaining. Moreover, employees probably felt that they were not violating a law by organizing labor unions. No legislative branch of government embodied into statutory law the doctrines established by the courts in the conspiracy cases.

The totality of economic and political forces encouraged the formation of labor unions. Many workers believed that intolerable conditions of employment could be erased only through the process of organization and collective bargaining. They interpreted the liberal political writings of the period as the philosophical justification for collective bargaining. In such a context the application of the conspiracy doctrine to labor unions appeared incongruous. So incensed were the workers against the courts that in 1836 in New York and Washington mass protest demonstrations were held. During these demonstrations two judges, who had previously convicted unionists as criminal conspirators, were burned in effigy.[24]

LABOR UNIONS DECLARED LAWFUL
ORGANIZATIONS IN 1842

Such were the prevailing circumstances when Chief Justice Shaw, of the Supreme Judicial Court of Massachusetts, handed down his decision in the celebrated case, *Commonwealth* v. *Hunt*.[25] Before the case received his attention, a lower court found a group of shoemaker unionists guilty of conspiracy. The workers were convicted in the lower court because they refused to work for an employer who hired a shoemaker not a member of their union. The indictment was that the action of the unionists interfered with the right of the nonunion shoemaker to practice his trade. Shaw struck sharply and repeatedly at the conception that labor unions are evil organizations. He did state that, like any other organization, a labor union may exist for a "pernicious" and "dangerous" purpose. But he emphatically affirmed that labor unions may also exist for a "laudable" and "public spirited" purpose. Rather than inflicting injury on society, a union may advance the general welfare of the community by raising the standard of life of the members of the union. In this connection, Shaw pointed out that labor organizations "might be used to afford each other assistance in times of poverty, sickness, or distress; or to raise their intellectual, moral, and social conditions; or to make improvements in their art."

For a union to be indicted and convicted under the conspiracy doctrine, Shaw contended, it must be shown that the objectives of the union are unlawful or that the means employed to gain a lawful end are unlawful. Unless this can be proved, a labor organization must be considered a lawful association. In the case at hand Shaw held that the prosecution did not prove that the conspiracy doctrine should be applied to the labor union. In addition, the Chief Justice pointed out that all union members are not responsible if some of the body engage in unlawful acts. The law should only result in the conviction of the guilty party and not the other members of the association. The fact that labor unions may adopt measures "that may have a tendency to impoverish another; that is, to diminish his gains and profits" does not constitute a reason for indictment of the organization. Accordingly, Shaw held that union members may agree not to work for an employer who hired workers not members of their association. By the same token he implied that the action of workers to raise their wages by collective bargaining does not justify the application of the conspiracy doctrine. Though such action could reduce employer profits or even increase prices of commodities, the ultimate purpose of collective bargaining was to advance the welfare of members of the union.

COMMONWEALTH v. HUNT: ITS SIGNIFICANCE

Commonwealth v. *Hunt* was a landmark in the development of the law of industrial relations. Its effect was to dissolve the identity between the conspiracy doctrine and labor unions. Labor organizations taken by themselves were declared lawful organizations, and unionists were no longer to be regarded as criminals in the eyes of the courts. In general, most other courts, though not bound by the Massachusetts decision, followed the doctrine established by Shaw. *Commonwealth* v. *Hunt* did not, however, mean that the courts were to withdraw from the area of industrial relations. Shaw did not even advocate the complete removal of the conspiracy doctrine from the affairs of labor unions. In fact, after *Commonwealth* v. *Hunt*, the conspiracy doctrine was still utilized to circumscribe particular labor union activities. The courts continued to scrutinize the affairs and operations of labor unions. Where the court in a particular labor case felt that a union was seeking an unlawful objective, or using unlawful means to gain a lawful objective, judicial action was undertaken to harass the labor organization. In 1806, the year in which the conspiracy doctrine was first applied to labor unions, the courts invaded the field of industrial relations. To this day they continue to influence profoundly the direction and character of labor relations.

FROM THE CONSPIRACY DOCTRINE TO THE LABOR INJUNCTION

As noted, the courts applied the conspiracy doctrine to labor unions after Shaw handed down his decision in the celebrated Massachusetts case. Although the conspiracy cases after 1842 did not involve the legal status of labor unions per se, the courts made use of the doctrine to restrain a number of union activities. Professor E. E. Witte of the University of Wisconsin reported there were actually more labor conspiracy cases in the second half of the nineteenth century than in the first half.[26] During the period from 1863 to 1880 alone, labor unions were involved in eighteen conspiracy trials. In one of these cases, decided by the Supreme Court of New Jersey in 1867, the facts were essentially the same as those in *Commonwealth* v. *Hunt*.[27] A group of employees formed a labor organization, a rule of which was that its members could not work alongside nonunion workers. The unionists took action against an employer to force him to dismiss two nonunion employees. The New Jersey court was not bound by Shaw's decision in *Commonwealth* v. *Hunt*. Nevertheless, the New Jersey court concurred "entirely . . . with the principles embodied in the opinion" of the Massachusetts case, but still held that the New Jersey case was "clearly distinguishable."

After 1880 the courts infrequently made use of the conspiracy doctrine in labor disputes. This development, however, did not result from a shift in the basic attitude of the courts toward collective bargaining. Subsequent years were to underscore the antipathy of the judiciary to the efforts of workers to better their economic position through collective action. Neither did this change in court policy result from a shift in employers' attitude. They still sought the aid of the judiciary in their conflicts with organized labor. Finally, the conspiracy doctrine did not fade away because of the slackening of the organizational efforts of workers. Organized labor in the latter period of the nineteenth century made significant progress. The Knights of Labor,[28] a militant labor organization which sought to organize "men and women of every craft, creed, and color," was formed in 1869. By 1886 the Knights of Labor claimed a membership of seven hundred thousand, representing the high-water mark of union membership in the United States since the first labor organization was formed in 1794. The organization engaged in many successful strikes, particularly on the railroads controlled by that great financier of the period, Jay Gould. After 1886 the Knights of Labor declined rapidly, but in its place arose the American Federation of Labor. Even in the period of its infancy, the AFL gave promise of an organization well equipped to expand and implement the process of collective bargaining.

Some employers utilized economic pressure, which often erupted into open violence between the competitive groups. During and after strikes organized employees were often confronted with serious obstacles in their collective bargaining activities. For example, in the famous Homestead strike of 1892, the Carnegie Steel Corporation hired 300 men from the Pinkerton Detective Agency to serve as strikebreakers.[29] Before the conflict was over, at least a dozen of the workers and detectives were killed and scores injured. In this framework of opposition to collective bargaining, it was to be expected that antiunion employers would seek the aid of the courts. The conspiracy doctrine, of course, could be utilized to discourage the spread of trade unionism. Prosecution of workers in conspiracy trials, however, was a rather cumbersome affair. Some of the trials lasted several days and during this time unionists could continue to damage the position of employers. It was increasingly more difficult to procure the witnesses to offer testimony against worker defendants. Even of greater importance was the trend toward jury sympathy to worker organizations seeking to raise their economic standards through collective bargaining. Jury requirements were becoming liberalized with the result that workers might be called upon to help decide labor conspiracy cases. In addition, some jurors, aware of the spread of industrialization and the growth of large corporations, were prone to side with unionists. It was necessary to seek a new legal weapon to discourage unionism. The technique should meet the requirements of speed, simplicity, and definiteness. Above all, if employers were to resist organization of their firms, it was mandatory to remove the labor dispute from the jurisdiction of a potentially sympathetic jury. All these requirements were met by the labor injunction.

SUMMARY

The application of the conspiracy doctrine to labor unions was an important factor in resisting the spread of the American labor union movement. Employers, concerned with the vitality of the early union movement, enlisted the courts as an ally in their challenge to organized labor. The courts proved a vehicle for use by employers resisting organization of their employees. Juries indicted unionists as criminal conspirators who, unless restrained, would do evil to the community. This conclusion was reached by assuming that the economy would function best if it were free of organizations that placed unnatural restrictions upon it. Such an assumption was then, as now, open to debate.

Commonwealth v. *Hunt* was a landmark labor law case because it dissolved the identity between the conspiracy doctrine and labor unions. However, by 1842, the year in which the case was decided, employers and judges were casting around for a more effective legal device to contain unions than the cumbersome and uncertain conspiracy trial. Moreover, union activities were still subject to the conspiracy doctrine after *Commonwealth* v. *Hunt*, even though unions in themselves were regarded as legal institutions.

NOTES

[1] Chester W. Wright, *Economic History of the United States* (New York: McGraw-Hill Book Company, 1949), p. 331.
[2] *Ibid.*, p. 319.

³ James A. Barnes, *Wealth of the American People* (New York: Prentice-Hall, Inc., 1949), p. 224.

⁴ *Ibid.*, p. 219.

⁵ Thomas C. Cochran and William Miller, *The Age of Enterprise* (New York: The Macmillan Company, 1943), p. 7.

⁶ *Ibid.*, p. 14.

⁷ John R. Commons and Associates, *History of Labour in the United States* (New York: The Macmillan Company, 1926), p. 418.

⁸ Barnes, *op. cit.*, p. 288.

⁹ *Ibid.*, p. 285.

¹⁰ Charles A. Beard and Mary Beard, *The Rise of American Civilization* (New York: The Macmillan Company, 1927), p. 316.

¹¹ Selig Perlman, *A History of Trade Unionism in the United States* (New York: The Macmillan Company, 1929), p. 5.

¹² John R. Commons and Eugene A. Gilmore, *A Documentary History of American Industrial Society* (Cleveland: The Arthur H. Clark Company, 1910), III, 64.

¹³ Thus *The Wealth of Nations*, written by Adam Smith, commonly recognized as the leading spirit of the classical school of economics, appeared in 1776.

¹⁴ Commons and Gilmore, *op. cit.*, III, 228.

¹⁵ *Ibid.*, III, 70.

¹⁶ For a treatment of the application of English law to labor unions in this early period, see James M. Landis and Marcus Manoff, *Cases on Labor Law* (Chicago: The Foundation Press, 1942), pp. 1–28.

¹⁷ Commons and Gilmore, *op. cit.*, III, 384.

¹⁸ *Ibid.*, III, 69.

¹⁹ *Ibid.*, III, 68.

²⁰ *Ibid.*, III, 233.

²¹ *Ibid.*, III, 261.

²² Perlman, *op. cit.*, p. 7.

²³ Grievances of workers in this period included the length of the working day, imprisonment for theft, the Pennsylvania compulsory military system under which rich people could avoid military duty, the failure of legislatures to enact machine lien laws to protect workers' wages in the event of employer bankruptcy, lack of free public education for children of workers, and general political and economic inequity between the rich and the workers.

²⁴ E. E. Witte, "Early American Labor Cases," *Yale Law Journal*, XXXV (1926), 827.

²⁵ *Commonwealth of Massachusetts* v. *Hunt*, Massachusetts, 4 Metcalf 3 (1842).

²⁶ "Early American Labor Cases," *supra.*

²⁷ *State of New Jersey* v. *Donaldson*, 32 NSL 151 (1867).

²⁸ For an interesting account of the Knights of Labor, see T. V. Powderly, *The Path I Trod* (New York: Columbia University Press, 1940). Powderly was the second "General Master Workman" of the Knights of Labor.

²⁹ Perlman, *op. cit.*, p. 134.

3

Nature and Use
of the Labor Injunction

The use of the labor injunction in labor disputes constitutes one of the most controversial issues in the area of industrial relations law. Representatives of management and organized labor sharply disagree on the use of the injunction in employer-employee conflicts. Parties not directly affiliated with either management or labor have added to the controversy by contributing divergent views on the subject. Jurists, scholars, legislators, and even laymen from time to time have condemned or praised the labor injunction. Fundamental to the controversy is that the labor injunction provides the basis for court entry into labor disputes. To some, court intervention in labor disputes is undesirable. They claim that the use of the injunction in labor disputes not only has interfered with the right of workers to collective bargaining, but has caused no end of disturbance in labor-management relations. Some contend that the state of industrial relations is improved to the degree that the court's power to issue the injunction is circumscribed. Opponents of the labor injunction further claim that the collective bargaining process is strengthened and promoted, and management and labor representatives will be more prone to reach a rapid and peaceful settlement of their controversies when they become aware that the courts are powerless to determine the outcome of labor disputes.

On the other hand, there are those who argue that the use of the labor injunction is necessary to protect the employer from the "lawlessness of labor unions." Its withdrawal from the field of labor-management relations would encourage the irresponsibility of organized labor. In addition, supporters of the labor injunction urge that it be retained to protect the public interest from unions, which threaten the health and safety of the community.

Passage of the Norris–La Guardia Anti-Injunction Act did not eliminate controversy over the labor injunction.[1] The issue was tossed to the forefront by passage of the Taft-Hartley Act. Some people, mostly labor leaders, indicted this legislation on the ground that it once again stimulated the use of the injunction in labor disputes. The injunction controversy largely prevented any change in the law during the first session of the 81st Congress. When it became apparent that any revision of Taft-Hartley would contain the procedure, representatives of unions lost interest in attempts to change the law. Organized labor was not interested in legislation that would empower the courts to restrain union activities during labor disputes through the issuance of injunctions.

This chapter will trace the development of the use of injunctions in labor disputes. The objective is to gain a better understanding of the instrument to facilitate an appraisal of its worth as a technique of government control of labor relations. In later chapters we shall deal with the character of legislation passed to curtail the use of injunctions in labor disputes, and we shall determine how Taft-Hartley and Landrum-Griffin influence its use in employer-employee conflicts.

THE NATURE OF INJUNCTIONS

An injunction is a court order directing a person, and if necessary his associates, to refrain from pursuing a course of action. In a comparatively small number of cases, the court may order affirmative action on the part of the people affected by the decree. Injunctions are issued in nonlabor cases as well as under circumstances where employer-employee relations are involved. More recently, injunctions have been used to restrain the circulation of libelous, indecent, or seditious material. During the prohibition era the instrument was employed to enforce laws forbidding the sale of liquor. In the great majority of injunction cases, however, in labor and nonlabor cases alike, the protection of property rights is the issue. In labor cases the issue of property rights is involved almost exclusively. Where the union seeks to obtain the injunction against employers, the property issue is not involved of course. Experience shows that unions have made little use of the injunction. Up to 1931 employers obtained 1,845 injunctions against unions while unions obtained 43 against employers.[2] The National Labor Relations Board, however, has stepped up the pace of injunction use against employers in recent years.

A special sort of court issues injunctions. In general, we think of a court in terms of a judge, jury, witnesses, cross-examination, and the like. This type of court is the familiar court of law, or trial court. In contrast, the court that issues injunctions is termed an "equity court." The distinguishing feature of an equity court is that the judge alone decides the case under controversy. There are no juries in equity courts. In cases involving the injunction, the judge alone decides whether or not the instrument shall be issued. This is true in both labor and nonlabor cases.

In injunction cases the judge alone decides all issues of fact and law. No jury influences the outcome of the proceedings. A person who violates an injunction is held in "contempt of court." It is essential to note that the judge who issues the injunction determines whether the injunction has been violated. Severe penalties can be inflicted on violators of injunctions, including the payment of heavy fines and imprisonment. One may question the entire injunction procedure. Is not the power of the judge of sweeping character? May he not abuse his power? Is it proper for the same man to act as judge, jury, and executioner? As a matter of fact, the injunction is a valuable part of our judicial system. An equity court can protect property before injury to property occurs. A trial court may award money damages to owners of property only after the damage to the property takes place. The equity court is preventive while the trial court is remedial. Of course, where the judgment of one man is the sole standard of reference, there is always possibility of abuse. Even though admitting this feature, one would hesitate to condemn the entire injunction procedure.

Suppose two owners of adjoining coal mine property disagree on the property line separating their respective mines. One owner proceeds to mine the coal in the disputed area. If later proceedings reveal that the man who mined the coal did not in fact own the area in dispute, he has caused serious, if not irreparable, damage to the other man's property. The injured party may, of course, sue for damages. But he would be greatly grieved if events proved that the wrongdoer had no funds to pay the damages awarded by a jury. The injunction procedure would have prevented these unhappy circumstances. The injured party could have applied for an injunction and the court probably would have ordered no coal mining until the dispute over the property line was settled. A court of law could not have served the cause of justice in this illustration. The injunction gives swift and definite protection to property. In its absence, the property in the illustration would suffer damage which even money obtained in the subsequent lawsuit could not likely remedy. Injunctions are issued when in their absence irreparable damage to property would occur, leaving the property owner with no adequate remedy in a law court to compensate for threatened injury.

FORMS OF INJUNCTIONS

A person who seeks an injunction will support his case at the outset with a series of sworn statements or affidavits. He will petition a court to issue an immediate order to prevent injury to his property. The plaintiff will contend that the matter is of such urgency that time does not permit a thorough investigation of the circumstances. There is no time for a full hearing, the questioning of witnesses, or other time-consuming judicial procedures. Frequently, the courts will heed the request of the plaintiff and issue what is termed a *temporary restraining order*. The purpose of this decree is to preserve the status quo until a full investigation is made of the circumstances. Temporary restraining orders are in effect injunctions. They prevent a person or persons from pursuing some contemplated course of action. Penalties for violating a temporary restraining order could be just as severe as those imposed for disobedience of a more permanent type of injunction. In addition, it should be carefully noted that the temporary restraining order is issued before the merits of the case are determined. The defendant or defendants are not provided with an opportunity to present their side.

A judge, in issuing the temporary restraining order, does not claim that the plaintiff is right and the defendant wrong. It is issued to preserve the status quo in order that property might not be irreparably damaged before the merits of the case are determined. The justification for the temporary restraining order is that the relative position of the parties will not be injured by the maintenance of the status quo. For example, in the coal illustration, the position of the parties would not have been affected materially by the issuance of a temporary restraining order. After the merits of the case were fully determined, the coal would still have been intact for the use of the victor in the injunction proceedings.

When a temporary restraining order is issued, the judge at the same time sets a date for a hearing. Under some circumstances courts will not issue a temporary restraining order. Instead, upon plaintiff's application for equity relief, a judge may set a date for a hearing. In either case, the court will direct that a hearing be held shortly after the temporary restraining order is issued or application for injunctive relief filed. The court is aware that the interests of the defendant may be injured by the temporary restraining order. Consequently justice demands that the defendant be given an opportunity to present his case soon after the court issues the temporary restraining order. Defendants, of course, have a better opportunity to be treated fairly if the court refuses to issue a temporary restraining order and instead orders a hearing to determine the facts of the case. However, courts frequently do issue the temporary restraining order, particularly under circumstances where irreparable damage to property appears imminent.

On the basis of the hearing, the court may dissolve or modify the temporary restraining order if one has been issued previously. If it is dissolved this action ends the matter. The defendant may then carry out the line of conduct from which he was enjoined by the temporary restraining order. On the other hand, as a result of this hearing the court may issue a second form of injunctive relief—the *temporary injunction*. The temporary injunction is a more permanent form of the injunction family than the temporary restraining order. However, the full merits of the case are not determined when this form of injunction goes into effect.

The reason for this involves the nature of the hearing prior to the issuance of the temporary injunction. It is true that the defendant may present affidavits and offer objections to the arguments of the plaintiff. Still, the full judicial procedure is not in operation. Witnesses are not ordinarily called, and no elaborate investigation of the case is made. There may be little opportunity for cross-examination, most important for testing the credibility of evidence. Both sides may be represented by counsel, but the judge still must determine "where the truth lies amid the contradictions of the affidavits presented by the contending parties, without opportunity to see or question any of the witnesses."[3] Despite these considerations, the temporary injunction demands the full obedience of the parties affected by the decree. Violators will be punished. Even if future investigation proves the defendant right and the plaintiff wrong, the defendant still may be punished if he violates the temporary injunction.

The final form of injunction is the *permanent injunction*. This form is issued after a full hearing on the merits of the case is held. Witnesses are called, questioned, and cross-examined. At this point the defendant has the opportunity to present his full case. The judge has had the opportunity to study carefully all documents and witnesses in the proceeding. The hearing on the permanent injunction may result in the dissolvement of the temporary injunction or the issuance of the permanent injunction. If the permanent injunction is issued, the defendants are permanently enjoined from engaging in certain action. The defendant may appeal the decision of the judge if there is a higher court available for appeal. When any appeal is made, however, the terms of the lower court's permanent injunction must be obeyed during the proceeding involving the appeal.

THE INJUNCTION IN LABOR DISPUTES

The brief description of the general injunction procedure provides a basis for discussion of the use of injunctions in labor disputes. Labor injunctions in the United States were frequently employed after 1895. The chief reason for this was that the Supreme Court in that year decided the celebrated *Debs* case,[4] and upheld the constitutionality of the labor injunction. One might speculate on the course of industrial relations had the high court held the use of the instrument to be unconstitutional. Such a circumstance would have had a most profound influence on the whole process of collective bargaining, industrial relations, and the development of labor unions.

The *Debs* case was indeed a landmark in the field of labor law. The case grew out of a dispute between the Pullman Car Company and the American Railway Union. In 1894 the workers of the Pullman Car Company struck in protest against a cut in wages and the discriminatory discharge of a number of union leaders. When it became apparent that the union could not win its strike by direct action, the workers through their union officers requested the railroads to boycott the use of Pullman sleeping cars. This the railroads refused to do. As a result the union induced a series of strikes against the railroads.

Such strikes immediately involved the government of the United States. The railroads are instrumentalities of interstate commerce,[5] carry the mails of the United States, and from time to time haul personnel and equipment of the armed forces of the United States. As a result officers of the United States government requested and obtained an injunction ordering the union, including its officers, to cease striking against the railroads. Eugene V. Debs, president of the union, and a number of other officers of the union were subsequently imprisoned for violating the terms of the injunction. The case was eventually appealed to the Supreme Court of the United States. In affirming the use of injunctions in labor disputes, the Supreme Court brushed aside the contention that the proper arm of government to suppress or control the action of the strikers was the executive branch, stating: "Is the army the only instrument by which rights of the public can be enforced and the peace of the nation preserved?" And the Court continued in this vein when it declared that "the right to use force does not exclude the right of appeal to the courts for judicial determination and the exercise of all their powers of prevention." Not only may labor disturbances or union activities be restrained by local police officers, state militia, federal troops, and the like, but the high court of the United States held that the injunction process likewise may be properly employed.

With the constitutionality of the labor injunction affirmed, the instrument became a potent factor in labor-management controversies. Professor Witte reported that prior to 1931 state and federal courts issued a total of 1,845 labor injunctions.[6] Data on the number of injunctions issued after that year are largely unavailable until 1947. As will be pointed out, Congress and some states enacted legislation in 1932 regulating the use of injunctions in labor disputes. In the light of this development, the number of injunctions issued in labor disputes from 1932 to 1947 decreased sharply. However, the injunction sections of the Taft-Hartley Act along with Landrum-Griffin in 1959 stimulated the increased use of the instrument. From August 23,

1947, the date on which the Taft-Hartley Act became effective, until June 30, 1949, there were 69 instances in which injunctions were sought against labor unions under the terms of the law. From 1950 through 1966 the National Labor Relations Board petitioned for 2,405 injunctions involving labor disputes. All of these were not directed against unions, but union actions account for a majority.[7]

THE CONCEPT OF "PROPERTY" IN
LABOR INJUNCTION CASES

As noted, injunctions are issued in labor disputes for the purpose of protecting property from "irreparable damage." It is therefore of considerable importance to determine the meaning of "property" for labor injunction purposes. If the term is defined narrowly, the opportunity for employing the labor injunction will be reduced. Conversely, if property is construed broadly, the possibilities for its use will be increased proportionately. The courts have attached a meaning to property which broadens the concept significantly. For purposes of court proceedings, the term includes much more than tangible items, such as machinery, land, buildings, physical goods, and the like. Courts in the United States have consistently held that the concept includes intangible items. The right to do business falls squarely within the meaning of the property concept. Likewise, the liberty to hire workers and sell goods to customers is included within the definition. In short, the freedom to run a business in a profitable manner falls within the boundaries of the concept.

Now the courts did not develop this definition of property merely to provide the basis for the labor injunction. This wide interpretation of the property doctrine was an integral part of American law long before the first labor injunction was issued. It was to be expected, therefore, that the courts would apply this concept of property to labor disputes. It is not difficult to see how the broad definition of the property concept would affect labor disputes. If a labor union interferes with the free access of an employer to labor and commodity markets, there is damage to property. Should a strike, picketing, or a boycott decrease the opportunities for profitable operation of the business, an injury to property arises. "Irreparable damage" to property can be inflicted, not only by violent destruction of physical items, but also by union activities calculated to interfere with the carrying out of the business function.

Some people contend that the courts were in error in applying the broad concept of property to labor disputes.[8] To support their views, they pointed to the practice in England. Courts in England for injunction purposes generally limited property to include only physical items. But the point of importance is that the restricted meaning of property applies to labor and nonlabor cases alike.[9] Logic demands that the courts apply the same meaning of property in all injunction cases. American courts hardly can be criticized for utilizing the property concept developed in nonlabor cases for labor controversies.

The argument has been raised that a more restricted definition of the term property would make the injunction in labor disputes appear more just. Only property in its tangible form should be used as the basis for labor injunctions. This contention rests on impracticable grounds. The broad concept of property is ingrained in the very marrow of judicial thought. It is extremely doubtful that legislation aimed in this direction could stand the test of constitutionality. In the *Debs* case, for example, the Supreme Court failed to distinguish between the authority of the judiciary to protect the right to control and use property and its right to protect injury to physical property. The implication is that the courts may extend protection to property under both circumstances. More important than the constitutional question, this viewpoint fails to recognize the basic objections to the labor injunction. The mere limitation of the property concept to include only physical objects would not result in the disappearance of these objections. The broad concept of property provides for the wider application of the labor injunction, but the wide concept in itself did not stimulate the historical abuses growing out of the use of the injunction in labor disputes. What has been the indictment against the labor injunction? Why do these objections proceed from a more fundamental basis than the mere concept of property as applied in labor cases?

ABUSES OF INJUNCTIONS

Several abuses of the injunction process were common prior to passage of the Norris–La Guardia Act. Some were more the result of the circumstances of the times than any conscious attempt to usurp power on the part of the judiciary.

Judges as Legislators

One abuse of the injunction was the legislative character of court action. Through its power to issue injunctions, the judiciary literally enacted legislation. Before a law is passed by Congress or a state legislature, there is ordinarily much debate on the measure. Public hearings are held on the more important of the proposed laws wherein any citizen has the right to be heard. Some citizens may object to a particular law enacted by a legislative body but one can be assured that the legislation was passed by the collective judgment of the people elected to represent their interests.

When judges issued labor injunctions, the standard of reference was their own social and economic predilections. No jury acted in injunction proceedings. In labor disputes, the judge alone decided whether an objective or activity of a labor union was lawful or unlawful. Judges outlawed many union activities. Strikes engaged in for certain purposes were stamped out by the force of the labor injunction. Some judges forbade the calling of strikes when they deemed their purpose unlawful. The "fairness" or "justice" of the strike's purpose is not the issue here. The point of importance is that the injunction procedure provided the court with the power to determine the legal and illegal boundaries of union activities. In the absence of legislation, the courts acted in labor disputes as the legislative branch of government. Clearly, the economic and social attitude of judges influenced their decisions. Every labor dispute had its social and economic ramifications. The manner in which judges interpreted their environment had an important bearing on whether or not an injunction would be issued. In equity cases, the judge alone, motivated by his own beliefs, attitudes, and prejudices decided the issues. The decisions did not indicate dishonesty or unfairness of the judiciary; but, rather, reflected their legal training, their social environment, and their lack of knowledge of industrial relations. Whatever the reason, the result was to favor the interests of the property group at the expense of labor groups. This was to be expected since the United States was short on capital relative to labor. A great deal of emphasis was placed on the accumulation of capital. Facilitation of capital expansion was deemed essential to economic growth. And it is necessary to note that the level of living in the United States was generally higher than in Europe—if not always in actuality, at least in hope and promise. With this in mind, the attitude of judges in labor disputes may be understood, not vindicated.

The Blanket Injunction

In the past labor injunctions frequently made acts illegal which standing alone were lawful and were applied to persons other than those immediately involved in a dispute. Even at the present time anti-injunction laws notwithstanding, some injunctions have this effect. Labor injunctions in many cases have been directed against "all other persons whomsoever" that may have aided workers in a labor dispute.[10] This meant an injunction was applied to persons other than those immediately involved in the controversy. People not directly concerned with the dispute, but nevertheless sympathetic to workers engaged in union activities, could not undertake action to support them. For example, such persons could have been enjoined from contributing money for strike relief when a court previously had declared a strike illegal. In addition, the labor injunction frequently outlawed activities which in themselves were legal. Thus the decrees often made it unlawful for workers and their sympathizers to "interfere in any way whatsoever" to further a labor dispute. Such language failed to make a distinction between activities commonly regarded as unlawful, such as violent destruction of property, and patterns of conduct commonly regarded as lawful, such as the exercise of the right to free speech. In 1911 the Supreme Court upheld an injunction which forbade anyone from speaking or writing to further a labor union activity.[11]

Sweeping or "blanket" terms such as "all other persons whomsoever" and "interfering in any way whatsoever" produced serious consequences. Lawful acts were made illegal. Participants in the dispute and nonparticipants were affected. Injunctions containing such all-inclusive terms could violate basic civil liberties guaranteed in the Constitution of the United States. Moreover, those terms were fundamentally devoid of definiteness in meaning. One rule which could have been followed in injunction cases was that the terms of the injunction should be clear. There was very little clarity in terms such as "whatsoever" and "whomsoever." The average person would scarcely have known under what circumstances he could have violated a court order. For example, did a church violate the terms of a *blanket injunction* because it provided free meals to workers that participated in a strike ruled unlawful by the courts? The matter grew more serious because of the enforcement procedure of injunctions. When the judge who issued the injunction subsequently interpreted and enforced it, the problem reached a magnitude disproportionate to its importance.

The Status Quo in Labor Disputes

The temporary restraining order and the temporary injunction were issued for the purpose of maintaining the status quo between the parties to the injunction proceedings. The effect was to stop at once action by the defendant until a hearing and investigation were conducted to determine fully the merits of the dispute. Justification of the procedure rested on the premise that the relative position of the parties would not be affected by the temporary injunction proceedings. If subsequent court investigations proved the conduct of the defendant was not unlawful, the injunction would have been terminated. The defendant would then be free to carry out the action he was pursuing, or had intended to pursue, before the court interfered with his plans. On the other hand, if the temporary restraining order or the temporary injunction were not issued, the defendant might have caused "irreparable damage" to the property of the plaintiff.

This line of reasoning, though generally valid in non-labor injunction proceedings, did not apply to labor disputes. Temporary injunction proceedings, regardless of the outcome of subsequent court action, had the effect of discriminating against the labor union. Events in labor disputes move swiftly. The ultimate outcome of strikes, then as now, could be determined in a few days. Interference with strike activities through the injunction process made it difficult for the union to carry out the strike to its successful termination.

Temporary injunction proceedings had a far-reaching effect on the general public. Public opinion tended to turn against the strikers once the court order was issued. Regardless of the merits of the cases and notwithstanding the eventual outcome of the full injunction proceedings, the court orders branded the workers as lawbreakers. Newspapers unfriendly to organized labor exploited the legal proceedings. Editorial and news commentators could use the court order as a basis for condemning the purpose of the strike and the conduct of the workers. Labor unions had a difficult task in winning a strike when general public opinion condemned the undertaking.

Injunction proceedings also lessened the chance of winning a strike by directing the energies of union leadership to the courtroom. In some cases the proceedings were conducted far from the locality of the strike. The strategy was to strip the rank and file of its leadership. Time spent in court proceedings endangered the success of strikes. In addition, the expense of combating injunctions was often considerable. Money paid out for lawyers' fees was not available for publicity, strike relief, or the purchase of food for strikers and their families.

Perhaps the greatest effect of the labor injunction was to dampen the enthusiasm of workers for the strike. They became fearful and confused by the court's intervention in the dispute. This was particularly so when the workers were engaged in their first strike or when they were relatively new in the labor union movement. The injunction procedure in labor disputes was a rather complex affair. Usually, workers did not understand such legal action and as a consequence the strike effort deteriorated.

In this connection, however, it should be pointed out that the effect of the injunction proceedings could work in the opposite direction. Cases are known wherein workers, after being served with court orders, tried even harder to win their strike. It was not unknown for "pickets" to have been imprisoned, only to return to the picket line after their release. Seasoned union leaders were not greatly disturbed by court proceedings or even by imprisonment because of injunction violations. Some of them viewed their experiences with pride rather than with alarm. In general, however, the fact remained that the entrance of the court in the labor dispute generated confusion and fear among the rank-and-file workers. This made the winning of a strike more difficult.

These observations repudiate the contention that the status of the parties remained the same during the period in which the temporary restraining order or the temporary injunction was in effect. If it stimulated fear and confusion among the workers, resulted in the dissipation of union funds, directed the energies of union leadership from the strike to the courtroom, and tended to turn public opinion against the strike, one can scarcely argue that the status quo between the parties had been maintained. Instead of protecting the employer's property against irreparable damage, temporary injunction proceedings could result in irreparable damage to the union's position. This was the usual result regardless of the outcome of future court proceedings.

Time Lags in Injunction Proceedings

Studies indicate that the courts made frequent use of the temporary restraining order. Frankfurter and Greene[12] reported that the temporary restraining order was involved in more than one-half of all federal labor injunction cases during 1901–1928.[13] Of the 118 officially reported federal labor injunction proceedings in this period, 70 involved the temporary restraining order. In 49 of the 118 cases, the courts actually issued the temporary restraining order.[14] In 45 labor injunction cases in the clothing trades in New York City during 1910 to 1927, the courts issued 26 temporary restraining orders.[15] Professor Witte, however, reported that in Massachusetts, in 234 applications for injunctions from 1898 to 1916, temporary restraining orders were issued in only 29 cases.[16] The defendant had no opportunity to present his case in temporary restraining order proceedings. The order was issued on the application of the plaintiff. The courts considered only the evidence submitted by the plaintiff, and defendants had no opportunity to challenge these allegations. Thus, in labor cases in which temporary restraining orders were issued, the union had no opportunity to answer the charges of the employer.

As noted, courts normally order a hearing concurrent with the issuance of the temporary restraining order. At this hearing the defendant has an opportunity to present his case. However, from the date the temporary restraining order is issued until the hearing is held, the order is in force and has to be obeyed by the defendants in the dispute. Obviously, the interests of the labor union would have been protected by a speedy hearing after the temporary restraining order was issued. A long delay caused irreparable damage to the labor union. For example, if a court enjoined a strike for any prolonged length of time, the strike was likely to be permanently broken regardless of further injunction proceedings. In nonlabor injunction cases, the lapse of time between the issuance of the temporary restraining order and the hearing ordinarily took from five to ten days. In the absence of injunction control legislation, the time lag in labor injunction cases was much longer. One study showed that out of 42 cases in which temporary restraining orders were issued, the intervening period was less than a month in only 16 cases. In one unusual case the period was one year.[17] Recognizing the inherent unfairness of such a long delay, subsequent labor injunction legislation limited the time between the issuance of temporary restraining orders and the hearings.

The hearing on the temporary restraining order could have resulted in its modification, continuance, or termination. If the court felt that activities of the labor union should continue to be restrained, the temporary injunction was issued. Actually, the hearing on the temporary restraining order did not offer a great amount of protection to the labor union. The union could offer counteraffidavits to challenge the allegations of the employer. But in general at these hearings "the usual safeguards for sifting fact from distortion or imaginings—personal appearance of witnesses and cross-examinations by opposing counsel—(were) lacking."[18] Thus the hearing was of dubious value to labor organizations. This conclusion is just as valid when the court denies the application for a temporary restraining order and instead directs a hearing to determine whether a temporary injunction should be issued.

Even today the full injunction procedure is rarely exhausted in labor cases. Labor unions generally contest a temporary restraining order. But the bulk of labor cases terminate with the issuance of the temporary injunction. Unions rarely continue injunction proceedings to the point where the court decides whether to issue a permanent injunction or dissolve or modify the temporary injunction. The reason for this is that frequently the strike is broken or some other settlement of the dispute is made before the full injunction procedure is exhausted.

It is only at the final stage of the injunction proceedings that the merits of the case are fully determined. At this level witnesses appear and there is the opportunity for cross-examination. But these safeguards are worthless in labor injunction cases for labor unions find little practicable value in exhausting the injunction procedure. These considerations moved Frankfurter and Greene to remark that

> in theory the final injunctive decree alone is an adjudication on the merits, temporary restraining orders and temporary injunctions are nominally provisional. In fact, however, the restraining order and temporary injunction usually register the ultimate disposition of a labor litigation, which seldom persists to a final decree. Lack of resources may frustrate pursuit on the litigation, or as is often the case, the strike has ended before the final stage is reached and ended not infrequently as a result of the injunction.[19]

Quality of Evidence in Injunction Proceedings

Judges issue injunctions only after considering evidence. This is equally true in labor and nonlabor cases. The character of the evidence presented is the real issue in the issuance of the labor injunction. "Character" does not mean the *amount* of evidence. Employers and unions alike support their positions with a considerable quantity of evidence. The challenge relates to the quality of the evidence. Affidavits constitute the chief—if not the exclusive—form of evidence which courts consider before ruling whether or not temporary restraining orders or temporary injunctions are to be issued.

Experience with the labor injunction has demonstrated that the affidavits submitted in labor cases are in large measure unreliable. One judge reflected this point of view when he stressed the "utter untrustworthiness of affidavits" and further asserted that "Such documents are packed with falsehoods, or with half-truths which in such a matter are more deceptive than deliberate falsehoods."[20] In some early cases courts decided injunction proceedings on the basis of affidavits sworn to by private detectives hired by employers to break strikes and unions. Such evidence, according to a former Justice of the Supreme Court, is particularly untrustworthy.

He declared in this connection that "all know that men who accept such employment commonly lack fine scruples, often willfully misrepresenting innocent conduct, and manufacturing charges."[21]

The point of importance is not that one side is basically more honest than the other in labor injunction proceedings. Both parties color their cases to suit their needs. This is to be expected. The chief objection is that the court must make an important decision, affecting the liberty and life of many people, on the basis of evidence that is often untrustworthy. Suppose an employer submitted a petition for temporary injunctive relief against a labor union. The petition attested that the union caused "irreparable damage" to the property of the employer. The sworn affidavits submitted to support the evidence alleged that workers have damaged or intend to cause destruction to physical property. In addition, they claim the union's action will interfere seriously with business operations. If this involves a temporary restraining order, the court makes its decision on the basis of the employer's evidence. Should the proceedings involve a temporary injunction, the labor union will normally deny each and every allegation of the employer. The union will support its position with a series of sworn affidavits. On the basis of this conflicting evidence, the court must make its decision. One judge squarely pointed up the difficulty of the problem when he stated, "I confess my inability to determine with any satisfaction from an inspection of inanimate manuscript questions of veracity. In disposing of the present rule, I am compelled to find, as best I may from two hundred thirty-five lifeless, typewritten pages of conflicting evidence, the facts which must determine respondents' guilt or innocence on the quasi-criminal charge of contempt."[22]

Some people brush aside the importance of the issuance of labor injunctions on the basis of evidence of this character. It is contended that the labor union will be reimbursed for damages resulting from an injunction issued on the basis of employer evidence subsequently proved false. Actually equity proceedings do recognize the possibility of injury to a defendant where an injunction is issued on the basis of unworthy evidence of the plaintiff. To provide for this possibility, the court normally will require the plaintiff to post a bond along with his application for an injunction. If an injunction is issued on the basis of the plaintiff's evidence and if the full injunction procedure reveals the plaintiff's evidence to be false, the court will award proceeds from the bond to the defendant. This award is supposed to compensate the defendant for damages occurring from the injunction proceedings.

Such an award has little bearing in labor injunction cases. The bond is not forfeited in any injunction case until the permanent injunction is denied. It has been pointed out that unions generally do not find it practicable to exhaust this procedure. In labor cases the temporary restraining order or the temporary injunction is usually the final stage of injunction proceedings. The injury which occurred to a labor union in an injunction proceeding could not be measured in dollars and cents. Much of the damage inflicted on unions by the labor injunction was of an intangible character. No monetary value could be placed on items such as loss of potential or actual membership, loss of prestige, undermining of the union, and the like. In actual labor injunction cases, some courts did not require the posting of bonds or they set the amount of bonds at very low levels. In the light of these factors, "it [was] not surprising that the recovery on the bond in labor cases [was] almost unknown."[23] Through 1928 unions were awarded damages in only three cases. And these awards only compensated the unions for court costs and attorney fees.

THE YELLOW-DOG CONTRACT AND
THE LABOR INJUNCTION

Organized labor in 1917 felt the full impact of the labor injunction on the right to self-organization and collective bargaining. In that year the Supreme Court of the United States handed down the celebrated *Hitchman* decision.[24] The Court held that the labor injunction could be employed to enforce the *yellow-dog contract*.[25] The yellow-dog contract was a device utilized by antiunion employers to stop the progress of the union movement. Its chief characteristic was the promise of a worker not to join a labor union while in the hire of an employer. A typical yellow-dog contract was involved in the *Hitchman* case:

> I am employed by and work for the Hitchman Coal & Coke Company with the express understanding that I am not a member of the United Mine Workers of America, and will not become so while an employee of the Hitchman Coal & Coke Company; that the Hitchman Coal & Coke Company is run non-union and agrees with me that it will run non-union while I am in its employ. If at any time I am employed by the Hitchman Coal & Coke Company I want to become connected with the United Mine Workers of America, or any affiliated organization, I agree to withdraw from the employment of said company, and agree that while I am in the employ of that company I will not make any efforts amongst its employees to bring about the unionizing of that mine against the company's wish. I have either read the above or heard the same read.[26]

The yellow-dog contract was first used in the 1870s by the stone manufacturers when combating the Molders' Union.[27] The Supreme Court in 1908[28] and in 1912[29] declared unconstitutional a federal and state statute designed to outlaw the use of these agreements. An analysis of this development is reserved for a future chapter.[30] However, the instrument did not come into widespread use until after the *Hitchman* decision. The yellow-dog contract was used mainly when unionization was attempting to gain a foothold. It is difficult to state just to what degree the union movement was retarded by the utilization of the instrument. One may be safe in concluding, however, that when it was employed the progress of unionization was seriously retarded. Though the device was used most extensively in the bituminous coal mines of West Virginia, Tennessee, and Kentucky, the yellow-dog agreement served to hinder the progress of collective bargaining in unionization in the coal, shoe, glass, full-fashioned hosiery, clothing, metal trades, and commercial printing industries.

Some may wonder why workers signed such agreements. Perhaps some signed because they were opposed to collective bargaining in principle and preferred to work in a nonunion shop. Another possible reason was that such contracts were signed under the force of economic necessity. Workers with families to support, and having no other employment opportunities, would be expected to execute the agreement. It was largely a question of "sign or starve." One may question whether an agreement signed under such conditions of duress was a legal contract. Although unemployment statistics are not entirely reliable in the period 1870–1917, the years in which the yellow-dog contract was becoming a factor in industrial relations, there is evidence that rather serious unemployment characterized the national economy. Paul H. Douglas estimated that for the years 1897–1918 about 10 percent of workers associated with manufacturing, transportation, building trades, and mining were unemployed.[31]

Such circumstances throw a considerable amount of doubt on the Supreme Court's declaration that the workers involved in the *Hitchman* case "voluntarily made the agreement and desired to continue working under it." Was it actually true, notwithstanding the language of the Court, that the yellow-dog contracts won the "unanimous approval of [the] employees"? Were these individual contracts signed in reality "with the free assent" of the employees?

On the face of it, the Court was correct in the belief that the contracts were "voluntarily made," but a deeper penetration of the problem leads to a different conclusion. A contract does not appear to be "voluntarily made" when one of the parties has no actual liberty to refuse to execute the agreement. One would expect a more profound analysis of the problem from a court of equity. Mr. Justice Pitney, who delivered the majority decision of the court in the *Hitchman* decision, remarked in this very case that "a court of equity . . . looks to the substance and essence of things and disregards matters of form and technical nicety." It appears that the Court failed to fulfill this worthwhile function when it concluded that the workers had actual liberty to refuse to sign the yellow-dog contract.

In the minority opinion, joined in by Justices Brandeis, Holmes, and Clarke, recognition was made of the realities of the proceedings. These men were aware that the inquiry of "the substance and essence of things" required a more practical view of the matter. In this respect the minority opinion, written by Brandeis, states: "If it is coercion to threaten to strike unless plaintiff consents to a closed union shop, it is coercion also to threaten not to given one employment unless the applicant will consent to a closed non-union shop. The employer may sign the union agreement for fear that labor may not be otherwise obtainable; the workman may sign the individual agreement for fear that employment may not be otherwise obtainable."

Additional economic circumstances surrounded the *Hitchman* case. In 1907 the United Mine Workers of America, the defendants in the *Hitchman* decision,[32] were organizing the miners in the states of Pennsylvania, Maryland, Virginia, and West Virginia. The union had successfully organized the mines in the so-called Central Competitive Area which included the states of Illinois, Indiana, and Ohio, and western Pennsylvania. Labor standards in the Central Competitive Area, however, were threatened by the unorganized mines of the eastern states. Unionized mines could not be expected to compete with the nonunion mines where labor standards were lower. Owners of unorganized mines could afford to sell coal more cheaply on the market than could the operators of the organized mines. Thus the United Mine Workers of America was vitally concerned with organizing the eastern mines and raising labor standards. The very existence of the union depended on organizing the nonunion mines. Either this was accomplished or the union in effect would be required to go out of business. Stimulated by these pressing circumstances, the United Mine Workers Union began an intensive organizing campaign in West Virginia. The Supreme Court was aware of these economic factors when it declared in the *Hitchman* case that "the plain effect of this action was to approve a policy which, as applied to the case, meant that in order to relieve the union mines of Ohio, Indiana, and Illinois from the competition of the cheaper product of the nonunion mines of West Virginia, the West Virginia mines should be organized. . . ." Apparently, the high court was fully conscious of these economic circumstances; nevertheless this knowledge did not control its decision.

The union knew of the yellow-dog contracts in existence at the Hitchman mine, located in West Virginia. Nonetheless, a labor organizer induced many of the miners to agree to join the union. Both the majority and minority of the Court made much of the difference of the terms "to join actually" and "to agree to join." Actually, the organizer did not "join up" miners who had signed the yellow-dog agreement. He merely requested them to agree to join. After a miner agreed to join, his name was written into a book. The plan of the union was first to gain the support of a majority of the miners, and then to call a strike at these mines. At the time of the strike the union probably would have issued union cards and the miners then would be actual members of the union. Brandeis argued in this connection that "there is evidence of an attempt to induce plaintiff's employees to *agree* to join the union; but none whatever of any attempt to induce them to violate their contract." The majority of the Court held no practical difference existed between "agreeing to join" and "actually joining." In this respect the Court was perfectly correct. Its shortcoming lay in the fact that it did not extend its "practical" view of things to the broader implications of the *Hitchman* case. When it served its purpose, the Court employed practical reasoning and looked to the "substance and essence of things"; but, at the point of decision, the Court abandoned this procedure and interpreted the facts and law of the case in a most narrow and technical fashion.

In reaching its decision, the Court held that the union attempted to "subvert the system of employment at the mine by coverted breaches of the contract of employment known to be in force there. . . ." The contract, reasoned the Court, was voluntarily made by the workers and the employer. The right to freedom of contract is a liberty enjoyed by all. This right as "any other legal right" is entitled to protection. By inducing a breach of contract, the labor organization was interfering with the right to contract. Hence the Court was constrained to enjoin the organization from further interference with the right to contract. The injunction was a proper remedy, and consequently this instrument was to be employed to protect and make effective the yellow-dog contract. Such was the reasoning of the Court. Not only was the yellow-dog agreement legal, but the Supreme Court was prepared to implement it through the injunctive process. What this meant to collective bargaining and unionization was indeed profound. Faced with an organization campaign, the employer made the execution of the yellow-dog contract a condition of employment. In periods of less than full employment, workers would be economically coerced into the agreement. The employer then applied for an injunction restraining any person who might encourage his workers to join a union. Any disobedience to the injunction was punishable as contempt of court.

The *Hitchman* decision was the low-water mark of the attitude of the Court toward collective bargaining and unionization. Not until 1932 was its effect eradicated. Its reversal came not by a change of attitude of the courts but by action of the legislative branch of government. From 1917 until 1932 the courts were a potent force in dealing with attempts to unionize. Not content with the fact that the bargaining power between employers and employees was inherently unequal, the Supreme Court in the *Hitchman* decision made the balance even less equal. The *Hitchman* doctrine clearly demonstrated the hostility of the courts to collective bargaining. It served clear notice that the courts were available to restrict union efforts at organization.

SUMMARY

The injunction is issued by equity courts. Normally, it is an order which directs a person and (where pertinent) his associates to refrain from pursuing a certain course of action. The application of the injunction to labor disputes stifled the growth and effective operation of unions. Through the injunction the courts denied to workers the opportunity to resort to collective action to improve their economic lot. In the *Debs* case the Supreme Court upheld the constitutionality of the labor injunction. The result was the widespread use of the instrument in labor disputes. Many union activities necessary for the effective operation of unionism were restrained by the courts. The judiciary served well the interests of the antiunion employer. The effects of the labor injunction on unionism were varied. However, organized labor felt the full impact of the labor injunction when the Supreme Court held that the instrument could be utilized to enforce the yellow-dog contract. The indiscriminate use of the injunction in labor disputes occurred along with the rapid progress of American industrialism. The courts via the injunction slowed down the drive toward collective action until society reached to limit the legislative character of the courts.

NOTES

[1] 47 Stat. 70 (1932).

[2] Edwin E. Witte, *The Government in Labor Disputes* (New York: McGraw-Hill Book Company, 1932), p. 234.

[3] *Ibid.*, p. 92.

[4] *In re Debs*, Petitioner, 158 U.S. 564 (1895).

[5] The Constitution of the United States, Article I, Section 8, provides the federal government with the power "to regulate commerce . . . among the several states. . . ."

[6] Witte, *op. cit.*, p. 84. The use of the labor injunction was first noted in the 1880s. However, its utilization became widespread after the constitutional question was settled.

[7] *National Labor Relations Act of 1949, Senate Report to Accompany S. 249*, 81st Congress, 1st sess., p. 8; National Labor Relations Board, *Annual Reports*, 1949–1966.

[8] See J. P. Frey, *The Labor Injunction* (Cincinnati: Equity Publishing Company, 1927). Also Witte, *op. cit.*, pp. 105–106.

[9] The injunction was first used in labor disputes in England in 1868. Since that time its application to labor disputes has been very infrequent. One reason for this is the more restricted meaning attached to the property concept. In this connection, see Charles O. Gregory, *Labor and the Law* (New York: W. W. Norton & Company, 1946), p. 97.

[10] The Supreme Court in the *Debs* case sustained an injunction the terms of which forbade "all other persons whomsoever" from encouraging the strike.

[11] *Gompers* v. *Bucks Stove and Range Company*, 221 U.S. 418 (1911). This case is discussed in more detail in Chapter 4.

[12] Felix Frankfurter and Nathan Greene collaborated to bring out the definitive study dealing with the abuses of the labor injunction. It is called *The Labor Injunction* (New York:

The Macmillan Company, 1930). At the time the book was written, Frankfurter was a professor of law at Harvard University. President Roosevelt subsequently appointed him to the Supreme Court of the United States. Undoubtedly, *The Labor Injunction* was a powerful force making for the enactment of labor injunction control legislation.

[13] Felix Frankfurter and Nathan Greene, "The Labor Injunction," *Encyclopedia of the Social Sciences*, VIII, 654.

[14] Frankfurter and Greene, *op. cit.*, p. 64, Appendix 1.

[15] P. F. Brissenden and C. O. Swayzee, "The Use of Injunctions in the New York Needle Trades," *Political Science Quarterly*, XLIV (1929), 548, 563.

[16] Witte, *op. cit.*, p. 90.

[17] *Ibid.*, p. 90.

[18] *Encyclopedia of the Social Sciences, op. cit.*, p. 655.

[19] *Ibid.*, p. 654.

[20] *Great Northern Railway Company* v. *Brosseau*, 286 Fed. 416 (1923).

[21] Justice McReynolds in *Sinclair* v. *U.S.*, 279 U.S. 749 (1929).

[22] *Long* v. *Bricklayers' Union*, 17 Pa. Dist. R. 984 (1929).

[23] Witte, *op. cit.*, p. 91.

[24] *Hitchman Coal Company* v. *Mitchell*, 245 U.S. 229 (1917).

[25] For a general treatment of the yellow-dog contract, see Joel Seidman, *The Yellow Dog Contract* (Baltimore: Johns Hopkins Press, 1932).

[26] *Hitchman Coal Company,* v. *Mitchell, op. cit.*

[27] Harry A. Millis and Royal E. Montgomery, *Organized Labor* (New York: McGraw-Hill Book Company, 1945), p. 511.

[28] *Adair* v. *U.S.*, 208 U.S. 161 (1908).

[29] *Coppage* v. *Kansas*, 236 U.S. 1 (1915).

[30] See Chapter 8.

[31] Paul H. Douglas and Aaron Director, *The Problem of Unemployment* (New York: The Macmillan Company, 1931), Chapter 2.

[32] During this period of time John Mitchell was president of the United Mine Workers of America.

The Struggle for a Labor Antitrust Policy   4

During the first thirty years of the twentieth century, industry became the dominant feature of American economic life. By 1930 nonagricultural occupations accounted for about 80 percent of the labor force. The number of workers attached to manufacturing increased over the thirty-year period from about 4.5 million to more than 8 million. In 1900 the total value of goods produced by industry was $11 billion. By 1930 the figure had increased to $70 billion. The nation was business oriented. Many believed that business, if left alone, would insure steady employment, an increased standard of living, and in general a better life. Calvin Coolidge once remarked that "the business of the United States is business." [1] Few would deny that the current American position of world industrial leadership largely reflects the emphasis which public policy placed on encouraging and strengthening competition. [2] The problem for debate—at the turn of the century as now—was how best to encourage and strengthen competition.

The early part of the twentieth century was an era of declining competition and increasing concentration of control of American industry. As markets became more fully exploited, business leaders rapidly saw the advantages of cooperation over competition. The result was the establishment of price agreements, trusts, pools, and trade associations. Each and every one of these devices was fashioned to stamp out competition between rivals. When the economic environment permitted, the business community renounced rigid competition as the regulator of industrial life for the greater certainty of cooperative control by the few. The elimination of competition meant the growth of huge and powerful corporations more capable of plotting their own destinies without the interdependencies occasioned by competition among many small firms.

The situation was characteristically described:

> Throughout the twentieth century the limitations upon economic opportunity and the concentration of economic power have increased rapidly in the United States. Economic individualism and personal freedom have declined. The language of free competition remains, but free competition has been circumscribed. Orthodox economics still speaks of *laissez faire*, but business itself has restricted the mechanism through which the principles of *laissez faire* can operate.[3]

The dominance of big business in American life did not go unnoticed. By the latter part of the nineteenth century, the public became somewhat concerned over the concentration of ownership into fewer hands. Business groups had formed huge trusts and combinations, the purpose of which was to monopolize the production and sale of vital products. Combinations operated in basic industries such as oil, sugar, tobacco, whiskey, and shoemaking machinery. The goal of the combinations was to eliminate competition. Once competition was stifled, it was a relatively simple matter to establish price levels that would maximize profit. To realize this objective, combinations regulated the rate of output, established market territories, imposed penalties on violators of combination policy, and eliminated outside sources of competition. Congress enacted the Sherman Antitrust Act in 1890 to eliminate monopolistic control of the nation's economy.[4] Predatory monopolistic practices endangered the traditional character of American economic life. Hence the law reflected the faith of the nation in free competition. It suggested that the American system of free enterprise did not exist for a few industrial giants. Rather, an economic system was to be maintained in which the small producer was to have an opportunity to enter into the economic affairs of the nation. The Sherman Act was based on the belief that competition and not monopoly advanced the interests of the nation.

APPLICATION OF SHERMAN ACT TO LABOR UNIONS

Whatever the effect of the antitrust laws on the business structure, the fact remains that their operation retarded the development of trade unionism. After the passage of the Sherman Act, labor unions felt its impact on many occasions. Unions were to learn that the law limited a variety of vital union activities. The prosecution of labor unions under the antitrust provisions stimulated controversy, centering on the fact that Congress made no specific reference to labor unions in the Sherman Act. Sections 1 and 2 of the law state:

> Every contract, combination, . . . or conspiracy, in restraint of trade or commerce among the several States, . . . is. . . illegal . . . every person who shall monopolize, or attempt to monopolize, or combine or conspire with any other person or persons, to monopolize any part of the trade or commerce among the several States . . . shall be guilty of a misdemeanor.

Central to the controversy was the fact that the two key sections did not specifically exclude unions. The question of importance was whether the words "combination" or "person" referred to unions as well as to business enterprises. Did Congress, by not mentioning unions, intend by omission that unions were to be included or excluded from the operation of the statute? Much has been written on this controversy. One representative study concluded that the intent of Congress was to exclude unions from the scope of the statute.[5] On the other hand, another study supported the opposite point of view.[6] Examination here on the intent of Congress would be of little practical value. The controversy was eventually resolved by the Supreme Court of the United States. It would be a barren academic exercise to inquire whether or not the Court was correct in holding labor unions subject to the Sherman Act. The fact is that the Court for many years applied the Sherman Act to unions. It is of greater importance to examine the manner in which the antitrust laws affected labor unions. What economic circumstances were involved in the application of the Sherman law to labor union cases? What labor union activities were restrained by action of the high court? How did the application of the Sherman law to labor organizations affect the development of the union movement?

Sherman Act Penalties

Before considering these problems, however, it is necessary to spell out the penalties provided for in the Sherman Act. Congress provided adequately for the enforcement of the law. The penalties were to apply equally to labor unions and to business enterprises convicted under the statute. The statute provides for three methods of enforcement. First, violators are guilty of a misdemeanor. Thus the courts may punish violators on conviction of the statute "by fine not exceeding five thousand dollars, or by imprisonment not exceeding one year, or by both."[7] Second, the Sherman law empowers the district attorneys of the United States "to institute proceedings in equity to prevent and restrain such violations." This means that the federal government may enforce the law by the injunction process. Finally, the law provides for damage suits against violators. Section 7 of the law states that "any person who shall be injured in his business or property by any other person or corporation, by reason of anything forbidden or declared to be unlawful by this Act, may sue therefor in any circuit court of the United States . . . and shall recover threefold the damages by him sustained, and the costs of the suit, including a reasonable attorney's fee." It is noteworthy that Section 7 provides for damages that are three times the actual damage caused by the violation. Such a provision could serve as a deterrent to anyone aware of the possibility of such a judgment for his actions.

Earliest Union Conviction Under Antitrust

Prosecution of labor unions under the Sherman Act started shortly after its enactment. In 1893 a federal court in Louisiana applied the antitrust statute to labor unions for the first time.[8] A group of unions in New Orleans engaged in a sympathetic strike, the purpose of which was to further the position of a draymen union's strike. The lower court declared that one of the results of the strike was "the forced stagnation of commerce which flowed through New Orleans." It was held that the action of the workers restrained trade within the meaning of the Sherman Act. In handing down its decision, the court brushed aside the contention that unions were excluded from the terms of the antitrust law. On this score the court held that although the statute had its origin in the "evils of massed capital," the intent of Congress was to "include combinations of labor, as well as capital: in fact, all combinations in restraint of commerce, without reference to the character of the persons who entered into them." The court issued an injunction which forbade further strike action. It is noteworthy that the injunction was the procedure utilized to enforce the Sherman Act in the first instance wherein the statute was applied to labor unions.

More commonly the Sherman Act in 1893–1894 was applied to a series of strikes involving the railroad industry.[9] In one of these early cases a federal district court suggested that any railroad strike was a violation of the Sherman Act. The court declared that

> in any conceivable strike upon the transportation lines of this country, whether main lines or branch lines or branch roads, there will be interference with and restraint of interstate or foreign commerce. This will be true also of strikes upon telegraph lines, for the exchange of telegraphic messages between people of different states is interstate commerce. In the presence of these statutes . . . it will be practically impossible hereafter for a body of men to combine to hinder and delay the work of the transportation company without becoming amenable to the provision of these statutes.[10]

This was a very important judicial observation. If every railroad strike restrained trade within the meaning of the Sherman Act, railroad employees could not engage in a lawful strike. The district judge referred to all strikes. He did not distinguish between those conducted peacefully and those carried out violently. There was no inquiry into the purpose of the strike. If this doctrine had been established into law, it would have profoundly affected the character of industrial relations and collective bargaining in the railroad industry and quite possibly of industry in general.

In re Debs

The *In re Debs* case in 1895 provided the Supreme Court the opportunity to decide the applicability of the Sherman law to railroad strikes.[11] The high court upheld an injunction restraining the Pullman strike. However, the Court did not rule on the applicability of the Sherman Act to labor disputes. Before the Supreme Court reviewed the *Debs* case, some circuit courts of appeals had approved injunctions in the Pullman strike, basing their action mainly on the Sherman law. For example, one court declared that "on July 2, 1890, Congress enacted a law that enlarged the jurisdiction of the federal courts and authorized them to apply the restraining power of the law for the purpose of checking and arresting all lawless interference with . . . the peaceful and orderly conduct of railroad business between the States."[12] Another court held that "it may be conceded that the controlling, objective point, in the mind of Congress, in enacting this statute, was to suppress what are known as 'trusts' and 'monopolies.' But, like a great many other enactments, the statute is made so comprehensive and far-reaching in its express terms as to extend to like incidents and acts clearly within the expression and spirit of the law."[13]

When the *Debs* case finally reached the attention of the Supreme Court, the injunction was sustained, as noted, but the Court based its action on the power of the federal government to regulate and promote interstate commerce. In this respect the Supreme Court declared: "We enter into no examination of the act of July 2, 1890 [Sherman Antitrust Act], upon which the Circuit Court relied mainly to sustain its jurisdiction. It must not be understood from this that we dissent from the conclusions of that court in reference to the scope of that act, but simply that we prefer to rest our judgment on the broader ground. . . . "[14] A railroad strike of the Pullman variety, which involved a great deal of violence, was unlawful with or without the Sherman law. The Supreme Court upheld the injunction on the powers of the federal government to regulate interstate commerce, and not because of the existence of the Sherman Act.

ECONOMIC ISSUES IN <u>DANBURY HATTERS</u> DOCTRINE

Labor unions may have drawn some comfort from the *Debs* case on the ground that the Supreme Court did not specifically hold the Sherman law applicable to labor unions. Thirteen years later, however, organized labor suffered a severe legal defeat in an antitrust case. In 1908 the Supreme Court of the United States decided the famous *Danbury Hatters* case,[15] and held that the Sherman law applied to labor unions. To the present time the *Danbury Hatters* case remains as a landmark in the law of collective bargaining.

The United Hatters of North America, the labor organization involved, claimed in 1908 a membership of about 9,000. It was affiliated with the American Federation of Labor. In those days the AFL possessed a total membership of approximately 1,400,000. The United Hatters in the early 1900s was in the process of organizing the felt hat industry. Out of the 82 firms manufacturing hats, the union successfully organized 70. In the organized firms, management recognized the union as the bargaining agent of the workers. Wages, hours, and other conditions of employment were determined through collective bargaining.

Collective bargaining did not operate in the nonunion shops. Conditions of work were not subject to negotiation. As a result labor standards in the nonunion shops presumably were lower than those in the organized firms. These circumstances provided a distinct competitive advantage to the nonunion firms. Operating with nonunion labor, employers could sell hats cheaper than those marketed by organized firms since the unorganized firms had greater flexibility in adjusting wage costs. The organized firms were not capable of withstanding the competition of the more viable nonunion firms for any prolonged length of time. The United Hatters recognized the necessity of organizing the nonunion plants in order to place the burden of competition on variables other than wages. Labor standards in the unionized firms were threatened to the extent that the national union was in danger of disintegration. Survival meant the standardization of employment conditions throughout the entire industry. Such an objective could not be attained short of the organization of each firm in the hat industry. The competitive advantages enjoyed by the nonunion firms, based on lower labor standards, could be erased only by expanding the collective bargaining process to the entire hat industry.

In 1902 the United Hatters undertook the task of organizing Loewe & Company, located in Danbury, Connecticut. The union requested that the company recognize it as the bargaining representative of its employees. Union officials further requested that only union members be permitted to work in the firm. The company refused the demands of the union. As a result, the union called 250 workers out on strike. The organizational strike fell short of its objective since the number of strikers constituted a minor percentage of the entire working force. In addition, the company found replacements for the striking workers and was able to operate successfully. In short, the organizational strike alone was not enough to achieve the union goal.

Faced with such circumstances, the United Hatters resorted to indirect economic pressure. It instituted a nationwide boycott against the products of Loewe & Company. By widespread publicity the union induced retailers not to handle the firm's hats. Similar pressure was placed on wholesalers. In addition, the general public was requested not to purchase any item from retailers or wholesalers handling Loewe's products. Under such pressures, many retailers and wholesalers ceased doing business with the company. Eventually the cooperation of the American Federation of Labor was attained. The AFL promoted the boycott by giving it wide publicity in leaflets, labor papers, and the daily press. Labor organizers toured the nation inducing unionists and dealers not to purchase Loewe's hats. The boycott was very successful. In one year the company claimed a loss of $85,000.

In the summer of 1903 the company sued the United Hatters and its members for damages under the Sherman law. After a circuit court of appeals found the union not in violation of the statute, the company appealed the case to the Supreme Court of the United States. On February 3, 1908, the Court handed down its decision. It held that the United Hatters and its members had violated the Sherman law. The boycott implemented by the union had the effect of restraining trade within the meaning of the Sherman law. On this score the Supreme Court declared,

> . . . The combination described in the declaration is a combination "in restraint of trade or commerce among the several states" in the sense in which those words are used in the act . . . and [this] conclusion rests on many judgments of this court, to the effect that the act prohibits any combination whatever to secure action which essentially obstructs the free flow of commerce between the States, or restricts in that regard, the liberty of a trader to engage in business.

The *Danbury Hatters* doctrine resulted in increased prosecution of labor unions under the Sherman law. Now that the Supreme Court held the law applicable to labor unions, a new weapon was available to combat trade unionism.

In addition, the doctrine established the principle that individual members were responsible for the actions of their officers. On January 5, 1915, approximately seven years later, the Supreme Court sustained a judgment of $252,000 against the United Hatters and its members. Justice Holmes, who wrote the opinion for the Court, declared that since "members paid their dues and continued to delegate authority to their officers unlawfully to interfere with the plaintiffs' interstate commerce in such circumstances that they knew or ought to have known, and such officers were in the belief that they were acting in the matters within their delegated authority, then such members were jointly liable. . . ."[16] The practical significance of the 1915 decision was that rank-and-file members as well as the union and its officers were liable for the payment of the judgment. It is noteworthy that the Taft-Hartley Act, enacted in 1947, though providing for a variety of ways in which labor organizations can be sued for damages, provides that damages can be recovered only from the assets of the unions and not from their members.

The *Danbury Hatters* doctrine also outlawed secondary boycott activity. A *secondary boycott* may be defined as the pressure placed on one business unit to force the firm to cease doing business with another business enterprise. It will be recalled that the United Hatters exerted pressure on the retailers and wholesalers to force them to cease trading with Loewe & Company. This action of the United Hatters fell within the secondary boycott category. The outlawing of secondary boycott action of unions resulted in a decline of effectiveness of the collective bargaining process. A broad and effective mode of economic action was no longer legally available to labor organizations. The struggle for recognition in the *Danbury Hatters* case demonstrated that the resort to the secondary boycott could have been the only alternative to extinction of the union and collective bargaining throughout the industry. The Supreme Court, however, was not persuaded by the economic circumstances that stimulated the action of the United Hatters. It was not sensitive to the fact that the boycott was instigated as a last resort in an effort to establish a bargaining relationship with the United Hatters. Essentially, the high court was of the opinion that "the liberty of a trader to engage in business" was equal to the liberty of workers to move to other economic endeavors to improve their standard of life if a particular pursuit was deemed unsatisfactory.

LABOR'S "MAGNA CHARTA" OR "ENIGMA"?

Organized labor vigorously condemned the *Danbury Hatters* doctrine. It was denounced in labor papers, leaflets, and at labor gatherings. Union leaders missed no opportunity to protest against the action of the Supreme Court. They objected to prosecution of organized labor under a statute which they considered was enacted to curtail business monopolies. Organized labor did more than merely denounce the *Danbury Hatters* doctrine. They resolved to change it. They were unsuccessful in attempts to obtain Supreme Court opinions favorable to the collective bargaining process. Supreme Court justices hold life tenure, if desired, and as a consequence were relatively insulated from whatever political pressures unions could bring to bear. Unions became aware that political action to influence elective officials was the only effective weapon at their disposal. If the Supreme Court held labor unions subject to the Sherman law, the proper course of action was to try to change the law to preclude prosecution of labor unions under the antitrust statute. This, of course, put unions into the political arena.

The American Federation of Labor became involved in politics at the beginning of the twentieth century. Legislation designed to promote a more favorable legal environment for collective bargaining was introduced regularly at sessions of Congress and state legislatures. Later discussion, however, will reveal that the courts nullified state laws favorable to organized labor.[17] On the federal level it was reported that "the labor bills were passed by the House of Representatives at several sessions of Congress, but invariably failed in the Senate. About 1904, owing to the activity of the National Association of Manufacturers and related organizations, labor influence was decreased in the House. The Federation resolved that it could no longer remain a purely economic organization. It was obliged to seek influence in elections."[18]

The <u>Gompers</u> Decision

After the *Danbury Hatters* decision, handed down in 1908, union efforts to influence elections were intensified. Reportedly, "In 1908 the method of 'questioning' was applied to the candidates of the two great parties, and the Democratic party was endorsed. At the elections of 1910 and 1912 the Democrats were again endorsed."[19] Stimulated to political activity by the Supreme Court's construction of the Sherman law, the labor movement in 1911 was further motivated to intensify its efforts. In that year the Supreme Court handed down the famous *Gompers* decision.[20] The Bucks Stove and Range Company refused to bargain or to recognize the Molders & Foundry Workers Union of North America, an affiliate of the American Federation of Labor. As a result the AFL placed the name of the company in the "We Don't Patronize" list of its publication, the *American Federationist*. The effect of the advertisement was to decrease the sales of the company's stoves. In addition, retail stores which handled Bucks stoves were boycotted and some retailers, to protect their own interests, refused to do business with the stove company. An injunction was obtained by the company against the officers of the AFL. Samuel Gompers, founder and first president of the AFL, along with the Federation, violated the injunction. The *American Federationist* continued to carry the company's name in the "We Don't Patronize" list.

For disobedience to the injunction, Gompers and two other AFL officers were sentenced to jail for terms ranging from six months to one year. The case was appealed to the Supreme Court. On purely technical grounds, the contempt charges against the union officials were dismissed. But the Supreme Court held that a boycott promoted by words and printed matter violated the Sherman Antitrust Act. The fact that the AFL spread the boycott by the exercise of speech and the use of printed matter did not make the action of the union officers any less unlawful. In this connection the Court declared:

> The court's protective and restraining powers extend to every device whereby property is irreparably damaged or commerce is illegally restrained. To hold that the restraint of trade under the Sherman Anti-Trust Act . . . could be enjoined but that the means through which the restraint was accomplished could not be enjoined, would be to render the law impotent. . . .

The Supreme Court of the United States relegated the constitutional guarantee of free speech and press to a secondary right in labor cases involving the Sherman law. A boycott restraining trade within the meaning of the Sherman law was unlawful and trade unionists who promoted such a boycott by either spoken or written words violated the Sherman law. They could not plead immunity on the ground that the exercise of free speech and press is protected by the Constitution of the United States.

The *Gompers* decision pushed unions toward greater efforts to influence election results. Unions intensified their political activities. In the congressional elections of 1908 and 1910 the unions managed to influence the election of some candidates who pledged their support to organized labor. In 1912 organized labor pledged its support to Woodrow Wilson for the presidency on the basis of campaign pledges approved by the AFL. In that year Woodrow Wilson was elected President, and the Democratic party showed majorities in both houses of Congress. For the first time in twenty years the Democratic party controlled the executive and legislative branches of the national government. The Democratic party acted swiftly to fulfill its obligations to organized labor. In October 1914 the Clayton Act became law.[21] Organized labor thought the Act was calculated to provide unions relief from the Sherman Antitrust Act. In the following section the provisions of the Clayton Act that were applicable to labor organizations will be discussed along with an assessment of the political intent of the Congress and President Wilson regarding the Clayton Act amendments to the Sherman Act.

Clayton Act Enigma

Celebrated Section 6 of the Clayton Act dealt with the application of antitrust statutes to labor unions. It provided:

> That the labor of a human being is not a commodity or article of commerce. Nothing contained in the anti-trust laws shall be construed to forbid the existence and operation of labor, agricultural, or horticultural organizations, instituted for the purpose of mutual help, and not having capital stock or conducted for profit, or to forbid or restrain individual members of such organizations, from lawfully carrying out the legitimate objects thereof; nor shall such organizations, or the members thereof, be held or construed to be illegal combinations or conspiracies in restraint of trade, under the anti-trust laws.

Labor leaders drew great comfort from Section 6. It stated that "the labor of a human being is not a commodity or article of commerce." It provided that "nothing contained in the anti-trust laws shall be construed to forbid the existence and operation of labor organizations." In addition, Section 6 proclaimed that labor organizations and their members shall not be held to be "illegal combinations or conspiracies in restraint of trade, under the anti-trust laws." There was a great celebration in the ranks of organized labor. Unionists felt that the courts no longer could apply the antitrust laws to labor unions. Samuel Gompers, president of the American Federation of Labor, jubilantly declared that Section 6 was labor's "Industrial Magna Charta upon which the working people will rear their construction of industrial freedom."[22]

Close consideration of Section 6 makes one wonder why labor leaders felt so jubilant about the Clayton Act. It is doubtful that President Wilson ever intended to exempt labor or any other group from the Sherman Act. He may have intended, during the campaign, to support governmental impartiality in labor disputes, but changed his mind after the election. One writer has argued that labor obtained minor gains during the early days of the administration such as the Sundry Civil Appropriation Bill which prevented the Justice Department from using appropriated funds for prosecuting labor violations under the Sherman Act.[23] However, such surface gains proved meaningless in reality since, for example, there was no law to keep the Justice Department from using other funds to prosecute unions. By 1913 the President attempted to end the animosity between his administration and the business community, which had developed during the 1912 campaign. At the same time he wanted to strengthen the antitrust provisions of the Sherman law in order to foster greater competition in the economy. The President was not to be deterred from his drive to obtain stronger laws against business monopolies. At the same time labor unions could not be ignored in the drive for better control over monopolies.[24] The political realities in the Congress would not have permitted both a stronger monopoly control law and a total exemption of unions from the antitrust provisions. Section 6 of the Clayton Act had the approval of organized labor when it was first introduced in the House, but union leaders later decided that the provision was not what they desired and sought amendment. There was no further support from the President since he considered the campaign pledges made to labor were fulfilled. Indeed, the President and leaders of the House resisted union pressures for outright exemption from the Sherman law.[25]

Labor pressures in the House led to an attachment to Section 6 which stated:

> Nor shall such organizations, or the members thereof, be held or construed to be illegal combinations or conspiracies in restraint of trade, under the anti-trust laws.

Some of the House leaders along with organized labor interpreted this amendment to mean union exclusion from the provisions of antitrust laws. It is probable that the "Magna Charta" statement of Gompers stemmed from this addition. However, this interpretation was not accepted by President Wilson or the Committee on the Judiciary.[26] No general agreement was reached in the House on either the labor exemption controversy or the meaning of the injunction section. The President along with the House and Senate agreed that Section 6 did grant labor the right to exist, but the Congress could not agree upon the interpretation of either Section 6, the exemption of labor from antitrust prosecution, or Section 20, the controversy over the power of the courts to issue injunctions. Therefore, "to him [Wilson] must go much of the responsibility for the failure of the Clayton Act to satisfy labor's demands. . . ." [27]

Organized labor wanted complete exemption from the antitrust laws. This could have been accomplished by a very simple provision: "nothing contained in the antitrust laws shall be construed to apply to labor organizations." But Congress and the President did not intend to exempt unions from the antitrust laws, and the proposal was rejected. If that were its intention, Congress would have adopted the proposal. Instead a relatively meaningless provision was enacted. Indeed, the President was convinced that the Clayton Act merely granted unions the legal right to exist. Some of the early testimony of Gompers before Congress indicated that such a right was his major objective. In the *Danbury Hatters* and *Gompers* decisions, the Supreme Court did not hold unions subject to the antitrust laws because labor was considered a commodity or an article of commerce. Unions were held to have restrained trade within the meaning of the Sherman Act because their boycott activities interfered with the interstate shipment of hats and stoves. The first sentence of Section 6 therefore did not change labor law. It was an empty phrase devoid of practical importance. Additional statements in Section 6 likewise should have made organized labor suspicious of the Clayton Act. Courts since 1842 held labor unions in themselves to be lawful organizations. In the antitrust cases the Supreme Court did not deny that employees had the right to form labor unions. As a consequence the statements "nothing contained in the antitrust laws shall be construed to forbid the existence and operation of labor organizations" and "nor shall such organizations or the members thereof, be held or construed to be illegal combinations or conspiracies in restraint of trade, under the antitrust laws" added nothing new to labor law. Labor unions were lawful organizations before the passage of the Sherman law, and they were lawful organizations after the Sherman Antitrust Act was passed.

Add to these phrases the statement that unions may "lawfully carry out the legitimate aspects thereof" and Section 6 appears worthless as a protective measure to labor unions. Who but the courts were to spell out when unions were lawfully carrying out their legitimate objectives? That was the crux of the problem in the Sherman Act antitrust cases. The Supreme Court declared that the implementation of a boycott by a labor union did not constitute a lawful activity under the Sherman law. All Section 6 did in this respect was to affirm the right of the courts to decide the questions of lawful and unlawful union activities and objectives.

Not only was the Clayton Act to prove worthless to labor unions, but their position was made much worse by the measure. Under the Sherman law only the government could obtain an injunction for the enforcement of that law. Employers had no right to obtain an injunction against a union on the ground of violation of the antitrust statute. They could sue unions for treble damages, but employers were not permitted to obtain injunctions under the 1890 law. The Clayton Act changed these circumstances. It provided that private parties as well as law-enforcement officers of the federal government could obtain injunctions in antitrust cases. This meant that the ability of employers to obtain injunctions against unions was considerably increased. If the government was not inclined to proceed against unions in injunction proceedings under the antitrust laws, employers after 1914 could petition the courts for injunctions themselves. Subsequently, unions were required to contest numerous antitrust injunction suits originating from employer action. One writer stated:

> Of a total of 64 proceedings of all kinds brought against labor under the Sherman Act after the passage of the Clayton Act, 34, or more than one-half, were private injunction suits. The law may thus be said to have more than doubled the chances that labor activities would be hampered by the Sherman Act. This is indeed a curious, though probably the most important consequence of a law which labor greeted as its great charter of industrial freedom.[28]

Actually, the changes of 1914 proved an enigma to organized labor.

RULE OF REASON:
DEVELOPMENT OF A DOUBLE STANDARD

The major purpose for enactment of the Sherman Act was to deal with growing business monopolies. It will be recalled that labor unions were not excluded from the provisions of the antitrust laws despite the confusion that stemmed from the legislative history of both laws. It remained for the Supreme Court to construct the degree to which the laws would be applied to both business and labor cases. The *rule-of-reason doctrine* was established and applied in business cases, but ignored in nearly all labor cases. Such a state of construction prompted Justice Brandeis in a 1927 case to imply a double standard had been developed between business and labor.[29] This section deals with the development of the double standard by focusing on the major business and labor cases which clearly point out the double treatment under the law.

Rule of Reason: Application to Business

In one of the first business cases arising under the Sherman law,[30] the Supreme Court served notice that the antitrust laws were not to prevent the growth of big business. The American Sugar Refining Company purchased the stock of independent refineries and as a result controlled 98 percent of all cane sugar refining capacity of the country. The Court held that the control of an industry gained by the purchase of stock did not restrain interstate commerce within the meaning of the Sherman law. In 1904, however, the Court ordered the dissolution of a railroad monopoly created through the purchase of stock.[31] A combination of two independent railroads was effected through stock acquisition manipulations. The Northern Securities Company, a holding company formed to effect the transaction, gained control of the Northern Pacific Railway and the Great Northern Railway. The roads had been competing with parallel lines, which serviced the northwestern states from St. Paul and Duluth to Seattle and Portland. In ordering the combination to dissolve, the Supreme Court held that the effect and purpose of the monopoly suppressed competition and restrained trade within the meaning of the antitrust law.

Those who supported the underlying philosophy of the Sherman law were pleased with the *Northern Securities Company* decision. They believed that the Supreme Court intended to interpret the antitrust statutes in a manner which would cut down industrial giants. The Supreme Court did not maintain a hard line, however, for in 1911 the Supreme Court established the celebrated rule-of-reason doctrine in the *Standard Oil* and *American Tobacco* decisions.[32] In those cases the Supreme Court distinguished between "reasonable" and "unreasonable" restraint of trade. Combinations which reasonably restrained commerce were not unlawful under the Sherman Act. Only those which unreasonably restrained trade were unlawful. Not *every* combination that suppressed competition was to be dissolved, but only those which unreasonably stamped out competition.

By introducing the rule-of-reason doctrine into the construction of the Sherman law, the Supreme Court precluded any possible objective interpretation of the statute. The terms *reasonable* and *unreasonable* admit to no precise definition. Obviously, the construction to be placed on the terms could vary with different persons. What may be reasonable to one individual may be unreasonable to another. In the *Standard Oil* and *American Tobacco* cases, the Supreme Court did rule that the monopolies unreasonably restrained commerce. The Standard Oil Company in the early 1900s refined between 85 to 90 percent of the country's output of oil.[33] On its part, the American Tobacco Company controlled, at the time of the case, about 97 percent of the production of domestic cigarettes and had a monopoly over most of the supply of other tobacco items, such as cigars, smoking tobacco, and snuff.[34]

The application of the rule of reason in subsequent antitrust cases, however, brought different results. In a case involving the United States Steel Corporation, the Supreme Court did not find a violation of the Sherman law.[35] Prosecution of the company was sought on the basis of monopolization under Section 2, not restraint of trade under Section 1. The decision was reached not to prosecute despite the fact that the steel corporation was organized as a holding company in 1901 for the purpose of acquiring the stock of independent operating companies. By 1920 the corporation controlled at least 50 percent of steel production in the nation. In addition, "from

1901 to 1911, when the government proceedings were instituted, there had been no price competition in the steel industry."[36] It was reported that "every stage in the production of iron and steel from the mining of ore and the manufacture of coke to the production of pig iron, as well as the manufacture of rails, bars, plates, sheets, tubes, rods, and other finished products, are under the control of the holding company."[37] Despite the facts presented, the Supreme Court ruled that the United States Steel Corporation was not in violation of the antitrust law. This was quite a contrast to the *Northern Securities* case.

In 1913 the Court likewise refused to apply the Sherman law to a shoe machinery combination.[38] The United Shoe Machinery Company, the defendant in the case, produced about 90 to 95 percent of all shoe machinery used in the nation. Four independent companies were united into one combination by the corporation. Promoters of the combination openly avowed their intent to control the entire production of shoe machinery equipment. This combination discouraged its customers use of any machine not controlled by the United Shoe Machinery Company. On the one occasion when the combination was threatened with competition, the assets of the would-be competitor were bought up by the combination.[39] Faced with this situation, the Supreme Court held that the combination merely effected a reasonable restraint of trade.

By now it appeared that the Supreme Court construed the term reasonable in a very broad manner. In addition, the Supreme Court, in a series of decisions, held that price and production control effected by trade associations did not violate the antitrust statute.[40] In this connection the Court declared:

> Persons who unite in gathering and disseminating information in trade journals and statistical reports on industry, who gather and publish statistics as to the amount of production of commodities in interstate commerce, and who report market prices, are not engaged in unlawful conspiracies or restraint of trade merely because the ultimate result of their efforts may be to stabilize prices or limit production. . . .[41]

Thus the rule of reason protected trade associations even though the net result of their activities resulted in artificial control of prices and production. After 1927 the application of the rule of reason in business cases was varied. The Court tended to rule illegal such activities as price fixing, market allocations, and the like without regard to the reasonable or unreasonable effect doctrine.

Rule of Reason: Application to Labor Organizations

Neither the passage of the Clayton Act nor the development of the rule-of-reason doctrine in business antitrust cases alleviated the position of labor unions under the Sherman law. In 1921 the Supreme Court of the United States had its first opportunity to deal with the application of the antitrust law to labor unions following enactment of the Clayton Act and the establishment of the rule-of-reason doctrine.[42] The Court decided the case squarely on the precedent of the *Danbury Hatters* and *Gompers* decisions. Labor's so-called Magna Charta pronouncement and the rule of reason did not influence the Court in its interpretation of congressional intent to apply the Sherman law to organized labor.

The 1921 case involved the International Association of Machinists, then an affiliate of the American Federation of Labor, and the Duplex Printing Press Company of Battle Creek, Michigan. At that time there were only three other companies manufacturing printing presses in the United States. All four firms were in active competition with each other. From 1909 until 1913 the machinists' union was successful in organizing all the firms with the exception of the Duplex Company. In the shops in which the union had won recognition, employers granted the eight-hour day, established a minimum-wage scale, and generally complied with other employment practices demanded by the union. On the other hand, the Duplex Company, which refused to recognize the union, operated on a ten-hour-day basis, refused to establish a minimum-wage scale, and disregarded the standards of work demanded by the union. Operating with lower labor standards, the Duplex Company represented a formidable competitive threat to the organized firms. So severe was this competition that two of the organized firms notified the union they would be obliged to terminate their agreements with it unless their competitor, the Duplex Company, also entered into an agreement with the union and thereby raised its labor standards. Organization of the Duplex Company was the prerequisite for standardization of labor costs and uniformity of competitive conditions within the industry.

Aware of the soundness of the argument of the organized firms, the International Association of Machinists attempted to organize the Duplex Company. Since the company refused to negotiate with the union on a voluntary basis, the IAM called an organizational strike. The strike proved totally unsuccessful because only a fraction of the workers responded to the strike call of the union. Out of the 250 employees of the Duplex Company, eleven engaged in the strike.

The union had two alternative courses of action. Either it could terminate its contract in the organized plants,thereby ending collective bargaining in the industry, or it could resort to economic action calculated to force the Duplex Company to recognize the organization. The union chose the latter course of conduct. Union action took the form of a secondary boycott directed against the products of the Duplex Company. Since New York City represented one of the most important markets for the products of Duplex, the International Association of Machinists aimed to prevent sale of the company's presses in the New York area. To accomplish the objective, the union implemented an elaborate program that included ordering members of the union located in New York not to install or repair Duplex presses; notifying a trucking company usually employed by Duplex customers to haul the presses not to do so; and warning customers not to purchase or install Duplex presses. These activities were designed to eliminate the Duplex Company from the New York market with the effect of encouraging Duplex customers to purchase presses manufactured by companies with which the union had contracts. The economic circumstances surrounding the *Duplex* case were strikingly similar to those involved in the *Danbury Hatters* affair. And, as in the latter case, the Court held that the action of the union violated the terms of the Sherman law. In the opinion of the Court there was no mention of the rule of reason which guided decisions in antitrust cases involving business enterprises.

Subsequent to the *Duplex* decision, the Court utilized the rule-of-reason doctrine in one case to find lawful a union activity that had the effect of restraining commerce.[43] Involved in the case with the labor organization was an employers' association, the National Association of Window Glass Manufacturers. This association was composed of firms which produced handmade glass. The union was the National Association of Window Glass Workers, which represented the workers engaged in the handmade glass industry. As the result of the advent of the automatic glass machine, the supply of handmade glass workers, a highly skilled craft, decreased by such an amount that there were not enough craftsmen to run all the handmade glass plants on a full-time basis. An industry-wide agreement was executed between the labor organization and the employers' association. To solve the labor-supply problem, the contract provided that half the factories would operate between September 15, 1922, and January 27, 1923, and the remaining half between January 29, 1923, and June 11, 1923.[44] After reviewing the economic factors involved in the case, the Court concluded "that we see no combination in unreasonable restraint of trade in the arrangement made to meet the short supply of men." With the exception of this one case, the Court never again utilized the rule of reason in labor cases.

The Court, though ignoring the rule-of-reason doctrine in the *Duplex* case, could scarcely bypass completely the Clayton Act. As stated previously, however, the law was interpreted in a fashion which afforded no relief to unions in antitrust cases. With respect to Section 6 of the Clayton Act, the Court in *Duplex* declared:

> There is nothing in the section to exempt such an organization or its members from accountability where it or they depart from its normal and legitimate objects and engage in an actual combination or conspiracy in restraint of trade. And by no fair or permissible construction can it be taken as authorizing any activity otherwise unlawful, or enabling a normally lawful organization to become a cloak for an illegal combination or conspiracy in restraint of trade as defined by the antitrust laws.

Thus the courts still claimed the power to determine whether or not a labor organization was "lawfully carrying out legitimate objects." Nothing in the Clayton Act, the Supreme Court contended, denied this right to the judiciary. As a consequence the Court ordered an injunction stamping out the secondary boycott instigated by the International Association of Machinists. The *Duplex* decision meant the position of organized labor under the Sherman law remained unchanged. Secondary boycott activities were still unlawful. The right to do business was still paramount to the right of workers to self-organization and effective collective bargaining.

After the decision was rendered, organized labor went before the Supreme Court of the United States in six antitrust cases.[45] Before 1921 the federal courts applied the antitrust statutes only to railroad strikes and union secondary boycott activities. After 1921 and the *Duplex* decision, courts applied the Sherman law to ordinary factory and coal strikes. The double standard between business and labor cases was to be developed further in the *Coronado* and *Bedford* cases.

The Coronado Doctrine: Continued Development
of the Double Standard

In the early part of the twentieth century, the United Mine Workers of America was confronted with a serious economic problem. The gains it had won through collective bargaining were threatened by the operation of nonunion mines. Intensive competition characterized the bituminous coal industry; unionized mines paying comparatively high wages and maintaining union standards of employment could not compete on even terms with nonunion mines operating with lower labor standards and lower costs. This differential, the union recognized, could only be erased by organization of the nonunion mines. Previously, we noted how the judiciary hindered the United Mine Workers from carring out its objective by enforcing the yellow-dog contract with the labor injunction.[46] Union efforts in the mines were further checked by the application of the Sherman law to its organizational activities. The *Coronado* cases were the outgrowth of union efforts to expand organization in the coal industry in the face of employer opposition.

The Coronado Coal Mine was controlled by the Bachne-Denman Coal Company, a corporation that controlled several coal mines in Sebastian County, Arkansas. In the spring of 1914 the company decided to operate its properties on an open shop and nonunion basis. This decision was made despite the fact that the United Mine Workers of America had valid contracts with the coal companies controlled by Bachne-Denman, including one with the Coronado Mine. To implement its decision, Bachne-Denman closed down a number of unionized mines and planned to open them on a nonunion basis. Aware of the possibility of violence, the company, while the mines were shut down, laid plans to operate them as open shops. Such preparation included the hiring of guards from the Burns Detective Agency, the purchase of rifles and ammunition, eviction of union members from company houses, and the stretching of cable around the mines. The coal company was aware of the threat of violence when the decision was reached in favor of operating the mines on a nonunion basis. In this connection, Bachne said, "To do this means a bitter fight, but in my opinion it can be accomplished by proper organization."[47]

Workers at the Coronado Mine expected the same pattern of action as at other mines of the Bachne-Denman Coal Company. To forestall such action, the workers at the Coronado Mine struck, but the company refused to submit to union demands and during the strike attempted to operate the Coronado Mine with nonunion workers. On April 6, 1914, about a month after the strike began, a union committee, along with a large crowd of union miners and sympathizers, visited the superintendent of the Coronado Mine with the intention of persuading the company to restore operations on a union basis. The company refused once again. As a result the crowd injured a number of nonunion employees, ran the guards off the premises of the mine, and flooded the mine, causing the cessation of all operations.

Violence erupted on July 17 when the unionists, equipped with rifles, attacked the mine in force. After a few hours the guards and nonunion employees were driven from the premises. Several of the nonunion employees were murdered. By the end of the day the entire mine was destroyed by dynamite and fire. A dialogue between the parties, which is a substantial attribute in an established collective bargaining relationship, was not available to alleviate the conflict.

Almost immediately the operators brought suit against the Mine Workers Union charging a violation under the Sherman law. They claimed that the union had caused $740,000 in damages, but asked for a judgment three times this sum since the Sherman law provides for treble damages. After prolonged litigation in the lower federal courts, the Supreme Court of the United States decided the first *Coronado* case on June 5, 1922, or about eight years after the strike took place.[48] The Supreme Court denied the company the damages it requested and ruled that the United Mine Workers of America did not violate the Sherman law. In reaching this conclusion, the Court held that "coal mining [was] not interstate commerce, and the power of Congress [did] not extend to its regulation as such." Since coal mining was not considered interstate commerce, the Sherman law, a federal statute, had no application to a strike effected in a coal mine. Owners of the coal company contended that the antitrust law applied because 75 percent of the output of their mines was delivered outside the state of Arkansas. This argument was rejected by the Court on the basis that the entire production of the Bachne-Denman mines, five thousand tons weekly, constituted an infinitesimal portion of the nation's entire coal production, about 10 to 15 million tons weekly.

The acts of violence during the strike were deplored by the Court, but it held that such unlawfulness in itself does not establish the jurisdiction of the Sherman law over a situation in which in the absence of violence the Act would not apply. Moreover, the Court was not convinced that the operation of the mine on a nonunion basis would have resulted in the sale of more coal by virtue of lower prices based upon lower labor costs. In this connection it declared that the company would not lower the price of coal, but "would probably pocket the profit" that a reduction of wages would make possible.

However, the main ground for the Court's decision in the *Coronado* case was that the company did not prove the union intended to monopolize or restrain interstate commerce within the meaning of the Sherman law. It was not sufficient to show that a strike may have indirectly reduced the amount of coal in commerce, but proof must be adduced that the unionists conspired to restrain trade or suppress competition. This type of evidence, the Court contended, was not produced by the plaintiff. The real purpose of the Coronado strike was well publicized. The United Mine Workers of America was on a campaign to stop nonunion coal from competing with union-mined coal. Since the Bachne-Denman Coal Company took action inconsistent with the union program, the union retaliated with a strike to implement its economic program. The Court recognized this, for in the *Coronado* opinion it declared that union leaders were stimulated "to press their unionization of nonunion mines not only as a direct means of bettering the conditions and wages of their workers but also as a means of lessening interstate competition for union operators which in turn would lessen the pressure of those operators for reduction of the union scale or the resistance to an increase."

The awareness of the general economic program of the Mine Workers Union, however, did not control the *Coronado* decision. The Court held that no evidence was produced to demonstrate that the strike standing alone was stimulated by a plot to suppress competition within the meaning of the Sherman law. If the union conspired to eliminate the marketing of nonunion coal, and hence restrain trade, the company had not proved such intent. If it could prove that the union intended to eliminate the sale of nonunion products, the company, the Court suggested, would win the case. This observation was an invitation to the company to hunt for such new evidence, and the company undertook a search for it. That the search was fruitful was demonstrated in 1925 in the second *Coronado* case.[49] This time the high court held that the 1914 strike at the Coronado Mine violated the Sherman law. It reversed its 1922 decision on the ground that the company now supplied "the links lacking at the first trial."

The company secured as a witness a former officer of the union who had been involved in the 1914 strike. This witness had been the secretary of the local union engaged in the strike, and worked as a checkweighman in the mine. He, along with others, was tried and imprisoned for engaging in the bloody 1914 strike. In his testimony, he claimed that the union undertook to prevent coal mined at the Coronado Mine while the strike was in progress "from getting into the market." He further testified that union officers and union members engaged in the Coronado strike instigated the acts of violence because they were aware that "if Bachne coal, scab-dug coal, got into the market it would only be a matter of time until every union operator in the country would have to close down his mine, and scab it, because the union operators could not meet Bachne competition." This testimony convicted the union, for the Court now held, in direct contrast to its position in 1924, "that the purpose of the destruction of the mines was to stop the production of nonunion coal and prevent its shipment to markets in states other than Arkansas, where it would by competition tend to reduce the price of the commodity and affect injuriously the maintenance of wages for union labor in competing mines. . . ."

An additional bit of new evidence also influenced the change on the part of the high court. As noted, in the first *Coronado* case, the estimate of the output of the Bachne-Denman mine was placed at five thousand tons weekly. In the second case, the company adduced evidence that supported its claim that the action of the union prevented the production of five thousand tons of coal daily. The company proved to the satisfaction of the Court that this larger figure justified the application of the Sherman law to the labor dispute. It is significant to note, however, that, despite the larger production estimate, the Court did not declare outright that coal mining constituted interstate commerce. Many years later the Supreme Court was again to rule that mining was not interstate commerce. Actually, the amount of coal in question was not too important in the *Coronado* case. When the Court concluded that a conspiracy existed to reduce the amount of coal in commerce, the conviction of the labor union was assured. This same verdict would have been handed down, no doubt, regardless of the amount of coal in question.

The effect of the *Coronado* decision was to deter the organizational campaign of the Mine Workers Union. After the decision, many nonunion operators, following the precedent of the Bachne-Denman Coal Company, brought suit against the union when faced with organizational campaigns. Uniformly, the complaint was always that the union conspired to suppress competition within the meaning of the Sherman Act by eliminating from commerce coal produced under nonunion conditions. Records indicate that the United Mine Workers of America was a defendant in antitrust proceedings more frequently than any other labor organization.[50] Not only did the *Coronado* decision stand as an obstacle to the efforts of the Mine Workers Union to organize the coal industry, but it served to dampen efforts of the entire labor movement. The Court held that unions, though unincorporated, could be sued as a body in the federal courts. It was not necessary for a plaintiff to proceed against each member of the union. The union as a body could be attacked in damage suits.

Of much greater significance, the *Coronado* doctrine shed doubt on the legality of any important strike. It is of importance to note that secondary boycott activities were not involved in the *Coronado* affair. Under the *Danbury Hatters* doctrine, repeated in the *Gompers* case, the Court applied the Sherman law because of the implementation of secondary boycott activity. In contrast, the union was convicted in the *Coronado* case because of a strike directed against the company immediately involved in the dispute. Organized labor was aware that every major strike had the effect of reducing the amount of products in commerce. The Supreme Court in the *Coronado* case declared that when the intent of those preventing "the manufacture of production is shown to be to restrain or to control the supply entering and moving in interstate commerce, or the price of it in interstate markets, their action is a direct violation of the Antitrust Act." So sweeping was this declaration that union leaders feared that any strike for any purpose that diminished the amount of products in interstate commerce would be unlawful under the Sherman law. Should a strike result in reduction of the supply of goods in commerce, all that remained to convict under the Sherman law would be to adduce evidence that the strikers "intended" to suppress interstate trade. To prove such intent, as the *Coronado* case indicated, would not be a very difficult task. Thus the testimony of a single witness was the chief ground for the conviction under the Sherman law of the union and workers involved in the *Coronado* affair. The decision generated uncertainty in the ranks of organized labor. Every important strike could be subject to the jurisdiction of the Sherman law by virtue of the far-sweeping implications of the *Coronado* doctrine.

In 1924, in another case, the legal atmosphere surrounding the application of the Sherman law to strikes against employers immediately involved in a labor dispute was somewhat clarified. In the spring of 1920 the United Leather Workers Union attempted to organize five Missouri corporations engaged in the manufacture and sale of leather goods and trunks. After the companies refused to bargain collectively, the labor organization called its members out on strike. Picket lines were thrown up at each of the factories for the purpose of persuading nonstriking workers to join in the strike and to force the company not to hire replacements for the strikers. Some of the tactics employed by the union to stop production in the plants were not lawful, but the record indicates that the strikers did not resort in any manner to the excess of lawlessness displayed by the workers in the *Coronado* case. In any event the union was successful in curtailing the operation of the factories, and the companies charged that the effect of the strike and the publicity prevented the manufacture and shipment of the products of their factories in interstate commerce. As a result the companies claimed the union restrained trade within the meaning of the Sherman law.

Here indeed was a test case involving the application of the Sherman law to a strike instigated against employers directly involved in a labor dispute. The union did not engage in secondary boycott activities, nor was the strike conducted in a context of lawlessness exemplified in the *Coronado* affair. Before the Supreme Court took jurisdiction of the case in 1924, lower federal courts dealt with the case. In November 1920 a district court judge issued a permanent injunction under the terms of the Sherman law stamping out the strike. The judge held that the union injured the interstate commerce of the companies within the meaning of the Act.[51] Upon appeal, the Eighth Circuit Court upheld the ruling of the district court judge by a 2-1 vote. The majority of the circuit court of appeals held that "the natural and inevitable effect of the prevention by the defendants of the making of the plaintiffs of the articles they had made interstate contracts to sell, make, and deliver, was the prevention of their performance of their contracts and the prevention or partial prevention of their interstate commerce, and this result was so evident and unavoidable that the defendants could not have failed to know, to propose, and to intend that this should be the result."[52] In short, any strike for any purpose was unlawful under the Sherman law, provided that the strike reduced the amount of goods in commerce. Particular evidence to show intent of the workers to restrain commerce, as was required in the *Coronado* case, was not essential for conviction under the Sherman law, for intent could be inferred from the action of the strikers. In effect, the district and circuit courts held that workers who struck and suppressed interstate commerce could not keep from knowing the result of their action.

Had the Supreme Court of the United States upheld the position of the lower court, the right of workers to strike would have been circumscribed to the degree of rendering their fundamental economic weapon ineffective and useless. The Supreme Court in a 6-3 decision reversed the judgment of the lower federal courts. The majority of the Supreme Court concurred with the dissenting judge in the circuit court of appeals who, in speaking of the majority opinion, declared: "The natural, logical, and inevitable result will be that every strike in any industry or even in any single factory will be within the Sherman Act and subject to federal jurisdiction provided any appreciable amount of its products enters into interstate commerce." In commenting on this statement, the majority of the high court declared, "We cannot think that Congress intended any such result in the enactment of the Antitrust Act. . . ." The Supreme Court overruled the lower federal court on the ground that the employers produced no evidence to indicate that the workers intended by their strike and picketing to restrain commerce. Even though the effect of their activities caused the reduction in the supply of products for interstate commerce, the Court contended, "The record is entirely without evidence or circumstances to show that the defendants in their conspiracy to deprive the complainant of their workers were directing their scheme against interstate commerce."[53] Thus the six members of the Supreme Court prevented the application of the Sherman law to every important strike. It is interesting to note that thirteen federal judges handled the *Leather Workers* case. Six held that the Sherman law outlawed every strike of any consequence. In short, the *Coronado* doctrine dramatized the Supreme Court's double standard in its extreme form.

THE <u>BEDFORD</u> <u>STONE</u> DECISION: EFFECT ON UNION TACTICS AND COMPLETION OF THE DOUBLE STANDARD

In 1927 organized labor felt the full measure of the double standard constructed under the Sherman law, for in that year the Supreme Court of the United States handed down the famous *Bedford Stone* decision.[54] This decision is a landmark in labor cases arising under the antitrust statutes. If organized labor sensed a new direction in decisions because of the *Leather Workers* decision, this attitude changed when the high court handed down its ruling in the *Bedford Stone* case. That decision, perhaps more than any other labor antitrust case, demonstrated to organized labor that the Sherman provisions provided a potent weapon to combat unionism and collective bargaining.

Arrayed against each other in the *Bedford Stone* case were an association of employers and an international labor union. The employers' association was composed of twenty-four corporations engaged in the business of quarrying and fabricating limestone in the Bedford-Bloomington area in Indiana. Their combined investment was about $6 million and their annual aggregate sales amounted to approximately $15 million, more than 75 percent in states other than Indiana. Together, the twenty-four corporations produced about 70 percent of all the cut stone in the nation. The local employers' association was affiliated with a national employers' organization, called the International Cut Stone & Quarryers Association. Thus the highly solvent employers in the *Bedford Stone* case banded together for their mutual benefit into an effective local employers' association, which was affiliated with a national employers' organization and dominated the cut stone industry of the nation. On the other hand, the labor organization, the Journeymen Stone Cutters Association, had a total membership of five thousand members in fifty local unions, or an average of thirty-three members in each local. The union jurisdiction extended to workers employed in quarries and affiliated quarry facilities and covered workers who installed cut stone in buildings.

Before 1921 the Bedford-Bloomington quarry operators recognized the Journeymen Stone Cutters Association as the bargaining agent of the workers employed in their quarries. As a result stone was quarried under collective bargaining conditions. In 1921, however, the employers' association refused to extend the trade agreement, and in its place set up a series of company-dominated unions. Later discussion will reveal that company-dominated unions do not perform the functions of collective bargaining. An effective union cannot serve the interests of employers and employees at the same time.[55] Company-dominated unions, under the influence of management, are not free to protect basic employment interests of workers. In spite of the protests of the Journeymen Stone Cutters Association, the operators resumed production under nonunion conditions. The Indiana quarries had to be organized once again, or the Journeymen Stone Cutters Association would for all intents and purposes disintegrate as a labor organization, since the Indiana area was the most important stone-producing region in the nation.

Stimulated by such considerations, the Journeymen Stone Cutters Association enacted a clause in its constitution which forbade its members to handle stone "cut by men working in opposition" to the labor organization. In other words, the members decided not to work with nonunion cut stone. This rule was implemented in states and cities in which the Bedford-Bloomington operators sold stone to building contractors. Customers of these operators were persuaded not to purchase Indiana stone for they were aware that, once purchased, the stone would not be installed in buildings by union members. For example, a building contractor in New York would hesitate to purchase nonunion Indiana stone when he knew the members of the Stone Cutters' Association would refuse to install the product.

The tactics of the Stone Cutters' Association were essentially the same as those employed by the labor organization involved in the *Duplex* affair. Both unions implemented a secondary boycott to force antiunion employers to recognize labor unions. Pressure was exerted on firms for the purpose of forcing them to cease doing business with companies directly involved in the labor dispute. Such pressure constitutes a secondary boycott. So impressed was the Court with the similarity of the *Bedford Stone* case with the *Duplex* decision that it declared "with a few changes in respect to the product involved, dates, names, and incidents, which would have no effect upon the principle established, the opinion in *Duplex Company* v. *Deering* might serve as an opinion in this case."

The Court was correct in establishing this similarity from the point of view of the weapon employed by the unions. Upon closer examination, the analogy is not as clear cut as indicated by the majority opinion, since in the *Duplex* case the union marshalled its forces against *one* employer, while in the *Bedford Stone* affair the union was arrayed against an employers' association of great wealth and power. In any event the Court, in the *Bedford Stone* case, held that the conduct of the union violated the antitrust act because "the strikes . . . preventing the use and installation of petitioners' products in other states, necessarily threatened to destroy and narrow petitioners' interstate trade by taking from them their customers."

Double Standard Implied

Organized labor suffered a reversal with the Supreme Court's decision in the *Bedford Stone* case. Before this Court reviewed the case, a district court and a circuit court of appeals refused to restrain the activities of the labor union. The high court's knowledge that the Stone Cutters Association was pitted against a powerful employers' association did not control the decision. The union conduct was peaceful and no violence of any sort occurred with implementation of the boycott. As a matter of fact, the union did not even engage in picketing. The sole activity of the workers was to refuse to handle nonunion stone for the purpose of defending their union against a powerful and wealthy employers' association. In addition, the union did not deter contractors from purchasing stone not quarried in the Bloomington-Bedford region. The boycott was instituted against nonunion stone, and there was no interference with the liberty of contractors to purchase union-made stone. The Court ruled that the union's action constituted an "unreasonable restraint of . . . commerce within the meaning of the Antitrust Act . . .," despite the character of the application of the rule of reason in business cases. Brandeis dissented vigorously from the majority on this issue and made it clear that the double standard had been fully developed and that development stopped just short of prohibiting strikes entirely. Justice Brandeis declared:

> If, on the undisputed facts of this case, refusal to work can be enjoined, Congress created by the Sherman Law and the Clayton Act an instrument for imposing restraints upon labor which reminds of involuntary servitude. The Sherman Law was held in *United States* v. *United States Steel Corporation* . . . to permit capitalists to combine in a single corporation 50 percent of the steel industry of the United States dominating the trade through its vast resources. The Sherman Law was held in *United States* v. *United Shoe Machinery Co.* . . . to permit capitalists to combine in another corporation practically the whole shoe-machinery industry of the country, necessarily giving it a position of dominance over shoe manufacturing in America. It would, indeed, be strange if Congress had by the same Act willed to deny to members of a small craft of workingmen the right to co-operate in simply refraining from work, when that course was the only means of self-protection against a combination of militant and powerful employers. I cannot believe that Congress did so.[56]

With the *Bedford Stone* decision the pattern of the application of the Sherman law to labor unions was completed. A law enacted presumably to check the growth of "big business" was more restrictive to union organization. It served as a fertile ground for the labor injunction and provided the basis for damage suits against labor unions. Secondary economic activity by unions when the alternative was disintegration of the labor organization was deemed unlawful. Such action was no less unlawful when its implementation was on a peaceful basis. The judiciary was prepared to coerce free men into "involuntary servitude," even though the refusal to work had as its fundamental purpose the raising of standards of living of workers by establishing, retaining, or widening the collective bargaining process. Strikes against employers directly involved in a labor dispute were likewise unlawful when proof could be adduced that the "intent" of the union was to suppress the amount of goods in commerce. The rule-of-reason doctrine, which proved of enormous benefit to business, did not alleviate the stern application of the Sherman law to labor unions. One standard was set for business enterprises and still another for labor unions. In addition, the high court brushed aside as worthless and unimportant the powerful economic and social forces that surrounded labor disputes in antitrust cases. Economic and social realism was rejected in favor of the standard of cold and legal formalism. This narrow legal approach invariably resulted in a restriction of collective action calculated to influence union members' economic and social status in life.

SUMMARY

The period around the turn of the twentieth century was one in which big business and monopolistic organization characterized the economic system. Congress became concerned with this turn of events and passed the Sherman Antitrust Act in 1890 and the Clayton Act in 1914 to legislate the nation's economy into a competitive pattern. The effort largely failed in terms of regulation of firm size, but had a stronger effect upon the activities of labor organizations. The application of the antitrust laws to organized labor made secondary boycotts illegal. This proved restrictive to union efforts to organize. The integration and interdependency of the economy made the secondary boycott a first-rate union weapon. The inability to use the weapon decreased union power to influence the outcome of economic struggles.

Out of the application of the antitrust laws to union activities arose several landmark labor cases: *Danbury Hatters, Gompers, Duplex, Coronado,* and *Bedford Stone.* A comparison of these cases with business cases such as *E. C. Knight, Northern Securities, Standard Oil,* and *United States Steel* make it clear that the Supreme Court developed a double standard in the application of antitrust provisions to the two groups. On the one hand, the Supreme Court in effect held that unionism was incompatible with the antitrust statutes. On the other hand, it ruled that the rule of reason would be applied in each business case to determine if there had been a reasonable or unreasonable restraint of interstate trade. The Sherman Act, passed primarily to check big business, was more effective in the control of the collective bargaining process.

NOTES

[1] Reported in Thomas C. Cochran and William Miller, *The Age of Enterprise* (New York: The Macmillan Company, 1943), p. 324.

[2] Reuben E. Slesinger, *National Economic Policy: The Presidential Reports* (Princeton, N. J.: D. Van Nostrand Co., Inc., 1968), p. 98.

[3] Cochran and Miller, *op. cit.*, p. 356.

[4] Sherman Anti-Trust Law, 26 Stat. 209, Act of July 2, 1890. On October 15, 1914, Congress enacted the Clayton Act, 38 Stat. 780, which in part purports to make the Sherman law more effective relative to the checking of monopoly control of industry.

[5] Edward Berman, *Labor and the Sherman Act* (New York: Harper & Brothers, 1930).

[6] A. T. Mason, *Organized Labor and the Law* (Durham, N. C.: Duke University Press, 1925).

[7] A 1955 amendment raised the maximum fine to $50,000.

[8] *United States* v. *Workingmen's Amalgamated Council*, 54 Fed. 994 (1893).

[9] Berman, *op. cit.*, p. 64.

[10] *Waterhouse* v. *Comer*, 55 Fed. 149 (1893).

[11] *In re Debs*, Petitioner, 158 U.S. 564 (1895).

[12] *United States* v. *Agler*, 62 Fed. 24 (1897).

[13] *United States* v. *Elliott*, 64 Fed. 27 (1898).

[14] *In re Debs, op. cit.*

[15] The official name is *Loewe* v. *Lawlor*, 208 U.S. 274 (1908). However, this landmark case is commonly referred to as the "Danbury Hatters" case, for the factory in question was located in Danbury, Connecticut. In 1915 the dispute was tried once more in the Supreme Court. The second case is officially cited as *Lawlor* v. *Loewe*, 235 U.S. 522 (1915).

[16] *Ibid.*

[17] See Chapter 8.

[18] J. R. Commons and Associates, *History of Labour in the United States* (New York: The Macmillan Company, 1926), p. 531.

[19] *Ibid.*, p. 532.

[20] *Gompers* v. *Bucks Stove and Range Company*, 221 U.S. 418 (1911).

[21] 38 Stat. 780 (1914).

[22] Edwin E. Witte, *The Government in Labor Disputes* (New York: McGraw-Hill Book Company, 1932), p. 68.

[23] Dallas L. Jones, "The Enigma of the Clayton Act," *Industrial and Labor Relations Review*, January 1957, p. 31.

[24] *Ibid.*, p. 207.

[25] *Ibid.*, p. 209.

[26] *Ibid.*, pp. 211–212.

[27] *Ibid.*, p. 221.

[28] Berman, *op. cit.*, p. 103.

[29] *Bedford Cut Stone Company* v. *Journeymen Stone Cutters' Association*, 274 U.S. 37 (1927).

[30] *United States* v. *E. C. Knight*, 156 U. S. 1 (1895).

[31] *Northern Securities Company* v. *United States*, 193 U.S. 199 (1904).

[32] *Standard Oil Company of New Jersey* v. *United States*, 221 U.S. 1 (1911). *United States* v. *American Tobacco Company*, 221 U.S. 106 (1911).

[33] Milton Handler, *Cases and Materials on Trade Regulations* (Chicago: The Foundation Press, 1937), p. 388.

[34] *Ibid.*, p. 401.

[35] *United States* v. *United States Steel Corporation*, 251 U.S. 417 (1920).

[36] Handler, *op. cit.*, p. 424.

[37] *Ibid.*, p. 422.

[38] *United States* v. *United Shoe Machinery Company*, 227 U.S. 32 (1913).

[39] Myron W. Watkins, "Trusts," *Encyclopedia of Social Sciences*, Vol. 15, p. 117.

[40] See Handler, *op. cit.*, pp. 256–385, for a discussion of the legal and economic aspects of trade associations.

[41] *Maple Flooring Manufacturers' Association* v. *United States*, 268 U.S. 563 (1925).

[42] *Duplex Printing Press Company* v. *Deering*, 254 U.S. 443 (1921).

[43] *National Association of Window Glass Manufacturers* v. *United States*, 263 U.S. 403 (1923).

[44] Berman, *op. cit.*, p. 150.

[45] *Ibid.*, p. 118.

[46] See Chapter 3.

[47] *United Mine Workers* v. *Coronado Coal Company*, 259 U.S. 344 (1922).

[48] *Ibid.*

[49] *Coronado Coal Company* v. *United Mine Workers of America*, 268 U.S. 295 (1925).

[50] Berman, *op. cit.*, p. 119.

[51] *Herbert and Meisel Trunk Company* v. *United Leather Workers International Union*, 268 Fed. 662 (1920).

[52] *United Leather Workers International Union* v. *Herbert and Meisel Trunk Company*, 284 Fed. 446 (1922).

[53] *United Leather Workers International Union* v. *Herbert and Meisel Trunk Company*, 285 U.S. 457 (1925).

[54] *Bedford Cut Stone Company* v. *Journeymen Stone Cutters' Association*, *op. cit.*

[55] See Chapter 7.

[56] *Bedford Cut Stone Company* v. *Journeymen Stone Cutters' Association*, *op. cit.*

III

GOVERNMENT ENCOURAGEMENT TO COLLECTIVE BARGAINING

PROLOGUE. *After 1932 collective bargaining flourished under the stimulus of a warm and friendly legal environment. What socioeconomic forces resulted in the change of the legal framework of collective bargaining? How did government implement this new policy? Is there a social and economic justification for a legal structure which nurtures unionism? Such problems demand an examination of the philosophy, mechanism, and results of the Norris–La Guardia and Wagner Acts. And then there must be discussion of the forces which produced Taft-Hartley, a law which changed the basic direction of national labor policy.*

5 Control of the Labor Injunction

THE CHANGING ECONOMIC AND POLITICAL SCENE

As demonstrated, the legal climate surrounding the collective bargaining process in the period 1806–1932 was restrictive. Theoretically, unions were lawful organizations; workers were legally free to join unions; and the right to strike as such was lawful. In practice, however, the courts controlled the right of workers to join unions and the liberty of labor organizations to engage in activities designed to make collective bargaining effective. The use of the injunction in labor disputes proved a most formidable obstacle to the expansion and implementation of trade unionism. Frequently, labor unions had the economic strength to deal with the antiorganizational activities of employers but fell before the labor injunction. When the courts held that the yellow-dog contract could be implemented by the labor injunction, the position of unions in an economic struggle was diminished immeasurably. The anomalous condition existed wherein workers legally free to join labor unions were prevented from doing this. Courts enforced the "yellow-dog" arrangement, which enabled employers to maintain shops closed to union workers, but frequently outlawed union tactics calculated to obtain shops closed to nonunion labor. The wide application of the Sherman law to labor unions likewise operated to constrain the union movement. Union action aimed to enforce bargaining demands against employers was deemed unlawful under the antitrust laws. In their interpretation of the Sherman law, the courts took the position that workers had the right to collective bargaining only insofar as there was no infringement of the right to do business. This right of employers was held paramount to the liberty of workers to engage in action to make collective bargaining work. For a time it appeared that all strikes of major proportions would be unlawful. That this condition did not result was attributable to the judgment of a few members of the Supreme Court. Had the composition of this Court been a shade different, it is likely that all strikes for any purpose which suppressed the shipment of goods in interstate commerce would have been deemed unlawful. In the light of all this evidence, it can scarcely be denied that courts served well the interests of antiunion employers. The judiciary proved to be a willing ally to employers in labor-management disputes. As a result, the level of union membership in 1930 amounted to about 3 million.[1]

Court construction of worker rights to collective bargaining may have continued indefinitely had it not been for the economic collapse of the 1930s. The depression in this period constituted the most severe economic debacle ever suffered by the nation. Unemployment totaled about 20 percent of the labor force. Widespread bankruptcy of business enterprises and bank failures characterized the period. Foreclosures of firms, repossession of personal property, and loss of homes added to the difficulties of the nation. Fear and deprivation characterized the American people. Never before in the history of the nation was the faith of the people at such low ebb.

About 15 million people tramped the streets looking for work. Life savings disappeared in the whirlwind of financial debacle. Farmers did what they could to save their land, but still farm after farm went on the auctioneer's block. Measures were supported to declare moratoriums on foreign debts and the nation debated the possibility of applying the same principle to its own debtors, who were losing their homes, farms, and other worldly possessions. Rightly or wrongly, the average American identified the misery of the depression with business, perhaps because of the emphasis placed on the role of capital in economic growth by students of the economic order.

The effects of the economic debacle could be multiplied indefinitely. School terms were reduced, and some schools and colleges even closed their doors. As educational appropriations were severely cut by economy-minded and debt-fearing legislators, teachers' salaries were usually decreased as far as possible. In Chicago teachers worked for months without pay, many walking to and from school, not even having the pennies for carfare. More than one Chicago teacher went without lunch, still trying to do the job in the face of a bankrupt city government. At the college level conditions were not much better. Scholars who devoted their life to research and university-level instruction found themselves without jobs, or with salaries cut to such a degree that life was barely possible. Other professional groups suffered in equal or even worse fashion. People had no funds to purchase the services of musicians, lawyers, artists, or architects. These people, as industrial workers, tramped the streets looking for whatever work could be found. Disease increased since money was not available for adequate—to say nothing of preventive—medicine. Ten thousand veterans of World War I marched on Washington in 1932, demanding immediate payment of their bonuses. They were dispersed with tanks, gas bombs, and bayonets. At that time the national government was not politically capable of invoking a fiscal and monetary policy to deal with such disturbances in the economy.

It was inevitable that the Great Depression would result in great changes in social thinking. Americans as never before were bewildered and disillusioned. Fear and uncertainty gripped the nation. The industrial and political leaders were searching for answers to deal with the breakdown of economic machinery. Hoover assured the American people that "the fundamental business of the country, that is production and distribution of commodities, is on a sound and prosperous basis," a statement calculated to alleviate the widespread hopelessness of the people until new policies and programs could be found. Still, these millions of insecure and poverty-stricken citizens questioned the soundness of society. Emphasis on such time-honored bywords as thrift, hard work, self-reliance, and personal initiative had a hollow ring in the midst of the economic holocaust. The people wanted more than doctrine; they wanted jobs, dignity, and security. Old values associated with the individual were on the wane as the effects of the economic catastrophe swept the nation. Industrialists had already abandoned the uncertainties of competition, when possible, many years before the depressed thirties. Now the common people, bewildered by the depression, questioned the social utility of widespread competition among individuals. The grimness of everyday life favored the readjustment of values. Veneration of business ceased. No longer did the profit-seeking businessman enjoy a special or privileged place in the affairs of the nation. Those in high places felt the wrath of the public.

Many aspects of the culture reflected the changing social stream of thought. The realities of the depression gave a new direction to literature and the arts. Books of social significance, such as *The Grapes of Wrath* and *Union Square*, claimed the public's attention. Such plays as *Waiting for Lefty* and *Of Mice and Men* highlighted the growing concern of the people with the imperfections of the economic order. The motion picture industry reflected somewhat the changing social thought. *The Grapes of Wrath* was filmed. *The River* and *The Plough That Broke the Plains* portrayed America in film. Depression-stimulated student organizations on the college campuses concerned themselves with problems of social and economic significance. Opposition to birth control was largely overcome as an increasing number of parents doubted the wisdom of rearing families in an unfavorable economic environment. Thus the depression reached even to the structure and composition of family life. As never before, the economy was subjected to critical intellectual appraisal. One thing was certain: The concept of economic Darwinism was dead. Society recognized that millions of its most fit members could survive only imperfectly in a depression economy. An increasing number of people recognized that institutional defects in the economic environment rather than personal inadequacies caused business failure, unemployment, and poverty.

EARLY REGULATION OF THE LABOR INJUNCTION

Organized labor had a long history of attempts to curb the use of injunctions prior to the period of turmoil of the 1930s. Political pressure by labor unions to obtain legislative relief from the labor injunction dates from the turn of the century. Impressed with the effects of the instrument in labor disputes, organized labor worked diligently to curtail the power of the courts to intervene in labor-management controversies. The spearhead of this legislative assault was the American Federation of Labor, the only national federation of labor unions in existance prior to 1935. Organized labor learned through experience the impact of the injunction on the collective bargaining process. Labor leaders pointed to the abuses of the instrument, asserting that the judiciary served as a potent ally to employers in labor disputes.

These abuses and their implications in industrial relations were examined in Chapter 3.

The American Federation of Labor conducted its legislative campaign on national and state levels. Its objective was to engineer the passage of state and federal legislation designed to provide protection from the equity power of the courts. This was a logical and necessary approach, for both state and federal courts issued labor injunctions. State control of the labor injunction antedated federal regulation. Thus it was on the state level that organized labor first succeeded in influencing the enactment of anti-injunction legislation. The rewards, however, were not destined to endure. Prior to October 15, 1914, the date on which Congress enacted the Clayton Act (which in part regulated the labor injunction), only six states passed legislation restricting the power of the state courts to issue injunctions in labor disputes. These states were California (1903), Oklahoma (1907), Massachusetts (1911), Kansas, Arizona, and Montana (1913).[2] The California and Oklahoma laws provided that acts which are not criminal when committed by a single person shall not be subject to the injunction when engaged in by a number of persons involved in a labor dispute. Massachusetts provided that its state courts could not enjoin peaceful picketing. The purpose of the Montana law was to prohibit discrimination against workers in equity proceedings. It provided that standards developed by the courts for the issuance of injunctions in nonlabor disputes should apply equally to labor disputes. In addition, the Oklahoma and Massachusetts laws granted persons involved in contempt cases the right to trial by jury.

Arizona and Kansas enacted legislation which closely resembled the injunction sections of the Clayton Act. The efforts of Arizona and Kansas may be regarded as the first genuine attempts to regulate by law the use of injunctions in labor disputes. While the laws of California, Oklahoma, Massachusetts, and Montana purported to control specific aspects of the labor injunction, Arizona and Kansas fashioned legislation calculated to remove the courts from this area of industrial relations. The laws of these two states prohibited judicial interference by injunction in controversies involving employers and employees growing out of a dispute concerning terms or conditions of employment. Such legislation removed the prerogative of the judiciary to declare what is lawful and unlawful in the carrying out of labor disputes. This restriction on the equity function of the courts marked a significant innovation in labor relations law. The judiciary had taken upon itself the full right to determine the legitimate boundaries of labor union activity. Arizona and Kansas endeavored to check the courts from exercising such sweeping power in the area of industrial relations. It was legislation of this character that the American Federation of Labor championed and hoped to have enacted by all states and the federal government.

Although the first visible results of its efforts appeared in state legislation, the American Federation of Labor consistently attempted to promote the passage of a federal anti-injunction labor law. Indeed, the use of the injunction in labor disputes along with the prosecution of unions under the Sherman law stimulated the entrance of organized labor into national politics. To induce the passage of favorable national legislation, organized labor openly supported candidates sympathetic to its legislative program and worked for the defeat of the "anti-labor" politician. To this day the union movement follows essentially this same political program, the foundation of which was laid down in the early 1900s. Organized labor had reason to believe its efforts to obtain national anti-injunction legislation bore fruit on October 15, 1914, for on this date Congress enacted the Clayton Act. Previously, we saw that labor's jubilation over the antitrust provisions of the Clayton act was premature. A careful analysis of Section 6 reveals that its terms added nothing new to the law of industrial relations. Actual experience with the law disclosed that the prosecution of labor organizations under the Sherman Act continued unabated.

The rejoicing of labor with respect to the injunction sections of the 1914 law appeared to be on firm ground. In general, the terms regulating the equity power of the federal courts in labor disputes seemed clear enough. The Clayton Act provided that the federal courts could not restrain employees involved in a labor dispute from engaging in peaceful picketing; from carrying out a strike in a peaceful manner; from engaging in a peaceful boycott; from attending any place where such employees may lawfully be; and from peacefully assembling in a lawful manner and for lawful purposes. These prohibitions are contained in Section 20 of the Clayton Act.[3] The terms "peaceful" and "lawful" defy objective construction and the Supreme Court was free to insert its own definition of what was lawful or peaceful. Patterns of union conduct previously interfered with by the federal courts were not immunized against the labor injunction.

Other sections of the Clayton Act closely regulated the procedure of issuing injunctions in labor disputes. Under circumstances wherein Section 20 did not operate to protect activities of labor unions, such as picketing attended with violence, the Clayton Act spelled out the procedure required to be followed by the federal courts. A temporary restraining order could not be granted without notice to the labor union unless irreparable injury to property appeared imminent, for which injury there was no adequate remedy at law. In addition, a temporary restraining order issued without notice to the labor organization must by its terms expire within a period of ten days after issuance. No preliminary injunction could be issued without notice to the trade union. Persons accused of violation of injunctions might, if they desired, be tried by jury. Employers applying for an injunction must post a bond for the indemnification of a union for court costs and damages if subsequent events proved the organization was wrongfully enjoined or restrained. Finally, the Clayton Act provided that every injunction or temporary restraining order must set forth in reasonable detail the specific acts to be enjoined.

Since the Clayton Act, on the one hand, forbade completely under certain circumstances the issuance of labor injunctions and, on the other hand, outlined carefully the procedure to be followed in the issuance of injunctions, unions felt that the law adequately protected organized labor. Inspired by its success on the federal level, organized labor concentrated on the task of obtaining the passage of state anti-injunction laws. Once again, the record reveals that its efforts were only moderately rewarded. Although the American Federation of Labor advocated legislation patterned after the Clayton Act in every state legislature in the nation, only five states prior to 1921 enacted laws duplicating the terms of the federal anti-injunction statute.[4] No progress on the state level was made after 1921. The basic reason for this was that the Supreme Court of the United States declared the Arizona law unconstitutional. The action of the high court reduced the incentive to work for the passage of state anti-injunction laws. Of what use would it be to enact such laws if they could not stand the test of constitutionality? Since the role of the Supreme Court in shaping the character of labor injunction control legislation is of conclusive importance, attention must be directed to the reaction of the courts to such statutes.

EARLY LABOR INJUNCTION LEGISLATION:
COURT ATTITUDES

The Clayton Act, as noted, did not operate to preclude the application of the Sherman law to labor unions. Once the Supreme Court took this position, it affirmed the use of the labor injunction to restrain unions found in violation of the antitrust statutes. This was the essence of the *Duplex* decision of 1921 and of the *Bedford* doctrine of 1927. Thus the principle was laid down that the injunction provisions of the Clayton Act were not operative when the judiciary found that labor unions restrained trade within the meaning of the Sherman law. As a consequence for many years the antitrust laws served as a basis for the issuance of labor injunctions.

In addition, in 1917 the Supreme Court affirmed the use of the injunction to make effective yellow-dog contracts. Despite the provisions against the use of labor injunctions in the Clayton Act, the high court in the *Hitchman* decision held that the equity power of the judiciary could be properly employed to implement agreements in which workers agreed not to join labor unions as a condition of employment. As a matter of fact, the Court did not make any reference to the Clayton Act in the *Hitchman* case, even though the terms of that law may have been reasonably construed to prohibit the issuance of labor injunctions in yellow-dog cases. The fundamental intent of the Clayton Act was to check the power of the federal courts to intervene by injunction in labor disputes growing out of controversies concerning terms and conditions of employment. A controversy as to whether or not workers form labor organizations for the purpose of collective bargaining falls squarely within the meaning of the injunction sections of the Clayton Act. In addition, Section 20 of the Clayton Act forbids the use of the injunction in labor disputes where the effect of the instrument would enjoin persons from "communicating information" or "from attending at any place where such persons may lawfully be. . . ." Even granted that the term "lawfully" is subject to no precise definition, the courts may have been guided by the intent of the legislation, as demonstrated in Chapter 4. Of course, this approach was precluded when the Supreme Court chose to hold that interference with a yellow-dog contract transgressed rights vouchsafed in the Constitution.

The high court was required to resolve an additional question. What of the application of the Clayton Act to cases in which violations of the antitrust statutes or yellow-dog contracts were not involved? Would the Court now construe the statute in a manner to provide a degree of protection to labor unions against the labor injunction? The answer to this question was found in the *American Steel Foundries* and *Truax* cases.

"ONE PICKET PER ENTRANCE"

In spite of the broad restrictions on the issuance of injunctions in labor disputes, the Supreme Court in the 1921 *American Steel Foundries* case[5] interpreted the law in a manner which sharply limited their application to labor-management controversies. The high court construction of the Clayton Act in this case meant the Act was to leave unchanged the law of industrial relations. This was subsequently recognized by the Court when it declared that the injunction sections of the Clayton Act "were merely declaratory of what had always been the law and the best practice in equity. . . ."

As a result of a strike over wages, a labor organization picketed a plant. The company obtained an injunction from a federal district court which stamped out all picketing. On review of the case, the Supreme Court modified the order, but limited union picketing to one picket per entrance of the factory. On this score Chief Justice Taft declared: "We think that the strikers and their sympathizers engaged in the economic struggle should be limited to one representative for each point of ingress and egress in the plant or place of business and that all others be enjoined from congregating or loitering at the plant or in the neighboring street by which access is had to the plant. . . ." Although these pickets (the Court termed them "missionaries") were to have the right of observation, communication, and persuasion, they could not approach nonstriking workers in groups, and their communication to these workers could not be abusive, libelous, or threatening. In addition, the Court held that a picket acting alone could not obstruct an unwilling listener by "dragging his step." It is noteworthy that the Court was concerned not only with the number of pickets but also with their conduct on the picket line.

A further limitation was attached to the picketing activities of labor unions. According to the Court, the Clayton Act provisions protected the activities only of employees of an employer on strike, or of ex-employees of an employer who might reasonably be expected to return to work for the employer. Other workers directly involved in a labor dispute, who are not in the present or past employment of the company but might still have a real economic interest in the working conditions of the firm, could not lawfully picket. This doctrine, it will be recalled, was first laid down in the *Duplex* case wherein Section 20 of the Clayton Act did not operate to make lawful union activities carried on by employees in one city to bring economic pressure against an employer located in another city. On this point, the Court in the *Duplex* case declared, "Congress had in mind particular industrial controversies, not a general class war." Following the *Duplex* decision, a narrow construction was placed on the Clayton Act in the *American Steel Foundries* case.

Unions learned that the Clayton Act was not to prevent the intervention of the courts by injunctions in labor disputes. Regardless of the purpose of union economic pressure and notwithstanding the peacefulness of picketing, the Supreme Court was not prepared to construe the Clayton Act as providing a greater area of freedom to labor unions than posting one picket per entrance to a plant. Even though the Court was careful to point out that "each case must turn on its own circumstances," the doctrine established in the *American Steel Foundries* case was followed by many courts. After this case the courts almost always limited the number of pickets who could be utilized in a labor dispute.

LABOR INJUNCTION CONTROL LEGISLATION UNCONSTITUTIONAL

Shortly after the *American Steel Foundries* case, the Supreme Court passed on the lawfulness of a state labor injunction control law. In the *Truax* case,[6] the high court held unconstitutional the Arizona labor injunction law. Previously, the Supreme

Court of Arizona approved its state law. Despite the construction by the state court, the Supreme Court of the United States held that the Arizona law violated the due process clause of the Fourteenth Amendment to the Constitution.[7]

Facts of the case disclose that the employees of a restaurant located in Bisbee, Arizona, became involved in a labor dispute with their employer over conditions and terms of employment. Since the employer refused to yield to their demands, some of the workers went on strike. The owners of the restaurant managed to operate without the strikers and, to retaliate, the striking employees carried on a vigorous boycott against the management. So successful was the boycott that the restaurant receipts dropped from $156 to $75 per day. The boycott was carried on by picketing the immediate premises of the restaurant. Although no violence was involved, the pickets carried banners containing statements against the restaurant and its owners, workers, and customers. According to the Supreme Court of the United States, the Arizona statute precluded the issuance of injunctions under circumstances of the *Truax* case. As a result, it held that the statute deprived the restaurant owners of their property without due process of law and accordingly violated the Constitution of the United States. "Property," of course, included the right to operate a business in a profitable manner, and a statute could not stand as a cloak behind which a labor organization could interfere with the employer's right to do business. On this score Chief Justice Taft, speaking for the majority of the Court, declared "a law which operates to make lawful such a wrong as is described in plaintiff's complaint deprives the owner of the business and the premises of his property without due process, and cannot be held valid under the Fourteenth Amendment." This reasoning was the opposite of that employed by the Arizona Supreme Court in giving its definition of property in the 1918 case. Union actions, it was argued, merely suggest to an owner the advisability of a change in business methods, but in no sense interfere with the methods of conducting business. The economic weapons could be both primary and secondary boycotts and, even more, "moral intimidation and coercion of threatening a boycott could be employed."[8] As noted, this liberality was not destined for long life after appeal to the United States Supreme Court.

A second reason for the declaration of unconstitutionality was the claim of the United States Supreme Court that the statute denied employers equal protection of the law. It contended that the Arizona statute provided employees with a right not enjoyed by employers. The Court declared:

> The necessary effect of [the Arizona law] is that the plaintiffs would have had the right to an injunction against such a campaign as that conducted by the defendants, if it had been directed against the plaintiffs, business and property in any kind of a controversy which was not a dispute between employer and former employees. If the competing restaurant-keepers in Bisbee had inaugurated such a campaign against the plaintiff and conducted it with banners and handbills of a similar character, an injunction would necessarily have been issued to protect the plaintiffs in the employment of their property and business.

"HOLMES AND BRANDEIS DISSENTING"

Holmes and Brandeis[9] teamed up to challenge the decision of the majority. Indeed, in many other circumstances, the dissenting opinions of these two men even-

tually became the holdings of the majority of the Court. On many matters of fundamental importance, the Supreme Court now refers to the dissenting opinions of
Holmes and Brandeis. History has demonstrated the wisdom of their views on the
utilization of social and economic data in legal proceedings, the proper relationship
between the legislative and judicial branches of government, and their over-all
approach to constitutional matters.

Holmes in the *Truax* case reaffirmed his belief that the legislative power of
government should be checked by the judiciary only under rare and unusual circumstances. He always held closely to the principle that state legislatures and the Congress
should be free from judicial restraint in their attempts to experiment in legislative
matters. This position was grounded on the proposition that the legislative arm of
government is subject to the direct control of the electorate. Representatives who
enact unpopular laws cannot expect re-election. Holmes refused to accept the proposition that the judiciary should constitute a forum for the invalidation of laws passed
by popularly elected legislators. Such an attitude squares with the viewpoint of those
who would see the democratic process strengthened. The containment of the legislative process by the judiciary could result in the checking of progress. Judges are
elected or appointed to their positions for comparatively long periods of time. For
example, members of the federal judiciary may hold office for life or, as the Constitution points out, "The Judges, both of the supreme and inferior Courts, should
hold their offices during good Behavior. . . ." This means that the judiciary, insulated
against changing personnel, could act as a permanent check against the legislative
will of the people. Such a circumstance is demonstrated clearly in the area of labor
law.

These considerations were underscored by Holmes in the *Truax* case when he
declared that

> there is nothing that I more deprecate than the use of the Fourteenth Amendment
> beyond the absolute compulsion of its words to prevent the making of social
> experiments that an important part of the community desires, in the insulated
> chambers afforded by the several states, even though the experiment may seem
> futile or even noxious to me and to those whose judgment I most respect.

Brandeis emphasized the principle that the legislative branch of the government
could properly limit the equity power of the courts in labor disputes without violating
the due process clause of the Constitution. He stressed the fact that injunction control
laws represented a reasonable exercise of legislative power and hence did not deprive
employers of their property without due process of law. Since experience with the
use of the injunction in labor disputes revealed the need for legislative restriction,
the enactment of such laws was neither unreasonable nor arbitrary. Changing needs of
society require the changing character of legislative approach to social and economic
problems. Workers chose to form labor unions to advance their economic welfare.
The courts through the injunction process threw the weight of the law on the side of
management in labor controversies. Legislators, aware of these circumstances and
basing their action on a plethora of data, decided to reduce the role of government in
collective bargaining by decreasing the power of courts to intervene.

The fact that many legislative bodies found that regulation of the injunction in
labor disputes would serve the public interest was given great weight by Brandeis. He
was deeply impressed by the careful accumulation of factual evidence which stimulated the advocacy and passage of injunction control legislation. As a matter of

fact, the contribution of Brandeis to the judicial process was his insistence that the courts weigh carefully the circumstances which produced legislation. He encouraged the courts to consider laws in their socioeconomic context and not to pass judgment on the basis of legal niceties or judicial precedent. In this manner Brandeis breathed life into the law. To him the law was not a dead, unresponsive, or unchanging institution. Courts must be aware of the swiftly moving events in the area of economic and social affairs. A law which may have been arbitrary a century ago at present may be a reasonable legislative approach to a particular problem because of the changing character of the needs of the public. This then was the creed of Brandeis: To penetrate behind the complex and intricate apparatus of the law and attach controlling weight to empirical data showing the necessity for legislation. That Brandeis was fully aware of the numerous abuses growing out of the use of the injunction in labor disputes is amply demonstrated by his statement in the *Truax* case. He declared that in labor injunction proceedings

> an alleged damage to property, always incidental and at times insignificant, was often laid hold of to enable the penalties of the criminal law to be enforced expeditiously without that protection to the liberty of the individual which the Bill of Rights was designed to afford; that through such proceedings a single judge often usurped the functions not only of the jury but of the police department; that in prescribing the conditions under which strikes were permissible and how they might be carried out, he usurped also the powers of the legislature; and that incidentally he abridged the constitutional rights of individuals to free speech, to a free press and to peaceful assembly.

As for the "equal-protection" argument of the majority of the Court, Brandeis contended that the state legislature may regulate the use of the labor injunction without violating the equal-protection clause of the Constitution. Such a conclusion was grounded on the commonplace legal principle that the states may set up reasonable classifications for legislative purposes. A classification between employers and employees, according to Brandeis, appeared reasonable and consequently to deny the use of the injunction to protect property rights in employer-employee disputes did not violate the equal-protection section of the Constitution, even though the same property rights would be protected by the injunction under circumstances where the parties did not stand in an employer-employee relationship. Thus Brandeis felt that the Arizona law neither denied employers the equal protection of the law nor deprived them of their property without due process of law. A labor injunction control law constituted a valid exercise of the legislative power of the states, for such a law was designed to correct a condition deemed evil by the collective judgment of the people of the commonwealth.

NOTE ON THE <u>TRUAX</u> DOCTRINE

In one respect the *Truax* decision appears inconsistent with the doctrine of the Supreme Court handed down in the *American Steel Foundries* case. The latter case was decided by the Court only a few weeks before the *Truax* matter. As noted, the principle established in the *American Steel Foundries* case greatly circumscribed the protective features of the Clayton Act. Unions involved in a labor dispute were to be permitted only one picket per entrance. On the other hand, the Supreme Court did not strike down the injunction sections of the Clayton Act as unconstitutional. The Court limited their application, but did not hold them to be violations of the Constitution. The Fifth Amendment to the Constitution states that Congress shall pass no law the effect of which would deprive a person of property without due process of law. This prohibition reflects the limitation placed on the states in the Fourteenth Amendment. Hence why did the Court, on the one hand, hold the Arizona law unconstitutional but, on the other hand, permit the injunction sections of the Clayton Act to stand? The provisions of the Arizona statute were duplicated practically word for word in the injunction sections of the Clayton Act.[10] Logic would appear to demand that both laws should be construed in essentially the same manner.

One labor law authority suggests that what the Court really meant in the *Truax* decision was that the Arizona law was unconstitutional insofar as it prohibited injunctions against unlawful picketing.[11] He holds that the Arizona anti-injunction act was valid "as long as it was properly construed and applied in the future." This may be a reasonable explanation, but the language of the Court appears much more sweeping. It declared that a law which prohibits the issuance of injunctions to restrain those union activities carried out in the *Truax* case "cannot be held valid under the Fourteenth Amendment." The Court's position appears clear. Since the Arizona law operated to prevent the use of the injunction to restrain union conduct deemed unlawful by the Court, the statute could not remain valid to limit the use of the injunction *under any circumstances*. Arizona law did not protect labor unions from the injunction after the *Truax* case.[12] Consequently, the conclusion is inescapable that the *Truax* decision completely nullified the Arizona anti-injunction statute.

In one sense the inconsistency of the *Truax* and *American Steel Foundries* decisions can be resolved. Both cases laid to rest statutes that could have provided relief to labor unions from the use of the injunction. In the *American Steel Foundries* case, though the injunction provisions of the Clayton Act were not held unconstitutional outright, the construction which the Court placed on them rendered the statute useless as a protective device for labor unions. In other words, the Court permitted the Clayton Act to stand in name only but erased the benefits organized labor expected from the statute. The Clayton Act, after the *American Steel Foundries* case, did not in any manner change the law of industrial relations. Hence the high court may just as well have held its injunction provisions unconstitutional in the face of the *American Steel Foundries* decision.

NORRIS–LA GUARDIA

The action of the Supreme Court checked any progress in the area of injunction control legislation. For about a decade no state attempted to regulate the use of the labor injunction. In addition, state supreme courts, following the precedent of the U.S. Supreme Court, construed those state anti-injunction labor laws passed subsequent to the Clayton Act in a manner to render them impotent. Since the rate of issuance of labor injunctions continued unabated, organized labor still desired legislative relief. The problem, however, was to fashion a law which would effectively limit the equity power of the courts in labor disputes *and* stand the test of constitutionality.

A congressional committee appointed a panel of experts to help in the drafting of legislation which would remove the abuses of the labor injunction, stand the test of constitutionality, and in general serve the cause of justice. In 1927 an anti-injunction bill was presented to the public for debate. In March 1932 the bill was finally passed by overwhelming majorities in both houses of Congress and shortly afterward was signed by Hoover. This bill was popularly termed the Norris–La Guardia Federal Anti-Injunction Act. What is the nature of this law, and how was it received by the judiciary?

Norris–La Guardia: Underlying Theory

Congress justified the Norris–La Guardia Act by pointing to the need for collective bargaining in modern society. This consideration is clearly stated in the provision of the law which spells out the public policy of the United States with respect to employer-employee relations. This section begins by pointing out that under prevailing economic conditions, developed with the aid of government authority for owners of property to organize in the corporate and other forms of ownership association, the individual unorganized worker is commonly helpless to exercise actual liberty of contract and to protect his freedom of labor. Such a statement reflects the current industrial environment. It appears that a job to a worker is infinitely more important than is a single worker to a modern corporation. The business enterprise would not be greatly disturbed if any single worker left his job because of dissatisfaction with working conditions. On the other hand, the job is of crucial importance to the worker and his family. To insure a flow of income, the individual worker may continue to work under conditions which he feels are unsuitable. He will be more prone to hold his job regardless of working conditions when there are no alternative job opportunities. Under such conditions it would be extremely difficult, if not impossible, to argue that the worker needs his job less than the corporation needs the single worker. Consequently, there exists no liberty of contract between single workers and employers in modern industry, as was assumed in litigated cases prior to 1932. If there is no actual liberty of contract, the single worker has little or no freedom in selling his labor. It is largely a case of holding a job regardless of working conditions. This is not to say that some workers do not quit jobs because of dissatisfaction with working conditions. Nor do these considerations deny the fact that some enterprising workers prepare themselves for better jobs by study and training. Despite these qualifications, the fact remains that in modern society the typical individual worker tends to remain at his job as long as the employer will keep him.

Workers tend to raise their bargaining strength by forming labor unions. An employer, though not greatly disturbed when one worker leaves his employment, must be vitally concerned when all workers cease working. Regardless of the rate of output, some costs of operation continue unabated. Production stoppage could result in the inability to fill orders and even in a permanent loss of customers. Since employers are aware that collective action of workers could result in the effective use of the strike, causing economic loss to the firm, they must listen with a degree of respect to the complaints and suggestions of organized workers. In short, by organizing into labor unions, workers are in a better position to sell their services: more in accordance with their conception of the standards of justice and fairness.

The Norris–La Guardia Act recognizes the helplessness of the individual worker in his employment relationship. It suggests that the formation of labor unions corrects the inherent inequality of bargaining power between employers and employees. Finally, it affirms that public policy of the United States sanctions collective bargaining and approves the formation and effective operation of labor unions.

Purpose Of Norris–La Guardia Act

If the foregoing represents an accurate assessment of the general philosophy of the Norris–La Guardia Act, the basic purpose of the law is easily understood. Collective bargaining is endorsed by the public policy of the United States. Consequently, logic would appear to demand that Congress implement this policy by checking a condition which had historically operated to retard the growth and effective operation of the union movement. Thus the fundamental purpose of Norris–La Guardia is to circumscribe sharply the power of the courts to intervene in labor disputes.

Since experience disclosed that the injunction constituted the bridge over which the courts entered the area of labor-management relations, Congress checked the prerogative of the courts to issue labor injunctions. The regulation of the injunction was incidental to the main purpose of Congress: to insulate industrial relations from the influence of the courts. If the facts had indicated that the courts interfered in labor-management relations in a manner other than the exercise of equity power, the approach of Congress would have been different. From the 1880s, however, the history of labor relations revealed that the injunction constituted the *modus operandi* of the judiciary. Hence regulation of the equity power of the courts was the proper approach to the problem.

It was the manner in which the courts wielded this power that stimulated congressional action. If evidence had revealed that the use of the injunction did not place government on the side of employers in labor disputes, there of course would have been no necessity for an anti-injunction law. However, close attention was directed to the abuses growing out of the labor injunction. These factors lead to an unmistakable conclusion: The use of the injunction placed the power of government on the side of management in labor disputes. The statute indicated that justice is advanced when government remains impartial. Accordingly, the judiciary had to behave as a neutral and not as an ally in labor disputes. These considerations would have been equally valid if the injunctive power of the courts had been utilized to make government an ally of trade unions in labor disputes. Regulation of the injunction under these circumstances would have been just as necessary as under the conditions which actually prevailed.

In reality, Norris–La Guardia did not provide labor unions with any new rights. It merely allowed them a greater area in which to operate free from court control. Naturally, this circumstance facilitated immeasurably the ability of labor unions to act as effective collective bargaining agencies. It is equally true that Norris–La Guardia encouraged the growth of the labor movement. The fact remains, however, that this growth was nurtured by the government only to the degree that Norris–La Guardia checked the power of the courts to interfere in labor-management disputes. It did not require workers to join unions, nor did it stop employers from preventing the development and operation of unions by methods other than the use of the injunction. Its underlying objective was to set up an area for industrial conflict in which the courts were forbidden to tread.

AREA OF INDUSTRIAL FREEDOM

Of all the abuses growing out of the use of the injunction in labor disputes, perhaps the outstanding one was that the courts had the power to make industrial relations law. Labor leaders denounced in no uncertain terms a procedure which permitted the judiciary to usurp the power of the legislature. In particular, they protested against an arrangement which empowered the courts to decide the lawful and unlawful areas of labor union activities. The cry of organized labor—"government by injunction!"—arose from the authority of the courts to decide by themselves, regardless of the existence of the legislative arm of government, the licit and illicit in industrial relations.

Such an arrangement served to raise the courts to a position of pre-eminence in the area of labor-management relations. By virtue of their authority to issue injunctions in labor disputes, the courts wielded a most extraordinary power over labor relations. The manner in which they exercised this power is a matter of public record. Overwhelming evidence indicates that the equity power of the courts served the interests of the employer in labor disputes. In the light of these considerations, and if the philosophy of the Norris–La Guardia Act is understood, it should be clear why the law set up a system of self-determination for labor unions. Congress stripped the federal courts of the power to restrain certain forms of union conduct. Regardless of the objective of the labor union in carrying out these activities, the authority of the federal courts to restrain such conduct was neutralized. In short, Congress immunized certain union conduct from the review of the courts. What are these activities which are insulated against court intervention?

Section 4 of Norris–La Guardia begins by declaring that no federal court shall have the power to issue any form of injunctive relief in any case involving a labor dispute, the effect of which would prohibit any person or persons participating or interested in such a dispute from doing, whether singly or in concert, any of a series of acts. The first of these acts immunized from court review is the right of workers to cease, or to refuse, to perform any work. Hence this provision is designed to deny federal courts the opportunity to interfere with the right of workers to strike. Illustrations were offered which revealed that some courts stamped out strikes when judges did not approve of the purpose for which they were carried out. For example, many courts restrained strikes for union security. Under the terms of Norris–La Guardia, the federal courts may not substitute their judgment for that of workers on strike phenomena. Judges may not restrain any strike regardless of its objective. This does not mean that strikes are never carried out for a purpose that is clearly antisocial. That such is the case is evidenced by that fact that some public-spirited labor leaders have advocated the outlawing of certain types of strikes. The point of importance here is that Norris–La Guardia deprives the judiciary of the power to utilize their own standards of reference to decide the lawfulness or unlawfulness of strikes. If strike control is deemed necessary in the public interest, this curtailment should be the work of the legislative branch of government. This is considered a superior approach to one in which judges, basing their decisions on their own socio-economic outlook, are empowered to limit the right of workers to strike.

Under the protection of the Norris–La Guardia Act, labor unions may provide workers engaged in a labor dispute with strike-relief funds or with anything else of value. In the past some judges forbade labor unions from providing strikers with strike-relief funds. Such a condition, of course, decreased a union's chance to win a strike. Workers on strike soon exhaust what savings they may have accumulated while at work. During a strike the worker still must meet his household expenses, insurance policy premiums, medical bills, rent, and the like. Some unions attempt to ease this burden by providing strikers with modest strike benefits. In most cases the sum is only a fraction of what the worker would have earned at the job. However, the money is of considerable importance in such a circumstance even if it means nothing more than improving the morale of the strikers. When unions supplement strike-relief funds with food tickets or with food itself, the lot of the striker is improved. Federal courts may no longer deny labor organizations the right to perform these functions.

Section 4 also checks the power of the courts to restrain the right of workers to picket or to give publicity to labor disputes. The law facilitates the ability of workers to win labor disputes by broadening considerably the lawful area of union publicity activities. No federal court may restrain picketing activities of unions as long as violence or fraud are not present. A comparison between the picketing sections of the Clayton Act and Norris–La Guardia is worthwhile. In the former law there is no mention of the term *picketing* or words denoting a similar meaning. The Norris–La Guardia Act, however, specifically states that nonviolent and fraud-free "patrolling" to publicize a labor dispute may not be enjoined. In the *American Steel Foundries* case, the Supreme Court, it will be recalled, held that the Clayton Act protected workers in their picketing function only to the extent of "one picket per entrance." In establishing this point of view, the Court no doubt was persuaded in part by the fact that the Clayton Act avoided use of specific language to protect picketing activities. Norris–La Guardia prevents such a limited construction of its provisions by utilizing the term "patrolling."

The law also permits workers engaged in labor disputes to advise and urge other employees to join the conflict. Frequently, some workers refuse to go out on strike even though a labor union may officially proclaim one. The position of the strikers would be greatly abetted if all workers joined the strike; for where all workers strike, the employer normally cannot produce at all, or can operate only at a very low rate of production. In the past courts were very careful to protect nonstrikers from the overtures of the workers engaged in the conflict. The decision of the Supreme Court in the *American Steel Foundries* case highlights this proposition. The effect of Norris–La Guardia is to provide more freedom to unions and their members to encourage all workers to strike. The action of the union in this respect is limited by the general restrictions in Section 4. Thus, whenever a union urges nonstrikers to join in the conflict, such a campaign must be free from violence or fraud.

Section 4 further forbids the issuance of a labor injunction when it would keep a union from aiding any person participating in or interested in any labor dispute who is being proceeded against, or is prosecuting, any action or suit in any court of the United States or of any state. Thus the resources of a labor organization may be utilized to defend members of the union, or the union itself, in court proceedings.

Sometimes, as an outgrowth of a labor dispute, legal action is taken against the officers of the union. Under such conditions, the organization may decide to come to the support of its officers and provide them with the services of expert and expensive legal talent. Such an activity of a union no longer can be enjoined by a federal labor injunction. Furthermore, under the protection of Norris–La Guardia, labor unions may conduct meetings or assemble peacefully to promote the interests of their members. On this point there is evidence that some courts actually forbade workers from holding peacefully conducted meetings. An injunction which produces such a result could cause irreparable damage to a labor organization involved in a labor dispute. During the course of a strike, a union frequently holds meetings involving all or a portion of the membership to discuss items of strike strategy or to vote on the issues of the conflict. No longer can the federal court restrain the right of a union to conduct such meetings.

To underscore the guarantees already discussed, Congress added a general provision to Section 4. It states that no court may issue an injunction to prevent workers from agreeing with each other to do any of the acts vouchsafed in Section 4. This section is intended to prevent the application of the conspiracy doctrine to those activities removed from the scope of the labor injunction. An act engaged in by one worker does not become unlawful when carried out by a group of workers. It was noted previously that the conspiracy doctrine operated to make group action unlawful even though the same activity would be lawful if carried out by one person. This general "anti-conspiracy" clause of Section 4 actually is rather superfluous. The general intent of the Norris–La Guardia Act would prevent the application of the conspiracy doctrine to labor activities protected from the injunction. However, in its zeal to block court intervention in labor disputes, Congress wrote this provision into Section 4. It wanted to be doubly sure that the right of workers to strike, give publicity to labor disputes, hold meetings to promote their interests, or come to the aid of their fellows by providing them with legal aid or strike benefits would not be circumscribed by the judiciary.

CONCEPT OF "LABOR DISPUTE"

It is clear that Congress immunized a variety of trade union activities from the application of the federal injunction. By checking the power of the courts, the Norris–La Guardia Act expanded the freedom of action of labor unions. In addition, the law protected labor union activities on a much broader basis, extending beyond a labor dispute involving an employer and his own employees. The guarantees of the law not only extend to such a limited situation, but its immunities also operate when the disputants do not stand in a proximate relationship of employer and employee. In short, for purposes of Norris–La Guardia, a *labor dispute* includes any controversy concerning terms of employment or concerning the representation of employees in collective bargaining, regardless of whether or not the disputants stand in the proximate relation of employer and employee.[13] By adopting a broad definition of a labor dispute, Congress expanded considerably the limits to which unions may lawfully operate. This conception of a labor dispute squares with the realities of modern industrial life. It recognizes that the successful operation of collective bargaining frequently requires the implementation of union pressure on an industry-wide or craft basis. Moreover, it recognizes that the brunt of union organizational activities of a plant may fall to workers other than those directly employed by the firm. No other concept of labor dispute would have made the anti-injunction law an effective check against the labor injunction. Not only was it necessary for Congress to guarantee that the courts would not interfere with basic union practices; it was also necessary to guarantee that labor organizations would have the opportunity to carry out these activities on a wide basis.

THE PASSING OF THE YELLOW-DOG CONTRACT

The Norris–La Guardia Act effected still another important change in the law of industrial relations. It declared that yellow-dog contracts are not enforceable in any court of the United States. In this manner the architects of Norris–La Guardia nullified the effect of the *Hitchman* decision, the case in which the Supreme Court upheld the validity and enforceability of the yellow-dog contract. Thus fifteen years elapsed before organized labor was released from the yellow-dog contract. Just as important is the observation that such relief came not from a change of attitude of the judiciary but from action of the legislative branch of government.

If one is aware of the effects of the yellow-dog contract on the collective bargaining process, it should be easy to understand why the instrument was declared unenforceable by Norris–La Guardia. No other single measure could exceed the effectiveness of a yellow-dog contract when enforced by an injunction. Section 3 of the law condemns the yellow-dog contract as inconsistent with the public policy of the United States. Norris–La Guardia identified public policy as support and endorsement of the collective bargaining process. Since the yellow-dog conflicts with such public policy, Congress denied federal courts the authority to enforce such promises.

It is noteworthy that the Norris–La Guardia Act does not outlaw the yellow-dog contract. It makes the federal courts unavailable for the enforcement of the instrument. In later years, however, the National Labor Relations Board (NLRB) held that an employer engages in an unfair labor practice if he demands that his employees execute such agreements. Thus the yellow-dog contract, the most complete of all antiunion measures, was laid to rest by action of Congress. No federal court is available for the enforcement of a contract, the terms of which require that a worker give up employment if he joins a union, nor can an employer require such agreements of his employees.

LABOR INJUNCTION: PROCEDURAL LIMITATIONS

Nothing could be more inaccurate than to conclude that the Norris–La Guardia Act forbids under every circumstance the issuance of federal injunctions in labor-management controversies. Certainly the law circumscribes sharply the power of courts to intervene in labor disputes. On the other hand, Congress did not prohibit altogether the issuance of labor injunctions. If a labor-management controversy does not fall within the labor dispute concept, the exercise of the equity power of the federal courts is not precluded. Despite the broad definition of labor dispute in Norris–La Guardia, there are circumstances in which a labor-management conflict does not fall within the scope of the law.[14] Injunctions can also be issued when union activities involve fraud and violence. Since the law does not distinguish between tangible property and the right to do business under proper conditions, the federal courts may protect by injunction both forms of property. Before any injunction can be issued, however, Norris–La Guardia sets up certain standards that must be adhered to by the federal courts.

Temporary Restraining Orders. In the first place, the law sets up several restrictions bearing on the issuance of temporary restraining orders. The authors of Norris–La Guardia were well aware of the abuses growing out of the use of the temporary restraining order. The law provides that a hearing must take place to determine whether or not the temporary restraining order should be issued. At such hearing the defendants in the case are to be provided with the opportunity to challenge the allegations of the complainant. On the other hand, Norris–La Guardia recognizes the possibility that the issuance of the temporary restraining order without such a hearing may be the only procedure whereby property may be protected from substantial and irreparable injury. For example, there would be no time to notify the defendant and hold a hearing when workers are inflicting serious damage to an employer's plant or machinery. Such circumstances demand that court intervention take place without delay. Under such pressing circumstances, the court may issue a temporary restraining order in the absence of such a hearing and the complainant must adduce testimony under oath the character of which, if sustained, would justify the court in issuing a temporary injunction upon the basis of a hearing participated in by the defendant.

If a temporary restraining order is issued in the absence of a hearing, the order by its own terms must expire within five days. This time limit was included to prevent the possibility of a temporary restraining order remaining in effect for a prolonged period. As noted, some courts, without requiring a hearing, issued temporary restraining orders which remained in force for long periods of time. When this occurred, the labor union suffered irreparable injury. The full injustice of this practice came to light when subsequent investigation proved the union guiltless of the crimes alleged by the complainant. Such a possibility is precluded under the Norris–La Guardia Act by virtue of the five-day limitation.

The law sets up another limitation on the issuance of temporary restraining orders. It provides that no temporary restraining order shall be issued except upon condition that the complainant submit a bond with the court to recompense those enjoined for any loss, expense, or damage caused by the erroneous issuance of such an order. The amount of the bond is to be fixed by the court. In this manner Norris–La Guardia recognizes that until a full investigation is made of a case, there is always a possibility that the defendants may be unjustly enjoined. If the court restrains a labor union from a course of conduct on the basis of employer-filed evidence and if subsequent investigation proves the evidence to be invalid, Norris–La Guardia provides for some compensation for the union organization.

Even though the posting of a bond may serve to deter employers from requesting temporary restraining orders based on false evidence, the fact remains that the baseless enjoinment of the labor union may result in irreparable damage to the organization, regardless of the subsequent recovery of money damages. Thus real protection of unions from the labor injunction is derived from other provisions of Norris–La Guardia, and only seemingly from the bond-posting requirement. Yet this feature makes for better injunction procedure than prevailed in the period before the Norris–La Guardia Act. Many courts failed to require the posting of any bond or set the figure at a very low level. Courts resorted to this practice even though the posting of bonds of reasonable amounts was required in nonlabor cases.

Temporary and Permanent Injunctions. Congress also established a series of standards to guide the federal courts in the issuance of temporary and permanent injunctions. Norris–La Guardia provides that no court may issue these forms of injunctive relief unless a hearing is held. Before the passage of the anti-injunction law, the courts held hearings prior to the issuance of temporary injunctions. However, the character of the hearing required by the terms of the Norris–La Guardia Act differs sharply from the typical hearing conducted prior to enactment. If an injunction is sought, witnesses must be produced to support allegations in the complaint. Thus federal courts may no longer issue temporary injunctions on the basis of mere sworn affidavits, a procedure proved inequitable in the pre–Norris–La Guardia period. In addition, the union must be permitted to produce witnesses to challenge the allegations. Both sides must be allowed the opportunity to cross-examine witnesses. Thus the court has a better basis to determine the facts of the case. An injunction issued after such precautions most likely is justified. It is important to note that these requirements apply equally to temporary and permanent injunction proceedings.

Federal courts may not grant injunctive relief unless the facts indicate that in the absence of the injunction substantial and irreparable injury to property will result. Moreover, the court prior to the issuance of a temporary or permanent injunction must be satisfied that greater injury will be inflicted upon the complainant by the denial of relief than will be inflicted upon the defendant by the granting of relief. This provision recognizes that a labor union may suffer from the issuance of an injunction. It further recognizes that an employer may be injured in the absence of an injunction. Only after the court balances these relative injuries may it exercise its equity power in labor disputes. Of course, the problem must be resolved largely on a subjective basis. In any event the requirement of balancing the relative damages to the disputants should serve the cause of justice.

In addition, under the terms of Norris–La Guardia the court prior to the granting of equity relief must be satisfied that the complainant has no adequate remedy at law. This means that no injunction will be issued against a labor union if the court finds that the employer may recover damages resulting from unlawful union activity in trial court proceedings. Considerations which would prompt a court to find that an employer has no adequate remedy at law include: (1) financial irresponsibility of the labor union; (2) the fact an employer would be required to file a multiplicity of suits to recover damages; and (3) the possibility that it would be difficult to obtain a jury that would not be sympathetic to the labor union. The latter factor would be important in a community that is a stronghold of unionism— the so-called "union town."

Still another finding of fact must be made by the court before Norris–La Guardia sanctions the granting of a temporary or permanent injunction. The facts must reveal that local police officers charged with the duty to protect the complainant's property are unable or unwilling to furnish adequate protection. This provision throws the responsibility for the protection of property on the local community. Many people would agree that such protection is the primary concern of local police officers. If the local police force is capable of providing such protection, it is undesirable for the federal goverment to exercise its authority in labor disputes. Most labor-management disputes have a local setting. It appears that local control of the matter will advance the long-run cause of industrial relations harmony. Local police officers frequently know personally the people involved in the dispute. Such law enforcement officers, as a result of this personal relationship, can frequently contain violence by resort to mere moral suasion. However, provided the other requirements of Norris–La Guardia are satisfied, federal courts may issue injunctions in labor disputes when local protection of property is lacking.

Elimination of the Blanket Injunction. Previous discussion revealed that one of the most flagrant abuses growing out of labor injunctions involved the blanket injunction. The chief characteristic of this abuse relates to the all-inclusive scope of the court order. Courts enjoined lawful as well as unlawful acts and directed injunctions at people not committing unlawful acts as well as those engaging in such conduct. The blanket injunction resulted from the utilization by the courts of catchall phrases. Unions found that the task of winning labor disputes was made difficult, if not impossible, when confronted with the blanket injunction.

Authors of Norris–La Guardia took these considerations into account when the provisions of the law were written. To eliminate the blanket injunction, the law requires that all injunctions issued by federal courts must be specific in their terminology. Persons or organizations enjoined in the carrying out of unlawful conduct must be spelled out. This provision eliminates the use of the typical ambiguous phrase, frequently found in the labor injunction before Norris–La Guardia: "all-other-persons-whomsoever." In addition, the federal courts now must clearly state the unlawful acts to be enjoined. Thus, the law requires that the labor injunction prohibit only "specific acts as may be expressedly complained of in the bill of complaint filed" as a result of a labor dispute. This standard eliminates the catchall phrase: "in any way interfering with the operation of the complainant's business." Such vague clauses were frequently contained in injunctions issued prior to the passage of Norris–La Guardia. In short, the law recognizes that, in the course of some labor disputes, some actions of unionists and their sympathizers may be unlawful and others lawful. The purpose of requiring specific wording by courts in injunctions is to eliminate only the performance of illegal conduct. The requirement for specific terminology applies equally to the temporary restraining order and the temporary or permanent injunction.

Promotion of the Collective Bargaining Process. Norris–La Guradia rests on the assumption that labor peace can best be achieved through the acceptance in good faith of the collective bargaining process. This feature of the law is best exemplified by its provision denying parties to a labor dispute the opportunity to obtain injunctive relief unless all possibilities of settling their controversies through collective bargaining have been exhausted. In short, the law places the primary responsibility for achieving industrial peace on management and labor. The equity powers of the judiciary are not available to any party to a labor dispute if the court finds it has not made reasonable efforts to settle the dispute by direct negotiation. When direct negotiation fails, the disputants are expected to make use, whenever appropriate, of mediation and voluntary arbitration.[15] Good faith in collective bargaining is further demonstrated by the willingness of the parties to comply with any law controlling the collective bargaining process. For example, a union does not qualify for injunctive relief if it has violated legislation regulating the collective bargaining process. Although labor unions make few applications for injunctions, the fact remains that a labor organization cannot avail itself of the advantages of the equity power of the judiciary when facts indicate that it has not complied with a law applicable to a labor dispute. Under Taft-Hartley, for instance, it is an unfair labor practice for a labor union to refuse to bargain collectively. If a union fails to fulfill this responsibility, the federal courts must act unfavorably on its application for equity relief.

Few people will find fault with this requirement of Norris–La Guardia. It is unwise to make available injunctive relief when facts indicate that the applicant has violated a law applicable to the labor dispute. Successful collective bargaining requires an honest attempt by both sides to reach a peaceful agreement. If any party to a labor dispute fails to bargain in good faith or refuses to comply with laws bearing on the collective bargaining process, it appears reasonable to deny to this party injunctive relief.

Violations of Injunctions. Two significant innovations for contempt-of-court proceedings are found in Norris–La Guardia. If a person is charged with contempt of court, the accused has the right to a "speedy trial and public trial by an impartial jury. . . ." Previously, it was pointed out that persons charged with contempt before Norris–La Guardia had no right to a jury trial. Such a procedure meant that the same judge who issued an injunction had the power to decide the issue of violation. In many cases, judges abused this prerogative and imposed penalties on highly questionable grounds. Particular abuse resulted when judges were biased against trade unions. Now a person charged with violation of a labor injunction may be tried by a jury of his peers. Such an opportunity will be denied defendants in a labor injunction proceeding under circumstances where contempts are committed in presence of the court or so near thereto as to interfere directly with the administration of justice. In the second place, a person charged with contempt of court may request a change of judge. Demand for the withdrawal of the judge, however, must be made prior to the hearing on the contempt proceeding. Upon the demand for the retirement of a judge, this person must withdraw from the case and another judge must be designated to conduct the proceeding. Obviously, this provision was inserted in the Norris–La Guardia Act to eliminate from contempt proceedings a judge possessing a strong anti-union bias. Persons charged with the violation of a labor injunction had no such privilege in the period before Norris–La Guardia.

JUDICIAL CONSTRUCTION OF NORRIS–LA GUARDIA

Historical evidence demonstrated that when the equity power of the courts was exercised in labor disputes, the power of government was on the side of employers. Norris–La Guardia was passed to eliminate this condition. By freeing certain union practices from the impact of the injunction and by regulating closely the procedure of issuing injunctions, Congress implemented its desire to neutralize the influence of the courts in labor-management controversies. Despite the law's clear terms, the judicial interpretation of the Norris–La Guardia Act was awaited with high interest, particularly by organized labor and employers. Both were aware of the possibility that the judiciary might nullify the second attempt of Congress to regulate the use of injunctions in labor disputes.

The first indication of the judicial fate of Norris–La Guardia involved the Supreme Court's construction of the Wisconsin anti-injunction law. In 1931 Wisconsin enacted an injunction law which foreshadowed Norris–La Guardia. In many respects, the Wisconsin law was similar to the 1939 federal anti-injunction measure. The terms of the state law were just as protective of labor unions as those subsequently contained in Norris–La Guardia. Consequently, what the Supreme Court had to say about the Wisconsin law would be applicable to Norris–La Guardia. If it found the state law unconstitutional or interpreted it in a manner which would drastically reduce its applicability, the same fate would be in store for the federal anti-injunction law. If, on the other hand, the high court upheld the constitutionality of the Wisconsin law and construed its terms in a liberal manner, the supporters of the federal law would be encouraged.

In addition, the character of the construction of the Wisconsin law would influence profoundly the effectiveness and progress of state anti-injunction laws. Passage of the Norris–La Guardia Act encouraged many state legislatures to enact laws patterned after the federal statute. If the high court treated the Wisconsin law unfavorably, these state laws would be rendered useless. Other states which might have been inclined to enact anti-injunction laws would be discouraged by an adverse construction of the Wisconsin statute. Thus, from the state and federal point of view, the nation awaited with deep interest the Supreme Court construction of the Wisconsin anti-injunction law.

The Tile-Laying Industry Case

The Wisconsin law was tested in 1937 in a case involving the tile-laying industry of Milwaukee.[16] For many years this industry had been in a depressed condition. Lack of building operations resulted in serious unemployment among tile layers. Severe competition also added to the problems of the industry. Some of the workers of the industry were organized and others were not. Labor standards in the unionized section were higher than those prevailing in the nonunion portion. To protect the union worker, the Tile Layers Union insisted that each employer with whom it had a contract employ only members of the union. In addition, the union required that no employer work on the job. This requirement was embodied in the following clause contained in each agreement:

> ARTICLE III. It is definitely understood that no individual, member of a partnership, or corporation engaged in the Tile Contracting Business shall work with the tools or act as Helper but that the installation of material . . . shall be done by journeymen members of the Tile Layers Union Local #5.

Obviously, the objective of the prohibition was to provide more jobs for union members. Widespread unemployment among tile layers and the fact that the tile-laying industry contained many employers who hired only a small number of employees induced the union to adopt a program to increase job opportunities for its members. A Mr. Senn became involved in a dispute with the union over the restriction contained in Article III.

Senn was in the contracting business in Milwaukee. His operations were very small. At peak seasons he employed only two journeymen tile layers and two helpers. He worked along with his employees and performed on-the-job work normally done by a journeyman tile layer or helper. The union wanted Senn to become a union contractor and requested that he sign an agreement which would deny him the opportunity to work personally on the job. He claimed that he would execute a union agreement provided that Article III did not appear in the agreement.

As expected, the union refused such a request. It pointed out the reasons for Article III and further declared that the granting of Senn's request would discriminate against all contractors who signed agreements which included Article III. Since the union could not grant Senn's request, he refused to sign the agreement or to unionize his small shop. As a result of his refusal, the union picketed his place of business. According to the record, the picketing was peaceful and was conducted without violence. The objective of the picketing was to persuade the public to cease doing business with Senn and to encourage the people of Milwaukee to take their business to employers under contract with the labor union.

The Wisconsin Anti-Injunction law, the statute in question, operated to protect the picketing activities of the union. Senn sought an injunction from the state courts to enjoin further picketing. He claimed that the picketing was injuring his business and that the objective of the union—to require him to refrain from working with his own hands—was unlawful. The state courts of Wisconsin refused his request, pointing to the provisions of the Wisconsin statute forbidding the courts to issue injunctions to enjoin peaceful picketing. Not content with the decision of the state court, Senn appealed his case to the Supreme Court of the United States. He claimed that the Wisconsin law was unconstitutional on the ground that it deprived him of his property without due process of law. As such, the charge against the Wisconsin statute duplicated the one leveled against the Arizona anti-injunction law, which was held unconstitutional in *Truax* v. *Corrigan*.

By a 5-to-4 vote, the Supreme Court upheld the constitutionality of the Wisconsin law. Brandeis delivered the majority opinion of the Court. He pointed out that the end sought by the union was not malicious or unlawful for the union rule was reasonable and "adopted by the defendant out of the necessities of employment within the industry and for the protection of themselves as workers and craftsmen in the industry." Brandeis conceded that the disclosure of the existence of the labor dispute by the union might be annoying to Senn. But, he declared, "such annoyance, like that often suffered from publicity in other connections, is not an invasion of the liberty guaranteed by the Constitution. Unions may request by picketing that the public withhold patronage from an employer 'unfair to organized labor' and bestow it on unionized firms." Brandeis showed the similarity of such union picketing to the advertisements of merchants who compete with one another by means of the press, by circulars, or by window displays. If the latter form of advertising does not violate the Constitution, Brandeis felt that a union publicity campaign, carried on peacefully and truthfully, was likewise lawful.

Other arguments were presented by Brandeis to support the Court's position. Members of the union and Senn had the right to strive to earn a living. Senn sought to do so through exercise of his individual skill and planning. It is not unlawful if workers by combination seek the same objective. The union did not desire to injure Senn, but the picketing was carried on to "acquaint the public with the facts, and, by gaining its support, to induce Senn to unionize his shop." Brandeis pointed out that Senn had the equal opportunity to "disclose the facts in such manner and in such detail as he deemed desirable, and on the strength of the facts to seek the patronage of the public." In any event, if the effect of the picketing prevented Senn from securing jobs, there was no invasion of constitutional rights for "a hoped-for job is not properly guaranteed by the Constitution."

Since the means of the union and the end it sought did not violate the Constitution, the Supreme Court held that the Wisconsin law which insulated the union activities from the injunction did not deprive Senn of his property without due process of law. In this connection Brandeis declared, "If the end sought by the unions is not forbidden by the Federal constitution the state may authorize working men to seek to attain it by combining as pickets, just as it permits corporations and employers to combine in other ways to attain their desired economic ends." The *Senn* decision marks a significant change in attitude on the part of the Supreme Court. Workers may take effective action to achieve their economic objectives. Such a program is not unlawful merely because it interferes with the right to run a business. Not only business people can organize for their mutual protection, but workers may likewise join in association and undertake action designed to implement the objectives of their associations. The *Senn* decision, which reflects the Brandeis philosophy, stands as a landmark in industrial relations law. It was a forerunner in a long line of court decisions which constructed a more favorable climate for the operation of effective collective bargaining.

The __Lauf__ Doctrine: Wide Application of Norris–La Guardia Assured

One year after the *Senn* decision, the Supreme Court decided the fate of Norris–La Guardia. For a time it appeared that the federal judiciary would repeat the Clayton Act performance and destroy the effectiveness of Norris–La Guardia. In spite of the unmistakable intent and written mandate of Congress, the lower federal courts held that the terms of the Norris–La Guardia Act did not apply to labor disputes when the disputants did not stand in a proximate relationship of employer and employee. Such an interpretation, wholly inconsistent with the terms of the law, if sustained by the Supreme Court, would destroy the effectiveness of Norris–La Guardia. It would allow a wide basis for the issuance of the labor injunction. The result would be a nullification of the second attempt of Congress to provide labor unions with a measure of relief from the restraining hand of the judiciary.

For these reasons all interested parties awaited the Supreme Court's ruling in the *Lauf* case with deep interest.[17] Like the tile-laying case, the locale was Milwaukee. Unlike that case, however, the industry was the retail meat markets of the city. The company in the dispute operated five meat markets. About thirty-five employees worked in them. None belonged to Local No. 73 of the AFL Butchers Union, the labor organization in question. The labor union attempted to organize the five stores. The union conducted an extensive picketing program, the objective of which was to condemn the company in the public's eyes as unfair to organized labor. Previously, the company refused the union demand to compel its workers to join the union as a condition of employment. It contended that its employees had their "own association and were perfectly well satisfied." There was speculation that the company sponsored the inside union with the objective of keeping it out of a nationally affiliated labor organization.

In any event, the picketing continued and subsequently the lower federal courts enjoined all picketing activities of the Butchers Union. The terms of the injunction provided that the union and its members were forbidden from (1) in any way picketing the premises of the complainant; (2) advertising, stating, or pretending that the complainant was in any way unfair to said defendants or organized labor generally; and (3) persuading or soliciting any customers or prospective customers of the said complainant to cease patronizing the complainant at its meat market.[18] As noted, the lower federal courts issued the injunction on the ground that the pickets were not employees of the company.

If the Supreme Court sustained the injunction, Norris–La Guardia would not afford much protection to labor unions conducting organizing campaigns. Unions grow through the organization of the unorganized. The job of organizing the nonunion plant is at times very difficult. For this reason experienced representatives of established international unions frequently spearhead organizational campaigns. Now such international representatives are not actual employees of the plants in the process of being organized. For this reason the lower federal courts which handled the *Lauf* case enjoined their activities. It follows from such a doctrine that nationally affiliated unions could not attempt to organize a nonunion area or a plant in which a company-dominated union is operating. Under such a construction of Norris–La Guardia, the public policy expressed in the statute—encouragement of the collective bargaining process—could not be implemented.

The Supreme Court refused to sustain the ruling of the lower federal courts. It found a labor dispute existed in the *Lauf* case, even though the disputants did not stand in proximate relationship of employer and employee. Such an interpretation is demanded by the terms of Norris–La Guardia. The members of the Butchers Union had a real economic interest in the outcome of the organizational drive of the nonunion retail meat markets. Higher labor standards prevailing in the union shops were imperiled to the extent that nonunion shops operated. If the Butchers Union did not organize each nonunion shop, it could be expected that union stores, once their collective bargaining contracts expired, would resist the execution of new ones, claiming inability to meet nonunion competition. As a result of these considerations, the Supreme Court held that a labor dispute within the meaning of Norris–La Guardia existed. Since the controversy constituted a labor dispute, the high court ordered dissolved the injunction which restrained the picketing. The Butchers Union was free to picket the nonunion meat markets even though they had no members working in the shops.

The *Lauf* decision affirmed the power of the Congress to define and limit the jurisdiction of the federal courts. It demonstrated that Norris–La Guardia was to apply to a wide area of industrial relations. Unions were to be protected in their activities regardless of whether or not the disputants were in the proximate relationship of employer and employee. The *Lauf* decision served to emphasize the fact that the way was clear for Congress to regulate the collective bargaining process.

The New Negro Alliance: Elasticity of
Norris–La Guardia Demonstrated

For the terms of the Norris–La Guardia Act to be applicable, a controversy must grow out of a dispute concerning the terms or conditions of employment, or be concerned with the association or representation of workers for collective bargaining. It is apparent that the protective features of the statute are in operation when there are disputes over wages, hours, working conditions, and the like. A short time after the *Lauf* decision, however, the Supreme Court applied the Norris–La Guardia Act to a controversy which in its technical sense involved neither conditions of employment nor the organization of employees for collective bargaining. The dispute grew out of the desire of Negroes for better treatment with respect to employment opportunities.

Washington, D. C., the nation's capital, was the locale of the dispute involving the application of the Norris–La Guardia Act to a group of Negroes who attempted to improve their employment opportunities. The Sanitary Grocery Company opened a branch store in a section of Washington populated by Negroes. The company refused to employ Negroes in this particular outlet, as well as in other branch stores patronized by Negroes. Such discriminatory tactics brought an organized protest from the Negroes of Washington. The protest issued from the New Negro Alliance, a corporation organized by Negroes for the advancement and improvement of its members and for the promotion of educational, civic, and charitable enterprises. The Alliance demanded from the Sanitary Grocery Company that it abandon its anti-Negro policy. It requested that in the normal course of labor turnover the company employ Negro help in the new branch store and others patronized chiefly by Negro people. The company refused to agree to these requests. As a result, the New Negro Alliance implemented a picketing campaign calculated to depress the business of the company. Workers patrolled in front of the company's stores carrying signs which read: "Do Your Part! Buy Where You Can Work! No Negroes Employed Here!"

A federal district court enjoined all picketing by the Alliance on the ground that there was no labor dispute within the meaning of the Norris–La Guardia Act. Later a circuit court of appeals sustained the decision of the district court. The New Negro Alliance appealed the case to the Supreme Court, claiming that the terms of Norris–La Guardia protected the activities of the Alliance from the injunction. In a split decision, the Supreme Court reversed the decision of the lower court and agreed with the Alliance that its picketing activities were immunized by the Norris–La Guardia Act.[19] The minority of the Court, composed of McReynolds and Butler, contended that this was a racial, not a labor, dispute. In addition, they agreed with the lower court that (1) there was no employer-employee relationship; (2) the Alliance was not a trade union but a social organization; (3) the controversy was not a labor dispute within the meaning of Norris–La Guardia, for the Alliance was not attempting to negotiate terms of employment (it was attempting to substitute Negro for white labor); and (4) if the Alliance were allowed to picket in this circumstance, its members might picket any private home in which white and non-Negro servants were employed.

The majority opinion of the Court rested on Section 13 of Norris–La Guardia. It was argued that the "labor dispute" section covered controversies between persons seeking employment and employers and that the law applied equally when the objective of a dispute was to improve the conditions of workers through the collective bargaining process or to promote employment opportunities for a racial group. As a result of this construction of Norris–La Guardia, the Supreme Court ordered that the injunction against picketing activities of the New Negro Alliance be dissolved.

RESULTS OF THE NORRIS–LA GUARDIA ACT

The Norris–La Guardia Anti-Injunction Act was to result in the near elimination of all labor union activities from antitrust liability. The Act virtually destroyed the ability of private parties to secure injunctions to influence the outcome of labor disputes. Injunctive use is not deterred in nonlabor dispute cases, even though a labor union is involved in the controversy. The key to interpretation is a determination of what constitutes a labor dispute. One federal court has held that a union's request to force an employer to pay a cost-of-living adjustment provided for in a collective bargaining contract did not constitute a labor dispute as defined by the Anti-Injunction Act since economic power was not involved in the case.[20] To be sure, interpretation of the statute by federal courts has not been without some confusion.

Some exceptions to the anti-injunction provisions resulted from particular provisions in the 1947 and 1959 amendments to the National Labor Relations Act of 1935. Governmental agencies have been granted greater authority to seek injunctions under certain conditions. For example, the National Labor Relations Board has the authority to request injunctions to enjoin either union or employer behavior described as unfair labor practices under the national labor laws. The Norris–La Guardia Act does not prevail in such instances. The parties to the dispute are not empowered to seek injunctive relief themselves.

Also, the Attorney General of the United States can seek 80-day injunctions in national emergency strikes. The Congress specifically legislated this exception to Norris–La Guardia in the Taft-Hartley Act. With only one exception, the federal courts have always granted injunctions when requested by an attorney general.

One provision in the amended Labor Management Relations Act provided that employers and unions could sue each other when breaches of collective bargaining contracts occurred. In June 1957 the United States Supreme Court held that the federal courts may apply the Taft-Hartley law to enforce arbitration clauses in labor contracts. When an employer refused to arbitrate a dispute arising under the contract (which provided for arbitration of all unresolved grievances), the United States Supreme Court issued an injunction to force the employer to arbitrate.[21] However, five years later in a 1962 case, *Sinclair Refining Company* v. *Atkinson*, the Court refused to enjoin a strike engaged in by a union during a contractual period.[22] This occurred despite the fact that the labor agreement contained no-strike and arbitration clauses. The union could have submitted the grievances which caused the strike to arbitration instead of striking. In its decision the Court reasoned that it could not issue an injunction to stamp out the strike on the grounds that it was forbidden to do so under the Norris–La Guardia Act. As such, the law, at that time, discriminated against employers, since they had to arbitrate unresolved grievances. In contrast, a union could bypass arbitration and strike free from the fear the courts would issue an injunction to stop the strike. However, it is doubtful that many unions would strike over grievances rather than use the arbitration process. In the interest of maintaining healthy union-management relationships, both parties normally attempted to honor the contractual arrangements.

A more recent case, *Avco Corporation* v. *Aero Lodge No. 735* (1968), decided by the United States Supreme Court generated considerable uncertainty regarding the legal effects of the *Sinclair* case, just discussed.[23] When an employer in interstate commerce obtained an injunction in a state court against a strike allegedly in violation of a no-strike clause, the union had the case removed to a federal district court. The employer defended on the premise that the federal court lacked jurisdiction since the Norris–La Guardia Act denied it the authority to grant injunctive relief. The district court claimed jurisdiction and dissolved the injunction, all of which was sustained by a court of appeals. Upon review, the Supreme Court ruled that *Sinclair* "meant only that the Federal district court lacked the general equity power to grant the particular relief." At this point, it is significant to note that the Court did not agree with the appeals court's ruling that "the remedies available in State courts are limited to the remedies under Federal law." In this regard the Court held that "we reserve decisions on those questions." However, as found in Chapter 15, this issue became moot because in 1970 the Supreme Court in *Boys Markets* v. *Retail Clerks* reversed the *Sinclair* doctrine.[24]

In January 1974 the coverage of Norris–La Guardia was reduced somewhat in a case involving a strike within the coal mining industry. At that time in *Gateway Coal* v. *United Mine Workers*, the United States Supreme Court sustained an injunction to stop a strike called by the union to protest what it believed to be unsafe working conditions. It was called during the time that a labor agreement was in effect. The contract contained an arbitration clause under which could be settled disputes concerning the application and the interpretation of the contract. The court held that the arbitration clause was broad enough to cover disputes involving safety considerations. Therefore, it said that such strikes are enjoinable despite the provisions of Norris–La Guardia. In any event, this was a rare and unusual instance where the law did not serve to forbid the use of injunctions in labor disputes.

It is clear that the full approval by the Supreme Court of Norris–La Guardia checked the use of the federal labor injunction. The action of the high court also stimulated the passage of state labor injunction control legislation. Twenty-five states and Puerto Rico now have enacted injunction control legislation.[25] The state statutes vary, but all have similarities to Norris–La Guardia. On the other hand, twenty-five have not enacted any law regulating the use of the labor injunction. It is likely that labor injunction procedures in these states have improved because of the existence of the federal law. However, the fact remains that the absence of state injunction control legislation provides the springboard for court intervention in labor disputes. Experience has conclusively demonstrated that such intervention has resulted in the placing of government on the side of employers in labor-management controversies. For example, some experience in Ohio, a state which by 1968 had not enacted injunction legislation, indicates that the equity power of the state courts proved harmful to the growth and effective operation of the collective bargaining process.[26]

If a great deal of labor violence followed the Norris–La Guardia Act, the legislation would not have been effective. Some people were fearful that this condition would result from the passage of the statute. However, there is no evidence that more violence accompanied labor disputes after Norris–La Guardia than took place before this law was passed. As a matter of fact, some of the most bloody strikes, such as Pullman and Homestead, occurred before 1932. It is noteworthy that in England labor violence has been less extensive than in the United States. This remains true even though the use of the labor injunction in Great Britain has been comparatively infrequent. It must be emphasized that violence is unlawful with or without injunctions. Overturning of automobiles, beatings, damage to machinery, and the like are not less unlawful because of the nonexistance of the injunction. On the other hand, as remarked previously, it is doubtful that an injunction will prevent violence if workers are bent on it.

One must be careful to distinguish between the violence of labor disputes and the use of organized labor's economic weapons. Implementation of the strike, picketing, and the boycott do not signify labor violence. In fact, Norris–La Guardia was passed to free these normal expressions of collective action from the restraining hand of the judiciary. The point of importance is that the anti-injunction law has not encouraged the carrying out of these trade union functions within a context of lawlessness and violence.

Nor should one point to the growth of the union movement as grounds for the condemnation of Norris–La Guardia. Indeed, the statute was passed to promote the union movement and collective bargaining. By regulating the use of the injunction in labor disputes, Norris–La Guardia provided a legal environment favorable to the growth of the union movement. One may quarrel with the objective of the law, but one scarcely can criticize the legislation because it has accomplished its goal. It is extremely doubtful that the growth of the union movement could have taken place in the absence of an effective law controlling the use of injunctions in labor disputes.

The Norris–La Guardia Act serves the public interest. In the modern industrial setting, characterized by the large and impersonal corporation, collective bargaining is widespread. If collective bargaining is deemed socially desirable, the Norris–La Guardia Act, calculated to promote the process, appears desirable. The statute can be justified from still another point of view. In a democracy it is essential that the organs of government remain impartial in conflicts between economic groups. Clearly, governments should check aggressions of any group, including trade unions, when it engages in conduct obviously unlawful and antisocial. However, the unrestrained court use of the labor injunction threw the government on the side of employers in labor disputes. Norris–La Guardia corrected this situation. Norris–La Guardia provided workers freedom to combine for their mutual advancement and refused to condemn union activity each and every time there was interference with the right to do business.

SUMMARY

The Great Depression of the thirties resulted in a profound change in the climate of social thought relative to the place of unions in contemporary society. As a result, Congress and some state governments passed legislation to provide a more favorable legal structure for the operation of unionism. The Norris–La Guardia Act was the first expression of this new legislative policy. It served to neutralize the power of the courts in labor disputes by regulating the substance and procedure of the labor injunction. Whereas the Clayton Act was interpreted into ineffectiveness by the Supreme Court, Norris–La Guardia was treated favorably by the courts. This was expected because the judiciary could not very well isolate itself from the forces of social thought.

Congress justified Norris–La Guardia by pointing to the need for collective bargaining in modern society. Since the abuse of the labor injunction operated to forestall unionism, it was proper to pass legislation to deprive employers of the opportunity to utilize the judiciary as an ally in labor-management disputes. The effect of Norris–La Guardia was to provide unions with a larger area in which to carry on their activities without interference by the courts. As such, the law conferred no new rights on workers. It merely neutralized the federal courts in labor disputes. The Supreme Court has been diligent in carrying out the congressional intent even in cases where it considered justice would have been better served by deviation from that intent.

The approach of Norris–La Guardia served to implement its basic objective: the containment of the influence of the courts in labor disputes. Among other things, it deprived the federal courts of the power to enforce the yellow-dog contract; denied them the right to enjoin peaceful and truthful picketing regardless of the purpose of the picketing; forbade courts to enjoin peaceful strikes regardless of the purpose of the strike; and established a carefully-drawn-up procedure to regulate the issuance of the injunction in labor disputes when the law did not forbid the instrument. Some states passed "little" Norris–La Guardia Acts to protect workers not covered by the national statute.

NOTES

[1] Florence Peterson, *American Labor Unions* (New York: Harper & Brothers, 1935), p. 56.

[2] Edwin E. Witte, *The Government in Labor Disputes* (New York: McGraw-Hill Book Company, 1932), pp. 270–273.

[3] See Appendix C for the exact language of Section 20.

[4] These states were Oregon, North Dakota, Utah, Washington, and Wisconsin.

[5] *American Steel Foundries* v. *Tri-City Central Trades Council*, 257 U.S. 312 (1921).

[6] *Truax* v. *Corrigan*, 257 U.S. 312 (1921).

[7] The Fourteenth Amendment to the Constitution states: "Nor shall any State deprive any person of life, liberty, or property, without due process of law; nor deny to any person within its jurisdiction the equal protection of the laws."

[8] Benjamin J. Taylor, *Arizona Labor Relations Law* (Tempe: Arizona State University, Occasional Paper Number 2, Bureau of Business and Economic Research, College of Business Administration, 1967), pp. 14–15.

[9] For an interesting and stimulating account of the life of Louis Dembitz Brandeis, see A. T. Mason, *Brandeis: A Free Man's Life* (New York: The Viking Press, 1946). On the life of Oliver Wendell Homes, Jr., see Silas Bent, *Justice Oliver Wendell Holmes* (New York: Vanguard Press, 1932).

[10] Taylor, *op. cit.*, p. 15.

[11] Charles O. Gregory, *Labor and the Law* (New York: W. W. Norton & Company, 1946), p. 173.

[12] *Ibid.*, pp. 15–16.

[13] See Chapter 6 for a discussion of the importance of the concept of labor dispute established in Norris–La Guardia relative to the application of antitrust laws to labor activities. Section 13 of Norris–La Guardia spells out the meaning of "labor dispute." See text of Norris–La Guardia in Appendix E for the exact language of Section 13.

[14] See, for example, *Carpenters and Joiners Union* v. *Ritter's Cafe*, 315 U.S. 722 (1942). The *Ritter* case is discussed in Chapter 19. The principle of the case is that picketing must be confined to the industry in which the labor dispute has arisen if the picketing is to be protected from the labor injunction.

[15] The nature of arbitration is discussed in Chapter 15.

[16] *Senn* v. *Tile Layers*, 301 U.S. 468 (1937).

[17] *Lauf* v. *Shinner & Company*, 303 U.S. 323 (1938).

[18] Harry A. Millis and Royal E. Montgomery, *Organized Labor* (New York: McGraw-Hill Book Company, 1945), p. 624.

[19] *New Negro Alliance* v. *Sanitary Grocery Company*, 303 U.S. 552 (1938). However, in 1950 the Supreme Court upheld a decision of the California Supreme Court which enjoined racial picketing in *Hughes* v. *Superior Court of California*, U.S. Supreme Court, May 8, 1950. The 1950 decision does not per se overrule the *New Negro Alliance* doctrine because the California case involved the state judiciary. In the *New Negro Alliance* case, the issue centered around the right of the federal courts to enjoin racial picketing. Still, it must be conceded that the 1950 decision represents a wide departure from the principles which the Supreme Court established in the *New Negro Alliance*.

[20] *Retail Clerks, Local 1222* v. *Alfred M. Lewis, Inc.*, 327 F. (2d) 442 (1964).

[21] *Textile Workers Union* v. *Lincoln Mills of Alabama*, 353 U.S. 448 (1957).

[22] *Sinclair Refining Company* v. *Atkinson*, 370 U.S. 195 (1962).

[23] *Avco Corp.* v. *Aero Lodge No. 735, International Association of Machinists*, 390 U.S. 557 (1968).

[24] *Boys Markets, Inc.* v. *Retail Clerks, Local 770*, 398 U.S. 235 (1970).

[25] United States Department of Labor, *Growth of Labor Law in the United States* (Washington, D.C.: U.S. Government Printing Office, 1967), p. 207.

[26] Glenn W. Miller, *American Labor and the Government* (Englewood Cliffs, N.J.: Prentice-Hall, Inc., 1948), pp. 107, 112.

Antitrust Prosecution
Since Norris–La Guardia 6

Norris–La Guardia did more than curb the labor injunction. It served to restrict labor union prosecution under the antitrust laws. Although the terms "Sherman Act" or "antitrust laws" do not appear in Norris–La Guardia, the background of the law reveals that this was the unmistakable intention of Congress. It was enacted to provide unions with the benefits they had hoped for under the Clayton Act. On this score the authors of the statute declared, "The purpose of the bill is to protect the right of labor in the same manner the Congress intended when it enacted the Clayton Act, which act, by reason of its construction and application by the Federal Courts, is ineffectual to accomplish the Congressional intent." [1] Along the same lines, the Supreme Court subsequently affirmed that "the Norris–La Guardia Act was a disapproval of *Duplex Printing Press* v. *Deering* and *Bedford Cut Stone Company* v. *Journeymen Stone Cutters' Association* as the authoritative interpretation of Section 20 of the Clayton Act. . . ." [2] Thus the Norris–La Guardia Act granted protection to labor unions from the application of the Sherman Act. How does Norris–La Guardia accomplish this purpose? How did the Supreme Court react to this new effort of Congress? What recent developments indicate a possible change in direction on the part of the Court regarding the extent of permissible union action in the pursuit of its own interests?

LABOR DISPUTE DEFINED BROADLY
IN NORRIS–LA GUARDIA

In writing Norris–La Guardia, Congress remedied the labor provisions of the Clayton Act. Section 20 [3] of the latter statute prohibits the federal courts from restraining certain activities of unions growing out of a labor dispute. However, Congress, in the Clayton Act, failed to define the meaning of *labor dispute*. The judiciary was obliged to define the term. The character of the construction was of paramount importance for the labor-dispute definition determined the practical effects of the Clayton Act. Thus an activity of a union growing out of a labor dispute could not be enjoined. But the very same activity—say peaceful picketing or an orderly strike— not arising out of a labor dispute is subject to the injunction.[4] The concept of labor dispute had particular importance for unions involved in antitrust proceedings. The last sentence of Section 20 provides that an activity of a labor union immunized by the statute could not be held to constitute a violation of any law of the United States. For practical purposes this means that where Section 20 protects a union activity from a labor injunction, the federal judiciary may not find such conduct to be a violation of any law of the United States, including the Sherman Act. On the other hand, this immunity does not apply when the act of the labor organization does not arise out of a labor dispute as that term has meaning for the purposes of the Clayton Act.

In the *Duplex* decision it was necessary for the Supreme Court to construe the meaning of labor dispute. Much to the disappointment of organized labor, the Court defined the concept in a very narrow fashion. It held that for a labor controversy to fall within the meaning of a labor dispute for purposes of the Clayton Act, the parties to the dispute must stand in proximate relationship of employer and employee. It will be recalled that with the exception of the *Coronado* affair the major antitrust cases resulting in legal setbacks to organized labor centered around secondary boy-cotts. In a secondary boycott a union exerts pressure against employers who have no direct controversy with the organization. Labor organizations have often exerted pressure on other firms for the purpose of winning their dispute with the employer with whom the union is embroiled in a controversy. Such was the logic of the secon-dary boycott activities instigated by unions in the *Danbury Hatters, Bucks Stove, Duplex,* and *Bedford Stone* affairs.

Organized labor hoped the Clayton Act would be interpreted to forbid the issuance of an injunction to restrain secondary boycott strikes. If this resulted, the courts would then be required to hold that the secondary economic pressure of unions did not violate any federal law, including the Sherman Act. These hopes were not realized; the high court excluded union secondary pressure activities from the protec-tion of Section 20 because the parties to the controversy did not stand in proximate relationship of employer and employee. The limitations in Section 20, the Court said, apply only to disputants in a labor controversy "who are proximately and substan-tially concerned as parties to an actual dispute respecting the terms or conditions of their own employment, past, present, or prospective." The Court refused to protect union activity directed against firms "wholly unconnected" with a company with which a union has a dispute over conditions of employment except "in the way of purchasing its products in the ordinary course of interstate commerce."

Brandeis vigorously denounced this point of view of the majority of the Supreme Court. He argued that the fundamental purpose of the Clayton Act was to broaden the legitimate area of union activities. Brandeis felt that Section 20 of the Clayton Act protected a secondary boycott from the injunction, and hence from the appli-cation of the Sherman Act, for "A statute of the United States declares the right of industrial combatants to push their struggle to the limit of the justification of self interest. . . ."

The authors of Norris–La Guardia were well aware of the various construc-tions placed on the term *labor dispute* by the judiciary. In the absence of legislative action, labor unions could not engage in secondary economic pressure activities, for the parties involved in such disputes do not stand in a proximate relationship of employer and employee. The task of Congress was to write a definition of labor dispute that would nullify the effect of the *Duplex* decision. It was necessary to spell out the concept in a manner that would legalize union secondary boycott activities. To accomplish this objective, Norris–La Guardia defines a labor dispute as any controversy concerning conditions of employment regardless of whether the disputants stand in proximate relationship of employee and employer.

JUDICIAL REACTION

In spite of the clear terms of Norris–La Guardia, organized labor was fearful that the courts would find some way to nullify the intent of Congress. Union leaders remembered the fate of the Clayton Act. Court construction would determine whether or not the new law was to provide benefits to labor unions. For these reasons the judicial construction of the law was awaited with much interest. The Supreme Court of the United States interpreted the Norris–La Guardia Act so as to conform with the intent of Congress. Its terms were broad enough, the Court held, to forbid the issuance of labor injunctions to restrain union secondary pressure tactics.

This principle was first established in the *Milk Wagon Drivers Union* case in 1940, and reaffirmed the next year in the more widely known *Hutcheson* decision. The members of the Milk Wagon Drivers Union, an American Federation of Labor affiliate, handled the bulk of the home milk deliveries in Chicago. With the advent of the depression, however, the "vendor system" of milk distribution was established. Under this depression-stimulated method, vendors purchased milk from nonunion dairies and sold the product to retail stores. As a result, the stores were able to sell milk at a price below that prevailing for milk delivered at home. To complicate the whole affair, the vendors organized themselves into a CIO union, but this feature of interunion rivalry did not influence the subsequent decision of the Supreme Court. The members of the Milk Wagon Drivers Union picketed the retail stores that handled milk under the new milk distribution method.

The action of the Milk Wagon Drivers Union constituted a secondary boycott, for pressure was placed on the retail stores not to deal with the vendors, the final result being that the vendors would not purchase milk from nonunion dairies. Interstate commerce was involved because the Chicago milk area includes the state of Wisconsin. After a federal district court refused to enjoin the action of the labor organization, an appeal was made to the Seventh Circuit Court of Appeals.[5] This court reversed the district court and held that the AFL union, by engaging in a secondary boycott, violated the terms of the Sherman Act. Finally, the Supreme Court, in a unanimous decision, held that Norris–La Guardia protected the action of the AFL union, for it was engaged in a labor dispute within the meaning of the law.[6]

In the *Hutcheson* case, Norris–La Guardia once more was interpreted in a manner that protected union secondary boycott activities.[7] In this matter an interunion jurisdictional problem was involved. It centered around a controversy involving the United Brotherhood of Carpenters and Joiners of America and the International

Association of Machinists. Both these labor organizations were affiliated with the AFL at the time of the conflict. The dispute was over the issue of which of these unions was to install and dismantle machinery in the Anheuser-Busch property in St. Louis.

When the Machinists Union was awarded the job by the company, the Carpenters Union called a strike, picketed the plant, and refused to permit its members to work on new construction taking place on Anheuser-Busch property. In addition, through letters and labor journals, the union called upon its members and friends to refrain from purchasing or selling Anheuser-Busch beer. In a split decision, three jurists dissenting, the Supreme Court held that the action of the Carpenters Union was protected by Norris–La Guardia. Despite the fact that the secondary boycott grew out of a jurisdictional dispute between two unions, the high court held that the terms of Norris–La Guardia were applicable. The controversy was a labor dispute within the meaning of the Act, and for this reason the federal courts were not permitted to restrain the activities of the labor organizations. Not only did the term labor dispute include controversies between an employer and his own employees, but the term was elastic enough to prohibit prosecution of a union involved in an inter-union jurisdictional dispute.

Roberts wrote the dissenting opinion in the *Hutcheson* case and contended that Norris–La Guardia did not preclude the application of the Sherman Act to union secondary boycott action. His position was that even though Norris–La Guardia might serve to protect unions against injunctions in such controversies, the union could be sued for damages or tried under the criminal provisions of the Sherman Act. It will be recalled that the Sherman Act provided for its enforcement along three lines—injunction, damage suits, and criminal prosecution. According to Roberts, the fact that the injunction might be prohibited in labor cases did not mean that the other two methods of enforcement could not be employed. He declared that

> what a reading of the [Norris–La Guardia] Act makes letter clear, is that the prosecution of actions for damages authorized by the Sherman Act, and of the criminal offenses denounced by the Act, are not touched by the Norris–La Guardia Act. By a process of construction never, as I think, heretofore indulged by this court, it is now found that, because Congress forbade the issuing of injunctions to restrain certain conduct, it intended to repeal the provisions of the Sherman Act authorizing actions at law and criminal prosecutions for the commission of torts and crimes defined by the antitrust laws.

Roberts' viewpoint, though on the surface tenable, appears wholly inconsistent with the intent of Norris–La Guardia. It is doubtful that Congress meant to restrain the issuance of injunctions in labor cases arising under the Sherman Act, only to permit unions to be attacked through damage suits and criminal prosecution. If the position of Roberts had prevailed, unions would have lost whatever benefits Congress intended that they should have from the operation of Norris–La Guardia in antitrust cases. Also, the law would protect secondary boycott activities from the labor injunction, but the government or employers could proceed against unions engaging in such conduct under the Sherman Act by initiating damage suits or criminal prosecutions.

The viewpoint of Roberts was brushed aside by the majority of the Court as constituting an erroneous interpretation of the Norris–La Guardia Act. Frankfurter, the jurist who wrote the majority opinion of the Court, contended that Norris–La Guardia reasserted the purpose of the Clayton Act and broadened its terms. If the judiciary did not interpret the Clayton Act so as to immunize labor union secondary boycott activities, Congress, by expanding the concept of labor dispute in the Norris–La Guardia Act, certainly meant to forbid the courts to enjoin such union conduct. If a secondary boycott can no longer be enjoined under the Norris–La Guardia Act, such an activity does not violate any law of the United States, including the Sherman Act. Section 20 of the Clayton Act immunizes labor unions from prosecution under any federal law when the judiciary may not restrain the conduct of the labor union by the labor injunction. Finally, Frankfurter challenged the view of Roberts that unions could still be subject to damage suits and criminal proceedings under the Sherman Act, even though Norris–La Guardia forbids the issuance of injunctions to restrain a particular pattern of union conduct. On this score Frankfurter declared:

> Congress expressed this national policy and determined the bounds of a labor dispute in an act explicitly dealing with the further withdrawal of injunctions in labor controversies. But to argue, as it was urged before us, that the *Duplex* case still governs for purposes of a criminal prosecution is to say that that which on the equity side of the court is allowable conduct may in a criminal proceeding become the road to prison. It would be strange indeed that although neither the Government nor Anheuser-Busch could have sought an injunction against the act here challenged, the elaborate efforts to permit such conduct failed to prevent criminal liability punishable with imprisonment and heavy fines.

THE <u>APEX</u> DOCTRINE NULLIFIES EFFECT OF <u>CORONADO</u> DECISION

Organized labor was permitted by the principles affirmed in the *Hutcheson* and *Milk Wagon Drivers Union* cases to undertake economic activities to expand the area of collective bargaining. Doctrines established by the Supreme Court in the *Danbury Hatters*, *Bucks Stove*, *Duplex*, and *Bedford Stone* cases were swept away by the impact of Norris–La Guardia. Only the *Coronado* cases appeared as a threat to labor unions in their Sherman Act relationship. In these cases, it will be recalled, the Supreme Court held that a labor union violated the antitrust provisions when it engaged in a strike, the effect and intent of which was to reduce the amount of goods in interstate commerce.

In 1940 the Supreme Court decided the *Apex* case,[8] a proceeding which in many respects duplicated the *Coronado* affair. Similar to the *Coronado* case, a great deal of violence surrounded the strike directed against the Apex Company of Philadelphia. The strike also had the effect of reducing the amount of nonunion goods in interstate commerce. The Apex Company engaged in the manufacture of hosiery, producing annually merchandise valued at approximately $5 million. It shipped in interstate commerce about 80 percent of its finished product. The company operated a nonunion shop and in April 1937 the hosiery workers' union demanded that the firm recognize the labor organization as the bargaining agent of its workers and employ only union members.

On May 6, 1937, about a month after the company refused to agree to the union's demands, members of the hosiery workers' union employed in the Apex plant, along with other members of the union employed in other hosiery factories in Philadelphia, gathered at the factory. Once more, the union officers demanded that the company operate the plant on a union basis. When this last ultimatum was refused, the officers of the union declared a "sit-down" strike. What occurred after the seizure of the plant by the union is described by the Supreme Court as follows:

> Immediately, acts of violence against the petitioner's plant and the employees in charge of it were committed by the assembled mob. It forcibly seized the plant, whereupon, under union leadership, its members were organized to maintain themselves on a sit-down strike in possession of the plant, and it remained in possession until June 23, 1937, when the strikers were forcibly ejected pursuant to an injunction ordered by the Court of Appeals of the Third Court. The locks in all gates and entrances of the petitioner's plant were changed: only strikers were given keys. No others were allowed to leave or enter the plant without permission of the strikers. During the period of the occupancy the union supplied them with food, blankets, cots, medical care, and paid them strike benefits. While occupying the factory, the strikers willfully wrecked machinery of great value, and did extensive damage to other property and equipment of the company. All manufacturing operations by petitioner ceased on May 6. As the result of the destruction of the company's machinery and plant, it did not resume even partial manufacturing operations until August 19, 1937. The record discloses lawless invasion of petitioner's plant and destruction of its property by force and violence of the most brutal and wanton character. . . .

Beyond causing such damage to plant and machinery, the union prevented the shipment of 130,000 dozen pairs of finished hosiery, of a value of about $800,000. Evidence proved that about 80 percent of this merchandise was scheduled for shipment outside the state of Pennsylvania. The company sued the union under the Sherman Act provisions and a trial court awarded it damages of $237,310. The trial judge utilizing his prerogative under the antitrust provisions trebled this figure to a sum exceeding $700,000. In 1940, after extensive litigation in the lower federal court, the case was finally reviewed by the Supreme Court.

The *Apex* decision was awaited with deep interest. After the district court awarded the Apex Company $700,000 damages, a wave of similar damage suits against labor unions was instituted under the Sherman Act. Professor E. B. McNatt stated:

> Two days after the Federal District Court awarded the $711,932 to the Apex Company in Philadelphia, three New England trucking companies filed an antitrust action against the International Brotherhood of Teamsters, asking for $90,000 damages resulting from a strike. And a few weeks later, on May 22, the Republic Steel Corporation filed a similar suit against the CIO and some 700 individuals asking for $7,500,000 treble damages under the Sherman Act for injuries suffered as a result of the Little Steel strike of 1937.[9]

In addition to deciding the outcome for these and other damage suits, the *Apex* decision would determine whether or not the Court would reaffirm the *Coronado* doctrine in a period of "liberalism." Would the Supreme Court, despite the enactment of legislation to encourage collective bargaining, utilize the Sherman Act to outlaw strikes carried out to force companies to recognize and bargain with labor unions?

The issue in the *Apex* case was not whether the action of the union was lawful or unlawful. As indicated, the Supreme Court spoke of the conduct of the unionists in terms of "lawless invasion of petitioner's plant and destruction of its property by force and violence of the most brutal and wanton character." Clearly, the union's conduct was unlawful. The state courts undoubtedly would have served as a forum in which the union could have been sued for damages. However, the company chose to sue the union for damages under the Sherman Act. Consequently, a fundamental question of the *Apex* case was whether or not violence made the Sherman Act applicable to a labor dispute, when in the absence of violence the statute would not have been applicable. The Supreme Court replied in the negative, for "restraints not within the [Sherman] Act when achieved by peaceful means are not brought within its sweep merely because, without other differences, they are attended by violence."

With this question clarified, the Court then proceeded to determine whether the Apex strike constituted restraint of trade within the meaning of the Sherman Act. Again the Court reached a negative conclusion and ordered the suit against the union dismissed. To support this decision, it declared that labor unions to function effectively must eliminate nonunion competition and action undertaken to achieve this objective does not violate the Sherman Act. The Court ruled that the intent of a labor union to eliminate nonunion competition by collective economic action did not violate the Sherman Act since "an elimination of price competition based on differences in labor standards is the objective of any national labor organization. But this effect in competition has not been considered to be the kind of curtailment of price competition prohibited by the Sherman Act."

In addition, the Court declared lawful for purposes of the Sherman Act strikes which have the effect of suppressing the amount of goods in commerce. Labor unions intend to stop production when they strike. Stoppage of production and a strike are one and the same thing. If a firm is engaged in interstate commerce, the amount of such commerce during the strike is reduced. Unions strike, however, not to reduce deliberately the amount of goods in commerce or influence their price, but to win disputes with companies. As the Supreme Court declared in the *Apex* case, if the lawfulness of strikes resulting in a diminution to commerce were questioned, the Sherman Act would threaten the legality of "practically every strike in modern industry."

Thus the effect of the *Apex* decision was to destroy the doctrine established in the *Coronado* cases. In this connection, it is noteworthy that even though the circumstances of *Apex* and *Coronado* were strikingly similar, the Supreme Court ruled on the action of the hosiery union without specifically overruling the *Coronado* doctrine. Even so, the *Apex* case established the principle that a strike, the effect and the intent of which is to reduce the goods in commerce, does not violate the Sherman Act, provided the strike is carried out for the purpose of furthering the interests of the labor organization.

The position of the Supreme Court in the 1940–1941 antitrust labor cases improved the legal position of organized bargaining agencies. The judiciary no longer utilized the Sherman Act to block organizing activities of unions. Secondary boycotts were deemed lawful, and the antitrust provisions no longer threatened the legality of major strikes undertaken to enforce demands against employers. On the other hand, labor unions were still subject to prosecution under the Sherman Act. In the *Apex* case the Court reaffirmed the principle that the antitrust statutes apply to labor organizations. In this connection, it was stated that for thirty-two years the Court in its efforts to determine the true meaning and application of the Sherman Act held that its terms "do enclose to some extent and in some circumstances labor unions and their activities."

At present, however, the Sherman Act outlaws union activities only when labor organizations combine with business groups to promote monopoly. The application of this rule is subject to interpretive change, as we shall see later in this chapter. The principle was emphasized in 1945 when the Supreme Court handed down its decision in the *Allen Bradley Company* case.[10] Local No. 3, affiliated with the International Brotherhood of Electrical Workers (AFL), had jurisdiction covering workers engaged in the manufacture of electrical equipment and in the installation of electrical products. Contractors operating in New York City agreed not to purchase electrical equipment from suppliers not under contract with Local No. 3. This meant that electrical product manufacturers outside of the city were excluded from a profitable market. On their part, manufacturers agreed not to sell electrical products to any contractor unless the contractor employed members of Local No. 3.

After a time the combination among the three groups proved highly successful to all concerned. The business of New York City electrical manufacturers increased sharply since they did not face any out-of-city competition. Jobs were available for members of Local No. 3 and their wages increased through the tripartite arrangement. Contractors likewise benefited from the arrangement. The effect of the arrangement is further indicated by the fact that the New York manufacturers sold their goods in the protected city market at one price and sold identical goods outside of New York City at a far lower price. All parties to the arrangement thereby benefited. But the tripartite agreement caused much hardship to the consuming public, to those electrical manufacturers denied the opportunity to sell in the New York market, and to electrical workers outside the city.

Such an arrangement, the Court held, violated the Sherman Act. It stated that "Congress never intended that unions could, consistent with the Sherman Act, aid nonlabor groups to create business monopolies and to control the mobility of goods and services." However, it is important to note that if the labor union alone, by strike or boycott, accomplished the same results, the Sherman Act would not be applicable. Thus one jurist of the Court stated, "If the union in this instance had acted alone in self-interest, resulting in a restraint of interstate trade, the Sherman Act concededly would be inapplicable." The violation of the law occurred when the union, manufacturers, and contractors of New York City combined to exclude from use in the city electrical equipment manufactured outside the city of New York. The *Allen Bradley* doctrine did not overrule the principles established in the *Hutcheson* and *Apex* decisions. Unions are free from prosecution under the Sherman Act, provided the Court is convinced that their activities are carried out for the sole purpose of advancing their own interests. The crime of the union in the *Allen Bradley* case was to combine with nonlabor groups for the purpose of monopolizing markets and effecting profits.

UNION MONOPOLY POWER AND DEBATE OVER
NEED FOR CONTROLS THROUGH ANTITRUST
AMENDMENTS

The post-Norris–La Guardia decisions and the changing structure of collective bargaining in recent years have led to the considerable debate over the desirability of labor union exclusion from the antitrust provisions. It is argued that Norris–La Guardia is outmoded as public law since unions have advanced from a relatively weak position in 1932 to one of excessive strength. Debate continues on whether or not the antitrust laws should be changed so as to stem union monopoly power. Discussion centers around four areas of concern: industry-wide collective bargaining, exclusive jurisdiction, featherbedding practices, and interferences with the product market.[11]

Industry-wide Collective Bargaining. Industry-wide collective bargaining as a labor device to control the labor market monopolistically is in reality a response to the rapid pace of technological advance in production. The proponents of eliminating such bargaining are actually more concerned with multiunit bargaining, which involves union negotiation with several plants under the control of a single firm such as General Motors, than with industry-wide bargaining. Industry-wide bargaining is more often characterized by small firms than the pattern bargaining of multiunit firms such as exists in the steel, coal, and automobile industries. In effect, the national union, not a local, negotiates the wage agreement for members of the several locals representing a firm's employees. The agreement reached usually sets the pattern for settlement with all other firms in the industry.

A union is compelled to seek essentially identical wage standards from all firms in order to eliminate wage competition so as to force competition to endure on the basis of efficiency and service as opposed to wage standards. It is the state of technology and extent of the market that dictates the bargaining practice. Legislation barring unions from multiunit or industry-wide bargaining would in effect emasculate free collective bargaining in an industry serving a national or international market. If a strike should occur in a particular plant, the firm need only shift production to another of its plants. In such a case the local labor organization would be without recourse. Multiunit agreements, therefore, have resulted from the very nature of the market itself. Curtailing the ability of unions to bargain with multiunit employers would result in destroying union organization of oligopolistic industries. A public policy to retain free collective bargaining, but destroying multiunit bargaining would of necessity result in the breakup of multiplant firms as well as the bargaining efforts of national unions.

Industry-wide bargaining prevails in industries such as the clothing industry. In such cases an association of small employers bargains with a single union or with multiple unions. Under such conditions union power is not as forceful as it is often assumed since unions are unable to single out an individual small employer and force their demands upon him. Hence, small as well as large unions benefit from this kind of bargaining.

Conclusive data are not available to justify applying antitrust provisions to unions merely because of the existence of multiunit or industry-wide bargaining. The lack of data is at the heart of the debate.

Exclusive Jurisdiction. Under the Taft-Hartley Act, a majority of employees in an appropriate unit may obtain exclusive rights to negotiate collective bargaining agreements and to otherwise represent its members with an employer. Once a union has been certified by the National Labor Relations Board, it is a monopoly to the extent that other unions are barred from competing to represent the same employees for a specified period of time. National labor legislation also permits a union shop arrangement whereby employees may be required to join a union as a condition of employment, after 30 days in general industry, and after 7 days in construction.

The general argument is that the union leadership will be more responsive to the desires of members if workers are free to join or refrain from joining a labor organization. Data are not available to conclusively show what effect such a prohibition would have on unions. It could be that a national labor policy restrictive on union security might result in an ineffectual union movement.

Featherbedding Practices. The rapid rate of technological change has resulted in the development of make-work rules and restrictions on output. Newspaper strikes have focused public attention on the "bogus" type requirements negotiated by the International Typographical Union. Certain type can be supplied to publishers already set without a need for work to be performed by a firm's employees. The union requires that all mats supplied a firm by other sources be duplicated by its members. After the work is performed the type is not used. There are many other examples, but the printing situation is one that is well known.

The application of antitrust provisions to featherbedding cases would place a burden on the courts with which they are not equipped to deal. Restrictions are placed on output throughout society for various purposes. Labor unions restrict output through make-work practices because of the fear of job losses. The particular restrictive practices are peculiar to all industries as to their nature. Such practices are intimately tied to most work relationships and policing could wind up in an impossible judicial task.

Product Market Controls. Some critics of union tactics point to their interference in product markets as justification for more rigid labor antitrust provisions. Essentially, unions often act as policemen over an entire industry or area covered by a collective bargaining contract. The maintenance of negotiated labor standards often requires that price cutting in the product market be prohibited. Unions, under some circumstances, have attempted to deal with such situations by refusing to work for a company that cuts prices, the reason being that price cutting may lead to such pressures on particular firms to survive that wages will be cut to advance their objectives. Success in preventing such company action tends to stabilize an area of competition, and greater certainty is afforded both workers and managers.

On occasion unions also control the number of firms that are permitted to compete in an area. They are able to control entry into the market when they are the sole source of labor supply to both existing and prospective firms. Again, such behavior is applauded by existing firms. This type of activity is detrimental to firms attempting to enter into competition.

Unions may also serve to restrict the amount of services a firm may supply its customers at a given price. A union can argue that its members will not perform more work at the same pay. If more services are to be provided, then increased remuneration must accompany the extra work.

The last example of union interference in the product market to be considered here is the attempt to restrict the areas of competition. Certain firms may be allotted certain geographic areas in which they may market their goods, and no more. In the past it has not been unusual to establish delivery routes by area, and no competitors were permitted to infringe on the allotted territory.[12]

The four situations mentioned are all enforceable by virtue of a union's ability to withhold labor. Usually, small highly competitive firms are characteristic of industries where such behavior is found. Union interference is often undertaken with employer approval.

The Attorney General's National Committee to Study Antitrust Laws issued a report in 1967 which summarized labor's immunity from such laws.[13] The view was expressed that only direct labor action to control the product market should be subject to antitrust action. The recommendation was made that Congress pass legislation to restrict efforts to control product market activities. It was clear in the report that the Committee was not in favor of restriction by private employer action, but by government action fashioned after the 1947 Taft-Hartley provisions as well as subsequent amendments to the federal labor laws.

Another study group—this time an independent study group comprised principally of university economics professors—concluded that the Congress should take action to include unions under the antitrust provisions when they interfere with the operation of the product market. In this regard it was recommended that:

> . . . agreements which contain direct links to the product market or activities to police the price structure of an industry would be violations of law. Thus, it would be illegal under our proposal for a union to condition work by its members on maintenance by the firm of a given price list or on the purchase of the firm's supplies from a given group of employers.[14]

The debate and recommendations continue with some apparent weakening of union position with the general public. There is need to cautiously review the consequences any potential antitrust amendments may have on the labor movement. There may be some merit in restricting union activities in the product market, not the labor market. While the debate continues the Supreme Court, not the Congress, has taken steps to expand the realm of review of union actions under the antitrust provisions.

LABOR UNIONS AND THE SHERMAN ACT: PRESENT APPLICATION

More recent labor cases before the Supreme Court highlight the broadening of the zone in which labor organizations can violate the Sherman Act. A new era of interpretation of labor union liabilities under the antitrust statutes appears to be developing. Two opinions were handed down on the same day, June 7, 1965, dealing with (1) limitations placed on the marketing hours of employers' products (*Jewel Tea* case)[15] and (2) industry elimination of small employers (*Pennington* cases).[16]

The Jewel Tea Case

In the *Jewel Tea* case collective bargaining negotiations involved a multi-employer association. The 1957 negotiations concluded with the signing of a pact by employers other than Jewel Tea and the National Tea Company to refrain from selling meat between the hours of 6:00 P.M. and 9:00 A.M. Jewel Tea contended that it signed the contract under duress of a union strike.

Jewel Tea brought suit in July 1958 seeking invalidation of the agreement under Sections 1 and 2 of the Sherman Act. It argued that the employer association and union agreed among themselves that all collective bargaining agreements would contain the same provisions. Further, the company contended it was placed under the duress of a strike vote since the rest of the industry had signed. This amounted to a conspiracy to force agreement that meat would not be sold between 6:00 P.M. and 9:00 A.M. with or without union members. Jewel Tea argued that it had no choice in the matter since a strike would have hampered its competitive position within the region. A federal district court ruled that the union acted in its own self-interest since the record was devoid of evidence of a conspiracy. The court of appeals, however, reversed the trial court and ruled that the agreement was a conspiracy whether or not it was called an agreement or a contract.

Upon review, the U.S. Supreme Court upheld the trial court, reversing the court of appeals. In a three-way split among the justices, it held that the parties were required to bargain on subjects intimately tied to wages, hours, and working conditions. The antitrust exemptions applied since the union action to limit marketing hours was undertaken in the union's own self-interest. The Court reviewed the history of bargaining in the industry to arrive at its decision. Historically, the union bargained on both working hours and operation hours of companies. It was reasoned that operations that continue beyond the agreed-upon working hours of union members would require someone other than union members to serve customers. Even if a self-service market was involved, union workers would be required to carry a heavier burden during working hours because of the increased demand to clean the work areas and package meat.

Justice Douglas entered a vigorous dissent opinion. He argued that the collective bargaining agreement itself was clear proof of a conspiracy between the union and employers to restrain operations in the product market. He saw no difference between an agreement to sell at fixed prices and one to limit the hours a store could market its products. In his opinion, the *Allen Bradley* case foreclosed the expansive view of labor exemption from the antitrust provisions. It was not necessary to review the bargaining history of the industry or to look at the effect marketing hours between 6:00 P.M. and 9:00 A.M. would have on the work standards of union members. In effect, he reasoned that any agreement that employers could not make between themselves under antitrust could not be justified because of the existence of a collective bargaining agreement.

The Pennington Case

The *Pennington* case, decided by the Supreme Court on June 7, 1965, the same day as the *Jewel Tea* decision, involved an antitrust suit for treble damages by a small coal-mining employer stemming from the National Coal Wage Agreement of

1950. Prior to 1950 the industry was notorious for the occurrence of frequent strikes and government seizure of mines. Relative peace was brought to the industry after the pact was signed in 1950.

An amendment to the 1950 agreement was negotiated in 1958 whereby company signatories agreed to pay 80 cents per ton on each ton acquired if the required 40 cents per ton had not already been paid into the United Mine Workers (UMW) Welfare and Retirement Fund. This clause was to discourage the leasing of coal fields to firms operating under wage standards inferior to those established by collective bargaining. Further, it was argued that the UMW collusively agreed to support mechanization of the large mines and to impose the terms of the wage agreement on all mines without regard to ability to pay. As support, the plaintiff identified the large investment outlays the union made to mechanize some of the mines.

Additionally, the UMW allegedly prevailed upon the Secretary of Labor to influence a prevailing wage determination, under the Walsh-Healey Act, which would eliminate the small operators from supplying coal to the Tennessee Valley Authority (TVA). It was argued that the small operators could not effectively enter competitive bids if they were forced to pay prevailing union wage rates.

When some of the operators failed to meet their payments to the Welfare Fund, the UMW brought suit for violation of the wage agreement. Several small firms retaliated by bringing suit against the UMW for entering into a conspiracy with the large operators to settle the general problem of overproduction by eliminating the marginal firms.

The Supreme Court upon review remanded the case for retrial in a federal district court in accordance with its decision on the case. It held that not every agreement arising out of collective provisions, merely because it involves a mandatory subject for bargaining, is exempt from the Sherman Act provisions. Exemption may not be claimed "when it is clearly shown that it [the union] has agreed with one set of employers to impose a certain wage scale on other bargaining units." This position was justified by holding that such an agreement restricted the freedom of unions to "respond to each bargaining situation as the individual circumstance might warrant." Mr. Justice White, in a footnote to his opinion for the Court, remarked that a union, if acting unilaterally, could seek to impose uniform wage standards on the entire industry even if it suspected some marginal operators could not compete if required to pay the union scale. The mere act of attempting to impose a uniform wage standard is not sufficient evidence to uphold a union-employer conspiracy charge. The intent to eliminate marginal firms has to be supported by specific and concrete evidence.

Justice Douglas, in a concurring opinion joined in by two other justices, interpreted the Court's opinion as meaning that an industry-wide collective bargaining agreement is obvious evidence of the existence of a conspiracy and no further investigation is required. He also wrote that a union may not agree on a wage scale in excess of the ability of some employers to pay when such agreement is for the purpose of forcing some of them out of business.

Retrial in Tennessee District Court

The 1965 retrial provided the guidelines within which the U.S. district court was required to solve the mining cases. The trial court reviewed the entire history of bargaining in the bituminous coal industry, similar to the *Jewel Tea* review, including the possibility of collusion on TVA bids to determine if the UMW was guilty of Sherman Act violations. It was found that the union was not in violation of the antitrust law. The trial court held on the basis of the *Hutcheson* case whereby a union, if acting alone and not in concert with nonlabor groups, is not in violation of the antitrust act. The concurring opinion of Justice Douglas was construed to mean that the agreement had to exceed the ability of some firms to pay and even then it had to be made for the purpose of putting some employers out of business. Also, the union investment in some companies did not in itself show collusive bidding. The trial court was convinced that the bids entered by the large companies were justified on the basis of productivity gains. Several studies have verified the validity of this position.[17]

Another Court's View

In 1968, two small coal operators sued the United Mine Workers in a federal district court charging they could not operate profitably under the terms of contract imposed on them by the union and Bituminous Coal Operators Association. A jury decided that the UMW had engaged in a conspiracy and intended to contract with the two small companies only on the terms provided in the national agreement. Thus, it was held that the union forfeited its exemption under the Sherman Act. Triple damages were awarded in the amount of $1,432,500 for one company and $67,500 for the other.

The decision was upheld by a federal appeals court. Unfavorable union treatment in the appellate court prompted the UMW to appeal to the U.S. Supreme Court. Review was denied without comment.

The trial court's action makes it clear that UMW's motives were considered to be different from that of the 1965 case. The jury was convinced that the union combined with an association of companies to prevent effective competition from a third party.

"Clear Proof" Not Required

The Supreme Court took another run at the antitrust implication of the 1950 Coal Agreement in *Ramsey* v. *Mineworkers*,[18] which was decided in 1971. In this case the high court took the position that union antitrust liability did not require the meeting of the standard of "clear proof" that is clearly specified in the Norris—La Guardia Act, but required only that parties making a complaint were required to establish their case only by a preponderance of the evidence. The Norris—La Guardia Act requires that no union shall be liable for acts of its officers who violated the antitrust laws, except on "clear proof" of the officers' "actual participation in or actual authorization of, such acts." In this respect, then, the standard-of-proof requirement to find unions in violation of the antitrust statutes has been eased.

Eighteen small coal mine operators in Tennessee filed suit in federal district court alleging UMW violation of the Sherman Act. It was charged that the UMW agreed not to oppose mine mechanization and, in turn, large producers with whom the union dealt agreed to wage increases and royalty payments to the union welfare fund. Basically, the charge was that there was a conspiracy with the large operators to drive the small unmechanized mines out of business by forcing them to pay wages and other benefits that they could not afford. The 1958 Protective Wage Clause Amendment to the 1950 Soft Coal Wage Agreement required the UMW not to enter into wage agreements applicable to employees covered by the contract on any basis other than those specified in the contract. In other words, the agreement was that the union would not permit other employers to sign a collective bargaining agreement with the UMW on terms different from those agreed to by the multiemployer group. The employer group constituted the larger mechanized operators in the industry.

The Federal District Court in Chattanooga, Tennessee, dismissed the suit. In so doing the judge interpreted the 1958 amendment in the context of Norris–La Guardia Act language. He decided that the law required "clear proof" not only that UMW officers actually participated in writing the amendment but also that the amendment itself constituted a violation of the Sherman Act. In the decision, the judge remarked that under the "preponderance of the evidence" rule that is applied to most antitrust cases the UMW implied agreement to an illegal conspiracy but when the "clear proof" standard is applied the UMW was not held to be liable under the antitrust laws. The trial court's opinion was affirmed by an Appellate Court.

The Supreme Court agreed to review the case. It held that the lower court was in error and remanded that case for retrial. The majority opinion was that the lower courts "read far too much" into the Norris–La Guardia Act's "clear proof" standard, which applies only to showing that union officers had authority to perform allegedly illegal acts. The acts themselves are to be judged on the preponderance of the evidence rule.

Justice Douglas, in dissent, was of the opinion that Congress intended that the "clear proof" standard should be applied broadly in antitrust suits dealing with the unions and because the majority of the court did not agree, their opinion amounted to a drastic rewriting of a part of the Norris–La Guardia Act.

The retrial held later in 1971 resulted in the trial judge instructing the jury that while the agreement between the UMW and the major operators was not in itself illegal, the agreement would on its face be a violation of the Sherman Act if the jury found proof that the agreement had been entered into with the intent of driving some coal mine operators out of business, or with the knowledge that it would have that effect.

The jury returned a "guilty" verdict requiring the UMW and one large company to pay triple damages. The lower court's decision was upheld by an appellate court and a request for review before the United States Supreme Court was refused without comment. The union and company asked the high court to decide the ultimate question of whether an agreement is on its face illegal when a union and an employer or group of employers agree to a basic contract that requires that the union insist on the same terms in its negotiations with other employers that have been imposed on the signatory employers.

CONSEQUENCES OF SUPREME COURT ACTION

A considerable amount of uncertainty has been thrust upon the legality of multiemployer bargaining because of the Supreme Court action. The most serious consequence is that the high court in particular has served notice that the judiciary is going to determine the motives of the parties to collective agreements on subjects of mandatory bargaining. The vigorous dissent of Justice Goldberg in *Pennington* indicates that the judiciary may once again be moving in a direction to set up its own socioeconomic philosophies over the congressional intent of how collective bargaining should work.

It is possible for both juries and trial judges to determine the motives of unions in seeking uniform contracts throughout an industry by imposing their own philosophies on whether a union acts unilaterally or in collusion with an employer group. Mere discussion at the bargaining table of the possible competitive effect of a wage package may be sufficient to prove the existence of a conspiracy. The development of such an application would in effect place the collective bargaining process in approximately the same state in which it existed prior to Norris–La Guardia. It has already been explained that unions do attempt to standardize wage settlements throughout an entire industry. Such a condition has generally accompanied successful union organization in several industries, one of which is coal. However, the UMW has had only limited success in such efforts, but it does make continued bids to standardize agreements throughout the areas it represents.

Another possible consequence of the cases is that the collective bargaining process itself is at stake. Guy Farmer, former chairman of the National Labor Relations Board, "reported that between 80 and 100 percent of the workers covered by union contracts" in several industries are under multiemployer contracts.[19] The concurring opinion of Justice Douglas indicated that both union and employers are liable when restraint-of-trade violations grow out of such agreements. If the one is found in violation, then the other cannot expect to escape. It is possible that employers will resist entering into multiemployer agreements with unions if marginal firms are permitted to resist signing agreements by bringing charges of collusion in the courts and collecting treble damages levied against both unions and large employers. Such a development would endanger the entire collective bargaining process. As mentioned, unions cannot organize successfully in the absence of a wage standard which it seeks to impose on all units in a particular competitive sphere.

Another possible consequence of the coal cases and the *Jewel Tea* case falls in the area of technological change. Small firms subject to multiemployer agreements may elect to utilize the antitrust provisions when they are unable to procure the most efficient techniques of production available to larger firms with greater access to the money market. If the more expansive application of antitrust to multiemployer agreements is taken by the courts, small firms could obtain release from industry-wide wage standards. In turn, they could set off explosive competition in the labor market, which might result in the eventual elimination of collective bargaining in the entire industry. It will be recalled that such a struggle was present in the *Danbury Hatters*, *Duplex*, *Coronado*, and *Bedford Cut Stone* cases of pre-Norris–La Guardia years.

The task is to fashion legislation that would protect the interest of the public without endangering the ability of labor unions to act as effective collective bargaining agents. The vehicle to accomplish this worthwhile objective should be in the form of new and proper labor legislation. As a matter of fact, Congress adopted this procedure when it amended the National Labor Relations Act in 1947 and 1959. It has been suggested that measures to amend the existing labor laws dealing with union abuses in the product market may lose support. It is argued that Congress is unlikely to proceed if the Court deals firmly with the subjects of their debate. It may be that political expediency would be furthered by a lack of legislative action if the felt abuses are cleared away by new antitrust applications in the federal courts.

SUMMARY

Other than curbing the labor injunction, Norris–La Guardia at first relieved labor unions from prosecution under the antitrust laws. To accomplish this objective, Congress defined the term *labor dispute* in a very broad fashion. It did this to overcome the basic shortcoming of the Clayton Act. In this law Congress failed to define the term, and the Supreme Court construed the meaning of labor dispute in a way which deprived unions of any protection in antitrust suits.

Some people felt, however, that the Supreme Court would nullify Norris–La Guardia, and the position of organized labor would be no better than it was before its passage. These fears proved groundless for the Court in the *Apex* and *Hutcheson* cases broadly construed Norris–La Guardia, providing unions with the opportunity to engage in activities calculated to effectuate the collective bargaining process.

Although the statute legalized union tactics formerly held objectionable under the antitrust laws, the Supreme Court in the *Allen Bradley* decision held that the Sherman Act still applies to unions when they conspire with employers to monopolize markets. Cases decided in 1965 and after have broadened the base of the antitrust laws so as to cover a wider area of labor activities. A great deal of uncertainty and speculation as to the eventual effect of these decisions has been generated. It seems very possible that the judiciary will take on an expanded role in determining how collective bargaining will work, at least in industries covered by multiemployer contracts.

NOTES

[1] House of Representatives, *Document No. 669*, 72nd Congress, 1st sess., p. 3.

[2] *United States* v. *Hutcheson*, 321 U.S. 219 (1941).

[3] Section 20, Clayton Act, reads as follows: "That no restraining order or injunction shall be granted by any court of the United States, or a judge or the judges thereof, in any case between an employer and employees, or between employers and employees, or between employees, or between persons employed and persons seeking employment, involving, or growing out of, a dispute concerning terms or conditions of employment, unless necessary to prevent irreparable injury to property, or to a property right, of the party making the application, for which injury there is no adequate remedy at law, and such property or property right must be described with particularity in the application, which must be in writing and sworn to by the applicant or by his agent or attorney.

"And no such restraining order or injunction shall prohibit any person or persons, whether singly or in concert, from terminating any relation of employment, or from ceasing to perform any work or labor or from recommending, advising or persuading others by peaceful means so to do; or from attending at any place where any such person or persons may lawfully be, for the purpose of peacefully obtaining or communicating information, or from peacefully persuading any person to work or to abstain from working; or from ceasing to patronize or to employ any party to such dispute, or recommending, advising, or persuading others by peaceful and lawful means so to do; or from paying or giving to, or withholding from, any person engaged in such dispute, any strike benefits or other moneys or things of value; or from peaceably assembling in a lawful manner, and for lawful purposes; or from doing any act or thing which might lawfully be done in the absence of such dispute by any party thereto; nor shall any of the acts specified in this paragraph be considered or held to be violations of any law of the United States."

[4] *American Federation of Musicians* v. *Stein*, 218 F. 2d 679 (1954); cert. denied 348 U.S. 873 (1955).

[5] *Milk Wagon Drivers' Union* v. *Lake Valley Farm Products*, 108 Fed. (2d) 436 (1939).

[6] *Milk Wagon Drivers' Union* v. *Lake Valley Farm Products*, 311 U.S. 91 (1940).

[7] *Hutcheson*, op. cit.

[8] *Apex Hosiery Company* v. *Leader*, 310 U.S. 409 (1940).

[9] E. B. McNatt, "Labor Again Menaced by the Sherman Act," *The Southern Economic Journal*, VI, No. 2 (October 1939), 208.

[10] *Allen Bradley Company* v. *Local Union No. 3, IBEW*, 325 U.S. 797 (1945).

[11] Herbert R. Northrup and Gordon F. Bloom, *Government and Labor* (Homewood, Ill.: Richard D. Irwin, Inc., 1963), pp. 29–39.

[12] Edwin Timbers, "The Problems of Union Power and Antitrust Legislation," *Labor Law Journal*, XVI, 9 (September 1965), 561.

[13] John C. Scott and Edwin S. Rockefeller, *Antitrust and Trade Regulation Today: 1967* (Washington, D.C.: The Bureau of National Affairs, Inc., 1967), p. 40.

[14] Committee for Economic Development, *The Public Interest in National Labor Policy* (New York: Committee for Economic Development, 1961), p. 139.

[15] *Local Union 189, Amalgamated Meat Cutters and Butcher Workmen of North America, AFL-CIO* v. *Jewel Tea Company Inc.*, 381 U.S. 676 (1965).

[16] *United Mine Workers of America* v. *James M. Pennington*, 381 U.S. 657 (1965); *Pennington* v. *United Mine Workers*, 257 F. Supp. 815 (1966).

[17] See Carroll L. Christenson and Richard A. Myren, *Wage Policy Under the Walsh-Healey Public Contracts Act: A Critical Review* (Bloomington, Ind.: Indiana University Press, 1966), pp. 194–198.

[18] *Ramsey* v. *Mineworkers*, U.S. Sup. Ct., No. 88 (February 24, 1971).

[19] Scott and Rockefeller, *op. cit.*, p. 43.

The Logic of Government Protection 7

THE PROBLEM

Commonwealth v. *Hunt* dissolved the identity between the conspiracy doctrine and the labor union. The decision established the lawfulness of labor organizations. However, by no means did the decision impose a respect for the right of workers to self-organization and collective bargaining. Workers were free to join labor unions, but there was no guarantee that they could exercise that right. In this connection, it should also be noted that Norris–La Guardia does not prevent interference with the collective bargaining rights of workers. The law restricts the power of courts in labor disputes, but sets up no prohibition on interferences with their right to engage in collective bargaining activities.

If there is freedom to utilize superior economic strength to prevent the organization and operation of labor unions, the fact that workers have the legal right to self-organization and collective bargaining has little practical value. A right, to be meaningful, must be respected. A democratic system provides for the right to freedom of worship. But if this right were not respected, the right to that freedom would have little practical significance. The same principle applies to the field of industrial relations. Of what value to workers is their right to collective bargaining if they are not free to exercise that right? Should the evidence reveal that there have been practices calculated to prevent workers from the enjoyment of this right, it would appear logical that the government protect the right of workers to self-organization and collective bargaining. Just as government has taken positive action to prevent the nullification of other rights enjoyed by citizens of the nation, it would seem equally valid for governments to protect the right of workers to collective bargaining. If, on the other hand, the record indicates that the right of workers to self-organization and collective bargaining has been respected, there is no occasion for government control.

Organs of government have declared that workers have the right to self-organization and collective bargaining. This recognition is grounded on the fact that labor unions fulfill a proper function in our economy. These considerations are underscored in a powerful statement made by former Chief Justice Taft:

> Labor unions are recognized . . . as legal when instituted for mutual help and lawfully carrying out their legitimate objects. They have long been thus recognized by the court. They were organized out of the necessities of the situation. A single employee was helpless in dealing with an employer. He was dependent on his daily wage for the maintenance of himself and family. If the employer refused to pay him the wages he thought fair, he was nevertheless unable to leave the employer and resist arbitrary and unfair treatment. Union was essential to give laborers an opportunity to deal on equality with their employer. They united to exert influence upon him and to leave him in a body in order by this inconvenience to induce him to make better terms with them. They were withholding their labor of economic value to make him pay what they thought it was worth. The right to combine for such a lawful purpose has in many years not been denied by any court.[1]

What remains to be seen is the extent to which the right of employees to self-organization and collective bargaining has been respected. Such an investigation must precede any recommendations for legislation calculated to protect this right of workers.

Several studies have dealt with efforts undertaken to forestall unionization of employees.[2] The most complete study dealing with antiunion tactics was conducted by the La Follette Committee. On June 6, 1936, Congress ordered a full-scale investigation of these antiunion techniques. Senator La Follette of Wisconsin headed up the committee authorized to make the study. The committee published 14 volumes of testimony. It conducted 58 days of hearings, at which some 245 witnesses testified. The committee later published a series of summary documents, which organizes and makes more readable the mass of evidence collected at the hearings.[3] Its findings highlight the intensity and thoroughness with which the union movement was challenged.

Care was taken by the committee to insure the accuracy of its reports. In the hearings of the committee, all of which were open to the public, witnesses were summoned from every group having an interest in the proceedings. The committee was careful not to accept at face value testimony of questionable truthfulness unless it could be verified from other sources. Consequently, its findings appear to be of unquestionable accuracy. Space limitations render it impossible to make a thorough report of the group's investigation. However, this volume—and, particularly, this chapter—could not be complete unless some consideration were given to the work of the La Follette Committee. Accordingly, while highlighting the patterns of antiunion conduct, we will direct attention to its results. Under present labor laws many of the antiunion tactics disclosed by the La Follette group are unlawful. This, however, does not render this investigation any the less important. Appreciation of present public policy rests upon the understanding of the factors producing such control.

PATTERNS OF ANTIUNION CONDUCT:
INDUSTRIAL ESPIONAGE

The La Follette Committee reported that industrial espionage was a common, if not the universal, practice in American industry. The purpose of industrial espionage was to prevent the organization and operation of a labor union. The industrial spy centered his work in the local union. A chief function of the spy was to provide the company with the names of union members. In particular, the employer wanted to ascertain the names of the workers most active in the labor union. Such information provided the basis for discharging these workers or otherwise isolating them from other employees. That these lists were used to influence the results of organizing campaigns is underscored by the following testimony of a former member of the National Labor Relations Board:

> I have never listened to anything more tragically un-American than stories of the discharged employees of the Fruehauf Trailer Co., victims of a labor spy. More often men in the prime of life, of obvious character and courage, came before us to tell of the blows that had fallen on him for his crime of having joined a union. Here they were—family men with wives and children—on public relief, blacklisted from employment, so they claimed, in the city of Detroit, citizens whose only offense was that they ventured in the land of the free to organize as employees to improve their working conditions. Their reward, as workers who had given their best to their employer, was to be hunted down by a hired spy like the lowest of criminals, and thereafter tossed like useless metal on the scrap heap.[4]

To obtain membership data, the spy could attend union meetings. A more effective method consisted of his election to some official position in the union, such as financial or recording secretary. In this capacity the spy could learn of every applicant for membership. At times, however, the ascertainment of the names of union members proved difficult. But, as the La Follette Committee reported, "In this, his initial task, the spy must not fail. If need be, therefore, he will bribe janitors or custodians, rifle files or desks, and burglarize offices to secure access to union records."[5]

Obviously, the operation of the industrial spy impaired the effective operation of a labor union. Workers were fearful that participation in union affairs—even the attendance of union meetings—might cost them their jobs. The following bit of testimony highlights this:

> *Senator La Follette:*   As a result of your experience, what would you say caused this fear of your organization when they became suspicious that a spy was in their midst?
>
> *Mr. Robertson* (a labor leader):   Because they felt to have their membership in our organization known to the company would place their jobs in jeopardy.[6]

Spy D-11 who operated in a plant in Hopewell, Virginia, also pointed out how spy activities result in union disintegration. After the workers of the plant became aware of his operations, he claimed that most of the workers wished "they would get out of the union if they knew just how to go about it."[7]

Industrial spies could cause the destruction of labor unions in ways other than the ascertainment of union membership lists. An effective method was to discredit union leaders in the eyes of the rank and file. A labor union's strength was sapped after the membership lost confidence in its officers. A classic example in this connection was the action of one spy who faked a photograph of the local union president leaning on the bar of a saloon and then preferred charges of drunkenness.[8] In another instance, a spy who managed election to the secretaryship of a local union affiliated with the International Association of Machinists brought charges of embezzlement of union funds against organizers of the union. Subsequently, the charges were proved to be false, but not until the local union had begun to disintegrate.[9] In addition, the spy might attack union officials on the basis of religion or nationality.

The industrial spy frequently assumed the role of an agent provocateur. In this role, "he incites the union to violence, preaches strikes, inflames the hot-headed and leads the union to disaster."[10] Many examples of this procedure are available. One spy sat in the meetings of the strike strategy committee of the Dodge Local of the United Automobile Workers in 1936 and urged the use of force and violence.[11] Another spy, operating in Kent, Ohio, in 1936 urged the unionists to dynamite a plant involved in a strike.[12] The strategy of these tactics, of course, was to goad the union into unlawful conduct, the effect being the stimulation of adverse public opinion, legal and military reprisal, and general disintegration of the labor union.

What was the source of supply of labor spies? A large number were furnished by private detective agencies. From 1933 to 1936 the Pinkerton Detective Agency claimed 309 industrial clients; Corporation Auxiliary Company, 499; National Corporation Service, 196; and the Burns Detective Agency, 440. Smaller detective agencies reported serving 497 clients. The La Follette Committee reports, "From motion-picture producers to steel makers, from hookless fasteners to automobiles, from small units to giant enterprises—scarcely an industry that is not fully represented in the list of clients of the detective agencies. Large corporations rely on spies. No firm is too small to employ them."[13] In the period 1933-1937, a total of $9,440,132.12 was expended by American firms to combat unions by means of industrial espionage and strike breaking.[14]

Frequently, ordinary workers were trapped by detective agencies into spying on the union activities of their fellow workers. In spy jargon such an individual was known as a "hooked man," an individual engaged in industrial espionage without knowledge that he was reporting to a detective agency or that his reports were going to an employer. Detective agency representatives who lured workers into spy activities were known as "hookers," and the process of entrapping workers to engage in spy activities was referred to as "hooking." Since most workers would refuse to spy on their fellow employees, the hooker used some pretext to induce a worker to write reports for the detective agency. The bait which the hooker used was money. A worker in financial difficulties would be an excellent prospect. The hooker might use a variety of pretexts to entrap an innocent worker. An outstanding example was the attempt of a representative of the Pinkerton Agency to hook the chairman of the grievance committee of a United Automobile Workers local. The representative posed as a federal officer to win the confidence of the worker. He asserted that he was an official of the government making an investigation of plant conditions.[15] Other hookers, to win the confidence of workers, posed as representatives of "minority stockholders," the "insurance setup," and the "financial house." One hooker even posed as a representative of a philanthropic agency which was working in the interests of the workers of the plant.

The use of industrial spies was one factor that made government protection of the right to collective bargaining appear reasonable. After industrial espionage was outlawed, the professional detective agencies terminated such activities. For example, the Pinkerton Agency, after the passage of the National Labor Relations Act, directed all its branch offices "to discontinue the furnishing of information to anyone concerning the lawful attempts of labor unions or employees to organize and bargain collectively, and not to undertake hereafter to furnish such information."[16] In addition, once industrial espionage was outlawed, the law was generally respected and its use declined. It is important to note, however, that spying terminated only after the passage of legislation. It is unlikely that industrial espionage would have ceased if it had not been outlawed.

PATTERNS OF ANTIUNION CONDUCT: ATTACK ON
UNION LEADERSHIP

As in every other organization, the successful functioning of labor unions depends in large part on leadership. How well labor union officials carry out their tasks will determine the success or failure of the trade union. Union leaders must of necessity bear the major burden of organizing drives. They are likewise instrumental in the successful implementation of strikes. In short, union leaders are the driving force of the union movement. If union leadership could be coerced into inactivity, the labor organization itself would become functionless and in time would wither away. Repeated attacks against union leadership could destroy its effectiveness and discourage others from assuming the role of the union leader.

The record is clear that union leaders have experienced both physical violence and intimidation. In addition, the record is equally clear that these individuals have been subjected to constant attacks against their character. The purpose of both of these approaches is to reduce the effectiveness of the union leader by frightening him into inactivity. Some people frighten more easily than others. This is as true of the union leader as of any other person. Consequently, it is difficult, if not impossible, to measure objectively the effect of the attacks on union leadership on the union movement. However, available evidence pointing up the character of the attacks would indicate that they have seriously retarded its progress.

In Cleveland, on September 21, 1937, at about 11:45 P.M., Vincent Favorito approached his parked automobile. He had just attended a union council meeting. The purpose of the meeting was to deal with problems arising in the "Little Steel" strike of 1937. Before he reached his automobile, Favorito was attacked by three men. He described this attack as follows:

> As I was walking toward my car, approaching my car I was about five feet from it there, I turned off the sidewalk to go to my car which was facing north on West Tenth. The man that was on my right side, the man that was walking toward me, hit me with a blackjack on the back of my head and the fellow that was coming toward me from the back end of my car hit me on the face with a gun, and I felt the man in back of me grapple me by the neck and put his knee on my back, and immediately then something come into my mouth like a gag, we can call it a gag because it was a rag, and I couldn't say a peep; and I was held on both arms by these two men that evidently wanted to knock me out, and didn't do it, and we struggled there. I happened to get loose some way and I get this man here that was in back of me and I throws him over me, but he went right on top of me, and I happened to hit the ground, and him on top of me, and I held him there.
>
> I was afraid that if I would get kicked in the head that it would be the end of me. I held onto him, and while I was holding onto him these other blokes or thugs were hitting me, kicking me, and swearing. While this was going on they also kicked the fellow that was up on top of me and he happened to let go and I hollered. As I hollered my brother-in-law and my sister heard me and come to my rescue.[17]

On December 13, 1936, Charles Doyle, a member of the Steel Workers Organizing Committee, was attacked. The assault took place after Doyle attended a union meeting in the back room of Marie's Grill on South Park Avenue in Buffalo, New

York. According to Doyle, he was pounced on by four men after he left the restaurant. He testified to the La Follette Committee that "someone hit me in the mouth from the front with his fist and immediately after that something hit me from behind, right on the ear at the side of the jaw."[18]

Testimony presented before the La Follette Committee also pointed up another attack in Cleveland against a union leader. This victim was Gerald Breads, an employee of the Otis Steel Company. Breads was active in organization work. His testimony is revealing:

> *Mr. Breads:* I was at the Bohemian National Hall on Broadway, I wouldn't know what number it was, it is right there at Pershing Road.
> *Senator La Follette:* When was that?
> *Mr. Breads:* That was on the night July 13, 1937. I had to go to work that night at 11 o'clock so I left that hall about 9 and another fellow by the name of Paul Chocky was with me. We started away from the hall to get the dinky that runs across the Clark Avenue Bridge, and just as we was going across Broadway—
> *Senator La Follette* (interposing): Was this while the strike was on?
> *Mr. Breads:* There was a car pulled away from the curb. I stepped in front of the car and got out in the streetcar tracks and I seen Dewey Jones and another fellow jumping in the car alongside.
> *Senator La Follette:* Did you recognize the other man?
> *Mr. Breads:* I couldn't; no. So I started through the gas station with the idea that if I got on the dinky they wouldn't follow me into there. I had an idea what was going to happen. Before I got to the dinky they had cut me off. Dewey Jones and the other fellow in the back seat jumped out and pulled revolvers on me.
>   One of them stuck one in the back of my neck and Jones was in front of me holding one in my stomach.
>   Well, words passed both ways, they called me names and I called them back, I guess, and I asked them what it was all about. They told me to never mind that I would get mine, that I would get what was coming to me, and they wanted to put me in the car and I said no. They tried to force me in the car and shoved me right against the car and the fellow who was riding in the back seat with Jones at the time the car stopped, he grabbed me and shoved me farther in. Then there was nothing I could do but get up on the seat. I don't know what route we took, or where we was, but I come to under the Clark Avenue Bridge, after I got bashed over the head a couple of times with a blackjack and revolver butt, and I was also hit on the arm too.[19]

Rough shadowing was also employed to intimidate union leadership. Rough shadowing was the practice of keeping union leaders under open surveillance. As such, the procedure differed from industrial espionage which was surreptitious in character. The objective of rough shadowing was to instill fear in the minds of union leaders. It also served the purpose of creating fear in the minds of workers who might have wanted to talk to union leaders. Rough shadowing may have been carried on during strikes, but most frequently was employed during preparation for strikes. One organizer claimed he was followed wherever he went. Another testified that even his home was kept under surveillance. This latter individual, attempting to lose his "shadowers," moved his residence and even changed his name. But this defense measure was only temporarily successful. He testified as follows:

> When we started our organizing campaign it was practically impossible to carry on any activity at the headquarters of our union. It was necessary to use our

homes as secret places where workers would be able to gather for the purpose of discussing the organizational problems. I lived at the time on the West Side, and about a week after I became a member of the staff several carloads of Republic stoolpigeons were parking at my house. They were there from 7 o'clock in the morning until about midnight and they had a special crew on some occasions that remained there overnight. I realized that my home cannot be used any more as a place where workers can be invited to come to talk about labor questions, so I had to move out of there. I also knew if I moved out of that place under my own name they would discover it just as soon. So I moved into another apartment under a different name, under "Stevens," and I was there about 2 weeks and these same people that were shadowing me before discovered the home where I lived and I had to move again, and from "Stevens" I stretched it to "Stevenson," and that is how I used that alias of "Stevenson" in order to make sure that my home will not be discovered.[20]

In addition to physical violence and intimidating tactics, union leaders endured attacks against their character. The purpose of such attacks was to break down the will of union leaders and to destroy the loyalty which connected the rank and file with union leadership. Nothing could be more damaging to a union than the discrediting of union leaders in the eyes of the membership. This objective could be achieved by the circulation of false rumors and stories about union leaders. As is well known, a rumor is difficult to combat. Attacks against the character of a labor leader might take many forms. He might be denounced as a "communist," "foreign element," "agitator," or "labor racketeer." During Would War II notices were posted throughout a plant, in one instance, suggesting that union organizers were a group of "intimidators," who threatened the "substitution of Nazi-ism for Americanism."[21] In another case also taking advantage of the wartime environment, the assertion was made that a union was "backed by Germans," the intent being to discourage membership in the labor union.[22]

PATTERNS OF ANTIUNION CONDUCT:
STRIKEBREAKING TACTICS

The purpose of strikebreaking was to destroy a union once it was formed. To carry out effective collective bargaining, a labor union must be able to strike successfully. Both the employer and the workers must be aware of this union capability. If a union cannot wage an effective strike, the employer need not pay much attention to its demands. Moreover, workers soon lose respect and interest in such an organization. This does not mean that unions should or do resort to the strike at every opportunity. Mature collective bargaining will diminish the need for industrial warfare. However, to function effectively at any stage of the collective bargaining process, a union must be capable of implementing effective strikes.

In the light of these considerations, it should occasion no surprise to learn that employers bent on the destruction of a labor union utilized every possible tactic to break a strike. Crushing of the strike dealt an irreparable blow to the labor union. This was particularly true where the issue in the strike was union recognition. Labor unions must first be recognized by employers as collective bargaining agencies before they can bargain collectively over economic issues. Since this is true, tactics were frequently employed calculated to break union recognition strikes.

This section points up some procedures that have been used to destroy labor unions by crushing strikes. Again, it must be kept in mind that many, if not all, of these practices are now not illegal. This fact, however, does not lessen the need for an analysis of strikebreaking procedures.

There are three major lines of approach to break strikes: (1) the fortification of a plant with munitions and private plant police, the latter hired not to protect property against theft, fire, and the like, but for the purpose of intimidating workers who would strike; (2) the hiring of professional strikebreakers; and (3) the breaking down of strikers' morale by instituting back-to-work movements.

A series of events which occurred in the spring of 1935 in Canton, Ohio, demonstrates the first procedure. The employees of a steel corporation organized a labor union. The corporation refused to recognize or bargain with the representatives of the union. As a result the union prepared to strike for recognition. Among other things this strike illustrated the propensity of workers to resort to economic force when other efforts to gain recognition failed. It also demonstrated the lack of a procedure to eliminate the need for those strikes called to force recognition of labor unions for collective bargaining purposes.

Aware of the imminence of the strike, the steel corporation made preparations to break it. The La Follette Committee describes the general character of these preparations as follows:

> The police department of [the] steel corporation reached the height of its activity during periods of union organization and in times of strike. As the first line of defense against labor organizations, it mobilized all the paraphernalia of military warfare. Manpower, munitions, and spies were all concentrated, deployed, and maneuvered with the objective of defeating organizing efforts, and of ambushing the union when it undertook the desperate step of calling a strike.[23]

More specific observations demonstrate the elaborate preparations for the strikebreaking. A few days before the strike the corporation mobilized its plant police from other cities. Thus fourteen men arrived from Buffalo; nineteen from Youngstown; one man from Chicago; twenty-five from Massillon; and twenty-one from Warren. The munitions arsenal of the corporation was also increased. A day or so before the strike, the corporation purchased sickening gas and gas equipment for $8,804.30[24] In addition, the company laid in a supply of pipes cut to club length, shotguns, small arms, and tear gas.

This preparation for a strike by a corporation was not an isolated example. The La Follette Committee reported even more extensive preparations, including the setting up of floodlights, the erection of electrically charged barbed wire around plant boundaries, and the use of armored trucks for the transportation of strikebreakers through picket lines. In addition, a corporation aware of an impending strike might work the plant overtime to build up inventory. If the company could fill orders during the course of the strike, it had a better chance to break the work stoppage.

The use of professional strikebreakers figured prominently in the pattern of strikebreaking. There is a considerable difference between the professional strikebreaker and the worker who merely refuses to strike. Workers should have the right to refrain from participating in a strike. If a union calls a strike and some employees refuse to strike, their decision should be respected. Although these workers tend to break a strike, they certainly are not professional strikebreakers. Individuals in this latter category, the La Follette Committee reported, had been supplied by the same agencies furnishing industrial spies.[25] In many cases the professional strikebreaker possessed a criminal record. Sam "Chowderhead" Cohen, a famous strikebreaker, while commenting on his long criminal record, declared, "You see, in this line of work they never asked for no references."[26] The job of the professional strikebreaker was to smash picket lines, to give the appearance that the plant was operating, and to incite violence so that the public authorities would take action against the unionists. For example, the strikebreaker might merely burn paper in a plant furnace so that the smoke of the chimney would give the appearance of plant production. The driving of empty trucks to and from the plant for the same purpose might also be performed by the strikebreaker. Actually, the professional strikebreaker frequently was incapable of carrying out the production duties performed by the ordinary worker. Generally, the strikebreaker would merely amuse himself in the plant to while away the time.

The record shows that the professional strikebreaker frequently provoked violence during strikes. For this reason these individuals were at times termed agents provocateurs. Unionists or strikers recall being spit at by such people. Stones were hurled into picket lines and other disorderly acts executed to incite the strikers to violence. If the strikers were goaded into violent action, the employer could then appeal to the public authorities. Frequently, arrests followed, jail sentences and fines were imposed, and in some cases the state militia or the National Guard were called to the scene of the strike. The presence of these groups was very demoralizing to the unionists. Moreover, action of public authorities against strikers condemned the unionists as lawbreakers in the eyes of the public.

Wages paid to strikebreakers ranged from $5 to $15 per day; at least these were the wage levels at the time that the La Follette Committee conducted its investigations. As stated, it was rare for strikebreakers to perform the duties of regular workers. Since this was the case, the employer realized no immediate profit from the use of strikebreakers. However, if the employment of these individuals could break a union, the employer presumably would profit in the long run. No union meant no collective bargaining. This in turn meant lower wages and lower labor standards.

Strikebreaking could be accomplished by pointing to the possibility of violence and to the effects of the strike on the business of the community, or by encouraging antilabor newspapers. All of these techniques, as well as others, were included in the celebrated "Mohawk Valley Formula." This organized system of strikebreaking was devised by James H. Rand, Jr., president of Remington Rand. By utilization of this formula, he was able to break strikes in six of his plants. The breaking of the strikes resulted in the destruction of the unions, for in each case the purpose of the strike was to force the company to bargain collectively. Since the formula proved so successful, the National Association of Manufacturers circulated its principles among members of the association. (See Appendix A for the complete Formula.)

The Mohawk Valley Formula was developed in meticulous detail. It represents careful thinking and shows a deep insight into social processes. It serves as one illustration of the extent to which union organization met resistance. Such tactics have since been condemned in the nation's labor laws.

PATTERNS OF ANTIUNION CONDUCT:
COMPANY UNIONS

The record of industrial relations indicates that some companies used more moderate procedures to forestall the development and operation of collective bargaining. One such technique consisted of the sponsoring of company unions.[27] The formation of such organizations, often referred to as employee representation plans, was due to the recognition by management of workers' desire to determine by organized action some of the elements of the employment relationship. Company unions provided for the expression of this deep-seated drive of workers. They also served to channel its implementation in a manner which lessened the threat to decision making that some firms consider managerial prerogative. This was the case because company unions were not independent from the control of management.

Company unions were not part of the labor union movement. They were not affiliated with either the AFL or the CIO. They were limited in membership to the workers in one company or one plant. Since company unions depended on their own resources, they could not utilize the resources, financial and otherwise, of international unions. They did not possess the backing of established and effective affiliates. Unlike regular unions, they could not avail themselves of experienced and capable labor leaders for the purpose of representation.

Collective bargaining implies the existence of labor unions free to act independently from the control of management. The process culminates in the execution of collective bargaining agreements, which are to be respected by both the labor union and the company. In addition, at times the collective bargaining function results in a strike. None of these basic features of real collective bargaining are found in company unions. On the contrary, employers dominated them by influencing the selection of officers, supervising their functions, and directing their activities to suit the interests of management. Collective bargaining contracts between company unions and the company did not exist. At most the activities of company unions consisted of calling minor grievances of workers to the attention of management. Officers of company unions had to take care that they did not vigorously prosecute major issues—such as the demand for higher wages, seniority systems, vacations, paid holidays, and the like. Such officers had to be careful how they spoke and acted before management representatives. If they appeared "unreasonable," management might discriminate against them with respect to layoffs, transfers, and promotions. In a regular labor union, union representatives are protected by collective bargaining agreements, and more effectively by the organization itself.

In still another respect, the company union failed to function as a true collective bargaining agent. In regular labor unions, officers hold their positions as long as they satisfy the rank and file. Union leaders must be responsive to the demands of the membership. To do otherwise would mean jeopardizing their positions. This is essentially true at both the local and international levels. Such responsiveness to the demands of the rank and file does not characterize the company union. Representatives of such an organization, enjoying little or no protection from possible discriminatory reprisal by management, had of necessity to curry the favor and good will of company officials. Since this was the case, company union representatives would prosecute desires of the rank and file only to the extent that their implementation did not conflict seriously with company policy. Such a situation scarcely squares with true collective bargaining.

Company unions were the creatures of management. If the interests of management would be advanced by their abolishment, this could be accomplished without much difficulty. In short, the continuity of company unions depended upon the pleasure of management. Company unions possessed no sovereignty and exerted only that authority bestowed on them by the employer. Since company unions attempted to serve two masters—the company and the workers—such organizations could not function as effective collective bargaining agencies. Labor unions, as defined by national labor policy, must represent and be responsible to their membership. This element was lacking in company unions. Consequently, they fell short of providing effective vehicles through which workers could engage in collective bargaining in accordance with national policy.

At times an independent local labor organization, free from the control of management, may function at the company or plant level. Such organizations have no affiliation with federations or international unions. Unlike company unions, these independent unions can perform the collective bargaining function. This is true because, though independent from federations or international unions, they are not subject to the control of the company. Such independent labor unions are controlled directly by the membership. Independent unions execute labor contracts, hold regular membership meetings, collect dues, elect their officers independent from the influence of management, and when necessary call strikes. Independent unions have at times affiliated with the international unions of the AFL-CIO. These international unions, have not, of course, issued charters to unions dominated by employers. Before application for such a charter was considered favorably, the company union had to rid itself of all evidences of employer control. As a matter of fact, in many cases company unions became regular labor unions by asserting their independence from management.

NEED FOR PUBLIC CONTROL

The foregoing brief discussion based largely on government documentation discloses that a variety of techniques have been used to interfere with the formation of labor unions and the exercise of the collective bargaining process. Thus workers have often been denied the right to engage in collective bargaining. Such a right was recognized by the government as lawful. Indeed, the Norris–La Guardia Act identifies collective bargaining with public policy. If the collective bargaining process was socially desirable, the utilization of antiunion techniques defeated the public purpose. It was necessary that society protect the right of workers to engage in collective bargaining. The alternative results in an incongruous situation: On the one hand, public policy grants workers the right to self-organization and collective bargaining and on the other hand, society silently approves by inaction and antiunion techniques. Consistency demanded that the government take appropriate action to provide protection to workers in the exercise of their right to collective bargaining. It appeared necessary that either the government should adopt this course of action or else denounce collective bargaining as an antisocial and unlawful institution.

An additional consideration highlighted the need for public protection of the workers' right to collective bargaining. Even though confronted with hostile opposition, some employees were still determined to engage in concerted activities. To check interference with organizational efforts, workers made use of their economic weapon—the strike. Employees resorted to the strike to force management to recognize their unions, to bargain collectively with their representatives, and to cease interfering with the organization and functioning of their unions. The record of industrial relations demonstrates that workers frequently made use of the organizational strike. During the period 1919–1933, union organizational issues, such as refusal to recognize or bargain with labor unions, alone or in a combination with other causes, accounted for 24 percent of all strikes. In 1934, 45.9 percent of all strikes resulted from the same causes.[28] It is noteworthy that the Supreme Court of the United States recognized the seriousness of this problem in industrial relations. The Court in 1937 declared: "Refusal to confer and to negotiate has been one of the most prolific causes of strife. This is such an outstanding fact in the history of labor disturbances that it is a proper subject of judicial notice and requires no citation of instances."[29] In a 1967 study one of the authors found that 94 percent of unfair labor practices filed against employers in one district office of the National Labor Relations Board stemmed from conduct arising directly out of union organizing campaigns.[30] Resistance to union organization, both past and present, seems to be the single most important cause of strife in the labor relations area.

Organizational strikes, like economic strikes (that is, strikes for wages, hours, vacations, and so on), interfere with effective operation of the national economy. A democratic government, responsive to the needs of the country, would be expected to deal with the problem. To reduce the frequency of organizational strikes, the nation could outlaw strikes calculated to force management to permit union organization and collective bargaining. Such an approach obviously would be more appropriate for nations in which freedom of association is more restrictive than in a democratic society. Outlawing of organizational strikes would be repugnant to a democracy. If legislation of this character could stand the test of constitutionality, the law of industrial relations would be turned back considerably. If workers were not permitted to strike for union recognition, the union movement could make little progress and, indeed, would likely disintegrate into ineffectual units. Under such a legal environment, the employer would need only to refuse to bargain with a union. If a labor organization, as a result of such conduct, would dare to strike, the penalties of law would come into operation. It appears clear enough that outlawing of union organizational strikes would result in the eventual destruction of the labor union movement.

Instead of outlawing the organizational strike, the public interest might be better served by legislation prohibiting the causes and abuses of such strikes. Specifically, Congress and state legislatures could forbid resistance to union organizational efforts. In addition, such legislation could require that employers bargain collectively with workers' unions when a majority of employees express such a desire through democratic standards of expression. Due care should be taken to balance the rights of both groups. Laws of this character do not confer any new rights or impose any new restrictions on anyone if properly administered by an impartial agency. Such legislation requires merely the respect of a right already possessed by both groups.

Such an approach would be in the public interest. Strikes for organizational purposes could be made unnecessary. Workers could utilize the remedial processes of the government if there were tamperings with their right to self-organization and collective bargaining. Since the frequency of such strikes should decrease, the public would be relieved from the inconveniences following in the wake of organizational strikes. Moreover, labor history demonstrates clearly that strikes for recognition purposes were usually bitter in character. Such strikes were frequently contested because management and workers were fully aware that the breaking of a recognition strike would result in the elimination of the labor union. The story of industrial relations is replete with instances of the bloody nature of the organizational strike. The circumstances of Memorial Day 1937 in Chicago highlight the point. Growing out of the context of an organizational strike carried out against a steel corporation, the record reveals a tragic pattern of events. Police attempted to disperse a large group of strikers and their sympathizers, and the result was violence. When the struggle ended, 10 strikers had been killed, 90 other unionists had been injured (30 by gunfire), and 35 of the police had sustained injury.[31]

Another example points up the violence which frequently followed in the wake of strikes undertaken to force management to recognize unions as representatives of their employees. On Monday, February 18, 1935, a union struck against an Ohio rubber company. The La Follette Committee reported that the strike resulted from the labor relations policy of the company which was "based upon a refusal either to enter into a written agreement with the union of its employees or to recognize that union as exclusive bargaining agent for its employees."[32] The company prepared to break the strike. Industrial spies were hired from professional detective agencies. At the time of the strike, the company had available a guard force of 133 men, a good share of whom were professional strikebreakers. About nine hundred workers were employed in the factory, the result being a ratio of about one guard to seven employees. This led one worker to draw a parallel between the environment of a prison and the company. He complained that a "free-born American citizen trying to work and make a living for my family" had to work in a "plant being infested with guards walking among us. . . ."[33] In addition, a supply of munitions was purchased. For $3,340.69 the company received tear gas and gas equipment, jumper-repeater tear gas rifles, three long-range field guns, and a large supply of shells.[34]

Such preparations were hardly conducive to peaceful strike conditions. As the La Follette Committee reported, "The company had created an explosive situation. The course of its activities preceding the strike can justly be construed as incendiary."[35] Despite the fact that strikers were given instructions "to conduct themselves in an orderly manner," violence characterized the strike from the beginning. When guards started shooting tear gas into the union's picket line, the strikers threw bricks. People not connected with either party were injured by the violence. The mayor of the town testified that some of the guards shot gas shells at some strikers near a school "and some of the school children near at the time got some of the gas."[36]

The strikers subsequently established a rest camp on an empty lot within sight of the factory. Shelter tents and a commissary wagon provided some protection against the winter cold. A few days after the camp was established the sheriff ordered the strikers to disperse. After the workers refused to break up their camp, the guards en masse "attacked the camp, gassed it, burned the shelter tent, and arrested about 40 strikers as violators of the peace."[37] Thus this illustration further underscores the need for effective laws to protect the rights of all parties concerned.

Not only do workers and the public benefit from such a legislative program, but employers also profit from such an arrangement. As stated, many employers have fully respected the collective bargaining process. Long before the Wagner Act, a good number of companies dealt in good faith with their employees' labor organizations. Many union-recognizing employers competed with companies which resisted the attempts of their workers to bargain collectively. Such a condition resulted in a competitive disadvantage to organized firms. This was usually the case because the nonunion companies could sell products at cheaper prices. Cheaper prices resulted from the lower labor standards of the nonunion firms. In view of these considerations, it could be expected that employers who dealt in good faith with their workers' unions would have welcomed a legal environment facilitating the organization of their nonunion competitors.

Some employers derived another advantage from a legal climate requiring respect of the workers' right to self-organization and collective bargaining. Such an arrangement provided an employer with an opportunity to engage in the collective bargaining process in good faith without losing the esteem of his business associates. It is possible that many employers combated labor unions because the *general* attitude of the business group advocated this course of action. In spite of personal inclinations to the contrary, an employer may have followed this line of procedure in order to maintain standing in his group. He may have been concerned that should he violate the "code" of his associates he might suffer social and economic reprisal. In a legal environment with firmly established rules, such an employer could have dealt in good faith with a labor union of his employees without fear of ostracism from his group. He would be afforded a valid basis for his action—in the event the law had required respect of the workers' right to self-organization and collective bargaining.

In the last analysis, legal protection of the right of workers to self-organization could be defended on the basis of the social desirability of collective bargaining. As long as the process is socially useful, the public interest is served to the degree that the right is respected. It follows therefore that the right of workers to collective bargaining must be protected against the invasions of those who would treat this right with contempt.

SUMMARY

Independent from aid given employers by the courts, government inquiry revealed that antiunion companies engaged in many tactics calculated to wipe out effective unionism. These activities were brought to light by many studies, including the celebrated findings of the La Follette Committee. Evidence revealed that spies, strikebreakers, and company unions were utilized in the attempt to destroy labor unions. Some employers attacked union leadership and set up systematic strikebreaking programs, such as the Mohawk Valley Formula, to accomplish the same objective.

Such activities stimulated long and bitter organizational strikes. These strikes would not have been necessary if there had been a recognition of the right of employees to engage in collective bargaining. This many, reportedly, refused to do; the result was industrial warfare. It became apparent that legislation was necessary to curb antiunion behavior so that the right of workers to engage in collective bargaining would be protected.

NOTES

[1] *American Steel Foundries Company* v. *Tri-City Central Trades Council*, 257 U.S. 184 (1921).

[2] For example, see *Report of the U.S. Commission on Industrial Relations*, 11 vols., Washington, 1916, and *Interchurch World Movement's Study of the Steel Strike of 1919*, with its special reports on espionage and strikebreaking carried on by the United States Steel Corporation. See also books such as *The Labor Spy*, by Sidney Howard and Robert Dunn; *I Break Strikes*, by Edward Levinson; and *Spies in Steel*, by Frank Palmer.

[3] *Violations of Free Speech and Rights of Labor, Report of the Committee on Education and Labor*, pursuant to S. Res. 266, 74th Congress, will be cited as La Follette Committee, Report No. . . .

[4] La Follette Committee, *Report on Industrial Espionage*, Report No. 46, pt. 3, 75th Congress, p. 39.

[5] *Ibid.*, p. 62.

[6] *Hearings*, pt. 4, pp. 1239–1240 (reference to the volumes of the hearings of the La Follette Committee will be designated throughout this chapter as *Hearings*).

[7] *Ibid.*, pt. 8, p. 3113.

[8] *Ibid.*, pt. 5, p. 1457.

[9] *Ibid.*, pt. 3, pp. 889–891.

[10] La Follette Committee, Report No. 46, *op. cit.*, p. 63.

[11] *Hearings*, pt. 4, p. 1266.

[12] La Follette Committee, Report No. 46, *op. cit.*, p. 63.

[13] *Ibid.*, p. 22.

[14] *Ibid.*, p. 79.

[15] *Hearings*, pt. 4, p. 1318.

[16] Pinkerton's National Detective Agency, Inc., Order 105—Business Accepting, dated April 20, 1937. Reported in La Follette Committee, Report No. 46, *op. cit.*, p. 122.

[17] La Follette Committee, *Private Police Systems*, Report No. 6, pt. 2, 76th Congress, 1st sess., p. 193.

[18] *Hearings*, pt. 26, p. 11058.

[19] *Ibid.*, pt. 26, pp. 11076–7.

[20] *Ibid.*, pt. 26, p. 10924.

[21] *Riecke Metal Products Company*, 40 NLRB 872 (1942).

[22] *Fred A. Snow & Company*, 41 NLRB 1292 (1942).

[23] La Follette Committee, Report No. 6, *op. cit.*, p. 126.

[24] *Ibid.*, p. 128.

[25] La Follette Committee, *Strikebreaking Services*, Report No. 6, 76th Congress, 1st sess., pp. 65, 74.

[26] R. R. R. Brooks, *When Labor Organizes* (New Haven: Yale University Press, 1937), p. 146.

[27] For an authoritative and interesting account of the character and operation of company unions, see Bureau of Labor Statistics Bulletin 634, *Characteristics of Company Unions* (Washington, D.C., 1938).

[28] *Monthly Labor Review*, XXXIX (July 1934), 75; XLII (January 1936), 162.

[29] *NLRB* v. *Jones & Laughlin Steel Corporation*, 301 U.S. 1 (1937).

[30] Benjamin J. Taylor, *The Operation of the Taft-Hartley Act in Indiana*, Indiana Business Bulletin No. 58 (Bloomington, Ind.: Bureau of Business Research, 1967), p. 27.

[31] For an account of the Memorical Day tragedy, see La Follette Committee, *The Chicago Memorial Day Incident*, Report No. 46, pt. 2.

[32] La Follette Committee, Report No. 6, *op. cit.*, p. 57.

[33] *Hearings*, pt. 21, p. 9218.

[34] La Follette Committee, Report No. 6, *op. cit.*, p. 60.

[35] *Ibid.*, p. 60.

[36] *Hearings*, pt. 21, exhibit 4243, p. 9349.

[37] La Follette Committee, Report No. 6, *op. cit.*, p. 62.

Precursors of the Wagner Act 8

THE BEGINNINGS OF LEGISLATIVE SUPPORT

The 1890s were years of transition for the American labor movement. The Knights of Labor was passing into oblivion and the young American Federation of Labor was seeking effective means of gaining societal acceptance. The financial panic of 1893 brought with it difficulties in expanding unionism into new areas. It was, however, the prevailing philosophy of the courts that proved the major obstacle to union progress. In 1895, in the *Debs* case, the Supreme Court sanctioned the use of the injunction in labor disputes. This procedure was followed by the courts and enlarged upon for several years, as mentioned in previous chapters. The lower federal courts in the middle 1890s were making widespread use of the Sherman Act to constrain union activities. The executive branch of the government upon occasion intervened in labor disputes. This was the case at both the federal and state levels. For example, in 1894 President Cleveland ordered federal troops to break the Pullman strike called by the American Railway Union. Cleveland took this action despite the protests of Governor Altgeld of Illinois. By 1900 the entire union membership in the nation totaled less than 1 million.

The legislative branch of government was beginning to demonstrate more concern for the union movement. There was a marked lag between the judicial and the legislative branches of government in the development of the law of collective bargaining. The legal aspects of the labor injunction illustrate the principle. State and federal attempts to control the injunction in labor disputes antedated the recognition by the courts that such control was necessary for industrial peace. A similar parallel between these two branches of government is noted with respect to positive legal protection of the right of workers to self-organization and collective bargaining. It may be worthwhile to emphasize the basic reason for such a lag. The tenure of office of the members of the judiciary is more secure than of the legislators. In addition, many judges receive their commissions by appointment and consequently are removed from the direct control of the electorate. As a result the legislator is more responsive to the changes in attitude of the people. It took the cataclysmic events of the 1930s plus the "court packing" threat by Roosevelt to change the structure of the Supreme Court to effect judicial approval of social legislation enacted by Congress and the states.

The first attempts of the legislative branch of government to provide a degree of protection to workers utilizing their right to self-organization and collective bargaining took place in the 1890s. Such efforts antedated labor injunction control legislation by about a decade; they came about fifty years after *Commonwealth* v. *Hunt*, the decision which marked the beginning of judicial approval of labor unions. And, as mentioned, this legislative attempt occurred during a period of almost total judicial control of the collective bargaining process.

THE EARLY LAWS: YELLOW-DOG CONTRACTS AND DISCRIMINATION UNLAWFUL

Fifteen states in the 1890s enacted laws calculated to provide protection of the right of workers to self-organization and collective bargaining: Massachusetts, Connecticut, New York, Pennsylvania, New Jersey, Ohio, Indiana, Illinois, Wisconsin, Minnesota, Kansas, Missouri, California, Idaho, and Georgia.[1] The statutes prohibited employers from discharging employees for joining labor unions or making the yellow-dog contract a condition of employment. The Indiana law of 1893 is characteristic of these early laws. It provided:

> It shall be unlawful for any individual, or member of any firm, agent, officer, or employee of any company or corporation to prevent employees from forming, joining and belonging to any lawful labor organization, and any such individual members, agents, officer, or employee that coerces or attempts to coerce employees by discharging or threatening to discharge from the employ of any firm, company or corporation because of their connection with such labor organization, and any officer or employer who exacts a pledge from workingmen that they will not become members of a labor organization as a consideration of employment, shall be guilty of a misdemeanor, and upon conviction thereof in any court of competent jurisdiction shall be fined in any sum not exceeding one hundred dollars ($100), or imprisoned for not more than six (6) months, or both, at the discretion of the court.

Thus the early laws attempted to eliminate two powerful antiunion weapons. Consideration has already been given to the yellow-dog contract. However, we must emphasize that no single antiunion procedure exceeded the effectiveness of the yellow-dog agreement. Workers could not exercise their right to self-organization and collective bargaining where employees were required to agree not to join labor unions as a condition of employment. Elimination of the effectiveness of the yellow-dog contract was a logical starting place to protect the collective bargaining process. Unlike Norris–La Guardia and some of the modern state anti-injunction statutes, the early laws outlawed the yellow-dog contract and made violators subject to fines and imprisonment if they should demand the execution of such agreements. Under Norris–La Guardia and state laws patterned after it, the method of rendering the yellow-dog contract ineffectual was merely to make the judiciary unavailable for the enforcement of such agreements. In this respect, the early laws may have been more effective than the more modern attempts to stamp out the yellow-dog contract. However, when the National Labor Relations Board was created, it held that coercion of employees to execute such agreements constituted an unfair labor practice. Failure to comply with an order of the NLRB could result in contempt-of-court proceedings.[2]

Discharge of workers because of union activities is another effective weapon to forestall unionization. In modern industry the worker's job is normally his sole means of support. Without a job the worker and his family are helpless. The fear of loss of job is a prominent factor in the discouragement of union membership. Should a few workers be discharged because of union activities, the remaining workers would possibly have little appetite for union affairs. Workers could scarcely enjoy their right to self-organization and collective bargaining if they were fearful that union activities could terminate their means of livelihood. These factors make the prohibition of discharge of workers for union activities appear feasible.

In 1898 Congress passed the Erdman Act. The purpose of the law was to promote interstate commerce. This objective was to be realized by setting up procedures designed to reduce labor conflict in the nation's railroads. Though the law provided for the mediation and arbitration of labor disputes, our concern at this point is with the provisions of the Erdman law that protected the right of railroad workers to self-organization and collective bargaining. The Erdman law in part resulted from the celebrated *Pullman* strike of 1894. Fundamentally, this strike was caused by the refusal of the Pullman Company to enter into collective bargaining negotiations with its workers. As noted, the strike eventually spread to the railroads themselves. Congress was aware that organizational strikes could again interrupt railroad traffic among the states. Such strikes could result from the demand by the railroads that workers execute yellow-dog contracts, and from the discharge of workers because of union activities. Congress reasoned that if these two antiorganizational practices could be eliminated, the necessity for organizational strikes on the railroads would be reduced. Consequently, the interstate commerce of the nation would thereby be promoted.

As a result of these considerations, the Erdman Act contained famous Section 10. It provided that it was a misdemeanor for railroad employers to "require any employee or any person seeking employment, as a condition of such employment, to enter into an agreement, either written or verbal, not to become or remain a member of any labor corporation, association, or organization; or to threaten any employee with loss of employment or unjustly to discriminate against any employee because of his membership in such labor corporation, association, or organization." Similar to the state laws mentioned previously, the Erdman Act outlaws the yellow-dog contract. On the other hand, the railroad law was more effective than the state laws, for it prohibited railroad employers from discriminating in any way against workers who exercised their right to self-organization and collective bargaining. The state laws prohibited only discrimination by discharge, but permitted other acts to discourage union activities, such as discriminating against union-minded workers with respect to promotions, layoffs, transfers, and the like. Under the Erdman Act all forms of discrimination against union employees were outlawed.

Compared to modern legislation, the early attempts to protect the rights of workers to self-organization and collective bargaining were ineffective. They did not prohibit the formation of company-dominated unions. Neither did they outlaw methods often used to break strikes and prevent the organization of labor unions. In addition, the early laws did not require that employers recognize their employees' unions and enter into collective negotiations with these unions. Finally, the method of enforcement of the statutes was ineffective. Enforcement was left entirely to court proceedings. This meant that violators of the law might avoid prosecution. The modern collective bargaining statute places the responsibility for enforcement on an expert administrative agency. This feature, as will be discussed in detail in later chapters, means the effective enforcement of such statutes.

Despite their obvious shortcomings, the early statutes were landmarks of industrial relations law. They reflected a growing awareness of the need for government action if the right of workers to self-organization and collective bargaining was to be effective. The early laws represented a beginning in the effective implementation of the collective bargaining process.

ATTITUDE OF THE JUDICIARY

The modest beginnings of legislative support of the collective bargaining process were rigidly controlled by the courts. The judiciary occasionally failed to give weight to the factors producing legislative action. Many of the state laws were declared unconstitutional by state supreme courts. However, the decisive factor came at the hands of the Supreme Court of the United States. In 1908 the Court invalidated Section 10 of the Erdman Act.[3] Seven years later the Kansas statute suffered a similar fate.[4] Observers should have expected these decisions. They were handed down in a period in which the Supreme Court was not convinced of the necessity for collective bargaining. The jurists were not impressed with the social and economic factors justifying the attempts of government to protect workers in their employment relationship. The position that the Constitution was to be protected from arbitrary invasions by the legislative branch caused the Supreme Court to rule against legislative action calculated to raise the collective bargaining power of the nation's workers. The record of the Supreme Court in the 1890s and in particular during the first two decades of the present century reveals unmistakably that the judiciary was not convinced that collective bargaining was a needed institution in light of its definition of individual property rights. The judges were determined that the economic welfare of worker groups could not be raised either by legislative action or workers' self-help activities. Economic welfare was determined by the manner in which property was utilized. Interference with the use of property could stifle competition and decrease the welfare of national trade.

In 1895 the Supreme Court sustained the use of the injunction in labor disputes.[5] In 1908 it applied the Sherman Act to labor union activities.[6] This decision set the precedent for subsequent prosecution of unions under the antitrust provisions. Such prosecution, as indicated, retarded the development of the American labor union movement. In 1917, two years after the Kansas attempt to outlaw the yellow-dog contract was held unconstitutional, the Supreme Court held that this agreement could be protected by the labor injunction.[7] In 1921 the Supreme Court interpreted the legislative intent of the Clayton Act and held unconstitutional the efforts of state governments to regulate the labor injunction.

Not only did the Court display this attitude toward labor relations legislation, but likewise it struck down laws designed to protect workers from the inexorable operation of the economic system. Thus, in 1918 and again in 1922, the Court held unconstitutional a congressional measure to control the use of child labor in American industry.[8] In 1923 the high court refused to sustain legislation that established a minimum wage for women employed in industry.[9]

Such was the record of the Supreme Court in the period in which legislative attempts were made to protect the right of workers to collective bargaining. In view of this pattern one scarcely could have expected the high court to sustain these legislative efforts. And the Supreme Court did not deviate from its established pattern of interpretation of protective labor relations law. Both the *Adair* and *Coppage* decisions were consistent with the overall personality of the Court.

In characteristic fashion the Supreme Court refused to give serious weight to the economic reasons that justified Section 10 of the Erdman Act. The Court could not see how Section 10 might prevent interruptions to interstate commerce by eliminating the need for strikes that resulted from the interference of railroad employers with the right of workers to self-organization and collective bargaining. In this connection the Court asked, "What possible legal or logical connection is there between an employee's membership in a labor organization and the carrying on of interstate commerce?" Such a statement reflects the Court's philosophy during this period. Many years elapsed before the judiciary decided that there was both a logical connection and a valid legal relationship between the promotion of interstate commerce and governmental protection of the right of workers to self-organization and collective bargaining.

Once the Court held that there was no positive relationship between the objectives of Section 10 and the promotion of interstate commerce, it found the section unconstitutional. The Court reached the conclusion that Section 10 deprived both the railroad operators and the industry workers of their property without due process of law. Freedom to contract is a liberty guaranteed by the Fifth Amendment to the Constitution. Congress may pass no law that deprives people of this liberty. Thus the Court declared that "such liberty and right embraces the right to make contracts for the sale of one's own labor." From this premise the Court held that workers and employers could agree on the execution of a yellow-dog contract. This was a freedom that could not be circumscribed by the legislature. The railroad employer had the right to establish conditions of employment and the employee had the right "to become or not, as he chose, an employee of the railroad company upon the terms offered to him." In other words, the Court said that if the railroad worker did not like the idea of signing a yellow-dog contract, he had the right not to accept employment under such conditions. The implication was that the employee was free to seek other employment. What the Court failed to consider was that the worker might have few alternative employment possibilities. Either he worked for the railroad or he was forced to seek another job, which might be an inferior alternative. The facts of economic life might have forced him to sign the agreement even though he objected vigorously to such an employment agreement. At this time the Court was more concerned with abstract and formal notions of law than with social and economic changes. Such an approach invariably resulted in harm to the interests of the nation's workers.

That portion of the Erdman Act forbidding the discharge of workers because of union activities was likewise held unconstitutional. The Court did not completely understand the new industrial life. The employer had the right to discharge a man for union activities in the same way that the individual worker had the right to quit the employment of an employer who persisted in the hiring of nonunion workers. The Court declared that "in all such particulars the employer and the employee have equality of right, and any legislation that disturbs that equality is an arbitrary interference with the liberty of contract which no government can legally justify in a free land." In short, the Court did not understand that the employer, who possesses infinitely greater economic power than the worker, could use his power to deny the worker his right to collective bargaining. It was assumed that there was already balanced power between the two groups. The worker was free to join a labor union. But that "freedom" was not realized if employers could deny workers their right to collective bargaining. If government would decide to protect this right against the arbitrary invasion of employers, it appears that the cause of freedom would be advanced and not limited. The conduct of the employer would be limited by government only insofar as such restriction permitted the worker to enjoy his exercise of a lawfully recognized right.

In the *Coppage* case, in which the Supreme Court invalidated the Kansas statute, essentially the same arguments that appeared in the *Adair* case were offered. Constant reference was made to the *Adair* opinion to support the *Coppage* decision. The Court utilized the *Adair* decision as a precedent to strike down the Kansas law. Thus the Court declared in the *Coppage* decision that "this case cannot be distinguished from *Adair* v. *United States*." Only changes in the formal approach appear in the *Coppage* decision. Since Kansas passed the statute under the authority of its police power, the Court was required to show that the statute had no relationship to the promotion of the general welfare of the people of the state. It accomplished this task by asking, "What possible relation has . . . the Act to the public health, safety, morals, or general welfare?" In the *Adair* case, the Court held that Section 10 of the Erdman Act did not constitute a valid exercise of the power of Congress to promote interstate commerce. In the *Coppage* proceeding, the Court held that the passage of a state law outlawing the yellow-dog contract and prohibiting discharge for union reasons was not "a legitimate object for the exercise of the police power." Similar to the *Adair* decision, the Court in the *Coppage* case held that the Kansas law deprived both employers and employees of their property and personal liberty without due process of law. In this respect the Court ruled on the Fourteenth Amendment (the constitutional provision that limits the power of the states) and not the Fifth Amendment (the one that checks the power of the Congress).

Justice Holmes dissented sharply from the viewpoint of the majority of the Court. Holmes, in the *Adair* case, upheld the right of Congress to fashion the public policy of the United States. He felt that there was a reasonable relationship between the promotion of interstate commerce and a law calculated to reduce the need for strikes in the railroads. Holmes felt that the Court, the judicial arm of government, should not overrule Congress, the legislative branch of government, in matters of public policy. He was even less impressed with the argument of the Court that Section 10 of the Erdman Act violated the Fifth Amendment to the Constitution. On this point he declared that Section 10 "is, in substance, a very limited interference with the freedom of contract, no more. The section simply prohibits the more powerful party to exact certain undertakings, or to threaten dismissal or unjustly discriminate on certain grounds against those already employed." Holmes's dissent in the *Coppage* case rested on his reasoning in the *Adair* proceeding. He made the simple statement that

> in present conditions a workman not unnaturally may believe that only by belonging to a union can he secure a contract that shall be fair to him. If that belief, whether right or wrong, may be held by a reasonable man, it seems to me that it may be enforced by law in order to establish the equality of position between the parties in which liberty of contract begins. Whether in the long run it is wise for the workingmen to enact legislation of this sort is not my concern, but I am strongly of opinion that there is nothing in the Constitution of the United States to prevent it, and that *Adair* v. *United States* . . . should be over-ruled.

This position was representative of Holmes. He consistently held that Congress and the states should be given wide latitude in legislative matters. The judiciary should respect the opinion of Congress and the state legislatures in matters of public policy. The Constitution should only be employed to check the legislative branch of government when a law flagrantly and unmistakably violated its terms.

EVENTS OF WORLD WAR I

By its position in the *Adair* and *Coppage* cases, the Supreme Court denied to legislative bodies the authority to protect the right of workers to collective bargaining. The effect of these decisions meant that government could not control their bargaining relationships. In a normal peacetime economy it was the considered opinion of the Court that legislative restraint in the collective bargaining process was necessary.

Had World War I not occurred, it is possible that legislative action in the area of collective bargaining would have been forestalled for many years. However, World War I served to focus the attention of the public on the state of the nation's labor relations policy. The need for uninterrupted production was essential. Any strike for any purpose was detrimental to the interests of the nation. In order to establish a procedure to eliminate wartime strikes, President Wilson called a conference of outstanding representatives of industry and organized labor. At the conference, employers and unions gave a no-lockout and no-strike pledge. To settle all labor-management disputes peacefully, the conference recommended the setting up of a war labor board. This proposal was accepted by President Wilson and on April 8, 1918, the National War Labor Board (NWLB) was established. To guide the operation of the Board, the conference adopted a series of principles agreed to by labor and management representatives. Our concern here is with only one of these principles. This involved the declaration by the conference representatives that the War Labor Board should protect employees in their right to self-organization and collective bargaining. The Board was to enforce the following policy: "The right of workers to organize in trade unions and to bargain collectively through chosen representatives is recognized and affirmed. This right should not be denied, abridged, or interfered with by the employers in any manner whatsoever. . . . Employers should not discharge workers for membership in trade unions, nor for legitimate trade union activities."[10]

By adopting this policy, it was hoped that strikes caused by employers' denial of employees' right to self-organization and collective bargaining would be sharply reduced. It is noteworthy that organizational strikes were not outlawed. To have adopted the latter course of action would have meant the disintegration of the union movement.

The National War Labor Board enforced in good faith the right of employees to self-organization and collective bargaining. The Board ordered the reinstatement of workers, with back pay, who were discharged because of union activities, required employers to bargain collectively with representatives of workers' labor unions, and ordered the polling of workers in elections to determine their choices of bargaining agents.[11] Many of these policies were to be embodied in the celebrated National Labor Relations Act passed by Congress in 1935. Although the National War Labor Board had no express authority to enforce its rulings, Wilson in practice did require compliance with the Board's orders through the exercise of his war powers. For example, Wilson seized the properties of the Western Union Telegraph Company because the carrier discharged workers who joined unions. Similarly, the Smith & Wesson Arms Company was seized when the firm refused to bargain collectively.[12]

Still another circumstance of World War I served to indicate the character of future public policy in industrial relations. With the entry of the United States into World War I, the federal government took over the operation of the nation's railroads. The task of supervising the operation of the railroads was lodged in the Railroad Administration. A director-general headed the agency. Early in 1918 the director-general issued General Order No. 8, which provided that "no discrimination will be made in the employment, retention, or conditions of employment of employees because of membership or nonmembership in labor organizations." In short, General Order No. 8 re-established the principle of Section 10 of the Erdman Act, and thereby conflicted directly with the doctrine of the Supreme Court laid down in the *Adair* decision. No one, however, chose to question the right of the federal government to protect collective bargaining rights in the railroad industry during World War I. Of course, the government, not private individuals, operated the roads. This may have had a bearing on any eventual court proceedings involving General Order No. 8.

The Railroad Administration recognized the railway unions as lawful bargaining agents. Of course, since the final determination of the conditions of work rested with the federal government, there was no actual collective bargaining in the industry during the war. Speculation as to whether or not there can be free collective bargaining in an industry owned or operated by the government continues to this day. It is known that the public, the vast majority of union leaders, and the rank-and-file worker frown on strikes when a plant or industry is owned or operated by the government under conditions of war. Free collective bargaining implies that workers have the moral and legal right to strike. Nevertheless, the Railroad Administration did entertain the demands of the railway unions. In many cases the administration granted such demands. From this point of view the railway unions performed an active role in shaping the conditions of work on the railroads during World War I.

Federal protection of the right of workers to collective bargaining during World War I served a dual purpose. In the first place, it demonstrated that a peaceful procedure could be instituted by government to decrease the need for the organizational strike. Such a wartime experiment was a harbinger of future labor relations policy. If protection of the right to collective bargaining during wartime promoted the cause of industrial peace, it appeared equally valid that the same result could follow from such a program during peacetime. In the second place, the favorable government policy toward organized labor during World War I stimulated the growth of the union movement. In 1917 union membership in all labor organizations totaled about 3 million. At the termination of World War I this figure was 4 million, an increase of 33 percent.

This increase in union membership reflects the profound effect of governmental policy on the collective bargaining process. It points up that a favorable legal environment stimulates union growth. After World War I ended, the National War Labor Board was abolished. This meant that once again the worker was left without government protection in his collective bargaining relationships. As a result union membership declined steadily; by 1933 membership was less than 3 million. The decline appears more serious if adjustment is made for the growth of the population and the labor force over the period 1919 to 1933. In 1920 the population of the United States was about 105 million; by 1930 the figure increased to approximately 123 million. The labor force increased from about 40 million in 1920 to about 47 million in 1930. In the same period there occurred a noticeable shift in the composition of the labor force. The number of people employed in agriculture declined sharply. In 1920 about 27 percent of the labor force was in agriculture, but in 1930 agriculture accounted for only 21 percent of the labor force. This meant that there was a shifting of workers to occupations more amenable to union organization. The agricultural worker for a variety of reasons was not easily organized. Despite the increase and change in the character of the labor force, the level of union membership was no higher in 1933 than it was in 1917.

The depression of the thirties contributed its share to thwart the progress of the union movement. Labor history does demonstrate that the strength of organized labor, in terms of numbers and bargaining power, is reduced in depression periods. Giving full weight to the depression of the thirties, the fact still remains that the chief factor preventing the growth of the union movement from World War I until the advent of the New Deal was the lack of legislative involvement. The union movement showed no progress, indeed actually declined in strength, during the relatively prosperous years of the twenties. In these years the level of unemployment averaged about 5 percent of the labor force. This figure does not represent a condition conducive to a decline in union membership, given the state of technology at the time. But, in spite of the relatively high level of employment, the union movement showed no progress and, if adjustment is made for changes in the size and composition of the labor force, organized labor actually lost ground in the twenties. The average union membership during these years was about 3.5 million.

Contrast this experience with that for the years 1932–1939. By 1939 the union movement claimed about 8 million members. Organized labor made this progress in the face of severe unemployment. Despite all efforts of the government to combat unemployment, the economy still suffered from serious unemployment until the entry into World War II. In 1939, for example, about 17 percent of the labor force was unemployed. Obviously, the better business conditions during the New Deal period as compared with the depression years of 1929–1932 had something to do with the growth of the union movement, but the most important factor is commonly held to be the positive support given by government to collective bargaining.

Some attribute this lack of progress in the prosperous years of the twenties to deficiencies in union leadership. Granted the importance of vigorous leadership to the union movement, the fact still remains that such leadership may not have been demonstrated because of the uncertainties of the environment. It is more than a coincidence that the split in the union movement occurred during a period in which the organs of government were sympathetic to organized labor. Organization of the mass-production worker by the CIO was a result of favorable government policy. It is difficult to contend that labor leaders of the twenties did not see the overall desirability of the organization of the mass-production worker into industrial-type unions. As a matter of fact, the same union leaders who were responsible for the rise of the CIO operated in the twenties. But in the twenties, despite the high level of employment, union leaders were not in agreement on the possibility of successfully concluding huge organizing drives. They were aware that efforts to organize the unskilled who did not possess well-entrenched skills would likely result in defeat. Why undertake such a venture if they were doomed to defeat? Clearly, the court experiences of the twenties dictated against such efforts. Industry's "open-shop" campaign of the period presented insurmountable obstacles to organization because of the relative ease of striker replacement. Moreover, the position of the judiciary on collective bargaining profoundly affected attitudes toward organizing activities. Some employers intensified their resistance to unions to the degree permitted by the organs of government. Rather than feeling that their techniques were antisocial in character, many employers considered that they were performing a public service by destroying the collective bargaining process. The prevailing attitude toward collective bargaining was in all probability a reflection of general public sentiment.

The worker himself was not isolated from the effects of the legal atmosphere. Some have attributed the decline in union membership in the twenties to the increasing real income of the workers. It is true that real income of workers did increase, but that should not have prevented some progress in the union movement. Workers may have refrained from union activities out of fear of loss of job because of open-shop tactics, because of the effectiveness of the labor injunction, or because of the disrepute of association with a labor union. Those who argue that the lack of progress of the union movement in the twenties resulted from increasing real income do not fully appreciate the profound effect of government on collective bargaining. Since the legal climate operated to prevent the demonstration of effective union leadership and inasmuch as the legal environment operated to discourage the unorganized worker from union activity, the union movement was bound to lose ground. Moreover, the real-income argument cannot be supported by empirical data. This conclusion is based on observation of the trend in real wages with the level of union membership. No actual investigation was made to test the thesis. Social phenomena are not to be explained solely by statistics. On the other hand, the record testifies to the imprisonment and fines imposed on workers for union activity, to the number of strikes broken as a result of the injunction, and to the antiorganizational activities of employers. Finally, the real-income explanation, if extended to its logical conclusion, would mean that there is no need for any labor union movement. From the dawn of history the worker has experienced a constantly increasing material standard of life. Fundamentally, this progress results from the advancing state of the arts of production. Since this progress is relentless, and if the real-income argument has validity, workers should show little propensity toward union organization. That such is not the case is demonstrated by the union movements of the western democracies.

On the basis of the foregoing observations, the conclusion must be reached that the character of the law of labor relations constitutes a most vital element influencing the growth of the union movement. The condition of the business cycle, the nature of union leadership, and the attitude of employers are of only contributory importance. An analysis of the union movement from World War I through the New Deal period supports this point of view. Given a favorable legal environment, the union movement will expand in numbers and in bargaining strength. Given a restrictive legal environment, the collective bargaining process will lose ground.

RAILROAD LEGISLATION

In 1926 Congress passed the Railway Labor Act.[13] The chief purpose of the law was to establish a variety of procedures, including mediation and voluntary arbitration, to reduce labor conflict in the railroads. These procedures, however, rested on the assumption that the workers would be represented by labor organizations. In short, Congress felt that industrial peace on the railroads could be achieved through the collective bargaining process. Accordingly, the Railway Labor Act of 1926 provided that "representatives . . . shall be designated by the respective parties in such manner as may be provided in their corporate organization or unincorporated association, or by other means of collective action, without interference, influence, or coercion exercised by either party over the self-organization or designation of representatives by the other." Briefly, both workers and management were to be free in the selection of their own representatives without interference. Once chosen, these representatives were to confer together to settle labor disputes. Thus Congress passed a law calculated to protect the railroad worker in his right to collective bargaining. The Railway Labor Act of 1926 provided for a greater degree of protection than Section 10 of the Erdman Act. In the 1926 law the railroad employers were required to negotiate with the freely selected collective bargaining representatives of their workers. This feature was not included in the Erdman Act.

Previous to the passage of the Railway Labor Act of 1926, the railroads had sponsored a number of company-dominated unions. Attention was given to the ability of these organizations to serve as true collective bargaining agencies. Since they were creatures of the company, they were not considered equipped to represent workers in collective bargaining. After the passage of the statute, the question immediately arose as to their legality. The law did not specifically proscribe company-dominated unions. On the other hand, these organizations did not appear to have received support from the new law. Under its terms workers were given the right to choose, freely, representatives for collective bargaining. A company-dominated union might not fall within this classification.

In 1930 the question of the legality of the company union merited the attention of the Supreme Court of the United States. Once again, the Court was to rule on the constitutionality of the law that protected the right of railroad workers to collective bargaining. The railroads contended that the *Adair* decision, handed down by the Court in 1908, controlled the present proceedings. The Texas & New Orleans Railroad, the railroad involved in the case, refused to recognize or bargain with the Brotherhood of Railroad Clerks, a labor union free from company influence. Instead, the railroad supported the company-sponsored-and-dominated "Association of Clerical Employees—Southern Pacific Line." The union claimed that the railroad violated the Railway Labor Act of 1926.

In a decision which contrasted in every respect with the *Adair* doctrine, the Supreme Court upheld the constitutionality of the Railway Labor Act of 1926.[14] It ordered the railroad to cease interfering with the right of workers to choose whatever bargaining agents they wished. In this case the Court held that promotion of the collective bargaining process was of the "highest public interest," for such a procedure prevents "the interruption of interstate commerce by labor disputes and strikes." In other words, the protection of the right of workers to collective bargaining promoted commerce among the states. The view was held that the need for organizational strikes was reduced, and the collective bargaining process itself provided the means for industrial peace.

With respect to the Railway Labor Act of 1926 violating the "due process" clause of the Constitution, the Court had this to say:

> The Railway Labor Act of 1926 does not interfere with the normal exercise of the right of the carrier to select its employees or to discharge them. The statute is not aimed at this right of the employers but at the interference with the right of employees to have representatives of their own choosing. As the carriers subject to the Act have no constitutional right to interfere with the freedom of the employees in making their selections, they cannot complain of the statute on constitutional grounds.

In effect, the Supreme Court overruled the *Adair* doctrine. It did not do so in so many words. For practical purposes it recognized that the *Adair* decision was no longer applicable in railroad disputes. This was not the last time the Court was to reverse itself on matters of labor legislation. For example, in 1937, in the *West Coast Hotel* case,[15] the Court reversed itself on the matter of minimum-wage laws. From 1923 the Court held such laws unconstitutional. Precedent is always a major factor in the decision-making process of the judiciary. On the other hand, factors such as changes in court personnel, political pressure, and fundamental changes in the economic and social environment at times overshadow the importance of precedent.

RAILWAY LABOR ACT AMENDED IN 1934

The *Texas & New Orleans Railroad* decision stands as a landmark in the law of industrial relations. For the first time, the Supreme Court of the United States recognized the authority of government to provide a measure of protection to the right of workers to self-organization and collective bargaining. It represented a clear-cut victory for those who contended that the collective bargaining process could not be carried out successfully without government encouragement. Moreover, the decision pointed up the possibility of additional legislation to implement the collective bargaining process.

In 1934 Congress strengthened the provisions of the Railway Labor Act. It enacted a series of important amendments to the 1926 law. Some of the new provisions added more protection to the right of workers to self-organization and collective bargaining. Despite the policy and provisions of the 1926 law, the collective bargaining process did not function as the Congress had intended. An investigation pointed up the following employer practices:[16]

1. Carrier officers have participated in or supervised, directly or indirectly, the formation of, and carrier managements have retained a measure of control over constitutions, by-laws, and other governing rules of organizations of their employees.
2. Carrier officers have supervised, or taken part in prescribing, the rules governing nominations and elections or other methods of choice of the representatives, committees and officers of such organizations.

Such practices of the railroads meant that their employees were being denied the right to select unions of their own choosing. Since the railroads sponsored company-dominated unions, the collective bargaining procedures provided for in the Railway Labor Act could not operate. The law was grounded on the belief that industrial peace and interstate commerce would be promoted to the degree that the collective bargaining process was utilized. Obviously, the objective of the statute could not be realized when the carriers interfered with the selection of workers' representatives.

Aware of these circumstances and encouraged by the outcome of the *Texas & New Orleans* case, Congress passed the 1934 amendments to strengthen collective bargaining in the railroad industry. Aimed at eliminating employer influence over the selection of workers' representatives for collective bargaining, the 1934 law forthrightly declares that "no carrier shall, by interference, influence, or coercion seek in any manner to prevent the designation by its employees as their representatives of those who or which are not employees of the carrier." It clearly established the right of officers of national unions to represent employees of the carrier. This was accomplished by providing that "representatives of employees for the purpose of this Act need not be persons in the employ of the carrier. . . ." In addition, it provided that railroad employers were prohibited from using funds to support any employee organization, or union representatives. They were also prohibited from deducting wages or collecting dues, fees, assessments, or contributions from employees transferable to labor organizations.

A National Mediation Board was established by the 1934 amendments. The Board was empowered to give meaning to the railroad employees' right to collective bargaining. It was authorized to conduct elections to determine which union the employees desired for collective bargaining purposes. A union receiving the majority of the votes was to be certified as the lawful representative. Railroad employers were required to bargain with the union obtaining certification.

As an adjunct to the law, Congress outlawed the yellow-dog contract on the railroads. This appeared superfluous for Norris–La Guardia, passed in 1932, made it ineffectual. However, Congress in its zeal to establish the collective bargaining process in the railroads outlawed the agreement to underscore its intent.

To enforce the provisions of the law, Congress provided severe penalties for violations. The law provided for fines up to $20,000 or imprisonment, or both, for willful violations of the terms of the Act. It became the duty of the various district attorneys of the United States to prosecute any person who violated the terms of the law. With such severe penalties backing up the clear statement of the law, company-dominated unions, as expected, declined sharply after the passage of the 1934 amendments.[17] Thus Congress was successful in eliminating employer interference with the right of the railroad employees to self-organization and collective bargaining. As will subsequently be noted, the Wagner Act drew heavily from the philosophy and techniques of the amended Railway Labor Act.

NATIONAL INDUSTRIAL RECOVERY ACT

In 1932 the nation was in the depths of the depression. After the election of Roosevelt, the federal government resorted to a variety of measures to promote recovery. Underlying all these attempts was a common purpose: to increase the purchasing power of the people. The New Deal aimed to promote economic recovery by bolstering the demand for goods. To this end, an extensive public works program was instituted. In keeping with the objective of increasing purchasing power, these projects were financed by government borrowing. An integral part of the scheme was the increase of workers' wages. If wages could be increased, workers would have more money to spend. Increase of expenditures would stimulate employment and promote economic recovery.

The general plan of the New Deal to promote recovery was contained in the National Industrial Recovery Act (NIRA). This law provided for the regulation of production and prices by groups of businessmen. The theory underlying the NIRA was that such control would provide balance in the economy. Businessmen in the various industrial facilities of the nation formed groups for the purpose of production and price control. Once formed, the group executed a "code." About 550 such codes were adopted during the NIRA era. The codes provided for industrial self-government by businessmen. Production and prices were not to be controlled by unregulated competition but through regulations adopted by the parties to the codes. Since such an arrangement violated the Sherman Antitrust Act, the NIRA provided that the antitrust statutes were not to apply to parties to the codes.

Congress required that two provisions pertaining to labor be included in every code. In the first place, each code was required to establish a minimum wage for the workers it covered. This was in keeping with the desire of the New Deal to increase purchasing power. Actually, the average minimum wage established by the codes was about 40 cents per hour. In the second place, the National Industrial Recovery Act required that its Section 7(a) be included in each and every code. Section 7(a) provided legal protection for the right of workers to collective bargaining. One reason for 7(a) was the desire of the New Deal to alleviate the causes of industrial relations warfare. Section 7(a), as will be shown below, made it mandatory that employers respect the right of employees to self-organization and collective bargaining. It was designed to outlaw practices adopted to frustrate the collective bargaining process. On the other hand, the economic motive of Section 7(a) cannot be disregarded. Legal protection of collective bargaining would mean stronger unions from the point of view of both numbers and bargaining capabilities. Such a condition might mean effective pressure by labor unions for higher wages. Thus a strong organized labor movement could serve the basic theory of the New Deal to promote economic recovery: the increase of national purchasing power.

From 1933, the year in which the NIRA and Section 7(a) was passed, until 1935, the year in which the NIRA was declared unconstitutional, union membership increased from 2,973,000 to 3,890,000—almost 33 percent.[18] These figures testify to the importance of labor relations law to the growth of the union movement.

SECTION 7(a): NATURE AND ENFORCEMENT

Section 7(a) contained two major principles: (1) that employees shall have the right to organize and bargain collectively through representatives of their own choosing, and shall be free from the interference, restraint, or coercion of employers of labor, or their agents, in the designation of such representatives or in self-organization or in other concerted activities for the purpose of collective bargaining or other mutual aid and protection; and (2) that no employee and no one seeking employment shall be required as a condition of employment to join any company union or to refrain from joining, organizing, or assisting a labor organization of his own choosing.

Thus for the first time during years of peace Congress declared that workers throughout industry were to be protected in their collective bargaining activities. In comparison with subsequent labor relations legislation, however, Section 7(a) contained many fundamental defects. Congress did not provide for a procedure to enforce the policy expressed in the section. Section 7(a) failed to specify the patterns of antiunion conduct that were illegal. It did not expressly declare that company-dominated unions were unlawful. It did not state that employers were required to bargain collectively with the freely chosen representatives of their employees. Nor did Section 7(a) forbid discrimination against employees for union activities.

These fundamental defects of Section 7(a) soon came to light. Employers did not accept the union argument that Section 7(a) outlawed the company-dominated union. In contrast, organized labor interpreted the section to mean that only regular labor organizations were to represent employees for collective bargaining purposes. The unions interpreted the intent of Congress as sanctioning a wide expansion of the labor union movement. Since Section 7(a) did not provide for its enforcement or its interpretation, and since employees and employers believed it to mean different things, a wave of strikes occurred during the summer of 1933. These strikes resulted from the intensity of organizational activities. To comply with Section 7(a), company unions were formed. Organized labor, feeling that these organizations did not reflect the policy of the government, struck for recognition of their own labor unions.

The National Labor Board

Since the wave of strikes impaired the nation's economic recovery, President Roosevelt created the National Labor Board to administer the labor policy of the NIRA. The Board was composed of three union representatives, three industry representatives, and one "impartial" person. It was established on August 5, 1933. At first the Board was successful in its attempts to regulate industrial relations. Almost immediately after its creation, it intervened in a hosiery strike in Berks County, Pennsylvania. More than ten thousand workers were involved in the strike, and every full-fashioned hosiery mill in the county was shut down. The National Labor Board settled the strike on the basis of a procedure known as the "Reading Formula." This formula provided that (1) the strike was to be called off; (2) the striking workers were to be reinstated on their jobs without prejudice or discrimination; (3) an election was to be held under the supervision of the National Labor Board to designate representatives for collective bargaining; and (4) representatives chosen in such elections were to be authorized to negotiate with employers with a view to executing agreements concerning wages, hours, and working conditions.[19] In all but eight of the forty-five mills, workers chose the Hosiery Workers Union as their collective bargaining representative. After the elections were held, a large number of mills in the area still refused to negotiate a contract with the union representatives. The National Labor Board ordered these employers to negotiate written agreements with the unions. Eventually, practically all firms executed collective bargaining agreements with the freely chosen representatives of their workers.

The success of the National Labor Board in the hosiery industry was repeated in other industries. On the basis of the Reading Formula, the Board peacefully settled disputes involving hundreds of thousands of workers in the wool, silk, clothing, street railways, and machine shop industries.[20] The high-water mark of the Board's operations was reached in November 1933. In this month the number of strikes subsided considerably. On November 22 and 23 it conducted the most extensive elections of its existence, involving some fourteen thousand workers of the captive coal mines. By November the Board established several regional boards. This decentralization permitted the national Board to deal with major controversies and, most important, permitted its members to reflect more carefully on matters of policy. A special study of the National Labor Board states that for a time "it seemed that, thanks to the Board's application of 7(a), an ideal of industrial democracy was in the process of realization in the field of industrial relations."[21] However, by the end of the year, it was apparent that the National Labor Board could not offer adequate remedies for violations of its orders. Since it could not function effectively, the Board did not serve the public interest, for unions resorted to the organizational strike to enforce Section 7(a).

A series of events operated to weaken the prestige and operating ability of the National Labor Board. The first blow was delivered by the Weirton Steel Company and the Budd Manufacturing Company. Both concerns refused to respect the principles of the Reading Formula. Determined in their positions, the corporations refused to agree to elections to determine the question of union representation. The Weirton Company refused to allow their workers to vote on whether or not they desired to be represented by the Amalgamated Association of Iron, Steel and Tin Workers, a regular labor union, or by a union created and sponsored by the company. Despite protests from the federal government, the Weirton Company held an election in which workers merely voted to designate representatives under the company union plan. This open conflict with the National Labor Board seriously impaired its prestige.

By February 1934, mainly as a result of its futile efforts to settle the *Weirton* and *Budd* disputes on the basis of the Reading Formula, the National Labor Board was on the verge of collapse. The example was set by Weirton and Budd for others to follow. Orders of the Board were not respected and its authority was disregarded. Because the peaceful procedures of the Board broke down, the frequency of organizational strikes sharply increased. Workers and employers were determined to prevail in organizational contests. Since the National Labor Board could not control by holding elections, employees resorted to the strike to gain their objective.

Aware of these circumstances, Roosevelt attempted to bolster the authority and prestige of the disintegrating National Labor Board. In February 1934 he issued two Executive Orders that increased the power of the Board.[22] These orders provided that the National Labor Board was to conduct elections to determine collective bargaining representatives of workers. If at such an election a majority of workers chose a particular labor union for representation, the employer would be required to recognize and negotiate with this union. If an employer should refuse, the National Labor Board was to refer the case to the Compliance Division of the National Recovery Administration and/or the office of the Attorney General of the United States. These agencies were to obtain compliance with the orders of the Board.

It appeared at first that the National Labor Board might now function as an effective organization. The intent of the President was clear. He clothed the Board with status and power. Heretofore the Board functioned on a more or less informal basis. It developed on its own initiative the Reading Formula, other policies, and administration procedures. Moreover, the great defect of the Board lay in its inability to enforce its decisions. Consequently, there was reason to believe that the Executive Orders of February 1934 would correct these shortcomings. This point of view, however, failed to materialize because of the intensity of the organizational conflicts.

Immediately after the President issued the Executive Orders, the "majority principle" laid down by the Orders was challenged. It was contended that this principle would deprive nonunion workers of their employment rights, for the National Labor Board held that an employer must bargain with a majority-selected labor union as the exclusive representative of all his employees. Unions argued that collective bargaining could not be carried out effectively if employers were free to make private deals with individual workers. When such an arrangement was established, it would not be difficult to undermine a labor union. This could be done by showing favoritism to the nonunion worker. To avail themselves of such benefits, it was argued, some workers might give up their union membership. Any sizable withdrawal from the labor union would mean its collapse. Once this occurred, the employer would then be free to determine employment conditions on a unilateral basis and need no longer show concern for the nonunion worker.

General Johnson and Donald R. Richberg, high-ranking officers of the National Recovery Administration, shared the employer point of view. This proved to be a determining factor in the decline of the National Labor Board. It could not implement the majority principle and assure parties to a dispute that its views were supported by all members of the government. Actually, the National Labor Board refused to heed the viewpoint of Johnson-Richberg; however, their position served to promote confusions in National Labor Board policy.

In March 1934 the National Labor Board suffered another blow to its prestige. During this month the nation was threatened with an industry-wide automobile strike. The automobile companies refused to recognize an automobile union which was then being organized under the sponsorship of the AFL. To prevent their workers from enjoying the benefits of true collective bargaining, the automobile manufacturers sponsored company-dominated unions. The AFL insisted on a free election to determine the bargaining desires of the automobile workers. The manufacturers refused and the AFL threatened to close down the nation's major automobile plants.

Such a strike, of course, would have seriously retarded the recovery efforts of the New Deal. The National Labor Board, aware of the implications of a nation-wide automobile strike, diligently attempted to settle the dispute on the basis of the Reading Formula. However, the Board failed to effect a settlement. President Roosevelt and Johnson, of the National Recovery Administration, then intervened in the dispute. This intervention made it clear to the public that the National Labor Board did not have the authority or the capability to settle important labor controversies. On March 25, 1934, President Roosevelt obtained a peaceful settlement of the dispute. The fact that White House pressure prevented the strike added further to the impairment of the National Labor Board's status as an effective labor agency.

The National Labor Board never recovered from this blow to its prestige. Employers and unions had little respect or faith in its procedures. Labor unrest again mounted in intensity as unions became aware of the impotence of the Board. Organized labor, convinced of National Labor Board inadequacies, undertook to enforce 7(a) through its own economic strength. Organizational strikes occurred during the early summer of 1934 in Toledo, Minneapolis, and San Francisco; and a nationwide steel strike was threatened by the Amalgamated Association of Iron, Steel and Tin Workers.[23] The National Labor Board did not prevent the outbreak of these strikes nor was it capable of obtaining settlement once they occurred. Its failure in this respect was inevitable. Its prestige was irreparably damaged by presidential intervention in the automobile dispute.

Finally, on May 29, 1934, the judiciary completed the cycle of Board humiliations. A district court refused to order the Weirton Steel Company to participate in a representation election to permit workers to choose freely their representatives for collective bargaining. Both the Reading Formula and the Executive Orders of February 1934 underscored the right of workers to make this choice. However, the district court refused to order the collective bargaining election. On the basis of such a judicial ruling, it is not difficult to see why both employers and unions lost confidence in its procedures.

Public Resolution No. 44: The First National Labor Relations Board

Congress recognized the shortcomings of the National Labor Board. Its failure stimulated members of Congress, particularly Senator Wagner of New York, to search for more effective protective procedures. Congress was alerted to the danger of relying on an inept agency to preserve industrial peace. Strikes for organizational purposes would continue in number and intensity to the degree that Congress failed to provide for the speedy and adequate enforcement of the free selection by workers of bargaining representatives. If the unions were reluctant to strike for recognition purposes prior to 1933, Section 7(a) completely changed this state of affairs. Collective bargaining had become a matter of public policy. The nation's workers were determined to engage in collective bargaining with or without government protection. As a result, 45.9 percent of all strikes in 1934 occurred wholly or in part from organizational issues.[24]

Congress, fully aware of this stream of events, undertook the task of providing the workers with adequate machinery to select bargaining representatives. Senator Wagner of New York led the drive for legislation to accomplish this objective. As early as February 1934, he introduced the so-called Wagner Labor Disputes Act.[25] Later he proposed still another law, the Industrial Adjustment Act, which would provide even broader protection for the collective bargaining process. Fundamental to Wagner's program was a streamlined method for enforcement. He would have set up a quasi-judicial agency, termed the "National Industrial Adjustment Board," empowering this agency to prevent employer antiunion practices. In addition, it was to have authority to conduct elections enabling workers to select bargaining representatives. Employers would be expected to recognize and negotiate with these representatives. Orders of the Board would be enforceable in the United States circuit courts of appeals. Unlike the ill-defined authority upon which the National Labor Board operated, the Wagner agency would derive its power from a statute of Congress. Its mandate would be clearly defined and, to obviate the possibility of disrespect for Board orders, as was the case with the National Labor Board, the Wagner Board could call upon the courts to enforce its decisions.

Despite the approval of the Wagner program by President Roosevelt, Congress did not enact the Wagner Labor Disputes Act or the Industrial Adjustment Bill. Congress adjourned without passing legislation to govern the nation's labor relations policy. However, the 73rd Congress did not adjourn without providing for the replacement of the defunct National Labor Board. For this purpose Congress on June 16, 1934, passed Joint Resolution No. 44. Three days later the Resolution was approved by the President.

The purpose of Joint Resolution No. 44 was to provide for the interpretation and enforcement of Section 7(a) of the National Industrial Recovery Act. Unlike the Wagner program, which would have set up a labor board on the basis of legislation independent of NIRA, the National Labor Relations Board, created by Joint Resolution No. 44, was tied to Section 7(a) of the NIRA. This Board expired with the decision that the National Industrial Recovery Act was unconstitutional.

The National Labor Relations Board appeared more fortified to provide adequate protection to the right of workers to self-organization and collective bargaining than the defunct National Labor Board. The spirit in which it was created demonstrated the desire of Congress for vigorous legal implementation of collective bargaining. More specifically, it was empowered to conduct representation elections to permit workers to choose their collective bargaining representatives. In addition, it was authorized to investigate alleged violations of Section 7(a).

On the other hand, this Board suffered from the defect which proved fatal to the National Labor Board; that is, the National Labor Relations Board did not have the power to enforce its own orders. Enforcement depended on the action of the Compliance Division of the National Recovery Administration or on the Department of Justice. This proved a serious barrier to the effective operation of the agency. In addition, employer antiunion practices, supposedly prohibited by Section 7(a), were not spelled out in Joint Resolution No. 44. This meant that the new Board, like its predecessor, had to establish its own principles. Joint Resolution No. 44 in effect placed the responsibility for establishing a national labor relations policy on the shoulders of a governmental agency. In any matter so important and complicated it is essential that Congress provide guides for an agency to follow. Section 7(a) declared in general terms that workers had the right to self-organization and collective bargaining without employer interference. But it did not spell out what constituted "employer interference." For example, as mentioned, it was not clear whether or not company-dominated unions were unlawful.

Vagueness with respect to the scope of authority of the National Labor Relations Board and division of responsibility for enforcement of its decisions constituted the two chief obstacles to effective operation of the agency. In short, Board orders were not respected. The Compliance Division of the NRA did order the removal of the

"Blue Eagle" from firms which ignored Board decisions. However, this technique of enforcement proved highly unsatisfactory. Consumers did not particularly care whether or not a company sported the Blue Eagle, the emblem showing compliance with the overall policy of the NIRA. The Department of Justice likewise did not provide an adequate vehicle for enforcement. The Board referred thirty-three cases to the Department of Justice. Of these the Department sought only one injunction for enforcement purposes.[26] Sixteen cases were sent back to the NLRB for additional evidence. In three other cases the Department exercised its prerogative to overrule the Board and held that no suit was justified. Finally, in the remaining cases, the Department of Justice for one reason or another refused to enforce orders of the Board.

Such an enforcement program did not enhance the prestige of the Board. Employers were not greatly impressed by its orders, for it was apparent that enforcement was a remote possibility. For effective operation an administrative agency must have the ability to enforce its decisions. Had the NLRB been authorized by Joint Resolution No. 44 to solicit the courts for enforcement orders, the record of the agency would have been more imposing. As a result the Board held that employers violated Section 7(a) in eighty-six instances during the first eight months of its operation, but in only thirty-four cases did employers comply with orders of the Board.

PASSAGE OF THE WAGNER ACT

When the 74th Congress assembled for the first time in 1935, Senator Wagner again led a drive for labor relations legislation. He was convinced that the National Labor Relations Board established under Joint Resolution No. 44 did not provide a sound basis for adequate protection of the collective bargaining process. Wagner's bill received support from the American Federation of Labor. President Roosevelt also gave his approval to the measure.

The factor that resulted in the speedy passage of Wagner's proposal, however, was the declaration by the Supreme Court that the entire National Industrial Recovery Act was unconstitutional.[27] As noted, Joint Resolution No. 44 and the National Labor Relations Board created under its terms were rooted in the NIRA. When this law was held invalid, the NLRB had no legal basis for its actions. Since its legislative authority was swept away, the orders of the Board had no legal validity. The Supreme Court's decision in the famous *Schecter* case was handed down on May 27, 1935. After this date all federal protection of workers' rights to self-organization and collective bargaining terminated. Section 7(a) and the National Labor Relations Board created under Joint Resolution No. 44 became dead letters.

After the *Schecter* decision the legislative pace quickened. Senator Wagner pushed for speedy passage of his bill, which by this time was popularly termed the "Wagner Act." House and Senate hearings on the measure were intensified. Members of these committees were well aware of the need for legislation to promote industrial peace. It was apparent that such peace could not be obtained in the absence of a law that would effectively establish the collective bargaining process in American industry. The American Federation of Labor pressed for new legislation. The campaign that the AFL conducted for the passage of the Wagner Act was centered around the Section 7(a) guarantees. Mass meetings to urge the passage of the Wagner Act were held under the sponsorship of the AFL and other labor groups. Organized labor made letter clear the character of its future political program. It threatened to work for the defeat of each and every senator or congressman who opposed the Wagner Act. Never before did organized labor conduct such an all-out campaign to urge the passage of a particular bill.

On June 27, 1935, the Wagner Act was passed by Congress.[28] Its technical name was the National Labor Relations Act but its popular name, and the one which will be used in this volume, is the Wagner Act. President Roosevelt approved the legislation on July 5, 1935, stating that

> this Act defines, as a part of our substantive law, the right of self-organization of employees in industry for the purpose of collective bargaining, and provides methods by which the Government can safeguard that legal right. It establishes a National Labor Relations Board to hear and determine cases in which it is charged that this legal right is abridged or denied, and to hold fair elections to ascertain who are the chosen representatives of employees. A better relationship between labor and management is the high purpose of this Act. By assuring the employees the right of collective bargaining it fosters the development of employment control on a sound and equitable basis. By providing an orderly procedure for determining who is entitled to represent the employees, it aims to remove one of the chief causes of wasteful economic strife. By preventing practices which tend to destroy the independence of labor, it seeks, for every worker within its scope, that freedom of choice and action which is justly his.[29]

With the passage of the Wagner Act, legislative approval of the collective bargaining process was reasserted. Here was a law passed specifically and deliberately for the purpose of protecting and encouraging the growth of the union movement. The law also set up an agency which appeared well fortified to implement the purpose of the statute. Public policy had changed considerably since the labor conspiracy cases of 1806. Society now declared that collective bargaining was socially desirable. Collective bargaining was to constitute the normal procedure for the establishment of the conditions of employment within American industry. As we shall see, there were many aspects to the Wagner Act, some of them complicated and controversial, but none more important than its social approval of the collective bargaining process.

SUMMARY

For many years the Supreme Court nullified the efforts of Congress and state legislatures to protect employees in their right to self-organization and collective bargaining. The attitude of the judiciary remained rooted in precedent even though the legislative branch of government recognized that the facts of industrial life made legal protection of the collective bargaining process a desirable public policy. The Supreme Court had difficulties balancing the constitutional property guarantees, as it interpreted them, with laws passed by Congress. The economic doctrines of the Constitution were subject to interpretation by all three branches of government. But the high court nullified legislative attempts to implement collective bargaining because of the social and economic predilections of the judges who composed the high court. The *Adair* and *Coppage* cases revealed a philosophy not conducive to an under-standing of the dynamics of the economic system. Only through speculation could one comment on the attitude of the majority of the electorate in the area of collective bargaining.

Despite such an attitude on the part of the judiciary, Congress passed legislation calculated to protect the right of the nation's railway workers to self-organization and collective bargaining. Part of this legislation was patterned after the principles estab-lished by the first National War Labor Board. The National Industrial Recovery Act, passed by Congress to implement economic recovery, attempted to extend federal protection to collective bargaining throughout all industry. This policy was set up in Section 7(a) of the NIRA. However, this section contained basic defects, which made its effective enforcement impossible. When the Supreme Court held the NIRA unconstitutional, Section 7(a) became a dead letter. Subsequently, Congress enacted the Wagner Act to protect employees in their right to self-organization and collective bargaining.

NOTES

[1] *Report of the Industrial Commission on Labor Legislation*, V (Washington, D.C.: U.S. Govern-ment Printing Office, 1900), 128.

[2] National Labor Relations Board, *Rules and Regulations and Statements of Procedure* (Wash-ington, D.C.: U.S. Government Printing Office, 1965), p. 63.

[3] *Adair* v. *U.S.*, 208 U.S. 161 (1908).

[4] *Coppage* v. *Kansas*, 236 U.S. 1 (1915).

[5] *In re Debs*, Petitioner, 158 U.S. 564 (1895).

[6] *Loewe* v. *Lawlor* (*Danbury Hatters* case), 208 U.S. 274 (1908).

[7] *Hitchman Coal & Coke Company* v. *Mitchell*, 245 U.S. 229 (1917).

[8] *Hammer* v. *Dagenhart*, 247 U.S. 251 (1918); *Bailey* v. *Drexel Furniture*, 259 U.S. 20 (1922).

[9] *Adkins* v. *Children's Hospital*, 261 U.S. 525 (1923).

[10] National War Labor Board, *Report, April, 1918, to May, 1919*, pp. 121–122.

[11] *Ibid.*, pp. 53–156.

[12] *Ibid.*, p. x.

[13] 44 Stat. 577 (1926).

[14] *Texas & New Orleans Railroad* v. *Brotherhood of Railroad Clerks*, 281 U.S. 548 (1930).

[15] *West Coast Hotel* v. *Parrish*, 300 U.S. 391 (1937).

[16] *Statement of Federal Co-ordinator of Transportation*, December 8, 1933, pp. 5–7.

[17] Twentieth Century Fund, Inc., *Labor and Government* (New York: McGraw-Hill Book Company, 1935), p. 88.

[18] Florence Peterson, *American Labor Unions* (New York: Harper & Brothers, 1945), p. 56.

[19] National Recovery Administration, Release No. 285, dated August 11, 1933.

[20] Lewis L. Lorwin and Arthur Wubnig, *Labor Relations Boards* (Washington, D.C.: Brookings Institution, 1935), p. 100.

[21] *Ibid.*, p. 102.

[22] Executive Order No. 6580, February 1, 1934; Executive Order No. 6612-A, February 23, 1934.

[23] Lorwin and Wubnig, *op. cit.*, p. 115.

[24] *Monthly Labor Review*, XLII, 162 (1935).

[25] S. 2926, 73rd Congress, 2d sess (1934).

[26] D. O. Bowman, *Public Control of Labor Relations* (New York: The Macmillan Company, 1942), p. 45.

[27] *Schecter Poultry Corporation* v. *United States*, 295 U.S. 495 (1935).

[28] 49 Stat. 449 (1935).

[29] *Public Papers and Addresses of Franklin D. Roosevelt* (New York: Random House, 1938–1950), pp. 294–295.

9 The Wagner Act

THE SOCIOECONOMIC RATIONALE OF
THE WAGNER ACT

The National Labor Relations Act, hereinafter referred to as the Wagner Act, provided a partial answer to changing problems of labor relations. It was a product of modern industrialism, rooted in the growth of big business and the corporate organization of industry. Supporters of the legislation recognized that the modern industrial environment rendered obsolete the concept of individual bargaining as the regulator of industrial relations. Social and economic change brought greater attention to the need for effective collective bargaining. Moreover, the Wagner Act recognized the incongruity of industrial autocracy in the context of political democracy. It appeared to Wagner Act supporters that the extension of the democratic process to the employment relationship was necessary and appropriate if the nation were to remain free and democratic. As Senator Wagner once put it, "Let men know the dignity of freedom and self-expression in their daily lives, and they will never bow to tyranny in any quarter of their national life."[1] The Wagner Act assumed democracy to be an indivisible process. Denial of the implementation of the process in any quarter of society would constitute a threat to survival of the economic system. The employer-employee relationship constituted one of the most common and important of all social phenomena. It was felt that if the nation was to be maintained as a going democracy, it was vital that the employment function be carried out in an environment of freedom and self-determination. Unchecked economic power lodged in a comparatively few corporate giants could lead to some form of despotism. An alternative to complete state control over the economic system, which could lead to loss of political freedom, was adjudged to be joint determination of labor policy by workers and employers. If concentrated economic power could be utilized to stifle self-expression in labor relations, this same power could be utilized to curtail the basic elements of democracy throughout the national life. Thus the Wagner Act reflected the dedication of the nation to democratic methods of decision making. Collective bargaining was to be the vehicle for extending democracy to the workplace.

The Wagner Act had still another express purpose. It was to act as an economic stabilizer for the nation. As mentioned, the New Deal, of which the statute was an integral part, resulted from the failure of traditional practices to provide the nation with economic prosperity. The theory of the New Deal was that sufficient purchasing power in the hands of the people would constitute one road to a healthy economic life. According to the architects of the New Deal, the nonunion employee did not possess actual liberty of contract. Such an employment relationship meant that an employer could keep for the firm a disproportionate share of its revenues under conditions of persistent excess supply of labor. This condition could contribute to and prolong a business cycle in the downturn stage, for the purchasing power to buy the commodities and services turned out by industry might not be available. Effective collective bargaining, according to New Deal policy, provided a way out of the difficulty. Through its implementation, wages would tend to increase, the result being the increase of effective demand for the products of American industry. One employer spokesman supported this approach to economic stability when he declared:

> It became obvious to the management of our company that no mass production could long be carried on unless there was increased purchasing power by the great masses of people. To us this meant there must be increases in wages and shortening of hours. This became the very fixed conviction of our management. The more difficult question was as to how this should be accomplished, and we arrived at the conclusion that collective bargaining by employer and employee . . . was the only means by which, under our system, any adjustment in the equitable distribution of income could be accomplished. We realized the difficulty of this method, but we felt that if this method did not accomplish the desired end, then the present capitalistic system would collapse. . . . There is a further and more selfish reason as to why we took the step which we did in co-operating with the organization of our plants. We felt that if the present economic system was to continue, it was inevitable that in the future there should be the organization of labor, and that real collective bargaining would eventually be made effective.[2]

Thus the fundamental purpose of the Wagner Act was economic in character. It sought to promote greater self-determination for workers, strengthen the democratic way of life, and improve the overall operation of the economy. The law was to accomplish these goals through the effective implementation of collective bargaining. It was necessary, therefore, for the law to stimulate the growth of strong unions, a prerequisite for effective collective bargaining. In short, the Wagner Act sought to establish a healthier socioeconomic life through strong unions and effective collective bargaining. The law did not promote strong unions as an end in itself. However, to accomplish the economic objectives of the Wagner Act, it was considered important to provide a legal climate in which the union movement could grow and operate effectively.

Under the provisions of the Constitution it was not sufficient for Congress to declare that the Wagner Act plan would serve the public interest by accomplishing its economic objectives. The national government is one of delegated powers.[3] This means that Congress had to find specific authority in the Constitution before it could enact a specific law. In the case of the Wagner Act, Congress, to meet the constitutional obligations, hooked the statute to the power of the federal government to regulate interstate commerce. Attention has already been directed to the large number of strikes engaged in by workers to force employers to accept the collective bargaining process. These strikes were bitterly contested. Frequently, they resulted in destruction of property, injuries, and even loss of life. Congress reasoned that such strikes, termed organizational strikes, obstructed interstate commerce by impairing the flow of raw materials and processed goods among the states, and causing diminution of employment and wages in such volume as to impair substantially the market for goods flowing from or into the channels of commerce. An organizational strike in the telephone and telegraph industry, for example, obviously would prevent the exchange of goods among the states. Businessmen rely on the telephone and telegram to effectuate the sale and purchase of goods. Likewise, an organizational strike in a factory would obstruct interstate commerce. Unless goods were first produced, they could scarcely enter the channels of interstate commerce. Finally, organizational strikes meant that wages of workers and profits of companies were either decreased or temporarily nonexistent. This resulted in the reduction of the sale and purchase of goods in interstate commerce. If organizational strikes resulted in such obstruction to commerce, the obvious inference was that reduction of the frequency of such strikes would promote trade among the states. The Wagner Act aimed to eliminate the cause of such strikes by outlawing employer antiunion practices.

Congress also believed that legal protection of the right of workers to self-organization and collective bargaining would result in a diminution in the number of nonorganizational strikes. In this connection the Wagner Act declared that "experience has proved that protection by law of the right to employees to organize and bargain collectively safeguards commerce from injury... by encouraging practices fundamental to the friendly adjustment of industrial disputes arising out of differences as to wages, hours, or other working conditions. . . ." By such a statement Congress meant that the collective bargaining process, once firmly established within the economy, could serve as a bridge to industrial harmony. The record of industrial relations testified to the fact that a labor union secure in its status was apt to be more responsible, more responsive to the problems of management, and more reasonable than one whose status was in a constant state of uncertainty. Studies pointing up the causes of industrial peace sponsored by the National Planning Association supported this observation.[4] Alternatively, management likewise would be more prone to reach a peaceful settlement in a labor dispute when dealing with a strong and secure labor union. If management felt that a union was so weak that it could not possibly withstand a serious challenge to its existence, the company officials could purposely force a showdown. Frequently the result was unnecessary industrial warfare. Collective bargaining, if it was to serve the cause of industrial peace, presupposed an arrangement in which the contesting parties possessed equality in bargaining power. Should one side be very weak and the other very strong, the possibilities for industrial warfare would be increased.

Beyond this reasoning, Congress could point to the history of industrial relations on the railroads to support the contention that employees had been denied the right of free collective bargaining. Despite the defects of the Railway Labor Act of 1926, the promotion of the collective bargaining process in the railroad industry by law did serve the cause of industrial peace. When Congress passed the Wagner Act, there was no conclusive evidence indicating how the 1934 amendments to the Railway

Labor Act of 1926 would function. The amendments were passed on June 31, 1934, and the Wagner Act was enacted one year later. However, in that one year, marked by a great amount of industrial warfare, the railroads were not affected by the wave of strikes. Railroad workers, secure in their right to self-organization and collective bargaining, had no occasion to resort to the organizational strike.

This then was the underlying philosophy of the Wagner Act. Industrial strife was promoted to the degree that employers denied to workers their right to self-organization and collective bargaining. The legal requirements of the Constitution were met by the Wagner Act, for interstate commerce was burdened by strikes resulting from such denial. In addition, Congress placed great faith in collective bargaining as the vehicle for industrial peace. Finally, it was hoped that the effect of economic depressions could be lessened by legal protection of the collective bargaining process, for this might mean more purchasing power for the nation's workers. That is, more purchasing power if unions possessed the economic power often attributed to them.

On the basis of such observations, Congress set forth the public policy of the United States, proclaiming:

> It is hereby declared to be the policy of the United States to eliminate the causes of certain substantial obstructions to the free flow of commerce and to mitigate and eliminate these obstructions when they have occurred by encouraging the practice and procedures of collective bargaining and by protecting the exercise by workers of full freedom of association, self-organization, and designation of representatives of their own choosing, for the purpose of determining the terms and conditions of their employment or other mutual aid or protection.

Opposition in some quarters was evident almost immediately after passage of the Act. Some employers attempted to prevent the effective operation of the law by seeking injunctions to restrain the activities of the National Labor Relations Board. Court actions were so numerous that the NLRB spent its first months of operation defending itself in court. However, it should be made perfectly clear at this point that a majority of employers either supported the Wagner Act provisions or offered no opposition to their implementation.

An event almost unique in the field of federal law stimulated injunctive attack against the NLRB. On September 5, 1935, a few months after the passage of the Wagner Act, the National Lawyer's Committee of the American Liberty League declared that the statute was unconstitutional.[5] This pronouncement was made long before the Supreme Court had an opportunity to review the legislation. The League pronouncement stimulated widespread violation of the Act's provisions. The National Labor Relations Board, commenting on this, declared,

> During its first months, and before the Board had opportunity even to announce its procedures, an incident occurred which was to stimulate injunction suits against the Board, and even to provide a sample brief for those wishing to attack the act. This was the publication by the National Lawyer's Committee of the American Liberty League, on September 5, 1935, of a printed assault on the constitutionality of the act. This document, widely publicized and distributed throughout the country immediately upon its issuance, did not present the argument in an impartial manner for the use of attorneys. It was not a review of the cases which might be urged for and against the statute. It was not a brief in any

case in court nor was it an opinion for any client involved in any case pending. Under the circumstances it can be regarded only as a deliberate and concentrated effort by a large group of well-known lawyers to undermine public confidence in the statute, to discourage compliance with it, to assist attorneys generally in attack on the statute, and perhaps to influence the courts.[6]

Soon after the National Lawyer's Committee circulated its anti-Wagner Act tract, the injunction proceedings began. The Board reported that the process was "like a rolling snowball." In a matter of weeks the legal attacks against the Board became uniform throughout the nation. Thus "the allegations or pleading filed by an employer in Georgia, for example, would show up in precisely the same wording in a pleading filed in Seattle."[7] Such a procedure testified to the organized attack against the Wagner Act. The pleas for injunctions were successful. In some cases the judges did not themselves understand the provisions of the National Labor Relations Act. Some judges, the NLRB reported, had the impression that the Act provided for mediation and arbitration. Others believed it was no more than a law of conciliation. The fact was that there were absolutely no features of conciliation or arbitration in the Wagner Act. In the first few months of the life of the Board, the federal district courts issued twenty injunctions restraining the operations of the NLRB. However, some judges, aware of the fact that NLRB orders could not be enforced except upon review by the circuit court of appeals and the Supreme Court, refused to act favorably upon employer applications for injunctions.

STATE OF AFFAIRS BEFORE <u>JONES & LAUGHLIN</u>

The attack against the Wagner Act, spearheaded by the National Lawyer's Committee, prevented the successful operation of the law. Its administrative agency, the National Labor Relations Board, could not effectively exercise the powers granted it by Congress. Criticized and ridiculed in the daily press, hamstrung by legal proceedings, the NLRB suffered crushing blows to its prestige. Organized labor began to lose faith in the law. Its purpose and provisions were clear enough. On paper it purported to permit employees to form—free from employer influence—labor unions and to utilize their organizations as collective bargaining agencies. In practice, however, it soon became obvious that neither the law nor the NLRB could operate as a protector of collective bargaining rights. Simultaneous with the decrease of workers' confidence in the law, the number of organizational strikes increased. From the summer of 1935, the period of the passage of the Wagner Act, until the spring of 1937, recognition and organizational strikes wholly or in part accounted for about 50 percent of all strikes.[8] Workers were impressed with the declaration by Congress that collective bargaining constituted the national policy of the United States. Their organizational efforts had their roots in the public approval of labor unions. These roots were nourished by the growing recognition of the possible effects of the collective bargaining process in the life of the nation. Citizens were engaged in a search for new answers to the financial ills plaguing the economy. Workers no longer were to be denied their right to self-organization and collective bargaining. If the NLRB could not enforce this right, the employees of the nation might resort to violence. Some regard the relatively large number of organizational strikes in the first years of the Wagner Act as demonstrating the failure of the law. Such an observation is without convincing support. The real reason for this great wave of strikes may have been the ineffective operation of the Wagner Act. Since the law's provisions were not widely accepted at first, employees may have resorted to organizational strikes to seek their objective of recognition of bargaining agents. Outward manifestations of employer resistance to collective bargaining were not checked by the NLRB in court proceedings. Thus the organizational strike and not the NLRB, an agency largely neutralized through early court proceedings, served to implement the public policy set forth in the Wagner Act.

Only a clear-cut declaration of constitutionality of the Wagner Act by the Supreme Court could effectuate the law. If the Court validated the Act, the legal proceedings against the NLRB would cease. The agency then could devote full energies to the enforcement of the statute. Voluntary compliance to the Wagner Act, indispensable to the successful operation of any law, would increase, since lengthy and costly legal proceedings against the NLRB would prove futile. Under such conditions the peaceful procedures of the Wagner Act would be substituted for industrial warfare. Labor leaders and workers alike could seek legal remedies for violations of the right to self-organization and collective bargaining. The need for the organizational strike would be reduced, if not virtually eliminated.

The effect of a validation of the Wagner Act by the Supreme Court appeared clear enough. What was doubtful was whether or not the high court would sustain the legislation. Would the Court hold the Wagner Act unconstitutional on the basis of the *Adair* decision? Or would the more recent *Texas & New Orleans* decision control the proceedings? Even the avid supporters of the Wagner Act recognized the strong possibilities for an adverse decision. The Railway Labor Act, sustained in the *Texas & New Orleans* decision, applied only to the railroad industry whereas the Wagner Act covered all workers engaged in interstate commerce. It was recognized that the Supreme Court could distinguish between a general statute and one very limited in scope.

The composition of the Court was a source of uncertainty to supporters of the Wagner Act. On the Court were Van Devanter, Sutherland, McReynolds, and Butler. Students of the Supreme Court were well aware of the social and economic philosophies of these men. Their philosophies were present in decisions denying the right of government to legislate for the benefit of the working population. The judges believed that the operation of the economic system provided payment to workers in accordance with their worth to their employers. They assumed that the forces of a competitive economy would protect the worker from exploitation. In short, this group believed that the type of economic system described by Adam Smith in 1776 was in operation in the 1930s. These men felt that the government should not protect the weak from the strong, but that workers should exercise their economic prerogatives to effect such protection. Thus, if a worker was dissatisfied with the conditions of work determined unilaterally by the employer, the man was free to quit and seek employment elsewhere. Characteristics of the contemporary economy—such as chronic unemployment, concentration of economic power, monopolistic control of product markets, formation of huge corporations, and the inherent disparity of bargaining power between the worker and the company—failed to impress these members of the Supreme Court. It was generally not recognized that Adam Smith advocated governmental intervention when necessary to restore competitive conditions to an economy.

Still another factor worried supporters of the Wagner Act. Even granted that the statute as such would be validated, the question still remained as to how far the Court would apply the law. The specific issue was whether or not the law would apply to manufacturing. Approximately 10 million workers were employed in manufacturing in 1935. These workers constituted a highly organizable group. If the Court upheld the Wagner Act but denied its application to manufacturing, the statute would not serve to expand significantly the area of unionization and collective bargaining. On the other hand, the application of the law to manufacturing facilities would result in the protection of the right of self-organization and collective bargaining for a group which could spearhead an expansion of the union movement. In addition, if manufacturing were included within the scope of the Wagner Act, the Court would establish a precedent that would likely result in the application of the statute to industries such as mining, foresting, fishing, finance, and some sectors of wholesale and retail trade. By denying the application of the law to manufacturing, even though upholding the general constitutionality of the law, the Supreme Court could limit its terms to interstate bus lines, truck and water transportation, and telephone and telegraph systems. The workers involved in these industries constituted a fraction of the nation's organizable workers.

In the light of judicial precedent there was some basis to believe that the Supreme Court might hold manufacturing beyond the scope of the Wagner Act. In 1894 the Court held that "commerce succeeds to manufacturing and is not a part of it."[9] In 1936, in the *Carter Coal* case, the Court could not see how regulating the labor relations of a coal company advanced and safeguarded interstate commerce.[10] Although the *Carter Coal* case did not involve the manufacturing industry, the 1936 decision represented a line of reasoning that indicated a limited construction of interstate commerce and caused considerable uncertainty about the future of the Act. Thus, in the *Carter* case, decided *after the passage of* the Wagner Act, the Court declared that

> mining brings the subject matter of commerce into existence. Commerce disposes of it. A consideration of the foregoing . . . renders inescapable the conclusion that the effect of the labor provision of the [Bituminous Coal Conservation Act], including those in respect of minimum wages, wage agreements, collective bargaining, and the Labor Board and its powers, primarily falls upon production and not upon commerce; and confirms the further resulting conclusion that production is a purely local activity. It follows that none of these essential antecedents of production constitutes a transaction in or forms any part of interstate commerce.

Such language of the Court appeared almost to preclude the application of the Wagner Act to manufacturing facilities.

Balanced against the foregoing, some factors served to support the view that the Wagner Act would be sustained and its terms applied to manufacturing. As noted, a great number of organizational strikes occurred after the employees of the nation became aware that the NLRB could not effectively carry out the provisions of the new labor policy. The vast majority of these strikes occurred in the nation's manufacturing facilities. Some of the strikes were unprecedented in scope, intensity, and destruction. They resulted in destruction of property, in physical injury, and in loss of life. Such developments were likely to have an effect on the Supreme Court. Moreover, the Court must have been impressed with the overwhelming reelection of Roosevelt in 1936. The result of the election, in which Roosevelt failed to receive the electoral votes of only Maine and Vermont, served to underscore the people's satisfaction with New Deal policies in that they were willing to experiment in areas previously considered best left alone. It was reasonable to believe that the Court would consider these election results. Finally, the threat of Roosevelt to "pack" the Supreme Court must have had some influence on its members. Impressed by his astounding success at the polls, Roosevelt was reluctant to permit the Supreme Court complete freedom to evaluate New Deal policies. He was determined to satisfy the demands of the people that social legislation be implemented. Accordingly, he proposed legislation which would have minimized the influence of the conservative element of the Supreme Court. Even though Congress refused to enact the law, the attempt undoubtedly left its mark on the members of the Court. Alternatively, it was clear from the legislative history of the Act exactly what Congress intended. This was not the case in much of the earlier legislation dealing with labor policy.

THE JONES & LAUGHLIN DECISION

Such was the environment in which the Supreme Court ruled on the Wagner Act. The nation was aware of the magnitude of the forthcoming decision and, as perhaps never before, anxiously awaited the high court's decision. Labor hoped for a clear-cut decision of constitutionality, for it would mean legal protection of bargaining rights. Many employers were hopeful of an opposite ruling, for that would mean little government influence in the collective bargaining process. The issue was settled in April 1937 in the case involving the Jones & Laughlin Steel Company.[11] By a slim majority of a single vote, the Supreme Court upheld the Wagner Act and, of equal importance, validated its application to the manufacturing sector of the American economy. On the majority were Chief Justice Hughes and Associate Justices Roberts, Stone, Cardozo, and Brandeis.

As some observers expected, the minority of the Court was composed of Sutherland, McReynolds, Van Devanter, and Butler. Once again, these men affirmed that constitutional prohibitions precluded the government from aiding and encouraging union organizations to establish collective bargaining. The minority group held that employers could utilize any antiunion tactic to defeat the collective bargaining process. The minority held that the *Texas & New Orleans* decision did not apply to a proceeding involving a manufacturing establishment. It was further avowed that the government could regulate the labor relations of the railroads, for this industry was considered a part of interstate commerce. But it was argued that Congress violated the Constitution by endeavoring to protect the right of workers to collective bargaining in manufacturing, for this industry was not a part of commerce. In short, whatever happened in the manufacturing industry did not directly affect trade among the states. Should a strike in manufacturing result from the discharge of workers because of union activities, or from the refusal of an employer to bargain collectively, the effect upon commerce was "far too indirect to justify congressional regulation." One may take issue with this point of view. For example, if the steel industry was shut down because of the relutance of the owners to recognize the steelworkers' union, there would likely be a real and substantial effect upon interstate commerce. The effect would depend upon the extent of stockpiling in anticipation of the work stoppage. On the other hand, the lack of worker income to expend upon consumer goods would have an indirect effect on commerce. Such a strike, for whatever reason, would mean that there would be no steel for shipment between the states. Production is as essential for interstate commerce as are the transportation facilities which carry the goods from one state to another. The breakdown of either production or transportation means that there is an effect on interstate commerce. On the basis of these practical observations, the position of the minority group in the *Jones & Laughlin* decision appears untenable and unrealistic. In any event the group held that the federal government could not lawfully regulate the labor relations of a manufacturing facility. Manufacturing, these members concluded, was not a part of interstate commerce and consequently the Constitution prohibited federal control over the steel industry.

This point of view was not shared by the majority of the Court. Chief Justice Hughes, speaking for the Court, declared that strikes in manufacturing facilities, such as in a steel mill, "would have a most serious effect upon interstate commerce." The majority argued that it was proper for Congress to take action to prohibit employers from interfering with the right of workers to bargain collectively because organizational strikes might result in "catastrophic" effects on commerce. In masterful language, Hughes struck at the contention of the minority that the effect of organizational strikes in commerce would be "indirect or remote." Thus Hughes remarked:

> We are asked to shut our eyes at the plainest facts of our national life and to deal with the question of direct and indirect effects in an intellectual vacuum. Because there may be but indirect and remote effects upon interstate commerce in connection with a host of local enterprises throughout the country, it does not follow that other industrial activities do not have such a close and intimate relation to interstate commerce as to make the presence of industrial strife a matter of the most urgent national concern. When industries organize themselves on a national scale, making their relation to interstate commerce the dominant factor in their activities, how can it be maintained that their industrial labor relations constitute a forbidden field into which Congress may not enter when it is necessary to protect interstate commerce from the paralyzing consequences of industrial war?

It was by use of such language that the Supreme Court upheld the Wagner Act's application to manufacturing. The entire theory of the authors of the law was given judicial approval. It was accepted by the Court that not only did organizational strikes involving the railroads or other instrumentalities of commerce burden trade between the states, but work stoppages in manufacturing, resulting from employer antiunion activities, likewise burdened interstate commerce. It was deemed proper therefore for Congress to eliminate the causes of such strikes because such action protected and promoted interstate commerce.[12]

Beyond dealing with the applicability of the Wagner Act to manufacturing, the Supreme Court directed its attention to another constitutional question. Did the statute violate the due process clause of the Fifth Amendment to the Constitution? Again the majority of the Court upheld the statute. It was held that the procedural provisions of the law adequately protected employers from the arbitrary action of the NLRB. Foremost in this connection, the Court stressed that the judiciary constituted the ultimate source of enforcement authority for the provisions of the law.

As will be pointed out below, an employer aggrieved with a decision of the Board has the right to appeal to the courts. Not only was the Wagner Act upheld with respect to the procedural aspects of due process, but the Court held also that the substance of the Wagner Act did not deprive an employer of his property or liberty without due process of law. On this point the majority leaned heavily on the *Texas & New Orleans* decision. Since manufacturing was deemed to fall within the concept of interstate commerce, the railroad decision was applicable. Thus the Court in the *Jones & Laughlin* decision reaffirmed the principle that law "cannot be considered arbitrary or capricious if it prohibits interference with the right of workers to self-organization."

It is important to stress that even if the Court held the law applicable to manufacturing, the Wagner Act could have been declared unconstitutional on the basis of interfering arbitrarily and unreasonably with the freedom of employers to run their businesses. However, the Court refused to hold unlawful a statute that protected the right of workers to collective bargaining. Since workers were extended the right to collective bargaining by both the judiciary and legislature, it appeared reasonable and prudent that government outlaw practices calculated to prevent self-organization and collective bargaining. Such was the conclusion of the Supreme Court.

Thus on April 12, 1937, the Supreme Court validated the Wagner Act. Not only were its terms consistent with the due-process clause of the Constitution, but the application of the law was to cover general industrial facilities. The *Jones & Laughlin* decision represented, perhaps, the most important pronouncement of the Supreme Court with respect to organized labor. At the time it constituted one of the most favorable decisions in the interest of the nation's workers. It made possible the implementation of public policy promoting collective bargaining.

SUBSTANTIVE PROVISIONS:
UNFAIR LABOR PRACTICES

The Wagner Act made collective bargaining a matter of public policy. Section 7 of the statute declared: "employees shall have the right to self-organization, to form, join or assist labor organizations, to bargain collectively through representatives of their own choosing, and to engage in concerted activities, for the purpose of collective bargaining or other mutual aid or protection." To make this right effective, Congress outlawed employer practices that operated to deny workers the freedom to carry out the collective bargaining function. In short, Congress was not content merely to state that workers have the right to self-organization and collective bargaining. It was determined to prohibit interference with the exercise of that right.

To accomplish the Section 7 objective, Section 8 of the Wagner Act sets forth five *unfair labor practices*. These practices were declared unlawful. Subsequently, attention will be devoted to methods by which the Wagner Act provides for remedies when employers violate the terms of Section 8. At this time we are concerned with the nature of the unfair labor practice.

Section 8 (a) (1). This section makes it an unfair labor practice for an employer to "interfere with, restrain, or coerce employees in the exercise of their rights under

Section 7. Independent interferences with employees' rights may occur exclusive of any other violation specified by Section 8 (a). The NLRB has held that violations of Section 8 (a) (1) exist when employees are: (1) threatened with the loss of their jobs or other reprisals; (2) granted wage increases timed to discourage union member-ship; and (3) questioned by employers about union activities under such circum-stances as will tend to coerce them in the exercise of their rights under Section 7.[13] Independent violations have also been declared when the working places or homes of employees were placed under surveillance by employers to the extent that reason-able communication regarding organization was restricted. In this regard the utili-zation of industrial spies constitutes a violation. An independent violation has been held when a sales manager, representing the employer, offered a more lucrative job in another city to an employee if he would drop his union activities.

Although the Wagner Act did not prevent an employer from utilizing his eco-nomic power to defeat a strike by peaceful means, the NLRB has ruled that a firm interfered with the right to self-organization by hiring strikebreakers for the purpose of provoking violence or creating fear in the minds of employees. When the NLRB held that the Mohawk Valley Formula,[14] a systematic procedure for breaking strikes, violated the Wagner Act, it stated, "Those activities were employed to defeat the strike, end the strike, rather than settling it through collective bargaining."[15] Inciting to violence against union organizers and members of labor organizations was also deemed an unfair labor practice. In one case the company violated the subsection of the law when a forelady incited to violence against a union organizer by suggesting to the employees in her section: "What do you say girls, we give her a beating?"[16]

Some of the unfair labor practices during World War II had a distinct wartime flavor. A number of employers utilized the wartime environment to interfere, re-strain, or coerce workers from exercising their right to self-organization and collec-tive bargaining. A violation of the National Labor Relations Act was found in which an employer posted notices throughout his plant suggesting that union organizers were a group of "intimidators" and threatened the "substitution of Naziism for Americanism."[17] Nor was an employer permitted to assert that a union was "backed by Germans" when the intent was to discourage unlawfully membership in the organization. A supervisor implicated his employer in an unfair labor practice by intimating that the company would not ask for occupational army service deferment for an employee if the worker persisted in union activities. Employers were not permit-ted to distribute "I am an American" buttons to their employees not wearing union buttons. The obvious inference that union members were not loyal Americans evidently prompted the Board's decision. Effecting the arrest of persons distributing union literature in a plant was deemed unlawful, even though the employer urged that the plant was engaged in secret war work and that the persons jailed might have been spies and saboteurs. It was noted that a labor union was organizing the plant's workers when the employer procured the arrest. Nor did the Board sustain the argument that employers could engage in unfair labor practices with impunity because the company was producing materials for the exclusive use of the govern-ment. The NLRB further ruled that an employer engaged in an unfair labor practice when he appealed to his workers' patriotism to defeat a union in a bargaining election by drawing a contrast between the hardships endured by men in the armed forces and the attempts of the employees to better their economic position through organization. On the other hand, the Board found no violation of the Wagner Act when union members were discharged because they had violated a Federal Bureau of Investigation domestic security measure. These employees were not permitted to utilize their union status as a bar to dismissal.

During the war period the NLRB established another source of subsection 1 violation. Wartime wage increases were prohibited unless approved by the National War Labor Board. Consequently, one of the most effective appeals that a trade union could make to maintain its membership was impaired for the duration of the war. To compensate in part for this wartime condition, the NLRB ruled that an employer violated the Wagner Act if he refused to consult with the representatives of his employees' labor organization before filing a wage increase application with the NWLB.

Section 8 (a) (1) of the act is so constituted that a violation of any of its sub-sections by clear implication is of necessity interference, restraint, or coercion in the exercise of Section 7 rights. A refusal-to-bargain violation, for example, is not only expressly in violation of Section 8 (a) (5), which makes it an unfair labor practice, but of necessity interferes with the Section 7 right to "bargain collectively through representatives of their own choosing." Such 8 (a) (1) infringements that also violate specific provisions of the Act are derivative violations.

Section 8 (a) (2). "Domination or interference with the formation or administration of a labor organization or contribution of financial or other support to it" is a viola-tion of Section 8 (a) (2). It has already been pointed out that a union that is the creature of an employer does not constitute a proper vehicle for the carrying out of the collective bargaining process. Congress was well aware of this fact and consequent-ly outlawed employer domination of labor unions. The NLRB, however, was required to spell out the circumstances under which an employer dominates a labor organiza-tion. Specifically, what are the characteristics of an employer-controlled union?

The Board has found a union to be company-dominated in a case where the employer told his employees that they should establish a union and indicated the form that the labor organization should take. If an employer or his representatives actively solicits members on behalf of a labor organization, such a union is illegal. A union may be company-dominated when the employer provides the union with bulletin boards, a company automobile, and stenographic service or office space.

The Board has held that, by advancing money to employees who were unable to pay membership dues, a company contributed support to a union and the organi-zation was ordered dissolved. Another union was held company-dominated because the employer permitted members of the organization to solicit members for the union on the employer's property during working hours and, most important, with the consent of the employer. In the case of the *Highway Trailer Company*,[18] employees were fired and threatened with discharge because of their refusal to join the organi-zation for which the employer had expressed his preference, and consequently the NLRB ordered the organization dissolved.

Other employer practices that indicate a labor organization is the creature of the company include those instances in which the employer has suggested the form of the constitution; in which a few hand-picked employees have been urged to create the organization; and in which management has been willing and eager to sign agreements with the organization it helped to create.

An important criterion in determining whether a labor organization is company-dominated may be the extent of collective bargaining between the union and management. The NLRB said:

> If the organization did not make any effort to meet with the employer concerned, and other features of the labor organization are indicative of company-domination, the Board may conclude, on the basis of the laxity in petitioning for a meeting on the part of the labor organization, that the employee's organization is the creature of the employer.[19]

Not only is neglecting to meet with management material evidence that the labor organization is company-dominated but, even though conferences do occur, the labor organization in question may be deemed company-dominated if the negotiations "be such as to reveal the employer's domination of the organization."[20]

On the other hand, the Board adopted a number of principles to determine whether an organization is independent of employer domination. Thus, if members of the organization hold regular meetings on property other than the company's; if members of the union pay dues; if the union has written agreements with the company; if the organization has contacts with other workers' organizations; if the union has the right to demand arbitration of differences whereby management abandons absolute veto power—the Board held such characteristics indicate clearly that the organization is its own master and is free to submit the real wishes of its members to management.

Discrimination in Hire or Tenure. Section 8 (a) (3) makes it an unfair practice for employers to discriminate "in regard to hire or tenure of employment on any term or condition of employment to encourage or discourage membership in a labor organization." This clause was directed against the most common and highly effective antiunion weapon—the discharge of workers who are union members or those who would promote the formation of a labor union. By adopting this provision, Congress endeavored to erase fear from the minds of union-conscious workers. Again, the Wagner Act charged the NLRB with the duty of interpreting and carrying out the terms of the provision. What constitutes discrimination? Is transferring an employee to an inferior job because of union activity discrimination within the meaning of the Act? Can union workers ever be discharged? What evidence will the Board consider material in determining whether an employer truly discriminated against workers for union activity?

The most common form of discrimination that the Board declared an unfair labor practice was discharge of an employee for union activity. When the evidence in a case proved that an employee was discharged because of union activity, the Board ordered his reinstatement. In most instances the employer denied that he discharged an employee, or otherwise discriminated against him, for union activity and consequently the NLRB would investigate to determine whether there really was discrimination prohibited by the Wagner Act. When an employer denied that discharges or other forms of claimed discrimination were within the meaning of the Act, the Board took into account the entire background of the case, reviewing the totality of circumstances to determine the nature of employer action against employees.

Not only will an employer usually maintain that he did not discriminate against an employee on the grounds of union activity, but in nearly all cases he will tender some reasons to the Board for discharging an employee. The most common alleged reason given for the discharge is the employer's claim that the worker was inefficient. In determining whether the employee was inefficient or whether this was a subterfuge for dismissal for union activities, the NLRB considers the following facts: (1) length of total employment; (2) experience in the particular position from which the employee was discharged; (3) efficiency ratings by qualified persons; (4) specific acts showing efficiency or inefficiency; and (5) comparison with other employees. Other reasons advanced for discharge include decrease in production, insubordination, infraction of company rules, fighting, and swearing. In all instances the NLRB will determine if the reasons have "color and substance" or whether they are only a convenient pretext designed to defeat the law.

An employer discriminates against an employee and thereby engages in an unfair labor practice if he refuses employment to persons because of their former or current membership in a labor organization. Moreover, an employer not only engages in an unfair labor practice by discriminating against an employee in regard to hire or tenure of employment, but discrimination can also occur in respect to other conditions of work. In one case the Board found the company discriminated against employees, transferring the men to a very difficult section of the firm as punishment for their union activities, or with the intention of making them quit. One union man would have had to move twenty to twenty-five cars of rock and dirt, and in so doing would have been forced to work for a month without pay. Another instance of discrimination occurred when an employer transferred a worker to another position in which he had no experience, with the motive of firing him for the inefficient work which would result.

The Board has also construed discrimination to include those instances in which an employer has temporarily laid off men for union activity. Refusal to reinstate employees because of union activity also is discrimination within the meaning of the Wagner Act. Other forms of discrimination include those cases in which an employer forces a man engaged in union activities to work the worst shifts; pays more wages to a nonunion man than to a union man doing equal work; violates seniority rules; discharges a man's wife because he is a union member.

A case before the U.S. Supreme Court involved the issue of whether an employer, Deering Milliken, owning several plants violated the discrimination provisions of the Act when he permanently closed down one of his plants for antiunion reasons.[21] The plant which was shut down was located in Darlington, S.C. The Darlington case was first taken before the NLRB as a result of unfair labor practices growing out of a plant shutdown after a vigorous company campaign to resist union organizational efforts. In March 1956, when the organizational campaign was initiated, the company interrogated employees and threatened to close the Darlington plant if the Textile Workers Union won the election. On September 6, 1956, the union prevailed in the Board-held election by a narrow margin. The decision was made to liquidate the plant. Employees were informed by the company that the reason for such a decision was the election result and encouragement was extended for employees to sign a petition disavowing the union. The Board found Darlington in violation of the discrimination provision of the Act. The Board ordered back pay for all employees until they obtained substantially equivalent work or were put on preferential hiring lists at the other Deering Milliken mills. Upon review, the second court of appeals denied enforcement and argued that a company had an absolute right to close out a part or all of its business regardless of antiunion motives.

The U.S. Supreme Court reviewed the case in 1965 and agreed partially with the court of appeals. It held that a single employer could go out of business completely for whatever reason he chose. But "a discriminatory partial closing may have repercussions on what remains of the business, affording employer leverage for discouraging the free exercise of Section 7 rights among remaining employees of much the same kind as that found to exist in the 'runaway shop' and 'temporary closing' cases."[22] The Court held that "a partial closing is an unfair labor practice under Section 8 (a) (3) if motivated by a purpose to chill unionism in any of the remaining plants of the single employer and if the employer may reasonably have foreseen . . . that effect."[23]

A more specific test was provided by the Court for resolving such cases. It stated that:

> If the persons exercising control over a plant that is being closed for antiunion reasons (1) have an interest in another business, whether or not affiliated with or engaged in the same line of commercial activity as the closed plant, of sufficient substantiality to give promise of their reaping a benefit from the discouragement of unionization in that business; (2) act to close their plant with the purpose of producing such a result; and (3) occupy a relationship to the other business which makes it realistically foreseeable that its employees will fear that such business will also be closed down if they persist in organizational activities, we think that an unfair labor practice has been made out.[24]

The Board had ruled only on the basis of the effect the plant closing had on Darlington employees. The Court test required that a determination be made regarding the effect such closing had on the employees in other plants owned and operated by the Deering Milliken group. In June 1967 the NLRB held that there was sufficient evidence to support the charge that the shutdown of the Darlington plant was for the purpose, at least in part, of discouraging union membership in other plants owned by Deering Milliken. It also found that the closing had a "chilling" effect on the other plant employees as far as union activity was concerned.

Discrimination with regard to hire or tenure will be held only if employees in other plants are affected by the antiunion behavior of an employer. A decision will have to be made in each case since a partial closing will not constitute a per se violation of the Act. However, it seems clear that multiplant firms cannot make antiunion decisions in one plant without intending the same result to spill over onto all the others.

Before concluding this section on discrimination, it may be of value to point out that an employer under the Wagner Act had the opportunity to discharge, or otherwise discriminate against his employees, for any reason except upon the grounds of union activity. It must not be forgotten that the employer retained his right to discharge an employee for other causes: disobedience, bad work, carelessness, drinking on duty, and so on. The law only forbade an employer from discriminating in any way against a worker solely for membership or activity in a union.

Protection of Board Integrity. Section 8 (a) (4) also prohibits employers from discharging or otherwise discriminating against an employee because he has filed charges or given testimony under the Wagner Act. Thus Congress provided protection for workers who might bring a charge against an employer alleging violation of the terms of the law. Moreover, since the procedures of the Wagner Act require hearings and court proceedings, it was reasonable to forbid discrimination against workers who would participate in such proceedings. The Board has in the past interpreted such employer behavior a violation of Section 8 (a) (3) as well.

Refusal to Bargain. Finally, Section 8 (a) (5) of the Wagner Act makes it an unfair labor practice for an employer to refuse to bargain collectively with the representatives of his employees. By this provision Congress intended partly to eliminate the need for the recognition strike. Since employers would be required to bargain collectively, workers would not find it necessary to strike for the recognition of the union. Moreover, this portion of Section 8 actually constitutes the heart of the Wagner Act, for it was enacted to promote the collective bargaining process once a bargaining unit was established. Once more the NLRB was required to implement public policy. Specifically, what must an employer do in order to fulfill his legal obligation to bargain collectively? The answer to this problem is embedded in scores of NLRB decisions and orders. A brief analysis of them will reveal the character of employer behavior that satisfies the requirement of the law.

In the first place, if an employer refuses to meet representatives of his employees, he has failed to bargain collectively and has engaged in an unfair labor practice. Of course, the labor organization must make a proper demand on the employer requesting collective bargaining. A demand to bargain must come from the proper source of the union and must be clearly presented to the representatives of the company who usually deal with matters concerning labor relations. A casual remark is not a sufficient demand, but a request for collective bargaining by registered letter is sufficient.

In practice employers have advanced various excuses for their refusal to meet or to bargain collectively with representatives of their employees. The Board held in this respect that an employer is not relieved of his duty to bargain collectively by the outbreak of a strike; by shutting down his factory (lockout); or by asserting that pension demands of the union are not proper subjects for negotiations.

A more definite action of some employers to avoid collective bargaining is evidenced in their attempts to undermine unions by engaging in other unfair labor practices. There is, of course, no duty to bargain if the union does not represent a majority of employees in the appropriate unit. Thus employers on occasion have attempted to evade their duty to bargain collectively by attempting to destroy the majority status of the union. The Board has ruled, however, that an employer who engages in unfair labor practices resulting in the destruction of the majority status of the labor organization is not relieved of his duty to bargain collectively with the representatives of that union.

Employers must do more than just meet with the representatives and merely go through the motions of bargaining. To satisfy the requirement of collective bargaining, an employer must bargain in "good faith."[25] In defining the term, the Board held that an employer to bargain in good faith "must work toward a solution, satisfactory to both sides, of the various problems under discussion by presentation of counter-proposals and other affirmative conduct."[26] In another case the Board declared that "the obligation of the Act is to produce more than a series of empty discussions, bargaining must mean more than mere negotiations. It must mean negotiations with a bona fide intent to reach an agreement if agreement is possible."[27]

The behavior of the employer at the meeting itself may indicate his desire to bargain in good faith. A conference completely dominated by the employer, with the representatives of the union mere auditors to the proceedings, has been held to constitute evidence that the employer does not desire to bargain collectively. If an employer makes no attempt to offer counter-proposals during the meeting, the Board has ruled that such action indicates that the employer refuses to bargain in good faith. "The Board has considered counter-proposals so important an element of collective bargaining that it has found the failure to offer counter-proposals to be persuasive of the fact that the employer has not bargained in good faith."[28]

In a series of decisions the NLRB has maintained that the nature of the employer's conduct after he was requested to bargain collectively is indicative of whether he desired to negotiate in good faith. An employer does not intend to bargain in good faith when he, after being asked to bargain collectively, restrains and interferes with the employees' right to self-organization; when he attempts to bargain with individual employees; and when he calls a general meeting of his employees, dominates such meetings, and therein attacks the union.

The Wagner Act declared that a labor organization designated by the majority of the employees in a unit appropriate for collective bargaining shall be the exclusive representative of all employees in such unit for the purposes of collective bargaining in respect to rates of pay, wages, hours, or other conditions of work. Thus the Board held early in its career that an employer engaged in an unfair labor practice when he refused to recognize a union as the exclusive representative of all the employees in the bargaining unit. Not only must an employer recognize a labor organization as the representative of all employees in the appropriate unit, but he must bargain collectively with the union for all the employees in the unit regardless of whether all are members of the union.

The Board established a rule that if an agreement between a company and a labor organization has been reached through discussion, such an agreement must be embodied in a written contract. In other words, an employer does not fulfill his obligation to bargain collectively and thereby engages in an unfair labor practice if he refuses to reduce an agreement reached orally into a written trade agreement. In dealing with the matter, the NLRB declared in one case that "an assertion that collective bargaining connotes no more than discussions designed to clarify employer policy and does not include negotiations looking toward a binding agreement is contrary to any realistic view of labor relations. The protection to organization of employees afforded by the first four subdivisions of Section 8 can have meaning only when the ultimate goal is viewed as the stabilization of working conditions through genuine bargaining and (written) agreement between equals."[29] Eventually, the Supreme Court of the United States upheld this policy of the NLRB.[30]

Although the NLRB imposed upon employers the duty to bargain collectively, the law does not require that the parties must reach an agreement. Consequently, when an impasse in the negotiations between an employer and the representatives of his employees occurs, the employer is not required to continue to bargain collectively. When differences develop between parties over substantial issues and the employer bargained in good faith, the NLRB has declared that an employer has fulfilled his collective bargaining obligations. If, however, the situation should change and new issues are introduced, the employer must resume the process of collective bargaining.

The *General Electric* case, decided by the NLRB on December 16, 1964, placed most of the required standards for good faith bargaining in perspective.[31] The General Electric Company was held in violation of the bargaining provision of the Act for its (1) failure to furnish at the proper time relevant information requested by the union, (2) attempts to bypass national negotiations by dealing separately with the local unions on matters at issue and soliciting their nonsupport of the national union's strike position, (3) manner of presentation of an insurance proposal on a take-it-or-leave-it basis, and (4) overall attitude or approach as evidenced by the totality of conduct.

The technique (known as "Boulwarism," named after a former vice-president, L. R. Boulware, who invented this form of bargaining) developed for national collective bargaining negotiations involved extensive year-round research into various items to determine what was "right" for employees. The company studied business conditions, competitive factors, and economic trends. It also studied employee needs and desires through independent employee attitude surveys. In addition to the attitude survey, comments made by employees at informative meetings were studied along with discussions supervisors held with employees.

The company argued that at the initial bargaining sessions it listened to union presentations and thereafter reviewed their demands along with all the other information collected earlier through its research efforts. A determination was then made by management regarding what was the "right" package for all its employees. The offer made to the unions and employees was its pat offer. The argument was advanced that nothing was held back to form the basis of trade or compromise in later bargaining sessions. However, the offer was not considered one of "take-it-or-leave-it" since the company professed a willingness to make adjustments if new information from any source could be presented to convince it that the offer fell short of being right. The company then proceeded to inform employees it would endure a strike before doing something it considered wrong.

The employer then developed an extensive communications campaign among its employees for the purpose of marketing its bargaining position to them. The campaign was calculated to bypass the international union and deal directly with the local unions. The Board held that the purpose of such action was "to seek to persuade the employees to exert pressure on the representative to submit to the will of the employer, and to create the impression that the employer rather than the union is the true protector of the employees' interest." As such the Board held that the employer failed to meet its statutory obligation "to deal with the employees through the union, and not with the union through the employees."

The employer's conduct at the bargaining table was also condemned by the Board. It held that the approach devised by the company was akin to entering "into negotiations with a predetermined resolve not to budge from an initial position." It was emphasized that the "auction" system of give-and-take bargaining had to exist as evidence that the parties were engaged in good-faith collective bargaining. Otherwise, the union role of statutory representative of employees would be reduced to merely an advisory role to the employer. In 1970, the Supreme Court refused to review the NLRB position on "Boulwarism," but the decision had little practical effect since, during a three-month strike in 1969, General Electric itself appeared to have departed from this form of bargaining.

Board Developed Union Responsibilities

Over the years in which the Wagner Act was in effect, the Board administered the unfair labor practice portion of the law in a vigorous manner. By checking employer antiunion practices, it gave substantial support to the growth of unions. The results of the Board's work in this direction are recorded in a following section of this chapter. However, as unions grew stronger, the attitude of the public toward them underwent a change. A growing number of people were becoming less tolerant toward organized labor. The changing climate of opinion was in part attributable to the antisocial activities of some unions. In some cases the growing power of unions was not matched by an increasing degree of social responsibility on the part of union leadership.

This changing attitude was felt at the NLRB. Its members were aware of the growing tide of antiunion sentiment in the nation. As a result the Board's policies in unfair labor practice cases underwent a significant change. It began to search for ways in which the Wagner Act could impose obligations on unions even though the law did not contain any unfair labor practices for unions. There was, however, another factor making for this change in NLRB policy. Undoubtedly the Board tried to make the statute appear more favorable to employers to forestall sweeping and fundamental changes in the Wagner Act.

There were several ways in which the NLRB utilized the Wagner Act to impose obligations on labor unions. In 1947 the NLRB handed down its decision in the celebrated *Times Publishing* case. It held that an employer was under no obligation to bargain with a labor organization which itself did not bargain collectively in good faith. In establishing this policy, the Board stated:

> The test of good faith in bargaining that the Act requires of an employer is not a rigid but a fluctuating one, and is dependent in part upon how a reasonable man might be expected to react to the bargaining attitude displayed by those across the table. It follows that, although the Act imposes no affirmative duty to bargain upon labor organizations, a union's refusal to bargain in good faith may remove the possibility of negotiation and thus preclude the existence of a situation in which the employer's own good faith can be tested. If it cannot be tested, its absence can hardly be found.[32]

In another case in 1947 the Board held that employees who participated in a strike, the purpose of which was to compel an employer to recognize and bargain with the union of the striking employees rather than with a certified labor organization, were not entitled to reinstatement.[33] Thus, to obtain the protection of the Wagner Act, unions and their members were not permitted to force employers to recognize one union when another organization had been certified for collective bargaining. During World War II, the Board under another set of circumstances refused to order the reinstatement of strikers. It happened that a union called a strike to force an employer to violate the wage stabilization orders and procedures of the National War Labor Board. The employer discharged the workers, and the NLRB held that they lost their reinstatement right under the Act because the union engaged in an illegal strike.[34]

EVOLUTION OF RACIAL DISCRIMINATION POLICY

During the Wagner Act years the Board attempted to induce labor organizations to cease the practice of racial discrimination. To this end, the NLRB refused to set up bargaining units on the basis of racial lines, stating, "The color or race of employees is an irrelevant and extraneous consideration in determining in any case the unit for collective bargaining."[35] Moreover, the NLRB often refused to certify labor organizations that engaged in discriminatory practices. On this issue the NLRB in 1943 declared, "We entertain grave doubts whether a union which discriminatorily denied membership to employees on the basis of race may nevertheless bargain as the exclusive representative in an appropriate unit composed in part of members of the excluded race."[36] The Wagner Act, however, did not make any conduct by a labor union unlawful. Prior to 1962 the Board had not utilized unfair labor practice provisions against employers for racial discrimination unless union activity was an integral part of the case.[37] In the *Miranda* case, the Board declared that Section 7 rights were inferred in the election provisions of the Act whereby employees have the right to be free from unfair treatment in matters affecting their employment.[38] Should an employer submit to union demands to treat an employee unfairly, the employer is in violation of Section 8 (a) (1) and 8 (a) (3) provisions. However, the Second Circuit denied enforcement on grounds that employer discrimination is not in violation of Section 8 (a) (3) if such is wholly unrelated to union activity. That is, the position was taken that Section 7 rights of employees to bargain collectively applied only in cases involving union conduct that encourages or discourages union membership. Essentially, the court was of the opinion that once bargaining representatives were established, the Section 7 rights of employees were assured. Section 8 (a) (1) and 8 (b) (1) (A) were interpreted as not guaranteeing employees the right to fair representation.[39] Thus the unfair labor practice provisions were not applicable in the day-to-day implementation of the collective bargaining agreement.

The U.S. Supreme Court declared in a 1944 case that Section 9 (a) of the Wagner Act imposed upon unions the duty to provide "fair representation" of all employees in an exclusive bargaining unit.[40] Neither the Wagner Act nor later amendments mentioned a duty of fair representation. Enforcement of this duty was recognized as falling within the exclusive jurisdiction of the courts until 1962 when the Board considered it had the responsibility to employees and union members to assure them of fair representation in all aspects of collective bargaining. As mentioned, the Second Circuit Court of Appeals disagreed with the Board and denied enforcement.

The Board was not deterred by the adverse treatment it received in *Miranda* and in a 1964 case involving racial discrimination it ruled that the union thereby refused to bargain, since a majority union has the statutory obligation to represent fairly all employees in a collective bargaining unit.[41] The *Hughes Tool Company* case arose when a local union comprising only white employees refused to consider a grievance filed by a member of a jointly certified local union comprised entirely of Negro employees. Refusal to process an employee's grievance was solely for reasons of race. Refusal to consider the grievance for processing was held to be, in effect, a situation where the local acted only for the benefit of its members. It had the *statutory duty* to represent all employees in the bargaining unit irrespective of membership. The Board further held that there was no statutory language limiting a union's bargaining obligation as owed only to employers. [42] The obligation to bargain was a duty owed equally to employees. The Board decision was not controlled by the *Miranda* reversal in the court of appeals, but by the Supreme Court opinion handed down after that case. Determination of the question of the duty of fair representation as redressable by unfair labor practice charges was held open by the Supreme Court.[43] The Board interpreted this as granting it the authority to rule on the issue. It was suggested in the case that the employer owed an obligation under Section 8 (a) (5) not to enter into contracts permitting invidious discrimination.

The Board further declared in a later case that perpetuation of discriminatory provisions in a collective bargaining agreement was "ground upon the irrelevant, invidious, and unfair considerations of race or union membership." Such a situation was adjudged in violation of union responsibility under the Act in that the labor organization caused an employer to discriminate against employees in violation of Section 8 (a) (3). It is clear that the Board does not intend to free employers from responsibility for attempting to alleviate racial injustice in employment.

In 1966 the Fifth Circuit Court of Appeals reviewed a determination by the NLRB that a labor union engaged in unfair labor practices when it refused to process grievances of Negroes in the bargaining unit.[44] Local 12 had been the exclusive bargaining agent for employees of a Goodyear Alabama plant since 1943. Three separate seniority lists had been maintained until 1962. Separate rolls were provided for white males, Negro males, and females. It was the custom that Negroes with greater seniority had no rights over white employees with less seniority with respect to promotions, transfers, layoffs, and recall. Separate facilities were also maintained on the basis of race. Eight Negroes approached the president of Local 12 and requested grievance action to remedy their being laid off while whites with less seniority remained on the job. Additionally, it was alleged that new employees were hired while they were still on layoff status. Back pay was asked for by the Negroes. The local union refused to process the grievances and the Board held that this was an unfair labor practice. The issue before the court of appeals was to determine whether a breach of the duty of fair representation in itself constituted an unfair labor practice within the framework of the National Labor Relations Act.

The Fifth Circuit Court of Appeals, contrary to the Second Circuit Court of Appeals, held that "the duty of fair representation was implicit in the exclusive representation requirement of Section 9 (a) of the act . . . as guaranteed in Section 7." As such, remedial action was considered available to the Board through the unfair labor practice provisions of national labor laws. Additionally, the Fifth Circuit Court argued that breaches of the duty to provide fair representation were within the primary jurisdiction of the Board.[45]

It is significant to note that the Fifth Circuit Court upheld the Board proposal to the employer in the *Rubber Workers* case to incorporate provisions in the collective bargaining contract aimed at prohibiting continued racial discrimination in terms and conditions of employment. It is obvious that the Board will invoke unfair labor practice charges against both unions and employers for the purpose of dealing with racial discrimination. The unfair labor practices of refusal to bargain and discrimination with regard to hire and tenure will be utilized to achieve the goal of racial justice in collective bargaining relations. It took the Board nearly thirty years to move forcibly into this area.

In a 1969 case the District of Columbia Circuit Court of Appeals upheld and went beyond a Board decision that the existence of racial discrimination was a proper subject for bargaining.[46] The federal court also ruled that discrimination may be an unfair labor practice in and of itself. The Supreme Court refused to review the decision. As noted above, the NLRB has long held that racial discrimination by unions violates the Taft-Hartley Act. The *Farmers' Cooperative Compress* case may mean that both employer and union racial discrimination cases can be decided by the NLRB.[47]

MODERN POLICY: EQUAL EMPLOYMENT OPPORTUNITY

Though discrimination problems have been handled by the NLRB, Civil Rights legislation endorsed by Congress constitutes the cornerstone of national policy calculated to provide equal opportunity in employment and union membership. The Civil Rights Act of 1964 was passed to deal with racial and sex discrimination in employment. Title VII of the 1964 law was not very effective because of the lack of enforcement machinery. It created an Equal Employment Opportunity Commission (EEOC), which is a five-person independent agency with appointments to it made by the President with the consent of the Senate.

The Equal Employment Opportunity Act of 1972 was passed to correct some of the deficiencies of the Civil Rights Act. The Equal Employment Opportunity Commission was reorganized along the lines of the NLRB. An independent General Counsel was named and made responsible for litigation. Three new groups of employers were also brought under the law. These were: (1) public and private educational institutions, (2) state and local governments, and (3) employers and unions with 15 or more members.

The Equal Employment Opportunity Commission set forth guidelines in 1965 to deal with discriminatory employment practices. These guidelines became far more meaningful because of the 1972 amendments to Title VII and will be used in all of the Commission's deliberations. The guidelines will be discussed briefly.

RECRUITMENT, SELECTION, AND CONDITIONS OF EMPLOYMENT

Title VII enjoins any advertisement that indicates a preference, limitation, specification, or discrimination based on sex. The EEOC holds it a violation for help-wanted advertisements to indicate a sex unless sex is a bona fide occupational qualification for the particular job involved. To place an ad in columns headed "Male" or "Female" is considered an expression of a preference, limitation, specification, or discrimination based on sex.

At first, the EEOC held it discriminatory to indicate on employment records a person's race, sex, or marital status. Later, it was realized that such information was necessary in order to develop statistical evidence of discrimination. Now such questions may be asked when a person fills out the initial employment application.

A requirement that a job applicant pass a physical examination is not discriminatory per se. The same holds under the Age Discrimination Act. For example, if 20/20 vision is required, an employer must show that the requirement is necessary for the person to perform a job or that it is a reasonable safety requirement. Physical requirements must be justified on the basis of the particular job to be performed. A minimal height may not be applied because women are generally shorter than men. Disqualification must be made on a case to case basis.[48]

A rule to hire unmarried women only is discriminatory unless there is a rule not to hire married men. Any rule that affects married women but not married men is discriminatory. The fact that such a rule does not affect all women does not eliminate sex as a factor in the employment decision.

Regarding testing and educational requirements, the basic case for guiding equal employment actions is *Griggs* v. *Duke Power Company*, a decision of the U.S. Supreme Court.[49] In it the Court held that the requirement to successfully pass an unvalidated ability test or to require a high school education as a condition of employment or prerequisite for promotion was in violation of Title VII because such requirements discriminate against blacks and are not job related.

More females than males have high school diplomas, which raises a question of whether such a requirement discriminates against males. Another question that is involved is do such requirements perpetuate discrimination that started in the past? The *Griggs* case set the stage for a great deal of litigation under the law. The lower courts will be faced with determining when hiring standards are discriminatory, even though set up in good faith.

Title VII authorizes pay differentials based upon (1) length of service, (2) merit, (3) an incentive system, (4) price rates, and (5) geographic locations. An employer cannot pay different rates of pay for the same job on the basis of sex or race. Violations of this standard transgress the Equal Pay Act of 1963 as well as Title VII of the Equal Employment Opportunities Act. The Wage and Hour Division enforces the Equal Pay Act of 1963 and it takes the position that the work need only be substantially the same in order to require equal pay. The EEOC guideline with respect to wages states that the Commission will give appropriate consideration to the interpretation of the Wage and Hour Division but it will not be bound thereby. A great deal more time will be needed to evaluate the direction that the EEOC will move in this category of equal employment opportunity.

The requirement of mandatory leave of absence in maternity cases is receiving a great deal of attention. The courts tend to attack the employer requirement of fixed maternity leaves, such as two months before the expected delivery date. The EEOC does not include this particular principle in its guidelines, but gets at the problem in a different manner. Pregnancy is treated as a form of sickness or accident. The EEOC guideline is: "disabilities caused or contributed to by pregnancy, miscarriage, abortion, childbirth, and recovery therefrom, for all job-related purposes, are temporary disabilities and should be treated as such under any health or temporary disability insurance or sick leave plan available in connection with employment. Written and unwritten employment policies and practices involving matters such as the commencement and duration of leave, the availability of extensions, the accrual of seniority and other benefits and privileges, reinstatement, and payment under any health or temporary disability insurance or sick leave plan, formal or informal, shall be applied to disability due to pregnancy or childbirth on the same terms and conditions as they are applied to other temporary disabilities." Thus, the EEOC guideline is that pregnancy will require the collecting of sick leave pay, and, therefore, it really does not matter when the leave begins or how long it lasts.

The EEOC prohibits disqualification of a prospective female employee on the ground that she is pregnant. She may not be refused employment on such a ground even though the pregnancy is illegitimate; is in the later stages of pregnancy; or is immediately eligible for sickness and accident benefits or that she has no intention of working permanently on the job. The basic consequence here is that industry may be required to finance every childbirth irrespective of any economic interest the firm may have within a particular industry. Obviously, labor costs will rise substantially under the above requirement with the effect that full employment definitions will have to be revised.

Title VII proscribes any seniority system that segregates females or minority groups in any way. A seniority system that perpetuates past discrimination will be held illegal. There are many questions that have to be worked out on this particular issue and only time will resolve such problems. One thing seems sure: The practices of the past will be altered.

Fringe benefits include medical, hospital, accident, life insurance, and retirement benefits. In addition, profit-sharing and bonus plans, leaves, and other terms, conditions, and privileges of employment are included in the guidelines. The EEOC makes it an unlawful employment practice for an employer to discriminate between men and women with regard to fringe benefits. This means that when an employer conditions benefits available to employees and their families on whether the employee is head of a household, or the principal wage earner in the family unit, it is assumed that the benefits tend to be available primarily to male employees and their families. As such, there is discrimination against the rights of female employees. Further, it is held that head of household or principal wage earner status bears no relationship to job performance and, consequently, such conditions discriminate against females. It is also an unlawful employment practice for an employer to make benefits available to wives and families of male employees where the same benefits are not made available to the husbands and families of female employees. In addition, the EEOC will not permit an employer to defend his practice under Title VII when charged with sex discrimination on the basis that the cost of such benefits is greater with respect to one sex than the other.

A person cannot be terminated because of his or her sex, or because of age if he or she is between 40 and 60 years. Maternity is not a ground for termination but must be treated as a leave of absence. Reinstatement poses a different situation. The problem is whether a female is entitled to the same precise job held when she left, or whether she is entitled to the vacancies that exist at the time of reinstatement. The circumstances of each case arising under the guidelines will undoubtedly provide the answer without a mechanistic approach.

Pension and retirement plans pose critical difficulties for employers. The problem with them is that, in fact, for their purposes men and women are not equal because women live longer. The Wage and Hour Division takes the position, under the Equal Pay Act, that there is no violation if the employer contribution for both sexes is equal, or if the benefits paid are equal even though the cost is different. However, the Wage and Hour Division has not prohibited different retirement ages for men and women. The EEOC does it differently. It states: "It shall be an unlawful employment practice for an employer to have a pension or retirement plan which establishes different optional or compulsory retirement ages based on sex, or which differentiates in benefits on the basis of sex."

The problems and difficulties with pensions and retirement plans are of such magnitude that the Congress may eventually have to clarify their intent with additional legislation. The other guidelines range from relatively simple to extremely difficult to implement. In most cases, there will be substantial changes in the labor market as the EEOC becomes more active in enforcement.

AFFIRMATIVE ACTION PROGRAMS

Affirmative action means active efforts toward voluntarily redressing any racial, sexual, or other minority imbalances that may exist in an employee work force. Executive Order 11246 and related regulations of the Office of Federal Contract

Compliance (OFCC) brought affirmative action programs into effect. The OFCC affirmative action program requirements apply to all contractors and sub-contractors of the federal government. Employers are not under a strict obligation to seek racial balance for its own sake. Neither must future job openings be necessarily reserved for minority groups. However, affirmative action requires employers to evaluate their work forces, analyze their employment needs, and actively solicit to obtain more minority employees. The primary requirement is a written stipulation of good faith efforts to achieve equal employment opportunity. As a minimum such efforts must include (1) an analysis of deficiencies of the utilization of minorities; (2) a timetable for correcting such deficiencies together with their expected goals; and (3) a coherent and reasonable plan for achieving those goals.

The analysis of the work force should include an analysis of all major job categories, by establishment, to determine where minorities are being underutilized along with an explanation as to why they are being underutilized and a further explanation as to how this can be corrected. Goals and timetables must be couched in terms of actual commitment. Also they must be cast in terms of correcting identifiable conditions, and support data must be furnished to show that the goals and timetables are realistic. Specific means set forth in a plan for reaching equal employment goals must include internal and external dissemination. Internally, the company should publicize its commitment to equal employment by placing appropriate notices on company bulletin boards and by setting forth its goals in company newspapers and by verbal expression during meetings held with company employees. Externally, a company must actively recruit employees from minority groups.

After a contractor with the federal government has established an affirmative action policy, he then must disseminate that policy as follows: One, meet with union officials to inform them of the policy and request their cooperation. Two, include nondiscrimination clauses in all union agreements and review all contractual provisions to insure that they are nondiscriminatory. Three, inform all recruiting sources, verbally and in writing, of company policy stipulating that those sources actively recruit and refer minorities for all positions listed. Four, incorporate the equal opportunity clause in all purchase orders, leases, contracts, and the like. Five, notify minority organizations, community agencies, community leaders, secondary schools, and colleges of company policy, preferably in writing. Sixth, a company must send written notification of company policy to all sub-contractors, vendors, and suppliers requesting appropriate action on their part. In 1971, the OFCC set up a number of factors that have to be considered in order to determine whether or not an employer is guilty of underutilization. These considerations are (1) the minority population of the labor area in the plant locale; (2) the size of the minority unemployment force in that locale; (3) the percentage of minority work force compared with the total work force of that locale; (4) the general availability of minorities with the necessary skills both in the immediate location and within a reasonable recruiting radius; (5) availability of promotable minorities within the employer's own work force; (6) anticipated expansion, contraction, and turnover of the employer's work force; (7) existence of training institutions capable of training minorities with the requisite skills; and (8) the amount of training that the contractor is reasonably able to undertake to make all job classifications available to minorities.

With respect to Item 8, there is no specific requirement in the law that clearly states that an employer must hire marginal employees. However, there is an affirmative duty to hire a candidate who can be trained to meet the degree of skill required within a reasonable amount of time even though there may be a candidate readily available who already possesses such skills.

A failure to develop an affirmative action program can lead to possible cancellation of existing contracts and debarment from future contracts. The OFCC will grant a conference to a contractor who has not developed an acceptable affirmative action program. The purpose of the conference is to make every effort to assist in developing an acceptable affirmative action program. If the contractor remains in noncompliance, the OFCC will move to set a hearing date that will serve to make the contractor ineligible for future contracts and sub-contracts. If there is no program at all or one that is unacceptable, the agency can issue notice, giving the contractor thirty days to show cause why enforcement proceedings should not be instituted. If the situation is not corrected within the thirty days, the compliance agency, with authorization, will commence formal proceedings leading to the cancellation or termination of existing contracts or sub-contracts.

Unions and Equal Employment Opportunity

There are four special problem areas which affect the American labor movement. These are (1) special problems of unions in the construction industry; (2) the dilemma posed by the seniority provisions of collective bargaining agreements; (3) the union's role and liability as co-defendant in fair representation cases; and (4) anomalies in the union's role in the reverse sex discrimination cases.

The hiring hall arrangement in building and trades collective agreements limit employers to hiring individuals referred by the union. The National Labor Relations Act requires referral unions to refer without discriminating between members and nonmembers, and further requires employers to hire those referred without discrimination. The law stipulates that it shall not be an unfair labor practice for a construction industry collective bargaining agreement to specify minimum training or experience qualifications for employment. As a result, construction industry collective bargaining agreements generally set up referral preference categories based on the extent of worker qualifications. These usually include the number of years of experience that a journeyman must have as a condition of employment. Such provisions have long been known to be discriminatory against blacks and other minority groups.

The Philadelphia Plan, the Washington Plan, and "Home Town" plans focus directly on federal construction project contractors. These plans require the contractor to use good faith efforts to meet specific minority hiring goals. These plans were designed to circumvent union control of federal construction employment by requiring the employer to insure adequate minority worker representation. The employer cannot meet the requirements merely because the union has refused to refer minority workers.

In 1970, the Office of Federal Contract Compliance announced that the Philadelphia Plan solutions would be imposed in nineteen cities unless those cities developed acceptable home town solutions.

The elimination of discriminatory hiring patterns has presented difficult enforcement problems under Title VII of the Civil Rights Act. It prohibits discriminatory exclusion from union membership, and precludes discriminatory classifications in the use of referral categories such as those traditionally employed by construction unions. It also prohibits discriminatory training in apprenticeship programs.

The effectiveness of Title VII in removing employment barriers is, however, limited by a section that permits employers to vary the terms and conditions of employment pursuant to a bona fide seniority or merit system. Courts normally have not invalidated this exception unless a past history of discrimination has been established.

The U.S. Supreme Court may ultimately remove employment barriers in the construction industry under the *Griggs* doctrine. Employment barriers that may be removed by lower courts on the basis of that decision include apprentice age restrictions, excessive formal education requirements, testing unless it shows a direct correlation between scores and the ability to perform the job, and restrictions on the size of union membership based on a projection of employment prospects and residence requirements. Attacks on the duration of apprenticeship training as being excessive may also be sustained in the courts.

Seniority Provisions

Seniority systems that maintain the results of past discrimination can place some unions in serious situations. If an employer attempts to champion the cause of the minority worker and proposes to revise long established discriminatory seniority systems, unions may face a dilemma.

Title VII prohibits seniority clauses in collective agreements that perpetuate discrimination against minorities where a history of discrimination has been shown. In *Griggs*, it was held that Title VII requires the removal of any artificial, arbitrary, and unnecessary barriers to employment. The Court stated that such barriers included not only those that are overtly discriminatory but also those that are fair on their face but discriminatory in practice. With respect to construction union employment barriers, the courts have indicated a willingness to require affirmative action in any situation where a deliberately discriminatory employment practice has been discovered.[50]

The Union's Role and Liability as Co-Defendant in Fair Representation Cases

Many years ago, the U.S. Supreme Court, in the *Steele* case established the doctrine on fair representation by unions of all employees in the bargaining unit.[51] It held that unions must fairly represent minority group employees denied union membership because of race. Since a union is the legal bargaining agent, the court held that it may not discriminate against any employee in the bargaining unit. This decision plus others of kindred types have provided the basis for union liability in discrimination cases under Title VII. When a union is a co-defendant in fair representation cases, and the evidence demonstrates that the union had violated the principle of fair representation, the courts have held that unions and employers are jointly liable for damages.

Reverse Discrimination

Male employees have filed a large number of complaints alleging sex discrimination under Title VII. For example, the EEOC has held that an employer hiring females with long hair may not discriminate against males with long hair.[52] A very controversial type of case involves pension and profit-sharing plans. These plans usually provide for different retirement ages for female and male employees. A circuit court of appeals held in *Rosen* v. *Public Service Electric Company* that males who were penalized by reduction in pension, if retiring before 65, were entitled to recover the amounts necessary to equalize them with females who were permitted to retire at age 62 on full pension without actuarial reductions.[53]

A critical problem in pension discrimination cases is that the number of female employees covered by such plans normally is comparatively small. To extend additional benefits to male employees has the effect of increasing benefits to a very high level. Because of the high cost involved in these benefit cases, employers faced with pension litigation seek to bring unions in as a co-defendant. Understandably unions do not desire to be involved in these cases despite the fact that they along with employees negotiated a pension plan favoring females. In any event, discrimination in pension plans that are favorable to women is not permitted under EEOC guidelines.

ARBITRATION AND TITLE VII RIGHTS

In 1972, in *Rios* v. *Reynolds Metals Company*,[54] a circuit court of appeals ruled that federal courts may defer to arbitration cases involving employees' rights protected by Title VII of the Civil Rights Act. The conditions set by the court of appeals for accepting arbitration awards for cases involving Title VII rights are more specific and demanding than the NLRB's.[55] These are:

> . . . first, there may be no deference to the decision of the arbitrator unless the contractual right coincides with rights under Title VII.

> Second, it must be plain that the arbitrator's decision is in no way violatant of the private rights guaranteed by Title VII, nor of the public policy which inheres in Title VII. In addition, before deferring, the District Court must be satisfied that (1) the factual issues before it are identical to those decided by the arbitrator; (2) the arbitrator had power under the collective agreement to decide the ultimate issue of discrimination; (3) the evidence presented at the arbitral hearing dealt adequately with all factual issues; (4) the arbitrator actually decided the factual issues presented to the Court; and (5) the arbitration proceeding was fair and regular and free of procedural infirmities. The burden of proof in establishing these conditions of limitation will be upon the respondent as distinguished from the claimant.

A question also raised in *Rios* involved whether an aggrieved employee may seek relief under Title VII without first invoking or exhausting available alternative legal or contractual remedies. That is, could an aggrieved employee submit his grievance to arbitration and also take it before the court? It was decided in *Caldwell* v. *National Brewing Company* that employees may seek relief under Title VII without invoking or exhausting available alternative legal or contractual remedies.[56] Not only that, but in *Hutchins* v. *United States Industries, Inc.* it was held that even where an employee does pursue an alternative remedy such as arbitration in cases involving Title VII rights the federal court is the final arbiter.[57] In *Rios*, however, the court stated that it does not follow, however, that the policies of Title VII require that an employee who has submitted his claim to binding arbitration must always be given an opportunity to relitigate his claim in court. In some instances such a requirement would not comport with elementary notions of equity for it would give the employee but not the employer a second chance to have the same issue resolved. . . .

In February 1974 the U.S. Supreme Court resolved the inconsistency created by the lower courts in *Rios & Hutchins*. At that time, in *Alexander* v. *Gardner-Denver*, the high court held that an arbitrator's decision is not final and binding when an employee claims that he was discharged because of racial reasons in violation of Title VII of the Civil Rights Act. An arbitrator sustained the discharge of a black employee on the grounds that he was terminated for just cause. A district court upheld the arbitrator's decision, and did not inquire into the question of whether or not the discharge was in violation of the Civil Rights Act. However, the U.S. Supreme Court remanded the case to the lower court with instructions that it make a determination as to whether the employee's rights under Title VII were violated. What *Alexander* means, therefore, is that even if an employee loses his case in arbitration, he may still seek relief from the courts provided that Title VII rights are involved.

SUBSTANTIVE PROVISIONS: THE PRINCIPLE OF MAJORITY RULE

It was necessary that Congress spell out the conditions under which employers refuse to bargain collectively with the representatives of their employees. Collective bargaining implies negotiations between representatives of management and representatives of employees. Consequently, it was indispensable for the Wagner Act to state the circumstances under which an employer refused to bargain collectively. To resolve this problem, Congress adopted the principle of majority rule. For purposes of the Wagner Act, an employer engaged in an unfair labor practice only when he refused to bargain with a union selected by a majority of his employees for purposes of collective bargaining. If a labor organization did not possess the support of the majority, an employer was under no legal compulsion to bargain.

Still another principle of industrial democracy was embodied in the Wagner Act. Under its terms a union selected by a majority of workers represented all workers in the bargaining unit regardless of membership status. This principle has been alluded to in the previous section on racial discrimination. A majority labor organization bargains equally for members and nonmembers in respect to rates of pay, hours of work, or other conditions of employment. Moreover, if a majority of the workers in a unit vote for a union, it must represent all workers in the unit regardless of whether they voted for the union, against it, or failed to vote.

Some have opposed the majority-rule principle on the ground that it violates the rights of minority groups. Suppose 75 percent of the workers in a plant select a labor organization as their bargaining representative. Under the Wagner Act the union not only was to represent this 75 percent, but also had to bargain for the remaining 25 percent. However, the fact that the labor organization chosen by the majority of workers represented all workers does not transgress the tenets of democracy. Nothing appears farther from the truth. In fact, the principle of majority rule implements the democratic way of life. In political life a Republican elected to the House of Representatives represents the Democratic members of his district as well as the Republicans. In addition, each Democratic member in the district is bound by decisions that the Republican representative might have made.

Not only is the principle of majority rule consistent with democracy, but it is justified on the basis of effective collective bargaining. If nonunion workers could make their own employment agreements with their employers, the labor union would soon collapse. It would be easy for an employer to favor the nonunion worker. He could pay him higher wages and this could lure other workers out of the organization. If a large number of workers withdrew from the union, the labor organization would soon cease to exist. With the disintegration of a union, an employer need not be so considerate of the nonunion worker.

There is still another value attached to the principle of majority rule from the viewpoint of effective collective bargaining. Suppose the workers of a factory choose among five labor organizations. Assume that one union received the support of the majority of employees while the others received a scattering of the workers' support. If the minority unions were given the right to bargain for the workers who voted for them, collective bargaining could hardly be conducted successfully. Such "Balkanization" of the bargaining unit would defeat the purpose of a law calculated to make collective bargaining effective. Thus, in this example, there would be five contract-negotiation sessions, five grievance committees, and five different chances for the plant to shut down because of disagreement over working conditions. Management as well as workers would suffer under such a system. Membership raiding among the unions would be incessant. Production could hardly be carried out effectively in such an environment. What worth would it be to management or the workers if the company negotiated contracts successfully with four of the unions, only to have the plant shut down because the fifth union called a strike over contract terms?

Thus it can readily be seen that the principle of majority rule satisfies the requirements of democracy and industrial harmony. Majority rule means the promotion of industrial democracy and orderly collective bargaining. Any other principle of representation would mean ineffective collective bargaining, retardation of the rate of production, and general industrial chaos.

UNFAIR LABOR PRACTICE PROCEDURE

The National Labor Relations Board was established by Congress to protect the rights prescribed by the Wagner Act. This includes the rights of employees, employers, unions, and the general public. The protection of these rights requires the remedying of unfair labor practices and the conduct of representation elections. *The procedures mentioned in this section include changes made by the Taft-Hartley Act.*

The NLRB responsibilities were not divided under the Wagner Act, but the Taft-Hartley amendments organized the agency into two divisions. One division, consisting of the general counsel and his staff, investigates and prosecutes unfair labor practice cases and conducts representation elections. It is the general counsel who maintains general supervision over the thirty-one regional offices and three subregional offices of the NLRB.

The second division is the five-member board that hears and decides the unfair labor practice cases prosecuted by the general counsel. The Board also hears and decides questions concerning representation elections referred to it by the regional offices.

The NLRB solicits neither unfair labor practices to remedy nor representation elections to conduct. Every case has its origin in one of the regional offices as a result of a charge or petition filed there by some individual or organization. Specific procedures guide the administration of the Wagner Act from the regional offices through the U.S. Supreme Court.

UNFAIR LABOR PRACTICE CHARGE

A charge must be filed with the Board before an unfair labor practice will be prosecuted. The charge must also be filed with the regional office in the territory in which the labor dispute occurred and must involve conduct defined by the National Labor Relations Act as an unfair labor practice.

After the charge is filed by an individual, union, employer, or any other person, the regional office must determine whether the Board has jurisdiction over the enterprise. The Board has established minimum standards indicating the volume of business that must be shown before it can exercise its power. These standards, expressed in terms of gross dollar volume of business or interstate transactions, differ for various categories of enterprises. Certain employers and employees are excluded from coverage under the Act. Once the jurisdictional dollar standards are met and it is determined that the employer and employees are covered by the Act, an investigation is conducted.

Investigation and Informal Settlement

An investigation is conducted by a field examiner or an attorney, who takes written statements and affidavits from available witnesses. When the investigation is completed, the case may be disposed of by withdrawal, settlement, or dismissal. If the case is not closed by one of these three methods, formal proceedings may be initiated if the regional director issues a complaint.

A charge may be withdrawn if the charging party feels that the case is without merit. Frequently, withdrawal is solicited by the regional office, but the charging party may take the initiative. A withdrawal, however, must be approved by the regional director; approval will be granted as long as it is not contrary to the purposes of the Act.

The regional director will dismiss a charge when evidence of a violation of the Act is lacking. Dismissals result if the charging party refuses to withdraw the charge voluntarily. If the regional director dismisses the charge, a request for review may be filed within ten days with the general counsel in Washington, who may approve or dismiss the regional director's action in the absence of settlement. The regional director must issue a complaint if his action is not upheld by the general counsel.

Board settlements are methods of closing cases in the regional offices by agreement of the parties and are frequently obtained after complaints are issued. Board settlements are of two types: all-party and unilateral. Both must be approved by the regional director.

All-party settlements permit the charged party, the regional office, and the party making the charge to bring about remedial action on a voluntary basis. This type of settlement does not involve prolonged formal action.

Unilateral board settlements are entered into without the charging party. This type of settlement is approved by the regional director if he considers that it fully remedies the unfair labor practice committed. Often, the charging party may have no objection to the agreement, but may simply not wish to sign because an individual involved in the charge may feel he was abandoned. The charging party may object to the regional director's actions and appeal to the general counsel within ten days, requesting a reconsideration of the case.

Non-Board settlements are those in which the Board is not a formal party to the agreement; the parties have settled their differences privately in a satisfactory manner. The settlement must be submitted to the regional director along with a withdrawal request, but the director is under no obligation to approve it. From 1936 until 1947, the years in which the Board administered the Wagner Act, the agency managed to settle 90.6 percent of all its cases involving unfair labor practice charges on an informal basis.[58] In this period of time, labor unions and employees filed with the NLRB 43,556 charges alleging employer violations of the Wagner Act. However, more than 50 percent of these cases were either dismissed by the Board or withdrawn by the filing party. Dismissal or withdrawal of cases resulted when the Board felt there was no violation of the Wagner Act. Thus these figures disclose that, on the basis of informal procedures, the NLRB dismissed more than 50 percent of all unfair labor practice cases alleging employer violations. These figures contradict allegations that the NLRB proceeded to prosecute each and every employer charged with violating the law.

In about 37 percent of the unfair labor practice cases filed in 1936–1947, the Board adjusted the disputes to the satisfaction of employers, employees, and labor unions. Again, no formal proceedings were involved in such adjustments. In many cases a field examiner, during an informal investigation of the case, merely advised an employer that he was violating the law. Frequently, the employer was not aware of his unlawful conduct and, when advised of it, immediately complied with the law.

The fact that the vast majority of the cases were settled on an informal basis by the NLRB speaks well of the Board, employers, unions, and employees. If a majority of the cases filed with the Board proceeded to formal hearings, investigations, and court proceedings, the administration of the law could not have been effective. By obtaining voluntary compliance with the law, by dismissing cases outright, and by urging labor unions to withdraw baseless charges, the NLRB was able to function successfully. Moreover, the informal settlement of cases resulted in a considerable saving of time and money for all parties involved in Wagner Act proceedings.

Settlement Notices

Board settlements provide for the posting of notices, which reassure employees of their rights under the Act and outline the action to be taken by the charged party as a condition for settlement. Notices are designed to cover the circumstances involved in each case and must remain posted for a period of sixty consecutive days on the employer's premises or in the union hall. In addition, settlements may require the accused to cease from illegal conduct in the future and provide for other remedial action, such as recognition of a labor organization, reinstatement, and the issuance of back pay to illegally discharged employees.

FORMAL PROCEEDINGS

Formal proceedings result if the parties are unable to resolve the dispute informally, or if the regional office feels the violation was flagrant and does not approve the informal settlement. The regional office may also refuse such approval if the charged party was a previous offender, or if the settlement agreed to by the parties does not realistically remedy the unfair labor practices.

The Complaint. A complaint is issued by the regional office in behalf of the general counsel; it is a formal charge by the government of violation of federal law. The complaint lists the provisions of the Act allegedly violated and the time and place of the hearing covering the unfair labor practice charges. The charged party must answer the complaint within ten days either by admitting, denying, or explaining the facts alleged in the complaint.

The Hearing. The hearing is the formal trial and is presided over by an administrative law judge (formerly called trial examiner), an agent of the five man Board in Washington, not of the general counsel. It is conducted in accordance with the rules of evidence and procedure that apply in the U.S. district courts. After the hearing the law judge issues a decision (called a recommendation), in which he summarizes the case and recommends its disposition to the Board. If a violation is found, the recommendations include an appropriate remedy. Any party that disagrees with the law judge's decision may appeal to the Board in Washington within twenty days.

Board Review. The recommendation report is normally adopted by the Board unless one of the parties files a written statement of exceptions. Board adoption refers to the acceptance of the findings, conclusions, and proposed order of the law judge. In the event exceptions are filed, the Board is under no obligation to accept the report, but may issue appropriate decisions and orders. The recommendation may be partially accepted or completely rejected. Law judges may be ordered to conduct new trials or the case may be dismissed entirely by the Board.

In the majority of cases a respondent complies with the Board's decision and order. If he does not comply, the Board may seek enforcement of its order through any U.S. court of appeals. Under some circumstances, it may seek enforcement even if the respondent does comply. Similarly, the party charged with a violation of the unfair labor practice provisions of the Wagner Act also may appeal the Board's decision to a U.S. court of appeals. Likewise, appeals may be made if the Board reverses a law judge's decision. If there is dissatisfaction with the circuit court decision, requests may be made for review to the U.S. Supreme Court. Once a circuit court order is finalized (by failure to seek review or denial thereof by the Supreme Court), the party charged must obey the Board order or face contempt-of-court proceedings.

Only 9.4 percent of all unfair labor practice cases filed with the Board from 1936 to 1947 involved formal proceedings. These proceedings were necessary when employers refused to comply with the law on an informal basis. They felt that their interests would best be served by not complying with informal recommendations tendered by Board officials. These employers in no sense can be censured, for it was their legal right to exhaust fully the procedures of the Wagner Act before complying with the law. The remarkable fact is that so few employers chose to bring into operation the formal procedures of the law. Undoubtedly those employers—or at least the majority of them—honestly felt that they had not violated the law even though an informal investigation may have pointed in that direction.

THE WAGNER ACT RECORD

How the Board discharged this responsibility is a matter of public record.[59] In the Wagner Act years, 1936–1947, the NLRB reinstated 76,268 workers who had been discharged because of union activities. Moreover, the Board awarded $12,418,000 in back pay. Congress recognized that reinstatement of workers discharged because of union activity without awarding them pay for time lost during their period of discharge would be an empty gesture. Accordingly, the Wagner Act provided that workers discharged because of union activities would be reinstated with back pay. In addition, the NLRB disestablished 1,709 company-dominated unions, ordered employers to post 8,156 notices stating that the company would henceforth comply with the Wagner Act, and on 5,070 occasions ordered employers to bargain collectively. Finally, the Board ordered 226,488 strikers reinstated on their jobs. Many of these workers struck because of employer unfair labor practices; and still others suffered discrimination at the termination of a strike. It has been a favorite union-busting technique for employers to refuse to reinstate strike leaders in their jobs after a strike ends. These figures stand as a testimonial to a law and agency dedicated to the promotion of collective bargaining and the union movement. This record underscores the proposition that the main source of criticism of the NLRB during its Wagner Act period resulted from the zeal of the agency to perform its duties in a positive and vigorous manner.

REPRESENTATION PROCEDURE

Representation cases must also follow a prescribed procedure before the Board is empowered to intervene and conduct elections. Representation elections, like unfair labor practices, are initiated by the filing of a petition. The petition may be for the purpose of obtaining initial recognition of a union or it may be to decertify the existing bargaining agent. The regional office is authorized to make an investigation of the petition.

The Investigation. An investigation is conducted in order to obtain information concerning the following: (1) whether the employer's operations meet the Board's jurisdictional standards; (2) the appropriateness of the unit of employees for purposes of collective bargaining (employees are grouped into units where similar interests exist); (3) the sufficiency of employee interest in representation by a labor organization (an election will usually be conducted by the Board if at least 30 percent of the employees indicate an interest in representation); and (4) whether the petition was filed at the proper time. An election may not be conducted if a valid election was held during the preceding twelve-month period. Complicated Board rules govern the conduct of elections when long-term collective bargaining agreements exist.

Representation petitions may be disposed of before a hearing by the same methods used in closing unfair labor practice cases—by withdrawal, dismissal, or settlement. If the petition has merit and no arrangements for a consent election have been made, the parties are entitled to a hearing. The Wagner Act entitles the parties to a representation hearing, which is a formal proceeding designed to obtain information to aid the regional director in deciding the adequacy of the petition. He must make a decision on the appropriateness of the bargaining unit, the timeliness of the petition, the sufficiency of employee interest, and other pertinent matters. The hearing is not held if the parties enter into a consent-election agreement since the matters that must be resolved in the hearing are by such agreement normally resolved voluntarily by the parties. The regional director, however, must approve consent elections before they are effective. During the Wagner Act years, the Board adjusted 42 percent of all representation cases through the consent-election procedure.

In hearing cases, the regional director reviews the record of the hearing and resolves eligibility, appropriateness of unit, and other requirements, then either directs an election or dismisses the petitions. His decision may be appealed to the Board in Washington. The hearing and appeal increase the time that elapses between the filing of a petition and the actual election. This procedure is available to the parties if they do not waive this action by entering into a consent agreement.

Actually, in the period 1936 to 1947, the Wagner Act years, the NLRB dismissed or caused the withdrawal of about 25 percent of all election petitions. The explanation for this action of the Board is simple enough. The Board does not want to waste the public's money and the time of its agents unless there is fairly good reason to believe that a union will poll the majority of votes in a representation election. In addition, such an election will prove a waste of time to workers and to the company when the investigation reveals that the union could not possibly win in an election.

Election Supervision. Personnel from the regional offices supervise the secret ballot elections after elections are ordered by the regional director or consented to by the parties. Representatives of both employers and unions are entitled to observe the procedure and challenge any employee who applies for a ballot. Challenges must be based on "reasonable cause." When the election results depend on the challenged ballots, the regional director must conduct an investigation and make a decision on the challenged votes.

Employer or union conduct affecting an election may be subject to objections within five days after the ballots are counted. Such objections must be investigated by the regional director and, if they are found to be justified, an election may be set aside and a new one ordered. This depends on the nature of the issues and the type of consent agreement executed by the parties. Challenges and objections may or may not be resolved on the basis of the investigation without a hearing. Depending on the circumstances, the ultimate decision on challenges or objections will be made by the regional director or the Board.

A representation petition may be withdrawn at any time—before the hearing, after the hearing, or after a second election has been ordered by the regional director or the Board. Once the election has been conducted and all the problems associated with it settled, its outcome must be certified. A certification of representatives occurs when a labor organization wins an election. Following certification of representatives, in the absence of an appeal, an employer is obligated to enter collective bargaining negotiations with the appropriate union. Should the labor organization lose, however, there is no certification of results and the employer is not required to bargain.

It is noteworthy that about 74 percent of all representation disputes were disposed of by the NLRB through informal procedures. Informal settlement meant a considerable saving of time and money for all parties involved in NLRB representation proceedings and, in addition, permitted the NLRB to conserve its energies for the proper disposition of difficult cases. If the full procedures of the Board were exhausted in each unfair labor practice and representation dispute, the operation of the Wagner Act would have been very ineffective.

STATISTICAL NOTE

During the period 1936–1947, the Wagner Act years, the NLRB was called upon to determine representatives for collective bargaining in 36,969 cases.[60] Labor unions won lawful bargaining rights in 30,110 instances and workers voted for "no union" in 6,859 cases. Slightly more than 9 million workers were eligible to vote in representation elections. Of this total 7,677,135 workers, 84.1 percent, actually cast ballots. Votes cast for labor unions amounted to 6,145,834 and votes against unions numbered 1,531,301.

These figures testify to the success of the Wagner Act in establishing an orderly manner for the selection of bargaining representatives. The law substituted the ballot box for industrial warfare. Workers in free secret-ballot elections had the opportunity to select or reject the process of collective bargaining. The Wagner Act established the principle of representative democracy in the nation's industrial life. Since our nation has progressed so admirably under a system of political democracy, it is inevitable that the application of the same principle to industrial life likewise must prove beneficial to workers, management, and the public.

WAGNER ACT DURING WORLD WAR II

The Wagner Act proved particularly beneficial to the nation during World War II.[61] The winning of a modern war requires maximum production. The Wagner Act provided workers with a peaceful and orderly procedure to adjust their organizational controversies. Instead of resorting to the organizational strike, the nation's employees could make use of the offices of the National Labor Relations Board.

Events proved that workers and labor unions in unprecedented numbers utilized the peaceful procedures of the Wagner Act. The NLRB handled a tremendous number of cases during the war period. Three factors accounted for this. In the first place, industry greatly expanded its facilities. As a result the level of employment reached unprecedented heights. By August 1945 the nation's labor force reached the level of 66,650,000. This number is compared with 54,230,000 reported for 1939. Moreover, unemployment was nearly wiped out during the war years. Whereas 7,300,000 were unemployed in 1939, there were only 830,000—these mostly "unemployables" —idle in August 1945. As might be expected, increased trade union activities followed the expansion of the level of employment. Whereas in 1940 membership in all the nation's labor force was reported at only 8,500,000, the figure soared to 13,750,000 in 1944. Such augmentation of union activities constituted the second factor making for the heavy workload of the NLRB during World War II. Finally, this increase was attributable to the confidence of the nation's workers and labor unions in the Wagner Act and in the NLRB. In prewar years the NLRB demonstrated its power and effectiveness in protecting the right of workers to self-organization and collective bargaining. As a result the Board entered its wartime career as an agency that had won the respect and admiration of the nation's workers. Obviously, if the unions and workers had held the NLRB in low esteem, they would not have utilized the Wagner Act as the vehicle whereby the right to self-organization and collective bargaining could be implemented.

Evidence indicating the large increase in the work of the NLRB during World War II may be briefly noted. Whereas the Board conducted only 3,386 representation elections or crosschecks during the years 1936–1940, in which 1,225,098 valid votes were cast, the NLRB during the war years, 1941–1945, administered 20,562 elections in which 4,889,627 workers cast valid ballots. In other words, more than 85 percent of all representation elections conducted by the Board during the first ten years of its operation were held in the war period. Workers resorted to the election procedures of the Wagner Act because, as noted, they had faith that once their unions were certified, the NLRB would guarantee that employers would recognize them as collective bargaining agencies. Actually, the NLRB issued 2,796 wartime orders requiring employers to bargain collectively with labor unions chosen by their employees. This figure is slightly in excess of the number of all such orders handed down by the NLRB during the years 1937 to 1941.

The major portion of the Board's activities during World War II involved the certification of bargaining representatives. By 1945 representation cases constituted 75.1 percent of the total of all cases and unfair labor practice cases accounted for 24.2 percent. In comparison, in 1936, the first full year of the Board's operation, unfair labor practice cases accounted for 81 percent of the total of all cases filed with the Board, whereas representation cases accounted for only 19 percent. These figures indicate that during World War II employers, instead of interfering with the right of employees to organize and bargain collectively, were more anxious to learn with whom they were required to bargain. The change in the comparative importance of representation cases indicated that after several years of the Wagner Act employers and employees alike recognized the role of collective bargaining in modern industry. However, it should not be overlooked that 18,187 unfair labor practice cases were filed with the Board during the period 1941–1945. This figure was only 932 less than the number of all unfair labor practice cases filed with the NLRB in the prewar years, 1936–1940. The wartime unfair labor practice cases involved 18,108,433 employees. Consequently, in war as in peace, legal protection of the right of workers to self-organization and collective bargaining is a prerequisite for industrial peace.

Another aspect of the wartime activities should be stressed. Much of the Board's wartime work involved basic war industries. More than 50 percent of all bargaining elections conducted by the NLRB were held in the nation's crucial war industries, which included those of iron and steel, machinery, food, chemicals, wholesale trade, electrical equipment, textiles, aircraft, and shipbuilding. Approximately 50 percent of all unfair labor practices likewise involved the same nine industries.

Literally millions of the nation's war production workers resorted to the machinery of the NLRB for adjustment of their organizational disputes. War production would have been seriously retarded if employees had not had the opportunity to settle their organizational controversies through the Board's peaceful and democratic procedures. Recognizing the importance of speedy disposition of wartime representation and unfair labor practice disputes, the NLRB streamlined its regulations under which disposition of the cases was made. By granting greater authority to its regional directors and by otherwise accommodating its procedures to the exigencies of war conditions, the NLRB decreased by several months the time required to process its cases. By lawful certification of bargaining agents and through speedy elimination of unfair labor practices, the NLRB hoped to abolish completely the justification for organizational strikes.

RESULTS OF THE WAGNER ACT

Organizational strike experience during World War II is one standard with which to evaluate the results of the Wagner Act. As noted, approximately 50 percent of all strikes that occurred during 1934 to 1936 resulted wholly or in part from organizational disputes.[62] These strikes involved about 43 percent of the workers who engaged in all strikes during this period. In comparison, in 1942, the first full year of World War II, organizational controversies wholly or in part caused 31.2 percent of all strikes.[63] In subsequent war years the organizational strike was of even less comparative importance. In 1943 organizational disputes, alone or in combination with other causes, resulted in 15.7 percent of all work stoppages; in 1944 they caused 16.3 percent of all strikes; and in 1945 they wholly or in part caused 20.5 percent of all work stoppages. From the point of view of the number of workers engaged in strikes during the war years (1942–1945), work stoppages carried out for organizational purposes alone or in combination with other causes involved approximately 18.5 percent of all workers who engaged in strikes during this period. In the light of the organizational strike experience of 1934 to 1936, it is likely that in the absence of the effective operation of the Wagner Act organizational strikes would have been of greater absolute and comparative importance during World War II.

A comparison of the frequency of organizational strikes during World War I with those during World War II might further indicate the extent to which the Wagner Act was successful in decreasing such work stoppages in World War II. The Bureau of Labor Statistics has faithfully throughout the years recorded the number of strikes resulting from the refusal of employers to recognize their employees' unions. Under the terms of the Wagner Act, an employer engages in an unfair labor practice if he refuses to recognize a certified labor organization as the exclusive representative of the workers in the bargaining unit. Accordingly, workers during World War II had little reason to engage in strikes to gain recognition for their labor unions, since their organizations could accomplish this objective by resorting to the peaceful machinery provided by the NLRB. During World War I, when there existed no agency similar to the NLRB, it is reported that 314 strikes and lockouts were caused by employers' refusal to recognize unions in 1917, and 221 such work stoppages took place in 1918. Expressed as a ratio, recognition strikes accounted for approximately 7 percent of all 1917 strikes and lockouts, and such interruptions to production resulted in 6.5 percent of all work stoppages in 1918. On the other hand, the Bureau reports that in 1942, the first full year of World War II, only 169 recognition-caused work stoppages occurred and that they accounted for 5.6 percent of all 1942 interruptions. In subsequent years the record indicates that the recognition strike continued to be of less importance, comparative and absolute, during World War II as compared to its importance in World War I.

Even though the lack of World War I data precludes a comparison of World War I and World War II recognition strikes on a "man-days lost" basis, it still appears that World War II employees and trade unions, able to utilize the NLRB procedures, resorted to the recognition strike less frequently than did World War I employees. In the light of these considerations, it is probable that the number of World War II recognition strikes would have been greater had there been no NLRB.

These figures underscore the contention that the Wagner Act was a powerful force making for industrial peace during World War II. They highlight the necessity for an orderly system calculated to provide effective and speedy protection of the right of workers to self-organization and collective bargaining. With the passage of years, it is likely that the Wagner Act would have contributed even more to the elimination of the organizational strike. Workers and unions, aware of the remedies of the NLRB, would have relied more on peaceful legal procedures than on the strike to make the right to collective bargaining effective.

The success of the Wagner Act in decreasing the number of organizational strikes cannot be denied. The trend during World War II removed all doubt on the issue. However, some people contend that the Wagner Act, though decreasing the number of organizational strikes, stimulated strikes for nonorganizational issues— wages, hours, pensions, vacations, and the like. The arguments run along the following lines. Under the protection of the Wagner Act, union membership increased, the union movement expanded into new areas, and general bargaining strength of labor unions sharply increased. These circumstances increased the number of nonorganizational strikes, for unions under the Wagner Act became a powerful force in the national economy. In other words, the Wagner Act did not promote industrial peace.

Close analysis of this argument will indicate its fundamental defects. In the first place, the Wagner Act was not passed to eliminate all types of strikes. It was enacted to reduce the number of organizational strikes. Unless we are prepared to make fundamental changes in the structure of a free-enterprise system, strikes over wages, hours, and the conditions of work will always characterize our national life. It is not fair to evaluate the Wagner Act on the basis of the number of all strikes arising during its operation. A valid basis for evaluating its contribution to industrial peace consists of the trend in organizational strikes.

Clearly, the Wagner Act stimulated the growth of the union movement. Union membership increased from about 4 million in 1935 to about 16 million in 1948. Under its protection, the CIO was able to organize the mass production industries on an industry-wide basis. Responding to the challenge of the CIO, the AFL likewise undertook important organizational activities. Obviously, the Wagner Act accomplished its objective of promoting collective bargaining. One may quarrel as to whether or not a large and strong labor union movement is good or bad for society. Whatever the answer to this question, the fact remains that the Wagner Act was very effective in stimulating the growth and strength of organized labor.

Other results of the Wagner Act appear equally impressive. Not only was the statute successful in reducing the number of organizational strikes and expanding the union movement, but the Wagner Act operated to increase greatly the number of effective collective bargaining agreements. In 1946, the last full year of the Wagner Act, the Bureau of Labor Statistics reported that the number of collective bargaining contracts in the nation totaled well over fifty thousand. In addition, during each year these contracts are rewritten in whole or in part. These figures underscore the contention that industrial peace and not industrial warfare is the result of the collective bargaining process. By far the vast majority of labor contracts are negotiated and signed without resort to the strike. The general public is not usually aware of this fact. Strikes are more often reported than peaceful settlement of agreements. Such a situation, however, is not limited to labor-management relations.

It is noteworthy that the Wagner Act stimulated an increase in the number of collective bargaining agreements. Moreover, it should be kept in mind that these contracts, once executed, often provided the basis for peaceful industrial relations for the life of the contract. Not only did they provide a peaceful procedure for the day-to-day relationship between employees and employer, but they also served to stabilize labor relations for long periods of time. The biggest hurdle to industrial peace is the execution of the first collective bargaining agreement. Recent Board experience supports such an assertion. After that is accomplished, and assuming a management and a union that recognize mutual problems and aspirations, long-run industrial peace should be anticipated.

SUMMARY

The Wagner Act sought to promote collective bargaining by denying the opportunity to interfere with the right of workers to self-organization and collective bargaining. Through this procedure Congress hoped to provide workers with a measure of social and economic justice, to promote a stable economic system, and to foster industrial peace. The law did not seek to promote strong unions as ends in themselves. Rather, the objectives of the Wagner Act were social in character, extending beyond the advancement of any particular economic group. Since the law effectively stopped antiunion conduct on the part of employers, the reaction of this group to the law was extremely unfavorable. Many employers attempted to nullify the law by enlisting the support of their old ally, the judiciary. However, by a majority of one, the Supreme Court of the United States in the *Jones & Laughlin* case upheld the constitutionality of the Wagner Act. The Court also assured wide coverage of the law by applying its terms to manufacturing.

The substance of the law centered around Section 7, which guaranteed the right of employees to self-organization and collective bargaining. To make this right meaningful, employers were required to bargain collectively with unions chosen by a majority of their employees and were forbidden to engage in other patterns of antiunion conduct. The National Labor Relations Board was established to enforce the Wagner Act. To sound out the collective bargaining desires of employees, the Board was required to conduct elections in appropriate bargaining units. In addition, it was empowered to prevent employer interference with the collective bargaining rights of the workers covered by the law. In recent years action has been taken to invoke the unfair labor practice provisions of the Act to eliminate racial discrimination.

Under the protection of the Wagner Act, the union movement made phenomenal progress. Union membership increased from about 4 million in 1935 to about 16 million in 1948. The effectiveness of the Wagner Act in this respect stimulated a great deal of employer hostility. However, the Wagner Act remained intact until 1947, the year of Taft-Hartley.

NOTES

[1] *New York Times* Magazine Section, May 9, 1937, p. 23.

[2] Statement of H. M. Robertson, General Counsel, Brown and Williamson Tobacco Corporation, in Senate Committee on Education and Labor, *Hearings on a National Labor Relations Board*, 74th Congress, 1st sess., 1935, p. 218.

[3] See Chapter 8.

[4] See studies on the *Causes of Industrial Peace Under Collective Bargaining*, National Planning Association (Washington, D.C., 1948–1950).

[5] National Labor Relations Board, *First Annual Report*, 1936, p. 46.

[6] *Ibid.*, p. 47.

[7] *Ibid.*, p. 48.

[8] *Monthly Labor Review*, XLII, 162, 1308; XLIV, 1230.

[9] *United States* v. *Knight*, 156 U.S. 12 (1894).

[10] 298 U.S. 238 (1935).

[11] *NLRB* v. *Jones & Laughlin Steel Corporation*, 301 U.S. 1 (1937).

[12] Since the *Jones & Laughlin* decision, the Supreme Court has widely construed the meaning of the interstate commerce clause for the purposes of national labor relations legislation. Decisions of the Supreme Court have empowered the NLRB to exercise jurisdiction over public utilities supplying energy to enterprises engaged in: interstate commerce, *Consolidated Edison Company* v. *NLRB*, 305 U.S. 197 (1938); national fraternal organizations, *Polish National Alliance* v. *NLRB*, 322 U.S. 643 (1944); a local transportation system in an industrial city, *NLRB* v. *Baltimore Transit Company*, 321 U.S. 796 (1944); a large retail department store, *NLRB* v. *J. L. Hudson Company*, 135 Fed. (2d) 380, certiorari denied by Supreme Court, October 11, 1943; and to a charitable hospital, *NLRB* v. *Central Dispensary and Emergency Hospital*, 324 U.S. 847 (1945). The Supreme Court has also held that a firm falls within the authority of the NLRB if it only exports goods into interstate commerce, *Santa Cruz Fruit Packing Company* v. *NLRB*, 303 U.S. 453 (1938); or only receives goods from other states, *Newport News Shipbuilding and Dry Dock Company* v. *Schauffler*, 303 U.S. 54 (1938). Moreover, in the *Fainblatt* case (*NLRB* v. *Fainblatt*), 306 U.S. 601 (1939), the Supreme Court rejected the criterion that an employer's operations must be large enough to be of great national importance in order to fall within the scope of the NLRB. It declared that the operation of the NLRB does not "depend on any particular volume of commerce affected more than that to which courts would apply the maximum *de minimis*." It should be noted here that this broad concept of interstate

commerce developed by the Supreme Court for purposes of the Wagner Act applies equally to NLRB operations when it administers the Taft-Hartley law.

[13] Benjamin J. Taylor, *The Operation of the Taft-Hartley Act in Indiana* (Bloomington, Ind.: Bureau of Business Research, Indiana University, 1967), p. 3.

[14] See Appendix A for the text of the Mohawk Valley Formula.

[15] National Labor Relations Board, *op. cit.*, p. 55.

[16] *Decisions and Orders of the National Labor Relations Board*, VII, 54.

[17] *Riecke Metal Products Company*, 40 NLRB 872 (1942).

[18] 3 NLRB 591.

[19] National Labor Relations Board, *Third Annual Report*, 1938, p. 115.

[20] 7 NLRB 877.

[21] *Textile Workers Union* v. *Darlington Mfg. Co.*, 380 U.S. 263 (1965).

[22] *Ibid.*, pp. 274–275.

[23] *Ibid.*, p. 275.

[24] *Ibid.*, pp. 275–276.

[25] National Labor Relations Board, *op. cit.*, p. 96.

[26] 2 NLRB 39.

[27] 3 NLRB 10.

[28] National Labor Relations Board, *op. cit.*, p. 97.

[29] 2 NLRB 39.

[30] *H. J. Heinz Company* v. *NLRB*, 311 U.S. 514 (1941). When Congress enacted Taft-Hartley, this principle established by the NLRB during the early years of its administration of the Wagner Act was incorporated in the legislation.

[31] *General Electric Company*, 150 NLRB 192 (1964).

[32] *Times Publishing Company*, 72 NLRB 676 (1947).

[33] *Thompson Products, Inc.*, 72 NLRB 888 (1947). See Chapter 17 to learn how such strikes are treated under the Taft-Hartley law.

[34] *American News Company*, 55 NLRB 1302 (1944).

[35] *United States Bedding Company*, 52 NLRB 382 (1943).

[36] *Bethlehem-Alameda Shipyards, Inc.*, 53 NLRB 1016 (1943).

[37] Robert W. Kapp, "Managements' Concern with Recent Civil Rights Legislation," *Labor Law Journal*, XVI, No. 2 (1965), 84.

[38] *Miranda Fuel Company*, 140 NLRB 181 (1962), enf. denied 326 F. (2d) 172 (CA, 1963).

[39] Section 8 (b) (1) (A) is a Taft-Hartley amendment to the Wagner Act and provides that "it shall be an unfair labor practice for a labor organization or its agents (1) to restrain or coerce (A) employees in the exercise of their rights guaranteed in section 7. . . . "

[40] *Wallace Corporation* v. *NLRB*, 323 U.S. 248 (1944).

[41] *Independent Metal Workers* (Hughes Tool Company), 147 NLRB 166 (1964).

[42] *Humphrey* v. *Moore*, 375 U.S. 335 (1964).

[43] *Local 1367, International Longshoremen's Assn.* (*Galveston Maritime Assn.*), 148 NLRB 897 (1965), enf. 368 F. (2d) 1010 (CA 5, 1966), cert. denied 389 U.S. 837 (1967).

[44] *Local 12, Rubber Workers* v. *NLRB*, 368 F. (2d) (CA 5, 1966), cert. denied 389 U.S. 837 (1967).

[45] See *San Diego Bldg. Trades Council* v. *Garman*, 359 U.S. 236 (1959), whereby the U.S. Supreme Court held that "when an activity is arguably subject to sections 7 or 8 of the Act, the states as well as the federal courts must defer to the exclusive competence of the National Labor Relations Board."

[46] *Farmers' Cooperative Compress* v. *United Packinghouse, Food and Allied Workers Union*, 416 F. (2d) 1126 (1969), cert. denied U.S. Sup. Ct. No. 448 (1969).

[47] *Farmers' Cooperative Compress*, 194 NLRB No. 3 (1972).

[48] *Bowe* v. *Colgate*, 2 FEP 223, 416 F. (2d) 711 (1969).

[49] 401 U.S. 424 (1971).

[50] *Heat, Frost and Asbestos Workers, Local 53* v. *Vogler*, 407 F. (2d) 1047 (1969).

[51] *Steele* v. *Louisville & Nashville Railroad*, 323 U.S. 197 (1944).

[52] EEOC Decision #6-8-6654 M EPG Section 6021 (1969).

[53] 409 F. (2d) 775 (1969).

[54] 467 F. (2d) 54 (1972).

[55] In Chapter 14, there is discussion of the circumstances under which the NLRB defers to arbitration under the *Collyer* and *Spielberg* doctrines.

[56] 443 F. (2d) 1044 (1971).

[57] 428 F. (2d) 303 (1970).

[58] National Labor Relations Board, *Twelfth Annual Report*, 1947, p. 86.

[59] *Ibid.*, pp. 83–90.

[60] *Ibid.*, p. 89.

[61] See Fred Witney, *Wartime Experiences of the National Labor Relations Board* (Urbana, Ill.: University of Illinois Press, 1949). This study points up the operation of the Wagner Act during World War II.

[62] See *Monthly Labor Review*, XLII, 162, 1308; XLIV, 1230. Although the Wagner Act was approved by Congress on June 27, 1935, and signed by President Roosevelt on July 5, 1935, the statute was not effective until the Supreme Court approved the legislation on April 1, 1937. Consequently, to ascertain the effectiveness of the Wagner Act in reducing organizational strikes, it appears appropriate to disregard 1935 and 1936, although the Act was technically in operation during these two years.

[63] *Monthly Labor Review*, LVI, 973.

The Taft-Hartley Act: General Observations
10

THE SHIFT IN GOVERNMENT POLICY

On June 23, 1947, Congress overrode a presidential veto and enacted the Taft-Hartley Act.[1] The law was far more controversial than both the Norris–La Guardia and Wagner Acts. This time, however, the positions of management and organized labor were reversed. Management defended the amendments while organized labor denounced congressional action. The controversy began while Congress was debating the law, and it increased in intensity after its enactment. With its passage management and labor joined in the battle with renewed vigor. Radio commentators, newspaper journalists, politicians, and students of industrial relations contributed their share to the controversy. The Taft-Hartley Act substantially changed the direction of industrial relations, and its effect was to produce a controversy never known to follow the passage of a single labor law.

Literally hundreds of articles and tracts have been written on the law. By December 1, 1949, the National Labor Relations Board reported a bibliography on the legislation that included about three hundred items. By no means did the list include all the material written or presented in speeches on the legislation. In scholarly publications, popular magazines, newspaper editorials, company and union tracts, public lectures, and radio debates, the people concerned with labor relations law analyzed the Taft-Hartley Act. If the legislation did nothing else, it underlined the importance of the state of industrial relations law to the functioning of the trade union and the collective bargaining process.

Proponents of Taft-Hartley

Defenders of the legislation generally direct their arguments along several lines. The law frees workers from the tyrannical hold of "union bosses"; it reduces the monopolistic position of labor unions; it protects the public from catastrophic strikes; it protects management from union abuses; it makes unions legally and financially responsible for their actions; it reduces communism within the union movement; it diminishes the power of "labor dictators"; and it promotes greater equality of bargaining power between management and labor. Additionally, defenders of the law, answering critics, vigorously argued that the Taft-Hartley Act does not: "enslave labor"; deprive workers of the legal protection of their right to self-organization and collective bargaining; destroy labor unions; reduce the bargaining power of labor unions; or interfere with the ability of labor to strike for better working conditions. Finally, the supporters of the law claimed that it "equalized" the legal position of employers and unions. The Wagner Act was appraised as one-sided, providing restrictions against unfair labor practices by management, but imposing no restraints on labor unions. Taft-Hartley, however, provided measures against union as well as employer unfair labor practices.

Management groups argued against the Wagner Act even before it was passed. One argument was that labor organizations should be under the same or equivalent limitations and responsibilities as were employers, or else management restrictions should be removed. The argument presented by management groups has been labeled the "doctrine of mutuality."[2] Between the passage of the Wagner Act and the Taft-Hartley amendments, mutuality was generally the basis for proposing amendments. The United States Chamber of Commerce proposed the addition of unfair labor practices of unions in 1937 after the Supreme Court upheld the constitutionality of the Wagner Act.

Criticism of the 1935 act was not limited to employer groups. The American Federation of Labor was not satisfied with some of the NLRB's policies and made proposals to change the law. It is important to note that the general public was not confronted by a labor movement united on the desirability of the law. Competition between the AFL and the CIO for members re-enforced the public's concern about a lack of union regulation.

A steel corporation, shortly after the passage of the Taft-Hartley Act, supplied each of its employees with a letter defending the law. In part the tract declared:

> The Taft-Hartley Act is designed to protect the rights of the *individual* worker. During the past few years the abuses of individual workers by some union bosses and some unions have become as great as those by the unscrupulous employers of the past era. The Taft-Hartley Act does *not* weaken the power of the Unions. It is aimed at insuring control of the Unions by the *individual* worker and protecting him from *abuse*—abuse in case he disagrees with his Union leaders.[3]

The same theme of protection of the union member from his labor organization was expressed by representatives in Congress. In this connection one senator declared: "I want to protect the worker. It seems to me he is the forgotten man. The individual worker is the man in trouble."[4] Only one more statement will be selected from a mountain of material turned out by Taft-Hartley defenders. The Joint Committee on Labor-Management Relations, established under the Taft-Hartley Act and headed in 1948 by former Senator Joseph H. Ball, reported that the law "is working well, without undue hardship upon employers or employees, and promoting the adjustment of labor problems equitably and in a more friendly and co-operative relationship."[5]

Opponents of Taft-Hartley

Organized labor regarded the Taft-Hartley Act in a much different light. Union representatives charged that it curtails the opportunities for the effective operation of the collective bargaining process. They claimed that the law gives aid and comfort to the employer who shows little or no inclination to bargain collectively. It was charged that the law seriously interfered with the right of labor to strike. On the basis of this assertion labor leaders denounced the statute as a "slave labor law," a claim which was vigorously denied. New organizational drives, it was claimed, were made more difficult or impossible by features of the statute. In general, labor leaders charged that the statute reduced the opportunities for effective collective bargaining, impaired free collective bargaining, promoted industrial strife, forestalled the expansion of unionism into new areas, and threatened the existence of the American labor union movement.

Selective observations of leading labor officials highlight the positions taken against the Taft-Hartley amendments. On June 20, 1947, the executive board of the CIO declared, "The sponsors of this legislation have attempted to commit the perfect crime. They seek to destroy labor unions, to degrade living standards, to extinguish and to cripple the exercise of basic rights and forever to prevent the great mass of those whose needs are thus to be sacrificed to reaction and privilege from shaking off this yoke of want and depression."[6]

Testifying before the Committee on Labor and Public Welfare, Arthur J. Goldberg, general counsel of the CIO, declared, "It is my contention that the Taft-Hartley Act is a strikebreaking law, that the Taft-Hartley Act can convert any legal strike into an illegal strike."[7]

Not to be outdone by the CIO, the AFL condemned the Taft-Hartley Act in an equally vigorous manner. In the AFL convention of 1947, the Executive Council of the Federation contended that the statute "seeks to weaken, render impotent, and destroy labor unions. It does so by striking a vital blow at free collective bargaining and substituting a process of government domination over employer-employee relationships."[8]

William Green, president of the AFL, declared, "The Taft-Hartley Act was passed over the strong opposition of labor. Workingmen and unions throughout the nation protested against the passage of this objectionable legislation. This opposition was based upon the knowledge of labor that it was impracticable, unworkable, and violated the common elemental rights of labor. Time and experience have shown that labor was right and the sponsors of the bill were wrong."[9]

The controversy concerning the law highlights the necessity for a careful approach to determining the factors primarily responsible for the new law. To this end we must be concerned with fact and experience. The controversial question must be appraised in terms of the record in order to pass judgment on the statute. Is the statute actually a "slave labor" law? Are unions really weakened by the statute? What about the issue of protecting the union member from his labor organization? Is it true that the statute substitutes government control of collective bargaining for free collective bargaining? Does Taft-Hartley seriously interfere with the right to strike? Does the employee still receive adequate protection of his rights to self-organization and collective bargaining? These problems as well as others merit close attention.

FACTORS RESULTING IN PASSAGE
OF TAFT-HARTLEY

The Taft-Hartley Act represents a significant change in the climate of industrial relations law. Before proceeding to an analysis of the issues growing out of the application of this statute, it is essential that attention be focused on the factors which partially explain enactment of Taft-Hartley. Laws do not spring from a vacuum; they are the result of definite conditions which give rise to legislative action. At this point our concern is not to criticize or commend Congress for the enactment of Taft-Hartley but merely to examine the circumstances that produced the statute. The mere presentation of the environmental framework which resulted in the passage of the legislation does not necessarily mean a stamp of approval or disapproval on the law. With these qualifications in mind an examination of some forces which influenced the passage of Taft-Hartley will prove profitable.

Perennial Opposition to the Wagner Act

Some employers and other special-interest groups never accepted the philosophy of the Wagner Act. They were not inclined to feel favorable toward a law that gave effective legal support to the collective bargaining process. The success of the Wagner Act in promoting a strong and expanding union movement served to intensify efforts to destroy the legislation. From the year in which the statute was enacted until the passage of Taft-Hartley, each session of Congress was marked by organized efforts calculated to repeal the Wagner Act.

Actually, opponents of the Wagner Act were successful on the state level long before they managed to alter the federal labor relations policy. As noted in the preceding chapter, the Wagner Act applied only to workers engaged in interstate commerce. Even after the Supreme Court decided to apply the law to manufacturing, millions of workers engaged in activities defined as intrastate received no benefits from the Wagner Act. One writer points out that in 1940 some 13 million nonagricultural workers were associated in industries not covered by the Wagner Act.[10] This category includes employees of beauty parlors, garages, cleaning establishments, and retail stores. Some state legislatures, aware of this situation, enacted "little Wagner Acts": to provide intrastate workers with legal protection of the right to self-organization and collective bargaining. In 1937, the year in which the Supreme Court validated the Wagner Act, such laws were passed in Utah, Wisconsin, New York, Pennsylvania, and Massachusetts. Rhode Island enacted a "little Wagner Act" in 1941 and the Connecticut legislature passed one in 1945. Except for minor differences these state laws resembled the national statute. Thus a considerable number of intrastate workers received legal protection of their organizational rights.

Organized labor desired that many more states would pass similar legislation. However, their hopes were not realized. Instead the trend was completely reversed and in place of laws favorable to unions many states enacted restrictive labor relations laws. In fact Wisconsin, Pennsylvania, and Utah repealed their little Wagner Acts and passed in their place legislation which provided for general restrictions on the activities of labor unions. In addition, the states of Michigan, Minnesota, Kansas, and Colorado passed legislation which likewise provided for the general regulation of labor unions. All these union-control laws were enacted before Taft-Hartley was passed by Congress. Wisconsin, Pennsylvania, Minnesota, and Michigan adopted such laws in 1939; Kansas and Colorado in 1943; and Utah in the spring of 1947.

The union-control acts of these states have little resemblance to the Wagner Act. In the place of statutes protecting the right of labor to self-organization and collective bargaining, they provided for the curtailment of the right of employees to strike, picket, boycott, and carry on organizational campaigns. Labor leaders bitterly denounced these laws. For example, Mr. Henry Ohl, chairman of the Wisconsin Federation of Labor, characterized the new Wisconsin law as the "most astounding and most vicious piece of legislation in his 40 years of experience."[11]

A. J. Biemiller, member of the Wisconsin legislature, likewise criticized the Wisconsin law, claiming that the bill would "strait-jacket" labor and would "allow employers to block the growth of unionism."[12] A Wisconsin newspaper viewed the concern of labor and concluded that "probably never before in the last two decades have labor leaders shown such alarm over a piece of legislation."[13]

Pressure groups that were successful in obtaining union-control laws on the state level also spearheaded the attack on the Wagner Act. The same criticisms voiced against the little Wagner Acts were leveled against the Wagner Act and the NLRB. For example, Mr. Milo R. Swanton, executive secretary of the Wisconsin Council of Agriculture, the special-interest group which ostensibly effected the passage of the Wisconsin union-control law,[14] appeared before the Senate Labor Committee and presented similar criticisms of the Wagner Act.[15]

Thus opponents of the Wagner Act type of legislation were successful on the state level prior to the amending of the national law. State union-control laws antedated by many years the amending of the Wagner Act and the enactment of Taft-Hartley. In fact, many of the provisions contained in the 1947 federal labor statute duplicate terms of previously enacted state laws. Such similarities should be expected for the same pressure groups which accepted neither the philosophy nor the objectives of the Wagner Act worked diligently to assert their philosophy of labor relations law on state and federal statute books. Organized labor did not present a united effort to forestall such pressures for change.

The Wagner Act: Popular Delusions

Perhaps no other law was so misunderstood by the public as the Wagner Act. It is possible that general misconceptions regarding the Wagner Act constituted an important factor in the enactment of Taft-Hartley. The public did not have much of an opportunity to understand the nature of the Wagner Act or of the duties and functions of the NLRB. In general, the law and the Board received a "bad press." Rulings of the NLRB consistent with the overall philosophy and purpose of the Wagner Act were highly criticized. Little effort was made by any group to relate administrative rulings to the basic philosophy and objectives of the Wagner Act. Board members rarely appeared to explain why the fundamental philosophy of the Wagner Act was consistent with the modern industrial relations environment.

In addition, the public was not adequately informed as to what the Wagner Act *did not* do. Popular misunderstandings grew up surrounding the law. Some people believed that the Wagner Act provided for mediation and conciliation and that the NLRB was a mediation agency. Nothing, of course, was farther from the truth. When President Roosevelt approved the Wagner Act on July 5, 1935, he declared that the NLRB "is an independent quasi-judicial body. It should be clearly understood that it will not act as a mediator nor as a conciliator in labor disputes. . . . Compromise, the essence of mediation, has no place in the interpretation and enforcement of the law."[16] Further, the public was not clearly informed that the Wagner Act and the NLRB did not: require workers to join labor unions; force agreement between management and labor; establish conditions and terms of employment; or prevent the discharge of employees for any reason other than for labor organization activities. The Wagner Act did not purport to eliminate *all* strikes, but merely *organizational* strikes; and the law did not *require* the closed shop, but merely permitted it when a majority-designated union and employer through collective bargaining agreed on such an arrangement.

The NLRB was portrayed as an agency unique in the federal legislative framework. It was charged that the NLRB acted as prosecutor, judge, and jury in unfair labor practice cases. What the public did not learn was that every Board decision was subject to review by the federal courts, including the Supreme Court of the United States. All federal administrative agencies were organized along the lines of the NLRB. In addition, the vast majority of cases of the NLRB were settled on a voluntary and informal basis without the necessity of proceeding to costly and time-consuming litigation. The public was led to believe that an employer, once charged with an unfair labor practice, had little opportunity to defend himself. It was not widely known that more than 50 percent of all charges alleging employer unfair labor practices were dismissed by the NLRB or withdrawn by the charging party at Board insistence. The debate over the need to amend the Wagner Act was interrupted by World War II. However, even the war years were not devoid of occurrences that conditioned the general public for changes in national labor policy.

Developments during World War II

From January 12, 1942, until June 25, 1943, wartime labor disputes were settled in accordance with the procedures outlined by the President of the United States. With one glaring exception, they proved successful in minimizing the effects of strikes on the operation of the nation's wartime economy. This exception involved the coal strikes which swept the nation during the early months of 1943. The United Mine Workers Union, led by John L. Lewis, defied the NWLB and would not cooperate with it to find a peaceful solution for the coal disputes. Its officers even refused to attend the coal-dispute hearings conducted by the Board. The coal strikes plus the defiant attitude of the officers of the UMW stimulated the passage of the controversial War Labor Disputes Act.[17] This law gave statutory authority to the President to seize war facilities; made it a criminal offense to instigate, direct, or aid a strike in a government-seized plant; gave the National War Labor Board statutory authority and defined its powers; prohibited labor organizations from contributing funds for political purposes; and, finally, outlawed strikes in privately operated war plants unless and until thirty-day strike notices had been filed and a strike vote taken to indicate the strike desires of war workers.

Both William Green, president of the AFL, and Philip Murray, president of the CIO, vigorously condemned the law. They contended that organized labor should not be punished by such legislation because the nation's unions had largely kept the no-strike pledge in good faith. Ultimately, President Roosevelt vetoed the bill, declaring that

> American labor as well as American business gave their "no-strike, no-lockout" pledge after the attack on Pearl Harbor. That pledge has been well kept except in the case of the leaders of the United Mine Workers. For the entire year of 1942, the time lost by strikes averaged only 5/100ths of 1 per cent of the total man hours worked. The American people should realize that fact—that 99 and 95/100 per cent of the work went forward without strikes and that only 5/100ths of 1 per cent of the work was delayed by strikes. That record has never before been equaled in this country.[18]

Congress, however, was not deterred by the President's arguments. It passed the War Labor Disputes Act over his veto. Actually, from the point of view of war-time production, there was little need for the War Labor Disputes Act. Even before its passage the President, by virtue of his constitutional war powers, had the authority to seize any plant or facility in the nation when operation of a firm was threatened or interfered with by a strike. As a matter of fact, at the time Congress was considering the law, the government had already seized the mines involved in the 1943 coal strikes, which stimulated the passage of the War Labor Disputes Act. Once the mines were seized, the miners returned to their jobs and production was resumed. Moreover, the law did not improve on the procedures for the settlement of wartime disputes. On the contrary, by providing for the strike-vote election, Congress actually encouraged wartime strikes.[19] As expected, workers voted to strike in the vast majority of ballots. This did not mean a work stoppage occurred every time a group of workers voted to strike. The effect of a favorable strike vote, however, served as a mandate to strike. Thus it scarcely can be argued that the War Labor Disputes Act promoted the nation's wartime production program. The statute was not needed to insure adherence of American labor to the no-strike pledge. Underlying the War Labor Disputes Act was a definite change in labor philosophy, which in postwar years contributed to the passage of national and state antiunion-control legislation.

That organized labor largely maintained its wartime no-strike pledge is borne out by the record. The average annual man-days lost to industry because of work stoppages during the war period, in relation to the number of man-days worked, was 11/100 of 1 percent. In comparison, an average of 27/100 of 1 percent was lost from total working time because of work stoppages in the years 1935–1939. Whereas the average duration of strikes was twenty-three days in 1939, twenty-one days in 1940, and eighteen days in 1941, the average duration of strikes was much less during the war years. In 1942 the average length of a strike was twelve days, in 1943 it was only five days; and in 1944 five and one-half days.[20] Of course, labor's no-strike pledge would not have been effective had the government failed to establish procedures calculated to adjust wartime disputes fairly and speedily. The overall plan for wartime labor peace was highly successful. In this plan the National War Labor Board played a leading role. During the war it settled approximately eighteen thousand disputes, which involved about 12 million workers. Assured that their disputes would be adjusted fairly and quickly by the NWLB when direct negotiations and mediation failed to result in a solution, the nation's unions in good faith maintained the no-strike pledge. However, the strike that did occur during World War II received widespread public attention and was not forgotten in the postwar period when national labor policy was reconsidered.

Another controversy arose during World War II which cannot be ignored in evaluating factors that led to enactment of the Taft-Hartley Act. "No issue presented to the War Labor Board precipitated more furious debate than union security."[21] Employer representatives contended that a dispute over union security should not be settled by the NWLB. On this point management declared that it believed "the board should not accept for arbitration or consideration the issue of the closed shop, requiring a person to become or remain a member of a labor organization if he is to get or hold a job."

Organized labor was just as emphatic in its belief that the Board should settle all disputes, including those arising out of union security. It was argued that if management's position on union security was accepted, workers, *pledged not to strike*, could not take effective action to protect their unions from antilabor conduct. In the light of these considerations, it is understandable why labor "hailed with delight" Roosevelt's decision that *all* disputes, including the union-security controversy, were to be within the jurisdiction of the NWLB.

Roosevelt's decision, however, did not settle the controversy. In fact the dispute over the issue in the conference merely foreshadowed the conflict that was to take place among the union and employer members of the NWLB. Employer representatives of the Board felt the government should not compel workers to join a union in order to work. They stated that "it is contrary to the principles of democratic government for this or any other governmental agency, to make union membership a condition of employment."[22] On the other hand, labor unions urged that the wartime industrial relations environment required that the NWLB direct the inclusion of union-security arrangements in labor agreements. One of the most important phases of the NWLB's work is related to the manner in which it settled the union-security controversy.

No great problem confronted the Board when union-security clauses were contained in labor agreements previous to World War II. Under such circumstances the Board usually ordered the same arrangement contained in contracts negotiated during the war years. In short, it directed the continuation of a closed shop or union shop when such an arrangement was previously included in a labor agreement. Labor unions were delighted with this policy. Since workers pledged not to strike, it is possible that union-security arrangements could have been eliminated in the absence of NWLB policy.

The Board, however, refused to order a closed shop or union shop when such arrangements had not characterized a firm's prewar labor-management relations program. This decision, bitterly denounced by labor union leaders, was in keeping with the principle laid down by President Roosevelt that "the Government of the United States will not order nor will Congress pass legislation ordering a so-called closed shop."[23] The Board interpreted the President's statement as extending to the union shop as well as closed shop. However, it did not feel that the President's policy was violated when it directed the continuation of the closed shop and union shop when these union-security arrangements were in effect before World War II.

If the NWLB had refused to grant some form of union security to a labor union that had not enjoyed such an arrangement before World War II, the government in effect would have frozen the open shop where it had existed previous to Pearl Harbor. Unions argued they would not be protected against members who dropped out of the organization for real or fancied reasons. The latter consideration assumed great significance in the light of the wartime wage stabilization program. A labor union's greatest appeal involves the contention it is able to obtain higher wages. During World War II increases in wage rates could be obtained only after governmental approval. Some union members, aware of these considerations, might have felt that union membership was not necessary and hence might have dropped out of the organization. This could have been particularly true when the union failed to obtain governmental approval for wage-rate increases.

In short, organized labor felt that the progress of the union movement during World War II turned on the union-security policy of the NWLB. Union leaders were fearful that in the absence of an adequate union-security program the union movement would become a wartime casualty. The NWLB was impressed by the position of organized labor. In particular, the Board was aware of labor's no-strike pledge. Some form of union security, it felt, was justified to balance the scales. Thus the public members of the Board declared that "the unions for the duration of the war gave up the use of their economic power with which to win increased security and increased wages. The nation should, in equity, provide the unions with a fair protection against disintegration both from the impacts and controls of war. . . ."[24]

Indeed, the NWLB was faced with dilemmas ! One was the union's position. The other involved the principle laid down by President Roosevelt. Clearly, it appears of questionable public policy for a government agency to force workers into labor unions. Such a policy appears as unjust as one that would result in the undermining of the union movement. To resolve this most perplexing problem, the NWLB utilized the *maintenance-of-membership arrangement*. This arrangement required that all present and future members of the union must remain members for the duration of the contract as a condition of employment. Actually, the NWLB did not "invent" the maintenance-of-membership arrangement. In 1941 the National Defense Mediation Board, an agency set up to help settle labor disputes in the pre–Pearl Harbor defense period, made use of the arrangement. Moreover, the National Defense Mediation Board did not itself create the maintenance-of-membership device. Such arrangements were used as union-security measures during the early 1930s in the chemical, meat-packing, and paper and pulp industries. Maintenance of membership, the NWLB reasoned, adequately reconciled the problem of individual freedom and union security. On this point it declared that the maintenance-of-membership arrangement

> is not a closed shop, is not a union shop, and is not a preferential shop. No old employee and no new employee is required to join the union to keep his job. If in the union, a member has the freedom for 15 days to get out and keep his job. If not in the union, the worker has the freedom to stay out and keep his job. This freedom to join or not to join, to stay in or get out, with foreknowledge of being bound by this clause as a condition of employment during the term of the contract, provides for both individual liberty and union security.[25]

To add further protection to the individual worker, the NWLB at one time required that maintenance of membership would not be ordered unless a majority of the members of a union voted for the inclusion of a maintenance-of-membership provision in a labor agreement. Such a referendum was secret and conducted under the supervision of the Board. This policy closely resembles the union-shop election feature provided by Taft-Hartley and later repealed in 1951. However, the NWLB conducted only one maintenance-of-membership election. An election was held in the *International Harvester* case. Out of a total of 10,751 ballots cast, 9,703, or 91 percent, voted in favor of the union-security arrangement. After the experience with this election, the Board dropped the procedure. It declared that "the technique had many disadvantages. It was expensive. When large companies were involved, it was time consuming and required the services of many trained people—far in excess of the Board's small staff. It created disturbances in the plant and interfered with war production."[26]

The principal ground upon which the agency declined to direct maintenance of membership was "union irresponsibility." The chief test for union "responsibility" rested on the degree to which labor unions kept in good faith labor's wartime no-strike pledge. Unions that violated the pledge did not obtain the coveted maintenance-of-membership arrangement. In the first case in which the NWLB refused to order maintenance of membership, the union involved clearly violated the no-strike pledge. While a renewal of the labor agreement was being negotiated with the company, the union repeatedly threatened to strike. Eventually, the union leaders recommended to the union members that they authorize a strike. This they did, and a strike took place. In denying the union's request for maintenance of membership, the NWLB pointed out that "the fact that the union leaders and membership authorized a strike instead of using peaceful means of settling the question under dispute indicated to the Board that the union was insincere in its no-strike pledge."[27]

By denying maintenance of membership to unions that arbitrarily violated labor's no-strike pledge, the NWLB obviously served the best interests of the nation. As noted, the NWLB awarded maintenance of membership to compensate organized labor for its surrender of the right to strike. Clearly, if a particular labor union violated this pledge and thereby endangered the *security of the nation*, it had no moral right to *union security*. In short the NWLB rewarded unions that maintained the no-strike pledge. Such a policy aided the nation's wartime production program and served the interests of industrial justice. The public followed the union-security issue during the war period and its concern was reflected in the eventual passage of state right-to-work laws and the Taft-Hartley Act. Both reflect the expressed concerns with closed- and union-shop arrangements. Debate over the desirability of such arrangements continue to this day.

Responsibility of Organized Labor

When the Wagner Act was passed, the labor movement was weak from the point of view of membership and bargaining strength. However, under the protection of government policy the union movement grew and prospered. With this growth it was inevitable that some unions and some union leaders would resort to practices of dubious social value. Some labor leaders, relatively new and inexperienced in their roles as officers, did not discharge their duties judicially. A few of the older union leaders, aware of their increased power, adopted courses of action which invited public criticism. For example, the coal strikes of early 1943, carried out during a critical period in the nation's war effort, were recalled with disfavor when strikes increased throughout industry in the early postwar period.

With the growing strength of organized labor, the public became more aware of the abuses of the labor movement. Aspects of the closed shop, the boycott, strikes of questionable moral justification, the discrimination of unions against minority groups, restrictions on output, and laxity in the administration of members' dues served to focus critical attention on the union movement. Actually, these features were part of the union movement long before the passage of the Wagner Act. However, with the growing power of labor unions, these abuses took on greater proportions in the public mind. People basically antiunion in thinking made the most of union shortcomings to point to the general undesirability of unions and collective bargaining.

The critical observer of organized labor is well aware of this area of union conduct. As a matter of fact, this aspect of organized labor is recognized by many union leaders. A labor union publication has this to say about antisocial practices of labor organizations:

> Every national union official, as well as the intelligent membership of organized labor, knows there are some things wrong in the trade union movement. In this respect trade unions differ, and they differ in accordance with their age and history, with the attitude of the industry with which they deal, with the type of their membership, and with respect to other factors.[28]

It is clear that the Wagner Act did not purport to deal with antisocial practices of labor unions. Its purpose was to equalize bargaining power between management and labor. It did not regulate union activities, even those which appeared injurious to the public. This omission was seized upon by opponents of the Wagner Act to brand the law unfair and one-sided. It was charged that the law regulated the activities of employers in the collective bargaining relationship but neglected to deal with any union practices. At the time the statute was enacted, such an argument received little attention. Union abuses were not considered a major problem because the country was more concerned with restoring prosperity. In short union-control legislation in 1935 was not of major concern. Legislation providing effective protection of the right of workers to self-organization and collective bargaining was essential if the collective bargaining process was to be strengthened and expanded. However, the argument of "one-sidedness" took on a different meaning after the union movement became a powerful factor in the national economy. There was a need for the Wagner Act. Its defect lay in the fact that it was not broadened from time to time to regulate union practices as abuses were recognized.

Organized labor was largely responsible for the failure of Congress to enact amendments to the Wagner Act that would correct outstanding abuses of the union movement. Representatives of organized labor refused to participate in any program calculated to preserve essentially the substance of the Wagner Act, but which would outlaw or regulate antisocial union activities. Unions wanted no change in the Wagner Act. For many years the stand-pat policy was effective. Until 1946 the nation sent Democratic majorities to both houses of Congress and re-elected F.D. Roosevelt three times, a record unprecedented in American history. Supported by organized labor, the Democratic congresses refused to alter the Wagner Act in any manner whatsoever. From 1935 to 1947 the law remained unaltered.

It may have been politically expedient over the long run if the union leaders had supported the enactment of periodic amendments to the Wagner Act. Such revisions, made by a sympathetic Congress, would have been moderate in character and designed in such a manner as to eliminate the necessity for sweeping changes with a single statute. Such changes, moreover, would have been directed at specific union abuses and likely would not have been as inclusive as the 1947 amendments.

The Strike Record of 1946

In the elections of 1946 the nation's representatives were aware of many problems growing out of World War II. People identified price control, shortages of consumer goods, and the general postwar inconveniences with the incumbent political party. The public was ready to deal with many of the accumulating problems that had received slight legislative attention because of the pressures of regulating a wartime economy.

Although the candidates fought the 1946 election campaign on a wide front, they made much of the wave of strikes that took place after the termination of World War II. Actually, the strike experience in 1946 was the worst the nation ever encountered. In that year 4,985 strikes occurred. Of greater importance, these strikes resulted in an unprecedented 116 million man-days of lost production. Estimated working time lost because of the 1946 strikes amounted to 1.43 percent. In comparison with the 1946 strike figures, the record for 1945 discloses 4,750 strikes and only 38 million man-days lost to production, the latter figure resulting in a loss to estimated working time of .47 percent.

The 1946 strike record was considered evidence of inadequacies in the Wagner Act. Actually, no labor law oriented toward free collective bargaining could have prevented the 1946 strike wave because 62.5 percent of all the strikes in this year were caused by disputes between employees and employers over wages, hours, and other working conditions. Since the organizational strike in 1946 accounted for only a fraction of all work stoppages, it was not correct to "blame" the Wagner Act for the 1946 strikes. This statute could be held accountable only from one point of view: it fostered a labor movement strong enough to take strike action in attempts to achieve collective bargaining objectives.

The 1946 strike wave had its roots in fundamental economic factors. With the end of the war the hours of work decreased from a wartime average of about 45 per week to a 1946 average of 40.4. Such a reduction of hours meant loss of overtime premiums and a sharp reduction in weekly earnings. To offset the reduction of the average work week, labor unions struck to increase hourly rates. Union pressure for higher wages in 1946 was also stimulated by the inflationary spiral of prices. General postwar shortages, the termination of rationing, reconversion problems, the unprecedented postwar public debt, the liberal credit policy of banks, and the foreign commitments of the United States all were important postwar inflationary factors. When price controls were removed in the summer of 1946, these inflationary forces produced an upward swing in the price level never before experienced in the nation. The cost-of-living index moved from 133.3 on June 15, 1946, to 153.3 on December 15, 1946 (1935–1939 = 100). Thus in a period of six months the cost of living increased by 15.04 percent. Caught between a reduction of take-home pay and rising prices, labor unions, pledged to protect the standard of living of their members, engaged in widespread strikes for higher rates of pay.

Consideration of the basic causes for the strikes of 1946 raises questions about the argument that the Wagner Act was the responsible factor for their outbreak. The Congress and the public were convinced that new labor legislation would alleviate many of the perceived abuses of organized labor.

After congressional debate, the Taft-Hartley Act was adopted in the House by a 320-79 vote, and the Senate voted in favor of the legislation, 68-24. When the law reached the desk of President Truman, he vetoed the legislation. This was expected;

in the summer of 1946 he had vetoed the "Case bill," a law that contained many of the provisions embodied in the Taft-Hartley law. While vetoing the Taft-Hartley Act, Truman in part declared:

> The bill taken as a whole would reverse the basic direction of our national labor policy, inject the Government into private economic affairs on an unprecedented scale, and conflict with important principles of our democratic society. Its provisions would cause more strikes, not fewer. It would contribute neither to industrial peace nor to economic stability and progress. It would be a dangerous stride in the direction of a totally managed economy. It contains seeds of discord which would plague this Nation for years to come.[29]

Despite the action of President Truman, the House and Senate overrode his veto and Taft-Hartley became the law of the land on June 23, 1947.

Thus Taft-Hartley supplanted the Wagner Act as the expression of the labor policy of the nation. Supporters of the legislation did not hesitate to affirm the fact that the law marked a significant shift in the attitude of government toward collective bargaining. In this connection Hartley declared that the bill was designed to reverse the basic direction of national labor policy. In fact, that was the primary intention of the authors of the measure.

TAFT-HARTLEY PROVISIONS

The Labor-Management Relations Act (Taft-Hartley) amended but did not displace the Wagner Act. The Wagner Act unfair employer practices were continued virtually word for word in the 1947 law. One significant change was that the closed shop (the arrangement requiring that all workers be union members at the time they are hired) was prohibited. In addition, the freedom of the parties to authorize the union shop (the employer may hire anyone he chooses, but all new workers must join the union after a stipulated period of time) was narrowed. Congressional intent in the passage of this amendment was to narrow even more the restrictions against employees with regard to hire or tenure of employment. Greater freedom of choice for employees to determine representation status free from both union and employer interference was intended.

The congressional attitude toward unions was expressed in other important provisions of the Taft-Hartley Act which dealt with: (1) union unfair labor practices; (2) the rights of employees as individuals; (3) the rights of employers; and (4) national emergency strikes. In addition, other provisions dealt with internal union affairs, the termination of modification of existing labor contracts, and suits involving unions.

UNION UNFAIR LABOR PRACTICES

Six union unfair labor practices were provided by the Taft-Hartley Act. Labor organizations operating in interstate commerce were to refrain from: (1) restraining or coercing employees in the exercise of their guaranteed collective bargaining rights;

(2) causing an employer to discriminate in any way against an employee in order to encourage or discourage union membership; (3) refusing to bargain in good faith with an employer regarding wages, hours, and other conditions of employment; (4) certain types of strikes and boycotts; (5) requiring employees covered by union-shop contracts to pay initiation fees or dues "in an amount which the Board finds excessive or discriminatory under all the circumstances"; and (6) "featherbedding," the requirement of payment by an employer for services not performed.

Two of the six provisions have perhaps had the greatest influence on collective bargaining—and undoubtedly a salutary one—in the 27 years since the enactment of Taft-Hartley. The first is the ban on union restraint or coercion of employees in the exercise of their guaranteed bargaining rights, which also entails a union obligation to avoid coercion of employees who choose to refrain from collective bargaining altogether. What constitutes such restraint or coercion? The myriad of rulings rendered by the NLRB and courts since 1947 has at least indicated that such union actions as the following will always run the risk of being found "unfair": communicating to an antiunion employee that the employee will lose his job should the union gain recognition; the signing of an agreement with an employer which recognizes the union as exclusive bargaining representative when in fact it lacks majority employee support; and the issuing of patently false statements during a representation election campaign. Union picket-line violence, threats of reprisal against employees subpoenaed to testify against the union at NLRB hearings, and activities of a similar vein are also unlawful.

This first unfair union practice also deals with coercion of an employer in his selection of a bargaining representative. Post-1947 rulings have stated, for example, that unions cannot refuse to deal with former union officers who represent employers, or insist on meeting only with the owners of a company rather than with the company's attorney. On the other hand, unions have every right to demand that the employer representative with whom they deal have sufficient authority to make final decisions on behalf of the company. The interpreters of public policy have clearly understood that to have this any other way would frustrate the entire process of bargaining.

The second Taft-Hartley provision makes it an unfair practice for a union to cause an employer to discriminate against an employee in order to influence union membership. There is a single exception to this prohibition. Under a valid union-shop agreement the union may lawfully demand the discharge of an employee who fails to pay his initiation fee and periodic dues. Otherwise, however, unions must exercise complete self-control in this area. They cannot try to force employers to fire or otherwise penalize workers for any other reason, whether these reasons involve worker opposition to union policies, failure to attend union meetings, or refusal to join the union at all. Nor can a union lawfully seek to persuade an employer to grant hiring preference to employees who are "satisfactory" to the union. Subject only to the union-shop proviso, Taft-Hartley sought to place nonunion workers on a footing equal to that of union employees.

Another restriction on union practices pertains to union refusal to bargain. This third Taft-Hartley restriction extended to labor organizations the same obligation that the Wagner Act had already imposed on employers. Prior to 1947 it was widely publicized that some unions merely presented employers with a list of demands on a take-it-or-leave-it basis. To many observers, however, the law's inclusion of this union bargaining provision has meant very little. Unions can normally be expected to pursue bargaining rather that attempt to avoid it. Nevertheless, the NLRB has used it to some extent in the years since Taft-Hartley to narrow the scope of permissible union action. The Board has, for example, found it unlawful under this section for a union to strike against an employer who has negotiated, and continues to negotiate, on a multiemployer basis with the goal of forcing him to bargain independently. It has also found that a union's refusal to bargain on an employer proposal for a written contract violates this part of the law. In short, some inequities seem to have been corrected by this good-faith bargaining provision.

The fourth unfair union practice has given rise to considerable litigation. Indeed, of all six Taft-Hartley union prohibitions the ban on certain types of strikes and boycotts has proven the most difficult to interpret. Even as "clarified" by Congress in 1959, this area remains a particularly difficult one for labor lawyers.

Briefly, Section 8(b)(4) of the 1947 act prohibits unions from striking or boycotting if such actions have any of the following three objectives: (1) forcing an employer or self-employed person to join any labor or employer organization or to cease dealing with another employer (secondary boycott); (2) compelling recognition as employee bargaining agent from another employer without NLRB certification; (3) forcing an employer to assign particular work to a particular craft.

Particularly in regard to the secondary boycott provision, it does not take much imagination to predict where heated controversy could arise. To constitute a secondary boycott, the union's action must be waged against "another" employer, one who is entirely a neutral in the battle and is merely caught as a pawn in the union's battle with the real object of its concern. But when is the secondary employer really neutral and when is he an "ally" of the primary employer? The Board has sometimes ruled against employers alleging themselves to be "secondary" ones on the grounds of common ownership with that of the "primary" employer and, again, when "struck work" has been turned over by primary employers to secondary ones. But Board and court rulings here have not been entirely consistent.

In its other clauses, too, the Taft-Hartley strike and boycott provisions have led to intense legal battles. When is a union, for example, unlawfully seeking recognition without NLRB certification and when is it merely picketing to protest undesirable working conditions (a normally legal action)? Is a union ever entitled to try to keep within its bargaining unit work that has traditionally been performed by the unit employees? On some occasions, but not all, the Board has ruled that there is nothing wrong with this. The histories of post-1947 cases on these issues constitute a fascinating study in the making of fine distinctions. At least, however, the large incidence of litigation might indicate that the parties have not been totally able to overlook the new rights and responsibilities placed upon them by Taft-Hartley (whatever these might be).

Last— and least in the magnitude of their effect— stand the relatively unenforceable provisions relating to union fees and dues and featherbedding.

The fifth union unfair practice prohibits charging workers covered by union-shop agreements excessive or discriminatory dues or initiation fees. The provision includes a stipulation that the NLRB should consider "all the circumstances" in determining discrimination or excess. Such circumstances, the wording of the Taft-Hartley Act continues, include "the practices and customs of labor organizations in the particular industry and the wages currently paid to the employees affected." Without further yardsticks and depending almost exclusively on the sentiments of individual employees rather than on irate employers for enforcement, this part of the Act has had little practical value. In one of the relatively few such cases to come before it thus far, the Board ruled that increasing an initiation fee from $75 to $250 and thus charging new members the equivalent of about four weeks' wages when other unions in the area charged only about one-eighth of this amount was unlawful. In another case it was held that the union's uniform requirement of a reinstatement fee for ex-members that was higher than the initiation fee for new members was *not* discriminatory under the Act.

The sixth and final unfair labor practice for unions has proved even less influential in governing collective bargaining. Taft-Hartley prohibits unions from engaging in *featherbedding*. The Board has ruled that this provision does *not* prevent labor organizations from seeking *actual* employment for their members, "even in situations where the employer does not want, does not need, and is not willing to accept such services." Mainly because of this latter interpretation, the antifeatherbedding provision has had little effect. A union would be quite willing to have work performed and the question of need is irrelevant. Employer spokesmen for some industries—entertainment and the railroads in particular—have succeeded in convincing the public that their unwanted—but performing—workers are featherbedding, but under current interpretation of the law such practices are not illegal.

THE RIGHTS OF EMPLOYEES AS INDIVIDUALS

In other areas, too, the Act attempted to even the scales of collective bargaining and the alleged injustices of the 1935–1947 period. Taft-Hartley, unlike the Wagner Act, recognized a need to protect the rights of individual employees *against* labor organizations. It explicitly amended the 1935 legislation to give a majority of the employees the right to *refrain* from, as well as engage in, collective bargaining activities. It also dealt more directly with the question of individual freedoms—even beyond its previously mentioned outlawing of the closed shop, union coercion, union-caused employer discrimination against employees, and excessive union fees.

Perhaps most symbolically, Taft-Hartley provided that should any state wish to pass legislation more restrictive of union security than the union shop (or, in other words, to outlaw labor contracts that make union membership a condition of retaining employment), the state was free to do so. Some states have enacted legislation to restrict the range of permissible union security. Nineteen states—mainly in the South and Southwest—now have so-called *"right-to-work" legislation*. Advocates of such laws have claimed that compulsory unionism violates the basic American right of freedom of association. Opponents of right-to-work laws have pointed out, among other arguments, that majority rule is inherent in our democratic procedure. Thus far, however, there has been an impressive correlation between stands on this particular question and attitudes about the values of unionism in general. Individuals opposed to collective bargaining have favored right-to-work laws with amazing regularity. Pro-unionists seem to have been equally consistent in their attacks on such legislation. It is still unproven at any rate that right-to-work laws have had much effect on labor relations in the states where they exist. One study points out, "The general pattern emerges that existing right-to-work laws have generally been unenforceable and have accomplished little."[30] The laws are, in short, considerably more symbolic than they are of real consequence.

Also designed to strengthen workers' rights as individuals was a Taft-Hartley provision allowing any *employee* the *right to present grievances directly* to the employer without union intervention. The union's representative was to have a chance to be present at such employer-employee meetings, but the normal grievance procedure (with the union actively participating) would be suspended. Few employees have thus far availed themselves of this opportunity. Clearly, the action can antagonize the union and since the *employer's* action is normally being challenged by the grievance itself, the employee may have a formidable task ahead.

Finally, the Act placed a major restriction on the fast-growing dues checkoff arrangement. Many employers had been deducting union dues from their employees' paychecks and remitting them to the union. Companies were thus spared the constant visits of dues-collecting union representatives at the workplace; unions had also found the checkoff an efficient means of collection. Under Taft-Hartley the checkoff was to remain legal, but only if the individual employee had given his own authorization in writing. Moreover, such an authorization could not be irrevocable for a period of more than one year. This restriction has hardly hampered the growth of the checkoff. Currently, the arrangement is provided for in approximately 80 percent of all labor contracts compared to an estimated 40 percent at the time of Taft-Hartley passage. The new legal provision has possibly minimized abuse of the checkoff mechanism.

THE RIGHTS OF EMPLOYERS

In still a third area Taft-Hartley circumscribed freedom of action of unions in the quest for industrial relations equity. It explicitly gave employers certain collective bargaining rights. For example, although employers were still required to recognize and bargain with properly certified unions, they could now give full freedom of expression to their views concerning union organization, so long as there was "no threat of reprisal or force or promise of benefit."

Thus an employer may now, when faced with a representation election, tell his employees that in his opinion unions are worthless, dangerous to the economy, and immoral. He may even, generally speaking, hint that the permanent closing of his plant would be the possible aftermath of a union election victory and subsequent high union wage demands. Nor will an election be set aside for that matter if he plays upon the racial prejudices of his workers (should these exist) by describing the union's philosophy toward integration or if he sets forth the union's record in regard to violence and corruption (should this record be vulnerable) and suggests that these characteristics would be logical consequences of the union's victory in his plant—although in recent years the Board has attempted to draw the line between dispassionate statements on the employer's part and inflammatory or emotional appeals.[31] An imaginative employer can in fact now engage in almost any amount of creative speaking (or writing) for his employees' consumption. The only major restraint on his conduct is that he must avoid threats, promises, coercion, and direct interference with worker-voters in the reaching of their decision. Two lesser restrictions also govern: the employer may not hold a meeting with his employees on company time within twenty-four hours of an election; and he may never urge his employees individually at their homes or in his office to vote against the union (the Board has held that he can lawfully do this *only* "at the employees' work area or in places where employees normally gather").

Under this section of Taft-Hartley, employers can also (1) call for elections to decide questions of representation (as noted earlier); (2) refuse to bargain with supervisors' unions (the Wagner Act protection was withdrawn for these employees, although they are not prohibited from forming or joining unions *without* the NLRB machinery and other safeguards of public policy); and (3) file their unfair labor practice charges against unions.

Understandably, such changes were received with favor by the employer community.

NATIONAL EMERGENCY STRIKES

Of most direct interest to the general public, but of practical meaning only to those employers whose labor relations can be interpreted as affecting the national health and safety, are the *national emergency strike provisions* which were enacted in 1947. As in the case of most Taft-Hartley provisions these remain essentially unchanged to this day.

Sections 206 through 210 of the Act provide for government intervention in the case of such emergencies. If the President of the United States believes that a threatened or actual strike affects "an entire industry or a substantial part thereof" in such a way as to "imperil the national health and safety," he is empowered to take certain carefully delineated action. He may appoint a Board of Inquiry to find out and report the facts regarding the dispute. The Board is allowed subpoena authority and can thus compel the appearance of witnesses. It cannot, however, make recommendations for a settlement. On receiving the Board's preliminary report, the President may apply through the Attorney General for a court injunction restraining the strike for sixty days. If no settlement is reached during this time, the injunction can be extended for another twenty days, during which period employees are to be polled in a secret-ballot election on their willingness to accept the employer's last offer. The Board is then to submit its final report to the President. Should the strike threat still exist after all these procedures, the President is authorized to submit a full report to Congress, "with such recommendations as he may see fit to make for consideration and appropriate action."

By 1973 the national emergency provisions had been invoked on thirty occasions. They had not always been effective in bringing about settlements, however. Rees conveys the majority opinion of detached observers in pointing out that "where the fact-finders have been successful in settling disputes it is often because they have been functioning as high-level mediators, commanding more respect from the parties than the mediators ordinarily furnished by government agencies."[32] There is also evidence that the eighty-day "cooling-off" period has sometimes done no more than delay the strike for that length of time. Such was the case in nine of the twenty-six times that injunctions were used. In addition, particularly in recent years, presidents have tended to avoid using the Taft-Hartley injunction procedures (often because unionists have viewed them as antilabor, as well as because of the more visible reason expressed above, that they have not been especially effective in set-tling disputes). Lyndon Johnson, for example, exhibited a notable reluctance to tap Sections 206–210 when basic steel bargaining reached an impasse in the late summer of 1965, achieving settlement extralegally through personal pressures and recommendations. A once-controversial issue regarding the national emergency strike provisions is no longer debatable, however. The United States Supreme Court, ruling against the Steelworkers union, found the provisions themselves constitutional in 1959.

OTHER TAFT-HARTLEY PROVISIONS

Other provisions of the Act, too, have caused some concern for union leaders. The 1947 legislation devoted attention to internal union affairs, the first such regulation in American history. Its impetus came not only from the previously cited communis-tic taints attached to several unions but also from the fact that, in the case of a few other labor organizations, lack of democratic procedures and financial irregularities (often involving employer wrongdoing as well) had become glaringly evident. Accord-ingly, the Act set new conditions for unions seeking to use the NLRB's services: (1) all union officers were obligated to file annual affidavits with the Board, stating that they were not members of the Communist party; (2) certain financial and con-stitutional information had to be annually filed by unions with the Secretary of Labor; and (3) unions (as well as corporations) could no longer contribute funds for political purposes in connection with any federal election. The affidavit requirement, judged to be ineffective, was repealed in 1959. The other stipulations were allowed to remain in force until that date, when they were only slightly amended and then substantially enlarged upon (as further discussion will indicate). Essentially, aside from what unionists vocally termed a nuisance value, the provisions are notable as the first recognition in public policy that some internal regulation of the union as an institution was in the public interest—and as a harbinger of more such regulation to come.

Another Taft-Hartley provision which has upset some union leaders involved the *termination or modification of existing labor contracts*. Applicable to both labor organi-zations and employers, it requires the party seeking to end or change the agreement to give a sixty-day notice to the other party. The law further provides that during this time period the existing contract must be maintained without strikes or lockouts. In addition, the Federal Mediation and Conciliation Service and state mediation services are to be notified of the impending dispute thirty days after the serving of the notice. Workers striking in violation of this requirement lose all legal protection as "employees" in collective bargaining, although the law also asserts that "such loss of status for such employee shall terminate if and when he is re-employed" by the employer.

In some instances leaders of labor organizations have found it both difficult and politically unpopular to restrain their constituents from violating this provision. Unionists have also on occasion frankly pointed out that the scheduling prerequisites for striking have deprived their organizations of some economic power, at least insofar as the element of surprise is concerned. Yet many representatives of both parties would undoubtedly agree with Falcone that "these provisions have slowed down the calling of strikes, enabled mediators to intervene before it is too late to help and have generally provided an orderly method for resolving disputes and reaching final settlements."[33] From the point of view of the public interest, it is clearly on this latter basis that the effectiveness of the notice provisions should be judged.

Finally, Section 301 of Taft-Hartley decreed that "*suits for violations of contracts* between an employer and a labor organization representing employees in an industry affecting commerce" could be brought directly by either party in any United States district court. Labor agreements, in short, were to be construed as being legally enforceable for the first time in American history. Damage suits are not calculated to increase mutual trust or offset misunderstandings between the parties in labor relations, however, and unions and management have generally recognized this. Consequently, relatively few such suits have come to the courts in the years since this provision was enacted. Many contracts today in fact contain agreements not to sue, a perfectly legal dodge of Section 301. The remedy of the suit—for employers confronted with union violations of no-strike clauses or for unions faced with management lockout inconsistent with no-lockout provisions, for example—nonetheless remains available for both parties in the absence of any restrictive covenants.

ENFORCEMENT PROCEDURES AND REMEDIES

The NLRB came under a great deal of criticism prior to Taft-Hartley. Particularly, the agency was accused of processing complaints too slowly. Even when cases were processed it was argued that the Board fulfilled the functions of issuing complaints, trying them, and then deciding the issues. Such authority was considered too inclusive for a single agency. The 1947 amendments reorganized the Board for the purpose of dealing with both complaints.

Agency Reorganization

Under the Wagner Act, the NLRB was a single agency with control of policy concentrated in the hands of a three-member Board. The Board then was empowered to delegate functions and decentralize operations for efficient administration of the national labor law.

The Congress decided to deviate from the structure established to govern all administrative agencies. The NLRB was divided into two authorities, the Board itself and the General Counsel. The Board was to function primarily as a court. It was to be concerned only with general policy to guide operations in the decentralized offices across the country. It was also given responsibility to make decisions on election and complaint cases. Its membership was increased from three to five to fulfill its function. Any or all of its powers could be delegated to any three members. The President of the United States was authorized to appoint members for a term of five years subject to Senate approval.

Under the Wagner Act, the General Counsel was employed by the Board to serve as its legal adviser for the purpose of directing litigation and supervising Board lawyers except the law judges. Taft-Hartley placed sole responsibility to investigate and prosecute unfair labor practice complaints and the conduct of elections in the hands of an independent General Counsel. The Board retained power to hear and decide appeals from the General Counsel's determinations. Term of office for General Counsel is four years and selection is by the President with Senate approval.

For the conduct of formal hearings in unfair labor practice cases, the NLRB employs law judges who hear and decide cases. Law judges are not subject to agency supervision and are appointed from a list established by the Civil Service Commission. When a law judge renders a decision, it may be appealed to the five man Board in Washington in the form of exceptions by one or all parties involved in the case. If no exceptions are taken to the decision, the statute provides that the recommended orders of law judges become orders of the Board; exceptions to the law judges' decision must be filed within twenty days.

The entire procedure involved in processing unfair labor practices and representation elections was discussed in the previous chapter and will not be repeated here. However, it is necessary at this point to review the record regarding Board performance in dealing with cases brought before it. The division of agency function and increase in Board membership did not immediately solve the problem of an increasing backlog of cases. Time was required to adjust to a new organizational structure. Taft-Hartley itself generated a larger volume of cases through an expansion of labor-management activity subject to governmental regulation.

In fiscal 1972 there were 41,039 cases including both unfair labor practices and election petitions filed in all the regional offices. In fiscal 1955 the case intake was 13,391 whereas the total load was 9,737 cases in 1945. Unfair labor practice charges alone amounted to 2,427 in 1945, but increased from 6,171 in 1955 to 26,852 in 1972.

Unions in 1972 were responsible for 61 percent of total unfair labor practices filed against employers. Individuals filed the remaining 39 percent. Employers filed 43 percent of the total charges against unions, and individuals accounted for 53 percent of the total. Unions were responsible for 4 percent of charges in this category by filing cases against other unions.

After unfair labor practice cases were filed in the appropriate regional office in fiscal 1972, adhering to the six-month limitation for filing charges after a violation occurs or is discovered, 83.3 percent were closed on an informal basis. The three informal methods were administrative dismissals, voluntary settlements or adjustments, and voluntary withdrawal of charges. Withdrawals by charging parties before complaints were issued by regional directors accounted for 35.2 percent of the total. Dismissals amounted to 33.1 percent of cases disposed of prior to issuance of complaints. Settlements and adjustments accounted for 25.0 percent of unfair labor practice cases closed in fiscal 1972. Nearly 5 percent (4.7 percent) of cases went to the Board in Washington for decision; 2.0 percent were closed by other methods.[34]

If a case is not settled on an informal basis by one of the methods mentioned, the regional director is obliged to issue a complaint. The median number of days required from the filing of charges to issuance of complaints is illustrated in the following table.

It is obvious that both the unfair labor practice case intake and the percentage deemed meritorious are rising annually. Despite the increased load on Board operations, the median days involved from filing of charges to issuance of complaints were

DISPOSITION OF UNFAIR LABOR PRACTICE CASES
1962–1972

Fiscal Year	Case Intake	Median No. of Cases Pending	Median Age of Pending Cases (days)	Merit Cases (percent)	Median Days from Filing to Complaint
1962	13,479	1,207.5	21.5	30.7	47
1963	14,166	1,322.0	22.3	32.3	49
1964	15,620	1,618.6	23.4	33.4	56
1965	15,800	1,674.5	24.8	35.5	59
1966	15,933	1,825.0	26.0	36.6	58
1967	17,040	2,035.0	27.0	36.2	61
1968	17,816	2,313.0	26.0	34.7	58
1969	18,651	2,234.0	25.0	32.3	58
1970	21,038	2,248.0	23.0	34.2	57
1971	23,770	2,803.0	25.0	31.2	59
1972	26,952	2,730.0	22.0	32.7	51

Source: Thirty-Seventh Annual Report of the National Labor Relations Board, 1972.

61 in fiscal 1967 and back to 51 in 1972. The record reveals decreased efficiency from fiscal year 1962 when 47 days were required for processing cases prior to issuance of complaints. Adjustment to the burden of increased demand for agency services during 1971–72 brought with it a decrease in the median days required to handle cases. It should be further noted that the median period reported includes fifteen days in which parties are permitted to adjust a case and remedy violations before proceeding to formal agency procedures.

Once a complaint is issued by the regional director, it may go the full course of litigation, through formal complaint, law judge's hearing, decision by the Board, to the U.S. Appeals Court for review or enforcement, and in a limited number of cases to the U.S. Supreme Court.

In 1972 the median days required to process a case from the initial filing to issuance of a complaint were 51. After the complaint is issued, the case proceeds to a hearing before a law judge unless an informal settlement is secured. At the hearing before the law judge, evidence is presented by both parties and is incorporated into a case record upon which the law judge's decision is made. If either party to the case is dissatisfied with the decision, appeal for review may be made to the five man Board in Washington, D.C. General Counsel does not have authority to advise the Board on how to handle the case. Cases accepted by the Board for review take a considerable period of time for final decision from the date of initial filing in a regional office. The average time required to obtain a Board decision (about one year) can have the effect of substantially impairing the effectiveness of bargaining-unit employees. Congress debated the desirability of granting authority to regional directors to decide and enforce their decisions, reserving only unusual cases for Board determination. Decentralization to this extent was rejected by Congress. The basic weakness of such a time lag is that the burden is placed on discharged employees when there are employer violations of the national labor laws. Then, too, weak labor organizations may disintegrate in the course of the year required to obtain a Board decision.

After a Board decision is rendered, a dissatisfied party may appeal to a circuit court of appeals and then to the U.S. Supreme Court. The time lag between the initial filing of a charge and final determination is uncertain once the federal courts are brought into the controversy. Several years are often required to take a case to the high court for final disposition. Board decisions have been upheld in the vast majority of labor cases reviewed by the Supreme Court. The basic difficulty is that labor organizations and individuals cannot normally be restored to their original positions in the presence of prolonged litigation. From 1955 to 1957 there were 1,821 Board decisions appealed to the courts. The Board was reversed in only 310 cases. To be sure, these cases established precedent but, in general, the Board is upheld in order to pursue its major responsibility of protecting the collective bargaining rights of employees.[35]

REPRESENTATION ELECTION TIME LAGS

A major complaint unions have made against the NLRB over the years has been the time lag involved from the date of filing petitions for representation elections to the final holding of elections to determine employee choice. The essential element for labor unions is the ability to expedite election proceedings in order to keep up bargaining-unit enthusiasm to vote for union representation. A majority of elections are conducted on a consent or stipulation basis, as explained in the previous chapter. In fiscal 1972, 80 percent of all elections held were by voluntary agreement of the parties.

In the absence of voluntary resolution of issues that may confront the parties dealing with technicalities of election procedures, a hearing is held in order to establish a record for purposes of deciding the issues. Prior to 1961 the entire record had to be sent to the five man Board in Washington for final decision on election issues. In 1958 and 1959 the median days required to process representation cases from the date of filing to the close of the hearing were 28. This number fell to 24 in both 1960 and 1961. However, the median days required to process the cases from the close of the hearing through the Board decision varied. In 1958 it took 54 days, but in 1961 the process required 65 days. In short, in 1959, from the date of filing to Board decisions on the controversial issues, the median days required were 89. A great deal of damage could have resulted to the bargaining unit during such an extended period of time. Unions were vociferous in their demands to decrease the time lag required to process cases through formal channels.

The Landrum-Griffin Act of 1959 granted the Board power to delegate to its regional directors full authority to handle and decide representation cases.[36] The authority was not delegated, however, until 1961. Despite the delegation of authority, the NLRB by its own motion and discretion may accept cases for review. Such cases as are accepted are novel and precedent-making since they provide the framework within which regional directors decide cases. A refusal of the Board to review a case results in the regional director's decision becoming finalized.

The trend at the hearing stage of the process continued in a downward direction after 1961 due to increased efficiency of NLRB operations generally. The Board load of representation cases has generally increased each year since 1961 except for a slight decline in 1963 and again in 1967 and 1968. Normally, it may be stated that there is a steady increase in demand on Board time to process representation election cases.[37] Despite this fact the median days required to process the increased load from date of filing to close of hearing were 23 days in 1962, 22 in 1964, 21 in 1966, and back to 22 in 1972. However, in 1962 there was no longer a requirement to send the hearing record to Washington, D.C., for final resolution of election issues. Regional directors assumed the function with the result that the median days required to resolve issues from the closing of hearings fell to 20 in 1972. In 1963 and 1964 a record low of 17 days was achieved, but since then the time requirement has been higher. At the close of fiscal 1972, 20 days were required for regional directors to resolve questions arising from elections. From the date of filing through regional director decisions, the days required to process cases were only 42 in 1972 as compared to 89 in 1961 when the Board performed the same functions.

It is obvious that the time required to process election petitions is currently less than half that of fiscal 1961. Greater speed in processing cases occurred despite the rapidly expanding number of cases before the Board throughout the period.

The record of representation elections does not reveal any special advantages to unions despite the decreased time between filing petitions and the election itself. In 1958 unions won 61 percent of elections and in 1959 they were successful in 63 percent of polls. The time lag between filing petitions and eventual resolution of issues was greatest in 1961 and union successes fell to 56 percent. However, it was fiscal 1966 before union success at the polls exceeded their record of 1958. In that year they won 62 percent of elections. In fiscal 1972 union successes dropped to 55 percent.

It seems reasonable to conclude that as the time lag is decreased between the time of filing election petitions to the actual poll itself, the more reflective results are likely to be of the actual desires of workers. They have less time to hear and receive conflicting propaganda from both sides. Despite the pros and cons of speedier solution to election requests, the record reveals that union successes remain roughly stable over the years.

ENFORCEMENT PROCEDURES

Taft-Hartley provides four kinds of remedies for violations of its provisions. The first is the remedial order designed to make the position of wronged parties the same as it was before the violation. Remedial measures include cease and desist orders when unfair labor practices are found, the posting of notices on employer property or in union halls, and the payment of back wages in discriminatory discharge cases. For example, in fiscal year 1965 back pay awarded to discriminatees amounted to $2,782,360. In fiscal 1967 it amounted to $3,286,460 and it was $6,448,640 in 1972.

The second sanction is imposed by courts for contempt of an injunction or restraining order. Taft-Hartley provided for injunctions or restraining orders in three types of situations. One required the General Counsel to seek an injunction to restrain unlawful strikes or boycotts after an investigation revealed apparent union violations. However, the General Counsel did not actively pursue this duty until well into the 1960s. The reason was a fear of obtaining a preliminary injunction to halt union action and then learning later the move was not justified. It will be recalled that injunctions can seriously impede unions to the point of making some impotent—particularly, small, relatively powerless labor organizations. More recently, the General

Counsel has given more attention to this duty. The second provides that General Counsel might seek a restraining order requiring compliance with the law while a case is pending before the Board. He is not required to do so, but he may do so. The purpose is to eliminate flagrant violations of the Act until Board orders can be invoked to deal with the situation. The third permits the Board to seek an injunction from a circuit court of appeals to enforce its order. The petitioned court may grant the injunction if it agrees with the order. The fourth statutory provision for an injunction permits the Attorney General to seek an injunction in national emergency strikes or lockouts.

The third kind of sanction provided by Taft-Hartley permits the loss of employee rights. For example, employees could lose their rights if they engaged in strikes prior to the end of the sixty-day waiting period required for contract renegotiations.

Still a fourth type of penalty called for fines or imprisonment when certain provisions of the Act were violated. Such sanctions could be invoked because of violations of the statutory ban on political contributions and activities by unions. In addition, a fine and imprisonment was possible for interferences with Board agents in the conduct of their duties.

Unions argue that remedies and penalties provided by Taft-Hartley are inadequate to enforce the national labor policy. Unions prefer more severe penalties for flagrant violations of the national labor laws: criminal penalties, triple back pay, and withdrawal of government contracts from firms engaged in activities calculated to destroy unions. Despite the desires of unions all existing sanctions provided have been used since 1947. Remedial orders constitute the most frequently used device for enforcing the Act. All the others are highly important also when occasions arise requiring more harsh measures to deal with violations of national labor policy.

"Make-Whole" Controversy

As noted previously, an employer engages in an unfair labor practice under Taft-Hartley when he refuses to bargain collectively. When this occurs, the normal NLRB remedy is to direct the employer to comply with the law and bargain with the union. However, this kind of remedy could be of no practical value because an employer may continue in his illegal conduct. In addition, such a Board order does not remedy the losses to employees who were placed at a disadvantage because of the employer's illegal conduct. These considerations prompted a union to request from the NLRB a more meaningful remedy to enforce the national policy.

In *Ex-Cell-O*,[38] the employer refused to bargain collectively for a long period of time after the union was victorious in a representation election. The union requested that the NLRB order the employer to pay to the employees wages and fringe benefits that arguably they would have obtained through collective bargaining had the employer bargained in good faith. An administrative law judge agreed with the union. In March 1967, two years after the union was certified as the legal bargaining agent, he stated that:

> Employers who promptly comply with their obligations are placed at an economic disadvantage and flouters of the national policy are primarily rewarded. These results are completely antithetical to the purposes of the law and call for a remedy which will help restore the situation to that which would have existed but for the unfair labor practices.

Accordingly, he not only ruled that the firm must bargain with the union, but also directed that it compensate the employees for the money value of the improved wages and benefits that it would be reasonable to conclude that the union would have been able to secure through collective bargaining except for the firm's refusal to bargain. To compute the amount due the employees, the law judge was prepared to compare the wages and benefits received in the plant in question with those prevailing in other plants owned by the company in the area and whose employees were covered by labor agreements negotiated by the same national union. To implement such a "make-whole" remedy other formulas for computation could be devised.

In other words, the objective of the law judge's decision was to take the profit out of stalling in collective bargaining, and make it expensive for a firm to refuse to bargain in good faith. In any event, whatever delight the employees and union received from this decision was short-lived because three years later the NLRB, by a 3–2 vote, held that it did not have the statutory power to grant such relief. Though the Board unanimously found that the employer violated the law by its refusal to bargain collectively, the majority (which included by this time two Nixon appointees) held that it could not compel an employer to put into effect wage increases that it had not agreed to make. What makes the majority decision somewhat questionable is that all five Board members stated that they were in "complete agreement that the customary remedies the NLRB imposes are inadequate." Also, as the minority members stressed, the NLRB under Taft-Hartley in Section 10(c) has the power "to take such affirmative action . . . as will effectuate the policies of this Act." It would seem that under proper circumstances a "make-whole" remedy would be proper to effectuate the law's policy for the promotion of collective bargaining.

Though the NLRB refused to order a "make-whole" remedy in *Ex-Cell-O*, some courts apparently believe that the Board has the legal power to do so. In *Tiidee Products*, a federal appeals court remanded a case back to the Board and instructed the agency that it had ample power to issue a "make-whole" remedy to "provide meaningful relief for employees unlawfully denied the fruits of collective bargaining." [39] Also, another federal court held in *J. P. Stevens*[40] that the Board has the power to direct the remedy. In remanding the case back to the NLRB to determine whether its narrow remedy was proper in light of the illegal conduct of the company, the court stated:

> although the courts will not lightly interfere with Board orders, the Board is under a complimentary obligation to set forth in valid fashion the relationship between the case and the remedy it orders.

Perhaps one reason for the remand is that J. P. Stevens is notorious for its illegal conduct in combating unions. Thus:

> J. P. Stevens is now in its 12th step in a long chain of litigation, each marked by a separate NLRB order to the company and each involving new problems arising against the background of the preceding step, but all of them relating to the basic controversy over unionization of the Company's numerous plants throughout the South. [41]

In any event, despite the judgment of the courts that the Board has the authority under Taft-Hartley to direct a "make-whole" remedy, the NLRB at this writing still refuses to do so. In January, 1972, the Board again refused to direct the remedy in the *Tiidee* case remanded to it by the federal court. [42] To support its position, the

NLRB relies heavily upon the United States Supreme Court decision in *H. K. Porter*.[43] In this case, the court ruled that the NLRB does not have the power to compel parties to adopt any contractual provision. Thus, the Board believes that by directing a "make-whole" remedy, it would in effect be writing contractual language. However, as the appeals court stated in *Tiidee*, the remedy does not require the inclusion of contract terms in a labor agreement, but it serves to compensate employees for past illegal conduct of the employer. When a labor agreement is actually negotiated, the parties would be free to adopt whatever wage structure that results from the collective bargaining process. The idea of the "make-whole" remedy is to award damages to employees to compensate them for previous illegal employer conduct. In view of the position of the NLRB, it would appear that congressional action, or a definitive decision of the United States Supreme Court, would be required if the "make-whole" remedy is deemed to be desirable public policy.

CHANGING NLRB PERSONNEL AND POLICIES

The National Labor Relations Board was created by Congress for the purpose of administering the National Labor Relations Act in accordance with public policy. Public policy in 1935, as now, was declared to be:

> ... to eliminate the causes of certain substantial obstructions to the free flow of commerce and to mitigate and eliminate these obstructions when they have occurred by encouraging the practice and procedure of collective bargaining and by protecting the exercise by workers of full freedom of association, self-organization, and designation of representatives of their own choosing, for the purpose of negotiating the terms and conditions of their employment or other mutual aid or protection.[44]

Obviously, the NLRB is charged with the duty of encouraging industrial peace and protecting the organizational rights of employees. The main functions of the agency in achieving that purpose are (1) to prevent and remedy unfair labor practices of both employers and labor organizations and (2) to conduct secret-ballot elections to determine if workers desire to be represented by labor organizations.

The National Labor Relations Board in its capacity as a quasi-judicial agency has been subject to criticism because of changing interpretations placed on the broad legal principles contained in the national labor laws. Charges cast at the Board for preferential treatment of some groups have never reached greater proportions than during the current debate regarding its usefulness in regulating labor-management relations.

Sources of criticism against the Board have not been limited to any single group. Academicians as well as labor, management, and the general public have all expressed opinions regarding the changing character of federal labor policy. Neil Chamberlain, for example, wrote that "one cannot speak of federal labor policy with definiteness since a policy which is enunciated today may be modified a year from today."[45] The reasons listed for changes in policies were (1) changing Board membership, (2) a realization that some policies are ineffective in practice, and (3) changing social norms. Each of the reasons enumerated, however, may be considered as reflective of the philosophies of Board members with policy changes coinciding with changing membership.

The effort of labor organizations to enlist members from smaller and smaller business operations may be the source of the rapidly expanding workload of the NLRB. As the workload of the agency has increased, there has been greater attention focused on revised Board policies. It is commonly recognized that in implementing the avowed public policy of the Act from 1935 to this date various administrations have been linked to the fluctuating philosophies of Board appointees. The Board of the Eisenhower era has been described as quite conservative in restricting employers in their free-speech policies during election campaigns as well as in other unfair labor practices. On the other hand, the Kennedy and Johnson boards have been more restrictive of employer activities. President Nixon appointed or reappointed five members to the Board. These are Edward B. Miller, Chairman; Ralph E. Kennedy; Howard Jenkins, Jr.; John A. Penello; and John H. Fanning. Fanning was reappointed to an unprecedented fourth term and Jenkins was approved for reappointment. Peter G. Nash was appointed General Counsel.

Labor organizations were critical of Board policies during the Eisenhower years and of certain policies since 1935. Employers have also taken exception to various policies since the existence of the agency. Both employers and unions approach labor relations from ideological standpoints. Due to the changing character of the five man Board in Washington, it has long been recognized that both groups are politically oriented toward a policy of generating pressures to attempt to influence decisions. Thus, even if one group had favorable experiences during one political administration, it may have had unfavorable ones during the next. So long as Board decisions are partially political, one must expect a political evaluation of the effectiveness of agency administration from parties that have a continuous relationship with it.[46]

Criticisms by some employer groups have currently gone far beyond the usual attitude of "keeping the pressure on" in order to influence policies. The Subcommittee on Separation of Powers, a part of the Senate Judiciary Committee, investigated the NLRB to determine how well it had performed its role. The Chamber of Commerce and the National Association of Manufacturers (NAM) at one time led a campaign both to rewrite the nation's basic labor laws and to abolish the National Labor Relations Board. It is proposed that the functions now performed by the Board be transferred to either a labor court or to federal district courts. The campaign was so intense that in 1965 the Chamber of Commerce and the NAM appointed a committee of 150 lawyers to draft changes in the National Labor Relations Act. The finished product is a 167-page report circulated under the title "Labor Management Relations Act." [47]

The general charge made against the Board by the pressuring employer groups is that policy is made by the five members who are not responsive to Congress or the people, but to labor unions. In this regard the interests of the American workingman are not served, but policies are being changed solely to promote the interests of labor union leaders.

There are several specific charges levied at the Board in support of attempts to eliminate it. The Senate Subcommittee Chairman, Sam J. Ervin, contends that court review of Board actions is too limited to eliminate erosion of the congressional intent in formulating statutory provisions.[48] As a result it has developed policies that have little relevance to statutory language. He remarks:

> Language defining bargaining rights, the duty to bargain, and the class of topics which are subject to bargaining has been "interpreted" by the Board in such a way that the statutory phrases now mean more than Congress intended or would have wished, or could have imagined. [49]

The major charge involved is the political sensitivity of the Board to change policy directions in response to changing political circumstances. The fact is that policies change with changing personnel and this is not new with quasi-judicial government agencies. Legislation dealing with broad social and economic problems can be interpreted and applied in many ways. NLRB policies have always changed to reflect the shifts in labor-management relations. Even if the Wagner Act had not been amended, most of the problems facing the agency today would probably have arisen for decision anyway. For example, it was inevitable that policies would have to be established to deal with racial discrimination in collective bargaining relationships. It is also obvious that employer and union election campaigns are different in large oligopolistic firms than is the case in small one-owner operations. The mere fact that effort is currently directed toward organizing smaller and smaller firms would have resulted in changing Board election policies with or without amendments to the basic 1935 statute.

The inconsistent NLRB and judicial decisions of recent years may be based to some extent on philosophical and political differences, but they also stem from the interpretive difficulties in the laws themselves. In this regard Justice Felix Frankfurter wrote in a 1957 case that:

> The judicial function is confined to applying what Congress enacted after ascertaining what it is that Congress enacted. But such ascertainment . . . is nothing like a mechanical endeavor. It could not be accomplished by the subtlest of modern "brain" machines. Because of the infirmities of language and the limited scope of science in legislative drafting, inevitably there enters into the construction of statutes the play of judicial judgment within the limits of the relevant legislative materials. Most relevant, of course, is the very language in which Congress has expressed its policy and from which the Court must extract the meaning most appropriate. [50]

The Board, out of necessity, must behave in the same fashion as it considers cases within the broad congressional language by extracting the meaning most appropriate to fit the situation at hand. The answer to the controversy over changing Board personnel and as a result changing policies cannot be resolved to the point of pleasing all who criticize the agency. It may well be that its responsiveness to political changes could be eliminated somewhat by a permanent NLRB membership. A permanent membership similar to the tenure policy of the federal judiciary, independent of the national political climate and staffed consistently with impartial members, could result in more consistent policies and procedures and thus more equitable treatment of those coming into contact with the agency. Elimination of the NLRB and shifting its function either to a labor court or the federal courts appears to be an inferior alternative either to maintaining the agency intact as it is or shifting to permanently tenured members.

UNION POLITICAL ACTIVITIES

For many years, unions under both the Railway Labor Act and the National Labor Relations Act took the position that they had the right to assist candidates for federal office. Business corporations were financially prohibited from making direct contributions to federal election candidates by the Federal Corrupt Practices Act of 1925.[51] The same restriction was placed on unions for the first time in the War Labor Disputes Act of 1943, which was in effect until the end of World War II. Nevertheless, the CIO organized the Political Action Committee (PAC) in July 1943, and received its initial financing from the treasuries of international unions. Thereafter PAC was financed by contributions from CIO membership. Expenditures to "get out the vote" were made, but direct contributions to candidates were not made. A Senate Special Committee on Campaign Expenditures reported in 1945 that there was no clearcut violation of the law because expenditures were made and these were not the same as contributions. The Senate Committee majority was not of the opinion that expenditures should be prohibited by amending the Corrupt Practices Act. The House Campaign Expenditures Committee in 1946 was of the opposite opinion.

Congress took a position on union political contributions and expenditures in 1947 when it passed the Taft-Hartley Act. Section 304 made it unlawful for corporations and unions to make contributions or expenditures in connection with a variety of federal election functions. However, the legislative history of Section 304 revealed that voluntary contributions from members to a separate political organization would not be unlawful. The section was written for the purpose of prohibiting unions from using member dues for political activities. Senator Taft's view prevailed that the First Amendment protected the voluntary right of individuals to engage in political functions.

Federal Election Campaign Act of 1971:
The Pipefitters Case

Congress clarified its position again in 1971 in a new statute. Two sections (205 and 610) were important in the interpretation of union rights to contribute or expend funds in federal election campaigns.

Representatives Crane and Hansen offered amendments to Section 610 that in their views would codify court decisions interpreting what unions or corporations could do in connection with a federal election. The use of voluntary money expended or contributed through COPE (AFL-CIO's Committee on Political Education) was not at issue. The basic difference between the two amendments involved the use of dues money for political endeavors. The Crane amendment would have forbidden the political use of dues money required of members for employment or union membership. The Hansen amendment, which prevailed and was written into law, has the effect of expanding union use of dues for political activities. It permitted the use of funds from the general treasury to establish, administer, and solicit contributions for political funds. In 1972, the U.S. Supreme Court in *Pipefitters* construed the Federal Election Campaign Act of 1971 as an expansion of statutory authority for unions to expend general dues money for political purposes.[52] A local union established a political fund contributed to by its members on an apparent voluntary basis. However, it used members' dues to establish and administer the fund. On this basis, lower federal courts held that the union violated the 1971 law. However, the high court in *Pipefitters* reversed the lower court, and established the following guidelines:

1. Voluntary political funds are legal so long as the contributions from members are segregated from union funds.
2. Contributors must not be coerced and must know that the fund is to be used for political purposes.
3. Union funds may be used to solicit, establish, and administer political funds. The fund need not be a separate entity from the union, but it must be segregated from the general treasury.
4. Political contributions and expenditures must not be made from dues and assessments paid by members as a condition of employment or union membership or from union commercial transactions.

It would appear that on net balance the new election law as applied by the U.S. Supreme Court strengthens the capability of organized labor to engage in the political arena. However, in Chapter 14 it will be pointed out that union members may claim a proportional return of their dues expended by a union for political activities when they are compelled to be union members as a condition of employment. That is, they are entitled to that portion of their dues used by a union for political purposes to which they object.

TAFT-HARTLEY AMENDMENTS

The Taft-Hartley Act remained in force for twelve years before controversy over its provisions resulted in congressional amendment in 1959. The amendments were contained in Title VII of a broader piece of legislation known officially as the Labor-Management Reporting and Disclosure Act of 1959, or more popularly the Landrum-Griffin Act. The first six titles deal with control of union affairs. The six labor-reform measures are dealt with in a later chapter. Our concern in this section is with the controversial provisions of Taft-Hartley that led to the Title VII amendments.

Unions had been pressuring to change certain provisions of Taft-Hartley since enactment in 1947. Specifically, they pushed to change the law regarding economic strikers, delete the oath and filing requirements, gain greater flexibility for hiring practices in the construction industry, legalize "hot cargo" contracts, neutralize state right-to-work laws, and liberalize the picketing and boycott provisions.[53] Management was determined to retain most of the Act, close picketing and boycott loopholes, and provide for greater implementation of state laws. There were areas where both agreed that changes were required, such as the federal-state jurisdiction problem, but they could not agree on the nature of the changes.

In structure, Title VII covers only a few pages of legislation; however, the relatively brief statements of national policy raise a multitude of problems. Some of them are raised because at points the draftsmanship of the legislation is vague and confusing. This reflects in part the haste and urgency of Congress to enact changes in Taft-Hartley through a law that had the major objective of controlling internal union and management affairs. Another source of confusion results from the fact that legislative history does not reveal, at several points, the intent of Congress.

There are features of Title VII which raise comparatively few problems and some are not controversial.[54] For instance, the President was provided authority to appoint a General Counsel of the NLRB when Congress is not in session,[55] the requirement that union officers file non-communist affidavits was eliminated and replaced with the proscription against communists holding union offices for a period of five years after persons terminate their communist affiliation.[56] In addition, the five man Board in Washington was permitted to delegate to regional directors full authority to handle and decide representation elections. The principal reason was to deal with the time-lag problem in processing cases.[57] The Supreme Court in 1971 upheld the Board's practice of only discretionary review of regional director determinations in representation proceedings even if unfair labor practices are involved.[58] *Magnesium Casting* settled the conflicting opinions of the U.S. Court of Appeals at Boston and at New York and upheld the Boston decision that Board review was not mandatory before bargaining orders can be issued by regional directors.

Another noncontroversial change was made which obligates the NLRB to give priority to unfair labor practice cases arising under Section 8 (a) (3), the antidiscrimination provision of Taft-Hartley.[59] This requirement reflects a continuing effort to provide speedy remedy to employees alleging they are discriminated against by employers for engaging in concerted activities.

Title VII of Landrum-Griffin had the effect of raising several controversial problems, which will be briefly reviewed here since they will be dealt with in detail in subsequent chapters. One problem stems from the effort of Congress to solve the federal-state jurisdiction dispute over labor cases falling within interstate commerce when the NLRB declines such cases for processing. The Tenth Amendment to the United States Constitution and Article 6 of the same document provide that laws enacted by Congress restrict contravention on the part of states. The Supreme Court, ruling on the issue in 1957, held that no state could take jurisdiction of a case unless that state's labor law was entirely consistent with the federal law.[60] This decision was based on Section 10 (a) of Taft-Hartley which required that the NLRB could cede jurisdiction to states only when state law was consistent with the federal law. Landrum-Griffin provided that states could assert jurisdiction over labor disputes declined by the NLRB. Restrictions were placed against the NLRB expanding the range of cases over which they would not assert national labor policy.

Landrum-Griffin also attempted to close loopholes in the original Taft-Hartley anti–secondary boycott provisions. These loopholes were bitterly criticized by the management community. Because of the wording of the original provisions, as construed by the NLRB and the courts, unions were legally free to engage in many kinds of secondary boycott activities. Later on we shall show how the 1959 law closed these loopholes. With the exception of the construction and garment industries, the 1959 law prohibits the so-called *"hot cargo" agreement,* an agreement of union and employer that the employer will not do business with another employer with whom the union has a dispute.

Special prehire arrangements were also extended to the construction industry. Due to the special nature of employment the usual union-security arrangements applicable to industry in general were not to apply. Construction unions were permitted to negotiate contracts with employers prior to hiring employees. This meant that no representation election is required. Employees in this industry work for several employers during the course of a year and may even change every few days or weeks. Prehire arrangements are possible when unions abide by Board-established hiring-hall guidelines.

The Act did not concentrate solely on actual and potential union misbehavior. The Senate investigations had unearthed rather flagrant instances of *employer wrongdoing* as well, including company bribery of union agents and particularly the hiring of outside agents by companies to stave off union organization by illegal means. Such agents, typically self-entitled "labor relations consultants," often acted as intermediaries in "buying off" the threat of unionization or as a last resort in ensuring that the union would at least extract only a minimum of concessions from the company.

Landrum-Griffin made employers responsible for reporting annually to the Secretary of Labor all company expenditures directed at influencing employee collective bargaining behavior. Employer bribery of union officers and other such blunt tactics had constituted federal crimes since the passage of Taft-Hartley, but the new Act expanded the list of *unlawful employer actions*. Payments by companies to their own employees in the exercise of their rights to organize and bargain collectively were now added to the list of prohibited actions. So, too, were many forms of employer payment aimed at procuring information on employee activities related to labor disputes.

Title VII also sought to redress a promanagement inequality that had been created by Taft-Hartley. Under the 1947 law workers who were out on "economic" strikes—those based on disagreements over wages or other economic benefits—were not eligible to vote in NLRB decertification elections. To some employers this provision had constituted an open invitation to provoke such a strike and then call for the decertification voting. Almost by definition their course of action (if unfair labor practices were not detected) could lead to the ousting of a union duly certified as the official bargaining agent. The only eligible voters were the strikers' replacements plus perhaps those few union members who had gone against the wishes of the majority of unionists by continuing to work. Landrum-Griffin amended the provision and economic strikers were now allowed to vote in NLRB elections if held during the period of a year following the start of the strike.

The last problem area to be mentioned here briefly is the recognitional and organizational picketing controversy. Title VII adds a seventh union unfair labor practice to the six provided by Taft-Hartley. Section 8 (b) (7) prohibits this form of picketing under certain circumstances. The chief difficulty involves that area of the law which provides that picketing cannot exceed thirty days without filing a petition for a representation election, except that informational or publicity picketing is not to be restricted. It was the intent of Congress to protect the integrity of NLRB election machinery and at the same time to permit unions to continue their historic practice of publicizing the existence of nonunion standards of some firms. The basic difficulty is that picketing often has both the objective of obtaining recognition and providing information at the same time. The Board and courts have to make the distinction.

SUMMARY

Public policy toward organized labor has changed significantly over the years. As demonstrated previously as well as in the current chapter, public policy has consecutively practiced repression (until 1932), strong encouragement (until 1947), modified encouragement coupled with regulation (until 1959), and detailed regulation (through at least 1970). It seems a safe prediction not only that further shifts in this public policy can be expected but that these changes—as was not always the case in earlier times—will depend for their direction strictly on the acceptability of current union behavior to the American public.

This latter point is particularly important to the unionists of today. Especially since 1937, when it held the Wagner Act wholly constitutional, the Supreme Court has permitted the legislative branch of government the widest latitude to shape public policy. Congress and the state legislatures are judicially free to determine the elements of the framework of labor law. To most citizens such a situation is only as it should be. The judiciary is expected to interpret law, but not to legislate it, and generally it is expected that actions of the legislative branch should be voided only when the particular statute clearly and unmistakably violates the terms of the Constitution. In recent years the electorate at the polls and not the courts constitute the forum in which public policies toward labor are determined, and actually the public is much more critical of union behavior. Such a development has the effect of forcing labor organizations to become increasingly conscious of the images they project.

Every law since Norris-La Guardia has expanded the scope of government regulation of the labor-management arena. Legislative control over collective bargaining started in 1932 when the judiciary was limited in the use of injunctions to deal with labor disputes. In 1935 Congress was concerned primarily with restricting employer conduct. The legislative branch attempted to balance the scales in collective bargaining in 1947 by placing limitations on union conduct and in 1959 it acted again by enacting legislation to deal with internal union affairs. Each time Congress has reviewed its enacted labor laws, it has increased the scope of regulation of collective bargaining. Future legislation can be expected to move further in the direction of governmental intervention into the collective bargaining process.

NOTES

[1] Act of June 23, 1947, Public Law 101, 80th Congress, Chapter 120, 1st sess. The official name of this law is the Labor-Management Relations Act, 1947. However, throughout this volume it will be referred to by its popular name—Taft-Hartley.

[2] Julius Rezler and S. John Insalata, "Doctrine of Mutuality: A Driving Force in American Labor Legislation," *Labor Law Journal*, XVIII, No. 5 (May 1967), 261.

[3] From the personal files of the author.

[4] *Hearings before the Committee on Labor and Public Welfare*, U.S. Senate, 80th Congress, 1st sess., on S. 55 and S. J. Res. 22, Part I, p. 73.

[5] *Report of the Joint Committee on Labor-Management Relations*, Senate Report No. 986. Part

I, March 15, 1948, p. 2. Title IV of Taft-Hartley created a joint committee to study and report on basic problems affecting friendly labor relations and productivity. This committee is officially termed the Joint Committee on Labor-Management Relations. It is composed of seven members of the Senate Committee on Labor and Public Welfare and seven members of the House of Representatives Committee on Education and Labor. The chairman of the first committee was Joseph H. Ball, who was defeated in 1948 for re-election as senator from Minnesota. The vice-chairman was Fred A. Hartley. The composition of this first committee, being appointed shortly after the passage of the law, though bipartisan, was dominated by supporters of Taft-Hartley. As indicated below, the minority group of the committee did not share the view of the majority relative to the operation of Taft-Hartley. As of 1950 this was the only report turned out by the committee.

[6] Congress of Industrial Organizations, *Taft-Hartley and You.*

[7] *Hearings before the Committee on Labor and Public Welfare*, 81st Congress, 1st sess. on S. 249, Part I, p. 436.

[8] *Monthly Labor Review*, LXV (November 1947), 529.

[9] *Hearings on S. 249, op. cit.*, Part IV, p. 1837.

[10] Charles C. Killingsworth, *State Labor Relations Acts* (Chicago: The University of Chicago Press, 1948), p. 3.

[11] *Green Bay Post Gazette*, February 17, 1939.

[12] *Ibid.*, March 2, 1939.

[13] *Ibid.*, February 20, 1939.

[14] Wisconsin Employment Relations Board, *First Annual Report* (1938), p. 2.

[15] Bureau of National Affairs, *Labor Relations Reporter*, IV (1939), 507.

[16] National Labor Relations Board, *First Annual Report* (1936), p. 9.

[17] 57 Stat. 163. The law was popularly termed the Smith-Connally Act.

[18] Bureau of National Affairs, *op. cit.*, XII (June 28, 1943), 632.

[19] The experience of the strike-vote election procedure of the War Labor Disputes Act was discussed in the previous chapter.

[20] Bureau of National Affairs, *op. cit.*, XVII (January 7, 1946), 604.

[21] National War Labor Board, *Termination Report*, Washington, D.C., I (1946), 81.

[22] *Ibid.*, p. 90.

[23] *Ibid.*, p. 82.

[24] *Humble Oil & Refining Company*, 15 War Labor Reports 380 (1944). The Bureau of National Affairs, a private publishing house, compiled all of the decisions of the National War Labor Board during World War II. It included these decisions in 28 volumes called the *War Labor Reports.* Consequently, cases of NWLB cited in this chapter as well as in the next refer to these volumes. For example, 15 War Labor Reports 380 means that the *Humble Oil & Refining* case will be found in the 15th volume of the War Labor Reports at page 380.

[25] *The Little Steel Cases*, 1 War Labor Reports 324 (1942).

[26] National War Labor Board, *op. cit.*, p. 84.

[27] *Ibid.*, p. 96.

[28] International Association of Machinists, *The Truth About the Taft-Hartley Law and Its Consequences to the Labor Movement* (April 1948), p. 29.

[29] *Congressional Record*, XCIII, 5703.

[30] Raymond L. Hilgert and Jerry D. Young, "Right-to-Work Legislation—Examination of Related Issues and Effects," *Personnel Journal* (December 1963), p. 559.

[31] See, particularly, the excellent article by Derek C. Bok, "The Regulation of Campaign Tactics in Representation Elections Under the National Labor Relations Act," *Harvard Law Review*, LXXVIII, No. 1 (November 1964), for a fuller discussion of these and various related organizational campaign legislative matters.

[32] Albert Rees, *The Economics of Trade Unions* (Chicago: The University of Chicago Press, 1962), p. 39.

[33] Nicholas S. Falcone, *Labor Law* (New York: John Wiley & Sons, Inc., 1963), p. 275.

[34] *Thirty-Seventh Annual Report of the National Labor Relations Board* (Washington, D.C.: Government Printing Office, 1972), p. 5.

[35] Hywell Evans, *Government Regulation of Industrial Relations* (New York State School of Industrial and Labor Relations, 1961), p. 58.

[36] Title VII, Section 701 (b), amending Section 3 (b) of Taft-Hartley.

[37] *Thirty-Second Annual Report of the National Labor Relations Board* (Washington, D.C.: Government Printing Office, 1969), p. 20.

[38] 185 NLRB 107 (1970).

[39] *IUE* v. *NLRB* (*Tiidee Products*), 426 F. (2d) 1243 (1970).

[40] *Textile Workers Union* v. *NLRB* (*J. P. Stevens*), CA DC No. 71–1469 (February 1, 1973).

[41] Department of Labor, Bureau of Labor Statistics, *Monthly Labor Review*, v. 96, No. 5 (May 1973), p. 54.

[42] 194 NLRB No. 198 (1972).

[43] *H. K. Porter Co.* v. *NLRB*, 397 U.S. 99 (1970).

[44] 49 Stat. 449 (1939).

[45] See Don R. Sheriff and Viola M. Kuebler, eds., *NLRB in a Changing Industrial Society*, Conference Series No. 2 (Iowa City: College of Business Administration, The University of Iowa, 1967), p. 43.

[46] Benjamin J. Taylor, *The Operation of the Taft-Hartley Act in Indiana*, Indiana Business Information Bulletin 58 (Bloomington, Ind.: Bureau of Business Research, Indiana University, 1967), p. 88.

[47] *Congressional Record* (Washington: Government Printing Office, August 2, 1968), p. S10118.

[48] *Congressional Record* (Washington: Government Printing Office, September 5, 1968), pp. S10288–89.

[49] *Ibid.*

[50] *Local 1976 Carpenters Union* v. *NLRB*, 357 U.S. 93–100 (1957).

[51] Section 313, 43 Stat. 1074.

[52] *Pipefitters Local Union No. 562* v. *United States*, 407 U.S. 385 (1972).

[53] R. W. Fleming, "Title VII: The Taft-Hartley Amendments," *Northwestern University Law Review*, LIV, No. 6 (January–February, 1960).

[54] See Fred Witney, "LMRDA Title VII: Its Problems and Their Development," in *Symposium on the Labor-Management Reporting and Disclosure Act of 1959*, ed. Ralph Slovenko (Baton Rouge: Claitor's Bookstore Publishers, 1960), p. 631.

[55] Title VII, Section 703, amending Section 3(d) of Taft-Hartley.

[56] As will be demonstrated in Chapter 20, this provision was declared unconstitutional.

[57] Title VII, Section 701 (b), amending Section 3 (b) of Taft-Hartley.

[58] *Magnesium Casting Co.* v. *NLRB*, 401 U.S. 137 (1971).

[59] Title VII, Section 706, amending Section 10 of Taft-Hartley.

[60] *Guss* v. *Utah Labor Relations Board*, 353 U. S. 1 (1957).

Jurisdiction of the National Labor Relations Board 11

At this point we are concerned with the jurisdiction of the NLRB. If the agency refuses to take jurisdiction over a case, the Taft-Hartley law is not available to the employer, the union, or the employees involved in the dispute. It is only when the NLRB exerts jurisdiction that the law comes into play.

Early in its career the NLRB decided that it would not deal with all cases which fall within the area of interstate commerce. As a federal agency, created by a federal law, the NLRB has the constitutional authority to take jurisdiction over any case which falls within the area of interstate commerce. However, because of budget considerations the NLRB, soon after it was established, refused to take cases which had only a minimal effect on commerce between the states. What with a growing case load and a staff limited in numbers by insufficient appropriations, the agency decided to concentrate upon cases which had a more important relationship to interstate commerce. Later on, the Board decided to restrict further its jurisdiction which resulted in the further curtailment of the operation of national labor policy.

It is the purpose of this chapter to review the evolutionary nature of the Board's self-imposed jurisdictional restrictions, the question of state control of labor relations in areas abnegated by the Board, and the impact of Landrum-Griffin in resolving the gray area of labor relations left by Board and Supreme Court actions.

SELF-IMPOSED RESTRICTIONS

The Wagner Act bestowed upon the NLRB authority to assume jurisdiction over unfair labor practices and questions of representation "affecting commerce." [1] Section 2 (7) described the phrase so broadly that the Supreme Court held the jurisdictional authority of the Board coextensive with the reach of Congress under the commerce power.[2] It will be recalled that the *Jones & Laughlin Steel Corporation* case decided the constitutionality of the Wagner Act and at the same time extended the commerce power of Congress to include the production process as well as distribution. The reach of Congress did not apply to manufacturing processes as late as 1935 when the National Industrial Recovery Act was ruled unconstitutional.[3] Once the Wagner Act was upheld it was the duty of the Board "to eliminate the causes of certain substantial obstructions to the free flow of commerce. . . ."[4] The Board's authority was established more clearly in a 1939 Supreme Court case construing the phrase when the Court held that it was obvious that it was the intent of Congress "to exercise whatever power is given to it to regulate commerce."[5]

This broad power of the NLRB to extend coverage of national labor policy in all possible situations was, however, never utilized. Authority of the agency to choose its own area of operation was approved by the courts; that is, the Board's jurisdiction did not depend on the volume of commerce involved in a particular situation. The NLRB had discretion as to what cases it would accept. Therefore, businesses having little effect on interstate commerce, as defined by the Board, were omitted from the national regulatory power of the agency on a case-to-case basis.

From its start the NLRB experienced a significant growing case load. Between 1937 and 1941 the Board case load expanded from 4,400 cases to 9,100.[6] Increased demands on the Board led it to decline jurisdiction of labor disputes on a case-to-case basis. The extent that it declined to accept labor cases for processing depended partly on the backlog of cases in process. The purpose given for such action, however, was that the policies of the Act would not be furthered if it accepted cases in which an employer's operation did not have a substantial impact upon interstate commerce.[7] The Board argued that the determining factor in establishing jurisdiction was the extent of interference a labor dispute might have on commerce.

Even before the Wagner Act was declared constitutional, the Board had to come to grips with the problem of jurisdiction. In its first year of operation it communicated to the public that under certain conditions retail trade or other purely local businesses did not fall within federal jurisdiction.[8]

The immediate postwar period, 1945–1947, was a particularly troublesome one for NLRB operations. The nation was in the process of changing to peacetime production of consumer goods, union organizational drives were more active than during the war years, unions were attempting to achieve gains they had foregone because of the war effort, and employer resistance to unions was rising rapidly. The Board's case load swelled to about fourteen thousand by 1947. Despite the increased demand for NLRB services, staff size was 800 in 1945, 990 in 1946, but only 720 in April 1947.[9] Because of insufficient appropriations during 1945–1947, jurisdictional control over marginal companies, in terms of their activities in interstate commerce, was declined. Lack of an adequate budget constituted the major reason why the Board declined jurisdiction over these cases.

The Taft-Hartley Act, passed in 1947, left the jurisdictional provisions of the 1935 law virtually unchanged. The new Act brought with it a difference in opinion between the Board and the General Counsel regarding the extent of Board obligation to assert jurisdiction over cases declined in the Wagner Act era. The result was that the Board did expand its control for a short period, but declined to do so on a permanent basis. The case-by-case method of asserting jurisdiction generated considerable uncertainty among some businesses and industries as to their status under the 1947 law.[10]

Publication of Jurisdictional Standards

Controversy over the uncertainties of Board behavior in providing interested parties protection from prohibited activities led to publication of some general guidelines clarifying Board jurisdictional policies in October 1950. The Board declared that it would take jurisdiction over firms clearly affecting commerce regardless of the channel from which the effect came. Included in the category of declared responsibility were public utility and transit companies, multistate firms meeting certain dollar standards of interstate commerce, and establishments affecting national defense.[11] The guidelines established in 1950, however, were destined for a short life.

A further curtailment of its jurisdiction was first revealed in a series of NLRB releases of Board member statements and subsequent decisions in the fall of 1953 and during the first part of 1954. Mr. Guy Farmer, chairman of the Board, in a speech after assuming office stated:

> I think perhaps the time has come to accept the proposition that it is not neces-sary or even desirable for the Federal Government to step into every labor dispute however insignificant it might be. It has always seemed to me, without engaging in any debate of the relative merits of state versus federal rights, that, regardless of the legal scope of the commerce clause the Federal Agencies should, as a matter of self-restraint, impose limits on their own power and thus provide the oppor-tunity for local problems to be settled on a local basis by the citizens of the com-munities in which these problems arise.[12]

In July 1954 the Board published a revised version of its 1950 jurisdictional dollar guidelines. Under the new "yardsticks," as the dollar standards are often called, many small business firms and their employees were removed from Taft-Hartley protection. The volume of business an enterprise must sell to firms in other states to qualify for coverage was raised from $25,000 to $50,000. Purchases from out-of-state-based firms by an enterprise seeking coverage were also raised from the 1950 level of $50,000 to a new high of $1 million. Trucking companies operating in intrastate commerce but linked to trade between the states under a franchise arrange-ment were required to do at least a $100,000 volume of business per year before Taft-Hartley would apply. Radio and television stations qualified only if their annual dollar volume of business totaled at least $200,000. A newspaper whose annual revenue fell below $500,000 per year was no longer subject to the law. Prior to 1954 the Board did not establish a dollar limitation for radio, television, or news-paper establishments whose operations affected commerce. Additionally, the Board declared that public utility and transportation systems would be subject to Taft-Hartley only if they grossed $3 million per year. There was also considerable con-traction of independent and chain retail store coverage as well as of many firms affecting national defense.[13]

All the Board members did not agree with the new jurisdictional standards. A minority dissented vigorously from the self-imposed restrictions of 1954. Labor and management groups entered the debate along with academicians. The most heated aspect of the debate centered on the authority of states to exercise jurisdiction over those business enterprises in interstate commerce denied coverage under federal law by the Board. One reason given for raising the jurisdictional standards in 1954 was the expectation that states would take the initiative by enacting state labor relations laws. However, fourteen years later, only seventeen states and Puerto Rico had done so. Major impetus for much of the recent state labor legislation has been the public employee organizational problem.[14]

The essential Board-stated purposes of decreasing federal authority over enterprises in interstate commerce were (1) the desire for states to regulate the area of labor relations abnegated by it, and (2) to encourage renewed state labor legislation patterned after the Taft-Hartley Act. It appears also that the Board assumed states had authority to exercise control over the rejected areas.

FEDERAL PREEMPTION: LEGISLATIVE ASPECTS OF TAFT-HARTLEY

When Congress passed the Taft-Hartley law, the national lawmakers were aware of the supremacy of federal law within interstate commerce. Aware of this state of affairs, but still desiring to provide the states with authority to deal with some labor relations problems within interstate commerce, Congress spelled out with precision those areas in which it desired state regulation to prevail. Perhaps the best illustration of the congressional approach to the federal-state jurisdictional problem involves the manner in which union security is treated in the national law. Whereas the federal law only outlaws the closed shop, the states under express provision of Taft-Hartley may prohibit any form of compulsory union membership.[15] At the time that Congress was considering the passage of Taft-Hartley, several states had already prohibited all forms of union security. Since Congress was determined to preserve this state action, it relinquished federal supremacy in this area of industrial relations. In the absence of such a clear statement of federal policy, Congress feared that state law prohibiting union security would have been invalidated because of federal supremacy in matters affecting commerce. In this connection the House Labor Committee declared:

> Since by the Labor Act Congress preempts the field that the act covers insofar as commerce within the meaning of the act is concerned ... the committee ... has provided expressly ... that laws and constitutional provisions of any state that restrict the right of employers to require employees to become or remain members of labor organizations are valid, notwithstanding any provision of the National Labor Relations Act.[16]

Other areas of Taft-Hartley spell out additional points at which Congress desired the states to control labor relations within interstate commerce. The meticulousness with which these areas are indicated lends additional support to the proposition that, in the absence of national legislation to the contrary, the states are forbidden to operate within interstate commerce once the federal government has occupied the field by the enactment of constitutional legislation. Thus the federal labor law requires that parties seeking to modify or terminate collective bargaining contracts must give notice of this fact not only to the Federal Mediation and Conciliation Service but also to any state agency that performs mediation services.[17] The director of the Federal Mediation and Conciliation Service is ordered to avoid attempting to mediate disputes that have only a minor effect on interstate commerce if state or other conciliation services are available to the parties.[18] In addition, the director of the federal mediation agency is empowered to establish suitable procedures for cooperation with state and local mediation agencies.[19] Under authority of another provision of the Taft-Hartley law, employers may sue unions in either federal or state courts for injuries suffered as a result of union action declared illegal in the national law.[20] Obviously, it is in these areas of labor relations that Congress desired the states to have concurrent jurisdiction with the national government. It recognized that the doctrine of national preemption would operate to exclude such state regulation of industrial relations within interstate commerce in the absence of clear and specific authority extended by the national government.

Not only does the Taft-Hartley law establish a system of concurrent federal-state jurisdiction within interstate commerce over certain specified areas of industrial relations, but it also provides that the NLRB, under certain limited conditions, can cede jurisdiction to state boards in unfair labor practice cases. This authority is in Section 10 (a) of the law.[21] This provision of the statute has crucial importance in the determination of the question of whether the states may lawfully occupy the area of interstate commerce vacated by the NLRB.

Section 10 (a) empowers the NLRB to prevent any person from engaging in any unfair labor practice affecting interstate commerce. It further provides that this power of the Board "shall not be affected by any other means of adjustment or prevention that has been or may be established by agreement, law, or otherwise." With the single exception that the law establishes a limited procedure whereby the NLRB may cede jurisdiction to the states, this section of Taft-Hartley showed the determination of Congress to reserve to the national labor agency full and exclusive power to enforce the terms of the national labor statute. No other enforcement agency, federal or state, regardless of the circumstances under which a case may arise before that forum, had any power to implement the provisions of the Taft-Hartley law. This was the clear and unmistakable meaning of Section 10 (a). With this one exception, Congress was anxious to insure the uniform application of national labor policy throughout interstate commerce. Uniform national labor policy within interstate commerce could not be realized if Congress had permitted a variety of federal and state courts or labor agencies to interpret and apply national labor policy. If Congress allowed a multiplicity of enforcement channels of the Taft-Hartley law to exist, there could be as many different versions of its meaning as there are law-enforcement forums within the nation. It was this state of affairs that Congress desired to avoid in 1947.

The determination of Congress to insure the uniform application of the federal law within interstate commerce is not lessened by the limited circumstances under which the NLRB could cede jurisdiction of unfair labor practice cases to state agencies. In the first place, Section 10 (a) clearly specified that the only way in which the federal agency could cede jurisdiction to the states is "by agreement." This meant that the Board could not cede jurisdiction to the states merely by declaring that it would not exercise its authority over a certain category of cases. Unless an agreement was entered into by the NLRB with state agencies, Section 10 (a) prohibits state exercise of control over labor relations within interstate commerce. Such an agreement was not implied merely by a decline of jurisdiction by the NLRB. Agreement was possible only if state law to be applied was identical with the federal law in both language and application stemming from interpretation.

Obviously, the reason why Congress included the consistency test within Taft-Hartley was to provide for the uniform application of national labor policy within interstate commerce. The objective of uniformity could not have been realized if federal and state law treated the same set of circumstances in an unlike manner. If the consistency standard were not included in the federal law, a situation could have arisen in which activities unlawful under federal law could be lawful under state law. It was this kind of confusion and conflict that Congress meant to avoid when it established the barrier to NLRB jurisdictional cession to the states. In this connection the Senate Labor Committee, which reported the Taft-Hartley law in 1947, stated: "The provision which has been added to this subsection permits the National Labor Relations Board to allow State labor-relations boards to take final jurisdiction of cases in border-line industries (that is, border line insofar as interstate commerce is concerned) provided the state statute conforms to national policy." [22]

FEDERAL PREEMPTION: THE SUPREME COURT

On several occasions, even before Taft-Hartley, the U.S. Supreme Court invalidated state laws when they conflicted with national labor legislation. In 1943 Florida enacted a union regulation law which, among other things, required that union officials obtain a license before operating within the state. [23] To satisfy the requirements for the license, a union official had to prove that he was a citizen of the United States, had resided in the United States for ten years, had not been convicted of a felony, and was of good moral character. The law also required that the applicant pay a fee before obtaining the license. In 1945 the Supreme Court held that the statute was invalid to the extent that it applied to the area of interstate commerce on the ground that it circumscribed the full freedom of choice that employees are given in the selection of bargaining representatives under national labor law. [24] In this connection the Court declared that "the full freedom of employees in collective bargaining which Congress envisioned as essential to protect the free flow of commerce among the states would be, by the Florida statute, shrunk to a greatly limited freedom." Thus the state of Florida could not use a state law to deprive workers of rights protected by the Wagner Act. [25]

The application of the principle of federal supremacy over state law within interstate commerce also involved a case dealing with bargaining rights of foremen. [26] In May 1943 the NLRB held that it would no longer extend the protection of the Wagner Act to foremen in the exercise of their collective bargaining rights. Specifically, the Board ruled that supervisors no longer constituted units appropriate for collective bargaining within the meaning of the national law. Under this policy unions of foremen could not be certified by the NLRB for collective bargaining purposes. However, while this NLRB policy was in effect, the New York State Labor Relations Board afforded the full protection of the New York State Labor Relations Act to foremen. Consequently, a union of foremen, denied access to the NLRB, petitioned and obtained a certification from the state labor agency for purposes of collective bargaining. When this case was heard by the Supreme Court of the United States, the state of New York argued that a state has the authority to act until federal power is actually exercised as to the particular employees. However, the Court rejected this argument, declaring that "the State argues for a rule that would enable it to act until the federal board had acted in the same case. But we do not think that a case-by-case test of federal supremacy is permissible here. The federal board has jurisdiction of the industry in which these particular employers engaged and has asserted control of their labor relations in general." The Supreme Court held that the state board did not have the power to permit supervisors to become a bargaining unit under a state labor law because the federal law denied them this right. Thus the decision demonstrated that a state could not endow employees covered by national labor law with rights not consistent with federal law.

In two cases involving state regulation of the right to strike, the Supreme Court again implemented the doctrine of federal supremacy in the field of labor relations. In both cases it held that the state laws interfered with the right of workers to strike as protected by the federal law. Accordingly, the Court invalidated these state laws to the degree that they applied to firms and employees covered by the Taft-Hartley law.

One of these cases involved the provision of the Michigan state labor law, which requires a strike-vote election before a work stoppage can legally take place.[27] Under the Michigan law a strike was not lawful unless authorized by a majority of the workers within a bargaining unit. In short, the Michigan statute made the lawfulness of a strike turn on the outcome of a strike poll. The second case dealt with the Wisconsin Public Utility Anti-Strike Law.[28] This statute outlawed strikes and lockouts in public utilities and substituted a system of compulsory arbitration to resolve disputes between employers and unions within the public utility field. Decisions of the arbitrators, subject to review by the courts, were binding upon the parties.

In 1948 the Supreme Court held that the Wisconsin Employment Relations Board did not have jurisdiction over a representation proceeding involving the bargaining representative of employees of a telephone company.[29] The company was engaged in interstate commerce within the meaning of federal legislation. However, a union involved in the case filed a petition with the state board requesting the agency to determine the collective bargaining representative. At the point of determination of bargaining representatives, there was no essential conflict between the federal and Wisconsin laws. The NLRB and the state agency both were equipped to dispose of the problem. Still, the Supreme Court held that the Wisconsin board could not deal with the question of representation in industries that fall within the area of interstate commerce. The fact that the NLRB had not taken jurisdiction of the controversy did not lessen the Court's determination to reserve for the national labor agency the jurisdictional area granted to it by national legislation enacted pursuant to the United States Constitution.

The principle of national preemption of the control of labor relations within interstate commerce was the basis for a Supreme Court decision involving unfair labor charges against an employer and a labor organization.[30] In this case a union utilized a variety of coercive techniques on a worker to force him to join the organization. He refused and the employer ultimately discharged him. Such tactics of the union and the discharge of the worker by the employer constituted unfair labor practices under the Wisconsin Labor Relations Act. Accordingly, the Wisconsin Employment Relations Board ordered reinstatement of the employee, and the Wisconsin Supreme Court subsequently enforced the action of the state board.

Ultimately, the Supreme Court of the United States reversed without opinion the ruling of Wisconsin's labor agency and Supreme Court. The United States Supreme Court merely cited the *Bethlehem Steel*[31] and *La Crosse Telephone*[32] decisions as the authority for its ruling in the case. Undoubtedly, the conduct of the union and the employer would have been illegal under the Taft-Hartley law. Still, the United States Supreme Court, mindful of the distribution of power between federal and state governments, did not permit the similarity between federal and state legislation to determine its decision.

In 1953 the Supreme Court handed down its decision in the celebrated *Garner* case,[33] and once again ruled that states were without authority to assume jurisdiction over labor relations disputes which fall within the area of the NLRB. Involved in this case was picketing by a labor organization which violated the laws of Pennsylvania. Without question the picketing was also unlawful under the Taft-Hartley Act. A Pennsylvania court held that the union conduct violated the Pennsylvania Labor Relations Act and enjoined the picketing. However, the Supreme Court of Pennsylvania upset the ruling of the lower court on the ground that the labor dispute fell within the exclusive jurisdiction of the NLRB. The United States Supreme Court upheld the high court of Pennsylvania declaring that in enacting the Taft-Hartley law "Congress did not merely lay down a substantive rule of law to be enforced by any tribunal competent to apply law generally to the parties. It went on to confide primary interpretation and application of its rules to a specific and specially constituted tribunal and prescribed a particular procedure for investigation, complaint and notice, and hearing and decision, including judicial relief pending a final administrative order."

The Guss Case and the "No Man's Land"

The *Garner* case seemed to serve notice that the Supreme Court did not look with favor upon state control of labor disputes falling within the scope of national labor legislation. However, it did not conclusively resolve the federal-state jurisdictional problem. It was not until 1957 that the Supreme Court clearly excluded the states from asserting control over cases declined by the NLRB. In the light of the language of Taft-Hartley and court precedent, it was only logical to expect such a decision of the high court.

In the *Guss* v. *Utah Labor Relations Board* case the Court held that when the Board has jurisdiction, even though it refuses to exercise it, states may assert their own laws only when the NLRB cedes jurisdiction under Section 10 (a) of the National Labor Relations Act.[34] It will be recalled that 10 (a) required that states had to apply law identical to that of the federal statute. Not a single state qualified to accept cases on conditions prescribed by Section 10 (a). Denial of state jurisdiction meant the creation of a "no man's land" within which labor relations were subject neither to federal nor state regulation.

The implications of the no man's land were several. First, when the agency declined jurisdiction, it meant that bargaining elections could not be conducted by use of Board machinery to determine whether collective bargaining representatives would be chosen. No method was available to the parties to resolve any conflict arising out of organizational issues. One of the basic purposes of the Wagner Act was to eliminate organizational strikes. The failure to assert control over some firms would result in strikes seeking to force recognition.

Second, the decision had the effect of allowing employers and unions to engage in activities illegal under national labor law without fear of intervention either by the NLRB or states. Employers could discharge workers for union activities, refuse to bargain with a majority union, and sponsor company-dominated labor organizations. On the other hand, unions were free to engage in such illegal activities as secondary-boycott strikes, jurisdictional strikes, and strikes for closed shops, and could refuse to bargain collectively without fear of restraint.

The Supreme Court was aware of the importance of its decision. It pointed out possible alternative solutions to the no-man's-land problem. One was congressional enactment of appropriate legislation. Another was that the Board could reassert its jurisdiction by reevaluating its dollar-volume guidelines.

The *Guss* decision created an immediate response from both Congress and the NLRB. In July 1958 Congress increased the Board's operating budget to permit a lowering of its dollar standards for the purpose of reducing a portion of the no-man's-land area. As a result the Board revised its jurisdictional standards in October 1958. The policies set forth in 1958 remain in effect at the present time.[35]

Despite the efforts of the Congress and Board, a gray area remained since many employers, unions, and employees engaged in interstate commerce, so far as judicial construction is concerned, were still outside the scope of national labor policy. Congressional action on the no man's land was certain since the controversy was not stilled by the greater budget and Board reevaluation of jurisdictional policies.

Impact of Landrum-Griffin: Title VII

In 1959 Congress attempted to deal with the no-man's-land problem. It enacted an amendment to Section 14 of Taft-Hartley. Two courses of congressional action were available to fill the gap. Congress could require the NLRB to take jurisdiction of all cases defined legally as falling within interstate commerce. Or it could permit states to exercise jurisdiction over those cases declined by the Board. President Eisenhower as early as January 1958 had recommended greater state control and his preference was known to Congress.

Section 14 (c) of the 1959 Landrum-Griffin amendments to Taft-Hartley contains the final decision made from among the alternatives facing the legislators. The section was designed to deal with the no man's land. It reads:

> (c) (1) (The NLRB is empowered, under certain conditions, to decline jurisdiction) where, in the opinion of the Board, the effect of such labor dispute on commerce is not sufficiently substantial to warrant the exercise of its jurisdiction. . . .
> (2) Nothing in this Act shall be deemed to prevent or bar any agency or the courts of any State or Territory (including the Commonwealth of Puerto Rico, Guam, and the Virgin Islands), from assuming and asserting jurisdiction over labor disputes over which the Board declines, pursuant to paragraph (1) of this subsection, to assert jurisdiction.[36]

Thus under the new law the NLRB at its discretion may decline to assert jurisdiction over any case when in its judgment the effect of the labor dispute on commerce is not sufficient to warrant the exercise of its jurisdiction. State courts and agencies have the authority to take jurisdiction of cases the Board declines. Nothing in the new law requires the states to take jurisdiction over these disputes. The law is merely permissive in this respect, not compulsory. It is not likely, however, that a state having a general labor relations law similar to Taft-Hartley will decline jurisdiction. But in states without such a law there is a different problem, the nature of which is discussed below.

The Board may expand its jurisdiction to reach all cases falling within the area of interstate commerce. To the extent that the federal agency should expand its jurisdiction, the states' rights to intervene in interstate commerce would correspondingly decline. Though the Board may lawfully increase the scope of its jurisdiction, it may not reduce its authority beyond that which was in force as of August 1, 1959. It is also important to note that under the new law the Board is authorized to decline jurisdiction over an entire industry. Congress provided this power to the Board because the Supreme Court in 1958 ordered the agency to take jurisdiction over the hotel and motel industry.[37] Before this time the Board refused to handle cases involving this industry. After the Supreme Court decision, the Board has exerted jurisdiction over motels and hotels provided the enterprise receives at least $500,000 in gross revenue in a year.[38] Making use of its authority to decline jurisdiction of an entire industry, the Board refuses to handle cases involving horse racing and dog racing.[39]

On the other hand, the Board has assumed jurisdiction over private colleges and universities.[40] Thus, the Board reversed *Columbia University*[41] in which it established its former policy that it would not take jurisdiction over private educational institutions. To be covered by Taft-Hartley, the school must gross at least $1,000,000 in annual revenue. The modesty of this amount assures that the vast majority of private universities and colleges now fall within the jurisdiction of the NLRB. Not only are nonacademic employees covered by the policy, but faculty members may also use the facilities of the NLRB for organizational purposes.[42] This policy should result in more organization and collective bargaining in colleges and universities. However, public colleges and universities are still excluded from the coverage of the federal law. State action would be required to provide the basis for collective bargaining in public schools.

Under current policy, the Board asserts jurisdiction over professional baseball[43]; and, since 1973, symphony orchestras with an annual revenue of at least $1,000,000 are now covered by the Taft-Hartley Act.[44] Previously, the NLRB assumed jurisdiction over the gambling industry, rejecting the contention of owners of a casino in Nevada that gambling in that state is essentially local in character.[45] In a case which involved the Christian Science Church, the NLRB held that a church as an employer is not entirely exempt from the coverage of Taft-Hartley.[46] Under this decision, the NLRB ruled that labor-management relations in commercial enterprises owned and operated by a church for profit are subject to its jurisdiction if the operations substantially affect interstate commerce, even if the profit is ultimately used to further religion. Rejecting the church's argument that NLRB intervention violates the First Amendment to the Constitution, it directed an election among employees who worked in commercial enterprises owned by the church. In addition, for many years unions as employers fell within the jurisdiction of the NLRB.[47] Under this policy, union organizers and office employees have formed unions of their own to bargain collectively with their union employers.

Problems flow from the congressional policy on jurisdiction. How can the parties determine whether the NLRB will take jurisdiction over a particular case? May the states apply state law, or may they pick and choose in this respect?

A party involved in a labor dispute may follow two procedures to determine whether the NLRB will accept or decline jurisdiction over a particular case. It may refer to the Board's published standards, which express in money volume the categories of cases the Board will take.[48] Perhaps a more definitive method is to seek an advisory opinion from the NLRB on whether it will take a particular case. The agency made such a procedure available shortly after the passage of the new law.[49] Such advisory opinions, however, deal exclusively with the issue of jurisdiction and will not relate to the merits of the dispute. In addition to the parties involved in a labor dispute, the Board will accept requests for advisory opinions from state courts and labor agencies. Advisory opinions may be filed only if a proceeding is currently pending before an agency or court. In general, the request for an opinion is expected to contain the general nature of the business of the employer involved in the dispute and present relevant data on commerce. The Board permits the party filing the request for an advisory opinion to withdraw it at any time before the Board issues the instrument.[50]

In regard to the body of law to be applied by a state court or labor agency, it is clear that state law may be applied. A Senate version would have required the states to apply only federal law in all cases affecting interstate commerce. The Conference Committee, however, rejected the Senate proposal so that state law may be applied.[51]

Beyond this clear fact, there exists an area of uncertainty. Nothing in the language of the law explicitly denies states the right to apply federal law. It is expected that states having state labor relations laws will apply state law. Not all states have enacted state laws to deal with labor relations. Many states are free to apply common law to labor disputes when federal jurisdiction is declined. Many employers, unions, and employees are denied the protection of federal statutes because of Board policies. Therefore considerable variation exists from state to state in the rights afforded all parties to labor disputes. Some employers and unions are dealt with more rigidly in one state than in another, even when the labor problems are identical. The analogy between the different state attitudes toward capital punishment may be well taken at this juncture. That is, a violation of the rights of parties to a labor dispute may be dealt with harshly in one state, but hardly at all in another. Some parties may lose their organizational rights almost completely in one state, but something less in another. It is very unlikely that the forces militating against enactment of such laws will be overcome by the stimulus provided by the 1959 labor law. In the meantime inequitable treatment of workers from one state to another is encouraged. Uniformity of treatment of all parties provides greater certainty than different methods of dealing with similar labor-management problems. States are free to apply their own statutory law, common law, or for that matter federal law if they so choose.

COVERAGE OF HOSPITAL EMPLOYEES

In 1967 the NLRB departed from its policy of declining jurisdiction over proprietary hospitals. In the *Butte Medical Properties* case, the Board established a new standard for hospitals that are privately owned with a profit orientation.[52] Jurisdiction is asserted if such hospitals have gross revenues of at least $250,000 per year.

The Board justified its action by noting that state regulation of privately owned hospitals is limited in the sphere of labor relations. Also, national health insurance companies and the federal government make considerable payments to proprietary hospitals for providing health protection. These payments were deemed to have a considerable impact on interstate commerce. Interstate commerce is also affected by substantial purchases of supplies and services from out-of-state sources.

Privately owned nursing homes, operating for a profit, were also placed under the National Labor Relations Act if the employer receives at least $100,000 in annual gross revenue.[53] The Board justified its action by applying the same reasoning used in the *Butte* case. Nonprofit hospital employees did not enjoy coverage of the national labor law. The Act denied coverage of such employees unless a part of the net earnings inured to the benefit of any private shareholder or individual.

The original language of Taft-Hartley and the 1967 change in Board jurisdictional policy over proprietary hospitals placed noncovered employees at a distinct bargaining disadvantage. The lack of parity in the bargaining rights of employees within the industry posed potentially explosive circumstances.

The relative wage and benefit discrepancies between hospital workers and those in other sectors are sufficient to ignite work stoppages. However, differential assertion of Board jurisdiction over essentially identical employees adds a new dimension to the entire process of collective bargaining. Since a large number of hospital employees are blacks or other minority group members, the demand of uncovered workers for bargaining rights has been plunged deep into the civil rights movement. Civil rights organizations placed increased pressures on nonprofit and public hospitals to conform essentially to the same labor relations standards the NLRB imposes on firms over which they assert jurisdiction. Bitter strikes resulted from the differential federal policy of guaranteeing bargaining rights for some hospital employees, but not for others.

These considerations prompted Congress to re-evaluate the policy of exempting employees of nonprofit hospitals from the coverage of Taft-Hartley. In July 1974 it amended the law and brought within the jurisdiction of the NLRB almost two million employees who work for nonprofit hospitals. Now, enjoying legal protection of their bargaining rights, it should not take too long before a good share of these employees are organized. One consequence of the new legislation is that recognition strikes are no longer necessary in the health-care industry. This serves the public interest since formerly many long and bitter strikes were undertaken by nonprofit hospital employees because hospital management refused to recognize their unions.

Since hospitals supply a critical public service, under this new legislation unions representing employees in proprietary and nonprofit hospitals are required to give ninety-days' notice before terminating or seeking to modify labor agreements, thirty days more than Taft-Hartley requires in other industries. In addition, a hospital union may not lawfully strike or picket unless it gives ten-days' notice. This provision was adopted to give hospital management an opportunity to make arrangements for the continuity of patient care. Furthermore, a labor dispute in a health-care institution is automatically subject to mediation by the Federal Mediation and Conciliation Service. Moreover, unlike its authority in other industries, the agency is empowered to appoint a fact-finding board to make recommendations to settle hospital labor disputes.

Undoubtedly, as collective bargaining becomes widespread in the health-care industry, labor costs will increase serving to increase already very high patient hospital bills. It should be recognized, however, that hospital employees are among the lowest paid in the nation. Though this was not its intent, it is quite possible that the new legislation will increase the chances for prompt enactment of a national health insurance program.

AGRICULTURAL WORKERS

Agricultural workers have always been excluded from the definition of *employee* within the meaning of the National Labor Relations Act. The Act does not define the term *agricultural workers* and has therefore since 1935 caused considerable disagreement over interpretation of the jurisdictional exemption. For example, at one time the federal courts ruled differently on the jurisdictional status of packinghouse workers. One court ruled that they were agricultural laborers[54] while another held that they were entitled to NLRB jurisdiction.[55]

Since 1946 the Congress has added a rider to the NLRB's annual appropriations. It specifies that the definition of *agricultural laborers* will be guided by the one set forth in the Fair Labor Standards Act. This law is administered and interpreted by the Department of Labor and the NLRB follows those interpretations whenever possible. Attempts to follow the Fair Labor Standards Act definition have resulted in reversal of some Board decisions rendered prior to 1947. Particularly, the NLRB and the courts have had considerable difficulty determining the exact status of packingshed workers.

Several cases declaring that certain agricultural workers are not exempt from NLRB jurisdiction point to factors such as: (1) whether the item processed was also grown by the employer; (2) whether the item was substantially changed after processing; (3) whether the employees worked in both the field and processing area or only in the field; and (4) the size of the incidental operation.[56] The "agricultural labor" exemption from NLRA coverage has continued through Board and court examination since 1935. The necessity to reevaluate policies in this industry attests to the continuous employment upheaval in agriculture and related operations.

A suit was brought by the NLRB against the United Farm Workers Union (UFW) in 1972 in federal district court in Fresno, California. The Board argued that there was reason to believe that the union was a labor organization within the meaning of the National Labor Relations Act. The Board moved in the picture against the union's secondary boycott activities because it contended the union might be attempting to organize industrial wine workers who fall under the Act. The case did not proceed to trial, however, because the Board and union settled informally. It was agreed that the union would not engage in illegal secondary boycott activities against companies selling nonunion-made California wine. Further, the union did not acknowledge that it is a labor organization within the meaning of the law or had engaged in unfair labor practices covered by the NLRA. These proceedings were consistent with longstanding NLRB and court decisions despite adverse publicity to the contrary. The secondary boycott is available to the UFW against agricultural employers not covered by the NLRA.

Public Law 78 and Related Developments

Public Law 78 permitted Mexican nationals (braceros) to cross the border and work in the United States as seasonal farm laborers. Prior to its termination at the end of 1964, braceros took the jobs of thousands of American farmworkers, most of whom were Mexican-Americans. Considerable pressure from labor leaders, religious leaders, and Mexican-American organizations led to the final demise of the practice. Despite the termination of Public Law 78, Mexican nationals still have the ability to cross the border into the United States to work on farms adjacent to Mexico.

The "Green Card" Holder

The exemption of most agricultural workers from NLRA coverage has not deterred AFL-CIO attempts to unionize this group of workers. Most union activity takes place in the state of California. Termination of Public Law 78 has not made the union organizer's job easier. Mexican nationals may continue to cross the border to work on American farms if they hold a permit known as a "Green Card." On a single day, January 11, 1967, 16,609 Green Card holders crossed the border to California. The use of such workers to replace American agricultural workers involved in a labor dispute was halted in 1967 by what one writer refers to as the "New Instant" NLRA.[57]

The 1967 rule requires the Immigration and Naturalization Service to invalidate the Green Card of Mexican workers who cross the border each day to work on farms certified by the Secretary of Labor as involved in a labor dispute. The new rule has the effect of providing federal protection of farm worker job rights when a labor dispute occurs. The determination of whether or not a laborer will work under "struck" conditions is made by the Secretary of Labor, not the individual.

Union fortunes in organizing farm workers have not been overly successful despite the new "National Labor Relations" law. There are other obstacles facing union drives in California. Pickets seeking to organize farm workers are not exempt from the general trespass laws, as is the situation in general industry. Conviction usually results in fines. Primary pickets are also subject to libel suits if they label the employer action as "unfair" or if they use other language commonly found on picket signs.

Unions have the right to engage in peaceful consumer picketing for the purpose of persuading customers of retail stores not to buy the struck product. Such secondary activity is legal as long as the union does not attempt to boycott all products sold by the retail establishment.

Secondary consumer boycott of California grapes has been picked up by non-union groups. Civil rights workers, high school and college students, and other groups have attempted to persuade housewives not to buy grapes in support of farm workers engaged in a labor dispute. Such efforts probably are successful. Thus, despite the growing coalition of unions and other concerned groups, the ultimate outcome of farm-worker attempts to organize rests with the consumer. To the extent that consumer secondary action is successful, the price of farm products in dispute should increase accompanied by greater pressure on employers to experiment with devices to substitute capital for labor. In any event, farm-worker attempts to unionize will not be highly successful without greater governmental support of their efforts. Either Taft-Hartley coverage or a new law dealing only with agricultural labor may be the only avenues of union organizational success. Former Secretary of Labor Hodgson favored some action in this field. He was of the opinion that new legislation should recognize that one-half of workers on farms are employed by large corporate farms.

State Reaction to Farm Organizing Attempts

Idaho, Kansas, and Arizona reacted relatively quickly to the organizing activities of the United Farm Workers Union. The Arizona law, which became effective August 13, 1972, has received the most attention. Secondary boycotts were prohibited and harvest time strikes were limited. An employer was authorized to apply to a state court for a restraining order to halt for ten days either a harvest strike or boycott. To obtain the restraining order, the employer must agree to binding arbitration after ten days and show that crops valued at $5,000 or more will be ruined or damaged.

An Agricultural Relations Board was created to administer the law. Board intervention can be made at the request of either party. Bargaining elections may be held and, in fact, the Board is authorized to even supervise union election of officers. When an election is authorized, the union no longer has a right to communicate with the workers. Eligibility to vote is decided by the employer. Even under NLRB procedures, the prospect of union election victory is small because farm workers ordinarily would not remain with an employer long enough to vote.

The Arizona law contains a ban on hot cargo provisions and one on consumer secondary boycotts when the object "is to induce, encourage, force or require" an employer to recognize a union or to bargain. The United Farm Workers Union correctly viewed the law as one that will make organizational drives very difficult if not virtually impossible. Standard union organizing techniques can hardly prevail against such restrictive legislation.

PROPOSALS FOR FEDERAL LEGISLATION

Various proposals for federal legislation have been made. General Counsel of the NLRB, Peter G. Nash, selected three of the most prominent ones and classified them as (1) the business proposal, (2) the agricultural labor proposal, and (3) the nonagricultural labor proposal.[58]

The nonagricultural labor proposal is advanced by the AFL-CIO. This proposal would eliminate the "agricultural laborer" exemption from the NLRB. The NLRB would deal with agriculture in the same framework as it does with industry in general.

The agricultural labor position is in the form of a bill brought before the House of Representatives in 1971. It is entitled "Farm Workers Bill of Rights" and essentially seeks to preserve the secondary boycott for organizing and bargaining use. It also seeks to invalidate state right-to-work law application to agriculture.

The third proposal, entitled the "Agricultural Labor Relations Act," is also in the form of a bill before the House of Representatives. Many features of the NLRA are included in the bill, but there are important differences. A separate three man Agriculture Labor Relations Board and a separate General Counsel are prominent features of the Act. *Agricultural employer* is defined to cover large firms and is essentially the same as the Fair Labor Standards Act definition. It estimated that the Fair Labor

Standards Act covers one percent of all farms or 45 percent of the total agricultural labor force.

Other provisions of the bill would require that a Board-held election would be necessary before bargaining could be required of an employer unless unfair labor practices caused the union to lose the election. In addition, a private party could obtain an injunction against unions for up to ten days while the agricultural board investigates charges of statutory violations. Either party to a dispute would also be required to give 20 days' notice of his intention to lockout or to strike or picket. The notice would be effective for one year. At any time during the year either party could serve the other with notice of intent to obtain mediation services from the Federal Mediation and Conciliation Service and the Agricultural Labor Relations Board. If mediation is not successful within 20 days, the parties would be required to choose an arbitrator under FMCS procedures. The arbitrator would recommend a collective bargaining agreement when the parties are unable to agree between themselves. Neither party may strike or lockout during the 20-day notice of intention period or the 40-day mediation period. Obviously, this latter proposal provides a great deal of protection for the large agricultural employers defined as coming within the proposed Act's jurisdiction. Work stoppages due to disputes would most likely be legislated out of existence during the busy season should this proposal pass the Congress. In any event, at this writing federal legislation has not been enacted.

SUMMARY

The NLRB decision to decline jurisdiction over cases has created a no man's land in the area of labor relations. In the *Guss* case the U.S. Supreme Court held that the states may not take jurisdiction over a case which falls within the area of interstate commerce. Though Congress attempted to close the gap in 1959, the effort has not dealt adequately with the problem. Currently, only seventeen states and Puerto Rico have enacted laws which are similar to the Taft-Hartley law. In the majority of states, however, the no-man's-land problem still exists and, what is more, there is still present the problem of uncertainty as to the kind of law which will be applied by the states in the area abnegated by the NLRB. In the last analysis, what the 1959 law has done is to destroy the principle of uniformity of labor relations law in the area of interstate commerce without doing very much to assure that all employers, employees, and unions engaged in interstate commerce have the opportunity to resort to a lawful forum in disputes covered by the Taft-Hartley Act.

The preponderance of minority group workers in hospitals and agriculture has led to a coalition of unions, civil rights organizations, religious organizations, and other interested groups. The NLRB has asserted jurisdiction over hospitals and nursing homes that meet certain annual dollar-volume tests, but has been required by Congress to eliminate agricultural laborers from coverage in accordance with the definitions contained in the Fair Labor Standards Act. Some members of Congress have proposed elimination of the NLRA agricultural exemption. Political pressures from the coalition may result in either federal or state legislation more favorable to farm worker organizations.

NOTES

[1] National Labor Relations Act, Sections 9(c) and 10(a), 49 Stat. 449, 453 (1935).

[2] *NLRB* v. *Jones & Laughlin Steel Corporation*, 301 U.S. 1 (1937).

[3] *Schecter Poultry Corporation* v. *United States*, 295 U.S. 495 (1935).

[4] National Labor Relations Act, Section 2 (7).

[5] *NLRB* v. *Fainblatt*, 306 U.S. 601, 607 (1939).

[6] Stephen S. Bean, "Federal-State Jurisdiction: An Analysis" in *Symposium on the Labor-Management Reporting and Disclosure Act of 1959*, ed. Ralph Slovenko (Baton Rouge, La.: Claitor's Bookstore Publishers, 1960), p. 660.

[7] *Yellow Cab & Baggage Company*, 17 NLRB 469 (1939).

[8] National Labor Relations Board, *First Annual Report* (1936), p. 135.

[9] Harry A. Millis and Emily C. Brown, *From the Wagner Act to Taft-Hartley* (Chicago: The University of Chicago Press, 1950), pp. 60–61.

[10] *Ibid.*, p. 401.

[11] The dollar standards established in 1950 were reported in National Labor Relations Board, *Sixteenth Annual Report* (1951), p. 16, as:

Enterprises producing or handling goods destined for out-of-state shipment, or performing services outside the state in which the firm is located valued at $25,000 a year;

Enterprises furnishing goods or services of $50,000 a year or more to concerns (dealing in commerce);

Enterprises with a direct inflow of goods or materials from out-of-state valued at $500,000 a year;

Enterprises with an indirect inflow of goods or materials valued at $1,000,000 a year;

Enterprises having such a combination of inflow or outflow of goods or services that the percentages of each of these (foregoing) categories, in which there is activity, taken together adds up to 100.

[12] NLRB Release R-428, October 21, 1953.

[13] Fred Witney, "NLRB Jurisdictional Policies and the Federal-State Relationship," *Labor Law Journal* (January 1955), p. 4.

[14] As of October 1968 states with labor relation laws were Colorado, Connecticut, Hawaii, Kansas, Maryland, Massachusetts, Michigan, Minnesota, New Jersey, New York, North Dakota, Oregon, Pennsylvania, Rhode Island, Utah, Vermont, Wisconsin, and Puerto Rico. See "State Laws," *Commerce Clearing House Labor Law Reporter* (October 18, 1968).

[15] Section 14 (b) of Taft-Hartley provides that nothing in the federal labor law "shall be construed as authorizing the execution or application of agreements requiring membership in a labor organization as a condition of employment in any State or Territory in which such execution or application is prohibited by State or Territorial law."

[16] House Report No. 245 on H.R. 3020, 80th Congress, 1st sess., p. 44.

[17] Section 8 (d) (3).

[18] Section 203 (b).

[19] Section 202 (c).

[20] Section 303 (b).

[21] Section 10 (a) of Taft-Hartley provides that "the Board is empowered, as hereinafter provided, to prevent any person from engaging in any unfair labor practice [listed in Section 8] affecting commerce. This power shall not be affected by any other means of adjustment or prevention that has been or may be established by agreement, law, or otherwise: Provided, that the Board is empowered by agreement with any agency of any State or Territory to cede to such agency jurisdiction over any cases in any industry [other than mining, manufacturing, communications, and transportation except where predominantly local in character] even though such cases involve labor disputes affecting commerce, unless the provision of the State or Territorial statute applicable to the determination of such cases by such agency is inconsistent with the corresponding provision of this Act or has received a construction inconsistent therewith."

[22] Senate Report No. 105 on Senate 1126, 80th Congress, 1st Sess. (1947), p. 26.

[23] Laws of Florida, 1943, Ch. 21968, p. 565.

[24] *Hill* v. *Florida*, 325 U.S. 538 (1945).

[25] Though this case arose under the Wagner Act, the principle set forth by the Supreme Court would, of course, have full application to Taft-Hartley.

[26] *Bethlehem Steel Company* v. *NYSLRB*, 330 U.S. 767 (1947).

[27] Public and Local Acts, Michigan, Section 423.9 (a), 1949; Michigan Statutes Annotated, Section 17.454 (1) (Cum. Supp. 1949).

[28] Wisconsin Statutes, 1947, Chapter 11.50.

[29] *La Crosse Telephone Corporation* v. *WERB*, 336 U.S. 18 (1948).

[30] *Plankinton Packing Company* v. *WERB*, 338 U.S. 953 (1950).

[31] Case cited at footnote 26.

[32] Case cited at footnote 29.

[33] *Garner* v. *Teamsters Union*, 246 U.S. 485 (1953).

[34] 353 U.S. 1 (1957).

[35] 1. *Nonretail enterprises:* $50,000 outflow or inflow, direct or indirect. Outflow and inflow may not be combined, but direct and indirect outflow or direct and indirect inflow might be combined to meet the $50,000 requirement. 2. *Office buildings:* Gross revenue of $100,000 or more of which $25,000 or more is derived from organizations that meet any of the standards. 3. *Retail concerns:* $500,000 gross volume of business. 4. *Instrumentalities, links, and channels of interstate commerce:* $50,000 from interstate (or linkage) part of enterprise, or from services performed for employers in commerce. 5. *Public utilities:* $250,000 gross volume or meet nonretail standards. 6. *Transit systems:* $250,000 gross volume. Taxicab companies must meet the retail standard. 7. *Newspapers and communications systems:* $100,000 gross volume for radio, television, telegraph, and telephone; newspapers, $200,000 gross volume. 8. *National defense:* Substantial impact on national defense. 9. *Business in the Territories and the District of Columbia:* The standards apply in the territories; all firms in the District of Columbia are covered. 10. *Associations:* Treated as single employer.

[36] Labor Management Reporting & Disclosure Act, Section 14 (c) (1959).

[37] *Hotel Employees Local 255* v. *Leedom*, 358 U.S. 99 (1958).

[38] *Floridian Hotel of Tampa*, 124 NLRB 261 (1959).

[39] *Los Angeles Turf Club*, 90 NLRB 20 (1950). In 1973, the Board reaffirmed this policy. NLRB, *Rules and Regulations*, Section 103 (April 17, 1973).

[40] *Cornell University*, 183 NLRB No. 41 (1970).

[41] 97 NLRB 424 (1951).

[42] *Fordham University*, 193 NLRB 134 (1971).

[43] *American League of Professional Baseball Clubs*, 180 NLRB 190 (1970).

[44] NLRB, *Rules and Regulations*, Section 103.2 (March 7, 1973).

[45] *El Dorado, Inc.*, 151 NLRB 579 (1965).

[46] *First Church of Christ. Scientist in Boston*, 194 NLRB No. 174 (1972).

[47] *Office Employees International Union, Local 11* v. *NLRB*, 353 U.S. 313 (1957).

[48] See 23 NLRB Annual Report 8–12 (1958), wherein these standards are discussed.

[49] New NLRB *Rule to Meet Amended Act*, 45 Labor Relations Report 49 (1959).

[50] Address of Stuart Rothman, NLRB General Counsel, before the Association of State Labor Relations Agencies, Detroit, Mich., November 18, 1959.

[51] Conference Report, House Report No. 1147, 86th Congress, 1st sess. (1959), 37.

[52] *Butte Medical Properties, d/b/a Medical Center Hospital*, 168 NLRB 52 (1967).

[53] *University Nursing Home*, 168 NLRB 53 (1967).

[54] *NLRB* v. *Campbell*, 159 F. (2d) 184 (1947).

[55] *North Whittier Heights Citrus Association* v. *NLRB*, 109 F. (2d) 76 (1940), cert. denied, 310 U.S. 632 (1940).

[56] *Bodine Produce Company*, 147 NLRB 832 (1964).

[57] Charles A. Rummell, "Current Developments in Farm Labor Law," *Labor Law Journal*, XIX, No. 4 (April 1968), pp. 235–236.

[58] Speech before the Fifteenth New Jersey Marketing Institute entitled "Bargaining in Agriculture: Current Trends in Labor Management Relations," November 30, 1972.

IV CONTROL OF COLLECTIVE BARGAINING

PROLOGUE.   *Taft-Hartley ushered in a new era regarding the role of government in peacetime collective bargaining. It further structured the freedom of unions and employers to fashion the collective bargaining relationship relative to the legislation preceding it. One objective of the law was to bring about a balance of employer-employee rights. How did the 1947 labor law accomplish this objective? Does government control over collective bargaining fulfill the aim of public policy? How do Taft-Hartley controls on collective bargaining affect the overall vitality of the American labor union movement? Such questions involve an analysis of the impact of the law on the bargaining unit, Board election policies, union security and revenue, and the enforcement of collective bargaining agreements.*

12

Election Policies of the NLRB

Establishment of a unit appropriate for collective bargaining, discussed in Chapter 13, is important for the purpose of carrying out the basic objective of the national labor legislation. Prior to mutual agreement on the part of the parties or a determination of the appropriate unit by the regional director and immediately prior to the actual poll, unions and employers are usually engaged in organizational campaigns attempting to sway workers either toward union membership or away from it. The campaign usually becomes more intense after the Board is petitioned to hold an election. The drive to enlist workers into unions is made both prior to petitioning the NLRB to conduct a representation election and thereafter to maintain or increase the proportion of workers who agree to cast ballots for the union when the poll is actually held. Unions seek to have bargaining authorization cards signed, which demonstrate the potential strength of the labor organization at the polls. At least 30 percent of an appropriate unit must sign bargaining authorization cards before the NLRB considers there is sufficient interest in collective bargaining to justify holding an election. It is considered that such a percentage raises a question of representation. Unions, on the other hand, normally try to obtain approximately 55 percent before they consider their chances at the poll adequate to petition for an election. The basic reason for this larger percentage is that once employers enter election campaigns, many workers often decide against supporting a union by the date secret ballots are cast. Some employers recognize unions and commence to bargain on the strength of the bargaining authorization cards signed by employees. Others refuse to accept such cards as evidence of employee desires. Since the enactment of the Wagner Act in 1935, the Board has had the responsibility of insuring the rights of employees to engage in collective bargaining through representatives of their own choosing.

Such a guarantee requires the development of a set of principles to govern the election conduct of unions and employers so as to provide maximum freedom for employees to choose or not to choose bargaining representatives. In short, the NLRB has the responsibility to reconcile or equate the legal rights of employees to organize and the constitutional right of employers to free speech. Absolute freedom does not exist for either group. This chapter will deal with the election policies developed by the Board and courts since 1935. Both administrative rules and statutory requirements are considered as they have developed and changed to the present time.

EMPLOYER FREE SPEECH UNDER THE
WAGNER ACT

Wagner Act Policies

During the early Wagner Act years, the economic position of employers was considered so superior to that of labor unions that employers were forbidden to take part in organizing campaigns.[1] The Board, in handing down its first decisions, contended that any words of employers during organizing campaigns, whether written or oral, constituted a force more powerful than peaceful persuasion. Thus employers were ordered to remain "neutral." The early rules were developed when both unions and the Board were in their infancy. Neither were very strong and employers often posed a formidable force when they defied union organizational efforts. Unemployment was widespread and the least employer utterance was often all that was required to frustrate employee efforts to organize into unions.

It did not take the Board and the U.S. Supreme Court long, however, to begin a search for criteria that would reveal what factors should be used to determine the coercive potential of employer communication, and for methods of equalizing the opportunities for employers and unions to present oral arguments to employees.[2] Absolute restriction on the right of employers to speak during pre-election campaigns was difficult to justify to a society with constitutional guarantees of freedom of speech.

In 1940, particularly, the courts were struggling to find a workable free-speech policy to guide employer activities during pre-election campaigns. In one well-known case, *Thornhill* v. *Alabama*, the Supreme Court in dealing with employee picketing rights held that "the dissemination of information concerning fact of a labor dispute must be regarded as within the area of free discussion that is guaranteed by the Constitution."[3] The statement by the Court was an indicator of what was to come in employer speech cases. The Sixth Circuit Court of Appeals in another case ruled that "the right to form opinions is of little value if it may not be communicated to those immediately concerned."[4] Obviously, the courts were driving toward the establishment of guidelines that would permit employers to enter pre-election representation campaigns, while at the same time remaining careful to insure employees their legal right to voluntarily choose representatives for collective bargaining.

The U.S. Supreme Court in a 1941 decision was confronted with the issue of determining employer rights to free speech under the First Amendment to the Constitution.[5] The *Virginia & Electric Power Company* case established the basic premise upon which the NLRB and the courts were to continue their attempts to structure free representation elections with balanced rights for all concerned parties. The Court in its decision made it clear that a per se approach to forbidding employer speech was not acceptable and stated that:

> The employer . . . is as free now as ever to take any side it may choose on this controversial issue. But, certainly, conduct, though evidenced in part by speech, may amount, in connection with other circumstances, to coercion within the meaning of the Act. And in determining whether a course of conduct amounts to restraint or coercion, pressure exerted vocally by the employer may no more be disregarded than pressure exerted in other ways.

Employer speech therefore was not necessarily coercive. Infringement of the rights of employees attempting to organize had to be evaluated in view of the totality of circumstances in each case. In a string of Board cases prior to Taft-Hartley enactment, it was established that employers could speak out if their words fell short of coercion, threats, or promises of economic benefits if employees would reject unionization. For example, antiunion speeches could not be delivered to *captive audiences*.[6] A captive audience refers to workers being ushered into a common meeting place on company time and property to listen to their employer on a subject determined solely by the employer. In the absence of a captive meeting, however, an employer was permitted to predict a decline in jobs if the union won the election. In still another case concerning employer speech, the Board ruled that "the consequences it prophesied from unionization carried no connotation that its own economic power would be used, if necessary, to make its prophecy come true."[7] Obviously, the NLRB was having difficulty in early cases in attempting to provide employees with the greatest possible freedom to determine their collective bargaining desires.

One writer has argued that the *totality-of-conduct doctrine* was in the process of development throughout the period 1941–1948.[8] The totality-of-conduct doctrine refers to an attempt to review actions within the totality of all circumstances. For example, a speech that seems harmless on the surface may in fact carry with it implied threats of which employees are very much aware because of some other recent event. In the *American Tube Bending* case, decided in 1943, the Board dealt with an employer's remarks to employees on company property regarding a forthcoming election. After delivering a captive-audience speech, the employer followed up by sending letters to workers on the same issue. The Board ruled that neither the speech nor the letters were coercive, but such employer activity interfered with employee free choice in the selection of bargaining representatives. The Second Circuit Court disagreed and reversed the Board decision.[9] By 1947, in the *United Welding Company* case, the NLRB held that an employer could send letters to individual employees for the purpose of communicating his own views regarding the issues at hand.[10] The context within which employers were permitted to respond to union organizational efforts was a difficult problem for the Board. The difficulty extends to this day, as we shall see shortly.

The issue of employer participation in election campaigns was before the Congress on at least two separate occasions. The House of Representatives appointed a Special Committee to Investigate the National Labor Relations Board; this committee published its results in 1940.[11] Among other things it recommended protection of employer expressions of opinion if not accompanied by acts of coercion. Legislation did not develop, however, because of the nation's concern with the war. Congressional hearings over employer free speech during representation election campaigns continued after World War II during debates over the Taft-Hartley Act. The Senate was generally of the opinion that the totality of conduct should determine the degree of employer participation in pre-election campaigns. Senate Report 105 of the 80th Congress proposed that "if . . . under all the circumstances [there is] no threat . . . of reprisal or force, or offer . . . of benefit . . . " employers should be permitted to express their views to employees or to answer union propaganda. Alternatively, the House of Representatives was not of the opinion that the totality-of-conduct doctrine should be controlling. It argued that there should be no rule restricting employer free speech. If a speech was in itself coercive, then it was not privileged. Otherwise it should not be restricted.

If the view of the House had prevailed, the speech itself would have controlled the resulting decision. A course of past conduct that restricted employee union activities could not be considered an integral aspect of any pre-election campaign culminating in a final employer speech. The speech in and of itself might be relatively harmless unless the content was correlated to past events for interpretation. Section 8 (c) of Taft-Hartley finally emerged from the debates. It requires that:

> The expressing of any views, argument, or opinion, or the dissemination thereof, whether in written, printed, graphic, or visual form, shall not constitute or be evidence of an unfair labor practice under any of the provisions of this Act, if such expression contains no threat of reprisal or force or promise of benefit.

It seems obvious that the law provides for many privileges in the area of free speech. One Board member remarked that the Taft-Hartley provision barred the agency "from even considering such statements in weighing the significance of other conduct." The National Association of Manufacturers wrote that the provision, if given a literal construction, "obviously would impose a harsher rule of evidence even than existed under common law rules in criminal cases."[12] It remained, however, for the Board and the courts to determine the substantive issues.

Construction of Taft-Hartley Provisions

The NLRB in a very early case following Taft-Hartley enactment ruled an election invalid in its famous *General Shoe* ruling because an employer read an "intemperate" statement to his employees.[13] It should be observed that the Board did not base its decision for ordering a new election on unfair labor practices. It held that:

> Conduct that creates an atmosphere which renders improbable a free choice in an election may invalidate the election even though such conduct may not constitute an unfair labor practice. . . . In election proceedings, it is the Board's function to provide conditions as nearly ideal as possible, to determine the uninhibited desires of the employees.[14]

The Board made it clear that the criteria applied in a representation proceeding to determine if certain activities interfered with elections need not be the same as those applied in unfair labor practice cases. The majority argued that Congress applied its provisions only to unfair labor practice situations. Representation cases were intended to be treated differently and as such the Board's own administrative standards were relevant in fulfilling the basic objectives of extending to employees freedom of choice in selecting bargaining representatives.

Even though the Board established its desire to set elections aside when it considered conditions had been inadequate for employees to make their selection, unions contended that the *General Shoe* doctrine provided inadequate remedies once their majority position had been undermined during the campaign. Labor unions argued that they should be certified as bargaining representatives on the basis of 50 percent of bargaining authorization cards signed within a bargaining unit when employer behavior resulted in union election losses. Their argument was based on the victory experience rate for subsequent elections after the setting aside of elections. They were not nearly as likely to win second elections as they were the first ones. The Board came to accept this argument in 1949, a special case of agency control over pre-election behavior which will be treated later in this chapter.

The Board was also confronted with the problem of misrepresentation of facts during pre-election campaigns on the part of both unions and employers. In the *Gummed Products* case the NLRB was required to establish guides for permissible action when facts are distorted.[15] Distortion of facts under certain situations prevents conditions of free choice for employees during a poll. The Board ruled that falsehoods, exaggerations, inaccuracies, partial truths, and name-calling can be excused as legitimate propaganda. However, the ultimate consideration for the Board turns on "whether the challenged propaganda has lowered the standards" of the campaign to the point where the uninhibited desires of the employees cannot be determined in an election. In the *Gummed Products* case the labor union misrepresented the wage rates paid employees by other employers that were represented by the same union. As such it was in a position to know the relative wage rates and a repeat of the same propaganda on election eve after the employer response to its first wage report lowered campaign standards to a position unacceptable to the Board. The union victory was set aside as a result of its action. The NLRB made it clear that it decides each case on an ad hoc basis and that at some point propaganda will result in the use of the *General Shoe* laboratory-of-conditions doctrine, which calls for the setting aside of an election and the holding of a new one.

In December 1973 the U.S. Supreme Court established another policy under which an election is to be set aside. A union promised employees that it would waive initiation fees for employees who signed union membership authorization cards before the election was held. The union won the election. In *NLRB* v. *Savair*, the high court set aside the election on the grounds that the waiver promise interfered with the conduct of a fair election. A short time later, however, the NLRB in *Lau Industries* held that a union may lawfully waive initiation fees provided that the waiver applied to *all* employees eligible to vote in the election, those who signed authorization cards and those who did not.

The "Futility Doctrine"

The Board has consistently stated that pre-election threats or promises that tend to influence employee action at the polls are grounds for setting aside elections. However, during the 1950s, the Board decided to distinguish between statements that constituted threats and those that merely stated an opinion or legal position. In 1953 the Board was confronted by a situation whereby the employer communicated to employees the futility of voting for a union since the situation would be taken into the courts in any event. Furthermore, the courts were alleged to be sympathetic to his stated position.[16] In the intervening years prior to a court determination of the issue, things would continue just as always. Selection of the union would result in bargaining on a "cold blooded" basis whereby workers would earn less than before if a union were selected. In its determination the Board held that the expression of a legal position did not warrant invalidating election results.

By 1962 Board personnel had changed and a similar case was once again brought before it for solution.[17] The employer in the *Dal-Tex* case made speeches informing employees that he could not be compelled to sign a collective bargaining agreement even if the Board ordered him to negotiate. The NLRB reviewed the totality of employer conduct and found that the speeches went beyond a mere statement of legal position. Reference was made to the probability of a strike, replacement of strikers, and the general futility of employee designation of bargaining representatives. Employer conduct was held to have destroyed the laboratory conditions within which the Board seeks to hold elections. The NLRB ruled that employer conduct that has long been considered an unfair labor practice violation cannot be protected merely because representation proceedings are involved. In short, the "free speech" protection of Taft-Hartley cannot be used currently to permit action during pre-election campaigns that would otherwise not be permissible under Board policy. Thus the "futility doctrine" of 1953 has been reversed to the extent that such communication, when taken in the context of all the circumstances present, reveals that freedom of employee choice to select bargaining representatives has been curtailed.

Economic Threats by Employers

Some statements made by employers during pre-election campaigns have been considered coercive of employee rights in and of themselves. A threat of economic retaliation if a bargaining unit is victorious in an election is perhaps one of the most damaging of statements with regard to free choice in selecting bargaining representatives. Free speech is considered protected by the First Amendment to the Constitution if it is in the form of an opinion on labor matters. However, the right is not protected when utterances impair the rights extended employees under the National Labor Relations Act.

During the Wagner Act years the Board held that an employer threat to move the plant to a new location to avoid bargaining obligations imposed under the Act was coercive in and of itself.[18] The courts upheld the Board determinations. During the 1950s, however, the new NLRB personnel changed the agency's position and ruled that employer statements that they might be forced to move the plant if a union won an election were not threats, but mere statements of prophesy. A mere statement that the company might have to move the plant was considered different from one stating that it would be moved. The laboratory conditions for holding elections were given a different interpretation from the one in the latter 1940s. Management was extended the greatest latitude in using its superior economic strength to influence election results. As stated, there can be no greater threat to a worker than the possibility of job loss.

In a 1961 case the Board changed its position once again and reverted to its pre-1950s position.[19] An employer assembled his workers prior to a scheduled election and stated:

> Now what I mean to bring out to you is simply this: that if by chance the union were to be voted into this shop, there is no doubt in my mind, because of the terrific demands that they are making, . . . there will be a strike. Somismo will not be able to cope with that problem; there will be a strike; whether we go out of business or not I am not saying right now. . . . I want to say that the demands of the union cannot and will not be met.

The law judge in the *Somismo* case ruled in favor of the company on the basis of the guidelines set by the Board during the 1950s. He held that the speech was a "mere prediction of the dire circumstances that would result from a union's policies." Upon review, the NLRB reversed the decision and held that the employer's speech interfered with employee free choice and set the election aside. Therefore, under Board policy, statements such as these constitute more than a mere prediction because of the fear instilled in employees that their jobs might be lost if they voted for union representation. The attempt to establish laboratory conditions for holding an election is not advanced, in the Board's opinion, by permitting such statements.

With the Nixon appointees in the majority, the current Board may alter or even reverse election policies. Note that in the Eisenhower administration, the *General Shoe* doctrine was eclipsed, providing employers with greater opportunity to defeat unions at the polls. A portent of what may be the future policy of the Board was revealed by Chairman Miller when he stated:

> In my opinion, the Board's role in policing pre-election campaigns is not to strip pre-election statements of the protection afforded by Section 8(c) of the Act simply because they stress the disadvantages of collective bargaining as drawn by the employer from his own experience.[20]

In *McLaughlin*, Miller was in the minority, but subsequently he was joined by Kennedy, another Nixon appointee, to constitute a majority over a third Board member to permit employers wider latitude to defeat unions at the polls.[21] In any event, at this writing the Nixon appointees have not reversed previous Board policies. It appears that they are chipping away at established doctrines, but as yet there has not been a total reversal. If the Nixon Board extends the "free speech" provision, Section 8(c), to cover virtually all employer statements, it would follow that the *General Shoe* laboratory-of-conditions doctrine would fall. Under these circumstances, employers would have a distinct advantage at the polls.

Racial Discrimination and Election Policies

Prior to 1962 the NLRB had never set aside an election in which statements had been made appealing to prejudices concerning race or religion. Any such statements were considered insufficient to warrant a new election.[22] Earlier Board policy was undoubtedly a reflection of general societal apathy regarding the position of minority groups in America's economic institutions. The agency had sufficient authority to establish guidelines for regulating election campaigns under its *General Shoe* doctrine calling for the establishment of laboratory conditions during election campaigns. It did not choose to deal with the controversial discrimination issue, possibly because of fear of repercussions that might result.

The *Sewell Manufacturing* case was placed before the Board in 1962; the case involved the issue of employer racial propaganda appealing to prejudices. The employer speech was alleged to have prevented a free election.[23] Involved were employer letters to employees with (1) a large picture showing a close-up of a Negro man dancing with a white lady and (2) a picture of a white man dancing with a Negro lady. Underneath both pictures were captions connecting them either with the union attempting to organize the local plant or the union movement in general. In still another letter sent out by the employer, union racial policies were linked to communism and the National Association for the Advancement of Colored People. The regional director ruled in accordance with past Board guidelines. That is, he did not consider the nature of the speech sufficient to warrant setting the election aside.

Upon appeal to the Board, a new policy was established. The Board ruled that if either a union or an employer uses racial propaganda during an election campaign and wins because of it, there will be a test to determine election interference. The test is that a party limit statements to those that truthfully set forth another party's racial attitudes and policies, and does not deliberately seek to overstress and exacerbate racial feelings by irrelevant, inflammatory appeals. The burden of proof rests upon the party making use of such arguments; he must establish that they are truthful and germane to an election campaign.

The major difficulty of the Board's policy is to draw the line between statements that are inflammatory and those that are not. The Board did not rule that parties are forbidden to discuss race in representation cases. The *Allen-Morrison Sign Company* case[24] was handed down on the same day as the *Sewell* case, which gave the broad structure for control of racial issues during election campaigns. In the *Allen-Morrison* case the Board refused to set aside an election despite the fact that the employer circulated a pre-election letter to employees advising them of union expenditures to help eliminate segregation. Enclosed with the letter was a newspaper excerpt concerning the union's position on racial issues.[25] The Board permits the utilization of racial propaganda if it is within a proper economic and social context. Advisement of the other party's true position is permissible even though it may have a determining impact on election results.

The proper economic and social context for permitting racial issues to be incorporated into campaigns is still in the process of development. In a 1967 case, *Baltimore Luggage*, an employer accused a union of improperly injecting racial propaganda in the pre-election campaign.[26] The Board refused to set the election aside on the ground that it could not justify prohibition of "reasonable, noninflammatory appeals to the solidarity and economic interests" of a racial group calculated to assist them in overcoming their social and economic disadvantage. The Board argued further that trade unions have traditionally "sought to unify groups of employees by focusing group attention on common problems and to further the acceptance of union spokesmen by emphasizing the extent to which the spokesmen have identified themselves with these problems." The Board argued that it would be discriminatory to disallow traditional union approaches to organizing workers merely because of the ethnic composition of the work force.

The Board's attempt to alleviate appeals to racial prejudices has not been well articulated. The standard for judgment turns on whether the information is intemperately presented to the electorate. In effect, the Board is itself rendering its racial policies ineffectual. The presentation of racial propaganda, when taken in the total context of each situation, is likely to have the same effect regardless of the media of communication used. It seems that all a party must do is present materials to some groups of workers containing racial overtones and the obvious basis for presentation in the first place is communicated. No inflammatory written words by either party are necessary. It may well be that the Board will yet have to articulate more inclusive criteria for its actions. The communication of racial materials to some groups, even if true, has the obvious effect of arousing hatred and retaliation against the minority groups rights at representation polls.

Captive-audience Doctrine

The captive-audience rules of the Board, in its attempts to provide a balanced opportunity for unions and employers to conduct their campaigns, have been particularly troublesome. Not only has the NLRB had to deal with the involuntary assembling of employees on company property during working time, but it has also had to establish some workable criteria for no-solicitation and no-distribution rules invoked by companies to regulate work and nonwork activity on company premises. A *privileged no-solicitation rule* refers to a condition whereby a union is prohibited from soliciting members on employer premises during both work and nonwork time. Bans against solicitation and distribution restrict oral attempts to encourage workers to join a union or passing out literature for the same purpose. Captive-audience policies are complex and a variety of approaches has been taken by the NLRB in attempts to equate employer and union rights. The complexity of the issues requires separate treatment of some of the evolving Board doctrines.

The captive-audience doctrine has been subject to considerable change as NLRB membership has shifted over the years. In 1946, prior to Taft-Hartley enactment, the Board dealt with employer meetings with employees on company premises prior to an election.[27] The Board ruled that a captive audience gave the employer an undue amount of control over the election and constituted an unfair labor practice. However, the Second Circuit Court of Appeals modified the Board order somewhat and argued that "we should hesitate to hold that he may not do this on company time and pay provided a similar opportunity to address them were accorded the union."[28] The case obviously provided equal time for the union's reply. The NLRB did not have time to work out the details involving equal time to reply to captive-audience speeches before the Taft-Hartley Act was passed. For example, it was not clear whether unions were to be afforded equal time on the company's premises and on company time or if some other method of reaching employees was to be devised.

The *Babcock & Wilcox* case was before the Board in 1948 after Taft-Hartley passage. It provided that the use of captive audiences could no longer form the basis for a ruling of unfair labor practices.[29] The decision was based on the Taft-Hartley provision dealing with employer free speech.[30] Union victories at the polls started to decline almost immediately. In fiscal 1947 union election victories amounted to 81.4 percent of cases reaching the election stage; by 1951 their victories declined to 71 percent of elections. Such a record may or may not reflect the impact of the captive-audience doctrine. It may well reflect the nature of bargaining units unions were attempting to organize by 1951. That is, possibly the units that were easier to organize were reflected in the 1947 victories, and union efforts were centered on more difficult smaller units by 1951. Whatever the reason, union victories started declining at about the same time the Board announced an easing of employer speech restrictions.

An equal opportunity for unions to reply to employer speeches under captive-audience conditions was also rejected by the NLRB in a 1950 case.[31] A new dimension to the captive-audience doctrine was added, however, the following year in the *Bonwit Teller* case.[32] A department store enforced a privileged no-solicitation rule and at the same time denied a union request for equal opportunity to address the company's employees. Employees were assembled by the employer during work time to hear an antiunion address. The union lost the election and filed an unfair labor practice charge. The Board ruled differently than it had in *Babcock & Wilcox*, holding that an unfair labor practice violation occurred because the employer had not provided the union an equal opportunity to rebut the employer's statements. The Board further ruled that when a company can lawfully enforce a privileged no-solicitation rule, it cannot use a captive audience unless it provides an equal opportunity for the union to reach employees. In short the NLRB introduced the equal-opportunity doctrine in any industry where a company can enforce a privileged no-solicitation rule. In 1952 the equal opportunity to respond when captive audiences were used was extended to industry in general with or without the presence of privileged no-solicitation rules. Obviously, the NLRB was attempting to equate the rights of unions and employers during election campaigns to fulfill its policy of providing laboratory conditions for representation polls.

Bonwit Teller was approved by the Second Circuit Court of Appeals to the extent that a *privileged no-solicitation rule* was in effect.[33] A privileged no-solicitation rule refers to a condition whereby a union is prohibited from soliciting members on employer premises during both work and nonwork time. Nonwork time refers to lunch periods and rest breaks and so on. However, the court held that if a union was permitted to solicit members during nonworking hours, an employer could deny a request for equal opportunity to address employees on company time and property.

In 1953, again with new personnel, the Board changed its rule and held that a union was not entitled to an equal opportunity to reply to a company's charges during a campaign unless an employer put into effect and enforced a privileged no-solicitation rule.[34] It reasoned that equal time qualified employer right of free speech. It held that

> if the privilege of free speech is to be given real meaning, it cannot be qualified by grafting upon it conditions which are tantamount to negation.

But the same year, 1953, the NLRB itself imposed conditions on employer free speech.[35] It held in *Peerless Plywood* that involuntary audience speeches could not be made within a twenty-four-hour period prior to a scheduled representation election. The restriction applies to both sides. However, reading materials may be distributed since employees are free to decide if they want to read printed handouts.

In 1958 the Supreme Court reviewed the captive-audience doctrine as related to a nonretail outlet.[36] It ruled that an employer's right to address an involuntary audience without extending an equal opportunity to a union should be considered in the context of alternatives facing a labor organization to reach employees. The high court was concerned with balancing the rights of both sides. The tendency of the Board to establish rigid rules was frowned on by the Court. Each case was to be reviewed in terms of all relevant evidence before a decision could be upheld by the high court.

In 1962 the Board composition was again changed as a result of the 1960 national election. In the *May Department Store* case[37] the NLRB reaffirmed the *Bonwit Teller* rule. Hence when employers put into effect a privileged no-solicitation rule—such as is common within the department store industry—and use a captive audience, the union must have equal time to reply. Speeches by employers to an involuntary audience would require an equal opportunity for unions to respond.

Captive-audience and No-distribution Rules:
Current Status

The no-distribution and no-solicitation rules have generated such changing Board opinions that the NLRB was forced to articulate its position more explicitly. In 1960 it was able to draw from Supreme Court decisions extending from 1945 to summarize the agency's position.[38] The quoted rules are:

1. No-solicitation or no-distribution rules which prohibit union solicitation or distribution of union literature on company property by employees during non-working time are presumptively an unreasonable impediment to self-organization, and are presumptively invalid both as to their promulgation and enforcement, however, such rules may be validated by evidence that special circumstances make the rule necessary in order to maintain production or discipline.
2. No-solicitation or no-distribution rules which prohibit union solicitation or distribution of union literature by employees during working time are presumptively valid as to their promulgation, in the absence of evidence that the rule was adopted for a discriminatory purpose; and are presumptively valid as to their enforcement in the absence of evidence that the rule was unfairly applied.
3. No-solicitation or no-distribution rules which prohibit union solicitation or distribution of union literature by nonemployee union organizers at any time on the employer's property are presumptively valid, in the absence of a showing that the union cannot reasonably reach the employees with its message in any other way, or a showing that the employer's notice discriminates against the union by allowing other solicitation or distribution.[39]

The enforcement of a no-distribution rule in a discriminatory fashion renders it illegal. Discrimination has been held to exist if one union is allowed to pass out literature while another is denied the privilege.[40] Also if the rule is applied to a union, but other forms of solicitation unrelated to union activity are permitted, the rule is then considered invalid.[41] For example, the Salvation Army may not go on an employer's premises and pass out literature or solicit donations and later the same right be denied to union attempts to organize.

In terms of the totality of conduct, such rules have been held discriminatory when adopted and enforced to discourage union membership or when the rules otherwise coincide with a union organizational drive.[42] Alternatively, special circumstances may exist that have the effect of validating seemingly invalid rules. For example, in the *May Department Stores* case, a no-solicitation rule was held valid at all times on the selling floor because solicitation for union membership would interfere with retail store sales. In a case involving the *Republic Aviation Corporation*, the U.S. Supreme Court made a distinction between a company rule applicable to working time and one applicable to employees outside of working hours but still on company property.[43] Prohibition of solicitation on nonworking time on company property was considered interference with employee organizational rights and as such constituted an unfair labor practice. Regarding department stores, no-solicitation rules have been held valid by the Board even in nonworking areas if they happen also to be areas open to the public.

Many years ago the U.S. Supreme Court established a policy dealing with the right of union organizers (nonemployees of the employer) to come on company property to solicit union members and to distribute union literature.[44] It held that union organizers may be barred from company property if by reasonable effort they can use other available channels of communication to reach employees. That is, union organizers can be barred if they can contact employees by mail, home visits, newspaper advertisements, radio and TV, or organize a meeting. If by reasonable effort they cannot use these methods of communication, it follows that an employer may not deny them access to plant property.

As with other policies established by the high court, the NLRB has the power and duty to apply it to the facts of a particular case. In recent years, it would appear that the NLRB is applying this doctrine to bar union organizers under questionable circumstances. One case involved a plant located just outside of Chicago. A union was denied access to the employer's parking lot. The physical layout of the plant made it very difficult, if at all possible, to contact employees before they arrived in the parking lot, or were in their cars and were starting to leave the lot. To and from the parking lot, employees used a short public road that connected directly with a busy four lane highway. This factor plus recognition of the difficulties of using alternative methods of communication in a large city to contact employees prompted a law judge to hold that the employer unlawfully denied the organizers access to the parking lot. The NLRB reversed the law judge.[45] In this respect, the NLRB stated that it rejected

> the claim that because the employees lived in a large metropolitan area, they were just as inaccessible as those employees who live and work wholly on employer's property. The Board finds it neither wise nor proper to adopt "a big city rule" and a different "small town rule" . . . or to attempt to determine how big a city must be to justify the professed differing application.[46]

In another instance, employees drove to and from the plant's parking lot over a viaduct that entered directly into a busy highway.[47] The employer denied union organizers the right to contact employees in the parking lot before they left, or to contact them when they arrived before the shift started. Among other reasons for upholding the employer position, the Board pointed out that an organizer could station himself at the viaduct area and jot down the license numbers of the employees' cars. Even if union organizers have sharp eyes, and could write very fast, the method would not be very effective because many employees arrange for car pools to come to work. Besides that, there is the burden of getting the drivers' names and addresses through their license numbers.

The remedial authority of the Board was further extended in another case involving coercive employer speeches before a captive audience.[48] The Board agreed with the union's argument that the holding of new elections and the posting of notices on company premises to inform employees of their right to be free from interference, coercion, and restraint were insufficient to cure employer unfair labor practices. The inadequacy of such traditional remedies was underscored by the success of the employer in bringing about a union loss at the poll. The Board ruled that it "must take measures designed to recreate the conditions and relationship that would have been had there been no unfair labor practice."[49] The particular remedy was equal time for the union to reply—during normal work time at company expense. Facilities were to be provided by the employer that were customarily used for employee meetings.

In early 1966 the Board delayed consideration of its *Livingston Shirt* rule in the *General Electric Company* case.[50] The *Livingston Shirt* case providing equal time to reply to antiunion speeches was limited to situations in which an unlawful or privileged no-solicitation rule prohibited union solicitation on nonworking time. The *General Electric* case did not involve a retail store and a no-solicitation rule was not involved. The union argued that the *Livingston Shirt* equal-time rule was not adequate and that the Board should return to its previous policy of 1951 holding that any employer antiunion speech on company time and property without equal opportunity to reply should constitute an unfair labor practice and as such provide grounds to set the election aside.

The Board was not willing to accept the union argument for equal time to campaign on employer premises at the time. However, the Board did defer a reconsideration of its *Livingston Shirt* policy until after the effects of its new *names-and-addresses rule* became known. In its new approach to dealing with equal opportunities, the Board initiated a procedural change in its election policies. The new requirement was that the names and addresses of bargaining unit employees eligible to vote had to be made available to all parties to an election proceeding at a specified time.

Names-and-addresses Policy

It will be recalled that the Supreme Court in 1941 implied that Board policies regarding elections should be evaluated in the context of all the circumstances involved in cases before it.[51] Also it called for balanced rights for all parties involved in labor disputes. The NLRB recognized that management possessed another avenue for communicating with employees that was not available to unions. Employers had in their possession the names and addresses of all workers included in the bargaining unit involved in the contest. Possession of such a list made it relatively simple to mail out propaganda dealing with union organizational attempts. Literature could be mailed out in the form of a regular weekly or monthly newsletter to employees or a special mailing enabling management to present its views on representation elections. Obviously, the greater accessibility of management to its employees placed unions at a distinct disadvantage in attempting to present views to prospective supporters.

The issue of union access to the names and addresses of employees involved in Board election proceedings was raised in the *Excelsior Underwear Inc.* case in 1966.[52] Essentially, the union request is merely another aspect of the equal-time-to-reply doctrine. The only difference is the opportunity to respond in writing as opposed to speeches before assembled groups of workers. Union representatives may also choose to visit employees in their homes as a device for communicating with potential members. The supplying of names and addresses to unions also permits the Board to establish election policies without requiring employers to extend use of their property to unions at company expense.

The Board is of the opinion that equal access to the names and addresses of eligible bargaining-unit voters "insure[s] the opportunity of all employees to be reached by all parties" even though unions may have other avenues by which they "might be able to communicate with employees." Employers may not decide for themselves whether a need for such a list exists.[53] What is required is that an employer place on file with regional directors the names and addresses of eligible voters within seven days after approval of elections by the various methods provided by law. That is, such information is required within seven days after consent agreements or a Board order directing the holding of elections.

Board policy requiring employers to file eligible voter names and addresses with regional directors was justified on the basis that Congress entrusted the NLRB alone to establish procedures and policies to conduct fair elections. Merely because employers were only required to file employee names in the past did not preclude the agency from requiring employers to furnish addresses. In addition, it was argued that the names and addresses of all registered voters are general public information in public elections. Also such information is required by law when proxy battles occur for corporation control. During proxy contests stockholder names and addresses must be either supplied the contestants or management must mail campaign materials for the other parties. The Landrum-Griffin Act of 1959 also requires that all candidates for union office have a right to have the union distribute campaign literature to all members.[54] In the past the Board has only required filing a list of eligible voter names. The list of names then were made available to all parties involved in election proceedings. In some cases unions were able to find out the addresses of persons on the lists, but certainly not all of them.

Knowledge of addresses in addition to names would have the effect of increasing employee ability to make a determination either for or against representation since greater communication is possible. The reason given by the NLRB was that an opportunity for both sides to reach all employees "is basic to a fair and informed election." Employer refusal to supply such information to the regional directors would be grounds for setting aside elections, if requested by unions.

The impact of the *Excelsior* case is important in resolving many of the captive-audience problems plaguing the Board in the past. For example, knowledge of eligible voter addresses as well as names not only permits unions to mail campaign literature to employees, but it also permits visitation to their homes. Home visits may be considered an equal opportunity for unions to reply to employer captive-audience speeches without requiring union equal time on employer time and property. At the same time the issue of violation of employer property rights may be precluded in general industry. More important to the NLRB, it can come closer to attaining its laboratory conditions for holding elections by providing unions with greater access to employees for informational purposes than previously.

During fiscal 1967, however, the Board was forced to seek enforcement of its subpoenas in cases before six district courts to require employers to supply regional directors with lists of names and addresses of employees eligible to vote in pending elections.[55] Unions do not have to proceed to elections when employers refuse to provide such lists as required by the Board. The NLRB argued in every case that it had the authority to make such rules, which are enforceable under the general equity powers of courts. The courts enforced the Board subpoenas in four of the six cases. The courts favoring the Board rule held that (1) the names-and-addresses requirement was within Board authority to prescribe election procedure; (2) no constitutional rights of employees were violated by supplying such lists; (3) employers were not obligated to hold employee lists as confidential; (4) the Board was behaving properly by making its lists available to unions; (5) union possession of lists would not interfere with employee rights to refrain from union activities; (6) chance of misuse of employee names and addresses was mininal and could be controlled by the Board in any event; and (7) the courts could use equity power to require such lists because the Board functions within the law in making such election requirements.

The U.S. Supreme Court upheld the Board's names-and-addresses policy in the *NLRB* v. *Wyman-Gordon Company* case decided in April 1969.[56] It was reasoned that the NLRB has

wide discretion to ensure the fair choice of bargaining representatives. The requirement that companies furnish worker lists to unions furthers the free-choice
objective of encouraging an informed employee electorate and by allowing unions
the right of access to employees that management already possesses.

Thus the Board now has clear authority to require employers to provide a list of
names and addresses of employees for union use in connection with representation
elections. The requirement is viewed as a part of the NLRB order directing that an
election be held.

BARGAINING ON THE BASIS OF AUTHORIZATION CARDS: THE GISSEL DOCTRINE

The Board has sole responsibility to establish policies governing pre-election conduct. It is also responsible for remedying violations of such policies that have the effect
of coercing, interfering with, or restraining employees in their free choice of bargaining
representatives. However, there is no legal requirement that unfair labor practices
must exist for a party to become subject to Board remedial action.

A Board policy that has generated considerable criticism from management
as well as other groups involves orders requiring employers to bargain with unions
even though election results do not favor unions. One section of the law enumerating
employer unfair labor practices requires an employer to bargain collectively with a
union designated as representative by a majority of employees in an appropriate
unit. To determine whether a union is the choice of a majority of employees, the
Board conducts elections. If the union wins in a validly conducted election, the
employer is required to bargain with it. But an election is not always necessary before
an employer is required to bargain. This is called the *Gissel* doctrine.

The Board policy requiring employers to bargain with a union based on a
bargaining authorization card count when unfair labor practices destroyed the
union's card-based majority was established in 1949. The *Joy Silk Mills* case involved
employer conduct such as the promise of benefits about one week before the election,
interrogation of employees concerning how they would vote, and implied threats of
reprisal if the union won the election or if employees voted for the union.[57] On the
basis of employer unfair labor practices in the *Joy Silk Mills* case, the Board refused
to order a new election, but instead ordered the company to bargain with the union.
The order to recognize and bargain was based on the evidence that the union did
represent a majority of employees in the unit prior to employer interference, restraint,
and coercion, which deprived the union of the margin of votes necessary to win at
the poll.

In still another case, decided in 1964, the Board overturned some prior decisions
regarding election policies.[58] The *Bernel Foam* case involved an employer refusal to
bargain upon request when the union offered to prove it represented a majority of
employees in the unit. The employer insisted upon a Board election as proof, but in
the meantime the company engaged in conduct designed to induce employees to
repudiate the union. After the union lost the election it filed unfair labor practice
charges. The company defended on the basis of a past Board rule requiring that a
union could not file unfair labor practices after elections were held if it had knowledge

of such practices prior to proceeding to the poll.[59] The NLRB overruled the previous policy on the ground that such a choice was difficult and dubious for a union to make, particularly since the choice was created by employer unlawful conduct. Thus a union that participates in an election despite employer refusals to bargain may, after losing the election, file refusal-to-bargain charges based on employer pre-election conduct. Three circuit courts subsequently approved the NLRB's decision.[60] The U.S. Supreme Court extended its approval in 1969, and this will be discussed subsequently.

As the law now stands there are three distinct ways by which unions may obtain Board certification without winning elections. First, there is the *Joy Silk* type of case. This involves unfair labor practices occurring concurrent with a refusal to honor union requests to bargain, destroying the labor organization's card-based majority. Unlike the actual *Joy Silk Mills* case, no election is held in this type of bargaining order. The mere existence of unlawful employer behavior is sufficient to justify a Board order to bargain with the labor organization.

Second, there is the *Bernel Foam* type of case. This type of case involves unfair labor practices existing concurrent with a refusal to bargain with the result that a union's card-based majority is destroyed. Also in cases of this nature an election was held and lost by the union, but the NLRB still compels collective bargaining. The NLRB justifies such a remedy on the basis that illegal employer action prior to a poll calculated to eliminate the union advantage is not appropriately remedied by forcing a labor organization to go through another campaign. There is no effective way of restoring a union to the same position it was in prior to the illegal conduct and as such a bargaining order is the only appropriate remedy—besides, unions usually lose the second or third election.

The third type of case is somewhat easier to understand. It is called a *Snow*-type case by the Board and involves only a refusal-to-bargain violation. No election has been held in these situations. The violation requiring Board bargaining orders is that in which the employer initially recognized the union on a demonstration that it represented a majority of employees in an appropriate unit, but subsequently reneged without a valid excuse. The validity of employer arguments for withdrawing union recognition after it is extended is subject to Board determination on the basis of the entire record. In 1970, the Board reaffirmed this policy.[61] In response to questions of the union representatives, the employer in this case had "agreed that the union represented a majority and agreed he would recognize the union." Subsequently, he reneged, and advised the union to seek an election. Under these circumstances, the NLRB held that he violated his obligations under the law and ordered the employer to bargain.

Before the Nixon Board became established, there was another way in which a union could gain bargaining rights without an election. Under these circumstances, the employer did not engage in any unfair labor practice. He merely refused to recognize or bargain with the union based upon a majority of signed union membership cards. However, the previous Board held that a bargaining order would be issued if the employer had knowledge of the union's majority status outside the cards.[62] For example, he could gain this knowledge by observation of his employees on a picket line during a strike. The Nixon Board reversed this policy.[63] It held that a bargaining order would not be issued solely on the basis of authorization cards. In *Summer*, a strike took place after the employer refused to recognize the union. Thus, the employer had opportunity to determine from events outside the cards that the union had majority support. In any event, the Board held that an employer should not be found guilty of a violation of Section 8(a) (5) (refusal to bargain collectively) solely on the basis of its refusal to accept evidence of majority status other than the results of a Board election.

It would seem that this policy of the Nixon Board is consistent with its objective to reduce the frequency of bargaining orders based on authorization cards. During fiscal year 1969 the Board had issued only half as many bargaining orders as in fiscal 1968, and in that year there were only 160 such orders issued.[64] Even during the Kennedy–Johnson administrations, the Board did not issue bargaining orders based upon authorization cards in a reckless fashion. In fiscal year 1967, the Board issued only 107 authorization card bargaining orders, compared with the holding of 8,183 elections.[65]

Most would agree that a secret election conducted by the NLRB is the best way to determine the desire of employees for collective bargaining. However, when an employer engages in serious unfair labor practices, and by this conduct makes a fair election unlikely, the Supreme Court of the United States stated in *Gissel* that authorization

> . . . cards may be the most effective—perhaps the only—way of assuring employee choice.[66]

In other words, the question arises as to why an employer should be rewarded for his illegal acts. If employers believe the authorization card method to be undesirable, all that they have to do to avoid it is to obey the law. In the absence of serious unfair labor practices, the NLRB will use the election as the sole method of determining the employer's obligation to bargain collectively.

POWER OF NLRB TO ORDER BARGAINING: CATEGORIES OF UNFAIR LABOR PRACTICES

In any event, the authorization card method has whipped up a storm of controversy that to this day has not subsided. It contains two major elements: the NLRB power to order bargaining on the basis of authorization cards, and the reliability of the authorization cards. Some argue that under Taft-Hartley, the NLRB is limited to the use of the election as the sole method upon which to base a bargaining order. However, the Supreme Court in *Gissel*, decided by an 8–0 vote, held that the law does not provide that the election is the sole method by which employees may select a union to represent them. It stated that it

> . . . was recognized that almost from the inception of the Wagner Act a union could establish majority status by other means as here by possession of cards signed by the majority of the employees authorizing the union to represent them for collective bargaining purposes.

After establishing the legal basis for bargaining orders based upon authorization cards, the Court determined the circumstances under which they may be used for this purpose. It established three categories of unfair labor practices that may be committed during an organizational campaign. In the first category are those acts that are so "pervasive" and "atrocious" as to call for an order even without inquiry into the union's card-based majority position. In other words, a bargaining order may be based under these circumstances even though the union did not obtain the signatures of a majority of the employees in the bargaining unit. The Court apparently believed that when the employer commits flagrant and atrocious unfair labor practices, most employees would be fearful of signing cards. In 1971 a federal appeals court upheld a Board order to compel J. P. Stevens, a firm notorious for its illegal conduct under the national labor code, to bargain with the Textile Workers Union even though the union never did possess a card majority.[67] This was the first time the NLRB ordered bargaining without the union possessing evidence of a majority status. Among other unfair labor practices, the record disclosed that J. P. Stevens' supervisors threatened that a union victory in an election would result in reduction of work, extensive discharges, and even closing the plant. Four union supporters were discharged to underscore the threats. Company officials engaged in "blatant surveillance" of union activities, and supervisors interrogated employees about union activities under circumstances which were "coercive and intimidating." Also, the firm promised benefits and actually granted certain benefits "calculated to undermine union strength." It is not likely that the NLRB will find frequent occasions to direct bargaining when a union has not secured a card majority since not many employers are likely to engage in conduct displayed by J. P. Stevens. It was in the second category that the Supreme Court placed those unfair labor practices that show a "lesser showing of misconduct." Under these circumstances the Court held that at one point in its campaign the union must demonstrate that it had the support of a majority of the employees. In other words, before a bargaining order would be issued under this category, the employer must be engaged in serious unfair labor practices and the union must have had a card-based majority. In the third category, the Court placed those minor employer violations that are likely to have a minimal impact on elections, and under these circumstances the NLRB will not issue a bargaining order.

Validity of Authorization Cards

In opposition to the authorization card method as the basis for bargaining orders, some argue that they are not reliable indications of employees' desires for collective bargaining. Indeed, the federal appeals court in Richmond, Virginia, stated that

> authorization cards are such unreliable indicators of the desires of employees that an employer is justified in withholding recognition pending the result of a certification election.

In this respect, it is argued that union organizers coerce employees to sign the cards; employees do not understand what they are signing; group pressure will prompt employees to sign; and union organizers will misrepresent the purpose of the card by telling employees that they are being used only to obtain an election from the NLRB and not for the purpose of authorizing the union to represent them in collective bargaining. As expected, the NLRB has established standards relating to the validity of the cards.[68] To count, a card must plainly state that the employee authorizes the union to represent him in collective bargaining and not to seek an election. Despite the language on the face of the card, if it can be proved that the employee was told that the card would be used solely for the purpose of obtaining an election, it will not be counted. Should the union organizer use coercive tactics, the card will not be deemed valid. As to the employee's intelligence, the Board stated that

> to assume that the employee does not understand what he is signing as long as he can read would be to downgrade his intelligence.[69]

Upon review of these standards, the Supreme Court held that they were sufficient to protect against abuse in the signing of authorization cards. It stated that when cards are obtained in conformance with the NLRB standards, there need be no fear of misrepresentation, and added that "employees should be bound by the clear language of what they sign."

In short, the Supreme Court endorsed the policy of issuing bargaining orders based upon authorization cards. It held that such a remedy is proper when employer illegal conduct makes it unlikely that a fair election could be held. In the absence of such a remedy, the Court stated that the employer

> could continue to delay or disrupt the election process and put off indefinitely his obligation to bargain; and any election held under these circumstances would not be likely to demonstrate the employees' true, undistorted desire.

What remains to be seen is how the NLRB applies the *Gissel* doctrine. It has the power to determine the character of unfair labor practices that would prompt a bargaining order. As stated above, it would appear that the Nixon Board is curtailing the use of the policy. All that the Supreme Court can do is establish the general policy, but it is up to the NLRB to implement it in practice. Finally, it should be stressed that employers have it within their control to assure that the *Gissel* doctrine is not used. If they obey the law, the NLRB will require an election to test the employees' desire for collective bargaining.

EMPLOYER INTERROGATION OF EMPLOYEES

Employer responses to union claims of representing a majority of employees are several. One well-known response over the years has been to interrogate employees regarding their union membership sentiments. Unions argue that such efforts reveal little since workers are unlikely to tell their employers their true sentiments due to fears of economic retaliation.

The Board, aware of the effects that employer interrogation might have on employee freedom to select bargaining representatives, established guidelines of permissible behavior. Its *Blue Flash Express* doctrine established that whether interrogation interferes with employees' rights depends upon "the record as a whole."[70] Factors evaluated by the Board included such items as the time, place, personnel involved, information sought, and the employer's known preference. The difficulty with such an approach has been employer uncertainty regarding permissible behavior.

The NLRB reconsidered its criteria regarding employer interrogation of employees in a 1967 case and established new guidelines.[71]

Except under unusual circumstances, employer interrogation of employees will be an unfair labor practice unless safeguards are observed. They are: (1) the poll must be for the purpose of determining the truth of a union's claim of a majority; (2) the purpose must be communicated to employees; (3) assurances against reprisals must be given; (4) employees must be polled by secret ballot; and (5) the employer must not have engaged in unfair labor practices or otherwise created a coercive atmosphere.

These rules tend to strengthen the Board's efforts to require bargaining without benefit of representation elections. Employer insistence upon an election may be supported by results of its own secret poll. Such a policy does not seem unreasonable since most present difficulties involve relatively small units of employees. At the same time there may be greater incidences of employer recognition of unions without the necessity of further burdening NLRB election machinery with resolving questions of representation. Settlement of such questions without waiting for Board elections should expedite the entire process of collective bargaining.

EMPLOYER ELECTION PETITIONS

During the first few years of experience with the Wagner Act, employers, regardless of the circumstances, were denied the opportunity to petition the NLRB for representation elections. Widespread discontent over such treatment was expressed in terms of unequal treatment between management and unions. In 1939 the Board permitted employers to petition for elections only when they were faced with two unions seeking recognition in the same bargaining unit. This included the right to petition the Board to hold an election when two unions sought recognition in overlapping units. Such a condition prevailed when one union's bargaining unit was defined so as to include workers claimed by a union in another unit. In such a situation management was faced with a dilemma; it could be charged with showing favoritism to any union with which it elected to bargain. Employers could also be subjected to union pressure for recognition when there was no evidence that it represented a majority of employees. Pressure could be applied in the form of recognitional picketing and boycotts. Some employers may have been forced to submit to economic pressures applied by unions which in fact represented only a minority of workers.[72]

The Taft-Hartley Act permits employers to file representation petitions even though only one individual or union demands recognition for collective bargaining purposes. It is required that exclusive recognition be demanded or else a claim of majority representation must be asserted. An employer cannot petition for an election before recognition is requested. This restriction prevents not only unions from requesting recognition before they in fact represent a majority of the bargaining unit, but it also keeps employers from obtaining elections before unions are ready to test their strength at the polls. Union attempts to enlist employees in its ranks often take a prolonged period of time. To permit management to petition for an election at any time it desires during a campaign could destroy union organizational activities for a period of one year. The Board will hold only one election in any twelve-month period, unless the one held was set aside due to unfair labor practice violations or under the *General Shoe* doctrine. The twelve-month ban on elections could become an effective antiunion device without restrictions on employer election requests. During the course of a year a union can disintegrate. Employers are not permitted to seek thc samc rcsult by soliciting employee signatures on election petitions requesting that representation elections be held.[73]

As it has with all other forms, the Board has significant control over employer election petitions. It is required to investigate petitions filed to determine if "a question of representation exists." An employer's right to seek an election is not a guarantee that it will obtain one in every case. The investigation provides the basis for the Board to reject an employer petition for an election at the close of the first anniversary of an incumbent bargaining agent when it is for the purpose of harassment. However, the employer's right to petition for an election at the close of a year on occasion reveals that a union is aware of its minority standing, and it may withdraw from the election. There is no requirement for a labor organization to subject itself to an election if it is unable to run even a close race in a poll. Withdrawal of an incumbent union from election proceedings, of course, relieves an employer from bargaining obligations.

DECERTIFICATION ELECTIONS

The Taft-Hartley Act establishes machinery whereby unions may be decertified.[74] Under its provisions an NLRB certification is valid for only one year. After that time employees within the bargaining unit can petition the Board for a decertification election. The Board will conduct such a poll when 30 percent of the employees sign a petition requesting a decertification election. If a labor union is defeated in such a referendum, it loses bargaining rights within the unit. In addition, once the Board conducts a decertification election, there can be no additional elections within the bargaining unit for one year. The statute permits only one election per year for certification purposes in a particular bargaining unit. Thus the defeat of a union in a decertification election relieves the employer from all legal obligation to bargain collectively for at least twelve months. During this period it is entirely possible that the union might completely disintegrate, thereby precluding collective bargaining on a permanent basis. The election must be free of unfair labor practices to obtain this result.

The decertification election procedure should be viewed in combination with the "free-speech" provision of the law. Employers who desire to avoid collective bargaining can be expected to campaign vigorously for the defeat of the union. As already demonstrated, the statute provides a wide basis for employer participation in the election process. Though the Board has refused to accept decertification petitions from an employer, it is possible for an employer to induce employees to request a decertification election. Once the petition is filed and a decertification election is ordered, management may utilize the opportunities provided by its right of free speech to conduct an antiunion campaign. Hence there can be abuse during the decertification election. On the other hand, the decertification election provides employees with the opportunity to get rid of a union in which they no longer have confidence.

Unions lose in the majority of these polls. In the first two years of Taft-Hartley operation, unions lost bargaining rights in 144 out of 229 decertification elections conducted.[75] This proportion of losses remained about the same down through the years.

A union member who files a decertification petition may be disciplined by a union. The worker may be expelled from membership, but he is not subject to a fine.[76] The rule permitting expulsion is an exception to general Board attempts to protect the integrity of Board processes. For example, the United States Supreme Court agrees that it is unlawful to discipline a member for filing unfair labor practices against a union.[77] The Board held that a decertification petition was a special situation justifying an exception to the general rule for two reasons. Expulsion or suspension is permitted because (1) the petition threatens the very existence of the union as an institution and (2) as a matter of self-defense the union cannot allow a member to lead an antiunion campaign while retaining the right to attend union meetings, obtain knowledge of union strategy, and even vote on union affairs. Expulsion is probably of little consequence to a member who files a decertification petition, but permitting fines in such cases would be punitive. Fines are enforceable in the courts in accordance with a 1967 Supreme Court decision.[78]

RUNOFF ELECTIONS

At times more than one union is on the election ballot. After the election it may be determined that no union received the majority of votes but, on the other hand, the employees did not by majority vote reject all unions in the election. Under these circumstances it is necessary to conduct a runoff election. Over the years the Board changed its policies regarding runoff elections, and the Taft-Hartley Act has established the current policy which the Board must follow in all cases.

Runoff elections were first permitted in 1937, affording an opportunity for employees to vote for or against the union receiving the largest vote in the first election when voters were presented with several choices on the first ballot.[79] A debate developed, however, regarding whether employees should be given an option to vote for no union or for neither in case of multiple unions on the ballot. In 1940 Board policy was adopted eliminating the "neither" choice from ballots and only the top two unions were presented to workers for their choice.[80] The policy did not prove effective because of the frequency of unions being selected by a minority of workers in the units. That is, unions are certified on the basis of a majority of those voting and in some cases a majority of the eligible voters do not cast ballots. When two unions were presented to those voting, the one receiving a majority of votes cast would be certified. Elections are held by the Board when 30 percent of the bargaining unit signs petitions seeking Board-held polls. Let us assume that only the 30 percent in fact cast ballots. Assume also that those ballots are almost equally split between two unions in runoff elections. The union receiving a majority of the votes cast qualifies as the Board-designated organization to represent all workers in the bargaining unit. However, in close elections, the representative may have been chosen on the basis of only slightly over 15 percent of all eligible voters in the bargaining unit. Such a situation placed the chances of an effective collective bargaining relationship in jeopardy from the very beginning. The Board responsibility of encouraging collective bargaining could have been doomed because of bargaining-unit antagonism against the union that won the election.

The Board's policy was then changed to require that runoff elections would carry the top two entries from the initial poll whether it involved two unions or one union and a neither option. If the neither option placed third in the initial election, it would not constitute a choice for voters in the runoff poll. Unions opposed the neither option in runoff elections. It was argued that a few antiunion workers could prevail in close elections where a majority of voters in fact desired union representation. On the basis of a public hearing held in 1943, the Board changed its policy once again to provide the no-union option only if it received the most votes in the initial election.[81] The basis for such a policy was that workers had demonstrated their desire for union representation by casting more votes for unions than for no representation. This, it was argued, was reflected in the no-union option ranking third or more from the top in votes received.

Congress considered the issue of runoff elections during its debate over Taft-Hartley. It provided that such elections should always carry the top two choices. If the no-union option ranks in the top two at the initial poll, it must go on the ballot in runoff cases. In some situations the Taft-Hartley policy yields excessively to a minority of bargaining-unit employees. For example, assume that four separate unions are involved in an initial election seeking to represent the entire unit in collective negotiations with management. It is not difficult to imagine a situation whereby the overwhelming majority of the unit splits its votes among the four labor organizations, but the solidified action of the no-union group is sufficient to rank that option either first or second in terms of votes on the first ballot. Since Taft-Hartley requires that the top two choices be presented to the bargaining unit for selection in the runoff poll, the range of choice facing workers is limited. Obviously, it has been demonstrated that a majority of the unit desired union representation but could not agree upon one to provide the function. The runoff election therefore may not provide the unit with an adequate alternative for making a choice since only one union appears on the ballot. A majority of workers may consider that particular union the least desirable of two unions receiving the most votes, but are prevented from making their preference known. They may well desire, however, the least desirable union to none at all. To the extent that this happens, workers are deprived of choosing a union desired by a majority of bargaining-unit members. The Taft-Hartley provision therefore has limited the range of worker choice in choosing bargaining representatives in runoff elections under these circumstances.

SUMMARY

It has been demonstrated that the NLRB has considerable responsibility for creating an election atmosphere that provides employees with the greatest range of freedom to select or reject collective bargaining representation. The agency attempts to balance employee-employer rights to engage in pre-election campaigns by establishing policies in the context of a totality of circumstances. Board policies as developed to date have been evolutionary in nature and not radical despite periodic changes in Board personnel and legislative enactment. Sole responsibility to establish effective representation election policies and to develop remedies for violations of such rules has been given the NLRB by Congress. The U.S. Supreme Court reviews Board actions in the last resort, but generally supports the agency in its implementation of congressional enactments. The high court does require a convincing articulation of Board-established rules in carrying out its legislative charge. Such a requirement is involved in establishment of an appropriate unit for purposes of collective bargaining and construction of employer free speech. Limitations may be placed on employer pre-election activities to the extent that free elections are advanced by doing so. Though the *Gissel* doctrine remains controversial, the Supreme Court permits bargaining orders based upon authorization cards. The Board may require equal time to respond to employer captive-audience speeches under certain circumstances; that names and addresses of eligible bargaining-unit voters be filed with regional directors within seven days after election orders or agreements; and orders to bargain on the basis of authorization cards when unfair labor practices undermine a card-based union majority. The effort to fulfill the *General Shoe* laboratory conditions for holding elections continues, and considerable progress has been made since enactment of the original National Labor Relations Act in 1935.

Employers have been extended the right to petition for elections after they are confronted with a request for recognition. Decertification elections are also possible for employees disenchanted with union representation. Such cases proceeding to the election stage result in union losses in over one-half of the polls. Runoff elections are also provided to determine employee preferences in selecting bargaining representatives. The top two choices of initial polls are currently carried over to the runoff election. Under some circumstances the requirement may limit the range of choice confronting eligible voters.

Election policies and procedures remain in a state of change. The Board and courts continue their search for workable policies ensuring the rights of all parties to election proceedings.

NOTES

[1] *Wickwire Brothers*, 16 NLRB 316 (1936).

[2] John E. Drotning, "Employer Free Speech: Two Basic Questions Considered by the NLRB and Courts," *Labor Law Journal*, XVI (March 1965), 131.

[3] *Ibid.*, p. 132.

[4] *Ford Motor Company* v. *NLRB*, 114 F. (2d) 905 (1940), cited in *ibid.*, p. 133.

[5] *NLRB* v. *Virginia Electric & Power Company*, 314 U.S. 469 (1941).

[6] *Clark Brothers Company, Inc.* v. *NLRB*, 163 F. (2d) 373 (1947).

[7] John M. Stochaj, "Free Speech Policies," *Labor Law Journal*, VIII, No. 8 (August 1957), 532.

[8] Drotning, *op. cit.*, p. 134.

[9] *NLRB* v. *American Tube Bending*, 134 F. (2d) 993 (1943). Cert. denied 320 U.S. 768 (1943).

[10] *United Welding Company*, 72 NLRB 954 (1947).

[11] House of Representatives, Special Committee to Investigate the National Labor Relations Board, *Intermediate Report*, House Report No. 1902, 76th Congress, 3rd sess., 1940, Part I, p. 83.

[12] *National Association of Manufacturers Law Digest 66* (1947).

[13] *General Shoe Corporation*, 77 NLRB 124 (1948).

[14] *Ibid.*

[15] *Gummed Products Company*, 36 LRRM 1156 (1955).

[16] *National Furniture Manufacturing Company*, 106 NLRB 1300 (1953).

[17] *Dal-Tex Optical Company*, 137 RLRB 1782 (1962).

[18] *NLRB* v. *American Pearl Button Company*, 140 F. (2d) 258 (1945).

[19] *Somismo, Inc.*, 133 NLRB 131 (1961).

[20] *McLaughlin Co.*, 187 NLRB 897 (1971).

[21] *Comet Rice Mills Division, Early California Industries*, 195 NLRB No. 117 (1972).

[22] *Sharney Hosiery Mills, Inc.*, 120 NLRB 102 (1958).

[23] *Sewell Manufacturing Company*, 138 NLRB 12 (1962).

[24] *Allen-Morrison Sign Company, Inc.*, 138 NLRB 73 (1962).

[25] *Twenty-eighth Annual Report of the National Labor Relations Board* (1963), p. 59.

[26] *Baltimore Luggage*, 162 NLRB 113 (1967).

[27] *Clark Bros. Company*, 70 NLRB 802 (1946), 163 F. (2d) 373 (1947).

[28] *Ibid.*

[29] *Babcock & Wilcox*, 77 NLRB 577 (1948).

[30] It will be recalled that Section 8 (c) provided that "the expressing of any views, arguments, or opinion, or the dissemination thereof, whether in written, printed, graphic, or visual form, shall not constitute or be evidence of an unfair labor practice under any of the provisions of this Act, if such expression contains no threat of reprisal or force or promise of benefit."

[31] *Sands Corrugated Paper Machinery Company*, 89 NLRB 1363 (1950).

[32] *Bonwit Teller, Inc.*, 96 NLRB 608 (1951).

[33] *Bonwit Teller, Inc.* v. *NLRB*, 197 F. (2d) 640 (1952).

[34] *Livingston Shirt Corporation*, 107 NLRB 400 (1953).

[35] *Peerless Plywood*, 107 NLRB 427 (1953).

[36] *NLRB* v. *United Steelworkers*, 357 U.S. 357 (1958).

[37] *May Department Stores*, 136 NLRB 797 (1962).

[38] *Walton Manufacturing Company*, 126 NLRB 697 (1960).

[39] *Ibid.*

[40] *NLRB* v. *Clark Brothers, op. cit.*

[41] *Victor Manufacturing & Gasket Company*, 79 NLRB 234 (1948).

[42] *Marion Mills*, 124 NLRB 56 (1959).

[43] *Republic Aviation Corporation* v. *NLRB*, 324 U.S. 793 (1945).

[44] *NLRB* v. *Babcock & Wilcox*, 351 U.S. 105 (1956).

[45] *Monogram Models*, 192 No. 99 (1971).

[46] National Labor Relations Board, *Thirty-Seventh Annual Report* (1972), p. 88.

[47] *Falk Corporation*, 192 NLRB No. 100 (1971).

[48] *H. W. Elson Bottling Company*, 155 NLRB 714 (1965).

[49] *Ibid.*

[50] *General Electric Company*, 156 NLRB 1247 (1966).

[51] *NLRB* v. *Virginia Electric & Power Company, op. cit.*

[52] *Excelsior Underwear, Inc.*, 156 NLRB 1236 (1966).

[53] *Swift & Company*, 162 NLRB 6 (1967).

[54] Section 481 (c).

[55] *Thirty-second Annual Report of the National Labor Relations Board* (Washington, D.C.: Government Printing Office, 1968), pp. 191–193.

[56] *NLRB* v. *Wyman-Gordon Company*, 394 U.S. 759 (1969).

[57] *Joy Silk Mills, Inc.*, 85 NLRB 1236 (1949); 185 F. (2d) 732 (1950); cert. denied 341 U.S. 914 (1951).

[58] *Bernel Foam Products Company*, 146 NLRB 1277 (1964).

[59] *Aiello Dairy Company*, 110 NLRB 1365 (1954).

[60] *Thirtieth Annual Report of the National Labor Relations Board* (Washington, D.C.: Government Printing Office, 1965), pp. 129–30.

[61] *Redmond Plastics, Inc.*, 187 NLRB 487 (1970).

[62] *Wilder Manufacturing*, 185 NLRB No. 76 (1970).

[63] *Summer & Company*, 190 NLRB No. 116 (1971).

[64] William J. Isaacson, "Discernible Trends in the 'Miller' Board—Practical Considerations for the Labor Counsel," *Labor Law Journal*, v. 43, No. 9, p. 540.

[65] *Hearings Before the Subcommittee on Separation of Powers, Congressional Oversight of Administrative Agencies (National Labor Relations Board)*, U.S. Senate, Nineteenth Congress, 2nd Session (1968), Part 1, p. 851. In commenting on the use of authorization cards, Frank McCulloch, former NLRB Chairman, stated: "How many Board decisions rest upon card-established majorities? The number is about a hundred in the same period that we conducted nearly 8,200 elections. And all the flak that this committee has had concerning Board's decisions based on card-established majorities relates to only about 1.2 or 1.3 percent of all NLRB cases in which a majority has been determined, mainly on the basis of a secret ballot election."

[66] *NLRB* v. *Gissel Packing Company*, 395 U.S. 575 (1969).

[67] *J. P. Stevens* v. *NLRB*, CA 5, No. 28631 and 29037 (March 22, 1971).

[68] *Cumberland Shoe Corporation*, 144 NLRB 1268 (1964); *Levi Strauss & Company*, 172 NLRB No. 57 (1968); *McEwen Manufacturing Company*, 172 NLRB 990 (1968).

[69] On this basis, the Board invalidated cards signed by Spanish-speaking employees. It determined that the employees could not speak, write, or read English (*Gate of Spain Restaurant*, 192 NLRB No. 161 (1971)).

[70] *Blue Flash Express*, 109 NLRB 591 (1954).

[71] *Struksnes Construction Company*, 165 NLRB 102 (1967).

[72] Harry A. Millis and Emily Clark Brown, *From the Wagner Act to Taft-Hartley* (Chicago: The University of Chicago Press, 1950), p. 529.

[73] *Serv-Air, Inc.* v. *NLRB*, 401 F. (2d) 363 (1968).

[74] Section 9 (c) (1) (A).

[75] National Labor Relations Board, *Thirteenth Annual Report* (1948), p.111; *Fourteenth Annual Report* (1949), p. 171.

[76] *International Molders & Allied Workers Local No. 125*, 178 NLRB 25 (1969).

[77] *NLRB* v. *Industrial Union of Marine and Shipbuilding Workers of America*, 391 U.S. 418 (1968).

[78] *NLRB* v. *Allis-Chalmers Manufacturing Company*, 388 U.S. 175 (1967).

[79] Millis and Brown, *op. cit.*, p. 135.

[80] *R. K. LeBlond Machine Tool Company*, 22 NLRB 465 (1940).

[81] Millis and Brown, *op. cit.*, p. 135.

13 Control of the Bargaining Unit

THE BARGAINING UNIT: ITS NATURE

Each collective bargaining contract covers a certain group of workers. When a labor contract is being negotiated, the representatives of labor and management are careful to spell out its terms to the affected workers. Workers covered by the agreement are said to constitute the bargaining unit. For example, in a contract between the United Steelworkers of America and Carnegie-Illinois Steel Corporation, the scope of the bargaining unit was set up in the following terms: ". . . this Agreement applies to all individuals occupying production, maintenance and hourly rated non-confidential clerical jobs employed in and about the Company's steel-manufacturing and by-product coke plant. . . ." Excluded from the bargaining unit, however, were those "individuals occupying salaried, watchmen, guard, confidential clerical or supervisory positions of foreman level and above." The significance of being part of the bargaining unit should be rather obvious. All workers within the bargaining unit have their conditions of work determined through the collective bargaining process. On the other hand, workers excluded from the unit are not represented by the labor union. They must adjust their employment problems on an individual basis or they may constitute a separate bargaining unit under certain conditions. At times both management and the union are in full agreement that certain workers shall be excluded from the bargaining unit (in the above illustration, both the steel company and the union agreed that foremen should not be included). Agreement is not always possible: employees such as those labeled craft or professional may feel that membership in a separate unit would enhance their bargaining positions. The NLRB has had to decide the basic criteria for the creation of separate bargaining units.

INFLUENCE OF THE WAGNER ACT

Before passage of the Wagner Act, representatives of labor and management had full authority to determine the scope and character of the bargaining unit. It was their exclusive responsiblity to decide problems relating to coverage of the labor agreement. This condition was altered after the passage of the National Labor Relations Act in 1935. The Wagner Act required that employers bargain collectively with unions selected by a majority of workers in the bargaining unit. This meant that the NLRB, the administrative agency of the Wagner Act, was required to poll workers to determine whether or not a majority of workers in a bargaining unit wanted a certain union to represent them in collective bargaining. Prior to the holding of such referendums, however, the NLRB set up the bargaining unit. All workers included were eligible to vote in the representation election. If a majority of workers participating in such a referendum cast ballots for a particular labor organization, the NLRB would normally certify this union as the representative of all workers in the bargaining unit. Should the labor union and the employer eventually negotiate a labor contract, the workers in the bargaining unit would be covered by it. Thus establishment of the bargaining unit by the NLRB serves a dual purpose: (1) it determines which workers are eligible to vote in a representation election; and (2) it sets up the group of workers to be covered by a labor contract resulting from negotiations with a certified labor organization.

ESTABLISHMENT OF THE BARGAINING UNIT: WAGNER ACT EXPERIENCE

Under the Wagner Act the NLRB had a considerable degree of freedom in the establishment of the bargaining unit. Congress merely instructed the Board to set up a bargaining unit that would be appropriate for the purposes of collective bargaining. Such a unit, according to the Wagner Act, should be of such character as would "insure to employees the full benefit of their right to self-organization and collective bargaining. . . ." Beyond this mandate the Wagner Act placed no restrictions on the NLRB. The agency was permitted to establish whatever unit it felt would further the cause of effective collective bargaining. To this end the NLRB was free to set up units along craft, employer, or industrial lines. In a particular case the NLRB might hold that collective bargaining would be furthered by the establishment of a craft unit. Under other circumstances the Board members might elect to establish an industrial unit. Whatever the character of the unit, the Board had to be convinced that the workers included in the unit constituted an appropriate group for the purposes of collective bargaining.

Character of Guides Utilized by the NLRB

The foregoing indicates that the NLRB possessed a considerable amount of power in the establishment of the bargaining unit. However, the Board early in its career established a series of guides to be employed. These guides had a common denominator, the setting up of a unit that would effectuate the collective bargaining process. In other words, the NLRB did not utilize its power in a capricious or arbitrary manner. Its decisions were related to the particular circumstances in each situation. Upon many occasions the Board declared that it would not apply "rigid rules to determine the appropriate unit in each case."[1] Instead the Board held that the "appropriate unit in each case must be determined in the light of the circumstances in the particular case."[2]

The character of the guides that the Board established was related to its fundamental objective: establishing units that would make the collective bargaining process effective. Factors which the agency considered in setting up units included: (1) the history, extent, and type of organization of employees in a plant; (2) the history of their collective bargaining; (3) the history, extent, and type of organization and the collective bargaining of employees in other plants of the same employer, or of other employers in the same industry; (4) the skill, wages, work, and working conditions of employees; (5) the desires of employees; (6) the eligibility of employees for membership in the union or unions involved in the election proceedings and in other labor organizations; and (7) the relationship between the unit or units proposed and the employer's organization, management, and operation of the plant.[3]

The Board exercised a considerable degree of freedom in its selection of bargaining-unit guides. Moreover, it employed them on a relatively consistent basis. In the vast majority of cases the bargaining unit was set up with a minimum amount of friction between labor unions, employers, and the Board. If the Board was capricious in its actions or utilized inappropriate guides, one would expect the setting up of bargaining units to stimulate a great deal of controversy among the parties to NLRB proceedings. As a matter of record, the Board during 1936–1947 settled about three-fourths of all cases involving the issue of the bargaining unit on an informal basis.[4] In other words, the Board, the employers, and the unions involved in these cases were of the same judgment as to the character of the bargaining unit.

Establishment of the Bargaining Unit: Controversial Issues

In bargaining-unit cases settled on an informal basis, the NLRB generally played the role of observer. All parties recognized the appropriateness of a particular collective bargaining unit. Under informal circumstances the Board merely approved a grouping that appeared logical to all concerned. However, in the cases which were decided only after formal action, the power of the NLRB to set up the bargaining unit assumed significant proportions. When differences of opinion between employers, unions, or the Board were involved, the agency finally resolved the dispute. Action of the NLRB in setting up the unit was conclusive and normally not reviewable in the courts.[5]

Controversy regarding the establishment of the bargaining unit could arise from several sources. Suppose an employer desires a unit which, if set up, will relieve him of any legal obligation to bargain with employee-designated representatives. Assume also that the enterprise is multiplant in character. The labor union has organized only one plant. It petitions the Board for certification. If the Board sets up a unit encompassing all the plants, the union likely will not win a representation election since the unorganized employees will overbalance the organized group. On the other hand, the labor union will stand a better opportunity to win the representation election if the bargaining unit is limited to the plant already organized by the union.

Conflict between craft and industrial unions constituted another basis for friction in the determination of bargaining units. This issue was kept before the public's eye by the American Federation of Labor, a federation composed of unions essentially craft in character. The AFL charged that the NLRB favored the industrial unions of the CIO. (It will be recalled that the AFL-CIO did not merge until 1955.) Such favoritism, the AFL contended, resulted in the loss of power and membership of its affiliated labor unions. The basis for the AFL grievances against the NLRB is described in the following illustration.

Suppose a group of twenty-five electricians, members of the International Brotherhood of Electrical Workers (AFL), worked in a factory which employed one thousand production workers. Suppose the NLRB set up a plant-wide bargaining unit. Such a unit included the twenty-five craft workers. In a bargaining election the production workers voted overwhelmingly for a CIO industrial union—say, the United Steelworkers of America. Under such circumstances the industrial union was certified by the NLRB. It became the legal representative of all workers in the bargaining unit, production workers and electricians alike. The employer bargained with the industrial union only. He was not required to recognize the craft organization as the bargaining agent of the twenty-five electricians. If the industrial union obtained a union-shop arrangement, the problem became even more crucial. Such a condition would require that the electricians join the CIO union, pay dues to it, and, as a condition of employment, maintain their membership in good standing. The electricians might feel that their interests were not properly considered in negotiations with the employer since the union was more concerned with the welfare of the larger group of production workers.

A final source of controversy relating to the establishment of the bargaining unit centered around the question of whether or not certain groups should be certified for collective bargaining purposes. Defining the bargaining unit is a prerequisite for election and certification purposes. In the absence of certification a group of workers could not enjoy legal protection of their right to collective bargaining. Under these circumstances it is doubtful that the workers could have obtained a collective bargaining contract. Attempts were often made to prevent the Board from setting up bargaining units containing certain classifications of workers.

The problem of the appropriateness of units containing certain groups of workers became particularly serious during World War II. Some employers contended that replacements for workers who had left for duty with the armed forces did not constitute units appropriate for the purposes of collective bargaining. These employers felt that replacements had no standing under the Wagner Act because their services would not be required once industry reconverted to peacetime activities. Rejecting this argument, the Board held that wartime replacements could constitute appropriate bargaining units.[6] A contrary ruling would have denied millions of wartime workers the opportunity to participate in the collective bargaining process.

Despite the objections of some employers, the NLRB in a 1942 case held that instructors employed to train groups of new wartime employees were to be included in the same bargaining unit as production workers.[7] In still another case a group of instructors hired to train army and navy personnel in the operation of war material produced by a company were considered eligible for inclusion in a unit for purposes of collective bargaining. Despite the fact that these instructors carried out their training duties in an area located many miles from the company's major plant, the NLRB held that they could constitute an appropriate bargaining unit. Another controversy centered around a group of nurses. An employer urged that a number of nurses, employed by the company for first-aid purposes, should be included in a production workers' bargaining unit. However, the Board classified them into a separate unit on the ground that the nurses constituted a well-defined professional group with interests and conditions of work dissimilar from the production workers.

Finally, the position of foremen and plant guards under the Wagner Act whipped up a storm of controversy. Employers argued that these two groups did not constitute units appropriate for the purposes of collective bargaining. In contrast, thousands of these employees felt that their economic positions would be advanced if they worked under the protection of collective bargaining contracts. They were aware that it would be much easier to obtain such agreements if the NLRB would certify their unions for purposes of collective bargaining. To this end they objected to the employer point of view and urged the NLRB to hold that they might be properly classified into collective bargaining units. The manner in which the Board resolved the foremen and plant guards problem at one time generated considerable controversy over Board action under the Wagner Act.

The Weight of the Evidence

Members of the NLRB were well aware of the significance of their authority to set up the appropriate bargaining unit. As the foregoing indicates, the determination of the bargaining unit can influence the structural pattern of collective bargaining. Whether industrial or craft unions shall prevail in a given industry can depend on the action of the NLRB. Again the unit could be determined in a manner that might relieve the employer of all responsibility to bargain collectively. Board decisions can be conclusive as to whether an industrial- or a craft-type union shall rule in a plant or within an industry. Finally, the manner in which the Board disposed of its duty to set up the bargaining unit determined whether certain classifications of workers were included in collective bargaining contracts.

Obviously, the NLRB was tackling a difficult job. There were no infallible standards for determining conclusively which groups of workers constituted appropriate bargaining units, given the complex and rapidly changing techniques of production in the American economy. Fundamentally, determination of the unit involved human judgment.

Even though the NLRB set up bargaining units under the Wagner Act, the American labor movement expanded to unprecedented proportions. With a few notable exceptions, employers did not find great fault with the manner in which the agency set up units. Employers may have objected to the entire philosophy of the Wagner Act, but they were not unduly critical of the way in which the Board set up bargaining units. In short, collective bargaining progressed under the structural arrangement of unionism, which was influenced by Board bargaining-unit decisions. The record leads to the conclusion that the Board under the Wagner Act carried out the mandate of Congress. It set up bargaining units which insured employees "the full benefits of their right to self-organization and collective bargaining."

PRESSURE FOR BARGAINING-UNIT LIMITATIONS

Congress, when it enacted the 1947 labor law, restricted the power of the Board to set up units for collective bargaining. Before examining the character of those restrictions, it is necessary to discuss several groups agitating for enactment of such legislative control over Board authority.

In the first place, some employers did not agree with the Board's bargaining-unit policies. They did not find fault with the guides the Board utilized to determine bargaining units. Nor did they object to the manner in which the agency employed these standards. Rather, they objected to the policy of extending the protection of the law to certain classifications of workers. In particular, these employers objected to the policy of placing foremen, plant guards, and partially organized plants into units for collective bargaining. As will be pointed out, the Board under the Wagner Act classified foremen and plant guards as eligible for bargaining-unit status. Likewise it set up bargaining units of unionized workers, the number of which included only a small part of the organizable workers of a plant.

As noted previously, the AFL protested against the treatment of its unions by the NLRB. Hence this national federation constituted the second force that sought to limit the authority of the Board to establish bargaining units. The objective of the AFL was to influence the passage of legislation that would require favoritism for craft workers. Unions of the AFL desired the passage of legislation that would separate craft workers from industrial unions. The AFL position was that craft workers, wherever employed, should be classified in units for collective bargaining separate from production workers. They should not be lumped together with unskilled or semiskilled workers. Thus if four plumbers work in a factory employing, say, two thousand unskilled and semiskilled workers, the plumbers should be classified in a separate unit for the purposes of collective bargaining. In this example, the AFL would have the four plumbers excluded from any labor agreement covering the unskilled and semiskilled workers and covered by a separate contract.

In addition to employers and the AFL, professional workers themselves agitated for restrictions on the Board's power to set up bargaining units. Similar to craft workers, professional workers wanted special consideration. Actually, under the Wagner Act, the Board, by administrative ruling, frequently classified professional workers into special bargaining units. The NLRB did this whenever it felt that collective bargaining would be advanced by the establishment of separate units for professional workers. However, this group was not satisfied with resolution of the problem by administrative ruling. It sought to fashion a law that would require the Board to separate the professional workers from others for purposes of collective bargaining. As in the case of craft workers, these employees would have separate contracts covering the professional workers. If there were a few professional workers in a firm employing hundreds of nonprofessional workers, the position of the former group was that the professional workers should not be affected by any collective bargaining contract covering the latter group, but that the terms of employment should be embodied into a special contract covering only the professional workers.

Greater detail regarding Board treatment of all the special-interest groups is required for a better understanding of the appropriate bargaining-unit problem. Special attention is now devoted to craft workers, foremen, plant guards, professionals, and the extent of organization. Finally, coordinated bargaining is treated as a special problem of unit determination.

TREATMENT OF CRAFT BARGAINING UNITS

Throughout the Wagner Act period, craft unions repeatedly alleged that the NLRB favored industrial unions. In weighing the contention of the AFL, we must look to the Board's record to determine whether or not the allegations made against it were valid. Some of the AFL antagonism undoubtedly springs from the results of NLRB elections in which craft and industrial unions were opponents on the same ballot. Returns show that industrial unions had won more of these elections than the AFL-affiliated craft unions. For example, during the period 1942–1945, the NLRB conducted 2,120 elections and crosschecks in which the sole contestants were AFL and CIO affiliates. In these elections workers selected CIO units in 53.9 percent of the cases, AFL affiliates in 38.9 percent of the cases, and rejected both in 7.2 percent. To charge that the Board had been biased because the industrial unions had won more representation elections is to lose sight of the nature of the democratic process. The Board was not the cause of workers selecting industrial units over craft representation. In this regard one writer stated that the craft criticism leveled against the Board was comparable "to an attack on the use of the voting machines because they record the victory of the party with the largest number of votes."[8]

Another source of AFL antagonism arose from circumstances inherent in dealing with large numbers of workers in an industrial setting. It is obvious that if craft workers are grouped within a large industrial unit, they may have difficulties obtaining separate bargaining rights. To have their own union the craft workers would have to be classified in a special bargaining unit. In practice the Board frequently included craft workers in a wide industrial unit, thereby denying them any opportunity for special representation.

Action of AFL. The objective of the AFL was to free the craft workers from the domination of industrial unions. To gain such an objective, the federation constantly sponsored amendments to the Wagner Act that would insure the autonomy of craft workers. The chief characteristic of such an amendment would be that when a craft exists, composed of one or more employees, such craft should constitute an appropriate collective bargaining unit and may designate collective bargaining representatives. Despite the pressure of the AFL, Congress for twelve years refused to give additional protection to craft workers. Such amendments as those sponsored by the AFL were rejected.

Had Congress agreed to the craft-union position, the effect on industrial relations would have been profound. In the normal plant and industry there are a variety of occupational groups. Some of the occupational groups fall within the jurisdiction of the craft unions affiliated with the AFL. Thus in, say, an auto parts firm, there would be a number of electricians, plumbers, tool-and-diemakers, painters, and carpenters, as well as other types of skilled craftsmen. According to the craft-union viewpoint, *each* of these skilled groups should constitute a separate bargaining unit. Any union certified for the purpose of representing the semiskilled and unskilled workers would have no bargaining rights over the craft groups. Such an environment appears conducive neither to effective collective bargaining nor harmonious industrial relations. In each plant there could be a number of labor unions with which the employer would be required to bargain collectively. Failure to reach an agreement with any one union could result in serious effects in the plant. It would indeed be incongruous for an entire plant to be shut down merely because no agreement could be reached with a small but vitally important group of craft workers. In addition, the setting up of a number of bargaining units in one plant would lead to a great deal of time diverted away from the productive process. Suppose ten unions are certified for collective bargaining purposes within one factory. Other than the ten possibilities for interruption to production, there would be ten different contracts to negotiate and ten separate grievance procedures. Each union grievance and negotiation committee would be composed of different workers since each group would represent a different labor union. Under such conditions management and unions would devote a disproportionate amount of time to union affairs. Production would inevitably suffer.

Apparently the craft organization did not give much attention to the implications and consequences of its proposals. The federation was merely concerned with the building up of its own membership. Congress was alert to the serious dangers inherent in the craft-unit proposal and refused to act favorably on AFL-sponsored amendments. This meant that the NLRB was free to set up industrial units when it believed that the interests of effective collective bargaining and sound industrial relations indicated the appropriateness of such groupings.

Concessions to Craft Groups by NLRB. However, the NLRB did make two major concessions to craft unions. In 1937 the Board established the *Globe* doctrine.[9] Under this doctrine the NLRB, under proper circumstances, afforded craft workers the opportunity to decide by secret ballot whether or not they desired to be included in an industrial unit before any bargaining unit was established. Thus the Board was conscious of the problem of the craft worker. It recognized that effective collective bargaining and sound industrial relations at times had to be balanced against the freedom of workers to select their own bargaining representatives. In practice the Board ordered the "Globe election" when it appeared that a group of craft workers constituted a "true" craft and that this group consisted of a substantial number of employees who had attempted to organize their own union. However, the Board reserved the right to deny craft workers the opportunity to select their own bargaining representatives. When the Board felt that a craft unit would retard effective collective bargaining or operate to impair sound industrial relations, it refused to implement the *Globe* doctrine.

In 1944 the NLRB established the *General Electric* doctrine,[10] and therein made a second major concession to craft organizations. Previously, the Board had held that craft workers, once included in a larger industrial unit, would be frozen indefinitely in the industrial classification.[11] This doctrine, bitterly criticized by the AFL, was established in 1939 in *American Can*. Abandoning this rule in a wartime case, the NLRB decided that it would entertain a representation petition from craft members included in a larger industrial unit when it could be shown that (1) the craft employees involved constituted a "true" craft and not a mere dissident faction; and (2) the craft members maintained their identity throughout the period of bargaining upon a more comprehensive unit and protested their inclusion in such a larger bargaining unit.

When craft members were able to satisfy these prerequisites, the Board was prepared to authorize an election to determine whether the craft workers desired a separate unit or whether they chose to remain in the industrial unit. Should such an election take place, and if the craft workers voted for their own union, the Board would certify the craft group as an appropriate bargaining unit. Under these conditions the craft group would be "carved out" of the wider industrial unit. The larger industrial unit would lose bargaining rights over the craft group, and the employer would be required to bargain with the new unit. Of course, the Board would not undertake to separate craft groups from an industrial unit when this would be inconsistent with effective collective bargaining and sound industrial relations.

Neither the *Globe* doctrine nor the principles that the NLRB established in the *General Electric* case satisfied the parent craft organization. In its 1944 convention AFL officers once more denounced the Board. The old charge was repeated that the Board functioned in the interest of industrial unions.[12] Clearly, there is an appropriate place in the American economy for both the craft type and the industrial type of labor organization. This fact was recognized by the NLRB. Under the Wagner Act craft membership almost doubled. The liberty of craft workers to select their own unions must be balanced against the setting up of an appropriate bargaining unit that will insure effective collective bargaining for *all* workers. In addition, the interests of management must not be overlooked. Consider the plight of an employer who is required to bargain with a host of labor unions! As far as possible the craft worker should be given freedom to choose his own union for representation purposes. However, this liberty should not be afforded at the expense of violating the basic principles of effective collective bargaining and sound industrial relations. It seems that the Board struck a justifiable balance in the *Globe* and *General Electric* doctrines.

CRAFT WORKERS UNDER TAFT-HARTLEY

Efforts of the AFL to win favor for the craft worker finally bore fruit in the Taft-Hartley Act. The 1947 labor law provides in Section 9 that the NLRB may not decide that any craft unit is inappropriate for collective bargaining on the ground that a different unit has been established by a prior Board determination, unless a majority of the employees in the proposed craft unit vote against separate representation. This provision reflects the Board policy established in the *General Electric* case. Congress merely wrote into law an administrative ruling of the agency. In effect the action of Congress is of prime significance. Personnel of administrative agencies change. With changing personnel the policies of administrative agencies are often modified. By making the *General Electric* doctrine a matter of law, Congress prevented the abolition of the policy by the Board regardless of its future composition. In addition, the NLRB would be expected to "lean over backward" to comply with the mandate of Congress. A policy established by administrative ruling does not have the force of a doctrine created by statute. Actually, the Board has granted more elections of the *General Electric* variety since the enactment of Taft-Hartley than in a comparable period before the passage of the statute. This is, of course, an expected consequence of the law. The intent of Congress is to provide more freedom to the craft worker if the basic intent of national labor policy is not damaged. The NLRB must pay full attention to the congressional objective in the administration of the statute.

Experience of NLRB with Craft-Union Provision. Under the terms of Taft-Hartley, the Board, however, has the right to deny to craft workers included in an industrial unit the opportunity to vote in a "self-determination" election. This point is illustrated in the *National Tube* case which the Board decided in the spring of 1948.[13] The agency refused to permit a group of bricklayers in a steel mill to vote in a craft election on the ground that inclusion of the bricklayers in the industrial unit was essential for the proper operation of the plant. It was pointed out that bricklaying operations are closely integrated into the steelmaking process. Separation of the bricklayers from the industrial unit, the Board concluded, would not be in the interest of sound industrial relations under collective bargaining. This decision underscores the fact that the Board membership considered it within its discretion to decide under what conditions a group of craft workers will be permitted to vote on the question of separate representation. The 1947 law was taken to mean that the NLRB may not deprive craft workers previously included in an industrial unit of the opportunity to vote in a craft election on the sole ground that the employees were classified in an industrial unit.

On other occasions the Board during the Truman years permitted workers, previously included within an industrial unit, to vote in special craft elections. In one case the NLRB directed a craft election for a group of electricians employed in a West Coast aircraft plant. This case underscores the fact that even though a group of workers belonging to a specific craft may be denied the opportunity to vote in a craft election, the Board under other different circumstances may permit other workers belonging to the same craft to vote in such elections. Previously, the NLRB denied to a group of electricians employed in a locomotive works the privilege of voting in a self-determination election. In sharp contrast to that ruling here the opportunity was made available to a group of electricians employed in an aircraft plant. The election was directed in the aircraft plant case on the ground that the electricians (1) performed highly skilled work; (2) engaged in no duties other than electrical work; and (3) worked under special supervision.

Upon another occasion the Board directed a self-determination election in part because the craft workers involved (machinists and millwrights) underwent a four-year training period before obtaining journeyman status. In cases in which craft elections were ordered, the Board refused to heed people opposing the elections who argued that (1) the employer as well as the industrial union objected to the election; and (2) the industrial union had bargained for the craft workers for periods as long as ten years.

In 1954 with a different Board membership the agency reversed its earlier *National Tube* decision with a new policy in the *American Potash* case.[14] The doctrine of integration established in *National Tube* was limited only to those industries where it had been previously established. Craft severance on an industry-wide basis was denied in basic steel, aluminum, lumber, and wet milling. Denial in the industries mentioned would continue because of the highly integrated production processes and the prevailing industrial pattern of bargaining. However, in the *American Potash* case the Board declared that in future cases craft units would automatically be permitted to break out of the industrial unit irrespective of their importance to the total production process.

Concern over the new craft policy of the Board generated a common concern among many observers that was generally expressed as:

> New uncertainty has been introduced by the Taft-Hartley Act which gives preference for craft bargaining units. This could threaten the industry-wide bargaining mechanism which has functioned so successfully in the industry as an instrument of industrial peace. In this complex industry as many as fifteen to twenty individual craft unions might become involved, each with its separate contract and possibly conflicting aspirations. Instead of single negotiations, there might be many negotiations to conduct jurisdictional rivalries, and greater possibilities of strikes.[15]

Two basic tests for craft severance were established. First, the employees had to constitute a true craft or departmental group. Second, the union seeking to carve out a craft or departmental unit had to be one that traditionally devoted itself to the special problems of the group. The Board, in its interpretation of congressional intent in Section 9 (b) (2), the section dealing with craft severance, was convinced that the interests of craft employees within larger industrial units should prevail. In this regard it stated in *American Potash* that ". . . it is not the province of this Board to dictate the course and pattern of labor organization in our vast industrial complex." The Board concluded that it did not have its traditional discretion to review all the facts and on the basis of findings to determine the appropriate unit for collective bargaining.

The Board remained firm in its *American Potash* decision despite a decision by the Fourth Circuit Court of Appeals.[16] In the *Pittsburgh Plate Glass* case before the circuit court, the employer argued that Board severance of crafts out of the industrial unit was discriminatory since such a development was disallowed in *National Tube* industries, but permitted in its own. The employer wanted to bargain with only one union, not several. The circuit court agreed with the employer and denied craft severance because of the highly integrated nature of the production process. The Board, however, refused to abandon its *American Potash* decision despite the court decision. The firmness of the Board was demonstrated in its *Kennecott Copper* case in 1962.[17] The agency ruled that it would not apply the integration doctrine to the copper industry. The force of the 1962 decision was that the Board, at least for the time, would continue to establish separate craft units in industries with integrated production processes.

The Mallinckrodt Doctrine. The NLRB reviewed the *American Potash* construction of Taft-Hartley Section 9 (b) (2) in *Mallinckrodt*, a 1966 case.[18] The different composition of Board membership led to a reevaluation of congressional intent on the craft severance problem. The Board held that Congress did not intend to deprive it of discretionary authority to find craft unions inappropriate for collective bargaining purposes under all circumstances. In *Mallinckrodt* the Board held that all relevant factors will be considered in each case. Not only will the interests of craft employees be considered, but also the effect that severance might have on the effectiveness of the industrial unit will be weighed before reaching any decision. In other words the

NLRB repudiated *American Potash* and no longer will permit craft employees to break away from an industrial unit on an automatic basis; they might or might not depending upon the particular circumstances of a case.

In *Mallinckrodt* the Board established some basic principles and standards to apply to all industries on a case-by-case basis, but it refused to restrict itself to only the ones mentioned because of the inappropriateness of purely mechanistic rules. Considerations described by the Board as relevant to such a decision were: (1) status of the employees as craftsmen working at their craft or of employees in a traditionally distinct department; (2) existing patterns of bargaining relationships, their stabilizing effect, and the possible effect of altering them; (3) separate identity of the employees within the broader unit; (4) history and pattern of bargaining in the industry; (5) degree of integration and interdependence of the production system; and (6) qualification and experience of the union seeking to represent the employees.

In a 1967 case the Board utilized the standards established in *Mallinckrodt* by denying tool-and-diemakers the privilege of establishing separate representation.[19] Evidence of overlapping job tasks along with the integral nature of the production process was sufficient for the Board to conclude that maintaining the existing unit outweighed the special interests of the tool-and-diemakers.

The Board continued to demonstrate in still another case that the integrated nature of the production process is but one factor to be considered in unit determinations.[20] The only time such a situation is sufficient in and of itself to preclude formation of separate craft units is when the functions, skills, and working conditions of all employees are so fused as to distort any meaningful lines of separate craft identity.

It is obvious from the new principles established to evaluate severance actions that the Board is attempting to evaluate the rights of all parties involved in such actions. The interests of craft employees are not controlling, but the impact on the larger industrial unit will now be given consideration. In addition, the possible disruptive effect of severance on employer ability to maintain production will also be weighed as a factor in the total situation. The Board also recognizes the effect that technological change has on collective bargaining. In this regard what is relevant and appropriate for evaluating the collective bargaining process at one point in time may change rapidly enough to render mechanistic rules inappropriate at another point in time.

TREATMENT OF FOREMEN

At one time foremen were endowed with a considerable degree of authority over many phases of industrial life. They were allowed a great deal of latitude in the settling of workers' wage rates, in hiring and discharging, and in matters of promotion, demotion, transfer, and discipline. In matters of production foremen likewise exercised a great deal of authority. Foremen resolved production issues relating to quality, scheduling, rate of output, and assignment of work. In both personnel and production matters foremen acted upon their own initiative and only rarely, if ever, sought the approval of their superiors in the performance of duties. Their judgment was normally accepted in the shaping of major company policy and little was done without their express approval.[21]

Technological improvements resulting in the modern specialized nature of production weakened the foreman's former status. As a result of general economic development the industrial process became highly departmentalized. Such specialization of production requires a central source of authority to integrate and coordinate all individual functions. Consequently, a new layer of officials arose between the foreman and top management. Production managers, plant supervisors, and superintendents of production were endowed with the responsibility of coordinating plant departments and accordingly were given authority over foremen. In order to meet production requirements, foremen were required to get the work out of their specialized departments in conformance to standards and to time deadlines as established by top authority. Such requirements are necessary in modern industry; the final product could scarcely be efficiently produced if minor, though vital, processes were delayed or completed incompetently. Consequently, though the foreman's authority over general production matters decreased, he was constantly being held to higher and higher standards of performance. Tolerances were reduced as the industrial process became more and more specialized. All parts of the product were required to reach the final assembly point at a specified time and, once there, had to fit accurately in relation to the whole. Thus "the routing and scheduling of production in each department so as to obtain the desired overall co-ordination necessarily deprives departmental foremen of their independence and authority to run their own departments."[22]

Accompanying the progress in technological matters was the centralization of the management function. Modern industrial plants employing hundreds and thousands of workers require a common personnel policy for all workers operating within a company's various specialized departments. Under these conditions it becomes impossible for each foreman, for example, to set wage rates inasmuch as this would probably result in as many different wage rates in the modern plant as there were foremen. Likewise, the foreman's former authority with respect to hiring, promoting, demoting, assigning work, and administering discipline was also materially weakened. It is necessary for top management to establish central control over all these matters, as well as over others, to insure uniformity and avoid worker dissatisfaction. Apart from such centralized control over personnel policies, the growth of trade unions similarly tended to diminish the foreman's authority in personnel matters. Thus the collective bargaining control ordinarily establishes in detail practically all terms and conditions of employment. Moreover, foremen, formerly the first and in most cases the last source of grievance adjustment, became subordinated to the grievance machinery that is typically set forth in the standard labor contract. The supervisor's prestige was further impaired when it became apparent that collective bargaining agreements were customarily executed by top management officials and top labor leaders. In short, development of the modern productive process, centralization of the management function, and the growth of trade unionism all have undermined the foreman's former high degree of authority and independence.

With this breakdown in their prestige and authority, foremen developed a specific set of grievances. These grievances were accentuated during World War II. Among the more important were those involving wages, sick pay, establishment of grievance machinery, lack of a clearly stated company personnel policy with respect to foremen, and the lack of support given by higher management to foremen in their dealings with rank-and-file workers and with trade union leaders. Evidence indicated, however, that insecurity was the most important grievance of foremen. This fear of layoff and demotion was sharply augmented during the war as the number of foremen greatly expanded with the increase of production. "The prospective reduction in the number of supervisors has introduced great insecurity into the lives of all foremen, both old and new. No one knows which supervisors will be kept after the war. The man of long service fears that he may be dropped in favor of younger supervisors with shorter services."[23] Both the new and old foremen apparently seem to have considered that a cornerstone of trade union policy is the protection of job security. If layoffs and demotions had to come, some foremen realized that adherence to a seniority policy, for example, would introduce a degree of security in their jobs. By organizing, some foremen assumed they would be able to insist upon some sort of security program.

In addition to increasing the insecurity factor, war conditions also caused a lag in adjustment of foremen wage rates commensurate with those of rank-and-file employees. The ordinary worker was sometimes paid one and one-half to two times more than the basic wage for working overtime or for giving up holidays. He also received an extra differential for night work. As a result of their supervisory status, foremen were usually paid a salary and performed such extra work without corresponding increases in compensation. A wartime study concluded that foremen's "wages failed to keep pace with increases secured by the production workers through collective bargaining agreements. The discrepancy became apparent during the war when foremen were required to work longer daily hours and on a seven-day week, without as high rate for overtime as paid to the men under their supervision."[24] In the light of the wartime wage stabilization program, such a discrepancy appears understandable. Labor organizations presented rank-and-file wage issues to the National War Labor Board, and top management attempted to protect the standard of living of the white-collar workers, including foremen, by instituting wage-increase applications. Nevertheless, foreman "take-home pay" fell proportionately behind the take-home pay of production workers.

Many a worker was promoted from the ranks to foreman status during the war. While a production worker, the employee was probably a member of a trade union. As such his conditions of employment frequently were rigidly defined in a collective bargaining agreement. Promoted to foreman, the former rank-and-file employee no longer had his rates of pay, hours, seniority, vacations, sick leave, promotions, demotions, or transfers set forth in a contract. Moreover, grievances over these matters had to be presented by the foreman to top management on an individual basis. It was generally recognized that such a situation could easily lead to discrimination against a supervisor. Individual bargaining affords an employer the opportunity to get rid of the "complainers" and "trouble-makers." Through collective bargaining the newly promoted foreman as well as the old supervisors recognized that conditions and terms of employment could be more definite and certain, and that grievances would be handled on a collective rather than on an individual basis.

Traditional Unions. Membership of foremen in labor organizations had long been a common practice in some industries. Specifically, nine old established unions are composed solely of persons of supervisory rank. Three constitute organizations of licensed maritime personnel, two include yardmasters and supervisors in the railroad industry, one is composed of master mechanics and foremen in navy yards, and three include supervisory personnel in the Postal and Railway Mail Service. In the printing industry membership of foremen in rank-and-file unions, as differentiated from those organizations composed only of supervisors, had been permitted or required since 1889. Apparently this practice in the printing industry was well established and was accepted by management and labor as a "matter of course."[25] On the other hand, there are generally two types of unions in the maritime industry, one for the officers and another for unlicensed seamen. In the building trades and in some metal trades industries, foremen are generally included in rank-and-file unions. Similarly, the inclusion of supervisory workers in ordinary unions has increased in British trade unions.[26]

FOREMEN UNDER THE WAGNER ACT

No legal barrier prevented foremen from organizing into labor organizations. All employees, regardless of their status in the industrial hierarchy, have had the legal right to organize into associations for the purpose of collective bargaining ever since *Commonwealth* v. *Hunt*. However, labor history has demonstrated this right could be impaired by interferences with the development of rank-and-file organizations. The character of such opposition was revealed in Chapter 7. Accordingly, foremen had reason to believe that employers would similarly resist the development and operation of their labor organizations. Under these conditions it was expected foremen would seek the support of the NLRB to protect them in their organizational activities. As the Board had prevented interference with the growth and activities of rank-and-file unions, foremen hoped that the Board would extend the same protection to their organizations.

There were two major reasons why foremen employed throughout general industry had reason to believe the Board would grant such protection. One was the fact that traditional foreman unions consistently received the full measure of the protection afforded by the Wagner Act. Hence the foreman employed in, say, manufacturing, felt that the NLRB would certify his organization for the purpose of collective bargaining in the same manner as the agency was prepared to set up bargaining units of foremen traditionally organized in labor unions.

In the second place, the NLRB did protect foremen engaged in general industry from discharge caused by their union activities. One typical case involved a construction superintendent of a mining company who had joined a rank-and-file labor organization. After repeated warnings to drop out of the union, the foreman was discharged. But inasmuch as the NLRB considered the supervisors as "employees" within the terms of the Wagner Act, the employer was directed to reinstate the foreman. On this point the NLRB stated that "it does not lie with the employer to advise his employees who happen to be foremen that they may not join unions or to discharge them if they do."[27] Hence the Board held that it would direct the reinstatement of any foreman who was discharged because of union activities. This ruling, it must be emphasized, was established *before* the Board was called upon to rule on whether it would set up bargaining units composed of supervisors employed throughout general industry. Since the Board was ready to protect any foreman discriminated against because of union activities, it was expected that the Wagner Act would cover all foremen who desired to be classified into bargaining units for collective bargaining purposes. According to this logic, foremen could not be covered by the Wagner Act for one of its purposes but excluded for another purpose. At least this line of reasoning buoyed up the hopes of those who desired the general application of the Wagner Act to foremen.

Original NLRB Position on Foreman Unions. On June 15, 1942, the NLRB held that foremen employed throughout general industry could constitute units appropriate for the purpose of collective bargaining.[28] When certified by the NLRB, a foreman union would be a statutory bargaining agent and the employer would be required by law to recognize the organization and to bargain collectively with its representatives. The foreman case decided by the NLRB on June 15, 1942, involved fifty-eight minor supervisors engaged in coal mining. The foremen organized an independent union, called the Mine Officials Union of America.

The NLRB decision attracted the attention of other supervisors. Guaranteed protection of their bargaining rights, the foreman labor movement made rapid progress, spearheaded by the Foreman's Association of America (FAA). The number of collective bargaining contracts covering foremen increased sharply. In general, the leadership of the young movement rested in efficient and militant hands. Actually, many of the officers of the foreman union movement were former officers of rank-and-file labor organizations. As noted, during the World War II period an unprecedented number of rank-and-file workers were promoted to the foreman level.

Reversal of Policy—the Maryland Drydock Decision. While foremen were enthusiastic about the Board decision of June 1942, many employers were concerned over it. Employers contended that organized foremen could not give management their undivided loyalty. One member of the NLRB, G. D. Reilly, supported the employer position. In fact, in the 1942 decision, Reilly dissented, and foremen obtained legal support of their bargaining rights by a 2-1 vote. In the spring of 1943 John M. Houston replaced William M. Leiserson as a member of the three man NLRB. In 1942 Leiserson and the late Harry A. Millis, wartime chairman of the NLRB, had teamed up against Reilly, the effect being that foremen employed throughout general industry could be classified in bargaining units for the purpose of collective bargaining.

Shortly after the new member, Houston, took office, he voted with Reilly to deny to foremen the opportunity to bargain collectively under the protection of the Wagner Act. The reversal of policy of the Board on foreman union policy was contained in the celebrated *Maryland Drydock* decision, handed down by the Board on May 11, 1943.[29] This decision prevented foremen from obtaining statutory protection while exercising their right of collective bargaining. However, the NLRB ruling did not outlaw foreman labor organizations. In spite of the *Maryland Drydock* doctrine foremen continued to organize in large numbers. The Foreman's Association of America grew from one chapter and 350 members in September 1941 to 281 chapters and 28,240 members in 1945. Though the *Maryland Drydock* decision was handed down in 1943, the FAA increased its membership from seven chapters and ten thousand members at the end of 1942 to 148 chapters and thirty-two thousand members at the end of 1944. As noted, its membership had dropped off considerably by the end of 1945.

Foreman Recognition Strikes. Notwithstanding employer contentions, some foremen still believed that collective bargaining offered a method for effectively adjusting their grievances. As they organized into unions, foremen, of course, wanted their associations to be recognized by top management. However, foremen were not eligible to obtain relief from the National Labor Relations Board. Therefore there was apparently but one alternative remedy to implement their right to collective bargaining—the utilization of the strike. By resorting to industrial warfare, foremen's unions, similar to the general practice of rank-and-file labor organizations in pre–Wagner Act years, might compel management to bargain collectively. Chairman Millis warned his colleagues that foreman organizational strikes would be encouraged by their refusal to protect foremen's collective bargaining rights. Actually, such collective bargaining strikes, rendered unnecessary by the Wagner Act, did take place.

One strike resulting from an employer's refusal to bargain with a foreman's union paralyzed the production of coal in the eastern mining area. To remedy this situation, the President of the United States seized many of the mines. Foreman organizational strikes that occurred in the Detroit industrial area also seriously disrupted war production in that region: "April, 1944 . . . foremen in thirteen industrial plants of six corporations walked out. Within two weeks of the start of the strike, Packard with its 35,000 employees closed down [for a few days] because its production did not measure up to Army specifications."[30] Additional evidence indicates that foremen, after the *Maryland Drydock* decision, made widespread use of the collective bargaining strike. The following table indicates the number of strikes for recognition purposes effected through industry in 1943 and 1944.[31]

COMPARISON OF RECOGNITION STRIKES

	1943	*1944*
Total Number Recognition Strikes	92	202
Workers Involved	14,440	169,958
Man-days Lost to War Production	71,168	853,118

As noted, the *Maryland Drydock* decision was handed down by the NLRB in 1943. In explaining the great increase in the frequency of these strikes in 1944 as compared with 1943, the Bureau of Labor Statistics reports:

> Work stoppages over questions of union recognition and bargaining rights increased in 1944 both numerically and proportionately. This was due in part to strikes over bargaining rights for foremen and supervisory workers. There were at least 30 such strikes in 1944, involving about 130,000 workers and over 650,000 man-days of idleness.[32]

Foremen recognition strikes, apparently encouraged by the *Maryland Drydock* decision, appear to have disrupted war production in 1944. Whereas the total number of recognition strikes in 1943 was comparatively small, the number increased considerably in 1944. And, as the Bureau of Labor Statistics concluded, the sharp increase in the number of workers involved in these strikes was largely attributable to foremen recognition work stoppages.

In the light of these considerations, it seems that many of the 1944 supervisors' recognition strikes would not have occurred had foremen been afforded the opportunity to settle their collective bargaining disputes with the aid of the National

Labor Relations Board. Legal protection of their right to self-organization and collective bargaining would have eliminated the causes of these work stoppages.

Final NLRB Position under Wagner Act. On March 26, 1945, the NLRB decided the famous *Packard Motor Car Company* case.[33] Therein the agency shifted its ground once again on the foreman union problem. Board member Houston changed his viewpoint and voted with Millis to afford legal protection to all foremen in the exercise of their right to collective bargaining. Supervisors throughout industry were again permitted to form labor organizations, and these unions would be designated as appropriate units for the purpose of collective bargaining. Employers who refused to negotiate with their representatives on an industry basis could be legally compelled to bargain collectively.

The consequences of the *Maryland Drydock* doctrine made the change in the foreman union policy of the NLRB almost inevitable. Bulking large as a causal factor in this change were the collective bargaining strikes engaged in by foremen. In this connection Millis and Houston declared that they could not "shut [their] eyes to these developments."

An additional factor involved the Board's policy on protection of foremen discriminated against for engaging in union activity. Even before the NLRB issued its first ruling dealing with the appropriateness of bargaining units of foremen, it held that foremen discharged because of union activities would be reinstated by the NLRB. This policy remained unchanged despite the Board's position in the *Maryland Drydock* case. According to the Board, foremen could not be discriminated against for participating in union activities but supervisors could not be classified in units for purposes of collective bargaining.

Such a position is inherently inconsistent. Either foremen should have been covered by the Wagner Act for all its purposes, or else they should have been stripped of all benefits of the law. In the *Maryland Drydock* case the Board took the position that foremen could not be classified into bargaining units under the Wagner Act because they did not fall within the law's definition of "employee." In other words foremen, for bargaining-unit purposes, were not employees, but actually fell in the employer category. However, when the issue of discrimination was involved, the Board held that these same foremen were no longer employers but employees. Hence in the *Packard* decision the Board held that foremen were covered by the Wagner Act for all its purposes. In the absence of strike activity of foremen following the *Maryland Drydock* decision, it is possible that the Board would have held that foremen lost all rights under the statute. Consistency could have been achieved by forfeiture of all benefits of the Wagner Act. However, the Board scarcely could have invited more industrial conflict during the war years.

Events Following the Packard Decision. Four important events followed in the wake of the doctrine the NLRB established in the *Packard Motor Car Company* case: (1) extension of the protection of the Wagner Act to foremen exercising considerable authority within industry; (2) permission to foremen to choose rank-and-file unions for bargaining representatives; (3) review of the *Packard* decision by the Supreme Court; and (4) agitation for congressional action. A brief discussion of each of these points follows.

After the *Packard* decision was handed down, the Board extended the protection of the Wagner Act to supervisors whose tasks involved a high degree of responsibility and discretion. In other words, the application of the Wagner Act was not to be limited to those foremen occupying the lower strata of the supervisory hierarchy.

Formerly, most of the cases involved foremen who carried out comparatively minor and routine supervisory tasks and exercised only a slight degree of authority within the plant. At one time the Board called these foremen the "traffic-cops" of industry. Once the *Packard* doctrine was established, however, the Board declared that "we do not believe that the application of the Act to foremen can or arbitrarily should be made to depend upon the type of industry involved, whether mass production or non-mass production, or upon the variation in the duties and responsibilities of foremen from company to company."[34] To illustrate this development, the details of one case may be examined.[35] Such a case involved a group of chain-store managers who organized a supervisors' union. Under the policy established by the company, the store managers exercised the authority to (1) hire and discharge all employees under their supervision; (2) set rates of pay, vacations, and hours of employment of such ordinary workers; (3) establish merchandising policies of their local stores; and (4) exercise general supervision over all operational activities of their respective stores. Thus the NLRB was prepared to make available the protection of the Wagner Act to supervisors who assumed considerable responsibility and exercised much authority within industry.

The second major event following the *Packard* decision attaches to the willingness of the NLRB to certify foreman unions for collective bargaining even though such organizations were associated with a parent union that represented production and maintenance workers. Actually, the Board established this doctrine before it handed down the *Maryland Drydock* doctrine.[36] Consequently, no great surprise accompanied the NLRB reaffirmation of this policy. Controlling factors which prompted establishment of the doctrine included: (1) the freedom of choice of bargaining agents is guaranteed by the Wagner Act to all employees; and (2) foremen are free to choose such a representative independent of the National Labor Relations Act. The NLRB pointed out that the Wagner Act provides full freedom to all employees to choose any labor organization as their bargaining agent. It further declared that foremen could seek to establish such a bargaining agent through the peaceful and democratic machinery of the NLRB, or else attempt to achieve this recognition by engaging in economic warfare. Thus the NLRB stated:

> By closing the door to the first of these alternatives, the Board would simply turn the direction of the struggle for union recognition from the ballot box to the economic battlefield. We would thus find ourselves in the anomalous position of promoting strikes for union recognition, the very kind of strikes which the Act intended to diminish.[37]

Many people, particularly employers, denounced the Board doctrine. Independent foreman unions, they claimed, interfered with the ability of management to operate their facilities. But foreman unions, affiliated with rank-and-file labor unions, seriously and actually impaired the management of the business enterprise. According to this view, foremen could not be loyal to management when they were organized in unions affiliated with rank-and-file organizations. Under such conditions, employers claimed, foremen would place the interests of the labor union members ahead of those of management.

The NLRB was aware of the different duties and interests of foremen and of the rank and file. For this reason it refused to lump together foremen and ordinary workers into one bargaining unit. It set up separate bargaining units for supervisors. However, once classified in such a unit, the NLRB held that foremen were free to elect the same bargaining agent as represented the rank-and-file workers of the plant. The fact that the Board made this distinction did not stay the storm of employer protest. Very few Board policies under the Wagner Act stimulated more controversy than the one authorizing foremen, though classified into separate units, to choose rank-and-file unions as their bargaining agent.

Shortly after the *Packard* case was decided, the Packard Motor Car Company carried the foreman battle into the federal courts. It charged that foremen could not be classified into units for collective bargaining purposes. In ruling that they could, the Board, the company contended, badly misinterpreted the Wagner Act. Actually, the Supreme Court, when it finally decided the case, had no legislative basis to determine the validity of the contention of management. Congress failed to deal with the position of foremen in the National Labor Relations Act. No mention of the problem appeared in congressional committee hearings or in the debate on the floors of Congress. No congressman, senator, witness before congressional hearings, or observer of labor relations brought the foreman problem to the attention of Congress before it passed the Wagner Act. Accordingly, the Supreme Court could not refer to legislative intent to determine whether or not the *Packard* doctrine was consistent or inconsistent with the terms of the Wagner Act.

On March 10, 1947, the Supreme Court of the United States sustained the position of the Board. [38] In upholding the authority of the NLRB to compel an employer to bargain collectively with a union composed of foremen, Justice Robert H. Jackson, speaking for the majority, stated that the fact that foremen were employees for purposes of the NLRB "is too obvious to be labored," and that there was nothing in the Wagner Act to indicate that Congress intended to deny benefits. By no means was the Supreme Court decision in the *Packard* case unanimous. The Court was divided 5-4 in its decision, the majority consisting of Associate Justices Jackson, Murphy, Black, Reed, and Rutledge, and the minority including Chief Justice Vinson and Associate Justices Frankfurter, Douglas, and Burton. The minority opinion echoed the fears of employers that the organization of foremen under the protection of the Wagner Act would "obliterate the line between management and labor."

The *Packard* decision focused the attention of Congress on the foreman union problem. Though the foreman union in the *Packard* case was independent and not affiliated with any production workers' union, many members of Congress felt that the organization of foremen constituted a threat to the effective operation of American industry. Consequently, in 1946, congressional action was taken to strip foremen of all legal protection of their right to self-organization and collective bargaining. In that year Congress enacted the Case Bill, a law that provided for the general regulation of labor unions. Included in the law was the provision that a foreman could not be considered as an "employee" for purposes of the Wagner Act. This meant the NLRB could not afford any protection to foremen in the exercise of their collective bargaining rights. Though the Case Bill, including the foreman provisions, passed both Houses of Congress, President Truman vetoed the entire measure. Congress lacked the necessary votes to pass the legislation over the President's veto. With respect to the section of the Case Bill dealing with foremen, President Truman in his veto message declared,

> This section would strip from supervising employees the right of self-organization and collective bargaining now guaranteed them under the National Labor Relations Act. I feel that this section would increase labor strife, since I have no doubt that supervising employees would resort to self-help techniques to gain the right now given them by law. [39]

FOREMEN UNDER TAFT-HARTLEY

When Congress enacted the 1947 labor law, foremen once more were stripped of all protection of their collective bargaining rights. Taft-Hartley effectively removed foremen from the jurisdiction of the NLRB. Under its terms the Board may not classify foremen in units for collective bargaining purposes. This means that employers have no legal obligation to bargain collectively with unions composed of supervisors. Although the Taft-Hartley law does not outlaw foreman labor organizations per se, the removal of legal protection limited the growth of the foreman union movement. The Foreman's Association of America rapidly felt the effects of the Taft-Hartley Act. Shortly after passage of the law, the Ford Motor Company declined to recognize the FAA and refused to renew the collective bargaining contract covering its foremen. As a result the FAA called an organizational strike. Although the strike lasted 47 days, the FAA lost it and by this defeat suffered irreparable damage. Many other companies refused to renew contracts, the result being that the FAA membership declined sharply.

In addition to relieving employers from any legal duty to bargain collectively with foreman unions, the Taft-Hartley Act permitted them to discriminate against foremen engaged in union activities. Thus employers can discharge or take any disciplinary action against foremen because of union activities. In this connection a federal circuit court declared, "It is clear that Congress intended by the enactment of the Labor Management Relations Act that employers be free in the future to discharge supervisors for joining a union, and to interfere with their union activities."[40] Subsequently, the Supreme Court sustained the decision of the lower federal court when it held that the foreman union provisions of Taft-Hartley are constitutional.[41]

Despite an NLRB policy to the contrary, the U.S. Supreme Court by a 5–4 vote in April 1974 held in *Bell Aerospace* v. *NLRB* that all managerial employees, even those who do not have the authority to formulate or carry out an employer's labor relations policy, are not employees for purposes of Taft-Hartley. Just like foremen, who are excluded from coverage by specific statutory language, all managers by this decision lose whatever protection the NLRB affords with respect to union activities. Note that Taft-Hartley does not by specific language exclude managerial employees from its coverage who have absolutely nothing to do with their employer's labor policy. In their dissent, four members of the high court charged that the majority unreasonably curtailed the scope of Taft-Hartley. The essence of their dissent is that if Congress intended to exclude all managerial employees from the coverage of the law, it would have adopted this policy in unambiguous language, as Congress did with respect to foremen.

OBSERVATIONS ON THE FOREMAN UNION
PROBLEM

The Taft-Hartley Act in effect wiped out the foreman labor union movement. This was the objective of the authors of the statute. Thus Hartley remarks, "No one had ever considered foremen and other types of supervisors as constituting proper personnel for union organizations."[42] However, the fact that about thirty thousand foremen elected to organize contradicts Hartley's viewpoint that *no one* had considered foremen as individuals suitable for collective bargaining. Foremen *themselves* apparently wanted to bargain collectively!

Some people contend that Taft-Hartley does not treat foremen unfairly because the statute does not *outlaw* foreman unions. It is said that the statute merely deprives them of their right to organize and bargain collectively under the protection of the NLRB. This liberty proves of little actual value to foremen who elect to engage in collective bargaining. Inherently, foremen possess little bargaining strength. The chief reason for this is that they represent a rather small percentage of all workers in a plant. Thus, in the event of a strike, their jobs can be covered fairly well by top supervisors or even by the rank and file. Actually, the FAA lost its 47-day Ford strike as a result of these factors. The point is that without legal support the foreman union movement cannot become effective. Supervisors cannot rely on their own economic strength to gain recognition. Even rank-and-file workers find this a difficult task in the absence of government protection. This is true even though the rank and file possess the necessary power to close down entire plants or important sections of firms. Supervisors do not possess this power. Foremen have insufficient economic strength to make organizational strikes effective. Such strikes are lost before they are begun. Their success during World War II was based on the tight wartime labor market and the willingness of some companies to make major concessions in the interest of wartime production and profits. In peacetime foremen have not resorted to the organizational strike because they are aware of the slim chance of gaining recognition through the utilization of economic power.

On the basis of these considerations the conclusion must be reached that Taft-Hartley removed foremen from effective union activities. Actually, the law's position on foreman unions appears inconsistent. If foreman unions are deemed undesirable from the public point of view, they should be outlawed. It is illogical for a statute to permit them to exist but to take away the only means of making them effective— legal support. Foremen have the permission to organize, but as a result of institutional factors are unable to do so without positive government support.

PLANT GUARDS

During World War II every plant of any significance employed a plant protection force. Before Pearl Harbor plant-security employees were ordinarily under the direct control of private employers. However, when the United States entered the war approximately two hundred thousand plant guards throughout the country became members of the civilian auxiliary to the military police. Many plant guards of both the militarized and nonmilitarized categories wanted to organize and bargain collectively under the protection of the National Labor Relations Board. Some employers, however, vigorously contended that plant guards had no standing under the Wagner Act. In general employers argued that guards were not "employees" within the meaning of the Wagner Act because of the nature of their duties. Thus the Board was compelled to decide whether plant guards, both militarized and nonmilitarized, could form appropriate units under the Wagner Act for collective bargaining purposes. It is reported that "few single questions have been contested in NLRB proceedings more often during [World War II] than union organization of plant guards."[43]

In a series of decisions the NLRB held that plant guards, similar to production and maintenance workers, enjoyed full protection of the National Labor Relations Act. Not only did the Board hold that nonmilitarized guards could select bargaining agents who did not represent production workers, but the NLRB also ruled that a plant guard's (nonmilitarized) union constituted an appropriate bargaining unit even though the union was affiliated with a production worker's union.

Principles established by the Board for the organization problem of nonmilitarized guards remained in force for guards who became members of the civilian auxiliary to the military police. Militarized guards' unions that were affiliated with production workers' labor organizations received as much protection from the Wagner Act as did independent militarized plant-protection unions. In a case in which the NLRB held that a production workers' labor organization could properly represent a unit of militarized guards, the Board declared: "Freedom to choose a bargaining agent includes the right to select a representative which has been chosen to represent the employees of the employer in a different bargaining unit."[44]

Though full protection of the Wagner Act was available to plant guards during World War II, the Board classified plant-protection employees in units separate from those that included rank-and-file workers. This distinction was deemed necessary because of the difference in functions of plant guards and production workers. Beyond this limitation security employees, classified in separate units, were afforded the opportunity to choose any bargaining agent as their representative. Thus a number of militarized plant-protection employees of the Chrysler Corporation selected the United Automobile Workers of America as their bargaining agent.

The Supreme Court of the United States upheld the ruling of the National Labor Relations Board. On May 19, 1947, the high court held that the provisions of the National Labor Relations Act were applicable to the collective bargaining activities of plant-protection employees. The decision of the Supreme Court established that plant-protection employees, whether or not militarized or deputized, may form labor organizations and bargain collectively under protection of the National Labor Relations Act. The Court held, moreover, that plant guards classified in separate bargaining units could select production and maintenance employees' labor organizations as their bargaining agent. In commenting on this issue, the Court declared that to prevent guards "from choosing a union which also represents production and maintenance employees is to make the collective bargaining rights of guards distinctly second class."[45]

The Supreme Court decisions were announced while a joint congressional committee was considering Taft-Hartley and directed immediate attention to the status of plant-protection employees. When the conference committee returned the bill to Congress, a provision was included which prevents the full application of the protective features of the Taft-Hartley Act to plant guards. Under the terms of the 1947 labor law, any union of plant guards affiliated with a rank-and-file organization may not be certified by the NLRB. Thus the Taft-Hartley Act nullified that decision of the Supreme Court which held that the NLRB could properly certify a single labor union as the appropriate bargaining agent for both plant guards and production workers.

In administering the plant-guard section of the Taft-Hartley Act, the Board adopted a literal interpretation. Shortly following the passage of the Act, the AFL chartered a union to represent plant guards and no other workers. But the NLRB refused to certify the plant guards' union on the ground that it was affiliated with the AFL, a parent body composed of production and maintenance workers' international unions.

The meaning of this decision for plant guards' unions is rather clear. To qualify for a certification of the NLRB, a labor organization of plant-protection employees must have no affiliation or connection with labor unions admitting production and maintenance workers. As a result the growth of plant guards' unions is limited. Denied the privilege of anchoring their unions to established production workers' labor organizations, plant guards' unions remain relatively isolated in attempts at collective bargaining.

In 1948 the Board expanded considerably the application of the definition of plant guards as contained in the Taft-Hartley Act. Thus it held in the *C. V. Hill* case that watchmen are guards within the meaning of the Act, regardless of whether they are armed, uniformed, or deputized.[46] In this case the watchmen were hourly-rated employees and wore the same badges as other employees. The effect of this ruling is to deprive a sizable group of employees of the benefits of collective bargaining. Only one qualification was made by the Board with respect to watchmen. The Board has directed that watchmen can be included in production and maintenance workers' units if not more than 50 percent of the time is devoted to watchman duties.[47]

More recently, in 1966, the Board was required to determine the employee status of individuals considered guards by an employer.[48] In the *American Telegraph* case the status of guards as employees within the meaning of Taft-Hartley Section 9 (b) (3) dealing with the problem had to be resolved since the individuals performed protective services by means of electric, electronic, and electromagnetic devices they installed and maintained. The employer argued that the performance of protective services and the servicing and installation of devices classified all such employees as guards because of the integrated nature of the work brought about by new detection techniques. The Board disapproved the employer's argument and held that employees that merely worked on the installation and maintenance of protective equipment did not come within the statutory definition of guards. *Guards* are those individuals engaged in enforcing rules to protect property or the safety of persons on the employer's premises.

In 1967 the Board ruled in *New England Tank Cleaning Company* to include employees in the general bargaining unit that merely performed guard duties on weekends, accounting for only 13 percent of their worktime.[49] The Board arrived at its decision by reasoning that at such times when the workers functioned in a protective capacity, other employees were not working and as such there was no conflict between loyalty to fellow union members and duty to the employer.

It is obvious in the cases cited that the Board is reviewing the plant-guard problem in terms of the totality of circumstances. The mere fact that a worker performs guard tasks on occasion will not automatically eliminate him from bargaining-unit status. Also new protective devices do not automatically require the status of plant guard merely because of the necessity for some workers to service those instruments.

CONCLUSIONS ON PLANT-GUARD
ORGANIZATION PROBLEM

The Taft-Hartley Act decreased the ability of plant guards to engage in collective bargaining. Standing alone, these workers possess very little bargaining strength. This condition results from two factors: (1) they are comparatively few in number in any one plant; and (2) plant guards perform tasks that can be learned rather readily by new employees. As a result of these two conditions, management can easily replace plant-protection employees. Since they are readily replaceable, plant guards cannot employ the strike effectively. This means that plant-guard unions, separated from production employees' labor organizations, cannot make effective use of their economic strength to win concessions. Plant guards may have their unions certified by the NLRB. Unlike foremen, they may be reinstated by the NLRB when they are discharged because of union activities.

An independent plant-guard international union was established soon after the passage of Taft-Hartley. This organization has been rather ineffective in promoting the organization of plant guards. The reason for this lack of success, as stated, rests upon the inherently weak bargaining strength of plant-guard unions separated from the established labor organizations.

Employers who sponsored the plant-guard limitations contained in the 1947 labor law contended that organized guards affiliated with production workers' unions were unable to carry out their duties in an effective and loyal manner. Nothing during World War II indicates that organized plant-protection employees, classified in units separate from production and maintenance workers affiliated with rank-and-file labor unions, could not perform their plant-security duties effectively. The Supreme Court dealt with this problem when it affirmed the position of the NLRB. It refused to regard as controlling the argument that unionized plant guards might be less loyal to management in the execution of their duties. Neither did the Court give much weight to the contention that rank-and-file labor organizations would make demands upon unionized plant guards or force agreements from management that would lessen the loyalty and efficiency of the guards. The Court stated that the process of collective bargaining is "capable of adjustment to accommodate the special function of plant guards." From this statement it appears that the Court would look with disfavor upon certification of a bargaining agent that interferes with the proper execution of duties of plant guards. In addition, it is clear that organized plant guards, discharged because of disloyalty to management, inefficiency, or failure to carry out their duties in an effective manner, would not be reinstated by the Board. The observations of the Supreme Court underscore the fact that guard unions affiliated with AFL-CIO labor organizations would not result in the consequences portrayed by some employers.

Plant guards, similar to ordinary production workers, develop a set of employment grievances. To adjust such complaints, some guards desire to organize and bargain collectively. Such collective bargaining activities cannot be carried out effectively where guard unions are denied the right to affiliate with established labor organizations. Taft-Hartley restriction on plant-guard labor organizations, in the words of the Supreme Court of the United States, "makes the collective bargaining right of guards distinctly second class."

PROFESSIONAL WORKERS

One section of Taft-Hartley provides that the NLRB may not set up a bargaining unit that contains both professional and nonprofessional employees unless a majority of the professional employees vote for inclusion in a combined unit.[50] As noted, agitation for this policy did not come from employers but from professional workers.

This group felt that its interests would be served through the setting up of independent professional worker units. Actually, the NLRB under the Wagner Act provided a considerable degree of freedom to professional workers to select their own unions. When a group of workers fell into the professional category, the Board frequently gave them the opportunity to select their own bargaining representatives provided they wanted separate representation.

Unlike the foreman, the professional worker may be reinstated by the Board if he is discharged by an employer because of union activities. Contrary to the plant guard, the professional worker may be represented in collective bargaining by rank-and-file labor organizations. The only restriction on the collective bargaining activities of professional workers contained in the new labor law is the prohibition of including them in the same bargaining unit with nonprofessional workers when a majority of the professional workers vote against inclusion.

The major problem confronting the Board in the administration of this section of the new labor law is the task of deciding which employees are professional workers. Although the Taft-Hartley Act sets up general standards for professional workers, the NLRB must decide which specific groups of employees are professional workers.[51]

The Board has held in one case that a worker to be classed as a "professional employee" does not need a specialized college degree. Thus the NLRB directed that a group of noncollege-trained plant engineers of a telephone company be polled on the question of whether they desired special representation. The Board in another case held that it is not the individual qualifications of employees but rather the character of the work required of them as a group that is determinative of professional status.[52]

Lawyers employed by an insurance company were also classified as professional workers. In this proceeding the Board rejected the employer's contention that professional employees were removed by the Taft-Hartley Act from the Board's jurisdiction. In a case involving a number of time-study men employed by a pump and machinery company, the Board held that these employees were not foremen, as the employer urged, but fell within the professional classification. An employer engaged in the designing and construction of office and industrial buildings contended that the "estimators" employed by the firm were not professional workers. The estimators of the company determine the amount of material to be required for the construction of a building and further compute the cost of the material. In rejecting the employer position, the NLRB held the estimators are included within the professional category on the ground that they must possess a high degree of intellectual ability and a substantial background of training, education, and experience. It was further decided that the estimators perform jobs that require the exercise of a considerable degree of judgment and discretion.

Four employees performing accounting work for a manufacturer of window glass were held by the Board as not falling within the professional classification. Three of the four employees performed cost analyses. Training for the job was attained at a local business school and supplemented by a special training course provided by the company. A fourth employee was engaged in appraising the employer's assets and surveying records with the objective of reorganizing the property record accounting system. Even though he had three years of college work and performed work requiring a high degree of intellectual ability, the Board held he was not a professional worker.

Upon another occasion a group of editorial employees of a newspaper were held not to be professional workers. In reaching this decision, the NLRB declared that the work they performed did not "require knowledge of an advanced type in a field of learning customarily acquired by a course of specialized intellectual instruction in an institution of higher learning as distinguished from a general academic education."[53] Thus a person with a general college education does not because of this fact alone fall within the professional classification, according to the NLRB. In another case involving the newspaper industry, the Board refused to classify special editors, rewrite men, and out-of-town reporters as professional workers. These groups, in the Board's opinion, perform essentially the same duties as regular newspaper reporters who are a nonprofessional group.

Radio announcers, singers, and continuity writers are not professional workers within the meaning of the Taft-Hartley Act. Although it was conceded that these groups are trained and skilled personnel, the Board refused to classify them as professional workers. The Board did not give any reasons for the decision. If a professionally trained worker does not perform the duties of his profession he will not be treated as a professional worker. In a case involving a professional chemist, the Board held that he was not a professional worker for purposes of the Taft-Hartley Act, on the ground that his job in the plant was the carrying out of duties relating to maintenance electrical work. As a result he was included in a bargaining unit of maintenance employees.

From the cases reviewed above, it can be seen that the problem of establishing which workers are professional employees for purposes of the Taft-Hartley Act is one fraught with difficulty since no objective standards are available to resolve the problem. The matter will be determined within the area of opinion. The Board has considerable latitude in deciding whether employees are professional or not. Once employees are given professional status, the Board must hold an election to determine if they desire to be included in a bargaining unit with nonprofessionals. The provision of Taft-Hartley requiring a poll of professionals will be enforced by the U.S. Supreme Court despite another provision of the same law intended to restrict judicial review of Board representation certifications.[54]

Section 9 (d) of the Act provides that the Board "shall decide in each case . . . the unit appropriate for the purposes of collective bargaining." The intent of Congress in giving such authority to the Board was to prevent unions and management from using the courts to delay the initiation of collective bargaining. The long delays that accompany litigation have the effect of frustrating the basic purpose of the Taft-Hartley Act. In this respect the Board argued in *Leedom* v. *Kyne* that it had exclusive jurisdiction in representation cases. In this case the NLRB did not poll a group of employees who were apparently professional within the meaning of Taft-Hartley and included them in a rank-and-file bargaining unit. When the Supreme Court heard the case, it held that the bargaining unit was defective and remanded the case back to the NLRB. While reversing the NLRB, the U.S. Supreme Court stated it could not "lightly infer that Congress does not intend judicial protection of rights it confers against agency action taken in excess of delegated powers." As the law now stands, it seems possible that a party dissatisfied with a Board bargaining-unit decision may resort to the courts for relief. Bargaining-unit efforts may be frustrated because a party is not satisfied with Board determinations.

"EXTENT OF ORGANIZATION"

A labor union instituting an organizing campaign in a plant may fail to induce all the workers to join the union. The union may be successful in organizing only a portion of the workers. When the NLRB administered the Wagner Act, it frequently granted legal protection to the collective bargaining rights of those actually organized. For example, in 1941 the Board held that a group of cutters employed by a company was an appropriate unit, although a large unit comprising all production employees might likewise constitute an appropriate unit. In reaching its decision, the NLRB declared:

> Self-organization among the Company's employees . . . has not extended beyond the limits of the unit proposed by the Union, nor is any organization here seeking to represent employees of the Company other than the cutters. Under these circumstances, we are of the opinion that the unit sought by the Union herein is appropriate. To find otherwise would deprive the cutters of the benefits of collective bargaining until the remaining production employees had organized. [55]

Thus when a group of workers, corresponding to the extent of organization, by majority vote elected to be represented for collective bargaining, the Board under the Wagner Act certified such a group for the purposes of collective bargaining. The employer was under legal obligation to bargain collectively with the union representing this group of employees. As noted, the NLRB based this policy on the ground that the organized workers should not be required to wait until a majority or more of all employees in the bargaining unit were unionized before enjoying the benefits of collective bargaining.

Under the terms of the Taft-Hartley Act, the NLRB may not consider the "extent of organization" as the controlling factor in the setting up of the appropriate bargaining unit. This means that the Board may not certify a union to represent a small group of workers of a large bargaining unit solely on the ground that a union has been successful in organizing a portion of the larger unit.

The insurance industry has received considerable attention in the last several years regarding the Section 9 (c) (5) congressional change that the extent of union organization shall not be the controlling factor in establishment of the appropriate unit for collective bargaining. In a 1944 case before the Board, it ruled that only a state-wide or company-wide unit of insurance employees was appropriate. [56] The inclusion of insurance employees in such an extensive unit was overruled in 1962 when the Board declared that a city-wide unit of insurance employees was more appropriate than the state- or company-wide situation. [57] It held that there was no longer a rational basis for applying different organizational rules to the insurance industry than are applied to other industries. For example, there has never been any requirement for a labor organization to organize all plants of a particular manufacturing firm operating within a particular state before a single plant of employees will be certified as a unit appropriate to bargain with an employer. In contrast, the insurance industry was treated differently when the Board required all offices within the state or within a particular company to be organized before bargaining would be permitted. Obviously, such a requirement made it virtually impossible for labor organizations to function. Some offices in distant cities might not want to organize and such a situation would prohibit employees in another city from bargaining collectively.

In a series of cases involving the Metropolitan Life Insurance Company, the

Board moved away from the state-wide unit to both single district offices and various geographic groupings of district offices in establishing bargaining units. The company challenged the Board and argued in various circuit courts that the extent of organization controlled the agency decision in violation of Taft-Hartley. The First Circuit agreed with the employer, but the Third and Sixth Circuits disagreed.[58] The Board appealed to the U.S. Supreme Court for a policy clarification.[59]

In its decision, the high court held that the NLRB may properly consider the extent of organization as one factor in the establishment of bargaining units, but not as the controlling factor. It stated:

> Although it is clear that in passing this amendment Congress intended to overrule Board decisions where the unit determined could only be supported on the basis of the extent of organization, both the language and legislative history of 9 (c) (5) demonstrate that the provision was not intended to prohibit the Board from considering the extent of organization as one factor, though not the controlling factor, in its unit determination.

However, it refused to sustain the Board's order in *Metropolitan Insurance* because of the agency's "lack of articulated reasons" for its establishment of the smaller bargaining units. The case was remanded to the Board for this purpose, and subsequently the agency articulated its reasons. It explained that each of the insurance company's individual offices constituted an administrative entity, and, therefore, an individual city-wide unit was appropriate for collective bargaining under Taft-Hartley. In other words, the controlling factor for the establishment of the smaller unit was its independence and autonomy from the parent company. The extent of organization was a subsidiary and not the controlling factor. So far, the administrative entity reason used as the basis for the Board's policy to establish smaller bargaining units has not been upset by the Supreme Court.[60]

Subsequently, the Board spelled out factors that would make a particular store, restaurant, or office of a parent company an administrative entity. In one case, a single restaurant in a chain operation constituted an appropriate bargaining unit because in the day-to-day operation of the restaurant, its manager ordered all of its supplies, contracted for major repairs, did about 60 percent of the hiring, fixed wage rates within the ranges established by central headquarters, trained employees, and had the authority to discharge employees.[61] In another instance, the Board held single stores of a drug chain to be a proper unit for bargaining primarily because of the relatively infrequent visits of representatives of the central management.[62] On the other hand, the Board refused to establish a single store as appropriate on the grounds that the parent corporation placed sharp limitations on store managers in the matter of personnel policies, considerable employee interchange between stores occurred, and district supervisors of the central headquarters had direct supervision over store departments.[63]

In short, the key to the establishment of a store or office of a chain operation as a bargaining unit is the autonomy and independence of the unit from control of central headquarters. When this finding is made, the Board applies its administrative entity principle. Each case will be determined on its own merits, since multistore or office operations differ widely in the amount of control exerted by the parent company. In any event, the *Metropolitan Insurance* doctrine has facilitated more organization among white collar and service employees. Union efforts can be concentrated on smaller units of these employees without the necessity of dealing with a large dispersed unit of identical workers of the same company. Thus, the task of organization is easier with industries such as insurance, chain drug, restaurants, supermarkets, banking, and in other kindred industries that operate on a multistore or office basis.

COORDINATED BARGAINING

Several labor organizations that deal separately with a single employer have found that their bargaining power might be enhanced if they are successful in establishing a joint bargaining relationship. That is, unions desire to collectively confront management at the same time on contractual issues of mutual interest. The term coordinated bargaining is not as yet well-defined and it may also refer to the presence of other unions' delegates on a non-voting basis in proceedings involving another union and the employer. The basic purpose is to prevent some bargaining units from approving settlements less desirable than those reached by some other units. This issue is critical when the labor movement is considered in its totality. For example, some firms such as General Electric bargain with a large number of unions representing workers in various parts of the country. The copper industry is still another example. All collective bargaining contracts may not be subject to negotiation at the same time. Because of the different expiration dates, a firm may successfully resist union demands in one plant located in one section of the country through its ability to increase output in another plant in a different region. This arrangement is especially convenient for management when unemployment rates are relatively high. This indicates that there may be considerable excess productive capacity within a firm. A decision to shift production from plant to plant is difficult to realize when there is relatively little excess capacity during periods of high demand for goods and services. Thus unions have opened a drive to change the historical pattern of bargaining in the last half of the 1960s as the economy neared relative full employment. They have achieved some successes from their efforts.

In 1968 the NLRB set a precedent in the *General Electric Company* case for future coordinated bargaining by permitting a union to include representatives of other unions on its negotiating committee.[64] Representatives of other unions included in the negotiations must belong to labor organizations having contracts with the involved firm. They are denied voting privileges even though they may sit in during negotiations. The Board, however, did not rule on several important issues in deciding the case. One is whether or not a company may refuse to bargain if participating unions enter into an agreement as to the circumstances under which they would sign a contract with the employer. Still another problem is involved if a company refuses to bargain when the unions continue to press their demand for joint bargaining.[65] The Board in a 1962 case upheld the legality of an interunion agreement that no single union would sign a contract providing less than the agreed-upon conditions without the consent of the other labor organizations.[66] Each union, however, was free to sign a collective bargaining agreement containing the common demands.

Essentially, the *General Electric* decision broadens the concept of bargaining-unit negotiations. Many decisions may now be made at interunion conferences and not at the bargaining table. This type of bargaining may be defended only on the basis that the problems and issues confronting one bargaining unit are the same as those which face all the others. Otherwise the NLRB with the approval of the U.S. Court of Appeals at New York City has permitted external union influence to shape the content of collective contracts.[67] The federal court was aware of the possibility of damage that could be done to bargaining-unit boundaries, but declared that the facts of the case did not demonstrate a clear and present danger to the bargaining process.

The NLRB has held interunion agreements unlawful that require that no labor organization will contract until all other unions have been offered the common demands. In 1972, the Board was overruled on this issue among others in *Phelps Dodge*.[68] During the 1967–68 negotiations Phelps Dodge dealt with the United Steelworkers of America and at least 25 other international unions. The unions through the Industrial Union Department of the AFL-CIO set up the Nonferrous Industry Conference to establish coalition bargaining. The Industry Conference set up joint union negotiating committees for each company. Phelps Dodge charged that the unions' objective was to obtain company-wide master agreements and common contract termination dates in the industry. The NLRB upheld the Phelps Dodge charge that the committee's insistence on the two items and delay of strike settlement until other company units reached agreements amounted to the same thing as demanding company-wide bargaining. The contract had been submitted to the Nonferrous Industry Conference for approval. Such behavior was viewed by the Board as illegal because it lay outside the mandatory bargaining category.

The Third Circuit Court of Appeals disagreed with the Board. It ruled that negotiations were conducted at separate locations and no bargaining in any unit involved discussion of terms and conditions of employment in other units. The appeals court also established that a union can strike for a limited no-strike clause and a "most favored nation" clause. Thus, a union is permitted to strike in support of workers in other bargaining units of the same employer under certain circumstances.

The Supreme Court refused to review the decision. This does not mean that the high court will not deal with the coalition bargaining issue at some future date. In the meantime, union efforts to expand the scope of bargaining beyond established units have been strengthened. Renewed activity to coordinate bargaining in other industries can be expected to follow the procedure used in the copper industry.

Labor history demonstrates that all bargaining units have a vital interest in collective agreements reached by any other unit that deals with a common firm. Indeed, the same interest exists regarding contracts signed in any given industry.

Both the *General Electric* and *Phelps Dodge* cases legally formalize a well-understood economic objective of labor unions. That is, in order to facilitate their efforts to standardize collective bargaining terms throughout an industry, unions attempt to coordinate bargaining among themselves. The final results on the issue are not yet decided; the Supreme Court can be expected to deal with coalition bargaining at some future date.

SUMMARY

Taft-Hartley has resulted in the nullification of many of the policies that the National Labor Relations Board established during World War II relating to the appropriate unit for collective bargaining. Under the force of the legislation the power of the Board to extend the process of collective bargaining is curtailed despite the fact that on several issues the Supreme Court of the United States upheld bargaining-unit policies of the NLRB. The authority of the Board to set up units of foremen for collective bargaining is nullified by the 1947 labor law. In addition, the Taft-Hartley Act operates to reduce the effectiveness of the plant guards' labor union movement by restricting the NLRB in certifying labor organizations of plant guards when they are associated with production and maintenance workers' labor unions. The law was once considered conducive to ineffective collective bargaining and strained industrial relations because it encouraged the disintegration of established industrial bargaining units and promoted competing and conflicting craft units. The Board, however, has been given authority by the Supreme Court to control such situations in order to effectuate the basic purpose of the Act. Finally, under the provisions of the Taft-Hartley Act, the NLRB was first restricted in granting legal protection of the right of workers to collective bargaining where a limited number of workers have been organized within an industrial facility. The extent-of-organization restriction has been extended beyond production worker units to white-collar employees, but litigation involving the latter is resulting in more realistic policies. The insurance company cases appear to have widened the area of Board authority to establish appropriate bargaining units.

Fresh legislation may yet be needed to correct the area of Taft-Hartley that bears on the appropriate-bargaining-unit problem. Any new legislation should have as its objective the widening of the area of authority of the NLRB to set up the appropriate bargaining unit for effective and peaceful collective bargaining. The curtailment of the Board's right to grant legal protection to workers in the exercise of their right to collective bargaining means that a considerable number of workers in American industry are unable to enjoy the benefits of collective action within the area of industrial relations.

NOTES

[1] National Labor Relations Board, *First Annual Report* (1936), p. 112.

[2] 2 NLRB 374 (1936).

[3] National Labor Relations Board, *Fourth Annual Report* (1939), p. 83.

[4] National Labor Relations Board, *Twelfth Annual Report* (1947), p. 87.

[5] *Pittsburgh Plate Glass Company* v. *NLRB*, 313 U.S. 146 (1941). In this case the Supreme Court held that the courts are forbidden to set aside a bargaining-unit determination by the NLRB as long as the NLRB exercises its power to designate the unit in a reasonable manner and supports its findings with evidence.

[6] *American Rolbal Corporation*, 41 NLRB 907 (1942).

[7] *General Steel Castings Corporation*, 41 NLRB 350 (1942).

[8] R. R. R. Brooks, *Unions of Their Own Choosing* (New Haven: Yale University Press, 1937), p. 164.

[9] *Globe Machine & Stamping Company*, 3 NLRB 294 (1937).

[10] *General Electric Company*, 58 NLRB 57 (1944).

[11] *American Can*, 13 NLRB 1252 (1939).

[12] Bureau of National Affairs, *Labor Relations Reporter*, XV (December 4, 1944), 396.

[13] *National Tube Company*, 76 NLRB 169 (1948).

[14] *American Potash & Chemical Corporation,* 107 NLRB 290 (1954).

[15] National Planning Association, *Causes of Industrial Peace Under Collective Bargaining,* Study No. 1, p. xv.

[16] *NLRB* v. *Pittsburgh Plate Glass Company,* 270 F. (2d) 26 (1959).

[17] *Kennecott Copper Company,* 138 NLRB 3 (1962).

[18] *Mallinckrodt Chemical Works,* 162 NLRB 48 (1966).

[19] *Holmberg,* 162 NLRB 53 (1967).

[20] *E. I. du Pont de Nemours & Company,* 162 NLRB 49 (1967).

[21] Bureau of National Affairs, "Report and Recommendations of the Panel," *War Labor Reports,* XXVI, 666–673. A panel headed by Professor Sumner Slichter was established by the National War Labor Board to determine the economic causes of foreman labor organizations and to make recommendations with respect to the problem. The panel conducted a most thorough analysis of the issues involved, and its report will probably stand as a significant contribution to economic literature.

[22] *Business Week,* December 16, 1939, p. 37.

[23] "Report and Recommendations of the Panel," *op. cit.,* p. 673.

[24] *Monthly Labor Review,* LXII (February 1946), 241.

[25] Bureau of Labor Statistics, *Union Membership and Collective Bargaining by Foremen,* Bulletin 745, p. 3.

[26] *Ibid.,* p. 5.

[27] *Golden Turkey Mining Company,* 34 NLRB 779 (1941).

[28] *Union Collieries Coal Company,* 41 NLRB 961 (1942).

[29] *Maryland Drydock Company,* 49 NLRB 733 (1943).

[30] *New York Times,* March 11, 1947.

[31] *Monthly Labor Review,* LX (May 1945), 968; LVIII (May 1944), 937.

[32] *Ibid.,* p. 967.

[33] *Packard Motor Car Company,* 61 NLRB 4 (1945).

[34] *L. A. Young Spring & Wire Corporation,* 65 NLRB 301 (1946).

[35] *Great Atlantic & Pacific Tea Company,* 69 NLRB 463 (1946).

[36] *Godchaux Sugar Company,* 44 NLRB 874 (1942).

[37] *Jones & Laughlin Steel Corporation,* 66 NLRB 400 (1946).

[38] *Packard Motor Car Company* v. *NLRB,* 67 S. Ct. 789 (1947).

[39] Bureau of National Affairs, *Labor Relations Reporter* (June 17, 1946), 123.

[40] *NLRB* v. *Budd Manufacturing Company,* 138 Fed. (2d) 86 (1948).

[41] 335 U.S. 908 (1949).

[42] Fred Hartley, *Our New National Labor Policy* (New York: Funk & Wagnalls Company, 1948), p. 56.

[43] *Labor Relations Reporter,* XV (January 1, 1945), 4.

[44] *Chrysler Corporation,* 44 NLRB 886 (1942).

[45] *NLRB* v. *Atkins & Company,* 331 U.S. 398 (1947); *NLRB* v. *Jones & Laughlin Steel Corporation,* 331 U.S. 416 (1947).

[46] *C. V. Hill,* 76 NLRB 24 (1948).

[47] *Steelweld Equipment Company,* 76 NLRB 116 (1948).

[48] *American District Telegraph Company,* 160 NLRB 1130 (1966).

[49] *New England Tank Cleaning Company,* 161 NLRB 1474 (1967).

[50] Section 9 (b) (1).

[51] Section 2 (12) defines a *professional employee* as follows:

(a) any employee engaged in work (i) predominantly intellectual and varied in character as opposed to routine mental, manual, mechanical, or physical work; (ii) involving the consistent exercise of discretion and judgment in its performance;

(iii) of such a character that the output produced or the result accomplished cannot be standardized in relation to a given period of time; (iv) requiring knowledge of an advanced type in a field of science or learning customarily acquired by a prolonged course of specialized intellectual instruction and study in an institution of higher learning or a hospital, as distinguished from a general academic education or from an apprenticeship or from training in the performance of routine mental, manual, or physical processes; or (b) any employee, who (i) has completed the courses of specialized intellectual instruction and study described in clause (iv) of paragraph (a), and (ii) is performing related work under the supervision of a professional person to qualify himself to become a professional employee as defined in paragraph (a).

[52] *Ryan Aeronautical Company*, 132 NLRB 1160 (1962).

[53] *Free Press Company*, 76 NLRB 152 (1948).

[54] *Boyd S. Leedom* v. *William Kyne*, 358 U.S. 184 (1958).

[55] *Crescent Dress Company*, 29 NLRB 351 (1941).

[56] *Metropolitan Life Insurance Company*, 56 NLRB 1635 (1944).

[57] *Quaker City Life Insurance Company*, 134 NLRB 960 (1962).

[58] *Metropolitan Life Insurance Company*. v. *NLRB*, 327 F. (2d) 906 (CA 1) denying enforcement of 142 NLRB 491; *Metropolitan Life Insurance Company* v. *NLRB*, 328 F. (2d) 820 (CA 3) enforcing 141 NLRB 337; *Metropolitan Life Insurance Company* v. *NLRB*, 330 F. (2d) 62 (CA 6) enforcing 141 NLRB 1074.

[59] *NLRB* v. *Metropolitan Life Insurance Company*, 380 U.S. 438 (1965).

[60] Federal courts have at times reversed the Board when they have found that there was not sufficient autonomy of the single store or office. For example, see *NLRB* v. *Purity Foods*, 376 F. (2d) 497, cert. denied 389 U.S. 959 (1967). This case and the subsequent action of the Supreme Court, however, should not be regarded as a reversal of the administrative entity doctrine. Rather, it should be regarded as an instance where the courts have disagreed with the Board's finding that the smaller unit was autonomous from the parent operation.

[61] *Haag Drug Company*, 169 NLRB 877 (1968).

[62] *Walgreen Company*, 198 NLRB No. 158 (1972).

[63] *Star Market*, 172 NLRB No. 130 (1968).

[64] *General Electric Company*, 173 NLRB 46 (1968).

[65] Stephen B. Goldberg, "Coordinated Bargaining: Some Unresolved Questions," *Monthly Labor Review*, XCII, No. 4 (April 1969), 56–58.

[66] *Standard Oil Company*, 137 NLRB 690 (1962) in *ibid.*, p. 57.

[67] *General Electric Company* v. *NLRB*, 358 F. (2d) 292 (1969).

[68] *AFL-CIO Joint Negotiating Committee for Phelps Dodge* v. *NLRB*, CA 3 No. 19199 (March 31, 1972).

14

Controls on the Substance of Bargaining

Government control over collective bargaining involves more than restrictions placed on certain economic weapons that may be used to obtain the particular contractual provisions desired by either management or unions. Control is extended also to restrictions placed on particular provisions that may be included in the collective bargaining agreement. Some union-security provisions are prohibited by law while many other items such as subcontracting are subject to bargaining. Impasses on some items may justify strikes or lockouts. Other subjects must be abandoned if the parties fail to reach agreement on them. That is, bargaining may take place voluntarily on some issues but in the absence of agreement the parties are forbidden from striking or locking out to influence the contractual result. This chapter focuses on the issues and forms of union security, checkoff provisions, and NLRB policy regarding good-faith bargaining. Mandatory and voluntary bargaining subjects are also considered.

UNION SECURITY: A CONTROVERSIAL ISSUE

Union security is a primary aim of most labor organizations and it usually involves some form of compulsory membership as a condition of employment. Automatic checkoff of union dues is a usual feature of such arrangements. Very few issues of collective bargaining are more controversial than the problem of union security. Union-security objectives include protection against employer discrimination, worker defection, and rival union raiding tactics.[1]

Unions contend that compulsory membership as a condition of employment precludes the possibility of some workers receiving the benefits of unionism without bearing the risks and obligations of union activities. It is also claimed that in the absence of some union-security arrangement union leaders must devote a large share of their time to organizing activities since there is of necessity a constant effort to enlist members. This means that there may be less time available for efforts to improve conditions of work in the bargaining unit. Alternatively, union officers occasionally admit that they may be more responsive to member and nonmember grievances which could have both a positive and a negative effect. The positive aspect involves a greater inclination to process worker grievances, which could bring about greater democracy in the bargaining unit. The negative factor exists because of the possibility of processing grievances that have little or no merit, resulting in a decline of grievance machinery integrity and efficiency.

Unions also argue that worker morale is improved when union membership is required. Freedom to remain outside the labor organization leads to conflict between union and nonunion workers. Union workers have historically preferred not to work with nonunion workers. It is argued that the production process could be carried out more efficiently if conflicts between the two could be avoided.

It is further contended that union security permits union discipline. A labor organization may be in a better position to enforce contractual provisions if it is able to discipline workers for violating the terms of the collective bargaining agreement. Enforcement is simpler if it is well known that expulsion from the union carries with it loss of job. Thus union-security clauses place unions in a better position to enforce internal organizational rules and regulations that result in a more disciplined organization. Essentially, the claim is that union security provides a greater degree of union responsibility. Demonstration of responsibility is considered necessary if favorable contractual provisions are to be won from management during negotiations. An inability to enforce agreements results in a loss of integrity for the entire collective bargaining process.

Arguments presented against compulsory union membership are several. One is that union security may make some union leaders unresponsive to the needs of members. Workers may receive less than the full amount of service they should receive from their union leaders.

Still another argument that is widely discussed in many public circles is that the requirement of union membership as a condition of employment deprives a person of the freedom to work. The influence of this argument on the general public is currently reflected in the "right-to-work" laws of nineteen states. At one time two additional states enacted such laws but later repealed these statutes.

The public has a considerable interest in the process of collective bargaining and over the years has taken action to minimize union management control over the freedom of individuals. Abuses of various forms of union security have been a part of the reason for increased regulation of permissible contractual provisions. The drive toward increased industry concentration and economic power has been another factor leading to greater governmental surveillance over labor-management negotiations. Large corporations and in turn large unions are often viewed as impersonal forces working to the detriment of individual workers. The presence of compulsory union membership arrangements therefore leaves the individual worker incapable of influencing the conditions under which he works in his place of employment. The monopoly issue rages in both the labor market and the product market. The elimination of compulsory union membership is advanced as one method of dealing with excessive union power.

Most debates over union security are largely emotional. Generalizations are made on the basis of limited and usually unrepresentative information. Until more adequate data are available, the debate will continue.

Forms of Union Security

Several union-security devices have come into being over the years. There are three primary arrangements that unions have used to fulfill the objective of union security: closed shop, union shop, and maintenance of membership. Although each arrangement has its own distinguishing characteristics, all are common in requiring continued union membership as a condition of employment. These forms differ, however, in the timing for the requirement of union membership and in the degree of freedom permitted workers to decide to join organizations.

The closed shop and union shop are dissimilar in that under the former the worker must belong to the union before obtaining a job. The latter requires union membership within a certain time period after the worker is hired. Under a maintenance-of-membership arrangement, the worker is free to elect whether or not he will join the union. Once he does join, however, he must maintain membership in the union for the duration of the contract period or forfeit employment.

Maintenance-of-Membership Compromise. The maintenance-of-membership device was utilized heavily by the National War Labor Board (NWLB) during World War II as a compromise device between the union security demands of organized labor and the principle laid down by President Roosevelt that "the Government of the United States will not order nor will Congress pass legislation ordering a so-called closed shop."[2] The President's statement was interpreted as extending also to the union shop. The union movement was demanding an acceptable form of security in return for its no-strike pledge. The NWLB struck a compromise with the maintenance-of-membership device. This arrangement required that all present and future members of the union had to remain members for the duration of the contract as a condition of employment. A fifteen-day escape period was provided union members.

The device was not created by the National War Labor Board. It was first utilized during the 1930s in the chemical, meat packing, and paper and pulp industries. In 1941 the National Defense Mediation Board, an agency set up to help settle labor disputes in the pre–Pearl Harbor defense period, made use of the arrangement. The National War Labor Board thereafter adopted it and made use of the device in cases where a closed-shop or a union-shop arrangement had not existed prior to World War II. The closed shop or union shop was continued where they had existed before the war.

At first the NWLB required that maintenance of membership would not be ordered unless a majority of the bargaining unit voted for its inclusion in the labor agreement. Voting was to be under NWLB supervision and by secret ballot. Only one election was held and involved International Harvester. About 91 percent of workers voted for the clause. Thereafter, the NWLB dropped the procedure because it was too expensive and it interfered significantly with the war effort.[3]

The maintenance-of-membership arrangement may have lessened the number of strikes which might otherwise have occurred over the union security issue. By 1945 nearly 30 percent of all workers were under collective bargaining agreements containing maintenance-of-membership provisions. However, unions considered the device as a short-run solution and by 1946 about one-half of workers under labor contracts were under closed- and union-shop arrangements.[4]

The maintenance-of-membership arrangement is still legal, but utilized relatively infrequently. After appearing in about one-quarter of all contracts in 1946, it declined in importance in the 1950s. Only 7 percent of all contracts studied in 1958–1959 contained the provision.[5] The decline is explained by the trend toward union-shop provisions since the substitute may have met little resistance from employers already acquainted with some form of union security. Employer resistance to union-security provisions is most prevalent the first time a particular type is negotiated.

Two other forms of union security are the agency shop and the preferential hiring arrangement. Both are used relatively infrequently and constitute compromises between the union's goal of greatest possible security and management's reluctance to grant such institutional status. The *agency shop* requires nonunion bargaining-unit workers to make a regular financial contribution to the labor organization, usually the equivalent of union dues and initiation fees. Under this arrangement no individual is required to join a union. Unions charge that some workers attempt to obtain their services without paying for them. This gives them a "free-ride" at the expense of the membership. The incentive for a worker to be a "free-rider" is reduced if he is required to contribute toward the cost of union representation to which he is entitled. The free-rider charge has been advanced because of the legal requirement for unions to represent all members of the bargaining unit without regard to membership.

A second form is the *preferential shop*, which gives union members preference in hiring, but allows the employment of nonunion members only if all union members are employed. Upon employment the worker must join the union. Section 8 (a) (3) of Taft-Hartley prohibits the preferential union shop, but permits the nondiscriminatory hiring hall arrangement. The hiring hall is widely used in the construction industry.[6]

The straight union shop appears to be the most popular form of union security, although some employers and unions have negotiated variations of this type of compulsory union membership. Under some contracts employees not union members when the union-shop agreement becomes effective are not required to join the union. Other agreements may exempt employees with comparatively long company service. Under other contracts old employees (only) are permitted to withdraw from the union at the expiration of the agreement without forfeiting their jobs. Under this arrangement there is a so-called *escape period* of about fifteen days. If an employee does not terminate his union membership within the escape period, he then must maintain his membership under the new arrangement. Newly hired workers, however, are required to join the union without this option.

Some negotiators have adopted variations of the straight union shop; others have devised a number of alternatives to the maintenance-of-membership arrangement. Only at the termination of the agreement are employees under most maintenance-of-membership arrangements permitted to withdraw from the union without forfeiting their jobs. This option is usually extended for only a fifteen-day period at the end of the contract. During this time the employee may terminate his union membership. Many agreements provide less than fifteen days for membership withdrawal. Some contracts permit more than the model fifteen days. If an employee fails to withdraw during this "escape" time, he must almost invariably remain in the union for the duration of the new collective bargaining agreement.

Under some labor agreements, maintenance-of-membership arrangements also provide for an escape period after the *signing* of the agreement to permit withdrawals of existing members from the union. Other agreements do not afford this opportunity to current members of the union, but restrict the principle of voluntary withdrawal to newly hired workers.

Still another variation of maintenance of membership was concluded in the basic steel industry in the early 1950s. Under this arrangement the contract required each new employee to sign an application for membership in the union upon being hired. Such an employee, however, had the option of canceling the application between the fifteenth and thirtieth day of employment. If the application was not canceled during this period, the employee was required to remain in the union as a condition of employment.[7]

Closed Shop. The *closed shop* is a system of union security that requires a worker to join a union before he can qualify for a job. Union membership is the prerequisite for employment. This device is prohibited by the Taft-Hartley Act. Under the closed-shop arrangement the right of management to select workers from the labor market is sharply restricted. The denial of a worker's right to join the organization is tantamount to preventing work in the occupation or plant covered by the closed shop. The *hiring hall* is commonly associated with the closed shop; this arrangement originated partially as a convenience for small employers unable to maintain permanent work crews adequately trained to perform the required tasks. Another reason for hiring halls was the desire on the part of unions to control entry into the craft or occupation and to spread available work equally among the entire membership. The maritime and construction industries illustrate the practice. Discrimination against some individuals and groups was widely publicized when such arrangements were permissible under the law.

The closed shop extended considerable power to labor unions to regulate the supply of labor. They could restrict the number of workers in a particular occupation to keep wage rates high relative to alternative occupations without benefit of such an arrangement. Racketeering has also been associated with unions having a long tradition of requiring the closed shop. It was not at all uncommon for business agents to require excessive fees from individuals seeking the union cards required for work in occupations such as those associated with the printing and construction industries.

Unfair denial by unions of the opportunity of a worker to join a labor union constitutes an antisocial policy, which is properly amenable to public regulation. For example, it was reported in 1949 that thirty-two international unions, comprising about 2.5 million members, discriminated against blacks.[8] It is not known precisely how much discrimination against this group persists in unions at this time. Since many of the unions engaging in this practice hold closed-shop contracts, the policy of discrimination operates to deprive thousands of qualified workers of the freedom to enter an occupation. Factors such as religion, sex, national origin, and ancestry were likewise utilized by some labor unions to deprive workers of the chance to join their organizations. Unreasonable apprenticeship limitations also operate to deny union membership to qualified employees. When labor unions charged excessive initiation fees, the effect again was to close the door to union membership. Professor Taft of Brown University found that some labor unions charged initiation fees which would appear excessive to the average worker.[9] This action reduced from membership a number of individuals capable of performing the work required. As a result union members were placed in a more favorable bargaining position because of the lesser supply of labor available to firms in the labor market.

Union control of the organized small-firm labor market is based on the closed shop and strict regulation of membership admission. Employers are often too small to maintain permanent work forces and thus worker identification is with the union or occupation. Workers usually move frequently from one job to another and are dependent upon the union for job information and protection. This permits local unions to control specific job territories and to do so for the benefit of members. Theoretically, a craftsman such as a union plumber could move from one local labor organization to another with the full job rights enjoyed by any other unionist. In practice, locals often discriminated against members of other locals if unemployment was prevalent in the territory subject to its control. Thus membership transfer from one local to another was abused since it was restricted by some union business agents.

Federal Control of the Closed Shop. Under the terms of the Wagner Act, the issue of the closed shop was left to the determination of the union-management negotiators. This law neither required nor forbade the closed shop. Its only element of control was that to be lawful the arrangement had to be executed with a union representing a majority of bargaining-unit workers. An employer could not give effect to the closed shop when the labor union did not represent a majority of workers in the bargaining unit. However, employers and majority-designated labor unions had full freedom to reject or accept the closed-shop arrangement. In short the Wagner Act provided that the closed-shop issue was to be resolved through collective bargaining. It was not permissible if the union had been dominated or assisted by the employer or if the union did not represent a majority of a unit appropriate for collective bargaining.

The closed shop was provided for in 33 percent of the nation's labor contracts in 1946.[10] With the passage of the Taft-Hartley Act in 1947, this freedom to contract was denied to employer and union negotiators. It is illegal under the terms of the 1947 law.[11] Unions and employers violate the law where a closed-shop arrangement causes the discharge of workers from a position, or where it prevents the hiring of a worker. The NLRB took an early position that it would not respect a contract that included a closed-shop provision. Such an agreement is made unlawful by the mere inclusion of any provision requiring union membership as the prerequisite for the obtainment of a job. Moreover, strikes or picketing for the closed shop is illegal. In 1950 the NLRB ruled that peaceful picketing or even the threat of it to coerce employers into hiring union members only violated Taft-Hartley.[12] There was no request for such a clause in the contract. About a year before this decision the Board held that a strike for a closed-shop clause in a union contract violates Taft-Hartley. The federal courts have upheld both of these Board decisions.[13]

Congress through this Act legislated out of existence a pattern of collective bargaining that over the span of years had become firmly entrenched in American industry. Events soon proved, however, that the closed-shop principle was so deeply rooted in the industrial relations environment that the passage of a law was not to cause its elimination. Working against the successful operation of the 1947 law on the closed-shop issue stood powerful institutional forces. At the time of the passage of the Taft-Hartley Act, millions of employees were working under closed-shop agreements. Some industries—such as printing, building, construction, and maritime—

have operated under the closed shop for scores of years. An elaborate study of 1,716 collective bargaining contracts, conducted in 1954 by the Bureau of Labor Statistics, revealed that less than 5 percent of all agreements sampled contained such a provision.[14] No exhaustive investigation on the subject has been made since 1954 but there is reason to suspect that the closed shop's decline is somewhat exaggerated in the Bureau's figures.

Many employers cooperated actively with unions to continue closed-shop arrangements after 1947. Companies refused to bring charges against unions when they demanded the closed shop. Instead many employers simply agreed to continue closed-shop provisions in collective bargaining contracts executed subsequent to Taft-Hartley passage. In this connection the Senate Committee on Labor and Public Welfare in 1949 reported that "notwithstanding the provisions of the Labor Management Relations Act, closed shop contracts continue to be observed over a wide area of industry."[15] This observation was supported in the Buffalo, New York, area by a careful study of the closed-shop experience. It was reported that "the most noteworthy fact of all presented by the experience in Buffalo is that the new labor law abolished the closed shop in neither form nor substance."[16] The NLRB deals with this illegal form of union security only when formal charges are filed dealing with the issue. The Board does not have the authority to seek out violators of the law.

On July 20, 1950, the NLRB partially "liberalized" the prohibition by Taft-Hartley of the union hiring hall.[17] A union of marine cooks and stewards proposed that a group of maritime employers hire all employees through the hiring hall. The union declared that it was prepared to administer the hiring hall without discrimination against nonunion workers. The Board ruled that such an arrangement would not violate the Taft-Hartley Act. It reached this conclusion even though the union demanded that preference in hiring be granted to employees currently employed by the employers and to those having seniority by reason of employment during the two years immediately preceding execution of the labor contract. The union claimed retention of membership would not be required for a worker to avail himself of the preference benefit.

This arrangement demonstrated the desire of unions to cling to a structure often supported by both labor and management. Board approval, however, appears to clash with the requirements of Taft-Hartley. One member dissented from the majority on the ground that the seniority clause and the hiring by the union in effect provided for preference to union members. The antidiscrimination proposal was labeled as mere "window-dressing."

Many other employers and labor unions, though not renewing closed-shop provisions outright, designed devices which in effect meant that only union members could be hired. Actually, these clauses were a subterfuge to avoid the closed-shop ban. One contract negotiated in 1948 provided that "the employers agree in the hiring of employees to prefer applicants who have previously been employed on vessels of one or more of the companies signatory to the contract."[18] Since the companies and the union, parties to the agreement, operated under a closed-shop contract for a number of years before the passage of Taft-Hartley, all "previously" employed workers were union members. The contract insured the continuation of the closed shop since all employees hired under it belonged to the labor union. Another contract negotiated in 1948 provided that only workers who successfully completed an apprentice training program conducted in a school sponsored by a labor organization were eligible for employment.[19] Such a contract clause effectively continued the closed-shop arrangement. In still another contract the employer gave the labor union the inside track in filling job vacancies.[20] It specified that the employer would give the union forty-eight hours' advance notice before interviewing any new applicants. The implication was that the union would send a qualified union member to apply for the position. Such a tactic obviously precluded hiring of nonunion workers.

These illustrations underline the support of employers for continuation of the closed-shop principle. Why have employers agreed to the closed shop even though the arrangement has been outlawed? Two factors are involved in the answer to this question: either employers have been satisfied with the closed shop or else they do not want to invite possible trouble, such as strikes, by denying union demands for the closed shop. This latter consideration is of considerable importance during periods of relatively high levels of economic prosperity such as existed in the first few years after the passage of Taft-Hartley. In short, employers did not want to risk interruption to production in a period of high profits. Despite the soundness of this argument, the fact remains that many employers favored the closed-shop arrangement. In the Buffalo study, previously noted, the investigation disclosed that in one industry an employer association spokesman said in support of the closed shop that "relations had been good and the closed shop worked satisfactorily."[21] Undoubtedly, many employers were of the opinion that the device was the prerequisite to harmonious labor relations. For these reasons they actively cooperated with labor unions to avoid the closed-shop ban of Taft-Hartley. The law is still evaded in some industries.

Brown-Olds Doctrine: A New Board Effort. By 1956 the NLRB was intent on destroying the closed shop. The opportunity was provided in the *Brown-Olds* case involving a collective bargaining agreement that contained several of the union's bylaws, working rules, and regulations requiring employees to obtain union clearance before seeking employment.[22] The union constitution and bylaws required members to obtain a union work order before accepting employment and gave the business agent power to remove members from the job for delinquency in paying dues and assessments.

The law judge ruled that the specific provisions constituted an unlawful closed-shop agreement in violation of Section 8 (a) (3) of Taft-Hartley. Upon review, the Board decided to use its remedial powers to correct union abuses of the closed-shop prohibitions. Union dues were to be returned to members to correct violations. It held that "the remedy of reimbursement of all such monies is appropriate and necessary to expunge the illegal effects of the unfair labor practices found here." A 1943 Supreme Court case in which a company union was held illegal by its very existence in that it was not formed by employee free choice was used as a precedent. Return of dues was one means of disestablishing the union.[23] The Board in the *Brown-Olds* case established the rule that a union would be required to reimburse employees for dues and assessments collected under illegal closed-shop agreements during a period beginning six months prior to the date unfair labor practice charges were filed. The doctrine was to fall upon both unions and management executing illegal closed-shop provisions.

It appears that the Board intended to invoke a financial penalty upon the parties to such contracts for the purpose of ending the closed-shop arrangement. Labor and management were put on guard that they would jointly be held responsible to reimburse all members for dues and other assessments paid from the time a remedial order was issued extending to six months previous to the filing of the charge. For example, if there were five hundred union members, all would be reimbursed for all monies paid during this period of time. Financially, the cost would run into the thousands of dollars. The doctrine was applied in many cases. The remedy was not deemed appropriate in all cases involving a defective union-security clause. It was applied when the condition of employment was prior union membership, which granted unions control over the hiring of employees.[24]

The Board later extended the remedy to hiring-hall arrangements even though they were not connected with a closed shop. The Board justified the extension by arguing that these arrangements had a coercive influence on work applicants to join the union.[25] That is, if an employee obtained workers exclusively through a hiring hall, the worker's first point of contact would be with the union. Both tacit and overt pressure could be applied to force union membership before a job opening would be made available. The Board decided to eliminate these pressures on workers.

The U.S. Supreme Court reviewed the *Brown-Olds* doctrine in 1961.[26] The case involved a collective bargaining contract with Mechanical Handling Systems, Inc,. of Indianapolis, Indiana. In it the company agreed to provisions requiring it to abide by the union rules and regulations requiring employment of only its members. The case arose when two job applicants, members of another union, were denied employment because they could not obtain referral from the union. The Board upon review applied its *Brown-Olds* doctrine requiring reimbursement to all employees of any assessments collected by the union starting from six months prior to the date unfair labor practice charges were filed.

Upon review, the Supreme Court ruled that the Board's *Brown-Olds* doctrine was punitive and not remedial in character. As such the Board exceeded its statutory powers. No evidence was presented indicating that a single union member had been coerced to join or remain in the labor organization. Indeed, all the workers may have been union members for many years. Thus the requirement to pay back all dues and assessments to members starting six months prior to the charge benefited union members and did not provide a remedy to persons denied work in the first place. Workers denied employment because of the labor contract were not benefited by the remedy. The Court held that the only power given the Board was that sufficient to remedy the harm done to persons denied work because of the illegal union-security provisions. It could only require a company to hire a worker that was denied employment and order back pay concerning lost wages and benefits. Any other construction of the law was not within the province of the NLRB. The Court could not agree with the implicit reasoning of the Board that the very existence of a closed-shop arrangement diminishes worker freedom of choice to join or refrain from joining unions guaranteed by Taft-Hartley. Board remedial policy could not be justified solely on its deterrent qualities. Thus the punitive financial aspect of *Brown-Olds* was held illegal by the Supreme Court.

Hiring-Hall Regulations. The key to the union-controlled and -administered hiring hall is the closed shop since, to avail himself of its services, a worker originally had to become a union member. A review of the legislative history of Taft-Hartley establishes the fact that its proponents meant to eliminate the union hiring hall. During debate on the law Senator Taft, in illustrating the scope of the prohibition of the closed shop, declared that its abolishment "is best exemplified by the so-called hiring halls in the west coast where shipowners cannot employ anyone unless the union sends him to them."[27]

Soon after Taft-Hartley passage the NLRB ruled that this traditional method for the organization of the labor market within industries of intermittent and casual employment violates the terms of the 1947 law. In *National Maritime Union* the controlling case on the hiring-hall issue, the NLRB held hiring halls unlawful because they result in unlawful discrimination against nonunion workers and provide illegal preference for union members.[28]

The union hiring hall was first outlawed in the maritime industry, but the rule applied throughout industry. While commenting on the scope of the prohibition, Mr. Denham, former General Counsel of the NLRB, declared that

> in the construction industry the matter of the union shop has been the source of much uneasiness ever since the Taft-Hartley Act went on the books. The union shop provision of the law definitely was designed to do away with the closed shop, under which a man was required to be a member of the contracting union before he could ever be considered for a job. Now, all of that is prohibited, as also is the use of the hiring hall, either directly or indirectly. There simply is no further such thing as the closed shop or the hiring hall, nor any legitimate way by which the employer can contract to prefer union members over non-union members in the matter of hiring.[29]

Despite the fact that the hiring-hall arrangement was at first considered per se illegal, the NLRB in a 1950 case held that the hiring-hall provisions of a labor contract did not violate the law.[30] The contract stated that hiring provisions would be administered without discrimination and that "no retention of membership is required in order for preference to be granted under the agreement." Essentially, the Board was attempting to preserve an arrangement that had a long history of accommodation in several industries. In 1958 the Board set forth rules to deal with hiring halls.

Mountain Pacific Doctrine. The NLRB ruled in 1958 that hiring-hall arrangements were not per se illegal if the union and company agreed to a number of specific safeguards. The agreement had to specifically provide that: (1) selection of applicants for referral to jobs shall be without regard to union membership requirements; (2) the employer shall retain the right to reject any applicant referred by the union; and (3) standards shall be posted in the hiring hall for employee inspection.

Essentially, the Board established that contractual hiring-hall arrangements without inclusion of the above safeguards would be subject to the *Brown-Olds* doctrine requiring reimbursement of all member dues and assessments from six months prior to the filing of unfair labor practice charges. The Supreme Court reviewed the Board's hiring-hall standards on the same day in 1961 that it reviewed the *Brown-Olds* doctrine.

In the case before the Court a union and a group of employers had agreed that casual employees would be hired only by union hiring-hall referral.[31] Also it was agreed that referral would be on the basis of seniority and without regard to an employee's union membership. The Board previously had ruled that the hiring arrangement was unlawful because it did not contain the *Mountain Pacific* safeguards.

The Supreme Court reversed the NLRB by holding it had exceeded its allowable powers. An exclusive hiring-hall arrangement was not per se illegal under the Act without specific safeguards imposed by the Board. The Court held that discrimination in hiring cannot be inferred from the face of the contract when it provides for nondiscriminatory action. Board authority was provided only for remedying cases where discrimination exists—to which Taft-Hartley is addressed. General categories do not permit a logical basis upon which the NLRB can properly remedy unfair labor practices where individuals are discriminated against with regard to hire or tenure of employment.

In short, the NLRB is required to examine the discriminatory nature of each hiring-hall arrangement formally presented to it. It cannot hold such arrangements as illegal per se if certain safeguards are not contained explicitly in the contract. The Supreme Court requires the Board to look at the administrative operation of each arrangement prior to reaching a decision. If the hiring hall reveals discriminatory hiring practices, each violation must be remedied separately and without broad remedial categories such as provided by the *Brown-Olds* doctrine. It is obvious that the Supreme Court tacitly gave approval to the traditional arrangements of some industries. It did not require a rigid adherence to Taft-Hartley if hiring halls are free from restrictive practices.

Landrum-Griffin Changes. The Congress gave special treatment to the building construction industry in 1959 when it amended Taft-Hartley. Section 8 (f) of Landrum-Griffin permits *prehire agreements* in the construction industry and permits compulsory union membership seven days after employment. In other industries union membership may be required only after a worker is employed thirty days. The reason for special treatment for the construction industry involves its short and intermittent nature of employment.

Prehire contracts are valid even though the majority status of the union has not been established at the time they are negotiated. Congress intended, however, that the prehire agreements apply only when a previous bargaining relationship had not existed.[32] This means that a contract may be negotiated before any employee is hired; the result is that employees do not have the opportunity to vote for bargaining agents. Even so, such agreements are valid when they require union membership after the seventh day of employment; when the union must be notified of vacancies and must be given the opportunity to refer workers; and when priority in employment is based on specified objective criteria. Though the short-term character of construction employment may justify this feature of the 1959 law, it still tends to conflict with the general public policy of permitting employees to choose their own unions.

A Board majority in *Smith Construction Co.* attempted to accommodate the prehire agreement authorization with other sections of the law.[33] It was held that Congress as evidenced by the final proviso to Section 8(f) intended to permit a test of majority status and unit appropriateness at any time during the contract and that prehire agreements did not prohibit examination through the litigation of refusal to bargain charges. Thus, an employer may break the prehire contract at will because the final proviso makes him immune from unfair labor practice liability. If employers wish to break such contracts, they may do so merely by challenging the union's representative status. According to the Board, either party may ignore the prehire agreement without the usual threat of statutory refusal to bargain violation remedies. Board and court guidelines requiring successor employers to assume a predecessor's contract do not apply because prehire agreements do not presume continuing majority status on the part of a union.[34]

The *Smith Construction Co.* ruling could result in more instability in the industry because of growing competition between union and nonunion firms. Prehire agreements are now unenforceable before the NLRB. The incident of future unilateral revocation of such contracts depends on the organization in the industry. Unions may also abuse contractual terms which could place relatively small contractors in jeopardy of being unable to survive, but, again, this depends on a relatively high level of union organization and the prospects that neither the Board nor the courts will change the rule.

THE UNION SHOP

The Taft-Hartley Act maintained the union-shop device as a permissible form of union security. The statute, however, closely controls the circumstances under which the arrangement may be incorporated into collective bargaining contracts and regulates its implementation. The only legal limitation contained in the Wagner Act was that the labor organization negotiating a union-security arrangement had to represent a majority of the bargaining unit. There was no other barrier to the type of agreement that could be included in the contract.

Taft-Hartley and the Union Shop

Under the terms of the 1947 law, employers and labor unions are permitted to execute a union-shop agreement requiring membership as a condition of continued employment on or after thirty days following their employment. Conditions, however, were attached to its legality.

Until 1951 the most demanding prerequisite for the union shop and the maintenance-of-membership arrangement as well was that a special authorization election had to be held by the NLRB. The referendum was known as the *union-shop election.* This election should not be confused with the representation or certification election. It will be recalled that a certification election refers to a poll to determine whether or not a labor union represents a majority of workers for the purpose of collective bargaining. The union-shop election was a special referendum to determine whether or not a majority of bargaining-unit workers approved of their union negotiating an agreement making union membership a condition of employment after the required waiting period. The Board would not conduct a union-shop election unless the labor organization petitioning for such an election represented a majority of workers in the bargaining unit.

Another distinction between representation and union-shop elections turns on the concept of majority. For purposes of representation a labor union was required only to win a majority of the votes cast. But for the union shop the union was required to receive the votes of a majority of those workers *eligible* to vote in the election.[35] This meant that a worker who did not cast a ballot actually voted against the union shop or, for that matter, the maintenance-of-membership provision if it were in question. Any worker who did not choose to vote or who was laid off or who failed to vote because of illness or any other reason was counted as voting against union security. It is obvious that Taft-Hartley went beyond normal election procedures to make it difficult for unions to obtain union-security provisions requiring membership as a condition of employment. Even if the union shop was authorized by a majority of the bargaining unit, there was no guarantee that it could be obtained. Authorization by union members merely gave the parties the right to negotiate on the issue.[36] Employers may have been in a position to resist successfully the union-shop demand despite the outcome of the election.

Not only were elections required to authorize the parties to negotiate union-shop terms, but employees had the right to petition the NLRB to hold deauthorization elections. A petition including a minimum of 30 percent of the bargaining unit was required. A union loss would mean that the union shop was no longer a valid provision in the collective bargaining agreement. Unions lose well over one-half of all such cases that proceed to the election stage. For example, in fiscal 1967 unions lost 67.2 percent of 67 elections involving 5,019 eligible voters.[37] This high percentage of deauthorization losses has held with considerable consistency throughout the years.

Labor unions were required also to satisfy several other conditions before they could use NLRB machinery to obtain the union shop. They were required to file financial statements and other documents such as bylaws and constitutions with the Secretary of Labor. Fulfillment of the statutory requirements was proved to the NLRB by receipt of a compliance number from that officer. This number in turn had to be filed with the Board along with non-communist affidavits signed by local and international union officers. All these materials were required in the regional office as well as the one in Washington, D.C. Employers were not required to meet the same standards to utilize Board facilities.[38] The compliance and filing requirements of Taft-Hartley were repealed in 1959.[39]

Repeal of Union-Shop Election Requirement. The assumption of Taft-Hartley that workers would reject a proposal that required union membership as a condition of employment if given an opportunity in a secret-ballot election was not realized in practice. The election requirement was repealed on October 22, 1951, by the Taft-Humphrey amendment of the Taft-Hartley law.[40]

During the four years and two months in which the union-shop election was required, the Board conducted 46,119 polls. Union-shop agreements were authorized in 44,795 of the referendums, or in 97 percent of those conducted. In the polls 6,542,564 workers were eligible to vote, of whom 5,547,478 or 84.8 percent cast valid ballots. Of those voting 5,071,988 or 77.5 percent of the workers voted in favor of union security.[41] In signing the October 1951 amendment, President Truman stated that union-shop elections "have involved expenditures in excess of $3,000,000 of public funds. Experience has proved them to be not only costly, and burdensome, but unnecessary as well."[42] The union-shop deauthorization provision of the 1947 law was not repealed and is still a feature of national labor policy.

The Aerospace Experience. In 1962 union-security disputes broke out in the aerospace industry involving a union demand for the union shop. The maintenance-of-membership device was still used in the industry located on the West Coast. President Kennedy was successful in obtaining agreement to have a special fact-finding board make recommendations to resolve the dispute. This group proposed that the NLRB conduct secret-ballot elections that would result in union victories if two-thirds of the employees voted for the union shop. The unions lost in every case.

The overwhelming percentages of votes cast for unions during the 1947–1951 union-shop election period were not duplicated in 1962. Various elements seem to have had an influence on the outcome of the elections. It is possible that the most important aspect, the provision dealing with wages and other economic terms, had already been settled. A vote for the union shop was not necessary on the part of workers to show the companies they backed the unions.[43] A later case in the same industry with all the issues the same as before, except that the union-shop vote was held before all the other issues were settled, resulted in a union victory at the polls. It may well be that labor organizations are increasingly viewed by workers as economic organizations with the responsibility of delivering an acceptable package of wage and related benefits. A determination that a union has little to offer at the time a union-security election is held will probably result in defeat for the organization.

Nonpayment-of-Dues Feature of Taft-Hartley. Section 8 (a) (3) of Taft-Hartley states that the only condition whereby a worker may lose his job for nonmembership in a union is for nonpayment of dues. It has been established by Board cases that unions do not have a right to prescribe rules that interfere with the relationship between employee and employer except for the nonpayment of dues.[44]

In 1955 the NLRB established a policy prohibiting discharge of a worker if, at any time before the discharge became effective, the employee made full and unqualified tender of dues to the union.[45] This rule was changed in 1962 when the Board held that employee delay of dues payment was at odds with the congressional purpose in permitting the parties to negotiate union-shop agreements.[46] An automatic determination was eliminated in that the Board decided to review the record to determine why an employee delayed dues payment under a valid union security agreement. In still another case the Board held that a union has the duty to inform members as to what their obligations are upon joining.[47] If workers are informed of their obligations at the time they become members, they have the responsibility to tender dues in accordance with union rules or run the risk of discharge.

An employee who offers to pay dues is not in violation of the Act even if the labor organization has expelled him for lack of conformity to internal union rules. Union-shop contracts therefore merely offer unions financial security. It will be recalled that employers are not forced to agree to such a provision. The same was true with union-shop elections; a union victory did not guarantee success in obtaining such a feature in the contract. In short, Taft-Hartley permits the union shop as a condition of employment and then proceeds to dilute its enforcement. The basic reason for this arrangement was to provide both employment rights for workers and financial security for unions. As early as 1949 the Board held that a worker does not have to join a union even though a union-shop arrangement exists. His only obligation under the law is his willingness to tender the dues and initiation fees required by the union. If a union imposes any other qualifications and conditions for membership with which an employee is unwilling to comply, the employee may be excluded from union membership, but not from his job.[48]

A clarification of union authority to deal with employees on a basis other than nonpayment of dues was set forth by the NLRB in a 1964 case.[49] One section of the law provides that "this paragraph shall not impair the right of a labor organization to prescribe its own rules with respect to the acquisition or retention of membership therein."[50] In *Wisconsin Motors* the United Auto Workers Union imposed production quotas upon its members which limited the amount of incentive pay they could earn through increased production. The union initiated suit in a state court to collect fines from violators of the rules, but did not seek assistance from the employer through the employment relationship. No attempt was made to adversely affect their status as employees.

The Board held the union action lawful since an attempt was made to enforce internal union policy only. It was pointed out that the union carefully restricted the enforcement of its rule to an area involving the status of the individual as a *member* rather than as an *employee*.[51]

It is important to note that the imposition of a fine by a union on a disobedient member and a subsequent refusal to pay it cannot be used by either the union or the employer as lawful grounds to fire him from his job. This holds even though the member is expelled from union membership. The only obligation of union membership under Taft-Hartley is payment of dues and initiation fees. The Board's *Wisconsin Motors* decision was widely criticized by the Ervin Subcommittee on Separation of Powers.[52] It stated that this "case is not an isolated instance of . . . brutal trampling on the statutory rights of employees in order to enhance union power." An appeals court upheld the NLRB. Four workers involved in the case went to the Supreme Court.

The production quota case was decided by the U.S. Supreme Court in 1969.[53] The NLRB's *Wisconsin Motors* case was upheld by a 7-1 decision in the *Scofield* v. *NLRB* case. The Court held that a union is free "to enforce a properly adopted rule which reflects a legitimate union interest, impairs no policy Congress has imbedded in the labor laws and is reasonably enforced against union members." Arbitrary rules of a union officer are probably unlawful. The ceiling rate on production had been indirectly involved in union-management negotiations regarding the *machine rate*. The machine rate was defined in the agreement as the production level of an "average competent operator working at a reasonable pace."

Implicit in the Court's decision was the *block-of-work doctrine*. Adherents of this philosophy contend that only so much work is available in the short run. Action on the part of workers to exceed production quotas could cause other workers to lose their jobs because of inadequate product demand. It was upon this argument that Justice White, speaking for the Court, held that the union had a legitimate interest in the situation.

Oddly enough, the Court stated that if ambitious workers were frustrated by union imposed ceilings on production, they were free to "leave the union." This pronouncement did not receive elaboration, but it may be of future interest because union membership is a requirement for continued employment at many plants. It may have meant that a disgruntled member may leave the union without loss of job if he continues to tender the required dues. This determination would be consistent with Supreme Court decisions previously discussed.

Landrum-Griffin added an additional protective feature for individual freedom. Union members are now permitted to file suit in a U.S. district court if they are thrown out of a labor organization for an unfair reason or by use of unfair procedures. The nonpayment-of-dues feature of Taft-Hartley, however, remains intact and is still applicable in the enforcement of national labor policy.[54]

The nonpayment-of-dues feature of Taft-Hartley tends to weaken the union-shop arrangement. The provision would be unnecessary to protect individual worker freedoms if labor organizations with contracts requiring membership were required to set up "watchdog" committees such as the one established by the United Auto

Workers.[55] The UAW committee is composed of an impartial outside membership with authority to review union action. If the union is held to have behaved unfairly, it can be required to bring about reinstatement of jobs and any back pay for time lost off the job. Union constitutions can provide for such committees.

Another method that could be used to protect the integrity of the union shop is a union constitutional change permitting arbitration of individual membership loss when requested. The judgment of the arbitrator would be final and binding.

Either the watchdog committee or ad hoc arbitration could eliminate the need for government to deal with discriminatory union action regarding the hire or tenure of workers. At the same time labor organizations could become more responsible to members, which should have the effect of strengthening the free collective bargaining process. However, as the law now stands expulsion from a union for any reason other than nonpayment of dues or initiation fees cannot result in loss of employment. The NLRB will order the reinstatement of an employee to his job with back pay in cases where the law is violated.

Board Control Over Union-Security Clauses. The NLRB established principles to guide it in determining the effect of union-security clauses on bargaining representation election petitions. The Board has consistently held that a valid collective bargaining contract will bar an election for at least a twelve-month period.

In 1958 the Board held that the existence of a contract would not stop it from holding an election if the agreement did not reflect the limitations placed on union security by Taft-Hartley.[56] However, this rule was not permitted to stand by the U.S. Supreme Court. In 1961 in two cases before it the Court held that such a mechanistic approach presumed illegality and amounted to a prejudgment of the labor organization.[57] The Board was forced to revise its rules regarding union-security clauses as bars to representation elections.

Revised rules were established in the same year, 1961, in the *Paragon Products Corporation* case.[58] It was deemed necessary for a union-security clause to be clearly unlawful on its face to permit a representation election before the end of a twelve-month period. The forms of unlawful union security include those which expressly and without doubt require that employers give union members preference in hiring, layoffs, and seniority. Also, unlawful provisions exist if employees are given less than the thirty-day grace period provided for union membership in Taft-Hartley. Contracts which require that employees pay the union money other than periodic dues and initiation fees required of all unionists are unlawful. Any other payments required as a condition of employment will not bar the holding of a representation election.

Ambiguous union-security clauses will not necessarily relax the twelve-month rule unless the provision is found illegal by the Board or a federal court. Each case therefore must be investigated and an appropriate remedy provided as a result of findings. Mechanical approaches to the problem of union security are discouraged by the U.S. Supreme Court.

SECTION 14 (b) AND RIGHT-TO-WORK LAWS

Right-to-work is a term normally used to describe state statutory or state constitutional provisions banning the requirement of union membership as a condition of employment. A significant feature of *right-to-work laws* is that they not only outlaw the execution of union-security arrangements in the area of intrastate commerce, but they also forbid the negotiation of compulsory union membership provisions within the area of interstate commerce. It will be recalled that Taft-Hartley outlawed the closed shop, but permitted negotiation of union shops or maintenance-of-membership arrangements. However, Section 14 (b) of the Act permits the states to enact laws applying to the area of interstate commerce that not only outlaw the closed shop, but that make any form of union security illegal. This provision of the Taft-Hartley Act states:

> Nothing in this Act shall be construed as authorizing the execution or application of agreements requiring membership in a labor organization as a condition of employment in any State or Territory in which such execution or application is prohibited by State or Territorial law.[59]

In this manner the federal government invited the states to legislate in the area reserved by the Constitution of the United States to the federal government.

Action of the states to eliminate union-security arrangements began several years before the passage of the 1947 law. In 1944 Arkansas and Florida amended their constitutions to outlaw all agreements making union membership a condition of employment.[60] The Florida amendment provided that "the rights of persons to work shall not be denied or abridged on account of membership in any labor union or labor organization."

After Florida and Arkansas set the pattern, Arizona, Nebraska, and South Dakota in 1946 passed amendments to their constitutions to prohibit all species of union-security arrangements.[61] In 1947 state prohibition of union security became even more widespread. During early 1947 seven states banned all forms of union security.[62] In these states the method of eliminating union security was the enactment of statutes instead of constitutional amendments. Thus at the time Taft-Hartley was passed twelve states had already prohibited all types of union security.

Without Section 14 (b) no state could lawfully enact right-to-work legislation applying to the area of interstate commerce, since such laws would conflict with the doctrine of national supremacy. National supremacy in the area of interstate commerce was established by the U.S. Supreme Court in 1819.[63]

If it desired, Congress when it passed Taft-Hartley could have made such state action inoperative in the area of interstate commerce. Even so a constitutional issue was advanced to test the ability of states to enact laws that in fact become superior to federal law in the area of interstate commerce. In 1949 the U.S. Supreme Court held that Section 14 (b) of Taft-Hartley and state right-to-work legislation enacted under its authority are compatible with the federal Constitution.[64]

Nineteen states now prohibit all forms of union security.[65] Two other states, Louisiana and Indiana, enacted such statutes; both repealed them either totally or in part. Louisiana maintains right-to-work legislation, but it is only applicable to agriculture. Organized labor has conducted a persistent campaign at both the national and state levels to repeal Section 14 (b) and the particular state laws in existence. The actual effect upon labor relations is highly debatable and is believed by some observers to be largely symbolic and political rather than economic and significant to the collective bargaining relationship.[66] Even so the United States Congress came close to repealing Section 14 (b) in its 1965–1966 sessions.[67] The effort failed. At the time of this writing organized labor continues its pressure to keep the issue before the Congress.

At the state level organized labor has launched extensive campaigns either to prevent passage of right-to-work laws or to repeal those already enacted. In 1958 six states voted on right-to-work proposals.[68] The issue was placed on the ballot in California, Colorado, Idaho, Kansas, Ohio, and Washington as a result of initiative petitions. In all states but Kansas the measure was defeated. Since 1944 ten states have defeated right-to-work measures by referendum.[69]

Union opposition was weak in Indiana when the law was enacted in 1957.[70] However, faced with the occurrence of such legislation or its threat in the several states, the labor movement stiffened its political opposition by intensified efforts to register voters for the 1958 elections. The defeat of Republican congressmen in Indiana and elsewhere has been credited partially to union efforts to increase voter participation at the polls.[71] The Indiana law was repealed in 1965.

In Arizona organized labor has not been successful in its political efforts to repeal the constitutional amendment that became effective November 25, 1946. However, the lack of enforcement provisions in the amendment rendered it relatively ineffectual for a short time. Bills were introduced in the state senate in 1947 for the express purpose of specifying which actions were illegal and prescribing penalties for those actions. On March 15, 1947, both houses of the legislature passed a law providing for enforcement of the amendment.

The law did not contain an emergency clause, which would have made it effective immediately if signed by the governor. Thus the law would become effective ninety days after the close of the regular legislative session. This pause between enactment and effectiveness provided time for political maneuvering. Organized labor circulated petitions to obtain voter signatures for the purpose of referring the law to the people at the polls. Filing of the referendum petitions with the Secretary of State automatically made the law ineffective until a final determination could be made at the polls.

The enforcement measure was carried at the polls by a greater margin than in 1946 when the original right-to-work amendment was approved. In fact there was a 4 percent increase in votes between November 25, 1946, and November 22, 1948.

Union political fortunes were at a low ebb in the period immediately after World War II. The merger of the AFL and CIO in 1955 was a partial reflection of such union fortunes. By 1958 unions were able to prevent enactment of right-to-work laws in five out of six states. In 1965–1966, as mentioned, Section 14 (b) was almost repealed by Congress. Regardless of the fate of right-to-work legislation, however, it seems possible that the issue of union security provisions will remain a controversial one for some time to come.

At the very least, Section 14 (b) has created unequal labor relations conditions among the several states. In states without right-to-work legislation forms of union security are often permitted that are outlawed in the nineteen states with restrictive legislation. These states are located primarily in the south and southwestern parts of the United States and use their restrictive laws on union security to support their competitive drives to attract industry from other sections of the country. The economic effect that these legal differences may have on industry location evades verification. But the Congress itself has imposed an atmosphere of potentially unequal competition for industry between the states. However, this is not the case in the railroad and airline industries whereby Congress in 1951 nullified state right-to-work laws as they apply to these two industries.

UNION SECURITY UNDER THE RAILWAY LABOR ACT

The Railway Labor Act was enacted in 1926 to regulate labor relations in the railroad industry. In 1936 it was amended to extend its coverage to air transportation. The act was amended in 1934 making all forms of compulsory union membership illegal and enforcing violations by imposing criminal penalties. The major support for prohibiting compulsory union membership came from the railway unions themselves. It was feared that any form of union security would diminish the ability of the railway unions to compete with company-supported labor organizations for members. By 1951 the contest between the two groups had been resolved sufficiently to change the attitude of railway unions toward compulsory union membership. Nearly 80 percent of railroad employees were members of labor unions free from company domination.

One amendment in 1951 to the Railway Labor Act provided that "union shop contracts could be entered into notwithstanding . . . any other statute or law . . . of any state."[72]

Some employees of the Union Pacific Railroad Company challenged the constitutionality of the Railway Labor Act's union security provision in the Nebraska courts.[73] Nebraska has a right-to-work provision in its constitution and the workers claimed that compulsory union membership was in violation of the state constitution. The labor contract signed by the company with the various railway unions required membership within sixty days that was to be maintained thereafter as a condition of continued employment.

The Nebraska trial court held that the union-shop agreement was a violation of the First Amendment to the U.S. Constitution since it deprived employees of their freedom of association and of the Fifth Amendment since members were required to pay for many things besides the cost of collective bargaining. No valid federal law superseded the right-to-work provision of the Nebraska Constitution for these reasons. The decision was upheld by the Nebraska Supreme Court. The U.S. Supreme Court reviewed the decision upon appeal.

The U.S. Supreme Court reversed the Nebraska courts and held that Congress had the authority to permit the union-shop arrangement notwithstanding any state laws to the contrary. Federal supremacy over interstate commerce eliminates the ability of states to regulate in this area unless legislation specifically cedes authority to them. Also the Court reasoned that the union-shop provision of the Railway Labor Act is only permissive. The parties were not compelled to reach agreement on these provisions. Should they desire to include the union shop in the collective bargaining contract, state right-to-work laws would not prevail over the will of Congress.

Thus Congress has established a dual standard regarding union security. The railway and airline industries are permitted to negotiate union-shop arrangements under the Railway Labor Act. Industry in general is prohibited from doing so where states enact restrictive laws in the form of right-to-work statutes or constitutional amendments. Political pressures account for these differences. There is no economic justification for or against the permissiveness extended railway and airline employees that could not be identically applied to employees under Taft-Hartley.

UNION SHOP AND UNION POLITICAL ACTIVITIES

The Supreme Court's decision in *Hanson* dealt with the contention that compulsory union membership forced workers into ideological and political conformity. In this case, the Court held that the charge was not supported by the record. However, the Georgia court held that when a union shop was in effect, the use of dues to support political activities was a violation of the U.S. Constitution.

Upon review the U.S. Supreme Court agreed that Congress had not intended to require workers to support union political activities to which they objected. However, the high court rejected the Georgia court's position that a union shop was illegal just because a union engaged in political activities. Instead the remedy was to either refund to a complaining member the proportion of the individual's dues money expended on such activities or to refund that proportion spent on activities to which the member advised the union he was opposed.[74]

The Court had occasion to deal with the matter again in 1963 under the Railway Labor Act. It held that a member could "contract out" of all union political activities and need not specify only those which were objectionable.[75] Not only would the member receive a refund of the proportion of his dues money (same proportion that union political expenditures were to total expenditures) spent on political matters, but his future dues would be reduced in the same proportion.

The remedy provided was for the purpose of eliminating the ideological and political conformity that a union shop might require if a member were not able to refrain from financial support of union political activities considered contrary to the belief of the individual. All members of the union were not granted the remedy, only those who actually objected to the use of funds for political purposes. Class action suits were eliminated. Thus, actual drain on a union treasury resulting from a court decision would probably be very small. Since the law of union security is now the same under the Taft-Hartley and Railway Labor Act, it follows that the U.S. Supreme Court decisions arising under the Railway Labor Act are applicable to Taft-Hartley.

THE AGENCY SHOP

The agency shop, along with the maintenance-of-membership arrangement, was first used during World War II when the National War Labor Board refused to extend closed-shop and union-shop arrangements to industries when they were not negotiated prior to the war. National labor policy required unions to represent all bargaining-unit workers, even those who are not union members. For this reason unions argue that there is an incentive for many workers to refrain from union membership since they are entitled to union benefits without paying their share of the financial costs. Such workers are referred to as "free-riders." The agency shop has been attractive to unions representing workers in right-to-work states. When the arrangement is successfully negotiated, an employee does not have to join a union but is required to pay a fee for union services as a condition of employment. The fee required is usually the equivalent of periodic dues and initiation fees required of members. The NLRB approved of the agency shop as a valid form of union security in a 1950 case.[76] However, this case involved a contract that had been negotiated prior to the enactment of Taft-Hartley. Two years later the Board ruled that Congress did not intend to outlaw the requirement for nonunion members to provide payment to unions for collective bargaining services when employers agree to such a provision.[77]

The agency-shop arrangement was seized upon by unions as a means of avoiding the financial afflictions of right-to-work laws. However, ten of the states explicitly prohibited the payment of union dues as a condition of employment.[78] The others were silent on the issue. Unions moved to obtain the agency shop in states that had not referred to the arrangement in their constitutions or statutes.

Agency-Shop Treatment in Indiana. The legality of the agency shop under the Indiana right-to-work law was presented to the Superior Court of Lake County, Indiana, in May 1958 soon after passage of the law.[79] A union demanded the agency-shop arrangement from an employer. The company refused and petitioned the court for an injunction to restrain the union from seeking the device, contending that it violated state law.

In refusing to grant the restraining order, the court held that the agency shop was legal because the Indiana right-to-work law did not specifically outlaw it. The court stated that "nowhere in the Indiana Act is there a specific prohibition against the payment of fees or charges to a labor organization" and that "while it prohibits agreements revolving around membership in a union, it is completely silent as regards the payment of fees, dues, or other charges to a labor organization." The court claimed that if the legislature intended to make the agency shop unlawful, it would have adopted appropriate language and its failure to do so cannot "be deemed to be accidental." This conclusion was reached after a careful review of the legislative history.

In further support of its position, the court pointed out that the majority of state right-to-work laws, beyond forbidding membership in a union as a condition of employment, also outlawed agreements requiring the payment of any fees to a labor organization. The Indiana court went one step further and suggested that no state could lawfully enact legislation prohibiting the arrangement within interstate commerce. It argued that Section 14 (b) of Taft-Hartley only gave the states permission to outlaw arrangements requiring membership in a union as a condition of employment. The law did not authorize the states to forbid arrangements requiring compulsory financial contributions to a labor organization. In this respect the court stated that a

> clear reading of that particular statute indicates that the only authority granted to the states was to outlaw agreements conditioning employment upon membership in a union. To the extent that an agency shop involves a totally different

concept, it would appear that any attempt by a state legislature to intervene in this field would be an usurpation of the federal regulation of commerce.[80]

In another state, Arizona, its Supreme Court had already implied that the agency shop was not an acceptable form of union security in the state. In 1957 it held that picketing for such a clause in a collective bargaining agreement was illegal; however, the agency-shop issue, as such, was not the question before the court for the issue had been abandoned since the trial court ruled it illegal in 1954.[81]

Attorney generals of five other states have rendered opinions on the legality of the agency shop.[82] Only North Dakota has permitted a limited form of the arrangement. In that state the fees paid to unions by nonmembers must be based solely on the cost of representation.[83]

The NLRB and U.S. Supreme Court Deal with the Issue. Because of the intensive struggle over the agency-shop issue in right-to-work states, the NLRB and the U.S. Supreme Court were ultimately involved in resolving the problem. Since the Board changes politically, confusion arose over the authority of states to decide the legality of agency-shop arrangements and then to enforce their decisions.

In February 1961 the NLRB, composed predominantly of Eisenhower appointees, ruled on the legality of agency-shop arrangements under the Taft-Hartley Act.[84] The Board held that an agency-shop clause in labor contracts was illegal because the device was different from a union shop. Since the parties engaged in collective bargaining were not free to require union membership as a condition of employment in right-to-work states, they also were not free to impose any lesser form of union security as a condition of employment. The two devices were held different because the agency shop did not require union membership as a condition of employment.

The Board reasoned that the agency shop forced workers to engage in union activities by forcing them to pay union dues. Thus such an agreement was seen as a clear violation of Section 7 of Taft-Hartley, which provides that employees have the right to refrain from all union activities except to the extent that they are required to join unions as a condition of employment. The obvious implication of the rule was that the agency shop was an illegal device under Taft-Hartley in every state and parties to collective bargaining agreements were not free to utilize the arrangement.

In September of the same year the Board, predominantly Kennedy appointees, decided to reconsider the same case.[85] The issue before the NLRB in the second *General Motors* case was the level of government that should control the negotiation of agency-shop agreements. The Board held that Taft-Hartley merely provided that the union shop was the maximum form of union security allowed. But the agency shop was held to be a lesser form of union security and therefore in the permissible bargaining category. Thus the agency-shop arrangement was held subject only to federal control. Such a decision, if permitted to stand, would have legalized the device in industries in all states subject to Taft-Hartley provisions, although the Board did not deal with the Section 14 (b) implication.

The Board rule was not destined for long life since in 1962 the Sixth Circuit Court of Appeals rejected the NLRB's reasoning in the second *General Motors* case.[86] The court held that the agency-shop device was not "something lesser" than a union shop but something "entirely different." Essentially, it restored the Board decision rendered in the first *General Motors* case and outlawed the agency-shop arrangement throughout the United States. The case was appealed to the U.S. Supreme Court.

Agency Shop before the U.S. Supreme Court. In June 1963 the high court had two cases before it involving the agency-shop issue. Both decisions were rendered on the same day. In the *General Motors* case the Court held that an agency-shop arrangement was a permissible form of union security under Taft-Hartley and could be negotiated any place in the United States where it was not illegal under state law.[87] The legislative history of the Act was reviewed and the conclusion was reached that the second proviso to Section 8 (a) (3) required that "the burdens of membership upon which employment may be conditioned are expressly limited to the payment of initiation fees and monthly dues." Thus, unlike the decision reached by the Board in the first *General Motors* case and the Sixth Circuit Court of Appeals' reasoning, the agency shop and union shop were held to be the same. The only reason an employee may be discharged under a valid union-security arrangement is for failure to tender periodic dues and initiation fees. Thus under Taft-Hartley the Court recognized that the only protection afforded a union is financial security. In this regard the two union-security devices were held to be the same thing for all practical purposes.

In the other case before the Supreme Court, *Schermerhorn*, the issue was raised regarding the authority of a state to outlaw the agency shop under Section 14 (b) of Taft-Hartley.[88] The union argued that states did not have the authority to do so since Section 14 (b) permits them only to outlaw arrangements demanding membership in a union as a condition of employment. The high court ruled that the agency shop was within the scope of Section 14 (b) and therefore could be prohibited by the state of Florida under its right-to-work law. It is interesting to note that unions were taking opposite positions in the two cases. In *Schermerhorn* it was argued that the agency shop was different from a union shop. In *General Motors* the union took the position that they were both the same. The result would have been a highly inconsistent labor policy if the Court had sustained both positions.

Another issue of *Schermerhorn* was whether the NLRB or the state courts had jurisdiction to enforce state prohibitions of union-security arrangements. A decision on the question was postponed until the next Court term. The Board presented its views on the subject as *amicus curiae* in the second *Schermerhorn* case before the Supreme Court.[89]

It was held that the state courts had the authority to issue injunctions to enjoin enforcement of union-security arrangements that are illegal under state law. However, a state court does not have jurisdiction to issue injunctions to halt union picketing for the purpose of forcing employers to execute union-security arrangements in violation of state law. Union behavior in this regard is considered an unfair labor practice within the exclusive jurisdiction of the NLRB.

Prevention is the exclusive authority of the NLRB. However, after agreement is reached, the state courts do have authority to issue injunctions to enforce their decisions upholding state law. In early 1971, the U.S. Supreme Court nullified a provision of the Georgia right-to-work statute that permits employees to revoke their checkoff authorizations at any time.[90] The Georgia statute was held to be in conflict with the National Labor Relations Act on that point because it would preclude a binding agreement, entered into voluntarily, which is permissible by federal law. Later in this chapter, Taft-Hartley controls on the checkoff will be discussed.

In summary, a consequence of the Supreme Court decisions on the agency shop is that the arrangement is lawful in any state that does not make it illegal. In addition, states may outlaw the agency shop under Section 14 (b) of Taft-Hartley. Thus, unions came out the best that they could given the provisions of the law. Indeed, had the high court held that the agency shop violated Taft-Hartley, it would be illegal in all states and not just in states in which it is prohibited by state law.

Additional State Efforts to Control Union Security

Section 14 (b) has another feature that invites the states to restrict the application of the federal formula to union security. Reference has been made to the fact that the national law no longer requires the union-shop election as a prerequisite to negotiation of a union-security arrangement. Several states, however, still provide for such elections. Before an employer in Wisconsin may lawfully execute a union-security arrangement, at least two-thirds of the voting employees must vote for the device in a secret-ballot election conducted by the state labor relations board. This two-thirds must constitute a majority of the bargaining-unit members. Prior to the two-thirds requirement, it was a three-fourths majority to legalize union-security clauses.

The states of Colorado and Kansas followed the Wisconsin precedent. The Colorado law requires a three-fourths vote, but Kansas requires only that a majority of an employer's workers vote in favor of the union-security arrangement. Still other states place different restrictions on union-security devices. Hawaii, for example, permits a union to negotiate arrangements requiring union membership as a condition of employment unless a majority of bargaining-unit workers vote to deny the right to so do.

Under the doctrine established by the Supreme Court in *Algoma Plywood*, it appears that state union-shop election requirements are valid despite the fact that this feature was eliminated from Taft-Hartley in 1951.[91] In this case the Court upheld the right of the Wisconsin State Labor Relations Board to enforce its requirement of a two-thirds vote for a union shop. This position was taken despite the fact that the NLRB had previously certified the union as bargaining agent for employees.

Prior to the *Algoma* case the Supreme Court had ruled that the federal standards for a union shop and not those of the states would prevail when a state merely regulated union-security agreements by requiring the union-shop election instead of outright prohibition of union security. Thus in one case the Board certified that the majority of employees had voted to authorize a union-shop agreement, and rejected the point of view that no such certification could be issued because Colorado law required a three-fourths vote.[92] The *Algoma Plywood* doctrine nullifies this NLRB position so that workers covered by Taft-Hartley will still have to meet state union-shop election requirements when they exist.

THE CHARACTER OF THE CHECKOFF

Early in the history of unionism, parties to the collective bargaining process found an effective method for the collection of union financial obligations. This system is popularly referred to as the *checkoff*. The checkoff procedure requires the employer to deduct from his employees' wages a sum equivalent to union dues and other obligations. The money is then turned over to the proper union officials. The chief feature of the checkoff is that the union member is relieved of the responsibility of making payment to his organization on an individual basis. His union financial obligations are simply deducted from his paycheck by the employer, who in turn forwards the money to his organization.

For the individual worker the checkoff provides a simple and convenient method for payment of union obligations. Assuming that the worker intends to remain in the labor union, he must meet his financial obligations under any circumstances. When membership in the union is made a condition of employment, the payment of union financial obligations becomes prerequisite to holding a job. If a union-security arrangement prevails, and in the absence of the checkoff, the worker who for some reason fails to make his required union payment might lose his job.

Unions generally favor the inclusion of a checkoff clause in the collective bargaining contract. It saves the organization a considerable amount of time and effort otherwise expended in the collection of dues. A checkoff arrangement, for example, would enable stewards to devote more attention to the enforcement of the collective bargaining contract and the processing of employees' grievances. The checkoff clearly serves the interests of some individual workers. Moreover, from the union point of view, the checkoff is desirable, for it removes the necessity of taking disciplinary action against workers who for some reason or other fail to carry out their union financial obligations. For example, when union membership is a condition of employment, the checkoff relieves the union from the job of requesting the discharge of delinquent members. Obviously, unions particularly favor the checkoff in plants that employ large numbers of workers.

Despite the advantages of the checkoff to unions, a few labor organizations favor the collection of financial obligations on an individual basis. These unions argue that this keeps union leadership in touch with the rank and file. Thus, if the shop steward visits each member monthly for the purpose of dues collection, the personal contact enables the union to keep a close relationship with the members. However, the typical labor union prefers the checkoff and probably devises other techniques to maintain a close personal relationship between union leadership and union members.

EMPLOYERS AND THE CHECKOFF

From the point of view of the employer, the checkoff becomes a first-rate problem. Contrary to popular notion, many employers favor the arrangement. They do so because in the absence of the checkoff the collection of union financial obligations normally is performed in or about the plant. Such a procedure could result in confusion and the diminution of production. In this connection the vice-president of the Allis-Chalmers Manufacturing Company once remarked, "We offered the checkoff to Local 248 because for selfish reasons we do not want a lot of collecting on the company premises."[93] A former General Counsel of the CIO likewise pointed up the value of the checkoff from the point of view of plant efficiency. He declared that in the absence of the checkoff the only alternative offered to the union is the collection of dues through its grievance men, its local union officers, and other similarly designated employees elected or appointed by their local groups. Virtually the only opportunity available to these representatives to make regular contact with all of the thousands of employees in any given plant, who may live over wide geographical areas, is while at work or in related periods at or near the plant. Most employers do not feel that it is advantageous for productive efficiency to have employees circulating, distributing dues stamps, collecting dues money, either during working hours or even during rest and lunch periods.[94]

Impressed with the value of the checkoff from the viewpoint of production efficiency, many employers have been as anxious as labor unions to incorporate checkoff provisions in collective bargaining contracts. As a result the Bureau of Labor Statistics reported that in 1946 approximately 6 million workers, or about 40 percent of all employees covered by collective bargaining agreements, were subject to the checkoff. By 1954 this percentage had increased to about 75 percent.[95] In 1958–1959 the percentage grew to 77 percent. In right-to-work states, 85 percent of workers under major agreements have checkoff provisions in their contracts. Outside these states 68 percent of workers were under such arrangements. One writer has concluded that "the less secure the union, the greater the impulse to negotiate" a checkoff agreement.[96] This may not be the case, however, since the checkoff is an efficient arrangement for all parties affected by the contract.

The employer's case against the checkoff involves three major elements. Some employers contend that it is the responsibility of the union to collect financial obligations from union members and not that of the company. In short, employers who take this position refuse to do the union's work. Other employers object to the checkoff on the ground that it places a financial burden on the company. Since productive efficiency is advanced somewhat through the checkoff, the expense of administering the procedure should be offset in whole or in part. If the expense to the company becomes excessive, the union might reimburse the company for the execution of these tasks. One collective bargaining contract provides that the company may retain as a service charge 5 percent of all money collected through the checkoff.[97] Finally, some employers may object to the checkoff because it enables the union to perform its tasks more effectively. When a company accepts the collective bargaining process in good faith, such an objection hardly exists. Under such conditions the employer might welcome a procedure that would permit union leadership to devote more attention to the proper administration of the collective bargaining contract and to the performance of the tasks that make for union and plant efficiency.

It appears that the checkoff serves to promote a sound collective bargaining relationship between management and labor. In this connection one labor union official remarked,

> if we assume that the employer has accepted in good faith the principles of collective bargaining ... there is utterly no excuse for a refusal to make the administration of the contract and the operation of the employees' organization as efficient and as simple as possible. If the employees, by contract negotiated through their representative, express the desire that the employer cooperate to the extent of making deductions ... , then a refusal on the part of the employer in the main can be born only of the desire to impede the union and unwillingness to render even a minimum aid to efficiency.[98]

CHECKOFF UNDER THE RAILWAY LABOR ACT

Congress first gave attention to the problem of the checkoff when it enacted the Railway Labor Act of 1926. Under the terms of this law the checkoff of union dues by railroad operators was forbidden. Such a prohibition was favored by organized labor and not opposed by the Railroad Brotherhoods. Likewise, the railway unions urged Congress to prohibit arrangements that require union membership as a condition of securing a job. Congress responded to these union requests and outlawed both the closed shop and the checkoff in the railroad industry.

Labor unions generally favored the closed shop and the checkoff for these arrangements enhanced union security and increased the bargaining effectiveness of the organizations. Why then did the railroad unions adopt a program that appears inconsistent with overall union policy? The answer to this question is found in the history of the growth of unionism in the railroads. Elsewhere it was noted that the company-dominated union characterized the industrial relations environment in the railroad industry. For many years railroad employers attempted to forestall genuine collective bargaining by sponsoring company-dominated unions. These employers were so determined that such unions receive the support of the workers that frequently membership in these organizations was made a condition of employment. Likewise, railroad management checked off a sum from the wages of each worker and turned the money over to the company-dominated unions. In other words railway employees were forced to join these company-sponsored unions, and they had no way to prevent the railroad employers from deducting from their wages a sum equivalent to the dues charged for "membership." In some railroads membership in the company union was not made a condition of employment, but the management nevertheless deducted membership dues from the workers' paychecks.

The checkoff and the requirement of membership as a condition of employment precluded the establishment of regular labor unions. Accordingly, the railroad workers sought relief from Congress. Hence the Railway Labor Act of 1926 stamped out the closed shop and the checkoff in the railroad industry. The policy of the Railway Labor Act with respect to the closed shop and the checkoff had a particular and limited origin. It was adopted to aid the collective bargaining efforts of workers.

The 1951 amendments to the Act legalized the checkoff arrangement. The status of standard railroad unions relative to company unions had changed as mentioned elsewhere in this chapter. Unlike Taft-Hartley there is no deauthorization machinery available to rescind union-security arrangements and therefore the checkoff holds a more certain position in railroading and in the airlines than in general industry. A dual set of federal labor laws tends to generate considerable dissatisfaction among the various unions. Basic conflicts in national labor policy provide one basis for continued agitation for balanced treatment.

CHECKOFF UNDER TAFT-HARTLEY

The reaction of organized labor to checkoff control legislation in general industry was quite different from that displayed by the railway labor unions. Unions opposed the efforts of Congress and state legislatures to outlaw or regulate the device. When Taft-Hartley was being considered, many labor leaders spoke out against its control. Despite their efforts, however, the 1947 labor law contained two important checkoff restrictions.[99] The effect is control over the ability of the union and management to negotiate checkoff arrangements; certain basic conditions must be met before a checkoff agreement can become effective.

First, each individual union member must sign an agreement authorizing the employer to deduct his union dues under the checkoff plan. In the absence of such an authorization, the employer may not deduct union dues despite the existence of a checkoff clause negotiated through the collective bargaining process. The second restriction applies to the length of time for which the authorization can be effective: No authorization of a worker can be irrevocable for more than one year or beyond the termination date of the contract, whichever is shorter. To illustrate: An authorization by a worker signed on January 1, 1970, becomes ineffective on December 31, 1970, regardless of the desires of the union, management, or the worker. Section 302 (d) provides that any employer who deducts union dues from the wages of his employees in violation of these restrictions may be imprisoned for one year and is subject to a fine of $10,000. As is the case with restrictions on union security, Taft-Hartley with respect to the checkoff overtly attempts to provide union members with protection against labor unions.

Soon after the Taft-Hartley law was enacted, the question arose as to the lawfulness of a collective bargaining provision under which an employer deducts initiation fees, special assessments, and fines as well as regular monthly membership dues. In addition, a question was raised as to whether it was required under the national law that each employee personally sign a new authorization card each year. On May 13, 1948, the Assistant Solicitor General of the United States issued an opinion that has served to clarify these questions somewhat.[100] He ruled that the term *membership dues*, as utilized in the law, includes initiation fees and assessments as well as regular periodic dues. On the other hand, he made no reference to fines assessed against union members for the violation of union rules. The Assistant Solicitor General further offered as his opinion the ruling that checkoff arrangements providing an employee the annual opportunity to rescind a written authorization did not appear to be a "willful" violation of the Taft-Hartley law. This meant that arrangements between employers and unions are valid if they give employees such an opportunity but they do not actually have to sign a new authorization each year.

As a result many checkoff provisions now allow for the deduction of initiation fees and assessments as well as for regular monthly membership dues. In addition, it is a common practice in industry for employees to sign one authorization card. However, under the latter arrangement, both the collective bargaining contract and the authorization card clearly state that the employee has an annual opportunity, usually lasting for fifteen days, to rescind his written authorization. If he does not avail himself of this opportunity, the authorization card remains in force for another year.

When bargaining-unit employees have deauthorized a union-security provision in a collective bargaining contract, they have the option of revoking checkoff authorizations.[101] The Second Circuit Court enforced the Board's *Penn Cork* rule that an employer's refusal to honor employee requests to revoke the checkoff constitutes support or assistance to the labor organization. The Board reasoned that employees who authorize a dues checkoff do so under the influence of union-security clauses;

otherwise they would not find it necessary to do so. It was also established in *Penn Cork* that rescission of a union-security clause resulting from a deauthorization election should serve to rescind checkoff provisions executed because of the union security clause.

Employees have the right to revoke their checkoff authorizations at any time after a union-security clause is deauthorized through a validly held election.[102] They are not required to adhere to the usual period of time provided each year to rescind authorization. However, deauthorization of a union-security clause does not automatically rescind the checkoff provision.[103] An employer cannot unilaterally change the checkoff provision since some bargaining-unit workers desire to remain union members and take advantage of the checkoff convenience. Also some arrangements contain provisions permitting new employees voluntarily to designate the checkoff as a method of paying union dues. Unilateral employer revocation of the checkoff would constitute a unilateral contractual change affecting new employees as well as old ones desiring the arrangement.[104]

From the foregoing it appears rather clear that though the checkoff is an important issue of collective bargaining, it does not normally constitute a crucial point of controversy between employers and unions. It does not contain the features of conflicting philosophy involved in the union-security problem. It has rarely by itself become a major strike issue since the stakes are not that high. As a matter of fact, though the checkoff serves the institutional needs of the union, employers often find some gain from the incorporation of the device in the collective bargaining agreement. This would be particularly true when the labor contract contains a union-security arrangement. Not only does the checkoff obviate the need of dues collection on company premises with the attendant impact upon the orderly operation of the plant, but it avoids the need of starting the discharge process for employees who are negligent in the payment of dues. Frequently, without a checkoff, an employee who must belong to a union as a condition of employment will delay paying his dues and the employer and union both are then faced with the task of instituting the discharge process, which is most commonly suspended when the employee (faced with loss of employment) pays his dues at the last possible minute. The checkoff eliminates the need for this wasted and time-consuming effort of busy employer and union representatives.

Even when the union shop is not in effect, moreover, the checkoff need not necessarily be given permanent status. The employee obligates himself to pay dues for one year only, and if he desires to stop the checkoff he may do so during the escape period. The escape period is different when deauthorization elections have occurred, as mentioned. But, under any circumstances, if the management believes the union is so irresponsible as not to deserve the checkoff, it need not agree to it as its part of the renegotiated contract and the mechanism is consequently also "revocable" from the company's point of view.

CONTROLS OVER GOOD-FAITH BARGAINING

The duty to bargain in good faith is a government requirement that predates the Wagner Act of 1935. However, "conclusions as to whether a given attitude or approach to collective bargaining constitutes 'good faith' will always have to be drawn."[105] The good-faith bargaining duty was advanced as early as 1921 in a case before the Railway Labor Board.[106] The Board, in its interpretation of requirements set forth in the Transportation Act of 1920, held that the negotiating parties must make an honest effort to decide all issues in conference. "If they cannot decide all matters in dispute in conference, it is their duty to then decide all that is possible. . . ."[107]

The National Labor Board, established by executive order to administer the National Industrial Recovery Act of 1933, could not ignore the good-faith bargaining issue. It held that Section 7 (a) placed an implicit reciprocal duty on employers to bargain.[108] This duty involved more than merely meeting and conferring with labor unions. During the 1930s it was assumed that unions as bargaining institutions would deal in good faith at the conference table. The Wagner Act was to require the same obligation of employers. Experiences under the 1935 law did not convince the public that unions proceeded in good faith at the conference table. This led to inclusion of a provision in Taft-Hartley that requires the same set of standards from unions as were required of employers under the earlier laws.[109]

Congress incorporated the Board's good-faith bargaining requirements into Section 8 (d) of the 1947 law. These requirements originated under earlier attempts of government to regulate labor relations. Section 8 (d) requires that

> for the purpose of this section, to bargain collectively is the performance of the mutual obligation of the employer and the representative of the employees to meet at reasonable times and confer in good faith with respect to wages, hours, and other terms and conditions of employment, or the negotiation of an agreement, or any question arising thereunder, and the execution of a written contract incorporating any agreement reached if requested by either party, but such obligation does not compel either party to agree to a proposal or require the making of a concession. . . .[110]

This requirement constituted the congressional framework for good-faith bargaining. The NLRB and the court took on the responsibility for giving substance to the broad legislative language.

Under the Wagner Act, as with Taft-Hartley, the major task for the Board in each case was to determine whether the parties entered into discussion "with an open and fair mind, and a sincere purpose to find a basis of agreement . . . and if found to embody it in a contract . . . which shall stand as a mutual guarantee of conduct, and as a guide for the adjustment of grievances."[111] Decisions are made after a review of the totality of bargaining conduct. Isolated behavior does not generally control the finding of unfair labor practices.

Good-faith conduct in bargaining requires an assessment of the state of mind of the negotiating parties; all the circumstances in a case must be reviewed to determine their motives. Even though the Wagner Act did not provide for union unfair labor practices, union conduct was reviewed by the Board before holding an employer in violation of the good-faith bargaining requirement. In one case, for example, the NLRB ruled that "a union's refusal to bargain in good faith may remove the possibility of negotiation and thus preclude the existence of a situation in which the employer's own good faith can be tested. If it cannot be tested, its absence can hardly be found."[112]

An assessment of the state of mind very often requires that the Board turn to circumstantial evidence to make a determination. Some circumstantial evidence, however, makes the intent of the party so evident that the lack of good faith may be logically inferred.

The Board and the courts, in their continuing quest to bring about statutory bargaining conformance, have built an enormous set of conditions for good-faith bargaining. These include:

1. There must be a serious attempt to adjust differences and to reach an acceptable common ground.
2. Counterproposals must be offered when another party's proposal is rejected. This must involve the "give and take" of an auction system.[113]
3. A position with regard to contract terms may not be constantly changed.[114]
4. Evasive behavior during negotiations is not permitted.[115]
5. There must be a willingness to incorporate oral agreements into a written contract.[116]

Many other rules on what constitutes good-faith bargaining have been advanced by the NLRB and sustained by the courts. The Board in a 1965 case set forth a substantial number of its good-faith bargaining standards in an evaluation of the General Electric "take-it-or-leave-it" approach to bargaining.[117] Most of the good-faith obligations mentioned can be traced back to Board decisions during the Wagner Act era. A close review of the *General Electric* case will highlight the recent treatment of the good-faith bargaining requirement.

General Electic and Boulwarism

Since the late 1940s General Electric Corporation has continuously pursued a policy of (1) preparing for negotiations by effecting what company representatives describe as "the steady accumulation of all facts available on matters likely to be discussed"; (2) modifying this information only on the basis of "any additional or different facts" it is made aware of, either by the union or from other sources, during the negotiations (as well as before them); (3) offering, at an "appropriate time" during the bargaining, "what the facts from all sources seem to indicate that we should"; and (4) changing this offer only if confronted "with new facts." Another aspect of this policy—known as Boulwarism after former General Electric Vice-President of Public and Employee Relations Lemuel R. Boulware—involves constant company communication to both its employees and the general citizenry of the various General Electric communities on the progress of the negotiations as they evolve.

The primary union that deals with the company—the International Union of Electrical Workers—attacked the policy on legal grounds and filed an unfair labor practice charge with the NLRB alleging bad-faith bargaining. In 1964 the Board upheld the union position and stated:

> It is inconsistent with this obligation [good-faith bargaining with the collective agent] for an employer to mount a campaign, as Respondent did, both before and during negotiations, for the purpose of disparaging and discrediting the statutory representative in the eyes of its employee constitutents, to seek to per-

suade the employees to exert pressure on the representative to submit to the will of the employer, and to create the impression that the employer rather than the union is the true protector of the employees' interests.

The Board reached its decision after a review of the totality of bargaining circumstances. The problem with the GE method was its "take-it-or-leave-it" approach. The NLRB has held such an approach illegal since the Wagner Act era.

General Electric took essentially the same bargaining stance during negotiations in 1969. However, the 1964 Board decision was appealed and reviewed by the Second Circuit Court of Appeals.[118] The Board had ruled that the totality of GE's conduct made it impossible for the union to respond to the company position. The court stated, however, that a "take-it-or-leave-it" approach, without other condemning evidence, is not an illegal bargaining tactic. What made GE conduct illegal was its publicity campaign that communicated to employees that GE, not the union, was their true representative. A firm is not permitted to deal with a union through employees, but is required to deal with employees through a union.

Thus, GE lost its appeal, but it was on its antiunion publicity campaign, and not on the basis of its "best offer first" approach. The appeals court did not require the making of concessions as an ingredient of good-faith bargaining. In any event, in 1973, GE abandoned "Boulwarism" in its entirety and a labor agreement was quickly negotiated with its unions that was hailed by all concerned as a satisfactory agreement.

Borg-Warner Categories

Probably Congress did not intend for the NLRB and the courts to interfere with the substance of collective bargaining. However, under the *Borg-Warner* doctrine, the Board with court approval plays an important role in determining what the parties may negotiate in their agreements. The *Borg-Warner* doctrine applies Section 8 (d) of Taft-Hartley to particular demands made by employers and unions during negotiations. It will be recalled that Section 8 (d) of Taft-Hartley requires the parties to confer on "wages, hours, and other terms and conditions of employment." But some terms and conditions of employment are outlawed by the Act. Many other items that might be of interest to unions or management may not fall within the bargaining items mentioned in Section 8 (d). The Board eventually resolved the question of what to do in such circumstances.

The *Borg-Warner* case, ultimately decided by the U.S. Supreme Court in 1958, involved "a 'ballot' clause calling for a pre-strike secret vote of employees (union and nonunion) as to the employer's last offer."[119] It also involved "a recognition clause which excluded, as a party to the contract, the International Union which had been certified by the National Labor Relations Board as the employees' exclusive bargaining agent, and substituted for it the agent's uncertified local affiliate."

The union refused to agree upon either of the company's demands as conditions of contract settlement. A strike resulted and the union did not prevail. Both clauses were subsequently included in the collective bargaining agreement. Prior to their inclusion the international union filed refusal-to-bargain unfair labor practice charges against the company.

The Board held the company violated the refusal-to-bargain provisions of Taft-

Hartley by insisting upon inclusion of these items in the contract. It classified bargaining demands into three major categories.

Illegal Items. One was the illegal category. If a demand was made by a negotiating party that was illegal under the Act, the Board would find it in violation of the refusal-to-bargain unfair labor practice provision.[120] For example, the Act prohibits the closed shop and compulsory dues checkoff. A demand for items such as these is prohibited by law. A refusal to bargain on them would not constitute an unfair labor practice. The Act itself withdrew certain subjects from the scope of bargaining.

Mandatory Items. The second category established by the Board and later the Court involved the mandatory group of items. It was in this category that the Board placed the Section 8 (d) items of "wages, hours, and other terms and conditions of employment."

Labor and management groups must bargain in good faith on items in the mandatory category and they may be bargained to an impasse without violating the unfair labor practice provisions of Taft-Hartley. Unions may strike to obtain mandatory items in the contract. Employers are authorized to refuse to sign a contract unless their version of items in the category is included in the agreement. The NLRB and the courts must ultimately decide what items fall within the meaning of wages, hours, and other terms and conditions of employment. Many issues have been designated as mandatory subjects for collective bargaining. Some of these include sub-contracting;[121] stock purchase plans;[122] profit-sharing plans;[123] pension and employee welfare plans;[124] rental of company housing;[125] Christmas bonuses;[126] work loads and production standards;[127] and plant rules.[128] In a significant decision, the U.S. Supreme Court held that employers may lawfully demand that promotions, discipline, and work scheduling be a matter of exclusive management control, and not subject to arbitration.[129]

Voluntary Items. The voluntary category includes items not labeled illegal or mandatory. One example might be a union demand to ratify promotions to the supervisor ranks as well as the right to ask for the dismissal of these employees. Voluntary items may be discussed at the bargaining table but they cannot be bargained to an impasse. Unions may not strike over the item. Employers cannot make the item a condition for signing a labor contract. If the NLRB finds that an item in the voluntary category is bargained to an impasse, it will hold that a *per se* violation of Section 8 (d) has taken place. No further inquiry will be made into the remaining bargaining conduct of the parties. It is a per se violation regardless of the other issues. Some union demands have been placed in the voluntary category. These include demanding that agricultural labor and supervision be included in the labor agreement;[130] requiring a company to contribute to an industry-wide promotion fund;[131] relating to strike insurance plans;[132] requiring a bank to continue a free investment counseling service for its employees that the bank terminated;[133] making the prices that an employer charged for food in its cafeteria and vending machines subject to joint determination;[134] and insisting that an employer association with which the union was negotiating abandon litigation concerning management of a trust fund.[135] In 1971, the U.S. Supreme Court held that unions have no right to bargain for pensions and other insurance programs for persons previously retired. It held that retired persons are not "employees" within the meaning of the law.[136] Previously the NLRB held that retired persons are employees under the law, and unions could bargain for them in the area of welfare benefits.[137] By this decision, unions have lost the opportunity to improve effectively the living standards of millions of retired persons.

Employer demands have also been placed in the voluntary category by the NLRB and the courts. These include demanding that a union withdraw fines previously imposed upon members who have crossed picket lines during a strike in violation of union rules;[138] insisting that a labor federation be party to the contract where a local union affiliated with the larger body is the lawful and certified bargaining representative;[139] granting the employer the right to use the union label;[140] requiring a union to post a performance bond;[141] and insisting that nonunion employees should have the right to vote upon the provisions of the contract negotiated by the union.[142] As stated previously in *Borg-Warner*, an employer demand that would require a strike vote election among employees before a strike occurs falls within the voluntary category.

Significance of Borg-Warner

Thus the NLRB has the authority to circumscribe and limit the area of free collective bargaining. As economic conditions change, employers and unions place greater emphasis upon some subjects and less on others. Some issues that may be of the utmost importance in 1975 may have required little attention in 1970. The Board has authority to classify such items in either the mandatory or voluntary categories. If the decision is made to place a subject in the voluntary category, neither party has the authority to insist upon its inclusion in a collective bargaining contract. A flat rejection of the issue by one of the parties ends the matter.

It is obvious that the NLRB has the authority to change the results of free collective bargaining. This constitutes a situation that may not have been intended by Congress. Nevertheless, the *Borg-Warner* doctrine placed the Board and the courts in the position of policing agencies over the collective bargaining process. There is no express provision in Taft-Hartley to provide the Board with such enormous power. Under this doctrine, it is not a question of who may benefit from a particular decision. Employers and unions may be treated favorably or unfavorably, depending upon the decision in a given situation. However, they both lose, since under *Borg-Warner* employers and unions have lost the full capability to deal with changing conditions in a climate of free collective bargaining. The NLRB is prepared to serve as a policeman to determine what may be included in a collective bargaining contract. Free collective bargaining would be advanced should the Board and the courts hold that, when an employer or union demand is not expressly illegal under Taft-Hartley, the demand is a mandatory issue of collective bargaining. To put it in other terms, the interests of employers, employees, and unions would be advanced if the voluntary category were eliminated.

Fibreboard Doctrine: Employer's Duty to Bargain

Once an issue falls within the mandatory category, the employer has the duty to bargain with the union over the issue when a collective bargaining contract is in effect. Section 8(d) of the law does not limit the obligation of the parties to bargain on the "terms and conditions of employment" only when a new contract is being negotiated. It also establishes an affirmative duty to bargain during the effective period of a collective bargaining contract. This problem arises when an employer desires to change employment conditions during a contract period. In order to promote efficiency or to reduce costs, the employer may desire to eliminate or modify a term or condition of employment.

Such an employer duty appeared to be settled under Taft-Hartley when the U.S. Supreme Court decided the *Fibreboard* case.[143] In that dispute, the employer sub-contracted certain maintenance work during the term of a labor agreement. He did so to save costs, and sub-contracted without consulting or bargaining with the union. As a result of the sub-contract, many employees lost their jobs. Upon its review of the case, the Supreme Court held that the employer refused to bargain collectively under Taft-Hartley. Not only did it find that sub-contracting is a mandatory issue of collective bargaining, but also the employer violated the law because it took action without consulting or bargaining with the union. As to the latter issue, the Supreme Court stated:

> . . . The facts of the present case illustrate the propriety of submitting the dispute to collective negotiation. The Company's decision to contract out the maintenance work did not alter the Company's basic operation. The maintenance work still had to be performed in the plant. No capital investment was contemplated; the Company merely replaced existing employees with those of an independent contractor to do the same work under similar conditions of employment. Therefore, to require the employer to bargain about the matter would not significantly abridge his freedom to manage the business.

After it made this decision, the Court held that the NLRB had the authority to order the employer to resume the maintenance operation that it had sub-contracted, and reinstate the laid off employees with back pay. In other words, the Board was authorized to restore the *status quo* because the employer failed to bargain with the union before it sub-contracted the work. As to the power of the Board to direct such a remedy, the Court pointed to Section 10(c) of Taft-Hartley which empowers the NLRB

> to take such affirmative action including reinstatement of employees with or without back pay, as will effectuate the policies of this Act.

To understand *Fibreboard*, it should be noted that the law does not forbid the employer to make a change in working conditions. He may make the change after he has bargained with the union to an impasse. After it appears that further bargaining would be fruitless, the employer may make the change. By bargaining to an impasse, he has discharged his duty to bargain in good faith under the terms of the law. In other words, an employer who has exhausted the bargaining process has the authority to make unilaterally the change in working conditions that was the subject of negotiations prior to the impasse.[144]

Some employers at times probably experienced difficulties under the *Fibreboard* doctrine. Before making a change, they had to wait until an impasse was reached. This prevented them from taking immediate advantage of the benefit that would result from the change. If the employer were faced with stiff economic competition, it is possible the doctrine could be burdensome. Also, the employer faced a risk under

Fibreboard in that the NLRB could subsequently find that no impasse had been reached. That is, the employer made the change after he believed that an impasse was reached in negotiations. Later on, the Board might find that an impasse was not reached. Though these appear to be valid criticisms of *Fibreboard*, it would be difficult, if not impossible, to obtain objective evidence to show that the doctrine was injurious to the business community. At times it is far easier to raise theoretical arguments against an NLRB policy than it is to obtain the economic data to evaluate the merits of the charge.

From **Fibreboard** to **Collyer**:
Deferral to Arbitration

In any event, it appeared that *Fibreboard* settled the employer's responsibility to bargain during the effective term of a collective bargaining contract. If an employer desired to change the terms and conditions of employment, he had the obligation to bargain with the union until an impasse was reached. After the impasse, he could lawfully change employment conditions. Under these circumstances, the union would not have a remedy under Taft-Hartley, but would be required to resort to arbitration if it believed the employer's action violated the terms of the labor agreement. However, if the employer failed to bargain to an impasse, the NLRB would find a violation of Taft-Hartley and order an appropriate remedy. In general, the agency would order that the previous condition of employment be restored and reinstatement and back pay for employees should they have lost their jobs or wages because of the employer's action. The key to understanding the *Fibreboard* doctrine is that the employer was compelled to bargain with the union *before he made a decision to change terms and conditions of employment.*

In 1971, however, the NLRB made a very significant change in this policy. By a 3–2 vote, the Board established the *Collyer* doctrine, one of the most controversial decisions announced by the agency in recent years.[145] In the majority were two Nixon appointees, Miller and Kennedy, and Brown, whose term was scheduled to expire in a few days after the decision was announced; Jenkins and Fanning constituted the minority. Under *Collyer*, an employer is permitted to make a change in the terms of employment without bargaining with a union provided that the labor agreement contains a final and binding arbitration provision and he is willing to arbitrate the dispute. In short, though the employer may commit an unfair labor practice by his refusal to bargain to an impasse, the NLRB held that the dispute concerning the change in working conditions should be settled in arbitration. In its decision, the majority stated:

> the contract clearly provides for the grievance and arbitration machinery; where the unilateral action taken is not designed to undermine the union and is not patently erroneous but rather is based on a substantial claim of contractual privilege, and it appears that the arbitral interpretation of the contract will resolve both the unfair labor practice issue and the contract interpretation issue in a matter compatible with the purposes of the Act, then the Board should defer to the arbitration clause conceived by the parties.

And:

> In our view, disputes such as these can better be resolved by arbitrators with special skill and experience in deciding matters arising under established bargaining relationships than by the application by this Board of a particular provision of our statute.

To justify its position, the Board majority pinned its decision to Section 203(d) of Taft-Hartley, which states:

> Final adjustment by a method agreed upon by the parties is hereby declared to be the desirable method of settlement of grievance disputes arising over the application or interpretation of an existing collective-bargaining agreement.

It is material that this provision appears in that section of the law which establishes the Federal Mediation and Conciliation Service. To carry out the policy expressed in the provision, the Federal Mediation and Conciliation Service makes available to employers and unions the names of qualified private arbitrators to enable them to use arbitration as a method for the final adjustment of disputes arising over the application and interpretation of a labor agreement. However, since the provision does not appear in those areas of the law which deal with unfair labor practices, it could be argued with validity that the Congress did not intend that Section 203(d) be used as a basis to dilute the exclusive power of the NLRB to prevent unfair labor practices.

In any event, at this writing two federal courts of appeals upheld the NLRB majority policy. In June 1973 the federal court of appeals in New York approved it in *Nabisco, Inc.* v. *NLRB*, and in February 1974 the federal appeals court for the District of Columbia reached the same conclusion in *Electrical Workers* v. *NLRB*. In the latter case, the court said:

> . . . The *Collyer* rule of deferral to grievance and arbitration procedures is clearly valid.

With unusual vigor, the minority criticized the majority position. Jenkins and Fanning charged that under *Collyer* the NLRB has abandoned its statutory duty to enforce the unfair labor practice feature of Taft-Hartley. They stated:

> Congress has said that arbitration and the voluntary settlement of disputes are the preferred method of dealing with certain kinds of industrial unrest. Congress has also said that the power of this Board to dispose of unfair labor practices is not to be affected by any other method of adjustment. Whatever these two statements mean, they do not mean that this Board can abdicate its authority wholesale.

> . . . The majority is so anxious to accommodate arbitration that it forgets that the first duty of this Board is to provide a forum for the adjudication of unfair labor practices. We have not been told that arbitration is the only method; it is one method.

In other words, the minority stressed that Congress established the NLRB to enforce the unfair labor practices of the law, and the power of the Board in this respect, as established in Section 10(a), is exclusive "and shall not be affected by any other means of adjustment or prevention that has been or may be established by agreement, law, or otherwise." In their view, private arbitrators do not have the authority under the law to decide unfair labor practice disputes, and the NLRB improperly conferred this right upon them. Once an unfair labor practice is filed, it is the duty of the Board to handle the case and not defer to arbitration. As one study states:

> The Board's contention that it should encourage the use of arbitration is laudable and may very well reflect the rather general, as well as the Congressional, sentiment that the arbitral process is the preferred way to settle contractual disputes, particularly if the alternative is economic strife. However, nowhere in the functions of the Board as described in the collective National Labor Relations Act, as amended, is there mention of encouragement of arbitration as one of those functions either prior to or after entertaining a charge of an unfair labor practice. To be blunt, once the unfair labor practice charge has been filed by one of the parties (in preference to arbitration) the Board should attend to the statutory business which Congress assigned it and leave the determination of arbitrability of a contractual dispute to the arbitrator, and review of the award to the courts.[146]

Cases Deferred

In the *Collyer* case itself, the employer unilaterally raised the wage rates of its skilled employees and reassigned certain job duties without consulting or bargaining with the union. Since that time the NLRB has deferred many other kinds of disputes to arbitration, rejecting the union claim that the NLRB should have jurisdiction over the disputes because of a refusal of the employer to bargain over changed conditions of employment. These cases included the reduction in crew sizes by an employer and his increase of the age of apprentices, and further required that they be high school graduates;[147] discontinuance of the distribution of "turkey" money at Thanksgiving and Christmas;[148] curtailment of the seniority unit for purposes of transfer and promotion;[149] establishment of a separate seniority list for part-time employees;[150] revoking of employee parking privileges;[151] lengthening of Saturday hours and elimination of paid lunch periods;[152] institution of a wage incentive system;[153] and cancellation of a union member's leave of absence to engage in union work.[154]

In these cases, the NLRB held that the employer's action was covered by some provision of the labor agreement and/or a past practice, and, therefore, the union involved was required to seek relief in arbitration. Under the *Collyer* doctrine, the employer was not compelled to bargain with the union to an impasse before the action was taken to change these working conditions. Beyond this group of cases, the NLRB has also deferred to arbitration in other types of disputes. These include the discharge of employees who alleged that their termination resulted from their participation in union activities. Under Taft-Hartley, employers are forbidden to discharge employees when they engage in protected union activities. When disputes of this kind arise, the NLRB customarily proceeds with the case to determine whether there was a violation of the law. To the extent that the NLRB departs from this normal procedure, the result is to deprive employees of their rights under law. As the minority members of the NLRB stated in one of the discharge cases:

> This case confirms our fears, and again illustrates the extent to which the majority is willing, by its policy of deferring to private tribunals, to abrogate the rights of individual employees under the act we administer.[155]

Cases Not Deferred

Though the Board has deferred to arbitration in an increasing number of cases, it should not be concluded that this has been done in every case. A dispute will not be deferred if the labor agreement does not contain a final and binding arbitration provision, or the employer refuses to agree to final and binding arbitration.[156] Also, the changed working condition must arguably be covered by some provision of the labor agreement or by a past practice. Probably this is not an important limitation to deferral since as the minority stated in *Collyer:*

> . . . Most unfair labor practices can be connected somehow to contract terms or existing practices, by broad construction of general clauses, by the necessary inquiry into existing practices, by "waiver," or otherwise.

In any event, before the NLRB defers, there must be a showing that the employer conduct arguably is based upon contractual provision or practice. If his action is not covered by any provision of the labor agreement or by a past practice, the Board will not defer to arbitration.

In addition, the Board will not defer to arbitration if the evidence shows that the bargaining history between a union and company has been marred by constant friction. In one case, a dispute was not deferred because of a considerable number of wildcat strikes, distrust for one another, and by continual bickering. For example, in one year, the union had filed 301 grievances.[157] Also, the Board will not defer when the employer has engaged in serious unfair labor practices. In one case of this type, the evidence showed the employer's "complete rejection of the principles of collective bargaining" and utter disregard for the organizational results of his employees.[158]

To understand the significance of *Collyer*, however, one should focus on the Board's desire to defer to arbitration rather than the limited number of times that it has refused to do so.

NLRB Holds Jurisdiction of Case

When the NLRB defers to arbitration, however, it holds jurisdiction of the case until after the arbitration award is issued. It may take jurisdiction of the case after the award is issued if the arbitrator did not conduct a fair hearing; where the employer refuses to abide by the award should the arbitrator find against him; if the arbitrator did not consider and determine the unfair labor practice issues involved in the case; or if the arbitrator's decision is repugnant to the policies of the NLRB. These are the so-called *Spielberg* standards, which are discussed more fully in the next chapter. Thus, the Board may take jurisdiction of a case that it deferred to arbitration if the arbitrator did not meet the standards contained in *Spielberg*.[159] As the General Counsel of the NLRB stated:

> If the dispute underlying the charge is not resolved amicably under the grievance procedure, and resort to arbitration proves necessary, the charging party may obtain a review of the arbitrator's final award by addressing a request for review to this Office. The request should be in writing and contain a statement of the facts and circumstances bearing on whether the arbitral proceedings were fair and regular; whether the unfair labor practice issues which gave rise to the charge were considered and decided by the arbitrator; and whether the award is consonant with the purposes and policies of the Labor Management Relations Act.[160]

Refusal to Enforce Arbitrator's Decision

Though the Board will review an arbitration decision under the *Spielberg* doctrine, it will not enforce an arbitrator's decision of cases in which it deferred to arbitration.[161] Once again, there was a bitter conflict between the members of the Board. As in *Collyer*, the Board split 3–2 on the issue. The majority held that if an employer refused to abide by an arbitrator's decision, the union had the opportunity to go to court for enforcement of the decision. This, of course, results in considerable delay and litigation expenses.

In contrast, the two minority members believed that the arbitrator's award should be enforced by the NLRB. They stressed that since the Board deferred to arbitration, it should enforce the award and not burden the union with court proceedings. In considering this issue, it should be noted that if the Board had not deferred to arbitration in the first place, it would direct a remedy under Taft-Hartley where the evidence demonstrated that the employer engaged in an unfair labor practice. On this basis, it would seem reasonable that when the Board defers to arbitration, it has the obligation to enforce the arbitrator's award. After all, it was the *Collyer* doctrine that forced the arbitration, and to complete matters, it would seem fair that the Board should enforce the arbitrator's award.

Impact on Labor Relations

One obvious result of the *Collyer* doctrine is that it stimulates more arbitration. Costs of arbitration are substantial. The average cost of a typical case in 1972 amounted to $590.12.[162] Even when the parties equally share the cost, as is customary, the charges are burdensome at least to the smaller unions. It is entirely possible that some unions, faced with these costs, would not proceed with arbitration with the result that employer conduct in violation of a labor agreement would not be contested. When a union or an employer charges a violation of Taft-Hartley, the charging party incurs no costs for the use of the NLRB services. In addition, the Board assumes a level of expertise among arbitrators that is not necessarily warranted. Arbitrators differ widely in terms of experience and professional capability. Unfortunately, some arbitrators, hopefully few in number, may decide cases on grounds other than on the evidence that is presented to them. In short, there are far more uncertainties in arbitration as compared with NLRB proceedings.

Beyond causing more arbitration, the *Collyer* doctrine has additional consequences on the state of labor-management relations. With the knowledge that the Board will likely defer to arbitration, it follows that some employers may be more aggressive in their labor practices. They could engage in conduct which arguably violates the labor agreement upon more occasions. Such conduct, when it occurs, would not be conducive to harmonious labor relations.

Perhaps the major consequence, however, is that *Collyer* precludes the union's input before an employer makes a change in working conditions. Since no consultation or bargaining is required, the employer is authorized to make a change before it solicits the views of the union. If bargaining were required, it is possible that the union may make suggestions that could be valuable to both sides. In other words, the change could be made in a way that would minimize the difficulties to the employees involved and still permit the employer to realize the intrinsic benefits of the change. There is, of course, no assurance that the union's input would result in this state of affairs. However, in the absence of consultation and bargaining, the possibility for a meaningful input by a union is precluded. After all, that is what collective bargaining is all about—it establishes a structure where both parties are able to resolve problems in a way that could be mutually beneficial to all concerned. In short, what *Collyer* really does is to impair the collective bargaining process, and this appears inconsistent in a law dedicated to the encouragement of the practice of collective bargaining.

THE **H. K. PORTER CO.** CASE

The U. S. Supreme Court in the *Porter* case took a strong position against Board orders "to compel a company or a union to agree to any substantive contractual provision of a collective bargaining agreement." [163] The *Borg-Warner* doctrine, of course, merely requires bargaining over mandatory items and does not require agreement. In *H. K. Porter*, the Board actually issued an order requiring the company to agree to checkoff union dues from employee paychecks. The order was based on the premise that Porter had refused to bargain on the checkoff in order to frustrate the bargaining process. An appeals court upheld the NLRB by agreeing that the order to include the checkoff provision in the contract was an appropriate remedy within the Board's statutory authority.

The U. S. Supreme Court reversed the appeals court and NLRB. Justice Black observed that "the parties to the instant case are agreed that this is the first time in the 35-year history of the Act that the Board has ordered either an employer or a union to agree to a substantive term of a collective bargaining agreement."

Thus, the NLRB has authority to require bargaining in certain categories and to restrict lockout and strike activity in accordance with certain categories. It does not have authority to make final settlement of the terms of collective bargaining agreements. The Board has authority to decide when an unfair labor practice occurs, but it cannot use its remedial powers to write the actual terms of a contract. However, under *Borg-Warner*, the NLRB can influence the content of labor agreements, though it may not directly insert provisions into them as was attempted in the *H. K. Porter* case.

SUMMARY

The NLRB and the courts have directly intervened with the substance of collective bargaining contracts. Government should establish general rules for the conduct of labor relations. The state should determine the limits of union and employer conduct. It may properly protect the right of workers to join unions, engage in collective bargaining, strike, and engage in other forms of concerted activities. It should limit union power and thereby confer protected rights upon employers, employees, and the public. This seems appropriate when unions engage in violence, violate collective bargaining contracts, and engage in strikes and picketing with an antisocial purpose. Government should not determine the substance of the contract that the parties negotiate in their own economic interest if bargaining takes place in good faith. Peaceful economic pressure is available to both and should not be interfered with unless there is clear evidence that such actions harm the public.

The *Borg-Warner* voluntary category of bargaining subjects deprives the parties to collective bargaining of the ability to apply economic pressure to influence the outcome of collective bargaining agreements. Restrictions of this type tend to frustrate the purpose of national labor legislation envisioned in the Wagner Act. The basic purpose of that law and of subsequent amendments in 1947 and 1959 was to balance the powers of labor and management. A balance-of-power approach was to ensure that the parties would be permitted to bargain on issues of interest without undue influence from external forces.

With respect to *Collyer*, it appears fair to conclude that the NLRB has abandoned its statutory duty to enforce the unfair labor practices of Taft-Hartley. Though it is probably true that some employers at times were placed at a disadvantage under *Fibreboard*, there is a lack of objective evidence to show that the doctrine injured the business community. Beyond that, public policy is paramount to the private interests of employers, employees, and unions. By deferral to arbitration, the NLRB has permitted employers to escape from an obligation established by federal law. The policy impairs the process of collective bargaining, and to this extent tends to undermine public policy dedicated to the encouragement of the practice of collective bargaining.

NOTES

[1] *Hearings before the Committee on Labor and Public Welfare*, 80th Congress, 1st sess., on S. 55 and S. J. Res. 22, Part III, p. 1204.

[2] National War Labor Board, *Termination Report*, Washington, D.C., I, 80.

[3] *Ibid.*, p. 84.

[4] Harry A. Millis and Emily Clark Brown, *From the Wagner Act to Taft-Hartley* (Chicago: The University of Chicago Press, 1950), p. 297.

[5] Theodore Rose, "Union Security and Checkoff Provisions in Major Union Contracts," *Monthly Labor Review*, LXXXII, No. 12 (December 1959), pp. 1348–1351.

[6] Irving Kovarsky, "Union Security, Hiring Halls, Right-to-Work Laws and the Supreme Court," *Labor Law Journal*, XV, No. 10 (October 1964), p. 660.

[7] After 1956 the basic steel labor agreement adopted a union security formula which requires all current union members to remain in the union and makes union membership compulsory for all newly hired workers.

[8] Joseph Shister, *Economics of the Labor Market* (Chicago: J. B. Lippincott Company, Philadelphia, 1949), p. 83.

[9] Philip Taft, "Dues and Initiation Fees in Labor Unions," *Quarterly Journal of Economics* (February 1946), p. 22.

[10] Theodore Rose, "Union Security Provisions in Agreements, 1954," *Monthly Labor Review*, LXXVIII, No. 6 (June 1955), p. 646.

[11] Sections 8 (a) (3) and 8 (b) (2).

[12] NLRB Release R-336, August 10, 1950.

[13] *NLRB* v. *National Maritime Union*, 175 F. (2d) 686 (1949).

[14] Rose, *op. cit.*

[15] *National Labor Relations Act of 1949*, Report No. 99 to accompany S. 249, 81st Congress, 1st sess., p. 20.

[16] Horace E. Sheldon, "Union Security and the Taft-Hartley Act in the Buffalo Area," New York State School of Industrial and Labor Relations, Cornell University Research Bulletin 4, p. 41.

¹⁷ *National Union of Marine Cooks & Stewards*, 90 NLRB 167 (1950).

¹⁸ Contract negotiated by the Sailors Union (AFL) with a number of shipping operators in 1948.

¹⁹ Contract between the New York Local of the International Typographical Union and publishers of that city (1948).

²⁰ Contract between the Milk Wagon Drivers Union and the Milk Industry Association of New York (1948).

²¹ Horace E. Sheldon, *op. cit.*, p. 43.

²² The plumbers' union was found in violation of Section 8 (b) (2) of Taft-Hartley, which prohibits a union from causing or attempting to cause an employer to discriminate against an employee in violation of subsection (a) (3) or to discriminate against an employee with respect to whom membership in such an organization has been denied or terminated on some ground other than his failure to tender the periodic dues and the initiation fees uniformly required as a condition of acquiring or retaining membership.

²³ *Virginia Electric Company* v. *NLRB*, 319 U.S. 533 (1943).

²⁴ *Nordberg-Selah Fruit, Inc.*, 126 NLRB 714 (1960).

²⁵ *Los Angeles-Seattle Motor Express, Inc.*, 121 NLRB 1629 (1958).

²⁶ *Carpenters, Local 60* v. *NLRB*, 365 U.S. 651 (1961).

²⁷ 93 *Congressional Record* 3952, April 23, 1947.

²⁸ *NLRB* v. *National Maritime Union of America, CIO*, 175 F. (2d) 686 (1949), cert. denied 338 U.S. 955 (1950).

²⁹ United States Congress, Hearings before the Senate Subcommittee on Labor-Management Relations, *Hiring Halls in the Maritime Industry*, 81st Congress, 2d sess., p. 168.

³⁰ *National Union of Marine Cooks & Stewards*, 90 NLRB 1099 (1950).

³¹ *Local 357, International Brotherhood of Teamsters, etc.* v. *NLRB*, 365 U.S. 667 (1961).

³² *Bricklayers and Masons International Local 3*, 162 NLRB 46, in *Thirty-Second Annual Report of the National Labor Relations Board, 1967* (Washington, D.C.: Government Printing Office, 1968), p. 132.

³³ *R. J. Smith Construction Company, Inc.* and *Local 150, Operating Engineers*, 191 NLRB No. 135 (1971).

³⁴ *Davenport Insulation*, 184 NLRB No. 114 (1970).

³⁵ Sections 8 (a) (3) and 9 (e) of Taft-Hartley.

³⁶ *Paragon Products Corporation*, 134 NLRB 86 (1961).

³⁷ *Thirty-Second Annual Report of the National Labor Relations Board, 1967* (Washington, D.C.: Government Printing Office, 1968), p. 237.

³⁸ Section 9 (f), (g), and (h).

³⁹ Labor Management Reporting and Disclosure Act of 1959, Section 201 (d).

⁴⁰ P.L. 189, 82d Congress, approved October 22, 1951.

⁴¹ NLRB, *Sixteenth Annual Report* (1951), p. 10.

⁴² *Monthly Labor Review* (December 1951), p. 682.

⁴³ Herbert R. Northrup and Gordon F. Bloom, *Government and Labor* (Homewood, Illinois: Richard D. Irwin, Inc., 1963), pp. 238–241.

⁴⁴ *International Union, United Automobile, Aircraft, and Agricultural Implement Workers*, 137 NLRB 104 (1962).

⁴⁵ *Aluminum Workers International Union, Local 135*, 112 NLRB 619 (1955).

⁴⁶ *General Motors Corporation, Packard Electric Division*, 134 NLRB 1107 (1962).

⁴⁷ *Philadelphia Sheraton Corporation*, 136 NLRB 888 (1962).

⁴⁸ *Union Starch & Refining Company*, 87 NLRB 779 (1949).

⁴⁹ *Local 283, UAW (Wisconsin Motor Corporation)*, 145 NLRB 1097 (1964).

⁵⁰ Proviso to Section 8 (b) (1) (A).

⁵¹ *Twenty-Ninth Annual Report of the National Labor Relations Board, 1964* (Washington, D.C.: Government Printing Office, 1965), p. 85.

[52] *Congressional Oversight of Administrative Agencies (National Labor Relations Board)*, Part II (Washington, D.C.: Government Printing Office, 1968), p. 1154.

[53] *Scofield* v. *NLRB*, 394 U.S. 423 (1969).

[54] Marten S. Estey, Philip Taft, and Martin Wagner, eds., *Regulating Union Government* (New York: Harper & Row, 1964), pp. 97–98.

[55] United Auto Workers, *A More Perfect Union* (Detroit: UAW Publications Department, 1958), pp. 5–6.

[56] *Keystone Coat, Apron & Towel Supply Company*, 121 NLRB 880 (1958).

[57] *NLRB* v. *News Syndicate Company, Inc., et. al.*, 365 U.S. 645 (1961); *Local 357, Teamsters* v. *NLRB (Los Angeles–Seattle Motor Express)*, 365 U.S. 807 (1961).

[58] *Paragon Products Corporation, op. cit.*

[59] 49 U.S. Stat. 499 (1947).

[60] Arkansas Constitutional Amendment No. 34, November 7, 1944; Florida Constitutional Declaration of Rights, No. 12, as amended November 7, 1944.

[61] Fred Witney, "Union Security," *Labor Law Journal*, IV, No. 2, (February 1953), p. 118.

[62] Georgia, Iowa, North Carolina, North Dakota, Tennessee, Texas, and Virginia.

[63] *McCulloch* v. *Maryland*, 4 Wheat. 316 (1819).

[64] *Lincoln Federal Labor Union* v. *Northwestern Iron & Metal Company*, 335 U.S. 525 (1949).

[65] Alabama, Arizona, Arkansas, Florida, Georgia, Iowa, Kansas, Mississippi, Nebraska, Nevada, North Carolina, North Dakota, South Carolina, South Dakota, Tennessee, Texas, Utah, Virginia, and Wyoming.

[66] John M. Glasgow, "The Right-to-Work Law Controversy Again," *Labor Law Journal*, XVIII, No. 2 (February 1967), 112.

[67] The repeal measure passed the House by a 20-vote margin, but a filibuster led by Senator Everett M. Dirksen of Illinois prevented the bill from being formally considered by the Senate. AFL-CIO officials nonetheless claimed that as many as 56 Senate votes, or more than the majority needed, would have been forthcoming in favor of repeal had the measure been brought to a vote.

[68] Paul E. Sultan, "The Union Security Issue," in eds. Joseph Shister, Benjamin Aaron, and Clyde W. Summers, *Public Policy and Collective Bargaining* (New York: Harper & Row, 1962), p. 93.

[69] In addition to the states mentioned, these are Maine (1948), Massachusetts (1948), New Mexico (1948), Oklahoma (1964), and Washington (1956, 1958).

[70] Fred Witney, *Indiana Labor Relations Law* (Bloomington, Ind.: Bureau of Business Research, Indiana University, 1960), p. 85.

[71] Sultan, *op. cit.*, p. 94.

[72] 68 Stat. 1238, 45 U.S.C. 152 Eleventh, Section 2.

[73] *Railway Employees' Dept.* v. *Hanson*, 351 U.S. 225 (1956).

[74] *Machinists* v. *Street*, 367 U.S. 740 (1961).

[75] *Brotherhood of Railway and Steamship Clerks* v. *Allen*, 373 U.S. 113 (1963).

[76] *Public Service Company of Colorado*, 89 NLRB 418 (1950).

[77] *American Seating Company*, 98 NLRB 800 (1952).

[78] Alabama, Arkansas, Georgia, Iowa, Mississippi, North Carolina, South Carolina, Tennessee, Utah, and Virginia.

[79] *Meade Electric Company* v. *Hagberg*, Indiana Superior Court, Lake County, May 19, 1958, No. 158–121. On June 19, 1959, the Second Northern Indiana Division, Indiana Court of Appeals, upheld the decision of the Superior Court.

[80] *Ibid.*

[81] *Baldwin* v. *Arizona Flame Restaurant, Inc.*, 82 Ariz. 385 (1957).

[82] Nebraska, Nevada, North Dakota, South Dakota, and Texas.

[83] Sultan, *op, cit.*, p. 109.

[84] *General Motors Corporation*, 130 NLRB 481 (1961).

[85] *General Motors Corporation*, 133 NLRB 21 (1961).

[86] *General Motors Corporation* v. *NLRB*, 303 F. (2d) 428 (1962).

[87] *NLRB* v. *General Motors Corporation*, 373 U.S. 734 (1963).

[88] *Retail Clerks International Association, Local 1625* v. *Schermerhorn*, 373 U.S. 746 (1963).

[89] *Retail Clerks, Local 1625* v. *Schermerhorn*, 373 U.S. 746 (1964).

[90] *Sea Pak* v. *Industrial, Technical and Professional Employees*, 400 U.S. 985 (1971).

[91] *Algoma Plywood & Veneer Company* v. *WERB*, 336 U.S. 301 (1949).

[92] *Safeway Stores*, 81 NLRB 387 (1949).

[93] *Hearings before the Committee on Labor and Public Welfare*, 80th Congress, 1st sess., on S. 55 and S. J. Res. 22, Part II, p. 839.

[94] *Ibid.*, Part II, p. 1151.

[95] Theodore Rose, "Union Security Provisions in Agreements, 1954," *Monthly Labor Review*, LXXVIII, No. 6 (June 1955), 657.

[96] Sultan, *op. cit.*, p. 91.

[97] Bureau of Labor Statistics Bulletin 908, *Union Security Provisions in Collective Bargaining*, (1947), p. 43.

[98] *Hearings before the Committee on Labor and Public Welfare*, 80th Congress, 1st sess., *op. cit.*, Part II, p. 1152.

[99] Section 302.

[100] "Coverage of Checkoff Under Taft-Hartley Act," *Monthly Labor Review*, LXVII (July 1948), 42.

[101] *Penn Cork & Closures*, 156 NLRB 411 (1965), enforced 376 F. (2d) 52 (1967).

[102] *Bedford Can Manufacturing Corporation*, 162 NLRB 133 (1967).

[103] *W. P. Ihrie & Sons, Division of Sunshine Biscuits*, 165 NLRB 2 (1967).

[104] *Keller Ladders Southern Subsidiary of Keller Industries*, 161 NLRB 21 (1966).

[105] Robben W. Fleming, "The Obligation to Bargain in Good Faith," in *Public Policy and Collective Bargaining*, ed. Joseph Shister, Benjamin Aaron, and Clyde W. Summers (New York: Harper & Row, 1962), p. 61.

[106] *In re International Association of Machinists*, 2 RLB 87 at 89 (1921) in *ibid.*

[107] *Ibid.*

[108] *Ibid.*, p. 62. Section 7 (a) required "that employees shall have the right to organize and bargain collectively through representatives of their own choosing."

[109] Section 8 (b) (3).

[110] 61 Stat. 142 (1947).

[111] *Globe Cotton Mills* v. *NLRB*, 103 F. (2d) 91, 94 (1939).

[112] *Times Publishing Company*, 72 NLRB 676 (1947).

[113] *Majure Transport Company* v. *NLRB* 198 F. (2d) 735 (1952).

[114] *NLRB* v. *Norfolk Shipbuilding & Drydock Corporation*, 172 F. (2d) 813 (1949).

[115] *Na-Mac Product Corporation*, 70 NLRB 298 (1946).

[116] *Southern Saddlery Company*, 90 NLRB 1205 (1950).

[117] *General Electric Company*, 150 NLRB 192 (1964).

[118] *NLRB* v. *General Electric Company*, 418 F. (2d) 736 (1969).

[119] *NLRB* v. *Wooster Division of Borg-Warner Corporation*, 356 U.S. 342 (1958).

[120] These are Section 8 (a) (5) for employers and 8 (b) (3) for unions.

[121] *Fibreboard Paper Products* v. *NLRB*, 379 U.S. 203 (1964).

[122] *Richfield Oil*, 110 NLRB 356 (1954) enforced 231 F. (2d) 717, cert. denied 351 U.S. 909 (1956).

[123] *Dicten & Masch Manufacturing*, 129 NLRB 112 (1960); *Kroger Company* v. *NLRB*, 399 F. (2d) 445 (1968).

[124] *Inland Steel Company*, 77 NLRB 1, enforced 170 F. (2d) 247 (1948), cert. denied 336 U.S. 960 (1949).

[125] *Lehigh Portland Cement*, 101 NLRB 1010 (1952).

[126] *NLRB* v. *Niles-Bemont Pond Company*, 199 F. (2d) 713 (1952).

[127] *Beacon Piece Dyeing & Finishing Company*, 121 NLRB 953 (1958).

[128] *Miller Brewing Company*, 166 NLRB 90 (1967).

[129] *NLRB* v. *American National Insurance*, 343 U.S. 395 (1952).

[130] *NLRB* v. *Retail Clerks International Association*, 203 F. (2d) 165 (1953).

[131] *Daelyte Service*, 126 NLRB 63 (1960).

[132] *Operating Engineers, Local No. 12 (Associated General Contractors of America)*, 187 NLRB 439 (1970).

[133] *Seattle First National Bank* v. *NLRB*, 450 F. (2d) 353 (1971) reversing 176 NLRB No. 97 (1969).

[134] *NLRB* v. *Package Machinery Company*, CA 1 No. 71-1344 (March 30, 1972).

[135] *NLRB* v. *United Brotherhood of Carpenters, Local 964*, 447 F. (2d) 643 (1971).

[136] *Allied Chemical Workers, Local 1* v. *Pittsburgh Plate Glass*, 404 U.S. 157 (1971).

[137] 177 NLRB 911 (1969).

[138] *Universal Oil Products* v. *NLRB*, 445 F. (2d) 155 (1971).

[139] *NLRB* v. *Taormina*, 207 F. (2d) 251 (1953) enforcing 94 NLRB 884 (1951).

[140] *Kit Manufacturing*, 150 NLRB 662 (1964) enforcing 365 F. (2d) 829 (1966).

[141] *Arlington Asphalt Company*, 136 NLRB 742 (1962).

[142] *NLRB* v. *Corsicana Cotton Mills*, 178 F. (2d) 344 (1959).

[143] *Fibreboard Paper Products Corporation* v. *NLRB*, 379 U.S. 203 (1964).

[144] *Television & Radio Artists* v. *NLRB*, 398 F. (2d) 319 (1968).

[145] *Collyer Insulated Wire*, 192 NLRB No. 150 (1971).

[146] D. J. Johannesen and W. Britton Smith, Jr., "*Collyer:* Open Sesame to Deferral," *Labor Law Journal*, v. 23, No. 12 (December 1972), p. 741.

[147] *Atlantic Richfield*, 199 NLRB No. 135 (1972).

[148] *Radioear*, 199 NLRB No. 137 (1972).

[149] *Western Electric*, 199 NLRB No. 49 (1972).

[150] *Southwestern Bell Telephone*, 198 NLRB No. 6 (1972).

[151] *Great Coastal Express*, 196 NLRB No. 129 (1972).

[152] *Coppus Engineering*, 195 NLRB No. 113 (1972).

[153] *Peerless Pressed Metal*, 198 NLRB No. 5 (1972).

[154] *Appalachian Power Company*, 198 NLRB No. 168 (1972).

[155] *Tyee Construction Company*, 202 NLRB No. 4 (1973).

[156] *Tulsa-Whisenhunt Funeral Homes*, 195 NLRB No. 20 (1972).

[157] *Borden Chemical*, 196 NLRB No. 172 (1973).

[158] *Mountain State Construction Company*, 203 NLRB No. 167 (1973).

[159] 112 NLRB 1080 (1955).

[160] National Labor Relations Board, Office of the General Counsel, "Arbitration Deferral Policy under *Collyer*, Revised Guidelines" (May 10, 1973), p. 59.

[161] *Malrite of Wisconsin*, 198 NLRB No. 3 (1972).

[162] Federal Mediation and Conciliation Service, *Twenty-Fifth Annual Report* (1972), p. 40.

[163] *H. K. Porter Company* v. *NLRB*, 397 U.S. 99 (1970).

15

Enforcement of the
Collective Bargaining Agreement

VIOLATIONS OF THE LABOR AGREEMENT

The typical collective bargaining contract is a complex document dealing with almost every phase of the employer-employee relationship. If the collective bargaining process is to serve its purpose, the rights and obligations in the labor contract must be respected. A seniority clause, designed to protect the job rights of long-service employees, for example, will have little value if employers give preference to the short-service workers. Likewise, employers will find very little value in the collective bargaining process when labor unions fail to perform their obligations as spelled out in labor contracts.

In the practical affairs of industrial relations, both unions and management frequently contend that the other party violated rights vouchsafed in the contract. These complaints—or "grievances," as they are commonly termed—are numerous and varied in character. Common grievances that labor unions file against employers involve such matters as the discharge and discipline of workers, seniority rights, job classifications, discrimination, safety and sanitation, defective machines, abuse by foremen, pay shortages, and speedup practices. Every time a labor organization files a grievance, it contends that management is violating some section or provision in the collective bargaining contract. Management also has occasion to charge that unions violate the terms of the collective bargaining contract. However, union complaints against management far exceed management complaints against unions. This circumstance arises from the fact that under most contracts the employer takes the initial action in the interpretation of the agreement. Once a complaint is raised, there must be some adequate provision to resolve disputes or the contractual terms are likely to deteriorate.

INTERNAL ENFORCEMENT PROCEDURE:
THE GRIEVANCE PROCEDURE

After a labor agreement is executed, management and the labor union bargain collectively on a day-to-day basis. Such bargaining does not involve negotiations for the purpose of fashioning a new labor contract. Neither is daily bargaining directed at altering the particular terms of the existing agreement. Collective bargaining on the day-to-day level is the process whereby the labor contract is made a living organism. Much of the day-to-day relations between management and labor involves the settling of disputes alleging violations of the provisions of the contract. Such settlement is achieved through the *grievance procedure*, a mechanism for self-enforcement of the contract contained in practically every collective bargaining agreement.

The grievance procedure provides an orderly system whereby the employer and the union can determine whether or not contractual terms have been violated. Only a relatively small number of violations involve willful disregard of the terms of the collective bargaining agreement. More frequently employers or unions pursue a course of conduct, alleged to be a violation of the collective bargaining agreement, which the party believes to conform with its terms. In any event the grievance procedure provides the mechanism to resolve misunderstandings. Through it the parties have an opportunity to determine whether or not the contract has actually been violated. Such a peaceful procedure permits enforcement of the contract and minimizes use of the strike or lockout. Each year thousands of grievances are filed alleging contract violations. Industry would indeed be in a chaotic state if the strike or the lockout were utilized to effect compliance with the contract instead of resorting to the peaceful procedures of the grievance mechanism. The economic costs of lost output could be substantial.

So that the collective bargaining contract will be enforced properly, labor and management rely on the grievance procedure. Both unions and management are aware that charges of contract violation will arise during the contract period. Every day-to-day problem or question that might arise cannot be anticipated in the collective bargaining agreement. The complexities of labor-management relations preclude the drawing up of such a contract. In addition, the provisions in an agreement are subject to conflicting interpretations, just as are laws enacted by legislative bodies. In this connection it should be emphasized that many charges involving contract violations arise merely because union and management representatives do not agree on the meaning of a particular contract provision. The grievance procedure provides management and unions with a mechanism to dispose of charges of contract violations in an orderly and equitable manner.

A chief characteristic of the grievance procedure is that it provides for several stages of settlement. Most agreements provide for three or four steps, exclusive of arbitration, and at each step the grievance will be discussed by different but specified representatives of the union and the company.

A typical four-step procedure might be one in which the foreman of the department in which the grievance arises and the employee in question, with or without a union steward, handle the problem at the first step. If a settlement is not reached at this stage, the second step might involve discussions by the general foreman and the chairman of the union grievance committee. Failing to reach agreement at the second step, the grievance would then go to the third stage, at which there could be deliberations by the local union president and the superintendent of the plant, perhaps together with other designated union and company representatives. Finally, if no settlement is reached, the fourth step of the grievance procedure is invoked. At this terminal step the grievance might be handled by the Director of Industrial Relations of the company and other key management representatives, and a representative of the international union and key representatives of the local union. This is only one illustration; it is not meant to be universal in character. Depending on the size of the plant, the customs of the union-management relationship, and the history of labor relations in the company, labor contracts will vary as to the number of steps in the grievance procedure and the personnel participating at each step.

Under many labor agreements or the customs of a particular plant, a worker's complaint is first discussed orally by the worker and the foreman. The employee's union steward or grievance committeeman may participate in the discussion. Only if settlement is not reached on an oral basis is the grievance formally written. A vast number of workers' complaints are settled on an oral basis to the satisfaction of all concerned.

A majority of grievance procedures specify definite time limits for each stage of grievance processing. For example, a contract may stipulate that a grievance must be filed within a certain number of days after the alleged violation of the contract takes place. Companies are required to give their answers within a certain number of days at each stage of the procedure. In addition, the union must appeal to the next stage of the procedure within a certain time limit if it is not satisfied with the answer of the company at any particular stage. Failure to comply with specified time limits may result in the forfeiture of the grievance by the union or the granting of it by the company. However, many companies and unions will grant extensions of time limits upon request.

By providing for time limits, the contract requires the company and the union to give speedy attention to the problem. In this manner grievances can be settled promptly, reducing or eliminating friction in the bargaining unit. A major problem in establishment of specified time limits is striking a balance between prompt and orderly progress of the grievance through the various steps of the grievance procedure and provision for a sufficient amount of time at each stage for the accumulation of all relevant facts so that the grievance can be discussed and settled in an intelligent manner. To accomplish this objective, many contracts provide a three-to-five-working-day interval between the various steps of the grievance procedure; others provide a somewhat longer interval.

CONTROL OF THE GRIEVANCE PROCEDURE: WAGNER ACT EXPERIENCE

Under the terms of the National Labor Relations Act, a labor union certified by the NLRB became the exclusive representative of all employees within the bargaining unit "for the purposes of collective bargaining in respect to rates of pay, wages, hours of employment, or other conditions of employment."[1] Consequently, an employer was in violation of the Wagner Act if he recognized the majority union as the representative of its members only. A certified labor organization negotiates for all workers within the unit regardless of their union membership status. Apart from conferring this exclusive status upon certified labor organizations, the Wagner Act provided that "any individual employee or a group of employees shall have the right at any time to present grievances to their employers."[2]

For several years the NLRB had no occasion to render an interpretation of this portion of the Wagner Act. Early in World War II, however, the North American Aviation Company believed that Section 9 (a) of the Act gave employees the right to present and adjust grievances individually regardless of the existence of a collective bargaining agreement.[3] The company had previously executed a contract with a union certified by the NLRB. Shortly afterward copies of the contract were distributed to the firm's employees. In addition each worker received a notice signed by the company's president which outlined a grievance procedure unilaterally prepared by the company. Such a procedure was inconsistent with the one set forth in the collective bargaining agreement. On the ground that the employer's conduct indicated a refusal to grant exclusive bargaining rights to the certified union, the NLRB subsequently found that he engaged in an unfair labor practice. But when the company appealed the Board's decision, a federal circuit court ruled that the "grievance provision" of the Wagner Act conferred upon employers the right to hear and to adjust any grievance presented by individual employees, notwithstanding the existence of a collective bargaining agreement.[4] It is noteworthy that the court construed the grievance provision to include not only "small out-of-mind grievances," but covered all grievances employees may wish to adjust. The court apparently indicated that an employer may lawfully adjust individual grievances relating to all conditions of employment regardless of the terms of a collective bargaining contract.

Beyond reversing the Board's decision, the court's ruling stimulated the first formal NLRB interpretation of the grievance provision. In general, the Board's General Counsel took the position that the provision means that an individual employee has the technical right to present grievances to his employer, but that representatives of the certified union must be present each time an employee makes such a presentation and must negotiate the settlement of the grievance. Under this construction the Wagner Act grievance provision extended to individual workers the mechanical right of presentation of grievances, but reserved to certified labor organizations the exclusive right to settle the grievances.

Such an interpretation appears to be supported by the legislative history of the Wagner Act. In discussing the right of individual workers to present grievances, Senator Walsh stated:

> I do not think it was the intent of the proponents of this legislation and I do not think it was the intent of the proponents of this language to permit groups to present grievances, nor was it intended to debar minority groups from sitting in on any negotiations or that they be separately heard by the employers and their grievances or their suggestions received and in turn presented by him to the majority group.[5]

Apparently, Senator Walsh believed that nothing in the National Labor Relations Act prohibited individual employees from presenting grievances, but indicated that majority unions must adjust them.

When the House of Representatives was considering the National Labor Relations Act, some thought was given to the clarification of the grievance provision by adding the following clause to Section 9 of the Wagner Act: "Provided, further, that if such grievances are presented to the employer, these grievances will be taken up by the employer and the representatives of the majority and be settled."[6] If this provision had been included in the Wagner Act, there would have been no area of controversy since grievances presented by individual workers could be adjusted only by agents of the certified labor organizations. However, Congress may have believed that the general nature of the Wagner Act indicated that majority unions should ultimately negotiate the settlement of all grievances and failed to include this clarifying provision.

Notwithstanding the rule of the federal court in the *North American* case, the NLRB adopted the interpretation of its General Counsel and ruled in a subsequent case that employers must settle grievances presented by individual workers with the majority union. In one instance the Board, in implementing this policy, declared that the right of employees to present grievances was not an "empty one." Such a right, according to the Board, insured to the individual employee that his grievances will not be ignored by the majority union.[7] When the exclusive bargaining agent refuses to participate in the adjustment of the grievances, the NLRB ruled that the employee may individually negotiate with his employer.

In another case the Board reaffirmed its policy even though the certified union involved in the controversy had not yet negotiated a contract. Accordingly, an unfair labor practice was found inasmuch as the employer ordered any individual with grievances to take them up directly with management. It is noteworthy that the National War Labor Board also ruled that final adjustment of grievances had to be made with majority unions and not upon an individual basis.[8]

GRIEVANCE PROCEDURE UNDER
TAFT-HARTLEY

The Taft-Hartley Act nullified the NLRB doctrine established under the Wagner Act dealing with the presentation and adjustment of grievances on an individual worker basis. Under the terms of Taft-Hartley, grievance procedure structures must be broad enough to meet two standards: (1) the individual worker must be permitted to present grievances to his employer on an individual basis; and (2) the employer must be permitted to make an adjustment of grievances so presented, provided the adjustment is not inconsistent with the terms of the collective bargaining agreement.[9]

The first requirement does not greatly change the rulings of the NLRB established under the Wagner Act. Individual workers had the opportunity to present grievances to employers. However, it was necessary for employers to invite representatives of the bargaining agent to be present at the time individual workers presented grievances to their employers. Under Taft-Hartley the labor union holding bargaining rights in the plant does not have to be involved in grievance adjustment, but must be given an opportunity to be present during the proceedings.

Actually, in this respect Taft-Hartley does not greatly alter collective bargaining procedures. Many collective bargaining contracts negotiated long before Taft-

Hartley was enacted provided that the individual worker could choose the method of presentation of his grievance. Scores of agreements gave the worker the freedom to (1) present his grievance on an individual basis; (2) elect to have a representative of the labor union present the grievance for him; or (3) go with a union representative to the proper management official for the presentation of the grievance. A comparatively small number of agreements went to the extremes of forbidding anyone but the union representative to present workers' grievances or requiring that the worker present his grievance on an individual basis.

On the other hand, the second grievance procedure standard of the 1947 law upsets traditional collective bargaining relationships. By providing that the employer may make adjustment of a grievance with a worker on an individual basis, Taft-Hartley destroyed the policies developed by the NLRB under the Wagner Act. As noted, the NLRB required that all grievances must be adjusted with the representatives of the workers' labor union. Only when the collective bargaining agency did not care to adjust a worker's grievance was it permissible for the employer to adjust grievances on an individual worker basis. Obviously, if a labor union refuses to do anything about a worker's grievance, the worker and the employer should have the right to make the adjustment. Any adjustment made through this arrangement since the Taft-Hartley enactment must be consistent with the terms of an existing collective bargaining contract. If individuals were permitted to reach agreements inconsistent with the contract, the entire process of collective bargaining would disintegrate rapidly. Most unions do not encourage individual processing of grievances because of the apparent implication that it is not capable of adequately functioning as bargaining agent. However, it should be recognized that some unions are much less than enthusiastic about processing nonmember grievances on a par with those raised by members. Regardless of attempts to discourage individual initiative in these matters, unions do not have legal authority to cause the discharge of employees for circumventing the labor organization and directly presenting grievances to employers.[10]

Should an employer adjust a worker's grievance in a fashion that violates the terms of the collective bargaining contract, unions may sue in the federal courts under Section 301 of Taft-Hartley. Generally, a union in such a position may prefer to resolve the issue through the grievance procedure. Often, however, an employer that violates the contractual terms of the agreement is aware of its action and union efforts to deal informally with the situation are not heeded. As the law now stands, dependent upon the grievance machinery provided in the contract, a dissatisfied union might submit the issue to arbitration, to the NLRB in the form of an unfair labor practice charge, or to the federal courts. The method will depend largely upon both the terms of the contract and the general nature of union-management relations in the bargaining unit.

The grievance sections of Taft-Hartley encourage individual bargaining and provide a vehicle for weakening the practice of collective bargaining. Government intervention in the collective bargaining process is made more prevalent by the provisions which were enacted in the first place to guarantee greater individual freedom to exercise rights regarding employment status. In the meantime the ability of the bargaining agent to act for the entire unit of employees is diminished. The grievance mechanism could arguably become so overburdened that productivity would decline as a result of delays in resolving problems.

Employee Recourse through NLRB. If a union which holds the position of exclusive bargaining representative of employees declines to process the grievance of a member of the bargaining unit, it has refused representation. Such a refusal constitutes restraint and coercion of the worker in his right to representation.[11] As stated in *Miranda*:

> ... Section 7 ... gives employees the right to be free from unfair or irrelevant or invidious treatment by their exclusive bargaining agent in matters affecting their employment. This right of employees is a statutory limitation on statutory bargaining representatives, and ... Section 8 (b) (1) (A) of the Act accordingly prohibits labor organizations, when acting in a statutory representative capacity, from taking action against any employee upon considerations or classifications which are irrelevant, invidious, or unfair.

Grievance handling is one aspect of an employee's right to fair and impartial treatment by exclusive bargaining agents.

Grievance processing is a part of the union's bargaining function. But it should be noted that refusal to process a grievance constitutes a breach of the union's duty to bargain with the employer under the Act's provisions. Any employee who feels aggrieved by a union's refusal to process his complaint may appeal his case to the NLRB.[12] This means that the Board must judge the substantive aspects of the collective bargaining agreement regarding the rights of employees to fair representation within the unfair labor practice provisions of Taft-Hartley.[13] The Board must evaluate the merits of the grievance and the union's action and motives for disposing of a situation so as to dissatisfy the worker. Failure to convince the NLRB that a worker's grievance was treated in the same fashion as those of other workers could result in unfair labor practice remedies. This unfair labor practice result holds since labor organizations have the statutory duty to represent all employees of a bargaining unit in a fair and nonarbitrary fashion. The courts have had a different set of circumstances under which they have dealt with labor contract enforcement.

The Common-Law Enforcement of Contracts through Court Proceedings. The Wagner Act did not provide for the enforcement of collective bargaining contracts. This aspect of labor relations was within the jurisdiction of the states to apply their common law. Essentially, the common law of contracts did not recognize collective bargaining agreements as legal instruments since unions did not offer employers the required considerations for their concessions. Labor power furnished the employer was provided by employees and not unions. Thus it was difficult for the courts to recognize any contract between employers and unions. Unions were without "legal personalities and as such it was difficult for them to sue or to be sued" under common-law rules.[14]

Essentially, the courts approached the issue of labor agreement enforcement in three separate theoretical fashions: custom and usage, agency, and third-party beneficiary.[15] The *custom-and-usage theory* provides one basis for court proceedings involving collective bargaining contracts. It provides an indirect basis for courts to recognize collective agreements. For example, an employee could sue an employer if he could show that the labor agreement was the contractual arrangement under which he was hired. Unions, however, acquired no rights under the agreement and as such the labor-management document was not considered a legal and binding contract. This meant that employers were often theoretically free to negotiate individually with employees regarding the terms and conditions of employment despite the existence of a collective bargaining agreement.

Actually, employers were not free to contract individually when labor-management agreements were signed with Board-certified bargaining-unit representatives. Recourse for such action was available through the NLRB, which has the authority to remedy such action through the unfair labor practice provisions of the National Labor Relations Act. Also the possibility of incurring economically devastating strikes often deterred employers from engaging in such unilateral action.

The *agency theory* provides a second method by which some of the courts reviewed collective bargaining contracts under common law. This theory provided that unions served as agents for employees in obtaining contractual terms and conditions of work for individual employees. The union, however, was not considered a party to the contract and as such could not seek court enforcement of its terms. Individual members of the labor organization were in a position to seek court enforcement of contractual terms if they desired to undertake individual court actions.

The third common-law category for enforcing collective bargaining agreements in the courts is the *third-party-beneficiary theory*. This theory provides that a union has entered into an agreement with management to cover the terms of work for all bargaining-unit members. In some cases the use of this theory permitted unions to obtain court recognition that they were parties to collective agreements. Suits brought in the courts, however, were generally viewed as cases on behalf of employees and not of the union itself.

In short, it was difficult for unions and employers to sue each other under the common law. Unions were not considered legally responsible organizations. Progress such as was made in this direction was slow prior to 1947.

Court Proceedings under Taft-Hartley. The Taft-Hartley Act makes it easier for parties to the collective bargaining process to sue each other in courts of law when alleged violations of the labor agreement occur. This is accomplished by expanding the jurisdiction of the federal court in labor contract violation cases.[16] Before the 1947 law was enacted, labor organizations could be sued for contract violations in the federal courts. However, two conditions had to prevail before the federal courts would assume jurisdiction of the case: (1) the parties involved were required to be citizens of different states; and (2) the amount of damages resulting from the breach of contract had to be at least $3,000. The Taft-Hartley Act removed both of these restrictions on the federal courts. Section 301 provided that "suits for violations of contract between an employer and a labor organization . . . may be brought in any district court of the United States having jurisdiction of the parties, without respect to the amount in controversy or without regard to the citizenship of the parties."

Proponents of this feature of the 1947 labor law argued that its effect would make labor unions more responsible in the discharge of their obligations under collective bargaining contracts—in particular, that unions would be more prone to respect their no-strike and no-slowdown obligations. In this respect the National Association of Manufacturers declared: "Now there is less danger that [workers] will suddenly be called out on strike while the contract is in effect."[17] Fearful of being sued in court for damages resulting from strikes violating the collective bargaining agreement, labor unions, it was felt, would exercise caution to prevent such work stoppages.

The Taft-Hartley Act expands considerably the jurisdiction of the federal courts over labor-management disputes. In addition, it sets up a concept of union responsibility quite different from the one in the Norris–La Guardia Act. Before the passage of Norris–La Guardia, the common-law rules of agency applied to federal court proceedings in which labor unions found themselves defendants. Under the common law a principal is liable for the unlawful acts of his agents whether or not the principal has knowledge of, has ratified, or has authorized the agents' actions. For purposes of labor relations, the union, under the common-law doctrine of agency, was responsible for actions of its members and officers.

Although the common-law doctrine of agency may be justified in many areas of judicial proceedings, its application to labor matters works a considerable hardship upon labor organizations. The fundamental reason for this rests upon the nature of the labor union as a functioning institution. Labor unions are composed of large numbers of members. In many unions there are hundreds—in some cases thousands—of officers but the employer chooses the union's membership. The union at best exercises a loose degree of discipline over its membership. The imposition of discipline by the union over union members and union officers is usually a difficult process. Union members are not "fired" out of the normal labor organization except after an elaborate procedure. This characteristic of the union movement is not criticized. On the contrary, adequate protection of a worker's union membership is necessary if democracy within the labor union is to be preserved. This merely highlights the fact that the status of union members and officers is well protected. Such insulation provides a basis for conduct that may be inconsistent with the terms of the labor contract.

Finally, it is pertinent to point out that the labor union does not have the control a business firm has in choosing its personnel. Agents of labor unions—such as union officers, stewards, and grievance committeemen—are elected by the membership. In contrast with the method employed by the union in obtaining its leadership, the company normally carefully selects representatives of management on the basis of education, experience, aptitude tests, and recommendations.

Congress was aware of these considerations when it passed Norris–La Guardia. It recognized that the application of the common-law rule of agency to labor relations operated to the serious disadvantage of the labor union. The complexities of modern industrial life and a realistic view of the labor union as a living organism militated for a different approach to the problem of union responsibility. As a result Section 6 of the Norris–La Guardia Act was adopted. This provision required actual authorization or ratification by labor organizations of agents' acts to establish union responsibility. Section 6 declared:

> No officer or member of any association or organization, and no association or organization participating or interested in a labor dispute, shall be held responsible or liable in any court of the United States for the unlawful acts of individual officers, members, or agents, except upon clear proof of actual participation in, or actual authorization of, such acts, or of ratification of such acts after actual knowledge thereof.

Thus Norris–La Guardia prevented the application of the common-law rule of agency to labor disputes. Under its terms a labor union, before it could be held liable for illegal action of its members or officers, must have authorized such conduct or ratified the action after it occurred. Proponents of Norris–La Guardia contend this conception of union responsibility was made necessary by the contemporary industrial relations environment.

Union Responsibility under Taft-Hartley. Under the terms of the 1947 labor law, it appeared at first that the rules of agency developed at common law would once again govern the issue of union responsibility. The law provides that in determining whether or not any person is acting as an agent of a labor organization so as to make the union responsible for his acts, "the question of whether the specific acts performed were actually authorized or subsequently ratified shall not be controlling." By this language the statute makes the labor union responsible for the activities of its members or officers, regardless of whether or not the union authorized or ratified the conduct. In this connection the International Association of Machinists pointed out that Taft-Hartley "makes the union responsible for the actions of irresponsible 'agents' who act without authorization. And it subjects the union to legal liability for such unauthorized actions."[18]

The officers of labor organizations must react responsibly when contractual violations occur or else they must be willing to subject their organizations to court actions.

At times strikes and other interruptions to production not authorized by the labor organization occur. These work stoppages, commonly known as *wildcat strikes*, are instigated by a group of workers, sometimes including union officers, without the sanction of the labor union. Under many labor agreements the employer has the right to discharge such employees or to penalize them otherwise for such activities.

An employer may sue a union because of a wildcat strike even though the union does not authorize or ratify it. As a result unions and employers have negotiated *nonsuability clauses*. Under these arrangements the company agrees that it will not sue a labor union because of wildcat strikes provided that the union fulfills its obligation to terminate the work stoppage. Frequently, the labor contract specifies exactly what the union must do in order to free itself from the possibility of damage suits. Thus, in some contracts containing nonsuability clauses, the union agrees to announce orally and in writing that it disavows the strike, orders the workers back to their jobs, and refuses any form of strike relief to the participants in such work stoppages.

Though an employer may sue a union for money damages under Section 301 when employees participate in a wildcat strike, the provision does not authorize employer suits against individual union members.[19] A certain labor agreement contained a no-strike clause that forbade work interruptions during the period of the contract. Despite this provision, employees went out on strike. The employer sued both the union and the individual employees for breach of contract and requested a federal court to assess money damages against the union and the employees. He argued that Section 301 established congressional intent that individual strikers, as well as the unions, be held responsible for damages suffered by employers as a result of unauthorized strikes. In rejecting the employer position, a federal appeals court stated:

> . . . The legislative history of the act indicates that the principal concern of Congress was with making unions, as parties to collective bargaining agreements, responsible for breaches of agreements and to avoid subjecting individual union members to fiscal ruin. . . .

In this regard, it should also be noted that union members as individuals are not responsible for damages levied against labor organizations. Section 301 provides that "any money judgment against a labor organization in a district court of the United States shall be enforceable only against the organization as an entity and shall not be enforceable against any individual member or his assets." In 1962, the U.S. Supreme Court maintained the integrity of this language when it held that "when a union is liable for damages for violation of the no-strike clause, its officers and members are not liable for these damages."[20]

What all this means is that union members and officers as individuals are not liable for money damages in the event of wildcat strikes. Action against individual employees is, therefore, limited to discharge or other forms of discipline. Employees who participate in a wildcat strike lose their status as employees for purposes of Taft-Hartley.[21] Thus, if an employer discharges such employees the NLRB will not direct their reinstatement.

Individual Suits in Federal Courts. Still another avenue is open to employees when a union does not represent them fairly in the collective bargaining process. They have the right to sue unions and employers in federal and state court jurisdictions under Section 301 of Taft-Hartley.[22] Thus employees who feel their rights have been violated under collective bargaining agreements may choose to seek relief from the courts or the NLRB. Unions have both the right and responsibility to represent all bargaining-unit members fairly by evaluating the merits of grievances filed. There is no requirement, however, that a union must process a grievance throughout the entire range of grievance machinery provided by the contract, including arbitration. The labor organization is required to accept a complaint for unbiased investigation before declining to proceed to advanced grievance stages. The Supreme Court stated that "to remove or gag the union in these cases would surely weaken the collective bargaining and grievance processes."[23]

Financial liability of unions even in cases where they may abandon a grievance improperly is not present merely because an employee may prove to the courts that it was a meritorious one. The test for holding labor organizations responsible in court suits is whether the employee can show "arbitrary or bad faith conduct on the part of the union in processing his grievance."[24] Unions have the authority to resolve issues with employers without having to obtain solutions no more advantageous to one employee than to another. Differences are inevitable within bargaining units. A suitable solution to one employee may well be unacceptable to another. Unions cannot bargain effectively with employers unless they can provide reasonable assurances their actions will not be destroyed legally by dissidents. The Supreme Court has ruled:

> A wide range of reasonableness must be allowed a statutory bargaining representative in serving the unit it represents subject always to complete good faith and honesty of purpose in the exercise of its discretion.[25]

Despite the probability that may exist against employees prevailing in the courts, the fact is that they have the right to file suits against employers and unions for alleged violations of rights under collective agreements. It is not likely the courts will be extensively used by workers dissatisfied with the way they are treated under collective bargaining contracts. The process is too expensive for most employees. Justice Goldberg in his concurring opinion felt that a breach of the duty of fair representation was one covered by Taft-Hartley and not the collective bargaining instrument.[26] The difference involves relief from the NLRB and not the courts. It was also the opinion of Justice Goldberg that unfair representation could be properly remedied through decertification elections. As such there would be no need to jeopardize the collective bargaining process by involving the courts in the grievance machinery. Undoubtedly, the entire issue turns on the protection of individual and minority rights relative to those of the majority.

Taft-Hartley has created the machinery whereby an individual may protest the decisions of the majority by bringing Section 301 suits before the courts. Unions and management are not as free as in prior years to determine by the terms of their contract what shall be the respective rights of the union and individual in its administration.[27] This procedure plunges the courts directly into a review of the substantive provisions of collective bargaining agreements, a task for which the courts in the past have had little competency. Their difficulties interpreting collective bargaining agreements are best illustrated in the complicated and inconsistent problems of grievance arbitration.

WHEN DIRECT NEGOTIATIONS FAIL:
ARBITRATION

The vast majority of disputes involving labor contract violations are settled by representatives of management and labor by direct negotiation. At one step or other in the grievance procedure union and company representatives usually find a workable solution for a dispute. However, some grievances are not resolved by direct negotiations. Both sides may feel that their positions are supported by the terms of the collective bargaining agreement. The question arises: What should be done about disputes in which labor and management cannot reach an agreement by direct negotiation?

A do-nothing policy would not serve the interests of sound labor relations. Unsettled contract violation disputes adversely affect plant morale and result in the general deterioration of labor-management relations. Ultimately, unresolved grievances could cause such serious tensions in the bargaining unit that effective implementation of the productive process would deteriorate. An accumulation of unsettled grievances could result in strikes and lockouts. All parties suffer from such work stoppages.

To avoid a breakdown in labor-management relations and to promote uninterrupted production during the life of a contract, a large number of unions and companies make use of a third party—called an "arbitrator" or an "umpire." The arbitrator makes the final settlement of disputes involving contract violations. His decision is binding on the two parties.

The method for selecting an arbitrator is normally provided for in the labor agreement. Both union and management must agree on the third party before the dispute is submitted to arbitration. Ordinarily, people who serve as arbitrators are strictly impartial and well versed in the fine points of collective bargaining. The function of the arbitration is to resolve the dispute in the light of the existing collective bargaining contract. The arbitrator has no power to add to, subtract from, or modify any provision of the collective bargaining agreement. His task is to determine whether or not a particular pattern of conduct constitutes a violation of the labor contract as it is written at the time of the arbitration. In short, the arbitrator applies the existing contract to the facts of the case and determines whether or not a violation has occurred.

Typical arbitration resembles a regular court of law in that a third party decides the dispute. Contrary to regular judicial proceedings, however, an atmosphere of informality characterizes the usual arbitration. Rules of procedure applicable to regular court proceedings are frequently ignored. The arbitrator may ask pertinent and searching questions to clarify points not presented adequately by the parties. In many arbitration proceedings each side will attempt to prove its case without the utilization of lawyers. The "judicial mind" is not necessarily an asset in arbitration proceedings. This is particularly the case when the arbitrator himself is not a member of the bar, a circumstance that is not uncommon.

Each side is responsible for preparation of its own case. If the labor union charges that a company violated a collective bargaining agreement, union representatives must come prepared to prove to the arbitrator that a violation actually did take place. In such circumstances company representatives must be prepared to prove that no violation occurred. Witnesses may be called, documents produced, and briefs submitted. Oral argument is effective provided that the speaker confines his remarks to the particular dispute and attempts to win his point by utilizing facts and not emotion.

When the arbitration proceedings are terminated, the arbitrator hands down a so-called *award*. The award contains the judgment of the arbitrator. However the arbitrator rules, his decision is final and binding on both parties. Obviously, the arbitration process is valuable for the peaceful settlement of industrial disputes. Certainly, contract violation disputes are better settled by arbitration than by resort to industrial warfare. Arbitration provides an orderly and peaceful mechanism to resolve grievances when direct negotiations fail.

The utilization of arbitration means that an outside party settles disputes. Although the arbitrator attempts to consider all aspects, the fact remains that all ramifications and the minutiae of a contract violation dispute are given greater attention when the controversy is resolved through direct negotiations. In short, the arbitration process means less flexibility in the adjudication of grievances because the opinion of an outside party prevails over the judgment of the parties to the collective bargaining process.

Sound collective bargaining relationships are established when union and management representatives assume the responsibility for effecting a solution to their mutual problems. Arbitration tends to weaken this responsibility. Frequent utilization of the arbitration process could cause a sharp setback to collective bargaining. Actually, this is the major count against arbitration. It operates to make an outside party responsible for the solution of day-to-day industrial disputes. Management and the union must assume this duty if collective bargaining is to accomplish its fundamental purpose—the establishment of sound industrial relations based on the meeting of minds of labor and management representatives on issues of mutual concern.

This shortcoming of arbitration for the settlement of contract violation disputes is indeed serious. Management and unions should be alert to the inherent damages of the arbitration process. Every effort should be made to settle grievances through direct negotiation. This is a fundamental responsibility of management and labor. However, there is no reason to believe that management and labor will settle all disputes through direct negotiation. It is therefore necessary that some peaceful and orderly mechanism be employed to finally settle grievances that management and labor have failed to resolve through direct negotiation. Arbitration serves this purpose.

As a result the typical labor agreement provides for the arbitration of contract violation disputes. One additional factor militates for the inclusion of an arbitration clause in the typical labor agreement. Unions will not agree to a no-strike provision unless a mechanism provides for the final settlement of grievances arising during the life of the contract. Organized labor feels that if it surrenders its right to strike during the contract period, it must be assured that a third party will break deadlocks over contract violation disputes. If arbitration were not provided for in a collective bargaining contract that contains a no-strike clause, a labor union could not take any economic or procedural action to effect a final settlement of grievances arising under the contract. Management representatives agree with organized labor that a contract containing a no-strike clause should also make provision for arbitration.

At present some 95 percent of all U.S. labor agreements provide for arbitration as the final step in the grievance procedure. This national percentage is significantly greater than it was in the early 1930s, when fewer than 8 to 10 percent of all agreements contained such a clause. And even by 1944 arbitration provisions had been included in only 73 percent of all contracts.[28]

Recent statistics involving arbitration caseloads have been of no small order of magnitude. In 1962, for example, neutrals were called upon to make awards in no less than fifteen thousand labor-management disputes and wrote an estimated million words in support of their opinions.[29] In an era of uncertainty as to the future growth of union membership totals, moreover, there is no collective job insecurity in the profession: according to the American Arbitration Association, the caseload of arbitrators keeps increasing at the rate of roughly 10 percent annually.[30]

ARBITRATION, THE COURTS, AND THE NLRB

Arbitration has long been held suspect by courts of law because the process is often viewed as a device to avoid court jurisdiction over contractual matters. The arbitration process is unique in industrial relations in that:

> it is the creation of the parties. It is created by them, and its limits, rules and regulations are established and may be changed by them. Its purpose is to provide an element of final action to the grievance procedure, so that when a given dispute is carried to the concluding step, the arbitration decision is the instrument that gives the final answer to the issue in dispute.[31]

The arbitration process is heavily utilized to resolve labor contract disputes partly because "the parties themselves maintain the power through collective bargaining to correct . . . errors that may appear in a decision."[32] Should issues in dispute go through the courts, correction of errors could be made only upon appeal to higher courts. The issue of jurisdiction of arbitrators or the courts to deal with issues under collective bargaining agreements remains a problem for the courts and arbitrators. The Supreme Court has taken steps to build a body of law to guide the courts when arbitration questions arise. However, the authority of arbitrators to deal with any grievance or dispute involving the interpretation or application of a collective bargaining contract is shared with the NLRB. This latter aspect is present since many contractual rights are also statutory rights under the National Labor Relations Act. The NLRB has statutory authority to resolve labor disputes. A review of the problems facing arbitrators, the state and federal courts, and the NLRB is necessary for a better understanding of the arbitration process itself.

THE SUPREME COURT AND ARBITRATION

Congressional inclusion of Section 301 in Taft-Hartley did not immediately resolve the common-law problems of collective bargaining agreement enforcement. No clarification was made of the substantive law applicable to labor contracts brought before the courts. Were the courts to apply state laws as was the previous practice or some yet undetermined federal law? If federal law would be applied, what would it be? Diverse court opinions were handed down dealing with the issue of state versus federal jurisdiction under Section 301. In addition, the question of whether issues could be arbitrated was one with which the courts had considerable difficulty. Could an arbitrator proceed to grant an award prior to court determination of the merits of the issue under the agreement? So long as these issues remained unresolved, the use of grievance arbitration was not likely to receive as much attention from union-management parties to collective bargaining agreements as might otherwise occur. There would be little incentive to utilize arbitration as the final step of grievance procedures if the courts continued to interfere with arbitration awards. Industrial warfare may have remained the alternative to peaceful resolution of contractual disagreements unless appropriate action was forthcoming from the courts to lend prestige and strength to the arbitration process.

In a 1947 decision a New York state court of appeals ruled that the court must decide the merits of a grievance raised under a contract before an arbitrator had the authority to issue an award.[33] It held that

> if the meaning of the provision sought to be arbitrated is beyond dispute, there cannot be anything to arbitrate, and the contract cannot be said to provide for arbitration.[34]

This attitude characterized the thinking of the courts, state and federal, until the 1960s. Even the U.S. Supreme Court was uncertain as to how collective bargaining contracts should be treated in the courts. The intent of Congress proved hard to determine in the light of the various laws involved.

UNIONS' ABILITY TO SUE IN FEDERAL COURTS

In 1955 the Supreme Court reviewed the Taft-Hartley Act's Section 301. The *Westinghouse* case dealt with the issue of how collective bargaining agreements were to be enforced.[35] This case provides the necessary background for appreciating the issues and results of arbitration questions before the courts. Indeed, it also provides a basis for understanding the Court's *Humphrey* v. *Moore* decision, which we previously discussed regarding individual employee rights to bring suit in the courts. The dilemma of common law remained despite the 1947 legislation.

The *Westinghouse* case resulted from a contractual provision for salaried employees to receive their full month's pay even if they missed working a day unless they were on furlough or leave of absence. The company deducted a day's pay from the salaries of four thousand employees who had missed work on a particular day of the month. The union contended a violation of the agreement had occurred and filed a suit in a federal district court under Section 301 of Taft-Hartley. The trial court dismissed the case because the union had not stated a reason for the absences in dispute. The union, however, was permitted to amend its complaint and the lower court ruled that the union had authority to file suit under the Taft-Hartley law.

Upon appeal to a court of appeals, the case was dismissed. The appellate court held that the individual employees were the proper ones to file suit, not the union. The union was considered without authority to sue for the employees under Taft-Hartley. It could sue only if a provision of the agreement between the union and management affected its rights exclusive of those employees. Rights not pertaining to employees—regarding such matters as wages, hours, and other terms and conditions of employment—were within the particular rights of unions. The result of this rule was that unions as organizations would not usually acquire many rights apart from those dealing with the contractual conditions under which employees work.

The U.S. Supreme Court was not able to deal adequately with the issue in 1955. Upon appeal, it sustained the appeals court, but on the basis of different logic. Justice Frankfurter, speaking for the Court, was of the opinion that suits brought in the district courts under Section 301 were to be disposed of by common law as it prevailed in the states. Also employees themselves, not unions, were to bring the suits against employers. If suits were initiated by employees, the Justice argued that they would have to be brought in the state courts unless there was a diversity of citizenship, in which case they could use the federal courts. But the case implied even more. Employees in cases such as *Westinghouse* could not use the federal courts because Section 301 permitted only actions between employers and unions, not litigation between employers and employees. The collective bargaining contract itself was not considered a sufficient basis for a union suit against employers.[36]

All the Supreme Court justices—those concurring and dissenting as well as Justice Frankfurther speaking for the majority—were obviously ill at ease with the decision. It was inevitable that a new approach to collective contract enforcement would be undertaken. The inconsistencies of the decision were pointed out by the justices. More study and thought would be required to establish law dealing with the complexities of labor relations. Two years passed before the high court had the opportunity to deal again with the constitutional issues of Section 301.

The Lincoln Mills Case. Refusal to abide by arbitration awards in a small number of cases kept the problem of collective bargaining contract enforcement before the federal courts. In June 1957 three separate Section 301 cases were decided by the U.S. Supreme Court.[37] The lower courts held in the *General Electric* and *Goodall-Sanford* cases that agreements to arbitrate collective bargaining disputes were enforceable in the federal courts under the federal arbitration act. However, an appellate court reviewing the *Lincoln Mills* case ruled differently. It ruled that there was no authority in federal or state law to require adherence to a labor contract provision calling for arbitration of future disputes. The *Lincoln Mills* case provided the Supreme Court with an opportunity to provide answers to the issue of how to deal with labor contracts.

The Supreme Court decided in *Lincoln Mills*, contrary to the *Westinghouse* case in 1955, "that the substantive law to apply in suits under Section 301 (a) is federal law, which the courts must fashion from the policy of our national labor laws." Thus arbitration provisions were deemed enforceable in the federal courts under federal law.

It was decided that the Norris–La Guardia Act did not bar injunctive relief since "the congressional policy in favor of the enforcement of agreements to arbitrate grievance disputes being clear, there is no reason to submit them to the requirements of Section 4 of the Norris–La Guardia Act." The existing law of the state in which the controversy arises is not used to resolve the dispute. However, the federal courts may use state law to resolve the issue if it "will best effectuate the federal policy." Such a pronouncement on the part of the Court meant that the federal courts would establish their own doctrine dealing with Section 301 as long as such doctrine remained consistent with national labor policies.

It should be observed that the state courts are not excluded from deciding Section 301 suits. They have concurrent jurisdiction with the federal courts in most cases. When the state courts are utilized by the parties, however, they must apply federal law.[38] Not all the justices agreed that the substantive law to be applied in a suit under Section 301 should be federal law. It was the opinion of some that an appropriate federal remedy could be fashioned without eliminating the ability of state courts to apply their own laws in many cases before them. Justice Frankfurter could not agree with the majority that common laws of the states would no longer provide the basic substantive law to be applied in these cases. He stated, "This plainly procedural section is transmuted into a mandate to the federal courts to fashion a whole body of substantive federal law appropriate for the complicated and touchy problems raised by collective bargaining. . . . This is more than can be fairly asked even from the alchemy of construction. . . ."

This decision of the Supreme Court to enforce agreements to arbitrate grievance disputes constituted a major impetus for growth in the use of arbitration. Considerably more prestige was provided the entire process as a result of the *Lincoln Mills* case. However, the drive toward establishment of a body of law under Section 301 has not proved a simple task. A long series of cases followed the *Lincoln Mills* case, which laid down some rules to guide the courts in enforcing both arbitration agreements and awards. These cases extended broad latitude to arbitrators under federal law and for this reason it is unlikely that future suits dealing with arbitration will be filed in the state courts.

THE "TRILOGY" CASES

On June 20, 1960, the U.S. Supreme Court handed down three other decisions, which provide even greater integrity to the arbitration process.[39] These decisions are commonly referred to as the "Trilogy" cases. Each involved the United Steelworkers of America and each demonstrates that the system of private arbitration in the United States has now received the full support of the highest court in the land.

In the *Warrior & Gulf Navigation* case the Court held that in the absence of an express agreement excluding arbitration it would direct the parties to arbitrate a grievance. To put this in other terms, the Court would not find a case nonarbitrable unless the parties specifically excluded a subject from the arbitration process. The Court stated that a legal order to arbitrate would thenceforth not be denied "unless it may be said with positive assurance that the arbitration clause is not susceptible to an interpretation that covers the asserted dispute. Doubts should be resolved in favor of coverage."

More precisely, the courts will not decide that a dispute is not arbitrable unless the parties have taken care to expressly remove an area of labor relations from the arbitration process. This could be accomplished by providing, for example, that "disputes involving determination of the qualifications of employees for promotion will be determined exclusively by the company and such decision will not be subject to arbitration."[40] But, needless to say, not many unions would agree to such a clause since management would then have the unilateral right to make determinations on this vital phase of the promotion process.

The *Warrior & Gulf Navigation* decision eliminated a course of action that some companies had followed. When faced with a demand by a union for arbitration, some employers had frequently gone to court and asked the judge to decide that the issue involved in the case was not arbitrable. On many occasions the courts had agreed with the company, sustaining the company position in the grievance and denying the union an opportunity to get a decision based on the merits of the case.

In the instant case the Warrior & Gulf Navigation Company employed forty-two men at its dock terminal for maintenance and repair work. After the company had subcontracted out some of the work, the number was reduced to twenty-three. The union argued in the grievance procedure that this action of the company violated certain areas of the labor agreement—the integrity of the bargaining unit, seniority rights, and other clauses of the contract that provided benefits to workers. The company claimed that the issue of subcontracting was strictly a management function and relied on the management rights clause in the contract which stated that "matters which are strictly a function of management should not be subject to arbitration." When the Supreme Court handled the case, it ordered arbitration because the contract did not specifically exclude such activity from the arbitration process. It stated:

> A specific collective bargaining agreement may exclude contracting-out from the grievance procedure. Or a written collateral agreement may make clear that contracting-out was not a matter for arbitration. In such a case a grievance based solely on contracting-out would not be arbitrated. Here, however, there is no such provision. Nor is there any showing that the parties designed the phrase "strictly as a function of management" to encompass any and all forms of contracting-out. In the absence of any express provision excluding a particular grievance from arbitration, we think only the most forceful evidence of a purpose to exclude the claim from arbitration can prevail, particularly where, as here, the exclusion clause is vague and the arbitration clause quite broad.

One additional important point on the significance of this court decision: It does not mean that private arbitrators do not have the authority to dismiss a grievance on the basis of its being nonarbitrable under a contract. Arbitrators before and after the decision have frequently held that a grievance is not arbitrable under the contract. Indeed, the authors at times after the *Warrior & Gulf Navigation* decision have upheld the arguments of companies that grievances were not arbitrable under the labor agreement. The major importance of the *Warrior & Gulf Navigation* doctrine is in its ruling that courts may not hold a grievance is not arbitrable unless specific and clear-cut language excludes it from the arbitration process. The private arbitrator is still fully empowered to dismiss a grievance on the basis of nonarbitrability.

In the second case, *American Manufacturing*, the issue of arbitrability was also involved, but in a somewhat different way from that of *Warrior & Gulf Navigation*. The American Manufacturing Company argued before a lower federal court that an issue was not arbitrable because it did not believe the grievance had merit. Involved was a dispute on reinstatement of an employee to his job after it was determined that the employee was 25 percent disabled and was drawing workmen's compensation. The lower federal court sustained the employer's position and characterized the employee's grievance as "a frivolous, patently baseless one, not subject to arbitration." When the U.S. Supreme Court reversed the lower federal court, it held that the federal courts are limited in determining whether the dispute is covered by the labor agreement and that they have no power to evaluate the merits of a dispute. It stated:

> The function of the court is very limited when the parties have agreed to submit all questions of contract interpretation to the arbitrator. It is then confined to ascertaining whether the party seeking arbitration is making a claim which on its face is governed by the contract. Whether the moving party is right or wrong is a question of contract construction for the arbitrator. In these circumstances the moving party should not be deprived of the arbitrator's judgment, when it was his judgment and all that it connotes that was bargained for.

Essentially, this means that the courts may not hold a grievance nonarbitrable even if a judge believes it is completely worthless. It is up to the private arbitrator to make the decision on the merits of a case. He may dismiss the grievance as being without merit, but this duty rests exclusively with him and not with the courts.

In the third case, *Enterprise Wheel & Car Corporation*, a lower federal court reversed the decision of an arbitrator on the grounds that the judge did not believe his decision was sound under the labor agreement. The arbitrator's award directed the employer to reinstate certain discharged workers and to pay them back wages for periods both before and after the expiration of the collective bargaining contract. The company refused to comply with the award, and the union petitioned for enforcement. The lower court held that the arbitrator's award was unenforceable because the contract had expired. The U.S. Supreme Court reversed the lower court and ordered full enforcement. In upholding the arbitrator's award, the Court stated:

> Interpretation of the collective bargaining agreement is a question for the arbitrator. It is the arbitrator's construction which was bargained for; and so far as the arbitration decision concerns construction of the contract, the courts have no business overruling him because their interpretation of the contract is different from his.

The significance of this last decision should be perfectly clear. It shows that a union or a company may not use the courts to set aside an arbitrator's award. The decision cuts both ways: It applies both to employers and labor organizations. Whereas the other two decisions definitely favor labor organizations, this one merely serves to preserve the integrity of the arbitrator's award. Thus, even if a judge believes an arbitrator's award is unfair, unwise, and inconsistent with the contract, he has no alternative but to enforce the award.

Thus the Trilogy cases demonstrate that the private arbitration system has been strengthened by the judiciary. They establish the full integrity of the arbitration process. As a result of these decisions companies and unions must be more careful in the selection of arbitrators. This is one reason they have increasingly voiced a desire to use seasoned and experienced arbitrators.

For arbitrators the decisions are equally meaningful. Private arbitrators bear an even greater degree of responsibility as they decide their cases. Not only are the posts ones of honor, in which the parties have confidence in arbitrators' professional competency and integrity, but arbitrators must recognize that for all intents and purposes their decisions are completely "final and binding" upon the parties. Indeed, if the system of private arbitration is to remain a permanent feature of the American system of industrial relations, arbitrators must measure up to their responsibilities. Should they fail, companies and unions may simply delete the arbitration clause from the contract and resolve their disputes by strikes or by going directly to the courts. These are not pleasant alternatives, but the parties may choose these routes if they believe that arbitrators are not discharging their responsibilities in an honorable, judicious, and professional manner.

NORRIS–LA GUARDIA INFLUENCE ON
NO-STRIKE PROVISIONS

Section 4 of the Norris–La Guardia Act was not immediately a problem at the time the Supreme Court handed down its *Lincoln Mills* decision and later the *Steelworkers* Trilogy.[41] Section 4 prohibits the federal courts—and for that matter state courts having little Norris–La Guardia acts—from issuing injunctions against unions engaged in strikes in violation of their contracts.

The *Lincoln Mills* and Trilogy cases established a *quid pro quo* approach to the enforcement of agreements. This was thought to have meant that an agreement to arbitrate disputes was entered into in exchange for a union agreement not to strike for the duration of the contract. These cases implied that the no-strike provision of collective contracts was subject to the same rules and treatment as any other contractual provision.[42] The question of enforcing no-strike provisions of a collective contract by use of the injunction was not put directly to the Court.

In 1962 the Supreme Court was required to decide the *Sinclair* case which involved a suit for breach of a no-strike contract.[43] The high court refused to enjoin a strike engaged in by a union during a contractual period despite the fact that the labor agreement contained no-strike and arbitration clauses. The union could have submitted the grievances that caused the strike to arbitration instead of striking. In its decision the Court reasoned that it could not issue an injunction to stamp out the strike on the grounds that it was forbidden to do so under the Norris–La Guardia Act. Section 301 of Taft-Hartley did not repeal the Norris–La Guardia Act of 1932. Therefore the law discriminated against employers since they had to arbitrate unresolved grievances. In contrast, a union could bypass arbitration and strike, free from fear that the courts would issue an injunction to stop the strike. It should be recognized, however, that most labor organizations would not strike over grievances rather than making use of the arbitration process.

An employer could sue for damages when unions breached no-strike agreements. Most employers were reluctant to carry a suit for damages through to a final court determination, however, because of the adverse effect it might have had on the bargaining relationship after the strike was terminated.[44] Workers involved in the illegal strikes were also subject to discharge or other discipline, but this was only a course of action available to employers after the strike was terminated.[45] If discharge action was communicated to discharged employees during the strike, the controversy may have been prolonged. Unfair treatment by management of some workers allegedly on strike could result in back pay awards. No effective action was available to the company for halting the strike and restoring the productive process. Action such as mentioned was usually available only after the fact. Very often, as a condition for ending the strike, discipline such as may be meted out to employees became minimal. Indeed, termination of the illegal strike was often conditioned on withdrawal of any pending breach-of-contract suit initiated by the employer.[46]

The enforcement of no-strike provisions was treated differently if the issue turned on an arbitration award. A federal appellate court distinguished between the use of an injunction for (1) a situation in which no arbitration award was involved and the court was asked to enjoin a union from violating a no-strike clause in a collective bargaining contract, and (2) a situation in which a trial court was requested to enforce an arbitration award.[47] The Fifth Circuit Court was of the opinion that the anti-injunction provisions of Norris–La Guardia did not prevent a federal court from enforcing an arbitrator's award requiring a union to cease and desist from striking in violation of a no-strike provision. This merely amounted to enforcement of an arbitrator's injunction that had been included in the collective agreement by unions and management. A court in honoring the request was merely enforcing a collective bargaining agreement and was not issuing an injunction in the form forbidden by the 1933 anti-injunction law. Once an arbitration award was made, a controversy ceased to be a labor dispute within the meaning of the Norris–La Guardia Act. However, a work stoppage incurred prior to submitting a controversy to arbitration and prior to an arbitrator's award was defined as a labor dispute and as such was protected activity under Section 4 of the 1933 law. The court order merely called for specific performance of the award.

The door was once again open for the Supreme Court to find an accommodation between the law that the Court established with regard to Section 301 of Taft-Hartley and the Section 4 anti-injunction provisions of the Norris–La Guardia Act. One writer contended that the *Sinclair* case did not preclude an injunction to enforce a no-strike agreement when an employer had proceeded to "arbitration in accordance with the terms of a mutually approved contract."[48] Failure of the courts to recognize that the ability of either party to refuse to arbitrate grievances in accordance with contractual provisions seriously weakened the integrity of the arbitration process. The parties themselves should have had the ability to determine which items would be subject to the process and which would be excluded. Indeed, some loopholes existed early which under certain restricted circumstances provided exceptions to the *Sinclair* decision. One was injunctive relief from state courts and the other was one-party arbitration proceedings.

Authority of State Courts. Original jurisdiction is extended the federal district courts in civil actions for breach of labor contracts under Section 301. However, the same action may be brought in state courts. It was not clear whether state courts without little Norris–La Guardia acts were deprived of injunctive use in Section 301 cases. It will be recalled that the Anti-Injunction Act restricted its use only in the federal courts.

The *American Dredging Company* case involved a situation in which a state court issued an injunction restraining a union from violating a no-strike clause in the collective agreement.[49] Prior to a hearing, the union had the case removed from the state court to a federal district court.

Removal of such cases from state to federal jurisdictions is permissible under the Removal Act of 1948.[50] It provides that

> (a) Except as otherwise expressly provided by Act of Congress, any civil action brought in a State court of which the district courts of the United States have original jurisdiction, may be removed by the defendant or the defendants, to the district court of the United States for the district and division embracing the place where such action is pending. . . .
> (c) Whenever a separate and independent claim or cause of action, which would be removable if sued upon alone, is joined with one or more otherwise nonremovable claims or causes of action, the entire case may be removed and the district court may determine all issues therein, or, in its discretion, may remand all matters not otherwise within its original jurisdiction.

The district court refused to remand the case back to the state court. The Third Circuit Court of Appeals reversed the district court's decision and held that its refusal to send the case back to the state court led to an "absurd consequence." This refusal constituted an injustice to the company because the federal court could not issue an injunction to stop the union's action. For this reason

> it rendered an injustice to the plaintiff in that it deprived it of the benefit of the temporary injunctive relief granted by the state court under state law . . . and foreclosed it from the available remedy of a permanent injunction; it ousted the state court from its jurisdiction to apply state law in a field not preempted by Congress, in contravention of the historic comity doctrine which proscribes avoidable direct conflicts between federal and state courts; and it thwarted the Congressional policy intended to have Section 301 (a) "supplement," "and not to displace" or to encroach upon the existing jurisdiction of the state courts in suits for violation of collective bargaining contracts in industries affecting interstate commerce.

The U.S. Supreme Court refused to review the case, but despite this refusal the lower federal courts were not following the *American Dredging* decision. Most continued to refuse state courts the authority to use injunctions in no-strike contract violations when their state laws permitted such action.[51]

Ex Parte Arbitration. Ex parte arbitration arises when one party to the dispute declares an issue not arbitrable and refuses to participate in the proceedings. Various motives exist from time to time that may encourage management or unions to refuse to arbitrate a controversy. For example, some employers may attempt to delay a decision to weaken a union's bargaining and financial position. Such a tactic may be used to discourage a labor organization from pursuing a particular issue that is of vital importance to management decision making—such as improper work assignments or compulsory overtime. These issues may mean little in terms of back pay when the controversy is eventually resolved since discharges and loss of income are not usually involved, but at the same time they could make some unions shy away from challenging the same type of situation in the future.

Unions may also breach their duty to arbitrate because of the knowledge that an award which involves some issue of vital concern to the rank and file will be against them. The issue may be so politically explosive for the union officers that they prefer to decline arbitration.

Whatever the reason may be for a party to refuse arbitration, a serious flaw existed when the courts refused to enforce the agreement negotiated by the parties themselves. If an arbitrator had been chosen in accordance with contractual terms, the refusal of a labor union to honor the no-strike provisions would be difficult to justify. Both the American Arbitration Association and the Federal Mediation and Conciliation Service have rules that provide for appointment of an arbitrator if one party refuses to engage in the process. Collective bargaining agreements often provide that the rules of one or both of the agencies will be followed in resolving controversies. [52] If there is adequate contract provision to proceed ex parte, the courts will usually uphold arbitration awards. [53] In such cases it appears that arbitrators should issue cease-and-desist orders (referred to previously as arbitrator's injunctions) to unions violating no-strike provisions and the courts should require specific performance by issuing injunctions.

SINCLAIR REVERSED BY U.S. SUPREME COURT

In any event, unions generally remained in a favored position because they could refuse to honor their no-strike agreements without fear of court enjoinment of their actions. The Supreme Court, in *Sinclair*, interpreted the use of injunctions in such cases to constitute a violation of Section 4 of the Norris–La Guardia Act. Yet, three courses of possible action might provide employers with relief. The first involved a Supreme Court determination of state court authority to issue injunctions under the *American Dredging* rule. The second involved congressional clarification of the issue. Congress could merely state that arbitration enforcement in the federal courts under federal law was not subject to the equity limitations of the Norris–La Guardia Act. The third approach depended upon the desire of unions and management to avoid industrial warfare. Collective bargaining agreements could have been constructed in a fashion that would subject both parties equally to the equity power of the courts. However, all these issues became moot in the light of the Supreme Court's decision in *Boys Markets* v. *Retail Clerks*.[54] On June 1, 1970, by a 5–2 vote, the court reversed *Sinclair Refining* and held that employers may obtain an injunction from the federal courts to stop a strike in violation of a no-strike clause. The Supreme Court stated that *Sinclair Refining* was "a significant departure from our otherwise consistent emphasis upon the Congressional policy to promote the peaceful settlement of labor disputes through arbitration."

Though the 1970 decision may be defended on the grounds that employees and unions should not strike to settle their grievances when arbitration is available, the decision nevertheless was sharply criticized because Congress did not change the

1962 policy although many bills were introduced in Congress to nullify *Sinclair Refining*. As the *Wall Street Journal* observed on June 5, 1970:

> As a matter of fact such legislation was introduced, but Congress so far has not seen fit to act. Congressional action, of course, would have been much the better way. However desirable the result, the Supreme Court still should restrain itself from assuming the tasks that properly belong to the legislators.

Thus, the source of the criticism of *Boys Markets* is the change in Supreme Court policy after an eight-year period during which Congress did not see fit to reverse the *Sinclair Refining* doctrine. Black, writing the minority opinion, stated:

> Nothing at all has changed, in fact, except the membership of the Court and the personal view of one justice.

(Nixon's first appointee to the Court, Burger, was Chief Justice at the time of *Boys Markets*, and Stewart was the Justice who changed his mind.)

In any event, the court has provided employers with a potent weapon to stop strikes that violate no-strike agreements. Though objective data indicating the frequency of *Boys Markets* injunctions are not available, it is safe to say that employers have used them on a widespread basis to terminate wildcat strikes. When the decision was announced, there was speculation that unions would refuse to agree to no-strike and arbitration clauses to avoid injunctions. Unless there is a no-strike and arbitration clause in a labor agreement, an employer may not obtain an injunction. These speculations were not realized. There is no evidence that contracts contain fewer no-strike and arbitration clauses.

Despite the advantage that employers receive from *Boys Markets*, federal courts have refused to issue injunctions under certain conditions. Before an injunction will be issued, the court must be satisfied that the issue is arbitrable under the labor agreement.[55] A federal appeals court refused to sustain an injunction issued by a district court because the employer refused to concede that certain work assignments were arbitrable under the labor agreement. The same principle made an injunction improper when employees belonging to one union in effect struck by refusing to cross a picket line maintained by employees of another union that represented employees in other plants of the same company. It was held that the issue which gave rise to the strike was not a grievance under the labor agreement. In other words, the issue that precipitated the employees' refusal to cross the picket line was not arbitrable under the contract.[56]

In another type of case, it was held that a *Boys Markets* injunction could not be issued when a strike took place before the parties agreed to a contract containing a no-strike and arbitration clause. During negotiations, they agreed to economic terms, but not to the arbitration clause. By the time of the negotiations, the previous labor agreement that contained an arbitration procedure had expired. The employer relied upon the expired agreement as a basis for his request for an injunction. A district court issued an injunction, but a federal appeals court held that it was not issued properly. It pointed out that at the time of the strike the parties were not bound by an agreement to arbitrate disputes.[57]

DUAL JURISDICTION OF ARBITRATORS AND NLRB

Despite the existence of no-strike and arbitration clauses in a labor contract, there are situations in which an arbitrator's award might not put an end to a dispute. There is a possibility that some cases may be relitigated before the NLRB if one party is disappointed with the award. These are cases in which Taft-Hartley issues are either directly or indirectly involved. For example, a union may prefer to use arbitration rather than the NLRB in cases which involve Taft-Hartley matters. But under certain circumstances the NLRB will hear the case if a union loses the arbitration award. Thus the union could get two chances to win its case. However, with certain important exceptions to be noted below, the NLRB as a matter of general policy defers to arbitration for the resolution of conflicts.[58]

The U.S. Supreme Court has extended considerable prestige to the voluntary arbitration process through *Lincoln Mills* and the *Steelworkers* Trilogy, as demonstrated previously. In these cases the Court recognized that Congress intended that "privately agreed-upon methods of settlement should be favored, the attempt being to restrict administrative supervision of bargaining as much as possible."[59] However, the NLRB needn't honor an arbitrator's award if Taft-Hartley unfair labor practices are involved in the case.[60] Thus the Trilogy doctrine will not preserve an arbitrator's decision if it does not conform with Taft-Hartley and its construction by the NLRB.

The Taft-Hartley Act granted the NLRB wide authority to deal with employer-employee relations. One federal court of appeals ruled that the NLRB has exclusive power over unfair labor practices and this authority "shall not be affected by any other means of adjustment or prevention that has been or may be established by agreement, law or otherwise."[61] The power of the Board in the context of existing law is greater than that of any other body in establishing employer and union regulations.[62] Indeed, when the NLRB takes a case after it has been arbitrated, it does so because statutory law is superior to a private labor agreement. In other words, Taft-Hartley is paramount to a labor agreement and unions, employees, or employers do not forfeit any statutory rights under labor agreements. Therefore the NLRB under certain circumstances will void an arbitrator's award if it finds the arbitrator deprived someone of rights guaranteed by statute.

Resolving unfair labor practices is the task of the Board. The interpretation and enforcement of collective labor contracts are normally left to arbitrators and the courts. Obviously, there is no clear-cut distinction between the two functions. For this reason the NLRB has established some guidelines the sense of which is that the NLRB may defer to an arbitrator's award even though matters of Taft-Hartley are involved in the case.

The *Spielberg* doctrine provides some of the rules by which it decides to accommodate arbitration awards.[63] Certain conditions must be met before the Board will defer to arbitration. These are: (1) the proceedings must appear to have been fair and regular; (2) the parties must have agreed to accept awards as final and binding; and (3) the award must not be a clear contradiction of the purposes and policies of the Board. Still a fourth rule was added in 1963.[64] The Board ruled that it would not permit relitigation of an arbitration award in NLRB proceedings if the award dealt with the statutory rights of the parties. Thus the award must spell out and resolve any statutory issues that may be brought out in the hearings. Failure to do so in accordance to Board- and Court-established policies could result in the NLRB permitting a party to make use of Board facilities to reconsider the same issue.

In a previous chapter it was pointed out in the discussion of the *Collyer* doctrine, the Board may take jurisdiction of a case even after it has deferred to arbitration. The *Collyer* doctrine has not reversed *Spielberg*, despite the willingness of the Board to defer to arbitration disputes that contain unfair labor practice elements.

It is obvious therefore that the NLRB will normally review the merits of each case presented to it. Arbitrators must take due care in rendering decisions. Not only are they subject to review by the courts, but by the NLRB as well. Both the courts and the NLRB attempt to give wide latitude to the process which provides a peaceful solution to labor disputes with a minimum of public interference. However, failure of an arbitrator to conform to Board guidelines could result in the reversal of his decision.

In any event the NLRB has been criticized for its willingness to review cases that have been arbitrated. It is argued that such a policy undermines arbitration and is in conflict with stable labor relations. Indeed, from time to time professional arbitrators have complained about the NLRB because it will review cases. Actually, as many other issues in labor law, there are two sides to the picture. On the one hand, there is some doubt that a party who has elected to arbitrate instead of going to the NLRB in the first place should be permitted to use the Board to upset an unfavorable arbitration award. The argument is that the party should not get two opportunities to win the same case. On the other hand, the fact is that statutory law is paramount to private labor agreements. Therefore the NLRB has the duty to reverse an arbitrator's award when it deprives an employee, employer, or union of rights guaranteed by Taft-Hartley. Probably there is no satisfactory solution to the problem, and the accommodation between the NLRB and arbitration will be resolved on a case-by-case basis.

BARGAINING OBLIGATION OF SUCCESSOR EMPLOYER

The NLRB, in 1970, issued a decision that required a successor employer to honor the collective bargaining agreement signed by the predecessor employer.[65] Lockheed Aircraft received security services from Wackenhut. The United Plant Guard Workers had prevailed in a Board-held election and was certified as bargaining agent for Wackenhut employees. A collective bargaining agreement was signed, but four months later Lockheed awarded the Burns International Detective Agency the contract to provide security services and was apprised of the fact of the collective bargaining relationship Wackenhut had with the United Plant Guard Workers. Burns employed 42 men on the Lockheed job, of which 27 had previously worked for Wackenhut. Burns had a bargaining contract with a different union with an accretion clause that was applied to workers on the Lockheed job. Charges were filed against Burns because it did not recognize the United Plant Guard Workers and honor the Wackenhut contract.

In reaching its decision in the *Burns* case, the Board relied on the Supreme Court decision in *John Wiley and Sons* v. *Livingston*.[66] In *Wiley* a small unionized company was merged into a larger nonunion organization. The union brought a Section 301 suit against the surviving firm to compel arbitration under the terms of agreement with the predecessor. The Supreme Court ordered arbitration, which left the question of applicability of other provisions of the labor contract to the surviving company. In the *Burns* case, the Board relied on the *Wiley* case to hold that Burns was obligated under Section 8 (a) (5) to honor the Wackenhut agreements. The Board reasoned that a collective bargaining agreement is not an ordinary contract but is a generalized code binding on successors who continue essentially the same enterprise.

Burns appealed the case. The court of appeals upheld the Board on the order to recognize the union, but refused to enforce that part of the order requiring Burns to honor the labor contract of the predecessor.[67] The Supreme Court affirmed the appellate court decision.[68] The high court reasoned

> . . . A potential employer may be willing to take over a moribund business only if he can make changes in corporate structure, composition of the labor force, work, location, task assignment, and nature of supervision. Saddling such an employer with the terms and conditions of employment contained in the old [labor] contract may make these changes impossible and may discourage and inhibit the transfer of capital . . .[69]

Problems Concerning Recognition

The Court ruled that for the predecessor union to obtain recognition, the Board must establish "that the new employer is the successor and that the bargaining unit remains intact."[70] To be a successor, the new employer must continue the same product lines, departmental organization, employee identity, and job functions.

The Supreme Court's decision in *Burns* did not resolve many questions that arose subsequent to the opinion.[71] Other questions concern a successor's duty to bargain, to abide by a pre-existing contract, and to honor existing employment conditions. In cases since *Burns*, the question of majority representation has been handled by simply determining if a majority of the successor's employees were previously employed by the predecessor.

An employer may raise good faith doubts concerning a union's majority in some circumstances. Board and court cases reveal that objective evidence must be presented to show that a union no longer represents a majority of employees.

The *Burns* case did not resolve the issue of when a successor employer can unilaterally institute changes. It was determined that he must recognize and bargain with the union. The NLRB was faced with facts somewhat different from those of *Burns*.[72] The union had never been certified by the Board, but had won an election supervised by the mayor of the town 14 years prior to the change of employers. It had a one-year contract with the predecessor employer that was based on an automatic renewal provision.

The successor employer refused to either accept the contract in existence or to negotiate a new one. An unfair labor practice was filed by the union. The Board ordered the successor employer to honor the old contract and to recognize and bargain with the union.

The court of appeals overruled the Board order to honor the old contract, but it required the successor employer to bargain. The Seventh Circuit Court of Appeals provided an answer to the issue of when a successor employer loses the right to make unilateral decisions. This right is lost at the moment it becomes clear that most of the predecessor's employees will retain their jobs if the nature of the business remains unchanged. The court held that

> . . . In the successor situation this generally means that a successor employer can set the initial terms upon which rehiring is conditioned since prior to the rehiring of a substantial proportion of his predecessor's employees there is no duty to bargain. The only instance in which the duty to bargain may precede the formal rehiring of employees is . . . where the new employer plans to retain all of the employees in the unit and in which it will be appropriate to have him initially consult with [the union] before he fixes terms.

The court majority reasoned that although there was no obligation to honor the old contract, the employer was not free to make unilateral changes until it had bargained to impasse. Otherwise, unilateral changes can only be made if the successor employer specified those changes which will be made at the time that job applications are given to predecessor employees. At that point, there is no certainty that the successor will employ most of them. If a new employer intends to retain the previous employer's workers, he cannot avoid an obligation to bargain about initial working conditions merely by making employment dependent upon acceptance of unilateral conditions.[73] If he plans to take all employees, bargaining with the incumbent is required before employment conditions are fixed.

In June 1974 unions lost some ground in the successor employer controversy. At that time, the U.S. Supreme Court held in *Howard Johnson* v. *Hotel and Restaurant Employees* that a successor employer did not have the obligation to arbitrate its refusal to hire employees of the seller's work force. In this case, the new employer discharged all supervisors and hired only a small number of the employees who had worked for the former employer.

There are many questions still unanswered under the *Burns* decision and it should be clear that the Supreme Court's 1972 opinion has not settled all of the issues being raised concerning successor employer obligations to bargain with a union which had a contract with his predecessor.

A very basic problem was raised in the Wachs article regarding the Supreme Court's *Burns* decision.[74] Many successors may find it advantageous to observe their predecessor's labor contract, but a union may not. Such a situation could make it very difficult for a new employer, particularly if he does not have substantial resources and the business is a good one.

SUMMARY

Enforcement of collective bargaining contracts has changed considerably since the Wagner Act era. Prior to the Taft-Hartley Act, unions generally had little legal recognition for entering into contracts with management. Individual employees obtained rights under collective bargaining contracts and as such were the appropriate ones to file suit in state courts under common law.

The 1947 labor law brought with it a recognition of union maturity and therefore recognition of their right to engage in collective bargaining contracts. Unions were permitted to sue and to be sued. Such suits are permitted in the federal courts as well as state courts, but federal law applies.

The U.S. Supreme Court is in the process of building a body of substantive law for the purpose of dealing with Section 301 suits. The *Lincoln Mills* and subsequent *Steelworkers* Trilogy cases brought substantial prestige to the arbitration process. Federal judges were instructed to stay away from the merits of arbitration cases and to sustain arbitrators unless clear violations of national labor policy occurred. At the same time it must be realized that alleged violations must be reviewed by the courts and this means the merits of a particular case must be evaluated, although in a context different from the normal law of contracts.

Reversing *Sinclair*, the Supreme Court in *Boys Markets* held that federal courts may issue an injunction terminating a strike in violation of a no-strike clause. The 1970 decision occasioned some surprise because Congress did not act to nullify *Sinclair*. In any event, *Boys Markets* clarifies the complex situation that developed as a result of the courts' attempts to accommodate the Norris–La Guardia Act to violations of union agreements not to strike during the term of a labor agreement. Though Congressional action would have been the better method to abolish the *Sinclair* doctrine, the result of *Boys Markets* is to provide employers with an effective method of making sure that unions will abide by their no-strike pledge when arbitration is available for the final settlement of contract disputes.

The NLRB has jurisdiction over unfair labor practices and at times this opens the possibility for relitigating an arbitration case if a party is dissatisfied with the award. The Board attempts to accommodate the arbitration process. In so doing, it has decided to defer to arbitration if certain conditions are met. The proceedings must have been fair and regular, the parties must have agreed to accept awards as final and binding, the award must not be a clear contradiction of the purposes and policies of the Board, and the award must deal with the statutory rights of the parties. The NLRB has the authority to decide if these four conditions have been met. This means that the Board, like the federal courts, makes a review of cases presented it to determine the merits of each case. In addition, under the *Collyer* doctrine, the Board decided to defer to arbitration disputes that contain unfair labor practice elements.

NOTES

[1] Section 9.

[2] Section 9 (a).

[3] *North American Aviation Company*, 44 NLRB 604 (1942).

[4] *NLRB* v. *North American Aviation Company*, 136 F. (2d) 899 (1943).

[5] *Hearings on S. 1958 Before the House Committee of Labor*, 74th Congress, 1st sess., Part III, p. 321.

[6] *Hearings on H. R. 6288 Before the House Committee on Labor*, 74th Congress, 1st sess., p. 211.

[7] *Hughes Tool Company*, 56 NLRB 981 (1944).

[8] *Douglas Aircraft Company*, 25 War Labor Reports 57 (1944).

[9] Section 9 (a).

[10] *Lakeland Bus Lines, Inc.* v. *NLRB*, 287 F. (2d) 888 (1960).

[11] *Miranda Fuel Company*, 140 NLRB 181 (1963).

[12] *Hughes Tool Company*, 147 NLRB 166 (1964).

[13] *Ibid.* Reference is made here to Section 8 (b) (3) of Taft-Hartley which requires that a labor organization or its agent commits an unfair labor practice by refusing "to bargain collectively with an employer, provided it is the representative of his employees subject to the provisions of section 9 (a)."

[14] Charles O. Gregory, *Labor and the Law*, 2nd ed. (New York: W. W. Norton & Company, Inc., 1961), p. 445.

[15] We are indebted to C. O. Gregory for this section, *ibid.*, pp. 446–447.

[16] Section 301.

[17] National Association of Manufacturers, *That New Labor Law*, p. 21.

[18] International Association of Machinists, *The Truth About the Taft-Hartley Law and Its Consequences to the Labor Movement* (April 1948), p. 26.

[19] *Sinclair Oil Corporation* v. *Oil, Chemical and Atomic Workers*, 452 F. (2d) 49 (1971).

[20] *Atkinson* v. *Sinclair Refining Company*, 370 U.S. 238 (1962).

[21] Section 8(d).

[22] *Humphrey* v. *Moore*, 375 U.S. 335 (1964).

[23] *Ibid.*

[24] *Vaca* v. *Sipes*, 386 U.S. 171 (1967).

[25] *Ford Motor Company* v. *Huffman*, 345 U.S. 330 (1953).

[26] *Humphrey* v. *Moore*, *op. cit.*

[27] Archibald Cox, "Rights Under a Labor Agreement," *Harvard Law Review*, LXIX (1956),601.

[28] "Arbitration Provisions in Collective Agreements, 1952," *Monthly Labor Review* (March 1953), pp. 261–266.

[29] Lawrence Stessin, "A New Look at Arbitration," *The New York Times Magazine*, November 17, 1963, p. 26.

[30] *Ibid.*

[31] Thomas J. McDermott, "Arbitrability: The Courts Versus the Arbitrator," *The Arbitration Journal*, XXIII, No. 4 (1968), 19.

[32] *Ibid.*

[33] *Cutler-Hammer*, 271 App. Div. 917, 67 N.Y. S. (2d) 317 (1947).

[34] *Ibid.*

[35] *Association of Westinghouse Salaried Employees* v. *Westinghouse Electric Corporation*, 348 U.S. 437 (1955).

[36] See Gregory, *op. cit.*, pp. 457–466, for an excellent and perceptive treatment of the *Westinghouse* case.

[37] These were *Textile Workers Union of America* v. *Lincoln Mills of Alabama*, 353 U.S. 448 (1957); *Goodall-Sanford,Inc.* v. *United Textile Workers of America*, 353 U.S. 550 (1957); and *General Electric Company* v. *United Electrical, Radio & Machine Workers of America*, 353 U.S. 547 (1957).

[38] *Dowd Box* v. *Courtney*, 368 U.S. 502 (1962).

[39] *United Steelworkers of America* v. *American Manufacturing Company*, 363 U.S. 564 (1960); *United Steelworkers of America* v. *Warrior & Gulf Navigation Company*, 363 U.S. 574 (1960); *United Steelworkers of America* v. *Enterprise Wheel & Car Corporation*, 363 U.S. 593 (1960).

[40] For other examples of such limiting language, see *To Protect Management Rights* (Washington, D.C.: U.S. Chamber of Commerce, 1961), pp. 7–22.

[41] Section 4 of Norris–La Guardia is readily available for review in its entirety in Appendix E.

[42] Thomas J. McDermott, "Enforcing No-Strike Provisions via Arbitration," *Labor Law Journal*, XVIII, No. 10 (October 1967), 1–2.

[43] *Sinclair Refining Company* v. *Atkinson*, 370 U.S. 238 (1962).

[44] John H. Kirkwood, "The Enforcement of Collective Bargaining Contracts," *Labor Law Journal*, XV (February 1964), 112.

[45] Evan J. Spelfogel, "Enforcement of No-Strike Clause by Injunction, Damage Action and Discipline," *Labor Law Journal*, XVII, No. 2 (February 1966), 77.

[46] McDermott, "Enforcing No-Strike Provisions via Arbitration," *op. cit.*, p. 2.

[47] *New Orleans Steamship Assn.* v. *Longshoremen (ILA), Local 1418*, 389 F. (2d) 369 (CA 5) (1968).

[48] McDermott, "Arbitrability" pp. 6–7.

[49] *American Dredging Company* v. *Local 25, Marine Division, Operating Engineers*, 338 F. (2d) 837 (1964), cert. denied, 380 U.S. 935 (1965).

[50] 28 U.S.C. Sections 1441–1450.

[51] See, for example, *Avco Corporation* v. *Aero Lodge 735 IAM*, 338 F. (2d) 837 (1964); *Oman Construction Company* v. *Local 327 Teamsters*, 263 F. Supp. 181 (1966).

[52] McDermott, "Arbitrability," pp. 31–32.

[53] *Ibid.*, p. 34.

[54] 398 U.S. 235 (1970).

[55] *Parade Publications* v. *Mailers Union* (CA) No. 71–1107 (May 1, 1972).

[56] *Amstar Corporation* v. *Meat Cutters* (CA 5) No. 72–1576 (November 6, 1972).

[57] *Emery Air Freight Corporation* v. *Teamsters, Local 295*, 356 F. (2d) 974 (1971).

[58] Jay W. Waks, "The 'Dual Jurisdiction' Problem in Labor Arbitration: A Research Report," *The Arbitration Journal*, XXIII, No. 4 (1968), 227.

[59] Labor Management Relations Act, Section 203 (d), cited in Richard I. Bloch, "The NLRB and Arbitration: Is the Board's Expanding Jurisdiction Justified?" *Labor Law Journal*, XIX, No. 10 (October 1968), 646.

[60] *NLRB* v. *Acme Industrial Company*, 385 U.S. 432 (1967).

[61] *NLRB* v. *Walt Disney Productions*, 146 F. (2d) 44 (1945), cited in Jay W. Waks, "Arbitrator, Labor Board, or Both?" *Monthly Labor Review*. Pronouncement was an exact quote from Section 10 (a) of the Taft-Hartley Act.

[62] *Shoreline Enterprises* v. *NLRB*, 262 F. (2d) 933 (1959).

[63] *Spielberg Manufacturing Company*, 112 NLRB 1080 (1955).

[64] *Raytheon Company*, 140 NLRB 883 (1963).

[65] *William J. Burns International Detective Agency*, 182 NLRB No. 50 (1970).

[66] 376 U.S. 543 (1964).

[67] *NLRB* v. *Burns International Detective Agency*, 441 F. (2d) 911 (1971).

[68] 406 U.S. 272 (1972).

[69] *Ibid.*, pp. 287–288.

[70] Robert E. Wachs, "Successorship: The Consequences of *Burns*," *Labor Law Journal*, Vol. 24, No. 4 (April 1973), p. 223.

[71] *Ibid.*, p. 221. An excellent treatment of the consequences of *Burns*.

[72] *NLRB* v. *Bachrodt Chevrolet Company*, 468 F. (2d) 963 (1972).

[73] *Howard Johnson Company*, 198 NLRB No. 98 (1972).

[74] Wachs, *op. cit.*, p. 233.

V

COLLECTIVE BARGAINING: AREA OF INDUSTRIAL CONFLICT

PROLOGUE. *The National Labor Relations Act, as amended, did not stop with regulation of the substance of collective bargaining. It also affects the economic weapons of management and unions: strikes, picketing, lockouts, and boycotts. What are the effects of the law on these activities? Are unions any worse off as a result of these legislative features? Are unions making progress in the Taft-Hartley era? What of the public policy of Taft-Hartley with respect to the impact on collective bargaining weapons? What loopholes arose under Taft-Hartley provisions, and in turn what were the results of Landrum-Griffin attempts to deal with the problem?*

Industrial conflict raises the problems of industrial peace under collective bargaining. What has government done to foster the peaceful settlement of labor disputes? Is there a solution for national emergency strikes?

16

Strikes, Lockouts, and Picketing

RECAPITULATION

It was established in earlier chapters that courts frequently limited the right of labor organizations to strike. Judges ruled that certain strikes, such as those for union security, were unlawful. The injunction constituted the vehicle whereby strikes were stamped out when deemed unlawful. The social and economic predilections of judges provided the basis for the injunction. No action of the legislative branch of government branded these strikes as unlawful. Nevertheless, the judiciary determined the legality of strikes. As the Massachusetts Supreme Court once put it:

> Whether the purpose for which a strike is instituted is or is not a legal justification for it is a question of law to be decided by the court. To justify interference with the right of others the strikers must in good faith strike for a purpose which the court decides to be a legal justification for such interference.[1]

Organized labor protested against a policy that permitted the courts to exercise their equity power in labor disputes. Union leaders charged that the government via the courts sided with management in labor disputes. They claimed that the indiscriminate use of the labor injunction made it difficult—and at times impossible—for workers to obtain economic concessions from employers.

The legislative branch afforded relief to the nation's labor unions. This was accomplished by stripping the courts of their power to enjoin strikes. In short, judges lost their power to decide whether or not the purposes of strikes were lawful. Peacefully conducted strikes, regardless of objective, were immunized from the injunction. Such a public policy was established by Norris–La Guardia and by a number of state anti-injunction laws. Not only did the federal anti-injunction law protect strikes from the injunction, but it also largely relieved labor unions from prosecution under the

397

antitrust laws. The Wagner Act added still more protection for labor's right to strike, outlawing a variety of strike-breaking practices engaged in from time to time by antiunion employers.

Thus Norris–La Guardia and the Wagner Act protected the right of employees to strike. Labor acclaimed these laws for the strike as by far the most effective of all of labor's economic weapons. After World War II the legal status of the strike underwent a change. A number of states and the federal government regulated and outlawed certain types of strikes. Once again labor was forbidden to engage in strikes calculated to gain certain objectives. This time, however, it was the legislative branch of government and not the judiciary which was responsible for the limitations on the exercise of the strike.

Our task in this chapter and the next three is to analyze Taft-Hartley and Landrum-Griffin changes regulating strike activity. How is this limitation accomplished? What enforcement techniques are provided in strike-control legislation? How do these laws affect the operation of collective bargaining? What forms of strikes are completely outlawed? Do these strike-control laws protect the basic interests of the public?

ECONOMIC STRIKER RIGHTS

The Taft-Hartley Act denied replaced economic strikers the right to vote in representation elections. Workers hired to replace economic strikers could vote, but economic strikers for whom the employer had found replacements were not eligible to cast ballots. Such a condition was established in a very short sentence in the law: "Employees on strike who are not entitled to reinstatement shall not be eligible to vote."[2] Organized labor immediately claimed that this fifteen-word phrase threatened the success of every economic strike. More important, union leaders charged that the representation voting policy of Taft-Hartley endangered the security of the entire union movement by providing employers with a potent antiunion weapon. In contrast, some people asserted that workers on an economic strike replaced by other employees had severed their employment relationship by the mere act of not reporting to work. Consequently, it was contended that these workers no longer had an interest in the outcome of representation elections.

Economic v. Unfair Labor Practice Strikes

So that the significance of the voting policy of Taft-Hartley may be fully understood, it is first necessary to distinguish between *economic strikes* and *unfair labor practice strikes*. Falling into the economic-strike category are strikes for higher wages, shorter hours, better working conditions, health and welfare plans, and so on. In contrast, an unfair labor practice strike is a work stoppage caused by employer tactics declared unlawful by national labor relations policy. In this classification fall such strikes as those for union recognition, discrimination against union members, refusal to bargain collectively, and interference by the employer with the right of workers to organize and bargain collectively. If a local union strikes because some of its officers are discharged for union activity, they would not be classified as economic strikers. Such a strike falls within the unfair labor practice category. It results from employer action declared unlawful under national law. The strike would not have occurred if the employer had not engaged in an unfair labor practice.

Reinstatement Rights of Strikers under the Wagner Act

Reinstatement rights of strikers differ depending upon the cause of the strike. Employees engaging in an unfair labor practice strike have unlimited right to reinstatement. This means that the NLRB has full authority to order the reinstatement of workers, including back pay awards when this category of strike occurs. Such strikers will be reinstated whether or not the employer replaced them with other workers. An employer must rehire these strikers even though their reinstatement results in the discharge of workers hired to take their jobs.

Indeed, in *Mastro Plastics* the U.S. Supreme Court held that employees are entitled to reinstatement even when they strike in violation of a no-strike clause in a labor agreement when they strike because of employer unfair labor practices.[3] In this case the Court, while upholding the NLRB, held that there is an

> inherent inequity in any interpretation that penalizes one party to a contract for conduct induced solely by the unlawful conduct of the other, thus giving advantage to the wrongdoer.

In the absence of such a policy the employer unfair labor practice section of national law would be rendered meaningless. Assume that employers would not be required to rehire unfair labor practice strikers. Now suppose an employer refuses to bargain collectively with a majority union. A strike results. During the course of the strike the employer permanently replaces the strikers with other workers. Under these conditions a strike resulting from employer noncompliance with national labor policy could have the effect of eliminating unions. It appears therefore as a matter of industrial justice that unfair labor practice strikers have the unlimited right to reinstatement. However, workers out on strike are generally not entitled to reinstatement when they engage in violence or coercive misconduct. It does not matter if an employer had committed unfair labor practices which either caused or prolonged the strike.[4]

In contrast with unfair labor practice strikers, employees who engage in economic strikes enjoy only a limited right to reinstatement. The NLRB will order their immediate reinstatement only when the employer does not fill their jobs with permanent replacements. In the event that economic strikers have been permanently replaced, the NLRB has no authority to direct their reinstatement. Hence permanently replaced economic strikers have no absolute legal right to reinstatement.

This policy was established in a case decided by the U.S. Supreme Court in 1938.[5] In *NLRB* v. *Mackay Radio & Telegraph*, the Court ruled that an employer could hire permanent replacements for economic strikers. The Wagner Act was interpreted as not prohibiting companies from protecting and continuing business operations when workers went on strike for economic reasons. If an employer was concerned with his business, he could continue to operate as long as this was for economic reasons and not for the purpose of destroying unions.

Later the same year, 1938, the NLRB was faced with the issue of whether replaced economic strikers could vote in Board-held representation elections. The NLRB held that workers could be deprived of their jobs by replacement, but not of their right to vote in such elections.[6] Both strikers and their replacements were extended the franchise. The Board was not satisfied with its rule, however, and reconsidered its position in the same case (*Sartorius*) about two months later. Replaced economic strikers were permitted to vote but their replacements were deprived of the right. The conflict of job interest of the two groups was offered as justification for changing the rule. The Board reasoned that two separate groups of employees should not be permitted to vote for representation or the lack of it within the same bargaining unit.

The Board was dissatistisfied with its rule change and made still another revision in 1941. In the *Rudolph Wurlitzer Company* case, it returned to its original *Sartorius* position.[7] Both economic strikers and their replacements were viewed as holding legal claims to their jobs and "both should have the same right to vote in a representation election." Considerable criticism was leveled at the Board for permitting replaced strikers to vote in representation elections. Essentially, it was often argued that only replacements should be permitted to vote since the strikers had no hope of returning to their jobs.

Taft-Hartley Act Innovation. It is obvious that the policy on reinstatement rights of strikers was not first established in 1947 by the Taft-Hartley Act. It was originally set up by the NLRB under the Wagner Act. The innovation of the 1947 labor law was that replaced economic strikers were denied the right to vote in any representation election held during the course of the work stoppage. Under the final Wagner Act position, the opportunity to vote was extended to this group of strikers as well as to their replacements. It did not distinguish between the voting rights of economic and unfair labor practice strikers.

This aspect of the law generated substantial concern on the part of unions. Suppose the workers of the XYZ Manufacturing Company strike for higher wages. This, of course, is an economic strike. The employer manages to find permanent replacements for the bulk of striking workers. The replacements eventually petition the NLRB for a bargaining election. Alternatively, they could have petitioned for a decertification election. A decertification election could provide the basis for eliminating the old bargaining-unit representative and stabilize replacement worker jobs. Even so a normal election petition may be filed. The Board conducts the election but permits only the replacements to vote. The replaced strikers are not eligible to cast ballots. This means that the replacements would win the election. As a consequence the strikers' union would lose bargaining rights and the employer would no longer need to recognize it or bargain with it. In fact, if the strikers now demand recognition the strike becomes unlawful in character. A union may not lawfully strike for recognition under Taft-Hartley when another organization has been certified.[8] This means that the employees might have to give up the strike.

In short, the nationally affiliated union involved in such a situation would be frozen out of the plant. It could no longer demand recognition. The strike is lost and the union is broken. The striking employees could not expect to be rehired. After an economic strike is terminated, a union that maintains its bargaining position invariably will demand that all strikers be reinstated. Such a demand is made as one condition for ending the strike. However, in the illustration, the striking union lost its status in the plant. It could not extend any protection whatsoever to the striking employees. The company would not be obligated to rehire any of the workers—even those with long years of service. The Board would not hold another election for at least one year. Periods marked by serious unemployment could have resulted in widespread union decline since worker risk of replacement for striking could have become more pronounced. Small bargaining units were particularly vulnerable under Taft-Hartley because of the relatively greater possibility of replacement than in larger units.

LANDRUM-GRIFFIN REVISION

Prior to the 1959 amendments of Taft-Hartley, recommendations were made by several persons to either eliminate the Section 9 (c) (3) feature or modify it so as to provide replaced economic strikers with some opportunity to vote in representation elections. Among these recommendations were those by President Dwight D. Eisenhower in a speech as early as 1952 and by Senator Robert A. Taft, one of the authors of the 1947 law.

Section 702 of Title VII changed the language of the 1947 statute. Under the new voting policy

> employees engaged in an economic strike who are not entitled to reinstatement shall be eligible to vote under such regulations as the Board shall find are consistent with the purposes and provisions of this act in any election conducted within twelve months after the commencement of the strike.

Congress was of the opinion that a replaced striker would usually not be interested in the bargaining-unit representative after a period of twelve months. It may also have been the view of Congress that they would have obtained other employment after such a long period. Yet it must be considered that many replaced strikers did retain a substantial interest in recapturing their former jobs. This was particularly the case of workers with long seniority with a company. Even if replaced workers did not possess long service records, their ages may have precluded them from finding comparable employment. Thus, if an employer managed to keep his business operating for more than one year by the use of replacements, unions and employees were no better off than they were before the Landrum-Griffin change was made. In any event unions received relief. It is probably true that not many employers could stand a work stoppage for more than a year.

For a time, the NLRB permitted replaced economic strikers to vote in elections that were held more than twelve months after a strike started.[9] The basis for this decision was that replaced strikers are employees and are entitled to vote for as long as they retain an expectation for future employment by the same employer. As noted later in this section, under the *Laidlaw-Fleetwood* doctrine, replaced economic strikers have a right to a job whenever a job becomes available for them. That is, they have permanent reinstatement rights.[10] The Board held that replaced economic strikers have permanent reinstatement rights, and an employer could not limit this right to a specific time period. It stated: "We likewise reject the contention that a time limit should be placed on the reinstatement rights of economic strikers." On this basis, the NLRB held in *Pioneer Flour Mills* that replaced economic strikers had the right to vote in elections regardless of when they were held. In 1972, however, the NLRB ruled that voting rights of replaced strikers are limited to one year.[11] It stated in *Wahl Clipper* that:

> It seems to us the most reasonable course, as well as the most reasonable interpretation of the statutory language, is to hold that replaced strikers are not eligible to vote in elections held more than 12 months after the commencement of an economic strike.

By this decision, though reasonable under the language of the 1959 law and its legislative history, there is greater opportunity for a motivated employer to get rid of a union with the resultant consequences to the employees.

The Board was required to establish regulations to implement the economic striker provision of the 1959 law. In 1960 it provided some rules to govern the new policy. The voting eligibility of economic strikers is to be determined by certain tests.[12] Voting privileges are to be forfeited when (1) the striker obtains permanent employment elsewhere before the election; (2) the employer eliminates his job for economic reasons; and (3) the striker is discharged or refused reinstatement for misconduct rendering him unsuitable for reemployment. These are not the only standards established to evaluate cases.

An economic striker must be on strike at the time of the election before he is entitled to vote.[13] But this does not mean that a new job will automatically forfeit his right to vote. Forfeiture of voting rights occurs only if the new job is substantially equivalent to the struck job.[14] Substantial equivalency depends upon such factors as pay, seniority, and working conditions. Even if the new job is substantially equivalent to the struck job, a replaced economic striker does not automatically lose voting rights. The replaced striker may retain the franchise despite the new job if he continues to picket or informs the new employer that he is on strike and intends to return to the struck job if given the opportunity.[15] Thus it is apparent that the Board weighs the economic gains and losses of replaced strikers when their ballots are challenged in Board-held elections. There is a recognition that these workers may have a substantial economic interest in their struck jobs. Voting privileges may afford an opportunity to recover the struck job.

Ordinarily, the Board directs that elections be held within thirty days from the date of the direction of election. The NLRB has determined that "permanent replacements for strikers are eligible to vote in elections even if they are employed [elsewhere] on the date of the election."[16] However, no more replacements than strikers are permitted to vote. This limitation is imposed despite any favorable changes in economic conditions between the time of replacement and the holding of the election. This rule is provided to eliminate any voting imbalance between the two groups competing for the same jobs. Furthermore, this restriction eliminates the possible creation of a situation whereby the union on strike can be placed at a voting disadvantage by a struck company. It would be a simple matter to hire a large number of workers for a short period in order to influence election results.

The election policies of the NLRB established to carry out the objectives of Landrum-Griffin provide some relief to unions and their members that engage in economic strikes. However, there is no certainty that they will prevail in elections should employers choose to continue operations after reaching bargaining impasses. Regardless of the administrative ruling or legislation prevailing at any given period of time, the issue of economic striker replacement will remain open to criticism. The position taken depends upon the economic gain or loss involved. Once a labor union loses an election under such conditions, the union is dissolved by law. Chance for job recovery is lost. The smaller the bargaining unit, the greater the chance that jobs will be lost permanently when economic strikes occur.

In 1968 the NLRB reversed its previous rule governing economic strikers. It held that those who had been permanently replaced still had to be reinstated if their jobs opened up again.[17] The new rule is based on a 1967 decision of the U.S. Supreme Court that requires a company to reinstate strikers not rehired at the termination of a strike because of the low level of production.[18] The Board, following the Supreme Court, reasoned that a striker remains an employee even though he is not reinstated immediately after the strike is concluded. This is called the *Laidlaw-Fleetwood* doctrine.

In 1971, the Board, however, modified the scope of this doctrine. In *United Aircraft* the union, as a condition of ending a long strike, "agreed" that reinstatement rights of the strikers would be limited to four and one-half months following the termination of the strike.[19] If they were reinstated after this time, they were to be treated as new employees. Under these circumstances, the employees would have lost the accumulated seniority and other contractual rights. As a matter of fact, 1,500 employees were not rehired at the end of the period. Under this agreement, they had lost reinstatement rights. In reviewing this situation, the NLRB, by this time dominated by Nixon appointees, held that the action of the employer in refusing to reinstate strikers after the four and one-half months, and to treat those rehired after this time as new hires, did not violate the law because the union "agreed" to this arrangement. The Board took the position that an agreement reached under the pressures to end a strike stands as a waiver of employee rights established by federal law. If the scenario in *United Aircraft* is used on a wide scale, the *Laidlaw-Fleetwood* doctrine would not be of much practical value.

JURISDICTIONAL STRIKES

A *jurisdictional strike* is a work stoppage resulting from a dispute between two or more unions over the assignment of work. At times unions strike because of inter-union conflict over the representation of workers. Such strikes do not fall within the jurisdictional strike category. These are representation and not jurisdictional strikes. As John T. Dunlop, a leading authority on labor relations, put it: "In the jurisdictional dispute proper the contending organizations are not seeking new members; they are demanding the work in dispute for existing members."[20] If the character of the jurisdictional strike is understood, it is not difficult to see why such strikes occur. Unions that extend their jurisdiction over new jobs increase their power. A jurisdictional strike does not increase the total amount of work available. It is merely a device to obtain work for one union at the expense of another.

The record reveals that jurisdictional strikes have been persistent features of the industrial environment. Despite this they have accounted for only a minor fraction of all strikes. However, their effect on employers, workers, and the public has been much greater than the figures reveal. In 1941 there were a total of 93 jurisdictional strikes, amounting to 2.2 percent of all strikes for that year. These strikes involved 37,410 workers and resulted in 260,985 man-days lost to production. This figure constituted 1.1 percent of all man-days lost to production because of strikes for 1941. In 1949 there were 94 jurisdictional strikes, accounting for 2.6 percent of all strikes. They involved 20,300 workers, and caused 143,000 man-days of idleness. This figure constituted .3 percent of all man-days lost to production because of 1949 strikes.[21] In 1965, however, strikes over work assignments numbered 392 and involved 39,600 workers. Jurisdictional strikes accounted for 10 percent of major work stoppages in that year. However, such stoppages were settled rapidly since only 174,000 man-days of idleness resulted, accounting for .7 percent of all man-days lost to production because of all 1965 strikes.[22]

During fiscal 1972 the NLRB reported 598 alleged union violations of the Taft-Hartley provision making union strikes against employer work assignments unfair labor practices.[23] Thus it is obvious that the continuing trend of technological change generates increased friction between unions regarding which one should perform assigned tasks. New materials and new production methods, particularly those affecting the building trades, will tend to continue interunion rivalry to obtain controversial work assignments for their own members.

Effects of Taft-Hartley

Disputes over the assignment of work should be settled before a work stoppage occurs. If the parties involved in such a dispute are unable or unwilling to resolve such disputes peacefully, it is proper for the government to take corrective measures. Employers and the public should not be victimized by interunion jurisdictional rivalries.

Taft-Hartley outlaws the jurisdictional strike.[24] Unions may not strike against a work assignment of an employer. As noted, jurisdictional strikes in the construction industry are particularly harmful because contractors usually work under specified time limits.

After the passage of Taft-Hartley the unions and employers involved in the construction industry established a National Joint Board. In addition to an impartial chairman, the Board is composed of an equal number of representatives of contractors and unions. Its purpose is to settle finally any jurisdictional dispute in the construction industry.[25] In February 1965 the National Joint Board for the Settlement of Jurisdictional Disputes was renegotiated and included all unions affiliated with the Building and Construction Trades Department, AFL-CIO, and employer members of the Associated General Contractors of America and the Participating Specialty Contractors Employers Associations. The new agreement provided new criteria and procedures to resolve jurisdictional disputes. An appeals board is provided when one party is dissatisfied with an award. An award at this stage is to be final and binding upon the disputants.

In large measure the unions and contractors established the National Joint Board with NLRB encouragement as a matter of self-protection. The Taft-Hartley Act empowered the NLRB to make final decisions in jurisdictional disputes in the event the parties failed to settle them peacefully. Fearful of the possible effects of intervention of an "outside party," the employers and unions adopted a procedure that would make intervention by the NLRB unnecessary. The National Joint Board changed its procedures again in 1970. Membership was increased from four to eight with half from management and half from labor. The new plan provides that the interest of the consumer should be considered when jurisdictional disputes come before the joint board.

Settlement of jurisdictional disputes in the construction industry is a difficult and complex task. If decisions are to be workable and equitable, they must conform to a large body of precedent established over a long period of time. In addition, arbiters of these disputes must have a firm knowledge of the entire construction industry. Obviously, the parties intimately connected with the construction industry are much better qualified to settle jurisdictional disputes than the NLRB. In this connection the General Counsel of the NLRB declared:

> We of the Board have plenty to do in the field with which we are familiar, and in which we are properly expected to serve as experts. We frankly do not want to be plunged into this new field that is strange territory to us, in which we would be compelled to become experts almost overnight, but we will do it if we must.[26]

The sponsors of Taft-Hartley had intended that one of its provisions would stimulate settlement of jurisdictional disputes outside the NLRB.[27] Further, it was intended that the settlement techniques would vary from industry to industry because of the uniqueness of each category. However, if an alleged violation of the law was filed with the Board, it was to hear and decide the dispute itself unless, within ten days after notice that an unfair labor practice had been filed, the parties to the dispute "submit to the Board satisfactory evidence that they have adjusted, or agreed upon methods for the voluntary adjustment of the dispute." The parties may arbitrate the dispute or settle the issue by use of another private method. Failure to comply with the private award or failure to settle the dispute would supposedly lead to a Board hearing on the unfair labor practice charge. If a violation were found, the Board should then issue a cease-and-desist order. Failure to comply at this stage would result in seeking enforcement of the Board order in a circuit court.[28]

However laudable the purpose of the 1947 labor law, the fact remains that it was not immediately enforced by the Board. The 1947 labor law provided for a very cumbersome procedure for settling jurisdictional disputes. It is one matter to outlaw jurisdictional strikes, it is another matter to settle the dispute. Outlawing the jurisdictional strike does not necessarily mean the adjudication of the dispute.

The Board, recognizing this, considered itself unqualified to deal with jurisdictional problems and thereby largely ignored such cases unless (1) an employer made a work assignment inconsistent with its certification of a union or (2) the assignment was inconsistent with the terms of the collective bargaining contract. This NLRB attitude left the actual determination of work assignment in the hands of employers. The possibility of unilateral action in this regard was precisely one of the situations the national labor laws had intended to eliminate.

Supreme Court Intervention

As noted, the Board viewed its function under Section 10 (k) as merely that of determining whether a striking union was entitled to the work in dispute under a preexisting Board order or certification, or under a collective bargaining contract. If the striking union was not entitled to the work on the basis of the two criteria just mentioned, the employer's assignment of work was regarded as decisive. Very often, however, neither the certifications nor the agreements clearly assigned work that employees represented by competing unions claimed. This type of problem could lead to constant disputes extending over a period of years. An employer forced to make an assignment would not be immune from work stoppages by dissatisfied labor organizations. It would attempt to satisfy all the unions involved, but usually would end up satisfying none. A strike by one of the unions would leave an employer no recourse but to file an unfair labor practice charge with the NLRB.[29]

These circumstances were presented the U.S. Supreme Court in a 1961 case.[30] The high court came down hard on the NLRB and explicitly informed it that it had not been carrying out its statutory duty to hear and resolve jurisdictional disputes in every case where the parties had not been able to resolve the problem themselves. The Board is required to decide any "underlying jurisdictional dispute on its merits and . . . make affirmative" awards of disputed work in every case before it if the parties have not set up their own machinery to so do within ten days.

The Board has responded in accordance with Supreme Court direction. The *Radio Engineers Union (Columbia Broadcasting System)* decision was required under the law. The legislative history of Section 10 (k) makes it obvious that Congress did not intend to permit the Board to ignore such cases.

The Supreme Court in 1971 was presented with the problem of NLRB authority to impose a jurisdictional dispute settlement when an employer refused to accept an award agreed to by the unions.[31] The issue centered on whether the employer was a "party" to the "dispute" within the meaning of Section 10(k). The Board has long held that a voluntary method of adjustment must include the employer as well as the unions to be valid. The two unions as members of the AFL-CIO's Building Trades Department were required to submit their dispute to the National Joint Board for Settlement of Jurisdictional Disputes. They did so and an award was made. The employers involved had contracts with the union losing the award and refused to accept the National Joint Board's determination. Picketing resulted and the companies filed unfair labor practice charges with the NLRB. The NLRB accepted the case and made its own award to the Tile Setters and not the Plasterers as did the National Joint Board. A lower federal court set aside the Board order and held that an employer was not a "party" to a dispute between rival unions.[32] This meant that the NLRB was without authority to settle the dispute. The Supreme Court upheld the NLRB and stated that "the LMRA requires that the Board defer only when all of the parties have agreed on a method of settlement." Otherwise the Board must settle the dispute.

The Board has established criteria that it usually observes in making work assignments. These factors of evaluation are the bargaining agreements and union constitutions, skills and work involved, industry custom and practice, and employer's past practice. However, it should be noted that these factors do not always permit an assignment. Conflicting results may be obtained when these four criteria are applied. This is particularly the case when "new work" is involved. The Board has on occasion relied upon novel factors to make work assignments. In the *Philadelphia Inquirer* case the NLRB applied "substitution of function" and "loss-of-jobs" tests in resolving a jurisdictional dispute.[33] Of critical concern to the Board was what would happen to a union's members if it assigned work to another organization. Another factor that impressed the Board was that one union had undertaken to retrain its members in the new technology. Yet similarity of the new techniques to prior processes would have required a different assignment of work.

Generally, however, the Board, when assigning disputed work, adheres to the tests of (1) bargaining agreements and union constitutions, (2) skills and work involved, (3) industry custom and practice, and (4) employer's past practice. Use of these tests provides a greater degree of stability than would determinations made without guidelines. The Board relies upon its "experience and common sense" when established tests fail to be adequate. Such an approach is consistent with the Supreme Court's *Columbia Broadcasting System* rule.

STRIKES AGAINST NLRB CERTIFICATION

The Wagner Act was based on the principle of majority rule. Unions selected by the majority of workers in a bargaining unit were to represent all employees within the unit. Employers were required to recognize and bargain with the majority union and with no other organization. An employer violated the statute if he granted any measure of recognition to a minority union. Some labor unions, however, violated the doctrine of majority rule. They refused to respect certifications awarded by the NLRB. Despite the evidence of the ballot box, a number of unions struck against certifications of the NLRB. These unions struck to force employers to violate their legal obligation to recognize majority-designated unions.

Such action resulted when unions were defeated in bargaining elections. Let us assume that Union A and Union B are rivals in a bargaining election. Union A polls a majority vote. Dissatisfied with the election returns, Union B strikes to force the employer to recognize it and not Union A, the majority-designated labor organization. Of course, the employer is under legal obligation to bargain with A. Under the law management would commit an unfair labor practice if it granted any recognition whatsoever to B, the defeated labor organization.

Such strikes are totally indefensible. They violate the most elementary principles of democracy. They are completely inconsistent with the spirit of the Wagner Act. The frequency of such strikes under the Wagner Act was not very great. In the vast majority of cases unions defeated in elections accepted the results of the polls in good faith. Frequently, this meant that workers were required to change union affiliations. It is to the credit of the union movement that such changes occurred without serious impairment to the productive process.

Ultimate Position of NLRB

Despite their limited frequency the fact remains that such strikes did take place in the Wagner Act era. When they did occur, employers and majority-designated unions were placed in an intolerable position. Ultimately, the NLRB did attempt to discourage strikes against its certifications. In the early part of 1947 the Board ruled that employees who participated in a strike, with the purpose of compelling an employer to recognize and bargain with the union of the striking employees rather than with a certified labor organization, were not entitled to reinstatement or back pay.[34] Since the Board held the purpose of this form of strike to be unjustified, the strikers were stripped of all benefits of the Wagner Act. This ruling was handed down by the NLRB at about the time the Wagner Act was to expire. The agency did not see fit to establish this policy earlier in the Wagner Act era.

Treatment Under Taft-Hartley

Even the ultimate position of the NLRB on minority strikes, however, was not sufficient to protect the principle of majority rule. At the very best it merely had the effect of discouraging such strikes. Under the Wagner Act the NLRB did not have the power to prevent them. In this respect the law was defective. The Board certified majority unions, but it did not have the authority to protect its certifications against strike action.

The principle of majority rule was included in the Taft-Hartley Act. As in the Wagner Act employers are required to bargain with majority-designated labor unions. However, Congress, when it passed the 1947 labor law, overcame the short-coming of the Wagner Act. It outlawed strikes for recognition when another union had been certified by the NLRB.[35]

Certification of a union as exclusive bargaining representative makes a primary strike for recognition by a union other than the one certified an unfair labor practice under Section 8 (b) (4) (C). Adequate enforcement procedures were adopted. Injunctions may be obtained against unions that engage in such strikes.

When strikes against NLRB certification occur, Section 10 (1) makes it mandatory for the Board to seek injunctions against the strikes. It must give priority to violations of this nature. In addition, whoever is injured by a minority recognition strike may sue the minority union for actual damages. Punitive damages are not permitted[36] under Section 301 permitting damage suits in federal and state courts.[37] However, adequate provision is now available to protect the bargaining rights of certified majority unions in most situations likely to arise.

LOCKOUT RIGHTS OF EMPLOYERS

The right of unions to strike to influence the outcome of bargaining demands has generally been considered as balanced by the right of employers to lock out employees for the same reason. The NLRB has not always been willing to permit the lockout, however, particularly when it can be identified as an offensive measure. It has never upheld the lockout as a legal form of economic pressure when used as an anti-union weapon. Purposes other than to destroy a union may qualify the weapon for legal use.

In 1951 the Board stated in *Betts Cadillac* that:

> An employer is not prohibited from taking reasonable measures, including closing down his plant, where such measures are, under the circumstances, necessary for the avoidance of economic loss or business disruption attendant upon a strike. This right may, under some circumstances, embrace the curtailment of operations before the precise moment the strike has occurred.... The nature of the

measures taken, the objective, the timing, the reality of the strike threat, the nature and extent of the anticipated disruption, and the degree of resultant restriction on the effectiveness of the concerted activity, are all matters to be weighed in determining the reasonableness under the circumstances, and the ultimate legality, of the employer's action.[38]

Essentially, the Board has established two situations under which it permits lockouts. One provides that the weapon is permissible as a defensive device to protect the employer against a sudden strike that might result in unusual economic losses. The other involves a lockout to preserve the institution of multicollective bargaining.

Unusual Economic Hardship

Unusual economic hardship might result for a company engaged in custom work that cannot afford to continue to operate on a day-to-day basis for an extended period after contract expiration. This is particularly the case when the timing of a possible work stoppage is not certain. Uncertainty regarding a work stoppage at a firm dealing with custom work could result in loss of considerable good will if it were caught with unexecuted orders on hand.

Unusual economic costs might also be involved for a firm that produces a perishable raw material. After a contract has expired a company may lock out if it has no knowledge of the timing of an expected union strike. Such action is regarded as defensive by the Board and as such would have nothing to do with an attempt to destroy a union.

Defense of Multibargaining Unit

The *Buffalo Linen* case was decided by the Supreme Court in 1956; the case involved a union, the Truck Drivers Local Union No. 449, and eight companies with which it bargained.[39] There was a history of multiemployer bargaining between the parties. The union struck one company and the remaining seven reacted by locking out their employees. The nonstruck companies reacted to prevent *whipsawing*. *Whipsawing* refers to successive strikes against one after another of the various members of an employers' association.

Whipsaw action can be highly beneficial to labor organizations in that they may strike one company while all the others continue operations. A single company cannot normally hold out for a long period of time if its competitors continue to supply the market for a particular product. Unions often strike the wealthiest companies first under these circumstances and then pick off the others at their discretion until all agree to approximately the same contractual terms.

The Board ruled in *Buffalo Linen* that the employers had the right to preserve the traditional multiemployer collective bargaining relationship, which was being threatened by the whipsawing action. A circuit court reviewing the case overruled the NLRB on the basis that it had expanded its "hardship doctrine," which permitted lockouts only if unusual economic costs were likely to be incurred. The U.S. Supreme Court reversed the lower court and upheld Board action on the theory that the pattern of multiemployer bargaining had been established for all purposes.

Actually, the doctrine established means that the lockout may be used to preserve a multiemployer bargaining arrangement, but only in cases where there is a history of it. The Board has had several occasions to implement the rule.

In a 1964 *A & P* case a recently formed employer association used the lockout to attempt to force a change in the pattern of bargaining. Traditionally, bargaining took place on a single-employer basis. During negotiations the association insisted upon a bargaining change from single units to a multiemployer unit. The union met with the group to discuss the issue and an impasse was reached in negotiations without agreement upon a change to a new procedure. The union struck one of the members whose contract had expired. The other employers locked out their employees as an offensive tactic to secure their objective. The Board held the employer action was outside *Buffalo Linen* limits since the lockout in such cases could be undertaken merely to preserve a multiemployer unit from attempted union destruction. This made the lockout an offensive weapon in the Board's view and as such was not permissible because of the effect it might have on unionism.

In another case, however, *Evening News Association*, the NLRB held that employer lockout action was protected within the *Buffalo Linen* principle since the result was to preserve the existing bargaining arrangement.[40] It was a defensive and not an offensive weapon.

Supreme Court Expansion of Employer Right to Lock Out and Continue Operations

The NLRB was persistent until 1965 in requiring a rigid interpretation regarding what constitutes defensive employer lockout behavior. In a 1962 case, *Brown Food Store*, the Board held that nonstruck employers in locking out their employees were exceeding the lawful defensive limits established in *Buffalo Linen* by continuing operations with temporary replacements.[41]

The Tenth Circuit Court of Appeals subsequently refused to enforce the Board's order and the Supreme Court agreed to hear the case. The high court rejected the Board's reasoning and held that it was not an unfair labor practice for the nonstruck members of a multiemployer unit to continue to operate by using temporary replacements.[42] It was permitted to do so as a response to a whipsaw strike against one of the association members. The Court reasoned that

> the continued operations . . . and their use of temporary replacements [no] more imply hostile motivation, nor [is it] inherently more destructive of employee rights, than is the lockout itself. Rather, the compelling inference is that this was all part and parcel [of the employers'] defensive measure to preserve the multi-employer groups in the face of the whipsaw strike.[43]

Thus multiemployer bargaining units have been extended considerable economic power to deal with labor organizations engaged in whipsaw action. They may temporarily lock out workers and replace them temporarily to preserve their bargaining-unit structure.

The Supreme Court was not entirely free to rule differently. It had already ruled in *Mackay Radio* that a struck employer could use replacements to keep its firm open.[44] Since the struck employer has such a right, then the other employers must also be entitled to do so or they would be placed at a competitive disadvantage relative to the struck firms. Thus a union may engage in whipsaw action but if it does, multiemployer unit firms do not have to suffer the economic consequences which would flow from a policy of permitting only a struck firm to continue its operations by replacing employees.

It should be noted, however, that the struck firm may permanently replace economic strikers whereas the nonstruck firms may replace only temporarily. Practically, this distinction means very little since one of the conditions of restoring the bargaining unit to normalcy would be reinstatement of all replaced workers.

Lockout as an Offensive Weapon

The Supreme Court's *American Ship Building* case provided employers with the right to lock out as a counterweapon to a strike.[45] However, such action is permissible only after a deadlock has been reached on mandatory bargaining items. *Lockouts* are not legal economic weapons if intended to discourage union membership.

When the lockout is used to support the legitimate bargaining demands of single employers, temporary or permanent replacements seemingly could not be used. Temporary replacements were permitted only to protect the integrity of multiemployer bargaining units where whipsaw action against the nonstruck firms may result.[46]

The lockout is viewed in a different fashion under single-employer bargaining arrangements than it is in multiemployer units. When a single employer acts in its own self-interest, the lockout is distinguished from union strike action in that it merely deprives the labor organization of the exclusive power to determine when a work stoppage will occur and how long it will last. Determination of the timing and duration of work stoppages were not rights extended to unions under the national labor law.

The real question that must be answered is to what extent the Court has balanced the strategic economic weapons that may be used by unions and employers in gaining desirable bargaining results. The high court in *American Ship Building* indicates that employers bargaining individually are only permitted to influence the timing and duration of the work stoppage by use of lockouts. This is viewed as the only difference between the strike and lockout. However, the decision is highly inconsistent with the *Mackay Radio* decision and Taft-Hartley itself. The inconsistency exists because economic strikers may be replaced under the Court's decision and under the 1947 law as well. *American Ship Building* establishes a law whereby permanent replacements for economic strikers may be hired if the union takes the initiative in determining the timing and duration of work stoppages. However, if the initiative is taken by employers, neither temporary nor permanent replacements may be used.

Under this doctrine a single employer could enhance its bargaining position and its weapons arsenal merely by permitting unions to take strike action instead of locking out workers. This may be accomplished with the employer in firm command of the timing element of the stoppage. That is, an employer may simply not agree to certain mandatory bargaining items. Variations of the *Brown* and *American Ship Building* rules developed. In *Inland Trucking*, an employer locked out employees after contract negotiations reached an impasse.[47] Temporary replacements were hired and the firm continued to operate. The Board and a federal appeals court held the employer in violation of Taft-Hartley. The court ruled that the lockout differed from *American Ship Building* and *Brown* because the use of temporary substitutes during a bargaining lockout was inherently destructive of employee statutory rights, a decision that was based on the Supreme Court's *Great Dane Trailers* case.[48] In addition, an appeals court was of the opinion that the employer's motives or reasons for using substitutes were unimportant. The desire to avoid a strike that might be called during the busiest season was insufficient by itself to justify use of temporary replacements. An employer's actions cannot be inherently destructive of important employee rights. For example, a union has a statutorily protected right to take initiative with respect to strikes because the right to strike and to refrain from striking are equally guaranteed under Section 7 of Taft-Hartley. Thus, the employer could not use the lockout to provoke a strike for the purpose of forcing agreement to a contract proposed by the employer and/or for the purpose of avoiding a strike that could be called during its busiest season.[49] In *U.S. Pipe* the company unilaterally reduced benefits and several weeks later locked out its workers when they refused to agree to the company's changes. This action was considered illegal.

In 1972, despite the federal court's decision in *Inland Trucking*, the Board position on use of temporary replacements during lockouts started to change. It was held in *Ottawa Silica* by a split vote that for a single firm to continue operation with temporary replacements was lawful as a means of getting locked out workers to act on the company's bargaining proposals.[50] The same circumstances occurred in a subsequent Board decision during the same year.[51]

The Board majority apparently interprets the Supreme Court's *Brown Food Store* decision as requiring an examination on a case-by-case basis, and the defensive nature of the lockout is one very relevant factor that permits use of temporary replacements. It appears that the NLRB has now started to expand employer use of temporary replacements after a bargaining impasse has been reached to include single firm bargaining arrangements. As a consequence, legitimate employer objectives may be interpreted to outweigh employee rights under the Act which in turn means that temporary replacements may be hired legally.[52] In so doing, a wave of complications should be expected to develop that include ultimately that the Supreme Court will have to review the permissiveness of temporary replacement use in light of its *American Ship Building* decision. It was in that case that the high court left the issue open when it stated that "we intimate no view whatever as to the consequences which would follow had the employer replaced its employees with permanent or even temporary help."[53]

EMPLOYEE CONDUCT ON THE PICKET LINE

The Taft-Hartley Act also regulates the conduct of workers participating in the picketing process. During strikes employees normally engage in picket-line activities. Hence the law of picketing cannot be divorced from strike action. One would look in vain for specific provisions of the law that deal with strike-related picketing. The NLRB has inferred from particular sections of the law that certain picketing patterns are unlawful. What are these sections?

Section 7 of Taft-Hartley provides that

employees shall have the right to self-organization, to form, join or assist labor organizations, to bargain collectively through representatives of their own choosing, and to engage in other concerted activities for the purpose of collective bargaining or other mutal aid or protection, *and shall have the right to refrain from any or all of such activities. . . .*[54]

The italicized phrase did not appear in the Wagner Act. Whereas the Wagner Act guaranteed to workers the right to engage in collective bargaining activities, such as striking and picketing free from employer interference, it did not protect workers in the right to refrain from such activities. The assumption of Taft-Hartley is that certain workers do not desire to bargain collectively, to strike, or to picket. Hence the law shields these workers from union tactics calculated to force them to participate in concerted employee activities.

Section 7 must be read in conjunction with another provision of Taft-Hartley to gain an understanding of the impact of the statute on picketing.[55] This additional section provides that it shall be unlawful for labor unions or their agents "to restrain or coerce employees in the exercise of the rights guaranteed in section 7." Thus labor unions violate the law if they coerce or restrain employees in their right to refrain from union activities. However, the Act also provides that "the paragraph shall not impair the right of a labor organization to prescribe its own rules with respect to the acquisition or retention of membership therein."[56]

The NLRB has held that certain picketing conduct of labor unions operates to deny workers their right not to engage in union activities. What is the general character of such unlawful picketing? Picketing is illegal under Taft-Hartley where the effect of the picketing denies to employees the opportunity to work during a strike. In short, employees have the protected right to work in face of a strike. The Board declared in October 1948 that "employees have a guaranteed right to refrain from striking. That right includes the right to go to and from work without restraint or coercion while a strike is in progress."[57] The legislative history of Taft-Hartley fully supports this position of the NLRB. In this connection Senator Taft declared that it outlaws "such restraint and coercion as would prevent people from going to work if they wished to go to work."[58] Thus picketing that prevents employees from working during a strike coerces and restrains workers in the exercise of their right not to engage in collective action. It must be noted, however, that the Taft-Hartley provisions that prohibit union coercion of employees extend beyond union interference with the right of employees to work during a strike. For example, in May 1950, the NLRB ruled unanimously that the Progressive Mine Workers Union violated the law by threatening to cause the discharge of two miners who favored the United Mine Workers of America as bargaining agent.[59]

The NLRB held in 1964 that a union has the authority to impose fines against members who cross picket lines while they are on strike.[60] This Board position was rejected by the Seventh Circuit Court of Appeals, however, and was accepted for review by the U.S. Supreme Court. The high court sustained the Board's position of 1964 in a close 5-4 decision.[61] In doing so it stated that the "economic strike against the employer is the ultimate weapon in labor's arsenal for achieving agreement upon its terms and the power to fine or expel strikebreakers is essential if the union is to be an effective bargaining agent. . . ." The Court argued further "that Congress did not propose any limitations with respect to the internal affairs of unions, aside from barring enforcement of a union's internal regulations to affect a member's employment status." Thus rules are legal that impose fines on members for crossing picket lines because unions have the right to preserve their integrity during a time of crisis. Section 7 does not insulate an employee from all consequences flowing from his choice of actions. He may legally cross a picket line to work during a strike but he may have to pay a fine for doing so if it is administered without discrimination by a labor organization. The ability to deal with a worker as a union member is therefore established by law. Unions on the other hand are not to interfere with a worker's status as an employee. The difference between the two is often difficult to determine. Court suits may be initiated by unions to collect fines assessed against members. This authority is found in Section 8 (b) (1) which states that "this paragraph shall not impair the right of a labor organization to prescribe its own rules with respect to the acquisition or retention of membership therein." This language prompted five Supreme Court justices to hold that a fine for crossing a picket line was a legitimate union action. However, the other four were of the opinion that such union action forced employees to engage in union activities against their will.

Though the high court held that a union may fine union members who work during a strike and sue such members for the collection of the fines in state courts, it stated that the amount of the fines must be "reasonable." The question arose as to whether or not the NLRB has jurisdiction to determine the reasonableness of a fine. Thus, if the Board has authority over such a problem, it could hold that a union would commit an unfair labor practice if the fine was deemed unreasonable. However, in 1973, the Supreme Court held that the NLRB is without authority to determine the reasonableness of such fines.[62] What this decision means is that state courts have jurisdiction to establish whether or not a fine levied against a union member for strikebreaking is reasonable. If a union member feels that the fine levied against him is too high, he must seek relief from the state courts and not from the Board.

In 1969 the Supreme Court carried its *Allis-Chalmers* rule a step further. It ruled in *Scofield* v. *NLRB* that a union is free to enforce a properly adopted internal rule which reflects a legitimate union interest.[63] A distinction must be made between internal and external enforcement of union rules to determine legality of such action. In *Scofield* the Court upheld union-imposed fines for exceeding a production ceiling. The high court observed that

> [t]he union rule here left the collective bargaining process unimpaired, breached no collective contract, required no pay for unperformed services, induced no discrimination by the employer against any class of employees, and presents no dereliction by the union of its duty of fair representation. In light of this, and the acceptable manner in which the rule was enforced, vindicating a legitimate union interest, it is impossible to say it contravened any policy of the act.

Thus *Scofield* made it clear that under federal law a union can fine members for violating certain rules. However, the collection of such fines is a matter of state and not federal law. But such fines are only enforced if a valid union-security clause is contained in the collective bargaining agreement. This was one feature of the *Allis-Chalmers* rule that was not made clear in 1967.

In June 1974 the *Allis-Chalmers* doctrine was applied to supervisors who are members of a union. At that time, the U.S. Supreme Court in *Florida Power and Light* v. *Electrical Workers* held that a union may properly fine supervisor-members who cross picket lines during a strike and perform bargaining unit work. However, such fines would not be lawful when supervisor-members represent their employer in collective bargaining or in the grievance procedure. To justify its decision, the court reasoned that supervisor-members do not carry out such collective bargaining duties when during a strike they take over the jobs normally performed by striking employees.

Severe criticism has been leveled at the *Allis-Chalmers* decision.[64] Since four Supreme Court justices believed that the majority was wrong, the criticisms obviously have a degree of validity. It is argued that union rules designed to prevent employees from crossing picket lines have an effect on their job status. To avoid a fine, they may not work, and, hence, lose wages. If they work, the union may fine them in the amount of the wages that they earned. Fines in this amount probably would be deemed reasonable by state courts. Under these circumstances, the union members would in effect work at their jobs without pay. On the other hand, the enforcement of a union rule against strikebreaking preserves the integrity of the union and the wishes of the majority during a strike.

In any event, probably the sharp criticisms against *Allis-Chalmers* prompted the Supreme Court in a subsequent case to undermine the policy. The question was whether or not a union may fine a union member who resigns from the union prior to the time that he crosses the picket line. In determining this important issue, the high court held by an 8–1 majority in *Granite State Joint Board* that a fine under these circumstances violates Taft-Hartley.[65] Thus, a union member who desires to engage in strikebreaking may simply resign from the union before he crosses the picket line, and the union may not fine him for this activity. Justice Blackmun, the sole dissenter, stated in his opposition to the majority:

> I cannot join the Court's opinion, which seems to me to exalt the formality of resignation over the substance of the various interests and national labor policies that are at stake here. Union activity, by its very nature, is group activity, and is grounded on the notion that strength can be garnered from unity, solidarity, and mutual commitment. This concept is of particular force during a strike, where the individual members of the union draw strength from the commitments of fellow members, and where the activities carried on by the union rest fundamentally on the mutual reliance that inheres in the "pact." . . .

One question, however, was not determined by the majority in *Granite State Joint Board*. The constitution of the union involved in that case did not expressly forbid resignations of members during a strike. It was silent on this issue. In its decision, the majority made special note of this omission. It stated: "We do not now decide to what extent the contractual relationship between union and member may curtail the freedom to resign." Thus, the high court indicated that it will subsequently determine the legality of fines when a union member by express constitutional provision of his organization is forbidden to resign during a strike.[66] If the court decides this issue against the unions, and in the light of *Granite State Joint Board*, the protection that unions received in *Allis-Chalmers* would be virtually destroyed.

Substance of Restraint and Coercion. To establish the full effect of the statute on picketing, the NLRB is required to spell out the meaning of the terms *restraint* and *coercion*. What are the circumstances in which a picket line restrains and coerces employees within the meaning of the law? Specifically, what patterns of picketing conduct prevent employees from working during a strike? Actually, this is a much more difficult problem to resolve than the mere establishment of the general character of unlawful picketing. This is necessarily the case because restraint and coercion mean different things to different people.

After the enactment of Taft-Hartley, the Board declared that picketing that forcibly blocks ingress and egress to a struck plant violates the Taft-Hartley Act.

For example, during one strike a union organized a picket line of between two hundred and three hundred members. The workers massed in front of the driveway leading to the struck plant's parking lot. When cars carrying nonstriking employees reached the driveway, they were blocked by the crowd. Three cars successfully drove into the parking lot, but only through the assistance of local police officers. Two other automobiles started to drive through the picket line but, when instructed by the plant superintendent not to attempt to go through, they drove away. Such picketing, the NLRB held, was unlawful.[67]

A case involving the United Furniture Workers of America is particularly helpful in determining the unlawful area of picketing. In this case the Board held unlawful a number of picketing tactics that operated to deny employees the right to work, free from restraint and coercion, during a strike. Such conduct included (1) the carrying of sticks by the pickets on the picket line; (2) the piling of bricks for use by the pickets; (3) the blocking of plant entrances by railroad ties, automobiles, raised gutter plates, and tacks; (4) the threat of violence toward nonstriking employees; (5) the warning given one nonstriking employee that "when we get in with the union you old fellows won't have a job"; (6) the placing of pickets in such a manner as to prevent nonstrikers from carrying out their assigned work of loading cabinets into railroad boxcars on a railroad siding located about a quarter of a mile from the plant; (7) the "goon-squad" mass assaults upon various nonstrikers; (8) the overturning of automobiles; and (9) the barring from the plant of a superintendent and a foreman by force and intimidation in full view of nonstriking employees.

Each and every one of the above acts of violence was held unlawful by the National Labor Relations Board.[68] They have been reaffirmed in subsequent cases.[69] However, a new philosophy toward picketing conduct has developed. Picket violence directed against employer property likewise constitutes unlawful coercion of employees. Thus during one work stoppage striking employees engaged in picketing broke more than 443 windows. This was accomplished by hurling stones, rocks, railroad tieplates, railroad spikes, clubs, and other objects through the windows. The union claimed its activities were not directed at employees but against the employer. Hence it contended that this action did not coerce or restrain employees in their right not to engage in union activities. This contention was flatly rejected by the Board. It held that the "atmosphere of terror" created by the union in the destruction of the property constituted a threat to employees. The Board observed that nonstrikers would have to risk physical violence if they attempted to enter the struck plant.[70]

Name-calling Lawful. About a year after Taft-Hartley was enacted the NLRB was called upon to decide whether or not pickets may lawfully abuse strikebreakers by calling them profane names. Pickets frequently call strikebreakers a variety of foul names as they come through the picket line. It was almost inevitable that the Board would be called upon to decide this problem. Its decision was handed down in a case that involved a number of women pickets and women strikebreakers. The facts indicate that six female employees who had chosen to abandon the strike and return to work were met at the plant gate by a large group of pickets. The Board reports that "[the strikebreakers] were vilified and verbally abused as scabs—deserters from the striker's ranks." Some of the pickets called the strikebreakers a variety of obscene epithets besides "scab" and "deserter."

The Board refused to find a violation of the Taft-Hartley Act, declaring that the abuse of the strikebreakers amounted only to name-calling.[71] Thus vocal resentment by pickets directed against strikebreakers is a form of peaceful picketing. Such picketing tactics, according to the Board, do not constitute coercion and restraint of employees within the meaning of the 1947 labor law. To support its position, the Board pointed to the section of Taft-Hartley which provides that

> the expressing of any views, arguments, or opinions, or the dissemination thereof, whether in written, printed, graphic, or visual form, shall not constitute or be evidence of an unfair labor practice under the provisions of this Act, if such expression contains no threat of reprisal or force or promise of benefit.[72]

Actually, this section, popularly termed the "free speech" clause, was inserted into the law to provide employers with greater opportunity to deliver speeches to employees.[73] It is noteworthy that the Board utilized this section to legalize name-calling on the picket line.

In June 1974 the opportunity to degrade nonmembers of a union was increased. At that time, in *Letter Carriers* v. *Austin* the U.S. Supreme Court held that publication in a union's newsletter of nonmembers' names in a "list of scabs" that also carried a highly pejorative definition of the term "scab" was protected under federal labor laws. Noting that such laws encourage "uninhibited, robust, and wide-open discussion," the court reversed the decision of the Supreme Court of Virginia which previously held that the publication was libelous under state law. State courts found that, under state law, the use of "scab" was libelous and awarded listed nonmembers $165,000 in damages.

In any event coercive conduct calculated to compel strike participation or observance of picket lines by employees remains illegal.[74] Threats of physical violence against nonstrikers and their families, likewise, do not constitute permissible behavior. A union is held liable for the coercive conduct of a striker if the threat is made in the presence of a union representative and is not repudiated by him.[75]

It should be noted, however, that if an employee refuses to cross a picket line at his place of employment and the picketing union is not his representative, he is usually protected, but not always. An employer may discharge employees who refuse to cross a picket line if motivation for refusal is fear alone and not because of sympathy toward the union cause.[76] If the individual refuses to cross another union's picket line because of both fear and sympathy for the union cause, an employer may not discharge him.[77] To do so would interfere with an employee's right to engage in concerted activities for the purpose of mutual aid or protection.

Nonviolent Mass Picketing Unlawful. Picketing by large numbers of workers is commonly termed *mass picketing*. This form of union activity poses no great legal problem when the picket line engages in acts of violence. As noted, the Board ruled that forcible blocking of the entrance to plants constitutes unlawful picketing. This would be true regardless of the number of workers picketing.

The perplexing legal problem, however, involves picketing in a peaceful manner by large numbers of workers. Strikebreakers must be allowed entry into the struck plant without violence or threats of violence to their persons or property. What then is the legal status of mass picketing carried out in a peaceful manner?

In 1949 the Board dealt with this extremely difficult problem. The case involved a picket line of some one thousand to two thousand persons. The pickets marched back and forth in front of a plant involved in a strike. Apparently, they did not engage in overt acts of violence. However, the Board held that such picketing was unlawful, declaring that "realistically viewed, restraint and coercion were the effect of the mass picketing."[78] It further observed that the "necessary effect of the manner in which the demonstration was conducted was to deny nonstriking employees access to the plant."

The effect of the Board's position is to outlaw nonviolent mass picketing. The Board has not, however, dogmatically stated how many workers can compose lawful picket lines. It avoids this problem by declaring that one definition of mass picketing cannot possibly fit all cases. Hence the substance of mass picketing must be determined by particular Board decisions. Each case will be decided on its own merits. For example, the Board did not find a violation in one case even though a picket line of about two hundred persons assembled near a plant during a strike. What is more, the pickets verbally denounced strikebreakers as they entered the plant. The Board pointed out that "there was no difficulty entering or leaving the plant. . . ."[79]

Despite its reluctance to set forth the exact number who may properly picket, the Board has regarded the number of workers on a picket line as relevant in determining the potential or calculated restraining effect of massed pickets in barring nonstrikers from entering or leaving the plant. It has held that some picket parades by mere force of numbers have the effect of coercing employees who want to enter a plant and work. The exact point at which peaceful picketing becomes "massed" and unlawful because of the number of pickets turns on the particular circumstances of each case.

Penalties for Unlawful Picketing. Both unions and employees are subject to penalties for unlawful picketing. Unions that sponsor unlawful picketing face injunction proceedings. Employees who engage in unlawful picketing lose reinstatement rights. Employers have no legal obligation to reinstate a striker found to have engaged in picketing held unlawful under Taft-Hartley. For example, the NLRB has held that workers engaging in violent picketing can expect no relief from the NLRB when discharged. A Puerto Rican firm discharged eighteen strikers who engaged in various acts of violence, threats of force against nonstrikers, and destruction of plant property. The NLRB refused to order the reinstatement of these workers.[80] Actually, the NLRB established this principle under the Wagner Act and has consistently utilized it. It refused to order the reinstatement of workers who committed extreme acts of violence while on strike. These workers were found guilty of offenses such as assault and battery, dynamiting, or murder. Under Taft-Hartley a worker engaging in any act of unlawful picketing loses reinstatement rights. The penalty is not reserved for extreme acts of violence. Thus the principle of denial of reinstatement has much wider application under Taft-Hartley than was true under the Wagner Act.

Neither unions nor employees engaged in unlawful picketing can prevent prosecution under Taft-Hartley by offering the defense that strikes are provoked by employer unfair labor practices. Even if company unfair labor practices provoke a strike, the Board for many years has held that unions and employees still violate the 1947 labor law when they prevent strikebreakers from entering a plant during a strike. In 1949 the Board rejected the "clean hands" doctrine in the enforcement of the statute. In this connection it declared:

> With respect to the "clean hands" defense, we find that the company's alleged unfair labor practices if established, do not lessen the need for vindicating and protecting employees rights under the Act, which the [union had] infringed.[81]

A CHANGE IN TAFT-HARTLEY PICKETING POLICY

Violent picketing should be outlawed. Though one can understand the cause for picket-line violence, the fact remains that unions should not be permitted to engage in acts of violence against persons or property calculated to keep strikebreakers out of struck plants. Thus far the NLRB has found violations of the law where picketing, judged by common-sense standards, has been obviously violent in character. Invariably, the patterns of picketing deemed unlawful have been already outlawed by state and local action. If federal prohibition adds to the elimination of violent picketing such a policy serves the public interest. The Taft-Hartley Act provides a penalty (denial of reinstatement rights of employees engaging in violent picketing) not available under state and local law. Furthermore, the national law has applicability in communities in which for some reason or other law-enforcement officers shut their eyes to overt acts of violence on the picket line.

However, the courts have apparently rejected the Board doctrine that employees always lose reinstatement rights when they engage in violence. As the law now stands, strikers who engage in violence or other misconduct are not automatically subject to discharge without possibility of Board reinstatement and back-pay orders. The reversal in policy came in 1962 in the *Kohler* case after the District of Columbia Court of Appeals rejected the Board's adherence to established standards rejecting reinstatement and back pay for strikers engaged in violence or other misconduct.[82]

When the *Kohler* case was first before the Board in 1960, it held that employer discharge of union members for violence and misconduct was legal. Relying upon *Thayer*, the federal court required the NLRB to reconsider its position.[83] The agency was required to weigh the character of the employer's unfair labor practice against the coercive misconduct of employees and determine on that basis whether or not employees were entitled to reinstatement.

Finding a flagrant employer violation of the law may result in a Board ruling that misconduct of strikers is excusable. This introduces the possibility that violence may be a protected activity of strikers and indeed may bring about a situation that the National Labor Relations Act was intended to eliminate. Violence on the picket line should not be excused regardless of employer action. Each violation of law should be punished. This recent doctrine could discourage the use of peaceful procedures in settling labor disputes. Two wrongs still do not make a right. Violence on the picket line should be treated in the same fashion that it is in the absence of employer unfair labor practices.

RECOGNITIONAL AND ORGANIZATIONAL PICKETING

Recognitional picketing is undertaken to obtain bargaining recognition from employers whereas organizational picketing is for the purpose of inducing workers to join the labor union. The history of organized labor makes it apparent that unions have long picketed nonunion employers as a means of organizing and obtaining bargaining recognition. Furthermore, although the primary aim has been to gain recognition and bargaining rights, unions have argued that they have been just as interested in maintaining union-established working standards. The economic interests of unions generally have required that they spread union organization throughout an entire industry to stabilize and protect working conditions in that industry. Failure to do so usually resulted in a deterioration of unionization.

The recognitional and organizational efforts of unions were protected activities under the Norris–La Guardia Act provisions as well as under the free-speech doctrines of the United States Supreme Court. The Wagner Act as well as the 1947 Taft-Hartley amendments did not alter this right even when picketing was undertaken by a minority union. Minority unions could picket even though another labor organization had been certified by the NLRB as the choice of a majority of employees.[84]

The NLRB attempted to deal with picketing of this nature under Taft-Hartley Section 8 (b) (4) (C). Under this provision a union engages in an unfair labor practice if it forces an employer to recognize or bargain with a labor organization as the representative of its employees if another labor organization has been certified as the representative of its employees.[85]

The Board used this provision of Taft-Hartley in 1956 to outlaw strikes and picketing even though there was no independent evidence available to show that the union had picketed for recognitional or organizational purposes. In *Lewis Food* the Board found a violation when a union struck to force an employer to reinstate employees who were previously discharged.[86] On the surface at least, the labor organization did not strike to force the employer to recognize it and bargain with it for all the employees in the bargaining unit. However, the Board ruled that recognition was the purpose of union action. It rejected the argument the union merely acted to require reinstatement of discharged workers since "the union's strike for such a purpose necessarily . . . is a strike to force or require the employer to recognize or bargain . . . as to this matter."

The NLRB attempted to utilize the broad language of Taft-Hartley to outlaw recognitional picketing.[87] Until it decided the *Curtis* case, peaceful picketing had not been considered coercive within the meaning of the union unfair labor practice provisions.[88] In *Curtis* a union lost an election conducted by the NLRB and immediately established picketing around the employer's premises. The Board ruled that recognitional and organizational picketing would tend to coerce workers to join a union in violation of their Section 7 right not to join. The U.S. Supreme Court reviewed the case and held that the NLRB did not have the authority to curb minority-union picketing undertaken to achieve recognition or organization.[89] If the situation had been left unchanged, the Board would have been incapable of restricting this type of union activity.

Landrum-Griffin Changes

The country was in the mood to change some of the picketing procedures used by unions in 1959. Attempts were made in the Landrum-Griffin Act to eliminate the weaknesses that had become apparent in the 1947 labor law.[90] Section 8 (b) (7) was created by Congress; this section makes it an unfair labor practice for a union to picket any employer for the purpose of either

> forcing or requiring an employer to recognize or bargain with a labor organization as the representative of his employees, or forcing or requiring an employee to accept or select such labor organization as their collective bargaining representative.

The restriction was designed to operate in three situations. They are: (1) when the employer has lawfully recognized another union and a representation question may not appropriately be raised; (2) when a valid election has been held by the NLRB within the preceding twelve months; or (3) when picketing has been conducted for a reasonable period of time, "not to exceed thirty days from the commencement of such picketing," without filing an election petition with the Board. These restrictions do not apply to unions that are the certified bargaining agents of employees.

The Act does not define a reasonable period of time; however, its language and legislative history indicate that a period of less than thirty days may be considered unlawful.[91]

In one case the Board reviewed employee conduct of picketing to decide that twenty-six days was more than a reasonable period for filing an election petition.[92] Pickets were engaged in conduct such as threatening physical violence, abusive and coercive language, and blocked ingress and egress to the struck premises.

Picketing at common construction sites may include the total picketing time even though the employer and employees at whom the activity is directed are absent part of the time.[93] The thirty-day period was computed on the basis of the record presented the Board.

The reasonable time period extended unions to petition for elections is generally set at thirty days. Extenuating circumstances may result in a shorter period of time, but as a general rule a fixed period of time is easier to administer than one that fluctuates.

Expedited Elections

Another important problem stimulated by the 1959 Taft-Hartley amendments involves the so-called *"quickie" election.* Expedited election procedure has practically no legislative history because of the circumstances under which it was adopted into the law. It came out of the Senate-House Conference Committee proceedings. When an election petition is filed under the terms of the recognitional and organizational picketing provisions, the Board is directed to process it under an expedited procedure. Essentially, this means that a prehearing election is held. The Board merely determines a unit appropriate for collective bargaining and holds the poll.

The NLRB ruled that labor unions should not be permitted to circumvent usual election procedures by maneuvering to obtain a prehearing election. It decided that it would direct a prehearing election under the recognitional and organizational picketing provisions only when a charge is filed alleging violation of the section. The General Counsel of the Board stated that

> any other interpretation would be deemed to have done by indirection what it [Taft-Hartley] refused to do directly—authorize pre-hearing elections generally. And picketing would be encouraged where it has not been used before.[94]

A federal district court in Michigan upheld the NLRB position and implemented it by refusing to direct a quickie election when an employee at the suggestion of his union filed an unfair labor practice charge against his own union. The court held that a charge for purposes of securing an expedited election is not valid when a union in effect files a charge against itself.[95]

Once the Board directs a quickie election, the union involved must be a party to the poll whether or not it wants to participate. Thus a union petitioned a federal district court to stop an expedited election arguing that it desired a hearing prior to the poll. The court denied the injunction request.[96]

The impact of expedited elections could be to force unions into premature polls. To the extent that this is so, an employer may be able to halt recognitional and organizational picketing for a period of twelve months. Alternatively, such elections could prove beneficial to labor organizations since they could decrease the time lag between petitioning for an election and holding of the actual vote. Less time is available to lose majority status, if indeed it has ever been attained. Many unions attempt to get 50 to 55 percent of bargaining-unit members to sign authorization cards before proceeding to polls under normal procedures. Expedited elections could permit some unions to prevail in representation proceedings with a minimum of authorization cards signed by employees.

When an election petition is filed under the terms of the provision, the law directs the Board to process the petition under an expedited procedure. The agency does not follow the general procedures that guide it in other elections. It does not require a showing that at least 30 percent of the bargaining unit supports the petitioning union as proof that it represents a substantial number of employees. However, the Board is required to make a rapid determination of bargaining-unit appropriateness for collective bargaining purposes. This is the so-called quickie election procedure required by Section 8 (b) (7).[97]

Landrum-Griffin does not prohibit all picketing beyond thirty days under all circumstances even though an election petition has not been filed with the Board. A union may picket beyond thirty days for the purpose of truthfully advising the public, including consumers, that an employer does not employ members of, or have a contract with, the labor organization engaged in picketing. However, this picketing is prohibited when it has the effect of interfering with services or the flow of goods to and from the picketed company. The NLRB is required to obtain federal court injunctions when violations occur.

Soon after the passage of Landrum-Griffin, controversy arose in the construction of its terms regulating recognitional and organizational picketing. The problem areas include (1) picketing objectives, (2) informational picketing, and (3) employer unfair labor practices.

Problem of Picketing Objectives

Soon after Section 8 (b) (7) became effective, the NLRB applied the provisions to a series of cases. As discussed in a previous chapter, changing NLRB personnel often brings with it a change in important policy areas. Prior to a transition from Eisenhower appointees to Kennedy appointees, the Board dealt with the new Landrum-Griffin provisions.

In the *Calumet Contractors* case a union contended that it picketed to protest that an employer was not paying the prevailing wage rates of the area.[98] Another union had been certified by the Board. It refused to accept the picketing union's disclaimer of intent to obtain recognition as bargaining agent. The NLRB was of the opinion that picketing to protest the employer's wage rates was an attempt to force recognition of the minority union. This meant that employees were coerced to accept the union as their bargaining agent. Thus the Board returned to its *Curtis* doctrine and the one established in the *Lewis Food* case. All picketing by minority unions was considered to be for recognitional and organizational purposes. For what other reason would a union picket when it represents only a minority of the bargaining unit?

Changes in Board personnel in 1961 led to a change in policy in another case involving the Calumet Contractors Association.[99] This time the Board refused to find a violation of Section 8 (b) (4) (C) wherein a union picketed to advertise the fact that an employer was not paying wage rates equal to those prevailing in the area. It will be recalled that a primary strike for the purpose of requiring recognition of a union other than the one certified is an unfair labor practice under Section 8 (b) (4) (C). Another union held NLRB certification as bargaining agent for bargaining-unit employees. Even so the newly constituted Board held that picketing for this purpose was not the same as that undertaken to obtain recognition. Picketing, taken by itself, did not prove that the minority union was in pursuit of such an objective. In this regard the Board ruled that:

> A union may legitimately be concerned that a particular employer is undermining area standards of employment by maintaining lower standards. It may be willing to forego recognition and bargaining provided subnormal working conditions are eliminated from area considerations. As this objective could be achieved without the employer either bargaining with or recognizing the union, we cannot reasonably conclude that the union's objective in picketing the employer was to obtain recognition or bargaining.

The finding that picketing by a minority union was for an object other than recognition left the Board only a short distance from overturning the previous Board's rule that all picketing by minority unions was for recognitional purposes. In *Fanelli Ford Sales* the new Board accomplished its objective under Section 8 (b) (7).[100] A minority union was permitted to picket for reinstatement of a discharged employee without at the same time seeking recognition within the meaning of the 1959 provisions. Reinstatement could be accomplished without consultation with the union. In still another case involving picketing to protest an employer's deviation from prevailing union standards, the Board held that "union standards" picketing is distinguished from that undertaken to force recognition.[101] The language on picket signs intended to inform the public of substandard working conditions is sufficient to permit minority unions to picket an employer's premises. Since picketing objectives are distinguishable, it is protected from the restrictions imposed by the 1959 law.

Realistically, it may be argued that any minority union that pickets an employer's premises is seeking bargaining rights. Otherwise it would not make the effort. If a union is successful in convincing the NLRB that it is not picketing for organizational or recognitional purposes, it may picket indefinitely.

Informational Picketing

A proviso to Section 8 (b) (7) (C) permits unions to picket for informational purposes. The expedited election procedure does not apply to picketing and other publicity undertaken to truthfully advise the public, including consumers, that an employer does not employ members of, or have a contract with, a labor organization.

To this provision there is added an exception. Even if a union engages in publicity or informational picketing, it becomes illegal under the law if it has an effect of inducing "any individual employed by any other person in the course of his employment, not to pick up, deliver or transport any goods or not to perform any services."

In its first effort to deal with this section, the NLRB held that picketing is unlawful even though picket signs reflect the statutory language of the 1959 law when an objective is recognition or organization.[102] Publicity picketing was held illegal because the Board decided that it was undertaken to achieve recognition from the employer or organization of employees. For picketing to fall within the protection of the publicity proviso, it had to be undertaken solely to inform the public that an employer did not employ members of the picketing union or have a contract with it. In the first *Crown* case the union truthfully advised the public that the employer was nonunion. However, upon examination the Board found that the union did not represent a majority of the employees and had picketed beyond a reasonable period of time without petitioning for an election. The employees of the picketed employer were neither represented by another union nor had they expressed their choice for representation in an NLRB poll within twelve months prior to the time picketing began. Dual-purpose picketing was considered illegal under the terms of the law. Informational or publicity picketing had to be completely divorced from any organizational or recognitional objective to be legal. Since recognition was viewed as one object of the action, it was held in violation of national labor policy. The decision in effect implied that all publicity picketing was undertaken for recognitional purposes. Also the decision implied that all picketing undertaken to inform the public that an employer does not employ union members has the purpose of organizing the nonmember workers.

Different Board personnel dealt with the same issue in the *Crown Cafeteria* case in 1962.[103] New NLRB personnel granted the union request to reconsider the decision of the replaced Board majority. This time the Board ruled differently. It held that the law clearly permits informational picketing even though organization, recognition, or bargaining is an implied objective. Thus, even if recognition is an object of the picketing, the Board will not find a violation provided that the picket-sign legends advise the public that the picketed employer does not employ members of the union engaged in the picketing or have a contract with it. In short, the 1962 *Crown Cafeteria* case declared picketing lawful after the thirty-day time period under two conditions. These were that (1) the picket-sign legends must inform the public only that the employer does not employ members of the picketing union and/or does not have a contract with it; and (2) such picketing must not unlawfully interfere with deliveries and services.

Informational picketing was therefore considered lawful as long as it did not stop pickups and deliveries of goods and services. In 1962, however, the Board held that when interference with deliveries or pickups is not sufficiently extensive as to disrupt, interfere with, or curtail the employer's business, then it has no effect on the employer's business.[104] Thus picketing will not be prohibited merely on the basis of a few isolated instances of drivers refusing to cross a picket line, or where an effect of the picketing resulted in one service stoppage or one temporary service delay.

The Board in the *Barker* case argued that a literal reading of the Act would render illusory the very protection Congress conferred upon labor's right to disseminate information to the public by engaging in publicity picketing. Such a restriction, it argued, might raise a serious constitutional question and do a disservice to the Congress. Thus the effect of publicity picketing is construed in "terms of the actual impact on the picketed employer's business." An employer must prove not only that delivery stoppages occurred, but also the extent to which such stoppages disrupted business.

The Ninth Circuit Court upheld the Board's decisions in both the *Barker Bros. Corporation* and *Crown Cafeteria* cases.[105] In *Barker Bros.* the federal court ruled that a "quantitative test concerning itself solely with the number of deliveries not made and/or services not performed is an inadequate yardstick for determining whether to remove informational picketing from" the protection of the publicity section of the law. The *Crown Cafeteria* case also resulted in court approval of Board action. The court reasoned that to rule that picketing undertaken to truthfully advise the public is illegal would render the publicity proviso meaningless.

Under current law there is no presumption that an original recognitional or organizational motive continues as the basic motive of unions after picketing becomes informational. There must be proof that the original motive remains the basic aim.[106] Proof may be available if a picket line is shifted from, for example, the public entrance to a restaurant to the employee entrance. A shift of the picket line provides a signal to employees to leave their job. Thus the Board will not protect picketing of this nature which is viewed as an appeal to other union members as opposed to consumers. The mere shift is deemed unlawful and the fact that employees do not leave their jobs does not control the decision.[107]

A minority union may picket indefinitely under the publicity proviso without filing an election petition. This means that the Board has construed the informational picketing provision so broadly that a union that does not represent a majority of bargaining-unit employees may picket for an indefinite period of time resulting in the possibility of eventually becoming the majority representative. This could be particularly the case when the union engages in other organizational activities simultaneously with the picket-line activity. It is often argued that such action was not the intent of Congress. Under this view the NLRB has taken on a legislative function in excess of its delegated authority.[108] On the other hand, the current Board policy can be defended on the grounds that Congress did not intend to prohibit informational picketing when such an activity does not seriously curtail an employer's business. A contrary policy could very well conflict with constitutional guarantees of free speech.

Employer Unfair Labor Practices

Shortly after the recognitional and organizational sections were enacted into law, the question was raised as to whether a union may picket toward this end, without violating the provisions, when employers commit unfair labor practices. Congress did not expressly permit a union to picket for recognitional or organizational purposes beyond thirty days without filing a representation petition even when an employer engages in unfair labor practices. The Eisenhower Board searched the legislative history of the 1959 law and concluded that Congress had not intended to permit recognitional and organizational picketing beyond thirty days even should employer unfair labor practices occur.[109]

Alternatively, it should be recalled that the U.S. Supreme Court held in *Mastro Plastics* that the Taft-Hartley penalties against a union striking during a contractual period do not apply when it strikes against an employer unfair labor practice.[110] In February 1961 the Board addressed itself to this problem.

In the *Blinne* case a union sought to represent three common laborers employed by a construction company.[111] All three had signed bargaining authorization cards. The employer allegedly transferred one worker to another building site in an effort to destroy the union's majority status. The labor organization afterward engaged in recognitional picketing for more than thirty days before it filed an election petition. Unfair labor practice charges were filed against the employer about three weeks after the picketing started. The union advanced the argument that the recognitional and organizational regulations should not be enforced when employer unfair labor practices are alleged.

The Board in its first consideration of *Blinne* held that the employer unfair labor practices did not legalize the union's picketing. Despite the merit of such charges, congressional intent was interpreted as opposed to lifting organizational and recognitional picketing prohibitions under such circumstances.[112]

The *Blinne Construction* case was reconsidered in 1962 after a change in Board personnel.[113] The new rule was only slightly changed from the one set forth in 1961. A union may picket beyond the thirty-day limit without filing an election petition only when an employer is in violation of the refusal-to-bargain provision of Taft-Hartley. Election petitions must be filed within the thirty-day limit when other unfair labor practices are committed. The NLRB set forth the reason for the distinction between unfair labor practices when recognitional and organizational picketing are involved. The reason is based entirely on Board procedure. For unfair labor practice charges other than refusal to bargain, the Board holds a representation petition in abeyance until the allegations have been remedied or dismissed. Under these circumstances the Board will accept an election petition and will not dismiss one already filed. However, the election will not be conducted until such time as the unfair labor practice charges have been resolved. Refusal-to-bargain charges are handled differently; an election petition will not be accepted or, if already submitted, will be dismissed. This distinction is based upon the idea that a representation petition assumes an unresolved question concerning representation. However, a refusal-to-bargain charge presupposes that no question of representation exists and that the employer is wrongfully refusing to recognize or bargain with a statutory bargaining representative.

SUMMARY

No rights extended to any of the parties to collective bargaining are absolute. Thus the complicated task of the Board and courts is to weigh the relative rights of each. The decisions resulting from this process often appear conflicting to many viewers. Indeed, they are if the criteria for evaluation is on the basis of precedent stemming from Board and Supreme Court cases. Essentially, the rule of precedent is followed consistently by the high court in regulating Board implementation of national labor policy. The totality of conduct must be reviewed in each case in reaching a decision in accordance with the *Virginia Electric Power* doctrine. If the Board is required to review the totality of circumstances that exist in each case, then the courts must do so too. It would be a strange doctrine indeed to require the NLRB to take one course of action in arriving at decisions while the courts use another.

The changing rules and regulations that exist in labor cases involving replacement of economic strikers, strikes against Board certification, striker conduct on picketing lines, lockout rights of employers, and recognitional and organizational picketing actually reflect the changing conditions and problems of American industry. Evolutionary changes in industry practices evade constancy in resolving conflict, which inevitably arises among the parties concerned. Not all decisions are immediately conducive to eliminating warfare in favor of more peaceful procedures for obtaining solutions. But the ability to make decisions on the basis of total conduct without necessarily adhering strictly to past decisions makes it easier to move toward solutions that are equitable to all parties.

NOTES

[1] Edwin E. Witte, *The Government in Labor Disputes* (New York: McGraw-Hill Book Company, 1932), p. 20.

[2] Section 9 (c) (3).

[3] *Mastro Plastics Corporation* v. *NLRB*, 350 U.S. 270 (1956).

[4] *NLRB* v. *Fansteel Metallurgical Company*, 306 U.S. 240 (1939).

[5] *NLRB* v. *Mackay Radio & Telegraph Company*, 304 U.S. 333 (1938).

[6] *A. Sartorius & Company, Inc.*, 10 NLRB 493 (1938).

[7] *Rudolph Wurlitzer Company*, 32 NLRB 163 (1941).

[8] See section entitled "Strikes Against NLRB Certification."

[9] *Pioneer Flour Mills*, 174 NLRB 1202 (1969).

[10] *Brooks Research & Manufacturing*, 202 NLRB No. 93 (1973).

[11] *Wahl Clipper Corporation*, 195 NLRB No. 104 (1972).

[12] *W. Wilton Wood, Inc.*, 127 NLRB 1675 (1960).

[13] *Bright Foods, Inc.*, 126 NLRB 553 (1960).

[14] *National Gypsum Company*, 133 NLRB 1492 (1962).

[15] *Twenty-Seventh Annual Report of the National Labor Relations Board, 1962* (Washington, D.C.: Government Printing Office, 1963), p. 80.

[16] *Tampa Sand & Material Company*, 47 LRRM 1166 (1961).

[17] *Laidlaw Corporation*, 171 NLRB 175 (1968).

[18] *NLRB* v. *Fleetwood Trailer Company*, 389 U.S. 375 (1967).

[19] *United Aircraft Corporation*, 192 NLRB No. 62 (1971).

[20] John T. Dunlop, "Jurisdictional Disputes," *Proceedings of New York University Second Annual Conference of Labor*, p. 479.

[21] *Monthly Labor Review*, LXX (May 1950), 503.

[22] Bureau of Labor Statistics, *Analysis of Work Stoppages 1965*, Bulletin No. 1525 (Washington, D.C.: Government Printing Office, 1966), p. 12.

[23] *Thirty-Seventh Annual Report of the National Labor Relations Board, 1972* (Washington, D.C.: Government Printing Office, 1972), p. 238.

[24] Section 8 (b) (4).

[25] See Dunlop, *op. cit.*, for an authoritative treatment of the work of the National Joint Board.

[26] Bureau of National Affairs, *Taft-Hartley After One Year* (1948), p. 101.

[27] Section 8 (b) (4) (D).

[28] Sections 10 (k) and (1).

[29] Section 8 (b) (4) (D) makes it an unfair labor practice for a union to strike or to refuse to perform services when the object is "forcing or requiring any employer to assign particular work to employees in a particular labor organization or in a particular trade, craft, or class rather than to employees in another labor organization or in another trade, craft, or class, unless such employer is failing to conform to an order or certification of the Board determining the bargaining representative for employees performing such work. . . ."

[30] *NLRB* v. *Radio Engineers Union,* 364 U.S. 573 (1961).

[31] *NLRB* v. *Plasterers' Local 79, Operative Plasterers (Texas State Tile and Terrazzo Company),* 404 U.S. 116 (1971).

[32] *NLRB* v. *Plasterers' Local 79, Operative Plasterers (Texas State Tile and Terrazzo Company),* 440 F. (2d) 174 (1971).

[33] *Philadelphia Typographical Union, Local No. 2 (Philadelphia Inquirer, Division of Triangle Publications, Inc.),* 142 NLRB 1 (1963).

[34] *Thompson Products, Inc.,* 72 NLRB 887 (1947).

[35] Section 8 (b) (4).

[36] *United Mine Workers* v. *Patton,* 211 F. (2d) 742 (1954),cert. denied, 348 U.S. 824 (1954).

[37] *Dairy Distributors, Inc.* v. *Western Conference of Teamsters,* 294 F. (2d) 348 (1961).

[38] *Betts Cadillac Olds, Inc.,* 96 NLRB 268 (1951).

[39] *NLRB* v. *Truck Drivers Local Union No. 449, et al. (Buffalo Linen Supply Company),* 353 U.S. 85 (1956).

[40] *Evening News Assn., Owner and Publisher of Detroit News,* 145 NLRB 996 (1964).

[41] *Brown Food Store,* 137 NLRB 73 (1962), enforcement denied 319 F. (2d) (7) (CA 10), cert. granted 375 U.S. 962 (1965).

[42] *NLRB* v. *Brown et al.* d/b/a/ *Brown Food Store, et al.,*380 U.S. 278 (1965).

[43] The Supreme Court used the *Buffalo Linen* case to arrive at its conclusion. A temporary layoff can be offset by temporary replacements.

[44] *NLRB* v. *Mackay Radio & Telegraph Company,* 304 U.S. 333 (1938).

[45] *American Ship Building Company* v. *NLRB,* 380 U.S. 300 (1965).

[46] This result is obtained from the *Buffalo Linen* and *NLRB* v. *Brown* cases, *op. cit.*

[47] *Inland Trucking Company* v. *NLRB,* 440 F. (2d) 562 (1971).

[48] *NLRB* v. *Great Dane Trailers,* 388 U.S. 26 (1967).

[49] *Local 155, International Molders and Allied Workers Union (U.S. Pipe and Foundry Company)* v. *NLRB,* 442 F. (2d) 742 (1971).

[50] *Ottawa Silica Company,* 197 NLRB No. 53 (1972).

[51] *Intercollegiate Press, Graphic Arts Division,* 199 NLRB No. 35 (1972).

[52] *Laclede Gas Company,* 187 NLRB No. 32 (1971).

[53] 380 U.S. 308.

[54] Italics added.

[55] Section 8 (b) (1).

[56] Section 8 (b) (1) (A).

[57] *Sunset Line & Twine,* 79 NLRB 1487 (1948).

58 *Congressional Record*, XCIII, 4563.

59 NLRB Release R-319, May 25, 1950.

60 *Local 248, UAW (Allis-Chalmers Manufacturing Company)*, 149 NLRB 67 (1964).

61 *NLRB* v. *Allis-Chalmers Manufacturing Company*, 388 U.S. 175 (1967), reversing 358 F. (2d) 656.

62 *NLRB* v. *Boeing*, U.S. Sup. Ct. No. 71-1607 (May 21, 1973).

63 *Scofield* v. *NLRB*, 394 U.S. 423 (1969).

64 Hearings before the Subcommittee on Separation of Powers, *Congressional Oversight of Administrative Agencies (National Labor Relations Board)*, Part II, U.S. Senate (Washington, D.C.: Government Printing Office, 1968), p. 1115.

65 409 U.S. 213 (1972).

66 In one case, a federal appeals court held that resignations are not forbidden by a constitution's provision prohibiting acceptance of employment in a strike-bound firm. It held that this provision dealt only with union member misconduct and not with resignations. *Boeing Company* v. *NLRB*, 459 F. (2d) 1143 (1972), cert. denied by the Supreme Court on December 18, 1972. U.S. Sup. Ct. No. 71-1563.

67 *Sunset Line & Twine, op. cit.*

68 81 NLRB 138 (1949).

69 *Local 761, International Union of Electrical, Radio & Machine Workers, AFL-CIO (General Electric Company)*, 126 NLRB 123 (1960).

70 *North Electric Manufacturing Company*, 84 NLRB 23 (1949).

71 *Sunset Line & Twine, op. cit.*

72 Section 8 (c).

73 Section 8 (c) of Taft-Hartley is popularly termed the "free speech" provision. It is discussed in Chapter 12.

74 *Local 761, International Union of Electrical, Radio & Machine Workers, AFL-CIO (Genral Electric Company)*, 126 NLRB 123 (1960).

75 *Chauffeurs, Teamsters & Helpers Local Union No. 795, etc. (Grant-Billingsley Fruit Company, Inc.)*, 127 NLRB 550 (1960).

76 *NLRB* v. *Union Carbide Corporation*, 440 F. (2d) 54 (1971).

77 *Virginia Stage Lines* v. *NLRB*, 441 F. (2d) 499 (1971).

78 *Cory Corporation*, 84 NLRB 110 (1949).

79 80 NLRB 47 (1948).

80 NLRB Release R-321, May 27, 1950.

81 84 NLRB 110 (1949).

82 *Local 833, United Automobile, Aircraft & Agricultural Implement Workers of America, UAW-CIO* v. *NLRB*, 300 F. (2d) 699 (1962), cert. denied 370 U.S. 911.

83 *NLRB* v. *Thayer Company*, 213 F. (2d) 748 (1954), cert. denied 348 U.S. 883.

84 Herbert S. Thatcher, "A Look at Section 8 (b) (7) and Problems Arising Thereafter," in Ralph Slovenko, ed., *Symposium on the Labor-Management Reporting and Disclosure Act of 1959* (Baton Rouge, La.: Claitor's Bookstore Publishers, 1961), pp. 939–40.

85 Section 8 (b) (4)(C) makes it unlawful for a union "by forcing or requiring any employer to recognize or bargain with a particular labor organization as the representative of his employees if another labor organization has been certified as the representative of such employees under the provisions of Section 9."

86 *Lewis Food Company*, 115 NLRB 890 (1956).

87 The Board used Section 8 (b) (1) (A) of Taft-Hartley which makes it an unfair labor practice for unions "to restrain or coerce employees" in the exercise of their right to engage in or refrain from concerted activities directed toward self-organization and collective bargaining.

[88] *Curtis Bros.*, 119 NLRB 232 (1957).

[89] *NLRB* v. *Drivers Local Union*, 362 U.S. 274 (1960).

[90] Section 704 (c) of the Labor Management Reporting and Disclosure Act of 1959, 73 Stat. 519, 544.

[91] *Twenty-Eight Annual Report of the National Labor Relations Board, 1963* (Washington, D.C.: Government Printing Office, 1964), p. 115.

[92] *District 65, Retail, Wholesale & Department Store Union* (*Eastern Camera & Photo Corporation*), 141 NLRB 85 (1963).

[93] *IBEW, Local 113* (*ICG Electric, Inc.*), 142 NLRB 145 (1963).

[94] Address of Stuart Rothman before the Section on Labor Law of the Association of the Bar of the City of New York, November 12, 1959.

[95] *Reed* v. *Ronmell*, 46 LRRM 2565 (E.D. Mich., 1960).

[96] *Local 1265, Dept. Store Employees* v. *Brown*, 45 LRRM 3101 (N.D. Col., 1960).

[97] See Fred Witney, "NLRB Membership Cleavage: Recognition and Organizational Picketing," *Labor Law Journal*, XIV, No. 5 (May 1963), pp. 434–458.

[98] *Calumet Contractors Association*, 130 NLRB 17 (1961).

[99] *Calumet Contractors Association*, 133 NLRB 57 (1961).

[100] *United Automobile Workers, Local 259* (*Fanelli Ford Sales, Inc.*), 133 NLRB 1468 (1961).

[101] *Claude Everett Construction Company*, 136 NLRB 321 (1962). Also see *Texarkana Construction Company*, 138 NLRB 102 (1962).

[102] *Crown Cafeteria*, 130 NLRB 570 (1961).

[103] *Crown Cafeteria*, 135 NLRB 124 (1962).

[104] *Retail Clerks, Locals 324 & 770* (*Barker Bros.*), 138 NLRB 54 (1962).

[105] *Barker Bros. Corporation* v. *NLRB*, 328 F.(2d)431 (1964); *Crown Cafeteria* v. *NLRB*, 327 F. (2d) 351 (1964).

[106] *Retail Clerks International Association, Local 344*, 136 NLRB 1270 (1962).

[107] *Atlantic Maintenance Company*, 136 NLRB 105 (1962).

[108] Hearings before the Subcommittee on Separation of Powers, *Congressional Oversight of Administrative Agencies* (*National Labor Relations Board*), Part I, *op. cit.*, pp. 34–35. U.S. Senate (Washington, D.C.: Government Printing Office, 1968), pp. 34–35.

[109] *Legislative History of the Labor Management Reporting and Disclosure Act of 1959*, II, 1383, 1384.

[110] *Mastro Plastics Corporation* v. *NLRB*, 350 U.S. 270 (1956).

[111] *C. A. Blinne Construction Company*, 130 NLRB 587 (1961).

[112] Discussion of Elliott bill as reported by the House, H.R. 8342, 86th Congress, 1st sess., 1959, and Kennedy-Irvin bill in the Senate, S. 1555, 86th Congress, 1st sess., 1959.

[113] *C. A. Blinne Construction Company*, 135 NLRB 121 (1962).

17 Secondary Boycott Pressures

In earlier chapters we investigated at considerable length the legal status of the secondary boycott strike under the antitrust laws. Reference was made to famous labor cases such as *Danbury Hatters*, *Duplex*, and *Bedford Cut Stone*. In all of these cases the Supreme Court held union secondary boycott activities unlawful under the Sherman Act. This meant that a union could not call a strike or induce a strike when the objective would be to force one employer to cease doing business with another employer. Frankfurter and Greene defined the device as "a combination to influence A by exerting some sort of economic or social pressure against persons who deal with A." [1] This definition of a secondary boycott is not nearly as simple as implied, as will be seen subsequently.

In developing the relationship of unions to the antitrust laws, close attention was paid to the economic factors that caused labor unions to resort to the secondary boycott. Consequently, there is no need to review these aspects again, except to point out that employees involved in the labor antitrust cases resorted to the secondary boycott to preserve the status of their labor unions. The alternative to the secondary boycott could have been the disintegration of labor unions.

Congress enacted the Clayton Act in 1914, but this legislation did not prove to be the Magna Charta it was hailed to be. The legal position of organized labor under the antitrust law of 1890 and the common law was not improved. It was not until the Norris–La Guardia Act was passed in 1932 that the union objective was realized. The law protected secondary boycott activities from prosecution under antitrust provisions. This protection remained until the Taft-Hartley Act was passed in 1947. Loopholes developed, however, because the NLRB and the courts were responsible for ensuring rights spelled out in other parts of the Act. Congress attempted to solve the problem again in Landrum-Griffin.

LEGAL STATUS UNDER TAFT-HARTLEY

The legislative history of the Taft-Hartley Act makes it clear that the congressional objective was to protect neutral employers and neutral employees from economically damaging union pressures stemming from labor-management disputes. Protection was to be extended to these groups only when they were neutral parties to the dispute.

In the Taft-Hartley hearings in 1947, Congress determined that the secondary boycott—the union practice of striking, picketing, or otherwise boycotting one employer in order to exert pressure on another employer—was an unjustifiable technique and should be removed from the labor scene. Congress drew up the Section 8 (b) (4) language to accomplish its objective. In the pertinent part the provision provided that:

> It shall be an unfair labor practice for a labor organization or its agents—(4) to engage in, or to induce or encourage the employees of any employer to engage in, a strike, or a concerted refusal in the course of their employment to use, manufacture, process, transport, or otherwise handle or work on any goods, articles, materials, or commodities, or to perform any services, where an object thereof is: (A) forcing or requiring ... any employer or any other person to cease using, selling, handling, transporting, or otherwise dealing in the products of any other producer, processor, or manufacturer, or to cease doing business with any other person.

The scope of the section was explained by Senator Taft during the debates. He stated:

> This provision makes it unlawful to resort to a secondary boycott to injure the business of a third person who is wholly unconcerned in the disagreement between an employer and his employees. ... It has been set forth that there are good secondary boycotts and bad secondary boycotts. Our committee heard evidence for weeks and never succeeded in having anyone tell us any difference between different kinds of secondary boycotts. So we have so broadened the provision dealing with secondary boycotts as to make them an unfair labor practice.[2]

The intent of Congress in enacting the provision is clear. However, the NLRB in applying the law opened up a large number of loopholes by permitting unions to continue using secondary boycotts under certain circumstances. In the years after the 1947 law was passed the NLRB and the courts had the occasion to deal with several sections of the law that were somewhat confusing. By 1953 a congressional committee was reviewing loopholes that were considered so large that "a truck can be driven through them."[3] The loopholes included:

1. Direct coercion of employers to cease doing business with another person. Strikes were not used to accomplish this end.
2. "Hot-cargo" contracts whereby employers agree not to do business with firms considered "unfair" by unions.
3. Exemption from the secondary boycott provision of "employers," "persons," and "employees" not considered as coming within the Act's definitions.

4. Union ability to influence the nonconcerted activities of employees. That is, the ability to deal with an employee as a single individual.
5. Union inducement to engage in consumer boycotts.
6. Union refusal to allow members to accept jobs from secondary employers.
7. Boycotts taking place at the location of the primary dispute.
8. Picketing trucks at secondary locations.
9. Boycotts of secondary employers who are allied with primary employers.[4]

One overwhelming difficulty that faced the Board and the courts in attempts to construct workable secondary boycott policies stemmed from other sections of the Act. Section 13 protects the right of employees to strike[5] and Section 7 guarantees employees the right to engage in concerted activity.[6] These sections show that Congress did not intend to outlaw all strikes or primary concerted activity. Neither did it intend to eliminate all secondary actions. A determination of what is primary activity and what is secondary activity has generated problems for the NLRB and the courts. Section 10 (1) of Taft-Hartley requires that the Board give priority to hearings dealing with secondary boycotts. Temporary injunctions may be obtained while the case is pending before the Board for determination. The Board is often reluctant to exercise its authority in this regard, however, because union action may subsequently be found legal. In such cases, when unions have not violated the law, the injunction damage usually evades remedy.

Congress reviewed the secondary boycott loopholes of Taft-Hartley during the Landrum-Griffin Act hearings. It reaffirmed its intention to outlaw a large percentage of secondary action. Senator John F. Kennedy, chairman of the Senate conferees on the Landrum-Griffin bill, explained the intent of the secondary boycott provision amendments as follows:

> The chief effect of the conference agreement, therefore, will be to plug loopholes in the secondary boycott provisions of the National Labor Relations Act. There has never been any dispute about the desirability of plugging these artificial loopholes.[7]

The loopholes that developed under Taft-Hartley were therefore supposedly closed by the 1959 amendments. Because of the complicated nature of the statutory language and subsequent Board and court interpretations, the loopholes of Taft-Hartley and Landrum-Griffin are treated together by major category of secondary activity.

ALLY DOCTRINE

The legislative history of Taft-Hartley makes it clear that Congress intended to prohibit union inducement of work stoppages for the purpose of forcing B to cease doing business with A only when B was in fact neutral in the dispute. The assumption implicit in the language of the law was that the two employers were independent.[8] Senator Taft during a debate on the section remarked that it "is not intended to apply to a case where the third party is, in effect, in cahoots with or acting as a part of the primary employer."[9]

The Board has consistently ruled that employers are allies where there is common ownership of capital as well as common management of two or more firms.[10]

In such cases secondary boycott violations are not found as a result of union actions. However, the *ally doctrine* is not applied merely because firms may have common owners[11] or because they may transact all business one with the other.[12]

The ally doctrine is also applicable when a primary employer is struck and it then subcontracts its work to another company that is aware of the existence of the labor dispute.[13] Indeed, this form of boycott was often permitted under the common law when other secondary activity was held unlawful. Unionists are permitted to protect themselves against such offensive employer actions. The primary employees have a self-interest in the work in dispute and do not have to sit idly by while their economic position deteriorates as a result of subcontracting.

The secondary employer in such cases is not completely powerless to resolve the underlying dispute. He could refuse to handle the struck work that is not handled by him under normal circumstances with the result that significant economic pressure is placed back on the first point of union concern. Since this is the case, it is deemed a primary employer by the Board. The ally doctrine has been consistently applied by the NLRB and was not a topic for 1959 remedial action by Congress. The ally doctrine is not and never was a loophole of the secondary boycott provisions of Taft-Hartley. The intent of Congress is made clear by the Conference Committee Report revealing that "no language has been included with reference to struck work because the committee conference did not wish to change the existing law as illustrated by such decisions as *Douds* v. *Metropolitan Federation of Architects*."[14] Thus existing law involving subcontracting of struck work was not changed by the 1959 amendments.

DEFINITION OF PERSONS AND INDIVIDUALS

Under the 1947 law, for secondary boycott activity to be unlawful, there had to be union pressure to induce the employees of the neutral employer in the course of their employment to engage in a concerted refusal to perform services. The refusal had to be for the purpose of interfering with a business relationship between the secondary and primary employer with whom the dispute existed. The basis for one loophole was the key words "induce the employees" of the neutral employer and "a concerted refusal" to perform services. Interpretation of this language had to be made within the statutory definition of *employer* under Taft-Hartley, which excluded such users of labor as agencies of federal, state, and municipal governments. In addition, nonprofit hospitals, railroads, and airlines were among the organizations not defined as being employers. Consequently, unions were permitted to lawfully exert pressure on the employees of these organizations for the purpose of effecting a secondary boycott. It would have been highly inconsistent to have ruled that some sections of law applied to these organizations while other sections did not. The Board and the courts responded to the total public policy and not to fragmented parts of it.

It was also lawful to exert pressure upon the secondary employer himself, or a supervisor, and even upon individual key employees hired by the neutral employer.[15] This situation was made clear by the Supreme Court in 1951. In the *International Rice Milling* case a union was seeking to organize a company's employees. The primary employer's premises were picketed. Two employees of a neutral employer, on a truck, refused to cross the picket line. The NLRB did not consider the action a secondary boycott forbidden by Taft-Hartley because picketing was limited to the situs of the primary employer. The Fifth Circuit Court of Appeals reversed the Board and held that the union deliberately discouraged the employees of neutral employers from supplying the primary employer.[16] The impact of this decision, if it had prevailed, would have been to outlaw most primary picketing if any other employer's employees refused to continue to perform their normal functions because of the existence of a picket line.

The U. S. Supreme Court ruled differently than both the Board and the lower court. The union action was deemed lawful since the refusal of two laborers to cross the picket line did not constitute "concerted activity" within the meaning of the Taft-Hartley Act. The two employees behaved merely as individuals in the face of a picket line.

On the basis of this decision in 1951, it became possible for unions to pressure a key employee of a secondary employer, such as a purchasing agent, not to deal with a company with whom the union had a dispute. Key employees could be told not to buy from particular employers until further notice. In some situations this action of a key employee of another firm could have prevented a primary employer from resisting union demands. Assume, for example, that a purchasing agent of a neutral employer constituted a source of significant business for an employer involved in a labor dispute. The mere fact that this sole employee honored union demands could have been enough to force the primary employer to yield to these demands. In some situations a union may be required to obtain the same cooperation from several key employees to obtain the same result. Even so the law did not forbid the labor organization from pursuing such a course of action since it did not amount to concerted activity.

Pressure could also be applied directly to the secondary employer since such action did not constitute concerted activity.[17] Thus unions could coerce a secondary employer not to buy struck work for the purpose of exerting economic pressure on the primary employer. This tactic was particularly effective when the union involved had a collective bargaining contract with the neutral employer. The union could threaten that failure to do as requested could result in an especially hard time when its own contract was due for renegotiation. In many situations this type of threat was all that was required to obtain the desired action from the neutral employer.

Additionally, the union was permitted to take other action. Because a union could legally pressure secondary employers, they could also effect a secondary consumption boycott.[18] Appeals to the public not to buy from a firm that had a business relationship with the primary employer were lawful since the union pressure was considered not to have been executed against the employees of the neutral employer but against the employer himself. This type of action often proved successful even in cases where the union did not have a collective bargaining relationship with the neutral employer.

Landrum-Griffin Changes

The Congress was intent upon closing the loopholes generated by the 1947 statutory language. Two clauses were adopted to achieve this end. Clause (i) of

Section 8 (b) (4) forbids unions to strike or to induce or encourage strikes or work stoppages by any individual employed by any person engaged in commerce or in an industry affecting commerce. Clause (ii) makes it unlawful for a union to threaten, coerce, or restrain any person engaged in commerce or in an industry affecting commerce for a secondary boycott objective.

It was the intent of Congress to prohibit a union from inducing "any individual employed by any person" to engage in a secondary boycott. "Any person" was to refer to government agencies and other organizations not defined as employers by Taft-Hartley. Thus such employers as the railroads, hospitals, and airlines are now covered by the law since they are persons even if they are not legally defined as employers. Also the new language outlaws union pressure on the secondary employer himself since now the pressure need not be exerted against the employees of an employer to fall within the unlawful area. It is now illegal when pressure is exerted either against the employees of the neutral employer or against the employer himself. The amendment also makes secondary consumer boycotts unlawful since such union pressure is directed against the secondary employer.

In short, Landrum-Griffin was intended to plug the loopholes of permitting unions to put pressure (1) directly on management, (2) directly on key individuals, and (3) directly on organizations not considered employers under Taft-Hartley. We shall see, however, that the NLRB and the courts found some loopholes even in the new language. However, despite these new loopholes, the opportunity for unions to engage in secondary boycotts is far less when compared to the situation prior to the adoption of the Landrum-Griffin changes.

Landrum-Griffin Loopholes

The Landrum-Griffin ban against inducing managerial employees to refuse to handle products of another employer came before the Board in the *Carolina* and *Servette* cases. In the *Carolina Lumber* case a union exerted pressure against the company's foreman by asking him not to buy from a nonunion shop.[19] The foreman held the job of project supervisor. The Board established two categories for interpreting the meaning of the two clauses added to the law in 1959. Clause (i) prohibits inducing an individual employed by persons. This aspect of the law was viewed by the Board as applying to low-level supervision. Since foremen were considered low-level supervision, the Board held it unlawful to induce them to follow union advice under the terms of this clause. The basic purpose of congressional enactment was viewed in this fashion because construction foremen are often union members and they may not be induced by the union. The foreman in the *Carolina* case was considered high-level management since he was solely responsible for the work being performed at the construction site. High-level management is covered by clause (ii). This clause permits unions to induce or encourage high-level management to assist them in obtaining objectives against primary employers, but they may not be coerced. That is to say, a union may approach high-level management and request it not to use nonunion products or labor since such action is detrimental to the union. It may not use coercion, however, since this would violate the terms of the provision.

The *Carolina* case generated considerable concern because a foreman, for example, is an individual under clause (i) and a person under clause (ii). He may be induced under one interpretation but not under another. Since he was considered top management in the instant case, he was a person. Board rejection of his inclusion under clause (i) means he was not an individual. Thus for purposes of the law he was a person and not an individual. This distinction permits unions to bring economic pressure on employers with whom they have a dispute through those neutral to it. The pressure may be made through top-level management when it is obtained through requests for cooperation and not coercion.

The U. S. Supreme Court dealt with the same issue in the *Servette* case in 1964.[20] The case involved a union's right to induce supervisors to cease handling the products of another employer. The union had induced managers of chain stores to discontinue handling merchandise supplied by Servette. The Board drew a distinction between high-level and low-level supervisors and held that store managers were high-level supervisors and not "individuals" as defined in the Act. Thus unions could induce them to refuse to handle Servette products. The NLRB continued the doctrine established in its *Carolina* case. A distinction was made between high- and low-level management and therefore between individuals and persons.

The Ninth Circuit Court of Appeals refused to accept the Board rule on the contention that the congressional purpose to ban such conduct was clear and unequivocal. The U. S. Supreme Court did not adopt the NLRB criteria for such cases, but did not ban such action either. It held that the crucial test for union action in approaching supervisors was whether the appeal was to the exercise of managerial discretion or was instead an appeal for them to cease performing employment services. An appeal to the exercise of managerial discretion is permissible action, but unions are not permitted to make appeals seeking neutral supervisors to cease performing employment services. It may well be that union "appeals" to management to pressure other employers, however politely stated, carry with them implicit threats of economic reprisal if refused. This is particularly the case if the union has a bargaining relationship with the supervisor to whom it makes an appeal.

In any event *Servette* opens a new loophole in the secondary boycott bans provided by Congress in 1959. Appeals may be made to management to exercise their discretion to heed union requests not to deal with other employers. The result reached by the Court has the same effect as the one reached by the Board. The Court did not attempt to distinguish between individuals and persons, but went directly to an examination of permissible union behavior.

On the other hand, the Board construed the word "person" to limit boycott activities in a dispute involving two divisions of the same parent corporation. In a case which concerned the *Hearst Corporation*, the NLRB forbade the picketing of one division of the enterprise when a union had a dispute with another division of the same corporation. Hearst owns a TV and a newspaper division. The direct labor dispute concerned the TV operation. During the dispute the union picketed the offices of the newspaper. The Board held that the picketing of the newspaper was illegal under the secondary boycott provisions of the law since it was calculated to solicit support of the newspaper employees to aid the union in its dispute with the TV station. In upholding the Board decision, a federal court stated that the two enterprises, though owned by the same parent corporation, were separate "persons" within the meaning of the law.[21]

On the basis of the record, the NLRB found that the divisions were separate and autonomous, with independent control vested in the officers of the respective divisions. Though the court acknowledged that the Hearst president could replace division heads, and had the power to approve large corporation expenditures, it also determined that in practice Hearst vested active control in the respective division heads. For example, the division heads set their own news policies, could reject news services offered by Hearst, handled collective bargaining on an independent basis, and established their own financial and accounting systems. In short, it was found that there was a sufficient degree of autonomous control to warrant their treatment as separate "persons" for purposes of the secondary boycott provision. In any event, the *Hearst* case has important implications for labor policy in these days of the conglomerate business enterprise. Though owned by the same parent corporation, different divisions of the same enterprise could be regarded as separate "persons" for purposes of the federal law.

COMMON-SITUS PICKETING

The phrase *common situs* refers to a location in labor dispute cases where employees of both primary and secondary employers perform their duties. For example, a construction site may consist of employees of ten to fifteen different employers. The term common situs is used to refer to an area where picketing occurs to place pressure on an employer with whom a labor dispute exists. Neutral employers are also present and working at the same location. The legislative history is void of any mention of this concept.[22]

In 1949 the NLRB dealt with the complex question of whether picketing at a common situs constitutes secondary boycott activity since secondary employers unavoidably feel the impact. In the *Pure Oil* case two oil companies operated refineries on adjacent premises.[23] They shared a common dock from which the employees of one of the companies originally performed shipment handling for both. Later the companies agreed that each would perform its own shipment services on the same dock by using separate personnel. A union became entangled in a dispute with one of the employers and picketed the dock with the result that the neutral employer's employees refused to cross the picket line to perform their usual duties.

The NLRB held that such action was primary picketing and not in violation of the secondary boycott provisions despite the fact that the neutral employees refused to perform work for the neutral employers. The Board based its decision on a distinction between primary and secondary picketing with regard to the physical location of the site. The physical layout within which picketing occurs must be viewed before an equitable determination of legality may be made. If the NLRB had held this picketing in violation of the secondary restrictions of the Act, it would have had to place severe restrictions on primary union activity, which is protected under national labor policy. The union had no alternative for picket action but that which it engaged in at the dock site. The physical location, according to the Board, was the proper variable to review in deciding the legality of union action at sites where several employees perform work.

In the same year, 1949, the Board had a similar situation before it in the *Ryan Construction* case.[24] In this case Ryan was performing construction work on the premises of a manufacturer against whom a strike occurred. The Board adhered to its use of physical situs as a criterion for deciding the legality of picketing the manufacturer. The primary employer established a separate entry and exit gate for the exclusive use of the neutral employees. The union on strike proceeded to picket the separate gate as well as the one used by employees of the primary employer. The neutral employees honored the picket line and refused to perform work for the neutral employer on the struck manufacturer's premises.

The Board refused to accept the argument that the area of dispute was enlarged due to picketing of the separate gate. The union action was deemed lawful picketing activity by the NLRB. Thus the doctrine that the physical site of the picketing is the most important determinant of picketing legality was established in 1949. In addition, this Board interpretation seems to have been approved by Congress in 1959 when it added two provisos to the secondary boycott section. The first proviso requires that "nothing contained in this clause shall be construed to make unlawful, where not otherwise unlawful, any primary strike or primary picketing."[25] The Supreme Court dealt with this issue after Landrum-Griffin was enacted.

Denver Building Trades Council. A somewhat confusing twist must now be viewed since it is often taken that the Supreme Court reversed the Board doctrine established in *Pure Oil* and *Ryan* cases. In 1951 the U. S. Supreme Court decided a case involving common-situs picketing of a secondary nature. In this situation the high court had to deal with a union that had undertaken picketing action to force a general contractor to cease doing business with a nonunion employer at the same location with union employers. Picketing of the site brought about a refusal to work by union members. The Supreme Court ruled that the use of economic pressure by unions against neutral employers at sites under their control was a violation of the law.

The dissenting justices pointed out that the general contractor was not a neutral party to the dispute. It had employed a nonunion subcontractor to perform work alongside union members, and the attitude of building trades unions toward working with nonunion members was widely known. Nevertheless, the minority view did not prevail. The Court held that the fact that the primary employer was operating at the same construction site with neutral employers was of no consequence.

On the surface it would appear that the doctrine set forth in 1949 by the Board had been overruled. This is not the situation since the Board did not permit common-situs picketing in the *Pure Oil* and *Ryan* cases with the motive of pressuring neutral employers. Picketing was undertaken against the primary employers, and the secondary employees only incidentally honored the picket line. No attempt was made to place pressure on the primary employer through the neutral one. The *Denver Building Trades* case was held to constitute secondary action because the general contractor in control of the site was neutral. Had he been deemed primary, the Court most likely would have permitted picketing at the site to continue.

"Reserve gate" doctrine. In the 1949 *Ryan* case the NLRB did not distinguish between picketing at a manufacturer's gate for general employees and at a gate reserved for construction workers of a neutral employer. It made this distinction in 1959. In the *Virginia-Carolina Chemical* case, a union that represented the production and maintenance employees of the company went out on strike and picketed the plant. The company had employed an outside construction company to work within the plant, but the work had not started prior to the strike. After the strike started the company erected a fence around the plant with four separate entrances. One of

the gates was set aside for the exclusive use of the other company's employees and this action was communicated to both the contractor and the union on strike. The union on strike ignored the reserved gate and picketed it anyway with the result that the construction workers honored the picket line.

The NLRB found the union in violation of the secondary boycott provisions because of its action at the reserved gate. The District of Columbia Circuit Court of Appeals enforced the Board order for the union to cease and desist from picketing activity at the reserve gate. [26]

The U. S. Supreme Court dealt with the Board's "separate gate" doctrine in 1961 in a case involving General Electric Company.[27] In the *General Electric* case the local union picketed the premises of the company with whom it had a labor dispute. It engaged in picketing not only at the gates utilized by General Electric's employees, but also at a gate reserved exclusively for independent contractors and their employees. The independent contractors regularly performed work in the manufacturer's plant. The NLRB held that picketing at the reserve gate constituted illegal secondary activity since it pressured the employees of neutral employers to join in the union action. This decision was sustained by a lower federal court.

The U. S. Supreme Court upheld the Board-established "reserve gate" doctrine, but qualified its position. It held that the "distinction between legitimate 'primary activity' and banned 'secondary activity'" is difficult to make. For this reason there must be an accommodation between a "union's right to picket and the interest of the secondary employer in being free from picketing." The key to resolving this issue in reserve gate cases is "found in the type of work that is being performed by those who use the separate gate." If independent contractors perform tasks "unconnected to the normal operations of the struck employer," then the Board could hold picketing at reserve gates to be secondary. However, if the work performed by employees using reserve gates is of the kind carried out by the regular employees of the plant, picketing would fall within the primary classification and hence be lawful. Thus the amount of bargaining-unit work performed while the strike is in process is the key to the legality of union picketing at the reserve gate. If employees of the outside contractor perform work which they would not normally carry out because of the strike, a union may lawfully picket the reserve gate. In addition, the reserve gate must be clearly marked as such or it will not be distinguished from any other gate leading to the primary employer's premises. [28]

Common Situs and Moore Dry Dock. When primary and neutral employers work on common premises during labor disputes, the NLRB must strike a "balance between the union's right to picket and the interest of the secondary employer in being free from picketing." In *Moore Dry Dock* a union was involved in a labor dispute with a shipowner.[29] It asked the dockowner for permission to enter the shipyard to picket the docksite where the primary employer operated, but the request was refused. The union established a picket line at the gate to the shipyard despite the fact that employees of other employers used the gate to reach their places of work in the shipyard. A secondary boycott unfair labor practice was filed against the union for its action.

The Board established four criteria for permitting picketing to take place at a site controlled by a neutral employer. It was forced to do so because the striking union could not exert effective economic pressure if a rigid rule were established regarding the effect of such action on neutral employers. In establishing the criteria for permissible activity, the Supreme Court upon review observed that these tests generated a shift in administrative policy involving common-situs problems. Physical location was no longer deemed the most important consideration to determine legality of union action. Now picketing is deemed legal at a neutral point if publicity is directed at the primary employer.

Thus picketing at a common situs is regarded as legal if (a) the picketing is strictly limited to times when the situs of the dispute is located on the secondary employer's premises; (b) at the time of the picketing the primary employer is engaged in its normal business at the situs; (c) the picketing is limited to places reasonably close to the location of the situs; and (d) the picketing discloses clearly that the dispute is with the primary employer. This test is applied to common-situs picketing in cases where other evidence does not clearly show the intent and purpose of union activity.

The case established a situation whereby picketing at the common situs may be undertaken if the test conditions are met. Picketing may be undertaken even if the effect is that employees of neutral employers refuse to cross the picket line. The secondary boycott effects are incidental to the right of labor unions to engage in primary picketing. As mentioned, *Moore Dry Dock* marked a departure from the earlier emphasis placed on the geographic location where picketing occurs as the guiding criterion for determining legality of union action to one emphasizing publicity. Thus an accommodation is established between the right of unions to engage in primary activity and that of secondary employers to be free from union pressure. Neither right is absolute.

Common Situs Policy Shifts: 1953–1962. A new Board membership achieved majority status in 1953 and immediately had the opportunity to review the common-situs rules of its predecessor. In the *Washington Coca Cola* case the Board altered the physical-location rule of prior decisions.[30] It held that if a primary employer maintained a place of business that presented no physical obstacles to picketing, a union could not lawfully picket some other location at which secondary neutral employees worked. In such situations picketing had to be confined to the easily accessible premises of the primary employer.

The Board meant that a union engaged in a labor dispute had to refrain from picketing the site where work is performed if the company had an office building or other facility at any other place in the community. It did not matter if the office building were located ten miles away from the site where nonunion workers and union workers were engaged side by side in work. It was reasoned that the mere presence of a picket sign is a signal to members of building trades unions to leave the job. This doctrine of 1953 was meant to eliminate the use of the signal and as such relieve pressure on neutral employers in labor disputes.

The doctrine of *Washington Coca Cola* was not destined for continued life and was reversed by a new Board majority in 1962. In the *Plauche Electric* case, a secondary neutral employer awarded a contract to the nonunion Plauche Electric Company to perform electrical work, along with other employers, on the premises of U. S. Tire, a manufacturing firm.[31] The nonunion contractor maintained an office to which its employees reported twice a day regardless of the project on which they were employed. The union did not choose to picket Plauche's place of business, as required under the *Washington Coca Cola* doctrine, but elected to picket the plant premises of U. S. Tire instead. The new Board found no violation of the secondary boycott provisions of the law and consequently reversed *Washington Coca Cola*. The revised position was justified on the ground that the standard established in 1953 was too rigid. Unions were viewed as unduly restricted in their efforts to picket employers that did not conform to union standards. There may be occasions when a primary employer's permanent place of business is adequate for a union to picket to seek its objective. However, a rigid rule requiring picketing only at permanent locations severely restricts the right of unions to engage in this action, as guaranteed by law. The place where work is performed is usually the only effective place where unions may exert economic pressure. Thus the law now permits unions to picket the physical location where the labor dispute is concentrated as opposed to a distant office maintained by an employer involved in a labor controversy. This policy permits unions to place the greatest economic pressure on a firm at the location where it is likely to have the greatest effect. The fact that neutral employers also work at the same location does not control the right of unions to engage in primary action. They must attempt to meet the tests provided in *Moore Dry Dock* unless other evidence clearly demonstrates to the Board the primary nature of union action. This aspect of Board policy may be considered a loophole in the law; however, it should be emphasized at this point that the NLRB has to balance the right of unions to strike with the right of neutral employers to be free from economic pressures when they have no power to influence the outcome of the dispute.

ROVING OR AMBULATORY SITUS

A deviation of the common-situs picketing standards involves union picketing of primary employer vehicles when they stop temporarily at neutral employer facilities. Such stops are for the purpose of picking up and delivering commodities. In trucking, drivers spend most of their time delivering or picking up shipments at various employer premises. This makes these workers ambulatory employees. In 1949 the NLRB recognized the nature of this type of work and permitted a union to picket a primary employer's trucks even during the time they were at a secondary employer's site of operations.[32] During the 1950s the Board adhered to its *Washington Coca Cola* doctrine whereby ambulatory picketing was almost totally eliminated.[33] Under this requirement a union had to picket the permanent place of business of a primary employer, if such existed, and refrain from such activity at sites where neutral employers operated. Thus the union tactic of truck following was not permissible unless it could show that a permanent place of business did not exist.

This prohibition was eliminated in 1961 when the NLRB set forth its *Carrier Corporation* ruling.[34] In *Carrier* a union picketed the company premises. The New York Central Railroad Company, a secondary employer, maintained a right of way on property next to Carrier Corporation property. The right of way was fenced in and trains moved through a gate to approach the Carrier plant to load and unload materials. The union picketed the gate to stop the secondary employer's workers from performing their usual jobs, involving the loading and unloading of Carrier Corporation products.

The NLRB held the picketing legal under secondary boycott provisions of the law since the secondary employer's business activity was "related to the normal plant operations of the primary employer with whom the union is in dispute." The union that had the dispute with Carrier had a clear economic interest in attempting to halt the movement of its goods to market. For clarity regarding the economic significance of the decision, let us assume that the Carrier Corporation maintained significantly high inventories at the time of the dispute. If its employees were unsuccessful in slowing down or stopping altogether the company's ability to supply users with its product, the union may have been unable to exert adequate economic pressure to support its position. However, if it were left free to peaceably induce employees of the other employer not to provide Carrier with their services, then it would be in a better position to require Carrier to bargain on items in dispute. This follows since the company would not be able to continue to supply other companies with its product despite high levels of inventories. Thus it is obvious that the railroad's employees were not neutral to the dispute since their services had vital implications for bargaining-unit employees on strike.

At the same time it should be realized that the *Moore Dry Dock* rules apply to ambulatory picketing as well as to that at stationary common sites. Pickets must clearly identify on their signs that their dispute is with a primary employer and not with those who are neutral. Due care must be taken not to appeal to neutral employees for the purpose of enmeshing them in an existing dispute. If such occurs the Board will outlaw picketing of vehicles as exceeding the permissible limits of primary picketing.[35]

These rules of *Moore Dry Dock* apply to ambulatory picketing cases unless there is evidence to the contrary revealing union motives such as in the *Carrier Corporation* case. If there is no clear evidence of the secondary employer's business relationship with the primary employer's normal operations, a picketing union becomes subject to the four rules of *Moore Dry Dock* in determining ambulatory picketing legality. Once again it is obvious that the difference between primary and secondary union activity is unclear at best. The lack of clear delineation between the two types of activity places the Board and courts in the position of attempting to draw conclusions on the basis of information gathered during investigation of charges filed as well as that brought out during formal Board hearings.

CONSUMER SECONDARY BOYCOTTS

Prohibited secondary boycott action includes activity calculated to induce work stoppages or to coerce any persons engaged in commerce in order to obtain an illegal object. One example of prohibited action is the forcing of any person to cease doing business with any other person. The law, however, is not as simple as it may first appear. A second proviso to the section states that

> for the purpose of this paragraph, only, nothing contained in such paragraph shall be construed to prohibit publicity, *other than picketing*, for the purpose of truthfully advising the public, including consumers and members of a labor organization, that a product or products are produced by an employer with whom a labor organization has a primary dispute and are distributed by another employer. (Emphasis added.)[36]

Unions have the ability to publicize a dispute with a primary employer at retail outlets selling the goods in dispute by using such tactics as handbilling, newspaper advertisements, and radio and television advertisements. The legality of picketing to induce customers not to buy "unfair" products is not entirely prohibited despite the language of the 1959 law. A consumer boycott depends mainly on publicity, but it is difficult to measure the effect of union efforts in most cases. Such activity is likely to be more successful in areas that are heavily populated with union members than in those with few if any members.

The NLRB held at first that Congress in 1959 had intended to outlaw all consumer picketing in front of a secondary store for the purpose of appealing to consumers not to buy the products in dispute.[37] Following its policy of holding all consumer picketing illegal, the Board held, in one highly important case destined for Supreme Court review, that union picketing was illegal when it picketed a retail outlet to appeal to customers on the grounds that it had a dispute with another employer whose product was sold by the retail store.[38]

The Court of Appeals for the District of Columbia reversed the Board and held that consumer picketing could not be found to "threaten, coerce or restrain the stores being picketed [without] affirmative proof that a substantial economic impact on the store had occurred, or was likely to occur as a result of the conduct." The case was remanded to the Board to look for this type of evidence. However, upon appeal, the U. S. Supreme Court established a different guideline for the Board to use when such cases come before it.

The Supreme Court ruled in the *Tree Fruits* case that the legislative history "does not reflect with the requisite clarity a congressional plan to proscribe all peaceful consumer picketing at secondary sites." The record merely revealed that such picketing was unlawful if the labor organization attempted to persuade customers not to buy any of the products on sale at the neutral store. Customers may be persuaded through picketing not to buy the struck product. Thus picketing confined to persuading customers to cease buying the product of the primary employer with whom the dispute exists is not prohibited secondary action. In most cases, the court reasoned, if secondary stores drop the item in dispute from their counters, they would not be hurt economically. This view of the Court may be correct in terms of grocery stores or department stores that merchandise a large range of goods. Presumably, the *Tree Fruits* doctrine rationale would not hold when specialty shops are involved. That is, a store that specializes in a particular good supplied by a single producer could quite logically be dealt a severe economic setback if consumer picketing were permitted in cases where suppliers were involved in labor disputes.

At the same time, however, it should be realized that unions may be legally within their rights to use forms of publicity other than picketing to appeal to customers not to patronize a secondary store at all. Consider this statement of the Court in *Tree Fruits*:

> Peaceful consumer picketing to shut off all trade with the secondary employer unless he aids the union in its dispute with the primary employer is poles apart from such picketing which only persuades his customer not to buy the struck product.

The Court said that picketing may not be used to stop all customer trade with a neutral employer, but other forms of publicity may be used even if it accomplishes this end. All that is required is that the information on handbills, for example, be truthful and not misleading to the public. Thus the area of labor dispute in accordance with this implication extends to all situations involving a struck product. This may flow from a manufacturer, to middlemen, and to retail outlets.

In short, the Supreme Court has held that all picketing of secondary employers is not per se illegal. This doctrine provides a basis for unions to exert secondary pressure and tends to create a loophole in the provisions of Landrum-Griffin. Carefully worded picket signs permit unions to effectuate consumer boycotts on particular goods.

In 1968 the District of Columbia Court of Appeals was faced with a consumer boycott issue that was somewhat less clear than the test provided by *Tree Fruits*.[39] A union had a primary dispute with a newspaper and picketed a restaurant which advertised regularly in the struck newspaper. The NLRB held the picketing to violate the secondary boycott provisions of Landrum-Griffin. Handbills were also passed out describing the union's dispute with the newspaper company in some detail. The question is: What part of the restaurant's product was the union permitted to ask customers not to buy?

The court of appeals upheld the NLRB rule in this case on the ground that *Tree Fruits* did not apply to the *Honolulu* case. This position was taken because a newspaper advertisement actually becomes incorporated into every product sold by the restaurant. The court of appeals ruled that "the struck product has become part of the retailer's entire offering, so that the product boycott will of necessity encompass the entire business of the secondary employer."

The Supreme Court's *Tree Fruits* decision upholds a limited boycott and will not support a total boycott. A total boycott spreads to and disrupts a retailer's entire trade. The Act protects a neutral employer from a boycott of its entire business.

The *Honolulu* case makes it clear that the Board and courts may not permit union picketing of a neutral employer whose entire product consists solely of the struck work. This would amount to a total boycott and the law prohibits picketing "to shut off all trade with the secondary employer. . . ."

Thus all peaceful consumer picketing at secondary sites is not forbidden by the Board and the courts. Total boycotts are clearly illegal. The U. S. Supreme Court has established a doctrine in the *Tree Fruits* case that appears equitable both to unions engaged in a dispute with a primary employer and to neutrals that sell its product. As long as the object of union picketing may be clearly identified as of a limited variety, consumer secondary boycotts are legal. Total boycotts against secondary retailers are forbidden even if one product, the struck product, is the only one sold by the store.

Unfair Lists

A union device often used to put economic pressure on employers with whom disputes exist is the *unfair list*. This list is circulated among the members of various local and national unions urging them not to buy particular goods or services. The desired result of unfair-list circulation is to induce consumers and secondary employers to cease doing business with struck employers so long as the dispute lasts. It is often asserted that unfair lists constitute secondary boycott activity if they do not clearly state that they are not designed to induce neutrals not to do business with primary employers.[40]

As early as 1949 the NLRB held that the mere placing of a primary employer's name on an unfair list and circulating the list among other locals did not induce secondary employees to withhold labor from neutral employers. Even if some employees of other employers withhold their services, it cannot be deemed the intent of unions using unfair lists to accomplish this end.[41] Members of other locals are merely encouraged not to purchase a struck employer's product. Other items on sale in retail stores, for example, are not in question and as such the secondary employer may feel little if any economic pressure as a result of the list.

Unfair lists merely provide a means for unions to publicize labor disputes. The list is a traditional device for accomplishing this objective. Neither Taft-Hartley nor the subsequent 1959 amendments outlawed its use and until specific language is provided by Congress to do so, the device is legal.[42]

There is no evidence to support any contention that unfair lists are very effective even among union members. Some ardent members may follow the advice given by unions not to purchase certain goods and services, but most may not. Further, it may well be that most individuals with longstanding union membership would be hard pressed to name just one unfair employer identified on any union unfair list circulated at any time during the past twenty years. The NLRB has not opened a secondary boycott loophole by permitting unfair lists since there is no evidence Congress intended to outlaw their use.

Products Produced Aspect of Publicity Exemption

Another aspect of the amended secondary boycott section provides that where the primary employer is the producer of a product, and that product is distributed by a secondary employer, the union may truthfully publicize that fact by means other than picketing so long as the publicity does not affect the performance of services at the establishment of the secondary employer. The NLRB has construed this provision in such a manner that widespread criticism of the agency has resulted. The basis of the criticism is that the Board provides an economic construction to the term *products produced*, and does not regard it in the sense that the primary employer must produce a physical product, such as an automobile. Instead the Board holds that the primary employer produces a product for purposes of the publicity section if he provides a service to the secondary employer.

In 1961 the *Lohman Sales*, *Middle South Broadcasting*, and *Great Western* cases came before the Board for interpretation of this proviso.[43] All three cases resulted in a determination that unions had the statutory right to handbill neutral employers.

In *Lohman* the primary employer with whom a labor dispute existed was Lohman Sales Company, a distributor. The Teamsters struck the company and then proceeded to pass out handbills in front of several drugstores to inform the public that these stores distributed items produced by a struck employer. The Board held that the wholesaler, Lohman, produced a product and thus handbilling of the drugstores was lawful. The products produced by Lohman Sales were deemed the candy and cigarettes it distributed. Essentially, the NLRB took this position because the distributor applied its labor to the product and this added value to it. Services constitute a part of a product since the national income accounts consider services at all stages of production and distribution in calculating final value.

This interpretation was carried over into the *Middle South Broadcasting* case. A union had a dispute with a radio station. A blacklist with the names of several firms that advertised over the station was circulated. One of the firms handbilled was an automobile agency that advertised over the Middle South station. The Board overruled a trial examiner and held that the radio station was a producer of the products it advertised. The Board justified its position by stating that

> as found in [Lohman Sales], labor is the prime requisite of one who "produces" and therefore an employer who applies his labor to a product, whether of an abstract or physical nature, or in the initial or intermediate stages of the marketing of the product, is one of the "producers" of the product.

Value is added at each stage of production and this includes the processes of supplier through manufacturing and ultimately final sales.

The Board utilized this same argument to uphold a union's action in a case involving a television station. The same criteria for product produced was used. The NLRB position was not sustained when presented to the Ninth Circuit Court of Appeals in the *Servette* case, but was later adopted by the U. S. Supreme Court upon review.[44] In economic terms the Board and the Supreme Court are correct. Value is added to a product at each stage of production and distribution. In this regard there is no loophole in secondary boycott prohibitions since the proper use of economic terms would logically lead to this conclusion. However, if Congress intended that products produced refers exclusively to physical products, it could be argued that the NLRB and the courts created a loophole in the 1959 amendment.

HOT-CARGO AGREEMENTS

Section 8 (e) of the amended Taft-Hartley Act makes it an unfair labor practice for an employer and a union to enter into any contract or agreement, express or implied, whereby such employer ceases or refrains, or agrees to cease or refrain, from handling, using, selling, transporting, or otherwise dealing in any of the products of any other employer, or to cease doing business with any other employer, or to cease doing business with any other person. *Hot-cargo agreements* refer to those made by an employer and union whereby it is promised that goods declared as unfair by the labor organization will not be handled by the company. Usually, unfair goods refer to those produced by nonunion shops. These agreements are considered effective in union attempts to organize nonunion employers. The arrangement has been used by unions for a considerable period of time and is considered highly effective in invoking economic pressure on nonunionized companies.

Originally, the NLRB held that not only may a union and employer execute a contract wherein the firm agrees not to handle work declared unfair, but that the labor organization could also apply economic pressure to enforce it.[45] Such action was deemed permissible despite the secondary boycott prohibitions of Taft-Hartley. However, new Board personnel changed the prior position and ruled in 1955 that hot-cargo agreements could be executed, but unions could not engage in prohibited secondary boycott activity to enforce the arrangement.[46] The Supreme Court upheld this position in 1958 in the *Sand Door* case.[47]

The Landrum-Griffin amendments to Taft-Hartley make hot-cargo arrangements unlawful throughout all industry except clothing and construction. Such agreements may not be made—either written or oral.

Attempts to Circumvent the Law

Some unions have been very active in attempts to get around the provisions of the 1959 law. Soon after the Taft-Hartley amendments became effective on November 13, 1959, a union attempted to circumvent the restrictions by obtaining a "Refusal to Handle" clause in the collective agreement. This required an employer to agree that it would not discharge or discipline any employee because he refused to work on nonunion or struck goods. The Board held that such clauses were an attempt to evade the law and as such were illegal.[48]

A "Struck Work" clause was also included in the case, which bound the employer not to assist or handle work from any employer on strike. This would have meant that any work of a struck employer, including that normally performed, would be prohibited. The Board held this language illegal because of its broad implications. The area of industrial conflict would be widened if such a clause had been permitted to stand.

In another case before the Board, a contractual clause forbade subcontracting to other employers of any work unless their employees "enjoy the same or greater wages" as the companies that were parties to the agreement paid.[49] The Board held the clause illegal because it went further than merely restricting subcontracting "for the purpose of the preservation of jobs and job rights of the unit employees." This type of clause was viewed as an attempt to prohibit an employer from doing business with another firm and as such violated the law.

Thus the NLRB has been steadfast in preventing unions from subverting the prohibitions against hot-cargo arrangements. It has carefully reviewed such clauses in the light of the intent of Congress and has repeatedly struck down subterfuges designed to circumvent the hot-cargo proscription. The ingenuity of unions has not been so sharp as to delude the Board into believing that violations did not exist.

CONSTRUCTION AND CLOTHING INDUSTRY
EXEMPTION

Congress extended special privileges to labor unions operating in the construction and clothing industries. This policy was motivated by the peculiarities of the industries.

The Construction Industry

In a qualification to Section 8 (e), the anti–hot-cargo provision, the law states that "nothing in this section shall apply to an agreement between a labor organization and an employer in the construction industry relating to the contracting or subcontracting of work to be done at the site of the construction, alteration, painting, or repair of a building, structure or other work." Several important problems are involved in this exemption. One concerns the interpretation of the phrase "at the site." Thus, may an employer and a construction union lawfully execute a hot-cargo arrangement for work that could be done at the site, or does the exemption apply only to work actually done at the site of construction?

A source of the problem is that in the construction industry certain work could be done at the site or in firms located off the construction site. These shops are frequently owned by employers not involved in the actual construction of the building site. Some work—such as the threading, bending, or fabrication of pipe, for example—could be done either in the shop or at the construction site. One of the Senate members of the Conference Committee debating the Landrum-Griffin changes of Taft-Hartley stated that the exemption was meant to apply to any work that "could be" done at the construction site.[50] Against this position, however, there is substantial evidence that the exemption was to apply only to work actually done at the site.

In 1963 the Board gave attention to the issue. It ruled that the hot-cargo exemption applies only to work done at the site.[51] Otherwise, the NLRB held, a subcontractor that performs work away from the site would be effectively deprived of its contract to fulfill a work assignment. A supplier of materials to an employer at the site was deemed the primary target of the union's conduct, which constituted secondary action. Thus nonunion labor may perform work off the site at lower wages even though the work could be done at the site. Contract clauses that attempt to cover subcontractor operation away from the site are unlawful. In this regard the Board has apparently carried out the intent of Congress despite the harm that may result to bargaining-unit workers.

Strikes to Obtain and Enforce Hot-cargo Clauses

The NLRB ruled initially that unions in the construction industry were forbidden from using economic force either to obtain or enforce agreements to cease doing business with nonunion contractors.[52] However, the Ninth Circuit Court, upon review, concluded that picketing to secure hot-cargo agreements was legal, but it was not legal to use economic pressure to enforce them.[53] This principle was explained fully in another court case involving the same issue:

> Secondary subcontracting clauses in the construction industry are lawful, under the proviso to Section 8 (e), and economic force may be used to obtain them not withstanding Section 8 (b) (4) (A), because Section 8 (b) (4) (A) incorporates that proviso by reference. But under Section 8 (b) (4) (B) such secondary clauses may be enforced only through lawsuits, and not through economic action. Primary subcontracting clauses, on the other hand, fall outside the ambit of Section 8 (e), as the Board concedes. Moreover, economic enforcement thereof is not proscribed by Section 8 (b) (4) (B) since they are not directed at involving neutral employers in a labor dispute "not their own."[54]

The language used by Congress in Section 8 (e) prompted the courts to construe the proviso as they did. Congress referred to the third qualification of the hot-cargo clause as "nothing in this Act shall prohibit the enforcement of any agreement that is within *the foregoing exception*." The exception referred to has been interpreted as the clothing industry and not the construction industry as well.

The Board and the courts may have viewed the situation in the construction industry more realistically. A law that permits economic pressure to obtain a clause dealing with subcontracting of work done on the site, but will not permit economic pressure for enforcement of it after agreement is reached renders the agreement largely ineffectual. A labor organization may bring suit in the courts to enforce such clauses, but the nature of the construction industry makes it readily apparent that most work will have been concluded by the time a judgment can be obtained. This state of affairs could weaken the ability of construction unions to maintain the integrity of bargaining-unit work under some circumstances. An important exception, however, is involved when a labor contract contains a so-called *work-preservation clause*.

Preservation of Bargaining-unit Work

The Board has long held with court approval that a union strike to preserve bargaining-unit work does not violate the secondary boycott prohibitions even though there may be consequences for neutral employers.[55] Work "historically and regularly" performed by employees is not involved in the secondary boycott proscription when a labor organization attempts to force an employer to abide by a contractual clause to preserve bargaining-unit work.[56]

In the *National Woodwork* case the NLRB and Supreme Court sustained the right of unions to enforce work-preservation clauses.[57] The carpenter's union had a clause in its contract which provided that union members would not handle or install prefitted doors. That is, the labor agreement provided that the carpenters on the site would fit the doors with the necessary hardware. Hence the union and the contractor agreed that such work fell under the jurisdiction of the union. It was a work-preservation clause. A strike was called to enforce the clause after the contractor purchased prefitted doors. The carpenters refused to install them.

The NLRB ruled in *National Woodwork* that a product boycott taken to enforce a work-preservation clause did not violate the hot-cargo or secondary boycott provisions of amended Taft-Hartley. Tne Board reasoned that union action was taken to preserve bargaining-unit work for members of the construction union and was not aimed at the suppliers of the prefabricated product. This was deemed legal even though the effect was to force the contractor to boycott the products of suppliers.

The Supreme Court in a 5-4 decision upheld the NLRB position. Thus the work-preservation doctrine of the Board and Supreme Court recognizes that a literal reading of the boycott prohibitions of Taft-Hartley would render unions helpless in attempts to protect bargaining-unit work at the job site. The Court reasoned that the clause was included in the contract for the sole benefit of bargaining-unit members and not directed against a secondary employer. The strike was provoked by the employer's unilateral decision to purchase prefabricated doors in violation of a collective bargaining agreement designed to protect the traditional job-site work of craftsmen against the inherent danger of factory-fitted building materials. There is no doubt that this interpretation may well slow down efforts to utilize new and improved materials and methods of production. However, unions must also be given the opportunity to attempt to prevent unilateral decisions to subcontract traditional work by use of economic pressure. A failure to distinguish between primary and secondary activity could indeed lead to a demise of union action that other portions of the same Act purports to protect. There is no absolute union right to preserve bargaining-unit work, but a labor organization's right should be protected in order to enable it to bargain effectively on problems vital not only to its existence, but to the jobs of members as well. The *National Woodwork* case permits strikes to preserve bargaining-unit work and as such is an important exception to the secondary boycott and hot-cargo prohibitions found in the amended Taft-Hartley Act.

Right-of-Control Test

The practical significance of *National Woodwork*, however, is related to the so-called "right-of-control" test that the NLRB stressed in the case. In the precedent case, the employer had the right to use either prefitted or unfitted doors. Thus, he controlled the kind of product that could be used. When the employer has no option as to the kind of product to be used, the NLRB has held that employees may not refuse to install the product called for by job specifications. In short, the right-of-control test establishes that if an employer controls the use of prefabricated products, union pressure tactics to stop use of the product are lawful. But if the owner of the building or general contractor specified a prefabricated product, the employer lacks control of its use and union pressures directed at him constitute illegal secondary boycott activity.

It is easy to see why the right-of-control test is significant in establishing the potential value of *National Woodwork*. To get around this decision, prefabricated materials could be specified in construction contracts. For example, the builder's architect could establish that prefitted doors be used. Under the right-of-control test, the employees assigned to the installation of the doors could not refuse to install them because their employer has no control over what kind of doors may be used. In fact, should the NLRB right-of-control test prevail, much of the protection that construction workers receive from *National Woodwork* would be lost. On the other hand, under this test, economies in construction could be realized by the use of prefabricated products. In this respect, an attorney for the Associated General Contractors warned that if the right-of-control test is abandoned that "you'll see housing costs go higher, since cheaper prefabricated material would be kept off the market."[58]

At this writing, the legality of the right-of-control test is in a somewhat confused state. Federal courts have reversed the NLRB when it has used the test to find union conduct illegal.[59] One federal court stated that the right-of-control test "is not of decisive significance." In spite of these court decisions, however, the NLRB continues to find union action illegal based upon the right-of-control test.[60] Undoubtedly, the issue will be determined by the United States Supreme Court.

Language Must Be Specific

For a work preservation clause to be valid, the language must be specific, and not written in a way to accomplish objectives other than preserving work traditionally performed by employees. Also, a work preservation clause will not protect union conduct if it is used in a manner other than to protect unit work. Two cases demonstrate these two conditions. In one case, the clause stated "all work . . . will be done on material, equipment, and apparatus owned by the Employer." The union argued that this clause preserved work for employees because ownership of the equipment would facilitate the contractor's control of the work assignments. In finding this provision invalid, the Board held that the language was too broad, aimed primarily to the ownership of equipment and not to work to be done at the job site.[61] In the second case, union conduct was held to be illegal in its use of the following clause: "all merchandise for resale which is delivered to a retail outlet owned by the Employer . . . shall be delivered from the warehouses of the Employer covered by the Collective Bargaining Agreement." The union involved used this clause to prevent retail outlets from purchasing soft drinks directly from a soft drink firm. In holding the union action illegal, the Board found that the provision was not being used to preserve work, but rather to force the employees of the soda pop companies to join the Teamsters union.[62] In the case, the Board was not impressed with the union's argument that its conduct did not cause the employer to terminate completely its business relationship with the soda pop company. By changing the point of delivery, the Board held that this would mean that the soda pop company would be required to reduce the number of its drivers. As the Supreme Court has held, Taft-Hartley does not require that a union demand a complete cessation of business before a secondary boycott violation can be found.[63]

In any event, the *National Woodwork* doctrine has been bitterly criticized in many circles. The criticisms became more intense as the doctrine was applied to several products. Work preservation clauses protected employees against the installation of prefabricated fireplaces,[64] precut steel bands,[65] and prefitted boilers.[66] As stated, the controversy involves job protection as against economy in construction. Ignoring employee concern for their jobs, the *Wall Street Journal* remarked:

> If the labor unions, with the labor board's help, continue successfully to plumb these depths of inefficiency, the outlook for even minor economies in construction seems very dim too. If their theories are sound, they ought to go all the way and come out foursquare for making things like nails by hand.[67]

The Clothing Industry

Congress treated the clothing unions in a more liberal fashion than the construction unions. Clothing unions may use economic pressure both to obtain hot-cargo clauses and to enforce them.

Unlike the situation with construction unions, Congress excepted clothing unions completely from the hot-cargo restrictions imposed in 1959. The congressional purpose for doing so was to permit unions to use such clauses to eliminate the so-called "sweatshop" conditions from the industry, which could prevail because of its highly competitive character. Clothing unions are exempt from secondary boycott provisions under three conditions. Exemption is permitted when an employer at which the union pressure is directed (a) works on the goods owned by a jobber or manufacturer; (b) works on the premises of a jobber or manufacturer; and (c) performs part of an integrated process of manufacture.

Congress has decreed that unions may use hot-cargo arrangements in attempts to stabilize the highly competitive conditions of the clothing industry, but evidently construction is not considered competitive enough to qualify to the same degree. On the other hand, industry in general is not afforded the luxury of negotiating any hot-cargo arrangements. Congress apparently must have been confused regarding whether or not competition is desirable or undesirable. Perhaps it is deemed desirable, but not too much so.

SUMMARY

Considerable attention has been directed by the Board and the courts on the various secondary boycott issues that come before them. It is often charged that they have opened up loopholes in the secondary boycott sections of the Act which Congress clearly intended to close and prohibit. Close examination of the entire law does not support such a conclusion. The major problem facing the Board and the courts is to distinguish between primary and prohibited secondary pressures.

Congress did not intend to outlaw primary strikes and picketing but this could be the actual result if all the secondary consequences which inevitably follow from pressures placed on employers with whom a dispute exists are prohibited.

The regulatory bodies must strike a balance between the right of unions to exert effective economic pressure to achieve their goals and the right of neutral employers to escape incidental pressure, which may derive from the primary action. It appears that the publicity provisos to the secondary boycott section of the Act were constructed broadly enough by Congress to permit unions to continue to act in their own self-interest. It may well be that some of the decisions set forth by the Board have been somewhat unrealistic regarding the conditions that prevail in a particular industry. For example, the rule that unions in the construction industry may picket to obtain hot-cargo clauses, but may not do so to enforce them does not appear reasonable. An exception to this policy is permissible when preservation of bargaining-unit work is an issue. Perhaps it would be more realistic either to permit both to occur or neither.

Regardless of the merits of Board and court action, if there are inconsistencies between their decisions and the will of Congress, it was Congress that created a jungle of highly inconsistent provisions and not the interpreting and enforcement authorities. Substance must be given to the broad congressional language that is both workable and equitable to all parties in labor disputes. After all the basic public policy continues to be to protect and encourage the institution of collective bargaining. The Board and the courts have the responsibility to do just that.

NOTES

[1] Felix Frankfurter and Nathan Greene, *The Labor Injunction* (New York: The Macmillan Company, 1930), p. 43.

[2] *Legislative History*, Taft-Hartley Act, p. 1106.

[3] *Hearings Before Committee on Education and Labor* on H.R. 115, 83d Congress, 1st sess., 1953, P. 3441.

[4] Melvin J. Segal, "Secondary Boycott Loopholes," *Labor Law Journal*, X, No. 3 (March 1959), 175.

[5] 61 Stat. 151 (1947).

[6] 61 Stat. 140 (1947).

[7] *Legislative History*, Landrum-Griffin Act, p. 1431.

[8] Section 8 (b) (4) (B) in part makes it an unfair labor practice for a union to induce a work stoppage in order to force a secondary employer to cease doing business with a primary employer.

[9] 95 Congressional Record 8709 (1947).

[10] *CIO-Longshoremen, Local 12 (Irwin-Lyons Lumber Company)*, 87 NLRB 54 (1949).

[11] *J. G. Roy & Sons Company* v. *NLRB*, 251 F. (2d) 771 (CA 1, 1958).

[12] *Teamsters, Local 20 (National Cement Products Company)*, 115 NLRB 1290 (1956).

[13] *AFL-CIO Brewery Workers Union (Adolph Coors Company)*, 121 NLRB 35 (1958).

[14] *Douds* v. *Metropolitan Federation of Architects*, 75 F. Supp. 672 (S. D. N.Y., 1948).

[15] *NLRB* v. *International Rice Milling Company*, 341 U.S. 665 (1951).

[16] 181 F. (2d) 21 (CA 5, 1950).

[17] *Texas Industries*, 112 NLRB 923 (1955).

[18] *NLRB* v. *Brewery Workers* (10th Cir., 1959).

[19] *Carolina Lumber Company*, 130 NLRB 148 (1961).

[20] *NLRB* v. *Servette, Inc.*, 337 U.S. 46 (1964).

[21] *Radio Artists, Washington-Baltimore Local* v. *NLRB*, CA DC No. 24, 641 (April 17, 1972).

[22] Hearings before the Subcommittee on Separation of Powers, *Congressional Oversight of Administrative Agencies (National Labor Relations Board)*, Part II (1968), p. 1146.

[23] *CIO-Oil Workers (Pure Oil Company, Toledo Refining Division)*, 84 NLRB 315 (1949).

[24] *CIO-Electrical Workers (Ryan Construction Company)*, 85 NLRB 417 (1949).

[25] Bernard Marcus, "Secondary Boycotts," in *Symposium on the Labor-Management Reporting and Disclosure Act of 1959*, ed. Ralph Slovenko (Baton Rouge, La.: Claitor's Bookstore Publishers, 1961), pp. 826–827.

[26] *Local 36, International Chemical Workers Union, AFL-CIO* v. *NLRB*, 47 LRRM 2493, cert. denied 366 U.S. 949 (1961).

[27] *Local 761, International Union of Electrical Workers* v. *NLRB*, 366 U.S. 667 (1961).

[28] This criteria was adopted from a lower federal court's test for reserve-gate picketing legality in *United Steelworkers of America* v. *NLRB*, 289 F. (2d) 591 (1961).

[29] *Sailors' Union of the Pacific (Moore Dry Dock Company)*, 92 NLRB 547 (1950), 366 U.S. 667.

[30] *AFL-Teamsters, Local 67 (Washington Coca-Cola Bottling Works, Inc.)*, 107 NLRB 299 (1953) enf. granted 220 F. (2d) 380 (CA DC, 1955).

[31] *Plauche Electric*, 135 NLRB 250 (1963).

[32] *Schultz Refrigerated Service*, 87 NLRB 502 (1949).

[33] *AFL-Teamsters, Local 67, op. cit.*

[34] *Carrier Corporation*, 132 NLRB 127 (1961).

[35] See, for example, *Highway Truck Drivers & Helpers, Local 107, IBT (Riss & Company)*, 130 NLRB 943 (1960).

[36] 29 U.S.C. S. 158 (b) (4).

[37] *Upholsterers Frame & Bedding Workers Twin City Local 61 (Minneapolis House Furnishings Company)*, 132 NLRB 40 (1961).

[38] *NLRB* v. *Fruit & Vegetable Packers & Warehousemen, Local 760, et al. (Tree Fruits, Inc.)*, 377 U.S. 58 (1964).

[39] *Honolulu Typographical Union No. 37* v. *NLRB*, 167 NLRB 150 (CA DC, 1968).

[40] Hearings before the Subcommittee on Separation of Powers, *Congressional Oversight of Administrative Agencies (National Labor Relations Board)*, Part II (1968), p. 1151. The controversy deals with Section 8 (b) (4) (A).

[41] *Grauman Company*, 87 NLRB 755 (1949).

[42] *Western, Inc.*, 93 NLRB 336 (1951).

[43] *Local 537, Teamsters (Lohman Sales Company)*, 132 NLRB 901 (1961); *Local 662, Electrical Workers (Middle South Broadcasting Company)*, 133 NLRB 1968 (1961); *Television & Radio Artists (Great Western Broadcasting Corporation)*, 134 NLRB 1617 (1961).

[44] *Local 848, Wholesale Delivery Drivers & Salesmen (Servette, Inc.)*, 133 NLRB 1501, 310 F. (2d) 659 (9th Cir., 1962) 377 U.S. 1964, p. 46.

[45] *Conway's Express*, 87 NLRB 972 (1949), affirmed, *Rabouin* v. *NLRB*, 195 F. (2d) 906 (2d Cir., 1952).

[46] *Local 1976, United Brotherhood of Carpenters (Sand Door & Plywood Company)*, 113 NLRB 1211 (1955), enforced *NLRB* v. *Local 1976*, 241 F. (2d) 147 (9th Cir., 1957), affirmed 357 U.S. 93 (1958).

[47] *United Brotherhood of Carpenters & Joiners* v. *NLRB*, 357 U.S. 93 (1958).

[48] *Brown* v. *Local No. 17, Amalgamated Lithographers of America (Employing Lithographers Division)*, 180 F. Supp. 294 (DCN, Calif.), 1960.

[49] *Meat & Highway Drivers, Local 710 (Wilson & Company)*, 143 NLRB 1221 (1964).

[50] 45 *Labor Relations Reporter* 132 (1959).

[51] *Ohio Valley Carpenters District Council (Cardinal Industries)*, 144 NLRB 91 (1963).

[52] *Construction, Production & Maintenance Laborers Union Local 383 (Colson & Stevens Construction Company)*, 137 NLRB 1650 (1963).

[53] *Ibid.*, 323 F. (2d) 422 (1964).

[54] *Building & Construction Trades Council of San Bernadino* v. *NLRB*, 328 F. (2d) 540 (1964).

[55] The proviso to Section 8 (b) (4) (B) reads: "Provided, that nothing contained in this clause (B) shall be construed to make unlawful, where not otherwise unlawful, any primary strike or primary picketing." See *International Association of Heat & Frost Insulators (Houston Insulation Contractors Association)*, 148 NLRB 866, sustained 386 U.S. 664 (1967).

[56] *Local 1332, ILA (Philadelphia Marine Trade Association)*, 151 NLRB 1447 (1965).

[57] *National Woodwork Manufacturers Association* v. *NLRB*, 386 U.S. 612 (1967).

[58] *Wall Street Journal*, June 26, 1972.

[59] *NLRB* v. *IBEW, Local 164*, 388 F. (2d) 105 (1968); *American Boiler Manufacturers Association* v. *NLRB*, 404 F. (2d) 547 (1968); *Beacon Castle Square Building Corporation* v. *NLRB*, 406 F. (2d) 188 (1969).

[60] *Carpenters, Local 742 (J. C. Simmons Company)*, 201 NLRB No. 8 (1973).

[61] *IBEW, Local 1186 (Pacific General Contractors)*, 192 NLRB No. 43 (1971).

[62] *Teamsters, Local 688 (Schnuck Markets)*, 193 NLRB No. 109 (1971).

[63] *NLRB* v. *Operating Engineers, Local 825*, 400 U.S. 297 (1971).

[64] *Bricklayers & Stone Masons, Local 8 (California Concrete Systems)*, 180 NLRB 43 (1969).

[65] *Houston Insulation Contractors Association*, 148 NLRB 866 (1966).

[66] *American Boiler Manufacturers Association*, 167 NLRB 602 (1967).

[67] *Wall Street Journal*, October 27, 1967.

State Picketing Policy
and the U.S. Supreme Court

18

Though we have considered in some detail the right of employees to picket under the Taft-Hartley Act, there is another feature of the law of picketing which warrants attention. This deals with the rights of the states to establish picketing policy either by legislation or through their courts. The crux of this problem is that the U.S. Constitution and its free-speech guarantees apply to all citizens of the United States. For this reason the United States Supreme Court has frequently tested state picketing policy in the light of the federal Constitution.

As this chapter demonstrates, the Court has not been wholly consistent in discharging this task. The chief reason for this is the Court's desire to accommodate a state policy as far as possible. Thus the Court has the difficult problem of viewing with sympathy state efforts to regulate picketing, but at the same time assuring that the standards of the federal Constitution are not breached by state action.

THE THORNHILL DOCTRINE: BASIC MEANING

In 1940 the Supreme Court of the United States handed down a picketing decision of momentous importance. It held that peaceful picketing is a form of free speech entitled to the protection of the federal Constitution. This doctrine at first seemed entirely different from the one reflecting the mature judgment of the Court that Congress and the states may regulate the use of the injunction in labor disputes. In the Norris–La Guardia cases, the Court held that the legislative branch of government may properly shield the picketing process from injunctions. It fully approved the limitation of the authority of the court in labor disputes, including those involving picketing. The 1940 innovation is that the free-speech guarantee of the Constitution operates to protect the peaceful picketing process under certain circumstances from the effect of antipicketing laws fashioned by either the legislative or judicial branches of government. Now the Court seemingly was not only prepared to approve legislative action calculated to give protection to picketing, but was ready to strike down legislation which endeavored to unduly forbid or to control picketing.

Picketing was identified with free speech by the Court in the celebrated *Thornhill* v. *Alabama* case.[1] The state of Alabama had passed a statute which outlawed all picketing. The statute did not distinguish between peaceful or violent picketing. It was not aimed merely at a particular form of picketing, such as the stranger or secondary boycott varieties. Rather the provisions of the law applied to the general picketing process, outlawing completely this form of union activity. Violators of the statute were subject to fines and imprisonment.

In striking down this statute, the Court declared that

> freedom of speech and of the press guaranteed by the Constitution embraces at least the liberty to discuss publicly and truthfully all matters of public concern without previous restraint or fear of subsequent punishment. . . . In the circumstances of our times the dissemination of information concerning the facts of a labor dispute must be regarded as within that area of free discussion that is guaranteed in the Constitution.

Here indeed was a most significant pronouncement! It operated to shed constitutional doubt on all legislative action calculated to control the peaceful picketing process. Actually, considerable misinterpretation of the meaning of the *Thornhill* decision resulted in the immediate belief that the Court meant to invalidate each and any federal or state action regulating peaceful picketing. No such conclusion was warranted by the *Thornhill* decision. The Court held that picketing is a form of free speech. It did not say, however, that all picketing, regardless of form and objective, would be protected by the guarantees of the Constitution. In fact, the Court declared in the *Thornhill* case:

> The right of employers and employees to conduct their economic affairs and to compete with others for a share in the products of industry are subject to modification or qualification in the interests of the society in which they exist. This is but an instance of the power of the State to set the limits of permissible contest open to industrial combatants. It does not follow that the states in dealing with the evils arising from industrial dispute may impair the effective exercise of the right to discuss freely industrial relations which are matters of public concern.

This statement appears clear enough. Thus the Court served notice that federal and state action restricting the picketing process must not infringe on the constitutional guarantee of free speech. At the same time it conceded that states have the right to regulate the peaceful picketing process. To grasp the understanding of subsequent picketing decisions of the Court, the basic meaning of the *Thornhill* doctrine must be kept in mind. In later cases the Court allowed the regulation of peaceful picketing. Such action is not inconsistent with *Thornhill* v. *Alabama* if one understands the fundamental limitations of the decision.

STRANGER PICKETING AND THE FREE-SPEECH
GUARANTEE

Subsequent to the *Thornhill* decision the Supreme Court held that picketing was protected by the constitutional guarantee to free speech in several other cases. The first of these, the *Swing* case, was decided in 1941.[2] It so happened that an AFL labor union operating in Illinois claimed jurisdiction over beauty shops. It attempted to organize a particular beauty shop. Failing in its efforts, the union picketed Swing's shop. The picket line was of the stranger variety; that is, in it were workers not employed by Swing. Displeased with these circumstances, Swing obtained an injunction from the Illinois courts which stamped out the picketing. The supreme court of the state upheld the injunction.

Upon review of the case, the Supreme Court of the United States declared that no court, state or federal, could suppress stranger picketing peacefully carried out. Such restraint violated the free-speech guarantees of the federal Constitution. The injunction restraining stranger picketing was invalid because

> a state cannot exclude workingmen from peacefully exercising the right of free communication by drawing the circle of economic competition between employers and workers so small as to contain only an employer and those directly employed by him. The interdependence of economic interest of all engaged under the same industry has become commonplace.

Thus in the *Swing* decision the Supreme Court shielded stranger picketing from the attack of legislative and court action. As a form of free speech, this type of picketing was privileged under the Constitution.

However, in 1957, the Supreme Court permitted the state of Wisconsin to enjoin peaceful stranger picketing contrary to its determined position of 1941.[3] In *Vogt* a union picketed a gravel pit for the express purpose of organizing the employees. The workers indicated they did not want to join the union and a lower court enjoined the union action. The action was held unlawful under a state law prohibiting peaceful picketing from coercing employers to force workers to join unions.

The U.S. Supreme Court ruled therefore that a state may place a statutory ban on peaceful picketing which conflicts with its public policy. Both state courts and their legislatures may constitutionally declare stranger picketing a violation of public policy. Seemingly, the injunction may be used every time stranger picketing occurs. All that is necessary is for a court to declare it illegal in cases before it and issue an injunction that specifically identifies the activity as contrary to public policy.

But, even in the absence of express legislative prohibition of picketing, state courts may take the initiative. The way is now paved for state courts dealing with cases under their jurisdictions to draw the circle of economic competition between employers and workers so small as to contain only an employer and those directly employed by him. Legislation at the state level would seemingly be required to control the courts in labor cases involved in intrastate commerce. They may also deal with cases rejected by administrative decree from coverage of the national labor laws. It will be recalled that this is permitted in accordance with the jurisdictional dollar guidelines of the NLRB.

It appeared for some time that specific enforcement of state public policy could lead to blanket prohibition of picketing, one situation at a time. Public policy need merely be established at the time a case reaches the court and specifically dealt with at that time. This direction in the high court's decisions seemed certain for a few years. Later in this chapter we shall see that this course was revised apparently in the quest for equity in establishing constitutional rights of all parties involved in labor disputes.

THE NEW YORK CASES: ABSENCE OF LABOR
DISPUTE NOT CONTROLLING

In 1942 and 1943 the Supreme Court again utilized the constitutional guarantee of free speech to afford protection to the picketing process. The locale of both these cases was the state of New York. The 1942 case, *Bakery & Pastry Drivers Union* v. *Wohl,* involved the picketing of a bakery drivers' union.[4] A number of employers of bakery wagon drivers engaged in activity calculated to decrease both their operating costs and the possibility of having to deal with unions. They wanted to avoid payment of social security taxes and workmen's compensation as well as liability insurance and vehicle upkeep. To accomplish this objective, they forced some drivers to drop out of the union and to purchase trucks which the employees were utilizing to make deliveries. The drivers were then expected to purchase the merchandise from their former employers and peddle the bakery goods on an independent basis. In effect, the tactics of the bakery owners made peddlers out of their employees. Experience soon proved that the "profits" which the newly created "businessmen" earned by this arrangement fell far below the amount they earned when they were mere "workers." Two of them, for example, earned about thirty-five dollars per week. In addition, they lost all protection of laws passed by Congress and the New York legislature calculated to protect the status of employees.

To prevent the spread of the peddler system, the bakery drivers' union conducted a widespread peaceful picketing campaign. The objective of the union was to stamp out this development before it undermined the economic standards of all the unionized employees. The union requested the peddlers to work only six days a week instead of seven and to hire an unemployed union member for the seventh day at wages of about six dollars to nine dollars per day. Obviously, the peddlers could not afford to agree to the demands of their former union. They scarcely earned enough on a seven-day week to get along. When the peddlers refused to comply, the union picketed the area of the bakeries where two of the peddlers (involved in the case) purchased their bakery goods. The picketing placards bore the names of these peddlers and highlighted in a true fashion the nature of the controversy. At times the union also ordered pickets to follow the trucks of the peddlers to induce customers not to buy from them. Actually, the peddlers felt the brunt of the union pressure, but the picketing tactics were fundamentally directed against the employers who for their own profit introduced the peddler system.

The 1943 case, *Cafeteria Employees Union* v. *Angelos,* involved the peaceful picketing of two restaurants by a labor organization composed of cafeteria workers.[5] The owners of the restaurants ran their establishments without any employees and were able to sell food at cheaper prices than the eating establishments hiring union employees. This was a situation which had to be rectified by the cafeteria workers' union lest the standards it had established in the organized restaurants be swept away. The objective of the picketing was to force the owners to hire union employees. The union appealed to the public to withhold patronage from the picketed restaurants.

In both of these cases New York courts issued injunctions stamping out the picketing. The New York Court of Appeals, the highest court of the state, upheld the injunctions. It ruled that the New York anti-injunction act, patterned after Norris–La Guardia, did not protect the picketing from the injunction. The court held that no "labor dispute" existed within the meaning of the statute; therefore the New York court could properly enjoin the picketing. The high court of New York rejected the union's argument that labor disputes did exist within the meaning of the state's anti-injunction statute.

Eventually, both cases were appealed to the Supreme Court of the United States. This Court did not quarrel with the state court's interpretation of the New York anti-injunction law. The Supreme Court of the United States respected the interpretation placed on state laws by the state judiciary. However, the Supreme Court reversed both of the state courts' decisions on the ground that the picketing of the two unions was protected by the federal Constitution's guarantee of free speech. The employees obtained protection from the fundamental document of the nation, though the state court felt that their picketing could be properly enjoined under state law. In short, the Supreme Court was not concerned with the manner in which the New York Court of Appeals construed the meaning of labor dispute for purposes of the state's anti-injunction law. It struck down the decisions because they infringed on guarantees contained in the federal Constitution.

The implications of the New York picketing cases were of crucial importance. The mere fact that a "labor dispute" prevailed under state law did not preclude the application of the free-speech guarantee to picketing. Once the Supreme Court holds the picketing to be protected by the Constitution, it is of no importance that under state law the activity can be restrained on the ground of the nonexistence of a labor dispute. Such picketing is protected under the immunities of free speech in the federal Constitution for, as the Court stated in the bakery drivers' case, "One need not be in a labor dispute as defined by state law to have a right under the Fourteenth Amendment to express a grievance in a labor matter unattended by violence, coercion, or conduct otherwise unlawful or oppressive." There is need to protect the union right to make known grievances to the public even if the cause is in accordance with law. The Court did not deny that states have the right to regulate peaceful picketing. It merely demonstrated its ability to decide when free speech is denied under the Fourteenth Amendment.

PEACEFUL PICKETING NOT PROTECTED BY THE GUARANTEE OF FREE SPEECH

Under certain circumstances the Supreme Court will not utilize the free-speech immunities to protect peaceful picketing from regulation by legislative and court action. Once again it must be stressed that this position of the Court is not inconsistent with the *Thornhill* doctrine. On the contrary, its refusal to hold all picketing beyond control supports the principle of the 1940 decision that the free-speech guarantee would not protect the picketing process under each and every circumstance that may arise.

Peaceful Picketing in a Context of Violence

On the same day that the Court handed down the *Swing* decision, it ruled the free-speech guarantee of the Constitution is not available to protect picketing carried on in a context of violence.[6] The Chicago Milk Wagon Drivers Union utilized violent tactics to prevent the Meadowmoor Dairies from utilizing the "vendor system" for the distribution of milk in the Chicago area. Under this system milk was sold by the dairy companies to vendors, operating their own trucks, who sold to retailers. The vendors departed from the working standards achieved by the union for its members as dairy employees. To force the company to abandon the vendor system, the union instituted a campaign of terror. It included window smashing, bombing, arson, wrecking of trucks, shootings, and beatings. This violence was directed against the Meadowmoor Dairies and the retail outlets which handled its products. As part of its general program, the union also employed peaceful picketing carried on in the vicinity of the stores handling Meadowmoor's products.

The Supreme Court of Illinois upheld an injunction which restrained all picketing conduct, peaceful or violent. All picketing, not merely the acts of violence, was enjoined. The milk wagon drivers' union appealed the case to the U.S. Supreme Court. The union argued that the state court imposed a blanket denial of picketing and contended further that the Illinois judiciary denied the exercise of the right to free speech when it enjoined the peaceful picketing activities.

The union's position was rejected by the Supreme Court. It held that peaceful acts of picketing when enmeshed with concurrent violent conduct can be properly enjoined. The Court took due care to distinguish the instant case from the *Thornhill* and *Carlson*[7] decisions. It declared, "We do not qualify the *Thornhill* and *Carlson* decisions. We affirm them. They involved statutes boldly forbidding all picketing near an employer's place of business. Entanglement with violence was expressly out of those cases." Thus peaceful picketing carried out in a general campaign of terror can be stamped out without violating the guarantee of free speech. Blanket injunctions may be issued to enjoin picketing undertaken in a context of violence.

In another case a union official's photographing of persons crossing a picket line was not deemed coercive conduct equivalent to threatening physical violence.[8] In the *Newell* case the Supreme Court referred to the free-speech doctrine of *Thornhill* in overturning a trial court decision that such photographing generated fear on the part of persons crossing the picket line that future violence would come to them. The context of violence was evidently not deemed sufficient to invoke the *Meadowmoor* doctrine as an exception to *Thornhill*.

In still another case, *Rainfair*, the Supreme Court was required to determine what is meant by Meadowmoor's context of violence for the purpose of enjoining all future picketing. The *Rainfair* case involved both peaceful picketing at a plant engaged in interstate commerce and a segregated group of strikers involved in violent action.[9] The employer obtained a blanket injunction in an Arkansas court outlawing all future picketing on the ground that violence was so enmeshed in peaceful picketing that it could not be free from violence.

The Supreme Court was not willing to permit the blanket enjoinment of all picketing. It found that the violence of the segregated group of strikers was not adequate justification for extending the injunction to the separate group of peaceful pickets. The state court was within its authority to specifically deal with illegal activity and that did not include a blanket stoppage of all picketing. Furthermore, even if the violent action had warranted enjoinment of all future picketing, it could not be permanently stopped by a state court. The reason is the NLRB preempts state courts from permanently enjoining any peaceful picketing unconnected with violence that is associated with some other group.

Thus, in the years after *Meadowmoor*, the Supreme Court has become more reluctant to permit blanket injunctions in cases involving peaceful picketing. There is greater reliance upon the *Thornhill* doctrine than seemed probable from the first few peaceful picketing cases immediately subsequent to its pronouncement.

The Area of the Industry

In 1942 the Supreme Court of the United States held that a state may confine peaceful picketing to the industry directly related to a labor dispute. This principle was established in *Carpenters & Joiners Union* v. *Ritter's Cafe*.[10] Even more than the *Meadowmoor* decision, the *Ritter* case demonstrates the fact that the legislative branch of government may regulate peaceful picketing. The carpenters' and painters' union of Houston peacefully picketed the restaurant owned by a Mr. Ritter. The union had no dispute with Ritter in his role as the proprietor of the café. No carpentry work was being performed at the restaurant at the time of the picketing. All of the restaurant employees were members of the Hotel and Restaurant Employees Union. There was no controversy between Ritter and his restaurant employees' union. Why then the picketing?

It so happened that Ritter made an arrangement with a contractor named Plaster for the construction of a building. The contract gave Plaster the right to make his own arrangements regarding the hiring of employees. He employed non-union carpenters and painters. The new building was being constructed about a mile and a half from the picketed café, and was wholly unconnected with the business of Ritter as a café proprietor.

The reason for picketing the café should now be clear. By damaging Ritter's restaurant business, the union hoped to force him to make arrangements for the employment of union men at the site of the business. The facts show that the picketing was very effective. Union truck drivers refused to cross the picket line or deliver food or other supplies to the restaurant. The restaurant workers' union out of sympathy with the carpenters' and painters' organizations called Ritter's employees out on strike. In short, the picketing resulted in a curtailment of 60 percent of Ritter's restaurant business.

The Texas judiciary held that peaceful picketing activities of the union were unlawful under state law. Accordingly, the union was enjoined from picketing Ritter's café. The injunction, however, neither forbade picketing elsewhere (including at the site of the new building under construction) nor communication of the fact of the dispute by any means other than the picketing of Ritter's restaurant.

Subsequently, the union appealed the matter to the Supreme Court of the United States. The union felt that its picketing activities were privileged under the free-speech guarantees of the federal Constitution. As such, state law could not be utilized to restrain the picketing of Ritter's café. It was not the task of the Supreme Court to determine whether or not the union in effect did violate Texas law. This question had already been answered in the affirmative by the Texas courts. As noted, the Supreme Court of the United States normally respects the construction which state courts place on state laws. This is a principle of constitutional law established early in the history of American jurisprudence. The problem facing the Supreme Court of the United States was to decide whether or not Texas law, as interpreted by the state judiciary, infringed on the free-speech guarantees of the Constitution.

The Court ruled that it did not. It held that free-speech immunities are not violated by a law which confines the peaceful picketing process to the industry directly involved in the dispute. Texas had the right to enjoin picketing of Ritter's restaurant because it was undertaken to win concessions in the construction industry. The union improperly picketed beyond the area of the industry involved in the basic dispute. In short, the legislative branch of government may restrict peaceful picketing to the area of the industry in which a labor dispute arises.

The *Ritter* decision was criticized.[11] The basis of objection to the Court was the free-speech decision of *Thornhill* v. *Alabama*. Such criticism was not warranted because the Court in the *Thornhill* decision did not state or imply that the legislative or judicial branch of government was without power to regulate peaceful picketing. It would have been inconsistent if the Court had ruled in *Thornhill* v. *Alabama* that all peaceful picketing, regardless of form or objective, was entitled to the protection of the free-speech immunity. The fact is, however, that the Court did no such thing. It carefully pointed out in the *Thornhill* case that the state has the power "to set the limits of permissible contest open to industrial combatants." Among others a state may restrict peaceful picketing by requiring that it be undertaken with (1) a reasonable number of pickets, (2) quietness, and (3) truthful placards. Also open ingress and egress to employer premises may be required along with suitable hours for picketing action. It may be found, for example, that a union's right to publicize a labor dispute is not impaired if it can picket only between the hours of 6:00 A.M. and 6:00 P.M.

Peaceful Picketing Which Violates a State's Antitrust Law

In 1949 the Court again reaffirmed the principle that a state may regulate the peaceful picketing process.[12] The State Supreme Court of Missouri found that picketing by a labor union violated the state's antitrust laws. Unlike the *Ritter* case, the picketing involved in the *Giboney* case took place in the area of the industry within which the labor dispute arose.

The Kansas City Ice and Coal Drivers Union undertook to organize all the peddlers of the city. The union claimed within its membership 160 of the 200 retail ice peddlers who drove their own trucks in selling ice from door to door in Kansas City. The objective of the union was to better the working conditions of all ice peddlers. However, most of the nonunion peddlers refused to join the organization.

To force them into the union, the organization attempted to obtain pledges from the Kansas City ice distributors not to sell ice to nonunion peddlers. It obtained such agreement from all but one ice company, the Empire Storage and Ice Company. It was determined to sell ice to union and nonunion peddlers alike. As a result the union picketed the premises of the company. Most of the truck drivers working for Empire's customers were members of the labor union. These union truck drivers refused to haul goods to or from Empire's place of business. Because of the picketing, Empire's business was reduced by about 85 percent. Faced with these circumstances, the company obtained an injunction under the provision of the state's antitrust laws to restrain the picketing.

The Supreme Court of Missouri held that the picketing was unlawful, and affirmed the injunction which stamped it out. The union appealed to the Supreme Court of the United States, claiming that its picketing activities were protected by the free-speech immunities of the federal Constitution. The Court rejected the union's position. It refused to apply the Constitution to shield the picketing from the application of the Missouri antitrust law. It pointed out that the picketing was part of an integrated plan calculated to violate a lawful purpose. Since it was unlawful in objective, the constitutional guarantee of free speech could not be employed to legalize the unlawful conduct. It declared that the pickets "were doing more than exercising a right of free speech or press. They were exercising their economic power together with that of their allies to compel Empire to abide by union rather than by state regulation of trade." Thus unions cannot utilize the constitutional guarantee of free speech to protect picketing undertaken to violate the provision of a state's antitrust law.

It is a long-established principle of American jurisprudence that legislative action should be regarded as valid unless it is so bad on its face that there is no mistaking its unconstitutionality. Few would disagree with the inherent value of such a principle. Congress and state legislatures should have the utmost freedom in the shaping of public policy. In the field of labor relations, the courts should be particularly careful to allow the widest latitude to shape policy. The fundamental philosophy of Holmes should not be ignored. Likewise, one is impressed with the wisdom of Brandeis when he declared:

> The condition developed in industry may be such that those engaged in it cannot continue their struggle without danger to the community. But it is not for judges to determine whether such conditions exist, nor is it their function to set the limits of permissible conduct and to declare the duties which the new situation demands. This is the function of the legislature which, while limiting individual and group rights to aggression and defense, may substitute processes of justice for the more primitive method of trial by combat.[13]

For many years the Supreme Court invalidated legislation passed by Congress and state legislatures calculated to improve the economic lot of the nation's workers. Statutes designed to protect the right to organize, to regulate the use of the injunction in labor disputes, and to impose minimum employment standards on industry failed to stand the test of constitutionality. These laws, however, are not prohibited by express provisions of the Constitution. The high court established their unconstitutionality only by resorting to their own ideas regarding how the economy should function. No provision of the Constitution denies to Congress or the states the right to pass legislation forbidding the discharge of a worker because of union activity. The Court therefore tends to permit the widest range of options to states when they deal with economic matters within their own jurisdictions.

In the case of antipicketing legislation, however, a different condition is attached. Specific constitutional provisions protect the right to free speech. Picketing transmits ideas, relays thoughts, and communicates concepts. As such, it falls within the embrace of the Constitution as a form of speech. Statutes which clearly and unmistakably suppress the picketing process transgress constitutional guarantees. Granting the unquestionable wisdom of a policy which allows the legislative arm of government wide freedom to determine the character of labor law, the fact remains that any statute, labor or otherwise, must necessarily fall if it is obviously prohibited by the express terms of the Constitution.

The Case of Gazzam. The greatest point of significance resulting from the *Giboney* case was that peaceful picketing is not protected if it seeks an objective that is illegal under a valid state law. The *Gazzam* decision was based on this declaration involving the state of Washington's "little Norris–La Guardia Act."[14] This law makes it illegal for an employer to coerce his employees in the designation of collective bargaining representatives.

A union organizer approached a small hotel operator and asked him to sign an agreement which would require his employees to join the labor organization. The request was refused; however, the employer did not interfere with the union's contacting of his workers. At a meeting of eleven workers with the union, nine voted against representation, one was neutral, and the other was not acceptable for membership. The union established a picket line to force the employer to yield to its demands. Since the hotel was small, it did not qualify for coverage under the National Labor Relations Act.

The employer filed a suit for damages and to obtain an injunction to halt picketing in a Washington court. The lower court granted the request. Subsequently, the Washington Supreme Court upheld the trial court decision. The U.S. Supreme Court was faced with the question of whether the First and Fourteenth Amendments permit a state to enjoin peaceful picketing on the basis of its own state policy.

The Court, as mentioned, relied upon the *Giboney* case to uphold the Washington Supreme Court. Prevention of peaceful picketing was held permissible if the injunction is "limited to the wrong being perpetrated, namely, 'an abusive exercise of the right to picket.'" Workers or organizations of workers have no more right to violate public policy than does the judiciary have a right to interfere with certain worker rights. A specific violation of state law was enjoined and there was no blanket attempt to ban all peaceful picketing. Thus specific violations of peaceful picketing are enjoinable by injunctive use, but blanket restrictions constitute an undue violation of constitutional rights to free speech. The ability of states to regulate peaceful picketing is not restricted to legislation, but may be accomplished through common law.

Peaceful Picketing in Violation of Common Law

In 1950 the high court upheld the right of state courts to restrict peaceful picketing in violation of its public policy as established by common law.[15] A significant deviation was made from *Thornhill* in the *Hughes* case which involved picketing of a grocery store by an association of blacks. The blacks requested the store to hire clerks of their race in proportion to the percentage that patronized the store. The store refused to honor the request, desiring to set hiring ratios by collective bargaining with the union with which it contracted. The black group picketed the Lucky Store and the operator went to court to obtain an injunction. It was granted but peaceful picketing continued. The California Supreme Court upheld the trial court decision to issue a limited injunction covering a specific violation.

The U.S. Supreme Court upheld the decision of the California courts. It held that

> the fact that California's policy is expressed by the judicial organ of the state rather than by the legislature we have repeatedly ruled to be immaterial.

It is apparent that the high court permitted the California courts to establish their own policy to deal with peaceful picketing in a labor dispute. The *Giboney* case was used as a precedent for permitting the judges to behave as they did. But the *Swing* case was ignored. It will be recalled that it was established in this case that stranger picketing was protected by the federal Constitution. Evidently, hiring on the basis of quotas set by a union dominated by whites was permissible but blacks could not picket peaceably to eliminate discrimination in hiring.[16] Nevertheless, judges were commissioned by the high court to set limits on peaceful picketing in accordance with their own views regarding how the economy should function.

Back to Court Pronouncement of Illegal Union Picketing Objectives?

Highly regarded legal scholars were concerned with the seeming return of the U.S. Supreme Court to its pre-1933 picketing doctrines.[17] There is no doubt that the courts have a constitutional responsibility to deal with changing socioeconomic problems as they come before them. By 1950 the country had not yet readjusted to union behavior that many citizens considered economically abusive during and immediately after World War II. Perhaps the courts are often more in tune with current sentiment than the other two branches of government and constitutionally have authority to deal with problems that their coequals are too slow to recognize. It is certain that many problems which occur in the state of New York are not necessarily pressing in the states of Indiana and Arizona. The Supreme Court seemed almost determined in 1950 to uphold local courts when they were dealing with local policy of their own making. The particular reason for this remains open for speculation.

Two cases with identical issues were decided by the high court; both involved the policy of state of Washington courts. Hanke and Cline were self-employed used-car dealers in Seattle, Washington.[18] Both dealers were picketed by different unions because they refused to observe the same hours of operation observed by organized dealers. Cline was requested additionally to hire a union member as salesman and to compensate him with 7 percent of gross sales. Refusal to agree resulted in a loss of sales from peaceful picketing. The Washington Supreme Court upheld a lower court's order of a permanent injunction.

The two unions were clearly engaged in primary and not secondary picketing. The courts under common law have traditionally attempted to distinguish between the two in issuing injunctions. The Washington courts did not do so.

The high court seemed uneasy in upholding the Washington Supreme Court decision. It was not only forced to review its rule in *Hughes* permitting the judiciary to proclaim state policy, but it had to go further and stated:

> We cannot conclude that Washington, in holding the picketing in these cases to be for an unlawful object, has struck a balance so inconsistent with rooted traditions of a free people that it must be found an unconstitutional choice.... Nor does the Fourteenth Amendment require prohibition by Washington also of voluntary acquiescence in the demands of the union in order that it may choose to prohibit the right to secure submission through picketing. In abstaining from interference with such voluntary agreements a state may rely on self-interest. In any event, it is not for this Court to question a State's judgment in regulating only where an evil seems to it most conspicuous.

The most obvious interpretation of *Hanke* and *Cline* is that the state courts were turned loose to decide once again the desirability of union objectives sought through peaceful picketing. If, for example, judges consider the picketing of small employers an unjustifiable weapon for the purpose of forcing compliance with union standards in a particular area, they may stop it when requested to do so. The decision moved dangerously close to bringing about a new era of conflict between unions and the judiciary regarding what economic activity is legal and what is illegal.

A state may not, however, regulate peaceful picketing in a field where the federal government has legislated.[19] This issue was dealt with in two separate cases involving a Wisconsin law prohibiting strikes by unions representing employees in public utilities. The state employment relations board obtained injunctions to perpetually forbid work stoppages after unions went out on strike. The U.S. Supreme Court refused to allow the injunction because the National Labor Relations Act covers public utilities. A state is forbidden to regulate when Congress establishes federal law covering the same field. Thus the marked decline of the *Thornhill* free-speech doctrine has greater relevance under state than under federal jurisdiction. A considerable body of federal legislation has been passed which restricts the freedom of the courts to deal with peaceful picketing. Many states, however, do not have adequate legislation in the labor field and for this reason their courts have considerable freedom to establish public policy.

FREE-SPEECH AND PRIVATE PROPERTY RIGHTS

In 1967 the Supreme Court was faced with a major issue involving state public policy and the right to picket peaceably.[20] The *Logan Valley Plaza* case was first presented to the Blair County, Pennsylvania, Court of Common Pleas. A union was engaged in a labor dispute with a nonunion supermarket. Peaceful picketing was initiated on privately owned shopping center premises. This activity was undertaken by six individuals and was restricted almost entirely to the parcel pickup area immediately adjacent to a supermarket with whom the dispute existed. The signs publicized that the market was nonunion and that wages and fringe benefits were substandard. There was no violence or threats involved in the action.

A trial court issued an injunction upon the request of the supermarket owner which prohibited the union from picketing and trespassing on private property. Peaceful picketing was not enjoined since the union still had the option of establishing its picket lines on public property off the shopping center premises. The union argued that the free-speech provision guaranteed by the First Amendment to the Constitution gave it the right to picket on shopping center grounds. The Pennsylvania Supreme Court denied this defense and upheld the injunction on the ground that state law prohibited trespassing on private property.

The U.S. Supreme Court reversed the Pennsylvania court. It held that owners of private property have the right to establish reasonable rules governing free-speech rights on private property. Regulations governing free speech on private property may be made through injunctions issued by state courts. However, limits were placed on the right of private property owners to restrict unions from peaceful picketing during labor disputes.

Absolute restriction of picketing on private property open to the public was held to infringe on that right. The Court distinguished between a private home and private property that is open and accessible to the public. Thus state rules regarding trespass do not apply to property used for business because the right of privacy is clearly not an issue.

The Court in establishing guidelines indicated that the free-speech rights may be subject to alteration if private property owners assert that peaceful picketing restrictions are necessary to protect normal business operations. No such evidence was presented in the *Logan Valley Plaza* case. Thus private shopping centers do not have access to the usual private property rights of homeowners to restrict normal union activities. In this regard the Court stated:

> The more an owner, for his advantage, opens up his property for use by the public in general, the more do his rights become circumscribed by the statutory and constitutional rights of those who use it.

State policy may not be used to place a blanket policy against all picketing. In this regard the *Logan Valley Plaza* case is consistent with *Gazzam*, *Vogt*, and *Hughes*. However, it is inconsistent in that the Supreme Court has questioned the specific prohibition of peaceful picketing in accordance with state policy which it had vowed not to do in *Hughes*, *Hanke*, *Cline*, *Gazzam*, and *Vogt*. However, in *Taggart* v. *Weinacker*, decided in 1970, Chief Justice Burger in an unusual concurring opinion to dismiss the case held the view that Congress has never undertaken to alter the power of states to protect private property.[21] It gave insight into the direction the Chief Justice would attempt to lead the court in the confused area of state and federal control over the right of unions to picket. The issue centers on union rights to free speech and employer rights to protect private property from trespass.

One step in the direction of giving states greater authority to control union picketing came in *Atlantic Coast Line*.[22] In a 5–2 decision, it was decided that a federal court does not have inherent power to enjoin state court proceedings merely because those proceedings interfere with a protected federal right. The Supreme Court relied on a 1793 law to hold that the lower federal courts cannot interfere with the state courts' proceedings. The only legal situations in which a lower federal court may enjoin a state court are to protect its judgments. When state and federal courts have concurrent jurisdiction, such as picketing rights, a party can simultaneously pursue claims in both court systems. Then if a state court issues an injunction to halt union picketing, a union must appeal through the state court system and ultimately to the U.S.

Supreme Court. Lower federal courts cannot directly review the decisions of state courts in such matters.

Essentially, the high court will now permit greater authority of state courts in the area of picketing if it is for the purpose of protecting the private property rights of employers from trespass. The National Labor Relations Act barred any court from enjoining peaceful picketing provided it was not aimed at an illegal object. The basic problem with *Atlantic Coast* is that it opened up permission for state courts to interfere with the right to picket when union activity is arguably protected by federal law. Unions may incur a great deal of damage before the Supreme Court resolves any state–federal conflict in picketing cases because of the appeals route unions must follow to obtain relief from state injunctions. *Logan Valley Plaza* has not been overruled by the high court, but some of its impact has been dampened by subsequent decisions.

In 1972, the Court held in *Lloyd Corp., Ltd.*, that nonemployees had access to a private parking lot only if a union had no other means to reach employees or if nonunion forces were free to use the lot.[23] The Supreme Court decided *Central Hardware Company* concurrently with *Lloyd*.[24] The high court went back to *NLRB* v. *Babcock & Wilcox*[25] as the precedent to rule on union organizational rights in contrast to employer property rights. In *Central Hardware*, the company had a no-solicitation rule against nonemployees on company property and ordered union organizers from its parking lots. The Board relied on *Logan Valley* to order the company to permit solicitation on Central Hardware's parking lots. The order was enforced by the court of appeals, and the Supreme Court agreed to review the decision. Relying on its *Babcock* decision, the Court remanded the case to the circuit court of appeals to determine if there was "no reasonable means of communication with employees . . . other than solicitation in Central Hardware's parking lots." In essence, the Court was trying to balance union organizational rights with employer property rights.

The *Lloyd* and *Central Hardware* cases make it legal for a retail merchant or shopping center owner to prohibit speech or organizational activity in a shopping center or parking lot under three circumstances. Prohibition may occur (1) if the activity is not directly related in its purpose to the use to which the store or the shopping center property is being put; (2) if other reasonable opportunities to communicate with the intended audience are available; and (3) if the rule prohibiting such activity has been enforced without discrimination.

The Board concluded on the basis of *Central Hardware* that a store manager was lawfully protecting his employer's property rights when he caused the arrest of nonemployee organizers who were picketing and passing out handbills in a private shopping center parking lot.[26] Thus, unions can expect less sympathy from the judiciary and the NLRB regarding the right to picket when employers make an issue of it on the basis of private property rights. The reason for this is that the Supreme Court redrew the line between property rights and free speech rights, with the result that *Logan Valley* was reinterpreted though not actually overruled.

SUMMARY

The U.S. Supreme Court attempts to yield as much authority as possible to state jurisdictions to establish policies that are peculiar to their own philosophies.

The federal system of government makes it difficult for the Court to articulate an unchanging body of law in a category as complicated as that which deals with labor disputes. This means, however, that the free-speech concept pronounced in the *Thornhill* case has no definitive limits or contents. Those skilled in the law have difficulties in understanding the free-speech protection of picketing and certainly have not defined it sufficiently to facilitate the understanding of others.

Peaceful picketing obviously is not exactly synonymous with free speech. This was made clear by Justice Douglas in the *Wohl* case when he stated that

> picketing by an organized group is more than free speech, since it involves patrol of a particular locality and since the very presence of a picket line may induce action of one kind or another quite irrespective of the nature of ideas which are being disseminated. [27]

It is obvious therefore that the Supreme Court has retreated somewhat from the *Thornhill* doctrine set forth in 1941. The chain of picketing cases since *Thornhill* makes it clear that the highest tribunal in the country continues to struggle with the problem of foregoing judicial legislation in order not to take exclusive control over matters that are of considerable local concern. This problem was best stated by Justice Frankfurter in the *Vogt* case when he wrote:

> It is inherent in the concept embodied in the Due Process Clause that its scope be determined by a gradual process of judicial inclusion and exclusion.

The process of gradual inclusion and exclusion is apparently the course of action that continues to dominate picketing cases reaching the Supreme Court. Precise definitions and limitations may not be logically set forth all at once.

NOTES

[1] 310 U.S. 88 (1940).

[2] *AFL* v. *Swing*, 312 U.S. 321 (1941).

[3] *International Brotherhood of Teamsters, Local 695, AFL* v. *Vogt, Inc.*, 354 U.S. 284 (1957).

[4] 315 U.S. 769 (1942).

[5] *Cafeteria Employees' Union* v. *Angelos*, 320 U.S. 293 (1943).

[6] *Milk Wagon Drivers' Union* v. *Meadowmoor Dairies, Inc.*, 312 U.S. 287 (1941).

[7] The Supreme Court decided the *Carlson* case (*Carlson* v. *California*, 310 U.S. 106) on the same day on which it handed down its ruling in the *Thornhill* case. In the *Carlson* case the court invalidated an antipicketing ordinance of Shasta County, California.

[8] *Chauffeurs, Teamsters & Helpers Local Union 795* v. *Richard Newell, d/b/a El Dorado Dairy*, 356 U.S. 341 (1958).

[9] *James E. Youngdahl* v. *Rainfair, Inc.*, 335 U.S. 131 (1957).

[10] 315 U.S. 722 (1942).

[11] For example, see Charles O. Gregory, *Labor and the Law* (New York: W. W. Norton & Company, Inc., 1946), pp. 357–362. See also International Juridical Association, *Monthly Bulletin*, XI (1942), 1–6.

[12] *Giboney v. Empire Storage & Ice Company*, 336 U.S. 490 (1949).

[13] *Duplex Printing Press Company v. Deering*, 254 U.S. 443 (1921).

[14] *Building Service Employees' Union v. Gazzam*, 339 U.S. 532 (1950).

[15] *Hughes v. Superior Court of the State of California*, 339 U.S. 460 (1950).

[16] Charles O. Gregory, *Labor and the Law*, 2nd. ed. (New York: W. W. Norton & Company, Inc., 1961), pp. 324–325.

[17] *Ibid.*, pp. 325–329.

[18] *International Brotherhood of Teamsters, Local 309 v. Hanke; Automobile Drivers & Demonstrators Local 882 v. Cline*, 339 U.S. 470 (1949).

[19] *Amalgamated Association of Street, Electric Railway & Motor Coach Employees of America, Division 998 v. Wisconsin Employment Relations Board; United Gas, Coke & Chemical Workers of America, CIO v. Wisconsin Employment Relations Board*, 340 U.S. 383 (1951).

[20] *Amalgamated Food Employees Union Local 590 v. Logan Valley Plaza, Inc.*, 391 U.S. 308 (1967).

[21] *Taggart v. Weinacker*, 397 U.S. 223 (1970).

[22] *Atlantic Coastline Railroad Company v. Locomotive Engineers*, U.S. Sup. Ct., No. 477 (June 8, 1970).

[23] *Lloyd Corporation, Ltd. v. Tanner*, 407 U.S. 551 (1972).

[24] *Central Hardware Company v. NLRB*, 407 U.S. 539 (1972).

[25] *NLRB v. Babcock & Wilcox Company*, 351 U.S. 105 (1956).

[26] *S. E. Nichols of Ohio, Inc.*, 200 NLRB No. 161 (1973).

[27] *Bakery & Pastry Drivers & Helpers Local, etc. v. Wohl*, 315 U.S. 769 (1940).

National Emergency Labor Disputes 19

CHARACTERISTICS OF
NATIONAL EMERGENCY DISPUTES

Strikes vary in their effect on the general public. A nationwide strike in the steel industry may cause more public concern than a work stoppage in a section of the garment industry. The effective functioning of the national economy may depend on the continuous operation of the nation's critical industries such as coal, oil, steel, ocean shipping, and transportation. Extensive strikes, however, in these industries may or may not imperil the nation's health and safety.

Widespread union organization of the nation's critical industries focused attention on the problem of national emergency strikes just after World War II. The public viewed unions as having the power to shut down the nation's vital industries. As a result Congress sought to protect the nation from such strikes by enacting the Taft-Hartley Act. Indeed, a fundamental aspect of this statute involves the procedures by which national emergency strikes are to be controlled. Such an attempt immediately raised fundamental questions. Are there strikes which actually constitute threats to the national health and safety? How effective are the national emergency strike provisions of Taft-Hartley? Are there alternative procedures available for the control of national emergency strikes?

This chapter deals with the economic effect of strikes in general industry, historical attempts to control strikes, legislation dealing with emergency disputes under Taft-Hartley, Railway Labor Act provisions, and alternatives that may be available to replace current laws. A national emergency dispute may be simply defined as a work stoppage that jeopardizes the health and safety of the general public. No general agreement exists on a precise workable definition of such disputes; however, broadly outlined procedures have been suggested from time to time to deal with national emergency disputes however they are defined.

DIFFICULTIES IN IDENTIFYING EMERGENCY DISPUTES

It is easier to name the nation's critical industries and define a national emergency strike than to spell out the circumstances which indicate that a strike imperils the nation's health and safety. In some of the critical industries a national emergency does not arise simultaneously with a strike. Stockpiles of coal and steel, for example, invariably exist at any one time. Stockpiles cushion the public for a time from the shock of nationwide strikes involving the critical industries. On the other hand, strikes in critical service industries, such as railroads, might result in a national emergency coincident with the work stoppage. Even here, however, the result may be more of an inconvenience to the public than a threat to the national health and safety.

Actually, there are no statistical or infallible rules to follow in the determination of national emergency strikes. The issue is much too complex for such a simple solution. However, certain criteria may be referred to in the determination of whether or not a strike is of national emergency proportions. The status of existing stockpiles may be taken into account. Vanishing stocks of critical items might at least indicate that a strike approaches a national emergency stage. The condition of the industries that depend on the struck product for their operation is another standard. If inadequate stockpiling is present among firms using a particular good as an import, for example, a work stoppage in a key industry may force shutdowns among firms not directly involved in the labor dispute. Such an assessment is difficult to make in the short period of time available to a President when these decisions are necessary.

An industry affected by a strike may supply a product or service essential to the personal comfort of the public. Coal and rail service may fall within this category. Thus the effect of a strike on the personal comfort of the general public is still another reference point in the determination of national emergency strikes. At a certain point during a strike involving a critical item, mere public *inconvenience* turns into public *suffering*. A national emergency does not exist when people do not have all the coal they would like to burn; this condition involves public inconvenience. However, the safety and health of the nation are imperiled when the people have little or no coal to warm their homes, schools, and hospitals. Consequently, the personal-comfort standard is perfectly valid provided a distinction is drawn between public inconvenience and a threat to national health and safety. Several studies have been undertaken in efforts to determine whether or not national emergencies have ever actually resulted from strikes and, if so, to what extent. A review of a few of these studies is appropriate before discussing the specific provisions for dealing with national emergency strikes.

The dilemma facing the public is that it is made fully aware of the strikes that stem from the collective bargaining process, but is less informed of the essentially peaceful character of the total process. The basic reason for this circumstance involves the relative newsworthiness of strikes as compared to the instances of industrial peace.

ECONOMIC EFFECT OF STRIKES

Contrary to public impression, the collective bargaining process in the over-whelming majority of cases results in the peaceful settlement of labor disputes. In 1946 the nation experienced the most serious strike wave in its history. Still, in that year, marked by significant postwar economic readjustments, there were about nine labor contracts renewed or revised peacefully for every one that resulted in a strike. The public was informed of the 4,985 work stoppages. What the public did not know, however, was that about forty-five thousand contracts were rewritten in whole or in part in 1946 without work stoppages. In 1968 there were a total of 4,950 work stoppages resulting in only 0.27 percent of total working time lost as a consequence. In total stoppages the record of 1946 was only slightly higher than 1968, and even this was the highest since 1953. The 1968 percent of total working time lost for the year was the highest since 1959 when it was 0.50.[1] In aggregate terms the impact of strikes at the close of the 1960s is less than it was at the close of World War II. Even so the public appears to remain unwilling to accept much inconvenience from work stoppages. It may well be that the inconveniences are more imagined than real since the mere possibility of them is enough to threaten the normal preference patterns of a significant proportion of the adult population. If the period 1933–1948 is considered, omitting 1946, a thoroughly abnormal year, the record of industrial peace under collective bargaining seems impressive. In this period the man-days of production lost due to strikes averaged 15 million per year. This amounted to approximately one-half of 1 percent of the man-days worked during this span of years. It is interesting to note that the man-days lost to strikes from 1940 to 1947 were less than the loss from work injuries on the job. Man-days of production lost from work injuries averaged 45 million per year. The average annual loss from strikes was 15 million.[2] Even so, the strike record of 1946 prompted Congress to include provisions to deal with strikes viewed by the President as threats to the national health and safety. After some experience with the law, several observers of the economy studied the impact of strikes in certain industries in an effort to evaluate the Taft-Hartley provisions.

Bituminous Coal Studies. C. Lawrence Christenson examined the bituminous coal industry in two separate studies. In one study it was shown that most output of coal supposedly lost due to strikes from 1933 to 1950 was offset before and after the stoppages.[3] This was possible because of excess capacity in the industry. Production of coal was moved from one operating period to another. The timing of production was shifted in two ways to offset the loss of production due to strikes. The one was anticipatory, the other was retroactive. That is, production was increased before strikes in anticipation of stoppages as well as afterward to catch up on any orders that may have been unfilled. It was also concluded that output foregone might be totally and immediately neutralized simply by a shifting of orders from firms involved in the dispute to firms not on strike. The rise of unionism in the industry, however, tended to weaken the transfer of orders from union to nonunion firms, thus spreading disputes over a larger area.

The same author in a 1955 study analyzed the impact of strikes on coal consumption.[4] Three consumer groups were classified in accordance with (1) purpose of use,

(2) availability of supplies for use, and (3) continuity of use. It was found that over 85 percent of the time, the strikes that occurred over two decades actually coincided with either seasonally falling demand for coal or a business recession. No evidence was found to support the contention that the steel industry, the general public, or other users such as the utilities were forced to curtail production because of inadequate coal supplies. A part of the reason was stockpiling by the individual companies, but the railroads were also important. They increased reserves sharply prior to the major disputes. This enabled them to continue deliveries once strikes went into effect.

Still another study of the bituminous coal industry set forth three economic tests for defining the term *national emergency*.[5] These were: "First, the strike must have an actual as distinguished from a potential effect; second, it must impose hardship rather than inconvenience; and, finally, its impact must be national rather than local." These tests were compared to their findings obtained from an analysis of the ten coal strikes that took place during the period 1937–1950. Not only did they analyze coal data, but they also studied output trends of the industry's major customers. It was then concluded that "none of the ten strikes studied created a national emergency." However, the two strikes that occurred in 1946 and 1949–1950 approached the emergency stage.[6]

Other Studies. Fifty-one highly unionized industries were studied by another observer to evaluate their national emergency potential.[7] The working definition of a national emergency was the same as the economic tests just mentioned.[8] The potential for creating a crisis when strikes occur was evaluated in terms of six tests. These were:

1. The industry must be highly unionized.
2. Its product or service must be essential.
3. It must have a national product market.
4. Its employees must be represented by a single labor organization, by several unions whose strike policies are coordinated, or by one or more craft organizations with power to shut down the industry.
5. Bargaining must be on an industry-wide basis in fact or in effect.
6. The collective bargaining agreements in the industry must expire on the same date.[9]

The author applied the tests just listed and concluded that

> only three of fifty-one highly unionized industries in the United States have a national emergency potential: coal, steel, and railroads. In the nine years following World War II there was a total of eight nationwide strikes in these industries— four in coal, three in steel, and one in railways. By applying the criteria of a national emergency . . . two of the eight (one steel and one railroad) were emergencies, four (three coal and one steel) were serious but failed to satisfy the criteria, and two (one coal and one steel) caused little inconvenience. The results leave little doubt that the national emergency problem, in so far as it is economic in character, has been much exaggerated.[10]

Several other studies have been conducted dealing with such industries as steel and public utilities.[11] Strikes in these industries were not deemed as constituting national emergencies. The Livernash study of the impact of steel strikes concluded that the economic effects "are usually seriously exaggerated." Similar to the Christenson study, it was found that excess capacity was an important factor to be considered in making any final judgment. An assessment of production foregone must be viewed "over a time span that encompasses a period prior to the strike, the period of the strike, and a period long enough following the strike to permit restoration of inventory." The secondary effects also must be viewed in terms of "inventory accumulation at several stages beyond basic steel itself." In these terms it was concluded that strikes generally can last much longer than is often believed before the economy is impaired.

Most studies that attempt to evaluate the effects of particular work stoppages reveal the difficulties associated with such tasks.[12] The major difficulty of assessing the impact of emergency strikes on the economy is the inability to find an invariant definition for emergency disputes. The lack of a standard leaves the question of legislative need open to continued debate. The provisions of the Taft-Hartley and the Railway Labor Acts and the use of them make it clear that the public continues with its concern about strikes in key industries. It is to an examination of these provisions that we now turn.

TAFT-HARTLEY PROCEDURES

Sections 206 through 210 of the Act provide for government intervention in cases that can be interpreted as affecting the national health and safety. If the President of the United States believes that a threatened or actual strike affects "an entire industry or a substantial part thereof" in such a way as to "imperil the national health or safety," he is empowered to take certain carefully delineated action. There are several steps to the action that may be taken if all legal measures in the Act are implemented.

Appointment of Board of Inquiry

The President of the United States is required to appoint a board of inquiry before he may proceed to deal with a situation that he feels will imperil the national health and safety. Since 1947 a board has been assembled on thirty occasions. The board, composed of qualified and disinterested parties, must be given the opportunity to investigate the dispute. After conducting the investigation, it is required to submit a report to the President; this report is submitted in writing and within a period of time determined by the Chief Executive. The board is to find out and report the facts of the dispute. It is allowed subpoena authority and can thus compel the appearance of witnesses. It cannot, however, make recommendations for a settlement. National emergency measures may not be taken by a President without use of the board.

The very fact that a board of inquiry is required procedure, however, has received criticism. If a strike or threat of it would actually threaten the national health and safety, the period of time required to investigate and report the findings could result in serious consequences. The President is unable to respond as promptly to the threat as may be called for under emergency conditions.[13] It should also be recognized that the board has insufficient time to uncover all the information needed to support a decision to forego or to proceed with use of the national emergency provisions.

The board of inquiry is also restricted in what it may report to the President. As mentioned, it is unable to provide recommendations from its findings. This may be a weakness in that the publication of recommendations could place public pressure on the parties to bargain within a particular framework whereby an acceptable solution could be found in a short period of time.

Neither does a board of inquiry have mediation authority. It appears that the framers of Taft-Hartley were concerned with the compulsory arbitration implication of such power.[14] The drawing of public attention to the mediation of disputes could have extended board power to approach that of binding arbitration of collective bargaining issues. Consequently, only the Federal Mediation and Conciliation Service has authority to mediate such disputes. The board of inquiry was viewed by Congress merely as a device for structuring public opinion. Public opinion was to be the force for effecting settlement. However, there have been but four occasions when the board has placed blame for a labor dispute on only one party to the proceedings. These have fallen exclusively on the coal and maritime industries.[15] Usually, the diverse positions of the parties are spelled out in the board's report, but no attempt is made to identify a "guilty party." Failure to attach some blame may have the effect of dampening public opinion and in turn decreasing pressure on a single party for settlement.

It has been recognized, however, that some boards have played a mediation role and have been successful. This occurred, for example, in the 1961 maritime industry dispute upon request of President John F. Kennedy. The same was done by the 1959 Basic Steel Industry Dispute Board under the chairmanship of George W. Taylor.[16] Other board mediation activities are credited with settling the 1962–1963 longshoremen's dispute and the 1967 Avco-UAW dispute.

Some other negative results are attributed to the very existence of boards of inquiry. One is that the bargaining parties relax their efforts to reach a settlement once a board has been appointed. Still another is the lack of respect held for such bodies by bargaining agents of labor and management. In short, the appointment of boards of inquiry before strikes actually occur may lead to a decline in efforts to reach agreement before a strike deadline.

As the law now stands, boards of inquiry may not be as effective as they could be. Criticism of board authority to deal effectively with bargaining parties is widespread. It is suggested that frequent use of Taft-Hartley machinery should be avoided.

After the Board Reports to the President

After the board of inquiry reports its findings, the President may decide the situation does not warrant intervention. Alternatively, he may direct the Attorney General of the United States to petition any U.S. district court having jurisdiction of the parties to enjoin a strike or lockout. An injunction may be issued for an eighty-day period.[17]

A district court is under no obligation to respond to the request for an injunction. In November, 1971, a Federal District Court refused to grant an 80-day injunction request for the first time.[18] The court reviewed the facts presented to it and held that the Port of Chicago did not handle sufficient volume to fulfill the Congressional intent that the dispute must affect ". . . an entire industry or a substantial part thereof . . ." and that the national health or safety had not been imperiled. It was concluded that the injunction request was made solely on an economic basis totally devoid of any threat to national defense or any war effort as such. With this single exception, carved out by a district court judge, no other federal court has denied an injunction requested by a President through his Attorney General.

On four occasions injunctions were not requested after receipt of board-of-inquiry reports. These involved the packing, telephone, and bituminous coal disputes of 1948 and the atomic energy dispute of 1954. President Truman declined to proceed with the Taft-Hartley provisions on three occasions and President Eisenhower declined to do so on only one. In total, Truman appointed ten boards of inquiry; Eisenhower, seven; Kennedy, six; Johnson, five; and Nixon, two. These presidents called for eighty-day injunctions on twenty-six occasions. On two of the twenty-six occasions, injunctions were requested from three different district courts.

During the eighty-day period the injunction is in force, the parties are required to continue to bargain in good faith, making every effort to adjust and settle their differences. They are assisted by the Federal Mediation and Conciliation Service. In five cases injunctions have been requested before strikes actually occurred. In a few instances, settlement was not reached until after the 80-day injunction period, but without a strike. In six other cases, all of which involved the maritime industry, some agreements were reached during the injunction period and some not until the injunction was lifted. On the west coast in 1972, the longshoremen struck after the 80-day injunction period. Congress passed special legislation in that year that would have required workers to return while a special arbitration board resolved the dispute if the parties failed to agree by a given date. An agreement was reached. (In total, six strikes occurred after the 80-day injunction period expired under the Taft-Hartley procedures.) This special legislation to resolve the dispute was the first time such action was taken by Congress, although President Truman requested seizure authority in 1950 after the coal industry failed to settle. Congress did not have to act on the coal dispute because of settlement, and the 1972 legislation never took effect because of agreement in longshoring before the date assigned by legislation.

The board of inquiry is reconvened by the President when an injunction is granted. If a settlement is not reached at the end of sixty days, the board is required to make a second public report to the President. This report does not carry with it recommendations for settlement. It includes the current status of the dispute, the positions of the parties, and "the employer's last offer of settlement."

Between the sixtieth and seventy-fifth day, the National Labor Relations Board is required to poll the employees to find out if they will accept the last offer of the employer. The results of the election are certified to the Attorney General within five days. By the close of eighty days the Attorney General must ask the federal court to dissolve the injunction. When the request is granted, the President makes a report of the entire proceedings to Congress together with any requests for legislation he may desire to make. Unless Congress acts, a strike may begin or resume because the emergency provisions of Taft-Hartley have been exhausted.

EXPERIENCES WITH TAFT-HARTLEY ACT
NATIONAL EMERGENCY PROVISIONS
1947–1974

Board of Inquiry Number and Dates	Dispute	President	Injunction Issued	Number Per Board	Employer Final Offer Vote	Strike Before Injunction	Strike After Injunction	Settlement Reached During Injunction
1. 1948	Atomic Energy	Truman	Yes	1	Rejected	No	No	
2. 1948	Meatpacking	Truman	No		No Vote	No		
3. 1948	Bituminous—Coal	Truman	Yes	1	No Vote	Yes	No	Yes
4. 1948	Telephone	Truman	No		No Vote	No	No	
5. 1948	Maritime Industry	Truman	Yes	3	Rejected	No	Pacific Coast	Except Pacific Coast
6. 1948	Bituminous—Coal	Truman	No		No Vote	No		
7. 1948	Dockworkers	Truman	Yes	1	Rejected	No	Yes	No
8. 1949–50	Bituminous—Coal	Truman	Yes	1	No Vote	Yes	No	Yes
9. 1951	Nonferrous Metals	Truman	Yes	1	Rejected	Yes	No	Yes
10. 1952	American Locomotive	Truman	Yes	1	No Vote	Yes	No	Yes
11. 1953	Longshoremen	Eisenhower	Yes	1	No Vote	Yes	No	Yes
12. 1954	Atomic Energy	Eisenhower	Yes	1	Rejected	Yes	No	No
13. 1954	Atomic Energy	Eisenhower	No		No Vote			
14. 1956–57	Longshoring	Eisenhower	Yes	1	Rejected	Yes	Yes	Yes
15. 1957	Atomic Energy	Eisenhower	Yes	1	Rejected	Yes	No	Yes
16. 1959	Longshoring	Eisenhower	Yes	1	Rejected	Yes	No	Yes
17. 1959	Steel	Eisenhower	Yes	1	Rejected	Yes	No	Yes
18. 1961	Maritime	Kennedy	Yes	1	Rejected	Yes	No	Yes
19. 1962	Maritime	Kennedy	Yes	1	No Vote	Yes	No	Yes
20. 1962	Aircraft (Republic)	Kennedy	Yes	1	No Vote	No	No	No
21. 1962	Longshoring	Kennedy	Yes	1	Rejected	Yes	No	No
22. 1962–63	Aircraft (Lockheed)	Kennedy	Yes	1	No Vote	Yes	No	Yes

Board of Inquiry Number and Dates	Dispute	President	Injunction Issued	Number Per Board	Employer Final Offer Vote	Strike Before Injunction	Strike After Injunction	Settlement Reached During Injunction
23. 1963	Aircraft (Boeing)	Kennedy	Yes	1	No Vote	No	No	No
24. 1964	Longshoring	Johnson	Yes	1	Rejected	Yes	No	No
25. 1966	General Electric Co.	Johnson	Yes	1	No Vote	Yes	No	Yes
26. 1966–67	Union Carbide	Johnson	Yes	1	No Vote	Yes	No	Yes
27. 1967	West Coast Shipyards	Johnson	Yes	1	No Vote	Yes	No	Yes
28. 1967	AVCO Corporation U.A.W.	Johnson	Yes	1	Rejected	Yes	No	Yes
29. 1968–69	Atlantic and Gulf Coast Longshore	Nixon	Yes	1	Rejected	Yes	Yes	No
30. 1971–72	Atlantic, Gulf and Pacific Coasts	Nixon	Yes	2 of 3 Requested	Rejected	Yes	Yes Pacific Coast Special Legislation Enacted	No (Atlantic and Gulf)

Source: Adapted from Federal Mediation and Conciliation Service, "Synopsis of Presidential Boards of Inquiry Created Under National Emergency Provisions of the Labor Management Relations Act, 1947," Washington, D.C., July, 1973.

THE LAST-OFFER VOTE RECORD

Last-offer ballots have been cast on fifteen occasions under the Taft-Hartley provisions. In every case employees have rejected the employer's last offer. The 1948 Maritime dispute proved even more disastrous for the procedure. The International Longshoremen's and Warehousemen's Union boycotted the balloting and not a single vote was cast. Balloting was engaged in through mailed ballots by other west coast unions, but the NLRB was not able to complete the procedure with offshore personnel before the end of the eighty-day injunction period. [19]

It has often been charged that one difficulty with the last-offer vote is the inability to draft the language of the employer's offer so employees can understand it. Congress intended that union members be given the opportunity to show if they preferred to take an employer's last offer rather than strike. Even if workers vote to accept the last offer, there is no legal requirement for union officers to abide by the results of a secret-ballot poll. Such a result, however, would obviously place union leaders in the position either of going along with the vote or having their political careers jeopardized as a consequence when union elections are held.

Unions instruct their members to reject the last offer presented to them. Actually, it is well known among workmen that there is no reason to accept the employer's last offer. The offer may always be accepted on the last day of the injunction. A refusal at the time of the NLRB-conducted poll is seen as automatic since employers may not make their best offer at that time. An early acceptance may also appear to be a repudiation of bargaining representatives engaged in negotiations with management. Union leaders and members are aware that employers know they will reject their last offer at the secret polls and for this reason the last offer will probably not be the best one. Experience since 1948 has led to this realization by the three parties involved in the process. This aspect of Taft-Hartley is useless and no rational basis exists to continue it. [20] This result was predicted shortly after the law was passed. [21]

SETTLEMENT RECORD DURING
THE INJUNCTION PERIOD

Strikes have not always been in progress at the time eighty-day injunctions were issued. It will be recalled that in four cases the President did not choose to proceed to the injunction stage. Of the remaining twenty-six cases, strikes were in progress in twenty-one when the injunction was granted. Only the United Mine Workers of America members refused to honor the injunction when it was issued during the 1949–1950 dispute. The union was subsequently found not guilty of ordering continuation of the strike. The miners themselves may have decided to continue the strike action despite the UMWA telegrams requesting them to return to work.

It has been charged that the entire procedure of dealing with national emergency disputes prolongs or delays serious bargaining.[22] The settlement record reveals that on fifteen of the twenty- six occasions that injunctions were issued, agreements were reached during the injunction period. In three other cases partial agreement was reached during the eighty-day period. The maritime industry was involved in all these cases in which some unions agreed to new collective bargaining contracts during the injunction period while others did not. The circumstances in all these cases were unusual in that the West Coast Longshoremen's Union has usually refused to settle before taking strike action after the injunction period.

In some cases settlements were obtained prior to the last-offer ballot. Indeed, of the fifteen cases resolved during the eighty-day period, only a few proceeded to the point where ballots were cast. This may mean that when the atmosphere is right for settlement of issues, the parties resolve them without regard to maneuvers moving them close to the midnight hour when a strike may either begin or resume. The weight of the particular issues such as the problem of containerization among longshoremen no doubt influences the dispute duration. In such cases the eighty-day period may merely prolong settlement. In most cases, however, the data do not support a suggestion that the parties play cat-and-mouse games until the very end of the eighty-day period. Even so it may well be that, in the absence of the eighty-day cooling-off period, greater pressure would exist to reach settlement.

Still another criticism of the injunction period is that workers are placed at a disadvantage because of the requirement to proceed with production for an eighty-day period. The various studies previously reviewed point out that production is increased both prior to and after the eighty-day period for the purpose of accumulating inventories. The existence of excess capacity in a particular industry engaged in a labor dispute increases employer power to withstand bargaining pressures. The requirement of continued production for eighty days may have the effect of raising inventory levels still higher and consequently increasing the possibility of strike action after an injunction is lifted. This ability obviously depends a great deal on the nature of an industry's product. Some products such as services cannot be accumulated. To the extent that they may be accumulated, however, the balance of power is placed in the hands of employers and eventual agreement to a contract may be prolonged. No actual penalty is imposed on employers during the eighty-day period. Employees, however, must continue to work at prestrike wages and other conditions of employment. This provides an incentive for employers to wait until near the end of the period before agreeing to new contract terms. Employers thus may discontinue bargaining efforts in cases where there is a reasonable chance that the government will intervene in the dispute.[23] The cost of continued operation of an industry seems to fall heaviest upon labor.

Another criticism of the injunction period involves the issue of threat to the public health and safety. If an actual threat is the reason the injunction was imposed in the first place, what is the situation after the eighty-day period? It will be recalled that six strikes have occurred after the injunction period. Taft-Hartley provides that the entire Congress may become involved at the close of the injunction. The President may submit recommendations to Congress regarding action such "as he may see fit to make for consideration and appropriate action." Congress may choose to deal with a particular situation on an ad hoc basis by enactment of specific legislation to alleviate the problem. Such legislation materialized once under Taft-Hartley. In 1969 some members of Congress desired to provide legislation to end the longshoremen's strike, which resumed after the Taft-Hartley emergency injunction was lifted. President Nixon responded, however, by indicating a preference for avoiding a legislative solution.[24]

Even if desirable, not much confidence may be placed in Congress to deal with such matters. It may well be that any legislation suggested by a President would be forthcoming only after a considerable period of time. The strike may be concluded with a more lasting solution by that time. A settlement imposed by government may not actually lead to an acceptable solution for the parties. To the extent that this is so, a final solution is again deferred to a later period of time. The possibility of further government intervention could retard the industry bargaining process. This is particularly the case if a government-imposed solution appears to one party as more desirable than one that might be reached in its absence.

Evidence is not available to support any contention that the public health and safety has been impaired as a result of resumed strikes after emergency injunctions. Until such evidence exists, it may be premature to invoke legislation to continue government intervention into labor disputes.

Another possible weakness of the Taft-Hartley procedures is that the injunction is viewed by unions as evidence the government is taking antilabor action against them. This injunction psychology is a carryover from the pre–Norris–La Guardia Act period. It is often argued that good-faith collective bargaining ceases at the time it appears likely an injunction will be issued. Unions take the position that better terms may be obtained by holding out longer. Employers are aware that a union is restrained from strike action and will not grant a more favorable offer. To the extent that an injunction psychology is generated, this constitutes a major defect in Taft-Hartley emergency procedures.

Last, it is frequently argued that the Taft-Hartley procedures are inflexible with the result that bargaining is adjusted to the next legal step and not to the critical issues in dispute.[25] A variety of approaches are viewed as unavailable and this has the effect of emasculating the objective of national emergency provisions. However, unsettled disputes may still be referred to Congress for specific action and any specific legislation that might be forthcoming from that body could leave the parties in a state of uncertainty.

CONSTITUTIONALITY OF
TAFT-HARTLEY PROVISIONS

The U. S. Supreme Court entertained the issue of constitutionality of the national emergency strike procedures in a 1959 case involving the steel industry. The United Steelworkers of America Union argued that Section 208 of Taft-Hartley, which vests jurisdiction in federal district courts to grant the federal government a temporary injunction against a national emergency strike in the steel industry, exceeded the constitutional limitations placed on the courts.[26] The Constitution prohibits courts from exercising powers of a legislative or executive nature. The union argued that the Court would be placed in the position of dual authority if the Act's provisions were permitted to stand. The Court would decide when to apply to law on the one hand and on the other it would determine the legislative standards to apply in each case. There was a second part to the union argument. It contended that if the Court viewed the law as valid, the emergency provisions should not be applied to the 1959 steel dispute because the national health and safety was not in jeopardy. Less than 1 percent of steel production was for defense purposes. Why should the entire industry be penalized when only about 1 percent could be classed as affecting "national safety"?

The U. S. Supreme Court ruled that the district courts have the constitutional authority to issue injunctions despite the fact that the Act "does not set up any standard of lawful or unlawful conduct on the part of labor [and] management." The Court reasoned that the law recognized the public has certain rights "to have unimpeded for a time production in industries vital to the national health or safety." Thus the Taft-Hartley law merely entrusts the courts with the power to decide on the basis of evidence if a national emergency dispute exists. The judiciary was viewed as functioning on the power extended it by Congress to implement one phase of the total procedure.

The second union argument that the total industry should not be placed under national emergency provisions was also rejected by the high court. It held that the statute did not require that

> the United States formulate a reorganization of the affected industry to satisfy its defense needs without the complete reopening of closed facilities.

The force of the Court's opinion was that an injunction against a part of an industry is not reasonable. The Court majority resolved the issue on the basis of national "safety," viewed broadly, and avoided the construction of national "health."

The Douglas Dissent

Justice Douglas dissented vigorously from the majority opinion. He reviewed the legislative history to determine the meaning Congress had intended to apply to the terms *health* and *safety*. It was argued that Congress had not intended that "national health" include the economic well-being or general welfare of the country. Senator Kennedy remarked in this regard that

> the proposal embraces two separate things, health and safety. Because the remedy is drastic these two, in my opinion are sufficient. I believe we should apply this remedy, when the strike affects health or safety, but not the welfare and interest, which may mean anything.

The Justice went further and argued that the word "welfare" should not be read into "health." He was of the opinion, however, that the Court majority had done just that.

The 1959 steel strike had not met the condition of placing "the national health and safety" in peril. When the board of inquiry was appointed, President Eisenhower stated that

> the strike has closed 85 percent of the nation's steel mills, shutting off practically all new supplies of steel. Over 500,000 steel workers and about 200,000 workers in

related industries, together with their families, have been deprived of their usual means of support. Present steel supplies are low and the resumption of full-scale production will require some weeks. If production is not quickly resumed, severe effects upon the economy will endanger the economic health of the nation.

Obviously, the President was concerned with economic health, which was contrary to the intent of Congress. Justice Douglas was concerned that this broad construction of the national emergency provisions would return the government to the strike-breaking role it played in the pre–Norris–La Guardia era. This was especially possible in the 1959 *Steelworkers* case since the mills that continued to operate accounted for at least 15 percent of the nation's steel production. Section 208 does not require that 100 percent of strikers *shall* be enjoined; this leaves the Court in the position to decide if only a portion would be covered by the injunction. Furthermore, a grant of jurisdiction to issue injunctions does not impose an absolute duty to do so under all circumstances. Justice Douglas concluded by arguing that an injunction covering all steel workers, when less than 1 percent were needed to supply defense needs, constituted inequitable treatment of workers relative to employers.

RAILWAY LABOR ACT EMERGENCY PROVISIONS

The Railway Labor Act provides a set of procedures for resolving national emergency disputes involving railroad and airline companies. The basic emergency provisions of the 1926 law were developed by union and management groups before Congress reviewed them. There was no hasty attempt to pass this type of legislation in the mid-1920s, which was the case when Taft-Hartley was debated about the time of the worst strike year (1946) in history.

The amended Railway Labor Act of 1926 provides several steps in dealing with emergency disputes in both the railroad and airline industries. First, when either the companies or unions desire to change existing contractual terms, and the private parties cannot agree upon terms, they may call for the mediation services of the National Mediation Board. Furthermore, the Board has the authority to enter the dispute without an invitation from either or both parties. The National Mediation Board, contrary to Taft-Hartley board-of-inquiry authority, may make recommendations for the parties to consider for settlement. There is no requirement, however, that such recommendations be accepted.

Failure to end the dispute with mediation services moves the National Mediation Board to a second stage. It urges the parties to submit disputes to voluntary arbitration. Acceptance of this proposal is rare among all unions, in or outside of rail and air. Arbitration is commonplace for resolving existing contractual problems, but not for the fixing of new contractual terms. Once arbitration is refused, the Board notifies the parties in writing that mediation has failed. Once notification is given, unilateral changes in wages, rules, or working conditions are prohibited for thirty days. Strikes are not permissible during this period.

At this point the National Mediation Board takes the initiative in dealing with a possible emergency in the rail and air industries. At any time during the thirty-day period that the Board feels the dispute threatens to "deprive any section of the country of essential transportation service," it notifies the President of the United

States. The President may then appoint an emergency board for the purpose of hearing the dispute and making recommendations for settlement. Within thirty days the Board must make a report to the President. During the thirty days, unilateral changes in the disputed issues are prohibited. Voluntary agreement is permitted, of course. Thus the Railway Labor Act provides a sixty-day period for postponing strike activity. After this period the parties are supposedly free to strike or otherwise make unilateral changes in contractual terms. No provision for controlling the dispute is spelled out after the sixty days expire.

The Railway Labor Act worked so well prior to 1941 that it was considered "model legislation." The airlines industry was placed under it in 1936. It has been estimated that emergency boards were appointed on twenty-one occasions in railroading from 1926 to 1941.[27] During the entire period of the law's operation, approximately 190 emergency boards have been developed to deal with transportation crises or an average of about four per year.[28]

Despite the rising incidence of strikes in rail and air transportation, the proportion of work time lost has been lower than for general industry.[29] A great deal of effort has been exerted by former presidents to "keep the rails operative." Seizure, use of injunctions, and requests for special legislation have been used by Roosevelt, Truman, and Kennedy. In the 1960s work rules were so prevalent an issue that the number of strikes increased substantially. For example, twenty-seven railroad strikes occurred in 1964, accounting for the largest number recorded in the then thirty-eight-year history of the Railway Labor Act. It was on August 28, 1963, that Congress approved a joint resolution requiring arbitration of two issues in a railroad dispute. Approval was based on a special message sent to Congress by the President seven days before a deadline was due to expire on July 29, 1963. The action by Congress constituted the first compulsory arbitration law ever passed by the federal government during a time of peace. In 1967 Congress again forbade a national rail strike and compelled the parties to arbitrate their differences. It has been suggested that this approach may have been largely responsible for breakdown of private negotiations.[30] The entire process of intervention has received widespread criticism.[31]

The courts have also intervened in railroad disputes. The Supreme Court held in *Chicago and Northwestern Railway Co.* that the Railway Labor Act requirement that every reasonable effort be made to reach agreement on wages and working conditions is enforceable by the courts.[32] As a consequence, the Norris–La Guardia Act will not prohibit injunctions under the Railway Labor Act if an employer or union alleges before a court that the other party bargained in bad faith. The threat of a strike and the economic pressure it may have in bringing agreement will be less effective in railway disputes from now on. The negative effect works on unions and management alike. Any party opposing change may now be less willing to compromise than before with the result that more and more government intervention in railway disputes is inevitable.

The courts have upset established patterns of bargaining by permitting rail unions to conduct selective strikes for the purpose of obtaining a national contract agreement. Selective strikes and lockouts are permitted provided the parties act in good faith.[33] Reasonable notice, defined as two weeks, of strikes and lockouts must be given. If national negotiations reach an impasse and all procedures of the act have been exhausted, a union may now whipsaw a few selected carriers in order to pressure the remainder to reach a national agreement. The result is that longstanding patterns of bargaining may now be unilaterally terminated after impasse and new patterns established. Thus, it appears that the courts have given impetus to possibly greater economic warfare in the railroad industry, which will increase intervention on the part of the other two branches of government.

GOVERNMENT POLICY IN THE RAILROAD INDUSTRY

Within the railroad industry successful collective bargaining has been seriously impaired because the federal government has affirmed that there will be no national work stoppages within this industry. In 1963, 1967, and 1970, the government prohibited stoppages in the railroad industry and by such action has made it perfectly clear that widespread strikes or lockouts within the railroad industry will not be tolerated. Except under the circumstances of World War II, this was the first time the United States government had prohibited strikes.

Despite the lack of agreement on the justification of outlawing widespread strikes in the railroad industry, the fact remains that the carriers and organizations well understand that from this time forward there will be no strikes of national character within this industry. Such strikes will not be tolerated, and this is a fact the parties must accept. The government justifies this policy on the grounds that outlawing widespread railroad strikes serves the public interest. It could be argued that such a policy serves the public *convenience*, but not necessarily the public *interest*. The latter could be identified with the preservation of free collective bargaining even though periodic railroad strikes would impose serious inconvenience to the public.

In short, consideration should be paid to the proposition that the genuine public interest is advanced to the extent to which employers and employees are permitted to strike and lock out. The railway experience now establishes a precedent that could easily be applied to other critical industries of the nation. Is the public interest preserved when the government destroys the free collective bargaining process? Short-run gains in terms of public convenience could eventually result in the domination of working conditions by government and the consequences involved in this policy. Once the government determines working conditions, it is only a short step to the determination of prices, profits, labor mobility, investment, and other critical features of the national economy. Granted that the public convenience is protected to the extent that the government outlaws important strikes, the question still arises as to whether or not the true public interest is promoted by a system of government domination of our economic life. Is security against strikes worth the loss of freedom? Where does the true public *interest* lie: in the preservation of free collective bargaining or state domination of our economic life?

Such issues and questions, however, are now academic within the railroad industry. Before the government outlawed the threatened strike in 1963, it painted a dismal picture of the consequences of a national railroad strike. To justify the outlawing of the strike, the Council of Economic Advisers predicted that such a strike would leave millions of commuters stranded in the large metropolitan centers;

certain industries which rely heavily upon rail transportation would have to close their operations after a few days; should the duration of the strike exceed thirty days, enough damage would be done to inflict a loss of about 13 percent or $75 billion on our GNP; after one month seven hundred thousand railroad employees would be unemployed in addition to six million other workers in affected industries. These were some of the dire predictions of the government, and they were used to justify the prohibition of the strike.

It is not known whether or not these predictions would actually have held up in real practice since the strike was not permitted to take place. Also it is not known how long the strike would have lasted, assuming one would have occurred. Moreover, if the government had refused to outlaw the strike and had informed the parties of this fact in clear and uncertain terms, would the carriers and the labor organizations then have proceeded to find a peaceful solution to their problems? If the government had stopped short of outlawing the strike, would the parties, faced with the stark realism that they alone had the full responsibility for settlement or strike, have found a peaceful formula for their dispute? If the government had not served as a crutch, would the parties have walked down the path of peaceful settlement?

The government was not prepared to give the institution of free collective bargaining a chance to resolve the issues in the railroad industry. There were only a lonely few within government who would give collective bargaining an opportunity to operate. The chairman of the House Commerce Committee, referring to the 1967 railroad situation, stated that if the government adopted a hands-off policy the carriers and the organizations "might be spurred to action on their own."

In any event the government outlawed the railroad strikes in 1963, 1967, and 1970 and in doing so established the clear precedent that it will follow the same action in the future. Whether or not the carriers and the organizations like it, whether or not the true public interest is promoted by this policy, the cold and inexorable fact is that from this time forward the federal government will not permit national railway strikes. The carriers and organizations must understand this and base their future actions on the basis of this incontrovertible proposition. No longer will the threat of a strike or lockout serve to stimulate and induce the parties to reach a settlement in genuine and good-faith collective bargaining. The government has removed the threat from the picture, and future policies and behavior of the carriers and the union organizations will take this into account.

COMPULSORY ARBITRATION AND COLLECTIVE BARGAINING

When the government outlawed the railway strikes in 1963, 1967, and 1970, it required the parties to arbitrate their disputes. That is, compulsory arbitration rather than collective bargaining is the federal policy within the railroad industry. Some government spokesmen attempted to identify the procedure in 1967 in terms of mediation. It was called "mediation to finality"—a sheer euphemism to cloak a procedure that was absolute compulsory arbitration.

By outlawing the strike and establishing a system of compulsory arbitration, the federal government has destroyed the collective bargaining process in the railroad industry. True, up to this point Congress has not yet passed a general compulsory arbitration law. The 1963 and 1967 disputes were dealt with on an ad hoc basis. However, the federal government has made it very clear that any threat of a future national railroad strike or lockout will be dealt with in the same manner. What the policy means is that the parties will not bargain in good faith and in a realistic manner. Why should they compromise their position in eventual arbitration by making concessions at the bargaining table? If it is argued that the carriers and the organizations do not live up to their responsibilities, the fact is that government laws brought about this state of affairs. If there is one fixed principle of labor relations, and one which is underscored by incontrovertible evidence, it is that a system of compulsory arbitration is incompatible with genuine collective bargaining. Realistic compromises, concessions, and counterproposals designed to reach settlement are simply not made out of the fear that by such action a party will prejudice its position before the arbitrator. It is a matter of gamesmanship to cling to the original position in order to protect a position destined for arbitration.

These observations are proved by the relationship between the carriers and the organizations in the 1963, 1967, and 1970 disputes. Once the parties understood that the government would not tolerate a national railroad work stoppage, there was no realistic collective bargaining. True, the parties met, discussed, and went through the rituals, but once they understood that there would be no strike or lockout, they made no serious attempt to reach a settlement. To argue that they did not meet their "responsibilities" ignores the realism of the situation. They did not meet their obligations because the government established an environment that produced the inevitable sterility in their negotiations. They understandably responded to a state of affairs that makes good-faith collective bargaining an impossibility. Why should the parties have bargained realistically when they were fully aware that failure to reach a settlement would not result in economic sanctions? Why should they make any genuine and serious effort to resolve their differences when they were aware that making concessions would serve to weaken their position in the eventual arbitration?

The events of the airline strike during the summer of 1966 and the 1970 dispute further establish proof that good-faith collective bargaining will not occur when the government makes it explicit that it will impose compulsory arbitration. Here was a wage dispute between the Machinists Union and most of the major airlines in the nation. Before the government made it clear that it would legislate compulsory arbitration, there was reason to believe that the parties would promptly reach an agreement. However, once the government in effect told the parties that compulsory arbitration was in the picture, realistic collective bargaining stopped. It may well be that the government prolonged the airline strike by its intervention.

If additional proof is needed, World War II experience with compulsory arbitration is squarely relevant. It is true, of course, that during World War II production had to go forward without interruption. No one quarrels with this point. However, it still remains true that the National War Labor Board was deluged with cases because the parties were aware that to bargain realistically would impair their position before the arbitration tribunal.

Not only does compulsory arbitration make genuine collective bargaining an impossibility, but the procedure also worsens the state of labor relations. This occurs because the parties may push to an impasse those issues they may have readily settled within the climate of free collective bargaining. Once again it is the gamesmanship of the parties that produces this state of affairs. If the dispute is going to wind up before the arbitrator, it is a matter of strategy to send to the tribunal as many issues as possible. For several years the state of Indiana had a compulsory arbitration law that applied to public utilities. In a study of the operation of the statute by one of the authors, the following observations were offered:

> Finally, in evaluating the operation of the Indiana law, it is quite plain that the parties submitted issues for decision in arbitration that they undoubtedly would have settled themselves within the climate of free collective bargaining. In general, in the absence of the requirement to arbitrate, there are ordinarily only a few issues remaining toward the close of negotiations. To avoid a strike, both parties normally make every effort to settle their differences and thereby eliminate all but a few particularly serious issues for final determination. However, under the Indiana law, great bulks of problems have been laid before the boards of arbitration. In one case, a board was required to make 30 separate decisions, and in others, arbitrators were called upon to decide cases involving from 10 to 18 separate problems. The smallest number of issues placed before a board was 7. Some of these items were quite insignificant, and would have been peacefully settled in one way or another without the compulsory arbitration statute.
>
>   Companies and unions frequently and deliberately refuse to settle items when they recognize that compulsory arbitration is involved. This is done on the grounds that some of these demands may be granted by a board of arbitration. They have nothing to lose by such a procedure, since the worst that can happen is to have the board reject these issues. In addition, the board may decide the major issue in favor of a party on the grounds that it disposed of some minor items against it. Once the arbitration process is interjected into a collective bargaining relationship, the parties will adopt appropriate strategy procedures to maximize their position if the case goes before a board. Parties hold on to demands that they would quickly dispose of under free collective bargaining. [34]

The same state of affairs can be expected within the railroad industry under a system of compulsory arbitration. Understandably, the parties will refuse to dispose of even minor issues, hoping that by this strategy their position in compulsory arbitration will be strengthened. It is a matter of gamesmanship between the parties under a system of compulsory arbitration.

After 15 months, the threat of a nationwide railroad strike was ended in April 1970 by special Congressional action. Essentially, four shopcraft unions reached tentative agreement on a contract in December 1969. The members of one union rejected the pact obtained by their negotiators because they were concerned that a work-rule change posed a threat to their job security. The Nixon administration lost hope of a settlement and in early March 1970 asked Congress to impose the December agreement on the railroads and four unions. The industry and three of the unions agreed with the Administration.

Congress was reluctant to impose an agreement upon the unwilling members of the fourth union and responded with a five-week strike moratorium. At the close of the period, an agreement still had not been voluntarily reached. The Congress reacted by imposing the December 1969 agreement upon the industry and the unions. Negotiators for the fourth union were in no position to accept the agreement privately because the members rejected the pact by a two-to-one margin. A legislated settlement usually will not be a lasting one in collective bargaining. The issue may be placed before the Congress at a future date.

Experiences with the national emergency provisions of both the Taft-Hartley and the Railway Labor Acts have led a large number of observers to suggest alternative procedures for dealing with such disputes. No agreement has been reached on the particular machinery needed to replace existing law. Indeed, agreement cannot even be reached on the definition of national emergencies or for that matter on whether economic emergencies have ever existed. Despite the lack of agreement suggestions for changes continue to be offered.

SUGGESTED ALTERNATIVES TO EXISTING EMERGENCY PROCEDURES ELIMINATE INTERFERENCE

Obviously, one approach to dealing with strikes previously subjected to national emergency provisions is to permit the parties to resolve their differences free from interference. Mediation services may be provided, but failure to reach agreement through this voluntary device should not prevent the parties from devising their own methods to resolve issues. The strike or lockout will settle the dispute. Many studies indicate the lack of an actual national emergency dispute since World War II. Continued outside interference with the collective bargaining process may destroy the freedom of the parties to bargain within an unrestricted framework. Inconvenience upon occasion may be the cost that is paid for the freedom to do so.

LABOR-MANAGEMENT ADVISORY COMMITTEE PROPOSAL

Several suggestions for Taft-Hartley changes were reported to President Kennedy by his Advisory Committee on Labor-Management Policy in 1962.[35] One committee proposal subject to little criticism was the elimination of the last-offer vote conducted by the NLRB between the sixtieth and the seventy-fifth day of the injunction period.

More controversial, however, was the proposal to eliminate the eighty-day injunction and replace it with presidential authority to order the parties to negotiate during a similar eighty-day cooling-off period. This proposal would supposedly take away the psychological aspect of the injunction. The primary argument that may be advanced for this change is that the parties will comply with a presidential request. It will be recalled that the Railway Labor Act does not provide for an injunction.

Still another suggestion dealt with the power of "emergency dispute boards" to make recommendations when deemed desirable by the President. This proposal carried with it a name change from the current "board of inquiry." In addition, it was advanced that appointment of boards be broadened to extend to any situation that might develop into a dispute threatening the national health and safety. The boards could be appointed to make recommendations at any time during the eighty-day period. This proposal differs from the procedure under the Railway Labor Act whereby recommendations are required at the beginning.

Essentially, the advisory committee sought to establish procedures making it easier to intervene in strikes and as a result increase the governmental role in the collective bargaining process. It has been suggested that the committee desired procedures similar to those of the Railway Labor Act to govern general industry.[36]

Some of the suggestions of the advisory committee have been tried at various times, both before and after the report was submitted to President Kennedy. Extralegal action was taken in the 1959 steel strike in which the board of inquiry succeeded in clearly defining the positions of management and the union for the first time. In addition, recommendations for settlement were made privately by the board. Still another mediation function was provided by then Vice-President Nixon and Secretary of Labor Mitchell. Extralegal action was also taken during the 1962 Lockheed-machinist dispute, the 1962–1963 longshoremen's dispute, and the 1967 Avco Corporation–UAW dispute. The boards of inquiry made recommendations in all these cases. Thus increasingly boards take on a conciliation role by making recommendations for dispute settlement. Clearly, the Taft-Hartley Act does not provide for such action.[37] This expanded extralegal role has been assumed in order to encourage bargaining, which tends to degenerate as soon as a panel is appointed by the President.

Presidential appointment of boards responsible for making recommendations follows closely the example of the Railway Labor Act. Yet it has been noted that the procedure used for the rail and airlines industries has broken down considerably over the past twenty years. Various reasons account for the breakdown. The most obvious is the featherbedding issue resulting from technological change. Related to this larger problem is the fact that the parties, particularly unions, have little respect for the boards. They have become routinely ignored. Unions have not fared so well from board recommendations since World War II. It may well be that the boards have been impressed with the alleged hardship pleas of the railroads and airlines. Continued governmental intervention has not provided the lasting solutions anticipated when the machinery was conceived. Public opinion was to be the factor that would force settlement, not the use of force by public officials.

COMPULSORY ARBITRATION

The major argument used against compulsory arbitration is that it ends free collective bargaining. Unions and management alike condemn this procedure. The weaker of the bargaining parties will tend to adhere to original positions since an outside party will ultimately decide the terms of settlement. This form of settlement is not usually as acceptable as one worked out by the parties themselves. Employers are also concerned that a practice of compulsory setting of wages, hours, and other terms and conditions of employment will lead to price fixing. After all this is done, there is no assurance that emergency strikes will be avoided. The absence of concrete evidence identifying economic costs imposed by strikes in key industries dictates against the use of compulsory arbitration by third parties not chosen by the negotiators themselves. The allocation of scarce resources may become less efficient by use of the procedure.

Not all observers are critical of compulsory arbitration in emergency cases. One argues that "our whole system of jurisprudence relies on the idea that anyone with a grievance is able to compel an antagonist to meet him peaceably at a public hearing where, after argument, a binding third party settlement is handed down."[38] Support was offered for this position from the history of labor relations. It was pointed out that a form of compulsory arbitration is used to resolve recognitional controversies by the National Labor Relations Board. The NLRB issues a decision in each case after following its own as well as legislated procedures.

Another use of grievance arbitration was also cited as support for compulsory arbitration. However, it is not widely accepted that there is a similarity between the two types. Grievance arbitration results from voluntary agreement to submit differences for resolution to a third party chosen by the parties themselves. This form of arbitration deals with disputes arising under an existing contract. Compulsory arbitration would deal predominantly with the terms of a new contract. There is a vast difference between the two methods.

Still another observer in favor of compulsory arbitration argued that an arbitrator could be required to make an award consistent with one of the final positions set forth by one party prior to applying this last resort measure.[39] It was suggested that good-faith bargaining could be obtained by providing penalties for bad-faith attempts to influence the final position submitted to arbitration.

Obviously, no single compulsory arbitration proposal receives unvarying devotion even from advocates of the mechanism. Perhaps the most definite argument against it is that both labor and management groups generally oppose it.

STATUTORY STRIKES

The *statutory strike* is known by various synonyms. It is also referred to as a semi-strike and a nonstoppage strike. This type of alternative to existing emergency dispute machinery requires that financial penalties be placed on unions, workers, and employers in lieu of strikes. Workers would be deprived of all or a part of their wages and benefits, unions would forego dues, and employers would lose all or part of their profits. Work would continue under this arrangement until settlement was reached.[40]

Various plans have been advanced to implement the proposal. The problems inherent in them, however, appear too formidable to result in a workable arrangement. Some suggest that workers may agree to strike, but a work stoppage is foregone in favor of a certain percentage deduction from wages which is matched by employers. All deductions would go to the public treasury and would be lost to the parties involved. The exact percentage deducted would be set by the President. In addition, a union treasury as well might be taxed—perhaps instead of workers. A more likely plan would be a tax on both workers and their unions. Periodic strike taxes would be collected. If settlement were obtained, for example, in between two collection periods, no further payment would be required. This has been held to provide an incentive to reach settlement.

Enforcement of all the conceived variations of the statutory strike would be most difficult. The heaviest penalty for unresolved disputes would fall on workers. Marginal firms might be an exception, but such firms would not likely be involved in a national emergency dispute. Income taxes, unemployment compensation, and other related adjustments would be involved in any such plan. No plan exists that would place an equal penalty on all parties to an emergency labor dispute. The impact that a payroll deduction of 40 percent might have on an individual worker may be reasonably calculated. But how does one impose an equal liability upon General Motors? Even if such a calculation can be made, there is no guarantee that workers will not engage in limited work stoppages such as slowdowns, or even resort to industrial sabotage. The end result of bargaining may be less equitable than if a strike were permitted, which would clear the air more completely.

SEIZURE

Government seizure of industry has occurred about seventy-one times in the history of the United States.[41] Sixty of these actions were taken under express statutory authority. The remaining eleven seizures were not supported by legislation. Seizure has been used by presidents either during or immediately before and after wars. Government behavior in the collective bargaining process varies widely in such cases. At times unions have been extended a wage and benefit package until settlement was reached with the employer. In other cases the government has merely taken measures to maintain production; no attempt has been made to influence the final package. Of course, unions lose their right to strike in such cases. President Truman used both seizures and injunctions to deal with the rail disputes in 1948, 1950, and 1951.

The last time seizure was used to deal with an emergency dispute was in steel in 1952. President Truman directed the Secretary of Commerce to take possession of and operate most of the steel mills engaged in the labor dispute. The Secretary complied and called upon the various company presidents to serve as operating managers of their firms. The companies brought suit against the United States charging that seizure was not authorized by either Congress or any constitutional provision.[42]

Upon review, the Supreme Court ruled in favor of the companies. It was made clear that if the other ten seizures without express legislative authority had been litigated, they would have been held unconstitutional. It is interesting to note that the steel crisis had passed by the time the Supreme Court handed down its decision in June 1952. Despite this fact, seizure since then has not been used by presidents even when they were convinced national emergencies existed.

Because of the New York transit strike in 1966, Senator Javits proposed a bill to amend Taft-Hartley, giving the President more authority to act during national emergency disputes. In essence, there were seven parts to the proposal. First, it was proposed that the President have authority to appoint a board of inquiry to make recommendations for settlement. No work stoppage would be permitted for thirty days after the report. The last-offer ballot and injunction would be eliminated under this procedure.

Second, the authority of the President would be expanded to permit intervention in disputes that "imperil the health or safety of a substantial part of the population." This provision would amend the Taft-Hartley and Railway Labor Acts, permitting application to disputes in transportation, transmission, or communications industries affecting commerce. It is interesting to note that this would apply even when the employer is a state or local government.

Third, failure to realize a settlement on the basis of the two techniques mentioned would set the stage for a more advanced move. Both labor laws would provide that the President could petition a federal district court to name a special receiver to take possession of the facility in dispute and to operate it.

Fourth, the court would take the initiative at this point and direct the receiver to make changes in wages or other employment conditions based on the court's discretion. Any changes would have to be on the basis of the earlier board of inquiry recommendations.

The fifth part of the proposal would permit the employer to choose whether or not he would accept any profits or losses incurred during the period of receivership. If not, he could elect to receive a "just, fair, and reasonable compensation" for use of his facilities. This latter choice would involve a government deduction from whatever standard of payment is used. The rationale is that the government should be compensated for keeping the facility in operation when it would otherwise have been closed by strike. Appeal to the courts would be permissible when an employer disagreed with the government's compensation offer.

Sixth, the receiver would not have authority to negotiate a labor contract. Bargaining would continue until a settlement was reached; then the facility would be returned to the employer within a thirty-day period.

The last provision proposed that a district court promote partial operation before permitting seizure. The court would be required to determine how much of the facility should be operated to protect the health and safety of the country. Failure of unions and management to agree to partial operation would result in a receiver operating only the portion of the facility identified by the court as necessary to protect health or safety. The crisis that called forth the Javits bill did not last long enough to stimulate Congress to accept it, or some other procedure, for dealing with emergency disputes.

Seizure and the States

Seven states at various times have passed seizure laws to deal with labor disputes.[43] Only five, however, actually used such laws and seized production facilities. Most of these laws dealt with strikes involving public utilities. The threat that these strikes may result in emergency situations is considerably less in 1970 than was the case immediately after World War II. Continued technological changes and the ability of supervisory personnel to operate facilities have contributed to diminishing the threat.

Most state laws designed to control strikes have been invalidated by the Supreme Court because of federal preemption in the area. This is the case with compulsory arbitration, strike-vote requirements, and fact-finding boards insofar as these devices apply to interstate commerce.[44]

The state of Missouri enacted legislation known as the King-Thompson Act to control public utility strikes. It provided that

> it shall be unlawful for any person, employer, or representative . . . to call, incite, support or participate in any strike or concerted refusal to work for any utility

> or for the state after any plant, equipment or facility has been taken over by the state . . . as a means of enforcing any demands against the utility or against the state.

Under this provision the governor of Missouri seized the Kansas City Transit, Inc., on November 13, 1961, the same day that a strike had begun. A permanent injunction was later obtained barring the continuation of the strike "against the State of Missouri." The union appealed the case to the Supreme Court of Missouri and argued that the King-Thompson Act conflicted with the National Labor Relations Act, which preempted the state in such matters. The Missouri court ruled in favor of the state.

The U. S. Supreme Court accepted the case for review and handed down its opinion in 1962.[45] It held that

> neither the designation of the state statute as "emergency legislation" nor the purported "seizure" by the State could make a peaceful strike against a public utility unlawful in direct conflict with Section 7 of the National Labor Relations Act, which guarantees the right to strike against a public utility, as against any employer engaged in interstate commerce.

State-owned and operated facilities are not covered by Taft-Hartley and may be controlled by state law. However, firms that meet the NLRB's jurisdictional dollar standards are not subject to state control. States are prohibited from dealing with so-called state emergencies despite the fact that they may be closer to the source of difficulty than federal officials and thus in a better position to judge the possible effect on local economies. It is often feared that a change in national labor policy extending greater authority to state governments to deal with local disputes would result in widespread abuse. The first issue that must be resolved in dealing with emergency disputes is a more adequate definition of what constitutes an emergency dispute. The definition of Taft-Hartley precludes the states from dealing with most strikes, whether actual or threatened.

PARTIAL INJUNCTION

The *partial injunction* has been suggested by several as an alternate method of dealing with national emergency disputes.[46] Essentially, it has been suggested on the one hand that the judiciary take the initiative in making a decision on what part of production or services should be continued. As opposed to this view, the Attorney General would be required to satisfy the judiciary of the need for certain production. Once a determination has been made, the injunction would be lifted, permitting the remainder of workers to strike or the company to lock out. A great deal of precise information would be required to implement this type of arrangement, and a more workable definition of national emergency would have to be worked out. Assuming that some workable solution could be reached on this issue, then other problems would still exist.

Some workers would enjoy full wages until the entire dispute was settled, whereas others would receive only strike benefits. Should employees supply the necessary labor on the basis of seniority or should those who normally perform specific tasks remain on the job? Often it may be impossible to single out a specific division and operate it to the exclusion of other sections of the firm.

Still other difficulties would have to be resolved before an operational plan could be developed to change the existing emergency procedure. In any event, if it is ever decided that the present methods do not adequately deal with emergency labor disputes, partial operation may provide an equitable approach to the problem.

CHOICE OF PROCEDURES

No single one of the devices mentioned have complete acceptance from observers of the labor scene. The *choice-of-procedures approach* would give the President a variety of weapons from which to choose in dealing with any given situation. Basically, advocates of this approach argue that the parties would be uncertain how to promote settlement and would attempt to settle their problems through collective bargaining. Among the weapons from which the President can select are (1) the injunction, (2) compulsory arbitration, (3) mediation, and (4) seizure or partial seizure. In addition, other approaches have been suggested.

It is not at all certain that the choice-of-procedures approach would provide an incentive for the parties to settle disputes prior to intervention. Recent presidents have used—or have threatened to use—a wide range of methods for dealing with particular industries. This does not seem to diminish the periodic concern with strikes in certain key industries. New legislation of the choice-of-procedures variety may merely formalize what already takes place in practice.

The state of Massachusetts enacted a choice-of-procedures law after a study by a committee headed by the late Sumner H. Slichter, but in actual practice it has not proved as successful as many had hoped. It has been reported that in some cases when the Slichter law was invoked the unions may have obtained a settlement in excess of what they were prepared to settle for earlier.[47] The Massachusetts law has been used sparingly by governors for political reasons. The law was passed without union backing by a Republican administration. Democratic governors have not generally favored its use. However, this may be a positive factor in that the law has not been overused, as may be the case with the provisions of both the Taft-Hartley and Railway Labor Acts.

THE NIXON ADMINISTRATION

George P. Shultz, President Nixon's first Secretary of Labor, favored the arsenal-of-weapons approach for dealing with national emergency disputes. Nixon, himself, favored having more options to deal with national emergency strikes. In addition, Shultz desired the repeal of the Railway Labor Act and inclusion of the railroad and airline industries under Taft-Hartley. As will be demonstrated in the next section, the Nixon administration called for the placing of all transportation industries under an amended Taft-Hartley Act which would provide for options to deal with disputes in the transportation industry. The present procedures of Taft-Hartley culminating in the 80-day injunction would continue to be applicable to all other industries.

During Nixon's first term in office, he established by Executive Order the Construction Industry Collective Bargaining Commission. It was authorized to intercede in any dispute with the construction industry which would have a significant impact on a particular locale or locales. The Commission is composed of twelve members. Four members each represent the public, labor, and management; the Secretary of Labor serves as chairman. A thirty-day cooling-off period may be imposed on the parties while mediation and related activities take place to settle issues. However, the Commission does not have the power to settle by compulsory arbitration the issues involved in a labor dispute. Rather, its role is limited to the encouragement of the parties to settle their disputes on a voluntary basis.

To carry out its responsibilities, the Commission established an operational policy. Fundamental to this policy was the group's determination not to intervene in nonsensitive labor disputes. It reserved its activities to those disputes, including strikes, which had a significant impact upon the construction industry in a particular locality. Another of its policies was to encourage the establishment of procedures within each branch of the construction industry to handle controversies between unions and employers. When such procedures were established, the national commission did not intervene provided the parties attempted to settle their controversies in good faith within the structure of the procedures adopted by the particular branch of the industry. In addition, the Commission refused to intervene in a dispute between two or more construction unions involving the issue of jurisdiction over work. As we know, jurisdictional disputes are a persistent problem within the construction industry. The Commission's policy not to intervene in such disputes was based upon the fact that the construction industry established the National Joint Board for settlement of these disputes, and further because the problem is handled fairly effectively under Taft-Hartley. These subjects were previously discussed in Chapter 16.

It is difficult to evaluate the success of the Construction Industry Collective Bargaining Commission. In general, it has kept a low profile, and it is speculative as to the impact of its intervention in construction disputes. Concrete evidence does not prove one way or the other whether its procedures have effectively aided the parties to settle their disputes. Also, in the light of the fact that over the years there have been many large construction strikes, it is safe to say that this Nixon experiment was not an overwhelming success.

PROPOSALS IN TRANSPORTATION INDUSTRY
PROTECTION ACT OF 1970

Work stoppages for the month of January 1970 accounted for 0.25 percent of estimated total working time, the highest for the month since 1950. This general industry record plus the approximately 15 months threat of a nationwide railroad strike led to the Nixon proposal of major legislation to deal with emergency disputes in the general transportation industry. Congress was asked to establish new procedures for settling disputes in the airline, longshore, maritime, railroad, and trucking industries that imperil the nation's health and safety.

The proposed legislation recognizes basic deficiencies in both the Railway Labor Act and the Taft-Hartley Act. As discussed previously in this chapter, much of the pressure for revision of existing law is political and reflects legislative concern for having to enact a special law to settle nationwide labor disputes in transportation.

Nixon requested that the emergency strike provisions of the Railway Labor Act be discontinued and that railroad and airline strikes and lockouts be subject to the Taft-Hartley Act. Other transportation industries are already subject to Taft-Hartley Act procedures. The President sought three new options under the 1947 law.

The first option would permit the Chief Executive to extend the cooling-off period for as long as 30 days beyond the 80-day injunction period. This option would be most useful if it were believed that the dispute were very close to settlement.

The second option would permit partial operation of the industry. This alternative would require appointment of a special board of three impartial members. The board would be charged with deciding the feasibility of requiring operation of an essential part of the industry or of requiring service to a special class of customers. Study of the problem could go on for up to 30 days during which strikes or lockouts are prohibited. Partial operation would be limited to six months. The special board would have the responsibility of choosing a level of operations that would impose economic hardships on the parties to the dispute. The presence of hardships would be the incentive for the parties to continue seeking an agreement.

The third option would be to invoke the procedure of final offer selection. If invoked, each of the parties would be given three days to submit either one or two final offers to the Secretary of Labor. Five additional days would then be provided to permit labor and management to meet and bargain over the submitted offers. If no agreement is forthcoming at the close of five days, a final offer selector group would make a selection of the final offers previously submitted by the parties. Three neutral members would make up the selector group and would be appointed by the disputants or the President if labor and management cannot agree on the individuals to be appointed. The offer selected would be final and binding on the parties. Nixon believed the final selection option different from arbitration because of the strong incentive for the parties to reach agreement themselves before an outside group imposes a settlement upon them.

The Chief Executive might also choose a fourth option. He could refer the entire issue to Congress for special action as is now required if agreement is not reached at the end of the 80-day injunction period.

Under the proposed bill, the President's choice of an option would be subject to either house of Congress or to the courts. Within a ten-day period, either house of Congress could void the President's recommendation. The courts would have authority to rule against the action if it were considered arbitrary and capricious.

Several other recommendations were included in the proposed legislation. A special study commission with a life span of two years was recommended to study those industries that are especially vulnerable to national emergency disputes. It would be known as the National Special Industries Commission and have the responsibility of identifying collective bargaining weaknesses in the various industries. It could also recommend corrective legislation to the President.

The National Railroad Adjustment Board would be abolished if Congress agrees that it is incapable of efficient resolution of disputes that come before it. The Railway Labor Act requires the NRAB to provide final arbitration of unresolved disputes. There is a backlog of several thousand cases which tend to frustrate labor relations harmony. In place of the NRAB, the parties themselves would be coaxed to establish grievance machinery including final arbitration in their contracts. This procedure is common under Taft-Hartley and experience shows that disputes arising under existing contracts are expeditiously resolved.

The tendency for negotiations to drag on indefinitely in the railroad and airline industries is partially due to the lack of an effective contractual termination date. Nixon recommended that this situation be reversed and that the same procedure of contractual termination be implemented as exists in general industry. A desire to change or terminate a contract would require a written notice to that effect sixty days in advance of the date the change is to go into effect. The contracting parties would have the incentive to engage in effective negotiations at an earlier date than is now the case with no termination dates.

The Federal Mediation and Conciliation Service would take on the mediation duties now performed by the National Mediation Board. The NMB currently determines representation of bargaining units as well as mediation. This dual function exists only for the airlines and railroad industries. Nixon was of the opinion that the FMCS is better equipped to provide the single function of mediation. The regulatory function would remain with the NMB, but a name change to the Railroad and Airline Representation Board would reflect the restricted function.

President Nixon emphasized the greater reliance upon private settlement of disputes that would come with the proposed legislation. It was his hope that the requested legislation would provide settlement of emergency disputes in the transportation industries that would be equitable to the public, industry, and labor. In the absence of emergency situations, an attempt is made to strengthen private collective bargaining efforts in the transportation industries. It may well be that the proposed legislation would eventually result in more harmonious labor relations than have been experienced during the last ten years. Considerable time would be required for such a result, however, because of the industries' inability to reach lasting settlements due to excessive intervention to prevent work stoppages. Some work stoppages seem inevitable if a lasting peace is to be achieved in the railroad industry during the decade of the seventies. At this writing, the Nixon proposals have not been enacted by Congress and with his resignation the fate of his proposals is speculative.

SUMMARY

It seems feasible to remark that the emergency strike provisions of Taft-Hartley were enacted more for political purposes than for any other reason. Congress intended that a narrow construction be placed on the meaning of national health and safety. Both Taft-Hartley and the Railway Labor Act emergency provisions receive an economic interpretation. Threats that a strike may impose an economic inconvenience upon the public are likely to be met by presidential use of national emergency provisions. Past studies reveal that disputes which arise in key industries have political implications as opposed to economic.

Intervention into labor disputes to protect the public from inconveniences may result in a higher economic cost than would have occurred if the parties were permitted to strike or lockout without restraint. At the time that it appears that presidential action may be forthcoming, the parties cease bargaining in good faith. Political settlements are achieved that may well be higher than if good-faith bargaining had been present throughout the entire period of negotiations. Extralegal action is used to secure political settlements. That is, presidents instruct boards of inquiry to make settlement recommendations even though Taft-Hartley forbids such behavior.

Compulsory arbitration is the political response, but the cost may be the tendency to forego greater economic efficiency over time. Several alternative national emergency procedures have been offered from time to time, but none has yet been accepted by Congress. There is no overwhelming evidence that national emergency dispute provisions were necessary on the occasions they were used in the past. It is unknown to what extent that workable machinery will be necessary in the future. Because of the uncertainty regarding future need, there is no reason to allow inadequate machinery to persist on the statute books. Before a new approach is accepted, however, there is need to study the available alternatives. The real purpose for such provisions should be clearly revealed. If the public is not to bear any inconvenience such as may be forthcoming from strikes in key industries, then there is no reason to deal with the matter under the guise of public health and safety. The new law should clearly state that the federal government is concerned with the national economic welfare, however it is defined. It may be that states have no more basis for dealing with so-called emergencies than the federal government. But if a level of government should move more into the strike arena, it should be the federal government. The probability is greater of a more balanced and uniform treatment of both parties at the federal rather than the state level.

NOTES

[1] *Monthly Labor Review*, XCII, No. 3 (March 1969), 75.

[2] Bureau of Labor Statistics, *Handbook of Labor Statistics* (Washington, D.C.: Government Printing Office, 1947), pp. 136, 163.

[3] C. L. Christenson, "The Theory of The Offset Factor: The Impact of Labor Disputes upon Coal Production," *American Economic Review*, XLIII, No. 4 (September 1953), 513–547.

[4] C. Lawrence Christenson, "The Impact of Labor Disputes upon Coal Consumption," *American Economic Review*, XLV, No. 1 (March 1955), 79–112.

[5] Irving Bernstein and Hugh G. Lovell, "Are Coal Strikes National Emergencies?" *Industrial and Labor Relations Review*, VI (April 1953), 353.

[6] *Ibid.*, p. 365.

[7] Irving Bernstein, "The Economic Impact of Strikes in Key Industries," in *Emergency Disputes and National Policy*, Irving Bernstein, Harold L. Enarson, and R. W. Fleming, eds. (New York: Harper & Bros., 1955), chap. 2.

[8] *Ibid.*, p. 25.

[9] *Ibid.*, p. 27.

[10] *Ibid.*, p. 44.

[11] See, for example, E. Robert Livernash, *Collective Bargaining in the Basic Steel Industry*, U.S. Department of Labor (Washington, D.C.: Government Printing Office, 1961); and Robert R. France and Richard A. Lester, *Compulsory Arbitration of Utility Disputes in New Jersey and Pennsylvania* (Princeton, N.J.: Industrial Relations Section, Princeton University, 1951).

[12] Donald E. Cullen, *National Emergency Strikes*, ILR Paperback No. 7 (Ithaca, N.Y.: New York School of Industrial and Labor Relations, Cornell University, 1968), p. 45.

[13] Senator Wayne Morse, Senate Joint Resolution 180, *Congressional Quarterly Weekly Report*, No. 30 (July 29, 1966), pp. 1636–1637.

[14] Arthur A. Sloane, "Presidential Boards of Inquiry in National Emergency Disputes, An Assessment After 20 Years of Performance," *Labor Law Journal*, XVIII (November 1967), 667.

[15] *Ibid.*, p. 669.

[16] *Ibid.*, p. 671.

[17] Section 210.

[18] *United States* v. *International Longshoremen's Association, Local 418*, D.C.—N.D. 111, No. 71 Civ. 2416 (November 3, 1971).

[19] Cullen, *op. cit.*, p. 58.

[20] Herbert Northrup and Gordon Bloom, *Government and Labor* (Homewood, Ill.: Richard D. Irwin, Inc., 1963), pp. 364–65.

[21] Harry A. Millis and Emily Clark Brown, *From the Wagner Act to Taft-Hartley* (Chicago: The University of Chicago Press, 1950), p. 578.

[22] *Ibid.*, pp. 581–82.

[23] Richard B. Peterson, "National Emergency Dispute Legislation—What Next?" *University of Washington Business Review*, 28, No. 1 (Autumn, 1968), 39.

[24] *Monthly Labor Review*, 92, No. 3 (March 1969), 2.

[25] Cullen, *op. cit.*, p. 64.

[26] *United Steelworkers* v. *U.S.*, 361 U.S. 39 (1959).

[27] Cullen, *op. cit.*, p. 70.

[28] *Ibid.*, p. 69.

[29] Jacob J. Kaufman, *Collective Bargaining in the Railroad Industry* (New York: King's Crown Press, 1954), pp. 78–80.

[30] Jacob J. Kaufman, "The Railroad Labor Dispute: A Marathon of Maneuver and Improvisation," *Industrial and Labor Relations Review*, 18, No. 2 (January, 1965), 201.

[31] *Ibid.*, pp. 211–12.

[32] *Chicago and Northwestern Railway Company* v. *United Transportation Union*, U.S. Sup. Ct. No. 189 (June 1, 1971).

[33] *Delaware and Hudson Railway Co.* v. *United Transportation Union*, U.S. Sup. Ct. No. 1634 (June 7, 1971).

[34] Fred Witney, *Indiana Labor Relations Law*, Indiana Business Report No. 30 (Bloomington, Ind.: Bureau of Business Research, Indiana University, 1960), pp. 72–73.

[35] *Free and Responsible Collective Bargaining and Industrial Peace*, Report of the President's Advisory Committee on Labor-Management Policy (Washington, D.C.: Government Printing Office, 1962).

[36] Northrup and Bloom, *op. cit.*, p. 429.

[37] Sloane, *op. cit.*, pp. 671–672.

[38] Orme W. Phelps, "Compulsory Arbitration: Some Perspectives," *Industrial and Labor Relations Review*, XVIII, No. 1 (October 1964), 81.

[39] Carl M. Stevens, "Is Compulsory Arbitration Compatible with Bargaining?" *Industrial Relations*, Vol. VI, No. 2 (February 1966), 45, 47.

[40] David B. McCalmont, "The Semi-Strike," *Industrial and Labor Relations Review*, XV, No. 2 (January 1962); Stephen H. Sosnick, "Non-Stoppage Strikes: A New Approach," *Industrial and Labor Relations Review*, XVIII, No. 1 (October 1964); also Cullen, *op. cit.*, pp. 102–106.

[41] John L. Blackman, Jr., *Presidential Seizure in Labor Disputes* (Cambridge, Mass.: Harvard University Press, 1967).

[42] *Youngstown Sheet & Tube Company* v. *Sawyer*, 353 U.S. 579 (1952).

[43] These states are Hawaii, New Jersey, North Dakota, Maryland, Massachusetts, Missouri, and Virginia.

[44] For example, see *International Union* v. *O'Brien*, 339 U.S. 454 (1950); *Amalgamated Association* v. *Wisconsin Employment Relations Board* 340 U.S. 383 (1951); *Grand Rapids City Coach Lines* v. *Howlett*, 137 F. Supp. 667 (1956).

[45] *Division 1287, Amalgamated Association of Street, Electric Railway & Motor Coach Employees of America et al.* v. *Missouri,* 374 U.S. 74 (1962).

[46] Senator Javits, "A Bill . . . ," Senate of the United States, 89th Congress, 2d sess., January 20, 1966; Committee for Economic Development, *The Public Interest in National Labor Policy* (New York, 1961), pp. 101–103.

[47] George P. Shultz, "The Massachusetts Choice-of-Procedures Approach to Emergency Disputes," *Industrial and Labor Relations Review,* X (April 1957), 364–365.

VI GOVERNMENT EFFORTS TO REGULATE INTERNAL UNION AFFAIRS

PROLOGUE. *In 1959 Congress enacted the Landrum-Griffin Act which is intended to deal with internal union practices that may deprive members of proper representation. The law establishes a "bill of rights" for members, requires union and employer reports to the Secretary of Labor, and enacts other features designed to control practices viewed as contrary to the public interest.*

Another feature of current concern is the organization of public employees into unions. Diverse approaches have been taken by the federal, state, and local governments in dealing with their employees. The following two chapters deal with these two features of labor relations law. Chapter 22 deals with problems that are attracting more attention in the area of labor relations law.

20 Labor-Management Reporting and Disclosure Act of 1959

The Labor-Management Reporting and Disclosure Act of 1959, commonly referred to as the Landrum-Griffin Act, is concerned primarily with the internal practices of unions.[1] Its major purpose is to protect union members from improper union conduct. Still another purpose of the law is to eliminate arrangements between unions and employers that would deprive members of proper union representation. A few provisions of the Act are directed at management. The 1959 law was the direct outgrowth of Senate investigations revealing unsatisfactory internal practices of a small but strategically located minority of unions. The first six of seven titles in the statute introduce controls on the powers that union officials exercise over funds, internal union affairs, and the membership.[2] This chapter reviews the background and treats the major areas of the 1959 law. They are (1) "the bill of rights," (2) reports to the Secretary of Labor, (3) union trusteeships, (4) conduct of union elections, and (5) financial safeguards.

BACKGROUND OF REGULATION OF INTERNAL UNION AFFAIRS

Growth of the U.S. labor movement from a position of relative weakness in the early 1930s to one of relative strength by the 1950s led to greater public attention devoted to internal union practices. Union membership grew from about 9 million in 1941 to 17 million in the 1950s. The logical extension of concern with strikes and picketing was to the perceived power of those directing such actions. The war years and the period of adjustment thereafter did not represent the first period of time the public was conscious of internal union operations. Concern with internal union affairs was prevalent even before the period of government protection of the right to organize and bargain collectively as provided by the Wagner Act of 1935.

By 1900 racketeering was revealed in the building trades, longshoremen, and teamsters unions. Graft, violence, extortion, and mishandling of funds by union leaders are some practices reported in these organizations. Labor organizations were also criticized for improper use of trusteeships, discrimination against blacks by barring them from membership or placing them in separate auxiliary locals, and lack of disciplinary protection of members.[3]

Scrutiny of union activities was intensified after World War II. In 1954 Congress began investigating the administration of employee benefit plans. Discovery of widespread abuses in the labor field led to the creation of the Senate Select Committee on Improper Activities in the Labor or Management Field, better known as the McClellan Anti-Racketeering Committee. Between 1957 and 1959 the McClellan committee held numerous hearings dealing with patterns of union behavior. Several findings and recommendations were presented as a result of the three-year effort. It should be noted that the committee concentrated its efforts on only five national unions of the 200 or so which operate in the nation. These were the International Brotherhood of Teamsters, Bakery and Confectionary Workers, United Textile Workers, Operating Engineers, and Allied Industrial Workers of America. Some attention was devoted to other unions, including those in the building trades, but the five mentioned accounted for the largest share of the committee's efforts. As a result of the inquiry, the Teamsters were expelled from the AFL-CIO, and, subsequently, its president, James Hoffa, was convicted and jailed for tampering with a jury and mail fraud. Prior to the 1972 national elections, President Nixon permitted Hoffa to leave prison, but he was forbidden to hold a union office until 1980.

McClellan Committee Findings and Recommendations

The labor movement anticipated government intervention into its internal affairs. In 1957 the AFL-CIO adopted a series of six codes of ethical practices to regulate the behavior of its affiliates. The codes dealt with paper locals, health and welfare funds, subversives and racketeers, business interests of union officials, union financial and proprietary activities, and union democratic processes.[4] The self-regulated effort proved too late. The McClellan committee, after many hearings and thousands of pages of testimony, uncovered these facts:

1. Rank-and-file members have no voice in union affairs, notably in financial matters, and frequently are denied secret ballot.
2. International unions have abused their right to place local unions under trusteeship by imposing the trusteeship merely to plunder the local's treasury or boost the ambitions of candidates for high office.
3. Certain managements have bribed union officials to get sweetheart contracts or other favored treatment.
4. Widespread misuse of union funds through lack of adequate inspection and audit.
5. Acts of violence to keep union members in line.
6. Improper practices by employers and their agents to influence employees in exercising the rights guaranteed them by NLRA.
7. Organizational picketing misused to extort money from employers or to influence employees in their selection of representation.
8. Infiltration of unions at high levels by criminals.

9. A no man's land in which employers and unions could not resort either to the NLRB or state agencies for relief.

On the basis of the findings the McClellan committee recommended legislation to deal with abuses in five areas. They were:

1. Legislation to regulate and control pension, health, and welfare funds.
2. Legislation to regulate and control union funds.
3. Legislation to insure union democracy.
4. Legislation to curb activities of middlemen in labor-management disputes.
5. Legislation to clarify the no man's land in labor-management disputes.[5]

Some of the findings and recommendations were dealt with in Title VII of the 1959 law and are discussed in previous chapters. The scope of the first six titles is broad and ambitious, as will be seen by a review of the important elements of the Act.

BILL OF RIGHTS OF MEMBERS OF LABOR ORGANIZATIONS

Senator McClellan was largely responsible for the "bill of rights" section that was written into the 1959 law. He stated that "racketeering, corruption, abuse of power and other improper practices on the part of some labor organizations" could not be prevented

> until and unless the Congress of the United States has the wisdom and the courage to enact laws prescribing minimum standards of democratic process and conduct for the administration of internal union affairs.[6]

The resulting bill of rights for union members is an ambitious and widesweeping one. It attempts to legislate into internal union constitutions and bylaws certain basic rights contained in the Bill of Rights of the United States Constitution. Title I provides for equality of rights concerning the nomination of candidates for union office, voting in elections, attendance at membership meetings, and participation in business transactions—all, however, "subject to reasonable union rules and regulations" as contained in constitutions and bylaws. It lays down strict standards to ensure that increases in dues and fees are responsive to the desires of the union membership majority. It affirms the right of any member to sue the organization once "reasonable" hearing procedures within the union have been exhausted. Provision is also made that no member may be fined, suspended, or otherwise disciplined by the union except for nonpayment of dues unless the member has been granted such procedural safeguards as being served with written specific charges, given time to prepare a defense, and being afforded a fair hearing. And it obligates union officers to furnish each of their members with a copy of the collective bargaining agreement, as well as full information concerning the Landrum-Griffin Act itself.

Considerable controversy broke out almost immediately after passage of the 1959 law. The underlying premise of the bill of rights was that labor organizations should function in a democratic fashion. The question was, however, could such a standard be imposed on unions externally? Union members are often viewed as apathetic to internal operations as long as they remain reasonably satisfied with collective bargaining results. Revolt against the leadership may be forthcoming only when there is a widespread feeling that contractual terms obtained are less than could have been received. Furthermore, some allege that union responsibility and internal democracy are often conflicting within the context of collective bargaining.[7]

Congress intended to give individual members the right to assert themselves more fully in matters dealing with their employment relationships. At the same time it recognized the union right to represent a majority of workers in collective bargaining matters. Unions must have authority to enforce a labor contract entered into with an employer. For this reason the exercise of individual rights is subject to "reasonable" union rules. Members have some responsibilities to the labor organization to which they belong. Recognition of this fact prompted Congress to provide that nothing in this section of the law should be construed to

> impair the right of a labor organization to adopt and enforce reasonable rules as to the responsibility of every member toward the organization as an institution and to his refraining from conduct that would interfere with its performance of its legal or contractual obligations.

The application of particular Title I provisions is somewhat complicated and for this reason each will be considered in turn.

EQUAL RIGHTS

The law grants equal rights and privileges to every union member with regard to nomination of candidates, voting in elections and referendums, attendance at union meetings, and voting at such meetings. The section makes no attempt, however, to regulate union admission standards. The procedural safeguards do not prohibit labor organizations from refusing membership or segregating members on the grounds of race, religion, color, sex, or national origin. This aspect was made clear by Congressman Landrum when he stated that

> we do not seek in this legislation, to tell the labor unions of this country whom they shall admit to their unions.[8]

Congressman Powell attempted to remedy this defect in Title I, but was unsuccessful by a vote of 215 to 160. A partial remedy to the problem was not available until it was provided by Title VII of the Civil Rights Act of 1964.[9]

Race is not the only form of discrimination permissible under Title I. The practice of *filial preference* has also been recognized as a basis for closing the door to union membership.[10] Only sons and close relatives are admitted under this practice and it has the blessing of the courts. The practice has been approved by the New York Court of Appeals.[11] Thus the law permits union action designed to restrict the supply of labor available under some circumstances. Union democracy is limited to the extent that membership may be denied to qualified applicants. The view is taken by many that unions are no longer voluntary associations, but quasi-public organizations. Prevailing technology, it is argued, does not lend itself to monopolistic control over labor supply. Thus the internal restrictive membership practices are viewed as antisocial because they work against public attempts to achieve and sustain high levels of employment.[12] On the other hand, it should be realized that restrictive admission practices have been in response to excessive unemployment in labor markets in which these unions operate. A public policy not committed to full employment through its monetary and fiscal policy cannot hope to attain it by changing union *admission* standards. *Discrimination* in any form, however, is unacceptable.

The Title I political rights of union members are closely connected with Title IV of Landrum-Griffin. Title I guarantees equal rights and privileges to nominate candidates and vote in union elections. Title IV extends members a reasonable opportunity to nominate candidates. It also provides that every member, subject to some qualifications, shall be eligible to hold office. The member also has the opportunity to support candidates and vote for them without interference or reprisals.

Benjamin Aaron reveals that the courts have given these titles narrow interpretations.[13] Title I rights may be enforced prior to the holding of elections, but Title IV rights are enforceable only after an election is held. After an election only the Secretary of Labor has authority to seek relief in the courts. The full range of litigation required to secure member rights may take so long that the full term of office in dispute may be served out completely before a decision may be obtained. Little practical relief from a violation therefore may be forthcoming.

A union has the authority to deprive members of their equal right to nominate, to vote, and to participate in internal affairs. It may do so by the way it frames its eligibility rules.[14] A union may do as was done by the National Marine Engineers' Beneficial Association. The association constitution provided that a member could nominate only himself for office, but no one was eligible to hold office unless he had been a member of the national union for five years. Also eligibility was conditioned by the requirement that a member had to have served at least 180 days at sea in two of the preceding three years prior to the election. Sea service had to be on ships covered by labor contracts with the national or its locals. The U.S. Supreme Court sustained a motion to dismiss the case filed against the union in *Calhoon* v. *Harvey*. This case has had the effect of substantially impairing the ability of members to participate fully in union political affairs.

FREEDOM OF SPEECH AND ASSEMBLY

Landrum-Griffin provides for both individual and organizational rights. Every member is granted the right to meet and assemble freely with other members to express views, arguments, and opinions. Such activity may be at union meetings or some other place. The rights of members are subject to two qualifications. One permits unions to apply their established and reasonable rules pertaining to the conduct of meetings. For example, time limits may be placed on debate and measures may be taken to maintain order. The ability to conduct business in an orderly fashion is necessary to efficient operation. Dissident members could call the tune at union meetings without this organizational safeguard. An inability to restrict member misbehavior could result in serious industrial strife. For example, wildcat strikes could be called by a vocal minority because of the inability of the majority to control normal union business.

The second limit placed on member rights to speech and assembly is that a union has the right "to adopt and enforce reasonable rules as to the responsibility of each member toward the organization as an institution and to his refraining from conduct that would interfere with its performance of its legal or contractual obligations." The union member therefore is extended the right to dissent from established or advocated union policies, but that right is not without limit.

It appears that the courts tend to rule in favor of individual speech and assembly rights as opposed to union rights. *Salzhandler* v. *Caputo* was a case posing the issue of whether a union member's allegedly libelous statements regarding the handling of union funds by union officers justified disciplinary action against the member.[15] The case also involved the issue of whether the union could exclude the member from any participation in union affairs for a period of five years, including speaking and voting at meetings and even attending meetings. A district court ruled in favor of the union. Upon appeal, the Second Circuit Court of Appeals reversed the lower court and remanded the case for further proceedings.

In upholding individual over organization rights, the appeals court stated:

> We hold that the LMRDA protects the union member in the exercise of his right to make such charges without reprisal by the union; that any provisions of the union constitution which make such criticism, whether libelous or not, subject to union discipline are unenforceable; and that the Act allows redress for such unlawful treatment.

The court pointed out that libelous statements may be made the basis of civil suit between those concerned, but a union governing board may not subject a member to disciplinary action for his statements. Libelous statements do not stand outside the law merely because they were made within the context of internal union affairs. The court merely established that other remedial action is available through civil suits. This approach appears to enhance democratic action within labor organizations. At the same time the individual member is still responsible for any libelous statements he may utter.

DUES, INITIATION FEES, AND ASSESSMENTS

Certain democratic procedures must be followed by a union, other than a federation of unions, in increasing dues, initiation fees, or assessments. This policy is intended to stop unscrupulous union officers from imposing higher dues upon members against their will. The McClellan committee hearings and reports had revealed such action of a few unions.

A local union has different procedural requirements than an international union. A local union may raise dues, initiation fees, or assessments by secret ballots in two ways. The determination is based on a majority of those members voting who are in good standing. The vote may be (1) taken at a membership meeting after reasonable notice that the issue will be put to the members or (2) in a membership referendum. Posted notices on bulletin boards in union halls and where work is performed as well as an announcement at one regular monthly meeting that a vote on the issue will be held at the next regular monthly meeting would meet the reasonable-notice requirement. There may be no better way to get a large membership turnout to a meeting than to announce that a vote will be taken to increase union dues. Union leaders have to present valid reasons for desiring an increase in dues. Failure to do so will inevitably lead to a rejection of the proposal.

An international union may use one of three different ways to increase its income from members. It may require (1) a majority vote of the delegates voting at a regular convention, or at a special convention held upon thirty-days' written notice to each local union; (2) a majority vote of the members voting by secret ballot in a membership referendum; or (3) a majority vote of the members of the executive board or similar governing body, if they are expressly granted such authority by the union's constitution and bylaws. The latter approach is subject to repeal at the next regular convention and for this reason may not be a politically feasible approach for increasing international union income.

Federations of national or international unions do not fall within the Landrum-Griffin prohibitions on increases of dues, initiation fees, and assessments.

In the *American Federation of Musicians* case, the U.S. Supreme Court was faced with the issue of whether the law prohibits the vote of delegates at a national convention of the union, in accordance with its constitution, to be weighed and counted according to the number of members in the local that the delegate represents.[16] The Court was of the opinion that the legislative history of the section makes it clear that weighted voting was not thought to be one of the abuses of union government found by the McClellan committee. Many large unions vary voting strength with the size of the locals.

The Court held that full and active participation of the rank and file in union affairs is the basic aim of Landrum-Griffin. The argument that a delegate may not vote in the same fashion as would the members questions the validity of representative government. Congress did not intend to impose a town-hall type of government upon labor unions. They were merely required to guarantee membership participation in fair elections.

In another case a U.S. district court held in 1965 that a union may not impose an increase in dues and assessments unilaterally and then proceed to obtain member ratification after the fact.[17] A union in violation of the procedural safeguards concerning dues and assessments must return the excess of dues unlawfully collected. An employer is not responsible for union action in the absence of proof that he conspired with the labor organization to illegally withhold the increased dues via the checkoff. The union must account for its own actions.

PROTECTION OF THE RIGHT TO SUE

Unions are prohibited from limiting the right of a member to bring suit against a labor organization even though the leaders may be involved. A member also has the right to petition a legislature or communicate with particular legislators without union-imposed limits. Congress, however, placed two qualifications on member rights to engage in such action. The first is that a member "may be required" to exhaust "reasonable hearing procedures (but not to exceed a four-month lapse of time) within such organization" before initiating action. The second qualification is:

> No interested employer or employer association shall directly or indirectly finance, encourage, or participate in, except as a party, any such action, proceeding, appearance, or petition.

The right of an individual union member to bring suit against an employer to enforce rights arising out of a collective bargaining contract is established under Section 301 of Taft-Hartley. This may well have the effect of relegating the second 101 (a) (4) qualification to a state of uselessness. No congressional expression on this aspect is revealed in the legislative history of the 1959 act and uncertainty exists regarding how a court might construe the qualification. Provision for individual action is contained elsewhere, and it may well be that this aspect of the section will remain untested.

By far the most important of the two qualifications, however, is the one dealing with the exhaustion of internal union hearing procedures. Typical union constitutions contain appeal procedures that provide for an appeal of local decisions to the international and then ultimately to the international convention. The section provides that a member may be required to exhaust internal remedies available within a four-month period before permitting suit against a union or its officers. Some questions arose immediately after the law was enacted. Does a member have to exhaust all internal remedies available within a four-month period before initiating proceedings? Does a member have the right to bring suit after four months of internal effort?

The legislative history of the Act sheds light on the issue of the members' right to bring suit after four months of internal effort to deal with a problem. Senator Kennedy was of the opinion that the section did not automatically permit a suit after a four-month period. He stated:

> The purpose of the law [was not] to eliminate existing grievance procedures established by union constitutions for redress of alleged violation of their internal governing laws. Nor is it the intent or purpose of the provision to invalidate the considerable body of State and Federal court decisions of many years standing, which require, or do not require, the exhaustion of internal remedies prior to court intervention depending on the reasonableness of such requirements in terms of the facts and circumstances of a particular case. So long as the union member is not prevented by his union from resorting to the courts, the intent and purpose of the "right to sue" provision is fulfilled, and any requirements which the court may then impose in terms of pursuing reasonable remedies within the organization to redress violation of his union constitutional rights will not conflict with the statute.[18]

The magnitude of the particular problem of a member and the appropriateness of internal-appeals machinery have a great deal to do with a court's judgment of particular cases. Some courts may require an exhaustion of internal remedies before allowing judicial relief whereas others may permit a suit despite the availability of internal procedures.

The issue of exhausting all internal remedies available within a four-month period has been litigated on several occasions since 1959. Congress intended to permit unions to correct their own wrongdoing by stimulating them to independently establish democratic appeal procedures.[19] A safeguard against union abuse was provided by not requiring exhaustion of union remedies if the procedures exceed four months in duration. However, as stated by Representative Griffin, "It should be clear that no obligation is imposed to exhaust procedures where it would obviously be futile or would place an undue burden on the union member."[20]

In 1961 an appellate court reversed a district court decision that imposed upon a union member an absolute duty to exhaust union remedies before applying to the federal courts.[21] In so doing it made a review of the legislative history of the section and held:

> Taking due account of the declared policy favoring self-regulation by unions, we nonetheless hold that where the internal union remedy is uncertain and has not been specifically brought to the attention of the disciplined party, the violation of federal law clear and undisputed, and the injury to the union member immediate and difficult to compensate by means of a subsequent money award, exhaustion of union remedies ought not to be required. The absence of any of these elements might, in light of Congressional approval of the exhaustion doctrine, call for a different result.

In a case decided by the U.S. Supreme Court in 1968, *Industrial Union of Marine & Shipbuilding Workers*, it was decided that the four-month period was not a grant of authority to unions to require exhaustion of internal remedies.[22] Instead it was merely a statement of policy that the courts or the NLRB may refuse to intervene for this period of time. Thus both the NLRB and the courts may prefer to consider if a procedure is reasonable and should be exhausted or if they should entertain the complaint. Each case therefore appears to evolve about the particular issues involved and the particular procedures available to which members may appeal.

The *Industrial Union of Marine & Shipbuilding Workers* case involved a public policy issue, however, and not one of individual rights. That is, the NLRB has jurisdiction over union unfair labor practices interfering with the right of individuals to engage in or to refrain from union activities. In the absence of a public policy granting an individual the statutory right to file an unfair labor practice charge, a union may regulate its legitimate internal affairs. If a union member gambles on the nature of public policy and is wrong when he fails to exhaust internal remedies, he may lose his union membership and in some situations even his employment as a result.

UAW Public Review Board

Many unions have responded to the discipline section by revising their constitutions to ensure conformance with the law. Still others have gone even further by establishing external procedures to be used by members choosing to do so.

In 1957 the United Automobile Workers dealt with the problem of abuse in the disciplinary procedure in a more unique manner. It established a Public Review Board, composed of seven citizens of respected reputation, impeccable integrity, and no relationship with the union. Usually, such men have been members of the clergy, the judiciary, or university faculties. The Board's membership in the past has included such outstanding names as Clark Kerr, former president of the University of California, the late Edwin E. Witte of the University of Wisconsin, the late Rabbi Morris Adler of Detroit, Bishop G. Bromley Oxnam of Washington, D.C., and Msgr. George G. Higgins, Director of the Social Action Department of the National Catholic Welfare Conference.

Under the amendment to the UAW constitution which established the plan, the president of the national union selects the Board members, subject to the approval of the national union's executive board and ratification by the national convention. Among other duties, the watchdog committee may reverse the decision of the executive board of the national union when it upholds the discipline of a union member. Experience shows that the Board has been quite willing to reverse the national union's executive board on the relatively few occasions when it has believed such a reversal was justified.

The Upholsterers International Union has followed the review board pattern set by the UAW. If each national union were to establish such an agency, and if each agency were allowed the same freedom to act that has been granted the UAW Public Review Board, there probably would be less need for legislation to protect the status of union members.

SAFEGUARDS AGAINST IMPROPER
DISCIPLINARY ACTION

Landrum-Griffin provides that a union member may not be "fined, expelled, or otherwise disciplined," except for nonpayment of dues, unless certain procedural steps are taken to ensure due process. The member must be "(A) served with written specific charges; (B) given a reasonable time to prepare his defense; (C) afforded a full and fair hearing." Where a union violates these standards, the union member has the right to challenge the action taken against him in the courts. In 1971, however, the U.S. Supreme Court held that the courts do not have the power to construe union rules to determine the offenses for which discipline may be imposed.[23] Previously, lower federal courts construed a union rule allowing expulsion of a union member for conduct against union interest so as to exclude expulsion for a personal altercation between a union member and a union official. When a union official did not refer a union member to an available job, the member struck the official. Subsequently, the union member was disciplined by his union, and the lower federal courts held that the union rule in question could not be used as the basis for expulsion. By its reversal of these decisions, the U.S. Supreme Court has held that unions may interpret union rules for which members may be disciplined. In other words, the law's protection is limited to the procedure for discipline and not to the substantive character of union rules and their interpretation by the organization.

Due-Process Rights for Whom? Early litigation dealing with the due-process rights of union members construed the section to apply only to the union-member relationship, not the employer-employee relationship with a union. The Act was also not construed to protect the union-officer relationship.[24]

The federal courts have been in conflict regarding the question of whether the members' rights provisions of the 1959 law apply equally to union members and union officials. In a 1962 case the Third Circuit Court of Appeals upheld the dismissal of a union business agent for exercising his membership rights.[25] The union brought charges against the officer and removed him from office. The court ruled that "it is the union-membership relationship, not the union-officer relationship that is protected" by the bill of rights. Furthermore, Section 609 of the 1959 law prohibiting disciplinary action against members in the exercise of their rights was not viewed as applicable to officers.

In another case a group of officials were summarily discharged from their offices because they actively supported an unsuccessful candidate for union office.[26] The court upheld the dismissed officers and ruled that

> nothing in the statutory language excludes members who are officers. Nor is there any intimation in the legislative history that Congress intended these guarantees of equal political rights and freedom of speech and assembly to be inapplicable to officer members.

The court in *Grand Lodge* did not rule that the 101 (a) (5) due-process section applied equally to both officers and members. The full and fair hearing was not necessary for removal from office because "Congress' primary concern was that [Section 101 (a) (5)] should not bar summary removal of union officials suspected of malfeasance. . . ." The U.S. Supreme Court denied review.

In a 1968 case before a federal district court, a distinction was made between the *Sheridan* and *Grand Lodge* cases when it held that

> the statutory distinction between officers and members of a union organization seems to be, for the most part, confined to the summary discharge of officers for alleged malfeasance. However, by contrast, when rights are asserted under [the bill of rights], no member "may be fined, suspended, expelled, or otherwise disciplined" without observance of . . . the due process section.[27]

It may well be therefore that an officer is entitled to the same due-process safeguards as any other member when he exercises his rights as a union member. However, for malfeasance he may receive summary treatment without regard to the due-process procedures of Section 101 (a) (5). This distinction may better serve the public interest in internal union democracy since officers are in the best position to generate competition for political office. To stifle their ability to challenge other officeholders could diminish the basic objective of the Act. During the decade of the 1960s national union presidents defeated in elections almost always lost to officers serving under them. One example was the loss of the United Steelworkers presidency by MacDonald to I. W. Abel, former secretary-treasurer of the national union. Also, in 1969, Joseph Yablonski, a United Mine Workers official for twenty-seven years, challenged W. A. (Tony) Boyle for the presidency. Mr. Yablonski lost the election and later his life along with the lives of his wife and daughter. The Secretary of Labor challenged the election after Mr. Yablonski's murder in what may prove to be one of the most notorious blots on recent union history. The fact that Mr. Yablonski was even successful in running for the UMW presidency is considered almost miraculous and marks the first attempt to challenge the incumbent president in the history of the UMW. In December 1972 Arnold R. Miller decisively defeated Boyle for the union presidency in an election ordered by the courts and supervised diligently by the Department of Labor. Miller, a reform candidate, headed an insurgent group called "Miners for Democracy." Several UMW officials who served under Boyle were convicted for the Yablonski murders, and subsequently Boyle was convicted for the crime.

ENFORCEMENT OF THE "BILL OF RIGHTS"

Civil actions may be brought by anyone whose rights have been affected by violations of the "bill of rights" provisions of the LMRDA of 1959. In contrast, the Secretary of Labor has administrative and enforcement responsibilities in connection with Titles II, III, and IV. There is no public remedy for violations of Title I. Most members do not have the financial resources to bring legal proceedings against labor organizations violating their rights. Also they may be subject to group pressure militating against their using court action.[28] In this way, the full benefits of the "bill of rights" section may not be available to union members. On the other hand, to permit the Secretary of Labor to intervene at the request of union members may result in an unreasonable amount of litigation, which could impair the effective operation of labor organizations. Dissident groups could use the section to harass union officers if union members did not bear the burden of enforcement. It was these considerations that prompted Congress to forbid the Secretary of Labor to enforce the "bill of rights" section. Despite the difficulty of union member enforcement, however, the fact is that private suits alleging violations of the "bill of rights" section are filed in court. Between 1959 and 1972, 1,360 private suits were filed by union members against their unions or officers, and a majority of them alleged violations of the "bill of rights" section.[29]

REPORTS TO SECRETARY OF LABOR

The LMRDA requires every labor organization to report its financial and administrative practices. Under certain conditions imposed by the Act, labor relations consultants, employers, union officers and employees, and surety companies must also file reports of their activities. The reports become public information and available to anyone for examination. Administrative responsibility is vested in the Secretary of Labor with most authority delegated to the Office of Labor-Management and Welfare-Pension Reports. The office is under the supervision of the Assistant Secretary for Labor-Management Services Administration.

The Secretary of Labor is authorized to establish regulations prescribing the form and publication of reports. The Act requires that all persons who file reports must maintain records for a period of five years from which the reports may be verified. Criminal sanctions are available to deal with persons who violate the reporting and disclosure provisions of the law. Civil enforcement is available to the Secretary of Labor.

REPORTS BY UNIONS

Every labor organization is required to file a copy of its constitution and bylaws with the Office of Labor-Management and Welfare-Pension Reports. A labor organization is defined as not only a union in the usual sense, but also employee representation groups, committees, and councils in an industry affecting commerce.[30] Such organizations fall within the Act's provisions if they deal with employers over grievances, rates of pay, and other terms and conditions of employment. A union comprised exclusively of government (federal or state) employees is not required to file reports. This exclusion does not apply to national bodies representing both government and nongovernment workers. State or local central bodies also do not have to file reports because their membership is made up of local unions or other subordinate affiliates.

The Initial Report

Within ninety days of the time a union first becomes subject to the 1959 law, it must file an initial report. The report must be signed by the principal union officers such as the president and secretary and include specific information on the following:

1. Union name and address and address where records are kept.
2. Names and titles of officers.
3. Initiation fees for new members or other fees for transferred members as well as for working permits.
4. Dues and fees required of members.

The union must also indicate where information may be found in documents filed that contain provisions and procedures for:

1. Membership qualifications.
2. Assessment levies.
3. Participation in insurance and other benefits.
4. Authorization for disbursement of funds.
5. Financial audits.
6. Calling of regular or special meetings.
7. Selection of officers and representatives.
8. Discipline or removal of officers or agents.
9. Imposition of fines, suspensions, and expulsion of members.
10. Authorization for bargaining demands.
11. Ratification of contract terms.
12. Strike authorization.
13. Issuance of work permits.

Any change in information filed in the initial report must be reported once a year when the annual financial report is filed. A union that is terminated for reasons such as merger or consolidation and dissolution must file a terminal report within thirty days after loss of identity or existence. The report must state (1) circumstances and effective date of termination; and (2) name and address of the union into which it was consolidated, merged, or absorbed.

Annual Financial Report

A labor organization is required to file an annual financial report within ninety days after the end of each fiscal year. The report must show:

1. Assets and liabilities at the beginning and end of the fiscal year.
2. Receipts of any kind and the sources thereof.
3. Salaries, allowances, and other direct or indirect payments to each officer, irrespective of amounts, and also to each employee who received a total of more than $10,000 during the year from the reporting organization and any other affiliated union.
4. Direct and indirect loans to any officer, employee, or member that aggregated more than $250 during the fiscal year, together with a statement of the purpose, security, and arrangments for repayment.
5. Direct and indirect loans to any business enterprise, together with a statement of the purpose, security, and arrangements for repayment.
6. Other disbursements made by it and the purposes thereof.

Simplified reports may be filed by small unions if (1) gross receipts total less than $30,000 per reporting year and (2) it is not in trusteeship. Terminal financial reports are required within thirty days after dissolution or consolidation, as are annual reports.

The requirement of reporting has not been a controversial matter. As of June 30, 1968, the Secretary of Labor had filed suit only against eleven unions seeking compliance with Section 201.[31] Congress required reports of small unions in order to deal with corruption and racketeering if it should arise. Debate over the exemption of small unions took place at a time when considerable attention was devoted to Teamster president James Hoffa. Thus small unions must maintain proper books and records.

Elimination of National Labor Relations Act Reports

Reporting requirements of the National Labor Relations Act were repealed by the 1959 law. The reports required prior to 1959 were filed with the National Labor Relations Board. Failure to comply resulted in a denial of the right to use the National Labor Relations Board procedures. This restriction on union access to the Board was eliminated by a change to making reports to the Secretary of Labor.

Some reporting changes were made in 1959, different from those required under the National Labor Relations Act. The aggregate compensation and allowances, when in excess of $5,000 per year, of three principal officers and any other officers had to be reported prior to 1959. Landrum-Griffin established a minimum of $10,000. Loans to officers or members in excess of $250 must now be reported, as compared to $500 required previously. The purpose, security, or repayment arrangements for such loans were first required in 1959. Also loans to business firms did not have to be reported individually prior to the 1959 changes.

It may well be that union reporting experiences prior to 1959 eased the way to greater acceptance of Landrum-Griffin provisions. However, the criminal penalties provided by the LMRDA cannot be ignored when evaluating the compliance record.

Availability of Information to Union Members

Section 201 (c) requires reporting unions to make information contained in reports available to all its members. The right of members to examine the union's books and records to verify the report is enforceable in any state court of competent jurisdiction or in an appropriate federal district court. The provision provides also that a union member successful in a court suit may be allowed to recover costs and reasonable attorney's fees. Thus proper administration of union funds is advanced because of the provision.

UNION OFFICER AND EMPLOYEE REPORTING

Every union officer or employee, other than those performing clerical or custodial services exclusively, is required to file an annual report within ninety days after the end of the fiscal year if he, his spouse, or his minor child had any specified financial transaction that might constitute a possible conflict of interest. The obvious reason for such a requirement was to discourage the kinds of transactions that might constitute a conflict of interest. Very few union officers engage in such questionable activity. Only one action has been brought against a union officer for refusal to file the necessary reports, and that occurred in 1964.[32] Union officers and employees who do engage in conflict-of-interest transactions must at least disclose their activity to the Office of Labor-Management and Welfare-Pension Reports.

Certain transactions are exempted from the reporting requirements. These include wages received as an employee, normal employee discount purchases, and investments in or income received from securities traded on an exchange covered by the Securities Exchange Act.

Violations of Reporting Requirements

In the light of the massive number of reports required of unions and their officers, the number of violations has been quite small. Between 1959 and 1972, over 700,000 reports were filed by about 52,000 labor organizations and their officers. Each labor organization averages about seven officers. This means that each year about 365,000 union officials are subject to criminal prosecution under the law. In the 13-year period, only 669 were convicted for *any* Landrum-Griffin offense.[33] As this chapter shows, beyond the reporting requirement, a union officer may be convicted under the law for many crimes, including the failure to secure union bonds; embezzlement; bribery; making of union loans to union officers or employees in excess of $2,000; the payment of any union fine imposed on a union officer or employee convicted of violating the law; depriving union members of their rights by coercion or violence; the wrongful transfer of funds of a local union under a trusteeship arrangement to the national union; and serving as a union official by a person convicted previously of specified crimes.

Of the 669 union officers convicted of any Landrum-Griffin offense—about 50 each year—the majority were convicted for reporting violations: the failure to report, filing of false reports, making false entries in union records, and destruction of union records. This analysis shows that the vast majority of union officers have not only complied faithfully with the reporting requirements, but have conformed with the other standards incorporated in the law. Since only a fraction of the estimated 365,000 union representatives are convicted of any Landrum-Griffin violation per year, it is safe to conclude that the labor movement viewed as a whole is largely free of corruption. The integrity of the union official and the deterrent of Landrum-Griffin have resulted in a very satisfactory record of union officer conduct.

EMPLOYER REPORTS

Employers are required to file reports in the fiscal years in which they engage in certain practices or incur certain expenditures. The law makes reporting mandatory for the following:

1. Any payment or loan, direct or indirect, of money or other things of value (including reimbursed expenses), or any promise or agreement thereof, to any labor organization or officer, agent shop steward, or other representative of a labor organization, or employee of any labor organization, except payments permitted under the Labor Management Relations Act and payments or loans made by any national or state bank, credit union, insurance company, savings and loan association or other credit institution.

2. Any payment (including reimbursed expenses) to any of the employer's employees, or any group or committee of such employees, for the purpose of causing such employee, group or committee to persuade other employees to exercise or not to exercise, or as to the manner of exercising, the right to organize and bargain collectively through representatives of their own choosing unless such payments were contemporaneously or previously disclosed to such other employees.

3. Any expenditure, during the fiscal year, where an object thereof, directly or indirectly, is to interfere with, restrain, or coerce employees in the exercise of the right to organize and bargain collectively through representatives of their own choosing, or is to obtain information concerning the activities of employees or a labor organization in connection with a labor dispute involving the employer, except for use solely in conjunction with an administrative or arbitral proceeding or a criminal or civil judicial proceeding. Provisions do not apply to expenditures to obtain information concerning labor dispute in which employer is not involved.

4. Any agreement or arrangement with a labor relations consultant or other independent contractor or organization pursuant to which such person undertakes activities where an object thereof, directly or indirectly, is to persuade employees to exercise or not to exercise, or persuade employees as to the manner of exercising, the right to organize and bargain collectively through representatives of their own choosing, or undertakes to supply the employer with information concerning the activities of employees or a labor organization in connection with a labor dispute involving the employer, except information for use solely in conjunction

with an administrative or arbitral proceeding or a criminal or civil judicial proceeding.

5. Any payment (including reimbursed expenses) pursuant to an agreement or arrangement described in (4) above.

Curiously, this language imposes on the employer the responsibility for determining whether his actions violate the Taft-Hartley unfair labor practice provisions or whether they are protected by the free-speech provisions of the law. Indeed, the law requires an employer to report expenditures made to dissuade employees from joining unions or to affect the results of collective negotiations. A free-speech problem could arise when an employer makes a publicity expenditure during a union organizing campaign. Some employer publicity has been held in violation of the Act's unfair labor practice prohibitions.[34] An employer cannot always be certain of the legality of his actions until a decision is rendered by the NLRB. Activities protected by the free-speech provisions are not exempt from the reporting requirements for that reason alone.[35] The employer must merely report such expenditures.

Reports must be made within ninety days after the end of the fiscal year. Willful violation is punishable by a fine of $10,000 and one year in jail. The number of actions against employers has been very small. For example, as of June 30, 1972, only nine actions had been filed against them, charging violations of the reporting requirements.[36] Most were settled by either voluntary dismissal by the charging party or by stipulation. In regard to five court suits brought by the Secretary of Labor against employers, three were settled by stipulation while two resulted in judgments in favor of the employer.[37] This record indicates that employers have complied with their obligations under the law.

LABOR RELATIONS CONSULTANTS

The law imposes a duty on an employer to report any arrangement and payment made to an outside consultant for the reasons specified. Section 203 (b) imposes the same duty on the consultant to report the arrangement and payment as well. Two separate reports are required of the consultant. One involves arrangements made with the employer and another is a report on receipts and disbursements if made during the fiscal year as a result of the arrangements. The report on arrangements must be filed within thirty days after entering into an agreement. It must contain:

1. Name under which the person making the report is engaged in doing business and the address of the principal office.
2. Detailed statement of the terms and conditions of the agreement or arrangement.

The basic reason for this requirement is to obtain reports from those consultants who agree to try to (1) influence employees regarding their organizational and bargaining rights or (2) supply an employer with information regarding union activities similar to those that employers are required to report.

The second report required of consultants is the annual financial report. It must be filed within ninety days after the end of the fiscal year during which payments were made under the agreement reached with an employer. Information must be supplied showing:

1. Receipts of any kind from employers on account of labor relations advice or services, and the sources of the receipts.
2. Disbursements of any kind in connection with labor relations services and the purposes thereof.

The question of the applicability of the Act's reporting requirements to attorneys who also function as labor relations consultants to employers has been raised on several occasions. Section 203 (c) exempts reports concerning services of the consultant when he merely gives advice to an employer. Also reports are exempted when persons represent employers before any court or other tribunal, or in collective bargaining negotiations. If a consultant undertakes activities which require a report within thirty days after an agreement, then an annual report thereafter must include receipts and disbursements in connection with advice as well as services. This is required despite the exemption provided in the first report. Attorneys are not exempt from the reporting requirements when information is communicated to employers in an attorney-client relationship. In one case a federal court ruled that an attorney who functions as a labor relations consultant for one or more employers must report income and expenditures made in connection with advice and services given to all of them.[38] In another case an appellate court held that since certain activities performed by attorneys were persuasive in nature, they were reportable.[39] More recently, the Fifth Circuit Court of Appeals reversed one of its earlier decisions and held that an attorney who engages in just one "persuader" activity must report all receipts and disbursements for labor relations services rendered all labor clients. This is the price an attorney must pay for engaging in such activities.[40]

Only twelve suits in this area had been presented to the courts at the close of fiscal 1972.[41] One case was lost by the Secretary and another was dismissed for lack of venue. Five were settled by stipulation or judgment that consultants submit reports. Two were pending at the close of the fiscal year. In all there has been relatively little challenge of the consultant filing requirements. Some major issues have not yet been resolved, but the trend appears to be toward requiring reports when an attorney advises and assists in a union-breaking campaign. Such activity falls in the persuader category and as such is not exempt from the reporting requirements of Landrum-Griffin.

SURETY COMPANY REPORTS

Bonding companies are required to file annual reports within 150 days after the close of the company's fiscal year. The report must include information on premiums and must itemize losses reported during the year. No civil actions have been initiated to require compliance.

CONTROL OF TRUSTEESHIPS

Trusteeships are normally used by national unions to prevent or eliminate malpractices in subordinate local unions. House Committee Report No. 741 explained the operation of trusteeships as follows:

> Constitutions of many international unions authorize the international officers to suspend the normal processes of government of local unions and other subordinate bodies, to supervise their internal activity and assume control of their property and funds. These "trusteeships" (or "receiverships" or "supervisorships," as they are sometimes called) are among the most effective devices which responsible international officers have to insure order within their organization. In general, they have been widely used to prevent corruption, mismanagement of union funds, violation of collective bargaining agreements, infiltration of Communists; in short, to preserve the integrity and stability of the organization itself.

The McClellan committee found, however, various misuses of the trusteeship arrangement. It was found that some national unions without justification imposed trusteeships. Some suppressed rank-and-file members who attempted to release their local from the national union. At times a local was taken over and its officers removed because the local union officers were opposed to the national union officers. Some national unions used the device to plunder local treasuries. Also the corrupt nature of the trusteeship arrangement was displayed in some instances wherein local union funds were diverted to national-union-appointed trustees for their personal use. Once the arrangement was imposed, some continued under national control for as long as thirty years.

The McClellan committee devoted a great deal of attention to the trusteeship abuses of three unions: the Bakery and Confectionery Union, Operating Engineers, and the Teamsters Union. Widespread publicity was devoted to union trusteeship abuses. The result is that the 1959 Landrum-Griffin Act provides three types of regulation of trusteeships. The first permits the establishment of trusteeships only if they are to achieve certain specific aims. These are:

1. Correct corruption.
2. Correct financial malpractices.
3. Assure the performance of union contracts.
4. Assure the performance of a bargaining representative's duty.
5. Restore democratic practices.
6. Carry out the legitimate objects of the labor organization.

The constitutions and bylaws of a union imposing a trusteeship must establish the administrative procedure to be used. This requirement limits the freedom of a parent body to impose its own rules as it pleases.

The second statutory regulation prohibits a local under trusteeship to cast votes at an international convention "unless the delegates have been chosen by secret ballot in an election in which all members in good standing . . . were eligible to participate." This restriction makes it more difficult for parent bodies to keep locals under their control to further their political objectives.

The third regulation is that parent unions are required to file reports on each trusteeship upon its imposition, periodically while it is in effect, and upon its termination. Once a labor organization imposes a trusteeship over a subordinate body, it must report the action within thirty days to the Secretary of Labor. Detailed information is required on the following:

1. Name and address of the subordinate body.
2. Date the trusteeship was established.
3. Detailed statement of reasons for establishing the trusteeship.
4. Nature and extent that the subordinate body's membership participates in regular or special conventions or other policy-making sessions.
5. Full and complete account of the financial condition of the local at the time the trusteeship was established.

Much of the information listed must be filed every six months while the trusteeship remains in effect. A trusteeship imposed in accordance with a parent union's constitution and bylaws and the allowable purposes enumerated above is presumed to be valid for a period of eighteen months. However, if union officials feel the arrangement should continue beyond the eighteen-month period, the presumption of validity is reversed, if challenged, and the national officers must show "clear and convincing proof" for the need to continue the device.[42] Even before a trusteeship arrangement may be considered valid for eighteen months, it must be ratified "after a fair hearing before the executive board or before such other body as may be provided in accordance with its constitution or bylaws."[43]

A regular annual financial report is required of the national union president, the treasurer, and the trustee to account for the use of the funds of the seized local.

A third type of report is required under the trusteeship provisions. A financial report must be filed at the time a trustee arrangement is terminated to protect the integrity of the finances of a trusteed organization. Violation of the provision dealing with transfer of funds is punishable by a maximum fine of $10,000 and one year of imprisonment.

A union may file a complaint with the Secretary of Labor alleging violation of the prohibitions regarding (1) transfer of funds, (2) delegate voting, or (3) improper imposition of the trusteeship. The Act requires an investigation when a complaint is filed alleging any violation of these three conditions. A civil suit is brought in a federal district court if the Secretary finds a violation. A complaining union member or a trusteed labor organization apparently has the right to bring suit in a federal district court.

Court cases are divided on the issue of whether a union member could choose between filing a complaint with the Secretary of Labor or filing suit in a district court. One court ruled that a review of trusteeship had to be made first through the Secretary of Labor as the primary remedy.[44] Another court, however, reasoned that a union member could seek relief from either source.[45] Remedies for trusteeship violations are available under state or local courts. However, if the Secretary of Labor files a complaint, his action takes precedence over one that may be pending in any other court.

On only very infrequent occasions has the Secretary of Labor instituted civil actions to compel compliance with Landrum-Griffin trusteeship provisions. All were settled in favor of the Secretary though one was appealed to a higher court in 1968.[46]

The latter case was particularly noteworthy because it dealt with a subterfuge to cloak an illegal trusteeship. A federal court ruled that a trusteeship is in effect merely by showing a suspension of autonomy "otherwise available to a subordinate body under its constitution and by-laws."[47] The court rejected a national union claim that a trusteeship was not in effect because arrangements other than suspension of autonomy were not imposed on the local. Undoubtedly, the court's judgment was influenced by the fact that the local had lost its autonomy for twenty years. This decision would indicate that the courts will sweep aside subterfuges calculated to conceal violations of the trusteeship provisions.

In 1973, however, a federal appeals court held that the courts do not have the authority to terminate a trusteeship when the subordinate body is limited to public employees.[48] The basis for the court's decision was its finding that the local union, composed solely of public employees, was not a "labor organization" within the meaning of the law. In one way, the decision seems somewhat strange because the national union itself, American Federation of State, County and Municipal Employees, is subject to the provisions of Landrum-Griffin.

It would appear that abuses involving the trusteeship arrangement have abated as a result of the legislation. In 1959, the year in which Landrum-Griffin was enacted, there were about 500 trusteeships in effect. It is quite possible that these involved abuses in at least some of the cases since the locals were placed in trusteeship prior to the law. By 1966, only 19 of the 500 were still under an active trusteeship arrangement.[49]

As noted, the law permits trusteeships for specified and legitimate purposes. Since the enactment of the law, national unions continued to place locals under this arrangement. Indeed, between 1959 and 1972, about 2,200 trusteeships were reported to the Secretary of Labor. However, by June 1972, only 351 of this number were still in effect.[50] This is not a large number when one considers that there are about 52,000 labor organizations in the nation; and, further, since they were put into effect under the stringent provisions of the law, it is very likely that national unions placed the subordinate bodies in trusteeship for lawful purposes.

CONDUCT OF UNION ELECTIONS

Landrum-Griffin deals with union elections. The section establishes requirements concerning the frequency of elections and sets forth minimum standards relating to such things as nomination and election procedures, candidate eligibility to vote, campaign rules, and fund expenditures. It also establishes provisions to enforce the requirements.

Background of Election Regulation

Concern with union officer election procedures predates the Taft-Hartley Act although the interest was at the state level and not in Congress. Indeed, in 1943 five states passed laws with the purpose of regulating election of officers among other internal practices.[51] One state supreme court held the election provisions unconstitutional (Texas), and another held them to be valid (Colorado).[52] However, most "state legislatures and courts were reluctant" to regulate internal union procedures prior to 1959.[53]

Malpractices in union election procedures were disclosed by the Bureau of Labor Statistics, the National Industrial Conference Board, and the McClellan committee. The committee found various violations of democratic principles in union elections. These were:

1. Disregard for the [union] constitutional provisions regulating elections.
2. Prevention of members from participating in elections.
3. Prevention of opponents from nomination by violence and intimidation.
4. Use of checkoff system to disfranchise membership.
5. Giving no advance notice to membership of balloting.
6. Not using secret ballots.
7. Use of union money for the election of incumbent officers.
8. Rigging elections by stuffing ballot box.
9. Removal of duly elected officers without due process.[54]

Two studies found that only a small percentage of unions were in violation of democratic internal practices. The 1958 Bureau of Labor Statistics study revealed that only 5 percent of unions did not hold presidential elections at least every five years.[55]

A study by Philip Taft was far more devastating to unions. He found that during the period 1900–1948 81 percent of 202 national presidential elections were uncontested. The reason was either lack of membership interest or political strength of incumbents.[56] Membership apathy therefore was an element in lack of membership participation in internal union affairs. The federal government proceeded to deal with the election abuses with the aim of establishing democracy in the election procedures used by unions.

The AFL-CIO acted to correct the election malpractices of its affiliates. It was successful in establishing an ethical code, but the effort to deal with its own problems was of little avail. As a matter of fact the Kennedy-Ervin bill mentioned the federation's code of ethical practices to support its contention that legislation was needed. In any event Congress intervened to regulate union election procedures.

ELECTION PROVISIONS

Frequency of Elections. Election provisions of Landrum-Griffin apply to national and international unions, intermediate bodies, and local unions. Federations and state or local central bodies were not included in its coverage. National or international unions are required to hold elections not less frequently than five years. Voting must be by secret ballot among members of good standing or at a convention of delegates chosen by secret ballot.

Local union elections must be held at least every three years. Secret balloting must proceed among members in good standing. Intermediate bodies must hold elections at least every four years. Balloting is on the same basis as that required of national unions. The credentials of convention delegates and all election records must be preserved for one year.

Many union constitutions and bylaws may call for more frequent elections than are required under the statute. Labor organizations may also legally establish stricter requirements for election of officers. Title IV merely provides minimum standards, not maximum. Also it would appear that the states under the federal preemption doctrine are forbidden to impose requirements stricter than those in Landrum-Griffin. Greater uniformity of internal union behavior is provided by federal control as opposed to state control of elections. For example, the too-frequent holding of elections could generate uncertainty in the collective bargaining process.

Minimum Election Procedures. A union's constitution and bylaws control elections if they are not in conflict with the following Landrum-Griffin standards:

1. An election notice must be mailed to the last known address of a member within at least 15 days prior to an election.
2. Each member in good standing is entitled to one vote.
3. No member shall be ineligible to vote or to be a candidate because of alleged default or delay in payment of dues if his dues have been withheld by the employer pursuant to a voluntary dues checkoff established in the labor agreement.
4. Votes by members of each local union must be counted and the results published, separately.
5. Election records must be kept for at least one year.
6. Any candidate has a right to have an observer at the polls and at the counting of ballots.
7. A reasonable opportunity must be given to nominate candidates and every member in good standing is eligible to be a candidate and entitled to vote without fear of reprisal.

Exceptions to Right to Hold Office. Congress prohibited some persons from holding office in Title V of the 1959 law. Persons are barred from holding most union offices and jobs for five years after the end of their imprisonment for such crimes as robbery, bribery, extortion, embezzlement, grand larceny, burglary, arson, violation of narcotics laws, murder, rape, assault with intent to kill, and assault that inflicts grievous bodily injury. The five-year ban on holding office runs from the date of prison sentence expiration, not from parole date.[57] A union office, however, may be held by a person prior to the end of the five-year period if either U.S. citizenship has been regained or a Certificate of Exemption has been issued by the Board of Parole, U.S. Department of Justice.

Also disqualified from being a union officer is any individual who is a member of the Communist party, and is excluded for five years after Communist party membership termination. The Landrum-Griffin anti-communist provision was intended to replace the provision of Taft-Hartley that required principal union officers to sign non-communist oaths before they could use National Labor Relations Board facilities. The labor movement fought such a requirement and argued that it stigmatized union leaders as anti-American. Furthermore, some critics argue that communists holding union offices could easily sign such an oath. Others, however, pointed out that refusal of known communist union leaders to sign the oath prevented their unions from using NLRB facilities. This paved the way for non-communist unions to raid their membership and therefore weaken the communist hold on the labor movement.

The non-communist oath requirement of Taft-Hartley was held constitutional by the U.S. Supreme Court in 1950.[58] The Court pointed out that Taft-Hartley merely denied the use of NLRB facilities to unions whose officers refused to sign the affidavit. The 1947 law did not deny them the right to hold office.

Landrum-Griffin, as mentioned, denied communists the right to hold union office for a five-year period after termination of party membership. The U.S. Supreme Court, however, held the provision unconstitutional in 1965.[59] The high court admitted that Congress has power to deal with the problem of communists occupying positions of power and trust in labor unions. It was not willing, however, to permit Congress to deal with Communist party members under criminal sanctions through general legislation.

Thus there are no longer prohibitions on a communist holding union office. It should be recognized, however, that the number of communists holding union offices has declined over the years. There is no apparent need for a statutory prohibition on such individuals. Should a threat arise, it appears that the Congress, despite the Supreme Court's decision, would have power to deal with specific abuses. As stated, the Court held the Landrum-Griffin communist provision unconstitutional because the law deals with communists as a class. Legislation designed to prevent communists or members of other subversive groups from holding union office would probably stand the test of constitutionality if a law established specific standards upon which to judge the fitness of such individuals to serve as union officers.

Candidates Not Limited to Prior Officeholders. Local 6, Hotel, Motel and Club Employees Union, established a requirement that candidates for office had to be prior officeholders as a condition of eligibility.[60] A district court held the requirement an unreasonable restriction on the right of union members to hold office and as such a violation of the Act. It refused, however, to set aside the election and order a new one because of lack of evidence that the prior officeholding requirement affected the election outcome. The trial court merely enjoined the local from using the requirement for candidacy in future elections. An appellate court deemed the union-imposed requirement reasonable and reversed the lower court.

The Supreme Court reversed the prior decisions and held that an eligibility requirement that rendered 93 percent of the membership ineligible for office could hardly be deemed reasonable. Further, exclusion of candidates from the ballot is prima facie evidence that the violation "may have affected the outcome." Disqualified candidates may have won an election. Such a restriction was viewed as a deviation from the congressional model for democratic union elections. The members themselves were deemed the best judges of candidacy qualifications as expressed in their actions at the polls.

Conduct of Campaign. A candidate for union office can be at a distinct disadvantage during a campaign if he does not have access to the membership on a par with all other candidates. The law therefore provides that within thirty days prior to an election a candidate can inspect a list of the last-known addresses of the union's members. Discrimination in the use of such lists is forbidden. The list must be available to all candidates at a union's main office. However, the right to inspect a list is not a right to copy it. If one candidate is permitted to copy the membership list, then all are afforded the same right.[61]

The distribution of campaign literature is treated in similar fashion. Unions subject to the Act must comply with any reasonable request by a candidate to distribute campaign literature. The candidate, however, must bear the expense. This applies both to the incumbent officers as well as to those who are challenging the present officers. Any distribution arrangement made on behalf of any candidate must be made available to all upon request.

Union funds and employer contributions cannot be used to promote any candidate for election. A labor organization, however, has authority to use its funds to operate election machinery. It may pay for such items as ballots and notices publicizing the election date, place, time, and candidates. It may even publish factual statements of election issues as long as the names of the candidates are not included.

On the basis of wholesale violations of these campaign standards, a federal court invalidated the 1969 United Mine Workers' election in which the incumbent Boyle defeated Yablonski, the challenger. It was determined that the union journal, financed wholly out of union member dues, gave extensive and favorable coverage during the election campaign to Boyle and his slate, with their speeches, statements, and pictures. At the same time, the journal, sent to all union members, did not even note the candidacy of Yablonski, or credit him for his efforts to secure the enactment of mine safety legislation. Union funds were used in other ways to support the election of the incumbents. Salary increases were provided to persons on the union's payroll to secure their support of Boyle and his slate. It was expected that these salary increases (union funds) would be turned over to Boyle to finance his campaign. Yablonski was denied the right to have observers at polling places. These and other serious campaign irregularities prompted Federal District Judge William Bryant to remark that

> to find for the union (Boyle) the court would be forced to swim upstream against the tide of evidence too strong to resist.[62]

Ironically, these were the same charges that Yablonski made before the 1969 election took place. If the government could have acted on these charges and had forbidden the election to take place, it is possible that the Yablonski murders would not have occurred. As it turned out, Yablonski was not alive to enjoy the fruits of victory when his supporters defeated Boyle in the 1972 court-ordered election. In any event, the law did provide the basis for the new election and the restoration of democracy in the union.

Removal of Officers. Elected union officers may be removed for serious misconduct. If a union's constitution or bylaws do not provide an adequate procedure for removal, the Act provides a procedure. A union member may file a complaint with the Secretary of Labor. The Secretary then holds a hearing to determine the adequacy of internal union machinery for such matters. If inadequate procedures are found, proper notice must be given that a hearing will be held on the charges. If the hearings disclose that serious misconduct occurred, a secret-ballot election will be held. The Secretary can force such an election in civil suits. If a court orders a vote, the Secretary certifies the results. The court will decide from the results whether or not an officer is removed.

Enforcement of Election Procedures. There are three preliminary steps involved in the enforcement of election provisions based on a union member's complaint to the Secretary of Labor. The steps are:

1. The complaining union member must have exhausted his internal union procedures, at local and parent union levels, or must have invoked them without a final decision within three calendar months from the time he invoked them.
2. The complaint must be filed within one calendar month thereafter.
3. The Secretary of Labor must investigate the complaint.

A challenged election is presumed valid unless found to the contrary. Elected officials perform their regular duties during the investigation. If the Secretary of Labor finds probable cause to believe a violation has occurred, he must file suit in a federal district court within sixty days after the complaint is filed. It is important to note that the union member must challenge an election through the Secretary of Labor and not through the courts. In 1973, a court held that regardless of wrongdoing by a union in election matters, the member may not directly solicit the courts for relief. He must file his charges with the Secretary of Labor and the government on his behalf will file suit in court.[63] Apparently, the only exception to this rule would be where a union arbitrarily denied members the right to vote in an election. Under this limited condition, members may seek relief directly from the courts.

One relief that may be requested in the suit is the setting aside of the challenged election and the conduct of another poll. The new election, if directed by the court, is held under the supervision of the Secretary of Labor. The court will void the challenged election and direct a new one if it is found that an election has not been held within the time period established by law or if a violation may have affected the election outcome.

The Secretary will not bring suit in every case where violations are found, but only in cases where he finds evidence that violations "may have affected the outcome of an election." The Department of Labor adopted this policy because a district court is required by law to make a similar finding before ordering a new election. An appeal of a district court's decision is available, but an ordered election must be held while the appeal is pending. Otherwise, the period required for final litigation could be—and usually is—longer than the term of office challenged.

The U.S. Supreme Court ruled that a district federal court must direct a new election when the Secretary of Labor has demonstrated that violations of Landrum-Griffin standards may have affected the outcome of an election. To assure compliance with the law, the Court also held that another election held by the union after the original one was challenged does not stay the Secretary of Labor's power to conduct one under his supervision. The Court stated:

> The intervention of an election in which the outcome might be as much a product of unlawful circumstances as the challenged election cannot bring the Secretary's action to a halt. Aborting the exclusive statutory remedy would immunize a proved violation from further attack and leave unvindicated the interests protected [by law].[64]

Thus a union may not eliminate a pending Title IV action by conducting an unsupervised election of officers after the original one was challenged.

In still another case before the Supreme Court, it was held that the Secretary of Labor is not limited in his investigative powers to the specifics of a union member's complaint. It stated:

> We reject the narrow construction adopted by the District Court and supported by respondent limiting the Secretary's complaint solely to the allegations made in the union member's initial complaint. Such a severe restriction upon the Secretary's powers should not be read into the statute without a clear indication of congressional intent to that effect . . . , the indications are quite clearly to the contrary.[65]

A union member may file a complaint based on incomplete information. The Secretary of Labor has machinery at his disposal to look at the totality of election conduct, and the Supreme Court upholds his right to do so. However, in 1971, the high court limited the power of the Secretary of Labor to police union elections.[66] It held that the Secretary can bring suit in court only against the union practices that a union member protests to his union before he files his charges with the Department of Labor. While investigating a member's complaint, it was discovered that the union allegedly committed another violation of the law. However, the union member did not attempt to correct this condition through internal union procedures as he did with respect to the complaint that he filed with the Labor Department. On this basis, the Supreme Court held that the district court could consider only that complaint that the union member unsuccessfully attempted to correct through internal union procedures. Thus, it was the judgment of the high court that a union should be given the opportunity to correct undemocratic procedures before a court takes action. If the Secretary of Labor could file suit against union practices that the union itself had not been given the opportunity to correct, the court stated that union "self-government . . . would be needlessly" weakened.

By far the election provisions of the 1959 law have been used more frequently by union members as compared to any other feature of Landrum-Griffin. Between September 14, 1959, and June 30, 1970, union members filed 1,246 complaints alleging violations of the election standards contained in the law.[67] Though this number appears substantial, it should be noted that there are about 52,000 labor organizations covered by the law. Since local unions must conduct an election at least once every three years, intermediate bodies at least once every four years, and national unions at least once every five years, it follows that in this time period more than 150,000 elections were held in union groups. Actual violations of the law were found in a small number of the cases alleging wrongdoing under the law. In only 316 cases were violations found that affected the outcome of elections. Of this amount, a total of 205 new elections were held, and in the other cases the unions involved agreed to correct election practices that were deemed in violation of the law, such as changing constitutional provisions establishing internal election procedures. In only 69 cases did the courts order a new election to be administered under the supervision of the Secretary of Labor.[68]

In short, in the light of the large number of elections held by union groups, it appears that the vast number of labor organizations hold regular and fair elections. Undoubtedly, union members frequently challenge elections because of internal political differences rather than on the basis of genuine wrongdoing by incumbent union officials. On these grounds, it is understandable why the AFL-CIO remarked that Landrum-Griffin election investigations "produced only harassment and disruption, with justifiable bitterness against unnecessary governmental intrusion into internal union affairs."[69] In any event, on net balance Landrum-Griffin election standards are salutory because an effective remedy is available whenever incumbent union officers fail to provide for a fair election. Also, the existence of the law serves as a deterrent to union officers who may be inclined to deprive members of the opportunity to elect officers of their own choice on a regular and fair basis.

FINANCIAL SAFEGUARDS FOR LABOR ORGANIZATIONS

Title V includes some of the most important provisions of Landrum-Griffin regarding internal union operations. It provides for (1) fiduciary responsibilities of union officers and employees; (2) general bonding; and (3) loan and payment-of-fines standards.

Fiduciary Responsibilities of Union Officers and Employees

Union officers and representatives occupy positions of trust in relation to the union and its members. For this reason they have a duty to use the union's money and property in accordance with its constitution and bylaws "solely for the benefit of the organization and its members."

A *fiduciary* may be defined as a person who undertakes to act in the interest of another person.[70] Congress codified the common law applicable to trust relations in Title V. Persons responsible for union funds must manage, invest, and expend such funds and property in strict accordance with a labor organization's constitution, bylaws, and governing body resolutions. They must refrain from (1) dealing with their own union as an adverse party and (2) holding or acquiring pecuniary or personal interests that conflict with the union's interests. Also such persons must account to the union for any profits received by them in any transaction conducted under their direction on behalf of the union. The prohibitions extend beyond money transactions but include other deals as well as some that could evolve out of the collective bargaining process. This basic language was intended "to aid members of labor organizations in their efforts to drive criminals from the trade union movement."[71] Judge Cardozo captured the primary fiduciary responsibility well when he stated:

> Many forms of conduct permissible in a workaday world for those acting at arm's length, are forbidden to those bound by fiduciary ties. A trustee is held to something stricter than the morals of the market place. Not honesty alone, but the punctilio of an honor the most sensitive, is then the standard of behavior. As to this there has developed a tradition that is unbending and inveterate. Uncompromising rigidity has been the attitude of courts of equity when petitioned to undermine the rule of undivided loyalty by the "disintegrating erosion" of particular exceptions. . . . Only thus has the level of conduct for fiduciaries been kept at a level higher than that trodden by the crowd.[72]

It is not at all strange in light of the attention that Congress devoted to the common law that a section was included preventing a union from freeing its personnel from liability of trust duties. Any attempt to do so by the inclusion of provisions in constitutions or bylaws is void as against public policy.

Congress made no attempt to tell unions how to spend their money. It merely intended that such funds and assets were used in accordance with the direction of the membership. Senator Kennedy made this clear when he remarked that

> the bill wisely takes note of the need to consider the special problems and functions of a labor organization in applying fiduciary principles to their officers and agents. [73]

A local union, for example, may pass a resolution to use union funds to pay an officer's defense in court litigation. Should a local do so, however, the courts may enjoin the resolution as *ultra vires* in violation of the Act's purpose.[74] The resolution itself does not have the effect of relieving a person from his trust duties.

The fiduciary feature of the law becomes more meaningful when considered in the light of the reporting features discussed in the earlier part of this chapter. As noted, union officers must report all expenditures of union funds and specify the purpose. If a union officer does not report such expenditures, or reports falsely, he would be subject to criminal penalties. If he expends funds not in the interest of the union, and reports the transaction, this information is available to union members. For example, suppose a union officer caused union funds to be spent for an item for his personal use, say a boat, and truthfully reports the expenditure. Under these circumstances, the union or its members can by suit in court force the union officer to return the money so expended to the union treasury. The suit would be based upon the charge that the union officer breached his fiduciary responsibilities.

Embezzlement of Union Funds. Under Landrum-Griffin it is a federal crime for anyone to embezzle, steal, or unlawfully and willfully convert union assets to his own or to someone else's use. The section goes farther than placing a limit on union officers. Any officer or employee who siphons off union funds to third parties violates the law. It is no violation of the section for a nonmember to behave in such fashion. However, it is unlikely that a nonmember would be in a position to violate the law without assistance from a member. A person convicted of such a violation may receive a maximum sentence of $10,000 fine or five years' imprisonment, or both. The basic issue involved at an embezzlement trial is whether an official misused union funds, not whether personal benefit was gained from the assets.[75] The courts deal sharply with officials convicted of Section 501 (c) violations. For example, a New York federal district court in 1963 fined a union official $25,000 on two counts of embezzlement and one for absconding with union fund records.[76] A five-year prison sentence was also imposed.

Recovery of Assets. Landrum-Griffin provides that in the event a labor organization or its governing board of officers refuses or fails to proceed against union agents who violate their fiduciary responsibilities, a union member may file a civil suit in a federal or state court for appropriate relief under certain circumstances. A request must first be made on officers and if they fail to correct the situation within a reasonable period of time the member may file suit. An individual suit may be brought only "upon leave of the court obtained upon verified application and for good cause shown. . . ." If a court permits an individual suit, it may be for damages, an accounting of the assets in question, or "other appropriate relief" for the benefit of the labor organization. Upon request, a trial judge may allot to an individual the counsel fees and expenses incurred in the litigation. Recovery of such costs to the individual are usually allotted from any recovery of assets resulting from the action. However, the District of Columbia Circuit Court of Appeals has ruled that Section 501 (b) of the Act does not limit the courts to the amount of assets recovered through litigation.[77] Thus unions that become lax in maintaining internal control over officers could find themselves liable for litigation costs that far exceed the value of assets in question. In still another case an appellate court held that the monetary recovery may constitute a source from which litigation costs of a member are paid.[78] The award of costs, in the court's view, should be based on the benefits realized by the union as a result of the suit.

A union member is not required to exhaust internal union remedies prior to bringing suit.[79] In *Giordani* the union argued that it had not refused or failed to sue its officers within a reasonable time after being requested to do so. Nearly a year had passed from the time of the member request of union officials to proceed to obtain appropriate relief. In another case, *Purcell* v. *Keane*, a trial judge relying on the *Giordani* case ruled that "since exhaustion of remedies is not mandatory, a court does not have to find exhaustion in order to find good cause."[80]

It is still not known exactly what is meant by "within a reasonable period of time," but the courts in the *Giordani* and *Purcell* cases referred to about one year. The period of time, however, could depend largely upon the procedures initiated by particular unions after members request action of them. Many union officers, particularly those who remember the court proceedings during and prior to the 1930s, prefer to keep union affairs out of court. This may account for some reluctance to initiate action. Some officers may have convinced their members to forget violations of fiduciary responsibility. The courts have proved themselves less kind in such matters.

General Bonding

All union personnel who "receive, handle, disburse, or otherwise exercise custody or control of the funds or other property of a labor organization or a trust in which a labor organization is interested" must be bonded. Union officers, agents, shop stewards or other representatives, and union employees are included in the requirement. Bonding is not required of personnel, however, if their union has property and annual financial receipts of less than $5,000. The amount of bond required of a person is not less than 10 percent of the funds handled by the person in the previous fiscal year. The law does not require any bond to exceed $500,000. If there was no previous fiscal-year experience upon which to calculate the bond, it shall be (1) not less than $1,000 in the case of a local union and (2) not less than $10,000 in the case of any other kind of union.

Bonds must be obtained from a surety company authorized by the Secretary of the Treasury as a surety on federal bonds. They cannot be obtained from a broker or surety company in which any labor organization or any union representative has a direct or indirect interest. The bond can be either individual or schedule in form. An individual bond is a single bond covering a single named individual. A schedule bond covers particular positions. A single position may be involved or the bond may designate several positions. Each position may carry quite different coverages in accordance with the amount of funds handled. Most unions prefer schedule bonds because under this system they are relieved from the expense and trouble of obtaining a new bond each time a new officer is elected or appointed to a position.

The bonding enforcement provision makes any person who willfully violates the requirements subject to a fine of not more than $10,000 or imprisonment for not more than one year, or both. Unintentional violations may merely result in a prohibition on an individual's function in a capacity for which bonding is required.

Loans and Payment of Fines

Landrum-Griffin limits the amount of loans unions can make to their personnel. It also forbids both unions and employers paying a fine of any officer or employee convicted of any willful violation of the Act.

Total indebtedness of union officers and employees cannot exceed $2,000. The safeguard was provided to eliminate the misuse of union assets under the guise of bona fide loans.

Employers and unions are prohibited from paying the fine of any officer or employee convicted of willfully violating the statute. Willful violations of the Section 503 bans are subject to fines up to $5,000 and imprisonment of up to one year.

SUMMARY

The basic aim of Landrum-Griffin is to assure fair treatment to union members, and guarantee to them rights that are expressed or contemplated by the United States Constitution. At this time, the law has been in effect for about fifteen years. Despite the original protest of organized labor against the law, and its continued opposition in some respects, unions have learned to live and adjust to the law. Its provisions have proved burdensome at times, and particularly with regard to the election standards, unions have been burdened with defending against false or trivial charges. However, when there is evidence of abuse and wrongdoing, and the interests of people are placed in jeopardy, it is commonplace that government does intervene.

For sure, the vast number of union leaders are honest and have integrity. As in any large institution, however, there are those who would use the union movement for their personal aggrandizement and not in the interest of the members. In this light, the law fulfills a public purpose and constitutes a valuable feature of our social fabric. No law, of course, can possibly result in a utopian kind of democracy where all participants are treated equally and fairly. Despite Landrum-Griffin, some corruption and undemocratic practices undoubtedly still exist in the union movement. However, the law has eliminated some of the more flagrant abuses, and at least has served to educate officers as to their responsibilities to the membership. Clearly, it has served as a deterrent to those unscrupulous union officers who would be inclined to treat the rights of members with contempt.

NOTES

[1] 73 Stat. 519.

[2] Charles O. Gregory, *Labor and the Law* (New York: W. W. Norton & Company, Inc., 1961), p. 573.

[3] Joel Seidman, "Emergence of Concern with Union Government and Administration," in *Regulating Union Government*, eds. Marten S. Estey, Philip Taft, and Martin Wagner (New York: Harper & Row, 1964), pp. 2–3.

[4] Robert D. Leiter, "LMRDA and Its Setting," in *Symposium on the Labor-Management Reporting and Disclosure Act of 1959*, ed. Ralph Slovenko (Baton Rouge, La.: Claitor's Bookstore Publishers, 1961), p. 13.

[5] Interim Report of the Senate Select Committee on Improper Activities in the Labor or Management Field, Report No. 1417, 85th Congress, 1958.

[6] 105 Congressional Record 5806 (daily ed.), April 22, 1959.

[7] C. Peter Magrath, "Democracy in Overalls: The Futile Quest for Union Democracy," *Industrial and Labor Relations Review*, XII (1959), 503.

[8] 105 Congressional Record 14389 (daily ed.), August 12, 1959.

[9] Benjamin Aaron, "Employee Rights and Union Democracy," *Monthly Labor Review*, XCII, No. 3 (March 1969), 50.

[10] *Ibid.*, p. 50.

[11] *Ibid.*

[12] *Phalen* v. *Theatrical Protective Union No. 1 International Alliance of Theatrical & Stage Employees, AFL-CIO*, 22 N.Y. (2d) 34 (1968).

[13] Aaron, *op. cit.*, pp. 50–51.

[14] *Calhoon* v. *Harvey*, 379 U.S. 134 (1964).

[15] *Salzhandler* v. *Caputo*, 316 F. (2d) 445 (1963).

[16] *American Federation of Musicians* v. *Wittstein*, 379 U.S. 171 (1964).

[17] *Peck* v. *Associated Food Distributors of New England*, 237 F. Supp. 113 (1965).

[18] 105 Congressional Record 16414 (daily ed.), September 3, 1959.

[19] Archibald Cox, "The Role of Law in Preserving Union Democracy," *Harvard Law Review*, LXXII (1959), 609, 615.

[20] 105 Congressional Record A7915 (daily ed.), September 4, 1959.

[21] *Detroy* v. *American Guild of Variety Artists*, 286 F. (2d) 75 (1961).

[22] *NLRB* v. *Industrial Union of Marine & Shipbuilding Workers, AFL-CIO, Local 22*, 391 U.S. 418 (1968).

[23] *Boilermakers* v. *Hardeman*, U.S. Sup. Ct. No. 123 (February 24, 1971).

[24] *Strauss* v. *L.B.T.*, 179 F. Supp. 297 (1959); *Jackson* v. *Martin Company and Local 738, UAW*, 180 F. Supp. 475 (1960); *Smith* v. *Local 467, General Truck Drivers, Warehousemen & Helpers*, 181 F. Supp. 14 (1960).

[25] *Sheridan* v. *United Brotherhood of Carpenters*, 306 F. (2d) 152 (1962).

[26] *Grand Lodge of International Association of Machinists* v. *King*, 335 F. (2d) 340 (1962), cert. denied 379 U.S. 920 (1964).

[27] *De Campli* v. *Greeley*, (November 1968); see *Monthly Labor Review*, XCII, No. 3 (March 1969), 62–63.

[28] Russell A. Smith, "The Labor-Management Reporting and Disclosure Act of 1959," *Virginia Law Review*, XLVI, No. 2 (March 1960), 210.

[29] U.S. Department of Labor, Labor-Management Services Administration, *Compliance, Enforcement and Reporting in 1972 under Labor-Management Reporting and Disclosure Act*, p. 25.

[30] *NLRB* v. *Cabot Carbon Company*, 360 U.S. 203 (1959).

[31] *Compliance, Enforcement and Reporting in 1968 Under the Labor-Management Reporting and Disclosure Act* (Washington, D.C.: Government Printing Office, 1968), p. 11.

[32] *Ibid.*, p. 11.

[33] *Compliance, Enforcement and Reporting in 1972, op. cit.*, p. 17.

[34] *Boston Mutual Life Insurance Company*, 110 NLRB 272 (1954).

[35] Regulations of Secretary of Labor, Part CDV, chap. iv, Title 29, December 27, 1963.

[36] *Compliance, Enforcement and Reporting in 1972, op. cit.*, p. 16.

[37] See, for example, *Wirtz* v. *National Welders Supply Company, Inc.*, U.S. District Court, Western District of North Carolina, No. 1725 (May 17, 1966).

[38] *Douglas* v. *Wirtz*, 353 F. (2d) 30 (1965), cert. denied 383 U.S. 909 (1966).

[39] *Fowler* v. *Wirtz*, 372 F. (2d) 315 (1966).

[40] *Price, Nelson, & Sears* v. *Wirtz*, *Federal Reporter*, CDXII, No. 2, 647–656.

[41] *Compliance, Enforcement and Reporting in 1972, op. cit.*, p. 16.

[42] Sar A. Levitan, "The Federal Law of Union Trusteeship," in *Symposium on the Labor-Management Reporting and Disclosure Act of 1959*, ed. Ralph Slovenko (Baton Rouge, La.: Claitor's Bookstore Publishers, 1961), p. 453.

[43] *Ibid.*

[44] *Rizzo* v. *Ammond*, 182 F. Supp. 456 (1960).

[45] *Local 28* v. *IBEW*, 184 F. Supp. 649 (1960).

[46] *Compliance, Enforcement and Reporting in 1972, op. cit.*, p. 15.

[47] *Lavender* v. *United Mine Workers of America*, 285 F. (2d) 869 (1968).

[48] *State, County, and Municipal Employees, New Jersey* and *Municipal Council 61* v. *State, County, and Municipal Employees* (CA 3), No. 72-1645 (May 4, 1973).

[49] U.S. Department of Labor, *Summary of Operations, 1966, LMRDA*, pp. 15–17.

[50] *Compliance, Enforcement and Reporting in 1972, op. cit.*, p. 5.

[51] The states were Colorado, Florida, Kansas, Minnesota, and Texas.

[52] See Julius Rezler, "Union Elections: The Background of Title IV of LMRDA," in Slovenko, ed., *op. cit.*, pp. 475–494.

[53] *Ibid.*, p. 482.

[54] *Ibid.*, pp. 485–486.

[55] *Ibid.*, p. 483.

[56] *Ibid.*, p. 483.

[57] *Serio* v. *Liss*, 189 F. Supp. 358 (1960), affirmed 300 F. (2d) 386 (1961).

[58] *American Communications Association* v. *Douds*, 339 U.S. 382 (1950).

[59] *United States* v. *Archie Brown*, 381 U.S. 437 (1965).

[60] *Wirtz* v. *Hotel, Motel & Club Employees Union, Local 6*, 391 U.S. 492 (1968).

[61] *Conley* v. *Aiello*, 276 F. Supp. 614 (1967).

[62] *Wall Street Journal*, April 3, 1972.

[63] *Schonfeld* v. *Raferty*, U.S. District Court, Southern District of New York, No. 67 Civ. 3147 (May 8, 1973).

[64] *Wirtz* v. *Local 153, Glass Bottle Blowers Association of the United States & Canada, AFL-CIO*, 389 U.S. 463 (1968).

[65] *Wirtz* v. *Local Union No. 125, Laborers International Union of North America, AFL-CIO*, 389 U.S. 477 (1968).

[66] *Hodgson* v. *Steelworkers, Local 6799*, 403 U.S. 333 (1971).

[67] U.S. Department of Labor, Labor-Management Services Administrator, *Union Elections under the LMRDA, 1966–1970*, p. 6.

[68] *Ibid.*, p. 120.

[69] AFL-CIO, *American Federationist*, v. 27, No. 11 (November 1970), p. 21.

[70] Albert B. Tarbutton, Jr., "The Fiduciary Responsibility of Officers of Labor Organizations Under the Common Law and LMRDA," in Slovenko, ed., *op. cit.*, p. 514.

[71] Samuel Duker, "Fiduciary Responsibility of Union Officials," in Slovenko, ed., *op. cit.*, p. 521.

[72] *Meinhard* v. *Salmon*, 249 N.Y. 464 (1928), cited at *ibid.*, p. 521.

[73] *History of the Labor-Management Reporting and Disclosure Act*, NLRB, II (1959), 1433.

[74] *Local 107, Highway Truck Drivers & Helpers* v. *Cohen*, 182 F. Supp. 608 (1960), affirmed 284 F. (2d) 162 (1960), cert. denied 365 U.S. 833 (1961).

[75] *United States* v. *Harrelson*, 223 F. Supp. 869 (1963).

[76] *United States* v. *Davis* (SD N.Y. 9/12/63), Nos. 63 Criminal 164 and 293.

[77] *Ratner* v. *Bakery Workers*, 394 F. (2d) 780 (1968).

[78] *Local 92, Iron Workers* v. *Norris*, 383 F. (2d) 735 (1967).

[79] *Giordani* v. *Hoffman*, 277 F. Supp. 722 (1967).

[80] *Purcell* v. *Keane*, 277 F. Supp. 252 (1967).

21 Labor Relations in the Public Sector

The issue of public employee collective bargaining reached unprecedented proportions in the decade of the sixties. The changing composition of employment in the United States has brought with it a rapid rise in government employment. In 1930 only about 6 percent of the civilian labor force was engaged in public employment. In 1972 government employees constituted nearly 17 percent of the nonagricultural work force. At the close of 1972 federal, state, and local governments employed a total of 12,202,000 workers.[1] Government employment has more than doubled since 1947 when it totaled 5,474,000.[2] However, the greatest gains have been at the state and local level—not in federal jobs, as is often mistakenly believed. About one-third of state and local employees are associated with education. Over the twenty-five-year period, federal employment rose by about 50 percent while state and local employment increased nearly 300 percent. State and local employment in 1972 accounted for 9,465,000 of the total of 12, 202,000 government employees.

The public sector has not been prepared to deal with the issues presented by increased employment. The lack of preparation is revealed in the diverse pattern of treatment of such workers in the fifty states and in the federal government. An appreciation of the critical collective bargaining issues existing in the government sector may be obtained by a review of (1) philosophies of government employee bargaining; (2) labor relations in federal employment; (3) state approaches to public employee bargaining. Many states have learned through experience that public workers will no longer refrain from collective action. Thus many states have had to review their traditional positions regarding state and local employees.

BASIS OF DENIAL OF GOVERNMENT EMPLOYEE
BARGAINING

The doctrine of sovereignty has been used by governmental bodies as a basis of denying the collective bargaining process to public employees. Sovereignty may be defined as the supreme, absolute, and uncontrollable power by which any independent state is governed. In the United States ultimate power reposes in the people but is exercised for them by their duly elected representatives. Elected representatives exercise sovereign power within the limits placed on them by constitutions and statutes. Unionization of government workers is viewed as interference with sovereign authority because it could lead to joint determination of wages, hours, and terms and conditions of employment. Union attempts to take away or share a sovereign power is therefore unlawful.

In public employment the extension to public employees of the right to join unions was traditionally viewed as a surrender of power and a dereliction of duty. President Franklin Roosevelt made a distinction between public and private bargaining rights in 1937 and he has often been quoted:

> The employer is the whole people, who speak by means of laws enacted by their representatives in Congress. Accordingly, administrative officials, and employees alike, are governed and guided, and in many instances restrained, by laws which establish policy procedures or rules in personnel matters.[3]

Both the Wagner Act and the Taft-Hartley Act deliberately excluded federal workers from coverage under their provisions. Public Law 330, 1955, makes a felony of federal employee strike activity.[4]

It has been advanced in recent years that a government has the authority to abandon traditional approaches to public employee bargaining. This may be done either by the legislative or executive branches of government. One writer concluded that

> the [sovereignty] doctrine does not preclude the enactment of legislation specifically authorizing the government to enter into collective bargaining relationships with its employees.[5]

Indeed, the concept of sovereignty has not prevailed as a hard and fast political concept over time. The federal government has long deviated from a policy of absoluteness.

Several arguments have evolved out of the sovereignty idea and are advanced to support denial of collective bargaining. One argument is that the public interest is not advanced by collective negotiations. The public pays the taxes that pay the wages and fringe benefits of the public employee. A work stoppage undertaken by such workers affects the public in two ways. First, taxes have to be increased to support the increased costs of labor. Collective bargaining therefore deprives citizens of their basic right to representation by elected officials only. Second, the public is also deprived of essential services such as transportation and garbage collection if strikes result from bargaining impasses. One member of the House Post Office and Civil Service Committee assessed the public-interest argument this way:

> The trouble with the "public interest" concept is that it is only triggered in time of crisis. There's no "public interest" generated ahead of time, no particular show of concern for meeting the genuine economic and social needs of the public employee—whether he's a teacher, a fireman, a policeman, a clerk or a laborer. It's not until there is a direct, adverse effect on the body politic that the "public interest" is invoked—and then, of course, it's invoked against the public employee and on the side of the public administrator.[6]

A second argument that is used to deny public employee collective bargaining is known as the *special status concept*. Such workers are viewed as virtually immune from unemployment imposed by business cycles. Furthermore, it is advanced that their pensions and other fringe benefits are superior to those available in the private sector.

In recent years public employee strikes have largely dispelled the special status argument. The general public often refuses to support wage increases of such groups, however, because of an increasing tax burden. The fact is that public workers have not been sharing proportionately in the economic growth of the United States. Teachers provide one example of this common problem.

The Bureau of Labor Statistics periodically prepares an intermediate budget for a family of four. The United States average in 1973 was $12,626. In January 1968 the Conference of Economic Progress reported that in the ten largest cities the minimum or starting salaries of public school teachers averaged 42 percent below the amount required to live at a moderate level within those cities. Also it was reported that 36 percent of all teachers earned less than the average of the thirty-nine metropolitan areas included in the budget. Teachers salaries have fallen below the 1968 level.

The doctrine of sovereignty is no longer capable of generating acceptance of the ancient denial of collective action in the public sector. Various approaches have been used to deal with the increased militancy of public employees.

COLLECTIVE BARGAINING AMONG FEDERAL EMPLOYEES

Unionization of federal employees reportedly existed as early as 1800 in naval yards.[7] The Departments of Defense and Interior have a long history of collective bargaining. Wage rate negotiation has occurred among various levels of TVA employees ranging from those classed as production workers through the professional ranks. Negotiations have occurred despite the general understanding that wages are set by law.

Federal policy toward employee organizations dates back to 1883 when the Pendleton Act was passed. That Act is commonly known as the Civil Service Act. Under its terms only Congress had the authority to regulate wages, hours, and other terms and conditions of employment.

President Theodore Roosevelt in 1902 banned federal employees from seeking legislation directly or indirectly through their associations that would benefit them except through the departments in which they were employed. A violation of the order was grounds for dismissal.[8] In 1906 President Roosevelt broadened the earlier order and stated that

> all officers and employees of the United States of every description, serving in or under any of the Executive Departments or independent Government establishments, and whether so serving in or out of Washington, are hereby forbidden, either directly or indirectly, individually or through associations, to solicit an increase of pay or to influence or attempt to influence in their own interest any other legislation whatever, either before Congress or its Committees, or in any way save through the heads of the Departments or independent Government establishments, in or under which they serve, on penalty of dismissal from the Government service.[9]

Congress took up the question of federal employee organization in 1912. It rejected the approach of President Theodore Roosevelt in the Lloyd–La Follette Act.[10] The statute became the basis for the principle that federal employees in general had the right to join any organization that does not assert the right to strike against the government.[11] If a literal interpretation is made, the Act limited protection of union membership to postal employees. Despite that fact other employees gained the right to organize on the basis of its language. The right to organize, however, is of limited value if procedures are not provided to guarantee an effective collective bargaining process. The Lloyd–La Follette Act did not provide such machinery.

Construction of the Alaskan railroad, which began in 1914, provided another boon to federal employee bargaining. Most of the construction workers on the railroad had already been organized prior to the time work was to start. The government negotiated its first written labor agreement in 1920.[12]

The Boston policemen's strike slowed the drive toward more effective collective bargaining machinery among all public employees—federal, state, and local alike. However, instances of collective bargaining arrangements occurred throughout the period of the thirties despite the damage of the Boston strike. Renewed efforts to obtain more favorable bargaining legislation started in the 1940s.

The Rhodes-Johnston Bill was introduced in 1949 as a measure to protect the right of unions to represent federal employees. It failed to pass in that year and was debated for fourteen years.[13] Essentially, the bill was designed primarily to provide for the resolving of grievances within the various federal agencies. A large number of weaknesses in the bill were partially responsible for its not being passed.

The Classification Act of 1949 contained a section that facilitates union influence on wages. It provides that wage board employees' compensation

> shall be fixed and adjusted from time to time as nearly as is consistent with the public interest in accordance with prevailing wages.

The provision makes it possible to affect the wage rate determined by surveys by negotiating on the items that determine the outcome. These are (1) the geographic area to be covered, (2) the firms to be included or excluded in the survey, (3) key jobs to be used as a basis for gathering wage information, and (4) the number of jobs to be surveyed. The 1949 provisions therefore enhanced the power of some unions to influence the wage rates paid their members.

COORDINATED FEDERAL WAGE SYSTEM

A new Coordinated Federal Wage System has been developed through consultation among unions, agencies, and the Civil Service Commission.[14] It became effective on June 30, 1970. The basic objective is to eliminate inequity in pay rates among federal blue-collar employees who do identical work in the same geographic areas.

A National Wage Policy Committee was established by the chairman of the Civil Service Commission to advise on the basic policies and procedures of the Coordinated Federal Wage System. Membership is composed of five from management, five from unions, and a chairman. Four of the union members are chosen by the president of the AFL-CIO and the other is named by the head of an independent union selected on a rotating basis. Three management representatives are from the Department of Defense. One each is from the Veterans Administration and the General Services Administration. The chairman is appointed by the chairman of the Civil Service Commission. The committee reviews and recommends basic policies and rules that govern the system.

The device gives unions a more definite role in determining wages than was provided through the wage board surveys of the past. Their new responsibilities include the recruiting and training of data collectors, recognition of weaknesses of the system, and the suggestion of changes to make the system more viable.

Essentially, wage determination begins with the designation of a lead agency by the Civil Service Commission. The designated agency is the largest employer of workers in the wage area. It in turn appoints an agency wage committee to advise it on the coverage of wage surveys and thereafter the development of a wage schedule.

The agency wage committee is composed of five members. The union exclusively representing the largest number of wage employees of the lead agency appoints two members. The other three are appointed by the lead agency. The committee functions in an advisory capacity.

Still other procedures are involved in establishing the prevailing wage in a particular area. The most important aspect of the Coordinated Federal Wage System is the involvement of unions at all phases of the wage-setting procedure. The system both formalizes and expands on an established practice of union involvement in wage board functions. If the device proves successful, other federal employee unions may obtain a voice in setting wage rates for their members in agencies not covered by wage boards. At least the precedent has been set for such behavior in the federal service.

EXECUTIVE ORDER NO. 10988

President Kennedy as a senator was involved in several unsuccessful attempts to pass the Rhodes-Johnston Bill. In 1961 after becoming President he appointed a six member task force to study the problem of employee-management relations in the federal service. The group, headed by Arthur Goldberg, submitted its findings on November 30, 1961, and reported in part that

> at the present time, the Federal Government has no Presidential policy on employ-ee-management relations, or at least no policy beyond the barest acknowledge-ments that such relations ought to exist. Lacking guidance, the various agencies of the Government have proceeded on widely varying courses. Some have established extensive relations with employee organizations; most have done little; a number have done nothing. The Task Force is firmly of the opinion that in large areas of the Government we are yet to take advantage of this means of enlisting the creative energies of Government workers in the formulation and implementation of policies that shape the conditions of their work.[15]

Thus it was deemed improper for the government to fail to extend to its own employ-ees the same privileges enjoyed by workers in private enterprise as a result of federal action. The task force expressed the opinion that responsible unions would strengthen and improve the federal service.[16]

In January 1962 President Kennedy responded to the report by issuing Executive Order No. 10988 which established the basic framework within which collective bargaining was to take place in agencies under the executive branch of government. In October 1969 President Nixon issued Executive Order No. 11491 which substan-tially changed President Kennedy's order. The new order became effective on January 1,1970. First we shall examine President Kennedy's executive order and then show how the new order changes the union organization and collective bar-gaining rights of federal employees. The key to an understanding of these orders is that for the first time federal employees have the protected right to join unions and engage in collective bargaining with certain federal agencies (Post Office Depart-ment, Department of Defense, Labor Department, Agriculture Department, and so on) for whom they work. These agencies under proper circumstances must recognize and bargain collectively with unions representing government employees. Thus the federal government has attempted to provide organizational and bargaining rights for its employees in essentially the same way as these rights are established for employ-ees in the private sector by Taft-Hartley.

Under Executive Order No. 10988 federal employees were free to decide to join or not to join any employee group. Union bargaining rights depended upon the extent of employee membership in the organizations. Three types of union recog-nition were provided. These were informal, formal, and exclusive.

Informal Recognition. This form was extended to any employee organization that did not qualify for either the formal or exclusive forms. Management was not required to seek the views of such organizations in personnel matters. Informal recognition therefore was not very effective since a union which secured this kind of recognition need not be consulted by government management in the establishment of conditions of employment. A head of a government agency on a voluntary basis might consult with such a union, but there was nothing compulsory about it. To secure informal recognition, a union did not have to show any specific amount of union member-ship. The AFL-CIO termed this form of recognition "virtually meaningless."[17]

Formal Recognition. Formal recognition was permitted if a union demonstrated a stable membership of at least 10 percent of employees in the bargaining unit. Unlike the condition that prevailed under informal recognition, a federal government agency was obligated to consult with a union securing formal recognition on matters of personnel policies and practices. In addition, such a union had the right to raise such matters for discussion with the appropriate management representatives. It follows therefore that formal recognition was a more meaningful form of recognition than the informal type.

Exclusive Recognition. The most meaningful type of recognition under Executive Order No. 10988 was exclusive recognition. To secure exclusive recognition for a group of federal employees, a union had to show that it represented at least 10 percent of the employees involved and then be selected or designated by a majority of employees within the bargaining unit. When a union obtained exclusive recognition, it represented all employees in the bargaining unit without regard to union membership. Of crucial importance such a union was authorized to negotiate collective bargaining contracts, and the government agency was compelled to meet with the labor organization in collective bargaining. Thus President Kennedy's order stated:

> When an employee organization has been recognized as the exclusive representative of employees of an appropriate unit it shall be entitled to act for and to negotiate agreements covering all employees in the unit and shall be responsible for representing the interests of all such employees without discrimination and without regard to employee organization membership. Such employee organization shall be given the opportunity to be represented at discussions between management and employees or employee representatives concerning grievances, personnel policies and practices, or other matters affecting general working conditions of employees in the unit. The agency and such employee organizations, through appropriate officials and representatives, shall meet at reasonable times and confer with respect to personnel policy and practices and matters affecting working conditions, so far as may be appropriate subject to law and policy requirements. This extends to the negotiation of an agreement, or any question arising thereunder, the determination of appropriate technique, consistent with the terms and purposes of this order, to assist in such negotiation, and the execution of a written memorandum or agreement of understanding incorporating any agreement reached by the parties.

To this extent unions which obtained exclusive recognition had some rights similar to those unions receive under the Taft-Hartley law. Also when exclusive recognition prevailed, the government agency had similar obligations as those imposed under Taft-Hartley for private employers.

ADDITIONAL CHARACTERISTICS OF EXECUTIVE ORDER NO. 10988

There were several other major characteristics of Executive Order No. 10988. An employees' association was not a lawful organization if it

1. asserted the right to strike against the United States government;
2. advocated the overthrow of the United States Constitution; or
3. discriminated with regard to membership on the basis of race, color, creed, or national origin. In other words, a union which did not conform to these standards has no rights or standing under the executive order.

If, for example, a union advocated the right to strike against the United States government, it could not represent federal employees, and a government agency would be forbidden to recognize such a union for the purposes of collective bargaining. Also the order prohibited any arrangement requiring union membership as a condition of employment. Thus under the order no government employee is obligated to join a union as a condition of employment. Note that in the private sector federal law permits the union-shop and maintenance-of-membership agreements. Other items were removed from the scope of collective bargaining under Executive Order No. 10988. It prohibited negotiations regarding the mission of a federal agency and its structural organization. Also forbidden were negotiations on the budget of an agency, the assignment of personnel, and the technology under which its work is carried out. For example, no union representing federal employees could negotiate an agreement limiting the right of a federal agency to automate its operation. As expected, negotiations may not result in changes of salaries or wages established by an act of Congress.

Despite limitations on the scope of collective bargaining, there was a considerable range of matters which could be lawfully negotiated and reduced to a collective bargaining contract. Indeed, even with the limitations mentioned, and the fact that federal employees and their unions are forbidden to strike, the issues negotiated and included in written collective bargaining agreements covering federal employees are truly impressive. Such issues included the following: overtime; call-back and call-in pay; shift differentials; upgrading of an entire job classification; rest periods; shift scheduling; apprenticeship programs and career development; qualifications for promotions and the posting of open jobs upon which employees may bid; transfers; vacation scheduling; safety programs; assignment of disabled employees; use of bulletin boards; and training programs for new employees and refresher courses for senior employees. Many of these items, of course, are included in labor agreements covering private employees.

Also, and of significance, is the fact that the voluntary checkoff of union dues was lawful under Executive Order No. 10988. Unions which held formal or exclusive recognition rights could negotiate dues checkoff arrangements. Federal employees, however, have the opportunity to rescind the checkoff authorization twice a year.[18] In contrast, under Taft-Hartley employees who authorized the checkoff of union dues may rescind their authorization only once per year.

President Kennedy's order also permitted the negotiation of a grievance procedure to apply the terms of an existing labor agreement. Not only could an employee or union protest that a government agency violated working conditions established by the contract, but they could also file a grievance protesting the discipline, including discharge, of a federal employee. In this respect there is a great similarity between private labor agreements and those negotiated for federal employees. However, there is an important difference between grievance procedures established in the private sector and those negotiated under Executive Order No. 10988. It will be recalled that the capstone of the grievance procedure under private contracts provides for final and binding arbitration. In contrast, the order establishes only *advisory* arbitration for federal employees. For example, if a union representing federal employees elected to arbitrate an unresolved grievance such as one protesting the discharge of an employee, the award would not have been final and binding on both parties. The proceedings of such an arbitration were similar to one taking place in the private sector, including the use of private arbitrators. However, the head of a government agency was not bound by an award issued by the private arbitrator. He looked at it only as a recommendation or as *advice*. If the agency head refused to honor an award issued by an arbitrator in favor of the discharged employee, there was no recourse for the employee or the union.

In two other ways the system of collective bargaining established for federal employees differed from that in the private sector. When a private employer and a union agree to a collective bargaining contract, it goes into effect without further approval (ratification by union members excepted). However, in the federal sector, the head of a government agency had the right to approve or rescind a labor agreement negotiated by a union and government agency representative. For example, the United States Postmaster General had the authority to rescind all or part of a labor agreement negotiated by a union and the postmaster of the post office located in Newark, Delaware. Under these circumstances the union would have no recourse from the decision of the Postmaster General.

Finally, the issue of handling an impasse in the negotiation of a labor agreement differed greatly as compared to the private sector. We know, of course, that a strike can take place when a private employer and a union reach an impasse in negotiations. In the private sector this is par for the course. However, federal employees are forbidden to strike and this weapon cannot be used to achieve a settlement of the issues in dispute. Moreover, arbitration of any kind—advisory or final and binding—was forbidden under Executive Order No. 10988 as a forum to break a deadlock in negotiations. Hence there was no effective way to break an impasse in negotiations. Mediation was permitted, but a recommendation by a mediator was not binding on the union or agency.

MEDIATION IN THE FEDERAL SERVICE

Even though Executive Order No. 10988 did not exactly encourage the use of mediation, the Federal Mediation and Conciliation Service (FMCS) has experimented with its use since 1965. The Civil Service Commission issued a bulletin in 1962 which emphasized that the FMCS was not assigned responsibility to mediate federal service disputes.[19]

Public employee unrest prompted the FMCS to reevaluate its lack of activity among federal employees. Discussion with Civil Service Commission personnel and union and agency representatives led to a policy and procedure for considering mediation requests. In part the policy included:

1. All requests for mediation had to be screened and decided upon at the FMCS office in Washington, D.C.
2. No request would be considered unless made jointly by both parties and usually in writing.
3. No request would be considered unless, following genuine bargaining efforts, both parties agreed that an impasse had been reached.
4. In the event a joint request was approved, the FMCS would select and assign the individual mediator.
5. The mediator assigned would be available only for a limited period of time on a limited number of joint meetings, as the situation dictated.[20]

This policy pronouncement resulted from the inadequate executive order provisions for dispute settlement. On the whole, mediation was only mildly successful in contract dispute cases because mediators faced a different set of circumstances than in private industry. The strike is not permitted by federal employees and thus the strike deadline is not available to assist mediation efforts. Some negotiations, moreover, had been in progress for as long as fifteen months before mediation efforts were initiated.[21] Another weakness was in the mediation policy itself. A single-party mediation request was not honored. In some cases one of the parties refused to enter into a joint request for mediation services. A more logical approach would have been to permit the FMCS to enter a case upon the request of either party.

DEFICIENCIES IN EXECUTIVE ORDER NO. 10988

A major weakness of meaningful bargaining in the federal service is the comparatively limited scope of bargaining subjects. Bargaining issues were limited not only by the 1962 executive order, but also by the Civil Service Commission and various agency rules and regulations. Even though the parties were forbidden to bargain on certain items, many of them are sources of employment irritation and could lead to unwholesome labor relations. As stated, many matters were considered as lawful issues of bargaining. However, those that were not imposed a limitation not found in the private sector. It is possible that bargaining on some of the subjects prohibited could be permitted without impairing the efficiency of the federal government.

Another important shortcoming was that no independent and impartial agency was established to administer and develop labor relations policies. The Civil Service Commission was entrusted with the responsibility of implementing labor-management policy under the order. Some observers contended that the Civil Service Commission is management-oriented and its responsibility for federal employee relations resembles a situation that could exist if the Board of Directors of General Motors had been entrusted with administration of the Taft-Hartley Act.[22]

The executive order was most defective, however, in the dispute settlement area. When mediation failed to bring about an agreement on the issues, the only available procedure was to appeal to a higher level of the agency's management. This has the effect of dampening meaningful negotiation.

Despite the weaknesses of the executive order, considerable activity has taken place among employee organizations. As of 1970 exclusive bargaining rights have been designated for 2,305 separate units in 35 agencies covering about 1,400,000 employees—52 percent of the federal labor force subject to the order. Organizational activity has been heaviest in the postal service where close to 90 percent of workers are members of unions with exclusive bargaining rights. The postal employees are by far the largest federal group of organized employees.[23]

EXECUTIVE ORDER NO. 11491

Executive Order No. 11491, styled "Labor-Management Relations in the Federal Service," became effective on January 1, 1970. It resulted from studies of the operation of President Kennedy's order which highlighted some areas for improvement.

In several ways the deficiencies of the original order have been corrected. In the first place, exclusive recognition is now provided only for unions representing federal employees. The informal and formal categories have been abolished. This is a wholesome change since these two types had little meaning. Under the present order a union, to gain exclusive recognition, must be selected by a majority of the employees in a bargaining unit through a secret election. Under the original order unions were able to secure exclusive recognition by the use of signed union membership authorization cards. This procedure has been eliminated and undoubtedly the reason for this change has been the criticism of the NLRB policy which permits the use of authorization cards under certain circumstances as the basis of bargaining orders. Note that the basis of the NLRB policy is employer unfair labor practices calculated to destroy a union's majority. Since government officials are not likely to engage in such practices, the requirement that the election be used as the sole basis of gaining bargaining rights is probably a valid policy.

As we have noted, under the original order the Civil Service Commission and the various federal agencies were given the power to oversee and implement the policies and procedures contained in the document. The new order creates a three-member Federal Labor Relations Council to administer the program, decide major policy matters, and issue rules and regulations. Thus it states: "This group is composed of the Chairman of the Civil Service Commission, the Secretary of Labor, and an official to be named from the President's Executive Office." In a way the Federal Labor Relations Council for purposes of the order stands in the same relationship as the NLRB for purposes of Taft-Hartley. It is likely that the Federal Labor Relations Council will be more objective and independent in its action than was the old system under which the Civil Service Commission and the government agencies interpreted and applied the former order.

In addition, the new order gives the Assistant Secretary of Labor for Labor-Management Relations authority to resolve disputes over the make-up of bargaining units and representation rights, to order and supervise elections, and to disqualify unions from recognition because of corrupt or undemocratic influences. Formerly, these matters were handled by the particular federal agency and their final judgment was not subject to appeal. Though there still may exist a "community of interest" between the Labor Department official authorized to make these determinations and the heads of federal agencies, it is a safe prediction that he will make his decision on a much fairer basis than when sole power was lodged in the federal agencies. Decisions of the Assistant Secretary for Labor-Management Relations may be appealed to the Federal Labor Relations Council.

Another entirely new feature is contained in the new order. Unions representing government employees are required to furnish essentially the same kind of information (election, bonding, and financial reporting) as required from unions operating in the private sector. In short, a good share of the information required in the Landrum-Griffin Act is now mandatory for government unions. Though there has been no evidence that such unions have been charged with corrupt or undemocratic practices, it may be argued that consistency demands that the Landrum-Griffin requirements be applied to unions representing federal employees. Since there is now assurance that government unions must operate free from corruption and undemocratic practices, it is questionable that the prohibition against the union shop should have been carried over to the new order. As before, government unions may not negotiate a requirement of union membership as a condition of employment. This means nonunion employees in the bargaining unit receive the same benefits as those federal employees who support the unions by membership and dues payments.

In the area of grievance arbitration, the new order strips federal agencies of the power to refuse to honor the award of an arbitrator. Now the Federal Labor Relations Council has the authority to issue binding arbitration decisions on grievance disputes and questions of interpretation of contracts. Private arbitrators still will be used to deal with grievances not settled by the parties. Under specified circumstances the decisions of the private arbitrators may be appealed to the council. The decisions of this body become final and binding. The new procedure overcomes one of the greatest defects of the original order. No longer is the head of a federal agency empowered to turn down an award issued by a private arbitrator. If there is to be any appeal from his award, it will go to the Federal Labor Relations Council. Though there still exists some difference even under the new order on grievance arbitration as compared to arbitration in the private sector, the present system certainly demonstrates improvement. At least it relieves from the head of a federal agency the power to refuse to abide by an arbitration decision when he feels inclined to do so. Of course, to make the new system work fairly and in a manner to maintain the integrity of the arbitration process, the Federal Labor Relations Council must act in a strictly judicial and objective manner on any appeal. If it acts in this fashion, it is entirely possible that in effect the decision of the private arbitrator will be final and binding.

Unfair labor practices for government unions and agencies are specified by the new order. In a way these unfair labor practices reflect those established in the Taft-Hartley law. For example, a government agency violates the terms of the order if it interferes with the right of employees to join unions; encourages or discourages membership in a union by discrimination in regard to hiring, tenure, promotion, or other conditions of employment; refuses to recognize a union qualified for recognition; and refuses to negotiate with a union which has secured exclusive bargaining rights. Under the new order a union engages in an unfair labor practice if it interferes with the right of employees not to join a union; coerces or fines a member as punishment for the purpose of impeding his work performance, his productivity, or his duties as a government employee; engages in strikes or slowdowns or fails to take appropriate action to prevent or stop a strike; and refuses to bargain collectively.

As stated, the Federal Labor Relations Council will interpret these unfair labor practices in the same way as the NLRB interprets the Taft-Hartley law. Undoubtedly, the council will use some of the precedents of the NLRB in the execution of this duty. For more than thirty-five years the NLRB has performed in the private sector the job now given to the Federal Labor Relations Council under the 1970 Executive Order. Hence there exists a large body of experience which the council could use in the interpretation of the unfair labor practices of the new order.

Finally, but of crucial importance, the new order establishes a procedure to break impasses in contract negotiation disputes. As stated, except for mediation the old order provided for no impartial procedure to break deadlocks in contract negotiation. Employees could not strike, and the old order strictly prohibited arbitration as a forum for the settlement of disputes. In fact, realistically viewed, the only procedure available under the old order was to have disputes of this kind resolved by the federal agency involved in the negotiations. It was the same as if a private employer would unilaterally determine contract negotiation disputes involving himself and the union!

Under the new order the President appoints members to a Federal Service

Impasse Panel. This group is authorized to consider negotiation impasses and "may take any action it considers necessary to settle an impasse." What this means is that if the Federal Mediation and Conciliation Service, which has the duty to mediate disputes in the federal sector under the order, is unable to mediate differences, the panel at its discretion may use arbitration to settle a contract negotiation dispute. Subject to appeals to the Federal Labor Relations Council, a decision of the Federal Impasse Panel is binding upon the union, employees, and agency involved. Since under the new order, as was true under the original order, federal employees are not permitted to strike, the system for final and binding arbitration is equitable and realistic.

It will be interesting to follow the activities of the Federal Service Impasse Panel. If unions and the federal agencies bargain realistically and in good faith, it is entirely possible that not many disputes will be referred to the group for final and binding arbitration. Another point to watch is the number of disputes the panel accepts for arbitration. Note that it is not compelled to arbitrate contract negotiation issues. It has the discretion to do so if in the judgment of its members such a procedure is deemed necessary. Clearly, the purpose and intent of the new system will be defeated if the panel refuses to arbitrate. On the other hand, it would be proper for the panel to refuse to arbitrate small and unimportant matters that the parties themselves should handle in direct negotiations. Finally, aside from the quantity of work of the panel, attention should be paid to the quality of its decisions. What kind of decisions will be handed down by the group? What standards will it use in the discharge of its arbitration function? Will it be judicial in its decisions, using accepted standards of arbitration, or will it be persuaded by considerations not relevant to the merits of a dispute?

On the whole the changes in the order were worthwhile. They did much to strengthen the right of federal employees to organize and bargain collectively. Complete evidence is not yet available as to the activities of the new groups established to implement the new order. In large measure how they operate will determine the success or failure of public policy to confer upon federal employees and their unions rights similar to those enjoyed by employees in the private sector. If the groups operate fairly and objectively, a long step forward will be taken by government to extend to its own employees the same rights which government has conferred on employees in the private sector.

EXECUTIVE ORDER 11616

When Executive Order 11491 was issued in 1969, President Nixon directed that a review and assessment of the Order be made after one year. In the meantime, the Postal Reform Act placed postal employees under a system separate from other federal employees in 1970. Still, over 1,000,000 federal workers are in exclusive units subject to the processes of the Order. The Federal Labor Relations Council issued the assessment report in June 1971.[24] The Council recommended that a revision of EO 11491 was necessary and Nixon responded with Executive Order 11616 in August 1971.

Several amendments of the new order warrant discussion. Previously, labor organizations that asserted the right to strike against the U.S. government or any agency thereof were not entitled to recognition. The new Order deleted "assert the right to strike" and replaced it with "assists or participates in a strike." The deletion did not alter the prohibition against the right to strike. Indeed, the Supreme Court subsequently ruled that no-strike statutes for federal employees were constitutional.[25]

Other general deletions included eliminating reference to informal and formal recognition and defining the roles of the Office of Management and the Budget, the Assistant Secretary of Labor for Labor-Management Relations, and the Civil Service Commission. Other amendments were more important.

Professional Groups

Professional groups were specified as lawful associations with which an agency may have a relationship. Professionals may vote to be included in a bargaining unit with nonprofessionals, but otherwise are left free to determine their role under a labor-management relations system. The amendment gave professional groups more freedom to deal with agencies on purely professional matters without agency fear of violating the rights of recognized labor organizations.

Unfair Labor Practice Processing

The Assistant Secretary of Labor for Labor-Management Relations was given responsibility for all unfair labor practice complaints. The amendment provides that when a complaint alleging an unfair labor practice arises and is also subject to a grievance procedure, required in all negotiated contracts, the complaining party may choose either procedure, but is forbidden to use both methods. Decisions under grievance or adverse action appeals are not considered as unfair labor practice decisions or as precedents for deciding future unfair labor practices. Statutory appeals procedures are outside the jurisdiction of the Assistant Secretary. An agency is no longer the final judge of its conduct, but now is subject to the Assistant Secretary of Labor for Labor-Management Relations and the Federal Labor Relations Council.

Grievance Procedures and Arbitration

The revised Order requires that a negotiated agreement for an exclusive unit must include a grievance procedure. The negotiated procedure must be the exclusive method for resolving contractual grievances. The procedure is limited to grievances regarding interpretation or application of the contract. Issues that arise over the application or interpretation of agency policy may not be processed through the grievance machinery. Matters subject to a statutory appeals system are also excluded from the grievance procedure. The net result of the limitations placed upon the grievance procedure may very well give rise to greater employee dissatisfaction and a backlog of appeals to the Federal Labor Relations Council. Greater formality was introduced into the system as a result of the changes, whereas informal settlement possibilities may have better served the parties. Civil Service Commission regulations need no longer be followed in structuring the grievance procedure.

Employees may present their own grievances under the contract. If a representative is chosen to present the grievance, it must be the exclusive union unless the agreement provides for other representation. If the grievance is not covered by the contract, it may not be presented through the negotiated procedure, but may proceed through any other available system. It would have been better to permit the parties to decide what could proceed through the grievance machinery. Instead, several routes have been established that will have the effect of rendering many grievances unsolvable.

Arbitration may be included in the grievance procedure, but must be limited to interpretation and application of the contract. Only the agency and union may invoke arbitration and may now do so without approval of the employee involved. The new procedure or arbitration eliminates the so-called distinction between employee grievances and union disputes. It was finally recognized that disputes arising under an agreement are, indeed, union matters.

The change on arbitration is not without debilitating features. The Assistant Secretary of Labor for Labor-Management Relations was authorized to decide whether an issue is grievable or arbitrable under the negotiated procedure. Because of this, the arbitration process is weakened under the amended Executive Order. Arbitration of an issue should be subject to the negotiated agreement without prior determination of the merits of the case. In this respect, the Task Force would have been better advised to follow the standards of arbitration developing in the courts as applied to private industry. The amended Order permits negotiation over cost sharing, but failed to permit complete utilization of a process that has worked well in the private sector.

Negotiable Item Changes

The requirement that contract negotiations could not take place on official time was changed and made a negotiable item within specified limits. The parties may agree to negotiate on official time up to 40 hours or to authorize up to one-half the time spent in negotiations during regular working hours for a reasonable number of employees, normally not to exceed the number of management representatives. The item should have been made completely negotiable.

Agencies are no longer required to recover the costs of union dues deductions. The item was made negotiable and without limits. Most agencies deduct charges for many benefits and it should not be a problem to add dues deduction without cost if the labor organization is able to convince management representatives to do so.

Assessment

Executive Order 11616 did not expand the scope of collective bargaining sufficiently to lead to effective labor relations in federal employment. There is little room for experimentation in the system and until it is encouraged, employee morale will be lower than is necessary. The entire collective bargaining operation under Executive Orders should be reviewed, and it should be done by persons external to the administration.

FEDERAL RESERVE SYSTEM

On May 9, 1969, the Board of Governors of the Federal Reserve System issued a statement of policies concerning employee-management relations within the system.[26] The statement was patterned after Executive Order No. 10988, but also took into account the special responsibilities of the system under the terms of the Federal Reserve Act and related statutes. It recognized the right of certain classes of employees to join or to refrain from joining labor organizations. Procedures were provided for recognition of labor organizations, bargaining-unit determinations, and elections. Grievance machinery was established along with a list of unfair labor practice prohibitions.

The Board of Governors issued its "Policy on Unionization and Collective Bargaining for the Federal Reserve Banks," because of the exclusion of the system from both the Taft-Hartley Act and Executive Order.

A few features of the policy require comment. Professional employees are given the right to organize as long as they belong to bargaining units separate from those which represent the other bank employees. Bank guards also have the right to organize into separate labor organizations. In this regard therefore some of the NLRB policies dealing with bargaining units have been incorporated into the policy statement.

Exclusive recognition of a labor organization is available after an election is held. At least 30 percent of employees of an appropriate bargaining unit must sign representation request cards. Once this is achieved, an election is held under the auspices of the American Arbitration Association. A union will receive exclusive recognition if a majority of at least 60 percent of eligible bargaining-unit employees cast votes for representation. Discontinuance of a labor organization's exclusive status is determined by the same procedure; however, only one election may be held in any unit in a twelve-month period.

Unfair labor practice prohibitions are fashioned after those contained in the National Labor Relations Act. Both parties are required to bargain collectively and are prohibited from interfering with employee organizational rights guaranteed by the system's policy.

Administration of the provisions is vested in a newly created three-member Federal Reserve System Labor Relations Panel. The Panel is fashioned after the Federal Labor Relations Council established by Executive Order No. 11491. Two of the panel members are of the Board of Governors and one is a public member. All three are selected by the Board of Governors. The panel is charged with the responsibility of establishing regulations and procedures similar to those applicable to unions and management in the private sector. The Board of Governors reserves the right to amend its labor relations policies without notice, provided that all labor organizations are informed of any changes. Amendments will not be applied retroactively.

The Federal Reserve System's labor relations policy has the strength of incorporating many of the essential features of both the National Labor Relations Act as amended and the Executive Order. The potentially most serious weakness is the possibility of considerable shifts in policy as the membership of the Board of Governors changes. It may well be that pressures will eventually be placed upon Congress to provide statutory rights for Federal Reserve employee collective bargaining as is the case with federal employees organized under Executive Order No. 11491 provisions.

COLLECTIVE BARGAINING AT THE
STATE AND LOCAL LEVELS

At the close of 1967 it was estimated that approximately 9.6 percent of state and local government employees were members of either unions or associations, excluding those in education.[27] In 1970, the estimate rose to 38 percent. The American Federation of State, County and Municipal Employees, an AFL-CIO affiliate, reached a membership of three hundred and thirty-one thousand in 1967 and 520,000 in 1971. The Assembly of Governmental Employees, a federation of thirty-six independent public employee associations, reached a total membership of five hundred and four thousand in 1968.[28] In 1970, only 828,000 state and local employees were members of unions, excluding association membership. Association membership was 1,180,000 in the same year.

Unions and associations compete for members. Traditionally, the latter have been less militant than the former on such issues as collective bargaining and strikes. More recently, the procedures and objectives of both have been converging. If the tendency toward common tactics continues, competition for members may depend largely upon the comparative pressure one group can bring upon public employers. This contest was encouraged by a 1969 circuit court of appeals decision.

Right of Public Employees to Join Unions

The Eighth Circuit Court of Appeals in 1969 gave its opinion of the right of public employees to join unions.[29] The issue presented to the appellate court in the *Woodward* case was whether public employees discharged because of union membership have a right to seek injunctions and sue those public officials for damages who discharged them. A solution to the basic issue required a determination of whether public employees have a constitutionally protected right to belong to a union.

The court ruled unanimously that union membership is protected by the right of association under the First and Fourteenth Amendments. The court quoted an earlier ruling that the right of assembly protects more than the right to attend a meeting. It includes

> the right to express one's attitudes or philosophies by membership in a group or by affiliation with it or by other lawful means.[30]

Public officials who violate the public employee's constitutional right of association are subject to court action for damages under Section 1 of the Civil Rights

STATE PROVISIONS FOR PUBLIC EMPLOYEE UNION ORGANIZATION (INCLUDES STATUTE, ADMINISTRATIVE DECLARATIONS, AND ATTORNEY GENERAL OPINIONS AS OF 1973)

State	Right to Organize	Bargaining Rights	Dispute Settlement Provisions	Prohibition of Right to Strike	Union Security Provisions	Detailed Recognition Provisions (Election) Certification
Alabama	Firemen	Right to present proposals on salaries and other conditions of employment.	None	All	None	None
Alaska	All employees	Required for state, local, police, and teachers.	Compulsory mediation and arbitration for state, local, and firemen, Board findings and mediation for teachers.	Prohibited for state, local, and firemen if essential; limited for semi-essential; and allowed for non-essential. Uncertain application to teachers.	Union shop permitted for state, local, and firemen. Negotiated agreements determine for teachers.	Exclusive for all. Labor Relations Agency conducts elections if question of representation. School board grants recognition to teachers if majority showing or holds election.
Arizona	All employees	Not specified	None	All	None	None
Arkansas		State may bargain. Local not required, but may bargain.	None	State	State-voluntary checkoff.	None

State						
California	All employees	State, local, and teachers required to meet and confer. Firemen have right to present grievances and recommendations.	Local and police may mediate subject to agreement. Tripartite committee reports findings for teachers non-binding recommendations.	Local, firemen, and police.	None	Exclusive for local and police. Employer will meet and confer with any employee organization certified by labor board. Teacher employee council. State employers bargain with members only. Union time is allotted commensurate with membership.
Colorado		None	None	None specified	None	None
Connecticut	Local, firemen, police, and teachers	Bargaining required for all except state.	Mediation for local, firemen, police, and teachers with non-binding fact-finding recommendations. Advisory arbitration may be requested by either party in education.	All	Dues deduction negotiation permitted for local, firemen, and police.	State Labor Relations Board may hold election for local, firemen, or police for exclusive recognition, or may be granted by municipal chief executive officer. Board of Education controls exclusive for teachers.

State	Right to Organize	Bargaining Rights	Dispute Settlement Provisions	Prohibition of Right to Strike	Union Security Provisions	Detailed Recognition Provisions (Election) Certification
Delaware	All employees	Bargaining required for all.	State Dept. of Labor and Industrial Relations mediates upon request except on wages and salaries for all except teachers. Teachers may request mediation by any method.	All	Dues deduction with employee.	Exclusive on basis of election conducted by SDLIR for all but teachers. Board of Education certifies majority representative for teachers.
Florida	All employees	Required for local, firemen, and police. Teachers may meet and confer. Prohibited for state by 1971 Executive Order but permitted by state court in 1969.	Firemen submit issues to advisory arbitration.	All	Dues deduction for teachers with employee authorization.	Exclusive for teachers.
Georgia	Firemen and teachers	Required for firemen. Permissive for teachers.	Fact-finding for firemen.	State, firemen, and teachers.	None	Exclusive for firemen after majority vote.
Hawaii	All employees	Required for all.	Parties may agree to binding arbitration. Public	Limited right to strike for all. Strikes endanger-	Service fees for exclusive representative	Exclusive for all upon certification of majority status

			Employment Relations Board appoints mediators, fact-finding boards.	ing public health and safety unlawful. Public Employment Relations Board determines strike legality.	for all. Dues deduction for all if authorized by employees.	by Public Employment Relations Board.
Idaho	Local, firemen, and teachers.	Local, firemen, and teachers may bargain.	Fact-finding with recommendations for firemen and teachers.	None	None	Exclusive for firemen and teachers upon selection by a majority.
Illinois	Local, firemen, and teachers.	Local and teachers may bargain.	Advisory arbitration for firemen.	All	None	None
Indiana	All employees	All may bargain.	Teachers mediation fact-finding arbitration.	All	None	Exclusive for teachers upon selection by majority.
Iowa	All employees	All may bargain.	None	All	None	None
Kansas	All employees	All required to meet and confer.	Mediation, fact-finding with recommendations, and voluntary arbitration for all except teachers.	All	None	Exclusive for all. Public Employee Relations Boards conduct elections for all but teachers. State Board of Education determines for teachers, but does not require election.

STATE PROVISIONS FOR PUBLIC EMPLOYEE UNION ORGANIZATION (Cont.)

State	Right to Organize	Bargaining Rights	Dispute Settlement Provisions	Prohibition of Right to Strike	Union Security Provisions	Detailed Recognition Provisions (Election) Certification
Kentucky	All employees	State and local have right to present proposals. Teachers may bargain. Firemen and police have authority and duty to bargain.	Mediation and fact-finding with recommendations for firemen.	All	Dues deduction required for firemen.	Exclusive for firemen.
Louisiana		None	None	None specified	Dues checkoff for all if authorized by employee and agreed to by employer.	None
Maine	All employees	Required for all except state.	State Employees Appeal Board mediates final settlements which are binding. Mediation, fact-finding, and arbitration for all others. Arbitration is advisory on salaries, pensions, and other money matters.	All	None	Exclusive for all except state (unspecified). Public Employee Labor Board determines.

Maryland	Teachers	Required for teachers.	Mediation for teachers.	Teachers prohibited. Silent on all others.	Dues checkoff with employee authorization for teachers.	Exclusive for teachers.
Massachusetts	All employees	Required for all.	Fact-finding and non-binding, recommendations upon request of parties for all.	All	Agency shop allowed for all. State silent.	Exclusive for all. Employer recognized unless a dispute; State Labor Relations Commission conducts election if necessary.
Michigan	All employees	Required for all.	Mediation and fact-finding for state and local. Compulsory final and binding arbitration for firemen, police, and teachers.	All	None	Exclusive for all. Michigan Employment Relations Commission Conducts election if necessary.
Minnesota	All employees	Required for all.	Mediation and binding arbitration for all. Decision binding for essential employees; binding at request of parties for non-essential employees.	All	Right to dues checkoff.	Exclusive for all.

STATE PROVISIONS FOR PUBLIC EMPLOYEE UNION ORGANIZATION (Cont.)

State	Right to Organize	Bargaining Rights	Dispute Settlement Provisions	Prohibition of Right to Strike	Union Security Provisions	Detailed Recognition Provisions (Election) Certification
Mississippi	None	None	None	None	None	None
Missouri	All employees	Required to meet, confer, and discuss for state, local, and firemen. Teachers have right to make proposals to school boards.	None	State, local, and firemen prohibited.	None	Exclusive for state, local, and firemen.
Montana	Teachers, nurses	Required	Impasse panel makes findings of fact and recommendations are made public for teachers.	Prohibited	None	Exclusive
Nebraska	All employees	Required for all except teachers. Teachers may meet and confer.	Mediation and fact-finding for all except teachers. Court of Industrial Relations may alter economic conditions. Ad hoc fact-finding board for teachers.	All	None	Exclusive for all.

State	Coverage	Bargaining	Impasse procedures		Union security	Representation
Nevada	All, except state	Required for all except state.	Mediation and fact-finding. Governor has authority to make fact-finding recommendations binding.	All except state.	None	Exclusive for all.
New Hampshire	State, police, and teachers	Required for state, police, and teachers.	Mediation and fact-finding.	All	Dues checkoff.	Exclusive
New Jersey	All employees	Required for all.	Mediation, fact-finding with recommendations, and voluntary arbitration.	All	None	Exclusive
New Mexico	State	May bargain.	Mediation, fact-finding, and arbitration.	State	Agency shop prohibited.	Exclusive. Consultation rights in absence of exclusive.
New York	All employees	Required for all.	Mediation and fact-finding. Legislature or committee thereof makes final determination if fact-finding recommendations not accepted.	All	Dues checkoff with employee authorization.	Exclusive for all.

STATE PROVISIONS FOR PUBLIC EMPLOYEE UNION ORGANIZATION (Cont.)

State	Right to Organize	Bargaining Rights	Dispute Settlement Provisions	Prohibition of Right to Strike	Union Security Provisions	Detailed Recognition Provisions (Election) Certification
North Carolina	None	None	None	None	None	None
North Dakota	All employees	May bargain for all except required for teachers.	Mediation. Fact-finding mediation for teachers.	All	None	Exclusive for teachers.
Ohio	None	None	None	All	None	None
Oklahoma	Local, police, and teachers	Required	Advisory arbitration. Arbitration binding if accepted by corporate authorities.	Prohibited for all except teachers.	None	Exclusive for local, police, and teachers.
Oregon	All employees	Required for all except teachers. Teachers required to confer, consult, and discuss.	Conciliation, mediation, fact-finding, and voluntary arbitration for state, local, firemen, and police. Mediation and fact-finding for teachers and nurses.	Prohibited for all except teachers.	None	Exclusive for all.
Pennsylvania	All employees	Required	Mediation, fact-finding, permis-	Limited right for state and local.	Dues checkoff and maintenance	Exclusive for state and local.

State							
Rhode Island	All employees	Required	...sible arbitration for state, local. Compulsory arbitration for firemen, police, and teachers. Conciliation and fact-finding for state. Binding arbitration except for salaries. Mediation, conciliation, and binding arbitration for local. Compulsory arbitration for firemen and police. Voluntary binding arbitration for education, although advisory on monetary matters.	Court determines if there is a clear and present danger or threat to health, safety, or welfare of public.	All	...of membership for state and local. Mandatory agency shops for state and police.	Exclusive for all.
South Carolina		None	None		All employees.	None	None
South Dakota	All employees	Required for all except firemen and police.	State Labor Commissioner decides.		State, local, and teachers.	None	Exclusive for all.
Tennessee		None	None		All employees.	None	None

STATE PROVISIONS FOR PUBLIC EMPLOYEE UNION ORGANIZATION (Cont.)

State	Right to Organize	Bargaining Rights	Dispute Settlement Provisions	Prohibition of Right to Strike	Union Security Provisions	Detailed Recognition Provisions (Election) Certification
Texas	Policemen and firemen	Declared against public policy for all except mutual obligation for policemen and firemen.	Mediation and binding arbitration.	All employees.	None	None
Utah	All employees	May bargain.	None	None	None	None
Vermont	All, except police	Required except police.	Mediation and fact-finding.	All employees.	Union shop permitted for local and firemen.	Exclusive, except police.
Virginia	Local, firemen, police, and teachers	May bargain.	None	All employees.	None	None
Washington	All employees and state university system	Required for all.	Decided by personnel board for state. Mediation service of State Department of Labor. Industries for local,	All except teachers.	Union shop and agency shop for nonmembership on religious grounds for state and university. May negotiate	Exclusive for all.

West Virginia		None	firemen, and police. Ad hoc committee decides for teachers.	None	None	None
					union shop at local level.	
Wisconsin	All employees	Required for all.	Mediation and fact-finding for state, local, and teachers. Mediation and final and binding arbitration for firemen and police.	All	Agency shop. All except state. Agency shop for state if authorized by referendum.	Exclusive for all.
Wyoming	Firemen	Required for firemen.	Compulsory arbitration.	None	None	Exclusive

Source: Adapted from U.S. Department of Labor, *Summary of State Policy Regulations for Public Sector Labor Relations: Statutes, Attorney Generals' Opinions and Selected Court Decisions*, Washington, D.C.: U.S. Government Printing Office, 1973.

Act of 1871. A different appellate court decision was quoted in reaching this conclusion. It stated:

> It is settled that teachers have the right of free association, and unjustified interference with teachers' associational freedom violates the Due Process clause of the Fourteenth Amendment. ... Public employment may not be subjected to unreasonable conditions, and the assertion of First Amendment rights by teachers will usually not warrant their dismissal. ... Unless there is some illegal intent, an individual's right to form and join a union is protected by the First Amendment.[31]

The guaranteed right to join a union may be important to a worker, but that right is not effective if there is a lack of procedure to protect it — such as required recognition of a labor organization representing a majority of bargaining-unit workers and thereafter good-faith collective bargaining. Also all the other appellate courts will not necessarily rule the same as the Seventh and Eighth Circuit Courts of Appeals. Conflicting rules may eventually result in a Supreme Court decision on the issue. In the meantime, however, the states vary widely in their interpretation of public employee collective bargaining rights.

STATUS OF STATE LAWS

Some states require bargaining for all categories of public employees. Twenty-nine states require the parties to bargain, but only ten of these adequately provide machinery to resolve questions of representation. Also, despite the fact that most states prohibit strikes, many do not have methods to settle disputes.

Dispute settlement provisions vary widely. Four states require compulsory arbitration if other methods fail. However, this requirement is often limited to certain groups such as policemen, teachers, and firemen. Four other states permit advisory arbitration, probably after the fashion of earlier federal executive orders. Final and binding arbitration is authorized by twelve states, although some employee classifications are excepted and it is not unusual to limit arbitrable items. Wages and salaries are often not subject to arbitration. Later in this section, it is pointed out that 60 percent of public employee strikes in 1970 were caused by disputes over economic issues. Consequently, for the majority of states, there is no adequate dispute settlement machinery designed to deal with the economic issues that trouble public employees most.

Bargaining is authorized but not required in ten states. There is no penalty, however, for refusals to bargain or for refusals to meet and confer. In nine states, there are no provisions whatever on either bargaining permissiveness or meeting and conferring. Obviously, some states, through silence, encourage power conflicts between public employers and employees. Work stoppages may result to force legislative action. Once meetings and conferences are held as a result of pressures, it may be more difficult to establish laboratory conditions within which constructive negotiations prevail.

Considerable uncertainty regarding bargaining rights faces public employees in a large number of states. In some cases rights are spelled out for certain categories of workers, but not for others. Even if public employees are dealt with uniformly in a particular state or lesser political jurisdiction, the mere difference of treatment in other states is enough to create instability in employment relations. Union organizers supply the comparative information to workers. This situation may be termed a demonstration effect. Public workers in a municipality in a state that does not protect collective bargaining become malcontents when bargaining rights are observed in other states among those performing similar tasks. Indeed, the ability of federal employees to engage in limited bargaining activities within the same state serves also to frustrate state and local employees deprived of the same right.

Agitation for equal bargaining rights is likely to persist among public employees as long as a relatively high level of employment continues in most labor markets. The loss of jobs because of union activities is less serious than would be the case if fewer job alternatives were available to such workers. Not only does a relatively high level of employment provide workers with more alternatives, it also has the effect of decreasing the number of job applicants from which public employers may choose. High turnover rates become especially damaging during such periods of high economic activity. Public pressure forces government agencies to maintain a constant flow of public services. Indeed, there is considerable pressure to expand and improve services when per capita income rises. It is difficult to adhere to traditional practices in the face of widespread employee dissatisfaction. Disruption of services could invoke the wrath of the general public which in turn could lead to losses at the polls and eventually to new public employers. These factors, including widespread strikes among public employees, probably will result in more and more recognition of public employee unions.

De Facto Bargaining

Despite the existence of restrictive laws or court and administrative decisions, state and local employees are exerting pressure on employers to obtain limited bargaining arrangements. The assassination of Martin Luther King in Memphis, Tennessee, was the essential ingredient that forced the city to yield to garbage collection employee demands for union recognition and collective bargaining. The Indiana University administration, as another example, decided to meet and confer with employee representatives although the same is not true among the other universities in that state. Thus even though specific legislation does not exist to support collective bargaining relationships in many jurisdictions, employee and third-party pressures are often enough to force employers to yield to certain pacifying demands. Civil rights groups devote considerable attention to public workers in urban areas. Such a situation has been described as multilateral bargaining.[32] Its very existence forces both unions and public employers to yield their traditional positions in favor of the demands of the special community interest groups. In the meantime a bargaining relationship is in the process of development. Such pressures have led to reconsideration of a wide range of traditional practices in the public sector.

Study Commissions

Some governors have responded to various pressures by appointing special commissions to study public employment relations. Governor Rockefeller of New York appointed the Taylor Commission on January 15, 1966, to study the public labor problems of the state. It was charged with the responsibility of proposing legislation which would protect the public from illegal strikes as well as the rights of workers to engage in union activities.[33] The crisis which climaxed the need for a revision of the outmoded Condon-Wadlin Act was the New York City Transit Authority employees strike in 1966. The commission's efforts resulted in recommendations which were included in the Taylor Act. Not only were employees given the right to organize but collective bargaining was required on a mandatory basis. The Public Employment Relations Board was created to administer the provisions of the New York act. It was also provided with machinery to deal with impasses.

The governors of Maryland, New Jersey, and Illinois have also utilized commissions to study public employment problems. This device should serve to bring special problems to the attention of the general public in an unbiased form whereby adequate legislation may result. Otherwise, the states will be increasingly forced into a crisis evaluation of the rights of the general public relative to those who provide public services. The explosive potential of public workers seems irreversible if machinery is not established to resolve disagreements before they arise.

THE RIGHT TO STRIKE

The right of public employees to strike is prohibited by statute, court decision, or attorney general opinion in all states except Alaska, Hawaii, Illinois, and Pennsylvania. Illinois has an Anti-Injunction Law that has been interpreted to permit public employees to refuse to work when a bargaining impasse has been reached and all other remedies have been exhausted. Alaska permits strikes by employees in the nonessential category and extends a limited right to semiessential workers. The problem is in the definition of which public employees are nonessential and which are essential or semiessential. Hawaii extends a limited right to strike; strikes endangering public health and safety are prohibited. The determination of which strikes endanger public health and safety is made by the Public Employment Relations Board. Thus, in Hawaii, strike legality depends on the basic philosophy of Board personnel which, of course, can change over relatively short periods of time. Pennsylvania law also extends a limited right to strike to state and local employees. The courts may prohibit strikes that they deem to constitute a clear and present danger or threat to health, safety, or welfare of the public.

It is obvious that the right to strike is not as liberal in Alaska, Hawaii, or Pennsylvania as might be thought on the face of the laws. Most public bodies with authority to decide strike legality will hold generally false conceptions of the effect that public employee strikes will have and prohibit them far beyond any real need to do so. In this respect, the politics of the moment will prevail over rational economic judgment. It has been demonstrated that because of technology, excess capacity, and the ability to substitute and postpone demand for services often performed by the public sector, most public employee strikes will impose little or no economic costs, only some inconvenience in substituting or in delay. State legislatures should spend more time developing strike safeguards instead of evading the problem by merely outlawing strikes.

An increasing number of unions and employee organizations are changing their traditional policy of no-strike pledges. In 1963 the American Federation of Teachers issued a policy statement supporting strikes under certain conditions. The American Federation of State, County and Municipal Employees Union followed this example in 1966. In one study it was found that of twenty unions composed primarily of public employees, eight have constitutional bans on strikes and eight others do not refer to the issue in their union constitutions.[34] In 1968 four unions representing federal employees dropped the no-strike pledge clauses in their constitutions. These were the National Association of Government Employees, the United Federation of Postal Clerks, the National Postal Union, and the International Association of Firefighters. As yet, however, none of the unions has formally asserted the right to strike because of the serious penalties against strikers and their unions in the federal government. The threatened strikes in 1967 of the postal and the air traffic employees did not materialize. Both groups engaged in strikes in 1970, however, because the grievances of 1967 still had not been resolved to their satisfaction. The postal strike started in New York City and spread to other parts of the country. The basic issue was wages, and strike action proved successful. Union representatives met with administration officials and reached a negotiated settlement. Congress approved the package. The air traffic employees were primarily concerned with working conditions and public safety. Their efforts have also been successful in turning inaction into action. Despite the prohibition of public employee strikes, such workers will engage in such activity if the issues linger long enough without resolution. At the federal level, public employees may assert the right to strike by virtue of the government's agreement in 1970 to dismiss a court case in which the constitutionality of the issue was contested. However, as noted, it is illegal for federal employees to strike. Their right "to assert" a strike is not the same as actually striking.

Public employee union leaders contend that without the right to strike employers will not negotiate in good faith. A former union official speaking for the International Association of Firefighters remarked:

> Certain arbitrary public officials knowing that we cannot and will not strike because we voluntarily gave up the right in 1918 when we were founded, have certainly taken advantage of the professional firefighters across the land. As a matter of fact, the record will show we have been exploited by such arbitrary public officials who oft time dared us to strike, knowing that we would not.[35]

Various penalties from time to time have been imposed upon striking employees. In 1947 New York passed the Condon-Wadlin Act which permitted reemployment of strikers, but eliminated pay increases for them for a period of three years. Reinstated strikers were also considered temporary employees for a period of five years. The 1967 New York Taylor Act eliminated the pay-raise-ban feature, but provided instead for dismissal or fines. A labor organization is subject to loss of dues checkoff privileges for as long as eighteen months and fines for engaging in strikes.

In Michigan state employees are subject to discharge or financial penalties for striking. Massachusetts provides that striking municipal workers may be fined $100. Most states reserve the right to discharge striking public employees although this is not clearly spelled out in legislation.[36]

Laws prohibiting public employee strikes have not been successful in their objective. In 1966, the first full year after Michigan amended its public employee relations act, there were twenty-three strikes in the public sector. This number of strikes was more than had occurred in the previous twenty years.[37] In the next year, 1967, the number of strikes in Michigan almost doubled. Other states have experienced increased strike threats even if actual work stoppages have not materialized.

Government employee strikes increased substantially between 1960 and 1970 from 36 to over 400. Local government workers accounted for most of the activity. Man-days of idleness increased ten times between 1960 and 1970. Total government employment rose by 50 percent during the eleven year period, but the number of workers involved in strikes rose by more. Strikers accounted for 0.3 percent of total government employment in 1960, and 2.7 percent in 1970.

Government work stoppages averaged 14.5 man-days in 1960 and 20.1 in 1970. Local stoppages due to strikes tend to be larger than at the state level. The 1970 experience was 7.9 days an average per strike among local workers and 5.1 days among state workers. The longer strikes usually centered on the issue of union organization and security, but economic issues were the cause of 60 percent of strikes in 1970. Public schools continue to account for the majority of strikes.[38]

By region, the Midwest was the scene of most government strike activity followed by the Northeast region. The states of Michigan and Ohio lead the nation in public employee strikes. Essentially, if strike activity is to decline in the public sector, solutions to teacher employment problems will have to be found. It is in public education that most strikes occur. Local school boards tend not to resolve teacher employment problems, but merely flap at the issues. Past practices of school boards will have to be altered if relative peace is to be achieved in public education.

UNION SECURITY

Union-security agreements are forbidden in the federal service under the provisions of Executive Order No. 11616. The same is true in the Federal Reserve System. Nine states specifically deal with the union security issue. Most, however, are silent on the subject. Alaska, Vermont, and Washington permit the union shop. In Washington, the agency shop is authorized for employees who object to union membership on religious grounds.

The states of Hawaii, Massachusetts, Rhode Island, and Wisconsin authorize the agency shop. New Mexico prohibits the arrangement. Pennsylvania law permits maintenance-of-membership for state and local employees. There may, in fact, be many other forms of union security negotiated at the state and local level, but they probably take the form of tacit understandings as opposed to written agreements in a majority of cases. It will be recalled that the union security issue is involved in the longer strikes involving public employees. It would seem, therefore, that the public interest would be best served if state legislatures would address themselves to this problem and authorize the agency shop in all of the states.

RESOLUTION OF DISPUTES

One of the most significant issues facing the public sector is machinery for resolving disputes in the face of prohibitions on the right to strike. Twenty-four states have some limited provisions for dispute settlement. Some limit machinery to specific categories of workers such as firemen or teachers. When legislation has been passed, it almost always states that there can be no conflict with civil service provisions or other statutes setting employment standards. The major difficulty seems to come from legislative bodies even when economic issues are negotiable. These bodies have to appropriate funds to cover the agreements and are usually unwilling to abide by decisions denied outside the traditional legislative processes.[39]

There are at least three types of disputes in the public employment field. The first, organizational, involves the issue of determining employee desires for union representation. Some states have labor relations boards to make bargaining-unit determinations.

The second type involves the terms and conditions of employment that are usually included in written collective bargaining agreements. Resolution may result from such devices as mediation or fact-finding boards with authority to offer recommendations.

The third type involves interpretation and enforcement of existing collective bargaining agreements. The usual method of resolving such disputes in private industry is an internal grievance procedure with impartial third-party arbitration as a final step.

It seems possible that strikes in the public sector could be decreased if certain steps are clearly provided. Some of the possible steps which may result in better labor-management relations are:

1. The right of employee representation by a union of their own choice.
2. Independent third-party mediation and fact-finding to deal with bargaining impasses.
3. Written contracts with detailed clauses dealing with wages and other working conditions.
4. Voluntary final and binding arbitration as the final step in a grievance procedure involving contractual interpretation.

Mediation and fact-finding boards are utilized by some states to resolve bargaining impasses. Connecticut made them available in its Municipal Employee Relations Act of 1965. Michigan also provides for fact-finding and nonbinding recommendations by its State Labor Mediation Board to resolve bargaining impasses. Wisconsin utilizes the fact-finding approach which may be initiated by its Employment Relations Board to break deadlocked negotiations.

What this chapter has shown is that the problem of public employee collective bargaining, and the growing restlessness among public employees, cannot be dealt with successfully simply by ignoring the problem. The results of inaction undoubtedly will be an increasing number of public employee strikes, a lowered morale among these employees, and the deterioration of services from government agencies. In the last analysis, the public will pay a stiff price if the federal and state governments do not face up to reality.

SUMMARY

The public sector has largely ignored its labor relations problems until confronted by crisis conditions. Not only has government at all levels become a relatively larger employer of labor than in the past, but there is every indication that the total will increase even more by 1975. Public workers do not accept the traditional attitudes used to describe their employment rights, such as "the sovereign can do no wrong." Unilateral determination of wages and employment conditions increasingly is being questioned by government employees. Employers are finding their decisions questioned not only by unions representing their employees, but also by associations that have traditionally been somewhat passive in the area of collective bargaining. Competition between unions and associations has resulted in the use of more aggressive tactics to obtain wages and other working conditions that more nearly approach those of the private sector.

Several years of sustained high levels of employment coupled with increased demand for public services have placed employers in a position whereby they must reevaluate their traditional management practices. The general public is intolerant of inconveniences resulting from stoppages in the flow of services performed by the various agencies of government. Placed in the middle of their employees and the general public, a growing number of state and local governments have been forced to spell out more clearly the collective bargaining rights of workers. Once the process begins, there is little possibility of reversing it. The rights established in one state may be expected to spill over into adjoining states and then spread farther from there. The process may be expected to continue for as long as relatively high levels of employment exist. Otherwise, work stoppages and high turnover rates may be expected to persist. The general public may react more against work stoppages than against the high turnover rates, although both are costly in terms of taxes. The public may not approve of government employee strikes and therefore may treat such workers in harsh fashion—but probably for a short period of time only. The greatest cost of a failure to provide a workable labor-management policy is likely to fall on the elected officeholders. Thus there are incentives for state and local governments to deal with their employees on a basis more comparable with the private sector.

NOTES

[1] *Monthly Labor Review,* v. 92 , No. 5 (May 1969), 99.

[2] *Ibid.*

[3] Committee on Public Employer-Employee Relations, *Employee Organizations in the Public Service*, National Civil Service League (New York, 1946), p. 16.

[4] 69 Stat. 624 (1965).

[5] Wilson R. Hart, *Collective Bargaining in the Federal Civil Service* (New York: Harper & Row, 1961), p. 44.

[6] *Collective Bargaining in the Public Sector, An Interim Report.* Prepared for Executive Board, AFL-CIO Maritime Trades Department, February 13, 1969, p. 10.

[7] H. Roberts, *A Manual for Employee-Management Cooperation in the Federal Service* (Honolulu, Hawaii: Industrial Relations Center, University of Hawaii, 1964), p. 4.

[8] Sterling Denhard Spero, *Government as Employer* (New York: Remsen Press, 1948), p. 122.

[9] Kurt L. Hanslowe, *The Emerging Law of Labor Relations in Public Employment*, ILR Paperback No. 4. (Ithaca, N.Y.: New York State School of Industrial and Labor Relations, Cornell University, 1967), p. 35.

[10] 5 U.S.C. 642 (1912).

[11] Charles B. Craver, "Bargaining in the Federal Sector," *Labor Law Journal*, XIX, No. 9 (September 1968), 570.

[12] *Ibid.*

[13] Hart, *op. cit.*, p. 168.

[14] Harry A. Donian, "A New Approach to Setting the Pay of Federal Blue-Collar Workers," *Monthly Labor Review*, XCII, No. 4 (April 1969), 30–34.

[15] Report of the President's Task Force on Employee-Management Relations in the Federal Service, *A Policy for Employee-Management Cooperation in the Federal Service* (Washington, D.C.: Government Printing Office, 1961), p. iii.

[16] Hanslowe, *op. cit.*, pp. 39–40.

[17] *AFL-CIO News* (November 11, 1967).

[18] Hanslowe, *op. cit.*, p. 46.

[19] Willoughby Abner, "The FMCS and Dispute Mediation in the Federal Government," *Monthly Labor Review*, XCII, No. 5 (May 1969), 27–29.

[20] *Ibid.*, p. 27.

[21] *Ibid.*, p. 28.

[22] Craver, *op. cit.*, p. 571.

[23] Hanslowe, *op. cit.*, p. 46.

[24] The Council on Labor Law and Labor Relations, "Federal Bar Association Task Force I Report—E.O. 11616," *Labor Law Journal* (July, 1972), pp. 414–24.

[25] *Postal Clerks* v. *Blount*, U.S. Sup. Ct. No. 32,97–69 (April 1, 1971).

[26] Federal Reserve Press Release, "Policy on Unionization and Collective Bargaining for the Federal Reserve Banks," May 9, 1969.

[27] James E. Young and Betty L. Brewer, *State Legislation Affecting Labor Relations in State and Local Government*, Labor and Industrial Relations Series No. 2 (Kent, Ohio: Kent State University Bureau of Economic and Business Research, 1968), p. 5.

[28] *Ibid.*, p. 8.

[29] *American Federation of State, County, & Municipal Employees, AFL-CIO* v. *Woodward*, 406 F. (2d) 137 (1969).

[30] *Ibid.*, at 139.

[31] *McLaughlin* v. *Tilendis*, 398 F. (2d) 287 (7th Cir., 1968).

[32] Kenneth McLennan and Michael H. Moskow, "Multilateral Bargaining in the Public Sector," *Monthly Labor Review*, v. 92, No. 4 (April 1969), 58–60.

[33] Hanslowe, *op. cit.*, p. 85.

[34] Young and Brewer, *op. cit.*, p. 16.

[35] William Buck, former president of the International Association of Fire Fighters, as

quoted by Eric Polisor in "Strikes and Solutions," Public Employee Relations Report No. 7, Public Personnel Association, 1968.

[36] Anne M. Ross, "Public Employee Unions and the Right to Strike," *Monthly Labor Review*, XCII, No. 3 (March 1969), 15.

[37] John Bloedorn, "The Strike and the Public Sector," *Labor Law Journal*, XX, No. 3 (March 1969), 157.

[38] U.S. Department of Labor, "Government Work Stoppages, 1960, 1969, and 1971," *Bureau of Labor Statistics Summary Report* (November 1971).

[39] *Collective Bargaining in the Public Sector, An Interim Report*, Executive Board, AFL-CIO Maritime Trades Department, 1969, p. 42.

22

Evolution and Problems of Labor Relations Law

From the inception of unionism in the United States until the advent of the New Deal era, organized labor operated in a legal environment that had not accepted unionism as a permanent and responsible institution. As a result unions played a minor role in the affairs of the nation. Union membership was small. With few exceptions the bargaining power of unions was weak. The basic industries were essentially nonunion. By 1932 unions were freed from the effects of the conspiracy doctrine as developed in the pre-*Commonwealth* v. *Hunt* period. However, the courts were still heavily utilizing the injunction. By use of the injunction the courts stamped out union economic activities calculated to influence and expand the collective bargaining process. Unions that engaged in secondary boycott activities risked prosecution under the Sherman Act, a statute ostensibly enacted to curb the growth of big business. The yellow-dog contract was still enforceable in the courts, owing to the pronouncement of the Supreme Court in the *Hitchman* decision.

While the courts blocked the progress of unions and collective bargaining, the legislative branch of government made some attempts to encourage the growth of unionism. Congress and some states passed laws calculated to prevent the employer from interfering with the right of employees to self-organization and collective bargaining. Congress limited its action to the railroad industry, though some states passed union protection legislation that applied to general industry. These laws forbade employers to discharge workers because of their membership in labor unions. To check abusive use of the labor injunction, Congress and some states attempted to curb the power of the judiciary. The injunction provided the means whereby government aided management at the most crucial points of industrial relations conflicts.

It is noteworthy that the legislative branch of government was more favorable to

organized labor than the courts. This condition resulted from the often more responsive character of the legislative branch to social change. Protected in tenure, the
judiciary was more concerned with legal formalism and precedent than with social
and economic realities. For many years the legislative and judicial branches of government were in sharp conflict over the labor issue. The employees of the nation
stood by, hoping for a favorable outcome to the struggle so that they might realize
a better socioeconomic existence. But for decades the courts refused to confirm legislation calculated to promote unions or, for that matter, any laws which promoted
the welfare of the working population. Social legislation was blocked by a Supreme
Court which ignored the most obvious facts of economic life. As late as 1937 there
was substantial reason to doubt that the Court would change its views on social
legislation and approve the Wagner Act.

However, the period 1929–1937 was characterized by sweeping changes in
the attitude of the American people relative to the proper role of government in
the area of economic activity. Stimulated by the effects of the Great Depression, the
climate of opinion of the nation underwent great change. Many people came to
believe that government had an important part to play if the national economy was
to be restored to conditions of relatively full employment. Previously, only a small
group held this view, the majority having faith in the operation of "natural" economic
laws to maintain a healthy industrial environment. Indeed, prior to the Great
Depression, the nation generally believed that "the government governs best that
governs least." The depression changed this attitude, and great segments of the
people welcomed government intervention in the economic sphere. The people saw
in this approach the cure for many of the problems of the national economy. In
short, the people became government-minded, supporting government efforts to
restore the national economy to a relatively higher level of operation.

This change in the climate of opinion had great implications for organized
labor. If weak unions did not prevent a depression, there was reason to believe that
a strong and widespread union movement might contribute to economic recovery.
A strong and growing union movement depended on the action of government. It
was necessary to establish a legal framework in which the collective bargaining
process could function effectively. This produced the logic underlying the Norris–
La Guardia and Wagner Acts, the laws which set the tone of the labor policy of the
New Deal. These laws were products of the Great Depression. They rested not only
on the assumption that effective unionism would insure workers a greater measure
of social justice, but on the idea that an effective and growing labor movement
would promote economic stability. In short, a strong union movement would fit
nicely into the scheme of New Deal economics, hence the unqualified support of
legislation calculated to protect the right of employees to self-organization and collective bargaining.

That the nation supported the bold ventures of the Roosevelt New Deal program
was clearly evidenced by the results of the 1936 national elections. The New Deal
program was endorsed by the people. Only the Supreme Court could stop its implementation. This the Court refused to do. The Wagner Act and some other New Deal
measures were—but by the narrowest margins—declared constitutional. Nonetheless,
the Court was not insulated from the spirit of the times and Norris–La Guardia
and the Wagner Act successfully overcame the constitutional hurdle.

Since 1937 the Supreme Court has permitted the legislative branch the widest
latitude to shape labor policy. Congress and state legislatures are judicially free to

determine the elements of the framework of labor law. Only upon rare occasions has the Court invalidated labor legislation on the ground of unconstitutionality. Actions of the legislative branch are struck down only when the statute clearly and unmistakably violates the terms of the Constitution.

Stimulated by the New Deal measures, unions grew in strength and number. They claimed about 10 million members in 1941 compared with less than 3 million in 1933. Union membership was on the upswing. This progress occurred despite the Great Depression and slow recovery thereafter. Unemployment remained serious at the outbreak of World War II. However, the favorable legal framework overcame the negative effects of an unfavorable economic environment, and the strength and membership of unions increased sharply. On the basis of this experience, the conclusion must be reached that the legal climate is a most important determinant of union progress. This principle of union growth was to be underscored after the passage of Taft-Hartley.

Organized labor made additional gains during the war period. The policies of the National War Labor Board encouraged the growth of unions. Moreover, the Wagner Act remained in force during the war period. The federal government did not dilute the protection afforded employees of their collective bargaining rights on the ground of wartime expediency. Organized labor pledged itself not to strike during World War II and largely kept that pledge, but nevertheless the effect of the favorable legal environment was to stimulate the growth of the union movement.

At the termination of World War II, the position of unions was stronger than ever. Union membership exceeded 15 million, an all-time high in the history of the American labor union movement. The basic industries were practically all organized. Collective bargaining policies made themselves felt throughout the entire economy. Indeed, unions played a foremost role in national affairs. Undoubtedly, some union leaders visualized a union movement which would include most of the nation's organizable workers.

Such was the status of organized labor in 1947. In that year Taft-Hartley became the law of the land, and many changes occurred in the character of national labor policy. A variety of factors produced this legislation, but not the least important was the fact that society felt that the power of unionism was excessive. The law was an effort to provide collective bargaining balance between unions and management. Unions were to be made more responsible.

The demand for more union responsibility did not end with the Taft-Hartley Act. Between 1957 and 1959 the McClellan Anti-Racketeering Committee held numerous hearings dealing with patterns of union behavior. Several findings and recommendations were presented to Congress as a result of the three-year effort. The Labor-Management Reporting and Disclosure Act was enacted in 1959. Its primary concern is with the internal practices of unions. The law attempts to protect union members from improper union conduct. Proper union representation is the vehicle by which labor organizations are expected to respond to the desires of members. The election provisions of Title IV have been utilized more heavily than other sections seeking to regulate internal union affairs. The loose organizational structure of the AFL-CIO resulted in governmental intervention into union internal affairs. Its adoption of six codes of ethical practices to regulate the behavior of its affiliates in 1957 proved to be too little, too late.

Continued public concern with the general operation of economic institutions is reflected in efforts other than Landrum-Griffin. President Kennedy issued Executive Order No. 10988 in 1962. This event touched off a wave of reexaminations of traditional attitudes toward public employee organization. President Nixon took advantage of experiences under the Kennedy order in Executive Order No. 11491. Attempts were made to make federal bargaining more effective. State and local jurisdictions continue their efforts to define the collective bargaining rights of their employees.

Repeated examination of government regulation of the collective bargaining process is evident from the changes discussed in this book. The policies forthcoming depend and have depended largely upon the public's view of the type of economic system it desires. Changing views of the economic system change the costs and benefits that may be associated with particular policies in the labor relations field.

Should national labor policy shift from private reliance upon statutory and administrative law to one which relies more upon informal pressure? Perhaps a shift toward informal pressure is attractive. The particular answers that one might come up with depend upon the objectives posed for the economic system. Various management groups have gone on record as desiring to change the basic national labor policy. They would radically change the laws of the past thirty years; the NLRB would be eliminated and replaced by special labor courts. Others would call for evolutionary changes from time to time as the old laws prove inadequate on particular issues. Indeed, changing views on how the economy should operate have led recent political figures to rely increasingly upon informal pressures to deal with labor-management disputes. For example, the wage-price guidelines were set forth in 1962 by the Council of Economic Advisors, which implied a policy shift from private to public interests when economic matters arise during collective bargaining negotiations. Certainly, the guidelines went beyond union-management matters, but they do represent a general policy shift at the national level on collective bargaining matters. Of course, the wage-price controls between August 15, 1971, and April 30, 1974, underscore this proposition.

Various pressures exist that illustrate the subtle debate over how the economy and collective bargaining should work. Brief mention of just a few will make the point more obvious.

ISSUES WITH POLICY IMPLICATIONS

National Labor Relations Act Coverage

For a variety of reasons, unions exerted greater efforts to organize in the latter 1960s and so far in the 1970s. Considerable organizational efforts have been expended on such groups as farm and hospital workers. Organized labor pressures Congress to expand the coverage of the National Labor Relations Act to include workers excluded from its protection. Indeed, state and local employees fall within the excluded list of workers not covered by national labor law. The eventual outcome of the coverage issue depends largely upon changing attitudes of how the economy should operate as expressed at the polls. Continued interruption of goods and services by strikes may bring public pressures to establish machinery to lessen the possible economic impact of work stoppages.

Former Secretary of Labor Shultz recommended that a considerable number of agricultural workers be covered by the National Labor Relations Act. However, it was recommended also that a separate three-member Farm Labor Relations Board be set up to conduct elections, determine bargaining units, and handle unfair labor practice cases. The NLRB was not to administer farm labor issues because of its thirty-nine years of established precedents that generally apply to industrial establishments. This proposal points up the rising public desire to reduce the labor problems confronting the agricultural industry in recent years. Farm labor problems are probably more of a nuisance to the public than a real economic threat, but there is a growing intolerance of dissent. The solution seems to be more public control of formerly private processes. Administrative decisions may be used in some cases to determine worker coverage under the National Labor Relations Act.

The Public Employee

Increased demand for public workers' services has found expression in changing approaches to resolve their grievances. Inclusion of such employees under the National Labor Relations Act does not seem as likely as may once have been the case. At the federal level employees receive increased attention to their bargaining desires. Growing dissatisfaction among public employees at all levels of government has resulted in changes in both legislation and administrative practices. Following the lead of Executive Orders Nos. 10988 and 11491, the Federal Reserve Board in 1969 established a policy to govern the collective bargaining rights of its workers. Many states have passed legislation dealing with the rights of workers. Still others are reviewing their traditional practices. It is widespread knowledge that the general public will not tolerate a great deal of inconvenience in the flow of services demanded from government. While some workers may find their jobs in jeopardy for participating in work stoppages, it is also certain that their public employers may also be subject to public wrath for the same reason. This situation represents a basic attitudinal change in the public's view of how the economy should work. Perhaps it may be said, at best, that the public has not completely decided how a particular institution in the economy should behave. One thing seems certain. The move may be toward accommodation of the various interest groups and not total support of one against all others. Such an accommodation may lead to greater stability than reliance upon strict traditional approaches. Continued crises and debates over public employee bargaining rights will fall upon the population for resolution. Ultimately, the various political jurisdictions will have to face the problems of public employment and seek solutions. The postal and airline strikes of early 1970 make this obvious.

White-Collar Unionization

Recent gains in unionizing teachers and other public employees have provided the incentive for labor organizations to step up their drive to organize office, sales, professional, and technical personnel. In the past unions have not been successful in organizing white-collar workers in any one particular industry. They have been the least successful in manufacturing industries, where only about 7 percent of such workers belong to unions.

Several factors indicate a change may occur in the near future. Among these are increasing union effort and sophistication in white-collar organization; depersonalization and routinization of many white-collar jobs with the advent of computer systems and company growth; gains in negotiated wages and fringe benefits in blue-collar and unionized white-collar situations; and increasing respectability of union membership in government and professional occupations. These considerations make it highly probable that unions and management will be engaged in considerable conflict over white-collar employees during the next several years.

Since there is current agitation of many special groups for collective bargaining, such as doctors, professional athletes, and musicians, the policy of Taft-Hartley denying legal protection to supervisors and other managerial personnel should be reviewed by Congress. Professional workers within an industrial setting have long been covered by the law. It would appear that supervisors and middle management under proper circumstances would have an interest in collective bargaining.

It is obvious that the entire question of employee coverage by the National Labor Relations Act is in a state of continuous examination. The issue will be a subject of considerable debate for the next few years.

National Emergency Strikes

The question of actual economic impact of strikes in general industry is unsettled. Studies such as have been made largely contend that the economic effects have been minimal at most. Thus the effective functioning of the national economy may or may not depend on the continuous operation of the nation's critical industries such as coal, oil, steel, ocean shipping, and transportation.

The Taft-Hartley and Railway Labor Act national emergency provisions seem to be utilized when the President feels that the threat of strikes may impose an economic inconvenience upon the public. Such intervention, however, tends to be drifting from legal to extralegal action. The result is political settlements. The cost of political settlements may well lead to a tendency to forego greater economic efficiency over time. Whatever economic costs are involved in the tendency to use political measures, the national emergency provisions and their uses clearly indicate the growing trend of placing the interests of the public over those of the private sector.

The trend in techniques of obtaining national emergency settlements makes it clear that there is a need to reexamine existing statutory provisions in the light of public demands. Failure to provide more realistic measures to deal with potentially inconvenient work stoppages will accelerate the tendency of collective bargaining representatives to seek political solutions to their problems. Collective bargaining differences can be settled by the private parties if an adequate framework is developed within which settlement responsibilities fall more heavily upon labor and management groups.

Categories for Bargaining

The ability of the government to limit and circumscribe the content of collective bargaining contracts is nowhere made as obvious as the NLRB authority to decide the mandatory and voluntary items of bargaining. Employers and unions upon occasion have attacked the NLRB for some of its bargaining orders. Pressures to eliminate or modify Board policies on bargainable items will undoubtedly accelerate over time. The search for a proper balance between worker and management rights will keep the issue of bargainable items active in the future. The NLRB has ruled, for example, that a company must bargain, if requested, on the level of benefits received by retired workers. The novel aspect of the ruling was that the order concerned workers who were not active members of the bargaining unit. The Board justified its decision partly by stating that active employees have considerable concern about retirement benefit adequacy. Actually, the basic concern of active employees regarding the general welfare of retirees reflects the economic welfare concerns of the general public. Since negotiated insurance plans often are set for postretirement enjoyment, the Board ruled that the terms of such benefits relate back to active employment. The Board found that collective bargaining is a suitable media for resolving health and welfare questions affecting retired workers. However, the Supreme Court reversed this policy.

The issue of bargaining rights for retired workers serves as an example of government authority to control the content and coverage of collective bargaining agreements. We believe the public interest would be served if Congress would mandate that bargaining issues not expressly declared unlawful by Taft-Hartley constitute mandatory issues.

Integrity of the NLRB

Greater public control over private interests is called for by most groups. Various tactics are deployed in attempts to influence results. Several employer groups attacked the NLRB fiercely during the Johnson and Kennedy years. It is not that employers—or unions either, for that matter—deplore public control of issues; it is merely that each attempts to direct that control to suit its own economic ends. Thus, during the Nixon years, organized labor believed the Board had treated employees unfairly. To avoid changes in national labor policy based upon political considerations of the moment, we believe permanent tenure for NLRB members would be in the national interest.

The pressures applied to change national labor policy can be expected to continue. Involved in the struggle is the basic issue of how the economy should function. The outcome of the battle will influence many of the basic economic decisions made in society—how the economy should function and for whom.

GENERAL VIEWS

The citizen should become more informed on the operation of trade unions and collective bargaining. Since he will determine the ultimate status of unions, judgment as to their merits should be based on accurate information and sound analysis. Too many people judge the overall program and functioning of unions by information purveyed by sources of doubtful reliability. The citizen owes it to his nation to gain the sound knowledge that will place him in a position wherein he can intelligently appraise the operation of unions and collective bargaining.

Such a search will not lead to the conclusion that legal curbs on unions are undesirable. On the contrary, some limitations on union activities are perfectly compatible with strong and militant unionism. However, the quest for accurate knowledge, if faithfully carried out, will lead to one obvious conclusion: In the modern profit economy, characterized by institutional forces not contemplated or given adequate weight by the classical or neoclassical school of economics, collective bargaining offers the American worker an effective means whereby he can realize social and industrial justice. This factor underlies the nation's labor union movement. It is the major justification for unions.

Unions themselves can do much to influence the climate of opinion and thereby the character of the law of labor relations. Acts of social irresponsibility on the part of unions will result in the enactment of restrictive measures. In some areas of organized labor the growth of union power has not been matched by the development of social responsibility. Unions that are socially responsible do not have to be servile or weak. Rather, union responsibility means the orientation of collective bargaining and union practices for the public good. Responsible unions are democratic unions. They scrupulously adhere to the letter and spirit of collective bargaining contracts that are in force. Such unions are vitally concerned with the overall prosperity of the firm, the industry, and the national economy. They recognize and understand the problems of management, and they expect management to recognize and understand the problems of the union and its members. Within the framework of effective collective bargaining, responsible unions are a force for national progress. In short, the responsible union is social-minded.

If this attitude of organized labor prevails, and if employers accept in good faith the principle of collective bargaining, the reliance upon law to enforce a viable and responsible collective bargaining system would decrease. If past history, however, is any guide, it is doubtful that such a desirable change of attitude on the part of unions and management will take place. At this writing, therefore, the safe prediction is for increasing government intervention in labor relations and the growing complexity of the law of labor relations.

THE MOHAWK VALLEY FORMULA

As noted in the text, the Mohawk Valley Formula was conceived by James H. Rand, Jr., president of Remington Rand. He utilized it successfully to defeat attempts of organization in his plant in 1936. The formula was also referred to as the Johnston Plan and was utilized with effectiveness during the steel strike of 1937. After the formula broke a strike in the Ilion, New York, plant of Remington Rand, Mr. Rand boasted: "Two million businessmen have been looking for a formula like this and business has hoped for, dreamed of, and prayed for such an example as you have set"—an example that "would go down into history as the Mohawk Valley Formula." Following is the complete formula reproduced from the Decisions and Orders of the National Labor Relations Board, II, 664–666.

* * *

First: When a strike is threatened, label the union leaders as "agitators" to discredit them with the public and their own followers. In the plant, conduct a forced balloting under the direction of foremen in an attempt to ascertain the strength of the union and to make possible misrepresentation of the strikers as a small minority imposing their will upon the majority. At the same time, disseminate propaganda, by means of press releases, advertisements, and the activities of "missionaries," such propaganda falsely stating the issues involved in the strike so that the strikers appear to be making arbitrary demands, and the real issues, such as the employer's refusal to bargain collectively, are obscured. Concurrently with these moves, by exerting economic pressure through threats to move the plant, align the influential members of the community into a cohesive group opposed to the strike. Include in this group, usually designated a "citizens committee," representatives of the bankers, real-estate owners, and businessmen, i.e., those most sensitive to any threat of removal of the plant because of its effect upon property values; and purchasing power flowing from payrolls.

Second: When the strike is called, raise high the banner of "law and order," thereby causing the community to mass legal and police weapons against a wholly imagined violence and to forget that those of its members who are employees have equal rights with the other members of the community.

Third: Call a "mass meeting" of the citizens to coordinate public sentiment against the strike and to strengthen the power of the citizens' committee, which organization, thus supported, will both aid the employer in exerting pressure upon the local authorities and itself sponsor vigilante activities.

Fourth: Bring about the formation of a large armed police force to intimidate the strikers and to exert a psychological effect upon the citizens. This force is built up by utilizing local police, state police, if the governor cooperates, vigilantes, and special deputies, the deputies being chosen if possible from other neighborhoods, so that there will be no personal relationships to induce sympathy for the strikers. Coach the deputies and vigilantes on the law of unlawful assembly, inciting to riot, disorderly conduct, etc., so that, unhampered by any thought that the strikers may also possess some rights, they will be ready and anxious to use their newly acquired authority to the limit.

Fifth: And perhaps most important, heighten the demoralizing effect of the above measures—all designed to convince the strikers that their cause is hopeless—by a "back-to-work" movement, operated by a puppet association of so-called "loyal employees" secretly organized by the employer. Have this association wage a publicity campaign in its own name and coordinate such campaign with the work of the "missionaries" circulating among the strikers and visiting their homes. This "back-to-work" movement has these results: It causes the public to believe that the strikers are in the minority and that most of the employees desire to return to work, thereby winning sympathy for the employer and an endorsement of his activities to such an extent that the public is willing to pay the huge costs, direct or indirect, resulting from the heavy forces of police. This "back-to-work" movement also enables the employer, when the plant is later opened, to operate it collectively with the strikers. In addition, the "back-to-work" movement permits the employer to keep a constant check on the strength of the union through the number of applications received from the employees ready to break ranks and return to work, such number being kept secret from the public and the other employees, so that the doubts and fears created by such secrecy will in turn induce still others to make applications.

Sixth: When a sufficient number of applications are on hand, fix a date for an opening of the plant through the device of having such opening requested by the "back-to-work" association. Together with the citizens' committee, prepare for such opening by making provision for a peak army of police, by roping off the areas surrounding the plant, by securing arms and ammunition, etc. The purpose of the "opening" of the plant is threefold: to see if enough employees are ready to return to work; to induce still others to return as a result of the demoralizing effect produced by the opening of the plant and the return of some of their number; and lastly, even if the maneuver fails to induce a sufficient number of persons to return, to persuade the public through pictures and news releases that the opening was nevertheless successful.

Seventh: Stage the "opening" theatrically, throwing open the gates at the propitious moment and having the employees march into the plant grounds in a massed group protected by squads of armed police, so as to give to the opening a dramatic and exaggerated quality and thus heighten its demoralizing effect. Along with the "opening" provide a spectacle—speeches, flag-raising, and praises for the employees, citizens, and local authorities, so that, their vanity touched, they will feel responsible for the continued success of the scheme and will increase their efforts to induce additional employees to return to work.

Eighth: Capitalize on the demoralization of the strikers by continuing the show of police force and the pressure of the citizens' committee, both to insure that those employees who have returned will continue at work and to force the remaining strikers to capitulate. If necessary, turn the locality into a warlike camp through the declaration of a state of emergency tantamount to martial law and barricade it from the outside world so that nothing may interfere with the successful conclusion of the "formula," thereby driving home to the union leaders the futility of further efforts to hold their ranks intact.

Ninth: Close the publicity barrage, which day by day during the entire period has increased the demoralization worked by all of these measures, on the theme that the plant is in full operation and that the strikers were merely a minority attempting to interfere with the "right-to-work," thus inducing the public to place a moral stamp of approval upon the above measures. With this, the campaign is over—the employer has broken the strike.

THE SHERMAN ANTITRUST ACT

Act of July 2, 1890, 26 Stat. 209, as Amended.

An Act

To protect trade and commerce against unlawful restraints and monopolies.

Be it enacted by the Senate and House of Representatives of the United States of America in Congress assembled,

CONTRACT, COMBINATION OR CONSPIRACY IN RESTRAINT OF INTERSTATE COMMERCE. SEC. 1. That every contract, combination in the form of trust or otherwise, or conspiracy, in restraint of trade or commerce among the several States, or with foreign nations, is hereby declared to be illegal: *Provided,* That nothing herein contained shall render illegal, contracts or agreements prescribing minimum prices for the resale of a commodity which bears, or the label or container of which bears, the trade mark, brand, or name of the producer or distributor of such commodity and which is in free and open competition with commodities of the same general class produced or distributed by others, when contracts or agreements of that description are lawful as applied to intrastate transactions, under any statute, law, or public policy now or hereafter in effect in any State, Territory, or the District of Columbia in which such resale is to be made, or to which the commodity is to be transported for such resale, and the making of such contracts or agreements shall not be an unfair method of competition under section 5, as amended and supplemented, of the Act entitled " An Act to create a Federal Trade Commission, to define its powers and duties, and for other purposes," approved September 26, 1914: *Provided further,* That the preceding proviso shall not make lawful any contract or agreement, providing for the establishment or maintenance of minimum resale prices on any commodity herein involved, between manufacturers, or between producers, or between wholesalers, or between brokers, or between factors, or between retailers, or between persons, firms, or corporations in competition with each other. Every person who shall make any contract or engage in any combination or conspiracy hereby declared to be illegal shall be deemed guilty of a misdemeanor, and, on conviction thereof, shall be punished by fine not exceeding $5,000, or by imprisonment not exceeding one year, or by both said punishments, in the discretion of the court.

MONOPOLIZING TRADE. SEC. 2. Every person who shall monopolize or attempt to monopolize, or combine or conspire with any other person or persons, to monopolize any part of the trade or commerce among the several States, or with foreign nations, shall be deemed guilty of a misdemeanor, and, on conviction thereof, shall be punished by fine not exceeding five thousand dollars, or by imprisonment not exceeding one year, or by both said punishments, in the discretion of the court.

TRUST IN TERRITORIES OF DISTRICT OF COLUMBIA. SEC. 3. Every contract, combination in form of trust or otherwise, or conspiracy, in restraint of trade or commerce in any Territory of the United States or of the District of Columbia, or in restraint of trade or commerce between any such Territory and another, or between any such Territory or Territories and any State or States or the District of Columbia, or with foreign nations, or between the District of Columbia and any State or States or foreign nations, is hereby declared illegal. Every person who shall make any such contract or engage in any such combination or conspiracy, shall be deemed guilty of a misdemeanor, and, on conviction thereof, shall be punished by fine not exceeding five thousand dollars, or by imprisonment not exceeding one year, or by both said punishments, in the discretion of the court.

EQUITY CASES. SEC. 4. The several district courts of the United States are hereby invested with jurisdiction to prevent and restrain violations of this act; and it shall be the duty of the several district attorneys of the United States, in their respective districts, under the direction of the Attorney General, to institute proceedings in equity to prevent and restrain such violations. Such proceedings may be by way of petition setting forth the case and praying that such violation shall be enjoined or otherwise prohibited. When the parties complained of shall have been duly notified of such petition the court shall proceed, as soon as may be to the hearing and determination of the case; and pending such petition and before final decree, the court may at any time make such temporary restraining order or prohibition as shall be deemed just in the premises.

ADDING PARTIES IN EQUITY CASES. SEC. 5. Whenever it shall appear to the court before which any proceeding under section four of this act may be pending, that the ends of justice require that other parties should be brought before the court, the court may cause them to be summoned, whether they reside in the district in which the court is held or not; and subpoenas to that end may be served in any district by the marshal thereof.

PROPERTY IN TRANSIT. SEC. 6. Any property owned under any contract or by any combination, or pursuant to any conspiracy (and being the subject thereof) mentioned in section one of this act, and being in the course of transportation from one State to another, or to a foreign country, shall be forfeited to the United States, and may be seized and condemned by like proceedings as those provided by law for the forfeiture, seizure and condemnation of property imported into the United States contrary to law.

TREBLE DAMAGE SUITS. SEC. 7. Any person who shall be injured in his business or property by any other person or corporation by reason of anything forbidden or declared to be unlawful by this act, may sue therefor in any district court of the United States in the district in which the defendant resides or is found, without respect to the amount in controversy, and shall recover threefold the damages by him sustained, and the costs of suit, including a reasonable attorney's fee.

DEFINITIONS. SEC. 8. The word "person," or "persons," wherever used in this act shall be deemed to include corporations and associations existing under or authorized by the laws of either the United States, the laws of any of the Territories, the laws of any State, or the laws of any foreign country.

APPENDIX C

THE CLAYTON ACT

Act of Oct. 15, 1914, 38 Stat. 731, as Amended.

An Act

To supplement existing laws against unlawful restraints and monopolies, and for other purposes.

Be it enacted by the Senate and House of Representatives of the United States of America in Congress assembled,

LEGITIMATE ACTIVITIES OF LABOR. SEC. 6. That the labor of a human being is not a commodity or article of commerce. Nothing contained in the antitrust laws shall be construed to forbid the existence and operation of labor, agricultural, or horticultural organizations, instituted for the purposes of mutual help, and not having capital stock or conducted for profit, or to forbid or restrain individual members of such organizations, from lawfully carrying out the legitimate objects thereof; nor shall such organizations, or the members thereof, be held or construed to be illegal combinations or conspiracies in restraint of trade, under the antitrust laws.

SUIT FOR INJUNCTION. SEC. 16. Any person, firm, corporation, or association shall be entitled to sue for and have injunctive relief, in any court of the United States having jurisdiction over the parties, against threatened loss or damage by a violation of the antitrust laws, including sections two, three, seven and eight of this Act, when and under the same conditions and principles as injunctive relief against threatened conduct that will cause loss or damage is granted by courts of equity, under the rules governing such proceedings, and upon the execution of proper bond against damages for an injunction improvidently granted and showing that the danger of irreparable loss or damage is immediate, a preliminary injunction may issue: *Provided*, That nothing herein contained shall be construed to entitle any person, firm, corporation, or association, except the United States, to bring suit in equity for injunctive relief against any common carrier subject to the provisions of the Act to regulate commerce, approved February fourth, eighteen hundred and eighty-seven, in respect of any matter subject to the regulation, supervision, or other jurisdiction of the Interstate Commerce Commission.

PRELIMINARY INJUNCTION AND TEMPORARY RESTRAINING ORDER. SEC. 17. That no preliminary injunction shall be issued without notice to the opposite party.

No temporary restraining order shall be granted without notice to the opposite party unless it shall clearly appear from specific facts shown by affidavit or by the verified bill that immediate and irreparable injury, loss, or damage will result to the applicant before notice can be served and a hearing had thereon. Every such temporary restraining order shall be endorsed with the date and hour of issuance, shall be forthwith filed in the clerk's office and entered of record, shall define the injury and state why it is irreparable and why the order was granted without notice, and shall by its terms expire within such time after entry, not to exceed ten days, as the court or judge may fix, unless within the time so fixed the order is extended for a like period for good cause shown, and the reasons for such extension shall be entered of record. In case a temporary restraining order shall be granted without notice in the contingency specified, the matter of the issuance of a preliminary injunction shall be set down for a hearing at the earliest possible time and shall take precedence of all matters except older matters of the same character; and when the same comes up for hearing the party obtaining the temporary restraining order shall proceed with the application for a preliminary injunction, and if he does not do so the court shall dissolve the temporary restraining order. Upon two days' notice to the party obtaining such temporary restraining order the opposite party may appear and move the dissolution or modification of the order, and in that event the court or judge shall proceed to hear and determine the motion as expeditiously as the ends of justice may require.

SECURITY ON ISSUANCE OF INJUNCTION. SEC. 18. That, except as other wise provided in section sixteen of this Act, no restraining order or interlocutory order of injunction shall issue, except upon the giving of security by the applicant in such sum as the court or judge may deem proper, conditioned upon the payment of such costs and damages as may be incurred or suffered by any party who may be found to have been wrongfully enjoined or restrained thereby.

REQUISITES OF INJUNCTION. SEC. 19. That every order of injunction or restraining order shall set forth the reasons for the issuance of the same, shall be specific in terms, and shall describe in reasonable detail, and not by reference to the bill of complaint or other document, the act or acts sought to be restrained, and shall be binding only upon the parties to the suit, their officers, agents, servants, employees, and attorneys, or those in active concert or participating with them, and who shall, by personal service or otherwise, have received actual notice of the same.

STATUTORY RESTRICTION. SEC. 20. That no restraining order or injunction shall be granted by any court of the United States, or a judge or the judges thereof, in any case between an employer and employees, or between employers and employees, or between employees, or between persons employed and persons seeking employment, involving, or growing out of, a dispute concerning terms or conditions of employment, unless necessary to prevent irreparable injury to property, or to a property right, of the party making the application, for which injury there is no adequate remedy at law, and such property or property right must be described with particularity in the application, which must be in writing and sworn to by the applicant or by his agent or attorney.

And no such restraining order or injunction shall prohibit any person or persons, whether singly or in concert, from terminating any relation of employment, or from ceasing to perform any work or labor, or from recommending, advising or persuading others by peaceful means so to do; or from attending at any place where any such person or persons may lawfully be, for the purpose of peacefully obtaining or communicating information, or from peacefully persuading any person to work or to abstain from working; or from ceasing to patronize or to employ any party to such dispute, or from recommending, advising, or persuading others by peaceful and lawful means so to do; or from paying or giving to, or withholding from, any person engaged in such dispute, any strike benefits or other moneys or things of value; or from peaceably assembling in a lawful manner, and for lawful purposes; or from doing any act or thing which might lawfully be done in the absence of such dispute by any party thereto; nor shall any of the acts specified in this paragraph be considered or held to be violations of any law of the United States.

CONTEMPT OF COURT. SEC. 21. That any person who shall willfully disobey any lawful writ, process, order, rule, decree, or command of any district court of the United States or any court of the District of Columbia by doing any act or thing therein, or thereby forbidden to be done by him if the act or thing so done by him be of such character as to constitute also a criminal offense under any statute of the United States, or under the laws of any State in which the act was committed, shall be proceeded against for his said contempt as hereinafter provided.

PUNISHMENT FOR CONTEMPT OF COURT. SEC. 22. That whenever it shall be made to appear to any district court or judge thereof, or to any judge therein sitting, by the return of a proper officer on lawful process, or upon the affidavit of some credible person, or by information filed by any district attorney, that there is reasonable ground to believe that any person has been guilty of such contempt, the court or judge thereof, or any judge therein sitting, may issue a rule requiring the said person so charged to show cause upon a day certain why he should not be punished therefor, which rule, together with a copy of the affidavit or information, shall be served upon the person charged, with sufficient promptness to enable him to prepare for and make return to the order at the time fixed therein. If upon or by such return, in the judgment of the court, the alleged contempt be not sufficiently purged, a trial shall be directed at a time and place fixed by the court: *Provided, however,* That if the accused, being a natural person, fail or refuse to make return to the rule to show cause, an attachment may issue against his person to compel an answer, and in case of his continued failure or refusal, or if for any reason it be impracticable to dispose of the matter on the return day, he may be required to give reasonable bail for his attendance at the trial and his submission to the final judgment of the court. Where the accused is a body corporate, an attachment for the sequestration of its property may be issued upon like refusal or failure to answer.

In all cases within the purview of this Act such trial may be by the court, or, upon demand of the accused, by a jury; in which latter event the court may impanel a jury from the jurors then in attendance, or the court or the judge thereof in chambers may cause a sufficient number of jurors to be selected and summoned, as provided by law, to attend at the time and place of trial, at which time a jury shall be selected and impaneled as upon a trial for misdemeanor; and such trial shall conform, as near as may be, to the practice in criminal cases prosecuted by indictment or upon information.

If the accused be found guilty, judgment shall be entered accordingly, prescribing the punishment, either by fine or imprisonment, or both, in the discretion of the court. Such fine shall be paid to the United States or to the complainant or other party injured by the act constituting the contempt, or may, where more than one is so damaged, be divided or apportioned among them as the court may direct, but in no case shall the fine to be paid to the United States exceed, in case the accused is a natural person, the sum of $1,000, nor shall such imprisonment exceed the term of six months: *Provided*, That in any case the court or a judge thereof may, for good cause shown, by affidavit or proof taken in open court or before such judge and filed with the papers in the case, dispense with the rule to show cause, and may issue an attachment for the arrest of the person charged with contempt; in which event such person, when arrested, shall be brought before such court or a judge thereof without unnecessary delay and shall be admitted to bail in a reasonable penalty for his appearance to answer to the charge or for trial for the contempt; and thereafter the proceedings shall be the same as provided herein in case the rule had issued in the first instance.

APPEAL IN CONTEMPT OF COURT CASES. SEC. 23. That the evidence taken upon the trial of any persons so accused may be preserved by bill of exceptions, and any judgment of conviction may be reviewed upon writ of error in all respects as now provided by law in criminal cases, and may be affirmed, reversed, or modified as justice may require. Upon the granting of such writ of error, execution of judgment shall be stayed, and the accused, if thereby sentenced to imprisonment, shall be admitted to bail in such reasonable sum as may be required by the court, or by any justice, or any judge of any district court of the United States or any court of the District of Columbia.

OTHER CASES OF CONTEMPT OF COURT. SEC. 24. That nothing herein contained shall be construed to relate to contempts committed in the presence of the court, or so near thereto as to obstruct the administration of justice, nor to contempts committed in disobedience of any lawful writ, process, order, rule, decree, or command entered in any suit or action brought or prosecuted in the name of, or on behalf of the United States, but the same, and all other cases of contempt not specifically embraced within section twenty-one of this Act, may be punished in conformity to the usages at law and in equity now prevailing.

THE RAILWAY LABOR ACT

Act of May 20, 1926, 44 Stat. 577, as Amended.

An Act

To provide for the prompt disposition of disputes between carriers and their employees, and for other purposes.

Be it enacted by the Senate and House of Representatives of the United States of America in Congress assembled, That

TITLE I

SEC. 1. DEFINITIONS; RAILWAY LABOR ACT. When used in this Act and for the purposes of this Act—

First. The term "carrier" includes any express company, sleeping-car company, carrier by railroad, subject to the Interstate Commerce Act, and any company which is directly or indirectly owned or controlled by or under common control with any carrier by railroad and which operates any equipment or facilities or performs any service (other than trucking service) in connection with the transportation, receipt, delivery, elevation, transfer in transit, refrigeration or icing, storage, and handling of property transported by railroad, and any receiver, trustee, or other individual or body, judicial or otherwise, when in the possession of the business of any such "carrier": *Provided, however,* That the term "carrier" shall not include any street, interurban, or suburban electric railway, unless such railway is operating as a part of a general steam-railroad system of transportation, but shall not exclude any part of the general steam-railroad system of transportation now or hereafter operated by any other motive power. The Interstate Commerce Commission is hereby authorized and directed upon request of the Mediation Board or upon complaint of any party interested to determine after hearing whether any line operated by electric power falls within the terms of this proviso. The term "carrier" shall not include any company by reason of its being engaged in the mining of coal, the supplying of coal to a carrier where delivery is not beyond the mine tipple, and the operation of equipment or facilities therefor, or in any of such activities.

Second. The term "Adjustment Board" means the National Railroad Adjustment Board created by this Act.

Third. The term "Mediation Board" means the National Mediation Board created by this Act.

Fourth. The term "commerce" means commerce among the several States or between any State, Territory, or the District of Columbia and any foreign nation, or between any Territory or the District of Columbia and any State, or between any Territory and any other Territory, or between any Territory and the District of Columbia, or within any Territory or the District of Columbia, or between points in the same State but through any other State or any Territory or the District of Columbia or any foreign nation.

Fifth. The term "employee" as used herein includes every person in the service of a carrier (subject to its continuing authority to supervise and direct the manner of rendition of his service) who performs any work defined as that of an employee or subordinate official in the orders of the Interstate Commerce Commission now in effect, and as the same may be amended or interpreted by orders hereafter entered by the Commission pursuant to the authority which is hereby conferred upon it to enter orders amending or interpreting such existing orders: *Provided, however,* That no occupational classification made by order of the Interstate Commerce Commission shall be construed to define the crafts according to which railway employees may be organized by their voluntary action, nor shall the jurisdiction or powers of such employee organizations be regarded as in any way limited or defined by the provisions of this Act or by the orders of the Commission.

The term "employee" shall not include any individual while such individual is engaged in the physical operations consisting of the mining of coal, the preparation of coal, the handling (other than movement by rail with standard railroad locomotives) of coal not beyond the mine tipple, or the loading of coal at the tipple.

Sixth. The term "representative" means any person or persons, labor union, organization, or corporation designated either by a carrier or group of carriers or by its or their employees, to act for it or them.

Seventh. The term "district court" includes the Supreme Court of the District of Columbia; and the term "circuit court of appeals" includes the Court of Appeals of the District of Columbia.

This Act may be cited as the "Railway Labor Act."

Sec. 2. General Purposes. The purposes of the Act are: (1) To avoid any interruption to commerce or to the operation of any carrier engaged therein; (2) to forbid any limitation upon freedom of association among employees or any denial, as a condition of employment or otherwise, of the right of employees to join a labor organization; (3) to provide for the complete independence of carriers and of employees in the matter of self-organization to carry out purposes of this Act; (4) to provide for the prompt and orderly settlement of all disputes concerning rates of pay, rules, or working conditions; (5) to provide for the prompt and orderly settlement of all disputes growing out of grievances or out of the interpretation or application of agreements covering rates of pay, rules, or working conditions.

GENERAL DUTIES

First. It shall be the duty of all carriers, their officers, agents, and employees to exert every reasonable effort to make and maintain agreements concerning rates of pay, rules, and working conditions, and to settle all disputes, whether arising out of the application of such agreements or otherwise, in order to avoid any interruption to commerce or to the operation of any carrier growing out of any dispute between the carrier and the employees thereof.

Second. All disputes between a carrier or carriers and its or their employees shall be considered, and, if possible, decided, with all expedition, in conference between representatives designated and authorized so to confer, respectively, by the carrier or carriers and by the employees thereof interested in the dispute.

Third. Representatives, for the purposes of this Act, shall be designated by the respective parties without interference, influence, or coercion by either party over the designation of representatives by the other; and neither party shall in any way interfere with, influence, or coerce the other in its choice of representatives. Representatives of employees for purposes of this Act need not be persons in the employ of the carrier, and no carrier shall, by interference, influence, or coercion seek in any manner to prevent the designation by its employees as their representatives of those who or which are not employees of the carrier.

Fourth. Employees shall have the right to organize and bargain collectively through representatives of their own choosing. The majority of any craft or class of employees shall have the right to determine who shall be the representative of the craft or class for the purposes of this Act. No carrier, its officers or agents, shall deny or in any way question the right of its employees to join, organize, or assist in organizing the labor organization of their choice, and it shall be unlawful for any carrier to interfere in any way with the organization of its employees, or to use the funds of the carrier in maintaining or assisting or contributing to any labor organization labor representative, or other agency of collective bargaining, or in performing any work therefor, or to influence or coerce employees in an effort to induce them to join or remain or not to join or remain members of any labor organization, or to deduct from the wages of employees any dues, fees, assessments, or other contributions payable to labor organizations, or to collect or to assist in the collection of any such dues, fees, assessments, or other contributions: *Provided,* That nothing in this Act shall be construed to prohibit a carrier from permitting an employee, individually, or local representatives of employees from conferring with management during working hours without loss of time, or to prohibit a carrier from furnishing free transportation to its employees while engaged in the business of a labor organization.

Fifth. No carrier, its officers, or agents shall require any person seeking employment to sign any contract or agreement promising to join or not to join a labor organization; and if any such contract has been enforced prior to the effective date of this Act, then such carrier shall notify the employees by an appropriate order that such contract has been discarded and is no longer binding on them in any way.

Sixth. In case of a dispute between a carrier or carriers and its or their employees, arising out of grievances or out of the interpretation or application of agreements concerning rates of pay, rules, or working conditions, it shall be the duty of the designated representative or representatives of such carrier or carriers and of such employees, within ten days after the receipt of notice of a desire on the part of either party to confer in respect to such dispute, to specify a time and place at which such conference shall be held: *Provided,* (1) That the place so specified shall be situated upon the line of the carrier involved or as otherwise mutually agreed upon; and (2) that the time so specified shall allow the designated conferees reasonable opportunity to reach such place of conference, but shall not exceed twenty days from the receipt of such notice: *And provided further,* That nothing in this Act shall be construed to supersede the provisions of any agreement (as to conferences) then in effect between the parties.

Seventh. No carrier, its officers or agents shall change the rates of pay, rules, or working conditions of its employees, as a class as embodied in agreements except in the manner prescribed in such agreements or in section 6 of this Act.

Eighth. Every carrier shall notify its employees by printed notices in such form and posted at such times and places as shall be specified by the Mediation Board that all disputes between the carrier and its employees will be handled in accordance with the requirements of this Act, and in such notices there shall be printed verbatim, in large type, the third, fourth, and fifth paragraphs of this section. The provisions of said paragraphs are hereby made a part of the contract of employment between the carrier and each employee, and shall be held binding upon the parties, regardless of any other express or implied agreements between them.

Ninth. If any dispute shall arise among a carrier's employees as to who are the representatives of such employees designated and authorized in accordance with the requirements of this Act, it shall be the duty of the Mediation Board upon request of either party to the dispute to investigate such dispute and to certify to both parties, in writing, within thirty days after the receipt of the invocation of its services, the name or names of the individuals or organizations that have been designated and authorized to represent the employees involved in the dispute, and certify the same to the carrier. Upon receipt of such certification the carrier shall treat with the representative so certified as the representative of the craft or class for the purposes of this Act. In such an investigation, the Mediation Board shall be authorized to take a secret ballot of the employees involved, or to utilize any other appropriate method of ascertaining the names of their duly designated and authorized representatives in such manner as shall insure the choice of representatives by the employees without interference, influence, or coercion exercised by the carrier. In the conduct of any election for the purposes herein indicated the Board shall designate who may participate in the election and establish the rules to govern the election, or may appoint a committee of three neutral persons who after hearing shall within ten days designate the employees who may participate in the election. The Board shall have access to and have power to make copies of the books and records of the carriers to obtain and utilize such information as may be deemed necessary by it to carry out the purposes and provisions of this paragraph.

Tenth. The willful failure or refusal of any carrier, its officers or agents to comply with the terms of the third, fourth, fifth, seventh, or eighth paragraph of this section shall be a misdemeanor, and upon conviction thereof the carrier, officer, or agent offending shall be subject to a fine of not less than $1,000 nor more than $20,000 or imprisonment for not more than six months, or both fine and imprisonment, for each offense, and each day during which such carrier, officer, or agent shall willfully fail or refuse to comply with the terms of the said paragraphs of this section shall constitute a separate offense. It shall be the duty of any district attorney of the United States to whom any duly designated representative of a carrier's employees may apply to institute in the proper court and to prosecute under the direction of the Attorney General of the United States, all necessary proceedings for the enforcement of the provisions of this section, and for the punishment of all violations thereof and the costs and expenses of such prosecution shall be paid out of the appropriation for the expenses of the courts of the United States: *Provided*, That nothing in this Act shall be construed to require an individual employee to render labor or service without his consent, nor shall anything in this act be construed to make the quitting of his labor by an individual employee an illegal act; nor shall any court issue any process to compel the performance by an individual employee of such labor or service, without his consent.

SEC. 3. NATIONAL RAILROAD ADJUSTMENT BOARD.

First. There is hereby established a Board, to be known as the "National Railroad Adjustment Board," the members of which shall be selected within thirty days after approval of this Act, and it is hereby provided—

(a) That the said Adjustment Board shall consist of thirty-six members, eighteen of whom shall be selected by the carriers and eighteen by such labor organizations of the employees, national in scope, as have been or may be organized in accordance with the provisions of section 2 of this Act.

(b) The carriers, acting each through its board of directors or its receiver or receivers, trustee or trustees or through an officer or officers designated for that purpose by such board, trustee or trustees or receiver or receivers, shall prescribe the rules under which its representatives shall be selected and shall select the representatives of the carriers on the Adjustment Board and designate the division on which each such representative shall serve, but no carrier or system of carriers shall have more than one representative on any division of the Board.

(c) The national labor organizations, as defined in paragraph (a) of this section, acting each through the chief executive or other medium designated by the organization or association thereof, shall prescribe the rules under which the labor members of the Adjustment Board shall be selected and shall select such members and designate the division on which each member shall serve; but no labor organization shall have more than one representative on any division of the Board.

(d) In case of a permanent or temporary vacancy on the Adjustment Board, the vacancy shall be filled by selection in the same manner as in the original selection.

(e) If either the carriers or the labor organizations of the employees fail to select and designate representatives to the Adjustment Board, as provided in paragraphs (d) and (c) of this section, respectively, within sixty days after the passage of this Act, in case of any original appointment to office of a member of the Adjustment Board, or in case of a vacancy in any such office within thirty days after such vacancy occurs, the Mediation Board shall thereupon directly make the appointment and shall select an individual associated in interest with the carriers or the group of labor organizations of employees, whichever he is to represent.

(f) In the event a dispute arises as to the right of any national labor organization to participate as per paragraph (c) of this section in the selection and designation of the labor members of the Adjustment Board, the Secretary of Labor shall investigate the claim of such labor organization to participate, and if such claim in the judgment of the Secretary of Labor has merit, the Secretary shall notify the Mediation Board accordingly, and within ten days after receipt of such advice the Mediation Board shall request those national labor organizations duly qualified as per paragraph (c) of this section to participate in the selection and designation of the labor members of the Adjustment Board to select a representative. Such representative, together with a representative likewise designated by the claimant, and a third or neutral party designated by the Mediation Board, constituting a board of three, shall within thirty days after the appointment of the neutral member, investigate the claims of the labor organization desiring participation and decide whether or not it was organized in accordance with section 2 hereof and is otherwise properly qualified to participate in the selection of the labor members of the Adjustment Board and the findings of such boards of three shall be final and binding.

(g) Each member of the Adjustment Board shall be compensated by the party or parties he is to represent. Each third or neutral party selected under the provisions of (f) of this section shall receive from the Mediation Board such compensation as the Mediation Board may fix, together with his necessary traveling expenses and expenses actually incurred for subsistence, or per diem allowance in lieu thereof, subject to the provisions of law applicable thereto, while serving as such third or neutral party.

(h) The said Adjustment Board shall be composed of four divisions, whose proceedings shall be independent of one another, and the said divisions as well as the number of their members shall be as follows:

First division: To have jurisdiction over disputes involving train- and yard-service employees of carriers; that is, engineers, firemen, hostlers, and outside hostler helpers, conductors, trainmen, and yard-service employees. This division shall consist of ten members, five of whom shall be selected and designated by the carriers and five of whom shall be selected and designated by the national labor organizations of the employees.

Second division: To have jurisdiction over disputes involving machinists, boilermakers, blacksmiths, sheet-metal workers, electrical workers, car men, the helpers and apprentices of all the foregoing, coach cleaners, power-house employees, and railroad-shop laborers. This division shall consist of ten members, five of whom shall be selected by the carriers and five by the national labor organizations of the employees.

Third division: To have jurisdiction over disputes involving station, tower, and telegraph employees, train dispatchers, maintenance-of-way men, clerical employees, freight handlers, express, station, and store employees, signal men, sleeping-car employees. This division shall consist of ten members, five of whom shall be selected by the carriers and five by the national labor organizations of employees.

Fourth division: To have jurisdiction over disputes involving employees of carriers directly or indirectly engaged in transportation of passengers or property by water, and all other employees of carriers over which jurisdiction is not given to the first, second, and third divisions. This division shall consist of six members, three of whom shall be selected by the carriers and three by the national labor organizations of the employees.

(i) The disputes between an employee or group of employees and a carrier or carriers growing out of grievances or out of the interpretation or application of agreements concerning rates of pay, rules, or working conditions, including cases pending and unadjusted on the date of approval of this Act, shall be handled in the usual manner up to and including the chief operating officer of the carrier designated to handle such disputes; but, failing to reach an adjustment in this manner, the disputes may be referred by petition of the parties or by either party to the appropriate division of the Adjustment Board with a full statement of the facts and all supporting data bearing upon the disputes.

(j) Parties may be heard either in person, by counsel, or by other representatives, as they may respectively elect, and the several divisions of the Adjustment Board shall give due notice of all hearings to the employee or employees and the carrier or carriers involved in any dispute submitted to them.

(k) Any division of the Adjustment Board shall have authority to empower two or more of its members to conduct hearings and make findings upon disputes, when properly submitted, at any place designated by the division: *Provided, however,* That final awards as to any such dispute must be made by the entire division as hereinafter provided.

(l) Upon failure of any division to agree upon an award because of a deadlock or inability to secure a majority vote of the division members, as provided in paragraph (n) of this section, then such division shall forthwith agree upon and select a neutral person, to be known as "referee," to sit with the division as a member thereof and make an award. Should the division fail to agree upon and select a referee within ten days of the date of the deadlock or inability to secure a majority vote, then the division, or any member thereof, or the parties or either party to the dispute may certify that fact to the Mediation Board, which Board shall, within ten days from the date of receiving such certificate, select and name the referee to sit with the division as a member thereof and make an award. The Mediation Board shall be bound by the same provisions in the appointment of these neutral referees as are provided elsewhere in this Act for the appointment of arbitrators and shall fix and pay the compensation of such referees.

(m) The awards of the several divisions of the Adjustment Board shall be stated in writing. A copy of the awards shall be furnished to the respective parties to the controversy, and the awards shall be final and binding upon both parties to the dispute, except insofar as they shall contain a money award. In case a dispute arises involving an interpretation of the award the division of the Board upon request of either party shall interpret the award in the light of the dispute.

(n) A majority vote of all members of the division of the Adjustment Board shall be competent to make an award with respect to any dispute submitted to it.

(o) In case of an award by any division of the Adjustment Board in favor of petitioner, the division of the Board shall make an order, directed to the carrier, to make the award effective and, if the award includes a requirement for the payment of money, to pay to the employee the sum to which he is entitled under the award on or before a day named.

(p) If a carrier does not comply with an order of a division of the Adjustment Board within the time limit in such order, the petitioner, or any person for whose benefit such order was made, may file in the District Court of the United States for the district in which he resides or in which is located the principal operating office of the carrier, or through which the carrier operates, a petition setting forth briefly the causes for which he claims relief, and the order of the division of the Adjustment Board in the premises. Such suit in the District Court of the United States shall proceed in all respects as other civil suits, except that on the trial of such suit the findings and order of the division of the Adjustment Board shall be prima facie evidence of the facts therein stated, and except that the petitioner shall not be liable for costs in the district court nor for costs at any subsequent stage of the proceedings, unless they accrue upon his appeal, and such costs shall be paid out of the appropriation for the expenses of the courts of the United States. If the petitioner shall finally prevail he shall be allowed a reasonable attorney's fee, to be taxed and collected as a part of the costs of the suit. The district courts are empowered, under the rules of the court governing actions at law, to make such order and enter such judgment, by writ of mandamus or otherwise, as may be appropriate to enforce or set aside the order of the division of the Adjustment Board.

(q) All actions at law based upon the provisions of this section shall be begun within two years from the time the cause of action accrues under the award of the division of the Adjustment Board, and not after.

(r) The several divisions of the Adjustment Board shall maintain headquarters in Chicago, Illinois, meet regularly, and continue in session so long as there is pending before the division any matter within its jurisdiction which has been submitted for its consideration and which has not been disposed of.

(s) Whenever practicable, the several divisions or subdivisions of the Adjustment Board shall be supplied with suitable quarters in any Federal building located at its place of meeting.

(t) The Adjustment Board may, subject to the approval of the Mediation Board, employ and fix the compensations of such assistants as it deems necessary in carrying on its proceedings. The compensation of such employees shall be paid by the Mediation Board.

(u) The Adjustment Board shall meet within forty days after the approval of this Act and adopt such rules as it deems necessary to control proceedings before the respective divisions and not in conflict with the provisions of this section. Immediately following the meeting of the entire Board and the adoption of such rules, the respective divisions shall meet and organize by the selection of a chairman, a vice-chairman, and a secretary. Thereafter each division shall annually designate one of its members to act as chairman and one of its members to act as vice-chairman: *Provided, however*, That the chairmanship and vice-chairmanship of any division shall alternate as between the groups, so that both the chairmanship and vice-chairmanship shall be held alternately by a representative of the carriers and a representative of the employees. In case of a vacancy, such vacancy shall be filled for the unexpired term by the selection of a successor from the same group.

(v) Each division of the Adjustment Board shall annually prepare and submit a report of its activities to the Mediation Board, and the substance of such report shall be included in the annual report of the Mediation Board to the Congress of the United States. The reports of each division of the Adjustment Board and the annual report of the Mediation Board shall state in detail all cases heard, all actions taken, the names, salaries, and duties of all agencies, employees, and officers receiving compensation from the United States under the authority of this Act, and an account of all moneys appropriated by Congress pursuant to the authority conferred by this Act and disbursed by such agencies, employees, and officers.

(w) Any division of the Adjustment Board shall have authority, in its discretion, to establish regional adjustment boards to act in its place and stead for such limited period as such division may determine to be necessary. Carrier members of such regional boards shall be designated in keeping with rules devised for this purpose by the carrier members of the Adjustment Board and the labor members shall be designated in keeping with rules devised for this purpose by the labor members of the Adjustment Board. Any such regional board shall, during the time for which it is appointed, have the same authority to conduct hearings, make findings upon disputes and adopt the same procedure as the division of the Adjustment Board appointing it, and its decisions shall be enforceable to the same extent and under the same processes. A neutral person, as referee, shall be appointed for service in connection with any such regional adjustment board in the same circumstances and manner as provided in paragraph (1) hereof, with respect to a division of the Adjustment Board.

Second. Nothing in this section shall be construed to prevent any individual carrier, system, or group of carriers and any class or classes of its or their employees, all acting through their representatives, selected in accordance with the provisions of this Act, from mutually agreeing to the establishment of system, group, or regional boards of adjustment for the purpose of adjusting and deciding disputes of the character specified in this section. In the event that either party to such a system, group, or regional board of adjustment is dissatisfied with such arrangement, it may upon ninety days' notice to the other party elect to come under the jurisdiction of the Adjustment Board.

SEC. 4. NATIONAL MEDIATION BOARD.

First. The Board of Mediation is abolished, effective thirty days from June 21, 1934, and the members, secretary, officers, assistants, employees, and agents thereof, in office on June 21, 1934, shall continue to function and receive their salaries for a period of thirty days from such date in the same manner as though this Act had not been passed. There is established, as an independent agency in the executive branch of the Government, a board to be known as the "National Mediation Board," to be composed of three members appointed by the President, by and with the advice and consent of the Senate, not more than two of whom shall be of the same political party. The terms of office of the members first appointed shall begin as soon as the members shall qualify, but not before thirty days after June 21, 1934, and expire, as designated by the President at the time of nomination, one on February 1, 1935, one on February 1, 1936, and one on February 1, 1937. The terms of office of all successors shall expire three years after the expiration of the terms for which their predecessors were appointed; but any member appointed to fill a vacancy occurring prior to the expiration of the term for which his predecessor was appointed shall be appointed only for the unexpired term of his predecessor. Vacancies in the Board shall not impair the powers nor affect the duties of the Board nor of the remaining members of the Board. Two of the members in office shall constitute a quorum for the transaction of the business of the Board. Each member of the Board shall receive a salary at the rate of $10,000 per annum, together with necessary traveling and subsistence expenses, or per diem allowance in lieu thereof, subject to the provisions of law applicable thereto, while away from the principal office of the Board on business required by this Act. No person in the employment of or who is pecuniarily or otherwise interested in any organization of employees or any carrier shall enter upon the duties of or continue to be a member of the Board.

All cases referred to the Board of Mediation and unsettled on June 21, 1934, shall be handled to conclusion by the Mediation Board.

A member of the Board may be removed by the President for inefficiency, neglect of duty, malfeasance in office, or ineligibility, but for no other cause.

Second. The Mediation Board shall annually designate a member to act as chairman. The Board shall maintain its principal office in the District of Columbia, but it may meet at any other place whenever it deems it necessary so to do. The Board may designate one or more of its members to exercise the functions of the Board in mediation proceedings. Each member of the Board shall have power to administer oaths and affirmations. The Board shall have a seal which shall be judicially noticed. The Board shall make an annual report to Congress.

Third. The Mediation Board may (1) appoint such experts and assistants to act in a confidential capacity and, subject to the provisions of the civil-service laws, such other officers and employees as are essential to the effective transaction of the work of the Board; (2) in accordance with the Classification Act of 1923, fix the salaries of such experts, assistants, officers, and employees; and (3) make such expenditures (including expenditures for rent and personal services at the seat of government and elsewhere, for law books, periodicals, and books of reference, and for printing and binding, and including expenditures for salaries and compensation, necessary traveling expenses and expenses actually incurred for subsistence, and other necessary expenses of the Mediation Board, Adjustment Board, Regional Adjustment Boards established under paragraph [w] of section 3, and boards of arbitration, in accordance with the provisions of this section and sections 3 and 7, respectively), as may be provided for by the Congress from time to time. All expenditures of the Board shall be allowed and paid on the presentation of itemized vouchers therefor approved by the chairman.

Fourth. The Mediation Board is hereby authorized by its order to assign, or refer, any portion of its work, business, or functions arising under this or any other Act of Congress, or referred to it by Congress or either branch thereof, to an individual member of the Board or to an employee or employees of the Board to be designated by such order for action thereon, and by its order at any time to amend, modify, supplement, or rescind any such assignment or reference. All such orders shall take effect forthwith and remain in effect until otherwise ordered by the Board. In conformity with and subject to the order or orders of the Mediation Board in the premises, any such individual member of the Board or employee designated shall have power and authority to act as to any of said work, business, or functions so assigned or referred to him for action by the Board.

Fifth. All officers and employees of the Board of Mediation (except the members thereof, whose offices are hereby abolished) whose services in the judgment of the Mediation Board are necessary to the efficient operation of the Board are hereby transferred to the Board, without change in classification or compensation; except that the Board may provide for the adjustment of such classification or compensation to conform to the duties to which such officers and employees may be assigned.

All unexpended appropriations for the operation of the Board of Mediation that are available at the time of the abolition of the Board of Mediation shall be transferred to the Mediation Board and shall be available for its use for salaries and other authorized expenditures.

SEC. 5. FUNCTIONS OF MEDIATION BOARD.

First. The parties, or either party, to a dispute between an employee or group of employees and a carrier may invoke the services of the Mediation Board in any of the following cases:

(a) A dispute concerning changes in rates of pay, rules, or working conditions not adjusted by the parties in conference.

(b) Any other dispute not referable to the National Railroad Adjustment Board and not adjusted in conference between the parties or where conferences are refused.

The Mediation Board may proffer its services in case any labor emergency is found by it to exist at any time.

In either event the said Board shall promptly put itself in communication with the parties to such controversy, and shall use its best efforts, by mediation, to bring them to agreement. If such efforts to bring about an amicable settlement through mediation shall be unsuccessful, the said Board shall at once endeavor as its final required action (except as provided in paragraph third of this section and in section 10 of this Act) to induce the parties to submit their controversy to arbitration, in accordance with the provisions of this Act.

If arbitration at the request of the Board shall be refused by one or both parties, the Board shall at once notify both parties in writing that its mediatory efforts have failed and for thirty days thereafter, unless in the intervening period the parties agree to arbitration, or an emergency board shall be created under section 10 of this Act, no change shall be made in the rates of pay, rules, or working conditions or established practices in effect prior to the time the dispute arose.

Second. In any case in which a controversy arises over the meaning or the application of any agreement reached through mediation under the provisions of this Act, either party to the said agreement, or both, may apply to the Mediation Board for an interpretation of the meaning or application of such agreement. The said Board shall upon receipt of such request notify the parties to the controversy, and after a hearing of both sides give its interpretation within thirty days.

Third. The Mediation Board shall have the following duties with respect to the arbitration of disputes under section 7 of this Act:

(a) On failure of the arbitrators named by the parties to agree on the remaining arbitrator or arbitrators within the time set by section 7 of this Act, it shall be the duty of the Mediation Board to name such remaining arbitrator or arbitrators. It shall be the duty of the Board in naming such arbitrator or arbitrators to appoint only those whom the Board shall deem wholly disinterested in the controversy to be arbitrated and impartial and without bias as between the parties to such arbitration. Should, however, the Board name an arbitrator or arbitrators not so disinterested and impartial then, upon proper investigation and presentation of the facts, the Board shall promptly remove such arbitrator.

If an arbitrator named by the Mediation Board, in accordance with the provisions of this Act, shall be removed by such Board as provided by this Act, or if such an arbitrator refused or is unable to serve, it shall be the duty of the Mediation Board, promptly, to select another arbitrator, in the same manner as provided in this Act for an original appointment by the Mediation Board.

(b) Any member of the Mediation Board is authorized to take the acknowledgment of an agreement to arbitrate under this Act. When so acknowledged, or when acknowledged by the parties before a notary public or the clerk of a district court or a circuit court of appeals of the United States, such agreement to arbitrate shall be delivered to a member of said Board or transmitted to said Board, to be filed in its office.

(c) When an agreement to arbitrate has been filed with the Mediation Board, or with one of its members, as provided by this section, and when the said Board has been furnished the names of the arbitrators chosen by the parties to the controversy it shall be the duty of the Board to cause a notice in writing to be served upon said arbitrators, notifying them of their appointment, requesting them to meet promptly to name the remaining arbitrator or arbitrators necessary to complete the Board of Arbitration, and advising them of the period within which, as provided by the agreement to arbitrate, they are empowered to name such arbitrator or arbitrators.

(d) Either party to an arbitration desiring the reconvening of a board of arbitration to pass upon any controversy arising over the meaning or application of an award may so notify the Mediation Board in writing, stating in such notice the question or questions to be submitted to such reconvened Board. The Mediation Board shall thereupon promptly communicate with the members of the Board of Arbitration, or a subcommittee of such Board appointed for such purpose pursuant to a provision in the agreement to arbitrate, and arrange for the reconvening of said Board of Arbitration or subcommittee, and shall notify the respective parties to the controversy of the time and place at which the Board, or the subcommittee, will meet for hearings upon the matters in controversy to be submitted to it. No evidence other than that contained in the record filed with the original award shall be received or considered by such reconvened Board or subcommittee, except such evidence as may be necessary to illustrate the interpretations suggested by the parties. If any member of the original Board is unable or unwilling to serve on such reconvened Board or subcommittee thereof, another arbitrator shall be named in the same manner and with the same powers and duties as such original arbitrator.

(e) Within sixty days after June 21, 1934, every carrier shall file with the Mediation Board a copy of each contract with its employees in effect on the 1st day of April 1934, covering rates of pay, rules, and working conditions. If no contract with any craft or class of its employees has been entered into, the carrier shall file with the Mediation Board a statement of that fact including also a statement of the rates of pay, rules, and working conditions applicable in dealing with such craft or class. When any new contract is executed or change is made in an existing contract with any class or craft of its employees covering rates of pay, rules, or working conditions, or in those rates of pay, rules, and working conditions of employees not covered by contract, the carrier shall file the same with Mediation Board within thirty days after such new contract or change in existing contract has been executed or rates of pay, rules, and working conditions have been made effective.

(f) The Mediation Board shall be the custodian of all papers and documents heretofore filed with or transferred to the Board of Mediation bearing upon the settlement, adjustment, or determination of disputes between carriers and their employees or upon mediation or arbitration proceedings held under or pursuant to the provisions of any Act of Congress in respect thereto; and the President is authorized to designate a custodian of the records and property of the Board of Mediation until the transfer and delivery of such records to the Mediation Board and to require the transfer and delivery to the Mediation Board of any and all such papers and documents filed with it or in its possession.

SEC. 6. PROCEDURE IN CHANGING RATES OF PAY, RULES, AND WORKING CONDITIONS. Carriers and representatives of the employees shall give at least thirty days' written notice of an intended change in agreements affecting rates of pay, rules, or working conditions, and the time and place for the beginning of conference between the representatives of the parties interested in such intended changes shall be agreed upon within ten days after the receipt of said notice, and said time shall be within the thirty days provided in the notice. In every case where such notice of intended change has been given, or conferences are being held with reference thereto, or the services of the Mediation Board have been requested by either party, or said Board has proffered its services, rates of pay, rules, or working conditions shall not be altered by the carrier until the controversy has been finally acted upon as required by section 5 of this Act, by the Mediation Board, unless a period of ten days has elapsed after termination of conferences without request for or proffer of the services of the Mediation Board.

SEC. 7. ARBITRATION.

First. Whenever a controversy shall arise between a carrier or carriers and its or their employees which is not settled either in conference between representatives of the parties or by the appropriate adjustment board or through mediation, in the manner provided in the preceding sections, such controversy may, by agreement of the parties to such controversy, be submitted to the arbitration of a board of three (or, if the parties to the controversy so stipulate, of six) persons: *Provided, however,* That the failure or refusal of either party to submit a controversy to arbitration shall not be construed as a violation of any legal obligation imposed upon such party by the terms of this Act or otherwise.

Second. Such board of arbitration shall be chosen in the following manner.

(a) In the case of a board of three the carrier or carriers and the representatives of the employees, parties respectively to the agreement to arbitrate, shall each name one arbitrator; the two arbitrators thus chosen shall select a third arbitrator. If the arbitrators chosen by the parties shall fail to name the third arbitrator within five days after their first meeting, such third arbitrator shall be named by the Mediation Board.

(b) In the case of a board of six the carrier or carriers and the representatives of the employees, parties respectively to the agreement to arbitrate, shall each name two arbitrators; the four arbitrators thus chosen shall, by a majority vote, select the remaining two arbitrators. If the arbitrators chosen by the parties shall fail to name the two arbitrators within fifteen days after their first meeting, the said two arbitrators, or as many of them as have not been named, shall be named by the Mediation Board.

Third. (a) When the arbitrators selected by the respective parties have agreed upon the remaining arbitrator or arbitrators, they shall notify the Mediation Board; and, in the event of their failure to agree upon any or upon all of the necessary arbitrators within the period fixed by this Act, they shall, at the expiration of such period, notify the Mediation Board of the arbitrators selected, if any, or of their failure to make or to complete such selection.

(b) The board of arbitration shall organize and select its own chairman and make all necessary rules for conducting its hearings: *Provided, however,* That the Board of arbitration shall be bound to give the parties to the controversy a full and fair hearing, which shall include an opportunity to present evidence in support of their claims, and an opportunity to present their case in person, by counsel, or by other representative as they may respectively elect.

(c) Upon notice from the Mediation Board that the parties, or either party, to an arbitration desire the reconvening of the board of arbitration (or a subcommittee of such board of arbitration appointed for such purpose pursuant to the agreement to arbitrate) to pass upon any controversy over the meaning or application of their award, the board, or its subcommittee, shall at once reconvene. No question other than, or in addition to, the questions relating to the meaning or application of the award, submitted by the party or parties in writing, shall be considered by the reconvened board of arbitration or its subcommittee.

Such rulings shall be acknowledged by such board or subcommittee thereof in the same manner, and filed in the same district court clerk's office, as the original award and become a part thereof.

(d) No arbitrator, except those chosen by the Mediation Board, shall be incompetent to act as an arbitrator because of his interest in the controversy to be arbitrated, or because of his connection with or partiality to either of the parties to the arbitration.

(e) Each member of any board of arbitration created under the provisions of this Act named by either party to the arbitration shall be compensated by the party naming him. Each arbitrator selected by the arbitrators or named by the Mediation Board shall receive from the Mediation Board such compensation as the Mediation Board may fix, together with his necessary traveling expenses and expenses actually incurred for subsistence, while serving as an arbitrator.

(f) The board of arbitration shall furnish a certified copy of its award to the respective parties to the controversy, and shall transmit the original, together with the papers and proceedings and a transcript of the evidence taken at the hearings, certified under the hands of at least a majority of the arbitrators, to the clerk of the district court of the United States for the district wherein the controversy arose or the arbitration is entered into, to be filed in said clerk's office as hereinafter provided. The said board shall also furnish a certified copy of its award, and the papers and proceedings, including testimony relating thereto, to the Mediation Board, to be filed in its office; and in addition a certified copy of its award shall be filed in the office of the Interstate Commerce Commission: *Provided, however,* That such award shall not be construed to diminish or extinguish any of the powers or duties of the Interstate Commerce Commission, under the Interstate Commerce Act, as amended.

(g) A board of arbitration may, subject to the approval of the Mediation Board, employ and fix the compensation of such assistants as it deems necessary in carrying on the arbitration proceedings. The compensation of such employees, together with their necessary traveling expenses and expenses actually incurred for subsistence, while so employed, and the necessary expenses of boards of arbitration, shall be paid by the Mediation Board.

Whenever practicable, the board shall be supplied with suitable quarters in any Federal building located at its place of meeting or at any place where the board may conduct its proceedings or deliberations.

(h) All testimony before said board shall be given under oath or affirmation, and any member of the board shall have the power to administer oaths or affirmations. The board of arbitration, or any member thereof, shall have the power to require the attendance of witnesses and the production of such books, papers, contracts, agreements, and documents as may be deemed by the board of arbitration material to a just determination of the matters submitted to its arbitration, and may for that purpose request the clerk of the district court of the United States for the district wherein said arbitration is being conducted to issue the necessary subpoenas, and upon such request the said clerk or his duly authorized deputy shall be, and he hereby is, authorized, and it shall be his duty, to issue such subpoenas. In the event of the failure of any person to comply with any such subpoena, or in the event of the contumacy of any witness appearing before the board of arbitration, the board may invoke the aid of the United States courts to compel witnesses to attend and testify and to produce such books, papers, contracts, agreements, and documents to the same extent and under the same conditions and penalties as provided for in the Act to regulate commerce approved February 4, 1887, and the amendments thereto.

Any witness appearing before a board of arbitration shall receive the same fees and milage as witnesses in courts of the United States, to be paid by the party securing the subpoena.

Sec. 8. Agreement to Arbitrate; Form and Contents; Signatures and Acknowledgement; Revocation. The agreement to arbitrate—

(a) Shall be in writing;

(b) Shall stipulate that the arbitration is had under the provisions of this Act;

(c) Shall state whether the board of arbitration is to consist of three or of six members;

(d) Shall be signed by the duly accredited representatives of the carrier or carriers and the employees, parties respectively to the agreement to arbitrate, and shall be acknowledged by said parties before a notary public, the clerk of a district court or circuit court of appeals of the United States, or before a member of the Mediation Board, and, when so acknowledged, shall be filed in the office of the Mediation Board;

(e) Shall state specifically the questions to be submitted to the said board for decision; and that, in its award or awards, the said board shall confine itself strictly to decisions as to the questions so specifically submitted to it;

(f) Shall provide that the questions, or any one or more of them, submitted by the parties to the board of arbitration may be withdrawn from arbitration on notice to that effect signed by the duly accredited representatives of all the parties and served on the board of arbitration;

(g) Shall stipulate that the signatures of a majority of said board of arbitration affixed to their award shall be competent to constitute a valid and binding award;

(h) Shall fix a period from the date of the appointment of the arbitrator or arbitrators necessary to complete the board (as provided for in the agreement) within which the said board shall commence its hearings;

(i) Shall fix a period from the beginning of the hearings within which the said board shall make and file its award; *Provided*, That the parties may agree at any time upon an extension of this period;

(j) Shall provide for the date from which the award shall become effective and shall fix the period during which the award shall continue in force;

(k) Shall provide that the award of the board of arbitration and the evidence of the proceedings before the board relating thereto, when certified under the hands of at least a majority of the arbitrators, shall be filed in the clerk's office of the district court of the United States for the district wherein the controversy arose or the arbitration was entered into, which district shall be designated in the agreement; and, when so filed, such award and proceedings shall constitute the full and complete record of the arbitration;

(l) Shall provide that the award, when so filed, shall be final and conclusive upon the parties as to the facts determined by said award and as to the merits of the controversy decided;

(m) Shall provide that any difference arising as to the meaning, or the application of the provisions, of an award made by a board of arbitration shall be referred back for a ruling to the same board, or, by agreement, to a subcommittee of such board; and that such ruling, when acknowledged in the same manner, and filed in the same district court clerk's office, as the original award, shall be a part of and shall have the same force and effect as such original award; and

(n) Shall provide that the respective parties to the award will each faithfully execute the same.

The said agreement to arbitrate, when properly signed and acknowledged as herein provided, shall not be revoked by a party to such agreement: *Provided, however,* That such agreement to arbitrate may at any time be revoked and canceled by the written agreement of both parties, signed by their duly accredited representatives, and (if no board of arbitration has yet been constituted under the agreement) delivered to the Mediation Board or any member thereof; or, if the board of arbitration has been constituted as provided by this Act, delivered to such board of arbitration.

SEC. 9. AWARD AND JUDGMENT THEREON; EFFECT OF CHAPTER ON INDIVIDUAL EMPLOYEE.

First. The award of a board of arbitration, having been acknowledged as herein provided, shall be filed in the clerk's office of the district court designated in the agreement to arbitrate.

Second. An award acknowledged and filed as herein provided shall be conclusive on the parties as to the merits and facts of the controversy submitted to arbitration, and unless, within ten days after the filing of the award, a petition to impeach the award, on the grounds hereinafter set forth, shall be filed in the clerk's office of the court in which the award has been filed, the court shall enter judgment on the award, which judgment shall be final and conclusive on the parties.

Third. Such petition for the impeachment or contesting of any award so filed shall be entertained by the court only on one or more of the following grounds:

(a) That the award plainly does not conform to the substantive requirements laid down by this Act for such awards, or that the proceedings were not substantially in conformity with this Act;

(b) That the award does not conform, nor confine itself, to the stipulations of the agreement to arbitrate; or

(c) That a member of the board of arbitration rendering the award was guilty of fraud or corruption; or that a party to the arbitration practiced fraud or corruption which fraud or corruption affected the result of the arbitration: *Provided, however,* That no court shall entertain any such petition on the ground that an award is invalid for uncertainty; in such case the proper remedy shall be a submission of such award to a reconvened board, or subcommittee thereof, for interpretation, as provided by this Act: *Provided further,* That an award contested as herein provided shall be construed liberally by the court, with a view to favoring its validity, and that no award shall be set aside for trivial irregularity or clerical error, going only to form and not to substance.

Fourth. If the court shall determine that a part of the award is invalid on some ground or grounds designated in this section as a ground of invalidity, but shall determine that a part of the award is valid, the court shall set aside the entire award:

Provided, however, That, if the parties shall agree thereto, and if such valid and invalid parts are separable, the court shall set aside the invalid part, and order judgment to stand as to the valid part.

Fifth. At the expiration of ten days from the decision of the district court upon the petition filed as aforesaid, final judgment shall be entered in accordance with said decision, unless during said ten days either party shall appeal therefrom to the circuit court of appeals. In such case only such portion of the record shall be transmitted to the appellate court as is necessary to the proper understanding and consideration of the questions of law presented by said petition and to be decided.

Sixth. The determination of said circuit court of appeals upon said questions shall be final, and, being certified by the clerk thereof to said district court, judgment pursuant thereto shall thereupon be entered by said district court.

Seventh. If the petitioner's contentions are finally sustained, judgment shall be entered setting aside the award in whole or, if the parties so agree, in part; but in such case the parties may agree upon a judgment to be entered disposing of the subject matter of the controversy, which judgment when entered shall have the same force and effect as judgment entered upon an award.

Eighth. Nothing in this Act shall be construed to require an individual employee to render labor or service without his consent, nor shall anything in this Act be construed to make the quitting of his labor or service by an individual employee an illegal act; nor shall any court issue any process to compel the performance by an individual employee of such labor or service, without his consent.

Sec. 10. Emergency Board. If a dispute between a carrier and its employees be not adjusted under the foregoing provisions of this Act and should, in the judgment of the Mediation Board, threaten substantially to interrupt interstate commerce to a degree such as to deprive any section of the country of essential transportation service, the Mediation Board shall notify the President, who may thereupon, in his discretion, create a board to investigate and report respecting such dispute. Such board shall be composed of such number of persons as to the President may seem desirable: *Provided, hoewver,* That no member appointed shall be pecuniarily or otherwise interested in any organization of employees or any carrier. The compensation of the members of any such board shall be fixed by the President. Such board shall be created separately in each instance and it shall investigate promptly the facts as to the dispute and make a report thereon to the President within thirty days from the date of its creation.

There is hereby authorized to be appropriated such sums as may be necessary for the expenses of such board, including the compensation and the necessary traveling expenses and expenses actually incurred for subsistence, of the members of the board. All expenditures of the board shall be allowed and paid on the presentation of itemized vouchers therefor approved by the chairman.

After the creation of such board and for thirty days after such board has made its report to the President, no change, except by agreement, shall be made by the parties to the controversy in the conditions out of which the dispute arose.

Sec. 11. Effect of Partial Invalidity of Chapter. If any section, subsection, sentence, clause, or phrase of this Act is for any reason held to be unconstitutional, such decision shall not affect the validity of the remaining portions of this Act. All

Acts or parts of Acts inconsistent with the provisions of this Act are hereby repealed.

SEC. 12. APPROPRIATION. There is hereby authorized to be appropriated such sums as may be necessary for expenditure by the Mediation Board in carrying out the provisions of this Act.

REPEAL OF PRIOR LEGISLATION; EXCEPTION. The Act of July 15, 1913, and the Act of February 28, 1920, providing for mediation, conciliation, and arbitration, and all Acts and parts of Acts in conflict with the provisions of this Act are repealed, except that the members, secretary, officers, employees, and agents of the Railroad Labor Board, in office on May 20, 1926, shall receive their salaries for a period of 30 days from such date, in the same manner as though this Act had not been passed.

TITLE II

Act of April 10, 1936, c. 166, 49 Stat. 1189

APPLICABILITY OF TITLE I. SEC. 201. All of the provisions of title I of this Act are extended to and shall cover every common carrier by air engaged in interstate or foreign commerce, and every carrier by air transporting mail for or under contract with the United States Government, and every air pilot or other person who performs any work as an employee or subordinate offical of such carrier or carriers, subject to its or their continuing authority to supervise and direct the manner of rendition of his service.

DEFINITION OF "CARRIER"; "EMPLOYEE." SEC. 202. The duties, requirements, penalties, benefits, and privileges prescribed and established by the provisions of title I of this Act shall apply to said carriers by air and their employees in the same manner and to the same extent as though such carriers and their employees were specifically included within the definition of "carrier" and "employee," respectively, in section I thereof.

JURISDICTION OF NATIONAL MEDIATION BOARD. SEC. 203. The parties or either party to a dispute between an employee or a group of employees and a carrier or carriers by air may invoke the services of the National Mediation Board and the jurisdiction of said Mediation Board is extended to any of the following cases:

(a) A dispute concerning changes in rates of pay, rules, or working conditions not adjusted by the parties in conference.
(b) Any other dispute not referable to an adjustment board, as hereinafter provided, and not adjusted in conference between the parties, or where conferences are refused.

The National Mediation Board may proffer its services in case any labor emergency is found by it to exist at any time.

The services of the Mediation Board may be invoked in a case under this title in the same manner and to the same extent as are the disputes covered by section 5 of title I of this Act.

CASES PENDING BEFORE NLRB. SEC. 204. The disputes between an employee or group of employees and a carrier or carriers by air growing out of grievances, or out of the interpretation or application of agreements concerning rates of pay, rules, or working conditions, including cases pending and unadjusted on April 10, 1936, before the National Labor Relations Board, shall be handled in the usual manner up to and including the chief operating officer of the carrier designated to handle such disputes; but, failing to reach an adjustment in this manner, the disputes may be referred by petition of the parties or by either party to an appropriate adjustment board, as hereinafter provided, with a full statement of the facts and supporting data bearing upon the disputes.

It shall be the duty of every carrier and of its employees, acting through their representatives, selected in accordance with the provisions of this title, to establish a board of adjustment of jurisdiction not exceeding the jurisdiction which may be lawfully exercised by system, or group of carriers by air and any class or classes of its or their employees; or pending the establishment of a permanent National Board of Adjustment as hereinafter provided. Nothing in this Act shall prevent said carriers by air, or any class or classes of their employees, both acting through their representatives selected in accordance with provisions of this title, from mutually agreeing to the establishment of a National Board of Adjustment of temporary duration and of similarly limited jurisdiction.

NATIONAL AIR TRANSPORT ADJUSTMENT BOARD. SEC. 205. When, in the judgment of the National Mediation Board, it shall be necessary to have a permanent national board of adjustment in order to provide for the prompt and orderly settlement of disputes between said carriers by air, or any of them, and its or their employees, growing out of grievances or out of the interpretation or application of agreements between said carriers by air or any of them, and any class or classes of its or their employees, covering rates of pay, rules, or working conditions, the National Mediation Board is hereby empowered and directed, by its order duly made, published, and served, to direct the said carriers by air and such labor organizations of their employees, national in scope, as have been or may be recognized in accordance with the provisions of this Act, to select and designate four representatives who shall constitute a board which shall be known as the "National Air Transport Adjustment Board." Two members of said National Air Transport Adjustment Board shall be selected by said carriers by air and two members by the said labor organizations of the employees, within thirty days after the date of the order of the National Mediation Board, in the manner and by the procedure prescribed by title I of this Act for the selection and designation of members of the National Railroad Adjustment Board. The National Air Transport Adjustment Board shall meet within forty days after the date of the order of the National Mediation Board directing the selection and designation of its members and shall organize and adopt rules for conducting its proceedings, in the manner prescribed in section 3 of title I of this Act. Vacancies in membership of office shall be filled, members shall be appointed in case of failure of the carriers or of labor organizations of the employees to select and designate representatives, members of the National Air Transport Adjustment Board shall be compensated, hearings shall be held, findings and awards made, stated, served, and enforced, and the number of compensation of any necessary assistants shall be determined and the compensation of such employees shall be paid, all in the same manner and to the same extent as provided with reference to the National Railroad Adjustment Board by section 3 of title I of this Act. The powers and duties prescribed and established by the provisions of section 3 of title I of this Act with reference to the National Railroad Adjustment Board and the several divisions thereof are hereby conferred upon and shall be exercised and performed in like manner and to the same extent by the said National Air Transport Adjustment Board, not exceeding, however, the jurisdiction conferred upon said National Air Transport Adjustment Board by the provisions of this title. From and after the organization of the National Air Transport Adjustment Board, if any system, group, or regional board of adjustment established by any carrier or carriers by air and any class or classes of its or their employees is not satisfactory to either party thereto, the said party, upon ninety days' notice to the other party, may elect to come under the jurisdiction of the National Air Transport Adjustment Board.

TRANSFER OF CASES AND RECORDS TO NATIONAL MEDIATION BOARD. SEC. 206. All cases referred to the National Labor Relations Board, or over which the National Labor Relations Board shall have taken jurisdiction, involving any dispute arising from any cause between any common carrier by air engaged in interstate or foreign commerce or any carrier by air transporting mail for or under contract with the United States Government, and employees of such carrier or carriers, and unsettled on the date of approval of this Act, shall be handled to conclusion by the Mediation Board. The books, records, and papers of the National Labor Relations Board and of the National Labor Board pertinent to such case or cases, whether settled or unsettled, shall be transferred to the custody of the National Mediation Board.

SEPARABILITY PROVISION. SEC. 207. If any provision of this title or application thereof to any person or circumstance is held invalid, the remainder of the Act and the application of such provision to other persons or circumstances shall not be affected thereby.

APPROPRIATIONS. SEC. 208. There is hereby authorized to be appropriated such sums as may be necessary for expenditure by the Mediation Board in carrying out the provisions of this Act.

THE NORRIS–LA GUARDIA ACT

Act of March 23, 1932, 47 Stat. 70

An Act

To amend the Judicial Code and to define and limit the jurisdiction of courts sitting in equity, and for other purposes.

JURISDICTION OF FEDERAL COURTS IN LABOR DISPUTES. SEC. 1. *Be it enacted by the Senate and House of Representatives of the United States of America in Congress assembled,* That no court of the United States, as herein defined, shall have jurisdiction to issue any restraining order or temporary or permanent injunction in a case involving or growing out of a labor dispute, except in a strict conformity with the provisions of this Act; nor shall any such restraining order or temporary or permanent injunction be issued contrary to the public policy declared in this Act.

DECLARATION OF PUBLIC POLICY IN LABOR CONTROVERSIES. SEC. 2. In the interpretation of this Act and in determining the jurisdiction and authority of the courts of the United States, as such jurisdiction and authority are herein defined and limited, the public policy of the United States is hereby declared as follows:

Whereas under prevailing economic conditions, developed with the aid of governmental authority for owners of property to organize in the corporate and other forms of ownership association, the individual unorganized worker is commonly helpless to exercise actual liberty of contract and to protect his freedom of labor, and thereby to obtain acceptable terms and conditions of employment, wherefore, though he should be free to decline to associate with his fellows, it is necessary that he have full freedom of association, self-organization, and designation of representatives of his own choosing, to negotiate the terms and conditions of his employment, and that he shall be free from the interference, restraint, or coercion of employers of labor, or their agents, in the designation of such representatives or in self-organization or in other concerted activities for the purpose of collective bargaining or other mutual aid or protection; therefore, the following definitions of, and limitations upon, the jurisdiction and authority of the courts of the United States are hereby enacted.

NONENFORCEABILITY OF UNDERTAKINGS IN CONFLICT WITH DECLARED POLICY— "YELLOW DOG" CONTRACTS. SEC. 3. Any undertaking or promise, such as is described in this section, or any other undertaking or promise in conflict with the public policy declared in section 2 of this Act, is hereby declared to be contrary to the public policy of the United States, shall not be enforceable in any court of the United States and shall not afford any basis for the granting of legal or equitable relief by any such court, including specifically the following:

Every undertaking or promise hereafter made, whether written or oral, express or implied, constituting or contained in any contract or agreement of hiring or employment between any individual, firm, company, association, or corporation, and any employee or prospective employee of the same, whereby

(a) Either party to such contract or agreement undertakes or promises that he will withdraw from an employment relation in the event that he joins, becomes, or remains a member of any labor organization or of any employer organization.

DENIAL OF INJUNCTIVE RELIEF IN CERTAIN CASES. SEC. 4. No court of the United States shall have jurisdiction to issue any restraining order or temporary or permanent injunction in any case involving or growing out of any labor dispute to prohibit any person or persons participating or interested in such dispute (as these terms are herein defined) from doing, whether singly or in concert any of the following acts:

(a) Ceasing or refusing to perform any work or to remain in any relation of employment;

(b) Becoming or remaining a member of any labor organization or of any employer organization, regardless of any such undertaking or promise as is described in section 3 of this act;

(c) Paying or giving to, or withholding from, any person participating or interested in such labor dispute, any strike for unemployment benefits or insurance, or other moneys or things of value;

(d) By all lawful means aiding any person participating or interested in any labor dispute who is being proceeded against in, or is prosecuting, any action or suit in any court of the United States or of any State:

(e) Giving publicity to the existence of, or the facts involved in, any labor dispute, whether by advertising, speaking, patrolling, or by any other method not involving fraud or violence;

(f) Assembling peaceably to act or organize to act in promotion of their interests in a labor dispute;

(g) Advising or notifying any person of an intention to do any of the acts heretofore specified;

(h) Agreeing with other persons to do or not to do any of the acts heretofore specified; and

(i) Advising, urging, or otherwise causing or inducing without fraud or violence the acts heretofore specified, regardless of any such undertaking or promise as is described in section 3 of this act.

DENIAL OF INJUNCTIVE RELIEF FROM CONCERTED ACTIONS. SEC. 5. No court of the United States shall have jurisdiction to issue a restraining order or temporary or permanent injunction upon the grounds that any of the persons participating or interested in a labor dispute constitute or are engaged in an unlawful combination or conspiracy because of the doing in concert of the acts enumerated in section 4 of this act.

RESPONSIBILITY FOR ACTS. SEC. 6. No officer or member of any association or organization, and no association or organization participating or interested in a labor dispute, shall be held responsible or liable in any court of the United States for the unlawful acts of individual officers, members, or agents, except upon clear proof of actual participating in, or actual authorization of, such acts, or of ratification of such acts after actual knowledge thereof.

Issue of Injunctions—When Permissible. Sec. 7. No court of the United States shall have jurisdiction to issue a temporary or permanent injunction in any case involving or growing out of a labor dispute, as herein defined, except after hearing the testimony of witnesses in open court (with opportunity for cross-examination) in support of the allegations of a complaint made under oath, and testimony in opposition thereto, if offered, and except after findings of fact by the court, to the effect—

(a) That unlawful acts have been threatened or will be committed unless restrained or have been committed and will be continued unless restrained, but no injunction or temporary restraining order shall be issued on account of any threat or unlawful act excepting against the person or persons, association, or organization making the threat or committing the unlawful act or actually authorizing or ratifying the same after actual knowledge thereof;

(b) That substantial and irreparable injury to complainant's property will follow;

(c) That as to each item of relief granted greater injury will be inflicted upon complainant by the denial of relief than will be inflicted upon defendants by the granting of relief;

(d) That complainant has no adequate remedy at law; and

(e) That the public officers charged with the duty to protect complainant's property are unable or unwilling to furnish adequate protection.

Such hearing shall be held after due and personal notice thereof has been given, in such manner as the court shall direct, to all known persons against whom relief is sought, and also to the chief of those public officials of the county and city within which the unlawful acts have been threatened or committed charged with the duty to protect complainant's property: *Provided, however,* That if a complainant shall also allege that, unless a temporary restraining order shall be issued without notice, a substantial and irreparable injury to complainant's property will be unavoidable, such a temporary restraining order may be issued upon testimony under oath, sufficient, if sustained, to justify the court in issuing a temporary injunction upon a hearing after notice. Such a temporary restraining order shall be effective for no longer than five days and shall become void at the expiration of said five days. No temporary restraining order or temporary injunction shall be issued except on condition that complainant shall first file an undertaking with adequate security in an amount to be fixed by the court sufficient to recompense those enjoined for any loss, expense, or damage caused by the improvident or erroneous issuance of such order or injunction, including all reasonable costs (together with a reasonable attorney's fee) and expense of defense against the order or against the granting of any injunctive relief sought in the same proceeding and subsequently denied by the court.

The undertaking herein mentioned shall be understood to signify an agreement entered into by the complainant and the surety upon which a decree may be rendered in the same suit or proceeding against said complainant and surety, upon a hearing to assess damages of which hearing complainant and surety shall have reasonable notice, the said complainant and surety submitting themselves to the jurisdiction of the court for that purpose. But nothing herein contained shall deprive any party having a claim or cause of action under or upon such undertaking from electing to pursue his ordinary remedy by suit at law or in equity.

EFFORT TO SETTLE DISPUTES. SEC. 8. No restraining order or injunctive relief shall be granted to any complainant who has failed to comply with any obligation imposed by law which is involved in the labor dispute in question, or who has failed to make every reasonable effort to settle such dispute either by negotiation or with the aid of any available governmental machinery of mediation or voluntary arbitration.

ISSUANCE OF INJUNCTIONS BASED ON FINDINGS OF FACT. SEC. 9. No restraining order or temporary or permanent injunction shall be granted in a case involving or growing out of a labor dispute, except on the basis of findings of fact made and filed by the court in the record of the case prior to the issuance of such restraining order or injunction; and every restraining order or injunction granted in a case involving or growing out of a labor dispute shall include only a prohibition of such specific act or acts as may be expressly complained of in the bill of complaint or petition filed in such case and as shall be expressly included in said findings of fact made and filed by the court as provided herein.

APPEALS—SECURITY FOR COSTS. SEC. 10. Whenever any court of the United States shall issue or deny any temporary injunction in a case involving or growing out of a labor dispute, the court shall, upon the request of any party to the proceedings and on his filing the usual bond for costs, forthwith certify as in ordinary cases the record of the case to the circuit court of appeals for its review. Upon the filing of such record in the circuit court of appeals, the appeal shall be heard and the temporary injunctive order affirmed, modified, or set aside with the greatest possible expedition, giving the proceedings precedence over all other matters except older matters of the same character.

JURY TRIAL IN CASES OF INDIRECT CONTEMPT. SEC. 11. In all cases arising under this act in which a person shall be charged with contempt in a court of the United States (as herein defined), the accused shall enjoy the right of a speedy and public trial by an impartial jury of the State and district wherein the contempt shall have been committed: *Provided*, That this right shall not apply to contempts committed in the presence of the court or so near thereto as to interfere directly with the administration of justice or to apply to the misbehavior, misconduct, or disobedience of any officer of the court in respect to the writs, orders, or process of the court.

REMOVAL OF JUDGE IN INDIRECT CONTEMPT CASES. SEC. 12. The defendant in any proceeding for contempt of court may file with the court a demand for the retirement of the judge sitting in the proceeding, if the contempt arises from an attack upon the character or conduct of such judge and if the attack occurred elsewhere than in the presence of the court or so near thereto as to interfere directly with the administration of justice. Upon the filing of any such demand the judge shall thereupon proceed no further, but another judge shall be designated in the same manner as is provided by law. The demand shall be filed prior to the hearing in the contempt proceeding.

DEFINITIONS. SEC. 13. When used in this act, and for the purposes of this act—

(a) A case shall be held to involve or to grow out of a labor dispute when the case involves persons who are engaged in the same industry, trade, craft, or occupation; or have direct or indirect interests therein; or who are employees of the same employer; or who are members of the same or an affiliated organization of employers or employees; whether such dispute is (1) between one or more employers or associations of employers and one or more employees or associations of employees; (2) between one or more employers or associations and one or more employers or associations of employers or; (3) between one or more employees or associations of employees and one or more employees or associations of employees; or, when the case involves any conflicting or competing interests in a "labor dispute" (as hereinafter defined) of "persons participating or interested" therein (as hereinafter defined).

(b) A person or association shall be held to be a person participating or interested in a labor dispute if relief is sought against him or it, and if he or it is engaged in the same industry, trade, craft, or occupation in which such dispute occurs, or has a direct or indirect interest therein, or is a member, officer, or agent of any association composed in whole or in part of employers or employees engaged in such industry, trade, craft, or occupation.

(c) The term "labor dispute" includes any controversy concerning terms or conditions of employment, or concerning the association or representation of persons negotiating, fixing, maintaining, changing, or seeking to arrange terms or conditions of employment, regardless of whether or not the disputants stand in the proximate relation of employer and employee.

(d) The term "court of the United States" means any court of the United States whose jurisdiction has been or may be conferred or defined or limited by Act of Congress, including the courts of the District of Columbia.

Separability Provision. Sec. 14. If any provision of this Act or the application thereof to any person or circumstance is held unconstitutional or otherwise invalid, the remaining provisions of the Act and the application of such provisions to other persons or circumstances shall not be affected thereby.

Repeal of Conflicting Acts—Sec. 15. All Acts and parts of Acts in conflict with the provision of this Act are hereby repealed.

APPENDIX F

WAR LABOR DISPUTES ACT

Act of June 25, 1943, 57 Stat. 163

An Act

Relating to the use and operation by the United States of certain plants, mines, and facilities in the prosecution of the war, and preventing strikes, lockouts, and stoppages of production, and for other purposes.

Be it enacted by the Senate and House of Representatives of the United States of America in Congress assembled, That this Act may be cited as the "War Labor Disputes Act."

DEFINITIONS. SEC. 2. As used in this Act—

(a) The term "person" means an individual, partnership, association, corporation, business trust, or any organized group of persons.

(b) The term "war contract" means—

(1) a contract with the United States entered into on behalf of the United States by an officer or employee of the Department of War, the Department of the Navy, or the United States Maritime Commission;

(2) a contract with the United States entered into by the United States pursuant to an Act entitled "An Act to promote the defense of the United States";

(3) a contract, whether or not with the United States, for the production, manufacture, construction, reconstruction, installation, maintenance, storage, repair, mining, or transportation of—

(A) any weapon, munition, aircraft, vessel, or boat;

(B) any building, structure, or facility;

(C) any machinery, tool, material, supply, article, or commodity; or

(D) any component material or part of or equipment for any article described in subparagraph (A), (B), or (C);

the production, manufacture, construction, reconstruction, installation, maintenance, storage, repair, mining, or transportation of which by the contractor in question is found by the President as being contracted for in the prosecution of the war.

(c) The term "war contractor" means the person producing, manufacturing, constructing, reconstructing, installing, maintaining, storing, repairing, mining, or transporting under a war contract or a person whose plant, mine, or facility is equipped for the manufacture, production, or mining of any articles or materials which may be required in the prosecution of the war or which may be useful in connection therewith; but such term shall not include a carrier, as defined in title I of the Railway Labor Act, or a carrier by air subject to title II of such Act.

(d) The terms "employer," "employee," "representative," "labor organization," and "labor dispute" shall have the same meaning as in section 2 of the National Labor Relations Act.

POWER OF PRESIDENT TO TAKE POSSESSION OF PLANTS. SEC. 3. Section 9 of the Selective Training and Service Act of 1940 is hereby amended by adding at the end thereof the following new paragraph:

"The power of the President under the foregoing provisions of this section to take immediate possession of any plant upon a failure to comply with any such provisions, and the authority granted by this section for the use and operation by the United States or in its interests of any plant of which possession is so taken, shall also apply as hereinafter provided to any plant, mine, or facility equipped for the manufacture, production, or mining of any articles or materials which may be required for the war effort or which may be useful in connection therewith. Such power and authority may be exercised by the President through such department or agency of the Government as he may designate, and may be exercised with respect to any such plant, mine, or facility whenever the President finds, after investigation, and proclaims that there is an interruption of the operation of such plant, mine, or facility as a result of a strike or other labor disturbance, that the war effort will be unduly impeded or delayed by such interruption, and that the exercise of such power and authority is necessary to insure the operation of such plant, mine, or facility in the interest of the war effort: *Provided*, That whenever any such plant, mine, or facility has been or is hereafter so taken by reason of a strike, lockout, threatened strike, threatened lockout, work stoppage, or other cause, such plant, mine, or facility shall be returned to the owners thereof as soon as practicable, but in no event more than sixty days after the restoration of the productive efficiency thereof prevailing prior to the taking of possession thereof: *Provided further*, That possession of any plant, mine, or facility shall not be taken under authority of this section after the termination of hostilities in the present war, as proclaimed by the President, or after the termination of the War Labor Disputes Act; and the authority to operate any such plant, mine, or facility under the provisions of this section shall terminate at the end of six months after the termination of such hostilities as so proclaimed."

TERMS OF EMPLOYMENT AT GOVERNMENT-OPERATED PLANTS. SEC. 4. Except as provided in section 5 hereof, in any case in which possession of any plant, mine, or facility has been or shall be hereafter taken under the authority granted by section 9 of the Selective Training and Service Act of 1940 as amended, such plant, mine, or facility, while so possessed, shall be operated under the terms and conditions of employment which were in effect at the time possession of such plant, mine, or facility was so taken.

APPLICATION TO WAR LABOR BOARD FOR CHANGE IN TERMS OF EMPLOYMENT AT GOVERNMENT-OPERATED PLANTS. SEC. 5. When possession of any plant, mine, or facility has been or shall be hereafter taken under authority of section 9 of the Selective Training and Service Act of 1940, as amended, the Government agency operating such plant, mine, or facility, or a majority of the employees of such plant, mine, or facility or their representatives, may apply to the National War Labor Board for a change in wages or other terms or conditions of employment in such plant, mine, or facility. Upon receipt of any such application, and after such hearings and investigations as it deems necessary, such Board may order any changes in such wages, or other terms and conditions, which it deems to be fair and reasonable and not in conflict with any Act of Congress or any Executive order issued thereunder. Any such order of the Board shall, upon approval by the President, be complied with by the Government agency operating such plant, mine, or facility.

INTERFERENCE WITH GOVERNMENT OPERATION OF PLANTS. SEC. 6. (a) Whenever any plant, mine, or facility is in the possession of the United States, it shall be unlawful for any person (1) to coerce, instigate, induce, conspire with, or encourage any person, to interfere, by lockout, strike, slow-down, or other interruption, with the operation of such plant, mine, or facility, or (2) to aid any such lockout, strike, slow-down, or other interruption interfering with the operation of such plant, mine, or facility by giving direction or guidance in the conduct of such interruption, or by providing funds for the conduct or direction thereof or for the payment of strike, unemployment, or other benefits to those participating therein. No individual shall be deemed to have violated the provisions of this section by reason only of his having ceased work or having refused to continue to work or to accept employment.

(b) Any person who willfully violates any provision of this section shall be subject to a fine of not more than $5,000, or to imprisonment for not more than one year, or both.

FUNCTIONS AND DUTIES OF THE NATIONAL WAR LABOR BOARD. SEC. 7. (a) The National War Labor Board (hereinafter in this section called the "Board"), established by Executive Order Numbered 9017, dated January 12, 1942, in addition to all powers conferred on it by section 1 (a) of the Emergency Price Control Act of 1942, and by any Executive order or regulation issued under the provisions of the Act of October 2, 1942, entitled "An Act to amend the Emergency Price Control Act of 1942, to aid in preventing inflation, and for other purposes," and by any other statute, shall have the following powers and duties:

(1) Whenever the United States Conciliation Service (hereinafter called the "Conciliation Service") certifies that a labor dispute exists which may lead to substantial interference with the war effort, and cannot be settled by collective bargaining or conciliation, to summon both parties to such dispute before it and conduct a public hearing on the merits of the dispute. If in the opinion of the Board a labor dispute has become so serious that it may lead to substantial interference with the war effort, the Board may take such action on its own motion. At such hearing both parties shall be given full notice and opportunity to be heard, but the failure of either party to appear shall not deprive the Board of jurisdiction to proceed to a hearing and order.

(2) To decide the dispute, and provide by order the wages and hours and all other terms and conditions (customarily included in collective-bargaining agreements) governing the relations between the parties, which shall be in effect until further order of the Board. In making any such decision the Board shall conform to the provisions of the Fair Labor Standards Act of 1938, as amended; the National Labor Relations Act; the Emergency Price Control Act of 1942, as amended; and the Act of October 2, 1942, as amended, and all other applicable provisions of law; and where no other law is applicable the order of the Board shall provide for terms and conditions to govern relations between the parties which shall be fair and equitable to employer and employee under all the circumstances of the case.

(3) To require the attendance of witnesses and the production of such papers, documents, and records as may be material to its investigation of facts in any labor dispute, and to issue subpenas requiring such attendance or production.

(4) To apply to any Federal district court for an order requiring any person within its jurisdiction to obey a subpena issued by the Board; and jurisdiction is hereby conferred on any such court to issue such an order.

(b) The Board, by its Chairman, shall have power to issue subpenas requiring the attendance and testimony of witnesses, and the production of any books, papers, records, or other documents, material to any inquiry or hearing before the Board or any designated member or agent thereof. Such subpenas shall be enforceable in the same manner, and subject to the same penalties, as subpenas issued by the President under title III of the Second War Powers Act, approved March 27, 1942.

(c) No member of the Board shall be permitted to participate in any decision in which such member has a direct interest as an officer, employee, or representative of either party to the dispute.

(d) Subsections (a) (1) and (2) shall not apply with respect to any plant, mine, or facility of which possession has been taken by the United States.

(e) The Board shall not have any powers under this section with respect to any matter within the purview of the Railway Labor Act, as amended.

NOTICE OF THREATENED INTERRUPTIONS IN WAR PRODUCTION, ETC. SEC. 8. (a) In order that the President may be apprised of labor disputes which threaten seriously to interrupt war production, and in order that employees may have an opportunity to express themselves, free from restraint or coercion, as to whether they will permit such interruptions in wartime—

(1) The representative of the employees of a war contractor, shall give to the Secretary of Labor, the National War Labor Board, and the National Labor Relations Board, notice of any such labor dispute involving such contractor and employees, together with a statement of the issues giving rise thereto.

(2) For not less than thirty days after any notice under paragraph (1) is given, the contractor and his employees shall continue production under all the conditions which prevailed when such dispute arose, except as they may be modified by mutual agreement or by decision of the National War Labor Board.

(3) On the thirtieth day after notice under paragraph (1) is given by the representative of the employees, unless such dispute has been settled, the National Labor Relations Board shall forthwith take a secret ballot of the employees in the plant, plants, mine, mines, facility, facilities, bargaining unit, or bargaining units, as the case may be, with respect to which the dispute is applicable on the question whether they will permit any such interruption of war production. The National Labor Relations Board shall include on the ballot a concise statement of the major issues involved in the dispute and of the efforts being made and the facilities being utilized for the settlement of such dispute. The National Labor Relations Board shall by order forthwith certify the results of such balloting, and such results shall be open to public inspection. The National Labor Board may provide for preparing such ballot and distributing it to the employees at any time after such notice has been given.

(b) Subsection (a) shall not apply with respect to any plant, mine, or facility of which possession has been taken by the United States.

(c) Any person who is under a duty to perform any act required under subsection (a) and who willfully fails or refuses to perform such act shall be liable for damages resulting from such failure or refusal to any person injured thereby and to the United States if so injured. The district courts of the United States shall have jurisdiction to hear and determine any proceedings instituted pursuant to this subsection in the same manner and to the same extent as in the case of proceedings instituted under section 24 (14) of the Judicial Code.

POLITICAL CONTRIBUTIONS BY LABOR ORGANIZATIONS. SEC. 9. Section 313 of the

Federal Corrupt Practices Act, 1925 (U.S.C., 1940 edition, title 2, sec. 251), is amended to read as follows:

"SEC. 313. It is unlawful for any national bank, or any corporation organized by authority of any law of Congress, to make a contribution in connection with any election to any political officer, or for any corporation whatever, or any labor organization to make a contribution in connection with any election at which Presidential and Vice Presidential electors or a Senator or Representative in, or a Delegate or Resident Commissioner to Congress are to be voted for, or for any candidate, political committee, or other person to accept or receive any contribution prohibited by this section. Every corporation or labor organization which makes any contribution in violation of this section shall be fined not more than $5,000; and every officer or director of any corporation, or officer of any labor organization, who consents to any contribution by the corporation or labor organization, as the case may be, in violation of this section shall be fined not more than $1,000 or imprisoned for not more than one year, or both. For the purposes of this section 'labor organization' shall have the same meaning as under the National Labor Relations Act."

TERMINATION OF ACT. SEC. 10. Except as to offenses committed prior to such date, the provisions of this Act and the amendments made by this Act shall cease to be effective at the end of six months following the termination of hostilities in the present war, as proclaimed by the President, or upon the date (prior to the date of such proclamation) of the passage of a concurrent resolution of the two Houses of Congress stating that such provisions and amendments shall cease to be effective.

SEPARABILITY. SEC. 11. If any provision of this Act or of any amendment made by this Act, or the application of such provision to any person or circumstance, is held invalid, the remainder of the Act and of such amendments, and the application of such provision to other persons or circumstances, shall not be affected thereby.

APPENDIX G

THE WAGNER ACT

Act of July 5, 1935, 49 Stat. 449

An Act

To diminish the causes of labor disputes burdening or obstructing interstate and foreign commerce, to create a National Labor Relations Board, and for other purposes.

Be it enacted by the Senate and House of Representatives of the United States of America in Congress assembled.

FINDINGS AND POLICY. SEC. 1. The denial by employers of the right of employees to organize and the refusal by employers to accept the procedure of collective bargaining lead to strikes and other forms of industrial strife or unrest, which have the intent or the necessary effect of burdening or obstructing commerce by (a) impairing the efficiency, safety, or operation of the instrumentalities of commerce; (b) occurring in the current of commerce; (c) materially affecting, restraining, or controlling the flow of raw materials or manufactured or processed goods from or into the channels of commerce, or the prices of such materials or goods in commerce; or (d) causing diminution of employment and wages in such volume as substantially to impair or disrupt the market for goods flowing from or into the channels of commerce.

The inequality of bargaining power between employees who do not possess full freedom of association or actual liberty of contract, and employers who are organized in the corporate or other forms of ownership association substantially burdens and affects the flow of commerce, and tends to aggravate recurrent business depressions, by depressing wage rates and the purchasing power of wage earners in industry and by preventing the stabilization of competitive wage rates and working conditions within and between industries.

Experience has proved that protection by law of the right of employees to organize and bargain collectively safeguards commerce from injury, impairment, or interruption, and promotes the flow of commerce by removing certain recognized sources of industrial strife and unrest, by encouraging practices fundamental to the friendly adjustment of industrial disputes arising out of differences as to wages, hours, or other working conditions, and by restoring equality of bargaining power between employers and employees.

It is hereby declared to be the policy of the United States to eliminate the causes of certain substantial obstructions to the free flow of commerce and to mitigate and eliminate these obstructions when they have occurred by encouraging the practice and procedure of collective bargaining and by protecting the exercise by workers of full freedom of association, self-organization, and designation of representatives of their own choosing, for the purpose of negotiating the terms and conditions of their employment or other mutual aid or protection.

DEFINITIONS. SEC. 2. When used in this Act—

(1) The term "person" includes one or more individuals, partnerships, associations, corporations, legal representatives, trustees, trustees in bankruptcy, or receivers.

(2) The term "employer" includes any person acting in the interest of an employer, directly or indirectly, but shall not include the United States, or any State or political subdivision thereof, or any person subject to the Railway Labor Act, as amended from time to time, or any labor organization (other than when acting as an employer), or anyone acting in the capacity of officer or agent of such labor organization.

(3) The term "employee" shall include any employee, and shall not be limited to the employees of a particular employer, unless the Act explicitly states otherwise, and shall include any individual whose work has ceased as a consequence of, or in connection with any current labor dispute or because of any unfair labor practice, and who has not obtained any other regular and substantially equivalent employment, but shall not include any individual employed as an agricultural laborer, or in the domestic service of any family or person at his home or any individual employed by his parent or spouse.

(4) The term "representatives" includes any individual or labor organization.

(5) The term "labor organization" means any organization of any kind, or any agency or employee representation committee or plan, in which employees participate and which exists for the purpose, in whole or in part, of dealing with employers concerning grievances, labor disputes, wages, rates of pay, hours of employment, or conditions of work.

(6) The term "commerce" means trade, traffic, commerce, transportation, or communication among the several States, or between the District of Columbia or any Territory of the United States and any State or other Territory, or between any foreign country and any State, Territory, or the District of Columbia, or within the District of Columbia or any Territory, or between points in the same State but through any other State or any Territory or the District of Columbia or any foreign country.

(7) The term "affecting commerce" means in commerce, or burdening or obstructing commerce or the free flow of commerce, or having led or tending to lead to a labor dispute burdening or obstructing commerce or the free flow of commerce.

(8) The term "unfair labor practice" means unfair labor practice listed in section 8.

(9) The term "labor dispute" includes any controversy concerning terms, tenure, or conditions of employment, or concerning the association or representation of persons in negotiating, fixing, maintaining, changing, or seeking to arrange terms or conditions of employment, regardless of whether the disputants stand in the proximate relation of employer and employee.

(10) The term "National Labor Relations Board" means the National Labor Relations Board, created by section 3 of this Act.

(11) The term "old Board" means the National Labor Relations Board established by Executive Order Numbered 6763 of the President on June 29, 1934, pursuant to Public Resolution Numbered 44, approved June 19, 1934 (48 Stat. 1183), and reestablished and continued by Executive Order Numbered 7074 of the President of June 15, 1935, pursuant to Title I of the National Industrial Recovery Act (48

Stat. 195) as amended and continued by Senate Joint Resolution 133 approved June 14, 1935.

NATIONAL LABOR RELATIONS BOARD

SEC. 3. (a) There is hereby created a board, to be known as the "National Labor Relations Board" (hereinafter referred to as the "Board"), which shall be composed of three members, who shall be appointed by the President, by and with the advice and consent of the Senate. One of the original members shall be appointed for a term of one year, one for a term of three years, and one for a term of five years, but their successors shall be appointed for terms of five years each, except that any individual chosen to fill a vacancy shall be appointed only for the unexpired term of the member whom he shall succeed. The President shall designate one member to serve as the chairman of the Board. Any member of the Board may be removed by the President, upon notice and hearing, for neglect of duty or malfeasance in office, but for no other cause.

(b) A vacancy in the Board shall not impair the right of the remaining members to exercise all the powers of the Board, and two members of the Board shall, at all times, constitute a quorum. The Board shall have an official seal which shall be judicially noticed.

(c) The Board shall at the close of each fiscal year make a report in writing to Congress and to the President stating in detail the cases it has heard, the decisions it has rendered, the names, salaries, and duties of all employees and officers in the employ or under the supervision of the Board, and an account of all moneys it has disbursed.

SEC. 4. (a) Each member of the Board shall receive a salary of $10,000 a year, shall be eligible for reappointment, and shall not engage in any other business, vocation, or employment. The Board shall appoint, without regard for the provisions of the civil-service laws but subject to the Classification Act of 1923, as amended, an executive secretary, and such attorneys, examiners, and regional directors, and shall appoint such other employees with regard to existing laws applicable to the employment and compensation of officers and employees of the United States, as it may from time to time find necessary for the proper performance of its duties and as may be from time to time appropriated for by Congress. The Board may establish or utilize such regional, local, or other agencies, and utilize such voluntary and uncompensated services, as may from time to time be needed. Attorneys appointed under this section may, at the direction of the Board, appear for and represent the Board in any case in court. Nothing in this Act shall be construed to authorize the Board to appoint individuals for the purpose of conciliation or mediation (or for statistical work), where such service may be obtained from the Department of Labor.

(b) Upon the appointment of the three original members of the Board and the designation of its chairman, the old Board shall cease to exist. All employees of the old Board shall be transferred to and become employees of the Board with salaries under the Classification Act of 1923, as amended, without acquiring by such transfer a permanent or civil-service status. All records, papers, and property of the old Board shall become records, papers, and property of the Board, and all unexpended funds and appropriations for the use and maintenance of the old Board shall become funds and appropriations available to be expended by the Board in the exercise of the powers, authority, and duties conferred on it by this Act.

(c) All of the expenses of the Board, including all necessary traveling and subsistence expenses outside the District of Columbia incurred by the members or employees of the Board under its orders, shall be allowed and paid on the presentation of itemized vouchers therefor approved by the Board or by any individual it designates for that purpose.

Sec. 5. The principal office of the Board shall be in the District of Columbia, but it may meet and exercise any or all of its powers at any other place. The Board may, by one or more of its members or by such agents or agencies as it may designate, prosecute any inquiry necessary to its functions in any part of the United States. A member who participates in such an inquiry shall not be disqualified from subsequently participating in a decision of the Board in the same case.

Sec. 6. (a) The Board shall have authority from time to time to make, amend, and rescind such rules and regulations as may be necessary to carry out the provisions of this Act. Such rules and regulations shall be effective upon publication in the manner which the Board shall prescribe.

RIGHTS OF EMPLOYEES

Sec. 7. Employees shall have the right to self-organization, to form, join, or assist labor organizations, to bargain collectively through representatives of their own choosing, and to engage in concerted activities, for the purpose of collective bargaining or other mutual aid or protection.

Sec. 8. It shall be an unfair labor practice for an employer—

(1) To interfere with, restrain, or coerce employees in the exercise of the rights guaranteed in section 7.

(2) To dominate or interfere with the formation or administration of any labor organization or contribute financial or other support to it: *Provided,* That subject to rules and regulations made and published by the Board pursuant to section 6 (a), an employer shall not be prohibited from permitting employees to confer with him during working hours without loss of time or pay.

(3) By discrimination in regard to hire or tenure of employment or any term or condition of employment to encourage or discourage membership in any labor organization: *Provided,* That nothing in this Act, or in the National Industrial Recovery Act (U.S.C. , Supp. VII, title 15, secs. 701–712), as amended from time to time, or in any code or agreement approved or prescribed thereunder, or in any other statute of the United States, shall preclude an employer from making an agreement with a labor organization (not established, maintained, or assisted by any action defined in this Act as an unfair labor practice) to require, as a condition of employment, membership therein, if such labor organization is the representative of the employees as provided in section 9 (a), in the appropriate collective bargaining unit covered by such agreement when made.

(4) To discharge or otherwise discriminate against an employee because he has filed charges or given testimony under this Act.

(5) To refuse to bargain collectively with the representatives of his employees, subject to the provisions of section 9 (a).

REPRESENTATIVES AND ELECTIONS. SEC. 9. (a) Representatives designated or selected for the purposes of collective bargaining by the majority of the employees in a unit appropriate for such purposes, shall be the exclusive representatives of all the employees in such unit for the purposes of collective bargaining in respect to rates of pay, wages, hours of employment, or other conditions of employment: *Provided*, That any individual employee or a group of employees shall have the right at any time to present grievances to their employer.

(b) The Board shall decide in each case whether, in order to insure to employees the full benefit of their right to self-organization and to collective bargaining, and otherwise to effectuate the policies of this Act, the unit appropriate for the purposes of collective bargaining shall be the employer unit, craft unit, plant unit, or subdivision thereof.

(c) Whenever a question affecting commerce arises concerning the representation of employees, the Board may investigate such controversy and certify to the parties, in writing, the name or names of the representatives that have been designated or selected. In any such investigation, the Board shall provide for an appropriate hearing upon due notice, either in conjunction with a proceeding under section 10 or otherwise, and may take a secret ballot of employees, or utilize any other suitable method to ascertain such representatives.

(d) Whenever an order of the Board made pursuant to section 10 (c) is based in whole or in part upon facts certified following an investigation pursuant to subsection (c) of this section, and there is a petition for the enforcement or review of such order, such certification and the record of such investigation shall be included in the transcript of the entire record required to be filed under subsections 10 (e) or 10 (f), and thereupon the decree of the court enforcing, modifying, or setting aside in whole or in part the order of the Board shall be made and entered upon the pleadings, testimony, and proceedings set forth in such transcript.

PREVENTION OF UNFAIR LABOR PRACTICES. SEC. 10. (a) The Board is empowered, as hereinafter provided, to prevent any person from engaging in any unfair labor practice (listed in section 8) affecting commerce. This power shall be exclusive, and shall not be affected by any other means of adjustment or prevention that has been or may be established by agreement, code, law, or otherwise.

(b) Whenever it is charged that any person has engaged in or is engaging in any such unfair labor practice, the Board, or any agent or agency designated by the Board for such purposes, shall have power to issue and cause to be served upon such person a complaint stating the charges in that respect, and containing a notice of hearing before the Board or a member thereof, or before a designated agent or agency, at a place therein fixed, not less than five days after the serving of said complaint. Any such complaint may be amended by the member, agent, or agency conducting the hearing or the Board in its discretion at any time prior to the issuance of an order based thereon. The person so complained of shall have the right to file an answer to the original or amended complaint and to appear in person or otherwise and give testimony at the place and time fixed in the complaint. In the discretion of the member, agent, or agency conducting the hearing or the Board, any other person may be allowed to intervene in the said proceeding and to present testimony. In any such proceeding the rules of evidence prevailing in courts of law or equity shall not be controlling.

(c) The testimony taken by such member, agent, or agency or the Board shall be reduced to writing and filed with the Board. Thereafter, in its discretion, the Board upon notice may take further testimony or hear argument. If upon all the testimony taken the Board shall be of the opinion that any person named in the complaint has engaged in or is engaging in any such unfair labor practice, then the Board shall state its findings of fact and shall issue and cause to be served on such person an order requiring such person to cease and desist from such unfair labor practice, and to take such affirmative action, including reinstatement of employees with or without back pay, as will effectuate the policies of this Act. Such order may further require such person to make reports from time to time showing the extent to which it has complied with the order. If upon all the testimony taken the Board shall be of the opinion that no person named in the complaint has engaged in or is engaging in any such unfair labor practice, then the Board shall state its findings of fact and shall issue an order dismissing the said complaint.

(d) Until a transcript of the record in a case shall have been filed in a court, as hereinafter provided, the Board may at any time, upon reasonable notice and in such manner as it shall deem proper, modify or set aside, in whole or in part, any finding or order made or issued by it.

(e) The Board shall have power to petition any circuit court of appeals of the United States (including the Court of Appeals of the District of Columbia), or if all the circuit courts of appeals to which application may be made are in vacation, any district court of the United States (including the Supreme Court of the District of Columbia), within any circuit or district, respectively, wherein the unfair labor practice in question occurred or wherein such person resides or transacts business, for the enforcement of such order and for appropriate temporary relief or restraining order, and shall certify and file in the court a transcript of the entire record in the proceeding, including the pleadings and testimony upon which such order was entered and the findings and order of the Board. Upon such filing, the court shall cause notice thereof to be served upon such person, and thereupon shall have jurisdiction of the proceeding and of the question determined therein, and shall have power to grant such temporary relief or restraining order as it deems just and proper, and to make and enter upon the pleadings, testimony, and proceedings set forth in such transcript a decree enforcing, modifying, and enforcing as so modified, or setting aside in whole or in part the order of the Board. No objection that has not been urged before the Board, its member, agent, or agency, shall be considered by the court, unless the failure or neglect to urge such objection shall be excused because of extraordinary circumstances. The findings of the Board as to the facts, if supported by evidence, shall be conclusive. If either party shall apply to the court for leave to adduce additional evidence and shall show to the satisfaction of the court that such additional evidence is material and that there were reasonable grounds for the failure to adduce such evidence in the hearing before the Board, its member, agent, or agency, the court may order such additional evidence to be taken before the Board, its member, agent, or agency, and to be made a part of the transcript. The Board may modify its findings as to the facts, or make new findings, by reason of additional evidence so taken and filed, and it shall file such modified or new findings, which, if supported by evidence shall be conclusive, and shall file its recommendations, if any, for the modification or setting aside of its original order. The jurisdiction of the court shall be exclusive and its judgment and decree shall be final, except that the same shall be subject to review by the appropriate circuit court of appeals if application was made to the district court as hereinabove provided, and by the Supreme Court of the United States and upon writ of certiorari or certification as provided in sections 239 and 240 of the Judicial Code, as amended (U.S.C., title 28, secs. 346 and 347).

(f) Any person aggrieved by a final order of the Board granting or denying in whole or in part the relief sought may obtain a review of such order in any circuit court of appeals of the United States in the circuit wherein the unfair labor practice in question was alleged to have been engaged in or wherein such person resides or transacts business, or in the Court of Appeals of the District of Columbia, by filing in such a court a written petition praying that the order of the Board be modified or set aside. A copy of such petition shall be forthwith served upon the Board, and thereupon the aggrieved party shall file in the court a transcript of the entire record in the proceeding, certified by the Board, including the pleading and testimony upon which the order complained of was entered and the findings and order of the Board. Upon such filing, the court shall proceed in the same manner as in the case of an application by the Board under subsection (e), and shall have the same exclusive jurisdiction to grant to the Board such temporary relief or restraining order as it deems just and proper, and in like manner to make and enter a decree enforcing, modifying, and enforcing as so modified, or setting aside in whole or in part the order of the Board; and the findings of the Board as to the facts, if supported by evidence, shall in like manner be conclusive.

(g) The commencement of proceedings under subsection (e) or (f) of this section shall not, unless specifically ordered by the court, operate as a stay of the Board's order.

(h) When granting appropriate temporary relief or a restraining order, or making and entering a decree enforcing, modifying, and enforcing as so modified or setting aside in whole or in part an order of the Board, as provided in this section, the jurisdiction of courts sitting in equity, shall not be limited by the Act entitled "An Act to amend the Judicial Code and to define and limit the jurisdiction of courts sitting in equity, and for other purposes," approved March 23, 1932 (U.S.C., Supp. VII, title 29, secs. 101–115).

(i) Petitions filed under this Act shall be heard expeditiously, and if possible within ten days after they have been docketed.

INVESTIGATORY POWERS

SEC. 11. For the purpose of all hearings and investigations, which, in the opinion of the Board, are necessary and proper for the exercise of the powers vested in it by section 9 and section 10—

(1) The Board, or its duly authorized agents or agencies, shall at all reasonable times have access to, for the purpose of examination, and the right to copy any evidence of any person being investigated or proceeded against that relates to any matter under investigation or in question. Any member of the Board shall have power to issue subpenas requiring the attendance and testimony of witnesses and the production of any evidence that relates to any matter under investigation or in question, before the Board, its member, agent, or agency conducting the hearing or investigation. Any member of the Board, or any agent or agency designated by the Board for such purposes, may administer oaths and affirmations, examine wit-

nesses, and receive evidence. Such attendance of witnesses and the production of such evidence may be required from any place in the United States or any Territory or possession thereof, at any designated place of hearing.

(2) In case of contumacy or refusal to obey a subpena issued to any person, any District Court of the United States or the United States courts of any Territory or possession, or the Supreme Court of the District of Columbia, within the jurisdiction of which the inquiry is carried on or within the jurisdiction of which said person guilty of contumacy or refusal to obey is found or resides or transacts business, upon application by the Board shall have jurisdiction to issue to such person an order requiring such person to appear before the Board, its member, agent, or agency, there to produce evidence if so ordered, or there to give testimony touching the matter under investigation or in question; and any failure to obey such order of the court may be punished by said court as a contempt thereof.

(3) No person shall be excused from attending and testifying or from producing books, records, correspondence, documents, or other evidence in obedience to the subpena of the Board, on the ground that the testimony or evidence required of him may tend to incriminate him or subject him to a penalty or forfeiture; but no individual shall be prosecuted or subjected to any penalty or forfeiture for or on account of any transaction, matter, or thing concerning which he is compelled, after having claimed his privilege against self-incrimination, to testify or produce evidence, except that such individual so testifying shall not be exempt from prosecution and punishment for perjury committed in so testifying.

(4) Complaints, orders, and other process and papers of the Board, its member, agent, or agency, may be served either personally or by registered mail or by telegraph or by leaving a copy thereof at the principal office or place of business of the person required to be served. The verified return by the individual so serving the same setting forth the manner of such service shall be proof of the same, and the return post office receipt or telegraph receipt therefor when registered and mailed or telegraphed as aforesaid shall be proof of service of the same. Witnesses summoned before the Board, its member, agent, or agency, shall be paid the same fees and mileage that are paid witnesses in the courts of the United States, and witnesses whose depositions are taken and the persons taking the same shall severally be entitled to the same fees as are paid for like services in the courts of the United States.

(5) All process of any court to which application may be made under this Act may be served in the judicial district wherein the defendant or other person required to be served resides or may be found.

(6) The several departments and agencies of the Government, when directed by the President, shall furnish the Board, upon its request, all records, papers, and information in their possession relating to any matter before the Board.

Sec. 12. Any person who shall willfully resist, prevent, impede, or interfere with any member of the Board or any of its agents or agencies in the performance of duties pursuant to this Act shall be punished by a fine of not more than $5,000 or by imprisonment for not more than one year, or both.

LIMITATIONS

Sec. 13. Nothing in this Act shall be construed so as to interfere with or impede or diminish in any way the right to strike.

SEC. 14. Wherever the application of the provisions of section 7 (a) of the National Industrial Recovery Act [U.S.C. , Supp. VII, title 15, sec. 707 (a)], as amended from time to time, or of section 77 B, paragraphs (1) and (m) of the Act approved June 7, 1934, entitled "An Act to amend an Act entitled 'An Act to establish a uniform system of bankruptcy throughout the United States' approved July 1, 1898, and Acts amendatory thereof and supplementary thereto" 48 Stat. 922, pars. (1) and (m), as amended from time to time, or of Public Resolution Numbered 44, approved June 19, 1934 (48 Stat. 1183), conflicts with the application of the provisions of this Act, this Act shall prevail: *Provided*, That in any situation where the provisions of this Act cannot be validly enforced, the provisions of such other Acts shall remain in full force and effect.

SEC. 15. If any provision of this Act, or the application of such provision to any person or circumstance, shall be held invalid, the remainder of this Act, or the application of such provision to persons or circumstances other than those as to which it is held invalid, shall not be affected thereby.

SEC. 16. This Act may be cited as the "National Labor Relations Act."

Approved, July 5, 1935.

LABOR MANAGEMENT RELATIONS ACT, 1947

Act of June 23, 1947, 61 Stat. 136, as Amended by Act of September 14, 1959, 73 Stat. 519.

KEY TO AMENDMENTS

Portions of the Act which have been eliminated by the Labor-Management Reporting and Disclosure Act of 1959, Public Law 86–257, are enclosed by black brackets; provisions which have been added to the Act are in italics; and unchanged portions are shown in roman type.

[Public Law 101—80th Congress]

An Act

To amend the National Labor Relations Act, to provide additional facilities for the mediation of labor disputes affecting commerce, to equalize legal responsibilities of labor organizations and employers, and for other purposes.

Be it enacted by the Senate and House of Representatives of the United States of America in Congress assembled,

SHORT TITLE AND DECLARATION OF POLICY

SEC. 1. (a) This Act may be cited as the "Labor Management Relations Act, 1947."

(b) Industrial strife which interferes with the normal flow of commerce and with the full production of articles and commodities for commerce, can be avoided or substantially minimized if employers, employees, and labor organizations each recognize under law one another's legitimate rights in their relations with each other, and above all recognize under law that neither party has any right in its

Section 201 (d) and (e) of the Labor-Management Reporting and Disclosure Act of 1959 which repealed Section 9 (f), (g), and (h) of the Labor Management Relations Act, 1947, and Section 505 amending Section 302 (a), (b), and (c) of the Labor Management Relations Act, 1947, took effect upon enactment of Public Law 86–257, September 14, 1959. As to the other amendments of the Labor Management Relations Act, 1947, Section 707 of the Labor-Management Reporting and Disclosure Act provides:

The amendments made by this title shall take effect sixty days after the date of the enactment of this Act and no provision of this title shall be deemed to make an unfair labor practice, any act which is performed prior to such effective date which did not constitute an unfair labor practice prior thereto.

relations with any other to engage in acts or practices which jeopardize the public health, safety, or interest.

It is the purpose and policy of this Act, in order to promote the full flow of commerce, to prescribe the legitimate rights of both employees and employers in their relations affecting commerce, to provide orderly and peaceful procedures for preventing the interference by either with the legitimate rights of the other, to protect the rights of individual employees in their relations with labor organizations whose activities affect commerce, to define and proscribe practices on the part of labor and management which affect commerce and are inimical to the general welfare, and to protect the rights of the public in connection with labor disputes affecting commerce.

TITLE I
AMENDMENT OF NATIONAL LABOR RELATIONS ACT

SEC. 101. The National Labor Relations Act is hereby amended to read as follows:

FINDINGS AND POLICIES

SEC. 1. The denial by some employers of the right of employees to organize and the refusal by some employers to accept the procedure of collective bargaining lead to strikes and other forms of industrial strife or unrest, which have the intent or the necessary effect of burdening or obstructing commerce by (a) impairing the efficiency, safety, or operation of the instrumentalities of commerce; (b) occurring in the current of commerce; (c) materially affecting, restraining, or controlling the flow of raw materials or manufactured or processed goods in commerce; or (d) causing diminution of employment and wages in such volume as substantially to impair or disrupt the market for goods flowing from or into the channels of commerce.

The inequality of bargaining power between employees who do not possess full freedom of association or actual liberty of contract, and employers who are organized in the corporate or other forms of ownership association substantially burdens and affects the flow of commerce, and tends to aggravate recurrent business depressions, by depressing wage rates and the purchasing power of wage earners in industry and by preventing the stabilization of competitive wage rates and working conditions within and between industries.

Experience has proved that protection by law of the right of employees to organize and bargain collectively safeguards commerce from injury, impairment, or interruption, and promotes the flow of commerce by removing certain recognized sources of industrial strife and unrest, by encouraging practices fundamental to the friendly adjustment of industrial disputes arising out of differences as to wages, hours, or other working conditions, and by restoring equality of bargaining power between employers and employees.

Experience has further demonstrated that certain practices by some labor organizations, their officers, and members have the intent or the necessary effect of burdening or obstructing commerce by preventing the free flow of goods in such commerce through strikes and other forms of industrial unrest or through concerted activities which impair the interest of the public in the free flow of such commerce. The elimination of such practices is a necessary condition to the assurance of the rights herein guaranteed.

It is hereby declared to be the policy of the United States to eliminate the causes of certain substantial obstructions to the free flow of commerce and to mitigate and eliminate these obstructions when they have occurred by encouraging the practice and procedure of collective bargaining and by protecting the exercise by workers of full freedom of association, self-organization, and designation of representatives of their own choosing, for the purpose of negotiating the terms and conditions of their employment or other mutual aid or protection.

DEFINITIONS. SEC. 2. When used in this Act—

(1) The term "person" includes one or more individuals, labor organizations, partnerships, associations, corporations, legal representatives, trustees, trustees in bankruptcy, or receivers.

(2) The term "employer" includes any person acting as an agent of an employer, directly or indirectly, but shall not include the United States or any wholly owned Government corporation, or any Federal Reserve Bank, or any State or political subdivision thereof, or any corporation or association operating a hospital, if no part of the net earnings inures to the benefit of any private shareholder or individual, or any person subject to the Railway Labor Act, as amended from time to time, or any labor organization (other than when acting as an employer), or anyone acting in the capacity of officer or agent of such labor organization.

(3) The term "employee" shall include any employee, and shall not be limited to the employees of a particular employer, unless the Act explicitly states otherwise, and shall include any individual whose work has ceased as a consequence of, or in connection with, any current labor dispute or because of any unfair labor practice, and who has not obtained any other regular and substantially equivalent employment, but shall not include any individual employed as an agricultural laborer, or in the domestic service of any family or person at his home, or any individual employed by his parent or spouse, or any individual having the status of an independent contractor, or any individual employed as a supervisor, or any individual employed by an employer subject to the Railway Labor Act, as amended from time to time, or by any other person who is not an employer as herein defined.

(4) The term "representatives" includes any individual or labor organization.

(5) The term "labor organization" means any organization of any kind, or any agency or employee representation committee or plan, in which employees participate and which exists for the purpose, in whole or in part, of dealing with employers concerning grievances, labor disputes, wages, rates of pay, hours of employment, or conditions of work.

(6) The term "commerce" means trade, traffic, commerce, transportation, or communication among the several States, or between the District of Columbia or any Territory of the United States and any State or other Territory, or between any foreign country and any State, Territory, or the District of Columbia, or within the District of Columbia or any Territory, or between points in the same State but through any other State or any Territory or the District of Columbia or any foreign country.

(7) The term "affecting commerce" means in commerce, or burdening or obstructing commerce or the free flow of commerce, or having led or tending to lead to a labor dispute burdening or obstructing commerce or the free flow of commerce.

(8) The term "unfair labor practice" means any unfair labor practice listed in section 8.

(9) The term "labor dispute" includes any controversy concerning terms, tenure or conditions of employment, or concerning the association or representation of persons in negotiating, fixing, maintaining, changing, or seeking to arrange terms or conditions of employment, regardless of whether the disputants stand in the proximate relation of employer and employee.

(10) The term "National Labor Relations Board" means the National Labor Relations Board provided for in section 3 of this Act.

(11) The term "supervisor" means any individual having authority, in the interest of the employer, to hire, transfer, suspend, lay off, recall, promote, discharge, assign, reward, or discipline other employees, or responsibly to direct them, or to adjust their grievances, or effectively to recommend such action, if in connection with the foregoing the exercise of such authority is not of a merely routine or clerical nature, but requires the use of independent judgment.

(12) The term "professional employee" means—

(a) any employee engaged in work (i) predominantly intellectual and varied in character as opposed to routine mental, manual, mechanical, or physical work; (ii) involving the consistent exercise of discretion and judgment in its performance; (iii) of such a character that the output produced or the result accomplished cannot be standardized in relation to a given period of time; (iv) requiring knowledge of an advanced type in a field of science or learning customarily acquired by a prolonged course of specialized intellectual instruction and study in an institution of higher learning or a hospital, as distinguished from a general academic education or from an apprenticeship or from training in the performance of routine mental, manual, or physical processes; or

(b) any employee, who (i) has completed the courses of specialized intellectual instruction and study described in clause (iv) of paragraph (a), and (ii) is performing related work under the supervision of a professional person to qualify himself to become a professional employee as defined in paragraph (a).

(13) In determining whether any person is acting as an "agent" of another person so as to make such other person responsible for his acts, the question of whether the specific acts performed were actually authorized or subsequently ratified shall not be controlling.

NATIONAL LABOR RELATIONS BOARD

Sec. 3. (a) The National Labor Relations Board (hereinafter called the "Board") created by this Act prior to its amendment by the Labor Management Relations Act, 1947, is hereby continued as an agency of the United States, except that the Board shall consist of five instead of three members, appointed by the President by and with the advice and consent of the Senate. Of the two additional members so provided for, one shall be appointed for a term of five years and the other for a term of two years. Their successors, and the successors of the other members, shall be appointed for terms of five years each, excepting that any individual chosen to fill a vacancy shall be appointed only for the unexpired term of the member whom he shall succeed. The President shall designate one member to serve as Chairman of the Board. Any member of the Board may be removed by the President, upon notice and hearing, for neglect of duty or malfeasance in office, but for no other cause.

(b) The Board is authorized to delegate to any group of three or more members any or all of the powers which it may itself exercise. *The Board is also authorized to delegate to its regional directors its powers under section 9 to determine the unit appropriate for the purpose of collective bargaining, to investigate and provide for hearings, and determine whether a question of representation exists, and to direct an election or take a secret ballot under subsection (c) or (e) of section 9 and certify the results thereof, except that upon the filing of a request therefor with the Board by any interested person, the Board may review any action of a regional director delegated to him under this paragraph, but such a review shall not, unless specifically ordered by the Board, operate as a stay of any action taken by the regional director.* A vacancy in the Board shall not impair the right of the remaining members to exercise all of the powers of the Board, and three members of the Board shall, at all times, constitute a quorum of the Board, except that two members shall constitute a quorum of any group designated pursuant to the first sentence hereof. The Board shall have an official seal which shall be judicially noticed.

(c) The Board shall at the close of each fiscal year make a report in writing to Congress and to the President stating in detail the cases it has heard, the decisions it has rendered, the names, salaries, and duties of all employees and officers in the employ or under the supervision of the Board, and an account of all moneys it has disbursed.

(d) There shall be a General Counsel of the Board who shall be appointed by the President, by and with the advice and consent of the Senate, for a term of four years. The General Counsel of the Board shall exercise general supervision over all attorneys employed by the Board (other than trial examiners and legal assistants to Board members) and over the officers and employees in the regional offices. He shall have final authority, on behalf of the Board, in respect of the investigation of charges and issuance of complaints under section 10, and in respect of the prosecution of such complaints before the Board, and shall have such other duties as the Board may prescribe or as may be provided by law. *In case of a vacancy in the office of the General Counsel the President is authorized to designate the officer or employee who shall act as General Counsel during such vacancy, but no person or persons so designated shall so act (1) for more than forty days when the Congress is in session unless a nomination to fill such vacancy shall have been submitted to the Senate, or (2) after the adjournment sine die of the session of the Senate in which such nomination was submitted.*

SEC. 4. (a) Each member of the Board and the General Counsel of the Board shall receive a salary of $12,000* a year, shall be eligible for reappointment, and shall not engage in any other business, vocation, or employment. The Board shall appoint an executive secretary, and such attorneys, examiners, and regional directors, and such other employees as it may from time to time find necessary for the proper performance of its duties. The Board may not employ any attorneys for the purpose of reviewing transcripts of hearings or preparing drafts of opinions except that any attorney employed for assignment as a legal assistant to any Board member may for such Board member review such transcripts and prepare such drafts. No trial examiner's report shall be reviewed, either before or after its publication, by any person other than a member of the Board or his legal assistant, and no trial examiner shall advise or consult with the Board with respect to exceptions taken to his findings,

* Pursuant to Public Law 854, 84th Congress, 2d Session, Title I, approved July 31, 1956, the salary of the chairman of the Board shall be $20,500 per year and the salaries of the General Counsel and each Board member shall be $20,000 per year.

rulings, or recommendations. The Board may establish or utilize such regional, local, or other agencies, and utilize such voluntary and uncompensated services, as may from time to time be needed. Attorneys appointed under this section may, at the direction of the Board, appear for and represent the Board in any case in court. Nothing in this Act shall be construed to authorize the Board to appoint individuals for the purpose of conciliation or mediation, or for economic analysis.

(b) All of the expenses of the Board, including all necessary traveling and subsistence expenses outside the District of Columbia incurred by the members or employees of the Board under its orders, shall be allowed and paid on the presentation of itemized vouchers therefor approved by the Board or by any individual it designates for that purpose.

Sec. 5. The principal office of the Board shall be in the District of Columbia, but it may meet and exercise any or all of its powers at any other place. The Board may, by one or more of its members or by such agents or agencies as it may designate, prosecute any inquiry necessary to its functions in any part of the United States. A member who participates in such an inquiry shall not be disqualified from subsequently participating in a decision of the Board in the same case.

Sec. 6. The Board shall have authority from time to time to make, amend, and rescind, in the manner prescribed by the Administrative Procedure Act, such rules and regulations as may be necessary to carry out the provisions of this Act.

Rights of Employees. Sec. 7. Employees shall have the right to self-organization, to form, join, or assist labor organizations, to bargain collectively through representatives of their own choosing, or to engage in other concerted activities for the purpose of collective bargaining or other mutual aid or protection, and shall also have the right to refrain from any or all of such activities except to the extent that such right may be affected by an agreement requiring membership in a labor organization as a condition of employment as authorized in section 8 (a) (3).

Unfair Labor Practices. Sec. 8. (a) It shall be an unfair labor practice for an employer—

(1) to interfere with, restrain, or coerce employees in the exercise of the rights guaranteed in section 7;

(2) to dominate or interfere with the formation or administration of any labor organization or contribute financial or other support to it: Provided, That subject to rules and regulations made and published by the Board pursuant to section 6, an employer shall not be prohibited from permitting employees to confer with him during working hours without loss of time or pay;

(3) by discrimination in regard to hire or tenure of employment or any term or condition of employment to encourage or discourage membership in any labor organization: Provided, That nothing in this Act, or in any other statute of the United States, shall preclude an employer from making an agreement with a labor organization (not established, maintained, or assisted by any action defined in section 8 [a] of this Act as an unfair labor practice) to require as a condition of employment membership therein on or after the thirtieth day following the beginning of such employment or the effective date of such agreement, whichever is the later, (i) if such labor organization is the representative of the employees as provided in section

9 (a), in the appropriate collective-bargaining unit covered by such agreement when made [and has at the time the agreement was made or within the preceding twelve months received from the Board a notice of compliance with section 9 (f), (g), (h)], and (ii) unless following an election held as provided in section 9 (e) within one year preceding the effective date of such agreement, the Board shall have certified that at least a majority of the employees eligible to vote in such election have voted to rescind the authority of such labor organization to make such an agreement: Provided further, That no employer shall justify any discrimination against an employee for nonmembership in a labor organization (A) if he has reasonable grounds for believing that such membership was not available to the employee on the same terms and conditions generally applicable to other members, or (B) if he has reasonable grounds for believing that membership was denied or terminated for reasons other than the failure of the employee to tender the periodic dues and the initiation fees uniformly required as a condition of acquiring or retaining membership;

(4) to discharge or otherwise discriminate against an employee because he has filed charges or given testimony under this Act;

(5) to refuse to bargain collectively with the representatives of his employees, subject to the provisions of section 9 (a).

(b) It shall be an unfair labor practice for a labor organization or its agents—

(1) to restrain or coerce (A) employees in the exercise of the rights guaranteed in section 7: Provided, That this paragraph shall not impair the right of a labor organization to prescribe its own rules with respect to the acquisition or retention of membership therein; or (B) an employer in the selection of his representatives for the purposes of collective bargaining or the adjustment of grievances;

(2) to cause or attempt to cause an employer to discriminate against an employee in violation of subsection (a) (3) or to discriminate against an employee with respect to whom membership in such organization has been denied or terminated on some ground other than his failure to tender the periodic dues and the initiation fees uniformly required as a condition of acquiring or retaining membership;

(3) to refuse to bargain collectively with an employer, provided it is the representative of his employees subject to the provisions of section 9 (a);

(4) (i) to engage in, or to induce or encourage [the employees of any employer] *any individual employed by any person engaged in commerce or in an industry affecting commerce* to engage in, a strike or a [concerted] refusal in the course of [their] *his* employment to use, manufacture, process, transport, or otherwise handle or work on any goods, articles, materials, or commodities or to perform any services [,]; *or* (ii) *to threaten, coerce, or restrain any person engaged in commerce or in an industry affecting commerce,* where in *either case* an object thereof is:

(A) forcing or requiring any employer or self-employed person to join any labor or employer organization or [any employer or other person to cease using, selling, handling, transporting, or otherwise dealing in the products of any other producer, processor, or manufacturer, or to cease doing business with any other person] *to enter into any agreement which is prohibited by section 8 (e) ;*

(B) *forcing or requiring any person to cease using, selling, handling, transporting, or otherwise dealing in the products of any other producer, processor, or manufacturer, or to doing business with any other person, or* forcing or requiring any other employer to recognize or bargain with a labor organization as the representative of his employees unless such labor organization has been certified as the representative of such employees under the provisions of section 9 [;]: *Provided, That nothing contained in this clause* (B) *shall be construed to make unlawful, where not otherwise unlawful, any primary strike or primary picketing;*

(C) forcing or requiring any employer to recognize or bargain with a particular labor organization as the representative of his employees if another labor organization has been certified as the representative of such employees under the provisions of section 9;

(D) forcing or requiring any employer to assign particular work to employees in a particular labor organization or in a particular trade, craft, or class rather than to employees in another labor organization or in another trade, craft, or class, unless such employer is failing to conform to an order or certification of the Board determining the bargaining representative for employees performing such work:

Provided, That nothing contained in this subsection (b) shall be construed to make unlawful a refusal by any person to enter upon the premises of any employer (other than his own employer), if the employees of such employer are engaged in a strike ratified or approved by a representative of such employees whom such employer is required to recognize under this Act [;]: *Provided further, That for the purposes of this paragraph (4) only, nothing contained in such paragraph shall be construed to prohibit publicity, other than picketing, for the purpose of truthfully advising the public, including consumers and members of a labor organization, that a product or products are produced by an employer with whom the labor organization has a primary dispute and are distributed by another employer, as long as such publicity does not have an effect of inducing any individual employed by any person other than the primary employer in the course of his employment to refuse to pick up, deliver, or transport any goods, or not to perform any services, at the establishment of the employer engaged in such distribution;*

(5) to require of employees covered by an agreement authorized under subsection (a) (3) the payment, as a condition precedent to becoming a member of such organization, of a fee in an amount which the Board finds excessive or discriminatory under all the circumstances. In making such a finding, the Board shall consider, among other relevant factors, the practices and customs of labor organizations in the particular industry, and the wages currently paid to the employees affected; [and]

(6) to cause or attempt to cause an employer to pay or deliver or agree to pay or deliver any money or other thing of value, in the nature of an exaction, for services which are not performed or not to be performed [.]; *and*

(7) *to picket or cause to be picketed, or threaten to picket or cause to be picketed, any employer where an object thereof is forcing or requiring an employer to recognize or bargain with a labor organization as the representative of his employees, or forcing or requiring the employees of an employer to accept or select such labor organization as their collective bargaining representative, unless such labor organization is currently certified as the representative of such employees:*

(A) where the employer has lawfully recognized in accordance with this Act any other labor organization and a question concerning representation may not appropriately be raised under section 9 (c) of this Act,

(B) where within the preceding twelve months a valid election under section 9 (c) of this Act has been conducted, or

(C) where such picketing has been conducted without a petition under section 9 (c) being filed within a reasonable period of time not to exceed thirty days from the commencement of such picketing: Provided, That when such a petition has been filed the Board shall

forthwith, without regard to the provisions of section 9 (c) (1) or the absence of a showing of a substantial interest on the part of the labor organization, direct an election in such unit as the Board finds to be appropriate and shall certify the results thereof: Provided further, That nothing in this subparagraph (C) shall be construed to prohibit any picketing or other publicity for the purpose of truthfully advising the public (including consumers) that an employer does not employ members of, or have a contract with, a labor organization, unless an effect of such picketing is to induce any individual employed by any other person in the course of his employment, not to pick up, deliver or transport any goods or not to perform any services.

Nothing in this paragraph (7) shall be construed to permit any act which would otherwise be an unfair labor practice under this section 8 (b).

(c) The expressing of any views, argument, or opinion, or the dissemination thereof, whether in written, printed, graphic, or visual form, shall not constitute or be evidence of an unfair labor practice under any of the provisions of this Act, if such expression contains no threat of reprisal or force or promise of benefit.

(d) For the purposes of this section, to bargain collectively is the performance of the mutual obligation of the employer and the representative of the employees to meet at reasonable times and confer in good faith with respect to wages, hours, and other terms and conditions of employment, or the negotiation of an agreement, or any question arising thereunder, and the execution of a written contract incorporating any agreement reached if requested by either party, but such obligation does not compel either party to agree to a proposal or require the making of a concession: Provided, That where there is in effect a collective-bargaining contract covering employees in an industry affecting commerce, the duty to bargain collectively shall also mean that no party to such contract shall terminate or modify such contract, unless the party desiring such termination or modification—

(1) serves a written notice upon the other party to the contract of the proposed termination or modification sixty days prior to the expiration date thereof, or in the event such contract contains no expiration date, sixty days prior to the time it is proposed to make such termination or modification;

(2) offers to meet and confer with the other party for the purpose of negotiating a new contract or a contract containing the proposed modifications;

(3) notifies the Federal Mediation and Conciliation Service within thirty days after such notice of the existence of a dispute, and simultaneously therewith notifies any State or Territorial agency established to mediate and conciliate disputes within the State or Territory where the dispute occurred, provided no agreement has been reached by that time; and

(4) continues in full force and effect, without resorting to strike or lockout, all the terms and conditions of the existing contract for a period of sixty days after such notice is given or until the expiration date of such contract, whichever occurs later:

The duties imposed upon employers, employees, and labor organizations by paragraphs (2), (3), and (4) shall become inapplicable upon an intervening certification of the Board, under which the labor organization or individual, which is a party to the contract, has been superseded as or ceased to be the representative of the employees subject to the provisions of section 9 (a), and the duties so imposed shall not be construed as requiring either party to discuss or agree to any modification of the terms and conditions contained in a contract for a fixed period, if such modification is to become effective before such terms and conditions can be reopened under the provisions of the contract. Any employee who engages in a strike within the sixty-day period specified in this subsection shall lose his status as an employee of the employer engaged in the particular labor dispute, for the purposes of sections 8, 9, and 10 of this Act, as amended, but such loss of status for such employee shall terminate if and when he is reemployed by such employer.

(e) It shall be an unfair labor practice for any labor organization and any employer to enter into any contract or agreement, express or implied, whereby such employer ceases or refrains or agrees to cease or refrain from handling, using, selling, transporting or otherwise dealing in any of the products of any other employer, or to cease doing business with any other person, and any contract or agreement entered into heretofore or hereafter containing such an agreement shall be to such extent unenforceable and void: Provided, That nothing in this subsection (e) shall apply to an agreement between a labor organization and an employer in the construction industry relating to the contracting or subcontracting of work to be done at the site of the construction, alteration, painting, or repair of a building, structure, or other work: Provided further, That for the purposes of this subsection (e) and section 8 (b) (4) (B) the terms "any employer," "any person engaged in commerce or an industry affecting commerce" and "any person" when used in relation to the term "any other producer, processor, or manufacturer," "any other employer," or "any other person" shall not include persons in the relation of a jobber, manufacturer, contractor, or subcontractor working on the goods or premises of the jobber or manufacturer or performing parts of an integrated process of production in the apparel and clothing industry: Provided further, That nothing in this Act shall prohibit the enforcement of any agreement which is within the foregoing exception.

(f) It shall not be an unfair labor practice under subsections (a) and (b) of this section for an employer engaged primarily in the building and construction industry to make an agreement covering employees engaged (or who upon their employment, will be engaged) in the building and construction industry with a labor organization of which building and construction employees are members (not established, maintained, or assisted by any action defined in section 8 [a] of this Act as an unfair labor practice) because (1) the majority status of such labor organization has not been established under the provisions of section 9 of this Act prior to the making of such agreement, or (2) such agreement requires as a condition of employment, membership in such labor organization after the seventh day following the beginning of such employment or the effective date of the agreement, whichever is later, or (3) such agreement requires the employer to notify such labor organization of opportunities for employment with such employer, or gives such labor organization an opportunity to refer qualified applicants for such employment, or (4) such agreement specifies minimum training or experience qualifications for employment or provides for priority in opportunities for employment based upon length of service with such employer, in the industry or in the particular geographical area: Provided, That nothing in this subsection shall set aside the final proviso to section 8 (a) (3) of this Act: Provided further, That any agreement which would be invalid, but for clause (1) of this subsection, shall not be a bar to a petition filed pursuant to section 9 (c) or 9 (e).*

* Section 8 (f) is inserted in the Act by subsection (a) of Section 705 of Public Law 86–257. Section 705 (b) provides:

> Nothing contained in the amendment made by subsection (a) shall be construed as authorizing the execution or application of agreements requiring membership in a labor organization as a condition of employment in any State or Territory in which such execution or application is prohibited by State or Territorial law.

REPRESENTATIVES AND ELECTIONS. SEC. 9. (a) Representatives designated or selected for the purposes of collective bargaining by the majority of the employees in a unit appropriate for such purposes, shall be the exclusive representatives of all the employees in such unit for the purposes of collective bargaining in respect to rates of pay, wages, hours of employment, or other conditions of employment: Provided, That any individual employee or a group of employees shall have the right at any time to present grievances to their employer and to have such grievances adjusted, without the intervention of the bargaining representative, as long as the adjustment is not inconsistent with the terms of a collective-bargaining contract or agreement then in effect: Provided further, That the bargaining representative has been given opportunity to be present at such adjustment.

(b) The Board shall decide in each case whether, in order to assure to employees the fullest freedom in exercising the rights guaranteed by this Act, the unit appropriate for the purposes of collective bargaining shall be the employer unit, craft unit, plant unit, or subdivision thereof: Provided, That the Board shall not (1) decide that any unit is appropriate for such purposes if such unit includes both professional employees and employees who are not professional employees unless a majority of such professional employees vote for inclusion in such unit; or (2) decide that any craft unit is inappropriate for such purposes on the ground that a different unit has been established by a prior Board determination, unless a majority of the employees in the proposed craft unit vote against separate representation; or (3) decide that any unit is appropriate for such purposes if it includes, together with other employees, any individual employed as a guard to enforce against employees and other persons rules to protect property of the employer or to protect the safety of persons on the employer's premises; but no labor organization shall be certified as the representative of employees in a bargaining unit of guards if such organization admits to membership, or is affiliated directly or indirectly with an organization which admits to membership, employees other than guards.

(c) (1) Whenever a petition shall have been filed, in accordance with such regulations as may be prescribed by the Board—

(A) by an employee or group of employees or any individual or labor organization acting in their behalf alleging that a substantial number of employees (i) wish to be represented for collective bargaining and that their employer declines to recognize their representative as the representative defined in section 9 (a), or (ii) assert that the individual or labor organization, which has been certified or is being currently recognized by their employer as the bargaining representative, is no longer a representative as defined in section 9 (a); or

(B) by an employer, alleging that one or more individuals or labor organizations have presented to him a claim to be recognized as the representative defined in section 9 (a);

the Board shall investigate such petition and if it has reasonable cause to believe that a question of representation affecting commerce exists shall provide for an appropriate hearing upon due notice. Such hearing may be conducted by an officer or employee of the regional office, who shall not make any recommendations with respect thereto. If the Board finds upon the record of such hearing that such a question of representation exists, it shall direct an election by secret ballot and shall certify the results thereof.

(2) In determining whether or not a question of representation affecting com-

merce exists, the same regulations and rules of decision shall apply irrespective of the identity of the persons filing the petition or the kind of relief sought and in no case shall the Board deny a labor organization a place on the ballot by reason of an order with respect to such labor organization or its predecessor not issued in conformity with section 10 (c).

(3) No election shall be directed in any bargaining unit or any subdivision within which, in the preceding twelve-month period, a valid election shall have been held. Employees [on] *engaged in an economic* strike who are not entitled to reinstatement shall [not] be eligible to vote [.] *under such regulations as the Board shall find are consistent with the purposes and provisions of this Act in any election conducted within twelve months after the commencement of the strike.* In any election where none of the choices on the ballot receives a majority, a run-off shall be conducted, the ballot providing for a selection between the two choices receiving the largest and second largest number of valid votes cast in the election.

(4) Nothing in this section shall be construed to prohibit the waiving of hearings by stipulation for the purpose of a consent election in conformity with regulations and rules of decision of the Board.

(5) In determining whether a unit is appropriate for the purposes specified in subsection (b) the extent to which the employees have organized shall not be controlling.

(d) Whenever an order of the Board made pursuant to section 10 (c) is based in whole or in part upon facts certified following an investigation pursuant to subsection (c) of this section and there is a petition for the enforcement or review of such order, such certification and the record of such investigation shall be included in the transcript of the entire record required to be filed under section 10 (e) or 10 (f), and thereupon the decree of the court enforcing, modifying, or setting aside in whole or in part the order of the Board shall be made and entered upon the pleadings, testimony, and proceedings set forth in such transcript.

(e) (1) Upon the filing with the Board, by 30 per centum or more of the employees in a bargaining unit covered by an agreement between their employer and a labor organization made pursuant to section 8 (a) (3), of a petition alleging they desire that such authority be rescinded, the Board shall take a secret ballot of the employees in such unit and certify the results thereof to such labor organization and to the employer.

(2) No election shall be conducted pursuant to this subsection in any bargaining unit or any subdivision within which, in the preceding twelve-month period, a valid election shall have been held.

[(f) No investigation shall be made by the Board of any question affecting commerce concerning the representation of employees, raised by a labor organization under subsection (c) of this section, and no complaint shall be issued pursuant to a charge made by a labor organization under subsection (b) of section 10, unless such labor organization and any national or international labor organization of which such labor organization is an affiliate or constituent unit (A) shall have prior thereto filed with the Secretary of Labor copies of its constitution and bylaws and a report, in such form as the Secretary may prescribe, showing—

(1) the name of such labor organization and the address of its principal place of business;
(2) the names, titles, and compensation and allowances of its three principal officers

and of any of its other officers or agents whose aggregate compensation and allowances for the preceding year exceeded $5,000, and the amount of the compensation and allowances paid to each such officer or agent during such year;

(3) the manner in which the officers and agents referred to in clause (2) were elected, appointed, or otherwise selected;

(4) the initiation fee or fees which new members are required to pay on becoming members of such labor organization;

(5) the regular dues or fees which members are required to pay in order to remain members in good standing of such labor organization;

(6) a detailed statement of, or reference to provisions of its constitution and bylaws showing the procedure followed with respect to, (a) qualification for or restrictions on membership, (b) election of officers and stewards, (c) calling of regular and special meetings, (d) levying of assessments, (e) imposition of fines, (f) authorization for bargaining demands, (g) ratification of contract terms, (h) authorization for strikes, (i) authorization for disbursement of union funds, (j) audit of union financial transactions, (k) participation in insurance or other benefit plans, and (1) expulsion of members and the grounds therefor;

and (B) can show that prior thereto it has—

(1) filed with the Secretary of Labor, in such form as the Secretary may prescribe, a report showing all of (a) its receipts of any kind and the sources of such receipts, (b) its total assets and liabilities as of the end of its last fiscal year, (c) the disbursements made by it during such fiscal year, including the purposes for which made; and

(2) furnished to all of the members of such labor organization copies of the financial report required by paragraph (1) hereof to be filed with the Secretary of Labor.]

[(g) It shall be the obligation of all labor organizations to file annually with the Secretary of Labor, in such form as the Secretary of Labor may prescribe, reports bringing up to date the information required to be supplied in the initial filing by subsection (f) (A) of this section, and to file with the Secretary of Labor and furnish to its members annually financial reports in the form and manner prescribed in subsection (f) (B). No labor organization shall be eligible for certification under this section as the representative of any employees, and no complaint shall issue under section 10 with respect to a charge filed by a labor organization unless it can show that it and any national or international labor organization of which it is an affiliate or constituent unit has complied with its obligation under this subsection.]

[(h) No investigation shall be made by the Board of any question affecting commerce concerning the representation of employees, raised by a labor organization under subsection (c) of this section, and no complaint shall be issued pursuant to a charge made by a labor organization under subsection (b) of section 10, unless there is on file with the Board an affidavit executed contemporaneously or within the preceding twelve-month period by each officer of such labor organization and the officers of any national or international labor organization of which it is an affiliate or constituent unit that he is not a member of the Communist Party or affiliated with such party, and that he does not believe in, and is not a member of or supports any organization that believes in or teaches, the overthrow of the United States Government by force or by any illegal or unconstitutional methods. The provisions of section 35 A of the Criminal Code shall be applicable in respect to such affidavits.]

PREVENTION OF UNFAIR LABOR PRACTICES. SEC. 10. (a) The Board is empowered, as hereinafter provided, to prevent any person from engaging in any unfair labor practice (listed in section 8) affecting commerce. This power shall not be affected by any other means of adjustment or prevention that has been or may be established by agreement, law, or otherwise: Provided, That the Board is empowered by agreement with any agency of any State or Territory to cede to such agency jurisdiction over any cases in any industry (other than mining, manufacturing, communications, and transportation except where predominantly local in character) even though such cases may involve labor disputes affecting commerce, unless the provision of the State or Territorial statute applicable to the determination of such cases by such agency is inconsistent with the corresponding provision of this Act or has received a construction inconsistent therewith.

(b) Whenever it is charged that any person has engaged in or is engaging in any such unfair labor practice, the Board, or any agent or agency designated by the Board for such purposes, shall have power to issue and cause to be served upon such person a complaint stating the charges in that respect, and containing a notice of hearing before the Board or a member thereof, or before a designated agent or agency, at a place therein fixed, not less than five days after the serving of said complaint: Provided, That no complaint shall issue based upon any unfair labor practice occurring more than six months prior to the filing of the charge with the Board and the service of a copy thereof upon the person against whom such charge is made, unless the person aggrieved thereby was prevented from filing such charge by reason of service in the armed forces, in which event the six-month period shall be computed from the day of his discharge. Any such complaint may be amended by the member, agent, or agency conducting the hearing or the Board in its discretion at any time prior to the issuance of an order based thereon. The person so complained of shall have the right to file an answer to the original or amended complaint and to appear in person or otherwise and give testimony at the place and time fixed in the complaint. In the discretion of the member, agent, or agency conducting the hearing or the Board, any other person may be allowed to intervene in the said proceeding and to present testimony. Any such proceeding shall, so far as practicable, be conducted in accordance with the rules of evidence applicable in the district courts of the United States under the rules of civil procedure for the district courts of the United States, adopted by the Supreme Court of the United States pursuant to the Act of June 19, 1934 (U.S.C. , title 28, secs. 723-B, 723-C).

(c) The testimony taken by such member, agent, or agency or the Board shall be reduced to writing and filed with the Board. Thereafter, in its discretion, the Board upon notice may take further testimony or hear argument. If upon the preponderance of the testimony taken the Board shall be of the opinion that any person named in the complaint has engaged in or is engaging in any such unfair labor practice, then the Board shall state its findings of fact and shall issue and cause to be served on such person an order requiring such person to cease and desist from such unfair labor practice, and to take such affirmative action including reinstatement of employees with or without back pay, as will effectuate the policies of this Act: Provided, That where an order directs reinstatement of an employee, back pay may be required of the employer or labor organization, as the case may be, responsible for the discrimination suffered by him: And provided further, That in determining whether a complaint shall issue alleging a violation of section 8 (a) (1) or section 8 (a) (2), and in deciding such cases, the same regulations and rules of decision shall apply irrespective of whether or not the labor organization affected is affiliated with a labor organization national or international in scope. Such order may further require such person to make reports from time to time showing the extent to which it has complied with the order. If upon the preponderance of the testimony taken the Board shall not be of the opinion that the person named in the complaint has engaged in or is engaging in any such unfair labor practice, then the Board shall state its findings of fact and shall issue an order dismissing the said complaint. No order of the Board shall require the reinstatement of any individual as an employee who has been suspended or discharged, or the payment to him of any back pay, if such individual was suspended or discharged for cause. In case the evidence is presented before a member of the Board, or before an examiner or examiners thereof, such member, or such examiner or examiners, as the case may be, shall issue and cause to be served on the parties to the proceeding a proposed report, together with a recommended order, which shall be filed with the Board, and if no exceptions are filed within twenty days after service thereof upon such parties, or within such further period as the Board may authorize, such recommended order shall become the order of the Board and become effective as therein prescribed.

(d) Until the record in a case shall have been filed in a court, as hereinafter provided, the Board may at any time, upon reasonable notice and in such manner as it shall deem proper, modify or set aside, in whole or in part, any finding or order made or issued by it.

(e) The Board shall have power to petition any court of appeals of the United States, or if all the courts of appeals to which application may be made are in vacation, any district court of the United States, within any circuit or district, respectively, wherein the unfair labor practice in question occurred or wherein such person resides or transacts business, for the enforcement of such order and for appropriate temporary relief or restraining order, and shall file in the court the record in the proceedings, as provided in section 2112 of title 28, United States Code. Upon the filing of such petition, the court shall cause notice thereof to be served upon such person, and thereupon shall have jurisdiction of the proceeding and of the question determined therein, and shall have power to grant such temporary relief or restraining order as it deems just and proper, and to make and enter a decree enforcing, modifying, and enforcing as so modified, or setting aside in whole or in part the order of the Board. No objection that has not been urged before the Board, its member, agent, or agency, shall be considered by the court, unless the failure or neglect to urge such objection shall be excused because of extraordinary circumstances. The findings of the Board with respect to questions of fact if supported by substantial evidence on the record considered as a whole shall be conclusive. If either party shall apply to the court for leave to adduce additional evidence and shall show to the satisfaction of the court that such additional evidence is material and that there were reasonable grounds for the failure to adduce such evidence in the hearing before the Board, its member, agent, or agency, the court may order such additional evidence to be taken before the Board, its member, agent, or agency, and to be made a part of the record. The Board may modify its findings as to the facts, or make new findings, by reason of additional evidence so taken and filed, and it shall file such modified or new findings, which findings with respect to questions of fact if supported by substantial evidence on the record considered as a whole shall be conclusive, and shall file its recommendations, if any, for the modification or setting aside of its original order. Upon the filing of the record with it the jurisdiction of the court shall be exclusive and its judgment and decree shall be final, except that the same shall be subject to review by the appropriate United States court of appeals if application was made to the district court as hereinabove provided, and by the Supreme Court of the United States upon writ of certiorari or certification as provided in section 1254 of title 28.

(f) Any person aggrieved by a final order of the Board granting or denying in whole or in part the relief sought may obtain a review of such order in any circuit court of appeals of the United States in the circuit wherein the unfair labor practice in question was alleged to have been engaged in or wherein such person resides or transacts business, or in the United States Court of Appeals for the District of Columbia, by filing in such court a written petition praying that the order of the Board be modified or set aside. A copy of such petition shall be forthwith transmitted by the clerk of the court to the Board, and thereupon the aggrieved party shall file in the court the record in the proceeding, certified by the Board, as provided in section 2112 of title 28, United States Code. Upon the filing of such petition, the court shall proceed in the same manner as in the case of an application by the Board under subsection (e) of this section, and shall have the same jurisdiction to grant to the Board such temporary relief or restraining order as it deems just and proper, and in like manner to make and enter a decree enforcing, modifying, and enforcing as so modified, or setting aside in whole or in part the order of the Board; the findings of the Board with respect to questions of fact if supported by substantial evidence on the record considered as a whole shall in like manner be conclusive.

(g) The commencement of proceedings under subsection (e) or (f) of this section shall not, unless specifically ordered by the court, operate as a stay of the Board's order.

(h) When granting appropriate temporary relief or a restraining order, or making and entering a decree enforcing, modifying, and enforcing as so modified, or setting aside in whole or in part an order of the Board, as provided in this section, the jurisdiction of courts sitting in equity shall not be limited by the Act entitled "An Act to amend the Judicial Code and to define and limit the jurisdiction of courts sitting in equity, and for other purposes," approved March 23, 1932 (U.S.C., Supp. VII, title 29, secs. 101–115).

(i) Petitions filed under this Act shall be heard expeditiously, and if possible within ten days after they have been docketed.

(j) The Board shall have power, upon issuance of a complaint as provided in subsection (b) charging that any person has engaged in or is engaging in an unfair labor practice, to petition any district court of the United States (including the District Court of the United States for the District of Columbia), within any district wherein the unfair labor practice in question is alleged to have occurred or wherein such person resides or transacts business, for appropriate temporary relief or restraining order. Upon the filing of any such petition the court shall cause notice thereof to be served upon such person, and thereupon shall have jurisdiction to grant to the Board such temporary relief or restraining order as it deems just and proper.

(k) Whenever it is charged that any person has engaged in an unfair labor practice within the meaning of paragraph (4) (D) of section 8 (b), the Board is empowered and directed to hear and determine the dispute out of which such unfair labor practice shall have arisen, unless, within ten days after notice that such charge has been filed, the parties to such dispute submit to the Board satisfactory evidence that they have adjusted, or agreed upon methods for the voluntary adjustment of the dispute. Upon compliance by the parties to the dispute with the decision of the Board or upon such voluntary adjustment of the dispute, such charge shall be dismissed.

(1) Whenever it is charged that any person has engaged in an unfair labor practice within the meaning of paragraph (4) (A), (B), or (C) of section 8 (b), *or section 8 (e) or section 8 (b) (7)*, the preliminary investigation of such charge shall be made forthwith and given priority over all other cases except cases of like character in the office where it is filed or to which it is referred. If, after such investigation, the officer or regional attorney to whom the matter may be referred has reasonable cause to believe such charge is true and that a complaint should issue, he shall, on behalf of the Board, petition any district court of the United States (including the District Court of the United States for the District of Columbia) within any district where the unfair labor practice in question has occurred, is alleged to have occurred, or wherein such person resides or transacts business, for appropriate injunctive relief pending the final adjudication of the Board with respect to such matter. Upon the filing of any such petition the district court shall have jurisdiction to grant such injunctive relief or temporary restraining order as it deems just and proper, notwithstanding any other provision of law: Provided further, That no temporary restraining order shall be issued without notice unless a petition alleges that substantial and irreparable injury to the charging party will be unavoidable and such temporary restraining order shall be effective for no longer than five days and will become void at the expiration of such period [.]: *Provided further, That such officer or regional attorney shall not apply for any restraining order under section 8 (b) (7) if a charge against the employer under section 8 (a) (2) has been filed and after the preliminary investigation, he has reasonable cause to believe that such charge is true and that a complaint should issue.* Upon filing of any such petition the courts shall cause notice thereof to be served upon any person involved in the charge and such person, including the charging party, shall be given an opportunity to appear by counsel and present any relevant testimony: Provided further, That for the purposes of this subsection district courts shall be deemed to have jurisdiction of a labor organization (1) in the district in which such organization maintains its principal office, or (2) in any district in which its duly authorized officers or agents are engaged in promoting or protecting the interests of employee members. The service of legal process upon such officer or agent shall constitute service upon the labor organization and make such organization a party to the suit. In situations where such relief is appropriate the procedure specified herein shall apply to charges with respect to section 8 (b) (4) (D).

(m) *Whenever it is charged that any person has engaged in an unfair labor practice within the meaning of subsection (a) (3) or (b) (2) of section 8, such charge shall be given priority over all other cases except cases of like character in the office where it is filed or to which it is referred and cases given priority under subsection (1).*

INVESTIGATORY POWERS

Sec. 11. For the purpose of all hearings and investigations, which, in the opinion of the Board, are necessary and proper for the exercise of the powers vested in it by section 9 and section 10—

(1) The Board, or its duly authorized agents or agencies, shall at all reasonable times have access to, for the purpose of examination, and the right to copy any evidence of any person being investigated or proceeded against that relates to any matter under investigation or in question. The Board, or any member thereof, shall upon application of any party to such proceedings, forthwith issue to such party

subpenas requiring the attendance and testimony of witnesses or the production of any evidence in such proceeding or investigation requested in such application. Within five days after the service of a subpena on any person requiring the production of any evidence in his possession or under his control, such person may petition the Board to revoke, and the Board shall revoke, such subpena if in its opinion the evidence whose production is required does not relate to any matter under investigation, or any matter in question in such proceedings, or if in its opinion such subpena does not describe with sufficient particularity the evidence whose production is required. Any member of the Board, or any agent or agency designated by the Board for such purposes, may administer oaths and affirmations, examine witnesses, and receive evidence. Such attendance of witnesses and the production of such evidence may be required from any place in the United States or any Territory or possession thereof, at any designated place of hearing.

(2) In case of contumacy or refusal to obey a subpena issued to any person, any district court of the United States or the United States courts of any Territory or possession, or the District Court of the United States for the District of Columbia, within the jurisdiction of which the inquiry is carried on or within the jurisdiction of which said person guilty of contumacy or refusal to obey is found or resides or transacts business, upon application by the Board shall have jurisdiction to issue to such person an order requiring such person to appear before the Board, its member, agent, or agency, there to produce evidence if so ordered, or there to give testimony touching the matter under investigation or in question; and any failure to obey such order of the court may be punished by said court as a contempt thereof.

(3) No person shall be excused from attending and testifying or from producing books, records, correspondence, documents, or other evidence in obedience to the subpena of the Board, on the ground that the testimony or evidence required of him may tend to incriminate him or subject him to a penalty or forfeiture; but no individual shall be prosecuted or subjected to any penalty or forfeiture for or on account of any transaction, matter, or thing concerning which he is compelled, after having claimed his privilege against self-incrimination, to testify or produce evidence, except that such individual so testifying shall not be exempt from prosecution and punishment for perjury committed in so testifying.

(4) Complaints, orders, and other process and papers of the Board, its member, agent, or agency, may be served either personally or by registered mail or by telegraph or by leaving a copy thereof at the principal office or place of business of the person required to be served. The verified return by the individual so serving the same setting forth the manner of such service shall be proof of the same, and the return post office receipt or telegraph receipt therefor when registered and mailed or telegraphed as aforesaid shall be proof of service of the same. Witnesses summoned before the Board, its member, agent, or agency, shall be paid the same fees and mileage that are paid witnesses in the courts of the United States, and witnesses whose depositions are taken and the persons taking the same shall severally be entitled to the same fees as are paid for like services in the courts of the United States.

(5) All process of any court to which application may be made under this Act may be served in the judicial district wherein the defendant or other person required to be served resides or may found.

(6) The several departments and agencies of the Government, when directed by the President, shall furnish the Board, upon its request, all records, papers, and information in their possession relating to any matter before the Board.

Sec. 12. Any person who shall willfully resist, prevent, impede, or interfere with any member of the Board or any of its agents or agencies in the performance of duties pursuant to this Act shall be punished by a fine of not more than $5,000 or by imprisonment for not more than one year, or both.

LIMITATIONS

Sec. 13. Nothing in this Act, except as specifically provided for herein, shall be construed so as either to interfere with or impede or diminish in any way the right to strike, or to affect the limitations or qualifications on that right.

Sec. 14. (a) Nothing herein shall prohibit any individual employed as a supervisor from becoming or remaining a member of a labor organization, but no employer subject to this Act shall be compelled to deem individuals defined herein as supervisors as employees for the purpose of any law, either national or local, relating to collective bargaining.

(b) Nothing in this Act shall be construed as authorizing the execution or application of agreements requiring membership in a labor organization as a condition of employment in any State or Territory in which such execution or application is prohibited by State or Territorial law.

(c) (1) *The Board, in its discretion, may, by rule of decision or by published rules adopted pursuant to the Administrative Procedure Act, decline to assert jurisdiction over any labor dispute involving any class or category of employers, where, in the opinion of the Board, the effect of such labor dispute on commerce is not sufficiently substantial to warrant the exercise of its jurisdiction: Provided, That the Board shall not decline to assert jurisdiction over any labor dispute over which it would assert jurisdiction under the standards prevailing upon August 1, 1959.*

(2) *Nothing in this Act shall be deemed to prevent or bar any agency or the courts of any State or Territory (including the Commonwealth of Puerto Rico, Guam, and the Virgin Islands), from assuming and asserting jurisdiction over labor disputes over which the Board declines, pursuant to paragraph (1) of this subsection, to assert jurisdiction.*

Sec. 15. Wherever the application of the provisions of section 272 of chapter 10 of the Act entitled "An Act to establish a uniform system of bankruptcy throughout the United States," approved July 1, 1898, and Acts amendatory thereof and supplementary thereto (U.S.C., title 11, sec. 672), conflicts with the application of the provisions of this Act, this Act shall prevail: Provided, That in any situation where the provisions of this Act cannot be validly enforced, the provisions of such other Acts shall remain in full force and effect.

Sec. 16. If any provision of this Act, or the application of such provision to any person or circumstances, shall be held invalid, the remainder of this Act, or the application of such provision to persons or circumstances other than those as to which it is held invalid, shall not be affected thereby.

Sec. 17. This Act may be cited as the "National Labor Relations Act."

Sec. 18. No petition entertained, no investigation made, no election held, and no certification issued by the National Labor Relations Board, under any of the provisions of section 9 of the National Labor Relations Act, as amended, shall be invalid by reason of the failure of the Congress of Industrial Organizations to have complied with the requirements of section 9 (f), (g), or (h) of the aforesaid Act prior to December 22, 1949, or by reason of the failure of the American Federation of Labor to have complied with the provisions of section 9 (f), (g), or (h) of the aforesaid Act prior to November 7, 1947: Provided, That no liability shall be imposed under any provision of this Act upon any person for failure to honor any election or certificate referred to above, prior to the effective date of this amendment: Provided, however, That this proviso shall not have the effect of setting aside or in any way affecting judgments or decrees heretofore entered under section 10 (e) or (f) and which have become final.

EFFECTIVE DATE OF CERTAIN CHANGES*

Sec. 102. No provision of this title shall be deemed to make an unfair labor practice any act which was performed prior to the date of the enactment of this Act which did not constitute an unfair labor practice prior thereto, and the provisions of section 8 (a) (3) and section 8 (b) (2) of the National Labor Relations Act as amended by this title shall not make an unfair labor practice the performance of any obligation under a collective-bargaining agreement entered into prior to the date of the enactment of this Act, or (in the case of an agreement for a period of not more than one year) entered into on or after such date of enactment, but prior to the effective date of this title, if the performance of such obligation would not have constituted an unfair labor practice under section 8 (3) of the National Labor Relations Act prior to the effective date of this title, unless such agreement was renewed or extended subsequent thereto.

Sec. 103. No provisions of this title shall affect any certification of representatives or any determination as to the appropriate collective-bargaining unit, which was made under section 9 of the National Labor Relations Act prior to the effective date of this title until one year after the date of such certification or if, in respect of any such certification, a collective-bargaining contract was entered into prior to the effective date of this title, until the end of the contract period or until one year after such date, whichever first occurs.

Sec. 104. The amendments made by this title shall take effect sixty days after the date of the enactment of this Act, except that the authority of the President to appoint certain officers conferred upon him by section 3 of the National Labor Relations Act as amended by this title may be exercised forthwith.

TITLE II
CONCILIATION OF LABOR DISPUTES IN INDUSTRIES AFFECTING COMMERCE; NATIONAL EMERGENCIES

Sec. 201. That it is the policy of the United States that—

(a) sound and stable industrial peace and the advancement of the general welfare, health, and safety of the Nation and of the best interest of employers and

*The effective date referred to in Sections 102, 103, and 104 is August 22, 1947.

employees can most satisfactorily be secured by the settlement of issues between employers and employees through the processes of conference and collective bargaining between employers and the representatives of their employees;

(b) the settlement of issues between employers and employees through collective bargaining may be advanced by making available full and adequate governmental facilities for conciliation, mediation, and voluntary arbitration to aid and encourage employers and the representatives of their employees to reach and maintain agreements concerning rates of pay, hours, and working conditions, and to make all reasonable efforts to settle their differences by mutual agreement reached through conferences and collective bargaining or by such methods as may be provided for in any applicable agreement for the settlement of disputes; and

(c) certain controversies which arise between parties to collective bargaining agreements may be avoided or minimized by making available full and adequate governmental facilities for furnishing assistance to employers and the representatives of their employees in formulating for inclusion within such agreements provision for adequate notice of any proposed changes in the terms of such agreements, for the final adjustment of grievances or questions regarding the application or interpretation of such agreements, and other provisions designed to prevent the subsequent arising of such controversies.

SEC. 202. (a) There is hereby created an independent agency to be known as the Federal Mediation and Conciliation Service (herein referred to as the "Service," except that for sixty days after the date of the enactment of this Act such term shall refer to the Conciliation Service of the Department of Labor). The Service shall be under the direction of a Federal Mediation and Conciliation Director (hereinafter referred to as the "Director"), who shall be appointed by the President by and with the advice and consent of the Senate. The Director shall receive compensation at the rate of $12,000* per annum. The Director shall not engage in any other business, vocation, or employment.

(b) The Director is authorized, subject to the civil-service laws, to appoint such clerical and other personnel as may be necessary for the execution of the functions of the Service, and shall fix their compensation in accordance with the Classification Act of 1923, as amended, and may, without regard to the provisions of the civil service laws and the Classification Act of 1923, as amended, appoint and fix the compensation of such conciliators and mediators as may be necessary to carry out the functions of the Service. The Director is authorized to make such expenditures for supplies, facilities, and services as he deems necessary. Such expenditures shall be allowed and paid upon presentation of itemized vouchers therefor approved by the Director or by any employee designated by him for that purpose.

(c) The principal office of the Service shall be in the District of Columbia, but the Director may establish regional offices convenient to localities in which labor controversies are likely to arise. The Director may by order, subject to revocation at any time, delegate any authority and discretion conferred upon him by this Act to any regional director, or other officer or employee of the Service. The Director may establish suitable procedures for cooperation with State and local mediation agencies. The Director shall make an annual report in writing to Congress at the end of the fiscal year.

---

* Pursuant to Public Law 854, 84th Congress, 2d Session, Title I, approved July 31, 1956, the salary of the Director shall be $20,500 per year.

(d) All mediation and conciliation functions of the Secretary of Labor or the United States Conciliation Service under section 8 of the Act entitled "An Act to create a Department of Labor," approved March 4, 1913 (U.S.C. , title 29, sec. 51), and all functions of the United States Conciliation Service under any other law are hereby transferred to the Federal Mediation and Conciliation Service, together with the personnel and records of the United States Conciliation Service. Such transfer shall take effect upon the sixtieth day after the date of enactment of this Act. Such transfer shall not affect any proceedings pending before the United States Conciliation Service or any certification, order, rule, or regulation theretofore made by it or by the Secretary of Labor. The Director and the Service shall not be subject in any way to the jurisdiction or authority of the Secretary of Labor or any official or division of the Department of Labor.

FUNCTIONS OF THE SERVICE

Sec. 203. (a) It shall be the duty of the Service, in order to prevent or minimize interruptions of the free flow of commerce growing out of labor disputes, to assist parties to labor disputes in industries affecting commerce to settle such disputes through conciliation and mediation.

(b) The Service may proffer its services in any labor dispute in any industry affecting commerce, either upon its own motion or upon the request of one or more of the parties to the dispute, whenever in its judgment such dispute threatens to cause a substantial interruption of commerce. The Director and the Service are directed to avoid attempting to mediate disputes which would have only a minor effect on interstate commerce if State or other conciliation services are available to the parties. Whenever the Service does proffer its services in any dispute, it shall be the duty of the Service promptly to put itself in communication with the parties and to use its best efforts, by mediation and conciliation, to bring them to agreement.

(c) If the Director is not able to bring the parties to agreement by conciliation within a reasonable time, he shall seek to induce the parties voluntarily to seek other means of settling the dispute without resort to strike, lockout, or other coercion, including submission to the employees in the bargaining unit of the employer's last offer of settlement for approval or rejection in a secret ballot. The failure or refusal of either party to agree to any procedure suggested by the Director shall not be deemed a violation of any duty or obligation imposed by this Act.

(d) Final adjustment by a method agreed upon by the parties is hereby declared to be the desirable method for settlement of grievance disputes arising over the application or interpretation of an existing collective-bargaining agreement. The Service is directed to make its conciliation and mediation services available in the settlement of such grievance disputes only as a last resort and in exceptional cases.

Sec. 204. (a) In order to prevent or minimize interruptions of the free flow of commerce growing out of labor disputes, employers and employees and their representatives, in any industry affecting commerce, shall—

(1) exert every reasonable effort to make and maintain agreements concerning rates of pay, hours, and working conditions, including provision for adequate notice of any proposed change in the terms of such agreements;

(2) whenever a dispute arises over the terms or application of a collective-bargaining agreement and a conference is requested by a party or prospective

party thereto, arrange promptly for such a conference to be held and endeavor in such conference to settle such dispute expeditiously; and

(3) in case such dispute is not settled by conference, participate fully and promptly in such meetings as may be undertaken by the Service under this Act for the purpose of aiding in a settlement of the dispute.

Sec. 205. (a) There is hereby created a National Labor-Management Panel which shall be composed of twelve members appointed by the President, six of whom shall be selected from among persons outstanding in the field of management and six of whom shall be selected from among persons outstanding in the field of labor. Each member shall hold office for a term of three years, except that any member appointed to fill a vacancy occurring prior to the expiration of the term for which his predecessor was appointed shall be appointed for the remainder of such term, and the terms of office of the members first taking office shall expire, as designated by the President at the time of appointment, four at the end of the first year, four at the end of the second year, and four at the end of the third year after the date of appointment. Members of the panel, when serving on business of the panel, shall be paid compensation at the rate of $25 per day, and shall also be entitled to receive an allowance for actual and necessary travel and subsistence expenses while so serving away from their places of residence.

(b) It shall be the duty of the panel, at the request of the Director, to advise in the avoidance of industrial controversies and the manner in which mediation and voluntary adjustment shall be administered, particularly with reference to controversies affecting the general welfare of the country.

NATIONAL EMERGENCIES

Sec. 206. Whenever in the opinion of the President of the United States, a threatened or actual strike or lockout affecting an entire industry or a substantial part thereof engaged in trade, commerce, transportation, transmission, or communication among the several States or with foreign nations, or engaged in the production of goods for commerce, will, if permitted to occur or to continue, imperil the national health or safety, he may appoint a board of inquiry to inquire into the issues involved in the dispute and to make a written report to him within such time as he shall prescribe. Such report shall include a statement of the facts with respect to the dispute, including each party's statement of its position but shall not contain any recommendations. The President shall file a copy of such report with the Service and shall make its contents available to the public.

Sec. 207. (a) A board of inquiry shall be composed of a chairman and such other members as the President shall determine, and shall have power to sit and act in any place within the United States and to conduct such hearings either in public or in private, as it may deem necessary or proper, to ascertain the facts with respect to the causes and circumstances of the dispute.

(b) Members of a board of inquiry shall receive compensation at the rate of $50 for each day actually spent by them in the work of the board, together with necessary travel and subsistence expenses.

(c) For the purpose of any hearing or inquiry conducted by any board appointed under this title, the provisions of sections 9 and 10 (relating to the attendance of witnesses and the production of books, papers, and documents) of the Federal Trade

Commission Act of September 16, 1914, as amended (U.S.C. 19, title 15, secs. 49 and 50, as amended), are hereby made applicable to the powers and duties of such board.

Sec. 208. (a) Upon receiving a report from a board of inquiry the President may direct the Attorney General to petition any district court of the United States having jurisdiction of the parties to enjoin such strike or lockout or the continuing thereof, and if the court finds that such threatened or actual strike or lockout—

(i) affects an entire industry or a substantial part thereof engaged in trade, commerce, transportation, transmission, or communication among the several States or with foreign nations, or engaged in the production of goods for commerce; and

(ii) if permitted to occur or to continue, will imperil the national health or safety, it shall have jurisdiction to enjoin any such strike or lockout, or the continuing thereof, and to make such other orders as may be appropriate.

(b) In any case, the provisions of the Act of March 23, 1932, entitled "An Act to amend the Judicial Code and to define and limit the jurisdiction of courts sitting in equity, and for other purposes," shall not be applicable.

(c) The order or orders of the court shall be subject to review by the appropriate circuit court of appeals and by the Supreme Court upon writ of certiorari or certification as provided in sections 239 and 240 of the Judicial Code, as amended (U.S.C. , title 29, secs. 346 and 347).

Sec. 209. (a) Whenever a district court has issued an order under section 208 enjoining acts or practices which imperil or threaten to imperil the national health or safety, it shall be the duty of the parties to the labor dispute giving rise to such order to make every effort to adjust and settle their differences, with the assistance of the Service created by this Act. Neither party shall be under any duty to accept, in whole or in part, any proposal of settlement made by the Service.

(b) Upon the issuance of such order, the President shall reconvene the board of inquiry which has previously reported with respect to the dispute. At the end of a sixty-day period (unless the dispute has been settled by that time), the board of inquiry shall report to the President the current position of the parties and the efforts which has (sic) been made for settlement, and shall include a statement by each party of its position and a statement of the employer's last offer of settlement. The President shall make such report available to the public. The National Labor Relations Board, within the succeeding fifteen days, shall take a secret ballot of the employees of each employer involved in the dispute on the question of whether they wish to accept the final offer of settlement made by their employer as stated by him and shall certify the results thereof to the Attorney General within five days thereafter.

Sec. 210. Upon the certification of the results of such ballot or upon a settlement being reached, whichever happens sooner, the Attorney General shall move the court to discharge the injunction, which motion shall then be granted and the injunction discharged. When such motion is granted, the President shall submit to the Congress a full and comprehensive report of the proceedings, including the findings of the board of inquiry and the ballot taken by the National Labor Relations Board, together with such recommendations as he may see fit to make for consideration and appropriate action.

COMPILATION OF COLLECTIVE-BARGAINING AGREEMENTS, ETC. SEC. 211. (a) For the guidance and information of interested representatives of employers, employees, and the general public, the Bureau of Labor Statistics of the Department of Labor shall maintain a file of copies of all available collective-bargaining agreements and other available agreements and actions thereunder settling or adjusting labor disputes. Such file shall be open to inspection under appropriate conditions prescribed by the Secretary of Labor, except that no specific information submitted in confidence shall be disclosed.

(b) The Bureau of Labor Statistics in the Department of Labor is authorized to furnish upon request of the Service, or employers, employees, or their representatives, all available data and factual information which may aid in the settlement of any labor dispute, except that no specific information submitted to confidence shall be disclosed.

EXEMPTION OF RAILWAY LABOR ACT. SEC. 212. The provisions of this title shall not be applicable with respect to any matter which is subject to the provisions of the Railway Labor Act, as amended from time to time.

TITLE III
SUITS BY AND AGAINST LABOR ORGANIZATIONS

SEC. 301. (a) Suits for violation of contracts between an employer and a labor organization representing employees in an industry affecting commerce as defined in this Act, or between any such labor organizations, may be brought in any district court of the United States having jurisdiction of the parties, without respect to the amount in controversy or without regard to the citizenship of the parties.

(b) Any labor organization which represents employees in an industry affecting commerce as defined in this Act and any employer whose activities affect commerce as defined in this Act shall be bound by the acts of its agents. Any such labor organization may sue or be sued as an entity and in behalf of the employees whom it represents in the courts of the United States. Any money judgment against a labor organization in a district court of the United States shall be enforceable only against the organization as an entity and against its assets, and shall not be enforceable against any individual member or his assets.

(c) For the purposes of actions and proceedings by or against labor organizations in the district courts of the United States, district courts shall be deemed to have jurisdiction of a labor organization (1) in the district in which such organization maintains its principal office, or (2) in any district in which its duly authorized officers or agents are engaged in representing or acting for employee members.

(d) The service of summons, subpena, or other legal process of any court of the United States upon an officer or agent of a labor organization, in his capacity as such, shall constitute service upon the labor organization.

(e) For the purposes of this section, in determining whether any person is acting as an "agent" of another person so as to make such other person responsible for his acts, the question of whether the specific acts performed were actually authorized or subsequently ratified shall not be controlling.

RESTRICTIONS ON PAYMENTS TO EMPLOYEE REPRESENTATIVES. SEC. 302. (a) It shall be unlawful for any employer *or association of employers or any person who acts as a labor relations expert, adviser, or consultant to an employer or who acts in the interest of an employer* to pay, *lend*, or deliver, or [to] agree to pay, *lend*, or deliver, any money or other thing of value—

(1) to any representative of any of his employees who are employed in an industry affecting commerce [.]; *or*

(2) to any labor organization, or any officer or employee thereof, which represents, seeks to represent, or would admit to membership, any of the employees of such employer who are employed in an industry affecting commerce; or

(3) to any employee or group or committee of employees of such employer employed in an industry affecting commerce in excess of their normal compensation for the purpose of causing such employee or group or committee directly or indirectly to influence any other employees in the exercise of the right to organize and bargain collectively through representatives of their own choosing; or

(4) to any officer or employee of a labor organization engaged in an industry affecting commerce with intent to influence him in respect to any of his actions, decisions, or duties as a representative of employees or as such officer or employee of such labor organization.

(b) (1) It shall be unlawful for any [representative of any employees who are employed in an industry affecting commerce] *person* to *request, demand,* receive, or accept, or [to] agree to receive or accept, [from the employer of such employees] *any payment, loan, or delivery* of any money or other thing of value[.] *prohibited by subsection (a).*

(2) It shall be unlawful for any labor organization, or for any person acting as an officer, agent, representative, or employee of such labor organization, to demand or accept from the operator of any motor vehicle (as defined in part II of the Interstate Commerce Act) employed in the transportation of property in commerce, or the employer of any such operator, any money or other thing of value payable to such organization or to an officer, agent, representative or employee thereof as a fee or charge for the unloading, or in connection with the unloading, of the cargo of such vehicle: Provided, That nothing in this paragraph shall be construed to make unlawful any payment by an employer to any of his employees as compensation for their services as employees.

(c) The provisions of this section shall not be applicable (1) [with] in respect to any money or other thing of value payable by an employer *to any of his employees whose established duties include acting openly for such employer in matters of labor relations or personnel administration or* to any representative *of his employees, or to any officer or employee of a labor organization* who is *also* an employee or former employee of such employer, as compensation for, or by reason of, his service[s] as an employee of such employer; (2) with respect to the payment or delivery of any money or other thing of value in satisfaction of a judgment of any court or a decision or award of an arbitrator or impartial chairman or in compromise, adjustment, settlement, or release of any claim, complaint, grievance, or dispute in the absence of fraud or duress; (3) with respect to the sale or purchase of an article or commodity at the prevailing market price in the regular course of business; (4) with respect to money deducted from the wages of employees in payment of membership dues in a labor organization: Provided, That the employer has received from each employee, on whose account such deductions are made, a written assignment which shall not be irrevocable for a period of more than one year, or beyond the termination date of the applicable collective agreement, whichever occurs sooner; [or] (5) with respect to money or other thing of value paid to a trust fund established by such representative, for the sole and exclusive benefit of the employees of such employer, and their families and dependents (or of such employees, families, and dependents jointly with the employees of other employers making similar payments, and their families and dependents):

Provided, That (A) such payments are held in trust for the purpose of paying, either from principal or income or both, for the benefit of employees, their families and dependents, for medical or hospital care, pensions on retirement or death of employees, compensation for injuries or illness resulting from occupational activity or insurance to provide any of the foregoing, or unemployment benefits or life insurance, disability and sickness insurance, or accident insurance; (B) the detailed basis on which such payments are to be made is specified in a written agreement with the employer, and employees and employers are equally represented in the administration of such fund, together with such neutral persons as the representatives of the employers and the representatives of [the] employees may agree upon and in the event the employer and employee groups deadlock on the administration of such fund and there are no neutral persons empowered to break such deadlock, such agreement provides that the two groups shall agree on an impartial umpire to decide such dispute or in event of their failure to agree within a reasonable length of time an impartial umpire to decide such dispute shall, on petition of either group, be appointed by the district court of the United States for the district where the trust fund has its principal office, and shall also contain provisions for an annual audit of the trust fund, a statement of the results of which shall be available for inspection by interested persons at the principal office of the trust fund and at such other places as may be designated in such written agreement; and (C) such payments as are intended to be used for the purpose of providing pensions or annuities for employees are made to a separate trust which provides that the funds held therein cannot be used for any purpose other than paying such pensions or annuities [.]; *or (6) with respect to money or other thing of value paid by any employer to a trust fund established by such representative for the purpose of pooled vacation, holiday, severance or similar benefits, or defraying costs of apprenticeship or other training programs; Provided, That the requirements of clause (B) of the proviso to clause (5) of this subsection shall apply to such trust funds.*

(d) Any person who willfully violates any of the provisions of this section shall, upon conviction thereof, be guilty of a misdemeanor and be subject to a fine of not more than $10,000 or to imprisonment for not more than one year, or both.

(e) The district courts of the United States and the United States courts of the Territories and possessions shall have jurisdiction, for cause shown, and subject to the provisions of section 17 (relating to notice to opposite party) of the Act entitled "An Act to supplement existing laws against unlawful restraints and monopolies, and for other purposes," approved October 15, 1914, as amended (U.S.C. , title 28, sec. 381), to restrain violations of this section, without regard to the provisions of sections 6 and 20 of such Act of October 15, 1914, as amended (U.S.C. , title 15, sec. 17, and title 29, sec. 52), and the provisions of the Act entitled "An Act to amend the Judicial Code and to define and limit the jurisdiction of courts sitting in equity, and for other purposes," approved March 23, 1932 (U.S.C. , title 29, secs. 101–115).

(f) This section shall not apply to any contract in force on the date of enactment of this Act, until the expiration of such contract, or until July 1, 1948, whichever first occurs.

(g) Compliance with the restrictions contained in subsection (c) (5) (B) upon contributions to trust funds, otherwise lawful, shall not be applicable to contributions to such trust funds established by collective agreement prior to January 1, 1946, nor shall subsection (c) (5) (A) be construed as prohibiting contributions to such trust funds if prior to January 1, 1947, such funds contained provisions for pooled vacation benefits.

Boycotts and Other Unlawful Combinations. Sec. 303. (a) It shall be unlawful, for the purpose [s] of this section only, in an industry or activity affecting commerce, for any labor organization to engage in [, or to induce or encourage the employees of any employer to engage in, a strike or a concerted refusal in the course of their employment to use, manufacture, process, transport, or otherwise handle or work on any goods, articles, materials, or commodities or to perform any services, where an object thereof is—]

[(1) forcing or requiring any employer or self-employed person to join any labor or employer organization or any employer or other person to cease using, selling, handling, transporting, or otherwise dealing in the products of any other producer, processor, or manufacturer, or to cease doing business with any other person;]

[(2) forcing or requiring any other employer to recognize or bargain with a labor organization as the representative of his employees unless such labor organization has been certified as the representative of such employees under the provisions of section 9 of the National Labor Relations Act;]

[(3) forcing or requiring any employer to recognize or bargain with a particular labor organization as the representative of his employees if another labor organization has been certified as the representative of such employees under the provisions of section 9 of the National Labor Relations Act;]

[(4) forcing or requiring any employer to assign particular work to employees in a particular labor organization or in a particular trade, craft, or class rather than to employees in another labor organization or in another trade, craft, or class unless such employer is failing to conform to an order or certification of the National Labor Relations Board determining the bargaining representative for employees performing such work. Nothing contained in this subsection shall be construed to make unlawful a refusal by any person to enter upon the premises of any employer (other than his own employer), if the employees of such employer are engaged in a strike ratified or approved by a representative of such employees whom such employer is required to recognize under the National Labor Relations Act.]

any activity or conduct defined as an unfair labor practice in section 8 (b) (4) of the National Labor Relations Act, as amended.

(b) Whoever shall be injured in his business or property by reason of any violation of subsection (a) may sue therefor in any district court of the United States subject to the limitations and provisions of section 301 hereof without respect to the amount in controversy, or in any other court having jurisdiction of the parties, and shall recover the damages by him sustained and the cost of the suit.

RESTRICTION ON POLITICAL CONTRIBUTIONS

Sec. 304. Section 313 of the Federal Corrupt Practices Act, 1925 (U.S.C. , 1940 edition, title 2, sec. 251; Supp. V, title 50, App. , sec. 1509), as amended, is amended to read as follows:

Sec. 313. It is unlawful for any national bank, or any corporation organized by authority of any law of Congress, to make a contribution or expenditure in connection with any election to any political office, or in connection with any primary election or political convention or caucus held to select candidates for any political office, or for any corporation whatever, or any labor organization to make a contribution or expenditure in connection with any election at which Presidential and Vice

Presidential electors or a Senator or Representative in, or a Delegate or Resident Commissioner to Congress are to be voted for, or in connection with any primary election or political convention or caucus held to select candidates for any of the foregoing offices, or for any candidate, political committee, or other person to accept or receive any contribution prohibited by this section. Every corporation or labor organization which makes any contribution or expenditure in violation of this section shall be fined not more than $5,000; and every officer or director of any corporation, or officer of any labor organization, who consents to any contribution or expenditure by the corporation or labor organization, as the case may be, in violation of this section shall be fined not more than $1,000 or imprisoned for not more than one year, or both. For the purposes of this section "labor organization" means any organization of any kind, or any agency or employee representation committee or plan, in which employees participate and which exists for the purpose, in whole or in part, of dealing with employers concerning grievances, labor disputes, wages, rates of pay, hours of employment, or conditions of work.

STRIKES BY GOVERNMENT EMPLOYEES

SEC. 305. It shall be unlawful for any individual employed by the United States or any agency thereof including wholly owned Government corporations to participate in any strike. Any individual employed by the United States or by any such agency who strikes shall be discharged immediately from his employment, and shall forfeit his civil-service status, if any, and shall not be eligible for reemployment for three years by the United States or any such agency.

TITLE IV
CREATION OF JOINT COMMITTEE TO STUDY AND REPORT ON BASIC PROBLEMS AFFECTING FRIENDLY LABOR RELATIONS AND PRODUCTIVITY

TITLE V
DEFINITIONS

SEC. 501. When used in this Act—

(1) The term "industry affecting commerce" means any industry or activity in commerce or in which a labor dispute would burden or obstruct commerce or tend to burden or obstruct commerce or the free flow of commerce.
(2) The term "strike" includes any strike or other concerted stoppage of work by employees (including a stoppage by reason of the expiration of a collective-bargaining agreement) and any concerted slow-down or other concerted interruption of operations by employees.
(3) The terms "commerce," "labor disputes," "employer," "employee," "labor organization," "representative," "person," and "supervisor" shall have the same meaning as when used in the National Labor Relations Act as amended by this Act.

SAVING PROVISION. SEC. 502. Nothing in this Act shall be construed to require an individual employee to render labor or service without his consent, nor shall anything in this Act be construed to make the quitting of his labor by an individual employee an illegal act; nor shall any court issue any process to compel the performance by an individual employee of such labor or service, without his consent; nor shall the quitting of labor by an employee or employees in good faith because of abnormally dangerous conditions for work at this place of employment of such employee or employees be deemed a strike under this Act.

Separability. Sec. 503. If any provision of this Act, or the application of such provision to any person or circumstance, shall be held invalid, the remainder of this Act, or the application of such provision to persons or circumstances other than those as to which it is held invalid, shall not be affected thereby.

APPENDIX I

LABOR-MANAGEMENT RELATIONS
IN THE FEDERAL SERVICE

Executive Order 11491 as Amended by Executive Order 11616, effective August 1971.

WHEREAS the public interest requires high standards of employee performance and the continual development and implementation of modern and progressive work practices to facilitate improved employee performance and efficiency; and

WHEREAS the well-being of employees and efficient administration of the Government are benefited by providing employees an opportunity to participate in the formulation and implementation of personnel policies and practices affecting the conditions of their employment; and

WHEREAS the participation of employees should be improved through the maintenance of constructive and cooperative relationships between labor organizations and management officials; and

WHEREAS subject to law and the paramount requirements of public service, effective labor-management relations within the Federal service require a clear statement of the respective rights and obligations of labor organizations and agency management:

Now, therefore, by virtue of the authority vested in me by the Constitution and statutes of the United States, including sections 3301 and 7301 of title 5 of the United States Code, and as President of the United States, I hereby direct that the following policies shall govern officers and agencies of the excutive branch of the Government in all dealings with Federal employees and organizations representing such employees.

General Provisions

SEC. 1. POLICY. (a) Each employee of the executive branch of the Federal Government has the right, freely and without fear of penalty or reprisal, to form, join, and assist a labor organization or to refrain from any such activity, and each employee shall be protected in the exercise of this right. Except as otherwise expressly provided in this Order the right to assist a labor organization extends to participation in the management of the organization and acting for the organization in the capacity of an organization representative, including presentation of its views to officials of the executive branch, the Congress, or other appropriate authority. The head of each agency shall take the action required to assure that employees in the agency are apprised of their rights under this section, and that no interference, restraint, coercion, or discrimination is practiced within his agency to encourage or discourage membership in a labor organization.

(b) Paragraph (a) of this section does not authorize participation in the management of a labor organization or acting as a representative of such an organization by a supervisor, except as provided in section 24 of this Order, or by an employee when the participation or activity would result in a conflict or apparent conflict of interest or otherwise be incompatible with law or with the official duties of the employee.

SEC. 2. DEFINITIONS. When used in this Order, the term—

(a) "Agency" means an executive department, a Government corporation, and an independent establishment as defined in section 104 of title 5, United States Code, except the General Accounting Office;

(b) "Employee" means an employee of an agency and an employee of a non-appropriated fund instrumentality of the United States but does not include, for the purpose of formal or exclusive recognition or national consultation rights, a supervisor, except as provided in section 24 of this Order;

(c) "Supervisor" means an employee having authority, in the interest of an agency, to hire, transfer, suspend, lay off, recall, promote, discharge, assign, reward, or discipline other employees or responsibly to direct them, or to evaluate their performance, or to adjust their grievances, or effectively to recommend such action, if in connection with the foregoing the exercise of authority is not of a merely routine or clerical nature, but requires the use of independent judgment;

(d) "Guard" means an employee assigned to enforce against employees and other persons rules to protect agency property or the safety of persons on agency premises, or to maintain law and order in areas or facilities under Government control;

(e) "Labor organization" means a lawful organization of any kind in which employees participate and which exists for the purpose, in whole or in part, of dealing with agencies concerning grievances, personnel policies and practices, or other matters affecting the working conditions of their employees; but does not include an organization which—

(1) consists of management officials or supervisors, except as provided in section 24 of this Order;

(2) assists or participates in a strike against the Government of the United States or any agency thereof or imposes a duty or obligation to conduct, assist, or participate in such a strike;

(3) advocates the overthrow of the constitutional form of government in the United States; or

(4) discriminates with regard to the terms or conditions of membership because of race, color, creed, sex, age, or national origin;

(f) "Agency management" means the agency head and all management officials, supervisors, and other representatives of management having authority to act for the agency on any matters relating to the implementation of the agency labor-management relations program established under this Order;

(g) "Council" means the Federal Labor Relations Council established by this Order;

(h) "Panel" means the Federal Service Impasses Panel established by this Order; and

(i) "Assistant Secretary" means the Assistant Secretary of Labor for Labor-Management Relations.

SEC. 3. APPLICATION. (a) This Order applies to all employees and agencies in the executive branch, except as provided in paragraphs (b), (c) and (d) of this section.

(b) This Order (except section 22) does not apply to—

(1) the Federal Bureau of Investigation;

(2) the Central Intelligence Agency;

(3) any other agency, or office, bureau, or entity within an agency, which has as a primary function intelligence, investigative, or security work, when the head of the agency determines, in his sole judgment, that the Order cannot be applied in a manner consistent with national security requirements and considerations; or

(4) any office, bureau, or entity within an agency which has as a primary function investigation or audit of the conduct or work of officials or employees of the agency for the purpose of ensuring honesty and integrity in the discharge of their official duties, when the head of the agency determines, in his sole judgment, that the Order cannot be applied in a manner consistent with the internal security of the agency.

(c) The head of an agency may, in his sole judgment, suspend any provision of this Order (except section 22) with respect to any agency installation or activity located outside the United States, when he determines that this is necessary in the national interest, subject to the conditions he prescribes.

(d) Employees engaged in administering a labor-management relations law or this Order shall not be represented by a labor organization which also represents other groups of employees under the law or this Order, or which is affiliated directly or indirectly with an organization which represents such a group of employees.

Administration

SEC. 4. FEDERAL LABOR RELATIONS COUNCIL. (a) There is hereby established the Federal Labor Relations Council, which consists of the Chairman of the Civil Service Commission, who shall be chairman of the Council, the Secretary of Labor, the Director of the Office of Management and Budget, and such other officials of the executive branch as the President may designate from time to time. The Civil Service Commission shall provide administrative support and services to the Council to the extent authorized by law.

(b) The Council shall administer and interpret this Order, decide major policy issues, prescribe regulations, and from time to time, report and make recommendations to the President.

(c) The Council may consider, subject to its regulations—

(1) appeals from decisions of the Assistant Secretary issued pursuant to section 6 of this Order;

(2) appeals on negotiability issues as provided in section 11 (c) of this Order;

(3) exceptions to arbitration awards; and

(4) other matters it deems appropriate to assure the effectuation of the purposes of this Order.

SEC. 5. FEDERAL SERVICE IMPASSES PANEL. (a) There is hereby established the Federal Service Impasses Panel as an agency within the Council. The Panel consists of at least three members appointed by the President, one of whom he designates as chairman. The Council shall provide the services and staff assistance needed by the Panel.

(b) The Panel may consider negotiation impasses as provided in section 17 of this Order and may take any action it considers necessary to settle an impasse.

(c) The Panel shall prescribe regulations needed to administer its function under this Order.

SEC. 6. ASSISTANT SECRETARY OF LABOR FOR LABOR-MANAGEMENT RELATIONS.

(a) The Assistant Secretary shall—

(1) decide questions as to the appropriate unit for the purpose of exclusive recognition and related issues submitted for his consideration;

(2) supervise elections to determine whether a labor organization is the choice of a majority of the employees in an appropriate unit as their exclusive representative, and certify the results;

(3) decide questions as to the eligibility of labor organizations for national consultation rights under criteria prescribed by the Council;

(4) decide unfair labor practice complaints and alleged violations of the standards of conduct for labor organizations; and

(5) decide questions as to whether a grievance is subject to a negotiated grievance procedure or subject to arbitration under an agreement.

(b) In any matters arising under paragraph (a) of this section, the Assistant Secretary may require an agency or a labor organization to cease and desist from violations of this Order and require it to take such affirmative action as he considers appropriate to effectuate the policies of this Order.

(c) In performing the duties imposed on him by this section, the Assistant Secretary may request and use the services and assistance of employees of other agencies in accordance with section 1 of the Act of March 4, 1915 (38 Stat. 1084, as amended; 31 U.S.C. §686).

(d) The Assistant Secretary shall prescribe regulations needed to administer his functions under this Order.

(e) If any matters arising under paragraph (a) of this section involve the Department of Labor, the duties of the Assistant Secretary described in paragraphs (a) and (b) of this section shall be performed by a member of the Civil Service Commission designated by the Chairman of the Commission.

Recognition

SEC. 7. RECOGNITION IN GENERAL. (a) An agency shall accord exclusive recognition or national consultation rights at the request of a labor organization which meets the requirements for the recognition or consultation rights under this Order.

(b) A labor organization seeking recognition shall submit to the agency a roster of its officers and representatives, a copy of its constitution and bylaws, and a statement of its objectives.

(c) When recognition of a labor organization has been accorded, the recognition continues as long as the organization continues to meet the requirements of this Order applicable to that recognition, except that this section does not require an election to determine whether an organization should become, or continue to be recognized as, exclusive representative of the employees in any unit or subdivision thereof within 12 months after a prior valid election with respect to such unit.

(d) Recognition of a labor organization does not

(1) preclude an employee, regardless of whether he is in a unit of exclusive recognition, from exercising grievance or appellate rights established by law or regulations; or from choosing his own representative in a grievance or appellate action, except when presenting a grievance under a negotiated procedure as provided in section 13;

(2) preclude or restrict consultations and dealings between an agency and a veterans organization with respect to matters of particular interest to employees with veterans preference; or

(3) preclude an agency from consulting or dealing with a religious, social, fraternal, professional or other lawful association, not qualified as a labor organization, with respect to matters or policies which involve individual members of the association or are of particular applicability to it or its members. Consultations and dealings under subparagraph (3) of this paragraph shall be so limited that they do not assume the character of formal consultation on matters of general employee-management policy, except as provided in paragraph (e) of this section, or extend to areas where recognition of the interests of one employee group may result in discrimination against or injury to the interests of other employees.

(e) An agency shall establish a system for intramanagement communication and consultation with its supervisors or associations of supervisors. These communications and consultations shall have as their purposes the improvement of agency operations, the improvement of working conditions of supervisors, the exchange of information, the improvement of managerial effectiveness, and the establishment of policies that best serve the public interest in accomplishing the mission of the agency.

(f) Informal recognition or formal recognition shall not be accorded.

SEC. 8. (Revoked)

SEC. 9. NATIONAL CONSULTATION RIGHTS. (a) An agency shall accord national consultation rights to a labor organization which qualifies under criteria established by the Federal Labor Relations Council as the representative of a substantial number of employees of the agency. National consultation rights shall not be accorded for any unit where a labor organization already holds exclusive recognition at the national level for that unit. The granting of national consultation rights does not preclude an agency from appropriate dealings at the national level with other organizations on matters affecting their members. An agency shall terminate national consultation rights when the labor organization ceases to qualify under the established criteria.

(b) When a labor organization has been accorded national consultation rights, the agency, through appropriate officials, shall notify representatives of the organization of proposed substantive changes in personnel policies that affect employees it represents and provide an opportunity for the organization to comment on the proposed changes. The labor organization may suggest changes in the agency's personnel policies and have its views carefully considered. It may confer in person at reasonable times, on request, with appropriate officials on personnel policy matters, and at all times present its views thereon in writing. An agency is not required to consult with a labor organization on any matter on which it would not be required to meet and confer if the organization were entitled to exclusive recognition.

(c) Questions as to the eligibility of labor organizations for national consultation rights may be referred to the Assistant Secretary for decision.

SEC. 10. EXCLUSIVE RECOGNITION. (a) An agency shall accord exclusive recognition to a labor organization when the organization has been selected, in a secret ballot election, by a majority of the employees in an appropriate unit as their representative.

(b) A unit may be established on a plant or installation, craft, functional, or other basis which will ensure a clear and identifiable community of interest among the employees concerned and will promote effective dealings and efficiency of agency operations. A unit shall not be established solely on the basis of the extent to which employees in the proposed unit have organized, nor shall a unit be established if it includes—

(1) any management official or supervisor, except as provided in section 24;

(2) an employee engaged in Federal personnel work in other than a purely clerical capacity;

(3) any guard together with other employees; or

(4) both professional and nonprofessional employees, unless a majority of the professional employees vote for inclusion in the unit.

Questions as to the appropriate unit and related issues may be referred to the Assistant Secretary for decision.

(c) An agency shall not accord exclusive recognition to a labor organization as the representative of employees in a unit of guards if the organization admits to membership, or is affiliated directly or indirectly with an organization which admits to membership, employees other than guards.

(d) All elections shall be conducted under the supervision of the Assistant Secretary, or persons designated by him, and shall be by secret ballot. Each employee eligible to vote shall be provided the opportunity to choose the labor organization he wishes to represent him, from among those on the ballot, or "no union." Elections may be held to determine whether—

(1) a labor organization should be recognized as the exclusive representative of employees in a unit;

(2) a labor organization should replace another labor organization as the exclusive representative; or

(3) a labor organization should cease to be the exclusive representative.

(e) When a labor organization has been accorded exclusive recognition, it is the exclusive representative of employees in the unit and is entitled to act for and to negotiate agreements covering all employees in the unit. It is responsible for representing the interests of all employees in the unit without discrimination and without regard to labor organization membership. The labor organization shall be given the opportunity to be represented at formal discussions between management and employees or employee representatives concerning grievances, personnel policies and practices, or other matters affecting general working conditions of employees in the unit.

Agreements

SEC. 11. NEGOTIATION OF AGREEMENTS. (a) An agency and a labor organization that has been accorded exclusive recognition, through appropriate representatives, shall meet at reasonable times and confer in good faith with respect to personnel policies and practices and matters affecting working conditions, so far as may be appropriate under applicable laws and regulations, including policies set forth in the Federal Personnel Manual, published agency policies and regulations, a national or other controlling agreement at a higher level in the agency, and this Order. They may negotiate an agreement, or any question arising thereunder; determine appropriate techniques, consistent with section 17 of this Order, to assist in such negotiation; and execute a written agreement or memorandum of understanding.

(b) In prescribing regulations relating to personnel policies and practices and working conditions, an agency shall have due regard for the obligation imposed by paragraph (a) of this section. However, the obligation to meet and confer does not include matters with respect to the mission of an agency; its budget; its organization; the number of employees; and the numbers, types, and grades of positions or employees assigned to an organizational unit, work project or tour of duty; the technology of performing its work; or its internal security practices. This does not preclude the parties from negotiating agreements providing appropriate arrangements for employees adversely affected by the impact of realignment of work forces or technological change.

(c) If, in connection with negotiations, an issue develops as to whether a proposal is contrary to law, regulation, controlling agreement, or this Order and therefore not negotiable, it shall be resolved as follows:

(1) An issue which involves interpretation of a controlling agreement at a higher agency level is resolved under the procedures of the controlling agreement, or, if none, under agency regulations;

(2) An issue other than as described in subparagraph (1) of this paragraph which arises at a local level may be referred by either party to the head of the agency for determination;

(3) An agency head's determination as to the interpretation of the agency's regulations with respect to a proposal is final;

(4) A labor organization may appeal to the Council for a decision when—

(i) it disagrees with an agency head's determination that a proposal would violate applicable law, regulation of appropriate authority outside the agency, or this Order, or

(ii) it believes that an agency's regulations, as interpreted by the agency head, violate applicable law, regulation of appropriate authority outside the agency, or this Order.

SEC. 12. BASIC PROVISIONS OF AGREEMENTS. Each agreement between an agency and a labor organization is subject to the following requirements—

(a) in the administration of all matters covered by the agreement, officials and employees are governed by existing or future laws and the regulations of appropriate authorities, including policies set forth in the Federal Personnel Manual; by published agency policies and regulations in existence at the time the agreement was approved; and by subsequently published agency policies and regulations required by law or by the regulations of appropriate authorities, or authorized by the terms of a controlling agreement at a higher agency level;

(b) management officials of the agency retain the right, in accordance with applicable laws and regulations—

(1) to direct employees of the agency;

(2) to hire, promote, transfer, assign, and retain employees in positions within the agency, and to suspend, demote, discharge, or take other disciplinary action against employees;

(3) to relieve employees from duties because of lack of work or for other legitimate reasons;

(4) to maintain the efficiency of the Government operations entrusted to them;

(5) to determine the methods, means, and personnel by which such operations are to be conducted; and

(6) to take whatever actions may be necessary to carry out the mission of the agency in situations of emergency; and

(c) nothing in the agreement shall require an employee to become or to remain a member of a labor organization, or to pay money to the organization except pursuant to a voluntary, written authorization by a member for the payment of dues through payroll deductions.

The requirements of this section shall be expressly stated in the initial or basic agreement and apply to all supplemental, implementing, subsidiary, or informal agreements between the agency and the organization.

SEC. 13. GRIEVANCE AND ARBITRATION PROCEDURES. (a) An agreement between an agency and a labor organization shall provide a procedure, applicable only to the unit, for the consideration of grievances over the interpretation or application of the agreement. A negotiated grievance procedure may not cover any other matters, including matters for which statutory appeals procedures exist, and shall be the exclusive procedure available to the parties and the employees in the unit for resolving such grievances. However, any employee or group of employees in the unit may present such grievances to the agency and have them adjusted, without the intervention of the exclusive representative, as long as the adjustment is not inconsistent with the terms of the agreement and the exclusive representative has been given opportunity to be present at the adjustment.

(b) A negotiated procedure may provide for the arbitration of grievances over the interpretation or application of the agreement, but not over any other matters. Arbitration may be invoked only by the agency or the exclusive representative. Either party may file exceptions to an arbitrator's award with the Council, under regulations prescribed by the Council.

(c) Grievances initiated by an employee or group of employees in the unit on matters other than the interpretation or application of an existing agreement may be presented under any procedure available for the purpose.

(d) Questions that cannot be resolved by the parties as to whether or not a grievance is on a matter subject to the grievance procedure in an existing agreement, or is subject to arbitration under that agreement, may be referred to the Assistant Secretary for decision.

(e) No agreement may be established, extended or renewed after the effective date of this Order which does not conform to this section. However, this section is not applicable to agreements entered into before the effective date of this Order.

SEC. 14. (Revoked)

SEC. 15. APPROVAL OF AGREEMENTS. An agreement with a labor organization as the exclusive representative of employees in a unit is subject to the approval of the head of the agency or an official designated by him. An agreement shall be approved if it conforms to applicable laws, existing published agency policies and regulations (unless the agency has granted an exception to a policy or regulation) and regulations of other appropriate authorities. A local agreement subject to a national or other controlling agreement at a higher level shall be approved under the procedures of the controlling agreement, or, if none, under agency regulations.

Negotiation Disputes and Impasses

Sec. 16. Negotiation Disputes. The Federal Mediation and Conciliation Service shall provide services and assistance to Federal agencies and labor organizations in the resolution of negotiation disputes. The Service shall determine under what circumstances and in what manner it shall proffer its services.

Sec. 17. Negotiation Impasses. When voluntary arrangements, including the services of the Federal Mediation and Conciliation Service or other third-party mediation, fail to resolve a negotiation impasse, either party may request the Federal Service Impasses Panel to consider the matter. The Panel, in its discretion and under the regulations it prescribes, may consider the matter and may recommend procedures to the parties for the resolution of the impasse or may settle the impasse by appropriate action. Arbitration or third-party fact-finding with recommendations to assist in the resolution of an impasse may be used by the parties only when authorized or directed by the Panel.

Conduct of Labor Organizations and Management

Sec. 18. Standards of Conduct for Labor Organizations.

(a) An agency shall accord recognition only to a labor organization that is free from corrupt influences and influences opposed to basic democratic principles. Except as provided in paragraph (b) of this section, an organization is not required to prove that it has the required freedom when it is subject to governing requirements adopted by the organization or by a national or international labor organization or federation of labor organizations with which it is affiliated or in which it participates, containing explicit and detailed provisions to which it subscribes calling for—

(1) the maintenance of democratic procedures and practices, including provisions for periodic elections to be conducted subject to recognized safeguards and provisions defining and securing the right of individual members to participation in the affairs of the organization, to fair and equal treatment under the governing rules of the organization, and to fair process in disciplinary proceedings;

(2) the exclusion from office in the organization of persons affiliated with Communist or other totalitarian movements and persons identified with corrupt influences;

(3) the prohibition of business or financial interests on the part of organization officers and agents which conflict with their duty to the organization and its members; and

(4) the maintenance of fiscal integrity in the conduct of the affairs of the organization, including provision for accounting and financial controls and regular financial reports or summaries to be made available to members.

(b) Notwithstanding the fact that a labor organization has adopted or subscribed to standards of conduct as provided in paragraph (a) of this section, the organization is required to furnish evidence of its freedom from corrupt influences or influences opposed to basic democratic principles when there is reasonable cause to believe that—

(1) the organization has been suspended or expelled from or is subject to other

sanction by a parent labor organization or federation of organizations with which it had been affiliated because it has demonstrated an unwillingness or inability to comply with governing requirements comparable in purpose to those required by paragraph (a) of this section; or

(2) the organization is in fact subject to influences that would preclude recognition under this Order.

(c) A labor organization which has or seeks recognition as a representative of employees under this Order shall file financial and other reports, provide for bonding of officials and employees of the organization, and comply with trusteeship and election standards.

(d) The Assistant Secretary shall prescribe the regulations needed to effectuate this section. These regulations shall conform generally to the principles applied to unions in the private sector. Complaints of violations of this section shall be filed with the Assistant Secretary.

Sec. 19. Unfair Labor Practices. (a) Agency management shall not—

(1) interfere with, restrain, or coerce an employee in the exercise of the rights assured by this Order;

(2) encourage or discourage membership in a labor organization by discrimination in regard to hiring, tenure, promotion, or other conditions of employment;

(3) sponsor, control, or otherwise assist a labor organization, except that an agency may furnish customary and routine services and facilities under section 23 of this Order when consistent with the best interests of the agency, its employees, and the organization, and when the services and facilities are furnished, if requested, on an impartial basis to organizations having equivalent status;

(4) discipline or otherwise discriminate against an employee because he has filed a complaint or given testimony under this Order;

(5) refuse to accord appropriate recognition to a labor organization qualified for such recognition; or

(6) refuse to consult, confer, or negotiate with a labor organization as required by this Order.

(b) A labor organization shall not—

(1) interfere with, restrain, or coerce an employee in the exercise of his rights assured by this Order;

(2) attempt to induce agency management to coerce an employee in the exercise of his rights under this Order;

(3) coerce, attempt to coerce, or discipline, fine, or take other economic sanction against a member of the organization as punishment or reprisal for, or for the purpose of hindering or impeding his work performance, his productivity, or the discharge of his duties owed as an officer or employee of the United States;

(4) call or engage in a strike, work stoppage, or slow-down; picket an agency in a labor-management dispute; or condone any such activity by failing to take affirmative action to prevent or stop it;

(5) discriminate against an employee with regard to the terms or conditions of membership because of race, color, creed, sex, age, or national origin; or

(6) refuse to consult, confer, or negotiate with an agency as required by this Order.

(c) A labor organization which is accorded exclusive recognition shall not deny membership to any employee in the appropriate unit except for failure to meet reasonable occupational standards uniformly required for admission, or for failure to tender initiation fees and dues uniformly required as a condition of acquiring and retaining membership. This paragraph does not preclude a labor organization from enforcing discipline in accordance with procedures under its constitution or bylaws which conform to the requirements of this Order.

(d) Issues which can properly be raised under an appeals procedure may not be raised under this section. Issues which can be raised under a grievance procedure may, in the discretion of the aggrieved party, be raised under that procedure or the complaint procedure under this section, but not under both procedures. Appeals or grievance decisions shall not be construed as unfair labor practice decisions under this Order nor as precedent for such decisions. All complaints under this section that cannot be resolved by the parties shall be filed with the Assistant Secretary.

Miscellaneous Provisions

SEC. 20. USE OF OFFICIAL TIME. Solicitation of membership or dues, and other internal business of a labor organization, shall be conducted during the nonduty hours of the employees concerned. Employees who represent a recognized labor organization shall not be on official time when negotiating an agreement with agency management, except to the extent that the negotiating parties agree to other arrangements which may provide that the agency will either authorize official time for up to 40 hours or authorize up to one-half the time spent in negotiations during regular working hours, for a reasonable number of employees, which number normally shall not exceed the number of management representatives.

SEC. 21. ALLOTMENT OF DUES. (a) When a labor organization holds formal or exclusive recognition, and the agency and the organization agree in writing to this course of action, an agency may deduct the regular and periodic dues of the organization from the pay of members of the organization in the unit of recognition who make a voluntary allotment for that purpose, and shall recover the costs of making the deductions. Such an allotment is subject to the regulations of the Civil Service Commission, which shall include provision for the employee to revoke his authorization at stated six-month intervals. Such an allotment terminates when—

(1) the dues withholding agreement between the agency and the labor organization is terminated or ceases to be applicable to the employee; or

(2) the employee has been suspended or expelled from the labor organization.

(b) An agency may deduct the regular and periodic dues of an association of management officials or supervisors from the pay of members of the association who make a voluntary allotment for that purpose, and shall recover the costs of making the deductions, when the agency and the association agree in writing to this course of action. Such an allotment is subject to the regulations of the Civil Service Commission.

SEC. 22. ADVERSE ACTION APPEALS. The head of each agency, in accordance with the provisions of this Order and regulations prescribed by the Civil Service Commission, shall extend to all employees in the competitive civil service rights identical in adverse action cases to those provided preference eligibles under sections 7511–7512 of title 5 of the United States Code. Each employee in the competitive service shall have the right to appeal to the Civil Service Commission from an adverse decision of the administrative officer so acting, such appeal to be processed in an identical manner to that provided for appeals under section 7701 of title 5 of the United States Code. Any recommendation by the Civil Service Commission submitted to the head of an agency on the basis of an appeal by an employee in the competitive service shall be complied with by the head of the agency.

SEC. 23. AGENCY IMPLEMENTATION. No later than April 1, 1970, each agency shall issue appropriate policies and regulations consistent with this Order for its implementation. This includes but is not limited to a clear statement of the rights of its employees under this Order; procedures with respect to recognition of labor organizations, determination of appropriate units, consultation and negotiation with labor organizations, approval of agreements, mediation, and impasse resolution; policies with respect to the use of agency facilities by labor organizations; and policies and practices regarding consultation with other organizations and associations and individual employees. Insofar as practicable, agencies shall consult with representatives of labor organizations in the formulation of these policies and regulations, other than those for the implementation of section 7(e) of this Order.

SEC. 24. SAVINGS CLAUSES. (a) This Order does not preclude—
    (1) the renewal or continuation of a lawful agreement between an agency and a representative of its employees entered into before the effective date of Executive Order No. 10988 (January 17, 1962); or
    (2) the renewal, continuation, or initial according of recognition for units of management officials or supervisors represented by labor organizations which historically or traditionally represent the management officials or supervisors in private industry and which hold exclusive recognition for units of such officials or supervisors in any agency on the date of this Order.
    (b) All grants of informal recognition under Executive Order No. 10988 terminate on July 1, 1970.
    (c) All grants of formal recognition under Executive Order No. 10988 terminate under regulations which the Federal Labor Relations Council shall issue before October 1, 1970.
    (d) By not later than December 31, 1970, all supervisors shall be excluded from units of formal and exclusive recognition and from coverage by negotiated agreements, except as provided in paragraph (a) of this section.

SEC. 25. GUIDANCE, TRAINING, REVIEW AND INFORMATION. (a) The Civil Service Commission, in conjunction with the Office of Management and Budget, shall establish and maintain a program for the policy guidance of agencies on labor-management relations in the Federal service and periodically review the implementation of these policies. The Civil Service Commission shall continuously review the operation of the Federal labor-management relations program to assist in assuring adherence to its provisions and merit system requirements; implement technical advice and information programs for the agencies; assist in the development of programs for training agency personnel and management officials in labor-management relations; and, from time to time, report to the Council on the state of the program with any recommendations for its improvement.
    (b) The Department of Labor and the Civil Service Commission shall develop

programs for the collection and dissemination of information appropriate to the needs of agencies, organizations and the public.

SEC. 26. EFFECTIVE DATE. This Order is effective on January 1, 1970, except sections 7 (f) and 8 which are effective immediately. Effective January 1, 1970, Executive Order No. 10988 and the President's Memorandum of May 21, 1963, entitled Standards of Conduct for Employee Organizations and Code of Fair Labor Practices, are revoked.

RICHARD NIXON

THE LANDRUM-GRIFFIN ACT

73 Stat. 519

Labor-Management Reporting and Disclosure Act of 1959

An Act

DECLARATION OF FINDINGS, PURPOSES, AND POLICY. SEC. 2. (a) The Congress finds that, in the public interest, it continues to be the responsibility of the Federal Government to protect employees' rights to organize, choose their own representatives, bargain collectively, and otherwise engage in concerted activities for their mutual aid or protection; that the relations between employers and labor organizations and the millions of workers they represent have a substantial impact on the commerce of the Nation; and that in order to accomplish the objective of a free flow of commerce it is essential that labor organizations, employers, and their officials adhere to the highest standards of responsibility and ethical conduct in administering the affairs of their organizations, particularly as they affect labor-management relations.

(b) The Congress further finds, from recent investigations in the labor and management fields, that there have been a number of instances of breach of trust, corruption, disregard of the rights of individual employees, and other failures to observe high standards of responsibility and ethical conduct which require further and supplementary legislation that will afford necessary protection of the rights and interests of employees and the public generally as they relate to the activities of labor organizations, employers, labor relations consultants, and their officers and representatives.

(c) The Congress, therefore, further finds and declares that the enactment of this Act is necessary to eliminate or prevent improper practices on the part of labor organizations, employers, labor relations consultants, and their officers and representatives which distort and defeat the policies of the Labor Management Relations Act, 1947, as amended, and the Railway Labor Act, as amended, and have the tendency or necessary effect of burdening or obstructing commerce by (1) impairing the efficiency, safety, or operation of the instrumentalities of commerce; (2) occurring in the current of commerce; (3) materially affecting, restraining, or controlling the flow of raw materials or manufactured or processed goods into or from the channels of commerce, or the prices of such materials or goods in commerce; or (4) causing diminution of employment and wages in such volume as substantially to impair or disrupt the market for goods flowing into or from the channels of commerce.

DEFINITIONS. SEC. 3. For the purposes of titles I, II, III, IV, V (except section 505), and VI of this Act—

(a) "Commerce" means trade, traffic, commerce, transportation, transmission, or communication among the several States or between any State and any place outside thereof.

(b) "State" includes any State of the United States, the District of Columbia, Puerto Rico, the Virgin Islands, American Samoa, Guam, Wake Island, the Canal Zone, and Outer Continental Shelf lands defined in the Outer Continental Shelf Lands Act (43 U.S.C. 1331–1343).

(c) "Industry affecting commerce" means any activity, business, or industry in commerce or in which a labor dispute would hinder or obstruct commerce or the free flow of commerce and includes any activity or industry "affecting commerce" within the meaning of the Labor Management Relations Act, 1947, as amended, or the Railway Labor Act, as amended.

(d) "Person" includes one or more individuals, labor organizations, partnerships, associations, corporations, legal representatives, mutual companies, joint-stock companies, trusts, unincorporated organizations, trustees, trustees in bankruptcy, or receivers.

(e) "Employer" means any employer or any group or association of employers engaged in an industry affecting commerce (1) which is, with respect to employees engaged in an industry affecting commerce, an employer within the meaning of any law of the United States relating to the employment of any employees or (2) which may deal with any labor organization concerning grievances, labor disputes, wages, rates of pay, hours of employment, or conditions of work, and includes any person acting directly or indirectly as an employer or as an agent of an employer in relation to an employee but does not include the United States or any corporation wholly owned by the Government of the United States or any State or political subdivision thereof.

(f) "Employee" means any individual employed by an employer, and includes any individual whose work has ceased as a consequence of, or in connection with, any current labor dispute or because of any unfair labor practice or because of exclusion or expulsion from a labor organization in any manner or for any reason inconsistent with the requirements of this Act.

(g) "Labor dispute" includes any controversy concerning terms, tenure, or conditions of employment, or concerning the association or representation of persons in negotiating, fixing, maintaining, changing, or seeking to arrange terms or conditions of employment, regardless of whether the disputants stand in the proximate relation of employer and employee.

(h) "Trusteeship" means any receivership, trusteeship, or other method of supervision or control whereby a labor organization suspends the autonomy otherwise available to a subordinate body under its constitution or bylaws.

(i) "Labor organization" means a labor organization engaged in an industry affecting commerce and includes any organization of any kind, any agency, or employee representation committee, group, association, or plan so engaged in which employees participate and which exists for the purpose, in whole or in part, of dealing with employers concerning grievances, labor disputes, wages, rates of pay, hours, or other terms or conditions of employment, and any conference, general committee, joint or system board, or joint council so engaged which is subordinate to a national or international labor organization, other than a State or local central body.

(j) A labor organization shall be deemed to be engaged in an industry affecting commerce if it—

1. is the certified representative of employees under the provisions of the National Labor Relations Act, as amended, or the Railway Labor Act, as amended; or
2. although not certified, is a national or international labor organization or a local labor organization recognized or acting as the representative of employees of an employer or employers engaged in an industry affecting commerce; or
3. has chartered a local labor organization or subsidiary body which is representing or actively seeking to represent employees of employers within the meaning of paragraph (1) or (2); or
4. has been chartered by a labor organization representing or actively seeking to represent employees within the meaning of paragraph (1) or (2) as the local or subordinate body through which such employees may enjoy membership or become affiliated with such labor organization; or
5. is a conference, general committee, joint or system board, or joint council, subordinate to a national or international labor organization, which includes a labor organization engaged in an industry affecting commerce within the meaning of any of the preceding paragraphs of this subsection, other than a State or local central body.

(k) "Secret ballot" means the expression by ballot, voting machine, or otherwise, but in no event by proxy, of a choice with respect to any election or vote taken upon any matter, which is cast in such a manner that the person expressing such choice cannot be identified with the choice expressed.

(l) "Trust in which a labor organization is interested" means a trust or other fund or organization (1) which was created or established by a labor organization, or one or more of the trustees or one or more members of the governing body of which is selected or appointed by a labor organization, and (2) a primary purpose of which is to provide benefits for the members of such labor organization or their beneficiaries.

(m) "Labor relations consultant" means any person who, for compensation, advises or represents an employer, employer organization, or labor organization concerning employee organizing, concerted activities, or collective bargaining activities.

(n) "Officer" means any constitutional officer, any person authorized to perform the functions of president, vice president, secretary, treasurer, or other executive functions of a labor organization, and any member of its executive board or similar governing body.

(o) "Member" or "member in good standing," when used in reference to a labor organization, includes any person who has fulfilled the requirements for membership in such organization, and who neither has voluntarily withdrawn from membership nor has been expelled or suspended from membership after appropriate proceedings consistent with lawful provisions of the constitution and bylaws of such organization.

(p) "Secretary" means the Secretary of Labor.

(q) "Officer, agent, shop steward, or other representative," when used with respect to a labor organization, includes elected officials and key administrative personnel, whether elected or appointed (such as business agents, heads of departments or major units, and organizers who exercise substantial independent authority), but does not include salaried nonsupervisory professional staff, stenographic, and service personnel.

(r) "District court of the United States" means a United States district court and a United States court of any place subject to the jurisdiction of the United States.

TITLE I

BILL OF RIGHTS OF MEMBERS OF LABOR ORGANIZATIONS

BILL OF RIGHTS. SEC. 101.(a)(1) EQUAL RIGHTS.—Every member of a labor organization shall have equal rights and privileges within such organization to nominate candidates, to vote in elections or referendums of the labor organization, to attend membership meetings, and to participate in the deliberations and voting upon the business of such meetings, subject to reasonable rules and regulations in such organization's constitution and bylaws.

(2) FREEDOM OF SPEECH AND ASSEMBLY.—Every member of any labor organization shall have the right to meet and assemble freely with other members; and to express any views, arguments, or opinions; and to express at meetings of the labor organization his views, upon candidates in an election of the labor organization or upon any business properly before the meeting, subject to the organization's established and reasonable rules pertaining to the conduct of meetings: *Provided,* That nothing herein shall be construed to impair the right of a labor organization to adopt and enforce reasonable rules as to the responsibility of every member toward the organization as an institution and to his refraining from conduct that would interfere with its performance of its legal or contractual obligations.

(3) DUES, INITIATION FEES, AND ASSESSMENTS.—Except in the case of a federation of national or international labor organizations, the rates of dues and initiation fees payable by members of any labor organization in effect on the date of enactment of this Act shall not be increased, and no general or special assessment shall be levied upon such members, except—

A. in the case of a local labor organization, (i) by majority vote by secret ballot of the members in good standing voting at a general or special membership meeting, after reasonable notice of the intention to vote upon such question, or (ii) by majority vote of the members in good standing voting in a membership referendum conducted by secret ballot; or

B. in the case of a labor organization, other than a local labor organization or a federation of national or international labor organizations, (i) by majority vote of the delegates voting at a regular convention, or at a special convention of such labor organization held upon not less than thirty days' written notice to the principal office of each local or constituent labor organization entitled to such notice, or (ii) by majority vote of the members in good standing of such labor organization voting in a membership referendum conducted by secret ballot, or (iii) by majority vote of the members of the executive board or similar governing body of such labor organization, pursuant to express authority contained in the constitution and bylaws of such labor organization: *Provided,* That such action on the part of the executive board or similar governing body shall be effective only until the next regular convention of such labor organization.

(4) PROTECTION OF THE RIGHT TO SUE.—No labor organization shall limit the right of any member thereof to institute an action in any court, or in a

proceeding before any administrative agency, irrespective of whether or not the labor organization or its officers are named as defendants or respondents in such action or proceeding, or the right of any member of a labor organization to appear as a witness in any judicial, administrative, or legislative proceeding, or to petition any legislature or to communicate with any legislator: *Provided,* That any such member may be required to exhaust reasonable hearing procedures (but not to exceed a four-month lapse of time) within such organization, before instituting legal or administrative proceedings against such organizations or any officer thereof: *And provided further,* That no interested employer or employer association shall directly or indirectly finance, encourage, or participate in, except as a party, any such action, proceeding, appearance, or petition.

(5) Safeguards Against Improper Disciplinary Action.—No member of any labor organization may be fined, suspended, expelled, or otherwise disciplined except for nonpayment of dues by such organization or by any officer thereof unless such member has been (A) served with written specific charges; (B) given a reasonable time to prepare his defense; (C) afforded a full and fair hearing.

(b) Any provision of the constitution and bylaws of any labor organization which is inconsistent with the provisions of this section shall be of no force or effect.

Civil Enforcement. Sec. 102. Any person whose rights secured by the provisions of this title have been infringed by any violation of this title may bring a civil action in a district court of the United States for such relief (including injunctions) as may be appropriate. Any such action against a labor organization shall be brought in the district court of the United States for the district where the alleged violation occurred, or where the principal office of such labor organization is located.

Retention of Existing Rights. Sec. 103. Nothing contained in this title shall limit the rights and remedies of any member of a labor organization under any State or Federal law or before any court or other tribunal, or under the constitution and bylaws of any labor organization.

Right to Copies of Collective Bargaining Agreements. Sec. 104. It shall be the duty of the secretary or corresponding principal officer of each labor organization, in the case of a local labor organization, to forward a copy of each collective bargaining agreement made by such labor organization with any employer to any employee who requests such a copy and whose rights as such employee are directly affected by such agreement, and in the case of a labor organization other than a local labor organization, to forward a copy of any such agreement to each constituent unit which has members directly affected by such agreement; and such officer shall maintain at the principal office of the labor organization of which he is an officer copies of any such agreement made or received by such labor organization, which copies shall be available for inspection by any member or by any employee whose rights are affected by such agreement. The provisions of section 210 shall be applicable in the enforcement of this section.

Information as to Act. Sec. 105. Every labor organization shall inform its members concerning the provisions of this Act.

TITLE II

REPORTING BY LABOR ORGANIZATIONS, OFFICERS AND EMPLOYEES OF LABOR ORGANIZATIONS, AND EMPLOYERS

REPORT OF LABOR ORGANIZATIONS. SEC. 201. (a) Every labor organization shall adopt a constitution and bylaws and shall file a copy thereof with the Secretary, together with a report, signed by its president and secretary or corresponding principal officers, containing the following information—

1. the name of the labor organization, its mailing address, and any other address at which it maintains its principal office or at which it keeps the records referred to in this title;
2. the name and title of each of its officers;
3. the initiation fee or fees required from a new or transferred member and fees for work permits required by the reporting labor organization;
4. the regular dues or fees or other periodic payments required to remain a member of the reporting labor organization; and
5. detailed statements, or references to specific provisions of documents filed under this subsection which contain such statements, showing the provision made and procedures followed with respect to each of the following: (A) qualifications for or restrictions on membership, (B) levying of assessments, (C) participation in insurance or other benefit plans, (D) authorization for disbursement of funds of the labor organization, (E) audit of financial transactions of the labor organization, (F) the calling of regular and special meetings, (G) the selection of officers and stewards and of any representatives to other bodies composed of labor organizations' representatives, with a specific statement of the manner in which each officer was elected, appointed, or otherwise selected, (H) discipline or removal of officers or agents for breaches of their trust, (I) imposition of fines, suspensions, and expulsions of members, including the grounds for such action and any provision made for notice, hearing, judgment on the evidence, and appeal procedures, (J) authorization for bargaining demands, (K) ratification of contract terms, (L) authorization for strikes, and (M) issuance of work permits. Any change in the information required by this subsection shall be reported to the Secretary at the time the reporting labor organization files with the Secretary the annual financial report required by subsection (b).

(b) Every labor organization shall file annually with the Secretary a financial report signed by its president and treasurer or corresponding principal officers containing the following information in such detail as may be necessary accurately to disclose its financial condition and operations for its preceding fiscal year—

1. assets and liabilities at the beginning and end of the fiscal year;
2. receipts of any kind and the sources thereof;
3. salary, allowances, and other direct or indirect disbursements (including reimbursed expenses) to each officer and also to each employee who, during such fiscal year, received more than $10,000 in the aggregate from such labor organization and any other labor organization affiliated with it or with which it

is affiliated, or which is affiliated with the same national or international labor organization;

4. direct and indirect loans made to any officer, employee, or member, which aggregated more than $250 during the fiscal year, together with a statement of the purpose, security, if any, and arrangements for repayment;

5. direct and indirect loans to any business enterprise, together with a statement of the purpose, security, if any, and arrangements for repayment; and

6. other disbursements made by it including the purposes thereof;

all in such categories as the Secretary may prescribe.

(c) Every labor organization required to submit a report under this title shall make available the information required to be contained in such report to all of its members, and every such labor organization and its officers shall be under a duty enforceable at the suit of any member of such organization in any State court of competent jurisdiction or in the district court of the United States for the district in which such labor organization maintains its principal office, to permit such member for just cause to examine any books, records, and accounts necessary to verify such report. The court in such action may, in its discretion, in addition to any judgment awarded to the plaintiff or plaintiffs, allow a reasonable attorney's fee to be paid by the defendant, and costs of the action.

(d) Subsections (f), (g), and (h) of section 9 of the National Labor Relations Act, as amended, are hereby repealed.

(e) Clause (i) of section 8(a)(3) of the National Labor Relations Act, as amended, is amended by striking out the following: "and has at the time the agreement was made or within the preceding twelve months received from the Board a notice of compliance with sections 9 (f), (g), (h)".

REPORT OF OFFICERS AND EMPLOYEES OF LABOR ORGANIZATIONS. SEC. 202. (a) Every officer of a labor organization and every employee of a labor organization (other than an employee performing exclusively clerical or custodial services) shall file with the Secretary a signed report listing and describing for his preceding fiscal year—

1. any stock, bond, security, or other interest, legal or equitable, which he or his spouse or minor child directly or indirectly held in, and any income or any other benefit with monetary value (including reimbursed expenses) which he or his spouse or minor child derived directly or indirectly from, an employer whose employees such labor organization represents or is actively seeking to represent, except payments and other benefits received as a bona fide employee of such employer;

2. any transaction in which he or his spouse or minor child engaged, directly or indirectly, involving any stock, bond, security, or loan to or from, or other legal or equitable interest in the business of an employer whose employees such labor organization represents or is actively seeking to represent;

3. any stock, bond, security, or other interest, legal or equitable, which he or his spouse or minor child directly or indirectly held in, and any income or any other benefit with monetary value (including reimbursed expenses) which he or his spouse or minor child directly or indirectly derived from, any business a substantial part of which consists of buying from, selling or leasing to, or otherwise dealing with, the business of an employer whose employees such labor organization represents or is actively seeking to represent;

4. any stock, bond, security, or other interest, legal or equitable, which he or his spouse or minor child directly or indirectly held in, and any income or any other benefit with monetary value (including reimbursed expenses) which he or his spouse or minor child directly or indirectly derived from, a business any part of which consists of buying from, or selling or leasing directly or indirectly to, or otherwise dealing with such labor organization;

5. any direct or indirect business transaction or arrangement between him or his spouse or minor child and any employer whose employees his organization represents or is actively seeking to represent, except work performed and payments and benefits received as a bona fide employee of such employer and except purchases and sales of goods or services in the regular course of business at prices generally available to any employee of such employer; and

6. any payment of money or other thing of value (including reimbursed expenses) which he or his spouse or minor child received directly or indirectly from any employer or any person who acts as a labor relations consultant to an employer, except payments of the kinds referred to in section 302(c) of the Labor Management Relations Act, 1947, as amended.

(b) The provisions of paragraphs (1), (2), (3), (4), and (5) of subsection (a) shall not be construed to require any such officer or employee to report his bona fide investments in securities traded on a securities exchange registered as a national securities exchange under the Securities Exchange Act of 1934, in shares in an investment company registered under the Investment Company Act of 1940, or in securities of a public utility holding company registered under the Public Utility Holding Company Act of 1935, or to report any income derived therefrom.

(c) Nothing contained in this section shall be construed to require any officer or employee of a labor organization to file a report under subsection (a) unless he or his spouse or minor child holds or has held an interest, has received income or any other benefit with monetary value or a loan, or has engaged in a transaction described therein.

REPORT OF EMPLOYERS. SEC. 203. (a) Every employer who in any fiscal year made—

1. any payment or loan, direct or indirect, of money or other thing of value (including reimbursed expenses), or any promise or agreement therefor, to any labor organization or officer, agent, shop steward, or other representative of a labor organization, or employee of any labor organization, except (A) payments or loans made by any national or State bank, credit union, insurance company, savings and loan association or other credit institution and (B) payments of the kind referred to in section 302(c) of the Labor Management Relations Act, 1947, as amended;

2. any payment (including reimbursed expenses) to any of his employees, or any group or committee of such employees, for the purpose of causing such employee or group or committee of employees to persuade other employees to exercise or not to exercise, or as the manner of exercising, the right to organize and bargain collectively through representatives of their own choosing unless such payments were contemporaneously or previously disclosed to such other employees;

3. any expenditure, during the fiscal year, where an object thereof, directly or indirectly, is to interfere with, restrain, or coerce employees in the exercise of the right to organize and bargain collectively through representatives of their

own choosing, or is to obtain information concerning the activities of employees or a labor organization in connection with a labor dispute involving such employer, except for use solely in conjunction with an administrative or arbitral proceeding or a criminal or civil judicial proceeding;

4. any agreement or arrangement with a labor relations consultant or other independent contractor or organization pursuant to which such person undertakes activities where an object thereof, directly or indirectly, is to persuade employees to exercise or not to exercise, or persuade employees as to the manner of exercising, the right to organize and bargain collectively through representatives of their own choosing, or undertakes to supply such employer with information concerning the activities of employees or a labor organization in connection with a labor dispute involving such employer, except information for use solely in conjunction with an administrative or arbitral proceeding or a criminal or civil judicial proceeding; or

5. any payment (including reimbursed expenses) pursuant to an agreement or arrangement described in subdivision (4);

shall file with the Secretary a report, in a form prescribed by him, signed by its president and treasurer or corresponding principal officers showing in detail the date and amount of each such payment, loan, promise, agreement, or arrangement and the name, address, and position, if any, in any firm or labor organization of the person to whom it was made and a full explanation of the circumstances of all such payments, including the terms of any agreement or understanding pursuant to which they were made.

(d) Every person who pursuant to any agreement or arrangement with an employer undertakes activities where an object thereof is, directly or indirectly—

1. to persuade employees to exercise or not to exercise, or persuade employees as to the manner of exercising, the right to organize and bargain collectively through representatives of their own choosing; or

2. to supply an employer with information concerning the activities of employees or a labor organization in connection with a labor dispute involving such employer, except information for use solely in conjunction with an administrative or arbitral proceeding or a criminal or civil judicial proceeding;

shall file within thirty days after entering into such agreement or arrangement a report with the Secretary, signed by its president and treasurer or corresponding principal officers, containing the name under which such person is engaged in doing business and the address of its principal office, and a detailed statement of the terms and conditions of such agreement or arrangement. Every such person shall file annually, with respect to each fiscal year during which payments were made as a result of such an agreement or arrangement, a report with the Secretary, signed by its president and treasurer or corresponding principal officers, containing a statement (A) of its receipts of any kind from employers on account of labor relations advice or services, designating the sources thereof, and (B) of its disbursements of any kind, in connection with such services and the purposes thereof. In each such case such information shall be set forth in such categories as the Secretary may prescribe.

(e) Nothing in this section shall be construed to require any employer or other person to file a report covering the services of such person by reason of his giving or agreeing to give advice to such employer or representing or agreeing to represent such employer before any court, administrative agency, or tribunal of arbitration or engaging or agreeing to engage in collective bargaining on behalf of such employer with respect to wages, hours, or other terms or conditions of employment or the negotiation of an agreement or any question arising thereunder.

(d) Nothing contained in this section shall be construed to require an employer to file a report under subsection (a) unless he has made an expenditure, payment, loan, agreement, or arrangement of the kind described therein. Nothing contained in this section shall be construed to require any other person to file a report under subsection (b) unless he was a party to an agreement or arrangement of the kind described therein.

(e) Nothing contained in this section shall be construed to require any regular officer, supervisor, or employee of an employer to file a report in connection with services rendered to such employer nor shall any employer be required to file a report covering expenditures made to any regular officer, supervisor, or employee of an employer as compensation for service as a regular officer, supervisor, or employee of such employer.

(f) Nothing contained in this section shall be construed as an amendment to, or modification of the rights protected by, section 8(c) of the National Labor Relations Act, as amended.

(g) The term "interfere with, restrain, or coerce" as used in this section means interference, restraint, and coercion which, if done with respect to the exercise of rights guaranteed in section 7 of the National Labor Relations Act, as amended, would, under section 8(a) of such Act, constitute an unfair labor practice.

ATTORNEY-CLIENT COMMUNICATIONS EXEMPTED. SEC. 204. Nothing contained in this Act shall be construed to require an attorney who is a member in good standing of the bar of any State, to include in any report required to be filed pursuant to the provisions of this Act any information which was lawfully communicated to such attorney by any of his clients in the course of a legitimate attorney-client relationship.

REPORTS MADE PUBLIC INFORMATION. SEC. 205. (a) The contents of the reports and documents filed with the Secretary pursuant to sections 201, 202, and 203 shall be public information, and the Secretary may publish any information and data which he obtains pursuant to the provisions of this title. The Secretary may use the information and data for statistical and research purposes, and compile and publish such studies, analyses, reports, and surveys based thereon as he may deem appropriate.

(b) The Secretary shall by regulation make reasonable provision for the inspection and examination, on the request of any person, of the information and data contained in any report or other document filed with him pursuant to section 201, 202, or 203.

(c) The Secretary shall by regulation provide for the furnishing by the Department of Labor of copies of reports or other documents filed with the Secretary pursuant to this title, upon payment of a charge based upon the cost of the service. The Secretary shall make available without payment of a charge, or require any person to furnish, to such State agency as is designated by law or by the Governor of the State in which such person has his principal place of business or headquarters, upon request of the Governor of such State, copies of any reports and documents filed by such person with the Secretary pursuant to section 201, 202, or 203, or of information and data contained therein. No person shall be required by reason of any law of any State to furnish to any officer or agency of such State any information included in a report filed by such person with the Secretary pursuant to the provisions of this title, if a copy of such report, or of the portion thereof containing such information, is furnished to such officer or agency. All moneys received in payment of such charges fixed by the Secretary pursuant to this subsection shall be deposited in the general fund of the Treasury.

RETENTION OF RECORDS. SEC. 206. Every person required to file any report under this title shall maintain records on the matters required to be reported which will provide in sufficient detail the necessary basic information and data from which the documents filed with the Secretary may be verified, explained or clarified, and checked for accuracy and completeness, and shall include vouchers, worksheets, receipts, and applicable resolutions, and shall keep such records available for examination for a period of not less than five years after the filing of the documents based on the information which they contain.

EFFECTIVE DATE. SEC. 207. (a) Each labor organization shall file the initial report required under section 201(a) within ninety days after the date on which it first becomes subject to this Act.

(b) Each person required to file a report under section 201(b), 202, 203(a), or the second sentence of 203(b) shall file such report within ninety days after the end of each of its fiscal years; except that where such person is subject to section 201(b), 202, 203(a), or the second sentence of 203(b), as the case may be, for only a portion of such a fiscal year (because the date of enactment of this Act occurs during such person's fiscal year or such person becomes subject to this Act during its fiscal year) such person may consider that portion as the entire fiscal year in making such report.

RULES AND REGULATIONS. SEC. 208. The Secretary shall have authority to issue, amend, and rescind rules and regulations prescribing the form and publication of reports required to be filed under this title and such other reasonable rules and regulations (including rules prescribing reports concerning trusts in which a labor organization is interested) as he may find necessary to prevent the circumvention or evasion of such reporting requirements. In exercising his power under this section the Secretary shall prescribe by general rule simplified reports for labor organizations or employers for whom he finds that by virtue of their size a detailed report would be unduly burdensome, but the Secretary may revoke such provision for simplified forms of any labor organization or employer if he determines, after such investigation as he deems proper and due notice and opportunity for a hearing, that the purposes of this section would be served thereby.

CRIMINAL PROVISIONS. SEC. 209. (a) Any person who willfully violates this title shall be fined not more than $10,000 or imprisoned for not more than one year, or both.

(b) Any person who makes a false statement or representation of a material fact, knowing it to be false, or who knowingly fails to disclose a material fact, in any document, report, or other information required under the provisions of this title shall be fined not more than $10,000 or imprisoned for not more than one year, or both.

(c) Any person who willfully makes a false entry in or willfully conceals, withholds, or destroys any books, records, reports, or statements required to be kept by any provision of this title shall be fined not more than $10,000 or imprisoned for not more than one year, or both.

(d) Each individual required to sign reports under sections 201 and 203 shall be personally responsible for the filing of such reports and for any statement contained therein which he knows to be false.

CIVIL ENFORCEMENT. SEC. 210. Whenever it shall appear that any person has violated or is about to violate any of the provisions of this title, the Secretary may bring a civil action for such relief (including injunctions) as may be appropriate. Any such action may be brought in the district court of the United States where the violation occurred or, at the option of the parties, in the United States District Court for the District of Columbia.

TITLE III

TRUSTEESHIPS

REPORTS. SEC. 301. (a) Every labor organization which has or assumes trusteeship over any subordinate labor organization shall file with the Secretary within thirty days after the date of the enactment of this Act or the imposition of any such trusteeship, and semiannually thereafter, a report, signed by its president and treasurer or corresponding principal officers, as well as by the trustees of such subordinate labor organization, containing the following information: (1) the name and address of the subordinate organization; (2) the date of establishing the trusteeship; (3) a detailed statement of the reason or reasons for establishing or continuing the trusteeship; and (4) the nature and extent of participation by the membership of the subordinate organization in the selection of delegates to represent such organization in regular or special conventions or other policy-determining bodies and in the election of officers of the labor organization which has assumed trusteeship over such subordinate organization. The initial report shall also include a full and complete account of the financial condition of such subordinate organization as of the time trusteeship was assumed over it. During the continuance of a trusteeship the labor organization which has assumed trusteeship over a subordinate labor organization shall file on behalf of the subordinate labor organization the annual financial report required by section 201(b) signed by the president and treasurer or corresponding principal officers of the labor organization which has assumed such trusteeship and the trustees of the subordinate labor organization.

(b) The provisions of section 201(c), 205, 206, 208, and 210 shall be applicable to reports filed under this title.

(c) Any person who willfully violates this section shall be fined not more than $10,000 or imprisoned for not more than one year, or both.

(d) Any person who makes a false statement or representation of a material fact, knowing it to be false, or who knowingly fails to disclose a material fact, in any report required under the provisions of this section or willfully makes any false entry in or willfully withholds, conceals, or destroys any documents, books, records, reports, or statements upon which such report is based, shall be fined not more than $10,000 or imprisoned for not more than one year, or both.

(e) Each individual required to sign a report under this section shall be personally responsible for the filing of such report and for any statement contained therein which he knows to be false.

Purposes for Which a Trusteeship May Be Established. Sec. 302. Trusteeships shall be established and administered by a labor organization over a subordinate body only in accordance with the constitution and bylaws of the organization which has assumed trusteeship over the subordinate body and for the purpose of correcting corruption or financial malpractice, assuring the performance of collective bargaining agreements or other duties of a bargaining representative, restoring democratic procedures, or otherwise carrying out the legitimate objects of such labor organization.

Unlawful Acts Relating to Labor Organization Under Trusteeship. Sec. 303. (a) During any period when a subordinate body of a labor organization is in trusteeship, it shall be unlawful (1) to count the vote of delegates from such body in any convention or election of officers of the labor organization unless the delegates have been chosen by secret ballot in an election in which all the members in good standing of such subordinate body were eligible to participate, or (2) to transfer to such organization any current receipts or other funds of the subordinate body except the normal per capita tax and assessments payable by subordinate bodies not in trusteeship: *Provided,* That nothing herein contained shall prevent the distribution of the assets of a labor organization in accordance with its constitution and bylaws upon the bona fide dissolution thereof.

(b) Any person who willfully violates this section shall be fined not more than $10,000 or imprisoned for not more than one year, or both.

Enforcement. Sec. 304. (a) Upon the written complaint of any member or subordinate body of a labor organization alleging that such organization has violated the provisions of this title (except section 301) the Secretary shall investigate the complaint and if the Secretary finds probable cause to believe that such violation has occurred and has not been remedied he shall, without disclosing the identity of the complainant, bring a civil action in any district court of the United States having jurisdiction of the labor organization for such relief (including injunctions) as may be appropriate. Any member or subordinate body of a labor organization affected by any violation of this title (except section 301) may bring a civil action in any district court of the United States having jurisdiction of the labor organization for such relief (including injunctions) as may be appropriate.

(b) For the purpose of actions under this section, district courts of the United States shall be deemed to have jurisdiction of a labor organization (1) in the district in which the principal office of such labor organization is located, or (2) in any district in which its duly authorized officers or agents are engaged in conducting the affairs of the trusteeship.

(c) In any proceeding pursuant to this section a trusteeship established by a labor organization in conformity with the procedural requirements of its constitution and bylaws and authorized or ratified after a fair hearing either before the executive board or before such other body as may be provided in accordance with its constitution or bylaws shall be presumed valid for a period of eighteen months from the date of its establishment and shall not be subject to attack during such period except upon clear and convincing proof that the trusteeship was not established or maintained in good faith for a purpose allowable under section 302. After the expiration of eighteen months the trusteeship shall be presumed invalid in any such proceeding and its discontinuance shall be decreed unless the labor organization shall show by clear and convincing proof that the continuation of the trusteeship is necessary for a purpose allowable under section 302. In the latter event the court may dismiss the complaint or retain jurisdiction of the cause on such conditions and for such period as it deems appropriate.

REPORT TO CONGRESS. SEC. 305. The Secretary shall submit to the Congress at the expiration of three years from the date of enactment of this Act a report upon the operation of this title.

COMPLAINT BY SECRETARY. SEC. 306. The rights and remedies provided by this title shall be in addition to any and all other rights and remedies at law or in equity: *Provided,* That upon the filing of a complaint by the Secretary the jurisdiction of the district court over such trusteeship shall be exclusive and the final judgment shall be res judicata.

TITLE IV

ELECTIONS

TERMS OF OFFICE; ELECTION PROCEDURES. SEC. 401. (a) Every national or international labor organization, except a federation of national or international labor organizations, shall elect its officers not less often than once every five years either by secret ballot among the members in good standing or at a convention of delegates chosen by secret ballot.

(b) Every local labor organization shall elect its officers not less often than once every three years by secret ballot among the members in good standing.

(c) Every national or international labor organization, except a federation of national or international labor organizations, and every local labor organization, and its officers, shall be under a duty, enforceable at the suit of any bona fide candidate for office in such labor organization in the district court of the United States in which such labor organization maintains its principal office, to comply with all reasonable requests of any candidate to distribute by mail or otherwise at the candidate's expense campaign literature in aid of such person's candidacy to all members in good standing of such labor organization and to refrain from discrimination in favor of or against any candidate with respect to the use of lists of members, and whenever such labor organizations or its officers authorize the distribution by mail or otherwise to members of campaign literature on behalf of any candidate or of the labor organization itself with reference to such election, similar distribution at the request of any other bona fide candidate shall be made by such labor organization and its officers, with equal treatment as to the expense of such distribution. Every bona fide candidate shall have the right, once within 30 days prior to an election of a labor organization in which he is a candidate, to inspect a list containing the names and last known addresses of all members of the labor organization who are subject to a collective bargaining agreement requiring membership therein as a condition of employment, which list shall be maintained and kept at the principal office of such labor organization by a designated official thereof. Adequate safeguards to insure a fair election shall be provided, including the right of any candidate to have an observer at the polls and at the counting of the ballots.

(d) Officers of intermediate bodies, such as general committees, system boards, joint boards, or joint councils, shall be elected not less often than once every four years by secret ballot among the members in good standing or by labor organization officers representative of such members who have been elected by secret ballot.

(e) In any election required by this section which is to be held by secret ballot a reasonable opportunity shall be given for the nomination of candidates and every member in good standing shall be eligible to be a candidate and to hold office (subject to section 504 and to reasonable qualifications uniformly imposed) and shall have the right to vote for or otherwise support the candidate or candidates of his choice, without being subject to penalty, discipline, or improper interference or reprisal of any kind by such organization or any member thereof. Not less than fifteen days prior to the election notice thereof shall be mailed to each member at his last known home address. Each member in good standing shall be entitled to one vote. No member whose dues have been withheld by his employer for payment to such organization pursuant to his voluntary authorization provided for in a collective bargaining agreement shall be declared ineligible to vote or be a candidate for office in such organization by reason of alleged delay or default in the payment of dues. The votes cast by members of each local labor organization shall be counted, and the results published, separately. The election officials designated in the constitution and bylaws or the secretary, if no other official is designated, shall preserve for one year the ballots and all other records pertaining to the election. The election shall be conducted in accordance with the constitution and bylaws of such organization insofar as they are not inconsistent with the provisions of this title.

(f) When officers are chosen by a convention of delegates elected by secret ballot, the convention shall be conducted in accordance with the constitution and bylaws of the labor organization insofar as they are not inconsistent with the provisions of this title. The officials designated in the constitution and bylaws or the secretary, if no other is designated, shall preserve for one year the credentials of the delegates and all minutes and other records of the convention pertaining to the election of officers.

(g) No moneys received by any labor organization by way of dues, assessment, or similar levy, and no moneys of an employer shall be contributed or applied to promote the candidacy of any person in an election subject to the provisions of this title. Such moneys of a labor organization may be utilized for notices, factual statements of issues not involving candidates, and other expenses necessary for the holding of an election.

(h) If the Secretary, upon application of any member of a local labor organization, finds after hearing in accordance with the Administrative Procedure Act that the constitution and bylaws of such labor organization do not provide an adequate procedure for the removal of an elected officer guilty of serious misconduct, such officer may be removed, for cause shown and after notice and hearing, by the members in good standing voting in a secret ballot conducted by the officers of such labor organization in accordance with its constitution and bylaws insofar as they are not inconsistent with the provisions of this title.

(i) The Secretary shall promulgate rules and regulations prescribing minimum standards and procedures for determining the adequacy of the removal procedures to which reference is made in subsection (h).

ENFORCEMENT. SEC. 402. (a) A member of a labor organization—

1. who has exhausted the remedies available under the constitution and bylaws of such organization and of any parent body, or
2. who has invoked such available remedies without obtaining a final decision within three calendar months after their invocation,

may file a complaint with the Secretary within one calendar month thereafter alleging the violation of any provision of section 401 (including violation of the constitution and bylaws of the labor organization pertaining to the election and removal of officers). The challenged election shall be presumed valid pending a final decision thereon (as hereinafter provided) and in the interim the affairs of the organization shall be conducted by the officers elected or in such other manner as its constitution and bylaws may provide.

(b) The Secretary shall investigate such complaint and, if he finds probable cause to believe that a violation of this title has occurred and has not been remedied, he shall, within sixty days after the filing of such complaint, bring a civil action against the labor organization as an entity in the district court of the United States in which such labor organization maintains its principal office to set aside the invalid election, if any, and to direct the conduct of an election or hearing and vote upon the removal of officers under the supervision of the Secretary and in accordance with the provisions of this title and such rules and regulations as the Secretary may prescribe. The court shall have power to take such action as it deems proper to preserve the assets of the labor organization.

(c) If, upon a preponderance of the evidence after a trial upon the merits, the court finds—

1. that an election has not been held within the time prescribed by section 401, or
2. that the violation of section 401 may have affected the outcome of an election,

the court shall declare the election, if any, to be void and direct the conduct of a new election under supervision of the Secretary and, so far as lawful and practicable, in conformity with the constitution and bylaws of the labor organization. The Secretary shall promptly certify to the court the names of the persons elected, and the court shall thereupon enter a decree declaring such persons to be the officers of the labor organization. If the proceeding is for the removal of officers pursuant to subsection (h) of section 401, the Secretary shall certify the results of the vote and the court shall enter a decree declaring whether such persons have been removed as officers of the labor organization.

(d) An order directing an election, dismissing a complaint, or designating elected officers of a labor organization shall be appealable in the same manner as the final judgment in a civil action, but an order directing an election shall not be stayed pending appeal.

Application of Other Laws. Sec. 403. No labor organization shall be required by law to conduct elections of officers with greater frequency or in a different form or manner than is required by its own constitution or bylaws, except as otherwise provided by this title. Existing rights and remedies to enforce the constitution and bylaws of a labor organization with respect to elections prior to the conduct thereof shall not be affected by the provisions of this title. The remedy provided by this title for challenging an election already conducted shall be exclusive.

Effective Date. Sec. 404. The provisions of this title shall become applicable—

1. ninety days after the date of enactment of this Act in the case of a labor organization whose constitution and bylaws can lawfully be modified or amended by action of its constitutional officers or governing body, or
2. where such modification can only be made by a constitutional convention of the labor organization, not later than the next constitutional convention of such labor organization after the date of enactment of this Act, or one year after such date, whichever is sooner. If no such convention is held within such one-year period, the executive board or similar governing body empowered to act for such labor organization between conventions is empowered to make such interim constitutional changes as are necessary to carry out the provisions of this title.

TITLE V

SAFEGUARDS FOR LABOR ORGANIZATIONS

Fiduciary Responsibility of Officers of Labor Organizations. Sec. 501. (a) The officers, agents, shop stewards, and other representatives of a labor organization occupy positions of trust in relation to such organization and its members as a group. It is, therefore, the duty of each such person, taking into account the special problems and functions of a labor organization, to hold its money and property solely for the benefit of the organization and its members and to manage, invest, and expend the same in accordance with its constitution and bylaws and any resolutions of the governing bodies adopted thereunder, to refrain from dealing with such organization as an adverse party or in behalf of an adverse party in any matter connected with his duties and from holding or acquiring any pecuniary or personal interest which conflicts with the interests of such organization, and to account to the organization for any profit received by him in whatever capacity in connection with transactions conducted by him or under his direction on behalf of the organization. A general exculpatory provision in the constitution and bylaws of such a labor organization or a general exculpatory resolution of a governing body purporting to relieve any such person of liability for breach of the duties declared by this section shall be void as against public policy.

(b) When any officer, agent, shop steward, or representative of any labor organization is alleged to have violated the duties declared in subsection (a) and the labor organization or its governing board or officers refuse or fail to sue or recover damages or secure an accounting or other appropriate relief within a reasonable time after being requested to do so by any member of the labor organization, such member may sue such officer, agent, shop steward, or representative in any district court of the United States or in any State court of competent jurisdiction to recover damages or secure an accounting or other appropriate relief for the benefit of the labor organization. No such proceeding shall be brought except upon leave of the court obtained upon verified application and for good cause shown, which application may be made ex parte. The trial judge may allot a reasonable part of the recovery in any action under this subsection to pay the fees of counsel prosecuting the suit at the instance of the member of the labor organization and to compensate such member for any expenses necessarily paid or incurred by him in connection with the litigation.

(c) Any person who embezzles, steals, or unlawfully and willfully abstracts or converts to his own use, or the use of another, any of the moneys, funds, securities, property, or other assets of a labor organization of which he is an officer, or by which he is employed, directly or indirectly, shall be fined not more than $10,000 or imprisoned for not more than five years, or both.

BONDING. SEC. 502. (a) Every officer, agent, shop steward, or other representative or employee of any labor organization (other than a labor organization whose property and annual financial receipts do not exceed $5,000 in value), or of a trust in which a labor organization is interested, who handles funds or other property thereof shall be bonded for the faithful discharge of his duties. The bond of each such person shall be fixed at the beginning of the organization's fiscal year and shall be in an amount not less than 10 per centum of the funds handled by him and his predecessor or predecessors, if any, during the preceding fiscal year, but in no case more than $500,000. If the labor organization or the trust in which a labor organization is interested does not have a preceding fiscal year, the amount of the bond shall be, in the case of a local labor organization, not less than $1,000, and in the case of any other labor organization or of a trust in which a labor organization is interested, not less than $10,000. Such bonds shall be individual or schedule in form, and shall have a corporate surety company as surety thereon. Any person who is not covered by such bonds shall not be permitted to receive, handle, disburse, or otherwise exercise custody or control of the funds or other property of a labor organization or of a trust in which a labor organization is interested. No such bond shall be placed through an agent or broker or with a surety company in which any labor organization or any officer, agent, shop steward, or other representative of a labor organization has any direct or indirect interest. Such surety company shall be a corporate surety which holds a grant of authority from the Secretary of the Treasury under the Act of July 30, 1947 (6 U.S.C. 6–13), as an acceptable surety on Federal bonds.

(b) Any person who willfully violates this section shall be fined not more than $10,000 or imprisoned for not more than one year, or both.

MAKING OF LOANS; PAYMENT OF FINES. SEC. 350. (a) No labor organization shall make directly or indirectly any loan or loans to any officer or employee of such organization which results in a total indebtedness on the part of such officer or employee to the labor organization in excess of $2,000.

(b) No labor organization or employer shall directly or indirectly pay the fine of any officer or employee convicted of any willful violation of this Act.

(c) Any person who willfully violates this section shall be fined not more than $5,000 or imprisoned for not more than one year, or both.

PROHIBITION AGAINST CERTAIN PERSONS HOLDING OFFICE. SEC. 504. (a) No person who is or has been a member of the Communist Party or who has been convicted of, or served any part of a prison term resulting from his conviction of, robbery, bribery, extortion, embezzlement, grand larceny, burglary, arson, violation of narcotics laws, murder, rape, assault with intent to kill, assault which inflicts grievous bodily injury, or a violation of title II or III of this Act, or conspiracy to commit any such crimes, shall serve—

1. as an officer, director, trustee, member of any executive board or similar governing body, business agent, manager, organizer, or other employee (other than as an employee performing exclusively clerical or custodial duties) of any labor organization, or
2. as a labor relations consultant to a person engaged in an industry or activity affecting commerce, or as an officer, director, agent, or employee (other than as an employee performing exclusively clerical or custodial duties) of any group or association of employers dealing with any labor organization,

during or for five years after the termination of his membership in the Communist Party, or for five years after such conviction or after the end of such imprisonment, unless prior to the end of such five-year period, in the case of a person so convicted or imprisoned, (A) his citizenship rights, having been revoked as a result of such conviction, have been fully restored, or (B) the Board of Parole of the United States Department of Justice determines that such person's service in any capacity referred to in clause (1) or (2) would not be contrary to the purposes of this Act. Prior to making any such determination the Board shall hold an administrative hearing and shall give notice of such proceeding by certified mail to the State, county, and Federal prosecuting officials in the jurisdiction or jurisdictions in which such person was convicted. The Board's determination in any such proceeding shall be final. No labor organization or officer thereof shall knowingly permit any person to assume or hold any office or paid position in violation of this subsection.

(b) Any person who willfully violates this section shall be fined not more than $10,000 or imprisoned for not more than one year, or both.

(c) For the purposes of this section, any person shall be deemed to have been "convicted" and under the disability of "conviction" from the date of the judgment of the trial court or the date of the final sustaining of such judgment on appeal, whichever is the later event, regardless of whether such conviction occurred before or after the date of enactment of this Act.

AMENDMENT TO SECTION 302, LABOR MANAGEMENT RELATIONS ACT, 1947. SEC. 505. Subsections (a), (b), and (c) of section 302 of the Labor Management Relations Act, 1947, as amended, are amended to read as follows:

"Sec. 302. (a) It shall be unlawful for any employer or association of employers or any person who acts as a labor relations expert, adviser, or consultant to an employer or who acts in the interest of an employer to pay, lend, or deliver, or agree to pay, lend, or deliver, any money or other thing of value—

"1. to any representative of any of his employees who are employed in an industry affecting commerce; or
"2. to any labor organization, or any officer or employee thereof, which represents, seeks to represent, or would admit to membership, any of the employees of such employer who are employed in an industry affecting commerce; or
"3. to any employee or group or committee of employees of such employer employed in an industry affecting commerce in excess of their normal compensation for the purpose of causing such employee or group or committee directly or indirectly to influence any other employees in the exercise of the right to organize and bargain collectively through representatives of their own choosing; or
"4. to any officer or employee of a labor organization engaged in an industry affecting commerce with intent to influence him in respect to any of his actions, decisions, or duties as a representative of employees or as such officer or employee of such labor organization.

"(b) (1) It shall be unlawful for any person to request, demand, receive, or accept, or agree to receive or accept, any payment, loan, or delivery of any money or other thing of value prohibited by subsection (a).

"(2) It shall be unlawful for any labor organization, or for any person acting as an officer, agent, representative, or employee of such labor organization, to demand or accept from the operator of any motor vehicle (as defined in part II of the Interstate Commerce Act) employed in the transportation of property in commerce, or the employer of any such operator, any money or other thing of value payable to such organization or to an officer, agent, representative or employee thereof as a fee or charge for the unloading, or in connection with the unloading, of the cargo of such vehicle: *Provided,* That nothing in this paragraph shall be construed to make unlawful any payment by an employer to any of his employees as compensation for their services as employees.

"(c) The provisions of this section shall not be applicable (1) in respect to any money or other thing of value payable by an employer to any of his employees whose established duties include acting openly for such employer in matters of labor relations or personnel administration or to any representative of his employees, or to any officer or employee of a labor organization, who is also an employee or former employee of such employer, as compensation for, or by reason of, his service as an employee of such employer; (2) with respect to the payment or delivery of any money or other thing of value in satisfaction of a judgment of any court or a decision or award of an arbitrator or impartial chairman or in compromise, adjustment, settlement, or release of any claim, complaint, grievance, or dispute in the absence of fraud or duress; (3) with respect to the sale or purchase of an article or commodity at the prevailing market price in the regular course of business; (4) with respect to money deducted from the wages of employees in payment of membership dues in a labor organization: *Provided,* That the employer has received from each employee, on whose account such deductions are made, a written assignment which shall not be irrevocable for a period of more than one year, or beyond the termination date of the applicable collective agreement, whichever occurs sooner; (5) with respect to money or other thing of value paid to a trust fund established by such representative, for the sole and exclusive benefit of the employees of such employer, and their families and dependents (or of such employees, families, and dependents jointly with the employees of other employers making similar payments, and their families and dependents): *Provided,* That (A) such payments are held in trust for the purpose of paying, either from principal or income or both, for the benefit of employees, their families and dependents, for medical or hospital care, pensions on retirement or death of employees, compensation for injuries or illness resulting from occupational activity or insurance to provide any of the foregoing, or unemployment benefits or life insurance, disability and sickness insurance, or accident insurance; (B) the detailed basis on which such payments are to be made is specified in a written agreement with the employer, and employees and employers are equally represented in the administration of such fund, together with such neutral persons as the representatives of the employers and the representatives of employees may agree upon and in the event the employer and employee groups deadlock on the administration of such fund and there are no neutral persons empowered to break such deadlock, such agreement provides that the two groups shall agree on an impartial umpire to decide such dispute, or in event of their failure to agree within a reasonable length of time, an impartial umpire to decide such dispute shall, on petition of either group, be appointed by the district court of the United States for the district where the trust fund has its principal office, and shall also contain provisions for an annual audit of the trust fund, a statement of the results of which shall be available for inspection by interested persons at the principal office of the trust fund and at such other places as may be designated in such written agreement; and (C) such payments as are intended to be used for the purpose of providing pensions or annuities for employees are made to a separate trust which provides that the funds held therein cannot be used for any purpose other than paying such pensions or annuities; or (6) with respect to money or other thing of value paid by any employer to a trust fund established by such representative for the purpose of pooled vacation, holiday, severance or similar benefits, or defraying costs of apprenticeship or other training programs: *Provided,* That the requirements of clause (B) of the proviso to clause (5) of this subsection shall apply to such trust funds."

TITLE VI

MISCELLANEOUS PROVISIONS

INVESTIGATIONS. SEC. 601. (a) The Secretary shall have power when he believes it necessary in order to determine whether any person has violated or is about to violate any provision of this Act (except title I or amendments made by this Act to other statutes) to make an investigation and in connection therewith he may enter such places and inspect such records and accounts and question such persons as he may deem necessary to enable him to determine the facts relative thereto. The Secretary may report to interested persons or officials concerning the facts required to be shown in any report required by this Act and concerning the reasons for failure or refusal to file such a report or any other matter which he deems to be appropriate as a result of such an investigation.

(b) For the purpose of any investigation provided for in this Act, the provisions of sections 9 and 10 (relating to the attendance of witnesses and the production of books, papers, and documents) of the Federal Trade Commission Act of September 16, 1914, as amended (15 U.S.C. 49, 50), are hereby made applicable to the jurisdiction, powers, and duties of the Secretary or any officers designated by him.

EXTORTIONATE PICKETING. SEC. 602. (a) It shall be unlawful to carry on picketing on or about the premises of any employer for the purpose of, or as part of any conspiracy or in furtherance of any plan or purpose for, the personal profit or enrichment of any individual (except a bona fide increase in wages or other employee benefits) by taking or obtaining any money or other thing of value from such employer against his will or with his consent.

(b) Any person who willfully violates this section shall be fined not more than $10,000 or imprisoned not more than twenty years, or both.

RETENTION OF RIGHTS UNDER OTHER FEDERAL AND STATE LAWS. SEC. 603. (a) Except as explicitly provided to the contrary, nothing in this Act shall reduce or limit the responsibilities of any labor organization or any officer, agent, shop steward, or other representative of a labor organization, or of any trust in which a labor organization is interested, under any other Federal law or under the laws of any State, and, except as explicitly provided to the contrary, nothing in this Act shall take away any right or bar any remedy to which members of a labor organization are entitled under such other Federal law or law of any State.

(b) Nothing contained in titles I, II, III, IV, V, or VI of this Act shall be construed to supersede or impair or otherwise affect the provisions of the Railway Labor Act, as amended, or any of the obligations, rights, benefits, privileges, or immunities of any carrier, employee, organization, representative, or person subject thereto; nor shall anything contained in said titles (except section 505) of this Act be construed to confer any rights, privileges, immunities, or defenses upon employers, or to impair or otherwise affect the rights of any person under the National Labor Relations Act, as amended.

EFFECT ON STATE LAWS. SEC. 604. Nothing in this Act shall be construed to impair or diminish the authority of any State to enact and enforce general criminal laws with respect to robbery, bribery, extortion, embezzlement, grand larceny, burglary, arson, violation of narcotics laws, murder, rape, assault with intent to kill, or assault which inflicts grievous bodily injury, or conspiracy to commit any of such crimes.

SERVICE OF PROCESS. SEC. 605. For the purposes of this Act, service of summons, subpena, or other legal process of a court of the United States upon an officer or agent of a labor organization in his capacity as such shall constitute service upon the labor organization.

ADMINISTRATIVE PROCEDURE ACT. SEC. 606. The provisions of the Administrative Procedure Act shall be applicable to the issuance, amendment, or rescission of any rules or regulations, or any adjudication, authorized or required pursuant to the provisions of this Act.

OTHER AGENCIES AND DEPARTMENTS. SEC. 607. In order to avoid unnecessary expense and duplication of functions among Government agencies, the Secretary may make such arrangements or agreements for cooperation or mutual assistance in the performance of his functions under this Act and the functions of any such agency as he may find to be practicable and consistent with law. The Secretary may utilize the facilities or services of any department, agency, or establishment of the United States or of any State or political subdivision of a State, including the services of any of its employees, with the lawful consent of such department, agency, or establishment; and each department, agency, or establishment of the United States is authorized and directed to cooperate with the Secretary and, to the extent permitted by law, to provide such information and facilities as he may request for his assistance in the performance of his functions under this Act. The Attorney General or his representative shall receive from the Secretary for appropriate action such evidence developed in the performance of his functions under this Act as may be found to warrant consideration for criminal prosecution under the provisions of this Act or other Federal law.

CRIMINAL CONTEMPT. SEC. 608. No person shall be punished for any criminal contempt allegedly committed outside the immediate presence of the court in connection with any civil action prosecuted by the Secretary or any other person in any court of the United States under the provisions of this Act unless the facts constituting such criminal contempt are established by the verdict of the jury in a proceeding in the district court of the United States, which jury shall be chosen and empaneled in the manner prescribed by the law governing trial juries in criminal prosecutions in the district courts of the United States.

PROHIBITION ON CERTAIN DISCIPLINE BY LABOR ORGANIZATION. SEC. 609. It shall be unlawful for any labor organization, or any officer, agent, shop steward, or other representative of a labor organization, or any employee thereof to fine, suspend, expel, or otherwise discipline any of its members for exercising any right to which he is entitled under the provisions of this Act. The provisions of section 102 shall be applicable in the enforcement of this section.

DEPRIVATION OF RIGHTS UNDER ACT BY VIOLENCE. SEC. 610. It shall be unlawful for any person through the use of force or violence, or threat of the use of force or violence, to restrain, coerce, or intimidate, or attempt to restrain, coerce, or intimate any member of a labor organization for the purpose of interfering with or preventing the exercise of any right to which he is entitled under the provisions of this Act. Any person who willfully violates this section shall be fined not more than $1,000 or imprisoned for not more than one year, or both.

SEPARABILITY PROVISIONS. SEC. 611. If any provision of this Act, or the application of such provision to any person or circumstances, shall be held invalid, the remainder of this Act or the application of such provision to persons or circumstances other than those as to which it is held invalid, shall not be affected thereby.

TITLE VII

AMENDMENTS TO THE LABOR MANAGEMENT RELATIONS ACT, 1947, AS AMENDED

FEDERAL-STATE JURISDICTION. SEC. 701. (a) Section 14 of the National Labor Relations Act, as amended, is amended by adding at the end thereof the following new subsection:

"(c)(1) The Board, in its discretion, may, by rule of decision or by published rules adopted pursuant to the Administrative Procedure Act, decline to assert jurisdiction over any labor dispute involving any class or category of employers, where, in the opinion of the Board, the effect of such labor dispute on commerce is not sufficiently substantial to warrant the exercise of its jurisdiction: *Provided,* That the Board shall not decline to assert jurisdiction over any labor dispute over which it would assert jurisdiction under the standards prevailing upon August 1, 1959.

"(2) Nothing in this Act shall be deemed to prevent or bar any agency or the courts of any State or Territory (including the Commonwealth of Puerto Rico, Guam, and the Virgin Islands), from assuming and asserting jurisdiction over labor disputes over which the Board declines, pursuant to paragraph (1) of this subsection, to assert jurisdiction."

(b) Section 3(b) of such Act is amended to read as follows:

"(b) The Board is authorized to delegate to any group of three or more members any or all of the powers which it may itself exercise. The Board is also authorized to delegate to its regional directors its powers under section 9 to determine the unit appropriate for the purpose of collective bargaining, to investigate and provide for hearings, and determine whether a question of representation exists, and to direct an election or take a secret ballot under subsection (c) or (e) of section 9 and certify the results thereof, except that upon the filing of a request therefor with the Board by any interested person, the Board may review any action of a regional director delegated to him under this paragraph, but such a review shall not, unless specifically ordered by the Board, operate as a stay of any action taken by the regional director. A vacancy in the Board shall not impair the right of the remaining members to exercise all of the powers of the Board, and three members of the Board shall, at all times, constitute a quorum of the Board, except that two members shall constitute a quorum of any group designated pursuant to the first sentence hereof. The Board shall have an official seal which shall be judicially noticed."

ECONOMIC STRIKERS. SEC. 702. Section 9(c)(3) of the National Labor Relations Act, as amended, is amended by amending the second sentence thereof to read as follows: "Employees engaged in an economic strike who are not entitled to reinstatement shall be eligible to vote under such regulations as the Board shall find are consistent with the purposes and provisions of this Act in any election conducted within twelve months after the commencement of the strike."

Vacancy in Office of General Counsel. Sec. 703. Section 3(d) of the National Labor Relations Act, as amended, is amended by adding after the period at the end thereof the following: "In case of a vacancy in the office of the General Counsel the President is authorized to designate the officer or employee who shall act as General Counsel during such vacancy, but no person or persons so designated shall so act (1) for more than forty days when the Congress is in session unless a nomination to fill such vacancy shall have been submitted to the Senate, or (2) after the adjournment sine die of the session of the Senate in which such nomination was submitted."

Boycotts and Recognition Picketing. Sec. 704. (a) Section 8(b)(4) of the National Labor Relations Act, as amended, is amended to read as follows:

"4. (i) to engage in, or to induce or encourage any individual employed by any person engaged in commerce or in an industry affecting commerce to engage in, a strike or a refusal in the course of his employment to use, manufacture, process, transport, or otherwise handle or work on any goods, articles, materials, or commodities or to perform any services; or (ii) to threaten, coerce, or restrain any person engaged in commerce or in an industry affecting commerce, where in either case an object thereof is—
　"A. forcing or requiring any employer or self-employed person to join any labor or employer organization or to enter into any agreement which is prohibited by section 8(e);
　"B. forcing or requiring any person to cease using, selling, handling, transporting, or otherwise dealing in the products of any other producer, processor, or manufacturer, or to cease doing business with any other person, or forcing or requiring any other employer to recognize or bargain with a labor organization as the representative of his employees unless such labor organization has been certified as the representative of such employees under the provisions of section 9: *Provided,* That nothing contained in this clause (B) shall be construed to make unlawful, where not otherwise unlawful, any primary strike or primary picketing;
　"C. forcing or requiring any employer to recognize or bargain with a particular labor organization as the representative of his employees if another labor organization has been certified as the representative of such employees under the provisions of section 9;
　"D. forcing or requiring any employer to assign particular work to employees in a particular labor organization or in a particular trade, craft, or class rather than to employees in another labor organization or in another trade, craft, or class, unless such employer is failing to conform to an order or certification of the Board determining the bargaining representative for employees performing such work:
Provided, That nothing contained in this subsection (b) shall be construed to make unlawful a refusal by any person to enter upon the premises of any employer (other than his own employer), if the employees of such employer are engaged in a strike ratified or approved by a representative of such employees whom such employer is required to recognize under this Act: *Provided further,* That for the purposes of this paragraph (4) only, nothing contained in such paragraph shall be construed to prohibit publicity, other than picketing, for the purpose of truthfully advising the public, including consumers and members of a labor organization, that a product or products are produced

by an employer with whom the labor organization has a primary dispute and are distributed by another employer, as long as such publicity does not have an effect of inducing any individual employed by any person other than the primary employer in the course of his employment to refuse to pick up, deliver, or transport any goods, or not to perform any services, at the establishment of the employer engaged in such distribution;".

(b) Section 8 of the National Labor Relations Act, as amended, is amended by adding at the end thereof the following new subsection:

"(e) It shall be an unfair labor practice for any labor organization and any employer to enter into any contract or agreement, express or implied, whereby such employer ceases or refrains or agrees to cease or refrain from handling, using, selling, transporting or otherwise dealing in any of the products of any other employer, or to cease doing business with any other person, and any contract or agreement entered into heretofore or hereafter containing such an agreement shall be to such extent unenforceable and void:*Provided,* That nothing in this subsection (e) shall apply to an agreement between a labor organization and an employer in the construction industry relating to the contracting or subcontracting of work to be done at the site of the construction, alteration, painting, or repair of a building, structure, or other work: *Provided further,* That for the purposes of this subsection (e) and section 8(b) (4) (B) the terms 'any employer', 'any person engaged in commerce or an industry affecting commerce', and 'any person' when used in relation to the terms 'any other producer, processor, or manufacturer', 'any other employer', or 'any other person' shall not include persons in the relation of a jobber, manufacturer, contractor, or sub-contractor working on the goods or premises of the jobber or manufacturer or performing parts of an integrated process of production in the apparel and clothing industry: *Provided further,* That nothing in this Act shall prohibit the enforcement of any agreement which is within the foregoing exception."

(c) Section 8(b) of the National Labor Relations Act, as amended, is amended by striking out the word "and" at the end of paragraph (5), striking out the period at the end of paragraph (6), and inserting in lieu thereof a semicolon and the word "and," and adding a new paragraph as follows:

"7. to picket or cause to be picketed, or threaten to picket or cause to be picketed, any employer where an object thereof is forcing or requiring an employer to recognize or bargain with a labor organization as the representative of his employees, or forcing or requiring the employees of an employer to accept or select such labor organization as their collective bargaining representative, unless such labor organization is currently certified as the representative of such employees:

"A. where the employer has lawfully recognized in accordance with this Act any other labor organization and a question concerning representation may not appropriately be raised under section 9(c) of this Act,

"B. where within the preceding twelve months a valid election under section 9(c) of this Act has been conducted, or

"C. where such picketing has been conducted without a petition under section 9(c) being filed within a reasonable period of time not to exceed thirty days from the commencement of such picketing: *Provided,* That when such a petition has been filed the Board shall forthwith, without regard to the provisions of section 9(c)(1) or the absence of a showing of a substantial interest on the part of the labor organization, direct an election in such unit as the Board finds to be appropriate and shall certify the results thereof: *Provided further,* That nothing in this subparagraph (C) shall be construed to prohibit any picketing or other publicity for the purpose of truthfully advising the public (including consumers) that an employer does not employ members of, or have a contract with, a labor organization, unless an effect of such picketing is to induce any individual employed by any other person in the course of his employment, not to pickup, deliver or transport any goods or not to perform any services.

"Nothing in this paragraph (7) shall be construed to permit any act which would otherwise be an unfair labor practice under this section 8(b)."

(d) Section 10(l) of the National Labor Relations Act, as amended, is amended by adding after the words "section 8(b)," the words "or section 8(e) or section 8(b)(7)," and by striking out the period at the end of the third sentence and inserting in lieu thereof a colon and the following: *"Provided further,* That such officer or regional attorney shall not apply for any restraining order under section 8(b)(7) if a charge against the employer under section 8(a)(2) has been filed and after the preliminary investigation, he has reasonable cause to believe that such charge is true and that a complaint should issue."

(e) Section 303(a) of the Labor Management Relations Act, 1947, is amended to read as follows:

"(a) It shall be unlawful, for the purpose of this section only, in an industry or activity affecting commerce, for any labor organization to engage in any activity or conduct defined as an unfair labor practice in section 8(b)(4) of the National Labor Relations Act, as amended."

BUILDING AND CONSTRUCTION INDUSTRY. SEC. 705. (a) Section 8 of the National Labor Relations Act, as amended by section 704(b) of this Act, is amended by adding at the end thereof the following new subsection:

"(f) It shall not be an unfair labor practice under subsections (a) and (b) of this section for an employer engaged primarily in the building and construction industry to make an agreement covering employees engaged (or who, upon their employment will be engaged) in the building and construction industry with a labor organization of which building and construction employees are members (not established, maintained, or assisted by any action defined in section 8(a) of this Act as an unfair labor practice) because (1) the majority status of such labor organization has not been established under the provisions of section 9 of this Act prior to the making of such agreement, or (2) such agreement requires as a condition of employment, membership in such labor organization after the seventh day following the beginning of such employment or the effective date of the agreement, whichever is later, or (3) such agreement requires the employer to notify such labor organization of opportunities for employment with such employer, or gives such labor organization an opportunity to refer qualified applicants for such employment, or (4) such agreement specifies minimum training or experience qualifications for employment or provides for priority in opportunities for employment based upon length of service with such employer, in the industry or in the particular geographical area: *Provided,* That nothing in this subsection shall set aside the final proviso to section 8(a)(3) of this Act:

Provided further, That any agreement which would be invalid, but for clause (1) of this subsection, shall not be a bar to a petition filed pursuant to section 9 (c) or 9(e)."

(b) Nothing contained in the amendment made by subsection (a) shall be construed as authorizing the execution or application of agreements requiring membership in a labor organization as a condition of employment in any State or Territory in which such execution or application is prohibited by State or Territorial law.

PRIORITY IN CASE HANDLING. SEC. 706. Section 10 of the National Labor Relations Act, as amended, is amended by adding at the end thereof a new subsection as follows:

"(m) Whenever it is charged that any person has engaged in an unfair labor practice within the meaning of subsection (a)(3) or (b)(2) of section 8, such charge shall be given priority over all other cases except cases of like character in the office where it is filed or to which it is referred and cases given priority under subsection (l)."

EFFECTIVE DATE OF AMENDMENTS. SEC. 707. The amendments made by this title shall take effect sixty days after the date of the enactment of this Act and no provision of this title shall be deemed to make an unfair labor practice, any act which is performed prior to such effective date which did not constitute an unfair labor practice prior thereto.

Bibliography

BOOKS

BARNES, JAMES A., *Wealth of the American People*. Englewood Cliffs, N.J.: Prentice-Hall, Inc., 1949.

BEARD, CHARLES A. AND MARY BEARD, *The Rise of American Civilization*. New York: The Macmillan Company, 1927.

BENT, SILAS, *Justice Oliver Wendell Holmes*. New York: Vanguard Press, 1932.

BERMAN, EDWARD, *Labor and the Sherman Act*. New York: Harper & Bros., 1930.

BLACKMAN, JOHN L. JR., *Presidential Seizure in Labor Disputes*. Cambridge, Mass.: Harvard University Press, 1967.

BOWMAN, D. O., *Public Control of Labor Relations*. New York: The Macmillan Company, 1942.

BROOKS, R. R., *Unions of Their Own Choosing*. New Haven: Yale University Press, 1937.

———, *When Labor Organizes*. New Haven, Conn.: Yale University Press, 1937.

CHRISTENSON, CARROLL L. AND RICHARD A. MYREN, *Wage Policy Under the Walsh-Healey Public Contracts Act: A Critical Review*. Bloomington, Ind.: Indiana University Press, 1966.

COCHRAN, THOMAS C. AND WILLIAM MILLER, *The Age of Enterprise*. New York: The Macmillan Company, 1943.

COMMONS, JOHN R. AND ASSOCIATES, *History of Labour in the United States*. New York: The Macmillan Company, 1926.

COMMONS, JOHN R. AND EUGENE A. GILMORE, *A Documentary History of American Industrial Society*. Cleveland: The Arthur H. Clark Company, 1910.

DOUGLAS, PAUL A. AND AARON DIRECTOR, *The Problem of Unemployment*. New York: The Macmillan Company, 1931.

ESTEY, MARTEN S., PHILIP TAFT, AND MARTIN WAGNER, eds., *Regulating Union Government*. New York: Harper & Row, 1964.

EVANS, HYWELL, *Government Regulation of Industrial Relations*. New York: Cornell University, New York State School of Industrial and Labor Relations, 1961.

FALCONE, NICHOLAS S., *Labor Law*. New York: John Wiley & Sons, Inc., 1963.

FRANCE, ROBERT R. AND RICHARD A LESTER, *Compulsory Arbitration of Utility Disputes in New Jersey and Pennsylvania*. Princeton, N.J.: Industrial Relations Section, Princeton University, 1951

FRANKFURTER, FELIX AND NATHAN GREENE, *The Labor Injunction*. New York: The Macmillan Company, 1930.

FREY, J. P., *The Labor Injunction*. Cincinnati: Equity Publishing Company, 1927.

GREGORY, CHARLES O., *Labor and the Law* (2nd rev. ed. with 1961 supplement). New York: W. W. Norton & Company, Inc., 1961.

HANDLER, MILTON, *Cases and Materials on Trade Regulations*. Chicago: The Foundation Press, 1937.

HART, WILSON R., *Collective Bargaining in the Federal Civil Service*. New York: Harper & Row, 1961.

HARTLEY, FRED, *Our New National Labor Policy*. New York: Funk & Wagnalls Company, 1948.

HERON, ALEXANDER R., *Beyond Collective Bargaining*. Stanford, Calif.: Stanford University Press, 1948.

HOWARD, SIDNEY AND ROBERT DUNN, *The Labor Spy*. New York: The Republic Publishing Company, 1921.

Interchurch World Movement's Study of the Steel Strike of 1919.

KAUFMAN, JACOB J., *Collective Bargaining in the Railroad Industry*. New York: King's Crown Press, 1954.

KILLINGSWORTH, CHARLES C., *State Labor Relations Acts*. Chicago: The University of Chicago Press, 1948.

LANDIS, JAMES M. AND MARCUS MANOFF, *Cases on Labor Law*. Chicago: The Foundation Press, 1942.

LEVINSON, EDWARD, *I Break Strikes: The Technique of Pearl L. Bergoff*. New York: R. M. McBride and Company, 1935.

LORWIN, LEWIS L. AND ARTHUR Wubnig, *Labor Relations Boards*. New York: Brookings Institution, 1935.

MASON, A. T., *Brandeis: A Free Man's Life*. New York: The Viking Press, 1946.

———, *Organized Labor and the Law*. Durham, N.C.: Duke University Press, 1925.

MILLER, GLENN W., *American Labor and the Government*. Englewood Cliffs, N.J.: Prentice-Hall, Inc., 1948.

MILLIS, HARRY A. AND EMILY C. BROWN, *From the Wagner Act to the Taft-Hartley*. Chicago: The University of Chicago Press, 1950.

——— AND ROYAL E. MONTGOMERY, *Organized Labor*. New York: McGraw-Hill Book Company, 1945.

NATIONAL CIVIL SERVICE LEAGUE, Committee on Public Employer-Employee Relations, *Employee Organizations in the Public Service*. New York, 1946.

NORTHRUP, HERBERT R. AND GORDON F. BLOOM, *Government and Labor*. Homewood, Ill.: Richard D. Irwin, Inc., 1963.

PALMER, FRANK, *Spies in Steel: An Exposé of Industrial Warfare*. Denver, Colo.: The Labor Press, 1928.

PERLMAN, SELIG, *A History of Trade Unionism in the United States*. New York: The Macmillan Company, 1929.

PETERSON, FLORENCE, *American Labor Unions*. New York: Harper & Bros., 1935.

POWDERLY, T. V., *The Path I Trod*. New York: Columbia University Press, 1940.

Public Papers and Addresses of Franklin D. Roosevelt. New York: Random House, 1938–1950.

REES, ALBERT, *The Economics of Trade Unions*. Chicago: The University of Chicago Press, 1962.

SCOTT, JOHN C. AND EDWIN S. ROCKEFELLER, *Antitrust and Trade Regulation Today: 1967*. Washington, D.C.: Bureau of National Affairs, 1967.

SEIDMAN, JOEL, *The Yellow Dog Contract*. Baltimore: Johns Hopkins Press, 1932.

SHISTER, JOSEPH, BENJAMIN AARON, AND CLYDE W. SUMMERS, eds., *Public Policy and Collective Bargaining*. New York: Harper & Row, 1962.

————, *Economics of the Labor Market*. Chicago: J. B. Lippincott Company, 1949.

SLESINGER, REUBEN E., *National Economic Policy: The Presidential Reports*. Princeton, N.J.: D. Van Nostrand Company, Inc., 1968.

SLOVENKO, RALPH, ed., *Symposium on the Labor-Management Reporting and Disclosure Act of 1959*. Baton Rouge, La.: Claitor's Bookstore, 1960.

SPERO, STERLING DENHARD, *Government as Employer*. New York: Remsen Press, 1948.

TAYLOR, BENJAMIN J., *Arizona Labor Relations Law*, Occasional Paper No. 2. Tempe: Arizona State University, Bureau of Business and Economic Research, College of Business Administration, 1967.

————, *The Operation of the Taft-Hartley Act in Indiana*, Indiana Business Bulletin No. 58. Bloomington, Ind.: Bureau of Business Research, 1967.

TWENTIETH CENTURY FUND, INC., *Labor and Government*. New York: McGraw-Hill Book Company, 1953.

UNITED STATES DEPARTMENT OF LABOR, *Growth of Labor Law in the United States*. Washington, D.C.: Government Printing Office, 1967.

WITNEY, FRED, *Indiana Labor Relations Law*. Bloomington, Ind.: Indiana University, Bureau of Business Research, 1960.

————, *Wartime Experiences of the National Labor Relations Board*. Urbana, Ill.: University of Illinois Press, 1949.

WITTE, EDWIN E., *The Government in Labor Disputes*. New York: McGraw-Hill Book Company, 1932.

WRIGHT, CHESTER W., *Economic History of the United States*. New York: McGraw-Hill Book Company, 1949.

ARTICLES

AARON, BENJAMIN, "Employee Rights and Union Democracy," *Monthly Labor Review*, XCII, No. 3, March 1969.

ABNER, WILLOUGHBY, "The FMCS and Dispute Mediation in the Federal Government," *Monthly Labor Review*, XCII, No. 5, May 1969.

"Arbitration Provisions in Collective Agreements, 1952," *Monthly Labor Review*, March 1953.

"Bargaining in Agriculture: Current Trends in Labor Management Relations," Speech before the Fifteenth New Jersey Marketing Institute, November 30, 1972.

BERNSTEIN, IRVING, HAROLD L. ENARSON, AND R. W. FLEMING, eds., "The Economic Impact of Strikes in Key Industries," *Emergency Disputes and National Policy*. New York: Harper & Bros., 1955.

———— AND HUGH G. LOVELL, "Are Coal Strikes National Emergencies?" *Industrial and Labor Relations Review*, VI, No. 3, April 1953.

BLOCH, RICHARD I., "The NLRB and Arbitration: Is the Board's Expanding Jurisdiction Justified?" *Labor Law Journal*, XIX, No. 10, October 1968.

BLOEDORN, JOHN, "The Strike and the Public Sector," *Labor Law Journal*, XX, No. 3, March 1969.

BOK, DEREK C., "The Regulation of Campaign Tactics in Representation Elections under the National Labor Relations Act," *Harvard Law Review*, LXXVIII, No. 1, November 1964.

BRISSENDEN, P. F. AND C. O. SWAYZEE, "The Use of Injunctions in the New York Needle Trades," *Political Science Quarterly*, XLIV (1929).

Bureau of National Affairs, "Report and Recommendations of the Panel," *War Labor Reports*, XXVI.

CHRISTENSON, C. L., "The Impact of Labor Disputes upon Coal Consumption," *American Economic Review*, XLV, No. 1, March 1955.

———, "The Theory of the Offset Factor: The Impact of Labor Disputes upon Coal Production," *American Economic Review*, XLIII, No. 4, September 1953.

COUNCIL ON LABOR LAW AND LABOR RELATIONS, "Federal Bar Association Task Force I Report—E. O. 11616," *Labor Law Journal*, July 1972.

"Coverage of Checkoff under Taft-Hartley Act," *Monthly Labor Review*, LXVII, July 1948.

COX, ARCHIBALD, "Rights under a Labor Agreement," *Harvard Law Review*, LXIX (1956).

———, "The Role of Law in Preserving Union Democracy," *Harvard Law Review*, LXXII (1959).

CRAVER, CHARLES B., "Bargaining in the Federal Sector," *Labor Law Journal*, XIX, No. 9, September 1968.

DONIAN, HARRY A., "A New Approach to Setting the Pay of Federal Blue-Collar Workers," *Monthly Labor Review*, XCII, No. 4, April 1969.

DROTNING, JOHN E., "Employer Free Speech: Two Basic Questions Considered by the NLRB and Courts," *Labor Law Journal*, XVI, No. 3, March 1965.

DUNLOP, JOHN T., "Jurisdictional Disputes," *Proceedings of New York University Second Annual Conference of Labor*.

FLEMING, R. W., "Title VII: The Taft-Hartley Amendments," *Northwestern University Law Review*, LIV, No. 6, January–February 1960.

GLASGOW, JOHN M., "The Right-to-Work Law Controversy Again," *Labor Law Journal*, XVIII, No. 2, February 1967.

GLASS, RONALD W., "Work Stoppages and Teachers: History and Prospect," *Monthly Labor Review*, XC, No. 8, August 1967.

GOLDBERG, STEPHEN B., "Coordinated Bargaining: Some Unresolved Questions," *Monthly Labor Review*, XCII, No. 4, April 1969.

HALL, JOHN T. JR., "Work Stoppages in Government," *Monthly Labor Review*, XCI, No. 7, July 1968.

HILGERT, RAYMOND L. AND JERRY D. YOUNG, "Right-to-Work Legislation—Examination of Related Issues and Effects," *Personnel Journal*, December 1963.

ISAACSON, WILLIAM J.,"Discernible Trends in the 'Miller' Board—Practical Considerations for the Labor Counsel," *Labor Law Journal*, Vol. 43, No. 9.

JOHANNESEN, D. J. AND W. BRITTON SMITH, JR., "Collyer: Open Sesame to Deferral," *Labor Law Journal*, Vol. 23, No. 12, December 1972.

JONES, DALLAS L., "The Enigma of the Clayton Act," *Industrial and Labor Relations Review*, X, No. 2, January 1957.

KAPP, ROBERT W., "Managements' Concern with Recent Civil Rights Legislation," *Labor Law Journal*, XVI, No. 2, February 1965.

KAUFMAN, JACOB J., "The Railroad Labor Dispute: A Marathon of Maneuver and Improvisation," *Industrial and Labor Relations Review*, XVIII, No. 2, January 1965.

KIRKWOOD, JOHN H., "The Enforcement of Collective Bargaining Contracts," *Labor Law Journal*, XV, No. 2, February 1964.

KOVARSKY, IRVING, "Union Security, Hiring Halls, Right-to-Work Laws and the Supreme Court," *Labor Law Journal*, XV, No. 10, October 1964.

McCALMONT, DAVID B., "The Semi-Strike," *Industrial and Labor Relations Review*, XV, No. 2, January 1962.

McDERMOTT, THOMAS J., "Arbitrability: The Courts Versus the Arbitrator," *The Arbitration Journal*, XXIII, No. 4 (1968).

———, Enforcing No-Strike Provisions via Arbitration," *Labor Law Journal*, XVIII, No. 10, October 1967.

McLENNAN, KENNETH AND MICHAEL H. MOSKOW, "Multilateral Bargaining in the Public Sector," *Monthly Labor Review*, XCII, No. 4, April 1969.

McNATT, E. B., "Labor Again Menaced by the Sherman Act," *The Southern Economic Journal*, VI, No. 2, October 1939.

MAGRATH, C. PETER, "Democracy in Overalls: The Futile Quest for Union Democracy," *Industrial and Labor Relations Review*, XII (1959).

PETERSON, RICHARD B., "National Emergency Dispute Legislation—What Next?" *University of Washington Business Review*, XXVII, No. 1, Autumn 1968.

PHELPS, ORME W., "Compulsory Arbitration: Some Perspectives," *Industrial and Labor Relations Review*, XVIII, No. 1, October 1964.

REZLER, JULIUS AND S. JOHN INSALATTA, "Doctrine of Mutuality: A Driving Force in American Labor Legislation," *Labor Law Journal*, XVIII, No. 5, May 1967.

ROSE, THEODORE, "Union Security and Checkoff Provisions in Major Union Contracts," *Monthly Labor Review*, LXXXII, No. 12, December 1959.

———, "Union Security Provisions in Agreements, 1954," *Monthly Labor Review*, LXXVIII, No. 6, June 1955.

ROSS, ANNE M., "Public Employee Unions and the Right to Strike," *Monthly Labor Review*, XCII, No. 3, March 1969.

RUMMELL, CHARLES A., "Current Developments in Farm Labor Law," *Labor Law Journal*, XIX, No. 4, April 1968.

SCHULTZ, GEORGE P., "The Massachusetts Choice-of-Procedures Approach to Emergency Disputes," *Industrial and Labor Relations Review*, X, No. 3, April 1957.

SEGAL, MELVIN J., "Secondary Boycott Loopholes," *Labor Law Journal*, X, No. 3, March 1959.

SLOANE, ARTHUR A., Presidential Boards of Inquiry in National Emergency Disputes, An Assessment After 20 Years of Performance," *Labor Law Journal*, XVIII, No. 11, November 1967.

SMITH, RUSSELL A., "The Labor-Management Reporting and Disclosure Act of 1959," *Virginia Law Review*, XLVI, No. 2, March 1960.

SONSNICK, STEPHEN H., "Non-Stoppage Strikes: A New Approach," *Industrial and Labor Relations Review*, XVIII, No. 1, October 1964.

SPELFOGEL, EVAN J., "Enforcement of No-Strike Clause by Injunction, Damage Action and Discipline," *Labor Law Journal*, XVII, No. 2 (1966).

STESSIN, LAWRENCE, "A New Look at Arbitration," *The New York Times Magazine*, November 17, 1963.

STEVENS, CARL M., "Is Compulsory Arbitration Compatible with Bargaining?" *Industrial Relations*, VI, No. 2, February 1966.

STOCHAJ, JOHN M., "Free Speech Policies," *Labor Law Journal*, VIII, No. 8, August 1957.

TAFT, PHILIP, "Dues and Initiation Fees in Labor Unions," *Quarterly Journal of Economics*, February 1946.

TIMBERS, EDWIN, "The Problems of Union Power and Antitrust Legislation," *Labor Law Journal*, XVI, No. 9, September 1965.

WACKS, ROBERT E., "Successorship: The Consequences of Burns," *Labor Law Journal*, Vol. 24, No. 4, April 1973.

WAKS, JAY W., "The Dual Jurisdiction Problem in Labor Arbitration: A Research Report," *The Arbitration Journal*, XXIII, No. 4 (1968).

WATKINS, MYRON W., "Trusts," *Encyclopedia of Social Sciences*, Vol. 15.

WEISENFELD, ALLEN, "Public Employees Are Still Second Class Citizens," *Labor Law Journal*, XX, No. 3, March 1969.

WITNEY, FRED, "NLRB Jurisdictional Policies and the Federal-State Relationship," *Labor Law Journal*, VI, No. 1, January 1955.

———, "NLRB Membership Cleavage: Recognition and Organizational Picketing," *Labor Law Journal*, XIV, No. 5, May 1963.

———, "Union Security," *Labor Law Journal*, IV, No. 2, February 1953.

WITTE, E. E., "Early American Labor Cases," *Yale Law Journal*, XXXV (1926).

ZANDER, ARNOLD S., "Trends in Labor Legislation for Public Employees," *Monthly Labor Review*, LXXXIII, No. 12, December 1960.

PAMPHLETS AND BOOKLETS

AFL-CIO Maritime Trades Department, *Collective Bargaining in the Public Sector, An Interim Report*. Washington, D.C.: Executive Board AFL-CIO Maritime Trades Department, 1969.

BUREAU OF NATIONAL AFFAIRS, *Taft-Hartley After One Year, 1948*.

COMMITTEE FOR ECONOMIC DEVELOPMENT, *The Public Interest in National Labor Policy*. New York, 1961.

CULLEN, DONALD E., *National Emergency Strikes*, ILR Paperback No. 7. Ithaca, N.Y.: Cornell University, New York State School of Industrial and Labor Relations, 1968.

HANSLOWE, KURT L., *The Emerging Law of Labor Relations in Public Employment*, ILR Paperback No. 4. Ithaca, N.Y.: Cornell University, New York State School of Industrial and Labor Relations, 1967.

INTERNATIONAL ASSOCIATION OF MACHINISTS, *The Truth About the Taft-Hartley Law and Its Consequences to the Labor Movement*, April 1948.

LIVERNASH, E. ROBERT, *Collective Bargaining in the Basic Steel Industry*. Washington, D.C.: Government Printing Office, 1961.

NATIONAL PLANNING ASSOCIATION, *Causes of Industrial Peace under Collective Bargaining*. Washington, D.C., 1948–1950.

POLISOR, ERIC, "Strikes and Solutions," Public Employee Relations Report No. 7, Public Personnel Association, 1968.

ROBERTS, H., *A Manual for Employee-Management Cooperation in the Federal Service*. Honolulu, Hawaii: Industrial Relations Center, University of Hawaii, 1964.

SHELDON, HORACE E., "Union Security and the Taft-Hartley Act in the Buffalo Area." Ithaca, N.Y.: Cornell University, New York State School of Industrial and Labor Relations Research Bulletin 4.

Sheriff, Don R. and Viola M. Kuebler, eds., *NLRB in a Changing Industrial Society*, Conference Series No. 2. Iowa City: College of Business Administration, The University of Iowa, 1967.

United Auto Workers, *A More Perfect Union*. Detroit: UAW Publications Department, 1958.

U.S. Chamber of Commerce, *To Protect Management Rights*. Washington, D.C., 1961.

Young, James E. and Betty L. Brewer, *State Legislation Affecting Labor Relations in State and Local Government*, Labor and Industrial Relations Series No. 2. Kent, Ohio: Kent State University, Bureau of Economic and Business Research, 1968.

GOVERNMENT DOCUMENTS AND PUBLICATIONS

Bureau of Labor Statistics, *Analysis of Work Stoppages 1965*, Bulletin No. 1525. Washington, D.C.: Government Printing Office, 1966.

———, *Characteristics of Company Unions*, Bulletin No. 634. Washington, D.C.: Government Printing Office, 1938.

———, *Handbook of Labor Statistics*. Washington, D.C.: Government Printing Office, 1968.

———, *Union Membership and Collective Bargaining by Foremen*, Bulletin No. 745. Washington, D.C.: Government Printing Office.

———, *Union Security Provisions in Collective Bargaining*, Bulletin No. 908. Washington, D.C.: Government Printing Office, 1947.

Congressional Quarterly Weekly Report, No. 30, July 29, 1966.

Congressional Record, various volumes. Washington, D.C.: Government Printing Office.

Federal Mediation and Conciliation Service, *Annual Reports*, 1947–1973.

La Follette Committee, *Private Police Systems*, Report No. 6, Pt. 2, 76th Cong., 1st sess.

———, *Report on Industrial Espionage*, Report No. 46, Pt. 3, 75th Cong.

———, *The Chicago Memorial Day Incident*, Report No. 46, Pt. 2, 75th Cong.

National Labor Relations Board, *Annual Reports*, Vols. 1–37. Washington, D.C.: Government Printing Office, 1936–1972.

———, Office of the General Counsel, "Arbitration Deferral Policy Under Revised Guidelines," *Collyer*, May 10, 1973.

———, *Decisions and Orders of the National Labor Relations Board*.

———, *History of the Labor-Management Reporting and Disclosure Act*, Vols. 1 and 2. Washington, D.C.: Government Printing Office, 1959.

———, *Legislative History of the Labor-Management Relations Act, 1947*, Vols. 1 and 2. Washington, D.C.: Government Printing Office, 1948.

———, *Rules and Regulations and Statements of Procedure*. Washington, D.C.: Government Printing Office, 1973.

National War Labor Board, *Report, April, 1918 to May, 1919*.

———, *Termination Report*. Washington, D.C.: I (1946).

———, *War Labor Reports*, 1942–1945.

Presidential Report, *A Policy for Employee-Management Cooperation in the Federal Service*, Report of the President's Task Force on Employee-Management Relations in the Federal Service. Washington, D.C.: Government Printing Office, 1961.

———, *Free and Responsible Collective Bargaining and Industrial Peace*, Report of the President's Advisory Committee on Labor-Management Policy. Washington, D.C.: Government Printing Office, 1962.

Report of the Industrial Commission on Labor Legislation. Washington, D.C.: Government Printing Office, 1900.

Report of the U.S. Commission on Industrial Relations, 11 vols. Washington, D.C.: Government Printing Office, 1916.

U.S. Congress, *Document No. 669*, 72nd Cong., 1st sess.

————, *Hearings Before the Committee on Education and Labor on H.R. 115*, 83rd Cong., 1st sess., 1953.

————, *Hearings Before the Committee on Labor and Public Welfare*, U.S. Senate, 80th Cong., 1st sess. on S. 55 and S.J. Res. 22, Part I and Part II, 1947.

————, *Hearings Before the Senate Subcommittee on Labor-Management Relations, Hiring Halls in the Maritime Industry*, 81st Cong., 2nd sess., 1950.

————, *Hearings Before the Subcommittee on Separation of Powers of the Committee on the Judiciary, Congressional Oversight of Administrative Agencies (National Labor Relations Board)*, United States Senate, Parts I and II. Washington, D.C.: Government Printing Office, 1968.

————, *Hearings on a National Labor Relations Board*, 74th Cong., 1st sess., 1935.

————, *Hearings on H.R. 6288 Before the House Committee on Labor*, 74th Cong., 1st sess., 1935.

————, *Hearings on S. 1958 Before the House Committee on Labor*, 74th Cong., 1st sess., Part III, 1935.

————, *Hearings on S. 249 (Labor Relations)*, III, Senate Committee on Labor and Public Welfare, 81st Cong., 1st sess., 1949.

————, *House Report No. 1147*, 86th Cong., 1st sess., 1959.

————, *House Report No. 245 on H.R. 3020*, 80th Cong., 1st sess., 1947.

————, *Intermediate Report, House Report No. 1902*, House of Representatives, Special Committee to Investigate the National Labor Relations Board, 76th Cong., 3rd sess., Part I, 1940.

————, *Report No. 99 to Accompany S. 249, National Labor Relations Act of 1949*, 81st Cong., 1st sess., 1949.

————, *Senate Report No. 1417, Interim Report of the Senate Select Committee on Improper Activities in the Labor or Management Fields*, 85th Cong., 2nd sess., 1958.

————, *Senate Report No. 105 on Senate 1126*, 80th Cong., 1st sess., 1947.

————, *Senate Report No. 986, Report of the Joint Committee on Labor-Management Relations*, Part I, March 15, 1948.

U.S. Department of Labor, *Compliance, Enforcement and Reporting in 1968 under the Labor-Management Reporting and Disclosure Act.* Washington, D.C.: Government Printing Office, 1968.

U.S. Department of Labor, "Government Work Stoppages, 1960, 1969, and 1971," Summary Report, November 1971.

U.S. Department of Labor, Labor-Management Services Administration, *Compliance, Enforcement and Reporting in 1972 under the Labor-Management Reporting and Disclosure Act.* Washington, D.C.: Government Printing Office, 1972.

U.S. Department of Labor, Labor-Management Services Administration, *Union Elections under the LMRDA, 1966–1970.*

NEWSPAPERS AND PERIODICALS

AFL-CIO, *American Federationist*

AFL-CIO News

Bureau of National Affairs, *Labor Relations Reference Manual*
Business Week
National Association of Manufacturers Law Digest
New York Times
Wall Street Journal

Index of Cases

For cases in which the United States or the NLRB is the moving party, the name of the other party is listed first. Thus, in *NLRB* v. *Smith*, the case is listed as *Smith* (*NLRB* v.). In addition, the full name of a union is reduced to show only the industry or craft of the union. Thus, in a case involving the International Association of Machinists and Aerospace Workers, the union's name is listed as *Machinists* v. *NLRB*.

General Index